p Price of a security
P Sales price per unit of product sold
P_o Present value
$P_{r,N}$ Present value of an annuity
P_s Probability of state-of-the-world *s*
PVIF Present value interest factor
PVIFA Present value interest factor for an annuity
Q Quantity produced or sold
r Interest rate (usually real rate)
R_M Return on the market portfolio
R_F Risk-free rate of interest
R_j Returns to individual firm or security
$\overline{R}$ Expected rate of return on new investment; also internal rate of return (IRR); also R is nominal interest rate
R^* Required rate of return
ρ_{jk} (rho) Correlation coefficient
s Subscript referring to alternative states-of-the-world
S Market value of a firm's common equity; also sales when indicated
S_N Compound sum
$S_{r,N}$ Sum of an annuity
σ (sigma) Standard deviation
σ^2 Variance; also Var ( )
T Marginal corporate income tax rate
t Time period
V Market value of a firm; also total variable costs
v Variable costs per unit
w Weights in capital structure or portfolio proportions
X Net operating income of the firm; also equals EBIT = NOI
Z Estimated salvage value

Managerial Finance

Seventh Edition

J. Fred Weston
Professor of Managerial Economics and Finance
University of California, Los Angeles

Eugene F. Brigham
Professor of Finance
University of Florida

The Dryden Press
Hinsdale, Illinois

Library of Congress Catalog Card Number: 80-65811

ISBN: 0-03-058186-9

International Edition is not for sale in the United States of America, its dependencies or Canada

Printed in the United States of America
4 -071-9876

Copy editing by Wanda Giles
Text and cover design by James Buddenbaum
Permissions by Jo-Anne Naples

Acquisitions Editor	*Glenn Turner*
Developmental Editor	*Anne Boynton-Trigg*
Project Editor	*Kathy Richmond*
Production Manager	*Peter Coveney*
Design Director	*William Seabright*

Preface

The seventh edition of Managerial Finance *was written during a period of increasing turbulence in the financial markets of the United States and the rest of the world. During early 1980, a steady stream of headlines in the financial press portrayed a developing financial crisis: the bond market in shambles . . . the prime rate at another new high . . . forecasts of recession coupled with a resurgent economy and higher inflation rates . . . crumbling Eurobond markets as money managers fled to gold and other commodities. In early April 1980, short-term interest rates peaked. The prime bank loan rate topped out at 20 percent and by late June dropped to 11.5 percent. Economic activity slowed, business loans at banks declined, and the volume of new bond offerings surged upward.*

Impacts of New Developments

The major developments have presented new challenges to financial managers. Corporate financial policies and practices have been greatly affected in most areas. These changes have also influenced the revisions made in this edition of Managerial Finance. *Besides the unusual state of events, academic scholars have continued to make significant advances, especially in the areas of capital budgeting, the cost of capital, and option pricing models. At the same time, business practitioners are making increasing use of financial theory, and feedback from the real world has led to revisions in such theory.*

Thus, there are many changes in the seventh edition. But this edition also continues the basic philosophy of previous editions, which is to provide users with coverage of all important areas of managerial finance and financial management, while providing flexibility in the use of the materials. This objective of flexibility has guided the placement of some new materials. Three important recent developments in finance are the Capital Asset Pricing Model (CAPM), the Option Pricing Model (OPM), and the State-Preference Model (SPM). The Capital Asset Pricing Model is presented in

Chapter 5. The Option Pricing Model has been set forth in Appendix A to Chapter 22. We utilize the State-Preference Model to provide a wrap-up of the discussion of financial leverage in Appendix E to Chapter 16. These and other materials continue the up-to-date coverage of Managerial Finance *while providing flexibility in the sequence they can be treated in and in the number and types of courses in which the topics are taught.*

Changes in the Seventh Edition

The seventh edition of Managerial Finance *incorporates these changes:*

1. *All materials that have a time aspect have been updated.*
2. *More than half of the end-of-chapter problems for the entire text have been changed. On all of the problems, the interest rate levels now reflect the changed conditions that the economy has experienced in recent years. We have also added new problems to round out the coverage of concepts and to provide appropriate emphasis on areas of central importance.*
3. *The listing of "Frequently Used Symbols" has been further developed. The symbols are intended to reflect the widest usage found in the journal literature. Another benefit of the listing is that it provides a perspective that allows some simplification and reduction in the number of symbols employed in* Managerial Finance.
4. *The overall organization has been changed. Chapters on "Risk and Return" and on "Valuation Relationships" are introduced early. The purpose is to provide an overview of these subjects as they relate to all subsequent topics. The reader who understands these materials early can use them repeatedly, increasing the mastery of these key topics.*
5. *The material on goals in Chapter 1 has been reoriented, and the discussion of managers versus stockholders has been placed in the agency-cost framework.*
6. *Chapter 2 adds a new part on the procedures involved in margin trading, in both long and short positions, with examples illustrating how this use of leverage by individuals also magnifies gains and losses.*
7. *Appendix A to Chapter 3 "Depreciation Methods," provides some further clarification and development of the declining balance methods.*
8. *Chapter 5, "Risk and Return," is completely rewritten material that provides an overview of the basic concepts.*
9. *Chapter 6, "Valuation Relationships," is also completely rewritten to reflect valuation in the most general "free cash flow" framework.*

10. *In Chapter 7, "Financial Ratio Analysis," studies on the determinants of a firm's required rate of return have suggested two more categories of financial ratios—growth measures and valuation measures. The two are logically related; they also provide a basis for integration with the later chapters on the cost of capital and valuation.*
11. *Appendix A to Chapter 7, "Adjustments for Changes in Price Levels," an appendix that carried a similar name in the sixth edition of* Managerial Finance, *has been completely rewritten to incorporate more recent materials, particularly FASB Statement No. 33, issued in December 1979.*
12. *Appendix B to Chapter 7, "Discriminant Analysis and Financial Ratios," is distinctive in providing a specific example with easily handled numbers to show how one can do discriminant analysis. There are, of course, canned computer programs for doing the calculations, but a reader who has worked through this relatively simple example gets a good understanding of what is involved in the actual calculations.*
13. *Chapter 9, "Financial Planning and Control," reflects the general reorganization of Part 2, "Financial Analysis, Planning, and Control," into related topics. The statement of financial position (sources and uses analysis) material is included in Chapter 8 on financial forecasting since it is often developed on a pro forma basis in connection with other kinds of financial projections. The cash budgeting materials are emphasized now in their Chapter 9 placement since the focus of that chapter is on budgeting. Breakeven analysis is used to open Chapter 9 in the general framework of an investment volume and returns analysis as a form of a broad, overall planning approach.*
14. *Chapter 10, "Working Capital Policy," contains more fully integrated materials on the term structure of interest rates and the use of short- versus long-term debt financing.*
15. *Chapter 11, "Current Asset Management," reflects articles on the analysis of credit policy decisions that have appeared in the journal* Financial Management *in recent years. Some corrections and extensions to the articles are made. The materials on inventory management are reworked, clarified, and moved entirely into the chapter, with the former appendix eliminated.*
16. *Appendix A to Chapter 11 simplifies and presents with illustrative applications the payments pattern approach to receivables management.*
17. *Appendix C to Chapter 11, "Credit Policy Decisions," is a somewhat more formal treatment of the several new articles on credit policy.*

18. *Appendix A to Chapter 13, "Additional Issues in Capital Budgeting Analysis," covers six topics that fit together logically. The materials on three of them in particular are reorganized and clarified. These topics are (1) projects of different scale, (2) projects of different lives, and (3) reinvestment rate considerations.*
19. *Chapter 14 and its Appendixes, which are materials on investment decisions under uncertainty, have been streamlined and regrouped. The appendixes have been reduced to four in number without omitting vital topics.*
20. *Chapter 16, "The Cost of Capital," summarizes and treats the Modigliani-Miller propositions as one of the approaches to measuring the cost of capital. The conditions under which the MM propositions do not hold are also noted.*
21. *Chapter 18, "Capital Markets: Institutions and Behavior," includes most of the relevant material from the similar sixth edition chapter, though the material on the timing of financial decisions is placed now in Chapter 10, "Working Capital Policy."*
22. *Appendix A to Chapter 20, "Refunding Decisions," summarizes and integrates contributions to the refunding literature. The literature on refunding both when interest rates have fallen and when they have risen is critically reviewed.*
23. *Chapter 23, "Mergers and Holding Companies," incorporates recent literature and data on mergers.*
24. *Chapter 24, "Reorganization and Bankruptcy," discusses the new bankruptcy law, effective October 1979.*
25. *Chapter 26, "International Business Finance," has been completely rewritten. The new end-of-chapter problems are particularly useful in summarizing the basic concepts.*
26. *In previous editions, we have rounded to the even number to avoid the bias of rounding upward. However, hand calculators are programmed to round upward. Since hand calculators are now so widely used, we have changed to rounding upward to avoid the discrepancies that would otherwise occur.*

Flexibility in Use of the Materials

Much of the specific content of the book is the result of our experience in executive development programs over a number of years. This experience, in addition to our consulting with business firms on financial problems and policies, has helped us to identify the most significant responsibilities of financial managers, the most fundamental problems facing firms, and the most feasible approaches to practical decision-making. Some topics are conceptually difficult, but so are the issues faced by financial managers. Business managers must be prepared to handle complex problems, and finding solutions to these problems necessarily involves the use of advanced tools and techniques.

We have not sought to avoid the many unresolved areas of business financial theory and practice. Although we could have simplified the text in many places by avoiding the difficult issues, we preferred to provide a basic framework based on the "received doctrine," then to go on (often in appendixes) to present materials on a number of important, but controversial issues. It is hoped that our presentation, along with the additional references provided at the end of each chapter, will stimulate the reader to further inquiry.

We acknowledge that the level and difficulty of the material is uneven. Certain sections are simply descriptions of the institutional features of the financial environment and, as such, are not difficult to understand. Other parts—notably the material on capital budgeting, uncertainty, and the cost of capital—are by nature rather abstract, and are therefore difficult for those not used to thinking in abstract terms. In some of the more complex sections, we have simply outlined procedures in the main body of the text, then justified the procedures in the chapter appendixes.

The appendixes permit great flexibility in the use of Managerial Finance. *The book can be used in a basic course by omitting selected appendix topics. If instructors wish to cover selected topics from the appendixes, they may do so, and the more interested or mature student may also choose to select appendix topics for independent study. Alternatively, the book may be used in a two-semester course, supplemented, as the instructor sees fit, with outside readings or cases, or both. At both UCLA and Florida we use the basic chapters plus a very few appendixes in the introductory course, then cover selected appendixes plus cases and some articles in the advanced course. In fact, some of the appendixes were written specifically to help bridge the gap between basic texts and journal literature.*

Several reviewers suggested that it might be desirable to reduce the total length of the book. While the idea was appealing, we did not follow the suggestion for several reasons. We want the book to cover the entire field of business finance and to deal with all the financial management functions. Eliminating institutional material and concentrating on theory and technique would give the student an unrealistic, sterile view of finance. Some of the more advanced theory and techniques could have been eliminated on the ground that they probably would not be covered in basic courses, but it is useful to show where this material fits into the scheme of things and to provide the student with a bridge to the journal literature. These factors, together with the fact that the book is structured so that instructors do not have to assign all the material, *caused us to forgo a marked reduction in the book's length.*

Ancillary Materials

Several items are available to supplement Managerial Finance. *First is the* Study Guide, *which many students will find useful. The* Study Guide *highlights the key points in the text and presents a comprehensive set of problems similar to those at the end of each chapter. Each problem is solved in detail, so a student who has difficulty working the end-of-chapter problems can be aided by careful use of the* Study Guide. *Second, a casebook is available,* Cases in Managerial Finance, *Fourth Edition, by Eugene Brigham, Roy Crum, Timothy Nantell, Robert Aubey and Richard Pettway. Third, books of readings can be used to supplement the text.* Issues in Managerial Finance, *Second Edition, edited by Eugene Brigham and Ramon Johnson is a particularly useful accompaniment to* Managerial Finance.

For the professor there is a very thorough 500-page Instructor's Manual. *It contains alternative subject sequences and teaching methods, course outlines, answers to all text questions, solutions to all text problems, and an extensive array of test questions and problems. Also available to the instructor is a comprehensive set of* Transparency Masters *featuring solutions to selected end-of-chapter problems. As a supplement to those in the text, an additional set of problems and solutions is available to adopters. These were developed with the assistance of Roger Bey, Keith Johnson and Ramon Johnson.*

In a further attempt to keep this text up-to-date we will begin publishing in 1981 an annual Newsletter. *This will be provided to all adopters and will contain among other things fresh problems, summaries of important new research, the latest changes in tax rates, and any other available material that is relevant to teaching corporate finance.*

Acknowledgments

In its several revisions, this book has been worked on and critically reviewed by numerous individuals, and we have received many detailed comments and suggestions from instructors and students using the book in our own schools and elsewhere. All this help has improved the quality of the book, and we are deeply indebted to the following individuals, and others, for their help: M. Adler, E. Altman, J. Andrews, R. Aubey, P. Bacon, W. Beranek, V. Brewer, W. Brueggeman, R. Carleson, S. Choudhur, P. Cooley, C. Cox, D. Fischer, G. Granger, R. Gray, J. Griggs, R. Haugen, S. Hawk, R. Hebre, J. Henry, A. Herrmann, G.Hettenhouse, R. Himes,

C. Johnson, R. Jones, D. Kaplan, M. Kaufman, D. Knight, H. Krogh, R. LeClair, W. Lee, D. Longmore, J. Longstreet, H. Magee, P. Malone, R. Moore, T. Morton, T. Nantell, R. Nelson, R. Norgaard, J. Pappas, R. Pettit, R. Pettway, J. Pinkerton, G. Pogue, W. Regan, F. Reilly, R. Rentz, R. Richards, C. Rini, R. Roenfeldt, W. Sharpe, K. Smith, P. Smith, R. Smith, D. Sorenson, M. Tysseland, P. Vanderheiden, D. Woods, J. Yeakel, and D. Ziegenbein for their careful reviews of this and previous editions.

We owe special thanks to Rolf O. Christiansen, Joel Dauten, S. Thomas Holbrook, Craig G. Johnson, Surendra Mansinghka, John Markese, Ronald W. Melicher, Howard L. Puckett, Kenneth L. Stanley, Peter Van den Dool, William Welch and Dennis P. Zocco for providing us with detailed reviews of the manuscript of this edition. We would like to thank C. Barngrover, S. Mansinghka, W. Eckardt, H. Rollins, H. Alway, D. Wort, and J. Zumwalt for their assistance in helping us develop the acetate program. We would also like to express our appreciation to Bob LeClair and to The American College for their help in preparing the transparencies, which are available from The Dryden Press.

The Universities of California and Florida and our colleagues on these campuses provided us with intellectual support in bringing the book to completion. Finally, we are indebted to the Dryden Press staff—principally Dick Owen, Glenn Turner, Anne Boynton-Trigg, Peter Coveney, Alan Wendt, and Kathy Richmond—for their special efforts in getting the manuscript into production and for following through to the bound book.

The field of finance will continue to experience significant changes. It is stimulating to participate in these exciting developments, and we hope that Managerial Finance *will contribute to continued advances in the theory and practice of finance.*

J. Fred Weston	*Los Angeles, California*
Eugene F. Brigham	*Gainesville, Florida*
December 1980	

Contents

Part One Fundamental Concepts of Managerial Finance

Part One
Fundamental Concepts of Managerial Finance

Part One consists of six chapters. Chapter 1, which describes the scope and nature of managerial finance, serves as an introduction to the book. Chapter 2 develops an overview of the total financial framework within which decisions are made. It deals with the role of the money and capital markets—their international dimensions and their major financing sources—and views the functions of financial managers in the perspective of this broad social framework. Chapter 3 examines the tax system. It emphasizes that since a high percentage of business income is paid to the government, taxes have an important influence on many kinds of business decisions—particularly the form of business organization chosen (proprietorship, partnership, or corporation). Chapter 4 examines the role of the interest rate, or time value of money, in financial decisions. Chapters 5 and 6 provide the risk, return, and valuation framework required for the analytical decision areas covered in the remainder of the book.

1
Scope and Nature of Managerial Finance

What is managerial finance? What is the finance function in the firm? What specific tasks are assigned to financial managers? What tools and techniques are available to them, and how can their performance be measured? On a broader scale, what is the role of finance in the U. S. economy, and how can managerial finance be used to further national goals? Providing at least tentative answers to these questions is the principal purpose of this book.

The Finance Function

Financial management is defined by the functions and responsibilities of financial managers. While the specifics vary among organizations, some finance tasks are basic. Funds are raised from external financial sources and allocated for different uses. The flow of funds in the operations of an enterprise is monitored. Benefits to the financing sources take the form of returns, repayments, products, and services. These key financial functions must be performed in all organizations—from business firms to government units or agencies, aid groups such as the Red Cross or Salvation Army, and other nonprofit organizations such as art museums and theater groups.

The main functions of financial managers are planning for, acquiring, and utilizing funds in ways that maximize the efficiency of the organization's operation. This requires knowledge of the financial markets from which funds are drawn and of how sound investment decisions are made and efficient operations stimulated. Managers must consider a large number of alternative sources and uses of funds in making their financial decisions. They must choose, for example, internal or external funds, long-term or short-term projects, long-term or short-term fund sources, and higher or lower rates of growth.

Up to this point, the discussion of the finance function has applied to all types of organizations. What is unique about business organizations is that they are directly and measurably subject to the discipline of the financial markets. These markets are continuously determining the valuations of business firms' securities, thereby providing measures of the firms' performance.[1] A consequence of the reassessment of managerial performance by the capital markets is the change in relative valuation levels of business firms. That is, changes in valuations signal changes in performance. Therefore, valuations stimulate efficiency and provide business managers with incentives to improve their performance. Testing the efficiency and performance of organizations other than business firms is more difficult because of the lack of financial markets for continuously placing valuations on them and assessing their performance.

Goals of the Firm

The objectives of financial management have been formulated in the context of the valuation processes of the financial markets. The primary goal of financial management is to maximize shareholder wealth. The discipline of the financial markets is implemented by formulating the firm's objectives in terms of the shareholders' interest. Thus firms that perform better than others have higher stock prices and can raise additional funds under more favorable terms. When funds go to firms with favorable stock price trends, the economy's resources are directed to their most efficient uses. Hence, throughout this book we operate on the assumption that management's primary goal is to maximize the wealth of its shareholders.

Most of the finance literature has adopted the basic postulate of maximizing the price of the firm's common stock over the long run. From this postulate, theories have been developed that receive considerable support from empirical tests. Shareholder wealth maximization also provides a basis for rational analysis and actions with respect to a wide range of financial decisions to be made by the firm. However, a number of issues have been raised with reference to the goal of maximizing shareholder wealth.

Profit versus Wealth Maximization

Suppose management is interested primarily in stockholders, making its decisions so as to maximize their welfare. Is profit maximization best for stockholders?

Total Profits. In answering this question, we must consider the matter of total corporate profits versus earnings per share. Suppose a firm raises capital by selling stock and then invests the proceeds in government bonds. Total profits will rise, but more shares will be outstanding. Earnings per share will probably decline, pulling down the value of each share of stock and, hence, the existing stockholders' wealth. Thus, to the extent that profits are impor-

1. The financial markets discussed in Chapter 2 provide valuations of firms whose shares are traded. The relationships between return and risk also provide the basis for the valuation of companies whose ownership shares are not actively traded.

tant, management should concentrate on earnings per share rather than on total corporate profits.

Earnings per Share. Will maximizing earnings per share also maximize stockholder welfare, or should other factors be evaluated? Consider the timing of the earnings. Suppose one project will cause earnings per share to rise by $.20 per year for five years, or $1 in total, while another project has no effect on earnings for four years but increases earnings by $1.25 in the fifth year. Which project is better? The answer depends on which project adds the most to the value of the stock, and this in turn depends on the time value of money to investors. In any event, timing is an important reason to concentrate on wealth as measured by the price of the stock rather than on earnings alone.

Risk. Still another issue relates to risk. Suppose one project is expected to increase earnings by $1 per share while another is expected to increase them by $1.20 per share. The first project is not very risky; if it is undertaken, earnings will almost certainly rise by about $1 per share. The other project is quite risky, so while the best guess is that earnings will rise by $1.20 per share, the possibility exists that there may be no increase whatever. If stockholders are averse to risk, the first project is probably preferable to the second.

Recognizing all these factors, managers interested in maximizing stockholder welfare seek to maximize the value of the firm's common stock. The price of the stock reflects the market's evaluation of the firm's prospective earnings stream over time, the riskiness of this stream, and a host of other factors. The higher the price of the stock, the better management's performance from the standpoint of the stockholders. Thus, market price provides a performance index by which management can be judged.[2]

Managers' versus Stockholders' Goals

A number of people argue that managers substitute their own objectives and welfare in place of those of the stockholders, who are the owners of the firm. They hold that managers come to know more about the firm than its shareholders do and that they control the machinery for electing the board of directors, thereby dominating the board, which in theory is supposed to represent the shareholders. In addition, they argue that managers are interested in the firm's growth or bigness because managers' salaries and other benefits are related to the size of the firm as measured by sales or total assets.

While there is some basis for this view of managerial control, counterarguments are made that managers operate in the interests of their firm's

2. A firm's stock price might, of course, decline because of factors beyond management's control. Accordingly, it is useful to look at comparative statistics. Even though a firm's stock declines by 10 percent, management has performed well if the stock of other firms in the industry declines over the same time period by 20 percent.

owners. One such argument is that the compensation arrangements for managers include bonuses tied to profits and stock options tied to the increasing value of the firm's common stock. A second is that the shareholders have the ultimate power to replace management and that they do, in fact, exercise this power. Just the threat of its use is enough to keep managers oriented to the best interests of the owners of their firm.

M. C. Jensen and W. H. Meckling have developed the most analytical treatment of the relationship between managers and owners.[3] In their formulation, an agency problem arises when a manager owns less than the total common stock of the firm. This fractional ownership can lead the managers to shirk—to enjoy a relaxed, easy life and not work as strenuously as in other circumstances—and to consume more perquisites (luxurious offices, furniture and rugs, company cars) because other owners bear part of the costs. The managers bear only part of the costs but enjoy the full benefits of their consumption activities.

To deal with such agency problems, additional expenditures would be required. These other forms of agency costs include: (1) auditing systems to limit this kind of management behavior, (2) various kinds of bonding assurances by the managers that such abuses will not be practiced, and (3) changes in organization systems to limit the ability of managers to engage in the undesirable practices.

In the Jensen-Meckling model the manager initially owns all of the firm's common stock. Since the model employs a one-period framework, the manager in it makes a single sale of stock to outsiders to finance favorable investment opportunities. But since the stock market expects managers to engage in more shirking and to consume more perquisites as the fraction of their ownership of the equity declines, this is reflected in a reduction in the price at which the shares can be sold.

But clearly everyone will be better off if a manager, as a fractional shareholder, can provide assurances against individual managerial shirking and perquisites. Since in the real world there is a multi-period time framework, managers have the opportunity to establish that they function in the best interests of the firm. One objective test of this is represented by the investment performance and related market evaluation of a firm's shares. E. F. Fama observes that these pressures are reinforced by the managerial labor market through its continuing reassessments of the value of the human capital of managers on the basis of the relationships between their potential or contracted performance and their actual performance.[4]

Many complex interrelationships are involved. Certainly the issue of

3. M. C. Jensen and W. H. Meckling, "Theory of the Firm: Managerial Behavior, Agency Costs and Ownership Structure," *Journal of Financial Economics* 3 (October 1976), pp. 350–360.

4. E. F. Fama, "Agency Problems and the Theory of the Firm," unpublished manuscript, November 1978, pp. 30–31.

agency costs must be taken into account in the theory of the firm. While these costs are an important variable to consider, empirical testing of the theories involved has been limited to date. Our own judgment is that the values of the securities of individual firms probably represent important disciplines for evaluating the performance of managers and other production agents. Also, the markets for the services for each type of contracting factor of production, as well as the competition among firms themselves, provide a discipline for efficient evaluation of the services of each type of contracting agent, including the firm's managers.

Stockholders and Bondholders

The investment decisions of the firm affect the riskiness of its income flows. A more risky investment program will benefit shareholders at the expense of bondholders. Bondholders buy the debt at a price and yield based on their best estimate of the riskiness of the firm's investment programs. If the firm subsequently changes to more risky investment activities, the required market yield on the bonds will rise, causing the current values of the bonds to fall. If the riskier investment programs turn out to be successful, the bondholders do not receive higher returns, but the stockholders benefit.[5]

E. F. Fama demonstrates two forces that help assure the predominance of the maximization of the value of the firm as a goal: the threats of possible takeovers and pricing pressures applied by the market.[6] If the firm has an investment rule other than to maximize the value of the firm, both the value of the bonds and the value of the stock will be lower than under the "maximize the value of the firm" investment rule. The bonds will have less value because they are perceived to be subject to future expropriation as a consequence of changes in the firm's investment programs. The value of the common stock will be lower because the value of the firm as a whole will be lower since the market will on average charge the firm in advance for changes in investment strategies the firm may possibly make. Unless the firm can establish assurance that it will not change its investment strategy in the future, the value of the firm will be lower than otherwise. Accordingly, the bondholders will require larger returns as compensation for the risks of changes in the firm's investment strategy. Outsiders who definitely establish that they will follow the goal of maximizing the value of the firm can then buy the common stock of the firm and increase both the value of the firm as a whole and the value of its common stock.

If the goal is to maximize the value of the firm as a whole, the value of its bonds and of its common stock will also be maximized. In the analysis of financial decisions in subsequent chapters, we will generally be guided by whether the value of the firm and the value of the common stock of the firm

5. The option pricing model discussed in the Appendix A to Chapter 22 formally demonstrates that an increase in the variance of the firm's returns will increase the value of the common stock and decrease the value of the bonds.

6. E. F. Fama, "The Effects of a Firm's Investment and Financing Decisions on the Welfare of its Security Holders," *American Economic Review* 68 (June 1978), pp. 272–284.

are maximized. When we state the goal "maximize the value of the firm's common stock price per share," it is in the sense that management is behaving as a responsible agent for both the shareholders and the bondholders. The goal "maximize share price," as used in this book, is intended also to convey "maximize the value of the firm" so that the value of common stock and debt will also be maximized. Importantly, "maximize share price" is not intended to imply that the managers or shareholders will do anything along the lines of changing investment strategies in the future to the detriment of other groups whose economic position is affected by the performance and value of the firm—bondholders, employees, consumers, and the like.

Maximizing Stockholder Wealth versus Other Goals

Thus far we have considered relationships between managers and stockholders and between stockholders and bondholders. Other factors that may influence the validity of our working hypothesis of the goal of maximizing shareholder wealth will be considered now.

Maximizing versus Satisficing

Consider *maximizing,* which involves seeking the best possible outcome, versus *satisficing,* which involves a willingness to settle for something less. Some argue that the management of a large, well-entrenched corporation can work to keep stockholder returns at a fair or "reasonable" level and then devote part of its efforts and resources to public service activities, employee benefits, higher management salaries, or golf.

Similarly, an entrenched management can avoid risky ventures even when the possible gains to stockholders are high enough to warrant taking the gamble. The theory here is that stockholders are generally well-diversified (holding portfolios of many different stocks), so if one company takes a chance and loses, the stockholders lose only a small part of their wealth. Managers, on the other hand, are not diversified, so setbacks affect them more seriously. Accordingly, some argue that the managers of widely held firms tend to play it safe rather than aggressively seeking to maximize the prices of their firms' stocks.

It is impossible to answer these questions definitively. More and more firms are tying management's compensation to the company's performance, and research suggests that this motivates management to operate in a manner consistent with stock price maximization. Additionally, in recent years tender offers and proxy fights have removed a number of supposedly entrenched managements; the recognition that such actions can take place has doubtless stimulated many firms to attempt to maximize share prices.[7] Finally, compet-

7. A tender offer is a bid by one company to buy the stock of another, while a proxy fight involves an attempt to gain control by getting stockholders to vote a new management group into office. Both actions are facilitated by low stock prices, so self-preservation can lead management to try to keep the stock value as high as possible.

itive pressures force firms to take actions that are reasonably consistent with shareholder wealth maximization. Thus, while other influences may be operating in addition to shareholder wealth maximization, it is a reasonable and useful working hypothesis to view the dominant goal of share price maximization as a basis for developing principles of financial management.

Maximizing Wealth versus Utility

In many formulations, the objective is stated in terms of utility—the satisfactions enjoyed by individuals that result in a set of preferences. But the utility patterns or utility functions of individuals vary greatly. For example, some individuals receive positive gratification from the excitement of exposure to risks; for other individuals even moderate risks cause nervousness or illness. Who is to determine or to interpret the risk attitudes of individual investors? What can the financial manager do if shareholders have widely divergent utility preferences?

Again the capital markets come to the rescue. Whatever the individual attitudes toward risk, the market returns in relation to various measures of risk establish that investors on the average exhibit risk aversion; they consider risk a bad rather than a good thing. Furthermore, capital market relationships make it possible to quantify the relationships between required returns and measures of risk. Methods of valuation are developed from these relationships.

Therefore, the decision criteria and decision rules for financial management are more operational and usable when the analysis is formulated in terms of the objective of shareholder wealth maximization rather than utility maximization.

Social Responsibility

Another viewpoint that deserves consideration is social responsibility. Should businesses operate strictly in stockholders' best interests, or are they also partly responsible for the welfare of society? This is a complex issue with no easy answers. As economic agents whose actions have considerable impact, business firms should take into account the effects of their policies and actions on society as a whole. No one—least of all large firms—can ignore the obligations of responsible citizenship. Furthermore, it may even help a firm's long-run wealth maximization if the firm is viewed as a good corporate citizen making substantial contributions to social welfare. Even more fundamentally, some amount of social responsibility on the part of business firms may be required for the survival of a private enterprise system in which they can operate.

But there are many different views on what is best for society. By what authority do businesses have the right to allocate funds in terms of their own views of the social good? In addition, if some firms attempt to be socially responsible and their costs thereby increase substantially, they will be at a disadvantage if their competitors do not incur the same additional costs. Because of these considerations, an argument can be made that social programs should be formulated through the processes of representative government in our democracy. This implies that most cost-increasing programs should be enacted by the government and put on a mandatory rather than a voluntary basis, at least initially, to ensure that their burden rests uniformly on all businesses.[8]

It is critical that industry and government cooperate in establishing rules for corporate behavior and that firms follow the spirit as well as the letter of the law in their actions. Thus constraints become the rules of the game, and firms should strive to maximize shareholder wealth within the constraints. Throughout the book, we shall assume that managements operate in this manner.

Changing Role of Financial Management

Financial management has undergone significant changes over the years. When finance first emerged as a separate field of study in the early 1900s, the emphasis was on legalistic matters such as mergers, consolidations, the formation of new firms, and the various types of securities issued by corporations. Industrialization was sweeping the country, and the critical problem businesses faced was obtaining capital for expansion. The capital markets were relatively primitive, and transfers of funds from individual savers to businesses were quite difficult. Accounting statements of earnings and asset values were unreliable, and stock trading by insiders and manipulators caused prices to fluctuate wildly; consequently, investors were reluctant to purchase stocks and bonds. In this environment, it is easy to see why finance concentrated so heavily on legal issues relating to the issuance of securities.

The emphasis remained on securities through the 1920s; however, radical changes occurred during the depression of the 1930s. Business failures during that period caused finance to focus on bankruptcy and reorganization, corporate liquidity, and government regulation of securities markets. Finance was still a descriptive, legalistic subject, but the emphasis shifted to survival rather than expansion.

During the 1940s and early 1950s, finance continued to be taught as a descriptive, institutional subject, viewed from the outside rather than from within the firm's management. However, some effort was devoted to budgeting and other internal control procedures, and, stimulated by the work of Joel Dean, capital budgeting began to receive attention.[9]

The evolutionary pace quickened during the late 1950s. While the right-hand side of the balance sheet (liabilities and capital) had received more attention in the earlier era, increasing emphasis was placed on asset analysis during the last half of that decade. Mathematical models were developed and

8. What is first imposed by government may be too much and too fast, and after some experience the requirements may be modified. An example is the initial requirement of seat belts interlocked so that a car could not be started until the seat belts were fastened. This requirement was later modified.

9. Joel Dean, *Capital Budgeting* (New York: Columbia University Press, 1951).

applied to inventories, cash, accounts receivable, and fixed assets. Increasingly, the focus of finance shifted from the outsider's to the insider's point of view, as financial decisions within the firm were recognized as the critical issues in corporate finance. Descriptive, institutional materials on capital markets and financing instruments were still studied, but these topics were considered within the context of corporate financial decisions.

The emphasis on decision making has continued in recent years. The first factor that accounts for this is the increasing belief that sound capital budgeting procedures require accurate measurements of the cost of capital. Accordingly, ways of quantifying the cost of capital now play a key role in finance. Second, capital has been in short supply, rekindling the old emphasis on ways of raising funds. Third, there has been continued merger activity, which has led to renewed interest in take-overs. Fourth, accelerated progress in transportation and communications has brought the countries of the world closer together; this in turn has stimulated interest in international finance. Fifth, inflation is now recognized as a critical problem, as so much of the financial manager's time is presently devoted to coping with high wages, prices, and interest rates while stock prices are relatively low. Finally, there is an increasing awareness of social ills such as air and water pollution, urban blight, and unemployment among minorities. Finding the firm's realistic role in efforts to solve these problems demands much of the financial manager's attention.

The Impact of Inflation on Financial Management

During the 1950s and 1960s prices rose at an average rate of about 1½ to 2 percent per year, but in the 1970s the rate of inflation in some years was more than 10 percent. The U.S. economy entered the 1980s with inflation again at a double-digit rate. This *double-digit inflation rate* has had a tremendous impact on business firms, especially on their financial operations. As a result, many established financial policies and practices have experienced dramatic changes, some of which are outlined here.

1. *Interest rates.* The rate of interest on U.S. government securities (called the default-free rate) consists of a "real rate of interest" of 1 to 3 percent plus an "inflation premium" that reflects the expected long-run rate of inflation. Accordingly, an increase in the rate of inflation is quickly translated into higher default-free interest rates. The cost of money to firms is the default-free rate plus a risk premium, so inflation-induced increases in the default-free rate are also reflected in business borrowing rates.
2. *Planning difficulties.* Businesses operate on the basis of long-run plans. For example, a firm builds a plant only after making a thorough analysis of expected costs and revenues over the life of the plant. Reaching such estimates is not easy under the best of conditions, but during rapid inflation, when labor and materials costs are changing dramatically, accurate forecasts are especially important yet exceedingly hard to make. Efforts are, of course, being made to improve forecasting techniques, and finan-

cial planners now realize that they must include more flexibility to reflect the increased level of uncertainty in the economy. The increased uncertainty in many industries tends to raise the risk premiums for firms in those industries, driving their costs of capital still higher.

3. *Demand for capital.* Inflation increases the amount of capital required to conduct a given volume of business. Sold inventories must be replaced with more expensive goods. The costs of expanding or replacing plants also increase, while workers demand higher wages. All these things put pressure on financial managers to raise additional capital. At the same time, in an effort to hold down the rate of inflation, the Federal Reserve System tends to restrict the supply of loanable funds. The ensuing scramble for limited funds drives interest rates still higher.

4. *Bond price declines.* Long-term bond prices fall as interest rates rise, so, in an effort to protect themselves against such capital losses, lenders are beginning (a) to put more funds into short-term rather than long-term debt, and (b) to insist on bonds whose interest rates vary with "the general level of interest rates" as measured by an index of interest rates. Brazil and other inflation-plagued South American countries have used such index bonds for years. Unless inflation in the United States is controlled, their use is likely to increase in this country.

5. *Investment planning.* High interest rates, as well as a general shortage of capital, are causing firms to be especially wary in planning long-term investment outlays. Indeed, headlines such as "ABC Company Cuts Spending Plans $106 Million Because of Difficulties in Raising Funds" or "XYZ Company to Fight Cash Shortage by Sale-Leaseback of Coal Equipment" have become commonplace. But as one financial executive expressed it, "Sure, we want to defer what we can, but we don't want to fall victim to a start-stop mentality. If we put off too much capital spending because of interest costs, we won't have capacity and labor-saving devices when the economy turns up."

6. *Accounting problems.* With high rates of inflation, reported profits are distorted. The sale of low-cost inventories results in higher reported profits, but cash flows are held down as firms restock with higher-cost inventories. Similarly, depreciation charges are inadequate, since they do not reflect the new costs of replacing facilities and equipment. If a firm is unaware of the shakiness of profits that reflect inaccurate inventory valuation and inadequate depreciation charges, and if it plans dividends and capital expenditures on the basis of such figures, then it can develop serious financial problems.

Inflation, particularly in the dramatically high and volatile proportions of the early 1980s, is a disturbing and challenging new experience for United States financial managers. If it continues, financial policies and practices will continue to be modified.

Organization of a Firm's Finance Department

In the typical firm, the chief financial officer, who has the title of vice-president for finance, reports to the chief executive officer; and two key officers, the treasurer and the controller, are accountable to the vice-president for finance. The treasurer's staff is responsible for raising capital, dealing with suppliers of capital, and forming the firm's credit policy. The controller's staff is responsible for the accounting and budgeting systems, including capital budgeting. In a sense, the treasurer handles the outside finance functions and the controller the inside functions, while the vice-president for finance has the overall responsibility for both.

Financial Decisions

Financial decisions affect the value of a firm's stock by influencing both the size of the earnings stream, or profitability, and the riskiness of the firm. These relationships are diagrammed in Figure 1.1. Policy decisions, which are subject to government constraints, affect both profitability and risk; these two factors jointly determine the value of the firm.

The primary policy decision is that of choosing the industry in which to operate—the product-market mix of the firm. When this choice has been made, both profitability and risk are determined by decisions relating to the size of the firm, the types of equipment used, the extent to which debt is employed, the firm's liquidity position, and so on. Such decisions generally affect both risk and profitability. An increase in the cash position, for instance, reduces risk; however, since cash is not an earning asset, converting other assets to cash also reduces profitability. Similarly, the use of additional debt raises the rate of return, or the profitability, on the stockholders' net worth; at the same time, more debt means more risk. The financial manager seeks to strike the particular balance between risk and profitability that will maximize the wealth of the firm's stockholders—called the *risk-return tradeoff*. As we shall see in subsequent chapters, most financial decisions involve such trade-offs.

Figure 1.1

Valuation as the Central Focus of the Finance Function

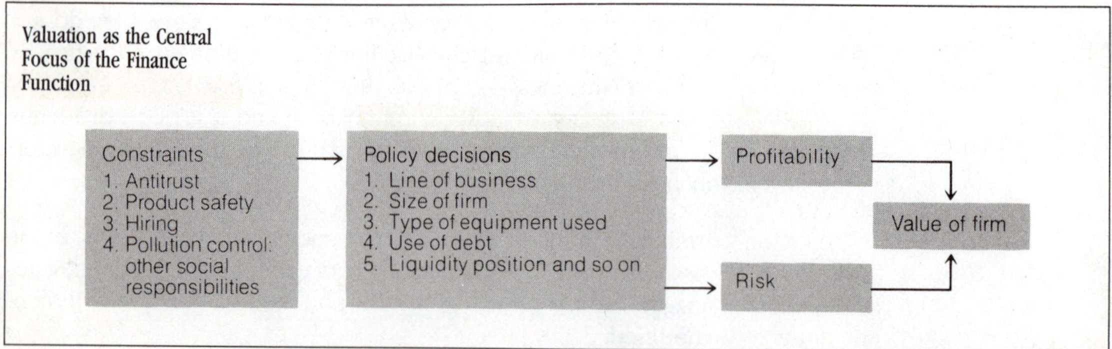

Organization and Structure of This Book

The optimal structure for a finance text must include a number of theoretical and applied factors. The order in which theory and application are presented is a decision problem. On the one hand, it is desirable to set out theoretical structures first, using the theory in later sections to explain behavior and to attack the problem of real-world decision making. On the other hand, it is easier to understand the theoretical concepts of finance if one has a working knowledge of certain institutional details. The seven parts of this book, outlined here, seek to balance both considerations. The parts are:

1. Fundamental concepts of managerial finance.
2. Financial analysis, planning, and control.
3. Working capital management.
4. Investment decisions.
5. Cost of capital and valuation.
6. Long-term financing.
7. Integrated topics in managerial finance.

To outline the logic of the flow of the materials, Part 1 includes basic tools such as tax laws and the use of interest rates. It also provides an overview of risk, return, and valuation relationships. Part 2 covers financial analysis, financial models of the firm, and planning and control systems. It provides a foundation for Part 3, which covers all aspects of working capital management.

Part 4 turns to the investment decisions of the firm in the framework of capital budgeting under certainty and under uncertainty. Part 5 takes up the cost of capital concepts required both for capital budgeting analysis and for the valuation of the firm.

With the analytic framework established, the long-term financing decisions of the firm are treated in Part 6. This part provides a review of the financial structure issues discussed in the cost of capital materials, but in a setting related to individual financial decisions. The increasingly important uses of warrants, convertibles, and other forms of options are developed. Finally, in Part 7, the general concepts and principles are applied in the areas of mergers, reorganization, small firm finance, and international business finance.

Questions

1.1 What are the main functions of financial managers?

1.2 Why is wealth maximization a better operating goal than profit maximization?

1.3 What role does utility maximization perform in finance theory?

1.4 What role does social responsibility have in formulating business and financial goals?

1.5 What have been the major developmental periods in the field of finance, and what circumstances led to the evolution of the emphasis in each period?

1.6 What is the nature of the risk-return trade-off faced in financial decision making?

Selected References

Anthony, Robert N. "The Trouble with Profit Maximization." *Harvard Business Review* 38 (November–December 1960), pp. 126–134.

Branch, Ben. "Corporate Objectives and Market Performance." *Financial Management* 2 (Summer 1973), pp. 24–29.

Ciscel, David H., and Carroll, Thomas M. "The Determinants of Executive Salaries: An Econometric Survey." *Review of Economics and Statistics* 62 (February 1980), pp. 7–13.

Cooley, Phillip L. "Managerial Pay and Financial Performances of Small Business." *Journal of Business* 7 (September 1979), pp. 267–276.

Davis, Keith. "Social Responsibility Is Inevitable." *California Management Review* 19 (Fall 1976), pp. 14–20.

De Alessi, Louis. "Private Property and Dispersion of Ownership in Large Corporations." *Journal of Finance* 28 (September 1973), pp. 839–851.

Donaldson, Gordon. "Financial Goals: Management versus Stockholders." *Harvard Business Review* 41 (May–June 1963), pp. 116–129.

Elliott, J. W. "Control, Size, Growth, and Financial Performance in the Firm." *Journal of Financial and Quantitative Analysis* 7 (January 1972), pp. 1309–1320.

Findlay, Chapman M., and Whitmore, G. A. "Beyond Shareholder Wealth Maximization." *Financial Management* 3 (Winter 1974), pp. 25–35.

Friend, Irwin. "Recent Developments in Finance." *Journal of Banking and Finance* 1 (October 1977), pp. 103–117.

Gerstner, Louis V., and Anderson, M. Helen. "The Chief Financial Officer as Activist." *Harvard Business Review* 54 (September–October 1976), pp. 100–106.

Grabowski, Henry G., and Mueller, Dennis C. "Managerial and Stockholder Welfare Models of Firm Expenditures." *Review of Economics and Statistics* 54 (February 1972), pp. 9–24.

Grossman, S. J., and Stiglitz, J. E. "On Value Maximization and Alternative Objectives of the Firm." *Journal of Finance* 32 (May 1977), pp. 389–415.

Hakansson, Nils H. "The Fantastic World of Finance: Progress and the Free Lunch." *Journal of Financial and Quantitative Analysis* 14 (November 1979), pp. 717–734.

Hill, Lawrence W. "The Growth of the Corporate Finance Function." *Financial Executive* 44 (July 1976), pp. 38–43.

Levy, Haim, and Sarnat, Marshall. "A Pedagogic Note on Alternative Formulations of the Goal of the Firm." *Journal of Business* 50 (October 1977), pp. 526–528.

Lewellen, Wilbur G. "Management and Ownership in the Large Firm." *Journal of Finance* 24 (May 1969), pp. 299–322.

Masson, Robert Tempest. "Executive Motivations, Earnings, and Consequent Equity Performance." *Journal of Political Economy* 79 (November–December 1971), pp. 1278–1292.

Mobraaten, William L. "Social Responsibility of the Treasurer." In *The Treasurer's Handbook.* Edited by J. Fred Weston and Maurice B. Goudzwaard. Homewood, Ill.: Dow Jones–Irwin, 1976, pp. 1144–1163.

Salamon, G. L., and Smith, E. D. "Corporate Control and Managerial Misrepresentation of Firm Performance." *Bell Journal of Economics* 10 (Spring 1979), pp. 319–328.

Scanlon, John J. "Bell System Financial Policies." *Financial Management* 1 (Summer 1972), pp. 16–26.

Trivoli, George W. "Evaluation of Pollution Control Expenditures by Leading Corporations." *Financial Management* 2 (Winter 1973), pp. 19–24.

Weston, J. Fred. "New Themes in Finance." *Journal of Finance* 24 (March 1974), pp. 237–243.

———. *The Scope and Methodology of Finance.* Englewood Cliffs, N. J.: Prentice-Hall, 1966.

———. "Toward Theories of Financial Policy." *Journal of Finance* 10 (May 1955), pp. 130–143.

2
The Financial Sector of the Economy

An important part of the environment within which financial managers function is the financial sector of the economy, which consists of financial markets, financial institutions, and financial instruments. This chapter will discuss each of the three aspects of the sector.

Financial Markets

In Figure 2.1, the financial manager is shown linking the financing of an organization to its financing sources via the financial markets. The major parts of this figure will be explained throughout the discussion of the finance function. Funds for conducting organizational operations are obtained from a wide range of financial institutions in such forms as loans, bonds, and common stocks. The financial manager has primary responsibility for acquiring funds and participates in allocating them among alternative projects and specific uses, such as inventories, plant, and equipment. The cash flow cycle must be managed. Payments must be made for labor, materials, and capital goods purchased from the external markets. Products and services that generate fund inflows must be created. In the management of cash inflows and outflows, some cash is recycled and some is returned to financing sources.

The financial manager functions in a complex financial network because the savings and investment functions in a modern economy are performed by different economic agents. For savings surplus units, savings exceed their investment in real assets, and they own financial assets. For savings deficit units, current savings are less than investment in real assets, so they issue financial liabilities. The savings deficit units issue a wide variety of financial claims, including promissory notes, bonds, and common stocks.

The transfer of funds from a savings surplus unit or the acquisition of funds by a savings deficit unit involves the creation of a financial asset and a financial liability. For example, when a person places funds in a savings account in a bank or a savings and loan association, the deposit represents a financial asset on the personal balance sheet, and the account holder adds it to real assets such as automobiles or household goods. The savings deposit is a liability account for the financial institution, representing a financial lia-

Figure 2.1

Financial Markets, the Financial Manager, and the Firm

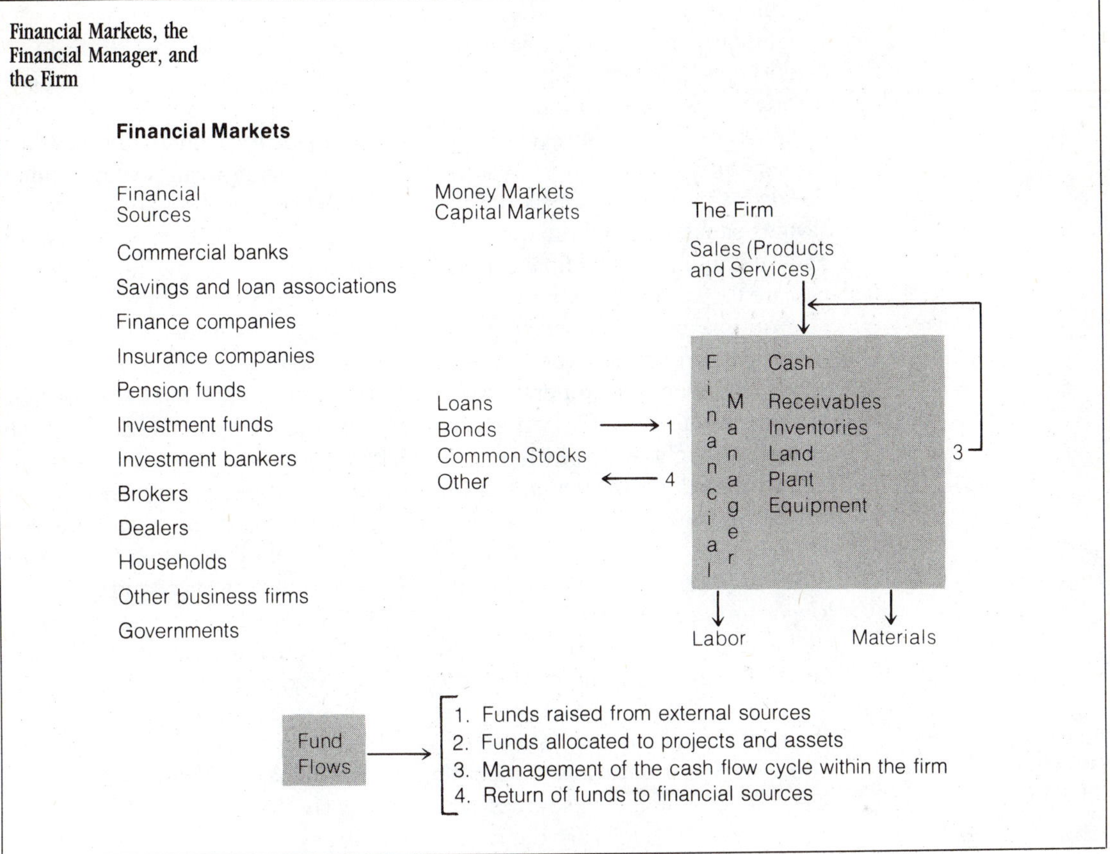

bility. When the funds are loaned to another person for, say, the purchase of a home, the loan by the financial institution represents a financial asset on its balance sheet. The borrower incurs a financial liability, represented by the loan owed to the financial institution. Consider another example. When a person buys goods on credit from a department store, the purchase price is added to "accounts receivable" on the store's books. The amount payable by the person who has purchased goods on credit represents a financial liability incurred by that person.

A financial transaction results in the simultaneous creation of a financial asset and a financial liability. The creation and transfer of such assets and liabilities constitute *financial markets.* The nature of financial markets can be further explained by analogy to the market for actual goods, such as automobiles. The *automobile market* is defined by all transactions in automobiles, whether they occur at auto dealers' showrooms, at wholesale auctions of used cars, or at individuals' homes. These transactions all constitute the automobile market because they make up part of the total demand and supply curves for autos.

Similarly, financial markets are comprised of all trades that result in the creation of financial assets and financial liabilities. Some trades are made through organized institutions such as the New York Stock Exchange or the regional stock exchanges. A large number are made through the thousands of brokers and dealers who buy and sell securities, comprising what is called the *over-the-counter market.* Individual transactions with department stores, savings banks, or other financial institutions also create financial assets and financial liabilities. Thus financial markets are not specific physical structures; nor are they remote. Everyone is involved in them to some degree.

Continuing the auto analogy, just as a distinction is made between a new car market and a used car market because somewhat different demand and supply influences are operating in each, different segments of the financial markets are also categorized and named. When the financial claims and obligations bought and sold have a maturity of less than one year, the transactions constitute *money markets.* When the maturities of the instruments traded are more than one year, the markets are referred to as *capital markets.* The latter term is somewhat confusing because real capital in an economy is represented by things—for example, plants, machinery, and equipment. But long-term financial instruments are regarded as ultimately representing claims on the real resources in an economy, and for that reason the markets in which these instruments are traded are referred to as capital markets.

Financing Sources and Financial Intermediation

The financial markets, composed of money markets and capital markets, provide a mechanism through which the financial manager obtains funds from a wide range of financing sources, shown in Figure 2.1.

Commercial banks are defined by their ability to accept demand deposits subject to transfer by depositors' checks. Such checks represent a widely accepted medium of exchange, accounting for over 90 percent of the transactions that take place. Savings and loan associations receive funds from passbook savings and invest them primarily in real estate mortgages that represent long-term borrowing, mostly by individuals. Finance companies are business firms whose main activity is making loans to other business firms and to individuals. Life insurance companies sell protection against the loss of income from premature death or disability. The insurance policies they sell typically have a savings element in them. Pension funds collect contributions from employees and/or employers to make periodic payments upon employees' retirement. Investment funds, which are also called mutual funds, sell shares to investors and use the proceeds to purchase already existing equity securities.

Investment bankers are financial firms that buy new issues of securities from business firms at a guaranteed agreed-upon price and seek immediately to resell the securities to other investors. Related financial firms that function simply as agents linking buyers and sellers are called investment brokers.

Investment dealers are those who purchase for their own account from sellers and ultimately resell to other buyers. While investment bankers (discussed in Chapter 18) operate in the new issues market, brokers and dealers engage in transactions in already issued securities. Other sources of funds are households, other business firms, and governments. At any point in time some of these will be borrowers and others lenders.

Financial intermediation is accomplished through transactions in the financial markets that bring the savings surplus units together with the savings deficit units so that savings can be redistributed into their most productive uses. The specialized business firms whose activities include the creation of financial assets and liabilities are called financial intermediaries. Without these intermediaries and the processes of financial intermediation, the allocation of savings into real investment would be limited by whatever the distribution of savings happened to be. With financial intermediation, savings are transferred to economic units that have opportunities for profitable investment. In the process, real resources are allocated more effectively, and real output for the economy as a whole is increased.

Financial managers have important responsibilities in the financial intermediation process. They are the part of the process by which funds are allocated to their most productive uses. Therefore, the functions of financial managers can now be restated in the perspective of this broader social framework. In the aggregate, business firms are savings deficit units that obtain funds to make investments to increase the supply of goods and services. Financial managers utilize financial markets to obtain external funds. How should the funds be acquired efficiently? What is the most economical mix of financing to be obtained? From what alternative sources and in what specific forms should the funds be raised? What should be the timing and forms of returns and repayments to financing sources?

Since funds are acquired as part of the process by which resources are allocated to their most productive uses, financial managers have the responsibility to use the funds effectively. To what projects and products should the funds be allocated? What assets and resources should the organization acquire in order to produce its products and services? What standards and controls should monitor the effective utilization of funds allocated among the segments of operating activities? How should the planning and control of funds be managed so that the organization will produce and sell its products and services most efficiently? The financial manager's major responsibility is to implement these choices in the various financial markets to meet the firm's capital requirements.

Types of Financial Assets

Financial institutions make use of three major types of financial assets: money, stock, and debt. *Money* is issued by the U.S. Treasury as coins and paper currency. The central bank, the Federal Reserve System, interacts with the commercial banking system in creating the demand deposits (the familiar checking accounts) by which about 90 percent of commercial transactions are conducted. *Stock* generally means common stock, which represents ownership of a firm. *Debt* represents a promise to pay to the creditor a specified amount plus interest at a future date.

The Federal Reserve System

Fundamental to an understanding of the behavior of the money and capital markets is an analysis of the role of the Federal Reserve System. The Fed, as it is called, has a set of instruments with which to influence the operations of commercial banks, whose loan and investment activities in turn have an important influence on the cost and availability of money. The most powerful of the Fed's instruments, hence the one used most sparingly, is changing reserve requirements (the percentage of deposits that must be kept in reserve with the Fed). The one most often used is changing the pattern of open-market operations (the Fed's buying and selling of securities, which expands and contracts the amount of funds in the public's hands).

Changes in the discount rate (the interest rate charged to commercial banks when they borrow from Federal Reserve Banks) are likely to have more psychological influence than direct quantitative effect. These changes represent an implicit announcement by Federal Reserve authorities that a change in economic conditions has occurred and that the new conditions call for a tightening or easing of monetary conditions. The data demonstrate that increases in the Federal Reserve Bank discount rate have been followed by rising interest rate levels and decreases by lowered levels. When the Federal Reserve System purchases or sells securities in the open market, makes changes in the discount rate, or varies the reserve requirement, this procedure changes the interest rates on most securities.

Fiscal Policy

The fiscal policy of the federal government has great impact on movements in interest rates. A cash budget deficit represents a stimulating influence by the federal government, and a cash surplus exerts a restraining influence. However, this generalization must be modified to reflect the way a deficit is financed and the way a surplus is used. To have the most stimulating effect, a deficit should be financed by a sale of securities through the banking system, particularly the central bank; this provides a maximum amount of bank reserves and permits a multiple expansion in the money supply. To have the most restrictive effect, the surplus should be used to retire bonds held by the banking system, particularly the central bank, thereby reducing bank reserves and causing a multiple contraction in the supply of money.

The impact of Treasury financing programs varies. Ordinarily, when the Treasury needs to draw funds from the money market, it competes with other potential users of funds; the result may be a rise in interest rate levels. However, the desire to hold down interest rates also influences Treasury and Federal Reserve policy. To ensure the success of a large new offering, Federal Reserve authorities may temporarily ease money conditions—a procedure that tends to soften interest rates. If the Treasury encounters resistance in selling securities in the nonbanking sector, it may sell them in large volume to the commercial banking system, a move that expands its reserves and thereby increases the monetary base. This change in turn tends to lower the level of interest rates.

Securities Markets

Within the framework of the broad functions of financial intermediation and the monetary and fiscal policies briefly summarized in the preceding sections is another important institution in the operation of the financial system—the securities markets. One basis for classifying securities markets is the distinction between *primary markets,* in which stocks and bonds are initially sold, and *secondary markets,* in which they are subsequently traded. Initial sales of securities are made by investment banking firms, which purchase them from the issuing firm and sell them through an underwriting syndicate or group. Subsequent transactions take place on organized securities exchanges or in less formal markets. The operations of securities markets provide a framework within which the nature of investment banking and the new issues market (discussed in Chapter 15) can be understood. Accordingly, the organized security exchanges, the over-the-counter markets, the third market, and the fourth market will be discussed in this section.

The major exchange is the New York Stock Exchange (NYSE), on which about 1,500 common stocks are listed, accounting for over 80 percent of the almost $200 billion of annual dollar volume of trading and somewhat less than 80 percent of the over 6 billion annual share volume of trading. The American Stock Exchange, with 1,300 stocks traded, is second in volume, accounting for under 10 percent of dollar volume and somewhat over 10 percent of share volume. Some 350 stocks are traded on one or more of the eleven registered regional exchanges, accounting for about 2 to 5 percent of volume in the three largest regional exchanges and less than 1 percent of total volume in the remaining eight.

The organized security exchanges are tangible physical entities. Each of the larger ones occupies its own building and has specifically designated members and an elected governing body—its board of governors. Members are said to have seats on the exchange (although everybody stands up). These seats, which are bought and sold, represent the right to trade on the exchange. In 1968, seats on the NYSE sold at a record high of $515,000; in 1974 they sold for about $85,000. During 1978 they ranged between $46,000 and $105,000.[1]

Most of the larger stockbrokerage firms own seats on the exchanges and

1. New York Stock Exchange, *1979 Fact Book* (New York: New York Stock Exchange, 1979), p. 54.

designate one or more of their officers as members of the exchange. The exchanges are open daily, and the members meet in a large room equipped with telephones and telegraphs that enable each brokerage house member to communicate with the firm's offices throughout the country.

Like other markets, a security exchange facilitates communication between buyers and sellers. For example, Merrill Lynch, Pierce, Fenner & Smith, which is the largest brokerage firm, may receive an order in its Atlanta office from a customer who wants to buy 100 shares of General Motors stock. Simultaneously, a brokerage house in Denver may receive an order from a customer wishing to sell 100 shares of GM stock. Each broker communicates by wire with the firm's representative on the NYSE. Other brokers throughout the country are also communicating with their own exchange members. Members with sell orders offer the shares for sale, and they are bid for by members with buy orders. Thus, the exchanges operate as *auction markets.*[2]

Benefits Provided by Security Exchanges

Organized security exchanges are said to provide at least four important benefits to businesses.

1. Security exchanges facilitate the investment process by providing a marketplace in which to conduct efficient and relatively inexpensive transactions. Investors are thus assured that they will have a place in which to sell their securities if they decide to do so. The increased liquidity provided by the exchanges makes investors willing to accept a lower rate of return on securities than they would otherwise require. This means that exchanges lower the cost of capital to businesses.
2. By providing a market, exchanges create an institution in which continuous transactions test the values of securities. The purchases and sales of securities record judgments on the values and prospects of companies. Those whose prospects are judged favorably by the investment community have higher values, which facilitate new financing and growth.
3. Security prices are relatively more stable because of the operation of the security exchanges. Organized markets improve liquidity by providing continuous markets that make for more frequent but smaller price changes. In the absence of organized markets, price changes are less frequent but more violent.
4. The securities markets aid in the digestion of new security issues and facilitate their successful flotation.

Although these benefits are important, not all firms can use them. However, some firms that cannot utilize the exchanges can get many of the same benefits by having their securities traded in the over-the-counter market.

The securities markets are in a state of flux. After four years of research

2. This discussion is highly simplified. The exchanges have members, known as *specialists,* who facilitate the trading process by keeping an inventory of shares of the stocks in which they specialize. If a buy order comes in at a time when no sell order arrives, the specialist may sell off some inventory. Similarly, if a sell order comes in, the specialist will buy and add to inventory.

and investigation, Congress enacted the Securities Acts Amendments of 1975.[3] This new law departs from the concept of self-regulation that had previously been followed in the relationships between the government and the securities industry. It states that no national securities exchange can impose a schedule of minimum fixed commission rates. While it is still too early to judge its impact, one likely effect of this law is the "unbundling" of joint services such as research reports from the buying and selling activities provided by brokerage firms.

The new law also provides for the development of a national market system. Two concepts of a central market system have emerged. One, sponsored by the NYSE, envisions a single trading exchange. The other sees competitive trading in a number of places linked together by a system of communications, including clearing and settlement facilities. The SEC is empowered to exercise leadership in developing a central market system.

Over-the-Counter (OTC) Security Markets

Over-the-counter security markets is the term used for all the buying and selling activity in securities that does not take place on a stock exchange. The OTC market includes stocks of all types and for all sizes of U.S. corporations, as well as some foreign issues. In the OTC market there are approximately 30,000 common stocks of public corporations, but only about 10,000 are actively traded. This is about three times the number of companies listed on the organized exchanges. In addition, the OTC market is where transactions take place in (1) almost all bonds of U.S. corporations; (2) almost all bonds of federal, state, and local governments; (3) open-end investment company shares of mutual funds; (4) new issues of securities; (5) most secondary distributions of large blocks of stock, regardless of whether they are listed on an exchange; and (6) stocks of most of the country's banks and insurance companies.

The exchanges operate as auction markets; the trading process is achieved through agents making transactions at one geographically centralized exchange location. On an exchange, firms known as specialists are responsible for matching buy and sell orders and for maintaining an orderly market in a particular security. In contrast, the OTC market is a dealer market—that is, business is conducted across the country by broker/dealers known as *market makers.* These dealers stand ready to buy and sell securities in a manner similar to wholesale suppliers of goods or merchandise. The exchanges are used to match buy and sell orders that come in more or less simultaneously. But if a stock is traded less frequently, perhaps because it is a new or a small firm, matching buy and sell orders might require an extended period of time. To avoid this problem, some broker/dealer firms maintain an inventory of stocks. They buy when individual investors want to sell and sell when investors want to buy. At one time these securities were kept in a safe; when they were bought and sold, they were literally passed over the counter.

3. The original Securities Acts of 1933 and 1934, which established the Securities and Exchange Commission (SEC) for federal regulation of the financial markets, are discussed in Chapter 18.

The brokers and dealers operating in the OTC markets communicate through a network of private wires and telephone lines and, since 1971, by an electronic quotation system called NASDAQ, whose letters stand for the National Association of Securities Dealers Automated Quotation system. NASDAQ is a computerized system that enables current price quotations to be displayed on terminals in subscribers' offices.

The term *third market* refers to OTC trading in listed securities by nonmembers of an exchange. It generally represents trades of large blocks of listed stocks off the floor of the exchange, with a brokerage house acting as intermediary between two institutional investors.

The *fourth market* refers to direct transfers of blocks of stock among institutional investors without an intermediary broker. A well known example is the arrangement between the Ford Foundation and the Rockefeller Foundation to exchange the common stocks of the Ford Motor Company and Standard Oil of New Jersey. Such transactions have led to the development of *Instinet,* a computerized quotation system with display terminals to provide communications among major institutional investors.

The development of the third and fourth markets reflects the increased importance of institutional investors in stock trading. During the decade of the 1960s, for example, the equity holdings of private, noninsured pension funds rose by over 500 percent, of state and local retirement funds by over 2,800 percent, and of investment companies (mutual funds) by over 300 percent. New York Stock Exchange studies indicate that by the mid-1970s these institutions held a third of NYSE-listed stocks and accounted for over half the dollar volume on the NYSE.

In terms of numbers of issues only, the majority of stocks are traded over the counter. However, because the stocks of larger companies are listed on the exchanges, it is estimated that two-thirds of the dollar volume of stock trading takes place on the exchanges. The situation is reversed in the bond market. Although the bonds of a number of the larger companies are listed on the NYSE bond list, over 95 percent of bond transactions take place in the OTC market. The reason for this is that bonds typically are traded among the large financial institutions (for example, life insurance companies and pension funds), which deal in very large blocks of securities. It is relatively easy for the OTC bond dealers to arrange the transfer of large blocks of bonds among the relatively few holders of the bonds. It would be impossible to conduct similar operations among the literally millions of large and small holders in the stock market.

Decision to List Stock

Firms must meet certain exchange requirements before their stock can be listed; these requirements relate to size of company, number of years in business, earnings record, number of shares outstanding and their market value, and the like. In general, requirements become more stringent if viewed on a spectrum ranging from the regional exchanges toward the NYSE.

The firm itself makes the decision on whether to seek to list its securities on an exchange. Typically, the stock of a new and small company is traded over the counter; there is simply not enough activity to justify the use of an auction market for such stocks. As the company grows and establishes an earnings record, expands its number of shares outstanding, and increases its list of stockholders, it may decide to apply for listing on one of the regional exchanges. For example, a Chicago company may list on the Midwest Stock Exchange and a West Coast company on the Pacific Coast Exchange. As the company grows still more and its stock becomes distributed throughout the country, it may seek a listing on the American Stock Exchange, the smaller of the two national exchanges. Finally, if it becomes one of the nation's leading firms, it may, if it qualifies, switch to the Big Board—the New York Stock Exchange.

Many people believe that listing is beneficial to both the company and its stockholders. Listed companies receive a certain amount of free advertising and publicity, and the status of being listed enhances their prestige and reputations. This probably has a beneficial effect on the sales of the firms' products, and it is advantageous in terms of lowering the required rate of return on the common stock. Investors respond favorably to increased information, increased liquidity, and increased prestige; by providing investors with these services in the form of listing their companies' stocks, financial managers lower their firms' costs of capital.[4]

Stock Market Reporting

Securities traded on the organized security exchanges are called *listed securities;* they are distinguished from *unlisted securities,* which are traded in the over-the-counter market.

Considerable information is available on transactions among listed securities, and the very existence of this information reduces the uncertainty inherent in security investments. This reduction of uncertainty, of course, makes listed securities relatively attractive to investors, and it lowers the cost of capital to firms. We cannot delve deeply into the matter of financial reporting (which is more properly the field of investment analysis), but we will attempt to explain the most widely used service—the New York Stock Exchange reporting system.

Figure 2.2 is a section of the stock market page taken from the *Wall Street Journal* reporting of NYSE-Composite Transactions, which include trades on five regional exchanges and those reported by the National Association of Securities Dealers and Instinet. Stocks are listed alphabetically, with those whose names consist of capital letters listed first. The items are explained by

4. Banks earlier had a tradition against listing their stocks. The historic reason was fear that a falling market price for their stocks could lead depositors to think a particular bank was in danger, causing a run on the bank. Some basis for such fears may have existed before the creation of the Federal Deposit Insurance Corporation in 1935, but that fear is no longer justified. The other reason for banks not listing has to do with the reporting of financial information. The exchanges require that quarterly financial statements be sent to all stockholders; banks have been reluctant to provide financial information. Increasingly, bank regulatory agencies are requiring public disclosure of additional financial information. As this trend continues, it is expected that banks will increasingly seek to list their securities on exchanges. A notable first is the Chase Manhattan Bank, which was listed on the New York Stock Exchange in 1965.

Figure 2.2

Stock Market Transactions

52 Weeks High	Low	Stock	Div.	Yld %	P-E Ratio	Sales 100s	High	low	Close	Net Chg.
		— A—A—A —								
43¼	27½	ACF	2.24	7.8	5	1353	28⅝	27½	28⅝	+1⅛
18⅜	11½	AMF	1.24	9.9	5	195	12½	12	12½	+ ⅝
20	12½	AM Intl	.28	1.8	..	253	15⅞	14⅝	15¾	+1¼
12¼	7⅞	APL	1	12.	30	16	8⅜	8⅛	8⅜	+ ¼
40⅛	24¾	ARA	1.82	6.5	5	163	28	26¾	28	+1¼
54⅞	24	ASA	3.15e	8.1	..	496	39⅝	38½	38⅞	+1⅜
12⅜	8⅛	ATO	.60	6.2	4	32	9⅞	9½	9¾	+ ⅛
31¾	17	AVX s	.32	1.4	11	195	23½	22½	23½	+2
43⅜	30¾	AbbtLb	1.20	3.0	13	290	39½	38⅝	39½	+1¼
34¼	17½	AcmeC	1.40	6.7	4	67	21¼	19¾	20¾	− ¾
4⅞	2¾	AdmDg	.04	1.4	5	9	3	2⅞	2⅞	− ⅛
14½	11	AdaEx	1.49e	13.	..	44	11⅝	11⅜	11⅝	+ ½
6⅛	3⅝	AdmMl	.20e	5.2	8	6	3⅞	3⅞	3⅞	− ⅛
46⅜	26⅞	AMD n		..	10	734	31¼	28½	30¾	+3¼
36⅞	28⅝	AetnLf	s2.12	6.1	5	1004	35	34½	35	+1⅜
28¼	15	Ahmans	1.20	7.0	3	16	17⅛	16¾	17⅛	+ ⅛
3¼	2	Aileen		..	..	11	2⅛	2⅛	2⅛	+ ⅛
43⅛	26½	AirPrd	.80	2.3	9	438	35¼	33	35¼	+2½
28¼	16⅛	AirbFrt	1.20	7.3	8	47	16½	16⅜	16½	.....
17½	7¾	Akzona	.80	8.1	6	36	9⅞	9⅜	9⅞	+ ⅜
8¼	5½	AlaP dpf	.87	12.	..	25	7	6¾	7	+ ¼
84	58½	AlaP pf	9	14.	..	z500	66	65¼	65¼	+ ½
15¾	13	Alagsco	1.48	11.	4	6	13¼	13¼	13¼	.....
55⅛	16	AlaskIn	.80	1.9	16	792	43	40¼	42⅞	+2⅞
36	23¼	Albany s	1	3.6	8	30	28½	27¾	27⅞	+ ⅝

Source: *Wall Street Journal*, April 23, 1980 (reporting transactions of April 22, 1980). Reprinted by permission of The Wall Street Journal. © Dow Jones & Company, Inc., 1980. All rights reserved.

reference to the information on Abbott Laboratories, a drug company. The two columns on the left show the highest and lowest prices at which the stocks have sold during the previous 52 weeks; Abbott has traded in the range from $30¾ to $43⅜ (or $30.75 to $43.375). The figure just to the right of the company's abbreviated name is the dividend rate based on the most recent regular quarterly payment. Abbott Labs was expected to pay $1.20 a share in 1980. This $1.20 dividend represents a yield percent of 3.0, based on the closing price of approximately $40. Next comes the price-earnings (P-E) ratio of 13, which is the current price of the stock divided by its earnings per share during the last year.

After the P-E ratio comes the volume of trading for the day; 29,000 shares of Abbott Labs stock were traded on April 22, 1980. Following the volume are the high and low prices for the day and the closing price. On April 22 Abbott traded as high as $39½ and as low as $38⅝, while the last trade was at $39½. The last column gives the change from the closing price on the previous day. Abbott Labs was up $1¼, so the previous close must have been $38¼ (since $38¼ + $1¼ = $39½, the indicated closing price on April 22). A set of footnotes giving additional information about specific issues always accompanies the stock market quotes.

Margin Trading and Short Selling

Margin trading and short selling are two practices that are said to contribute to the securities markets' efficiency. *Margin trading* involves the buying of securities on credit. For example, when margin requirements are 60 percent, 100 shares of a stock selling for $100 a share can be bought by putting up, in cash, only $6,000, or 60 percent of the purchase price, and borrowing the remaining $4,000. The stockbroker lends the margin purchaser the funds, retaining custody of the stock as collateral. Margin requirements are determined by the Federal Reserve Board. When the Fed judges that stock market activity and prices are unduly stimulated by easy credit, it raises margin requirements and thus reduces the amount of credit available for the purchase of stocks. On the other hand, if the Fed wants to stimulate the market as part of its overall monetary policy operations, it reduces margin requirements.

Short selling means selling a security that is not owned by the seller. Suppose you own 100 shares of ZN, which is currently selling for $80 a share. If you become convinced that ZN is overpriced and that it is going to fall to $40 within the next year, you will probably sell your stock. Now suppose you do not own any ZN, but you still think the price will fall from $80 to $40. If you are really convinced that this drop will occur, you can, through a lending arrangement with a broker, *go short* in ZN, or *sell ZN short.*

Margin trading is a form of leverage that, whether used in a long or a short position, magnifies the gains and losses from a given percentage of price swings in securities. We provide here some brief examples to illustrate how this happens. First we will illustrate the effects of margin trading through an example that starts with a 100 percent investment and then shifts to 50 percent margin.

Walter Smith buys 100 shares of Provo Company's stock at $20 per share. He will hold the stock for one year and then sell it. The brokerage costs and transfer taxes represent 2 percent of the transaction value. The stock pays a single year-end dividend of $1. Since Mr. Smith makes a 100 percent payment, his total investment would be equal to $2,040.

$$\begin{aligned}\text{Total cash outlays} &= \text{Purchase price} + \text{Transaction cost}\\ &= (\$20 \times 100) + (\$20 \times 100 \times 0.02)\\ &= \$2{,}000 + \$40\\ &= \$2{,}040.\end{aligned}$$

Initially, we assume the stock is sold for $25 per share at year end when total cash inflows are:

$$\begin{aligned}\text{Total cash inflows} &= \text{Selling price} - \text{Transaction costs} + \text{Dividend earned}\\ &= (\$25 \times 100) - (\$25 \times 100 \times 0.02) + (\$1 \times 100)\\ &= \$2{,}500 - \$50 + \$100\\ &= \$2{,}550.\end{aligned}$$

We can now calculate the return on Smith's investment.

$$\begin{aligned}\text{Return on investment} &= (\text{Net cash inflows})/(\text{Initial cash outlays}).\\ &= (\$2{,}550 - \$2{,}040)/\$2{,}040\\ &= \$510/\$2{,}040\\ &= 25\%.\end{aligned}$$

On the other hand, if the year-end stock price dropped by \$5 to \$15 per share, Smith would experience a loss.

$$\begin{aligned}\text{Total cash inflows} &= \text{Selling price} - \text{Transaction cost} + \text{Dividend earned}\\ &= (\$15 \times 100) - (\$15 \times 100 \times .02) + (\$1 \times 100)\\ &= \$1{,}500 - \$30 + \$100\\ &= \$1{,}570.\end{aligned}$$

The net cash inflows are now negative; and in relation to Smith's investment, they represent a return on his investment of a negative 23 percent.

$$\begin{aligned}\text{Return on investment} &= (\text{Net cash inflows})/(\text{Initial cash outlays})\\ &= (\$1{,}570 - \$2{,}040)/\$2{,}040\\ &= -\ \$470/\$2{,}040\\ &= -23\%.\end{aligned}$$

Next we consider the impact of a purchase on margin by Smith. Suppose the present legal margin requirement is 50 percent and Smith invests on a 50 percent margin basis. It is assumed that interest rate levels are such that the broker will charge a rate of 10 percent on Smith's unpaid balance. Smith's cash outlays or investment will be \$1,020, calculated as follows:

Total cash outlays

$$\begin{aligned}&= (\text{Margin requirements}) \times (\text{Purchase price} + \text{Transaction cost})\\ &= (0.50)[(\$20 \times 100) + (\$20 \times 100 \times 0.02)]\\ &= (0.50)(\$2{,}040)\\ &= \$1{,}020.\end{aligned}$$

If the stock is sold at year end at \$25 per share, the net cash flow will be the same as before except for the interest paid to the broker, which causes a net cash inflow decline from \$510 to \$408. Since Smith's cash investment is \$1,020, his return on investment is calculated by dividing his net cash inflows by his initial cost outlays:

$$\begin{aligned}\text{Return on investment} &= (\text{Net cash inflows})/(\text{Initial cash outlays})\\ &= (\$2{,}448 - \$2{,}040)/\$1{,}020\\ &= \$408/\$1{,}020\\ &= 40\%.\end{aligned}$$

The 40 percent is much higher than the 25 percent return on investment when Smith put up 100 percent of the transaction.

If the price of the stock declines to \$15 per share, the loss of \$470 will be increased by \$102 interest, making the total loss \$572. We can then calculate Smith's new return on investment:

$$\begin{aligned}\text{Return on investment} &= (\text{Net cash inflows})/(\text{Initial cash outlays})\\ &= (\$1{,}468 - \$2{,}040)/\$1{,}020\\ &= -\$572/\$1{,}020\\ &= -56\%.\end{aligned}$$

Smith experiences a loss of 56 percent on this investment, compared with a loss of 23 percent on the full 100 percent investment.

Thus the use of debt by an investor will increase gains as well as make losses larger: Both gains and losses are magnified. The use of debt makes investment returns riskier since the range of probable returns is extended in both the positive and negative directions. The magnification of the amplitude of gains and losses caused by the use of leverage applies not only in individual transactions but to investments by business firms as well. In fact, leverage decisions by business firms will be one of the central issues of financing to be discussed in subsequent chapters.

Next we will illustrate the concept of short selling, using the same example except that this time Walter Smith is selling short instead of buying on margin. Smith believes that the ABC stock, which is currently selling at \$20 per share, will be worth only \$15 one year from now. He does not now own any shares of ABC stock, so he sells 100 shares short. What happens is a procedure in which Smith borrows from a broker 100 shares of "street name" stocks which were purchased on margin by an investor named Jones, who left them registered in the broker's name. Smith sells these borrowed ABC stocks at \$20 per share with a margin of 50 percent to yet a third investor, named Brown, hoping to buy them back at \$15 per share one year later. Smith will be charged no interest by the broker, since the net proceeds and cash he has invested represent a positive balance.

Smith needs to meet the *maintenance requirements* established by his brokerage firm for short sales on margin. These requirements vary with brokerage firms. One practice would be the requirement of at least a 50 percent margin on the proceeds of \$2,000 at the time of the sale, with additional cash deposits on short sales for each 2.5 point rise in the price of the stock that has been sold short. Thus Smith would be required to put up \$1,000 at the time of the short sale; this assumes that the 50 percent is not applied to the transaction costs. Then if the stock sold by Smith at \$20 rises to \$22.50, the 2.5 point rule would call for his depositing additional cash of \$125 (again not including the transaction costs). A less stringent maintenance requirement calls for additional cash when his \$1,000 margin deposit falls to below 30 percent of the purchase price of the stock. Under this rule, if the price of the stock rises to above \$33.33, Smith will be required to deposit more cash so that the 30 percent maintenance requirement is not violated.

Another technical point is the need to cover two sets of dividends. One is for Jones, whose stock was borrowed to make the short sale. The other is for Brown, who bought the stock on Smith's short sale. One dividend will be paid by the ABC Company; the other dividend will have to be paid by the short seller.

Suppose the stock price one year later is \$25 instead of \$15. The gain (loss) for Smith on this investment would be:

$$\begin{aligned}\text{Total gain (loss)} &= \text{Net selling price} - \text{Dividends} - \text{Net purchase price}\\ &= (\$2{,}000 - 0.02 \times \$2{,}000) - \$100\\ &\qquad - (\$25 \times 100 + \$25 \times 100 \times 0.02)\\ &= (\$2{,}000 - \$40) - \$100 - (\$2{,}500 + \$50)\\ &= \$1{,}960 - \$100 - \$2{,}550\\ &= -\$690.\end{aligned}$$

Smith's investment is $\$2{,}000 \times 0.5 = \$1{,}000$.[5] The result will be $-\$690/\$1000 = -69\%$, a substantial loss.

If the stock were repurchased at \$15 per share as Smith had hoped, the gain would be $(\$2{,}000 - \$40) - \$100 - (\$15 \times 100 + \$15 \times 100 \times 0.02) = \$1{,}960 - \$100 - \$1{,}530 = \$330$. The return would be $\$330/\$1{,}000 = 33\%$.

As can be seen from the above example, a short sale with margin could generate cash gains if the stock price actually falls as predicted. Otherwise, if the stock price goes up after the short sale, the short seller will suffer a loss. Again, the use of debt (or a margin of less than 100 percent) magnifies the gains and losses. The upside gain on the short sale (the price of the stock declines) is reduced by the obligation to pay a second dividend by the seller in a short position.

Insofar as margin trading and short selling do make a more continuous market, they encourage stock ownership and have two other beneficial effects: (1) they broaden ownership of securities by increasing the ability of people to buy them, and (2) they provide for a more active market—and more active trading makes for narrower price fluctuations. However, when a strong speculative psychology grips the market, margin trading can be a fuel that feeds the speculative fervor, while short selling can aggravate pessimism on the downside. The downside effects of short selling are somewhat restricted, however, since the SEC has ruled that a short sale cannot be made at a price lower than that of the last previously recorded sale. If a stock is in a continuous decline, short selling cannot occur; hence it cannot be used to push the stock down. In the 1920s, before this rule was put into effect, market

5. If Smith had been required to deposit additional cash as the stock increased in price, he might have been required to deposit 0.5(\$500) = \$250 more.

manipulators could and did use short sales to drive prices down. Today more short selling occurs when stocks are rising rapidly, and this has a stabilizing influence.

Financial Instruments

Within the framework of the financial markets and financial institutions we have described, financial managers have a wide range of possibilities with respect to financial instruments in which they can invest and forms of financing by which they can raise funds. The range of financial instruments is illustrated in Table 2.1, which is organized by issuer, maturity, and other such characteristics.

Government Securities

The first category of financial instruments consists of those issued by governments. They exist in wide variety and in very substantial amounts. The total amount of U.S. Treasury debt held by private investors at the end of 1979 was

Table 2.1

Overview of Securities Traded in Financial Markets

I. Government Securities
    A. Treasury bills
    B. Treasury coupon issues
    C. Agency issues
    D. Municipal bonds
II. Corporate Issues
    A. Short-term
        1. Commercial banks
            a. Federal funds
            b. Certificates of deposit (CDs)
            c. Bankers acceptances
            d. Prime rate loans
        2. Finance companies
            a. Direct commercial paper
            b. Dealer commercial paper
        3. Other corporations
            a. Commercial paper
            b. Bank loans
    B. Long-term (utilities and industrials)
        1. Term loans
        2. Bonds
        3. Mortgages
III. International Instruments
    A. Eurocurrency deposits
    B. Eurocurrency CDs
    C. Euromarket bonds

$535 billion. The total amount of federal agency debt privately held at the end of 1979 was $225 billion.

Treasury Bills. Treasury bills are debts of the federal government with maturities of less than one year. At the end of 1979, privately held Treasury bills totaled $168 billion. These bills are issued, quoted, and traded on a discount basis. The computation is based on the actual number of days, using 360 days per year. The following formula is used to compute the discount basis and dollar price:

$$D = \frac{M}{360} B$$

$$P = \$100 - D$$

where:

D = full discount
M = days to maturity
B = discount basis
P = dollar price

For example, calculate the dollar price for a Treasury bill due in 275 days on an 8 percent discount basis.

$$D = \frac{275}{360} \times 8\%$$

$$D = 6.111\%$$
$$P = \$100 - D$$
$$= \$100 - \$6.111$$
$$D = \$93.889 \text{ (the dollar price on an 8\% discount basis).}$$

Income from Treasury bills is subject to all federal taxes. The difference between the purchase price and the sale price or maturity value is treated as ordinary income, not a capital gain or loss.

Coupon Issues. Treasury notes carry maturities of not less than one year and not more than ten years. Treasury bonds generally have an original maturity of over ten years. Offerings of notes and bonds are usually announced one to three weeks before the issue date. Until a set deadline, the books are open for entering subscriptions at the offering price set by the Treasury or for submitting bids if the price is to be set by auction. Bidding is usually in terms of yield rather than price.

Agency Issues. A number of government sponsored activities do their own financing. Privately held agency issues outstanding at the end of 1979 totaled over $225 billion. The three largest categories of issuers among federally sponsored agencies are the Federal Home Loan Banks, the Federal National Mortgage Association (known as Fannie Mae), and other housing and farm credit agencies. Besides Fannie Mae, two other issuers of housing credit are the Government National Mortgage Association (Ginnie Mae) and the Federal Home Loan Mortgage Corporation (Freddy Mac). These agencies help develop a national market for mortgages, which increases the availability of mortgage financing and reduces regional differences in mortgage rates.

Municipal Bonds. The debt issues of state and local government units are called municipal bonds. Interest on such bonds is exempt from federal income taxes, which means that the "muni's" can be sold at interest rates lower than those paid by business firms and often lower than those paid by the federal government itself.

Three main types of municipal bonds are available. *General obligation bonds* are backed by the total taxing power of the government unit that issues them. *Revenue bonds* are related to specific projects from which the interest and principal are to be paid. Particular sections of highways may be financed by revenue bonds. Interest and principal are then repaid from tolls charged for the use of the highways. *Industrial development bonds* are used to build plants to attract business firms to a local area. The business firms that occupy such plants pay rent that is used to pay off the interest and principal on the bonds. The tax-exempt feature of the bonds enables the local government to subsidize business firms with low-cost financing.

Interest-Bearing Business Securities

Many types of financial instruments and securities are provided by business firms. The issuers include banks, finance companies, and other business corporations.

Short-Term Financial Instruments

Federal Funds. Trading in federal funds has developed as a way of adjusting the reserve position of commercial banks. Commercial banks that are members of the Federal Reserve System account for over three-fourths of the bank deposits in the United States. Their required reserves are held on deposit in the Federal Reserve Banks. In the daily ebb and flow of commercial transactions throughout the United States, funds are withdrawn from some sectors and accumulated in others. Some banks accumulate more deposits with the Federal Reserve Banks than they need to meet their reserve requirements, while others need to increase their deposits to meet their reserve requirements.

The federal funds market represents purchases and sales of member bank deposits held at the Federal Reserve Banks. A sale of federal funds is a loan by one bank to another. The basic trading unit is $1 million, and the volume of such loans can be in excess of $20 billion per day. Transactions in federal funds can be accomplished within minutes by wire. The loans are for overnight or over the weekend.

The interest rate on federal funds is the most sensitive of money market rates. It is not unusual for it to fluctuate as much as 25 percent on either side of its average level for the day. The federal funds rate reflects the many changes taking place in the economy and in the financial markets. It provides a highly sensitive index of the impact the Fed has on the money markets. Sharp movements in the rate may reflect the market's judgment that the Fed has embarked on a shift in its policies with regard to tightening or relaxing conditions in the money markets.

Certificates of Deposit. In early 1961 major New York commercial banks began to issue interest-bearing negotiable certificates of deposit (CDs) to domestic business corporations. These certificates are a form of savings deposit, except that they cannot be withdrawn before their maturity date. However, since they are negotiable, they can be sold in the money market prior to maturity—and there is an active secondary market for them. CDs give banks an opportunity to compete for corporate and other funds that in the past were invested in Treasury bills and other types of short-term paper. They bear rates of interest in line with money rates at the time of issuance. However, during periods of tight money market conditions, when banks are aggressively seeking to add to their deposits, CD rates may rise sharply.

Bankers Acceptances. A bankers acceptance is a debt instrument created by the creditor and arising out of a self-liquidating business transaction. It arises mainly from import and export activity. For example, a U.S. coffee processor may arrange with his U.S. commercial bank for the issuance of an irrevocable letter of credit in favor of a Brazilian exporter with whom the U.S. processor has negotiated a transaction. The letter of credit covers the details of the shipment and states that the Brazilian exporter can draw a time draft for a specified amount on the U.S. bank. On the basis of the letter of credit, the exporter draws a draft on the bank and negotiates the draft with a local Brazilian bank, receiving immediate payment. The Brazilian bank then forwards the draft to the United States for presentation to the bank that issued the letter of credit. When this bank stamps the draft "accepted," it accepts the obligation to pay the draft at maturity, thereby creating an acceptance. Typically the acceptance is then sold to an acceptance dealer, and the proceeds are credited to the account of the Brazilian bank. The shipping documents are released to the U.S. importer against a trust receipt, enabling the U.S. company to process and sell the coffee.

The proceeds of the coffee sales are deposited by the importer at the accepting bank in time to meet the required payment on the draft at maturity. The holder of the acceptance at maturity presents it to the accepting bank for payment, and that completes the transaction. The cost of the acceptance reflects the discount in the dealer's bid plus the accepting bank's commission rate. The cost can be paid by either of the parties to the transaction in accordance with the agreement made with the accepting bank. It reflects the trade-offs involved in the selling price of the goods (which is related to provisions for bearing the risks that may be involved in the transaction) and the payment of fees for various instruments created by the transaction (such as the acceptance itself).

Prime Rate Loans. Prime rate loans are loans made by commercial banks to customers who qualify for the best rate available on short-term bank lending. The result of direct negotiation between the bank and the borrower, they usually are part of a continuing financial relationship. Commercial bank rates to borrowers other than those qualifying for the prime rate are usually higher than that rate. Prime rate loans compete on a rate basis with commercial paper borrowing.

Commercial Paper. Commercial paper is unsecured promissory notes issued by firms to finance short-term credit needs. In recent years the issuance of commercial paper has become an increasingly important source of short-term financing for many types of corporations, including utilities, finance companies, insurance companies, bank holding companies, and manufacturing companies. It is used increasingly, not only to finance seasonal working capital needs but also as a means of interim financing of major projects such as bank buildings, ships, pipelines, nuclear fuel cores, and plant expansion.

Some commercial paper—especially the large volume of it issued by finance companies—is sold directly to investors, including business corporations, commercial banks, insurance companies, and state and local government units. At the end of 1976 about 60 percent of the commercial paper outstanding had been sold directly to investors. The remainder represented that sold through commercial paper dealers, who function as intermediaries in the commercial paper market.

The commercial paper market is generally available only to firms with the best credit ratings. Commercial paper sold through dealers is rated as to quality by Moody's or Standard & Poor's. Surprises do occur, however; witness the Penn Central bankruptcy in 1970, which took place with over $80 million of commercial paper outstanding. In March 1978, when Standard & Poor's reduced its rating on the senior long-term debt of Chrysler Corporation from Bbb to Bbb−, S&P maintained its existing ratings on the company's short-term instruments, including commercial paper. While commercial paper rates are generally somewhat higher than the rates on Treasury bills, they are somewhat lower than the prime bank loan rate.

Long-Term Corporate Borrowing

Like government units and financial institutions, nonfinancial business firms issue various forms of long-term debt. Some forms are arranged with financial institutions such as banks or insurance companies; others are sold with the help of investment bankers to a wider range of buyers. The many different kinds of corporate bonds are discussed in Chapter 18.

Technically, bonds are any form of long-term debt. When secured by real estate, they are referred to as mortgage bonds or simply mortgages. The long-term loans on individual residences are referred to as mortgages, but mortgage financing exists for commercial properties as well. The federal government has established a number of organizations that provide a secondary market in mortgages by purchasing them from the financial institutions that originally made the loans. In the mortgage and related fields considerable interaction exists between private financial institutions and government agencies.

International Markets

We turn next to the increasingly important international dimensions of financial markets and the instruments that have been developed. The international dimension of financial markets has been stimulated through the mechanism of the *Eurocurrency market.* The Eurocurrency deposit is created when a banking office in one country accepts a deposit denominated in the currency of another country. The development of this market began in the late 1950s, and by the mid-1970s the volume of Eurocurrency accounts had grown to over $250 billion, at least three-fourths of it in U.S. dollars. The Eurocurrency market denominated in dollars is referred to as the Eurodollar market. While the main instrument of the Eurocurrency market is the deposit, other forms include certificates of deposit, bankers acceptances, commercial paper, and loans of various maturities.

A bank, corporation, or government unit owning foreign currency in excess of its working needs will seek to earn interest on these temporary surplus funds. If the amount is large, it is worthwhile for the financial manager to seek the best rate available. This may include the use of a banking office in a foreign country and the deposit of funds in that country. When foreign money markets provide more favorable terms than U.S. markets, the lender and the banking office that accepts the deposit exchange letters detailing the terms of the deposit, and the transfer of funds is acknowledged. The normal deposit unit is 1 million currency units. The lender who needs short-term funds prior to the maturity of the deposit can become a borrower for the necessary period by initiating an offsetting transaction in the Eurocurrency market.

The rate paid on these deposits among the largest and best-known international banks is called the London Inter-Bank (LIBO) rate. Deposit rates are generally fixed for shorter-term deposits but may float on longer-term deposits. Floating rates are usually adjusted twice each year in response to changes in the LIBO short-term rate to which they are tied.

Participants in the Eurocurrency market are located throughout the world; transactions are negotiated by Telex, cable, and telephone. Trading is normally done for settlement on the second business day following the trade date. Funds are transferred either directly through correspondent banks in the home country of the currency involved or according to the broker's instructions against delivery of the required instrument.

In addition to conventional interbank deposits, there are Eurodollar certificates of deposit (similar to the CDs in our domestic market), negotiable instruments that enjoy an active secondary trading market. Many branches of U.S. banks compete for Eurodollar funds through the issuance of Eurodollar certificates of deposit.

Besides placing temporary surplus funds in Eurocurrency deposits or Eurodollar CDs, many U.S. firms utilize the Euromarket as borrowers. The rates on long-term borrowing in the Euromarket are sometimes below the rates on comparable securities in the United States. The relative rates depend on supply and demand conditions in the U.S. capital market as compared with conditions in the Euromarket. A situation that illustrates this point developed at the end of 1976: "Fierce competition among banks across the Atlantic for loan business is driving down the cost of credit to the point where U.S. corporations and their overseas subsidiaries can now borrow five-year money in Europe for nearly the same price that they have to pay for short-term bank loans at home."[6] Of course, if interest rates are relatively lower in Europe, the increased borrowing abroad tends to bring other rates back into balance. Sometimes foreign firms find it attractive to sell " 'Yankee' bonds—bonds issued by foreign governments and corporations but sold in the U.S. and denominated in U.S. dollars."[7]

Increasingly the financial manager, whether in the United States or in a foreign country, looks at the whole world as a relevant financial market. Responding to changes in political, economic, and financial conditions throughout the world, the financial manager is sometimes an investor and sometimes a borrower abroad. Transportation and communication systems now link nations directly and closely together. For this reason further analysis of the international dimensions of financial markets will be developed later, in Chapter 26.

Summary

The financial sector of the economy, an important part of the financial manager's environment, is comprised of financial markets, financial institutions, and financial instruments.

Financial markets involve the creation and transfer of financial assets and liabilities. The financial manager uses these markets to obtain needed funds for the operation and growth of the business and to employ funds temporarily not needed by the business. Funds are provided by savings surplus units to be used by savings deficit units. This transfer of funds creates a financial

6. "Big Loan Bargains in the Euromart," *Business Week,* December 13, 1976, pp. 10–11.
7. " 'Yankee' Bonds Are Doing Just Dandy," *Business Week,* December 6, 1976, pp. 76–77.

asset for the surplus unit and a financial liability for the deficit unit. Transfers can be directly between a surplus and a deficit unit or can involve a financial intermediary, such as a bank. Intermediaries take on financial liabilities in order to create financial assets, typically profiting from their expertise in packaging these assets and liabilities. The operations of intermediaries and financial markets in general bring about a more efficient allocation of real resources.

The money markets involve financial assets and liabilities with maturities of less than one year, and the capital markets involve transfers for longer periods. Since most businesses are savings deficit units, the financial manager is concerned with the choice of financial markets, intermediaries, and instruments best suited to the needs of the firm and with the decision of how best to employ excess funds for short periods.

The initial sale of stocks and bonds is known as the primary market; subsequent trading takes place in the secondary market—the organized exchanges. The over-the-counter market, the third market, is a dealer market where broker-dealers throughout the country act as market makers. Sometimes large blocks of stock are traded directly among institutional investors, which represent the fourth market.

In addition to the ordinary purchase or sale of stocks or bonds, margin trading involves borrowing to increase the size of the investment. Margin requirements, set by the Fed, change from time to time. Short selling is the practice of borrowing securities and selling them immediately, while anticipating an opportunity to repurchase them later at a lower price to repay the loan. (That is, the short seller benefits if the price of stock falls.) Short selling and margin trading make the stock market more active and thus may contribute to the ability to buy or sell securities with smaller price swings than otherwise would occur.

Two major forms of financing are used by business firms: equity financing through common stock and various forms of debt financing. Numerous alternative types of debt instruments exist; they differ in duration and in the degree of risk that the borrower (the issuer of the debt) will become unable to meet the obligation.

International financial markets extend the range of alternatives available to financial managers. Surplus funds can be invested at advantageous rates in the many different types of international financial instruments. Financing can be obtained in the Eurocurrency market for short-term borrowing or in the Eurobond market for longer-term debt financing.

Questions

2.1 What activities of financial managers are depicted by Figure 2.1?

2.2 What are financial intermediaries, and what economic functions do they perform?

2.3 How could each tool of the Fed be used to slow down expansion?

2.4 Evaluate each of the arguments in favor of organized securities exchanges relative to OTC markets a hundred years ago versus today.

2.5 One day the New York Stock Exchange reporting system showed XYZ Corporation as follows:

49 27 XYZ 1.20 8 60 33 30 32 +1

a. Is XYZ trading near its high or its low for the year?

b. What was yesterday's closing price?

c. In terms of the closing price, what is the expected dividend yield on XYZ stock?

d. Based on the information given in the report, what would you estimate XYZ's annual earnings to be?

2.6 Why might an investor want to sell short?

2.7 As the financial manager of a business, what factors would you want to consider in deciding how to invest some temporary surplus funds?

2.8 If your firm needs more long-term capital, can you think of a situation where you might want to use a short-term source of funds?

Problems

2.1 John Adams buys a hundred shares of CDL Corporation common stock at a price of $40 per share and holds the stock for one year. Brokerage costs and transfer taxes are 2 percent of the transaction value. What is the percentage gain or loss on the funds he has invested if the stock pays a single year-end dividend of $2? The brokerage firm charges Adams 10 percent on his unpaid balance for the year.

a. What is the percentage gain or loss on the funds invested by Adams if the stock is sold for $50 per share and the cash he provides is

1. 100 percent of the sum of the purchase price plus brokerage expenses?
2. 70 percent of the sum of the purchase price plus brokerage expenses?
3. 50 percent of the sum of the purchase price plus brokerage expenses?

b. What is the percentage gain or loss on the funds invested by Adams if the stock is sold for $30 per share under the same three margin percentages?

c. What is the effect of using debt on the percentage gain or loss to Adams?

2.2 Assume the same facts as in Problem 2.1 with the exception that Adams sells the stock short. Answer the same questions as in Problem 2.1.

2.3 Select a recent issue of the *Federal Reserve Bulletin* and locate the table giving information on margin requirements for margin stocks, convertible bonds, and short sales.

a. Does *margin requirements* refer to the percentage of borrowing to market value of the collateral or to the percentage of funds provided by the investor?

b. Are the requirements always the same for the three types of securities?

c. What has been the trend in margin requirements since March 11, 1968?

d. What are current margin requirements?

2.4 Using a recent issue of the *Wall Street Journal,* answer the following questions with respect to General Electric Company common stock:

a. On what exchange is it listed?

b. What is the annual dollar amount of dividends based on the last quarterly or semiannual distribution?

c. What percentage yield is represented by this dollar amount of dividend based on the closing price of the stock?
d. How does this compare with the rate of interest the same funds could earn in a savings account?
e. What is the indicated price-earnings ratio of the stock based on the closing price and the most recent twelve months' earnings?
f. By what percentage is the closing price below the high price for the previous fifty-two weeks?
g. By what percentage is the closing price above the low price for the previous fifty-two weeks?
h. Would you say that the common stock of General Electric has experienced high, low, or moderate volatility during the previous fifty-two weeks?

2.5 Using a recent issue of the *Wall Street Journal,* answer the following questions about the $8^1/_2$ percent bonds of the Dow Chemical Company maturing 2006.
a. On what exchange are they listed?
b. What is their current yield?
c. What was their closing price?
d. Was their closing price below or above their par value of 100?

Selected References

Andersen, Leonal C. "Is There a Capital Shortage: Theory and Recent Evidence." *Journal of Finance* 31 (May 1976), pp. 257–268.

Freund, William C. "The Dynamic Financial Markets." *Financial Executive* 33 (May 1965), pp. 11–26, 57–58.

Friedman, Milton. "Factors Affecting the Level of Interest Rates." In *Savings and Residential Financing.* Chicago: U.S. Savings and Loan League, 1968, pp. 10–27.

Gibson, William E. "Price Expectations Effects on Interest Rates." *Journal of Finance* 25 (March 1970), pp. 19–34.

Grossman, Herschel I. "The Term Structure of Interest Rates." *Journal of Finance* 22 (December 1967), pp. 611–622.

Henning, Charles N.; Pigott, William; and Scott, Robert Haney. *Financial Markets and the Economy.* Englewood Cliffs, N. J.: Prentice-Hall, 1975.

Heslop, Alan, ed. *The World Capital Shortage.* Indianapolis, Ind.: Bobbs-Merrill, 1977.

Johnson, Ramon E. "Term Structures of Corporate Bond Yields as a Function of Risk of Default." *Journal of Finance* 22 (May 1967), pp. 313–345.

Kaufman, George G. *Money, the Financial System, and the Economy.* 2d ed. Chicago: Rand McNally, 1977.

Kessel, Reuben A. *Cyclical Behavior of the Term Structure of Interest Rates.* New York: National Bureau of Economic Research, 1965.

Macaulay, Frederick R. *Some Theoretical Problems Suggested by the Movements of Interest Rates, Bond Yields, and Stock Prices in the United States since 1856.* New York: National Bureau of Economic Research, 1938.

Malkiel, Burton G. *The Term Structure of Interest Rates.* Princeton, N.J.: Princeton University Press, 1966.

Murphy, J. Carter. *The International Monetary System: Beyond the First Stage of Reform.* Washington, D.C.: American Enterprise Institute Studies in Economic Policy, 1979.

Polakoff, Murray E., et al. *Financial Institutions and Markets.* Boston: Houghton Mifflin, 1970.

Pyle, David H. "On the Theory of Financial Intermediation." *Journal of Finance* 26 (June 1971), pp. 737–747.

Van Horne, James C. *Financial Market Rates and Flows.* Englewood Cliffs, N.J.: Prentice-Hall, 1978.

Wachtel, Paul; Sametz, Arnold; and Shuford, Harry. "Capital Shortages: Myth or Reality." *Journal of Finance* 31 (May 1976), pp. 269–286

Winchester, Mark B., ed. *The International Essays for Business Decision Makers.* Vol. 4. Dallas, Tex.: The Center for International Business, 1979.

3

The Tax Environment and Forms of Business Organization

The federal government is often called the most important stockholder in the U.S. economy. While this is not literally true, since the government does not own corporate shares in the strict sense of the word, the government is by far the largest recipient of business profits. Income of unincorporated businesses is subject to tax rates ranging up to 70 percent (50 percent on earned income), while corporate income in excess of $100,000 is taxed at a 46 percent rate. Furthermore, dividends received by stockholders are subject to personal income taxes at the stockholders' individual tax rates. State and sometimes city or county taxes must be added to these federal taxes.

With such a large percentage of business income going to the government, it is not surprising that taxes play an important role in financial decisions. To lease or to buy, to use common stock or debt, to make or not to make a particular investment, to merge or not to merge—all these decisions are influenced by tax factors. This chapter summarizes some basic elements of the tax structure relating to financial decisions.

Corporate Income Tax

The tax law of 1978 adopted the following rates, effective 1979, for the corporate income tax:

Rate Structure

First $25,000	17%
Second $25,000	20%
Third $25,000	30%
Fourth $25,000	40%
Over $100,000	46%

This chapter has benefited from the assistance of R. Wendell Buttrey, tax attorney and lecturer on taxation at the University of California, Los Angeles.

Table 3.1

Marginal and Average Corporate Tax Rates, 1979

Taxable Corporate Income (in Dollars)	Marginal Tax Rate (Percent)	Incremental Taxes Paid	Total Taxes Paid[a]	Average Tax Rate (Percent)[a]
0–25,000	17	4,250	4,250	17.00
25,001–50,000	20	5,000	9,250	18.50
50,001–75,000	30	7,500	16,750	22.33
75,001–100,000	40	10,000	26,750	26.75
100,001–200,000	46	46,000	72,750	36.38
200,001–1,000,000	46	368,000	440,750	44.08
1,000,001–11,000,000	46	4,600,000	5,040,750	45.83
11,000,001–111,000,000	46	46,000,000	51,040,750	45.98

a. Based on upper limit of income range

For example, if in 1979 a corporation has a taxable net income of $110,000, its tax will be computed as follows:

$$
\begin{aligned}
0.17(\$25{,}000) &= \$\ 4{,}250 \\
0.20(\$25{,}000) &= \quad 5{,}000 \\
0.30(\$25{,}000) &= \quad 7{,}500 \\
0.40(\$25{,}000) &= \quad 10{,}000 \\
0.46(\$10{,}000) &= \quad \underline{4{,}600} \\
\text{Total tax} &= \$31{,}350
\end{aligned}
$$

Thus the corporation's effective tax rate will be $31,350÷$110,000=28.5 percent. However, on any amount over $100,000, the tax rate on this incremental income will be 46 percent. Table 3.1 shows that the average corporate income tax is moderately progressive up to $11 million, after which it becomes virtually a flat 46 percent.

This relatively simple tax structure has wide implications for business planning. Because the tax rate increases sharply when corporate income rises above $100,000, it clearly will seem advantageous to break moderate-sized companies into two or more separate corporations in order to make the lower corporate income tax rates applicable. This was, in fact, done for many years by a number of firms, with some groups (such as retail chains and small loan companies) having literally thousands of separate corporations. However, from a tax standpoint, the Tax Reform Act of 1969 eliminated the advantages of multiple corporations.

Accelerated Depreciation

Depreciation charges are deductible in computing federal income taxes; the larger the depreciation charge, the lower the actual tax liability. The tax laws specify the methods for calculating depreciation for purposes of computing federal income taxes. When tax laws are changed to permit more rapid, or accelerated, depreciation, this reduces tax payments and stimulates business investments.[1]

A number of different depreciation methods are authorized for tax purposes: (1) straight line, (2) units of production, (3) sum-of-years'-digits, and (4) double declining balance. These methods are explained in Appendix A to this chapter. The last two methods listed are generally referred to as accelerated depreciation methods; ordinarily, they are more favorable than straight line depreciation from a tax standpoint.

The fiscal policy implications of depreciation methods stem from two factors: (1) accelerated depreciation reduces taxes in the early years of an asset's life, thus increasing corporate cash flows and making more funds available for investment; and (2) faster cash flows increase the profitability, or rate of return, on an investment. The second point is discussed in the context of capital budgeting in Chapter 13.

Depreciation methods, like tax rates, are determined by Congress and are occasionally altered to influence the level of investment and thereby to stimulate or retard the economy. The most sweeping changes were made in 1954, when the accelerated depreciation methods listed above were first permitted, and in 1962 and 1970, when the depreciable lives of assets for tax purposes were reduced.

Investment Tax Credit

The concept of an investment tax credit was first incorporated into the federal income tax laws in 1962. Under the investment tax credit program, business firms could deduct, as a credit against their income tax, a specified percentage of the dollar amount of new investment in each of certain categories of assets. Under the rules existing in 1978, the tax credit amounted to 10 percent of the amount of new investment in assets having useful lives of seven years or more, two-thirds of 10 percent for assets having lives of five or six years, one-third of 10 percent for assets having lives of three or four years, and no tax credit for assets having useful lives of fewer than three years. Thus, if a firm that otherwise will have a $100,000 tax bill purchases an asset costing $200,000 and having a twenty-year life, it will receive a tax credit of $20,000 (10 percent of $200,000), and its adjusted tax bill will be $80,000.

The investment tax credit, like tax rates and depreciation methods, is subject to congressional changes. During the economic boom in the early part of 1966, the investment tax credit was suspended in an effort to reduce investment; it was reinstated later that year, then removed again in 1969 and reinstated in 1971. The Revenue Act of 1978 makes the investment tax credit, including a $100,000 used-property limitation, permanent. The amount of tax liability that can be offset is the first $25,000 plus a fraction of the amount over $25,000. The fractional amount rises from 50 percent by 10 percentage points a year, beginning in 1979 and reaching 90 percent by 1982. The pro-

1. Federal tax statutes also consider the time over which assets must be depreciated. A reduction in that period has the same stimulating effect on the economy as does a change in permitted depreciation methods that speeds up depreciation expenses for tax purposes.

visions are somewhat more liberal for railroad and airline companies and some utilities.

Corporate Capital Gains and Losses

Corporate taxable income consists of two components: profits from the sale of capital assets and all other income (defined as *ordinary income*). *Capital assets* (for example, security investments) are defined as assets not bought and sold in the ordinary course of a firm's business. Gains and losses on the sale of capital assets are defined as capital gains and losses, and under certain circumstances they receive special tax treatment.[2] Real and depreciable property used in the business is not defined as a capital asset, although the Internal Revenue Code specifies that such property is treated as a capital asset in the event of a net gain. (However, the recapture of depreciation provisions may eliminate much of this benefit.) If there is a net loss, the full amount can be deducted from ordinary income without any of the limitations described below for capital loss treatment.[3]

Until 1977, the distinction between short-term and long-term capital gains was based on a six-month holding period. Assets held six months or less gave rise to short-term capital gains or losses on their sale. If held more than six months, the gain or loss was considered long-term. The Tax Reform Act of 1976 increased the period over which assets must be held for purposes of determining long-term capital gain or loss from six months to nine months in 1977 and to twelve months thereafter. Thus, from 1978 on, the sale of a capital asset held for twelve months or less gives rise to a short-term capital gain or loss. When held for more than twelve months, its disposal produces a long-term gain or loss. Short-term capital gains less short-term capital losses equal net short-term gains, which are added to the firm's ordinary income and taxed at regular corporate income tax rates. For net long-term capital gains (long-term gains less long-term losses), the tax is limited to 28 percent plus a minimum tax factor on part of a corporation's gains, making the maximum rate on corporate capital gains slightly higher. For example, if a corporation holds the common stock of another corporation as an investment for more than twelve months and then sells it at a profit, the gain is subject to a maximum tax of 28+ percent. Of course, if income is below $50,000, regular tax rates of 17 or 20 percent apply.

Depreciable Assets

If a building is subject to depreciation, its tax cost is defined as the original purchase price less allowable accumulated depreciation. To illustrate, suppose a building cost $100,000, and $40,000 of (allowable) depreciation has been taken on it. Its book value, by definition, is $100,000 − $40,000 = $60,000.

2. Corporate capital gains and losses (as well as most other tax matters) are subject to many technical provisions. This section and the others dealing with tax matters include only the most general provisions. For special cases see *Federal Tax Course* (Englewood Cliffs, N.J.: Prentice-Hall, 1980).

3. The special treatment of depreciable properties should be kept in mind in connection with the material in Chapter 13 on capital budgeting. The difference between the book value of an asset and its salvage or abandonment value (if lower than book value) can be deducted from ordinary income; thus the full amount of this difference is a deductible expense.

A building cannot be depreciated by an accelerated method to transfer ordinary income to capital gains. Thus a problem may arise when it is bought, depreciated by an accelerated method, and subsequently sold. If the sale is at a price above book value, the difference between straight line and accelerated depreciation is not allowable for determining the capital gain or loss. To illustrate: In the above example, if straight line depreciation had been $25,000, then $15,000 of the $40,000 depreciation would be recaptured. Thus the tax cost for figuring a capital gain would be $75,000 ($100,000−$25,000). If the asset were sold for $85,000, a long-term capital gain of $10,000 ($85,000−$75,000) would result. The $15,000 difference between allowable depreciation and depreciation claimed would be taxed as ordinary income. This rule is intended to prevent firms from converting regular income to capital gains by accelerated depreciation in order to avoid payment of some income tax.

In the case of personal property such as machinery, the entire gain is recaptured as ordinary income up to the amount of the depreciation taken, regardless of the method employed. In the case of depreciation of buildings, the recapture provisions apply only to the excess of depreciation deducted over straight line depreciation.

Deductibility of Capital Losses

A corporation's net capital loss is not deductible from ordinary income. For example, if in 1979 a corporation had ordinary income of $100,000 and a net capital loss of $25,000 (that is, capital losses for the year exceeded capital gains for the year by $25,000), it still paid a tax of $26,750 on the $100,000 ordinary income. The net capital loss, however, can be carried back three years and forward five years and can be used to offset capital gains during that period.

Dividend Income

Another important rule is that 85 percent of the dividends received by one corporation from another are exempt from taxation.[4] For example, if Corporation H owns stock in Corporation J and receives $100,000 in dividends from that corporation, it must pay taxes on only $15,000 of the $100,000. Assuming H is in the 46 percent tax bracket, the tax is $6,900, or 6.9 percent of the dividends received. The reason for this reduced tax is that subjecting intercorporate dividends to the full corporate tax rate would eventually lead to triple taxation. First, Corporation J would pay its regular taxes. Then, Corporation H would pay a second tax. Finally, H's own stockholders would be subject to taxes on their dividends. The 85 percent dividend deduction thus reduces the multiple taxation of corporate income.

4. If the corporation receiving the dividends owns 80 percent or more of the stock of a dividend-paying firm, it can file a consolidated tax return. In this situation there are no dividends as far as the Internal Revenue Service is concerned, so there is obviously no tax on dividends received. The internal books of the related corporations may show an accounting entry entitled "dividends," which is used for transferring funds from the subsidiary to the parent; but this is of no concern to the IRS.

Deductibility of Interest and Dividends

Interest payments made by a corporation are a deductible expense to the firm, but dividends paid on its own stock are not. Thus, if a firm raises $100,000 and contracts to pay the suppliers of this money 7 percent, or $7,000 a year, the $7,000 is deductible if the $100,000 is debt. It is not deductible if the $100,000 is raised as stock and the $7,000 is paid as dividends.[5] This differential treatment of dividends and interest payments has an important effect on the manner in which firms raise capital, as later chapters will show.

Payment of Tax in Installments

Firms must estimate their taxable income for the current year and, if reporting on a calendar year basis, pay one-fourth of the estimated tax on April 15, June 15, September 15, and December 15 of that year. The estimated taxes paid must be identical to those of the previous year or at least 80 percent of actual tax liability for the current year, or the firm will be subject to penalties. Any differences between estimated and actual taxes are payable by March 15 of the following year. For example, if a firm expected to earn $100,000 in 1980 and to owe a tax of $26,750 on this income, then it had to file an estimated income statement and pay $6,688 on the 15th of April, June, September, and December of 1980. By March 15, 1981, it must have filed a final income statement and paid any shortfall (or received a refund for overages) between estimated and actual taxes.

Net Operating Loss Carrybacks and Carryovers

Any ordinary corporate operating loss can be carried back three years and forward seven. Previous to the Tax Reform Act of 1976 the carryover was only five years, and the loss had to be carried back to the earliest year. But now operating losses do not have to be carried back. For example, an operating loss in 1980 can be used to reduce taxable income from 1977 through 1987 or 1981 through 1987.

The purpose of permitting this loss averaging is to avoid penalizing corporations whose incomes fluctuate widely. To illustrate: Suppose the Ritz Hotel made $100,000 before taxes in all years except 1978, when it suffered a $600,000 operating loss. The Ritz could utilize the carryback feature to recompute its taxes for 1975, using $100,000 of the operating losses to reduce the 1975 profit to zero and recovering the amount of taxes paid in that year; that is, in 1979 the Ritz would receive a refund of its 1975 taxes because of the loss experienced in 1978. Since $500,000 of unrecovered losses would still be available, it could do the same thing for 1976 and 1977. Then, in 1979, 1980, and 1981, it could apply the carryover loss to reduce its profits to zero in each of these years. Alternately, the Ritz could have chosen to start this procedure in 1979.

The Tax Reform Act of 1976 limits the use of a company's net operating losses in periods following a change in its ownership. The carryover is disallowed if the following conditions exist: (1) 50 percent or more of the corpo-

5. Limits have been placed on the deductibility of interest payments on some forms of securities issued in connection with mergers.

ration's stock changes hands during a two-year period as a result of purchase or redemption of stock, and (2) the corporation changes its trade or business. (There are other important restrictions on the acquisition of a loss company, but they are too complex to be covered in this brief summary.)

Improper Accumulation

A special surtax on improperly accumulated income is provided for by Section 531 of the Internal Revenue Code, which states that earnings accumulated by a corporation are subject to penalty rates *if the purpose of the accumulation is to enable the stockholders to avoid the personal income tax.* The penalty rate is 27.5 percent on the first $100,000 of improperly accumulated taxable income for the current year and 38.5 percent on all amounts over $100,000. Of income not paid out in dividends, a cumulative total of $150,000 (the balance sheet item of retained earnings) is prima facie retainable for the reasonable needs of the business; this benefits small corporations. Of course, most companies have legitimate reasons for retaining earnings over $150,000, and they are not subject to the penalty.

Earnings retention can be justified if the firm is paying off debt, financing growth, or increasing marketable securities to seek to provide the corporation with a cushion against possible cash drains caused by losses. How much a firm should properly accumulate for uncertain contingencies is a matter of judgment. Fear of the penalty taxes that can be imposed under Section 531 may cause a firm to pay out a higher rate of dividends than it otherwise would.[6]

Sometimes Section 531 stimulates mergers. A clear illustration is provided by the purchase of the Toni Company (home permanents) by the Gillette Safety Razor Company.[7] The sale was made at a time when Toni's sales volume had begun to level off. Since earnings retention might have been difficult to justify, Toni's owners—the Harris brothers—were faced with the alternatives of paying penalty rates for improper accumulation of earnings or of paying out the income as dividends. Toni's income after corporate taxes was $4 million a year; with the Harris brothers' average personal income tax of 75 percent, only $1 million a year would have been left after they had paid personal taxes on dividends. By selling Toni for $13 million, they realized a $12 million capital gain because their book value was $1 million. After paying the 25 percent capital gains tax on the $12 million—$3 million—the Harrises realized $10 million after taxes ($13 million sale price minus $3 million tax). Thus Gillette paid the equivalent of three and one-quarter years' after-corporate-tax earnings for Toni, while the Harris brothers received ten years'

6. See materials in James K. Hall, *The Taxation of Corporate Surplus Accumulations* (Washington, D.C.: Government Printing Office, 1952), especially app. 3.

7. See J. K. Butters, J. Lintner, and W. L Cary, *Effects of Taxation on Corporate Mergers* (Boston: Harvard Business School, 1951), pp. 96–111. The lucid presentation by these authors has been drawn on for the general background, but the data have been approximated to simplify the illustration. The principle involved is not affected by the modifications of the facts.

after-personal-income-tax net income for it. The tax factor made the transaction advantageous to both parties.

The broad aspects of the federal corporate income tax have now been covered. Because the federal income tax on individuals is equally important for many business decisions, the individual tax structure will now be examined and compared with the corporate tax structure. This will provide a basis for making an intelligent choice as to which form of organization a firm should elect for tax purposes.

Personal Income Tax

Of some 5 million firms in the United States, over 4 million are organized as sole proprietorships or partnerships. The income of these firms is taxed as personal income to the owners or the partners. The net income of a proprietorship or partnership provides a basis for determining the individual's income tax liability. Thus, as a business tax, the individual income tax can be as important as the corporate income tax.

The personal income tax is conceptually straightforward, although many taxpayers find it confusing. Virtually all the income a person or family receives goes into determining the tax liability. For tax purposes income is classified as earned (wages or salary) and nonearned (primarily capital gains, rents, interest, and dividends). Under existing tax laws different kinds of income may be taxed in different ways or at different rates.

Total income from all sources is called gross income. All taxpayers are permitted to deduct part of their gross income before computing any tax. These deductions are of two types: standard deductions and personal exemptions.

Deductions. State and local taxes, medical expenses, interest payments, and charitable contributions are tax deductible expenses. The standard deduction can be claimed in lieu of these actual expenses. Since 1979, the standard deduction has been $3,400 for joint returns of married couples and $2,300 for single taxpayers. Taxpayers with actual expenses in excess of the standard deduction reduce the amount of taxable income by itemizing their deductible expenses.

Personal Exemptions. A $1,000 deduction is allowed for the taxpayer and each of that person's dependents. The deduction is doubled for any taxpayer who is over sixty-five years old or blind. In 1979, a family of four—husband, wife, and two dependent children, none blind or over sixty-five—had personal exemptions totaling $4,000. The apparent intent of the personal exemption is to exempt the first part of income from taxation, thereby enabling the family to obtain the basic necessities of life, such as food and shelter. The same intent appears in the form of the graduated income tax, where the highest tax rates are levied against "discretionary" income.

The following classifications are used in connection with calculating an individual's income tax liability:

Income
Wages, salaries, tips, and so on
Interest income
Dividends less exclusion
Business income
Applicable capital gains or losses
Pensions, annuities, rents, royalties, partnerships, and so on
Alimony received
Other categories

Total income (the sum of the above)

Adjustments to income
Moving expenses
Employee business expenses
Payments to an individual retirement arrangement
Alimony paid
Other categories

Total adjustments (the sum of the above)

Adjusted gross income =
Total income less adjustments to income

Less: Number of personal exemptions times $1,000

Less: Excess itemized deductions (itemized deductions in excess of the applicable standard deduction)

Equals taxable income

A number of aspects of tax liability have significance for corporate financial policy. Among the itemized deductions that enable gross income to be reduced is interest paid on borrowings by individuals. Thus, for both corporations and individuals, interest expenses paid are deductible for tax purposes.

Tax Rates for the Personal Income Tax. Tax rates that became effective with the Revenue Act of 1978 are indicated in Table 3.2. The tax rates presented are for the joint return of a married couple or surviving spouse. The taxable income is adjusted gross income less personal exemptions less the excess of itemized deductions over the applicable standard deduction. The average tax rate rises relatively slowly, but the marginal rate reaches 49 percent for taxable income of $60,000. For other than earned income, the marginal tax goes

Table 3.2

Marginal and Average Personal Income Tax Rates, 1979

Taxable Income		Tax Liability		
Over (1)	Not Over (2)	Tax (3)	Percent of Excess over Column 1 (4)	Average Percent Tax on Upper Limit of Bracket (5)
$ 3,400	$ 5,500	$ 0	14	5.35
5,500	7,600	294	16	8.29
7,600	11,900	630	18	11.80
11,900	16,000	1,404	21	14.16
16,000	20,200	2,265	24	16.20
20,200	24,600	3,273	28	18.31
24,600	29,900	4,505	32	20.74
29,900	35,200	6,201	37	23.19
35,200	45,800	8,162	43	27.77
45,800	60,000	12,720	49	32.80
60,000	85,600	19,678	54	39.14
85,600	109,400	33,502	59	43.46
109,400	162,400	47,544	64	50.16
162,400	215,400	81,464	68	54.55
215,400	and over	117,504	70	—[a]

The table shows a joint return for a married couple or surviving spouse.
[a]Not calculable.
Source: *Revenue Act of 1978* (Washington, D.C.: Government Printing Office, 1978).

up to a maximum of 70 percent on income of $215,400. Table 3.2 will be used in subsequent comparisons of sole proprietorships, partnerships, and corporations.

Individual Capital Gains and Losses

As with corporations, the distinction between short-term and long-term gains and losses is the twelve-month holding period. Net short-term gains are taxed at regular rates. The tax on net long-term capital gains is computed by deducting 60 percent of the amount, with the remaining 40 percent subject to tax at the marginal tax rate on ordinary income.

Dividend Income

The first $100 of dividend income received by an individual stockholder is excluded from taxable income. If stock is owned jointly by a husband and wife, the exclusion is $200. If only one spouse owns stock, however, the total exclusion is generally only $100.

To illustrate, if a family's gross income consists of $12,000 of salary and $500 of dividends on stock owned by the husband, the gross taxable income (before deductions) is $12,400. However, if the stock is jointly owned, the gross taxable income is $12,300, because $200 of the dividend income is excluded.

Choices among Alternative Forms of Business Organization

Taxes are an important influence in choosing among alternative forms of business organization. In the following sections the nature of the various alternatives and their advantages and disadvantages will be described. Then the tax aspects will be considered.

From a technical and legal standpoint, there are three major forms of business organization: the sole proprietorship, the partnership, and the corporation.[8] In terms of numbers, 70 percent of business firms are operated as sole proprietorships, 8 percent are partnerships, and 14 percent are corporations. By dollar value of sales, however, about 80 percent of business is conducted by corporations, about 13 percent by sole proprietorships, and about 7 percent by partnerships. The remainder of this section describes and compares the characteristics of these alternative forms of business organization.

Sole Proprietorship

A sole proprietorship is a business owned by one individual. Going into business as a sole proprietor is very simple; a person merely begins business operations. However, cities or counties may require even the smallest establishments to be licensed or registered. State licenses may also be required.

The proprietorship has key advantages for small operations. It is easily and inexpensively formed, requires no formal charter for operations, and is subject to few government regulations. Further, it pays no corporate income taxes, although all earnings of the firm are subject to personal income taxes, regardless of whether or not the owner withdraws the funds for personal use.

The proprietorship also has important limitations. Most significant is its inability to obtain large sums of capital. Further, the proprietor has unlimited personal liability for business debts; creditors can look to both business assets and personal assets to satisfy their claims. Finally, the proprietorship is limited to the life of the individual who creates it. For all these reasons, the sole proprietorship is limited primarily to small business operations. However, businesses frequently are started as proprietorships and then converted to corporations when their growth causes the disadvantages of the proprietorship form to outweigh its advantages.

Partnership

When two or more persons associate to conduct a business enterprise, a partnership is said to exist. Partnerships can operate under different degrees of

8. Other less common forms of organization include business trusts, joint stock companies, and cooperatives.

formality, ranging from an informal oral understanding to a written partnership agreement to a formal agreement filed with the state government. Like the proprietorship, the partnership has the advantages of ease and economy of formation as well as freedom from special government regulations. Partnership profits are taxed as personal income in proportion to the partners' claims, whether or not they are distributed to them.

One of the advantages of the partnership over the proprietorship is that it makes possible a pooling of various types of resources. Some partners contribute particular skills or contacts, while others contribute funds. However, there are practical limits to the number of co-owners who can join in an enterprise without destructive conflict, so most partnership agreements provide that the individual partners cannot sell their share of the business unless all the partners agree to accept the new partner (or partners).

If a new partner comes into the business, the old partnership ceases to exist and a new one is created. The withdrawal or death of any of the partners also dissolves the partnership. To prevent disputes under such circumstances, the articles of the partnership agreement should include terms and conditions under which assets are to be distributed upon dissolution. Of course, dissolution of the partnership does not necessarily mean the end of the business; the remaining partners may simply buy out the one who left the firm. To avoid financial pressures caused by the death of one of the partners, it is a common practice for each partner to carry life insurance naming the remaining partners as beneficiaries. The proceeds of such policies can be used to buy out the investment of the deceased partner.

A number of drawbacks stemming from the characteristics of the partnership limit its use. They include impermanence, difficulty of transferring ownership, and unlimited liability (except for limited partners). Partners risk their personal assets as well as their investments in the business. Further, under partnership law, the partners are jointly and separately liable for business debts. This means that if any partner is unable to meet the claims resulting from the liquidation of the partnership, the remaining partners must take over the unsatisfied claims, drawing on their personal assets if necessary.[9]

Corporation

A corporation is a legal entity created by a state.[10] It is a separate entity, distinct from its owners and managers. This separateness gives the corporation three major advantages: (1) it has an unlimited life—it can continue after its original owners and managers are dead; (2) it permits limited liability—stockholders are not personally liable for the debts of the firm; and (3) it

9. However, it is possible to limit the liabilities of some partners by establishing a limited partnership, wherein certain partners are designated general partners and others limited partners. Limited partnerships are quite common in the area of real estate investment.

10. Certain types of firms (for example, banks) are also chartered by the federal government.

permits easy transferability of ownership interest in the firm—ownership interests can be divided into shares of stock, which can be transferred far more easily than partnership interests.[11]

While a proprietorship or a partnership can commence operations without much paperwork, the chartering of a corporation involves a complicated, but routinized, process. First, a certificate of incorporation is drawn up; in most states it includes the following information: (1) name of proposed corporation, (2) purposes, (3) amount of capital stock, (4) number of directors, (5) names and addresses of directors, and (6) duration (if limited). The certificate is notarized and sent to the secretary of the state in which the business seeks incorporation. If it is satisfactory, the corporation officially exists.

The actual operations of the firm are governed by two documents, the charter and the bylaws. The corporate charter technically consists of a certificate of incorporation and, by reference, the general corporation laws of the state. Thus the corporation is bound by the general corporation laws of the state as well as by the unique provisions of its certificate of incorporation. The bylaws are a set of rules drawn up by the founders of the corporation to aid in governing the internal management of the company. Included are such points as (1) how directors are to be elected (all elected each year or, say, one-third each year, and whether cumulative voting will be used); (2) whether the preemptive right is granted to existing stockholders in the event new securities are sold; and (3) provisions for management committees, such as an executive committee or a finance committee, and their duties. Also included is the procedure for changing the bylaws themselves should conditions require this.

Tax Aspects of the Forms of Organization

To a small, growing firm, the advantage of the corporate form of organization is that the tax rate is low for income up to $100,000. There is "double taxation" of dividends, but salaries paid to the principals in the corporation are a tax-deductible expense and so are not subject to double taxation. The income of a proprietorship or partnership is subject to the personal tax at rates up to 70 percent unless it is paid out in salaries qualifying as earned income, which is subject to a maximum tax rate of 50 percent (a rate only 4 percent higher than the highest corporate tax rate). Thus the influence of taxes involves more than just a comparison of the personal tax rates with the corporate tax rates.

A specific example will illustrate the application of the several factors influencing the amount of taxes under alternative forms of business organiza-

11. In the case of small corporations, the limited liability feature is often a fiction, since bankers and credit managers frequently require personal guarantees from the stockholders of small, weak businesses.

tion. Craig Vernon, a married man with two children, is planning to start a new business, CV Manufacturing. He is trying to decide between a corporation or a sole proprietorship as the form of organization. Under either form, he will initially own 100 percent of the firm. Tax considerations are very important to him because he plans to finance the expected growth of the firm by drawing a salary sufficient for living expenses for his family (about $30,000) and plowing the remainder back into the enterprise.

Vernon will have no outside income, since he is liquidating all his investments in order to initially finance CV Manufacturing. He estimates that his itemized deductions will be $5,800 in excess of the standard deduction. He expects the following income before deducting his salary:

1979	$ 50,000
1980	80,000
1981	100,000

To determine whether Vernon should form the new business as a corporation or a proprietorship, we will first calculate the total taxes to be paid if it is organized as a corporation (see Table 3.3). Then we will calculate total taxes on the basis of a proprietorship (see Table 3.4).

By comparing Tables 3.3 and 3.4, we see that the taxes are lower for a corporation in each of the years. The reason is that the corporate form of ownership enables Vernon to split his income so that it is taxed at low marginal rates (most of it at less than 30 percent). But under the single proprietorship, much of the income is subject to higher rates.

We can compare the results and see that the corporate form of organization will yield Vernon the greatest bottom-line profits.

	1979	1980	1981
Taxes paid as a proprietorship	$10,312	$25,186	$36,216
Taxes paid as a corporation	6,673	12,523	18,523
Advantage as a corporation	$ 3,639	$12,663	$17,693

However, the advantage to the corporate form of organization is somewhat illusory. The figures shown for the corporation deal with dollars that have not yet come into the hands of the shareholders. If the earnings are distributed as a dividend, there will be further taxes to be borne by the shareholders individually. If a shareholder sells his or her stock and gets the benefit of corporate earnings in the form of a capital gain, the person will have to pay a capital gains tax. The extent of the ultimate additional tax is currently unknown, but the shareholder does benefit from having at least temporary use of the tax dollars saved.

Table 3.3

Total Taxes for CV as a Corporation

	1979	1980	1981
Income before salary and tax	$50,000	$80,000	$100,000
Less salary	−30,000	−30,000	−30,000
Taxable income, corporate	$20,000	$50,000	$ 70,000
Corporate taxes:			
$25,000 at 17%	3,400	4,250	4,250
$25,000 at 20%	0	5,000	5,000
Balance at 30%	0	0	6,000
Total corporate tax	$ 3,400	$ 9,250	$ 15,250
Salary	$30,000	$30,000	$ 30,000
Less exemptions	−4,000	−4,000	−4,000
Total	$26,000	$26,000	$ 26,000
Less excess deductions	−5,800	−5,800	−5,800
Taxable income, personal	$20,200	$20,200	$ 20,200
Total personal tax	3,273	3,273	3,273
Combined total tax	$ 6,673	$12,523	$ 18,523

Table 3.4

Total Taxes for CV as a Sole Proprietorship

	1979	1980	1981
Total income	$50,000	$80,000	$100,000
Less exemptions	−4,000	−4,000	−4,000
Total	$46,000	$76,000	$ 96,000
Less excess deductions	−5,800	−5,800	−5,800
Taxable income	$40,200	$70,200	$ 90,200
Tax liability	$10,312	$25,186	$ 36,216

Of course, for a large enterprise with income of several hundred million dollars, the "tax splitting" effect does not have as great an influence. However, in that case, the corporation's effectiveness in raising large sums of capital from a large number of sources becomes the major consideration in selecting the corporate form of organization.

While broad generalizations are not possible, these are factors that should at least be taken into account in making the decision about the form of organization for any business enterprise.

Summary

This chapter provides some basic background on the tax environment within which business firms operate. The corporate tax rate structure is relatively simple. The tax rate is 17 percent on income up to $25,000; 20, 30, and 40 percent respectively on the next three increments of $25,000; and 46 percent on all income over $100,000. Estimated taxes are paid in quarterly installments during the year in which the income is earned; when the returns are filed, the actual tax liability results either in additional payments or in a refund due. Any operating loss incurred by the corporation can be carried back three years and forward seven years against income in those years. The firm can elect not to employ the carryback provision.

Assets that are not bought and sold in the ordinary course of business are subject to capital gains tax on disposition. If an asset is held more than twelve months, any gain on the sale is classified as long-term and taxed at a maximum rate of 28+ percent. Gains on assets held fewer than twelve months are subject to taxation at the company's regular rate. Capital losses can be offset against capital gains to arrive at net long-term gains and net short-term gains. These losses can be carried back against gains for three years and carried forward for five years but cannot be offset against ordinary income.

Of the dividends received by a corporation owning stock in another firm, 85 percent are excluded from the receiving firm's taxable income, but the firm must pay full taxes on the remaining 15 percent. Dividends paid are not treated as a tax-deductible expense. Regardless of the size of its earnings, a corporation does not have to pay dividends if it needs funds for expansion. If, however, the funds are not used for a legitimate purpose—if earnings are retained merely to enable stockholders to avoid paying personal income taxes on dividends received—the firm is subject to an improper accumulations tax. Interest received is taxable as ordinary income; interest paid is a deductible expense.

Unincorporated business income is taxed at the personal tax rates of the owners. Personal income tax rates for both individuals and married persons filing jointly are progressive—the higher the income, the higher the tax rate. The rates start at 14 percent of taxable income and rise to either 50 percent or 70 percent, depending on whether the income is considered earned income.

The holding period for long-term capital gains and losses is twelve months, which is similar to that for corporations. Short-term gains are taxed as ordinary income, and 40 percent of long-term gains are taxed at the regular tax rate.

The information presented here on the tax system is not designed to make a tax expert of the reader. It merely provides a few essentials for recognizing the tax aspects of business financial problems and for developing an awareness of the kinds of situations that should be dealt with by tax specialists. These basics are, however, referred to frequently throughout the text, because income taxes are often an important factor in business financial decisions.

Sole proprietorships and partnerships are easily formed. All earnings are taxed as regular income at the rate of the owner or partner. Owners and partners are also personally liable for the debts of the business.

The corporation has the advantage of limiting the liability of the participants, but it is generally more expensive to organize. Once organized a corporation provides an easy means to transfer ownership to others. Corporate earnings paid as dividends are subject to double taxation. The other tax differences between corporations and proprietorships or partnerships depend on the facts of individual cases.

Questions

3.1 Compare the marginal and the average tax rates of corporations for taxable incomes of $5,000, $50,000, $500,000, and $50,000,000. Can you make such a comparison for sole proprietorships or for partnerships?

3.2 Which is the more relevant tax rate—the marginal or the average—in determining the form of organization for a new firm? Have recent changes in the tax laws made the form of organization more or less important than formerly? Explain.

3.3 For tax purposes, how does the treatment of interest expense compare with the treatment of common stock dividends from each of the following standpoints: a firm paying the interest or dividends, an individual recipient, and a corporate recipient?

3.4 What is the purpose of the Internal Revenue Code provision dealing with improper accumulation of corporate surplus revenue?

3.5 Why is personal income tax information important for a study of business finance?

3.6 How do the tax rates for capital gains and losses affect an individual's investment policies and opportunities for financing a small business?

3.7 What are the advantages and disadvantages of the use of a sole proprietorship versus a partnership for conducting the operations of a small business firm?

3.8 Under what circumstances does it become advantageous for the small business to incorporate?

3.9 In what sense is the corporation a person?

3.10 Would it be practical for General Motors to be organized as a partnership?

Problems

3.1 A corporation had net income of $60,000 in 1980.
   a. How much income tax must the corporation pay?
   b. What is the marginal tax rate?
   c. What is the average tax rate?

3.2 The Dolmite Corporation had net income from operations of $40,000. It also had $20,000 of interest expense and $35,000 of interest revenue during the year.
   a. How much income tax must the corporation pay?
   b. What is the marginal tax rate?
   c. What is the average tax rate?

3.3 The Triangle Corporation had net income of $130,000 in 1980, including $30,000 in dividend income on stocks of various major publicly held corporations.
   a. How much tax must the corporation pay?
   b. What is the average tax rate on net income?
   c. What is its marginal tax rate?

3.4 Determine the effective marginal and average income tax rates for a corporation earning (a) $10,000; (b) $100,000; (c) $1,000,000; and (d) $100,000,000.

3.5 The taxable income of the Pennock Corporation, formed in 1974, is indicated below. (Losses are shown as minuses.)

Year	Taxable Income
1974	−$80,000
1975	60,000
1976	50,000
1977	70,000
1978	−120,000

What is the corporate tax liability for each year?

3.6 Victor Stone has operated his small machine shop as a sole proprietorship for several years, but recent changes in the corporate tax structure have led him to consider incorporating. Stone is married and has two children. His only income, an annual salary of $40,000, is from operating the business. He reinvests any additional earnings in the business. In addition to the applicable personal exemptions, he has $6,100 of itemized deductions in excess of the standard deductions already incorporated in the tax tables (e.g., in Table 3.2). Stone estimates that his proprietorship earnings before salary and taxes for the period of 1979 to 1981 will be:

Year	Income before Salary and Taxes
1979	$50,000
1980	70,000
1981	90,000

a. What will his total taxes be under:
   1. a proprietorship?
   2. a corporate form of organization?

b. Should Stone incorporate? Discuss.

Selected References

Comiskey, Eugene E., and Hasselback, James R. "Analyzing the Profit-Tax Relationship." *Financial Management* 2 (Winter 1973), pp. 57–62.

Dyl, Edward A. "Capital Gains Taxation and Year-End Stock Market Behavior." *Journal of Finance* 32 (March 1977), pp. 165–175.

Federal Tax Course. Englewood Cliffs, N.J.: Prentice-Hall, 1980.

Maer, C. M., Jr., and Francis, R. A. "Whether to Incorporate." *Business Lawyer* 22 (April 1967), pp. 127–142.

The Revenue Act of 1978 and the Energy Tax Act of 1978. Englewood Cliffs, N.J.: Prentice-Hall, 1978.

Skadden, Donald H., ed. *A New Tax Structure for the United States.* Indianapolis, Ind.: Bobbs-Merrill, 1978.

Smith, D. T. *Effects of Taxation: Corporate Financial Policy.* Boston: Graduate School of Business Administration, Harvard University, 1952.

Appendix A to Chapter 3

Depreciation Methods

The four principal methods of depreciation—straight line, sum-of-years'-digits, double declining balance, and units of production—and their effects on a firm's taxes are illustrated in this appendix. We will begin by assuming that a machine is purchased for $1,100 and has an estimated useful life of ten years or ten thousand hours. It will have a scrap value of $100 after ten years or ten thousand hours of use, whichever comes first. Table 3A.1 illustrates each of the four depreciation methods and compares the depreciation charges of each method over the ten-year period.

Table 3A.1

Comparison of Depreciation Methods for a 10-Year, $1,100 Asset with a $100 Salvage Value

Depreciation Methods

Year	Straight Line	Sum-of-Years'-Digits	Units of Production[a]	Double Declining Balance
1	$ 100	$ 182	$ 200	$ 220
2	100	164	180	176
3	100	145	150	141
4	100	127	130	113
5	100	109	100	90
6	100	91	80	72
7	100	73	60	58
8	100	55	50	46
9	100	36	30	42
10	100	18	20	42
Total	$1,000	$1,000	$1,000	$1,000

a. The assumption is made that the machine is used the following number of hours: first year, 2,000; second year, 1,800; third year, 1,500; fourth year, 1,300; fifth year, 1,000; sixth year, 800; seventh year, 600; eighth year, 500; ninth year, 300; tenth year, 200.

Straight Line

With the straight line method, a uniform annual depreciation charge of $100 a year is provided. This figure is arrived at by simply dividing the economic life into the total cost of the machine minus the estimated salvage value:

$$\frac{(\$1{,}100 \text{ cost} - \$100 \text{ salvage value})}{10 \text{ years}} = \$100 \text{ a year depreciation charge.}$$

If the estimated salvage value is not in excess of 10 percent of the original cost, it can be ignored, but we are leaving it in for illustrative purposes.

Sum-of-Years'-Digits

Under the sum-of-years'-digits method, the yearly depreciation allowance is determined as follows:

1. Calculate the sum of the years' digits; in our example, there is a total of 55 digits: 1 + 2 + 3 + 4 + 5 + 6 + 7 + 8 + 9 + 10 = 55. This figure can also be arrived at by means of the sum of an algebraic progression equation where N is the life of the asset:

$$\text{Sum} = N\left(\frac{N+1}{2}\right)$$
$$= 10\left(\frac{10+1}{2}\right) = 55.$$

2. Divide the number of remaining years by the sum-of-years'-digits and multiply this fraction by the depreciable cost (total cost minus salvage value) of the asset:

$$\text{Year 1: } \frac{10}{55}(\$1{,}000) = \$182 \text{ depreciation.}$$

$$\text{Year 2: } \frac{9}{55}(\$1{,}000) = \$164 \text{ depreciation.}$$

$$\text{Year 10: } \frac{1}{55}(\$1{,}000) = \$18 \text{ depreciation.}$$

Units of Production

Under the units of production method, the expected useful life of 10,000 hours is divided into the depreciable cost (purchase price minus salvage value) to arrive at an hourly depreciation rate of ten cents. Since, in our example, the machine is run for 2,000 hours in the first year, the depreciation in that year is $200; in the second year, $180; and so on. With this method, depreciation charges cannot be estimated precisely ahead of time; the firm must wait until the end of the year to determine what usage has been made of the machine and hence its depreciation.

Double Declining Balance

The double declining balance method (DDB) is a special case of the declining balance methods. The depreciation charge is calculated in DDB by multiplying a fixed rate times the cost less accumulated depreciation. Since the undepreciated balance becomes smaller in each successive period, the amount of depreciation declines during each successive period. The rate applied to the undepreciated balance is fixed. The rate most commonly used is the maximum permitted for income tax purposes—usually twice the straight line method. Hence it is called the double declining balance method.

In DDB, the estimated salvage value is not usually subtracted from the cost of the asset in making the depreciation calculation, though that practice is followed in other depreciation methods. The DDB method is illustrated for the data of our example in Table 3A.2.

Table 3A.2

Illustration of DDB Method

Year (1)	Net Book Value ($1,000 − Column 3 of Previous Year) (2)	DDB Depreciation (0.20 × Column 2) (3)	Accumulated Depreciation (Sum of Column 3) (4)	Test of Straight Line Method (5)	Adjusted Accumulated Depreciation (6)
1	$1,100	$220	$220		
2	880	176	396		
3	704	141	537		
4	563	113	650		
5	450	90	740		
6	360	72	812		
7	288	58	870		
8	230	46	916	$43[a]	
9	184	37	953	42[b]	$ 958
10	147	29	982	42	1,000

a. $1,100 − $100 − $870 = $130 ÷ 3 = $43.
b. $1,100 − $100 − $916 = $84 ÷ 2 = $42.

Column 2 is the net book value subject to depreciation. It is the purchase price of the asset less the depreciation taken. For the second year, the depreciation rate is applied to $1,100 less $220, or $880. Then 20 percent of $880 is

$176, the amount of depreciation for Year 2; and this procedure continues for each successive year.

The company makes a switch from DDB to straight line whenever straight line depreciation on the remaining net book value of the asset exceeds the depreciation amount under the DDB method. In Table 3A.2, we test for this in the eighth year, but DDB depreciation is still somewhat higher. In the ninth year, the depreciable amount of $1,000 less accumulated depreciation of $916 equals $84, which is $42 per year for the remaining two years. The switch is made at this point so that the adjusted accumulated depreciation as shown in Column 6 is the full $1,000 net depreciable value of the asset.

Thus, although the salvage value is not initially taken into account in applying the DDB method, it is not ignored. The method we have illustrated is used when the salvage value is relatively small. Strictly applied, the salvage value has a substantial impact on the depreciation rate applied. The formula for computing the rate under the declining balance method when the salvage value is relatively large is:

$$\text{Depreciation rate} = 1 - \left(\frac{Z}{I}\right)^{1/N}$$

where

N = Estimated periods of service life,
Z = Estimated salvage value,
I = Purchase price of the asset.

Thus for $N = 8$ years, $Z = \$2{,}000$, and $I = \$12{,}000$, we have

$$\text{Depreciation rate} = 1 - \left(\frac{2{,}000}{12{,}000}\right)^{1/8} = 1 - 0.80 = 0.20 = 20\%.$$

If N is changed to 4 years, we have

$$\text{Depreciation rate} = 1 - \left(\frac{2{,}000}{12{,}000}\right)^{1/4} = 1 - 0.64 = 0.36 = 36\%.$$

Thus although the depreciation rate under the declining balance method is applied to the full investment cost before the estimated salvage value is deducted, the amount of the depreciation and its time pattern under the declining balance are affected by the amount of the estimated salvage value.

Effect of Depreciation on Taxes Paid

The effect of the accelerated methods on a firm's income tax payment is easily demonstrated. If a firm chooses in the first year to use the straight line method, it can deduct only $100 from its earnings to arrive at earnings before taxes (the amount of earnings to which the tax rate applies). However, using any one of the other three methods, the firm would have a much greater deduction and, therefore, a lower tax liability.

Changing the Depreciable Life of an Asset

The Treasury Department of the federal government establishes certain guidelines that set legal limits on the minimum life of classes of assets; by lowering these limits, the government can accomplish ends similar to permitting accelerated depreciation methods. Halving the minimum depreciable life of an asset, for example, would effectively double the annual rate of depreciation.

Problems

3A.1 The Altmont Corporation has purchased an asset for $5,200; it has an estimated salvage value of $200 at the end of its five-year life. Calculate the annual depreciation expense under each of the following methods:
a. Straight line method
b. Double declining balance method
c. Sum-of-years'-digits method

3A.2 The Rudd Corporation has purchased for $8,500 a machine with an expected useful life of eight years or 6,000 hours. It has an expected salvage value of $500. The annual usage of the machine is estimated as follows:

Year	Hours of Usage
1	1,500
2	1,200
3	1,000
4	800
5	500
6	400
7	300
8	300
	6,000

a. Calculate the annual depreciation expense under each of the following methods:
1. Straight line method
2. Sum-of-years'-digits method
3. Units of production method
4. Double declining balance method

b. Add the depreciation expenses for the first two years and rank each method in descending order of the amount of tax deductible depreciation expenses.

3A.3 Assume the same facts as in the above problem except for a four-year life, salvage value of $2,500, and hours of usage per year of:

Year	Hours of Usage
1	2,000
2	1,800
3	1,200
4	1,000
	6,000

Answer the same questions asked in problem 3A.2, a and b.

4
The Time Value of Money

A clear view of the time value of money is essential to an understanding of many topics throughout this book. Financial structure decisions, lease versus purchase decisions, bond refunding operations, security valuation techniques, and the whole question of the cost of capital are subjects that cannot be understood without a knowledge of compound interest.

Many people are afraid of the subject and simply avoid it. It is certainly true that many successful business persons—even some bankers—know very little about it. However, as technology advances, as more engineers become involved in general management, and as modern business administration programs turn out more highly qualified graduates, this pattern—success in spite of yourself—will become more difficult to achieve. Furthermore, a fear of compound interest relationships is quite unfounded; the subject matter is not inherently difficult. Almost all problems involving compound interest can be handled with only a few basic formulas.

Compound Value

A person invests $1,000 in a security that pays 10 percent interest compounded annually. How much will this person have at the end of one year? To treat the matter systematically, let us define the following terms:

P_0 = Principal, or beginning amount, at time 0.
r = Interest rate.
P_0r = Total dollar amount of interest earned.
V_t = Value at the end of t periods.

When t equals 1, V_t can be calculated as follows:

$$\begin{aligned} V_1 &= P_0 + P_0r \\ &= P_0(1 + r). \end{aligned} \tag{4.1}$$

Equation 4.1 shows that the ending amount (V_1) is equal to the beginning amount (P_0) times the factor $(1 + r)$. In the example, where P_0 is \$1,000, r is 10 percent, and t is one year, V_t is determined as follows:

$$V_1 = \$1,000\,(1.0 + 0.10) = \$1,000\,(1.10) = \$1,100.$$

Multiple Periods

If the person leaves the \$1,000 on deposit for five years, to what amount will it have grown at the end of that period? Equation 4.1 can be used to construct Table 4.1, which indicates the answer. Note that V_2, the balance at the end of the second year, is found as follows:

$$V_2 = V_1\,(1 + r) = P_0\,(1 + r)\,(1 + r) = P_0\,(1 + r)^2.$$

Similarly, V_3, the balance after three years, is found as:

$$V_3 = V_2\,(1 + r) = P_0\,(1 + r)^3.$$

Table 4.1

Compound Interest Calculations

Period	Beginning Amount ×	$(1 + r)$ =	Ending Amount (V_t)
1	\$1,000.0	1.10	\$1,100.0
2	1,100.0	1.10	1,210.0
3	1,210.0	1.10	1,331.0
4	1,331.0	1.10	1,464.1
5	1,464.1	1.10	1,610.5

In general, V_t, the compound amount at the end of any year t, is found as:

$$V_t = P_0\,(1 + r)^t. \tag{4.2}$$

Equation 4.2 is the fundamental equation of compound interest. Equation 4.1 is simply a special case of Equation 4.2, where $t = 1$.

While an understanding of the derivation of Equation 4.2 will help in understanding much of the remaining material in this chapter (and in subsequent chapters), the concept can be applied quite readily in a mechanical sense. Tables have been constructed for values of $(1 + r)^t$ for wide ranges of r and t. (See Table A.1 in Appendix A at the end of the book.)

Letting CVIF (compound value interest factor) = $(1 + r)^t$, we can write Equation 4.2 as $V_t = P_0$ (CVIF). It is necessary only to go to an appropriate interest table to find the proper interest factor. For example, the correct interest factor for the illustration given in Table 4.1 can be found in Table A.1. Look down the period column to 5, then across this row to the appropriate number in the 10 percent column to find the interest factor, 1.6105. Then, using this interest factor, the compound value of the $1,000 after five years is:

$$V_5 = P_0\,(\text{CVIF}) = \$1{,}000(1.6105) = \$1{,}610.5.$$

This is precisely the same figure that was obtained by the long method in Table 4.1.

Graphic View of the Compounding Process: Growth

Figure 4.1 shows how the interest factors for compounding grow as the compounding period increases. Curves can be drawn for any interest rate, including fractional rates; we have plotted curves for 0 percent, 5 percent, and 10 percent from data in Table A.1.

Figure 4.1 also shows how $1 (or any other sum) grows over time at various rates of interest. The higher the rate of interest, the faster the rate of growth. The interest rate is, in fact, the growth rate; if a deposited sum earns 5 percent, then the funds on deposit grow at the rate of 5 percent per year.

Figure 4.1

Relationships among Compound Value Interest Factors, Interest Rates, and Time

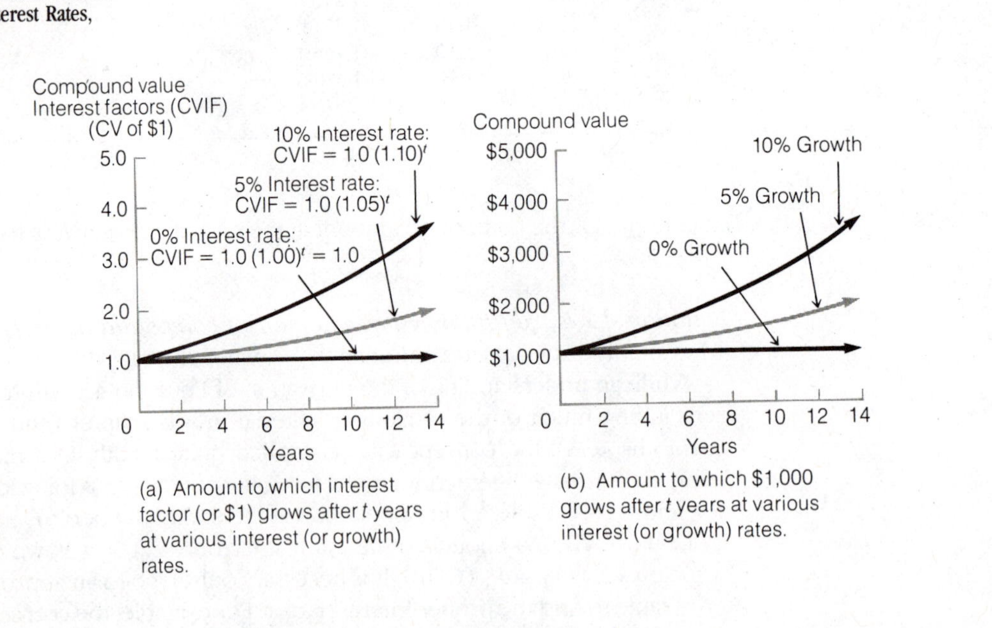

(a) Amount to which interest factor (or $1) grows after *t* years at various interest (or growth) rates.

(b) Amount to which $1,000 grows after *t* years at various interest (or growth) rates.

Present Value

Suppose you are offered the alternative of either $1,610.50 at the end of five years or X dollars today. There is no question that the $1,610.50 will be paid in full (perhaps the payer is the United States government). Having no current need for the money, you deposit it in a savings association paying a 10 percent dividend; the 10 percent is your *opportunity cost.* How small must X be to induce you to accept the promise of $1,610.50 five years hence?

Table 4.1 shows that the initial amount of $1,000 growing at 10 percent a year yields $1,610.50 at the end of five years. Thus, you should be indifferent about the choice between $1,000 today and $1,610.50 at the end of five years. The $1,000 is the present value of $1,610.50 due in five years when the applicable interest rate is 10 percent. The subscript zero in the term P_0 indicates the present. Hence present value quantities can be identified by either P_0 or *PV.*

Finding present values (*discounting,* as it is commonly called) is simply the reverse of compounding, and Equation 4.2 can readily be transformed into a present value formula.

$$\text{Present value} = P_0 = \frac{V_t}{(1+r)^t} = V_t\left[\frac{1}{(1+r)^t}\right]. \qquad (4.3)$$

Tables have been constructed for the bracketed term for various values of r and t. (See Table A.2 in Appendix A at the end of the book.) For the case being considered, look down the 10 percent column in Table A.2 to the fifth row. The figure shown there, 0.6209, is the present value interest factor (PVIF) used to determine the present value of $1,610.50 payable in five years, discounted at 10 percent.

$$\begin{aligned} P_0 &= V_5\,(\text{PVIF}) \\ &= \$1{,}610.50\,(0.6209) \\ &= \$1{,}000. \end{aligned}$$

Graphic View of the Discounting Process

Figure 4.2 shows how the interest factors for discounting decrease as the discounting period increases. The curves in the figure, plotted from data in Table A.2, show that the present value of a sum to be received at some future date decreases (1) as the payment date is extended further into the future and (2) as the discount rate increases. If relatively high discount rates apply, funds due in the future are worth very little today; even at relatively low discount rates, funds due in the distant future are not worth much today. For example, $1,000 due in ten years is worth $247 today if the discount rate is 15 percent, but it is worth $614 today at a 5 percent discount rate. Similarly, $1,000 due in ten years at 10 percent is worth $386 today, but the same amount at the same discount rate due in five years is worth $621 today.[1]

1. Note that Figure 4.2 is not a mirror image of Figure 4.1. The curves in Figure 4.1 approach ∞ as t increases; in Figure 4.2, the curves approach zero, not $-\infty$, as t increases.

Figure 4.2

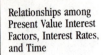

Relationships among Present Value Interest Factors, Interest Rates, and Time

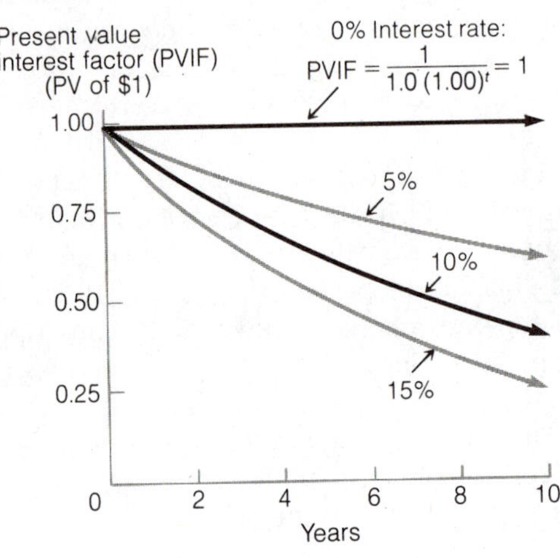

Compound Value versus Present Value

Because a thorough understanding of compound value concepts is vital to understanding the remainder of this book and because the subject gives many students trouble, it will be useful to examine in more detail the relationship between compounding and discounting.

Notice that Equation 4.2, the basic equation for compounding, is developed from the logical sequence set forth in Table 4.1; the equation merely presents in mathematical form the steps outlined in the table. The present value interest factor ($PVIF_{r,t}$) in Equation 4.3 (the basic equation for discounting or finding present values) is the reciprocal of the compound value interest factor ($CVIF_{r,t}$) for the same r,t combination:

$$PVIF_{r,t} = \frac{1}{CVIF_{r,t}}.$$

For example, the *compound value* interest factor for 10 percent over five years is seen in Table A.1 to be 1.6105. The *present value* interest factor for 10 percent over five years must therefore be the reciprocal of 1.6105:

$$PVIF_{10\%,\ 5\ years} = \frac{1}{1.6105} = 0.6209.$$

The PVIF found in this manner must, of course, correspond with the PVIF shown in Table A.2 at the end of this book.

The reciprocal nature of the relationship between present value and compound value permits us to find present values in two ways—by multiplying or by dividing. Thus the present value of $1,000 due in five years and discounted at 10 percent can be found as:

$$P_0 = \text{PV} = V_t\,(\text{PVIF}_{r,t}) = V_t\left(\frac{1}{1+r}\right)^t = \$1{,}000\,(0.6209) = \$620.90$$

or

$$P_0 = \text{PV} = \frac{V_t}{\text{CVIF}_{r,t}} = \frac{V_t}{(1+r)^t} = \frac{\$1{,}000}{1.6105} = \$620.90.$$

In the second form, it is easy to see why the present value of a given future amount (V_t) declines as the discount rate increases.

To conclude this comparison of present and compound values, compare Figures 4.1 and 4.2. Notice that the vertical intercept is at 1.0 in each case, but compound value interest factors rise while present value interest factors decline. The reason for this divergence is, of course, that present value factors are reciprocals of compound factors.

Compound Value of an Annuity

An *annuity* is defined as a series of payments of a fixed amount for a specified number of years. Each payment occurs at the end of the year.[2] For example, a promise to pay $1,000 a year for three years is a three-year annuity. If you were to receive such an annuity and were to invest each annual payment in a security paying 10 percent interest, how much would you have at the end of three years? The answer is shown graphically in Figure 4.3. The first payment is made at the end of Year 1, the second at the end of Year 2, and the third at the end of Year 3. The last payment is not compounded at all; the next

Figure 4.3

Graphic Illustration of an Annuity: Compound Sum

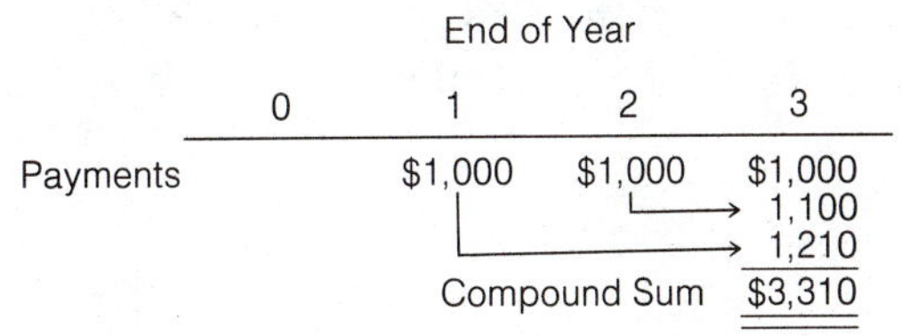

	End of Year			
	0	1	2	3
Payments		$1,000	$1,000	$1,000
			└→	1,100
		└→		1,210
		Compound Sum		$3,310

2. Had the payment been made at the beginning of the period, each receipt would simply have been shifted back one year. The annuity would have been called an *annuity due;* the one in the present discussion, where payments are made at the end of each period, is called a *regular annuity* or, sometimes, a *deferred annuity.*

to the last is compounded for one year; the second from the last for two years, and so on back to the first, which is compounded for $t - 1$ years. When the compound values of each of the payments are added, their total is the sum of the annuity. In the example, this total is \$3,310.

Expressed algebraically, with S_t defined as the compound sum, a as the periodic receipt, t as the length of the annuity, and CVIFA as the compound value interest factor for an annuity, the formula for S_t is:

$$\begin{aligned} S_t &= a(1+r)^{t-1} + a(1+r)^{t-2} + \cdots + a(1+r)^1 + a(1+r)^0 \\ &= a[(1+r)^{t-1} + (1+r)^{t-2} + \cdots + (1+r)^1 + (1+r)^0] \qquad (4.4) \\ &= a\,[\text{CVIFA}]. \end{aligned}$$

The expression in brackets, CVIFA, has been given values for various combinations of t and r. To find these, see Table A.3 in Appendix A. To find the answer to the three-year, \$1,000 annuity problem, simply refer to Table A.3, look down the 10 percent column to the row for the third year and multiply the factor 3.3100 by \$1,000. The answer is the same as the one derived by the long method illustrated in Figure 4.3:

$$\begin{aligned} S_t &= a \times \text{CVIFA} \\ S_3 &= \$1{,}000 \times 3.3100 = \$3{,}310.00. \end{aligned}$$

Notice that the CVIFA for the sum of an annuity is always *larger* than the number of years the annuity runs.

Present Value of an Annuity

Suppose you were offered the following alternatives: a three-year annuity of \$1,000 a year or a lump-sum payment today. You have no need for the money during the next three years, so if you accept the annuity you will simply invest the funds in a security paying 10 percent interest. How large must the lump-sum payment be to make it equivalent to the annuity? Figure 4.4 helps explain the problem.

The present value of the first receipt is $a[1/(1+r)]$, that of the second is $a[1/(1+r)]^2$, and so on. Defining the present value of an annuity of t years as PV_{at} and the present value interest factor for an annuity as PVIFA, we can write the following equation:

$$\begin{aligned} \text{PV}_{at} &= a\left[\frac{1}{1+r}\right] + a\left[\frac{1}{1+r}\right]^2 + \cdots + a\left[\frac{1}{1+r}\right]^t \\ &= a\left[\frac{1}{(1+r)} + \frac{1}{(1+r)^2} + \cdots + \frac{1}{(1+r)^t}\right] \qquad (4.5) \\ &= a[\text{PVIFA}]. \end{aligned}$$

Again, tables have been worked out for the PVIFA, the term in the brackets. (See Table A.4 in Appendix A.) From Table A.4, the PVIFA for a three-year, 10

Figure 4.4

Graphic Illustration of an Annuity: Present Value

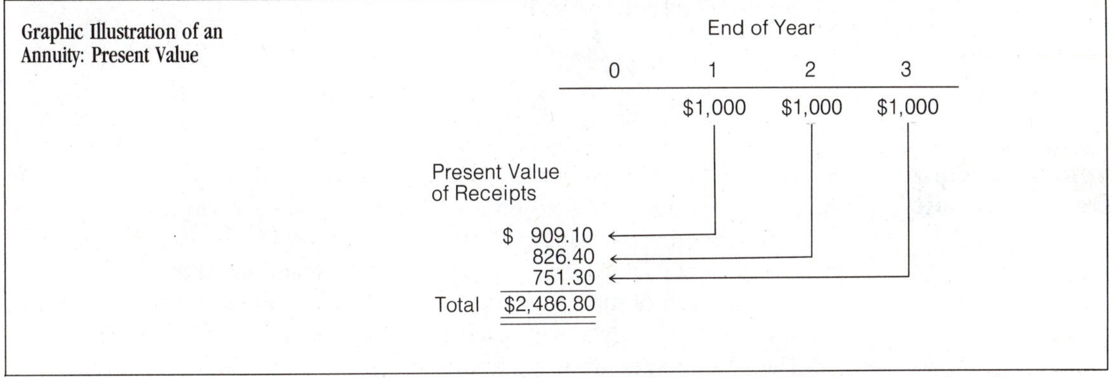

percent annuity is found to be 2.4869. Multiplying this factor by the $1,000 annual receipt gives $2,486.90, the present value of the annuity:

$$\begin{aligned} PV_{at} &= a \times \text{PVIFA}. \\ PV_{a3} &= \$1{,}000 \times 2.4869 \\ &= \$2{,}486.90. \end{aligned} \tag{4.6}$$

Notice that the PVIFA for the present value of an annuity is always less than the number of years the annuity runs, whereas the CVIFA for the sum of an annuity is larger than the number of years.

Annual Payments for Accumulation of a Future Sum

Thus far in the chapter all the equations have been based on Equation 4.2. The present value equation merely involves a transposition of Equation 4.2, and the annuity equations simply take the sum of the basic compound interest equation for different values of t. We now examine some additional modifications of the equations.

Suppose we want to know the amount of money that must be deposited at 10 percent for each of the next five years in order to have $10,000 available to pay off a debt at the end of the fifth year. Dividing both sides of Equation 4.4 by the CVIFA, we obtain:

$$a = \frac{S_t}{\text{CVIFA}}.$$

Looking up the sum of an annuity interest factor for five years at 10 percent in Table A.3 at the end of the book and dividing that figure into $10,000 we find:

$$a = \frac{\$10{,}000}{6.1051} = \$1{,}638.$$

Thus, if $1,638 is deposited each year in an account paying a 10 percent return, at the end of five years the account will have accumulated $10,000. The procedure is called setting up a sinking fund; such funds are used, for example, to provide for bond retirements.

Annual Receipts from an Annuity

Suppose that on September 1, 1980, you receive an inheritance of $7,000. The money is to be used for your education and is to be spent during the academic years beginning September 1981, 1982, and 1983. If you place the money in a bank account paying 10 percent annual interest and make three equal withdrawals on each of the specified dates, how large can each withdrawal be to leave you with exactly a zero balance after the last one has been made?

The solution requires application of the present value of an annuity formula, Equation 4.6. Here, however, we know that the present value of the annuity is $7,000, and the problem is to find the three equal annual payments when the interest rate is 10 percent. This calls for dividing both sides of Equation 4.6 by the PVIFA to make Equation 4.7.

$$\text{PV}_{at} = a \times \text{PVIFA}. \tag{4.6}$$

$$a = \frac{\text{PV}_{at}}{\text{PVIFA}}. \tag{4.7}$$

The interest factor (PVIFA) is found in Appendix A, Table A.4 to be 2.4869. Substituting this value in Equation 4.7, we find the three equal annual withdrawals to be $2,814.75 a year:

$$a = \frac{\$7{,}000}{2.4869} = \$2{,}814.75.$$

This particular kind of calculation frequently is used in setting up insurance and pension plan benefit schedules; it is also used to find the periodic payments necessary to retire a loan within a specified period. For example, if you want to retire a $7,000 bank loan, bearing interest at 10 percent on the unpaid balance, in three equal annual installments, the amount of each payment is $2,814.75. In this case, you are the borrower, and the bank is "buying" an annuity with a present value of $7,000.

Determining Interest Rates

In many instances the present values and cash flows associated with a payment stream are known, but the interest rate is not known. Suppose a bank offers to lend you $1,000 today if you sign a note agreeing to pay the bank $1,762.30 at the end of five years. What rate of interest would you be paying on the loan? To answer the question, we use Equation 4.2:

$$V_t = P_0\,(1 + r)^t = P_0\,(\text{CVIF}). \tag{4.2}$$

We simply solve for the CVIF, then look up this value of the CVIF in Table A.1 under the row for the fifth year:

$$\text{CVIF} = \frac{V_5}{P_0} = \frac{\$1{,}762.30}{\$1{,}000} = 1.7623.$$

Looking across the row for the fifth year, we find the value 1.7623 in the 12 percent column; therefore, the interest rate on the loan is 12 percent.

Precisely the same approach is taken to determine the interest rate implicit in an annuity. For example, suppose a bank will lend you $2,401.80 if you sign a note in which you agree to pay the bank $1,000 at the end of the next three years. What interest rate is the bank charging you? To answer the question, we solve Equation 4.6 for the PVIFA and then look up the PVIFA in Table A.4:

$$\text{PV}_{at} = a \times \text{PVIFA}. \tag{4.6}$$

$$\text{PVIFA} = \frac{\text{PV}_{a3}}{a} = \frac{\$2{,}401.8}{\$1{,}000} = 2.4018.$$

Looking across the third-year row, we find the factor 2.4018 under the 12 percent column; therefore, the bank is lending you money at 12 percent interest.

Linear Interpolation

The tables give values for even interest rates (such as 8 percent or 9 percent). Suppose you need to find the present value of $1,000 due in ten years and discounted at 8¼ percent. The appropriate PVIF is not in the tables, but a very close approximation to the correct factor can be estimated by the method of *linear interpolation.* The PVIF for 8 percent, ten years, is 0.4632; that for 9 percent is 0.4224. The difference is 0.0408. Since 8¼ is 25 percent of the way between 8 and 9, we can subtract 25 percent of 0.0408 from 0.4632 and obtain 0.453 as the PVIF for 8¼ percent due in ten years. Thus, if the appropriate discount rate is 8¼ percent, $1,000 due in ten years is worth $453 today.

In general, the formula used for interpolation is as follows:

$$\text{IF for intermediate interest rate} = \left(\frac{r - r_L}{r_H - r_L}\right)(\text{IF}_H - \text{IF}_L) + \text{IF}_L. \tag{4.8}$$

Here r is the interest rate in question, r_L is the interest rate in the table just lower than r, r_H is the interest rate in the table just higher than r, and IF_H and IF_L are the interest factors for r_H and r_L, respectively. Using the equation with the preceding example, we have:

$$\text{PVIF for } 8\tfrac{1}{4}\% \text{ due in 10 years} = \left(\frac{8.25 - 8}{9 - 8}\right)(0.4244 - 0.4632) + 0.4632$$
$$= \left(\frac{0.25}{1}\right)(-0.0408) + 0.4632 = 0.453,$$

which is the PVIF found before. The equation can be used for each type of factor expression, PVIF, CVIF, PVIFA, or CVIFA.

Interpolation can also be used to determine interest rates if interest factors are provided. For example, suppose an investment that costs $163,500 promises to yield $50,000 per year for four years, and we want to know the rate of return on the investment. We use Equation 4.6 to find the PVIFA:

$$\text{PVIFA} = \frac{\$163{,}500}{\$50{,}000} = 3.27.$$

Looking this value up in Table A.4, Period 4, we see that it lies between 8 and 9 percent. Applying the interpolation formula, but solving for r, we have:[3]

$$\text{PVIFA for } r\% = 3.27 = \left(\frac{r - 8}{9 - 8}\right)(3.2397 - 3.3121) + 3.3121$$
$$3.27 = (r - 8)(-0.0724) + 3.3121$$
$$-0.0421 = -0.0724r + 0.5792$$
$$0.0724r = 0.6213$$
$$r = 8.58\%.$$

Present Value of an Uneven Series of Receipts

The definition of an annuity includes the words *fixed amount;* in other words, annuities deal with constant, or level, payments or receipts. Although many financial decisions do involve constant payments, many others (especially those dealt with in the next chapter) are concerned with uneven flows of cash. Consequently it is necessary to expand our analysis to deal with varying payment streams. Since most of the applications call for present values, not compound sums or other figures, this section is restricted to the present value (PV).

To do the calculating procedure, suppose someone offers to sell you a series of payments consisting of $300 after one year, $100 after two years, and $200 after three years. How much will you be willing to pay for the series, assuming the appropriate discount rate (interest rate) is 10 percent? To determine the purchase price, we simply compute the present value of the series;

3. Alternatively, the interest factors can be calculated using the formulas at the top of each table. For example, using an 8.25 percent interest rate and a ten-year period:

$$\text{CVIF} = (1 + k)^n = 1.0825^{10} = 2.2094.$$
$$\text{PVIF} = 1/(1 + k)^n = 1/1.0825^{10} = 0.4526.$$
$$\text{CVIFA} = [(1 + k)^n - 1]/k = (1.0825^{10} - 1)/0.0825 = 14.6594.$$
$$\text{PVIFA} = \frac{1 - \dfrac{1}{(1 + k)^n}}{k} = \frac{1 - \dfrac{1}{1.0825^{10}}}{0.0825} = 6.6350.$$

In this book, the formulas will be used for interest rates not given in the tables.

the calculations are worked out in Table 4.2. The receipts for each year are shown in the second column; the discount factors are given in the third column; and the product of these two columns, the present value of each individual receipt, is given in the last column. When the individual present values in the last column are added together, the sum is the present value of the investment—$505.63. Under the assumptions of the example, you should be willing to pay this amount for the investment.

Table 4.2

Calculating the Present Value of an Uneven Series of Payments

Period	Receipt ×	Interest Factor (PVIF) =	Present Value (PV or P_0)
1	$300	0.9091	$272.73
2	100	0.8264	82.64
3	200	0.7513	150.26
		PV of investment	$505.63

If the series of payments are somewhat different—say $300 at the end of the first year, $200 at the end of the second year, then eight annual payments of $100 each—we will probably want to use a different procedure for finding the investment's present value. We can, of course, set up a calculating table such as Table 4.2, but because most of the payments are part of an annuity, we can use a short cut. The calculating procedure is shown in Table 4.3, and the logic of the table is diagramed in Figure 4.5.

Table 4.3

Calculating Procedure for an Uneven Series of Payments That Includes an Annuity

1. PV of $300 due in one year = $300 (0.9091) =	$272.73
PV of $200 due in two years = $200 (0.8264) =	165.28
2. PV of eight-year annuity with $100 receipts	
a. PV at beginning of Year 3: $100 (5.3349) = $533.49	
b. PV of $533.49 = $533.49 (0.8264)	440.88
3. PV of total series	$878.89

Section 1 of Table 4.3 deals with the $300 and the $200 received at the end of the first and second years, respectively; their present values are found to be $272.73 and $165.28. Section 2 deals with the eight $100 payments. In Part a, the value of a $100, eight-year, 10 percent annuity is found to be $533.49. However, the first receipt under the annuity comes at the end of the third year, so it is worth less than $533.49 today. Specifically, it is worth the present value of $533.49, discounted back two years at 10 percent, or $440.88. This

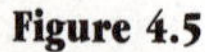

Figure 4.5

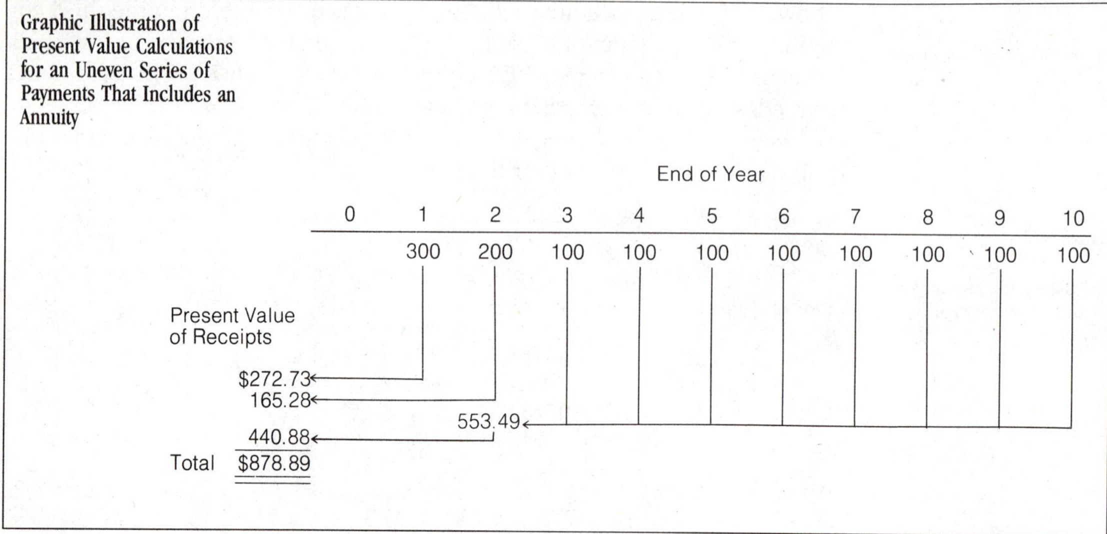

Graphic Illustration of Present Value Calculations for an Uneven Series of Payments That Includes an Annuity

calculation is shown in Part b of Section 2.[4] When the present values of the first two payments are added to the present value of the annuity component, the sum is the present value of the entire investment, or $878.89.

Semiannual and Other Compounding Periods[5]

In all the examples used thus far, it has been assumed that returns were received annually. For example, in the section dealing with compound values, it was assumed that the funds earned 10 percent a year. However, suppose the earnings rate had been 10 percent compounded semiannually (that is, every six months). What would this have meant? Consider the following example.

You invest $1,000 in a security to receive a return of 10 percent compounded semiannually. How much will you have at the end of one year? Since semiannual compounding means that interest is actually paid each six months, this fact is taken into account in the tabular calculations in Table 4.4. Here, the annual interest rate is divided by two, but twice as many compounding periods are used because interest is paid twice a year. Comparing the amount on hand at the end of the second six-month period, $1,102.50, with what would have been on hand under annual compounding, $1,100.00, shows that semiannual compounding is better for the saver. This result occurs, of course, because the saver earns interest on interest more frequently.

4. The present value of the annuity portion, $440.88, could also have been found by subtracting the PVIFA for a two-year annuity from the PVIFA for a ten-year annuity, then multiplying the result by $100.
5. This section can be omitted without loss of continuity.

Table 4.4

Compound Interest Calculations with Semiannual Compounding

Period	Beginning Amount (P_0)	× (1 + r) =	Ending Amount (P_t)
1	$1,000.00	1.05	$1,050.00
2	1,050.00	1.05	1,102.50

General formulas can be developed for use when compounding periods are more frequent than once a year. To demonstrate this, Equation 4.2 is modified as follows:

$$V_t = P_0(1 + r)^t. \tag{4.2}$$

$$V_t = P_0\left(1 + \frac{r}{q}\right)^{qt}. \tag{4.9}$$

Here, q is the number of times per year that compounding occurs. When banks compute daily interest, the value of q is set at 365, and Equation 4.9 is applied.

The interest tables can be used when compounding occurs more than once a year. Simply divide the nominal, or stated, interest rate by the number of times compounding occurs, and multiply the years by the number of compounding periods per year. For example, to find the amount to which $1,000 will grow after five years if semiannual compounding is applied to a stated 10 percent interest rate, divide 10 percent by two and multiply the five years by two. Then look in Table A.1 at the end of the book under the 5 percent column and in the row for the tenth period, where you will find an interest factor of 1.6289. Multiplying this by the initial $1,000 gives a value of $1,628.90, the amount to which $1,000 will grow in five years at 10 percent compounded semiannually. This compares with $1,610.50 for annual compounding.

The same procedure is applied in all the cases covered—compounding, discounting, single payments, and annuities. To illustrate semiannual compounding in finding the present value of an annuity, for example, consider the case described in the section on present value of an annuity; $1,000 a year for three years, discounted at 10 percent. With annual discounting or compounding the interest factor is 2.4869, and the present value of the annuity is $2,486.90. For semiannual compounding, look under the 5 percent column and in the Year 6 row of Table A.4 to find an interest factor of 5.0757. Then multiply by half of $1,000, or the $500 received each six months, to get the present value of the annuity, $2,537.85. The payments come a little more rapidly (the first $500 is paid after only six months), so the annuity is a little more valuable if payments are received semiannually rather than annually.

By letting q approach infinity, Equation 4.9 can be modified to the special case of *continuous compounding.* Continuous compounding is extremely useful in theoretical finance, and it also has practical applications. For example, some banks and savings and loan associations pay interest on a continuous basis.

A Special Case of Semiannual Compounding: Bond Values[6]

Most bonds pay interest semiannually, so semiannual compounding procedures are appropriate for determining bond values. To illustrate: Suppose a particular bond pays interest in the amount of $50 each six months, or $100 a year. The bond will mature in ten years, paying $1,000 (the principal) at that time. Thus, if you buy the bond you will receive an annuity of $50 each six months, or twenty payments in total, plus $1,000 at the end of ten years (or twenty six-month periods). What is the bond worth, assuming that the appropriate market discount (or interest) rate is (a) 10 percent; (b) higher than 10 percent, say 12 percent; and (c) lower than 10 percent, say 8 percent?

At 10 Percent Interest

Step 1. You are buying an annuity plus a lump sum of $1,000. Find the PV of the interest payments:

1. Use $r/q = 10\%/2 = 5\%$ as the "interest rate."
2. Look up the PVIFA in Table A.4 for 20 periods at 5 percent, which is 12.4622.
3. Find the PV of the stream of interest payments:

$$\begin{aligned}\text{PV of the interest} &= \$50\,(\text{PVIFA}) \\ &= \$50\,(12.4622) \\ &= \$623.11.\end{aligned}$$

Step 2. Find the PV of the $1,000 maturity value:

1. Use $r/q = 10\%/2 = 5\%$ as the "interest rate."
2. Look up the PVIF in Table A.2 for 20 periods at 5 percent, which is 0.3769.
3. Find the PV of that value at maturity:

$$\begin{aligned}\text{PV of the maturity value} &= \$1{,}000\,(\text{PVIF}) \\ &= \$1{,}000\,(0.3769) = \$376.90.\end{aligned}$$

Step 3. Combine the two component PVs to determine the value of the bond:

$$\text{Bond value} = \$623.11 + \$376.90 = \$1{,}000.01.$$

At 12 Percent Interest. Repeating the process, we have:

Step 1. $12\%/2 = 6\% =$ the "interest rate."

$$\begin{aligned}\text{PVIFA from Table A.4} &= 11.4699. \\ \text{PVIF from Table A.2} &= 0.3118.\end{aligned}$$

6. This section can be omitted without loss of continuity. The topic is also covered in Chapter 15.

Step 2. Bond value = \$50 (11.4699) + \$1,000 (0.3118)
= \$573.50 + \$311.80
= \$885.30.

Notice that the bond is worth less when the going rate of interest for investments of similar risk is 12 percent than when it is 10 percent. At a price of \$885.30, this bond provides an annual rate of return of 12 percent; at a price of \$1,000, it provides an annual return of 10 percent. If 10 percent is the coupon rate on a bond of a given degree of risk, then whenever interest rates in the economy rise to the point where bonds of this degree of risk have a 12 percent return, the price of our bond will decline to \$885.30, at which price it will yield the competitive rate of return, 12 percent.

At 8 Percent Interest. Using the same process produces the following results:

Step 1. 8%/2 = 4% = the "interest rate."
PVIFA from Table A.4 = 13.5903.
PVIF from Table A.2 = 0.4564.

Step 2. Bond value = \$50 (13.5903) + \$1,000 (0.4564)
= \$679.52 + \$456.40
= \$1,135.92.

The bond is worth *more* than \$1,000 when the going rate of interest is less than 10 percent, because then it offers a yield higher than the going rate. Its price rises to \$1,135.92, where it provides an 8 percent annual rate of return. This calculation illustrates the fact that when interest rates in the economy decline, the prices of outstanding bonds rise.

Appropriate Compounding or Discounting Rates

Throughout the chapter, assumed compounding or discounting rates have been used in the examples. Although we provided some background in Chapter 2, it is useful at this point to summarize what the appropriate interest rate for a particular investment might be.[7]

The starting point is, of course, the general level of interest rates (for each type of investment) in the economy as a whole, which is set by the interaction of supply and demand forces.

There is no single rate of interest in the economy; at any given time, there is an array of different rates. The lowest rates are set on the safest investments and the highest rates on the most risky ones. Usually, there is less risk on investments that mature in the near future than on longer-term investments, so higher rates are usually associated with long-term investments.

7. For convenience, in this chapter we speak of *interest rates,* which implies that only debt is involved. In later chapters the concept is broadened considerably, and the term *rate of return* is used in place of *interest rate*.

People who have money to invest can buy short-term United States government securities and incur no risk whatever. However, they generally must accept a relatively low yield on investment. Those willing to assume a little more risk can invest in high-grade corporate bonds and get a higher fixed rate of return. And people willing to accept still more risk can move into common stocks to obtain variable (and, they hope, higher) returns (dividends plus capital gains) on investment. Still other alternatives are bank and savings and loan deposits, long-term government bonds, mortgages, apartment houses, land held for speculation, and various forms of international securities and investments.

Risk Premiums

With only a limited amount of money to invest, one must pick and choose among investments, the final selection involving a trade-off between risk and return. Suppose, for example, that you are indifferent about the choice of a five-year government bond yielding 10 percent a year, a five-year corporate bond yielding 12 percent, and a share of stock on which you can expect a 15 percent return. Given this situation, the government bond is assumed to be a riskless security, and a 2 percent risk premium is attached to the corporate bond, while a 5 percent risk premium is attached to the share of stock. Risk premiums, then, are the added returns that risky investments must command over less risky ones if there is to be a demand for them. (The concept of the risk premium is discussed in more detail in Chapters 5, 14, and 16.)

Opportunity Costs

Although there are many potential investments available in the economy at any given time, individual investors actively consider only a limited number of them. After making adjustments for risk differentials, they rank the various alternatives from most attractive to least attractive. Then, presumably, they put their available funds into the most attractive investment. If they are offered a new investment, they must compare it with the best of the existing alternatives. If they take the new investment, they must give up the opportunity of investing in the best of the old alternatives. *The yield on the best of the alternatives is defined as the opportunity cost of investing in the new alternative.* For example, suppose you have funds invested in an asset that pays 10 percent. Now someone offers you another investment of equal risk. To make the new investment, you must withdraw funds from the asset; therefore, 10 percent is the opportunity cost of the new investment.

Summary

A knowledge of compound interest and present value techniques is essential to an understanding of many important aspects of finance: capital budgeting, financial structure, security valuation, and many other topics.

Compound value *(V_t)*, or compound amount, is defined as the sum to which a beginning amount of principal (P_0) will grow over t years when interest is earned at the rate of r percent a year. The equation for finding compound value is:

$$V_t = P_0 (1 + r)^t.$$

Tables giving the compound value of $1 for a large number of different years and interest rates have been prepared. The compound value of $1 is called the compound value interest factor (CVIF), given in Appendix Table A.1.

The present value of a future payment (PV) is the amount that, if we had it now and if we invested it at the specified interest rate *(r),* would equal the future payment *(V_t)* on the date the future payment is due. For example, if a person were to receive $1,610 after five years and then decided 10 percent was the appropriate interest rate (called the *discount rate* when computing present values), then that person could find the present value of the $1,610 by applying the following equation:

$$\text{PV} = V_t\left[\frac{1}{(1 + r)^t}\right] = \$1{,}610\,(0.6209) = \$1{,}000.$$

The term in brackets is called the present value interest factor (PVIF), and values for it have been worked out in Appendix Table A.2.

An *annuity* is defined as a series of payments of a fixed amount *(a)* for a specified number of years. The compound value of an annuity is the total amount one will have at the end of the annuity period if each payment is invested at a certain interest rate and is held to the end of the annuity period. For example, suppose we have a three-year, $1,000 annuity invested at 10 percent. There are formulas for annuities, but tables are available for the relevant interest factors. The CVIFA for the compound value of a three-year annuity at 10 percent is 3.3100, and it can be used to find the present value of the illustrative annuity:

$$\text{Compound value} = \text{CVIFA} \times \text{Annual receipt} = 3.3100 \times \$1{,}000 = \$3{,}310.$$

Thus, $3,310 is the compound value of the annuity.

The present value of an annuity is the lump sum we would need to have on hand today in order to be able to withdraw equal amounts *(a)* each year and end up with a balance exactly equal to zero at the end of the annuity period. For example, if we wish to withdraw $1,000 a year for three years, we could deposit $2,486.90 today in a bank account paying 10 percent interest, withdraw the $1,000 in each of the next three years, and end up with a zero balance. Thus, $2,486.90 is the present value of an annuity of $1,000 a year for three years when the appropriate discount rate is 10 percent. Again, tables are available for finding the present value of annuities. To use them, we simply look up the interest factor (PVIFA) for the appropriate number of years and interest rate, then multiply the PVIFA by the annual receipt:

$$\text{PV of annuity} = \text{PVIFA} \times \text{Annual receipt} = 2.4869 \times \$1{,}000 = \$2{,}486.90.$$

All interest factors given in the tables are for $1; for example, 2.4869 is the PVIFA for finding the present value of a three-year annuity at 10 percent. It must be multiplied by the annual receipt ($1,000 in the example) to find the actual value of the annuity. Students—and even financial managers—sometimes make careless mistakes when looking up interest factors by using the wrong table for the purpose. This can be avoided by recognizing the following sets of relations:

1. *Compound value, single payment.* The CVIF for the compound value of a single payment, with normal interest rates and holding periods, is *always* more than 1.0 but seldom more than about 3.0.
2. *Present value, single payment.* The PVIF for the present value of a single payment is *always* less than 1.0 (for example, 0.6209 is the PVIF for 10 percent held for five years). CVIF is, of course, more than 1.0.
3. *Compound value of an annuity.* The CVIFA for the compound value of an annuity is *always* greater than the number of years the annuity has to run. (For example, the CVIFA for a three-year annuity is greater than 3.0, while the CVIFA for a ten-year annuity is greater than 10.0.) Just how much greater depends on the interest rate. At low rates the interest factor is slightly greater than the number of years; at high rates it is very much greater.
4. *Present value of an annuity.* The PVIFA for the present value of an annuity is always less than the number of years it has to run. (For example, the PVIFA for the present value of a three-year annuity at 10 percent is less than 3.0; at high rates it is very much less than 3.0.)

The four basic interest formulas can be used in combination to find such things as the present value of an uneven series of receipts. The formulas can also be transformed to find (1) the annual payments necessary to accumulate a future sum, (2) the annual receipts from a specified annuity, (3) the periodic payments necessary to amortize a loan, and (4) the interest rate implicit in a loan contract.

It is crucial to use the appropriate interest rate in working with compound interest problems. The true nature of the interest rates to be used with business problems can be understood only after examining the chapters dealing with the cost of capital. Risk premiums and opportunity costs are important considerations in determining the most attractive investments.

Questions

4.1 What kinds of financial decisions require explicit consideration of the interest factor?

4.2 Compound interest relationships are important for decisions other than financial ones. Why are they important to marketing managers?

4.3 Would you rather have a savings account that pays 5 percent interest compounded semiannually or one that pays 5 percent interest compounded daily? Why?

4.4 For a given interest rate and a given number of years, is the interest factor for the sum of an annuity greater or smaller than the interest factor for the present value of the annuity?

4.5 Suppose you are examining two investments, A and B. Both have the same maturity, but A pays a 6 percent return and B yields 5 percent. Which investment is probably riskier? How do you know?

Problems

4.1 Which amount is worth more at 10 percent: $1,000 today or $2,000 after ten years?

4.2 The current production target for the five-year plan of the Bowden Company is to increase output by 9 percent a year. If the 1980 production is 5.81 million tons, what is the target production for 1985?

4.3 At a growth rate of 8 percent, how long does it take a sum to double?

4.4 You need $129,200 at the end of seventeen years. You know that the best you can do is to make equal payments into an account on which you can earn 9 percent interest compounded annually. Your first payment is to be made at the end of the first year.

a. What amount must you plan to pay annually to achieve your objective?

b. Instead of making annual payments, you decide to make one lump-sum payment today. To achieve your objective of $129,200 at the end of the seventeen-year period, what should this sum be? (You can still earn 9 percent interest compounded annually on your account.)

4.5 You can buy a note for $12,835. If you buy it, you will receive ten annual payments of $2,000, the first payment to be made one year from today. What rate of return, or yield, does the note offer?

4.6 You can buy a bond for $1,000 that will pay no interest during its eight-year life. It will, however, have a value of $2,144 when it matures. What rate of interest will you earn if you buy the bond and hold it to maturity?

4.7 A bank agrees to lend you $1,000 today in return for your promise to pay back $2,773 nine years from today. What rate of interest is the bank charging you?

4.8 If last year's earnings were $2.83 a share, while seven years earlier they were $1, what has been the rate of growth in earnings?

4.9 The Zimmer Company's sales last year were $200,000.

a. Assuming that sales grow 24 percent a year, calculate sales for each of the next six years.

b. Plot the sales projections.

c. If your graph is correct, your projected sales curve is nonlinear. If it had been linear, would this have indicated that the growth rate was constant, increasing, or decreasing in percentage? Explain.

4.10 The Broxton Company's common stock paid a dividend of $1 last year. Dividends are expected to grow at a rate of 10 percent for each of the next six years.

a. Calculate the expected dividend for each of the next six years.

b. Assuming that the first of these six dividends will be paid one year from now, what is the present value of the six dividends? (Given the riskiness of the dividend stream, 10 percent is the appropriate discount rate.)

4.11 a. What amount will be paid for a $1,000 ten-year bond that pays $40 interest semiannually ($80 a year) and that yields 10 percent, compounded semiannually?

b. What will be paid if the bond is sold to yield 8 percent?

c. What will be paid if semiannual interest payments are $50 and the bond yields 6 percent?

4.12 On December 31, Frank Ferris buys a building for $80,000, paying 20 percent down and agreeing to pay the balance in fifteen equal annual installments that are to include principal plus 10 percent compound interest on the declining balance. What are the equal installments?

4.13 The Peyton Company has established a sinking fund to retire a $900,000 mortgage that matures on December 31, 1988. The company plans to put a fixed amount into the fund each year for ten years. The first payment was made on December 31, 1979; the last will be made on December 31, 1988. The company anticipates that the fund will earn 9 percent a year. What annual contributions must be made to accumulate the $900,000 as of December 31, 1988?

4.14 You have just purchased a newly issued $1,000 five-year Vanguard Company bond at par. This bond (Bond A) pays $60 in interest semiannually ($120 a year). You are also negotiating the purchase of a $1,000 six-year Vanguard Company bond that returns $30 in semiannual interest payments and has six years remaining before it matures (Bond B).

a. What is the going rate of return on bonds of the risk and maturity of the Vanguard Company's bonds?

b. What should you be willing to pay for Bond B?

c. How will your answer to Part b change if Bond A pays $40 (instead of $60) in semiannual interest but still sells for $1,000? (Bond B still pays $30 semiannually and $1,000 at the end of six years.)

4.15 An investment of $1,000 earns 8 percent interest per year for three years. A second $1,000 investment earns 1 percent for the first and second years and 22 percent the third year.

a. What is the average (arithmetic) of the returns on each of the investments over the three years?

b. Compute the terminal value of each investment. Which is larger?

c. What is the compound rate of interest at which the initial $1,000 rises to the terminal value of each investment?

d. What is the geometric mean of the returns on each project?

e. How do your results in Part d compare with your results in Part c? Comment on the implications.

Selected References

Cissell, R.; Cissell, H.; and Flaspohler, D. C. *Mathematics of Finance.* 5th ed. Boston: Houghton Mifflin, 1978.

U.S. Department of Commerce. *Handbook of Mathematical Functions.* Edited by M. Abramowitz and I. A. Stegum. Washington, D.C.: Government Printing Office, December 1972.

Vichas, Robert P. *Handbook of Financial Mathematics, Formulas and Tables.* Englewood Cliffs, N.J.: Prentice-Hall, 1979.

Appendix A to Chapter 4

Continuous Compounding and Discounting

Continuous Compounding

In Chapter 4 we implicitly assumed that growth occurs at discrete intervals—annually, semiannually, and so forth. For some purposes it is better to assume instantaneous, or *continuous,* growth. The relationship between discrete and continuous compounding is illustrated in Figure 4A.1. Figure 4A.1a shows the annual compounding case, where interest is added once a year; in Figure 4A.1b compounding occurs twice a year; in Figure 4A.1c interest is earned continuously.

We developed Equation 4.9 in Chapter 4 to allow for any number of compounding periods per year:

$$V_t = P_0\left(1 + \frac{r}{q}\right)^{qt}. \tag{4.9}$$

Figure 4A.1

Annual, Semiannual, and Continuous Compounding

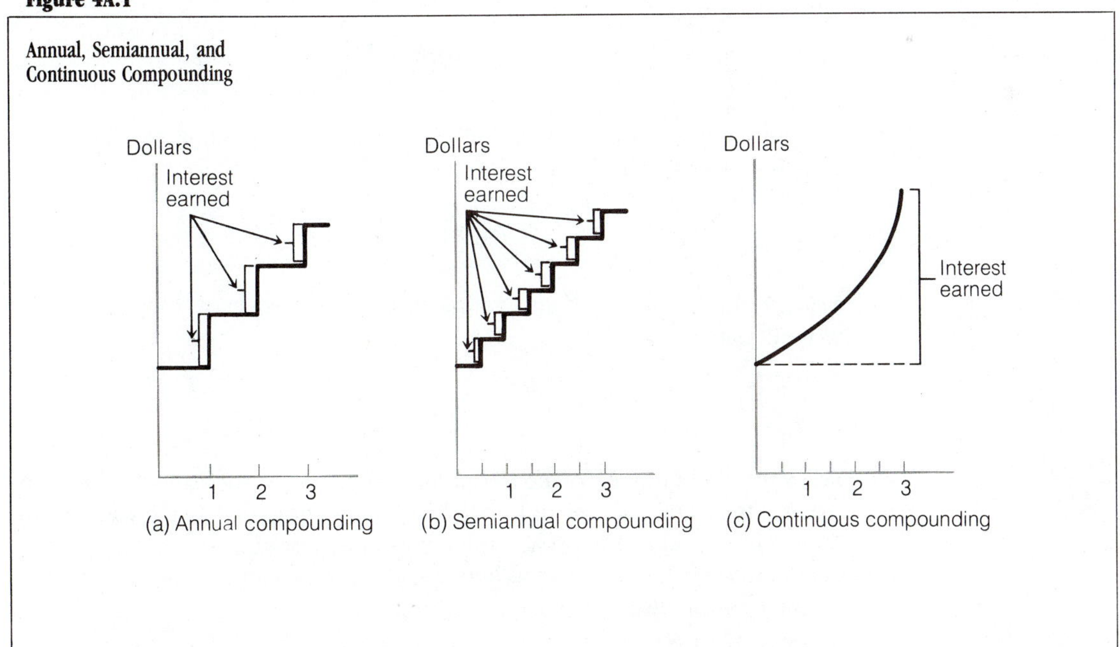

Equation 4.9, in turn, can be modified to allow for continuous compounding. The steps in this modification are developed below. In the literature of finance, where continuous compounding is employed, t is used for years (time). In the same financial language, r is an interest rate, discount rate, or growth rate and is also denoted by k, which is used in the following material.

Step 1. First, assume that k, the interest or growth rate, is 100 percent (k = 100 percent = 1.0); that is, assume that with annual compounding the initial principal (P_0) will double each year.

$$\begin{aligned} V_t &= P_0\,(1 + k)^t \\ &= P_0\,(1 + 1)^t \\ &= P_0\,(2)^t. \end{aligned}$$

Step 2. Now suppose that $P_0 = 1$ and that k remains at 100 percent, but compounding occurs q times per year. The value after one year will be

$$V_1 = \left(1 + \frac{1}{q}\right)^q. \tag{4A.1}$$

If $q = 1$, $V = 2$; if $q = 2$, $V = 2.25$; if $q = 3$, $V = 2.37$. Thus, V increases as q is increased.

Step 3. Returning to Equation 4.9, the general case of compound growth (but using the new notation), we can develop an equation for the special case of continuous compounding. Starting with

$$V_t = P_0\left(1 + \frac{k}{q}\right)^{qt} \tag{4.9}$$

and noting that, since we can multiply qt by k/k, we can set $qt = (q/k)(kt)$ and rewrite Equation 4.9 as

$$V_t = P_0\left[\left(1 + \frac{k}{q}\right)^{(q/k)}\right]^{(kt)}. \tag{4A.2}$$

Step 4. Defining $m = q/k$ and noting that $k/q = 1/(q/k) = 1/m$, we can rewrite Equation 4A. 2 as

$$V_t = P_0\left[\left(1 + \frac{1}{m}\right)^{m}\right]^{kt}. \tag{4A.3}$$

Step 5. As the number of compounding periods, q, increases, m also increases; this causes the term in brackets in Equation 4A.3 to increase. At the limit, when q and m approach infinity (and compounding is instantaneous, or continuous), the term in brackets approaches the value 2.718 ⋯. The value e is defined as this limiting case:

$$e = \lim_{m \to \infty} \left(1 + \frac{1}{m}\right)^m = 2.718 \cdots. \qquad (4A.4)$$

Thus, we may substitute e for the bracketed term, rewriting Equation 4A.3 as

$$V_t = P_0 e^{kt} \qquad (4A.5)$$

for the case of continuous compounding (or continuous growth).

Step 6. Interest factors (IF) can be developed for continuous compounding; developing the factors requires the use of natural, or Naperian, logarithms.[1] First, letting $P_0 = 1$, we can rewrite Equation 4A.5 as

$$V_t = e^{kt}. \qquad (4A.6)$$

Setting Equation 4A.6 in log form and noting that *ln* denotes the log to the base e, we obtain

$$ln\ V_t = kt\ ln\ e. \qquad (4A.7)$$

Since e is defined as the base of the system of natural logarithms, $ln\ e$ must equal 1.0 (that is, $e^1 = e$, so $ln\ e = 1.0$). Therefore,

$$ln\ V_t = kt. \qquad (4A.8)$$

One simply looks up the product kt in a table of natural logarithms and obtains the value V_t as the antilog. For example, if t = five years and k = 10 percent, the product is 0.50. Looking up this value in Appendix B at the end of the book, we find in this table of natural logs that 0.5 lies between 0.49470 and 0.50078, whose antilogs are 1.64 and 1.65 respectively. Interpolating, we find the antilog of 0.5 to be 1.648. Thus, 1.648 is the interest factor for a 10 percent growth rate compounded continuously for five years; $1 growing continuously at this compound rate would equal $1.648 after five years.

Since continuous compounding is not commonly applied in practice, we have not provided a table of continuous interest factors.[2] It should be noted, however, that the $1.648 obtained for five years of *continuous* compounding compares closely with $1.629, the figure for semiannual compounding, and with the $1.611 obtained with annual compounding. Thus, continuous compounding does not produce values materially different from semiannual or annual compounding. As was pointed out earlier, the importance of continuous compounding is its convenience in theoretical work where calculus must be employed.

1. Recall that the logarithm of a number is the power, or exponent, to which a specified base must be raised to equal the number; that is, the log (base 10) of 100 is 2 because $(10)^2 = 100$. In the system of natural logs the base is $e \approx 2.718$.
2. Continuous compounding is used extensively in theoretical work. In practice, the major use is by banks and savings and loan associations as a competitive tactic to raise the effective rate on deposits permitted by regulators.

Continuous Discounting

Equation 4A.5 can be transformed into Equation 4A.9 and used to determine present values under continuous compounding. Using *k* as the discount rate (again, this is the standard notation: *k* is used as the discount rate, and *g* as the growth rate for compounding), we obtain

$$PV = \frac{V_t}{e^{kt}} = V_t e^{-kt}. \quad (4A.9)$$

Thus, if \$1,648 is due in five years and if the appropriate *continuous* discount rate *k* is 10 percent, the present value of this future payment is

$$PV = \frac{\$1{,}648}{1.648} = \$1{,}000.$$

Continuous Compounding and Discounting for Annuities

The treatment of continuous compounding for single values is more complex than that for discrete compounding. Still, it involves nothing more than algebra. For continuously compounding and discounting *streams* of payments ("annuities"), however, elementary integral calculus must be employed. The procedures involved are outlined below.

Step 1. First, observe Figure 4A.2a. An amount a is received at the end of each year. The amount received grows at the rate g; thus the accumulated sum of the receipts at the end of any year N is

$$\begin{aligned} S_t &= a(1+g)^0 + a(1+g)^1 + a(1+g)^2 + \cdots + a(1+g)^{t-1} \\ &= a + a(1+g)^1 + a(1+g)^2 + \cdots + a(1+g)^{t-1} \\ &= \sum_{t=1}^{N} a(1+g)^{t-1}. \end{aligned}$$

S_t is the accumulated sum of the receipts, and it is equal to the sum of the rectangles in Figure 4A.2a; this is the area under the discontinuous curve formed by the tops of the rectangles.

Step 2. Exactly the same principle is involved in finding the accumulated sum of the continuous equivalent of an annuity, or a stream of receipts received continuously. The accumulated sum is again represented by the area under a curve, but now the curve is continuous as in Figure 4A.2b. In the discrete case, the area under the curve was obtained by adding the rectangles; in the continuous case, the area must be found by the process of integration.

Note that the stream of receipts (or the value of a_t) is found by taking the initial receipt a_0 rather than a_1. It grows at the continuous rate g.

$$a_t = a_0 e^{gt}. \quad (4A.10)$$

Figure 4A.2

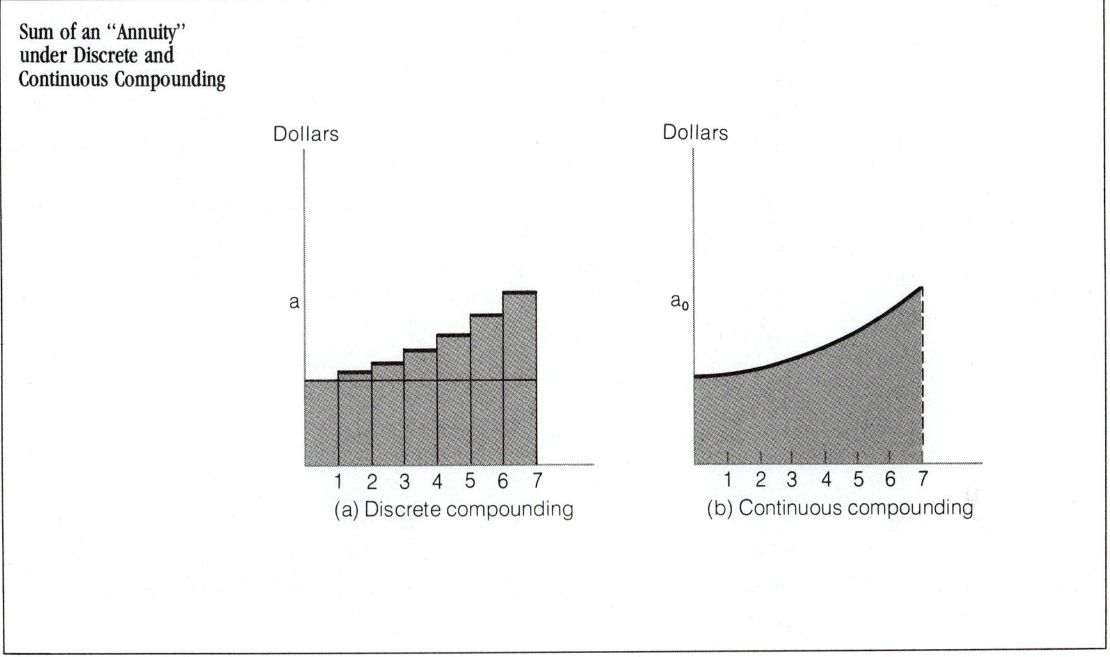

Sum of an "Annuity" under Discrete and Continuous Compounding

(a) Discrete compounding

(b) Continuous compounding

Equation 4A.10 defines the curve, and the area under the curve (S_t) is represented by the integral

$$S_t = \int_{t=0}^{N} a_0 e^{gt}\, dt = a_0 \int_{t=0}^{N} e^{gt}\, dt. \tag{4A.11}$$

Step 3. Given a discrete series of receipts such as those shown in Figure 4A.2a and a discount rate, *k,* we find their PV as

$$\text{PV} = \sum_{t=1}^{N} a_t(1 + k)^{-t}.$$

If the receipts accrue continuously, as do those in Figure 4A.2b, we must find the present value of the stream of payments by calculus. First, note that by Equation 4A.9 we find the PV of the instantaneous receipt for period t as

$$\text{PV} = a_t e^{-kt}. \tag{4A.9}$$

The present value of the entire stream of receipts is given as the integral

$$\text{PV} = \int_{t=0}^{N} a_t e^{-kt}\, \text{dt}. \tag{4A.12}$$

Step 4. Although the primary equations (4A.11 and 4A.12) developed thus far in this section are seldom used individually, the basic dividend model is developed by combining them.

First, note from Equation 4A.10 that $a_t = a_0e^{gt}$. Next, substitute this value into Equation 4A.12, obtaining

$$PV = \int_{t=0}^{N} a_0e^{gt}e^{-kt}\,dt. \tag{4A.13}$$

Now remove the constant term a_0 from within the integral and combine the exponents of the e term, obtaining

$$\begin{aligned} PV &= a_0\int_{t=0}^{N} e^{gt-kt}\,dt \\ &= a_0\int_{t=0}^{N} e^{-(k-g)t}\,dt. \end{aligned} \tag{4A.14}$$

Therefore, the integration of Equation 4A.14 yields an indefinite integral of the form

$$PV = \frac{a_0e^{-(k-g)t}}{k-g}$$

that, when evaluated at $t = \infty$, is equal to 0 and when evaluated at $t = 0$, is equal to

$$-\frac{a_0}{k-g}.$$

Subtracting the lower bound from the upper (which is 0) yields:

$$\begin{aligned} PV &= 0 - \left[-\frac{a_0}{k-g}\right] \\ &= \frac{a_0}{k-g}. \end{aligned} \tag{4A.15}$$

Equation 4A.15 is thus the present value of a continuous stream of receipts growing at rate g and discounted at rate k. This is the basic dividend valuation model, discussed further in Chapter 17.

5

Risk and Return

We have found that the time value of money has a substantial impact on the value of an asset. A perpetual return of $20 per year capitalized at 10 percent is worth $200; capitalized at 5 percent, it is worth $400. The capitalization rate—the applicable discount or interest factor—performs a crucial role in finance. Recall that in Chapter 1 we formulated the maximization of value as the goal of the firm. The applicable discount factor has a great impact on the value that will result from a future stream of receipts.

The Nature of Risk

It is widely agreed that the major determinant of the required return on an asset (or the rate to be applied to a stream of receipts to capitalize its value) is its degree of risk. Risk, defined most generally, is the probability of the occurrence of unfavorable outcomes. But risk has different meanings in different contexts. We are interested in the effects of risk on the valuation of assets or securities—claims on assets. In this context, risk refers to the probabilities that the returns and therefore the values of an asset or security may have alternative outcomes.

Alternative outcome probabilities are fundamentally related to relative frequencies. If you flipped a fair coin for a large number of times (say 1,000), the probability is that it would turn up heads about 50 percent of the time and tails about 50 percent of the time. These percentages represent the relative frequencies of heads or tails. We also say that the probability of heads is 50 percent, or 0.5, and that the probability of tails is 50 percent, or 0.5. We note that the sum of the alternative probabilities is exactly 1.0 (0.5 + 0.5). The relative frequency from tossing coins is limited to heads or tails since those are the only alternatives. In the financial markets, many outcomes are possible. The dominant influence on financial events is the general state of the economy. For illustration, reading the annual reports of business, we will often find statements such as, "The general state of the economy was depressed last year, causing our company's earnings to decline."

The relationship between the expected future state of the economy and the performance of individual firms enables a relationship to be set forth between the state of the economy and the returns from investments in firms. (Returns are defined as the dividend yield plus the capital gain or loss.) The relationship between different levels of returns and their relative frequency is called a probability distribution. We could formulate a probability distribution for the relative frequency of a firm's annual returns by analyzing its historical returns over the previous years. But we know that history never repeats itself exactly. Hence, after analyzing relative frequencies of historical returns for the individual company, we can form a probability distribution based on historical data plus our analysis for the outlook for the economy, the outlook for the industry, the outlook for the firm in its industry, and any other factors we deem relevant as inputs for our judgments. For example, as the U.S. economy was entering a recession in late 1979, the outlook for the auto industry deteriorated. All four of the major U.S. auto companies reported operating losses from U.S. operations for the third quarter of 1979. But the outlook for Chrysler was much more unfavorable than for General Motors.

Suppose then, based on historical experience and the best analysis of all relevant factors for the economy, industry, and firms, we formulate the following probability distributions for individual Firms A and C:

State of the Economy	Probability of the State Occurring	Rate of Return to Firm A If This State Occurs	Rate of Return to Firm C If This State Occurs
Down	0.2	−0.20	−0.15
Average	0.5	+0.18	+0.20
Up	0.3	+0.50	+0.10
	1.0		

A number of formal methods of analyzing the riskiness represented by the probability distributions for Firms A and C will be performed. The first is simply the visual representation of the probability distributions as shown in Figure 5.1

We can readily see that the probable returns are spread apart more widely for Firm A. In a down economy, the loss to Firm A would be greater than the loss to Firm C. With an upswing in the state of the economy, the positive return from Firm A would be larger than the positive return from Firm C. The magnitude of the spread of the probability distributions of returns from different investments is one rough indicator of the degree of risk involved. In the framework of the mean-dispersion approach we are using here, we seek to evaluate alternative investments by their return-risk relationships. To do so requires more formal methods of analyzing and characterizing the probability distributions.

Figure 5.1

Graph of Two Probability Distributions

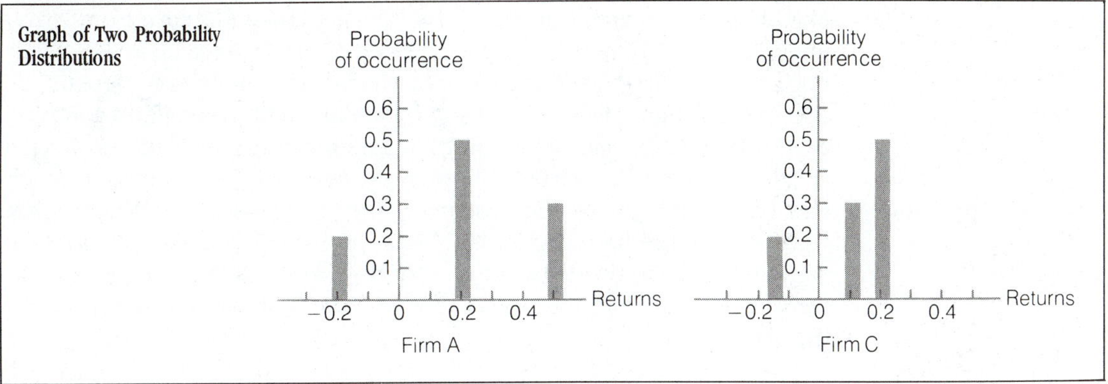

Expected Return and Standard Deviation

Two measures developed from the probability distribution have been used as initial measures of return and risks. These are the mean and the standard deviation of the probability distribution. Calculations of the mean and standard deviation of returns for Firm A are shown in Table 5.1.

Table 5.1

Calculations of the Standard Deviation for Firm A

State of the Economy	P_s	$\tilde{R}_a$	$P_s\tilde{R}_a$	$(\tilde{R}_a - \overline{R}_a)$	$(\tilde{R}_a - \overline{R}_a)^2$	$P_s(\tilde{R}_a - \overline{R}_a)^2$
Down	0.2	−0.20	−0.04	−0.40	0.1600	0.0320
Average	0.5	0.18	0.09	−0.02	0.0004	0.0002
Up	0.3	0.50	0.15	0.30	0.0900	0.0270
			$\overline{R}_a = 0.20$			$\sigma_a^2 = 0.0592$
						$\sigma_a = 0.2433$

In equation form, the expected rate of return or mean return is:

$$\text{Expected rate of return } E(R_a) = \overline{R}_a = \sum_{s=1}^{S} P_s\tilde{R}_a . \quad (5.1)$$

In Equation 5.1, the expected return is expressed either with the expectation operator, E, as $E(R_a)$ or with the bar as $\overline{R}_a$. It is simpler to use the bar, and we shall do so generally; but the forms can be used interchangeably. P_s is the probability of a state occurring, and $\tilde{R}_a$ is the associated return from Firm A under that state. Calculation of the expected return is the same as the calculation of the ordinary arithmetic mean of a frequency distribution. Here the frequency distribution is expressed by probabilities and so is called a probability distribution. In calculating an arithmetic mean, we sum the product of frequencies times associated values and divide by the number of frequencies (observations). We do essentially the same thing in calculating the weighted average here. We multiply each probability and associated return. We then total. We divide by the sum of the probabilities, which is one. We really have nothing further to do after we have multiplied by the probabilities and totaled:

$$\begin{aligned} \overline{R}_a &= P_1(R_1) + P_2(R_2) + P_3(R_3) \\ \overline{R}_a &= 0.2(-0.20) + 0.5(0.18) + 0.3(0.50) \\ \overline{R}_a &= -0.04 + 0.09 + 0.15 = 0.20. \end{aligned} \tag{5.1a}$$

We have now calculated the expected return. We need to relate this return or reward to some measures of risk. We begin with the basic statistical measure of the dispersion of the probability distribution, the standard deviation, which is generally referred to by the Greek symbol σ (sigma). The standard deviation is the square root of the variance. The variance is computed by (1) calculating the deviations from the mean, (2) squaring the deviations, (3) summing the squared deviations, and (4) dividing by the total number of observations. For the probability distribution of returns, the probabilities total to 1, so this step is performed by multiplying the squared deviation by the probability before summing. The square root of the variance is the standard deviation. The general expression for the variance is shown in Equation 5.2.

$$\text{Variance} = \sigma_a^2 = \sum_{s=1}^{S} P_s(R_a - \overline{R}_a)^2 \tag{5.2}$$

$$\sigma_a^2 = P_1(R_{a_1} - \overline{R}_a)^2 + P_2(R_{a_2} - \overline{R}_a)^2 + P_3(R_{a_3} - \overline{R}_a)^2.$$

Using the data for Firm A, we have

$$\sigma_a^2 = 0.2(-0.40)^2 + 0.5(-0.02)^2 + 0.3(0.30)^2 = 0.0592$$

$$\sqrt{\sigma_a^2} = \sigma_a = 0.2433.$$

These results reflect the calculations in Table 5.1.

We have now defined and set forth the procedures for calculating two parameters (summarizing measures) of the probability distributions of prospective returns: the mean and standard deviation. In general, these two measures enable us to sketch the full probability distribution. We make the further assumption that the probability distribution is continuous, implying that probabilities can be estimated for a large number of values so that we may draw an unbroken curve through all the indicated rates of return. For example, consider two assets, or investment opportunities, D and E, with the distribution of returns shown in Tables 5.2 and 5.3.

Table 5.2

Distribution of Returns from Asset D

Probability	Indicated Return, R_d	
0.05	0.05	Mean = 0.1625
0.20	0.10	$\sigma_d = 0.063$
0.50	0.15	
0.20	0.25	
0.05	0.30	

Table 5.3

Distribution of Returns from Asset E

Probability	R_e	
0.03	−0.40	Mean = 0.0505
0.04	−0.30	$\sigma_e = 0.160$
0.06	−0.20	
0.08	−0.10	
0.10	0.00	
0.15	0.05	
0.20	0.10	
0.15	0.15	
0.10	0.20	
0.05	0.25	
0.04	0.30	

The probability distributions for Assets D and E from Tables 5.2 and 5.3 are graphed in Figure 5.2.

The graph of Asset D exhibits two features of a more favorable investment. First, it has a higher expected return. In addition, the frequency distribution is bunched closer together, indicating less dispersion, one of the measures of risk.

Figure 5.2

Graph of Continuous Probability Distributions

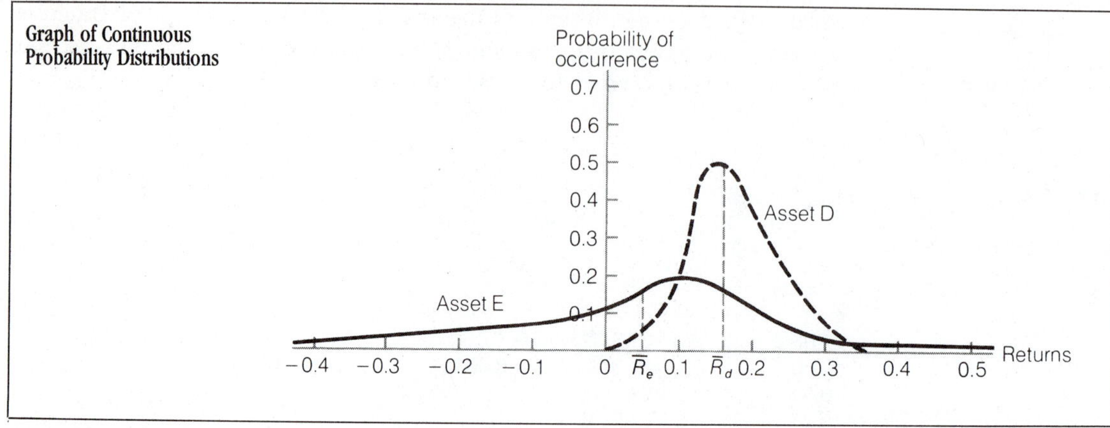

The Mean-Variance Criterion and Risk Aversion

From the data on Assets D and E it would appear that Investment D is preferable to Investment E. Investment D has a higher expected return and a lower standard deviation than does Investment E. This illustrates the fundamental basis for the mean-variance criterion: People prefer more return to less return and less risk to more risk. The mean-variance criterion is based on the general pattern that investors are, on average, risk averse. In making investment decisions, a trade-off between expected returns and risks is made. From this it would seem to follow that riskier securities would require higher expected returns than less risky securities. But that expectation covers only part of the story. We need to proceed further to consider more closely how risk is measured and to attempt to develop some quantitative relationships between levels of risk and required returns.

The Coefficient of Variation as a Measure of Risk

Asset D will be preferred to Asset E because it has a higher expected return and a lower standard deviation. But suppose we were comparing Assets G, H, and I with characteristics as shown in Table 5.4.

Table 5.4

Calculation of the Coefficient of Variation

	Expected Return	Standard Deviation of Returns	Coefficient of Variation (CV_j)
Asset G	0.12	0.10	0.83
Asset H	0.20	0.22	1.10
Asset I	0.15	0.10	0.67

Asset G has the same standard deviation of returns as Asset I, but it has a lower expected return. Asset H has both a higher expected return and a higher standard deviation than Asset I. Can we make comparisons of the relative risks of the different assets?

One procedure that can be used is to standardize the risk per unit of return. This is the concept of the coefficient of variation (CV), which is the standard deviation (σ_j) divided by the mean or expected return $(\overline{R}_j)$:

$$CV_j = \frac{\sigma_j}{R_j}.$$

The measures of the coefficient of variation have been calculated in the final column of Table 5.4. By the criterion of the coefficient of variation, Asset I is less risky than Asset G, which in turn is less risky than Asset H. Thus although Asset G has the same standard deviation as Asset I, its standard deviation per unit of return is higher. Asset H has both a higher expected return and a higher standard deviation. Its risk, as measured by the standard deviation per unit of return, is the highest of the three assets exhibited. If the standard deviation is to be used as a measure of risk for investments viewed in isolation, as individual investments, the normalization obtained by dividing through by the mean return to obtain the coefficient of variation should be used.

Risk in a Portfolio Framework

We have seen that the standard deviation is not a complete measure of risk, since the measure needs to be standardized per unit of return. In addition, another fundamental consideration that must be taken into account is that assets or investments are held not in isolation but jointly with other assets or investments. Hence, the riskiness of an asset can be influenced by the interaction of the pattern of its return with the patterns of return of the other assets it is held in combination with. This leads us to a consideration of portfolio risk.

To illustrate the basic idea, let us consider the pattern of returns for Firm B, as indicated by Table 5.5.

Table 5.5

Calculation of the Expected Return and Standard Deviation of Firm B

State of the Economy	P_s	$\tilde{R}_b$	$P_s\tilde{R}_b$	$(\tilde{R}_b - \overline{R}_b)$	$(\tilde{R}_b - \overline{R}_b)^2$	$P_s(\tilde{R}_b - \overline{R}_b)^2$
Down	0.2	0.50	0.10	0.37	0.1369	0.02738
Average	0.5	0.18	0.09	0.05	0.0025	0.00125
Up	0.3	−0.20	−0.06	−0.33	0.1089	0.03267
			$\overline{R}_b = 0.13$			$\sigma_b^2 = 0.06130$
						$\sigma_b = 0.2476$

Firm B is assumed to have exactly the same returns as Firm A, but their state pattern is exactly reversed. When the state of the economy is strong, Firm B's earnings are negative; when the state of the economy is weak, its earnings are strong. We have taken an extreme illustration to emphasize the point. However, the example is not completely unrealistic: Loan and finance companies tend to do better in a downturn, when people may need to borrow money. Also, the returns from gold mining companies have historically tended to move inversely with the general pattern of business activity.

We observe from Table 5.5 that the expected return from Firm B is 13 percent and the variability of its returns is about the same as for Firm A. The variance is about 6 percent, and the standard deviation is somewhat over 24 percent.

Now we want to examine what happens when we combine securities of A and B into a portfolio. A *portfolio* simply represents the practice among investors of having their funds in more than one asset: The combination of investment assets is called a portfolio. Here we have a two-asset portfolio. The first thing we seek to determine is how the returns *co-vary* between Firm A and Firm B. The calculations are shown in Table 5.6.

Table 5.6

Covariance of Returns of Firm A with Returns of Firm B

P_s	$(\tilde{R}_a - \bar{R}_a)(\tilde{R}_b - \bar{R}_b)$	$P_s(\tilde{R}_a - \bar{R}_a)(\tilde{R}_b - \bar{R}_b)$
0.2	$-0.40 \times 0.37 = -0.1480$	-0.0296
0.5	$-0.02 \times 0.05 = -0.0010$	-0.0005
0.3	$0.30 \times -0.33 = -0.0990$	-0.0297
	$\text{Cov}(R_a, R_b) =$	-0.0598
		≈ -0.06

For each of the firms, we simply take the deviations of the returns from the mean and multiply them, as shown in the second column of Table 5.6. We then multiply by the frequencies (in this case by the probabilities since we have probability distributions). Ordinarily, we would then divide by the sum of the frequencies, but for probabilities the sum is 1. Therefore, after multiplying the product of the deviation by the probabilities, we simply sum. We find that the covariance between the returns of Firms A and B is approximately −6 percent.

We can now proceed to analyze the prospective return and standard deviation for this two-security portfolio. Let us assume initially that the invested sums are distributed equally between Firm A and Firm B. In general, the return for a portfolio will be determined by the relationships set forth in Equation 5.3:

$$\bar{R}_p = w_a\bar{R}_a + w_b\bar{R}_b. \tag{5.3}$$

Equation 5.3 indicates that the portfolio return is the proportion of each asset in the portfolio multiplied times its return summed over all assets in the portfolio. Using the expected returns previously calculated, we can determine the portfolio return from Equation 5.3a:

$$\bar{R}_p = 0.5\bar{R}_a + 0.5\bar{R}_b = 0.5(0.20) + 0.5(0.13) = 0.1 + 0.065 = 0.165. \quad (5.3a)$$

We now turn to the calculation of the portfolio standard deviation. The expression for the portfolio standard deviation when the portfolio is composed of two assets is shown in Equation 5.4:

$$\sigma_p = (w_a^2\sigma_a^2 + w_b^2\sigma_b^2 + 2w_a w_b \text{Cov}_{ab})^{1/2}. \quad (5.4)$$

We illustrate the application of this expression in

$$\begin{aligned}\sigma_p &= [0.25(0.06) + 0.25(0.06) + 2(0.25)(-0.06)]^{1/2} \quad (5.4a)\\ &= (0.015 + 0.015 - 0.03)^{1/2} = 0.\end{aligned}$$

We observe that the portfolio's standard deviation has been reduced to zero. This is an extreme case, as the data assumed perfect inverse correlation between the returns for Firms A and B. In addition, the portfolios were equally weighted with the two securities. Although this is a special case, it does illustrate the power of diversification. Simply by combining the two assets in equal proportion, we eliminated risk as measured by the portfolio standard deviation.

We may also examine another aspect of the relationship between the two securities. This aspect is defined by the correlation between the returns from the two securities. It is another measure of how the returns co-vary. The measure is standardized so that the range of values for the correlation coefficients is constrained, limited between +1 and −1. The general expression for the covariance between two assets is set forth in Equation 5.5.

$$\text{Cov}(R_a, R_b) = \rho_{ab}\,\sigma_a\,\sigma_b\,. \quad (5.5)$$

The nature of the correlation coefficient is indicated by the equation. When we solve for the correlation coefficient, we obtain Equation 5.5a:

$$\rho_{ab} = \frac{\text{Cov}(R_a, R_b)}{\sigma_a\sigma_b}. \quad (5.5a)$$

As Equation 5.5a shows, the correlation coefficient is simply the covariance measure standardized by dividing by the product of the two standard deviations. Utilizing the data already developed, we can calculate the correlation coefficient between the returns for Assets A and B as shown in Equation 5.5b.

$$\rho_{ab} = \frac{-0.06}{(0.2433)(0.2476)} = \frac{-0.06}{0.06} = -1.0. \quad (5.5b)$$

But perfectly negative correlation between the returns from two securities is a rather extreme case. Let us therefore turn our attention to the more common pattern of relationships. In general, the returns from most securities tend to be positively correlated—but with a correlation coefficient that is something less than 1. Let us therefore consider Security C. The pattern of returns and the indicated expected return, variance, and standard deviation for Security C are shown in Table 5.7.

Table 5.7

Calculation of the Expected Return and Standard Deviation of Firm C

P_s	$\tilde{R}_c$	$P_s\tilde{R}_c$	$\tilde{R}_c - \overline{R}_c$	$(\tilde{R}_c - \overline{R}_c)^2$	$P_s(\tilde{R}_c - \overline{R}_c)^2$
0.2	−0.15	−0.03	−0.25	0.0625	0.01250
0.5	0.20	0.10	0.10	0.0100	0.00500
0.3	0.10	0.03	0.00	0.0000	0.00000
		$\overline{R}_c$ = 0.10			σ_c^2 = 0.01750
					σ_c = 0.1323

The expected return for Firm C is 10 percent, and its standard deviation is about 13 percent. When Firm C is combined with Firm A, the portfolio return is 15 percent, shown by Equation 5.6:

$$\overline{R}_p = 0.5\overline{R}_a + 0.5\overline{R}_c = 0.5(0.20) + 0.5(0.10) = 0.15. \qquad (5.6)$$

Next we seek to calculate the correlation coefficient between the two firms. To do this we need to calculate their covariance. The covariance is calculated in Table 5.8 in the same way that it was calculated for Firms A and B. The covariance between the two securities is approximately 2 percent.

Table 5.8

Calculation of Covariance of Returns of Firm A with Returns of Firm C

P_s	$(\tilde{R}_a - \overline{R}_a)(\tilde{R}_c - \overline{R}_c)$	$P_s(\tilde{R}_a - \overline{R}_a)(\tilde{R}_c - \overline{R}_c)$
0.2	−0.40 × −0.25 = 0.1000	0.0200
0.5	−0.02 × 0.10 = −0.0020	−0.0010
0.3	0.30 × 0.00 = 0.0000	0.0000
		$\text{Cov}(\tilde{R}_a, \tilde{R}_c)$ = 0.0190

We can then proceed to calculate the portfolio standard deviation as shown in Equation 5.7:

$$\sigma_p^2 = 0.25(0.0592) + 0.25(0.01750) + 2(0.25)(0.0190)$$

$$= 0.0148 + 0.004375 + 0.00950 = 0.028675. \qquad (5.7)$$

$$\sigma_p = \sqrt{\sigma_p^2} = \sqrt{0.02868} = 0.169.$$

The portfolio standard deviation is 16.9 percent. The simple average is: (0.2433 + 0.1323)/2 = 18.8 percent. The portfolio standard deviation is below a straight average by 1.9 percentage points. It is below a straight average by the extent to which the correlation coefficient between the two securities is less than 1. In the present instance we can calculate the correlation between the returns from Firms A and C. This is shown in Equation 5.8:

$$\rho_{ac} = \frac{\text{Cov}(\tilde{R}_a, \tilde{R}_c)}{\sigma_a \sigma_c} = \frac{0.0190}{(0.2433)(0.1323)} = \frac{0.0190}{0.0322} = 0.59. \quad (5.8)$$

The correlation coefficient between the returns from the two firms is 0.59. Since it is less than 1, it has the effect of bringing down the standard deviation for the portfolio to something below a straight average of standard deviations for the individual firms. Thus, combining individual securities into portfolios changes the nature of their riskiness.

Three influences reduce portfolio risk in relation to the standard deviation of individual securities in isolation: (1) the extent to which the correlation between the returns from the individual securities is less than 1, (2) the number of securities in the portfolio, and (3) the proportions or weights of the individual securities in the portfolio in relation to their correlations among one another. The effects of these three influences combined can be determined by relating individual securities to all securities—the market portfolio. We can obtain the most general relationship by relating the pattern of returns from an individual security to the pattern for the market as a whole. The *market as a whole* is defined as the portfolio of the total of all types of investment opportunities available.

We illustrate two methods for calculating the market parameters. One is based on historical data; the other uses probability estimates of market returns under alternative states. The market return is measured in the same way as returns to individual assets; it is the sum of the capital gain (loss) plus the dividend return for the period. The expected return and standard deviation for the market as a whole can also be calculated as we did for the individual securities by using a probability distribution of market returns. (This is shown later in Table 5.10.)

Much empirical work has been performed on the estimates of the market parameters. Some of the literature represents formal scholarly studies analyzing the empirical validity of the capital asset pricing model (described in a later section).[1] Other estimates of market parameters are available from such

1. M. H. Miller and M. Scholes, "Rates of Return in Relation to Risk: A Re-examination of Some Recent Findings," in *Studies in the Theory of Capital Markets,* ed. M. C. Jensen (New York: Praeger, 1972), pp. 47–78; F. A. Black, M. C. Jensen, and M. Scholes, "The Capital Asset Pricing Model: Some Empirical Tests," in *Studies in the Theory of Capital Markets,* pp. 79–124; E. F. Fama and J. MacBeth, "Risk, Return and Equilibrium: Empirical Tests," *Journal of Political Economy* 81 (May–June 1973), pp. 607–636; I. I. Friend and M. Blume, "Measurement of Portfolio Performance under Uncertainty," *American Economic Review* 60 (September 1970), pp. 561–575; N. I. Jacob, "The Measurement of Systematic Risk for Securities and Portfolios: Some Empirical Results," *Journal of Financial and Quantitative Analysis* 6 (March 1971), pp. 815–834.

financial firms and services as Merrill Lynch, Pierce, Fenner & Smith, Wells Fargo Bank, and Value Line. The sophisticated methodologies utilized include analysis over a number of periods; typically the intervals are one month, but some services use intervals as short as one week or one day.

The nature of the sophisticated procedures for estimating the market parameters is conveyed by the data in Table 5.9, which provides an approximation to the market parameters for a seventeen-year period. The percent returns listed in Column 5 are obtained by adding the dividend yield in Column 4 to the capital gain calculated in Column 3 from the information on the Standard & Poor's 500 stock price index data listed in Column 2. Using the data in Column 5, we obtain the mean market return of approximately 8 percent over

Table 5.9

Estimates of Market Parameters

Year	S&P 500 Price Index	Percent Change in Price	Dividend Yield	Percent Return	Return Deviation	Market Variance	Risk-Free Return
(t)	P_t	$\frac{P_t}{P_{t-1}} - 1$	$\frac{D_t}{P_t}$	R_{Mt} (3) + (4)	$(R_{Mt} - \overline{R}_M)$ (5) $- \overline{R}_M$	$(R_{Mt} - \overline{R}_M)^2$ $(6)^2$	R_F
(1)	(2)	(3)	(4)	(5)	(6)	(7)	(8)
1	55.85						
2	66.27	0.1866	0.0298	0.2164	0.1371	0.018796	0.03
3	62.38	(0.0587)	0.0337	(0.0250)	(0.1043)	0.010878	0.03
4	69.87	0.1201	0.0317	0.1518	0.0725	0.005256	0.03
5	81.37	0.1646	0.0301	0.1947	0.1154	0.013317	0.04
6	88.17	0.0836	0.0300	0.1136	0.0343	0.001176	0.04
7	85.26	(0.0330)	0.0340	0.0010	(0.0783)	0.006131	0.04
8	91.93	0.0782	0.0320	0.1102	0.0309	0.000955	0.05
9	98.70	0.0736	0.0307	0.1043	0.0250	0.000625	0.05
10	97.84	(0.0087)	0.0324	0.0237	(0.0556)	0.003091	0.07
11	83.22	(0.1494)	0.0383	(0.1111)	(0.1904)	0.036252	0.06
12	98.29	0.1811	0.0314	0.2125	0.1332	0.017742	0.05
13	109.20	0.1110	0.0284	0.1394	0.0601	0.003612	0.05
14	107.43	(0.0162)	0.0306	0.0144	(0.0649)	0.004212	0.07
15	82.85	(0.2288)	0.0447	(0.1841)	(0.2634)	0.069380	0.08
16	85.17	0.0280	0.0431	0.0711	(0.0082)	0.000067	0.06
17	102.01	0.1977	0.0376	0.2353	0.1560	0.024336	0.06
				1.2682		0.215826	0.81

$R_F = 0.81/16 = 0.051$

$\overline{R}_M = 1.2682/16 = 0.0793 \approx 0.080$

$\text{Var}(R_M) = 0.215826/15 = 0.0144$

Sources: Columns 2 and 4 from individual issues of *Economic Report of the President,* and Column 8 from individual issues of the *Federal Reserve Bulletin.*

the period. Column 6 lists the deviations from the market return. In Column 7 the deviations are squared, then summed and divided by 15 to obtain the 0.0144 estimate of market variance.[2]

The risk-free return is estimated by use of the six-month Treasury bill rate. The averages for the years indicated are listed in Column 8. These average annual values are summed and divided by 16 to obtain an estimate of 5.1 percent for the risk-free return for the time period covered.

Studies of the market behavior over more extended time periods, utilizing monthly rather than annual intervals, suggest a range of about 9 to 11 percent for market returns. Thus our 8 percent dominated by the weak market in recent years is slightly low. Most previous studies of market parameters utilize at least 60 months of returns as compared with the 16 observations in Table 5.9. Of course, a large number of observations will reduce the variance measured, so the longer term studies suggest that 1 percent is, on the average, a good estimate of market variance. Inspection of Column 8, which contains the risk-free return measures, indicates a range of from 3 percent to 8 percent. Thus the higher values of R_F have predominated in the later years. Hence, to make current estimates of the cost of equity or to make estimates for use for future periods, a 5 to 6 percent range of estimates of the risk-free return would be plausible.

The indicated return on the market in Table 5.10 is 9 percent. The variance of the market returns is approximately 1 percent, and the standard deviation of the market is 10 percent.

The pattern of data in Table 5.10 facilitates the calculation of the covariance of the returns on an individual security with the market returns. For each state of the economy, the deviation of the return for each security from its mean is multiplied by the deviation of the market return from the mean return on the market. The probabilities of the alternative states are then multi-

Table 5.10

Calculation of Market Returns and Variance

State of the Economy	P_s	$\tilde{R}_M$	$P_s\tilde{R}_M$	$(\tilde{R}_M - \overline{R}_M)$	$(\tilde{R}_M - \overline{R}_M)^2$	$P_s(\tilde{R}_M - \overline{R}_M)^2$
Down	0.2	−0.10	−0.02	−0.19	0.0361	0.00722
Average	0.5	0.10	0.05	0.01	0.0001	0.00005
Up	0.3	0.20	0.06	0.11	0.0121	0.00363
			$\overline{R}_M = 0.09$			$\sigma_M^2 = 0.01090 \approx 0.01$
						$\sigma_M = 0.1044 \approx 0.1$

2. We divide by 15 rather than 16 since one degree of freedom has been lost because the calculation of the variance involves the use of the mean return on the market, which has already been calculated.

plied by each of these products, and the results are summed. The calculations are shown in Table 5.11.

Table 5.11

Calculation of Covariances

Asset A

P_s	$(\tilde{R}_a - \bar{R}_a)(\tilde{R}_M - \bar{R}_M)$	$P_s(\tilde{R}_a - \bar{R}_a)(\tilde{R}_M - \bar{R}_M)$
0.2	$-0.40 \times -0.19 = 0.0760$	0.0152
0.5	$-0.02 \times 0.01 = -0.0002$	−0.0001
0.3	$0.30 \times 0.11 = 0.0330$	0.0099
		$\text{Cov}(\tilde{R}_a, \tilde{R}_M) = 0.0250$

Asset B

P_s	$(\tilde{R}_b - \bar{R}_b)(\tilde{R}_M - \bar{R}_M)$	$P_s(\tilde{R}_b - \bar{R}_b)(\tilde{R}_M - \bar{R}_M)$
0.2	$0.37 \times -0.19 = -0.0703$	−0.01406
0.5	$0.05 \times 0.01 = 0.0005$	0.00025
0.3	$-0.33 \times 0.11 = -0.0363$	−0.01089
		$\text{Cov}(\tilde{R}_b, \tilde{R}_M) = -0.02470$

Asset C

P_s	$(\tilde{R}_c - \bar{R}_c)(\tilde{R}_M - \bar{R}_M)$	$P_s(\tilde{R}_c - \bar{R}_c)(\tilde{R}_M - \bar{R}_M)$
0.2	$-0.25 \times -0.19 = 0.0475$	0.0095
0.5	$0.10 \times 0.01 = 0.0010$	0.0005
0.3	$0.0 \times 0.11 = 0.0000$	0.0000
		$\text{Cov}(\tilde{R}_c, \tilde{R}_M) = 0.0100$

With the covariance as calculated in Table 5.11, we can readily calculate the beta for each asset, defined as:

$$\text{Beta of an asset} = \left[\begin{matrix}\text{Covariance with} \\ \text{market returns}\end{matrix}\right] \Big/ \left[\begin{matrix}\text{Variance of the} \\ \text{market returns}\end{matrix}\right].$$

We can utilize the data from the appropriate table to obtain:

(5.9)

$$\beta_j = \frac{\text{Cov}(R_j, R_M)}{\sigma_M^2}$$

$$\beta_a = \frac{0.0250}{0.01} = 2.5$$

$$\beta_b = \frac{-0.0247}{0.01} = -2.47$$

$$\beta_c = \frac{0.0100}{0.01} = 1.00.$$

We have now constructed all of the building blocks to make use of some general market relationships between return and risk.

The Capital Asset Pricing Model and the Security Market Line

The riskiness of assets or securities held in portfolios can be measured by their contribution to the portfolio risk. This relationship is measured by the covariance of the asset or security returns with the returns on the market as a whole. From the portfolio approach to the measurement of risk, the capital asset pricing model (CAPM) sets forth a theory of the relationship between the risk of an asset and the required risk adjustment factor.

The relationship is expressed in the security market line (SML) as:

$$\overline{R}_j = R_F + \lambda \text{Cov}(\tilde{R}_j, \tilde{R}_M) \tag{5.10}$$

$E(R_j) = \overline{R}_j$ = "Expected" return on Asset J ("expected" return *required* by the security market line relationships)

R_F = Risk-free return

$\text{Cov}(\tilde{R}_j, \tilde{R}_M)$ = Covariance between the returns on Asset J and the returns on the market

λ = Price of risk for securities $= \dfrac{\overline{R}_M - R_F}{\sigma_M^2}$.

In the above formulation, the market risk premium $(\overline{R}_M - R_F)$ is normalized by dividing it by the variance (a measure of market risk) of the market returns. Alternatively, the normalization can be applied to the covariance measure of the riskiness of the individual Asset J. The security market line (SML) is then expressed:

$$\overline{R}_j = R_F + (\overline{R}_M - R_F)\beta_j$$

where: (5.11)

$$\beta_j = \text{Cov}(\tilde{R}_j, \tilde{R}_M)/\sigma_M^2$$

and is a measure of the volatility of the individual investment's returns relative to the market returns.

The logic of the security market line equation is that the required return on an investment is a risk-free return plus a risk adjustment factor. The risk adjustment factor is obtained by multiplying the risk premium required for the market return by the riskiness of the individual investment. If the returns on the individual investment fluctuate by exactly the same degree as the returns on the market as a whole, the beta for the security is 1. In this situation the required return on the individual investment is the same as the required return on the total market. If the variation in the returns of an individual investment is greater than the variation in the market returns, the beta of the individual investment is greater than 1, and its risk adjustment factor is greater than the risk adjustment factor for the market as a whole.

Figure 5.3

Graph of the Security Market Line

$E(R_j)$ (Percent)

16
14
12
$E(R_M)$
10
8
$R_F = 6$
4
2
0

SML

$9\% - 7\% = 2\%$

$0.6 - 0.2 = 0.4$

0.2 0.4 0.6 0.8 1.0 1.2 1.4 1.6 1.8

β_j

$$\text{Slope of SML} = \frac{\Delta E(R_j)}{\Delta \beta_j} = \frac{2\%}{0.4} = 5\%$$

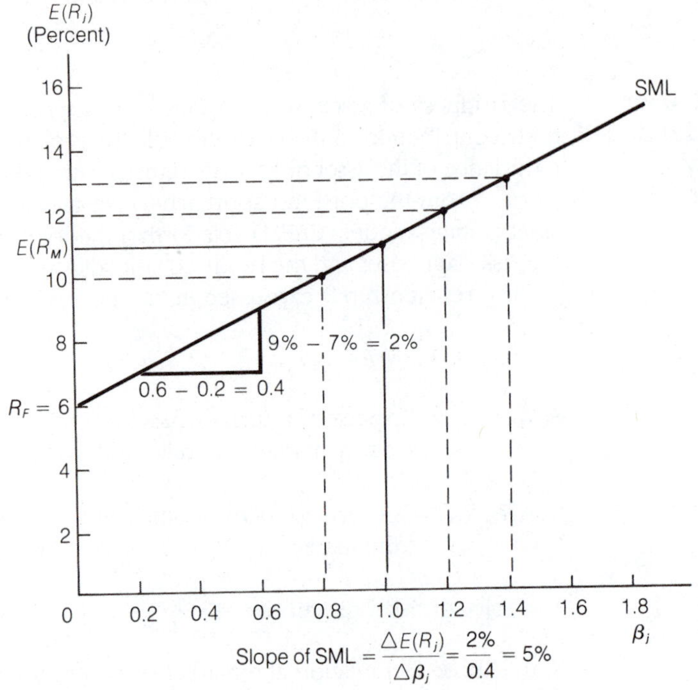

The relationship between the riskiness of an individual investment, as measured by its beta, and the risk adjustment factor is illustrated in Figure 5.3. The risk-free return is given as 6 percent. If we use 11 percent as the long-term average return on the market, the market risk premium is 11 percent minus 6 percent, which is 5 percent, the slope of the SML. If the risk-free return is 6 percent, the required return on the market is 6 percent plus a risk adjustment factor of 5 percent, totaling 11 percent.

The required return on an individual investment depends on the size of its beta, which measures the variations in its returns in relation to the returns on the market. If the beta of an individual investment is 1.2, its risk adjustment factor is 1.2 times the market risk adjustment factor of 5 percent. The risk adjustment factor for the individual investment is therefore 6 percent, and its required return is 12 percent. If the beta measure of an investment is 1.4, its risk adjustment factor is 7 percent, and its required return is 13 percent. An investment with a beta of 0.8 has a risk adjustment factor of 4 percent and a required return of 10 percent.

The advantages of the security market line approach to measuring the risk adjustment factor and the required return on an investment are that the relationships can be quantified and that they have been subjected to considerable statistical testing. But it would be premature to discard the earlier approach that analyzes the risk of an individual investment by its standard deviation and coefficient of variation. There are a number of reasons for keeping both approaches:

1. Some studies have found that the standard deviation does in fact have an influence on the required return of a security.
2. Empirical studies of the SML confirm a positive relationship between risk and return, but the observed SML appears to be tilted clockwise from the theoretical line, as shown in Figure 5.4. Low beta assets earn more than the CAPM would predict, and high beta assets earn less than the CAPM would predict.

Figure 5.4

Theoretical versus Statistical Estimates of the SML

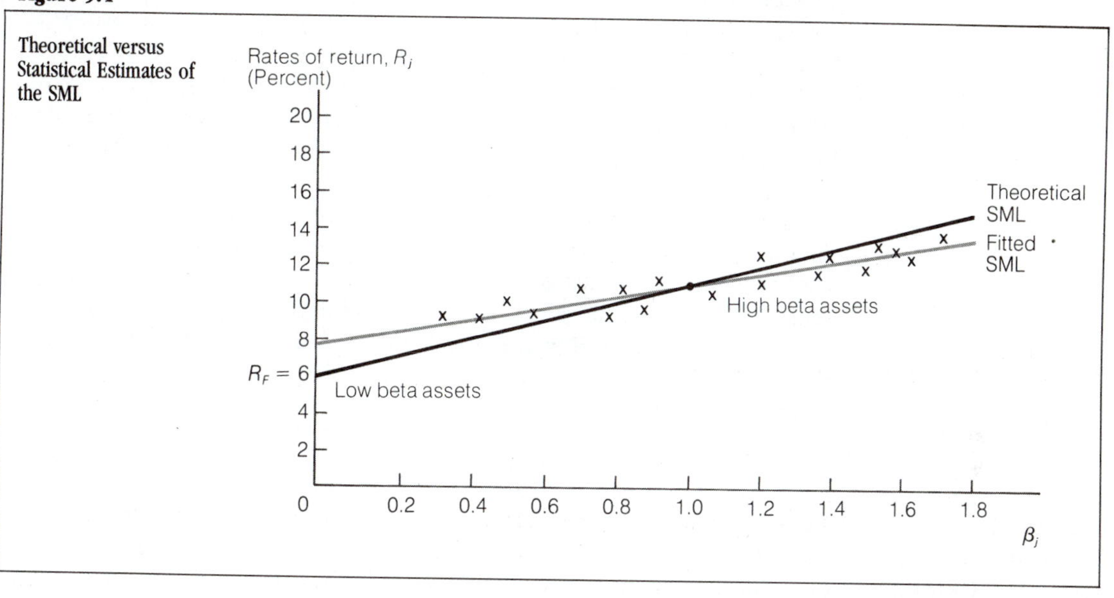

3. The CAPM utilizes historical data, and all the terms in the SML can be different, depending on the time period selected for measurement. Thus, for some time periods, the average return on the market may be as low as 5 to 6 percent (or even negative). The risk-free rate may rise or fall, depending on the expected rate of inflation. Note, however, that if the rate of inflation causes the risk-free rate and market return to rise by the same number of percentage points, the market risk adjustment factor is unchanged. For example, suppose that with an expected rate of inflation of 3 percent per year, the risk-free rate is 5 percent and the market rate of return 10 percent. With an expected rate of inflation of 8 percent, the risk-free rate may rise to 10 percent and the market rate of return to 15 percent. In both cases, the market risk adjustment factor remains at 5 percent.

4. The β for an individual security reflects industry characteristics and management policies that determine how returns fluctuate in relation to variations in overall market returns. If the general economic environment is stable, if industry characteristics remain unchanged, and if management policies have continuity, the measure of β will be relatively stable when calculated for different time periods. However, if these conditions do not exist, the value of β will vary as the characteristics of investments or securities change in their relationship to the total market.

Nevertheless, alternative measures of risk are subject to similar or even more serious limitations. The great attractiveness of the SML is that it provides a quantitative relationship between risk and required return. While the relationship is subject to some errors in measurement, at least we have a first approximation that may be used as a basis for further analysis. Further, while the SML estimates of the relationship between risk and return are subject to change over time, they provide one useful approach. SML measures must be combined with estimates reached through individual judgments to arrive at financial decisions. In formulating judgments, the alternative measures of risk —the standard deviation and its normalized form, the coefficient of variation —may also aid in the decision process.

In addition, these formal measures of risk-return relationships should be supplemented by techniques such as decision tree formulations, sensitivity analysis, and the simulation of the consequences of alternative estimates of critical variables in the calculations. These additional approaches will be described in Chapter 14. However, the formal measures—the SML and standard deviation relationships—are useful for initial quantification of return and risk relationships.

Effects of Inflation on Required Returns

A major factor that has had serious impact on the level of nominal returns has been the persistence since the late 1960s of worldwide inflation. The nature of the impact can be conveyed by analyzing the patterns of interest rates and returns before the impact of inflation. Three major influences determine the levels of interest rates and returns: the real productivity rate in the economy, a positive differential for greater risk, and a positive differential for longer maturities. Here we will abstract from short-term demand and supply conditions, which sometimes push short-term interest rates above long-term interest rates. The real productivity rate is the basic rate of growth in the economy; it provides the source of payment to savers for postponing their consumption from the present to the future. The basic real interest rate reflecting the productivity rate in the economy is 2.5 to 3 percent per annum. This is also the rate of interest on short-term government securities free of the risk of nonpayment at maturity. For longer-term government securities, the rate rises with the length of maturity, reflecting the greater risk of interest rate fluctuations. This adds 1.5 to 2 percent to the basic 2.5 to 3 percent interest rate.

For prime short-term business debt such as commercial paper, we add 1 to 1.5 percent to the government short-term debt rates. For longer-term corporate debt, we add about the same 1 to 1.5 percent differential to rates on longer-term government securities. Since common stocks of corporations carry still greater risk, we add risk adjustment premiums of 2 to 3 percentage points to the corporate bond rates.

To each of the interest rates and common stock returns we must also add a factor based on the expected rate of inflation, so that real returns are maintained after adjusting for inflation. Taking inflation into account, the pattern of rates appears something like this:

		Price Level Rise per Year		
	Basic Rates	2%	5%	10%
Short-term government bills	2.5–3%	4.5–5%	7.5–8%	12.5–13%
Long-term government bonds	4–5	6–7	9–10	14–15
Short-term business debt	3.5–4.5	5.5–6.5	8.5–9.5	13.5–14.5
Long-term corporate bonds	5–6.5	7–8.5	10–11.5	15–16.5
Common stocks of corporations	7–9.5	9–11.5	12–14.5	17–19.5

Technically, we adjust nominal yields or returns for inflation by the procedures indicated in Table 5.12. Column 1 shows data on the rates of interest on short-term business debt for a period of years. Column 2 gives a measure of the price level for each year. Column 3 calculates the purchasing power of the currency as compared to the previous year. Column 4 multiplies Columns 1 and 3 to obtain the real interest rate (plus 1). Note that the real interest rate on short-term business loans has remained constant, although nominal interest rates have risen from 10 percent to 14 percent over the period of years.

Table 5.12

Calculation of Real Interest Rates on Short-Term Business Debt

Year	One Plus Nominal Returns (1)	Price Index (P_t) (2)	$\frac{P_{t-1}}{P_t}$ (3)	One Plus Real Rate of Return (1) × (3) (4)
19X1		100		
19X2	1.10	106	0.94	1.03
19X3	1.11	114	0.93	1.03
19X4	1.12	124	0.92	1.03
19X5	1.13	136	0.91	1.03
19X6	1.14	151	0.90	1.03

Table 5.13

Calculation of Real Returns on Common Stocks

	One Plus Nominal Returns	Price Index (P_t)	$\frac{P_{t-1}}{P_t}$	One Plus Real Rate of Return (1) × (3)
Year	(1)	(2)	(3)	(4)
19X1		100		
19X2	1.10	102	0.98	1.08
19X3	1.11	106	0.96	1.07
19X4	1.12	116	0.91	1.02
19X5	1.13	130	0.89	1.01
19X6	1.14	148	0.88	1.00

The impact of inflation in recent years has been unfavorable to U.S. business firms. In fact, it is doubtful whether their level of real returns on common stocks has been maintained. The situation is indicated in Table 5.13; following the same methodology as in Table 5.12, we see that while nominal returns have risen from 10 to 14 percent, real returns have declined from 8 percent to 0. The impact of inflation on different industries has varied, but it tends to be unfavorable for the following reasons. Firms in a given industry with fixed assets and inventories acquired at lower historical costs are able to offer severe price competition because they are operating from a lower historical cost basis. Since accounting is predominantly based on the expiration of historical costs, the higher current replacement costs of fixed assets and inventories may not be reflected in the prices charged by firms in industries such as paper, cement, and steel. As a consequence, even the nominal profits in inflated dollars reported by some individual companies may be severely depressed.

Summary

In this chapter, the basic risk and return relationships that we shall be using throughout subsequent topics have been presented in overview. The quantification of the basic relationships between risk and return is provided by the security market line (SML).

$$\bar{R}_j = R_F + (\bar{R}_M - R_F)\beta_j.$$

These relationships apply to forms of financing with different risks as well as to a given class of securities with variations in risk for different issuers of the securities. They are illustrated in Figure 5.5.

Short-term government securities are relatively free from both default risk and purchasing power risk. When we move from the government sector

Figure 5.5

Risk-Return Relationships for a Range of Securities

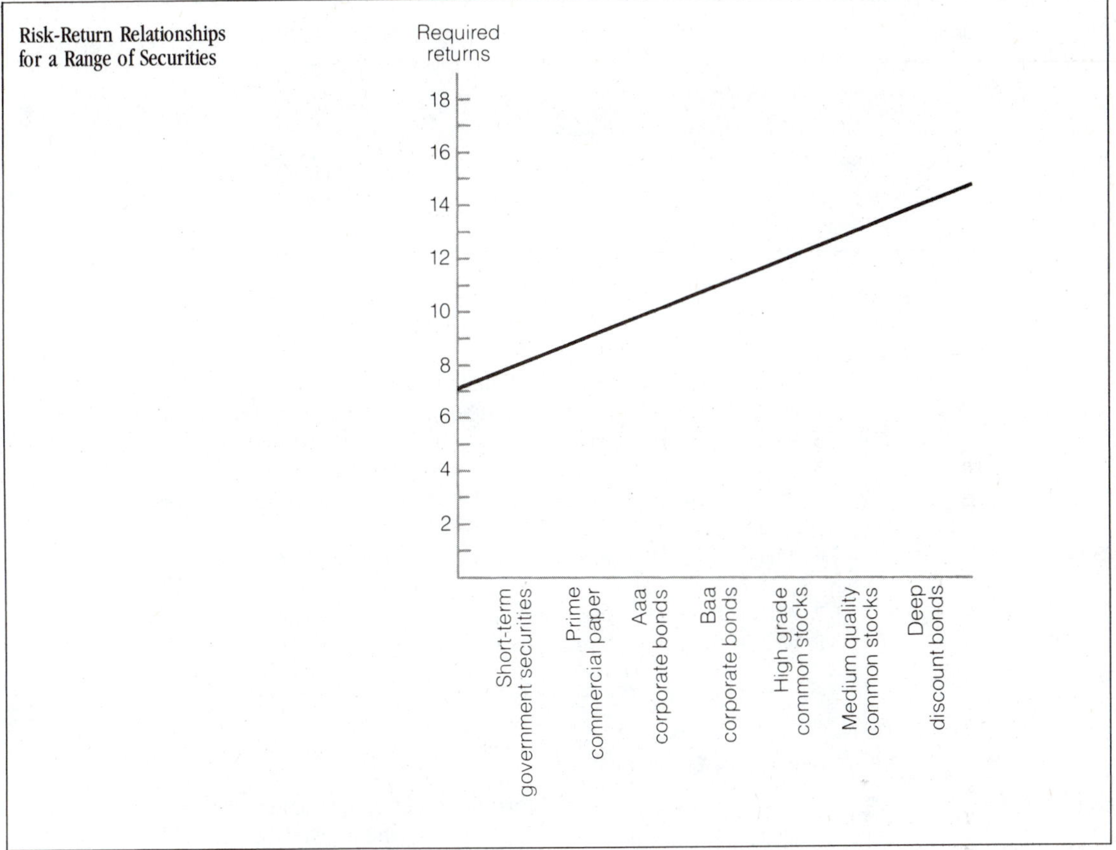

to private corporations as issuers of securities, we encounter some default risk. The highest quality corporate issues are short-term commercial paper. For longer maturity obligations, the highest quality corporate securities would be Aaa corporate bonds. Lower grade corporate securities carry ratings of B, C, or D, varying with the classification system employed.

The relationship between the risk of the security and the indicated required return shown on the vertical axis varies with the state of money and capital market conditions. The relationships depicted in Figure 5.5 are illustrative only.

From the SML, as modified by other factors discussed in this and subsequent chapters, we can develop some fundamental relationships required for the analysis of financial decisions. We then have the pattern shown in Figure 5.6. Valuation represents the payoff of the interaction of the variables. We therefore turn to this key management goal.

Figure 5.6

Variables Influencing Valuation

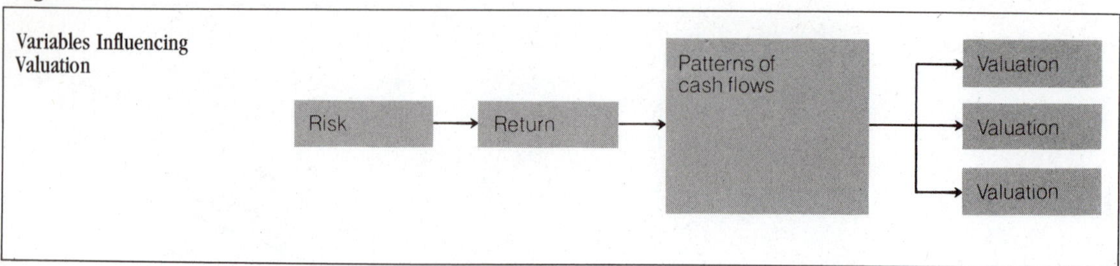

Questions

5.1 Describe the nature of risk. Of uncertainty.

5.2 How is the alternative state approach used in handling uncertainty?

5.3 What is the mean-variance approach to risk and uncertainty?

5.4 What is the coefficient of variation, and why is it used as a measure of risk?

5.5 How is the concept of risk measured when assets are viewed in the framework of the portfolio?

5.6 What is the relationship between covariance, the correlation coefficient, and the beta measure?

5.7 What is the basic underlying logic of the security market line equation?

5.8 What is the effect of inflation on the required return?

Problems

5.1 Based on the following historical market data, calculate the expected return on the market, the variance of the returns on the market, the standard deviation of the returns on the market, and the expected risk-free returns.

Year	S&P 500 Price Index	Dividend Yield	R_F
1	55.85		0.035
2	66.27	0.0298	0.032
3	62.38	0.0337	0.035
4	69.87	0.0317	0.039
5	81.37	0.0301	0.042
6	88.17	0.0300	0.051
7	85.26	0.0340	0.049
8	91.93	0.0320	0.056
9	98.70	0.0307	0.068
10	97.84	0.0324	0.065
11	83.22	0.0383	0.064
12	98.29	0.0314	0.086
13	109.20	0.0284	0.099
14	107.43	0.0306	0.119

5.2 Assuming the following probability distribution of market returns, calculate the $E(R_M)$, $\text{Var}(R_M)$, and σ_M.

State	Probability	Market Return (R_M)
1	0.12	−0.10
2	0.26	0.15
3	0.44	0.20
4	0.18	0.25

5.3 The Barfield Company has a new investment project. The project returns are estimated as follows:

Year	Project Return (R_j)
1981	0.10
1982	0.17
1983	0.24
1984	0.20
1985	0.14

Calculate:
a. The expected return on the investment.
b. The variance of returns.
c. The standard deviation of returns.
d. The coefficient of variation of returns.

5.4 The McCoy Company has developed the following data regarding a project to add new production facilities.

State (s)	Probability (P_s)	Market Return (R_M)	Project Return (R_j)
1	0.05	−0.20	−0.30
2	0.25	0.10	0.05
3	0.35	0.15	0.20
4	0.20	0.20	0.25
5	0.15	0.25	0.30

Calculate:
a. The expected return on the project.
b. The variance of the project returns.
c. The standard deviation of project returns.
d. The coefficient of variation of project returns.
e. The covariance of the project returns with the market returns.
f. The correlation coefficient between the project returns and the market returns.

5.5 The expected returns for two firms, A and B, are as follows:

State (s)	P_s	Return of Firm A	Return of Firm B
1	0.1	−0.05	−0.10
2	0.4	0.10	0.15
3	0.3	0.25	0.10
4	0.2	0.30	0.18

Firm A has a total investment in assets of $75,000,000, three times the size of Firm B.

Assume that a new firm, C, is formed through a merger between Firms A and B. The share of A and B in the portfolio represented by the new Firm C is based on the ratio of their total assets prior to the merger.

Calculate:

a. The expected return and standard deviation of Firms A and B before the merger.
b. The covariance—Cov *(ab)*—and correlation coefficient (ρ_{ab}) between the returns for Firms A and B before the merger.
c. The expected return of Firm C, $\bar{R}_c$.
d. The standard deviation of returns, σ_c.

Selected References

Arditti, Fred D. "Risk and the Required Return on Equity." *Journal of Finance* 22 (March 1967), pp. 19–36.

Black, F. "Capital Market Equilibrium with Restricted Borrowing." *Journal of Business* 45 (July 1972), pp. 444–454.

Black, F.; Jensen, M. C.; and Scholes, M. "The Capital Asset Pricing Model: Some Empirical Tests." In *Studies in the Theory of Capital Markets.* Edited by M. C. Jensen. New York: Praeger, 1972.

Brennan, M. J. "Capital Market Equilibrium with Divergent Borrowing and Lending Rates." *Journal of Financial and Quantitative Analysis* 6 (December 1971), pp. 1197–1205.

———. "Investor Taxes, Market Equilibrium and Corporate Finance." Ph.D. dissertation, Massachusetts Institute of Technology, June 1970.

Brigham, E. F., and Pappas, J. "Rates of Return on Common Stock." *Journal of Business* 42 (July 1969), pp. 302–316.

Carlson, John A. "Expected Inflation and Interest Rates." *Economic Inquiry* 17 (October 1979), pp. 597–608.

Cooley, Philip L.; Roenfeldt, Rodney L.; and Modani, Naval K. "Interdependence of Market Risk Measures." *Journal of Business* 50 (July 1977), pp. 356–363.

Evans, J. L., and Archer, S. H. "Diversification and the Reduction of Dispersion: An Empirical Analysis." *Journal of Finance* 23 (December 1968), pp. 761–767.

Fama, E. F. "Efficient Capital Markets: A Review of Theory and Empirical Work." *Journal of Finance* 25 (May 1970), pp. 383–417.

———. "Risk, Return, and Equilibrium." *Journal of Political Economy* 79 (January–February 1971), pp. 30–55.

Fama, E. F., and MacBeth, J. "Risk, Return and Equilibrium: Empirical Tests." *Journal of Political Economy* 81 (May–June 1973), pp. 607–636.

Fama, E. F., and Miller, M. H. *The Theory of Finance.* New York: Holt, Rinehart and Winston, 1972.

Firth, Michael. "The Relationship between Stock Market Returns and Rates of Inflation." *Journal of Finance* 34 (June 1979), pp. 743–749.

Fisher, Lawrence. "Determinants of Risk Premiums on Corporate Bonds." *Journal of Political Economy* 67 (June 1959), pp. 217–237.

Friend, I.; Landskroner, Yoram; and Losq, Etienne. "The Demand for Risky Assets under Uncertain Inflation." *Journal of Finance* 31 (December 1976), pp. 1287–1297.

Gehr, Adam K., Jr. "Risk and Return." *Journal of Finance* 34 (September 1979), pp. 1027–1030.

Hagerman, Robert L., and Kim, E. Han. "Capital Asset Pricing with Price Level Changes." *Journal of Financial and Quantitative Analysis* 11 (September 1976), pp. 381–392.

Hakansson, N. "Capital Growth and the Mean-Variance Approach to Portfolio Selection." *Journal of Financial and Quantitative Analysis* 6 (January 1971), pp. 517–558.

Hakansson, Nils H., and Miller, Bruce L. "Compound-Return Mean-Variance Efficient Portfolios Never Risk Ruin." *Management Science* 22 (December 1975), pp. 391–400.

Hamada, R. S. "Portfolio Analysis, Market Equilibrium and Corporation Finance." *Journal of Finance* 24 (March 1969), pp. 13–22.

———. "The Effect of the Firm's Capital Structure on the Systematic Risk of Common Stocks." *Journal of Finance* 27 (May 1972), pp. 435–452.

Haugen, Robert A., and Heins, A. James. "Risk and the Rate of Return on Financial Assets." *Journal of Financial and Quantitative Analysis* 10 (December 1975), pp. 775–784.

Hirshleifer, J. "Efficient Allocation of Capital in an Uncertain World." *American Economic Review* 54 (May 1964), pp. 77–85.

———. *Investment, Interest and Capital.* Englewood Cliffs, N.J.: Prentice-Hall, 1970.

Hsia, C. C. "Inflation Risk and Capital Asset Pricing." Unpublished manuscript, University of California, Los Angeles, 1973.

Ibbotson, Roger G., and Sinquefield, Rex A. "Stocks, Bonds, Bills, and Inflation: Simulations of the Future (1976–2000)." *Journal of Business* 49 (July 1976), pp. 313–338.

Jacob, N. "The Measurement of Systematic Risk for Securities and Portfolios: Some Empirical Results." *Journal of Financial and Quantitative Analysis* 6 (March 1971), pp. 815–834.

Jaffe, Jeffrey F. "Corporate Taxes, Inflation, the Rate of Interest and the Return to Equity." *Journal of Financial and Quantitative Analysis* 13 (March 1978), pp. 55–64.

Jensen, M. C. "Capital Markets: Theory and Evidence." *Bell Journal of Economics and Management Science* 3 (Autumn 1972), pp. 357–398.

———. "Risk, the Pricing of Capital Assets, and the Evaluation of Investment Portfolios." *Journal of Business* 42 (April 1969), pp. 167–247.

———. "The Performance of Mutual Funds in the Period 1945–1964." *Journal of Finance* 23 (May 1968), pp. 389–416.

———, ed. *Studies in the Theory of Capital Markets.* New York: Praeger, 1972.

Lintner, J. "The Aggregation of Investors' Diverse Judgment and Preferences in Purely Competitive Securities Markets." *Journal of Financial and Quantitative Analysis* 4 (December 1969), pp. 347–400.

———. "Security Prices, Risk, and Maximal Gains from Diversification." *Journal of Finance* 20 (December 1965), pp. 587–616.

———. "The Valuation of Risk Assets and the Selection of Risky Investments in Stock Portfolios and Capital Budgets." *Review of Economics and Statistics* 47 (February 1965), pp. 13–37.

Litzenberger, R. H., and Budd, A. P. "Secular Trends in Risk Premiums." *Journal of Finance* 27 (September 1972), pp. 857–864.

Litzenberger, R. H., and Rao, C. U. "Portfolio Theory and Industry Cost-of-Capital Estimates." *Journal of Financial and Quantitative Analysis* 7 (March 1972), pp. 1443–1462.

Long, J. B., Jr. "Consumption-Investment Decisions and Equilibrium in the Securities Market." In *Studies in the Theory of Capital Markets.* Edited by M. C. Jensen. New York: Praeger, 1972.

McEnally, Richard W. "A Note on the Return Behavior of High Risk Common Stocks." *Journal of Finance* 29 (March 1974), pp. 199–202.

Markowitz, H. M. *Portfolio Selection: Efficient Diversification of Investments.* New York: Wiley, 1959.

———. "Portfolio Selection." *Journal of Finance* 7 (March 1952), pp. 77–91.

Mayers, David. "Nonmarketable Assets, Market Segmentation, and the Level of Asset Prices." *Journal of Financial and Quantitative Analysis* 11 (March 1976), pp. 1–12.

———. "Non-marketable Assets and the Determination of Capital Asset Prices in the Absence of a Riskless Asset." *Journal of Business* 46 (April 1973), pp. 258–267.

Melicher, Ronald W., and Rush, David F. "Systematic Risk, Financial Data, and Bond Rating Relationships in a Regulated Industry Environment." *Journal of Finance* 29 (May 1974), pp. 537–544.

Modigliani, Franco, and Pogue, Gerald A. "An Introduction to Risk and Return." *Financial Analysts' Journal* 30 (March–April 1974), pp. 68–80; 30 (May–June 1974), pp. 69–86.

Mossin, J. "Security Pricing and Investment Criteria in Competitive Markets." *American Economic Review* 59 (December 1969), pp. 749–756.

———. "Equilibrium in a Capital Asset Market." *Econometrica* 34 (October 1966), pp. 768–783.

Norgaard, Richard L. "An Examination of the Yields of Corporate Bonds and Stocks." *Journal of Finance* 29 (September 1974), pp. 1275–1286.

Robichek, Alexander A., and Cohn, Richard A. "The Economic Determinants of Systematic Risk." *Journal of Finance* 29 (May 1974), pp. 439–447.

Roll, R. "Investment Diversification and Bond Maturity." *Journal of Finance* 26 (March 1971), pp. 51–66.

———. "Bias in Fitting the Sharpe Model to Time Series Data." *Journal of Financial and Quantitative Analysis* 4 (September 1969), pp. 271–289.

Rubinstein, M. E. "A Mean-Variance Synthesis of Corporate Financial Theory." *Journal of Finance* 28 (March 1973), pp. 167–181.

Schall, Lawrence D. "Asset Valuation, Firm Investment, and Firm Diversification." *Journal of Business* 45 (January 1972), pp. 11–28.

Sharpe, W. F. *Portfolio Theory and Capital Markets.* New York: McGraw-Hill, 1970.

———. "Capital Asset Prices: A Theory of Market Equilibrium under Conditions of Risk." *Journal of Finance* 19 (September 1964), pp. 425–442.

———. "A Simplified Model for Portfolio Analysis." *Management Science* 9 (January 1963), pp. 277–293.

Thompson, Donald J. II. "Sources of Systematic Risk in Common Stocks." *Journal of Business* 49 (April 1976), pp. 173–188.

Tobin, J. "Liquidity Preference as Behavior toward Risk." *Review of Economic Studies* 25 (February 1958), pp. 65–85.

Treynor, J. L. "How to Rate Management of Investment Funds." *Harvard Business Review* 43 (January–February 1965), pp. 63–75.

6
Valuation Relationships

We have seen how the level of risk affects the size of the required return, or discount factor. The greater the risk, the higher the discount factor and the lower the resulting capitalized value. We now consider the influence of the pattern of the future inflows or receipts on valuation or capitalized values. We can distinguish among four major types of cash inflows or receipts as indicated by Table 6.1.

Table 6.1

Patterns of Future Cash Net Inflows

Pattern of Growth	Duration of Receipts	Examples
No growth	Infinite or perpetual	Consols, preferred stock, common stock
No growth	Finite time period	Notes and bonds
Constant growth	Infinite or perpetual	Common stock
Temporary growth	Finite time period for growth, followed by a subsequent pattern to infinity	Common stock

In this overview, we shall distinguish between bonds and common stocks. We discuss two basic categories for bonds—consols with infinite maturities and other bonds with finite maturities.

Valuation of Bonds

The valuation formula for a consol is quite simple, as shown in Equation 6.1.

$$B = \frac{c}{r}, \tag{6.1}$$

where:

B = Value of a bond
c = Annual cash payment on the bond which continues forever
r = Required return or capitalization rate applicable to the risk of the bond.

Thus if the annual coupon were \$100 and the required return on the bond were 10 percent, the value of the bond, B, would be \$1,000. If the required return falls to 8 percent, the value of the bond rises to \$1,250. If the required return on the bond rises to 12 percent, the value of the bond falls to \$833.33.

For a bond of finite maturity, the applicable valuation formula is:

$$B = \sum_{t=1}^{N} \frac{c_t}{(1+r)^t} + \frac{M}{(1+r)^N}, \tag{6.2}$$

where:

c_t = Annual coupon for years 1, 2, ⋯, N
N = Year in which the bond matures
M = Maturity value of the bond.

The first term of Equation 6.2 can be restated:

$$\sum_{t=1}^{N} \frac{c_t}{(1+r)^t} = c_t \sum_{t=1}^{N} \frac{1}{(1+r)^t} = c_t \times \text{PVIFA}_{r,N}.$$

The second term can also be restated:

$$\frac{M}{(1+r)^N} = M \frac{1}{(1+r)^N} = M \times \text{PVIF}_{r,N}.$$

A bond with an annual coupon of \$100 for 10 years that pays \$1,000 at maturity and has a required yield of 10 percent will have a present value of \$1,000:

$$\begin{aligned} B &= \$100(\text{PVIFA}_{10\%,\ 10\ \text{yrs.}}) + \$1{,}000(\text{PVIF}_{10\%,\ 10\ \text{yrs.}}) \\ &= \$100(6.1446) + \$1{,}000(0.3855) \\ &= \$614.46 + \$385.50 \\ &= \$1{,}000. \end{aligned} \tag{6.2a}$$

If we let the required yield fall to 8 percent, the expression for the value of the bond will become:

$$\begin{aligned} B &= \sum_{t=1}^{10} \frac{\$100}{(1.08)^t} + \frac{\$1{,}000}{(1.08)^{10}} \\ &= \$100(\text{PVIFA}_{8\%,\ 10\ \text{yrs.}}) + \$1{,}000(\text{PVIF}_{8\%,\ 10\ \text{yrs.}}) \\ &= \$100(6.7101) + \$1{,}000(0.4632) \\ &= \$671.01 + \$463.20 \\ &= \$1{,}134.21. \end{aligned} \tag{6.2b}$$

The value of the bond rises to \$1,134.21, or 13.4 percent. For the consol, the decline in the required yield to 8 percent results in a 25.0 percent rise in value. When the required yield rises to 12 percent, the value of the bond becomes:

$$\begin{aligned} B &= \sum_{t=1}^{10} \frac{\$100}{(1.12)^t} + \frac{\$1{,}000}{(1.12)^{10}} \\ &= \$100(\text{PVIFA}_{12\%,\,10\text{ yrs.}}) + \$1{,}000(\text{PVIF}_{12\%,\,10\text{ yrs.}}) \\ &= \$100(5.6502) + \$1{,}000(0.3220) \\ &= \$565.02 + \$322.00 \\ &= \$887.02. \end{aligned}$$

The value of the bond has fallen to \$887.02, a decline of 11.3 percent. This compares with a decline of 16.7 percent for the consol. We see that for the same required yield, the bond with a shorter maturity has less price change volatility in response to variations in required yield. However, the degree of bond price volatility is influenced by factors other than maturity alone.[1]

Bond valuation applies the two interest rate concepts of (1) the present value of an annuity to discount the annual coupon payments and (2) the present value factor to discount the maturity value of the bond to its present value. A final aspect of bond valuation is the concept of yield to maturity. Suppose we are presented with an offer to buy bonds at a specified market price. What will our investment earn? As an example, we can suppose a bond paying \$1,000 at maturity and with 10 years to run pays an annual coupon of \$100 and is offered at \$1,134.21. It would have an effective yield to maturity of 8 percent. An 8 percent interest rate would satisfy the following equation:

$$B = \$1{,}134.21 = \sum_{t=1}^{10} \frac{\$100}{(1.08)^t} + \frac{\$1{,}000}{(1.08)^{10}}.$$

We know the answer is 8 percent because when we solved the problem before, with 8 percent as the required yield, the result was the value calculated as \$1,134.21 in Equation 6.2b. In the present example, we were given a value of \$1,134.21, and with everything else given, we solved for the required yield to maturity. This is the interest rate, or discount factor, that satisfies the basic bond valuation equation for a finite maturity bond (as shown in Equation 6.2). We next consider the valuation of common stocks.

Valuation of Common Stocks

In this overview of the valuation of common stocks we shall limit ourselves to firms financed entirely by equity, using no debt in their capital structure.[2] Our point of view is that of a stockholder analyzing the value of the firm's earnings. Table 6.2 provides the opportunity to consider a concrete example of a company's balance sheet and income statement.

1. An important influence is the concept of *duration,* which is influenced by yield levels as well as by years to maturity of the bond.
2. The influences of the use of debt (leverage) and other complications are discussed in subsequent chapters. Our aim here is to present as simple an overview as possible.

Table 6.2

Financial Statements, Marshall Company

Balance Sheet, December 31, 1980

Total Assets	$3,500,000	Stockholders' Equity	$3,500,000

Income Statement for the Year Ended December 31, 1980

Sales	$7,000,000
Cost of goods sold	4,900,000
Gross profit margin	$2,100,000
Other operating expenses	1,500,000
Net operating income (NOI, X)	$ 600,000
Income taxes at 40%	240,000
Net income	$ 360,000

We focus on the results of the operating activity of the firm as measured by its net operating income (NOI). For brevity, this is also referred to as X.[3] For a firm whose net operating income (X) does not grow, the valuation model is similar to that for any uniform amount of a perpetuity. The form is the same as shown in Equation 6.1; however, the discount factor is that associated with common stock rather than with bonds. The valuation formula for common stock with no growth is shown in Equation 6.3.

$$V_u = \frac{X(1-T)}{k_u} = S, \tag{6.3}$$

where:

V_u = Value of an unlevered firm
X = Net operating income of the firm
k_u = Cost of capital of an unlevered firm
k_s = Cost of capital of stockholders' equity
S = Value of the stockholders' equity in the firm
T = Applicable corporate tax rate.

Since the firm uses no debt, $S = V_u$, because the total value of the firm is represented by the value of the stockholders' equity. The capitalization factor is the cost of capital for an unlevered firm. Since an unlevered firm has only stockholders' equity, $k_u = k_s$. However, the expression in Equation 6.3 is technically correct for an unlevered firm. In the present situation, $k_u = k_s$, but it would not be a correct representation for a k_s situation where leverage is employed. We shall maintain the subscript to indicate the cost of capital for an unlevered firm in order to be consistent with a usage in subsequent chapters where the firm uses debt financing as well as equity financing.

3. When we discuss the use of debt in later chapters, we sometimes refer to net operating income as earnings before interest and taxes (EBIT). We still refer to this income measure as X.

In the model expressed in Equation 6.3, taxes are taken into account, whereas taxes were not considered in the bond valuation model. A difference in the viewpoint reflected in bond valuation models as compared with stock valuation models is the reason this happens. In the bond valuation models, the point of view is that of the bondholders who have received income. The bondholders receive the number of dollars represented by a coupon interest rate on the bond. The firm does not have to pay taxes on its income until bond interest has been deducted. But in valuing the equity or common stock of the firm, we begin with the net operating income *(X)* of the firm. We must take into account what portion of this income flow is available to the owners of the firm, and therefore provision for payment of taxes must be taken into account.

We can illustrate the valuation model shown in Equation 6.3 by using the balance sheet and income statement data in Table 6.2. From that data we know that $X = \$600{,}000$ and $T = 40$ percent; we can assume that $k_u = 12$ percent.

The value of the common stock equity of the firm would be:

$$V_u = S = \frac{\$600{,}000(0.6)}{0.12} = \frac{\$360{,}000}{0.12} = \$3{,}000{,}000. \qquad (6.3a)$$

The valuation model is basically the same in form as for any level perpetual annuity. The capitalization factor reflects a rate appropriate to the risk of the equity position in the firm.

We next consider a firm whose net operating income *(X)* is growing at some rate. The valuation model for a firm whose net operating income is growing at a constant rate forever is:

$$V = \frac{X_0(1-T)(1-b)(1+g)}{k_u - g}, \qquad (6.4)$$

where:

b = Ratio of net investment *(I)* in period t to the after-tax NOI in period t = $I_t/X_t(1-T)$
g = Growth rate of $X(1-T) = b\bar{R}$
$\bar{R}$ = Internal profitability rate of investment in the firm = $\Delta X(1-T)/I$.

Since the firm is growing, the source of its growth must be taken into account. The source of the firm's growth is represented by a combination of its investment activity and its favorable internal profitability rate.

For investment to take place, the firm's internal profitability rate, $\bar{R}$, must be greater than its cost of capital, in this case k_u. Otherwise, the firm will not make any new investment. Hence, in general, growth requires that $\bar{R}$ exceed k.

In the model expressed in Equation 6.4, it can be shown that $g = b\bar{R}$. The growth in X or $X(1-T)$ is exactly the product of the investment rate times the internal profitability rate. So $\bar{R}$ must exceed k for growth to occur. Since this model is for an infinite time period, g must not equal or exceed k_u. Otherwise, the firm would grow to infinite size and value or have a meaningless negative value.

We now have the background for using the constant growth stock valuation model. Let us assume the same value as before for X, T, and k_u. In addition, let $b = 0.5$ and $\overline{R} = 16$ percent. Note that in the numbers we are using, $\overline{R}$ exceeds k_u, and $b\overline{R} = g = 8$ percent, which is less than a k_u of 12 percent. The resulting valuation is shown in Equation 6.4a.

$$V = \frac{\$600{,}000(0.6)(0.5)(1.08)}{0.12 - 0.08} = \frac{\$194{,}400}{0.04} = \$4{,}860{,}000. \qquad (6.4a)$$

The value of the firm and the value of the shareholders' equity which represents the firm's total ownership now rises from the previous \$3,000,000 to \$4,860,000.

Common Stock Valuation—Temporary Supernormal Growth

We next consider the valuation of common stock when supernormal growth occurs for a finite time period. Let us first develop the background of this type of growth situation. In a competitive economy, each firm tries to develop some areas of investment with above-average profitability. But such success is likely to stimulate imitation by other firms. Hence, the probable duration of investment activities that achieve above-average profitability is only a limited number of years. This is the economic rationale behind the model for valuing firms financed entirely by common stock whose earnings grow at an above-average rate for a limited number of years.

To develop the model for *temporary supernormal growth,* we must also specify what occurs at the end of the period of supernormal earnings. A wide range of plausible earnings patterns could be imagined, and the nature of the assumptions in each pattern could be reflected in the resulting model. For present purposes, it is convenient to make only two assumptions, both of which have been covered in the earlier part of this chapter. We will assume either no growth or growth at a constant rate, for which formulas have already been developed. In Equation 6.5 we present the model for the valuation of temporary supernormal growth followed by no growth:

$$V = X_0(1 - T)(1 - b)\sum_{t=1}^{N} \frac{(1 + g_s)^t}{(1 + k_u)^t} + \frac{X_0(1 - T)(1 + g_s)^N}{k_u(1 + k_u)^N}, \qquad (6.5)$$

where:

g_s = Rate of supernormal growth
N = Years of supernormal growth.

Equation 6.5 is composed of two terms. The first term covers the period of supernormal growth. In front of the summation term is the after-tax *free cash flow* (FCF), which represents the NOI after taxes and after provision for investment requirements. This initial free cash flow grows each year at g_s and is discounted at k_u. The numerator in Equation 6.4 also contains this FCF term (multiplied by $[1 + g]$ to begin discounting at the end of period 0).

The second term on the right-hand side of Equation 6.5 brings together a number of pieces, each of them already discussed. We begin with the after-tax net operating income, $X(1 - T)$. This has grown for N years at g_s. The product, therefore, is the level of net operating income after the N years of supernormal growth. This level of income is discounted at k_u, exactly as in Equation 6.3. Finally, the resulting value is discounted back to the present by the present value factor $1/(1 + k_u)^N$.

In supernormal growth there are no restrictions on the relationship between g and k_u. This is in contrast to the constant growth formula, for which a number of restrictions were noted. We can now proceed to apply Equation 6.5. The only new data required are g_s and N. Let us assume that g_s equals 30 percent and N equals 5 years. We then proceed to place all of the appropriate numbers in Equation 6.5 to form Equation 6.5a.

$$V_u = \$600{,}000(0.6)(0.5) \sum_{t=1}^{5} \frac{(1.30)^t}{(1.12)^t} + \frac{\$600{,}000(0.6)(1.30)^5}{0.12(1.12)^5}. \qquad \textbf{(6.5a)}$$

We begin the computations with the term

$$\sum_{t=1}^{5} \frac{(1.30)^t}{(1.12)^t} = \sum_{t=1}^{5} (1.16)^t = (1.16)^1 + (1.16)^2 + \cdots + (1.16)^5.$$

This is a sum of an annuity expression except that the first term should be 1, which can be obtained by factoring:

$$\sum_{t=1}^{5} (1.16)^t = 1.16[1 + (1.16) + (1.16)^2 + \cdots + (1.16)^4]$$

$$= 1.16\left[\frac{(1.16)^5 - 1}{1 + 0.16 - 1}\right] = 1.16\left[\frac{(1.16)^5 - 1}{0.16}\right] = 1.16\text{CVIFA}_{16\%,\ 5\text{ yrs.}}.$$

We can then make use of the relationship involved for a geometric series expressed most generally by the following:

$$\sum_{t=1}^{N} (1 + \text{h})^t = (1 + \text{h}) \times \text{CVIFA}_{h,N}.$$

For our data

$$(1 + \text{h})\text{CVIFA}_{16\%,\ 5\text{ yrs.}} = (1.16)(6.8771).$$

Similarly, for $(1.30)^5$ divided by $(1.12)^5$ we have $(1.16)^5$. Because the CVIF (the compound sum factor) is found by $(1 + \text{h})^t$, our result of $(1.16)^5$ is equal to $\text{CVIF}_{16\%,\ 5\text{ yrs.}}$, or 2.1003. We now have all the numbers needed to complete the calculations initially expressed in Equation 6.5a.

$$\begin{aligned} \text{V} &= \$180{,}000(1.16)(6.8771) + \$3{,}000{,}000(2.1003) \qquad \textbf{(6.5b)} \\ &= \$1{,}435{,}938 + \$6{,}300{,}900 \\ &= \$7{,}736{,}838. \end{aligned}$$

The first term starts with the \$180,000, the free cash flow that first appeared in

Equation 6.4a. We then multiply by (1 + h) times $CVIFA_{h,N}$, where h = 0.16 and $N = 5$. The second term is the valuation result for the no growth case multiplied by the compound sum factor at the supernormal growth rate of 30 percent for 5 years. Thus, the value of the firm with 5 years of supernormal growth at 30 percent with no growth thereafter rises to over $7.7 million.

An alternative assumption for the period following the limited duration of supernormal growth is the assumption of continued growth at a constant rate under the restrictions previously set forth. The general expression for this situation is set forth in Equation 6.6. All the elements of Equation 6.6 have previously been discussed.

$$V = X_0(1-T)(1-b)\sum_{t=1}^{N}\frac{(1+g_s)^t}{(1+k_u)^t} + \frac{X_0(1-T)(1-b)(1+g)}{k_u - g}\times\frac{(1+g_s)^N}{(1+k_u)^N} \quad (6.6)$$

$$= \$1{,}435{,}938 + \$4{,}860{,}000(2.1003) = \$11{,}643{,}396.$$

The first term in the valuation model is exactly what we had in Equation 6.5. The second term simply utilizes materials from the constant growth formula set forth in Equation 6.4. We can, therefore, readily perform the numerical calculations for Equation 6.6. The value for the first term is exactly as we observed in Equation 6.5b. The second term takes the valuation result of the constant growth case and multiplies it by the compound sum growth factor. The resulting value is $11.643 million.

This overview of the influence of growth on valuation provides a basis for establishing some other relationships as well, and these relationships are illustrated in Table 6.3. In the table we first summarize for the four categories of growth the valuation of the firm that we previously developed for each of

Table 6.3

Effects of Growth on Price-Earnings Ratios and Market to Book Relations

	Valuation of the Firm and Valuation of Shareholders' Equity[a] (1)	Price to Earnings Ratio[b] (2)	Market to Book Ratio[c] (3)
1. No growth	$3,000,000	8.3*X*	0.86 to 1
2. Constant growth ($g = 0.08$)	$4,860,000	13.5*X*	1.4 to 1
3. Temporary super growth ($g_S = 0.3$)			
A. Subsequent no growth	$7,736,838	21.5*X*	2.2 to 1
B. Subsequent constant growth ($g = 0.08$)	$11,643,396	32.3*X*	3.3 to 1

a. The cost of capital, k_U, is 12 percent for all these examples.
b. Recall that initial earnings after tax were $360,000.
c. Recall that accounting book value of total assets is $3,500,000.

the growth situations. These valuations can then be related to the initial after-tax earnings, which were $360,000. The resulting price to earnings ratios are shown in Column 2. Clearly, there is a relationship between these ratios and the underlying growth pattern of the earnings. The higher the growth, the higher the ratio. However, a higher price-earnings ratio does not necessarily mean that the firm's cost of capital is lower or higher. The cost of capital that was employed for the unlevered firm throughout all these examples was 12 percent.

In Column 3 we utilize the valuations of Column 1 and relate them to the accounting book value of total assets stated in Table 6.2, which was $3,500,000. Again, the more favorable the underlying growth pattern, the more favorable the resulting market to book ratio. When net operating income is assumed to have no growth, the firm is likely to have a market value less than its book value. For more favorable growth assumptions the market to book ratio rises above 1.

Thus, we have developed a basis for judging how effectively the management of a firm has achieved favorable valuation performance for the firm. One measure of favorable valuation performance is the price-earnings ratio. Another is the market to book relationship. The market to book relationship indicates that value can be created above the initial investment outlay. This favorable increase in value rises with growth.

Summary

Given the pattern of cash flows from an asset or security, risk characteristics determine the required return or capitalization factor to be applied in calculating its valuation. For bonds we have the following:

Consols $$B = \frac{c}{r}.$$

Finite maturity bonds $$B = \sum_{t=1}^{N} \frac{c_t}{(1+r)^t} + \frac{M}{(1+r)^N}.$$

For the valuation of the ownership shares of stockholders we have:

Pattern of Cash Flows	Valuation Models
1. No growth	$V_u = S_0 = \dfrac{X(1-T)}{k_u}$
2. Constant growth ($\overline{R} > k$; $g = b\overline{R}$; $g < k$)	$V_u = S_c = \dfrac{X(1-T)(1-b)(1+g)}{k_u - g}$
3. Temporary supernormal growth followed by no growth (for $t > N$, $\overline{R} = k$)	$V_u = S_{s0} = X_0(1-T)(1-b)\displaystyle\sum_{t=1}^{N} \frac{(1+g_s)^t}{(1+k_u)^t} + \frac{X_0(1-T)(1+g_s)^N}{k_u(1+k_u)^N}$

4. Temporary supernormal growth followed by constant growth

$$V_u = S_{sc} = X_0(1 - T)(1 - b)\sum_{t=1}^{N} \frac{(1 + g_s)^t}{(1 + k_u)^t} + \frac{X_0(1 - T)(1 - b)(1 + g)}{k_u - g)} \times \frac{(1 + g_s)^N}{(1 + k_u)^N}$$

The valuation of the above four expressions involves a limited number of modules, as demonstrated by our numerical examples:

$$X_0(1 - T) = \$600{,}000(0.6) = \$360{,}000$$

$$X_0(1 - T)/k_u = \$360{,}000/0.12 = \$3{,}000{,}000$$

$$X_0(1 - T)(1 - b) = \$360{,}000(0.5) = \$180{,}000$$

$$b\overline{R} = g = 0.5(0.16) = 0.08$$
$$k_u - g = 0.12 - 0.08 = 0.04$$

$$\left(\frac{1 + g_s}{1 + k_u}\right) = \left(\frac{1.30}{1.12}\right) = (1 + \text{h}) = 1.16.$$

$$\sum_{t=1}^{5}\left(\frac{1 + g_s}{1 + k_u}\right)^t = 6.8771.$$

$$\left(\frac{1 + g_s}{1 + k_u}\right)^5 = 2.1003.$$

We can observe a clear pattern of relationships between these valuation expressions:

$$S_0 = \frac{X_0(1 - T)}{k_u}$$

$$S_c = \frac{X_0(1 - T)(1 - b)(1 + g)}{k_u - g} = \frac{\text{FCF}(1 + g)}{k_u - g}$$

$$S_{s0} = \text{FCF}(1 + \text{h})\text{CVIFA}_{h,N} + S_0\,\text{CVIF}_{h,N}$$
$$S_{sc} = \text{FCF}(1 + \text{h})\text{CVIFA}_{h,N} + S_c\,\text{CVIF}_{h,N}$$

We can then combine the numerical relationships and the fundamental valuation terms to obtain the valuation results which follow:

1. No growth $S_0 = \frac{X(1 - T)}{k_u} = \frac{\$360{,}000}{0.12} = \$3{,}000{,}000.$

2. Constant growth $\overline{R} > k;\ g = b\overline{R};\ g < k$ $S_c = \frac{X(1 - T)(1 - b)(1 + g)}{k_u - g} = \frac{\text{FCF}(1 + g)}{k_u - g} = \frac{\$180{,}000(1.08)}{0.04} = \$4{,}860{,}000.$

3. Temporary supernormal growth followed by no growth

$$\begin{aligned} S_{s0} &= \text{FCF}(1 + \text{h})\text{CVIFA}_{\text{h}N} + S_0\text{CVIF}_{\text{h}N} \\ &= \$180{,}000(1.16)(6.8771) + \$3{,}000{,}000(2.1003) \\ &= \$1{,}435{,}938 + \$6{,}300{,}900 \\ &= \$7{,}736{,}838. \end{aligned}$$

4. Temporary supernormal growth followed by constant growth

$$\begin{aligned} S_{sc} &= \text{FCF}(1 + \text{h})\text{CVIFA}_{\text{h}N} + S_c\,\text{CVIF}_{\text{h}N} \\ &= \$1{,}435{,}938 + \$4{,}860{,}000(2.1003) \\ &= \$1{,}435{,}938 + \$10{,}207{,}458 \\ &= \$11{,}643{,}396. \end{aligned}$$

These exercises should clarify the nature of the valuation relationships so that the basic valuation framework for use in the following chapters will be firmly in hand.

Questions

6.1 What are the different kinds of growth that are likely to have an influence on the valuation relationship?

6.2 What is the valuation formula for an asset whose returns exhibit no growth although they continue perpetually?

6.3 What are the main components influencing the value of a bond with a finite maturity date?

6.4 Explain verbally the valuation model for a firm whose net operating income is growing at a constant rate forever.

Problems

6.1 A consol bears a coupon rate of 8 percent.

a. When market yields are 10 percent, what is its price?

b. When market yields are 5 percent, what is its price?

6.2 A twenty-year bond with a coupon of 9 percent is selling to yield 12 percent.

a. What is its price?

b. If the yield basis on which it sells becomes 10 percent, what is its new price?

6.3 A preferred stock pays a $9 dividend per year. If yields on preferred stocks of similar risk and other characteristics are 10 percent, at what price will the preferred stock sell?

6.4 A fifteen-year bond carries a coupon of 8 percent; its market price is $85. What yield to maturity does it provide?

6.5 Bonds A and B both carry coupon rates of 8 percent and both require a yield to maturity of 8 percent. Bond A has five years to maturity, while Bond B has ten years to maturity. The required market yield for each bond rises by 2 percentage points. Compare the percentage price change for the two bonds.

6.6 Bonds C and D both carry coupon rates of 6 percent and both require a yield to maturity of 16 percent. Bond C has twenty years to maturity, while Bond D has thirty years to maturity. The required market yield for each bond rises by 2 percentage points. Compare the percentage price change for the two bonds.

6.7 Compute the rate of return you will earn on the following investments.

a. A U.S. Treasury bill which has a current price of $900 and will pay $1,000 at maturity one year from now.

b. A U.S. Treasury bill which has a current price of $940 and will pay $1,000 at maturity six months from now.

c. A U.S. Treasury note selling at its maturity value ($1,000), paying 9 percent coupon interest per year and maturing in five years.

d. A bond with a current price of $90, paying 8 percent coupon interest, maturing in twenty years.

6.8 You are evaluating the following two United States government bonds:

Coupon	Maturity	Current Prices ($100 Maturity Value)
7%	10 years	$80
9%	10 years	$100

Your income tax rate is 40 percent and your capital gains tax rate is 20 percent. Capital gains taxes are paid at maturity on the difference between the purchase price and maturity value. What will be your after-tax yield to maturity (rate of return after taxes) from owning these bonds to maturity?

6.9 The Olson Company has a beta of 1.4. The expected return on the market is 12 percent, the risk-free rate is 7 percent, and the market variance is 1 percent. The net operating income of the Olson Company for the year just completed was $5 million, with an applicable corporate tax rate of 40 percent.

a. Assuming no growth in Olson's NOI is expected, what would be the value of the firm?

b. Next assume that the internal profitability rate, $\overline{R}$, of Olson is 18 percent and that b, the ratio of investment to after-tax net operating income, averages 0.50. What would be the value of Olson under these new assumptions?

c. Compare the price to after-tax earnings ratios under no growth and constant growth.

6.10 The Pelman Company has a required return of 15 percent. Its net operating income, now $4 million, is expected to grow at a rate of 26.5 percent for the next eight years with a ratio of investment to after-tax net operating income of 0.20. The applicable tax rate is 40 percent.

a. If, after the period of supernormal growth, the net operating income of Pelman has zero growth, what is the current value of the firm?

b. If, after the period of supernormal growth, the net operating income of Pelman grows at 10 percent per year, what is the current value of the firm?

c. Compare the price to after-tax earnings ratios for the two alternative assumptions with respect to the growth of net operating earnings after the period of supernormal growth.

Selected References

Brennan, Michael. "A Note on Dividend Irrelevance and the Gordon Valuation Model." *Journal of Finance* 26 (December 1971), pp. 1115–1123.

Brigham, Eugene F., and Pappas, James L. "Duration of Growth, Changes in Growth Rates, and Corporate Share Prices." *Financial Analysts' Journal* 24 (May–June 1966), pp. 157–162.

Elton, Edwin J.; Gruber, Martin J.; and Lieber, Zvi. "Valuation, Optimum Investment and Financing for the Firm Subject to Regulation." *Journal of Finance* 30 (May 1975), pp. 401–425.

Gordon, Myron J. *The Investment, Financing and Valuation of the Corporation.* Homewood, Ill.: Richard D. Irwin, 1962.

Haugen, Robert A. "Expected Growth, Required Return, and the Variability of Stock Prices." *Journal of Financial and Quantitative Analysis* 5 (September 1970), pp. 297–308.

Holt, Charles C. "The Influence of Growth Duration on Share Prices." *Journal of Finance* 17 (September 1962), pp. 465–475.

Malkiel, Burton G. "Equity Yields, Growth, and the Structure of Share Prices." *American Economic Review* 53 (December 1963), pp. 467–494.

Mao, James C. T. "The Valuation of Growth Stocks: The Investment Opportunities Approach." *Journal of Finance* 21 (March 1966), pp. 95–102.

Miller, Merton H., and Modigliani, Franco. "Some Estimates of the Cost of Capital to the Electric Utility Industry." *American Economic Review* 56 (June 1966), pp. 333–391.

———. "Dividend Policy and Market Valuation: A Reply." *Journal of Business* 36 (January 1963), pp. 116–119.

———. "Dividend Policy, Growth, and the Valuation of Shares." *Journal of Business* 34 (October 1961), pp. 411–433.

Robichek, Alexander A., and Bogue, Marcus C. "A Note on the Behavior of Expected Price/Earnings Ratios over Time." *Journal of Finance* 26 (June 1971), pp. 731–736.

Stapleton, Richard C. "Portfolio Analysis, Stock Valuation, and Capital Budgeting Decision Rules for Risky Projects." *Journal of Finance* 26 (March 1971), pp. 95–118.

Stone, B. K. "The Conformity of Stock Values Based on Discounted Dividends to a Fair-Return Process." *Bell Journal of Economics* 6 (Autumn 1975), pp. 698–702.

Turnbull, Stuart M. "Market Value and Systematic Risk." *Journal of Finance* 32 (September 1977), pp. 1125–1142.

Van Horne, James C., and Glassmire, William F., Jr. "The Impact of Unanticipated Changes in Inflation on the Value of Common Stocks." *Journal of Finance* 27 (December 1972), pp. 1081–1092.

Walter, James E. "Dividend Policies and Common Stock Prices." *Journal of Finance* 11 (March 1956), pp. 29–41.

———. *Dividend Policy and Enterprise Valuation.* Belmont, Calif.: Wadsworth, 1967.

———. "Dividend Policy: Its Influence on the Value of the Enterprise." *Journal of Finance* 18 (May 1963), pp. 280–291.

Wendt, Paul F. "Current Growth Stock Valuation Methods." *Financial Analysts' Journal* 33 (March–April 1965), pp. 3–15.

Part Two
Financial Analysis, Planning, and Control

Part 2 contains chapters on financial planning and control systems in firms. They provide the framework for planning the firm's growth and the development of financial controls for efficiency. While these areas of finance do not have the sophistication of the formal models that will be used in later chapters, they are vital to the firm's healthy profitability. Chapter 7 examines the construction and use of the basic ratios of financial analysis; through this ratio analysis, we can pinpoint the firm's strengths and weaknesses.

Chapter 8 takes up financial forecasting: Given a projected increase in sales, how much money must the financial manager raise to support this level of sales? The statement of changes in financial position, or sources and uses of funds analysis, is also considered in a planning context.

Chapter 9 begins with the broad planning framework of the relations among revenues, volume, and profits in a breakeven analysis. The chapter then goes on to more detailed consideration of budget systems and controls for decentralized operations.

Finance deals, in the main, with very specific questions: Should we lease or buy the new machine? Should we expand capacity at the Hartford plant? Should we raise capital this year by long-term or short-term debt or by selling stock? Should we go along with the marketing department, which wants to expand inventories, or with the production department, which wants to reduce them? Such specific questions, typical of those facing the financial manager, are considered in the remainder of the book. But Part 2 takes an overview of the firm. Because all particular decisions are made within the context of the firm's overall position, this overview is critical to an understanding of any individual proposal.

7
Financial Ratio Analysis

Planning is the key to the financial manager's success. Financial plans may take many forms, but any good plan must be related to the firm's existing strengths and weaknesses. The strengths must be understood if they are to be used to proper advantage, and the weaknesses must be recognized if corrective action is to be taken. For example, are inventories adequate to support the projected level of sales? Does the firm have too heavy an investment in accounts receivable, and does this condition reflect a lax collection policy? The financial manager can plan future financial requirements in accordance with the forecasting and budgeting procedures we will present in succeeding chapters, but the plan must begin with the type of financial analysis developed in this chapter.

Basic Financial Statements

Because ratio analysis employs financial data taken from a firm's balance sheet and income statement, it is useful to begin with a review of these accounting reports. For illustrative purposes, we shall use data taken from the Walker-Wilson Manufacturing Company (W-W), a manufacturer of specialized machinery used in the automobile repair business. Formed in 1961, when Charles Walker and Ben Wilson set up a small plant to produce certain tools they had developed while in the army, Walker-Wilson grew steadily and earned the reputation of being one of the best small firms in its line of business. In December 1978, both Walker and Wilson were killed in a crash of their private plane, and for the next two years the firm was managed by Walker-Wilson's accountant.

In 1980 Mrs. Walker and Mrs. Wilson, the principal stockholders in Walker-Wilson, acted on the advice of the firm's bankers and attorneys and engaged David Thompson as president and general manager. Although Thompson is experienced in the machinery business, especially in production and sales, he does not have a detailed knowledge of his new company, so he has decided to conduct a careful appraisal of the firm's position and, on the basis of this position, to draw up a plan for future operations.

Table 7.1

Walker-Wilson Company
Illustrative Balance Sheet
(Thousands of Dollars)

Assets	Dec. 31, 1979		Dec. 31, 1980	
Cash		$ 52		$ 50
Marketable securities		175		150
Receivables		250		200
Inventories		355		300
Total current assets		$ 832		$ 700
Gross plant and equipment	$1,610		$1,800	
Less depreciation	−400		−500	
Net plant and equipment		1,210		1,300
Total assets		$2,042		$2,000

Claims on Assets	Dec. 31, 1979		Dec. 31, 1980	
Accounts payable		$ 87		$ 60
Notes payable (at 10%)		110		100
Accruals		10		10
Provision for federal income taxes		135		130
Total current liabilities		$ 342		$ 300
First mortgage bonds (at 8%)[a]		520		500
Debentures (at 10%)		200		200
Common stock (200,000 shares)	$600		$600	
Retained earnings	380		400	
Total net worth		980		1,000
Total claims on assets		$2,042		$2,000

a. The sinking fund requirement for the mortgage bonds is $20,000 a year.

Balance Sheet

Walker-Wilson's balance sheet, given in Table 7.1, shows the value of the firm's assets, and of the claims on these assets, at two particular points in time, December 31, 1979, and December 31, 1980. The assets are arranged from top to bottom in order of decreasing liquidity; that is, assets toward the top of the column will be converted to cash sooner than those toward the bottom of the column. The top group of assets—cash, marketable securities, accounts receivable, and inventories, which are expected to be converted into cash within one year—is defined as *current assets.* Assets in the lower part of the statement—plant and equipment, which are not expected to be converted to cash within one year—are defined as *fixed assets.*

The right side of the balance sheet is arranged similarly. Those items toward the top of the claims column will mature and have to be paid off fairly soon; those further down the column will be due in the more distant future. Current liabilities must be paid within one year; because the firm never has to pay off common stockholders, common stock and retained earnings represent permanent capital.

Income Statement

Walker-Wilson's income statement is shown in Table 7.2. Sales are at the top of the statement; various costs, including taxes, are deducted to arrive at the net income available to common stockholders. The figure on the last line represents earnings per share (EPS), calculated as net income divided by number of shares outstanding.

Table 7.2

Walker-Wilson Company Illustrative Income Statement for Year Ended December 31, 1980

Net sales		$3,000,000
Cost of goods sold		2,555,000
Gross profit		$ 445,000
Less operating expenses:		
Selling	$22,000	
General and administrative	40,000	
Lease payment on office building	28,000	90,000
Gross operating revenue		$ 355,000
Depreciation		100,000
Net operating income (NOI)		$ 255,000
Plus other income and expenses except interest		
Royalties		15,000
Earnings before interest and taxes (EBIT)		$ 270,000
Less interest expenses:		
Interest on notes payable	$10,000	
Interest on first mortgage	40,000	
Interest on debentures	20,000	70,000
Net income before income tax		$ 200,000
Federal income tax (at 40%)		80,000
Net income, after income tax, available to common stockholders		$ 120,000
Earnings per share (EPS)		$ .60

Statement of Retained Earnings

Earnings can be paid out to stockholders as dividends or retained and reinvested in the business. Stockholders like to receive dividends, of course; but if earnings are plowed back into the business, the value of the stockholders' position in the company increases. Later in the book we shall consider the pros and cons of retaining earnings versus paying them out in dividends, but for now we are simply interested in the effects of dividends and retained earnings on the balance sheet. For this purpose, accountants use the statement of retained earnings, illustrated for Walker-Wilson in Table 7.3. Walker-Wilson earned $120,000 during the year, paid $100,000 in dividends to stockholders, and plowed $20,000 back into the business. Thus the retained earnings at the end of 1980, as shown both on the balance sheet and on the statement of retained earnings, is $400,000, which is $20,000 larger than the year-end 1979 figure.

Table 7.3

Walker-Wilson Company Statement of Retained Earnings for Year Ended December 31, 1980

Balance of retained earnings, December 31, 1979	$380,000
Plus net income, 1980	120,000
	$500,000
Less dividends to stockholders	−100,000
Balance of retained earnings, December 31, 1980	$400,000

Relationships among the Three Statements

It is important to recognize that the balance sheet is a statement of the firm's financial position *at a point in time,* whereas the income statement shows the results of operations *during an interval of time.* Thus, the balance sheet represents a snapshot of the firm's position on a given date, while the income statement is based on a flow concept, showing what occurred between two points in time.

The statement of retained earnings indicates how the retained earnings account on the balance sheet is adjusted between balance sheet dates. Since its inception, Walker-Wilson had retained a total of $380,000 by December 31, 1979. In 1980 it earned $120,000 and retained $20,000 of this amount. Thus, the retained earnings shown on the balance sheet for December 31, 1980, are $400,000.

A firm that retains earnings generally does so to expand the business—that is, to finance the purchase of assets such as plant, equipment, and inventories. As a result of operations in 1980, Walker-Wilson has $20,000 available for that purpose. Sometimes retained earnings are used to build up the cash account, but as shown on the balance sheet, they are *not* cash. Through the years they have been invested in bricks and mortar and other assets, so they are not available for any expenditure now. The earnings *for the current year* may be available for investment, but the *past retained earnings* have already been employed.

Stated another way, the retained earnings balance sheet item simply shows how much of their earnings the stockholders, through the years, have elected to retain in the business. Thus, the retained earnings account shows the additional investment the stockholders as a group have made in the business over and above their initial investment at the inception of the company and through any subsequent issues of stock.

Basic Types of Financial Ratios

Each type of analysis has a purpose or use that determines the different relationships emphasized. The analyst may, for example, be a banker considering whether to grant a short-term loan to a firm. Bankers are primarily interested in the firm's near-term, or liquidity, position, so they stress ratios that measure liquidity. In contrast, long-term creditors place far more emphasis on earning power and operating efficiency. They know that unprofitable operations erode asset values and that a strong current position is no guarantee that funds will be available to repay a twenty-year bond issue. Equity investors are similarly interested in long-term profitability and efficiency. Management is, of course, concerned with all these aspects of financial analysis; it must be able to repay its debts to long- and short-term creditors as well as earn profits for stockholders.

It is useful to classify ratios into six fundamental types:

1. *Liquidity ratios,* which measure the firm's ability to meet its maturing short-term obligations.
2. *Leverage ratios,* which measure the extent to which the firm has been financed by debt.
3. *Activity ratios,* which measure how effectively the firm is using its resources.
4. *Profitability ratios,* which measure management's overall effectiveness as shown by the returns generated on sales and investment.
5. *Growth ratios,* which measure the firm's ability to maintain its economic position in the growth of the economy and industry.
6. *Valuation ratios,* which are the most complete measure of performance because they reflect the risk ratios (the first two) and the returns ratios (the following three). Valuation ratios are of great importance since they relate directly to the goal of maximizing the value of the firm and shareholder wealth.

Specific examples of each ratio are given in the following sections, where the Walker-Wilson case history illustrates their calculation and use.

Liquidity Ratios

Generally, the first concern of the financial analyst is liquidity: Is the firm able to meet its maturing obligations? Walker-Wilson has debts totaling $300,000 that must be paid within the coming year. Can these obligations be satisfied? Although a full liquidity analysis requires the use of cash budgets (described in Chapter 9), ratio analysis, by relating the amount of cash and other current assets to the current obligations, provides a quick and easy-to-use measure of liquidity. Two commonly used liquidity ratios are presented here.

Current Ratio. The current ratio is computed by dividing current assets by current liabilities. Current assets normally include cash, marketable securities, accounts receivable, and inventories; current liabilities consist of accounts payable, short-term notes payable, current maturities of long-term debt, accrued income taxes, and other accrued expenses (principally wages). The current ratio is the most commonly used measure of short-term solvency, since it indicates the extent to which the claims of short-term creditors are covered by assets that are expected to be converted to cash in a period roughly corresponding to the maturity of the claims.

The calculation of the current ratio for Walker-Wilson at year-end 1980 is shown below.

$$\text{Current ratio} = \frac{\text{Current assets}}{\text{Current liabilities}} = \frac{\$700{,}000}{\$300{,}000} = 2.3 \text{ times.}$$

$$\text{Industry average} = 2.5 \text{ times.}$$

The current ratio is slightly below the average for the industry, 2.5, but not low enough to cause concern. It appears that Walker-Wilson is about in line with most other firms in this particular line of business. Since current assets are near maturity, it is highly probable that they could be liquidated at close to book value. With a current ratio of 2.3, Walker-Wilson could liquidate current assets at only 43 percent of book value and still pay off current creditors in full.[1]

Although industry average figures are discussed later in the chapter, it should be stated at this point that the industry average is not a magic number that all firms should strive to maintain. In fact, some well-managed firms are above it, and other good firms are below it. However, if a firm's ratios are very far removed from the average for its industry, the analyst must be concerned about why this variance occurs; that is, a deviation from the industry average should signal the analyst to check further.

Quick Ratio or Acid Test. The quick ratio is calculated by deducting inventories from current assets and dividing the remainder by current liabilities. Inventories are typically the least liquid of a firm's current assets and the assets on which losses are most likely to occur in the event of liquidation. Therefore, this measure of the firm's ability to pay off short-term obligations without relying on the sale of inventories is important.

$$\text{Quick ratio or acid test} = \frac{\text{Current assets} - \text{Inventory}}{\text{Current liabilities}} = \frac{\$400{,}000}{\$300{,}000}$$

$$= 1.3 \text{ times.}$$

$$\text{Industry average} = 1.0 \text{ times.}$$

1. (1/2.3) = 0.43, or 43 percent. Note that (0.43) ($700,000) ≈ $300,000, the amount of current liabilities.

The industry average quick ratio is 1, so Walker-Wilson's 1.3 ratio compares favorably with other firms in the industry. Thompson knows that if the marketable securities can be sold at par and if he can collect the accounts receivable, he can pay off his current liabilities without selling any inventory.

Leverage Ratios

Leverage ratios, which measure the funds supplied by owners as compared with the financing provided by the firm's creditors, have a number of implications. First, creditors look to the equity, or owner-supplied funds, to provide a margin of safety. If owners have provided only a small proportion of total financing, the risks of the enterprise are borne mainly by the creditors. Second, by raising funds through debt, the owners gain the benefits of maintaining control of the firm with a limited investment. Third, if the firm earns more on the borrowed funds than it pays in interest, the return to the owners is magnified. For example, if assets earn 10 percent and debt costs only 8 percent, a 2 percent differential accrues to the stockholders. Leverage cuts both ways, however; if the return on assets falls to 3 percent, the differential between that figure and the cost of debt must be made up from equity's share of total profits. In the first instance, where assets earn more than the cost of debt, leverage is favorable; in the second, it is unfavorable.

Firms with low leverage ratios have less risk of loss when the economy is in a downturn, but they also have lower expected returns when the economy booms. Conversely, firms with high leverage ratios run the risk of large losses but also have a chance of gaining high profits. The prospects of high returns are desirable, but investors are averse to risk. Decisions about the use of leverage, then, must balance higher expected returns against increased risk.[2]

In practice, leverage is approached in two ways. One approach examines balance sheet ratios and determines the extent to which borrowed funds have been used to finance the firm. The other approach measures the risks of debt by income statement ratios designed to determine the number of times fixed charges are covered by operating profits. These sets of ratios are complementary, and most analysts examine both.

Total Debt to Total Assets. The ratio of total debt to total assets, generally called the *debt ratio,* measures the percentage of total funds provided by creditors. Debt includes current liabilities and all bonds. Creditors prefer moderate debt ratios, since the lower the ratio, the greater the cushion against creditors' losses in the event of liquidation. In contrast to the creditors' preference for a low debt ratio, the owners may seek high leverage to magnify earnings or because raising new equity means giving up some degree of control. If the debt ratio is too high, there is a danger of encouraging irresponsibility on the part of the owners. The owners' stake can become so small that speculative activity, if it is successful, will yield them a substantial percentage

2. The problem of determining optimum leverage for a firm with given risk characteristics is examined extensively in Chapters 15 and 16.

return. If the venture is unsuccessful, however, they will incur only a moderate loss because their investment is small.

$$\text{Debt ratio} = \frac{\text{Total debt}}{\text{Total assets}} = \frac{\$1{,}000{,}000}{\$2{,}000{,}000} = 50\%.$$

$$\text{Industry average} = 33\%.$$

Walker-Wilson's debt ratio is 50 percent; this means that creditors have supplied half the firm's total financing. Since the average debt ratio for this industry is about 33 percent, Walker-Wilson would find it difficult to borrow additional funds without first raising more equity capital. Creditors would be reluctant to lend the firm more money, and Thompson would probably be subjecting the stockholders to undue risk if he sought to increase the debt ratio even more by borrowing.[3]

Times Interest Earned. The times interest earned ratio is determined by dividing earnings before interest and taxes (EBIT) from Table 7.2 by the interest charges. The ratio measures the extent to which earnings can decline without resultant financial embarrassment to the firm because of inability to meet annual interest costs. Failure to meet this obligation can bring legal action by the creditors, possibly resulting in bankruptcy. Note that the before-tax profit figure is used in the numerator. Because income taxes are computed after interest expense is deducted, the ability to pay current interest is not affected by income taxes.

$$\text{Times interest earned} = \frac{\text{Earnings before interest and taxes}}{\text{Interest charges}}$$

$$= \frac{\text{Profit before taxes} + \text{Interest charges}}{\text{Interest charges}}$$

$$= \frac{\$270{,}000}{\$70{,}000} = 3.9 \text{ times.}$$

$$\text{Industry average} = 8.0 \text{ times.}$$

Walker-Wilson's interest charges consist of three payments totaling $70,000 (see Table 7.2). The firm's gross income available for servicing these charges is $270,000, so the interest is covered 3.9 times. Since the industry average is 8 times, the company is covering its interest charges by a minimum margin of safety and deserves only a poor rating. This ratio reinforces the conclusion

3. The ratio of debt to equity is also used in financial analysis. The debt to assets *(B/A)* and debt to equity *(B/S)* ratios are simply transformations of one another:

$$B/S = \frac{B/A}{1 - B/A} \quad \text{and} \quad B/A = \frac{B/S}{1 + B/S}.$$

Both ratios increase as a firm of a given size (total assets) uses a greater proportion of debt, but *B/A* rises linearly and approaches a limit of 100 percent while *B/S* rises exponentially and approaches infinity.

based on the debt ratio that the company is likely to face some difficulties if it attempts to borrow additional funds.

Fixed Charge Coverage. The fixed charge coverage ratio is similar to the times interest earned ratio, but it is somewhat more inclusive in that it recognizes that many firms lease assets and incur long-term obligations under lease contracts.[4] As we show in Chapter 21, leasing has become widespread in recent years, making this ratio preferable to the times interest earned ratio for most financial analyses. Fixed charges are defined as interest plus annual long-term lease obligations, and the fixed charge coverage ratio is defined as follows:

$$\text{Fixed charge coverage} = \frac{\text{Profit before taxes} + \text{Interest charges} + \text{Lease obligations}}{\text{Interest charges} + \text{Lease obligations}}$$

$$= \frac{\$200{,}000 + \$70{,}000 + \$28{,}000}{\$70{,}000 + \$28{,}000} = \frac{\$298{,}000}{\$98{,}000}$$

$$= 3.04 \text{ times.}$$

$$\text{Industry average} = 5.5 \text{ times.}$$

Walker-Wilson's fixed charges are covered 3.04 times, as opposed to an industry average of 5.5 times. Again, this indicates that the firm is somewhat weaker than creditors would prefer it to be, and it points up the difficulties Thompson would likely encounter if he attempted additional borrowing.

Cash Flow Coverage. Suppose Walker-Wilson had preferred stock that required payment of dividends of \$12,000 per year; further suppose the firm had to make annual payments of principal on its various debt obligations of \$42,000 per year. To the numerator of the previous ratio we will add depreciation. To the denominator we shall add the two additional items on a before-tax basis. We divide each by $(1 - T)$ because neither is a tax deductible expense. Hence there must be enough cash flow so that after taxes are paid, the firm can meet all cash flow obligations.

$$\text{Cash flow coverage} = \frac{\text{Cash inflows}}{\text{Fixed charges} + \dfrac{\text{Preferred stock dividends}}{(1 - T)} + \dfrac{\text{Debt repayment}}{(1 - T)}}$$

$$= \frac{\$298{,}000 + \$100{,}000}{\$98{,}000 + 12{,}000/0.6 + 42{,}000/0.6} = \frac{\$398{,}000}{\$188{,}000}$$

$$= 2.1 \text{ times.}$$

While there are no generally published industry standards on this ratio, logic

4. Generally, a long-term lease is defined as one extending at least three years into the future. Thus, rent incurred under a one-year lease would not be included in the fixed charge coverage ratio, but rental payments under a three-year or longer lease would be defined as fixed charges.

suggests that a firm should achieve a cash coverage ratio of at least two times. This allows for a substantial decline in cash inflows before the firm encounters a cash solvency problem. W-W meets this standard minimally.

Activity Ratios

Activity ratios measure how effectively the firm employs the resources at its command. These ratios all involve comparisons between the level of sales and the investment in various asset accounts. They presume that a proper balance should exist between sales and the various asset accounts—inventories, accounts receivable, fixed assets, and others. As we shall see in the following chapters, this is generally a good assumption.

Inventory Turnover. The inventory turnover, defined as sales divided by inventory, follows:

$$\text{Inventory turnover} = \frac{\text{Sales}}{\text{Inventory}} = \frac{\$3{,}000{,}000}{\$300{,}000} = 10 \text{ times.}$$

Industry average = 9 times.

Walker-Wilson's turnover of 10 times compares favorably with an industry average of 9 times. This suggests that the company does not hold excessive stocks of inventory. Excess stocks are, of course, unproductive; they represent an investment with a low, or even zero, rate of return. The company's high inventory turnover also reinforces Thompson's faith in the current ratio. If the turnover was low—say 3 or 4 times—Thompson would wonder whether the firm was holding damaged or obsolete materials not actually worth their stated value.

Two problems arise in calculating and analyzing the inventory turnover ratio. First, sales are at market prices; if inventories are carried at cost, as they generally are, it is more appropriate to use cost of goods sold in place of sales in the numerator of the formula. However, established compilers of financial ratio statistics, such as Dun & Bradstreet, use the ratio of sales to inventories carried at cost. Therefore, to develop a figure that can be compared with those developed by Dun & Bradstreet, it is necessary to measure inventory turnover with sales in the numerator, as we do here.

Second, sales occur over the entire year, whereas the inventory figure is for one point in time. This makes it better to use an average inventory, computed by adding beginning and ending inventories and dividing by 2. If it is determined that the firm's business is highly seasonal, or if there has been a strong upward or downward sales trend during the year, it is essential to make some such adjustment. Neither of these conditions holds for Walker-Wilson; to maintain comparability with industry averages, Thompson did not use the average inventory figure.

Average Collection Period. The average collection period, which is a measure of the accounts receivable turnover, is computed in two steps: (1) annual sales are divided by 360 to get the average daily sales,[5] and (2) daily sales are divided into accounts receivable to find the number of days' sales tied up in receivables. This is defined as the average collection period, because it represents the average length of time the firm must wait to receive cash after making a sale. The calculations for Walker-Wilson show an average collection period of 24 days, slightly above the 20-day industry average.

$$\text{Sales per day} = \frac{\$3{,}000{,}000}{360} = \$8{,}333.$$

$$\text{Average collection period} = \frac{\text{Receivables}}{\text{Sales per day}} = \frac{\$200{,}000}{\$8{,}333} = 24 \text{ days.}$$

$$\text{Industry average} = 20 \text{ days.}$$

This ratio can also be evaluated by comparison with the terms on which the firm sells its goods. For example, Walker-Wilson's sales terms call for payment within 20 days, so the 24-day collection period indicates that customers on the average are not paying their bills on time. If the collection period over the past few years had been lengthening while the credit policy had not changed, this would have been even stronger evidence that steps should be taken to expedite the collection of accounts receivable.

One additional financial tool should be mentioned in connection with accounts receivable analysis—the *aging schedule,* which breaks down accounts receivable according to how long they have been outstanding. The aging schedule for W-W is given below.

Age of Account (Days)	Percent of Total Value of Accounts Receivable
0–20	50
21–30	20
31–45	15
46–60	3
Over 60	12
Total	100

The 24-day collection period looks bad by comparison with the 20-day sales term, and the aging schedule shows that the firm is having especially serious collection problems with some of its accounts: 50 percent are overdue, many for over a month; others pay quite promptly, bringing the average down to only 24 days. But the aging schedule shows this average to be somewhat misleading.

Fixed Assets Turnover. The ratio of sales to fixed assets measures the turnover of plant and equipment.

5. Because information on credit sales is generally unavailable, total sales must be used. Since firms do not all have the same percentage of credit sales, there is a good chance that the average collection period will be somewhat in error. Also, note for convenience that the financial community generally uses 360 rather than 365 as the number of days in the year for such purposes as these.

$$\text{Fixed assets turnover} = \frac{\text{Sales}}{\text{Net fixed assets}} = \frac{\$3{,}000{,}000}{\$1{,}300{,}000} = 2.3 \text{ times.}$$

$$\text{Industry average} = 5.0 \text{ times.}$$

Walker-Wilson's turnover of 2.3 times compares poorly with the industry average of 5 times, indicating that the firm is not using its fixed assets to as high a percentage of capacity as are other firms in the industry. Thompson should bear this in mind when his production people request funds for new capital investments.

Total Assets Turnover. The final activity ratio, which measures the turnover of all the firm's assets, is calculated by dividing sales by total assets.

$$\text{Total assets turnover} = \frac{\text{Sales}}{\text{Total assets}} = \frac{\$3{,}000{,}000}{\$2{,}000{,}000} = 1.5 \text{ times.}$$

$$\text{Industry average} = 2.0 \text{ times.}$$

Walker-Wilson's turnover of total assets is well below the industry average. The company is simply not generating a sufficient volume of business for the size of its asset investment. Sales should be increased, some assets should be disposed of, or both.

Profitability Ratios

Profitability is the net result of a large number of policies and decisions. The ratios examined thus far reveal some interesting things about the way the firm operates, but the profitability ratios give final answers about how effectively the firm is being managed.

Profit Margin on Sales. The profit margin on sales, computed by dividing net income after taxes by sales, gives the profit per dollar of sales.

$$\text{Profit margin} = \frac{\text{Net income}}{\text{Sales}} = \frac{\$120{,}000}{\$3{,}000{,}000} = 4\%.$$

$$\text{Industry average} = 5\%.$$

Walker-Wilson's profit margin is somewhat below the industry average of 5 percent, indicating that the firm's prices are relatively low, that its costs are relatively high, or both.

Return on Total Assets. The ratio of net profit to total assets measures the return on total investment in the firm (ROI).[6]

6. In calculating the return on total assets, it is sometimes desirable to add interest to net profits after taxes to form the numerator of the ratios. The theory is that since assets are financed by both stockholders and creditors, the ratio should measure the productivity of assets in providing returns to both classes of investors. We have not done so at this point because the published averages we use for comparative purposes exclude interest. Later in the book, however, when we deal with leverage decisions, we will add back interest. This addition has a material bearing on the value of the ratio for utilities (which have large amounts of fixed assets financed by debt), and the technically correct ratio is the one normally used for them.

$$\text{Return on total assets} = \frac{\text{Net income}}{\text{Total assets}} = \frac{\$120{,}000}{\$2{,}000{,}000} = 6\%.$$

$$\text{Industry average} = 10\%.$$

Walker-Wilson's 6 percent return is well below the 10 percent average for the industry. The low rate results from the low profit margin on sales and from the low turnover of total assets.

Return on Net Worth. The ratio of net profit after taxes to net worth measures the rate of return on the stockholders' investment.

$$\text{Return on net worth} = \frac{\text{Net income}}{\text{Net worth}} = \frac{\$120{,}000}{\$1{,}000{,}000} = 12\%.$$

$$\text{Industry average} = 15\%.$$

Walker-Wilson's 12 percent return is below the 15 percent industry average but not as far below as the return on total assets. In a later section of this chapter, where the Du Pont method of analysis is applied to the Walker-Wilson case, we shall see why this is so.

The annual reports of business firms will generally include a section of historical data on selected financial items. These can be used to develop the growth and valuation ratios. The data for Walker-Wilson are presented in Table 7.4.

Table 7.4

Some Historical Data for Walker-Wilson Company

	1975	1976	1977	1978	1979	1980	Growth Rates (Industry Norm)
Sales (in thousands)	$2,100	$2,200	$2,500	$3,000	$3,200	$3,000	7.2%
Net income (in thousands)	100	120	150	180	160	120	7.8
Earnings per share	$ .50	$ .60	$ .75	$ .90	$ .80	$ .60	8.2
Dividends per share	.10	.12	.12	.12	.12	.12	6.4
Market price per share, common stock—High	5.00	7.00	8.00	9.00	5.00	6.00	
—Low	4.00	5.00	6.00	7.00	4.00	3.00	
—Average	4.50	6.00	7.00	8.00	4.50	4.50	2.0
Book value of common stock, year-end	4.10	4.30	4.40	4.70	4.90	5.00	7.0

Growth Ratios

Growth ratios measure how well the firm is maintaining its economic position in the general economy and in its own industry. During the recent period of inflation, the interpretation of growth ratios has become more difficult than previously. Since the early 1970s, nominal growth rates have increased greatly. The growth of the economy, as well as that of industries and firms, has reflected the inflation factor as well as the underlying real growth. Before the onset of persistent inflation in the late 1960s, real growth rates were about 3 to 3½ percent per year, with an inflation rate of 2 to 3 percent. This made for a total growth rate in the 5 to 7 percent range. However, since the early 1970s, the inflation rate has been in the 7 to 10 percent range, while real growth has declined to the 1 to 2 percent range. Thus nominal growth from 8 to 12 percent has occurred, but real growth has been much lower.

Since reported figures are reflected in nominal terms, the growth rate reference standards we shall employ will include the inflation factor. However, as a part of the further internal analysis, business firms need to make a separation between growth coming from the inflation influence alone—which just changes the measuring stick—and the underlying real growth, which reflects the basic productivity of the economy.

Table 7.5

Growth Rate Data

	Five-Year Growth Rates, 1975–1980	
	Walker-Wilson	Industry
Sales	7.4%	7.2%
Net income	3.7	7.8
Earnings per share	3.7	8.2
Dividends per share	3.7	6.4
Market price, average	0.0	2.0
Book value per share	4.0	7.0

From the basic data in Table 7.4 we have calculated, in Table 7.5, the 5-year growth rates for six items for Walker-Wilson covering the years 1975–1980. We have calculated growth by dividing the last period figure by the first period figure, a process that gives a compound sum interest factor. Then, by referring to the compound interest tables at the end of the book, we can determine the percent growth represented by the ratio. We observe that the growth rate in sales for Walker-Wilson was about the same as for the industry. However, net income, which is the measure of the profitability performance of the firm, has grown at about half the rate of the industry standard.

Next we turn to per share growth analysis. First, we consider earnings per share, a factor that reflects the methods of financing the firm's overall growth. Here again Walker-Wilson's growth rate is less than half that of the industry. Dividends per share have grown at the same rate as earnings per share. However, we note from Table 7.4 that the total dividend growth came in the first year, while the earnings growth has been declining, particularly during the two most recent years.

Market price represents the results of the valuation of the firm's earnings.

Market price growth for the industry as a whole has been weak, only 2 percent. But the market price change for Walker-Wilson has been zero. While its average price increased from $4.50 in the early years to $8, it declined again to $4.50 in the two most recent years.

Book value per share indicates the resources in the company per share of stockholder investment. This value grew at a 7 percent rate for the industry but at only a 4 percent rate for Walker-Wilson. Again, the weakened performance of the last two years has pulled down the growth rate in the book value per share. Thus the growth performance of Walker-Wilson has been relatively weak, a situation that should have some implications for the valuation ratios as well.

Valuation Ratios

Valuation ratios are the most comprehensive measures of performance for the firm, as they reflect the combined influence of risk ratios and return ratios. We have calculated two valuation ratios and summarized their pattern in Table 7.6.

Table 7.6

Valuation Relations

		1975	1976	1977	1978	1979	1980
Price to earnings ratios—	Company	9.0	10.0	9.3	8.9	5.6	7.5
	Industry	7.0	8.0	8.0	8.0	9.0	8.0
Market to book ratios—	Company	1.1	1.4	1.6	1.7	0.9	0.9
	Industry	0.9	1.0	1.0	1.2	1.1	1.0

We first analyze trends in the price to earnings ratios. At the beginning of the period they were higher for the company than for the industry. By the end of the period, however, they were higher for the industry than for the company, reflecting the company's poor performance in the last two years.

Price to earnings ratios have to be interpreted with caution. Note that between 1979 and 1980 the price-earnings ratio for the company rose from 5.6 to 7.5. However, the average market price of the company stock stayed at $4.50. The price-earnings ratio rose only because earnings dropped while the average price remained the same.

The market to book ratio is also an important valuation ratio. In some sense it indicates the value the financial markets attach to the management and the organization of the company as a going concern. In some sense, book value represents the historical costs of the physical assets of the company. A company with a strong management and an organization that has learned to function efficiently should have a market value in excess of its costs of physical assets.

As we see from Table 7.6, in the early years the market to book ratio of Walker-Wilson exceeded 1. In fact, by 1978 it had become 1.7. The industry did not perform as well, but in most years it had a market to book ratio of at least slightly over 1. During the last two years, however, while the market to book ratio for the industry has remained at 1 or better, it has declined below 1 for Walker-Wilson.

Summary of the Ratios

The individual ratios, which are summarized in Table 7.7, give Thompson a reasonably good idea of Walker-Wilson's main strengths and weaknesses. First, the company's liquidity position is reasonably good; its current and

Table 7.7

Summary of Financial Ratio Analyses

Ratio	Formula for Calculation	Calculation	Industry Average	Evaluation
Liquidity				
Current	$\frac{\text{Current assets}}{\text{Current liabilities}}$	$\frac{\$700,000}{\$300,000}$ = 2.3 times	2.5 times	Satisfactory
Quick ratio or acid test	$\frac{\text{Current assets} - \text{Inventory}}{\text{Current liabilities}}$	$\frac{\$400,000}{\$300,000}$ = 1.3 times	1 time	Good
Leverage				
Debt to total assets	$\frac{\text{Total debt}}{\text{Total assets}}$	$\frac{\$1,000,000}{\$2,000,000}$ = 50 percent	33 percent	Poor
Times interest earned	$\frac{\text{EBIT}}{\text{Interest charges}}$	$\frac{\$270,000}{\$70,000}$ = 3.9 times	8 times	Poor
Fixed charge coverage	$\frac{\text{EBIT plus other fixed charges}}{\text{Fixed charges}}$	$\frac{\$298,000}{\$98,000}$ = 3.04 times	5.5 times	Poor
Cash flow coverage	$\frac{\text{Cash inflows}}{\text{Fixed charges} + (\text{Other cash outflows})/(1 - T)}$	$\frac{\$398,000}{\$188,000}$ = 2.1	2	Fair
Activity				
Inventory turnover	$\frac{\text{Sales}}{\text{Inventory}}$	$\frac{\$3,000,000}{\$300,000}$ = 10 times	9 times	Satisfactory
Average collection period	$\frac{\text{Receivables}}{\text{Sales per day}}$	$\frac{\$200,000}{\$8,333}$ = 24 days	20 days	Satisfactory
Fixed assets turnover	$\frac{\text{Sales}}{\text{Fixed assets}}$	$\frac{\$3,000,000}{\$1,300,000}$ = 2.3 times	5 times	Poor
Total assets turnover	$\frac{\text{Sales}}{\text{Total assets}}$	$\frac{\$3,000,000}{\$2,000,000}$ = 1.5 times	2 times	Poor
Profitability				
Profit margin on sales	$\frac{\text{Net income}}{\text{Sales}}$	$\frac{\$120,000}{\$3,000,000}$ = 4 percent	5 percent	Fair
Return on total assets	$\frac{\text{Net income}}{\text{Total assets}}$	$\frac{\$120,000}{\$2,000,000}$ = 6 percent	10 percent	Poor
Return on net worth	$\frac{\text{Net income}}{\text{Net worth}}$	$\frac{\$120,000}{\$1,000,000}$ = 12 percent	15 percent	Fair
Growth				
Sales	$\frac{\text{Ending values}}{\text{Beginning values}} = \text{CVIF}_{r,5}$	$\frac{\$3,000}{\$2,100}$ = 1.4286; r = 7.4 percent	7.2 percent	Satisfactory
Net income	$\frac{\text{Ending values}}{\text{Beginning values}} = \text{CVIF}_{r,5}$	$\frac{\$120}{\$100}$ = 1.2; r = 3.7 percent	7.8 percent	Poor
Earnings per share	$\frac{\text{Ending values}}{\text{Beginning values}} = \text{CVIF}_{r,5}$	$\frac{\$0.60}{\$0.50}$ = 1.2; r = 3.7 percent	8.2 percent	Poor
Dividends per share	$\frac{\text{Ending values}}{\text{Beginning values}} = \text{CVIF}_{r,5}$	$\frac{\$0.12}{\$0.10}$ = 1.2; r = 3.7 percent	6.4 percent	Poor
Valuation				
Price to earnings ratio	$\frac{\text{Price}}{\text{Earnings}}$	$\frac{\$4.50}{\$0.60}$ = 7.5 times	8 times	Fair
Market to book ratio	$\frac{\text{Market value}}{\text{Book value}}$	$\frac{\$4.50}{\$5.00}$ = 0.9 times	1.0 times	Poor

quick ratios appear to be satisfactory by comparison with the industry averages. Second, the leverage ratios suggest that the company is rather heavily indebted. With a debt ratio substantially higher than the industry average, and with coverage ratios well below the industry averages, it is doubtful that Walker-Wilson could do much additional debt financing except on relatively unfavorable terms. Even if Thompson could borrow more, to do so would be subjecting the company to the danger of default and bankruptcy in the event of a business downturn.

The activity ratios show an inventory turnover and average collection period that indicate good control of Walker-Wilson's current assets. But the low fixed asset turnover suggests that there has been too heavy an investment in fixed assets. This low turnover means, in effect, that the company probably could have operated with a smaller investment in fixed assets. Had the excessive fixed asset investment not been made, the company could have avoided some of its debt financing and would now have lower interest payments. This in turn would have led to improved leverage and coverage ratios.

The profit margin on sales is low, indicating that costs are too high, prices too low, or both. In this particular case, the sales prices are in line with those of other firms; high costs are, in fact, the cause of the low margin. Further, the high costs can be traced to high depreciation charges and high interest expenses, both of which are in turn attributable to the excessive investment in fixed assets.

Returns on total investment and net worth are also below the industry averages. The relatively poor results are directly attributable to the low profit margin on sales, which lowers the numerators of the ratios, and to the excessive investment, which raises the denominators.

Sales growth of Walker-Wilson is satisfactory in relation to the industry standard. However, all the profitability growth measures are weak, and valuation relationships are also unfavorable. Additional perspective on the growth performance of Walker-Wilson is provided by the trend analysis, which supplements the single measure provided by the growth percentage.

Trend Analysis

While the preceding ratio analysis gives a reasonably good picture of Walker-Wilson's operation, it is incomplete in one important respect—it ignores the time dimension. The ratios are something like single frames in a motion picture. They capture one point in time. But trends may be in motion that will, over more time, either erode a good present position or improve a weak one.

The method of trend analysis is illustrated in Figure 7.1, which shows graphs of Walker-Wilson's sales, current ratio, debt ratio, fixed assets turnover, and return on net worth. The figures are compared with industry averages. Industry sales have been rising steadily over the entire period, and the industry average ratios have been relatively stable throughout. Thus, any trends in the company's ratios are due to its own internal conditions, not to environmental influences on all firms. In addition, Walker-Wilson's deterioration since the 1978 death of the two principal officers is quite apparent. Prior

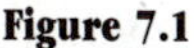

Figure 7.1

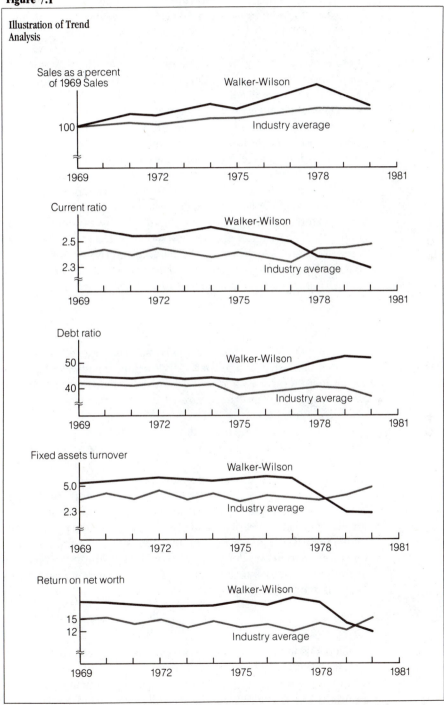

Illustration of Trend Analysis

to 1978, the company was growing more rapidly than the average firm in the industry; during the following two years, however, sales actually declined.

Walker-Wilson's liquidity position, as measured by its current ratio, has also gone downhill in the past two years. Although the ratio is only slightly below the industry average at the present time, the trend suggests that a real liquidity crisis may develop during the next year or two unless corrective action is taken immediately.

The debt ratio trend line shows that Walker-Wilson followed industry practices closely until 1976, when the ratio jumped to a full 10 percentage points above the industry average. Similarly, the fixed assets turnover declined during 1976, even though sales were still rising. The records reveal that the company borrowed heavily during 1976 to finance a major expansion of plant and equipment. Walker and Wilson had intended to use this additional capacity to generate a still higher volume of sales and to retire the debt out of expected high profits. Their untimely deaths, however, led to a decrease rather than an increase in sales, and the expected high profits that were to be used to retire the debt did not materialize. The analysis suggests that the bankers were correct when they advised Mrs. Walker and Mrs. Wilson of the need for a change in management.

Du Pont System of Financial Analysis

The Du Pont system of financial analysis has achieved wide recognition in American industry, and properly so. It brings together the activity ratios and profit margin on sales and shows how these ratios interact to determine the profitability of assets. The nature of the system, modified somewhat, is set forth in Figure 7.2.

The right side of the figure develops the turnover ratio. It shows how current assets (cash, marketable securities, accounts receivable, and inventories) are added to fixed assets to give total investment. Total investment divided into sales gives the turnover of investment.

The left side of the figure develops the profit margin on sales. The individual expense items plus income taxes are subtracted from sales to produce net profits after taxes. Net profits divided by sales give the profit margin on sales. When the asset turnover ratio on the right side of Figure 7.2 is multiplied by the profit margin on sales developed on the left side of the figure, the product is the return on total investment (ROI) in the firm. This can be seen from the following formula:

$$\frac{\text{Profit}}{\text{Sales}} \times \frac{\text{Sales}}{\text{Investment}} = \text{ROI}.$$

Walker-Wilson's turnover was 1.5 times, as compared to an industry average of 2 times; its margin on sales was 4 percent, as compared to 5 percent for the industry. Multiplied together, turnover and profit margin produced a return on assets equal to 6 percent, a rate well below the 10 percent industry aver-

Figure 7.2

Modified Du Pont System of Financial Control Applied to Walker-Wilson

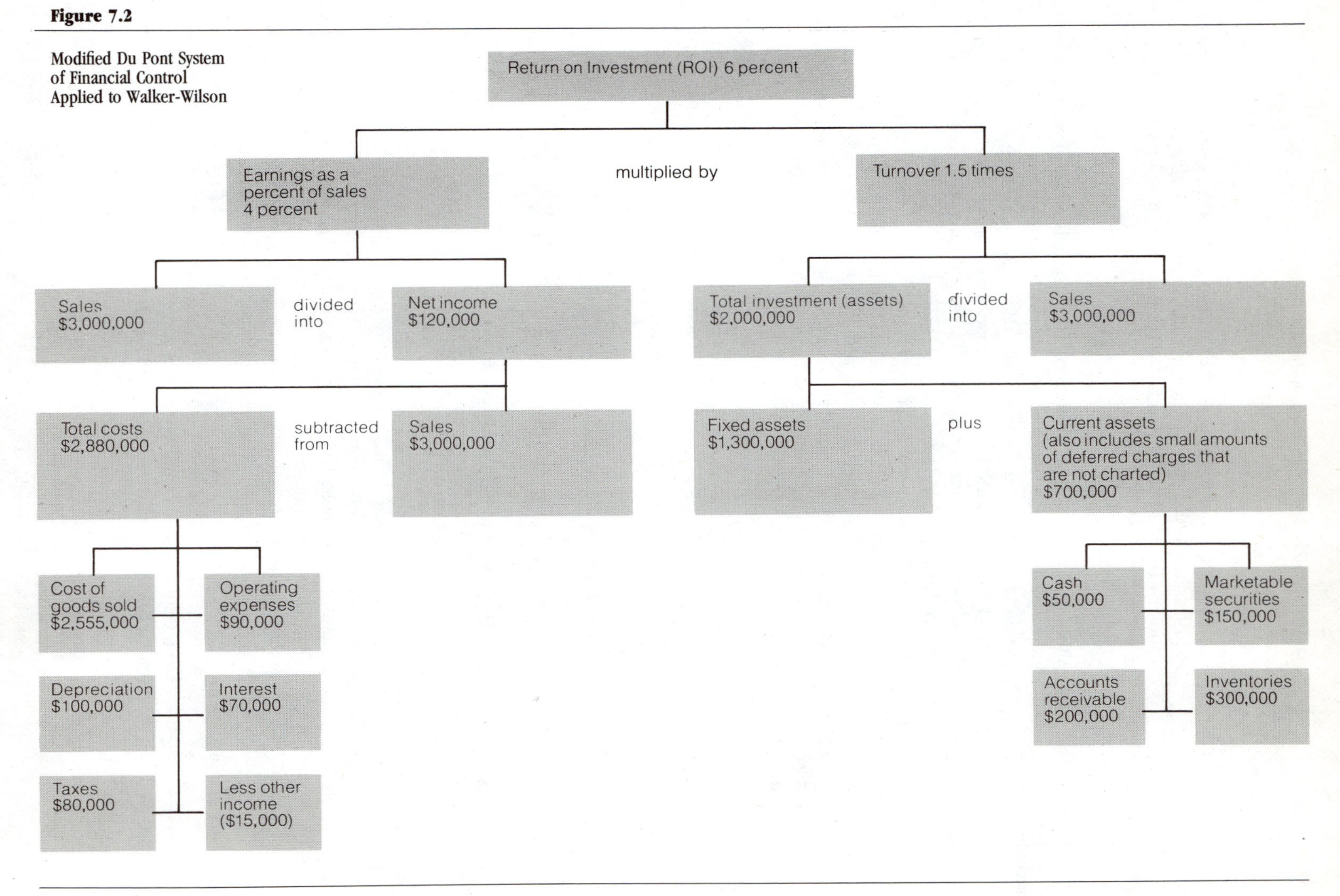

age. If Thompson is to bring Walker-Wilson back to the level of the rest of the industry, he should strive to boost both his profit margin and his total asset turnover. Tracing back through the Du Pont system should help him in this task.

Extending the Du Pont System to Include Leverage

Although Walker-Wilson's return on total assets is well below the 10 percent industry average, the firm's 12 percent return on net worth is only slightly below the 15 percent industry average. How can the return on the net worth end up so close to the industry average when the return on total assets is so far below it? The answer is that Walker-Wilson uses more debt than the average firm in the industry.

Only half of Walker-Wilson's assets are financed with net worth; the other half are financed with debt. This means that the entire 6 percent return on assets (which is computed after interest charges on debt) goes to the common stockholders, so their return is boosted substantially. The precise formula for measuring the effect of financial leverage on stockholder returns is shown below:

$$\text{Rate of return on net worth} = \frac{\text{Return on assets (ROI)}}{\text{Percent of assets financed by net worth}}$$

$$= \frac{\text{Return on assets (ROI)}}{1.0 - \text{Debt ratio}}.$$

Calculation for Walker-Wilson:

$$\text{Return on net worth} = \frac{6\%}{1.0 - 0.50} = \frac{6\%}{0.5} = 12\%.$$

Calculation for the industry average:

$$\text{Return on net worth} = \frac{10\%}{1.0 - 0.33} = \frac{10\%}{0.67} = 15\%.$$

This formula is useful for showing how financial leverage can be used to increase the rate of return on net worth.[7] But increasing returns on net worth by using more and more leverage causes the leverage ratios to rise higher and higher above the industry norms. Creditors resist this tendency, so there are limitations to the practice. Moreover, greater leverage increases the risk of bankruptcy and thus endangers the firm's stockholders. Since Mrs. Walker and Mrs. Wilson are entirely dependent on income from the firm for their support, they will be in a particularly bad position if the firm goes into default. Consequently, Thompson would be ill-advised to attempt to use leverage to boost the return on net worth much further.

7. There are limitations on this statement: Specifically, the return on net worth increases with leverage only if the return on assets exceeds the rate of interest on debt, after considering the tax deductibility of interest payments. This whole concept is explored in detail in Chapter 15, which is devoted entirely to financial leverage.

Rates of Return in Different Industries

Would it be better to have a 5 percent margin on sales and a total asset turnover of 2 times or a 2 percent sales margin and a turnover of 5 times? It makes no difference; in either case the firm has a 10 percent return on investment. Actually, most firms are not free to make the kind of choice posed in this question. Depending on the nature of its industry, the firm *must* operate with more or fewer assets, and its turnover will depend on the characteristics of its particular line of business. In the case of a dealer in fresh fruits and vegetables, fish, or other perishable items, the turnover should be high—every day or two is most desirable. In contrast, some lines of business require heavy fixed investment or long production periods. A hydroelectric utility company, with its heavy investment in dams and transmission lines, requires heavy fixed investment; a shipbuilder or an aircraft producer needs a long production period. Such companies necessarily have a low asset turnover rate but a correspondingly higher profit margin on sales.

If a grocery chain has a high turnover and a chemical producer, with its heavy investment in fixed assets, a low turnover, should there be differences in their profit margins on sales? In general, yes. The chemical producer should have a considerably higher profit margin to offset its lower turnover. Otherwise, the grocery industry would be much more profitable than the chemical, investment would flow into the grocery industry, and profits in this industry would be eroded to the point where the rate of return was about equal to that in the chemical industry.

We know, however, that leverage must be taken into account when considering the rate of return on net worth. If the firms in one industry have a somewhat lower return on total assets but use slightly more financial leverage than do those in another industry, both sets of firms may end up with approximately the same rate of return on net worth.[8]

Table 7.8

Turnover, Profit Margins, and Returns on Net Worth

	Sales to Total Assets (Times)	×	Profit to Sales (Percent)	=	Profit to Total Assets (Percent)	Debt to Total Assets (Percent)	Profit to Net Worth (Percent)[a]
All manufacturing firms	1.40		5.65		7.91	49.8	15.8
Crown-Zellerbach (forest products)	1.30		4.76		6.19	52.3	13.0
Kroger (food retailer)	5.08		0.94		4.78	64.6	13.5

a. The figures in this column can be found as:

$$\text{Profit to net worth} = \frac{\text{Profit to total assets}}{1 - \text{Debt to total assets}}.$$

Sources: FTC quarterly financial reports and company annual reports for 1979.

8. The factors that make it possible for firms to use more leverage are taken up in Chapters 15 and 16. It can be stated now, however, that the primary factors favoring leverage are sales and profit stability.

These points, which are all necessary for a complete understanding of ratio analysis, are illustrated in Table 7.8. There we see how turnover and profit margins interact with each other to produce varying returns on assets and how financial leverage affects the returns on net worth. Crown-Zellerbach, Kroger, and the average of all manufacturing firms are compared. Crown-Zellerbach, with its very heavy fixed asset investment, is seen to have a relatively low turnover; Kroger, a typical chain food store, has a very high sales-to-assets ratio. Crown-Zellerbach, however, ends up with about the same rate of return on assets because its high profit margin on sales compensates for its low turnover. Both Kroger and Crown-Zellerbach use financial leverage to increase their return on net worth.

Sources of Comparative Ratios

In our analysis of the Walker-Wilson Company, we frequently used industry average ratios. Where are such averages obtained? Some important sources are listed below.

Dun & Bradstreet

Probably the most widely known and used of the industry average ratios are those compiled by Dun & Bradstreet. D&B provides fourteen ratios calculated for a large number of industries; samples and explanations are shown in Table 7.9. The complete data give the fourteen ratios, with the interquartile ranges, for 800 types of business activity based on the firms' financial statements.[9] The compilations are based on 400,000 companies. The figures are also grouped by annual sales into three size categories. The comprehensive data are presented in Dun & Bradstreet's *Key Business Ratios.*

Robert Morris Associates

Another group of useful ratios can be found in the annual *Statement Studies* compiled and published by Robert Morris Associates, the national association of bank loan officers. These are representative averages based on financial statements received by banks in connection with loans made. Ratios are calculated for manufacturing, wholesaling, retailing, contractors, and the finance industry. Asset items are all expressed as a percent of total assets. Income statement data are expressed as a percent of net sales. Data are presented for four size categories as well as for all the firms in the industry. The industry names are related to the Standard Industrial Classification (SIC) numbers of the U.S. Bureau of the Census. Sixteen ratios are presented, along with the total dollar amount of net sales and total assets for each category covered.

9. The median and quartile ratios can be illustrated by an example. The median ratio of current assets to current debt of manufacturers of airplane parts and accessories, as shown in Table 7.9, is 1.98. To obtain this figure, the ratios of current assets to current debt for each of the 30 concerns were arranged in a graduated series, with the largest ratio at the top and the smallest at the bottom. The median ratio of 1.98 is the ratio halfway between the top and the bottom. The ratio of 2.73, representing the upper quartile, is one-quarter of the way down from the top (or halfway between the top and the median). The ratio 1.69, representing the lower quartile, is one-quarter of the way up from the bottom (or halfway between the median and the bottom).

Table 7.9

Dun & Bradstreet Ratios for Selected Industries

Manufacturing Line of Business (and Number of Concerns Reporting)[a]	Current Assets to Current Debt	Net Profits on Net Sales	Net Profits on Tangible Net Worth	Net Profits on Net Working Capital	Net Sales to Tangible Net Worth	Net Sales to Net Working Capital	Collection Period	Net Sales to Inventory	Fixed Assets to Tangible Net Worth	Current Debt to Tangible Net Worth	Total Debt to Tangible Net Worth	Inventory To Net Working Capital	Current Debt to Inventory	Funded Debts to Net Working Capital
	Times	Percent	Percent	Percent	Times	Times	Days	Times	Percent	Percent	Percent	Percent	Percent	Percent
2873	2.43	3.76	27.05	58.31	8.51	12.91	91	16.5	98.5	161.0	224.1	139.4	311.8	95.6
Agricultural Chemicals,	*1.47*	*1.45*	*10.91*	*6.92*	*4.61*	*5.10*	*49*	*7.3*	*74.1*	*90.2*	*104.8*	*81.1*	*140.4*	*44.7*
Nitrogenous (43)	1.01	.54	2.05	3.64	2.10	3.17	27	3.8	26.7	39.2	46.7	30.5	78.3	48.6
3724	2.73	5.20	17.90	38.81	6.12	8.65	61	11.6	83.0	95.5	105.8	91.0	157.9	89.8
Airplane Parts &	*1.98*	*4.09*	*14.11*	*19.21*	*3.41*	*5.89*	*50*	*8.0*	*56.2*	*49.8*	*79.6*	*69.1*	*114.6*	*49.7*
Accessories (30)	1.69	1.08	.01	3.92	1.98	3.06	33	4.6	29.8	27.2	38.3	55.2	72.7	26.4
2051	3.32	7.35	58.82	108.94	10.17	29.26	25	53.3	155.1	99.6	167.9	105.2	383.0	241.4
Bakery Products,	*1.75*	*3.01*	*16.95*	*21.05*	*6.21*	*10.45*	*17*	*33.3*	*91.2*	*43.0*	*69.7*	*50.5*	*229.7*	*72.7*
Bread, Cake (135)	1.08	.96	4.90	11.47	3.47	2.91	11	20.9	47.3	15.9	24.1	9.2	104.0	2.0
3312	2.79	7.84	31.90	67.00	8.82	9.68	57	17.9	181.3	205.5	306.3	107.0	318.4	146.8
Blast Furnaces, and	*1.76*	*4.32*	*17.08*	*20.29*	*3.68*	*4.23*	*44*	*7.1*	*84.8*	*85.1*	*109.3*	*80.1*	*130.7*	*65.8*
Steel Mills (71)	1.06	1.84	5.90	5.60	2.25	.95	31	4.5	37.6	32.3	51.2	28.8	74.9	12.2
2331	2.79	4.96	43.40	50.98	15.23	17.68	57	19.5	44.3	220.3	269.2	139.5	250.6	92.8
Blouses & Waists:	*1.69*	*2.60*	*23.72*	*24.86*	*8.51*	*8.44*	*34*	*8.4*	*17.1*	*103.6*	*122.6*	*83.0*	*140.6*	*46.6*
Women's & Misses' (216)	1.36	.91	9.14	7.01	4.44	4.93	15	5.5	4.2	36.4	53.5	42.7	86.3	10.2
2731	6.61	11.46	37.94	41.49	5.53	7.44	72	14.0	65.4	83.8	131.8	100.6	239.8	133.8
Book Publishing (266)	*2.70*	*4.97*	*15.94*	*19.45*	*2.93*	*3.33*	*44*	*5.8*	*23.6*	*33.3*	*50.2*	*69.9*	*99.1*	*38.0*
	1.47	1.49	6.33	4.20	1.29	1.38	26	2.7	8.7	9.3	14.0	30.1	35.4	9.0
2211	4.94	10.14	27.85	46.80	8.57	8.38	61	16.2	71.0	137.2	191.8	100.4	202.8	95.2
Broad Woven Fabrics,	*2.57*	*3.84*	*17.16*	*22.85*	*3.76*	*5.08*	*42*	*8.8*	*37.4*	*43.0*	*65.5*	*62.5*	*85.8*	*42.5*
Cotton (103)	1.43	2.36	9.37	10.78	2.70	3.07	24	5.0	19.8	16.8	21.8	35.1	47.0	16.3
2033	2.64	4.77	23.23	34.06	7.80	15.00	34	8.4	109.2	187.0	226.0	272.4	143.5	115.0
Canned Fruits &	*1.54*	*2.45*	*11.63*	*15.23*	*4.31*	*6.64*	*24*	*4.2*	*66.0*	*84.7*	*111.4*	*111.0*	*101.6*	*51.6*
Vegetables (115)	1.15	1.10	6.32	.99	2.61	2.52	15	3.3	39.6	29.5	52.6	48.0	60.2	9.0

a. Standard Industrial Classification (SIC) categories.
Source: Excerpted from "The Ratios," *Dun's Review,* October 1979, p. 149. Reprinted with the special permission of Dun's Review, October 1979. Copyright, 1979, Dun & Bradstreet Publications Corporation.

Quarterly Financial Report for Manufacturing Corporations

The Federal Trade Commission (FTC) publishes quarterly financial data on manufacturing companies. Both balance sheet and income statement data are developed from a systematic sample of corporations. The reports are published perhaps six months after the financial data have been made available by the companies. They include an analysis by industry groups and by asset size and financial statements in ratio form (or common-size analysis) as well. The FTC reports are a rich source of information and are frequently used for comparative purposes.

Individual Firms

Credit departments of individual firms compile financial ratios and averages on their customers in order to judge their ability to meet obligations and on their suppliers in order to evaluate their financial ability to fulfill contracts. The First National Bank of Chicago, for instance, compiles semiannual reports on the financial data for finance companies. NCR gathers data for a large number of business lines.

Trade Associations and Public Accountants

Financial ratios for many industries are compiled by trade associations and constitute an important source to be checked by a financial manager seeking comparative data. These averages are usually the best obtainable. In addition to balance sheet data, they provide detailed information on operating expenses, which makes possible an informed analysis of the firms' efficiency.

Use of Financial Ratios in Credit Analysis

We have analyzed a rather long list of ratios, determining what each ratio is designed to measure. Sometimes it is unnecessary to go beyond a few of these calculations to determine that a firm is in very good or very bad condition, but often what one ratio will not indicate, another may. Also, a relationship vaguely suggested by one ratio may be corroborated by another. For these reasons, it is generally useful to calculate a number of different ratios.

In numerous situations, however, a few ratios tell the story. For example, a credit manager who has a great many invoices flowing across her desk each day may limit herself to three ratios as evidence of whether the prospective buyer of goods will pay promptly. She may use (1) either the current or the quick ratio to determine how burdened the prospective buyer is with current liabilities, (2) the debt to total assets ratio to determine how much of the prospective buyer's own funds are invested in the business, and (3) any of the profitability ratios to determine whether the firm has favorable prospects. If the profit margin is high enough, it may justify the risk of dealing with a slow-paying customer (profitable companies are likely to grow and thus to become better customers in the future). However, if the profit margin is low in relation to other firms in the industry, if the current ratio is low, and if the debt ratio is high, a credit manager probably will not approve a sale involving an extension of credit.[10]

Of necessity, the credit manager is more than a calculator and a reader of financial ratios. Qualitative factors may override quantitative analysis. For instance, in selling to truckers, oil companies often find that the financial ratios are adverse and that if they based their decisions solely on financial ratios, they would not make sales. Or, to take another example, profits may have been low for a period, but if the customer understands why and can remove the cause of the difficulty, a credit manager may be willing to approve a sale to that customer. This decision is also influenced by the profit margin of the selling firm. If it is making a large profit on sales, it is in a better position to take credit risks than if its own margin is low. Ultimately, the credit manager must judge each customer on character and management ability, and intelligent credit decisions must be based on careful consideration of conditions in the selling firm as well as in the buying firm.

Use of Financial Ratios in Security Analysis

We have emphasized the use of financial analysis by the financial manager and by outside credit analysts. However, this type of analysis is also useful in security analysis—the analysis of the investment merits of stocks and bonds. When the emphasis is on security analysis, the principal focus is on judging the long-run profit potential of the firm. Profitability is dependent in large part on the efficiency with which the firm is run; because financial analysis provides insights into this factor, it is useful to the security analyst.

Some Limitations of Ratio Analysis

Although ratios are exceptionally useful tools, they have some limitations and must be used with caution. Ratios are constructed from accounting data, and these data are subject to different interpretations and even to manipulation. For example, two firms may use different depreciation methods or inventory valuation methods; depending on the procedures followed, reported profits can be raised or lowered. Similar differences can be encountered in the treatment of research and development expenditures, pension plan costs, merg-

10. Statistical techniques have been developed to improve the use of ratios in credit analysis. One such development is the discriminant analysis model reported by Edward I. Altman in "Financial Ratios, Discriminant Analysis, and the Prediction of Corporate Bankruptcy," *Journal of Finance* 23 (September 1968), pp. 589–609. In his model, Altman combines a number of liquidity, leverage, activity, and profitability ratios to form an index of a firm's probability of going bankrupt. His model has predicted bankruptcy quite well one or two years before it occurs. See also Edward I. Altman, Robert G. Haldeman, and P. Narayanan, "ZETA Analysis: A New Model to Identify Bankruptcy Risk of Corporations," *Journal of Banking and Finance* 1 (June 1977), pp. 29–54.

ers, product warranties, and bad-debt reserves. Further, if firms use different fiscal years, and if seasonal factors are important, this can influence the comparative ratios. Thus, if the ratios of two firms are to be compared, it is important to analyze the basic accounting data on which the ratios were based and to reconcile any major differences.

A financial manager must also be cautious in judging whether a particular ratio is good or bad and in forming a composite judgment about a firm on the basis of a set of ratios. For example, a high inventory turnover ratio could indicate efficient inventory management, but it could also indicate a serious shortage of inventories and suggest the likelihood of stock-outs. When financial ratio analysis indicates that the patterns of a firm depart from industry norms, this is not an absolutely certain indication that something is wrong with the firm. Such departures provide a basis for questions and further investigation and analysis. Additional information and discussions may establish sound explanations for the differences between the pattern for the individual firm and industry composite ratios. Or the differences may reveal forms of mismanagement calling for correction.

Conversely, conformity to industry composite ratios does not establish with certainty that the firm is performing normally and is well managed. In the short run many tricks can be used to make a firm look good in relation to industry standards. The analyst must develop first-hand knowledge of the operations and management of the firm to provide a check on the financial ratios. In addition, the analyst must develop a sixth sense—a touch, a smell, a feel—for what is going on in the firm. Sometimes it is this kind of business judgment that uncovers weaknesses in the firm. The analyst should not be anesthetized by financial ratios that appear to conform with normality.

Ratios, then, are extremely useful tools. But as with other analytical methods, they must be used with judgment and caution, not in an unthinking, mechanical manner. Financial ratio analysis is a useful part of an investigation process. But financial ratios alone are not the complete answer to questions about the performance of firms.

Summary

Ratio analysis, which relates balance sheet and income statement items to one another, permits the charting of a firm's history and the evaluation of its present position. It also allows the financial manager to anticipate reactions of investors and creditors and thus to gain insight into how attempts to acquire funds are likely to be received.

Ratios are classified into six basic types: liquidity, leverage, activity, profitability, growth, and valuation. Data from the Walker-Wilson Manufacturing Company are used to compute each type of ratio and to show in practice how a financial analysis is made. An almost unlimited number of ratios can be calculated, but in practice a limited number of each type is sufficient.

A ratio is not a meaningful number in and of itself; it must be compared with something before it becomes useful. The two basic kinds of comparative analysis are (1) trend analysis, which involves computing the ratio of a particular firm for several years and comparing the ratios over time to see if the firm is improving or deteriorating, and (2) comparisons with other firms in the same industry. These two comparisons are often combined in the graphic analysis illustrated in Figure 7.1.

The Du Pont system shows how the return on investment is dependent on the profit margin and asset turnover. The system is generally expressed in the form of the following equation:

$$\frac{\text{Profit}}{\text{Sales}} \times \frac{\text{Sales}}{\text{Investment}} = \text{ROI}.$$

The first term, the profit margin, times investment turnover equals the rate of return on investment. The kinds of actions discussed in this chapter can be used to effect needed changes in turnover and the profit margin and thus improve the return on investment.

The Du Pont system can be extended to encompass financial leverage and to examine the manner in which turnover, sales margins, and leverage all combine to determine the rate of return on net worth. The following equation is used to show this relationship:

$$\text{Rate of return on net worth} = \frac{\text{Return on assets (ROI)}}{1.0 - \text{Debt ratio}}.$$

The extended Du Pont system shows why firms in different industries—even though they have widely different turnovers, profit margins, and debt ratios —may end up with very similar rates of return on net worth. In general, firms dealing with relatively perishable commodities are expected to have high turnovers but low profit margins; firms whose production processes require heavy investments in fixed assets are expected to have low turnover ratios but high profit margins.

Questions

7.1 "A uniform system of accounts, including identical forms for balance sheets and income statements, would be a most reasonable requirement for the SEC to impose on all publicly owned firms." Discuss this statement.

7.2 We have divided financial ratios into six groups: liquidity, leverage, activity, profitability, growth, and valuation. We could also consider financial analysis as being conducted by four groups of analysts: management, equity investors, long-term creditors, and short-term creditors.

a. Explain the nature of each type of ratio.

b. Explain the emphasis of each type of analyst in dealing with the ratios.

7.3 Why can norms with relatively well defined limits be stated in advance for some financial ratios but not for others?

7.4 How does trend analysis supplement the basic financial ratio calculations and their interpretation?

7.5 Why should the inventory turnover figure be more important to a grocery store than to a shoe repair store?

7.6 How can a firm have a high current ratio and still be unable to pay its bills?

7.7 "The higher the rate of return on investment (ROI), the better the firm's management." Is this statement true for all firms? Explain. If you disagree with the statement, give examples of cases in which it might not be true.

7.8 What factors would you, as a financial manager, want to examine if a firm's rate of return (a) on assets or (b) on net worth was too low?

7.9 Profit margins and turnover rates vary from industry to industry. What industry characteristics account for these variations? Give some contrasting examples to illustrate your answer.

7.10 Which relation would you, as a financial manager, prefer: (a) a profit margin of 10 percent and a capital turnover of 2, or (b) a profit margin of 20 percent and a capital turnover of 1? Can you think of any firm with a relationship similar to b?

Problems

7.1 Fill in the blanks to complete the balance sheet and sales information for the Burke Company, using the following financial data:

Debt/Net worth: 50 percent
Acid test ratio: 1.2
Total asset turnover: 2.0 times
Days' sales outstanding in accounts receivable: 30
Gross profit margin: 30 percent
Sales to inventory turnover: 5 times

Balance Sheet

Cash	______	Accounts payable	______
Accounts receivable	______	Common stock	$25,000
Inventories	______	Retained earnings	$35,000
Plant and equipment	______	Total liabilities and capital	______
Total assets	______		
Sales	______	Cost of goods sold	______

7.2 The following data were taken from the financial statements of the Lawson Furniture Company for calendar year 1979. The norms given below are based on averages for the "wood household furniture and upholstered" industry.

a. Fill in the ratios for the Lawson Furniture Company.

b. Indicate by comparison with industry norms the possible errors in management policies reflected in these financial statements.

Lawson Furniture Company Balance Sheet as of December 31, 1979

Assets		Liabilities	
Cash	$ 11,000	Accounts payable	$ 45,000
Receivables	104,000	Notes payable (at 10%)	21,000
Inventory	250,000	Other current liabilities	39,000
Total current assets	$365,000	Total current liabilities	$105,000
Net fixed assets	110,000	Long-term debt (at 9%)	115,000
		Net worth	255,000
Total assets	$475,000	Total claims on assets	$475,000

Lawson Furniture Company Income Statement for Year Ended December 31, 1979

Sales		$752,000
Cost of goods sold:		
Material	$240,000	
Labor	210,000	
Heat, light, and power	25,000	
Indirect labor	30,000	
Depreciation	22,000	527,000
Gross profit		$225,000
Selling expense	$ 80,000	
General and administrative expense	110,000	190,000
Net operating profit (EBIT)		$ 35,000
Less interest expense		−12,450
Net profit before tax		$ 22,550
Less federal income tax (at 1979 rates)		−3,834
Net income		$ 18,716

Lawson Furniture Company Analysis

Ratio	Ratio	Industry Norm
Current assets / Current liabilities	________	3.1 times
Debt / Total assets	________	50%
Times interest earned	________	4.8 times
Sales / Inventory	________	6.2 times
Average collection period	________	46 days
Sales / Total assets	________	2.0 times
Net profit / Sales	________	3.0%
Net profit / Total assets	________	6.0%
Net profit / Net worth	________	12.0%

7.3 The following data were taken from the financial statements of Lennon Drug Company, a wholesaler of drugs, drug proprietaries, and sundries, for calendar year 1979. The norms given below are the industry averages for wholesale drugs, drug proprietaries, and sundries.

Lennon Drug Company Balance Sheet as of December 31, 1979 (Thousands of Dollars)

Assets		Liabilities	
Cash	$ 200	Accounts payable	$ 300
Receivables	800	Notes payable (at 10%)	200
Inventory	600	Other current liabilities	300
Total current assets	$1,600	Total current liabilities	$ 800
Net fixed assets	600	Long-term debt (at 10%)	600
		Net worth	800
Total assets	$2,200	Total claims on assets	$2,200

Lennon Drug Company Income Statement for Year Ended December 31, 1979 (Rounded to Nearest Thousands of Dollars)

Sales	$4,000	
Cost of goods sold	3,400	
Gross profit		$600
Selling expenses	$ 250	
General and administrative expenses	200	450
Net operating income (NOI)		$150
Interest expense		80
Income before taxes		$ 70
Federal income taxes (at 1979 rates)		15
Net income		$ 55

Lennon Drug Company Analysis

Ratio	Ratio	Industry Norm
Current assets / Current liabilities	______	1.97 times
Debt / Total assets	______	60%
Times interest earned	______	3.79 times
Sales / Inventory	______	6.7 times
Average collection period	______	36 days
Sales / Total assets	______	2.94 times
Net profit / Sales	______	1.14%
Net profit / Total assets	______	3.35%
Net profit / Net worth	______	8.29%

a. Fill in the ratios for Lennon Drug Company.
b. Indicate by comparison with the industry norms the possible errors in management policies reflected in these financial statements.

7.4 Silicon Valley Electronic Supply Company, a closely held family manufacturer of electric components, has, since the death of its founder/president Marilyn Hickley two years ago, been managed by her nephew Ron, formerly a company salesman. Ed Smith, the account manager at the firm's bank, has received from the family numerous complaints about Ron's actions and has asked you to evaluate Ron's performance. The company's most recent financial statements are reproduced below.

a. Calculate the relevant financial ratios for this analysis.
b. Apply a Du Pont chart analysis to Silicon Valley.
c. Evaluate Ron's performance and list specific areas that need improvement.

Industry Average Ratios

Current ratio: 2.2
Quick ratio: 1.0
Debt to total assets: 50%
Times interest earned: 5.2 times
Inventory turnover: 5.1 times
Average collection period: 52 days
Fixed assets turnover: 9.25 times
Total assets turnover: 1.85 times
Net profit on sales: 3.19%
Return on total assets: 5.90%
Return on net worth: 10.8%.

Common-Size Balance Sheet for Electronic Components Industry, 1979

Assets (in Percentages)		Liabilities (in Percentages)	
Cash	5.8%	Due to banks—short term	7.6%
Marketable securities	3.5	Due to trade	11.3
Receivables, net	25.9	Income taxes	2.3
Inventory, net	34.8	Current maturities—long-term debt	2.3
All other current	2.5	All other current	8.5
Total current	72.5%	Total current debt	32.0%
Fixed assets, net	25.0	Long-term debt	17.7
All other noncurrent	2.5	Tangible net worth	50.3
Total assets	100.0%	Total claims on assets	100.0%

Common-Size Income Statement for Electronic Components Industry, 1979

Net sales	100.0%	
Cost of sales	77.9	
Gross profit		22.1%
Selling and delivery expenses	4.2%	
Officers' salaries	2.5	
Other general administrative expenses	8.5	
All other expenses, net	1.1	
Operating expenses		16.3
Earnings before interest and tax		5.8%
Interest expense		1.1
Taxes		1.5
Net income		3.2%

Silicon Valley Electronic Supply Company Balance Sheet as of December 31, 1979 (Thousands of Dollars)

Assets		Liabilities		
Cash	$ 90	Accounts payable	$450	
Marketable securities	40	Notes payable (at 11%)	380	
Receivables	1,550	Other current liabilities	280	
Inventory	1,190	Total current liabilities		$1,110
Total current assets	$2,870	Long-term debt (at 9%)		880
Net fixed assets	1,130	Total liabilities		$1,990
		Net worth		2,010
Total assets	$4,000	Total claims on assets		$4,000

Silicon Valley Electronic Supply Company Income Statement for Year Ended December 31, 1979 (Thousands of Dollars)

Sales		$6,200
Cost of goods sold:		
Materials	$2,470	
Labor	1,540	
Heat, light, and power	230	
Indirect labor	370	
Depreciation	140	4,750
Gross profit		$1,450
Selling expenses	$490	
General and administrative expenses	530	1,020
Net operating income (=EBIT)		$ 430
Less interest expense		−121
Income before taxes		$ 309
Less federal income taxes (at 1979 rates)		−123
Net income		$ 186

7.5 Quality Cannery is a medium-sized firm whose products—canned fruits, vegetables, and juices—are sold to distributors throughout the midwestern states. Seasonal working capital needs have been financed primarily by loans from a Kansas City bank, and the current line of credit permits the cannery to borrow up to $360,000. In accordance with standard banking practices, however, the loan agreement requires that the bank loan be repaid in full at some time during the year, in this case by February 1980. Interest expense for 1979 was $48,000.

A limitation on prices of canned goods, coupled with higher costs, caused a decline in Quality's profit margin and net income during the last half of 1978 and during most of 1979. Sales increased during both these years, however, because of the cannery's aggressive marketing program.

The First National Bank of Kansas City has a newly instituted computer loan analysis program, which recently alerted Robert Mitchell, loan officer, to the deteriorating financial position of one of his clients, Quality. Consulting the analysis run on Quality three months earlier, Mitchell saw that certain of Quality's ratios were showing downward trends and were dipping below the averages for the canning industry. Mitchell sent David Tinsley, president of Quality, a copy of the computer output, together with a note voicing his concern.

Tinsley received a copy of Mitchell's latest computer analysis, showing that Quality Cannery was in technical violation of the financial standards specified in the loan agreement. Quality's balance sheets and income statements for 1976–1979 are shown below, together with the industry norms.

Quality Cannery Balance Sheets

	Year Ended December 31			
	1976	1977	1978	1979
Cash	$ 51,000	$ 76,500	$ 35,700	$ 25,500
Accounts receivable	204,000	306,000	346,800	484,500
Inventory	255,000	382,500	637,500	1,032,800
Total current assets	$510,000	$ 765,000	$1,020,000	$1,542,800
Land and building	76,500	61,200	163,200	153,000
Machinery	102,000	188,700	147,900	127,500
Other fixed assets	61,200	35,700	10,200	7,600
Total assets	$749,700	$1,050,600	$1,341,300	$1,830,900
Notes payable, bank	—	—	$ 127,500	$ 357,000
Accounts and notes payable	112,200	$ 122,400	193,800	382,500
Accruals	51,000	61,200	71,400	96,900
Total current liabilities	$163,200	$ 183,600	$ 392,700	$ 836,400
Mortgage	76,500	56,100	51,000	45,900
Common stock	459,000	459,000	459,000	459,000
Retained earnings	51,000	351,900	438,600	489,600
Total liabilities and equity	$749,700	$1,050,600	$1,341,300	$1,830,900

Quality Cannery Income Statements

	Year Ended December 31 1977	1978	1979
Net sales	$3,315,000	$3,442,500	$3,570,000
Cost of goods sold	2,694,500	2,782,900	2,873,000
Gross operating profit	$ 620,500	$ 659,600	$ 697,000
General administration and selling	255,000	280,500	306,000
Depreciation	102,000	127,500	153,000
Miscellaneous	51,000	107,100	153,000
Net income before taxes	$ 212,500	$ 144,500	$ 85,000
Taxes (40%)	85,000	57,800	34,000
Net income	$ 127,500	$ 86,700	$ 51,000

Canning Industry Ratios (1979)[a]

Quick ratio	1.0
Current ratio	2.7
Inventory turnover[b]	7 times
Average collection period	32 days
Fixed asset turnover[b]	13.0 times
Total asset turnover[b]	2.6 times
Return on total assets	9%
Return on net worth	18%
Debt ratio	50%
Profit margin on sales	3.5%

a. Industry average ratios have been constant for the past three years.
b. Based on year-end balance sheet figures.

Mitchell stated that the bank would insist on immediate repayment of the entire loan unless Quality presented a program showing how its poor current financial picture could be improved.

a. Calculate the key financial ratios for Quality and plot trends in the firm's ratios against the industry averages.
b. What strengths and weaknesses are revealed by the ratio analysis?

7.6 Chrysler Corporation experienced financial difficulties in 1978 and 1979. Below are data taken from the financial statements of the corporation for the year ended December 31, 1978. Also given are industry norms for the automobile industry.

a. Fill in the ratios listed on page 172 for Chrysler Corporation.
b. Indicate by comparison with the industry norms the possible weaknesses reflected in these financial statements.

Chrysler Corporation and Consolidated Subsidiaries Consolidated Balance Sheet, December 31, 1978

Assets	
Current Assets:	
Cash	$ 100
Time deposits	250
Marketable securities—at lower of cost or market	150
Accounts receivable (less allowance for doubtful accounts: 1978—$16.7 million)	850
Inventories—at the lower of cost (substantially first-in, first-out) or market	2,000
Prepaid insurance, taxes and other expenses	100
Income taxes allocable to the following year	50
Refundable taxes on income	50
Total current assets	$3,550
Investments and Other Assets:	
Investments in and advances to associated companies outside the United States	450
Investments in and advances to unconsolidated subsidiaries	900
Other noncurrent assets	50
Total investments and other assets	$1,400
Property, Plant and Equipment:	
Land, buildings, machinery and equipment	$3,400
Less accumulated depreciation	−1,960
	1,440
Unamortized special tools	600
Net property, plant and equipment	$2,040
Cost of Investments in Consolidated Subsidiaries in Excess of Equity	10
Total assets	$7,000

Liabilities and Shareholders' Investment	
Current Liabilities:	
Accounts payable	$1,710
Accrued expenses	700
Short-term debt	49
Payments due within one year on long-term debt	10
Taxes on income	1
Total current liabilities	$2,470
Other Liabilities and Deferred Credits:	
Deferred incentive compensation	2
Other employee benefit plans	90
Deferred taxes on income	108
Unrealized profits on sales to unconsolidated subsidiaries	60
Other noncurrent liabilities	100
Total other liabilities and deferred credits	$ 360

(continued)

Chrysler Corporation and Consolidated Subsidiaries Consolidated Balance Sheet, December 31, 1978 (Continued)

Long-Term Debt:	
Notes and debentures payable	$1,100
Convertible sinking fund debentures	100
Total long-term debt	$1,200
Obligations under Capital Leases	15
Minority Interest in Net Assets of Consolidated Subsidiaries	5
Shareholders' Investment	
Represented by	
Preferred Stock—no par value	200
Common Stock—par value $6.25 a share	400
Additional paid-in capital	700
Net earnings retained for use in the business	1,650
Total shareholders' investment	$2,950
Total liabilities and shareholders' investment	$7,000

Chrysler Corporation and Consolidated Subsidiaries Consolidated Statement of Net Earnings for Year Ending December 31, 1978

Net sales	$13,600
Equity in net earnings of unconsolidated subsidiaries	20
Net earnings from European and certain South American operations	30
	$13,650
Costs, other than items below	12,650
Depreciation of plant and equipment	150
Amortization of special tools	200
Selling and administrative expenses	600
Provision for incentive compensation	—
Pension plans	250
Interest expense—net	100
	$13,950
Earnings (loss) before taxes on income	(300)
Taxes (credit) on income	(100)
Net earnings (loss)	$ (200)
Dividends on preferred shares (includes amortization of discount)	20
Net earnings (loss) attributable to common stock	$ (220)
Earnings (loss) per share of common stock	$ (3.54)
Average number of common shares outstanding during the year (in millions)	62

Chrysler Corporation Ten-Year Financial Summary

	1978	1977	1976	1975	1974	1973	1972	1971	1970	1969
Summary of Operations (Dollar Amounts in Millions)										
Net sales	$13,600	$13,050	$12,250	$8,600	$8,400	$9,000	$7,750	$6,450	$5,600	$5,800
Net income	(220)	160	420	(260)	(50)	260	220	80	(10)	100
Cash dividends	52	54	18	—	79	69	47	30	29	95
Stockholders' equity at year end	2,950	2,900	2,800	2,400	2,650	2,750	2,500	2,250	2,150	2,150
Average number of shares of capital stock outstanding (in millions)	62	60	60	60	56	53	52	50	49	47
Per Share Data (in Dollars)										
Net income	$ (3.54)	$ 2.71	$ 7.02	$ (4.33)	$ (0.92)	$ 4.80	$ 4.27	$ 1.67	$ (0.15)	$ 2.09
Cash dividends	0.85	0.90	0.30	—	1.40	1.30	0.90	0.60	0.60	2.0
Stockholders' equity at year end	42.06	48.51	46.73	40.09	44.89	50.10	47.54	44.53	43.55	44.94
Common stock price range: High	$13\frac{3}{4}$	22	$22\frac{3}{8}$	$14\frac{1}{2}$	$20\frac{1}{8}$	$44\frac{1}{4}$	$41\frac{5}{8}$	$33\frac{3}{8}$	$35\frac{3}{4}$	$57\frac{7}{8}$
Low	$8\frac{1}{8}$	$12\frac{3}{8}$	$10\frac{3}{8}$	$7\frac{3}{8}$	7	$14\frac{3}{4}$	28	$24\frac{1}{2}$	$16\frac{1}{8}$	$31\frac{5}{8}$

Ratio	Chrysler Corporation Ratio					Auto Industry Norm
I. Liquidity						
Current ratio						1.65 times
Quick ratio						0.93 times
II. Leverage						
Total debt to total assets						0.44 times
Times interest earned						7.36 times
Fixed charge coverage						7.36 times
III. Activity						
Inventory turnover						8.00 times
Average collection period						29 days
Fixed assets turnover						6.58 times
Total assets turnover						1.85 times
IV. Profitability						
Profit margin on sales						4.90%
Return on total assets						9.14%
Return on net worth						16.35%
V. Growth						
a. Five-year compounded (1973–1978)						
Sales						7.29%
Net income						8.81%
Earnings per share						4.35%
b. Nine-year compounded (1969–1978)						
Sales						8.65%
Net income						9.09%
Earnings per share						6.10%
Dividends per share						3.84%
VI. Valuation						
	1974	1975	1976	1977	1978	
P/E ratio						
High						
Low						
Norm (DJIA)	6.2	11.3	10.3	9.3	8.5	
Market to book value of equity per share:						
High						
Low						
Norm (DJIA)	0.85	1.10	1.00	0.88	0.82	

7.7 The following are financial data and reference standards for four American steel companies for 1978. Evaluate the comparative performance of the four companies.

Ratios	Norm[a]	U.S. Steel	National Steel	Republic Steel	Bethlehem Steel
I. Liquidity					
1. Current ratio	1.7 times	1.7	1.7	2.0	1.6
2. Quick ratio	1.0 times	1.1	1.0	1.0	1.0

Ratios	Norm[a]	U.S. Steel	National Steel	Republic Steel	Bethlehem Steel
II. Leverage					
3. Total debt to total assets	45–50 percent	50	47	45	52
4. Times interest earned	7 times	2.3	4.9	8.2	4.6
5. Fixed charge coverage	7 times	2.3	4.9	8.2	4.6
III. Activity					
6. Inventory turnover	8.0 times	8.8	6.5	7.4	9.7
7. Average collection period	40 days	47	43	35	39
8. Fixed assets turnover	2.8 times	1.8	2.3	2.4	2.1
9. Total assets turnover	1.4 times	1.0	1.2	1.3	1.3
IV. Profitability[a]					
10. Net income to sales	5.0 percent	2.2	3.0	3.2	3.6
11. Net income to net worth	16.0 percent	4.6	8.4	8.3	9.5
12. Net income plus after-tax interest to total assets	9.0 percent	3.8	4.8	5.5	6.1
V. Growth: Nine-Year Compounded (1969–1978)[a]					
13. Sales	7 percent	9.6	13.2	9.8	8.7
14. Net income	7 percent	1.2	4.1	3.8	4.1
15. Earnings per share	7 percent	0.7	2.3	3.7	4.2
16. Dividends per share	5 percent	0.0	0.0	(1.4)	(6.0)
VI. Valuation[a]					
17. Price to earnings ratio (1974–1978 average)	9.1 (DJIA)	10.5	8.76	6.38	5.52
18. Market to book ratio (1974–1978 average)	0.93 (DJIA)	0.60	0.57	0.34	0.55

a. Since some steel industry ratios have been chronically low, we have used "all manufacturing industries" norms for profitability and growth and the ratios for the Dow-Jones Industrials Average (DJIA) for valuation relationships.

Selected References

Beaver, William H. "Financial Ratios as Predictors of Failure." In *Empirical Research in Accounting: Selected Studies in Journal of Accounting Research* (1966), pp. 71–111.

Branch, Ben. "The Impact of Operating Decisions on ROI Dynamics." *Financial Management* 7 (Winter 1978), pp. 54–60.

Helfert, Erich A. *Techniques of Financial Analysis.* 3d ed. Homewood, Ill.: Richard D. Irwin, 1972.

Horrigan, James C. "A Short History of Financial Ratio Analysis." *Accounting Review* 43 (April 1968), pp. 284–294.

———. "The Determination of Long-Term Credit Standing with Financial Ratios." In *"Empirical Research in Accounting: Selected Studies"* in *Journal of Accounting Research* (1966), pp. 44–62.

Johnson, W. Bruce. "The Cross-sectional Stability of Financial Ratio Patterns." *Journal of Financial and Quantitative Analysis* 14 (December 1979), pp. 1035–1048.

Laurent, C. R. "Improving the Efficiency and Effectiveness of Financial Ratio Analysis." *Journal of Business, Finance and Accounting* 6 (Autumn 1979), pp. 401–413

Lev, Baruch, and Taylor, Kenneth W. "Accounting Recognition of Imputed Interest on Equity: An Empirical Investigation." *Journal of Accounting, Auditing and Finance* 2 (Spring 1979), pp. 232–243.

Theil, Henri. "On the Use of Information Theory Concepts in the Analysis of Financial Statements." *Management Science* 15 (May 1969), pp. 459–480.

Appendix A to Chapter 7
Adjustments for Changes in Price Levels

Immediately after World War II, with the removal of price controls that had held prices to arbitrary levels, came a burst of inflation. Annual price increases thereafter stayed mostly within 3 to 5 percent per annum until the escalation of hostilities in Southeast Asia in 1966, when inflation again erupted in the United States. In 1971, the United States departed from the convertibility of the dollar into gold, and the major nations adopted floating exchange rates in place of nominally fixed exchange rates. Double digit inflation, as measured by the wholesale price index or consumer price index, has been an actuality or a threat in the United States for more than a decade.

It has been pointed out that in a period of inflation, distortions will result from the use of the historical cost postulate. Assets are recorded at cost, but revenue and other expense flows are in dollars of different purchasing power. The amortization of fixed costs does not reflect the current cost of the assets. Furthermore, net income during periods when assets are held does not reflect the effects of management's decision to hold the assets rather than sell them. Assets are not stated on the balance sheet at their current values, so the firm's financial position cannot be accurately evaluated. When assets are sold, gains or losses are reported during the period of sale, even though the results reflect decisions in prior periods to hold the assets.

As a consequence of a continued high rate of inflation, proposals have been made to modify accounting procedures to recognize that the traditional postulate of a stable measuring unit is no longer valid. In December 1974, the Financial Accounting Standards Board (FASB) issued an exposure draft of a proposed statement entitled "Financial Reporting in Units of General Purchasing Power." On March 23, 1976, the Securities and Exchange Commission issued Accounting Series Release No. 190. That release requires disclosure of replacement costs for inventory items and depreciable plant from registrants with $100 million or more (at historical cost) of gross plant assets and inventories constituting 10 percent or more of total assets.

In September 1979, the FASB issued Statement No. 33, "Financial Reporting and Changing Prices." It issued a related publication, "Illustrations of Financial Reporting and Changing Prices," in December 1979. FASB Statement No. 33 requires major companies to disclose the effects of both general inflation (purchasing power) and specific price changes (current costs) as supplementary information in their published annual reports. It applies to public enterprises having either (1) inventories and property, plant, and equipment (before deducting accumulated depreciation) amounting to more than $125 million, or (2) total assets amounting to more than $1 billion (after deducting accumulated depreciation). Statement No. 33 is effective for fiscal years ended on or after December 22, 1979.[1]

Inflation-adjusted profits may be substantially below reported income. The nature of such an impact is indicated by Table 7A.1. Note that for building materials and paper and forest products the inflation-adjusted profits are about half of reported profits. For the steel industry, inflation-adjusted profits go from positive to negative. Thus if a steel company reported profits of $100 million, its inflation-adjusted profits would be a negative $39 million. More generally, rising inflation appears to greatly overstate corporate earnings. This is illustrated by Figure 7A.1. For example, in 1978 after-tax profits as reported were over $120 billion. However, after adjustment they were about $85 billion. This represents a decline of over one-fourth.

The impact of inflation on reported profits and the way in which FASB Statement No. 33 proposes to make the necessary adjustments can be indicated by the following illustrative example. The example is not intended to be

Table 7A.1

The Varying Impact of Inflation on Profits

	Inflation-Adjusted Profits (Percent of Reported Income)[a]	
Industry	1974–1978	1978
Computers	93%	90%
Retailers	81	82
Drugs	78	83
Food	71	71
Machinery	66	67
Chemicals	62	64
Industrial company composite	61	65
Autos	59	71
Building materials	51	51
Paper and forest products	48	49
Steel	−26	−39

a. Net income less after-tax adjustments for inventory profits and the difference between reported depreciation and depreciation based on the replacement cost of plant and equipment.

Source: Data from Kidder, Peabody & Co. Financial Quality Profile, in "Inflation Accounting," *Business Week*, October 15, 1979, p. 69. Used by permission.

1. In its Accounting Series Release No. 271, issued shortly after the publication of FASB Statement No. 33, the Securities and Exchange Commission ruled that companies giving supplemental current-cost information in accordance with the FASB Statement need not provide the SEC with replacement cost information.

Figure 7A.1

How Rising Inflation Distorts Corporate Earnings

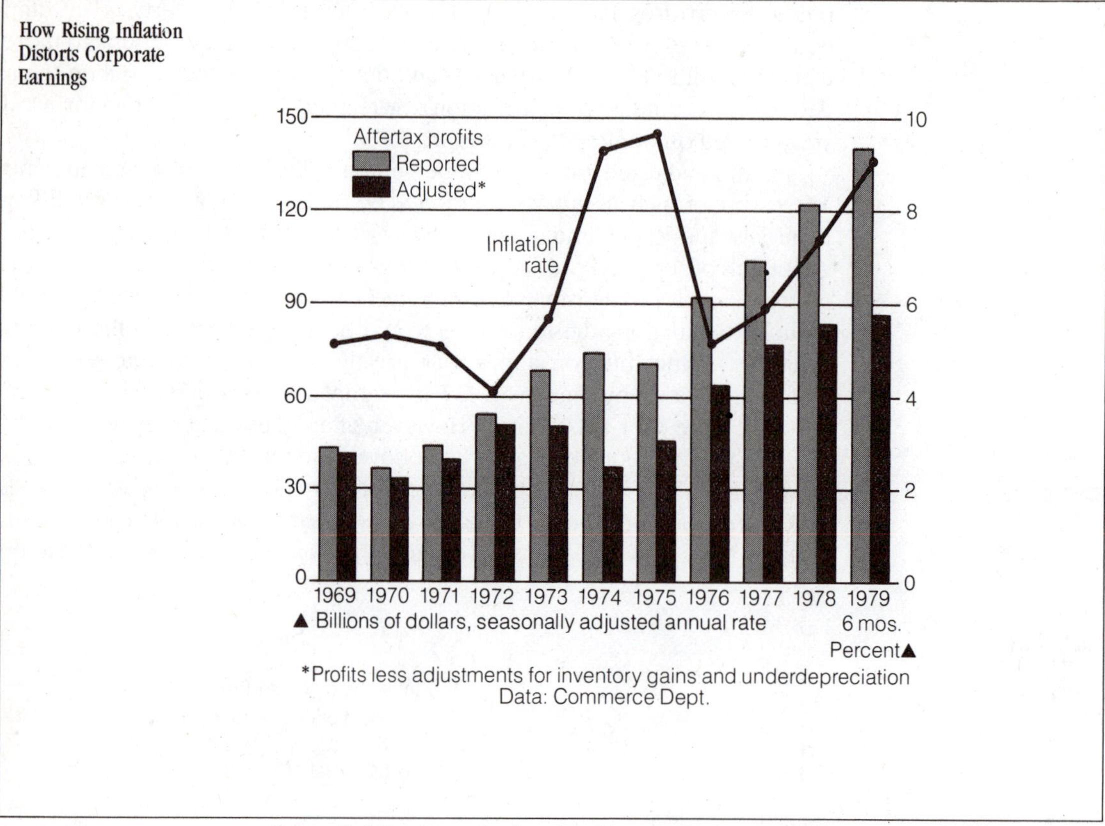

Source: "Inflation Accounting," reprinted from the October 15, 1979, issue of *Business Week*, p. 68, by special permission.

precisely accurate; it is oversimplified in order to make clear the nature of the basic adjustments involved.

We begin with Table 7A.2, a simplification of Schedule B (p. 33) of FASB Statement No. 33.

Table 7A.2 starts with a statement of income as reported and then indicates the nature of the adjustments to reflect general inflation and changes in specific prices. Table 7A.3 presents balance sheet data with information on the effects of changing prices. In Table 7A.3 it is assumed that during the preceding year inventories rose in value by 20 percent to reflect the general inflation. They rose another $40,000, reflecting the effects of changes in specific prices. Net fixed assets are similarly affected. It is assumed that the assets are exactly 50 percent depreciated, so that gross fixed assets are $1 million and the reserve for depreciation is $500,000. It is assumed that, on average, since the fixed assets were acquired (from 1 to 15 years earlier), they have doubled in price because of the effects of general inflation.

Table 7A.2

Statement of Income from Continuing Operations Adjusted for Changing Prices for the Year Ended December 31, 1980

	As Reported	Adjusted for General Inflation	Adjusted for Changes in Specific Prices (Current Costs)
1. Sales	$2,000,000	$2,000,000	$2,000,000
2. Cost of goods sold	1,600,000	1,660,000	1,700,000
3. Depreciation expense	100,000	200,000	280,000
4. Other operating expense	100,000	100,000	100,000
5. Net operating income	200,000	40,000	(80,000)
6. Interest expense	30,000	30,000	30,000
7. Net income before income taxes	170,000	10,000	(110,000)
8. Provision for income taxes at 40%	68,000	68,000	68,000
9. Income (loss) from operations	102,000	(58,000)	(178,000)
10. Gain from decline in purchasing power of net amounts owed		48,000	48,000
11. Increase in specific prices (current costs) of real assets held during year		Inventories	100,000
		Net fixed plant	200,000
			300,000
12. Effect of increase in general price level	Inventories	60,000	
	Net fixed plant	90,000	
		150,000	
13. Excess of increase in specific prices over increase in the general price level			$150,000

Source: Adapted from Schedule B of FASB Statement No. 33, September 1979, p. 33. Copyright by the Financial Accounting Standards Board, High Ridge Park, Stamford, Connecticut 06905 U.S.A.

In addition, a further increase in specific prices raises gross fixed assets to $2,800,000, so that net fixed assets are $1,400,000. This information is then used in making the adjustments in the Table 7A.2 statement of income. In Line 1, sales are carried as reported. Line 2 is the cost of goods sold; it includes the cost of inventories used. The column for the adjustment for general inflation is increased by $60,000 to reflect the effect of general inflation, which is not carried in the cost of goods sold as reported. Then a further $40,000 represents an adjustment for changes in the specific prices of the inventories. The numbers themselves are arbitrary and are presented purely for illustrative purposes.

Line 3 presents depreciation expense. The balance sheet data reflect the changes between the historical costs of fixed assets and prices reflecting general inflation and specific asset values over a period of years. However, only a portion of the effects of general inflation and specific price changes is reflected in the particular year under analysis. Hence, the adjustment for general inflation and depreciation expense is assumed to represent the same ten-year life or 10 percent of the gross fixed assets, assumed to be $2 million.

Table 7A.3

Balance Sheet with Adjustments Shown for Effects of Changing Prices as of December 31, 1980

	As Reported	Effect of General Inflation	Effect of Changes in Specific Prices
Monetary Assets			
Cash	$ 100,000		
Receivables	200,000		
Nonmonetary Assets			
Inventories	300,000	$ 360,000	$ 400,000
Net fixed assets	500,000	1,000,000[a]	1,400,000[a]
Total assets	$1,100,000		
Monetary Liabilities			
Current liabilities			
(Short-term interest bearing liabilities—$100,000 at 10%)	340,000		
Long-term debt at 10%	200,000		
	$ 540,000		
Nonmonetary Liabilities			
Common stock	200,000		
Retained earnings	360,000		
Net worth	$ 560,000		
Total claims	$1,100,000		

a. The increases in net fixed assets are accumulated increases over years. They are different from those shown in Lines 11 and 12 in Table 7A.2, which are the increases in net fixed assets only for the one accounting year discussed.

Source: Adapted from Schedule B of FASB Statement No. 33, September 1979.

Thus the depreciation expense adjusted for general inflation is $200,000. Taking the effect of changes of specific prices into account, the depreciation expense is 10 percent of the value of gross fixed assets, or 10 percent of $2,800,000. The depreciation expense is therefore $280,000. Other operating income is assumed to be unchanged at $100,000 throughout.

The net operating income as reported is therefore $200,000. The interest expense represents 10 percent of the long-term debt based on the balance sheet in Table 7A.3 and 10 percent of the $100,000 interest bearing debt portion of current liabilities. Thus, 10 percent of $300,000 yields $30,000 interest expense throughout; and as reported, net income before income taxes is therefore $170,000. Assuming an effective tax rate of 40 percent, the provision for income taxes is $68,000. The income from operations is therefore $102,000.

Now we consider the next column, which makes an adjustment for general inflation. Since inventory costs, which are assumed to be fully absorbed by the cost of goods sold, have increased by $60,000, and since depreciation expense has increased by $100,000, the net operating income is reduced by $160,000 and becomes $40,000. With the same interest expense of $30,000, net income before income taxes is $10,000. However, the income tax laws do not take these cost adjustments into account, so the provision for income taxes remains at $68,000. Thus, the loss from operations taking the price level adjustments into account is $58,000.

We then go to the final column of Table 7A.2. Inventory costs are increased by another $40,000 to represent the effects of changes in specific prices. Thus the cost of goods sold becomes $1,700,000. Depreciation expense is 10 percent of the gross fixed assets of $2,800,000, or $280,000. Net operating income is therefore a negative $80,000. Adding interest expense to this loss gives a net income before income taxes of a negative $110,000. The provision for income tax still remains at $68,000. Hence the loss from operations is $178,000.

Some offsetting inflation effects are then taken into account. First, we analyze the gain from the decline in the purchasing power of the net amounts owed. The calculations are shown in Table 7A.4. The $48,000 figure obtained in Table 7A.4 corresponds to Line 10 in Table 7A.2, which is the gain from the decline in purchasing power of the net amounts owed.

Table 7A.4

Analysis of Gains or Losses from Net Monetary Position

Monetary liabilities	$540,000
Monetary assets	300,000
Net monetary debtor position	240,000
Price index, year end / Price index, beginning of year	1.20
Net debt in year-end $	288,000
Gain from net debt position	48,000

Source: Adapted from Schedule B of FASB Statement No. 33, September 1979, p. 74. Copyright by the Financial Accounting Standards Board, High Ridge Park, Stamford, Connecticut 06905 U.S.A.

We next consider the gain from the rise in specific prices over the effect of the increase in the general price level. The total gain in inventory value is $100,000. The rise in inventory value from the general price level effect was $60,000, so the specific gain is $40,000. It is assumed that in the particular year just passed, the gain in the specific value of fixed plant was $200,000. However, the rise in the fixed plant value because of the general price level effects is assumed to be $90,000, so the gain is only $110,000. Hence the total excess of the increase in specific prices over the increase in the general price level for real assets is $150,000.

A number of these changes and their interrelationships are summarized in Table 7A.5. The new income statement begins with the loss from operations of $178,000. Since the provision for income tax is $68,000, the adjusted pre-tax loss is $110,000. This is the same as the amount on Line 7 of Table 7A.2, in the final column of the table. We next take into account the $48,000 gain from the decline in the purchasing power of the debt obligations plus the gain of $150,000 represented by the increase in the values of specific prices of assets over the increase in the general price level. The readjusted pre-tax income, therefore, becomes a positive $88,000. With provision for income tax at 40 percent, income taxes are $35,200. Hence adjusted net income after taxes is $52,800.

Table 7A.5

Illustrative Adjusted Income from Operations and Related Adjusted Tax Collections

1. Income (loss) from operations	(178,000)
2. Add: Provision for income taxes	68,000
3. Adjusted pre-tax income	(110,000)
4. Gain from decline in purchasing power of debt obligations	48,000
5. Increase in values of specific prices of assets over the increase in the general price level	150,000
6. Readjusted pre-tax income	88,000
7. Provision for income taxes at 40%	35,200[a]
8. Adjusted net income after taxes	$ 52,800

a. Actual provision required is $68,000, so adjusted net income after actual taxes is $88,000 − $68,000 = $20,000.

Source: Adapted from Schedule B of FASB Statement No. 33, September 1979. Copyright by the Financial Accounting Standards Board, High Ridge Park, Stamford, Connecticut 06905 U.S.A.

We can now survey the effects of the numerous adjustments on the reported income position of the firm. The firm initially reported an after-tax income of $102,000. The adjustments we made were to increase the cost of goods sold by the higher values of inventories and to increase the depreciation expense based on the higher current values of gross fixed assets. These represent cost increases and reduce reported income after taxes. Offsetting the increases in costs are two gains from balance sheet effects. One is the gain from the net monetary debtor position of the firm during the period of rising prices. The other is the increase in the current values of real assets represented by inventories and fixed plant. The amounts we have illustrated for these two items total $150,000.

In Table 7A.5 we show that if income taxes had been based on the price adjusted net income figure, which is $88,000, income taxes would have been $35,200 instead of $68,000. The adjusted net income after taxes would then have been about $52,800 rather than $20,000 when provision was made for payment of income taxes of $68,000. It has been suggested that one of the benefits of firms' making full price-level adjustments to report their "true" income is that the income tax laws might in time reflect these new accounting procedures. If the income tax laws were based on price-level-adjusted income, and if the effect of the adjustments were to reduce reported income, there would be a reduction in taxes that are otherwise based on lower historical costs and higher reported profits. Lower taxes would increase the net cash flow of the firm.

But changes in reported profits alone do not affect actual cash flows so long as the accounting changes do not affect other company actions, such as production and pricing decisions. To the extent that income taxes are reduced as shown by this illustration from $68,000 to $35,200, there is a substantial improvement in the actual cash flow position of the firm. The impact on the firm's real cash flow position is one of the major forces making for a movement toward more realistic presentation of income from operations during a period of general inflation and sharp changes in the prices of specific assets.

The nature of the five-year comparison data required by FASB Statement No. 33 is shown by Table 7A.6, which duplicates Schedule C of FASB Statement No. 33 (p. 34). Income (loss) from continuing operations is calculated by adjusting for both general inflation and current cost information. Furthermore, all data are expressed in average 1980 dollars, from which we infer that the average Consumer Price Index for 1980 is divided into the figures for 1976 through 1979. The two gains from balance sheet adjustments—(1) the excess of the increase in specific prices over the increase in the general price level and (2) the gain from the decline in purchasing power of net amounts owed—are also presented. Cash dividends per share and market price per share are presented after they are deflated by the 1980 price index. FASB Statement No. 33 does not provide information on how the schedules are developed. They are presented simply to illustrate the format that may be used to disclose the information required.

An illustration of the presentation of the impact of inflation before the FASB Statement No. 33 requirement is provided by the General Motors Annual Report for 1978. Table 7A.7 presents material based on GM's data in its Annual Report (page 18). We added the Consumer Price Index figures taken from *Economic Indicators,* December 1979 (p. 23). We also converted the Consumer Price Index from a 1967 base to a 1973 base by dividing through by the 1973 index of 133.1 percent. For example, the 1978 value of 195.4 on the 1967 base becomes 146.8 on the 1973 base. When the 1978 earnings per share of $12.24 are divided by the 146.8 percent, we obtain the $8.34 shown in Table 7A.7.

The GM figures in Table 7A.7 do not make adjustments for either general purchasing power or prices of specific assets in calculating the net income figures. The GM data use the net income measurements as conventionally calculated, and the report expresses them in 1973 dollars.

Table 7A.6

Five-Year Comparison of Selected Supplementary Financial Data Adjusted for Effects of Changing Prices (In Thousands of Average 1980 Dollars)

	Years Ended December 31				
	1976	1977	1978	1979	1980
Net sales and other operating revenues	$265,000	$235,000	$240,000	$237,063	$253,000
Historical cost information adjusted for general inflation					
Income (loss) from continuing operations				(2,761)	(2,514)
Income (loss) from continuing operations per common share				(1.91)	(1.68)
Net assets at year-end				55,518	57,733
Current cost information					
Income (loss) from continuing operations				(4,125)	(8,908)
Income (loss) from continuing operations per common share				(2.75)	(5.94)
Excess of increase in specific prices over increase in the general price level				2,292	5,649
Net assets at year-end				79,996	81,466
Gain from decline in purchasing power of net amounts owed				7,027	7,729
Cash dividends declared per common share	$ 2.59	$ 2.43	$ 2.26	$ 2.16	$ 2.00
Market price per common share at year-end	$ 32	$ 31	$ 43	$ 39	$ 35
Average Consumer Price Index	170.5	181.5	195.4	205.0	220.9

Source: Adapted from Schedule C of FASB Statement No. 33, September 1979, p. 34. Copyright by the Financial Accounting Standards Board, High Ridge Park, Stamford, Connecticut 06905 U.S.A. Reprinted with permission. Copies of the complete document are available from the FASB. This reprint does not include the appendixes to FASB Statement No. 33. These appendixes are an integral part of the document.

The adjustments are relatively modest; yet they convey important information. Sales as reported increased by 77 percent between 1973 and 1978. In constant dollars, however, they increased by only 20 percent. Net income as reported increased by 46 percent over the five-year period. Expressed in constant 1973 dollars, however, it declined by $7.3 million. Earnings per share in 1978 were unchanged from 1973 earnings per share when expressed in constant dollars. Since sales in constant dollars increased by 20 percent while net income remained flat, the profit margin measured by net income to sales declined from 6.7 percent in 1973 to 5.5 percent in 1978.

Table 7A.7

General Price Level Adjustment for Inflation ($ in Millions Except per Share Amounts)

	1978	1977	1976	1975	1974	Base Year 1973
Sales, as reported	$63,221.1	$54,961.3	$47,181.0	$35,724.9	$31,549.5	$35,798.3
Percent increase (decrease) over 1973	77%	54%	32%	0%	(12%)	—
Sales in constant dollars[a]	43,086.2	40,305.0	36,831.6	29,497.4	28,430.9	35,798.3
Percent increase (decrease) over 1973	20%	13%	3%	(18%)	(21%)	—
Net income, as reported	3,508.0	3,337.5	2,902.8	1,253.1	950.1	2,398.1
Percent increase (decrease) over 1973	46%	39%	21%	(48%)	(60%)	—
Net income in constant dollars[a]	2,390.8	2,447.5	2,266.1	1,034.7	856.2	2,398.1
Percent increase (decrease) over 1973	0%	2%	(6%)	(57%)	(64%)	—
Profit margin, as reported	5.5%	6.1%	6.2%	3.5%	3.0%	6.7%
Earnings per share—($ per share)						
As reported	12.24	11.62	10.08	4.32	3.27	8.34
Constant dollars[a]	8.34	8.51	7.86	3.56	2.95	8.34
Consumer Price Index (1967 = 100)	195.4	181.5	170.5	161.2	147.7	133.1
Consumer Price Index (1973 = 100)	146.8	136.4	128.1	121.1	111.0	100.0

a. Adjustment to constant dollar basis has been determined by applying the Consumer Price Index to the data for 1974 through 1978 with 1973 as the base year.
Source: General Motors Annual Report, 1978, p. 18.

Thus the mere expression of sales, net income, and earnings per share in constant dollars after deflating by some base year price index provides additional information. The adjustments called for by FASB Statement No. 33 will provide further understanding of business performance during a period of a continued high rate of inflation.

Selected References

Agrawal, Surendra P.; Hallbauer, Rosalie C.; and Perritt, Gerald W. "Measurement of the Current Cost of Equivalent Productive Capacity." *Journal of Accounting, Auditing and Finance* 3 (Winter 1980), pp. 163–173.

Brinkman, Donald R., and Prentiss, Paul H. "Replacement Cost and Current-Value Measurement: How to Do It." *Financial Executive* 43 (October 1975), pp. 20–26.

Davidson, S., and Weil, R. L. "Replacement Cost Disclosure." *Financial Analysts' Journal* 32 (March–April 1976), pp. 57–66.

———. "Inflation Accounting and 1974 Earnings." *Financial Analysts' Journal* 31 (September–October 1975), pp. 42–54.

———. "Predicting Inflation-Adjusted Results." *Financial Analysts' Journal* 31 (January–February 1975), pp. 27–31.

Dhavale, Dileep G., and Wilson, Hoyt G. "Breakeven Analysis with Inflationary Cost and Prices." *Engineering Economist* 25 (Winter 1980), pp. 107–122.

Financial Accounting Standards Board. *Illustrations of Financial Reporting and Changing Prices: Statement of Financial Accounting Standards No. 33.* Stamford, Conn.: Financial Accounting Standards Board, December 1979.

———. *Statement of Financial Accounting Standards No. 33: Financial Reporting and Changing Prices.* Stamford, Conn.: Financial Accounting Standards Board, September 1979.

———. *Summary Statement of Financial Accounting Standards No. 33: Financial Reporting and Changing Prices.* Stamford, Conn.: Financial Accounting Standards Board, September 1979.

Hong, Hai. "Inflationary Tax Effects on the Assets of Business Corporations." *Financial Management* 6 (Fall 1977), pp. 51–59.

Ovadia, Arie, and Ronen, Joshua. "General Price-Level Adjustment and Replacement Cost Accounting as Special Cases of the Index Number Problem." *Journal of Accounting, Auditing and Finance* 3 (Winter 1980), pp. 113–137.

Runser, Robert J. "Opinion: The Conceptual Framework and Inflation Accounting." *Financial Executive* 47 (April 1979), pp. 30–40.

Weston, J. Fred, and Goudzwaard, Maurice B. "Financial Policies in an Inflationary Environment." In *The Treasurer's Handbook.* Edited by J. Fred Weston and Maurice B. Goudzwaard. Homewood, Ill.: Dow Jones–Irwin, 1976, pp. 20–42.

Appendix B to Chapter 7

Discriminant Analysis and Financial Ratios

Financial ratios give an indication of the financial strength of a company. The limitations of ratio analysis arise from the fact that the methodology is basically univariate; that is, each ratio is examined in isolation. The combined effects of several ratios are based solely on the judgment of the financial analyst. Therefore, to overcome these shortcomings of ratio analysis, it is necessary to combine different ratios into a meaningful predictive model. Two statistical techniques—regression analysis and discriminant analysis—have been used for this purpose. *Regression analysis* uses past data to predict future values of a dependent variable, while *discriminant analysis* results in an index that allows classification of an observation into one of several a priori groupings. Edward I. Altman has applied discriminant analysis in predicting bankruptcy. The purpose of this appendix is to give the reader a brief description of discriminant analysis and its applications.

Classification of Observations by Discriminant Analysis

The general problem of classification arises when an analyst has certain characteristics of an observation and wishes to classify that observation into one of several predetermined categories on the basis of the characteristics. For example, a financial analyst has on hand various financial ratios of an enterprise and wishes to use these ratios to classify the firm as either bankrupt or nonbankrupt. Discriminant analysis is a statistical technique that allows such classification.

Basically, discriminant analysis consists of three steps:

1. *Establishing mutually exclusive group classifications.* Each group is distinguished by a probability distribution of the characteristics.
2. *Collecting data for each of the groups.*
3. *Deriving linear combinations of the characteristics that* best *discriminate between the groups.* By *best,* we mean those discriminations that minimize the probability of misclassification.

For simplicity, let us consider the case in which two variables X_1, X_2 are used to discriminate between two groups of individuals—B and NB. For example, we use the working capital to total assets ratio (X_1) and the earnings before interest and taxes to total assets ratio (X_2) to classify firms into bankrupt and nonbankrupt groups. Let

$$Z = V_1X_1 + V_2X_2 \tag{7B.1}$$

be a linear combination of X_1 and X_2. The problem is to determine the values of V_1 and V_2 by means of past data and some criterion that makes Z useful as an index for discriminating among members of the two groups. In terms of probability distributions, the means for X_1 and X_2 are different, but their standard deviations may be so large that there is a region of overlap, also called the zone of ignorance, as shown in Figure 7B.1. Observations in this region of overlap are classified with a greater likelihood of error.

The results of classification are shown in the form of a classification matrix:

Actual Group Membership	Predicted Group Membership: B	Predicted Group Membership: NB
B	C_1	I_1
NB	I_2	C_2

The actual group membership is equivalent to the *a priori* groups, and the model attempts to classify the individuals correctly. The C and I stand for correct and incorrect classifications, respectively. If the model were a perfect predictor, then $I_1 = I_2 = 0$.

It is clear that we should try to minimize the number of misclassifications. We seek to separate the values of Z for the two groups as widely as possible

Figure 7B.1

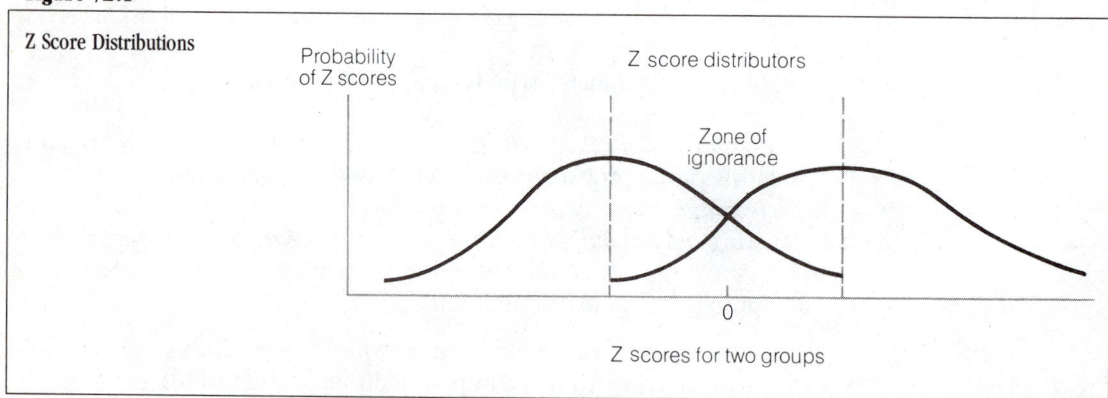

Z Score Distributions

relative to the variations of Z within the groups. We seek values of V_1, V_2 that maximize the function

$$G = \frac{(\overline{Z}_1 - \overline{Z}_2)^2}{\sum_{i=1}^{2} \sum_{j=1}^{n_i} (Z_{ij} - \overline{Z}_i)^2} \tag{7B.2}$$

where the numerator represents the separation of two groups and the denominator is a measure of the variation of Z within the groups. Z_{ij} is the Z value of the jth individual in the ith group ($i = 1, 2$); n_i is the number of individuals in Group i ($i = 1, 2$); and $\overline{Z}_i$ is the mean of the Z values in Group i ($i = 1, 2$).

By partial differentiation, we find that the values of V_1 and V_2 can be determined by the following linear equations:

$$V_1 S_{11} + V_2 S_{12} = d_1 \tag{7B.3}$$
$$V_1 S_{21} + V_2 S_{22} = d_2 \tag{7B.4}$$

where

$$S_{pq} = \sum_{i=1}^{2} \sum_{j=1}^{n_i} (X_{pij} - \overline{X}_{pi})(X_{qij} - \overline{X}_{qi})$$

$$d_p = \overline{X}_{p1} - \overline{X}_{p2}$$
$$p = 1, 2$$
$$q = 1, 2$$

and

n_i = Number of members of Group i, $(1, 2, \ldots, n)$
X_{pij} = Value of X_p for the jth member of Group i
$\overline{X}_{pi}$ = Mean value of X_p for the n_i members of Group i

There is no unique set of V's maximizing G, and any multiple of a set of V's satisfying the pair of linear equations will do equally well. This is because the two sets of Z's would merely be multiplied by this constant factor and would therefore be equivalent as far as discriminating between the two groups.[1]

An Illustration of Discriminant Analysis

As an illustration, let us apply the above analysis to a hypothetical sample of 20 firms, of which 10 went bankrupt and the other 10 did not. The two variables used to characterize the firms are the working capital to total assets ratio (X_1) and the EBIT to total assets ratio (X_2). The data are presented in Table 7B.1.

1. Paul G. Hoel, *Introduction to Mathematical Statistics*, 3d ed. (New York: Wiley, 1954), p. 183.

Table 7B.1

Data and Calculations for Two Groups of Firms[a]

Group 1: Bankrupt Firms

Number	X_{11j} (1)	X_{21j} (2)	$(X_{11j} - \overline{X}_{11})$ (3)	$(X_{11j} - \overline{X}_{11})^2$ (4)	$(X_{21j} - \overline{X}_{21})$ (5)	$(X_{21j} - \overline{X}_{21})^2$ (6)	$(X_{11j} - \overline{X}_{11})(X_{21j} - \overline{X}_{21})$ (7)	Z Score (8)
1	−30	−40	−18.4	338.56	−18	324	331.2	−122.79
2	−26	−36	−14.4	207.36	−14	196	201.6	−109.51
3	−22	−32	−10.4	108.16	−10	100	104.0	−96.23
4	−18	−28	−6.4	40.96	−6	36	38.4	−92.95
5	−14	−24	−2.4	5.76	−2	4	4.8	−69.67
6	−10	−20	1.6	2.56	2	4	3.2	−56.39
7	−6	−16	5.6	31.36	6	36	33.6	−43.12
8	−2	−12	9.6	92.16	10	100	96.0	−29.84
9	4	−8	15.6	243.36	14	196	218.4	−14.56
10	8	−4	19.6	384.16	18	324	352.8	−1.28
	−116 $= \sum X_{11j}$	−220 $= \sum X_{21j}$		1,454.4 $= \sum (X_{11j} - \overline{X}_{11})^2$		1,320 $= \sum (X_{21j} - \overline{X}_{21})^2$	1,384.0 $= \sum (X_{11j} - \overline{X}_{11})(X_{21j} - \overline{X}_{21})$	

$\overline{X}_{11} = -11.6.$

$\overline{X}_{21} = -22.$

Table 7B.1 (continued)

Group 2: Nonbankrupt Firms

Number	X_{12j} (1)	X_{22j} (2)	$(X_{12j} - \overline{X}_{12})$ (3)	$(X_{12j} - \overline{X}_{12})^2$ (4)	$(X_{22j} - \overline{X}_{22})$ (5)	$(X_{22j} - \overline{X}_{22})^2$ (6)	$(X_{12j} - \overline{X}_{12})(X_{22j} - \overline{X}_{22})$ (7)	Z Score (8)
11	20	10	−18	324	−4.5	20.25	81	43.20
12	24	11	−14	196	−3.5	12.25	49	49.52
13	28	12	−10	100	−2.5	6.25	25	55.84
14	32	13	−6	36	−1.5	2.25	9	62.16
15	36	14	−2	4	−0.5	0.25	1	68.48
16	40	15	−2	4	0.5	0.25	1	74.80
17	44	16	6	36	1.5	2.25	9	81.12
18	48	17	10	100	2.5	6.25	25	87.43
19	52	18	14	196	3.5	12.25	49	93.75
20	56	19	18	324	4.5	20.25	81	100.07
	380 $= \sum X_{12j}$	145 $= \sum X_{22j}$		1,320 $= \sum (X_{12j} - \overline{X}_{12})^2$		82.50 $= \sum (X_{22j} - \overline{X}_{22})^2$	330 $= \sum (X_{12j} - \overline{X}_{12})(X_{22j} - \overline{X}_{22})$	

$\overline{X}_{12} = 38.$

$\overline{X}_{22} = 14.5.$

a. X_{11j} refers to the value of the first variable (WC/TA) for Firm J in Group 1, the bankrupt firm group (recall that $j = 1, 2, \ldots 10$). X_{21j} refers to the value of the second variable (EBIT/TA) in Group 1. X_{12j} refers to the value of the first variable (WC/TA) for Firm J in Group 2, the nonbankrupt firm group. X_{22j} refers to the value of the second variable (EBIT/TA) in Group 2.

$\overline{X}_{11}$ is the mean value of the first variable for all the firms in Group 1.

$\overline{X}_{21}$ is the mean value of the second variable for all the firms in Group 1.

$\overline{X}_{12}$ is the mean value of the first variable for all the firms in Group 2.

$\overline{X}_{22}$ is the mean value of the second variable for all the firms in Group 2.

$(X_{11j} - \overline{X}_{11})^2$ is the squared deviations from the mean for the first variable for the firms in Group 1.

$(X_{21j} - \overline{X}_{21})^2$ is the squared deviations from the mean for the second variable for the firms in Group 1.

$(X_{11j} - \overline{X}_{11})(X_{21j} - \overline{X}_{21})$ is the product of the deviations from the mean for the first and second variables of the firms in Group 1.

$(X_{12j} - \overline{X}_{12})^2$ is the squared deviations from the mean for the first variable for the firms in Group 2.

$(X_{22j} - \overline{X}_{22})^2$ is the squared deviations from the mean for the second variable for the firms in Group 2.

$(X_{12j} - \overline{X}_{12})(X_{22j} - \overline{X}_{22})$ is the product of the deviations from the mean for the first and second variables of the firms in Group 2.

From the data in Table 7B.1 we make the following calculations needed to obtain the V's.

For Group 1

$$\bar{X}_{11} = \frac{\sum_{j=1}^{10} X_{11j}}{10} = \frac{-116}{10} = -11.6.$$

$$\bar{X}_{21} = \frac{\sum_{j=1}^{10} X_{21j}}{10} = \frac{-220}{10} = -22.$$

$$\sum_{j=1}^{10} (X_{11j} - \bar{X}_{11})^2 = 1{,}454.4.$$

$$\sum_{j=1}^{10} (X_{21j} - \bar{X}_{21})^2 = 1{,}320.$$

$$\sum_{j=1}^{10} (X_{11j} - \bar{X}_{11})(\bar{X}_{21j} - \bar{X}_{21}) = 1{,}384.$$

For Group 2

$$\bar{X}_{12} = \frac{\sum_{j=1}^{10} X_{12j}}{10} = \frac{380}{10} = 38.$$

$$\bar{X}_{22} = \frac{\sum_{j=1}^{10} X_{22j}}{10} = \frac{145}{10} = 14.5.$$

$$\sum_{j=1}^{10} (X_{12j} - \bar{X}_{12})^2 = 1{,}320.$$

$$\sum_{j=1}^{10} (X_{22j} - \bar{X}_{22})^2 = 82.5.$$

$$\sum_{j=1}^{10} (X_{12j} - \bar{X}_{12})(X_{22j} - \bar{X}_{22}) = 330.$$

We use the above results to obtain the S's and d's needed to solve for the V's.

$$S_{11} = \sum(X_{11j} - \bar{X}_{11})^2 + \sum(X_{12j} - \bar{X}_{12})^2 = 1{,}454.4 + 1{,}320 = 2{,}774.4.$$

$$S_{12} = \sum(X_{11j} - \bar{X}_{11})(X_{21j} - \bar{X}_{21}) + \sum(X_{12j} - \bar{X}_{12})(X_{22j} - \bar{X}_{22}) = 1{,}384 + 330 = 1{,}714.$$

$$S_{21} = \sum(X_{21j} - \bar{X}_{21})(X_{11j} - \bar{X}_{11}) + \sum(X_{22j} - \bar{X}_{22})(X_{12j} - \bar{X}_{12}) = S_{12} = 1{,}714.$$

$$S_{22} = \sum(X_{21j} - \overline{X}_{21})^2 + \sum(X_{22j} - \overline{X}_{22})^2 = 1{,}320 + 82.5 = 1{,}402.5.$$
$$d_1 = \overline{X}_{11} - \overline{X}_{12} = -11.6 - 38 = -49.6.$$
$$d_2 = \overline{X}_{21} - \overline{X}_{22} = -22 - 14.5 = -\ 36.5.$$

The values of V_1 and V_2 are given by the solutions of:

$$V_1 S_{11} + V_2 S_{12} = d_1 \tag{7B.3}$$

and

$$V_1 S_{21} + V_2 S_{22} = d_2. \tag{7B.4}$$

Inserting our calculations,

$$2{,}774.4\ V_1 + 1{,}714\ V_2 = -49.6 \tag{7B.3a}$$

and

$$1{,}714\ V_1 + 1{,}402.5\ V_2 = -36.5. \tag{7B.4a}$$

Therefore, $V_1 = -0.00735$, $V_2 = -.01705$, and $Z = -0.00735X_1 - 0.01705X_2$.

For the purpose of computing values of Z, it is convenient to have either V_1 or V_2 be equal to 1.[2] It seems more natural for the bankrupt firms to have negative values. So we divide the above equation by the V_1 value of -0.00735. This gives us Equation 7B.5:

$$Z = X_1 + 2.3197X_2. \tag{7B.5}$$

We next use the discriminant function in Equation 7B.5 with the data for X_1 and X_2 for Groups 1 and 2 in Table 7B.1 to calculate the Z values in column 8 of the table. We can then plot the Z value results to see the relationships visually as shown in Figure 7B.2.

Figure 7B.2

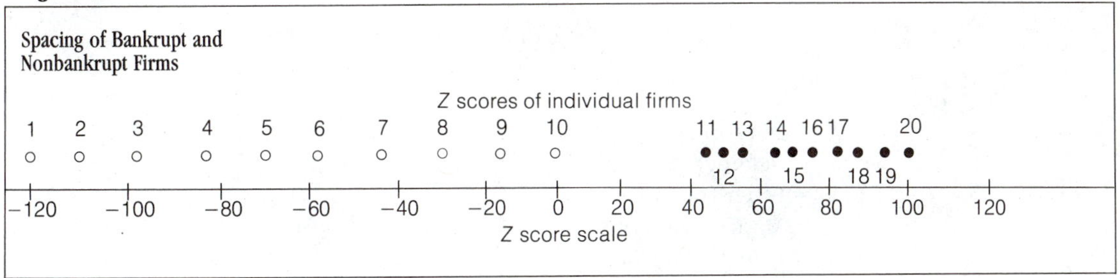

○ = Bankrupt firms
● = Nonbankrupt firms.

Firms with negative Z values are classified as bankrupts, while those with positive Z values are nonbankrupts. The classification matrix for this model is:

2. Ibid., p. 184.

Actual Group Membership	Predicted Group Membership	
	Bankrupt	Nonbankrupt
Bankrupt	10	0
Nonbankrupt	0	10

For this hypothetical example, the model classifies the two groups perfectly. We see that the two groups of firms are completely separated by the magnitudes of the Z values of their members. In practice, some of the Z values of bankrupt firms may be positive, just as some of the Z values of nonbankrupt firms may be negative. In that case, some misclassifications may occur, and we should choose a cutoff value of Z (other than zero) such that the possibility of misclassification is minimized. For this particular sample, instead of zero, we may select the cutoff value, Z_c, to be the mean value of the Z values of Firms 10 and 11. In that case,

$$Z_c = 1/2(43.20 - 1.28) = 20.96.$$

Using the cutoff value, we could infer that any firm outside the original sample is a potential bankrupt if $Z < 20.96$ and a potential nonbankrupt if $Z > 20.96$.

Altman's Applications of Discriminant Analysis

In 1968 Altman used discriminant analysis to establish a model for predicting bankruptcy of firms. His sample was composed of sixty-six manufacturing firms, half of which went bankrupt. From their financial statements (one period prior to bankruptcy for the bankrupt firms), Altman obtained twenty-two financial ratios, five of which were found to contribute most to the prediction model. The discriminant function Z was found to be

$$Z = 0.012\,X_1 + 0.014\,X_2 + 0.033\,X_3 + 0.006\,X_4 + 0.999\,X_5$$

where

X_1 = Working capital/Total assets (in percent)
X_2 = Retained earnings/Total assets (in percent)
X_3 = EBIT/Total assets (in percent)
X_4 = Market value of equity/Book value of debt (in percent)
X_5 = Sales/Total assets (times)

We illustrate in Table 7B.2 how this discriminant function can be used by applying it to the group means reported by Altman for his groups of bankrupt and nonbankrupt firms. The resulting Z values are as follows:

	X_1	X_2	X_3	X_4	X_5	Z
Z_{br} =	− 0.0732	− 0.8764	− 1.0494	+ 0.2406	+ 1.4985	= − 0.2599.
Z_{nbr} =	+ 0.4968	+ 0.4970	+ 0.5082	+ 1.4862	+ 1.8981	= +4.8863.

Table 7B.2

Group Means for Bankrupt and Nonbankrupt Firms

	Bankrupt	Nonbankrupt
X_1	−6.1%	41.4%
X_2	−62.6%	35.5%
X_3	−31.8%	15.4%
X_4	40.1%	247.7%
X_5	1.5*X*	1.9*X*

Source: Reprinted by permission of the publisher from *Corporate Bankruptcy in America* by Edward I. Altman (Lexington, Mass.: Lexington Books, D. C. Heath and Company, copyright 1971, D. C. Heath and Company).

The largest contributor to group separation of the discriminant function was found to be the profitability ratio X_3, followed by X_5, X_4, X_2, and X_1 in descending order. The model correctly classifies 95 percent of the total sample, with the following accuracy matrix:

	Predicted Group Membership	
Actual Group Membership	Bankrupt	Nonbankrupt
Bankrupt	31	2
Nonbankrupt	1	32

The zone of ignorance—that is, the range of Z values where misclassifications can be observed—lies between 1.81 and 2.67. To establish a guideline for classifying firms in this zone, a cutoff value for Z is chosen: 2.675, the midpoint in the range of values of Z that results in minimal misclassifications. Thus a firm with a Z score of greater than 2.675 is classified as a nonbankrupt firm, while a score of less than 2.675 classifies the firm as bankrupt.

By applying the above discriminant function to data obtained two to five years prior to bankruptcy, Altman found that the model correctly classified 72 percent of the initial sample two years prior to failure. A trend analysis shows that all five observed ratios, $X_1, \ldots, X_5$, deteriorated as bankruptcy approached and that the most serious change in the majority of these ratios occurred between the third and second years prior to failure.

In 1977, Altman, along with R. G. Haldeman and P. Narayanan, constructed a new bankruptcy classification model, the ZETA model, based on discriminant analysis. This model differs from the earlier one in two major aspects. First, the sample is a larger one that includes not only manufacturing firms but also retailers. Second, the basic data of the sample are adjusted to take into consideration several accounting modifications, such as the capitalization of leases, reserves, minority interests, and other liabilities on the balance sheet, captive finance companies and other nonconsolidated subsidiaries, goodwill and intangibles, capitalized research and development costs, capitalized interest, and certain other deferred charges.

From an initial list of twenty-seven variables, the authors selected seven variables that best classify the sample firms:

X_1 = EBIT/Total assets

X_2 = Normalized standard error of estimate of EBIT/Total assets

X_3 = Log (EBIT/Total interest payments)

X_4 = Retained earnings/Total assets

X_5 = Current ratio

X_6 = Common equity/Total capital (Common equity is measured by a five-year average of the market value)

X_7 = Total assets

The most important contributor to the discriminating power of the model was found to be X_4, the cumulative profitability ratio; and the least important was X_1. This is a major departure from the earlier model, in which X_4 and X_1 ranked fourth and first respectively out of five variables considered.

For proprietary reasons, the discriminant function Z of the ZETA model is not given. However, a distribution of Z values shows that the overlap area is relatively small—from -1.45 to 0.87. By specifying the costs of misclassifications, the authors arrived at several cutoff values of Z, ranging from -2.11 to 1.43.

We have so far discussed the role of discriminant analysis only in the context of bankruptcy prediction. Other uses of the discriminant model can be made. First, since the model contains many of the variables common to business loan evaluation, it may serve, in conjunction with other considerations, as a useful tool in credit evaluation. For example, if the Z value of a firm is over 3 (using the 1968 model), then perhaps less time and effort need be spent on investigating the loan applicant. Second, by applying the discriminant model periodically to a firm, analysts may be able to predict corporate problems early enough that management can take corrective measures to avoid failure. From this point of view, the model is a potentially useful internal control method.

Selected References

Altman, Edward I. "Examining Moyer's Re-examination of Forecasting Financial Failure." *Financial Management* 7 (Winter 1978), pp. 76–79.

———. "Financial Ratios, Discriminant Analysis and the Prediction of Corporate Bankruptcy." *Journal of Finance* 23 (September 1968), pp. 589–609.

Altman, Edward I., and Eisenbeis, Robert A. "Financial Applications of Discriminant Analysis: A Clarification." *Journal of Financial and Quantitative Analysis* 13 (March 1978), pp. 185–195.

Altman, Edward I.; Haldeman, Robert; and Narayanan, P. "ZETA Analysis: A New Model for Identifying Bankruptcy Risk." *Journal of Banking and Finance* 1 (June 1977), pp. 29–54.

Eisenbeis, Robert A. "Pitfalls in the Application of Discriminant Analysis in Business, Finance, and Economics." *Journal of Finance* 32 (June 1977), pp. 875–900.

Eisenbeis, Robert A., and Avery, Robert B. *Discriminant Analysis and Classification Procedures: Theory and Applications.* Lexington, Mass.: D. C. Heath, 1972.

Johnson, Craig C. "Ratio Analysis and the Prediction of Firm Failure." *Journal of Finance* 25 (December 1970), pp. 1116–1168. (See also Edward I. Altman, "Reply," pp. 1169–1172.)

Joy, O. Maurice, and Tollefson, John O. "On the Financial Applications of Discriminant Analysis." *Journal of Financial and Quantitative Analysis* 10 (December 1975), pp. 723–739.

Lachenbruch, Peter A. *Discriminant Analysis.* New York: Hafer Press, 1972.

Moyer, R. Charles. "Forecasting Financial Failure: A Re-examination." *Financial Management* 6 (Spring 1977), pp. 11–17.

———. "Reply to 'Examining Moyer's Re-examination of Forecasting Failure.'" *Financial Management* 7 (Winter 1978), pp. 80–81.

Perreault, William D.; Behrman, Douglas N.; and Armstrong, Gary M. "Alternative Approaches for Interpretation of Multiple Discriminant Analysis in Marketing Research." *Journal of Business Research* 7, No. 2 (1979), pp. 151–173.

Scott, Elton. "On the Financial Application of Discriminant Analysis: Comment." *Journal of Financial and Quantitative Analysis* 13 (March 1978), pp. 201–205.

Terbough, George. "Inflation and Profits." *Financial Analysts' Journal* 30 (May–June 1974), pp. 19–23.

Tollefson, John O., and Joy, O. Maurice. "Some Clarifying Comments on Discriminant Analysis." *Journal of Financial and Quantitative Analysis* 13 (March 1978), pp. 197–200.

8
Financial Forecasting

The planning process is an integral part of the financial manager's job. As we shall see in subsequent chapters, long-term debt and equity funds are raised infrequently and in large amounts, primarily because the cost per dollar raised by selling such securities decreases as the size of the issue increases. Because of these considerations, it is important that the firm have a working estimate of its total needs for funds for the next few years. It is therefore useful to examine methods of forecasting the firm's needs for funds, and this is the subject of the present chapter.

Cash Flow Cycle

We must recognize that firms need assets to make sales; if sales are to be increased, assets must also be expanded. Growing firms require new investments—immediate investment in current assets and, as full capacity is reached, investment in fixed assets as well. New investments must be financed, and new financing carries with it commitments and obligations to service the capital obtained.[1] A growing, profitable firm is likely to require additional cash for investments in receivables, inventories, and fixed assets. Such a firm can, therefore, have a cash flow problem. The nature of this problem, as well as the cause and effect relationship between assets and sales, is illustrated in the following discussion, in which we trace the consequences of a series of transactions.

Effects on the Balance Sheet

1. Two partners invest a total of $50,000 to create the Glamour Galore Dress Company. The firm rents a plant; equipment and other fixed assets cost $30,000. The resulting financial situation is shown by Balance Sheet 1.

2. Glamour Galore receives an order to manufacture 10,000 dresses. The receipt of an order in itself has no effect on the balance sheet, but the preparation for the manufacturing activity often does. Say that the firm buys $20,000

1. *Servicing* capital refers to the payment of interest and principal on debt and to dividends on common stocks.

worth of cotton cloth on terms of net 30 days. Without additional investment by the owners, total assets increase by $20,000, financed by the trade accounts payable to the supplier of the cotton cloth.

After the purchase, the firm spends $20,000 on labor for cutting the cloth to the required pattern. Of the $20,000 total labor cost, $10,000 is paid in cash and $10,000 is owed in the form of accrued wages. These two transactions are reflected in Balance Sheet 2, which shows that total assets increase to $80,000. Current assets are increased; net working capital—total current assets minus total current liabilities—remains constant. The current ratio declines to 1.67, and the debt ratio rises to 38 percent. The financial position of the firm is weakening. If it should seek to borrow at this point, Glamour Ga-

Balance Sheet 1

Assets		Liabilities	
Current Assets		Capital stock	$50,000
Cash	$20,000		
Fixed Assets			
Plant and equipment	30,000		
Total assets	$50,000	Total liabilities and net worth	$50,000

Balance Sheet 2

Assets		Liabilities	
Current Assets		Accounts payable	$20,000
Cash	$10,000	Accrued wages payable	10,000
Inventories		Total current liabilities	$30,000
Work in process			
Materials	20,000	Capital stock	50,000
Labor	20,000		
Total current assets	$50,000		
Fixed Assets			
Plant and equipment	30,000		
Total assets	$80,000	Total liabilities and net worth	$80,000

Balance Sheet 3

Assets		Liabilities	
Current Assets		Accounts payable	$20,000
Cash	$ 5,000	Notes payable	15,000
Inventory		Accrued wages payable	10,000
Finished goods	60,000	Total current liabilities	$45,000
Total current assets	$65,000		
		Capital stock	50,000
Fixed Assets			
Plant and equipment	30,000		
Total assets	$95,000	Total liabilities and net worth	$95,000

lore could not use the work-in-process inventories as collateral, because a lender could find little use for partially manufactured dresses.

3. In order to complete the dresses, the firm incurs additional labor costs of $20,000 and pays in cash. It is assumed that the firm desires to maintain a minimum cash balance of $5,000. Since the initial cash balance is $10,000, Glamour Galore must borrow an additional $15,000 from its bank to meet the wage bill. The borrowing is reflected in notes payable in Balance Sheet 3. Total assets rise to $95,000, with a finished goods inventory of $60,000. The current ratio drops to 1.4, and the debt ratio rises to 47 percent. These ratios show a further weakening of the financial position.

4. Glamour Galore ships the dresses on the basis of the original order, invoicing the purchaser for $100,000 within 30 days. Accrued wages and accounts payable have to be paid now, so Glamour Galore must borrow an additional $30,000 in order to maintain the $5,000 minimum cash balance. These transactions are shown in Balance Sheet 4.

Balance Sheet 4

Assets		Liabilities	
Current Assets		Notes payable	$ 45,000
Cash	$ 5,000	Total current liabilities	$ 45,000
Accounts receivable	100,000	Capital stock	50,000
Total current assets	$105,000	Retained earnings	40,000
		Total net worth	$ 90,000
Fixed Assets			
Plant and equipment	30,000		
Total assets	$135,000	Total liabilities and net worth	$135,000

Note that in Balance Sheet 4, finished goods inventory is replaced by receivables, with the markup reflected as retained earnings. This causes the debt ratio to drop to 33 percent. Since the receivables are carried at the sales price, current assets increase to $105,000 and the current ratio rises to 2.3. Compared with the conditions reflected in Balance Sheet 3, most of the financial ratios show improvement. However, the absolute amount of debt is large.

Whether the firm's financial position is really improved depends upon the credit worthiness of the purchaser of the dresses. If the purchaser is a good credit risk, Glamour Galore may be able to borrow further on the basis of the accounts receivable.

5. The firm receives payment for the accounts receivable, pays off the bank loan, and is in the highly liquid position shown by Balance Sheet 5. If a new order for 10,000 dresses is received, it will have no effect on the balance sheet, but a cycle similar to the one we have been describing will begin.

Balance Sheet 5

Assets		Liabilities	
Current Assets		Capital stock	$50,000
Cash	$60,000	Retained earnings	40,000
Fixed Assets			
Plant and equipment	30,000		
Total assets	$90,000	Total liabilities and net worth	$90,000

6. The idea of the cash flow cycle can now be generalized. An order that requires the purchase of raw materials is placed with the firm. The purchase in turn generates an account payable. As labor is applied, work-in-process inventories build up. To the extent that wages are not fully paid at the time labor is used, accrued wages will appear on the liability side of the balance sheet. As goods are completed, they move into finished goods inventories. The cash needed to pay for the labor to complete the goods may make it necessary for the firm to borrow.

Finished goods inventories are sold, usually on credit, which gives rise to accounts receivable. As the firm has not received cash, this point in the cycle represents the peak in financing requirements. If the firm did not borrow at the time finished goods inventories were at their maximum, it may do so as inventories are converted into receivables by credit sales. Income taxes, which were not considered in the example, can add to the problem. As accounts receivable become cash, short-term obligations can be paid off.

Financing Patterns

The influence of sales on current asset levels has just been illustrated. Over the course of several cycles, the fluctuations in sales will be accompanied in most industries by a rising long-term trend. Figure 8.1 shows the consequences of such a pattern. Total permanent assets increase steadily in the form of current and fixed assets. Increases of this nature should be financed by long-term debt, by equity, or by "spontaneous" increases in liabilities, such as accrued taxes and wages and accounts payable, which naturally accompany increasing sales. However, temporary increases in assets can be covered by short-term liabilities. The distinction between temporary and permanent asset levels may be difficult to make in practice, but it is neither illusory nor unimportant. Short-term financing for the financing of long-term needs is dangerous. A profitable firm may become unable to meet its cash obligations if funds borrowed on a short-term basis have become tied up in permanent asset needs.

Figure 8.1

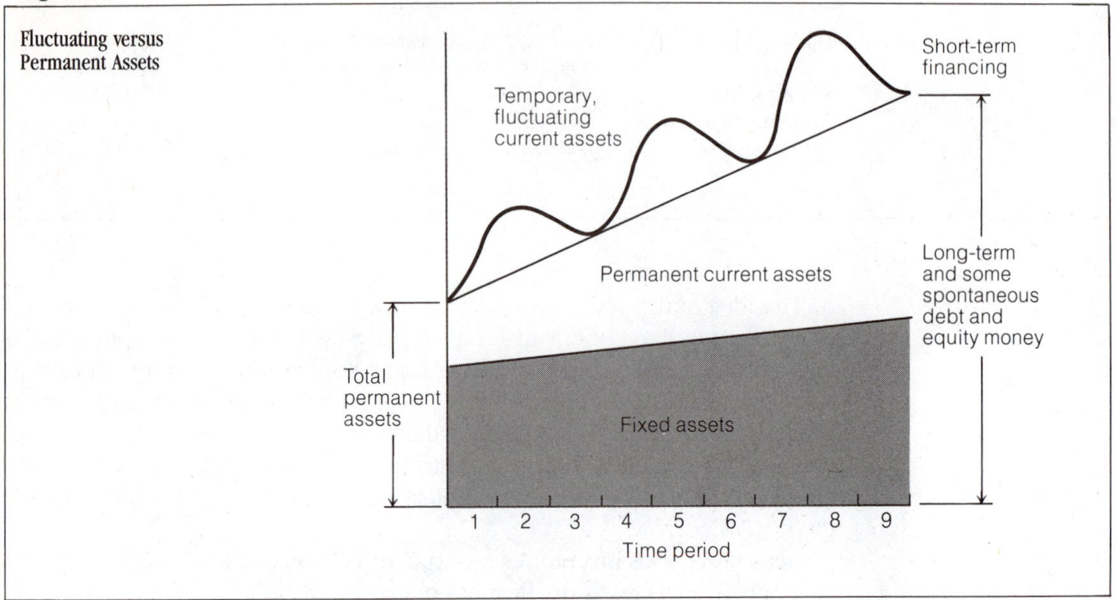

Fluctuating versus Permanent Assets

Percent of Sales Method

It is apparent from the preceding discussion that *the most important variable that influences a firm's financing requirements is its projected dollar volume of sales. A good sales forecast is an essential foundation for forecasting financial requirements.* In spite of its importance, we shall not go into sales forecasting here; rather, we simply assume that a sales forecast has been made, then estimate financial requirements on the basis of this forecast. The principal methods of forecasting financial requirements are described in this and the following sections.

The simplest approach to forecasting financial requirements expresses

Table 8.1

The Moore Company Balance Sheet as of December 31, 1980

Assets		Liabilities	
Cash	$ 10,000	Accounts payable	$ 50,000
Receivables	85,000	Accrued taxes and wages	25,000
Inventories	100,000	Mortgage bonds	70,000
Fixed assets (net)	150,000	Common stocks	100,000
		Retained earnings	100,000
Total assets	$345,000	Total liabilities and net worth	$345,000

the firm's needs in terms of the percentage of annual sales invested in each individual balance sheet item. As an example, consider the Moore Company, whose balance sheet as of December 31, 1980, is shown in Table 8.1. The company's sales are running at about $500,000 a year, which is its capacity limit; the profit margin after tax on sales is 4 percent. During 1980, the company earned $20,000 after taxes and paid out $10,000 in dividends, and it plans to continue paying out half of net profits as dividends. How much additional financing will be needed if sales expand to $800,000 during 1981? The calculating procedure, using the percent of sales method, is explained below.[2]

First, isolate those balance sheet items that can be expected to vary directly with sales. In the case of the Moore Company, this step applies to each category of assets—a higher level of sales necessitates more cash for transactions, more receivables, higher inventory levels, and additional fixed plant capacity. On the liability side, accounts payable as well as accruals may be expected to increase as sales do. Retained earnings will go up as long as the company is profitable and does not pay out 100 percent of earnings, but the percentage increase is not constant. However, neither common stock nor mortgage bonds will increase spontaneously with an increase in sales.

The items that can be expected to vary directly with sales are tabulated as a percentage of sales in Table 8.2. For every $1.00 increase in sales, assets must increase by $.69; this $.69 must be financed in some manner. Accounts payable will increase spontaneously with sales, as will accruals; these two items will supply $.15 of new funds for each $1.00 increase in sales. Subtract-

Table 8.2

The Moore Company Balance Sheet as of December 31, 1980

Assets (Percent)		Liabilities (Percent)	
Cash	2.0	Accounts payable	10.0
Receivables	17.0	Accrued taxes and wages	5.0
Inventories	20.0	Mortgage bonds[a]	—
Fixed assets (net)	30.0	Common stock[a]	—
		Retained earnings[a]	—
Total assets	69.0	Total liabilities and net worth	15.0
Assets as percent of sales			69.0
Less: Spontaneous increase in liabilities			15.0
Percent of each additional dollar of sales that must be financed			54.0

a. Not applicable.

2. We recognize, of course, that as a practical matter, business firms plan their needs in terms of specific items of equipment, square feet of floor space, and other factors, and not as a percentage of sales. However, the outside analyst does not have access to this information; even though the information on specific items is available, a manager needs to check forecasts in aggregate terms. The percent of sales method serves both these needs surprisingly well.

ing the 15 percent for spontaneously generated funds from the 69 percent funds requirement leaves 54 percent. Thus, for each \$1.00 increase in sales, the Moore Company must obtain \$.54 of financing either from internally generated funds or from external sources.

In the case at hand, sales are scheduled to increase from \$500,000 to \$800,000, or by \$300,000. Applying the 54 percent developed in the table to the expected increase in sales leads to the conclusion that \$162,000 will be needed.

Some of that need will be met by retained earnings. Total revenues during 1981 will be \$800,000; if the company earns 4 percent after taxes on this volume, profits will amount to \$32,000. Assuming that the 50 percent dividend payout ratio is maintained, dividends will be \$16,000 and \$16,000 will be retained. Subtracting the retained earnings from the \$162,000 that was needed leaves a figure of \$146,000—the amount of funds that must be obtained through borrowing or by selling new common stock.

This process may be expressed in equation form:

$$\text{External funds needed} = \frac{A}{TR}(\Delta TR) - \frac{B}{TR}(\Delta TR) - bm\,(TR_2). \quad \textbf{(8.1)}$$

Here

$\frac{A}{TR}$ = Assets that increase spontaneously with total revenues or sales as a percent of total revenues or sales

$\frac{B}{TR}$ = Those liabilities that increase spontaneously with total revenues or sales as a percent of total revenues or sales

ΔTR = Change in total revenues or sales

m = Profit margin on sales

TR_2 = Total revenues projected for the year

b = Earnings retention ratio

For the Moore Company, then,

$$\begin{aligned}\text{External funds needed} &= 0.69\,(\$300{,}000) - 0.15\,(\$300{,}000)\\ &\quad - 0.5\,(0.04)\,(\$800{,}000)\\ &= 0.54\,(\$300{,}000) - 0.02\,(\$800{,}000)\\ &= \$146{,}000.\end{aligned}$$

The \$146,000 found by the formula method must, of course, equal the amount derived previously.

Notice what would have occurred if the Moore Company's sales forecast for 1981 had been only \$515,000, or a 3 percent increase. Applying the formula, we find the external funds requirements as follows:

$$\begin{aligned}\text{External funds needed} &= 0.54\,(\$15{,}000) - 0.02\,(\$515{,}000)\\ &= \$8{,}100 - \$10{,}300\\ &= (\$2{,}200).\end{aligned}$$

In this case, no external funds are required. In fact, the company will have \$2,200 in excess of its requirements; it should therefore plan to increase dividends, retire debt, or seek additional investment opportunities. The example shows that while small percentage increases in sales can be financed through internally generated funds, larger percentage increases cause the firm to go into the market for outside capital. In other words, small rates of sales growth can be financed from internal sources, but higher rates of sales growth require external financing.[3]

Note that the sales level equals $(1 + g)TR_1$, where g equals the growth rate in sales. The increase in sales can therefore be written:

$$\Delta TR = (1 + g)TR_1 - TR_1 = TR_1(1 + g - 1) = gTR_1.$$

Let us next take the expression for external funds needed, Equation 8.1, and use it to derive the percentage of the increase in sales that will have to be financed externally (percentage of external funds required, or PEFR) as a function of the critical variables involved. In Equation 8.1 let $\left(\frac{A}{TR} - \frac{B}{TR}\right) = I$, substitute for ΔTR and TR_2, and divide both sides by $\Delta TR = gTR_1$.

$$PEFR = I - \frac{m}{g}(1 + g)b. \qquad \textbf{(8.2)}$$

Using Equation 8.2, we can now investigate the influence of factors such as an increased rate of inflation on the percentage of sales growth that must be financed externally. Based on the relationships for all manufacturing industries, some representative values of the terms on the right hand side of the equation are: $I = 0.5$, $m = 0.05$, and $b = 0.60$.

During the period that preceded the onset of inflation in the United States after 1966, the economy was growing at about 6 to 7 percent per annum. If a firm was in an industry that grew at the same rate as the economy as a whole and if a firm maintained its market share position in its industry, the firm grew at 6 to 7 percent per annum as well. Let us see what the implications for external financing requirements would be. With a growth rate of 6 percent, the percentage of an increase in sales that would have to be financed externally would be as follows:

$$PEFR = 0.5 - \frac{0.05}{0.06}(1.06)(0.6)$$

$$= 0.50 - 0.53 = -0.03 = -3\%.$$

3. At this point, one might ask two questions: "Shouldn't depreciation be considered as a source of funds, and won't this reduce the amount of external funds needed?" The answer to both questions is no. In the percent of sales method, we are relating fixed assets, net of the reserve for depreciation, to sales. This process implicitly assumes that funds related to the depreciation policies are used to replace assets to which the depreciation is applicable. The net fixed assets related to sales already have the reserve for depreciation (which is a cumulative sum of each year's depreciation expense charge) deducted from gross fixed assets.

At 7 percent growth, the PEFR would be:

$$\text{PEFR} = 0.5 - \frac{0.05}{0.07}(1.07)(0.6)$$

$$= 0.50 - 0.46 = 0.04 = 4\%.$$

Thus at a growth rate of 6 percent the percentage of external financing to sales growth would be a negative 3 percent. In other words, the firm would have excess funds which it could use to increase dividends or increase its investment in marketable securities. With a growth rate of 7 percent, the firm would have a requirement of external financing of 4 percent of the sales increase.

Following 1966 the inflation rate in some years was in the two digit range; that is, 10 percent or more. Suppose we add sufficient percentage points per annum of an inflation rate to the previous 6 to 7 percent growth rate to obtain a growth rate of 15 or 20 percent for a firm. Then the external financing requirements will be as follows:

$$\text{PEFR} = 0.5 - \frac{0.05}{0.15}(1.15)(0.6)$$

$$= 0.50 - 0.23 = 0.27 = 27\%.$$

$$\text{PEFR} = 0.5 - \frac{0.05}{0.20}(1.20)(0.6)$$

$$= 0.50 - 0.18 = 0.32 = 32\%.$$

With a growth rate in sales of 15 percent, external financing rises to 27 percent of the firm's sales growth. If inflation caused the growth rate of the firm to rise to 20 percent, then the external financing percentage would rise to 32 percent. The substantial increase in the growth rate of sales of firms measured in inflated dollars in recent years points up why external financing has become more important for firms. It underscores also why the finance function in firms has taken on increased importance in recent years. There is just a much bigger job to be done, particularly in requirements for using external financing sources to maintain the sales growth of a firm. Even if the firm were not growing in real terms, an inflation rate of 10 percent, for example, would make it necessary for the firm to raise external financing of 17 percent of its growth in sales of inflated dollars—even though the real growth of the firm was zero. This, again, underscores why financing has come to the fore as an important function in the firm.

The percent of sales method of forecasting financial requirements is neither simple nor mechanical, although an explanation of the ideas requires simple illustrations. Experience in applying the technique in practice suggests the importance of understanding (1) the basic technology of the firm and (2) the logic of the relation between sales and assets for the particular firm in question. A great deal of experience and judgment is required to apply the technique in actual practice.

The percent of sales method is most appropriately used for forecasting relatively short-term changes in financing needs. It is less useful for longer term forecasting for reasons best described in connection with the regression method of financial forecasting discussed in the next sections.

Scatter Diagram, or Simple Regression, Method

An alternative method used for forecasting financial requirements is the *scatter diagram,* or *simple regression,* method. A scatter diagram is a graphic portrayal of joint relations. Proper use of the scatter diagram method requires practical, but not necessarily statistical, sophistication.

We will use data for the Standard Oil Company of California (SOCAL) to illustrate the basic concepts involved. Table 8.3 presents data on sales and inventories for the Standard Oil Company of California for the ten years 1969 through 1978. The data are graphed in Figure 8.2. Using a hand calculator, the *line of best fit for the points,* or the regression line, was calculated to be:

$$\text{Inventories} = \$216 \text{ million plus } 0.05 \text{ sales.}$$

This regression line was then drawn in on Figure 8.2. As can be seen, the points are all relatively close to the calculated regression line. The correlation coefficient between sales and inventories for these data is 0.9745, indicating only a relatively small scatter of the actual data off the regression line.

The relationship appears to be a straight line. A number of offsetting influences seem to be operating. From the economic order quantity formula discussed in Chapter 11, inventories increase as the square root of sales. The line would be curved downward somewhat. Also, the greater efficiencies in

Table 8.3

Inventory to Sales Relationships for SOCAL for 1969–1978 (Millions of Dollars)

	Inventory (*Y*)	Sales (*X*)	Inventory to Sales Ratio (*Y/X*)
1969	$403	$ 4,560	0.088
1970	461	4,962	0.093
1971	506	5,728	0.088
1972	507	6,477	0.078
1973	665	8,480	0.078
1974	1,087	17,924	0.061
1975	1,165	17,524	0.066
1976	1,278	20,181	0.063
1977	1,438	21,752	0.066
1978	1,216	24,106	0.050

Source: *Moody's Industrial Manual* (New York: Moody's Investors Services, 1979). Used by permission.

Figure 8.2

Inventory to Sales Relationships for SOCAL for 1969–1978

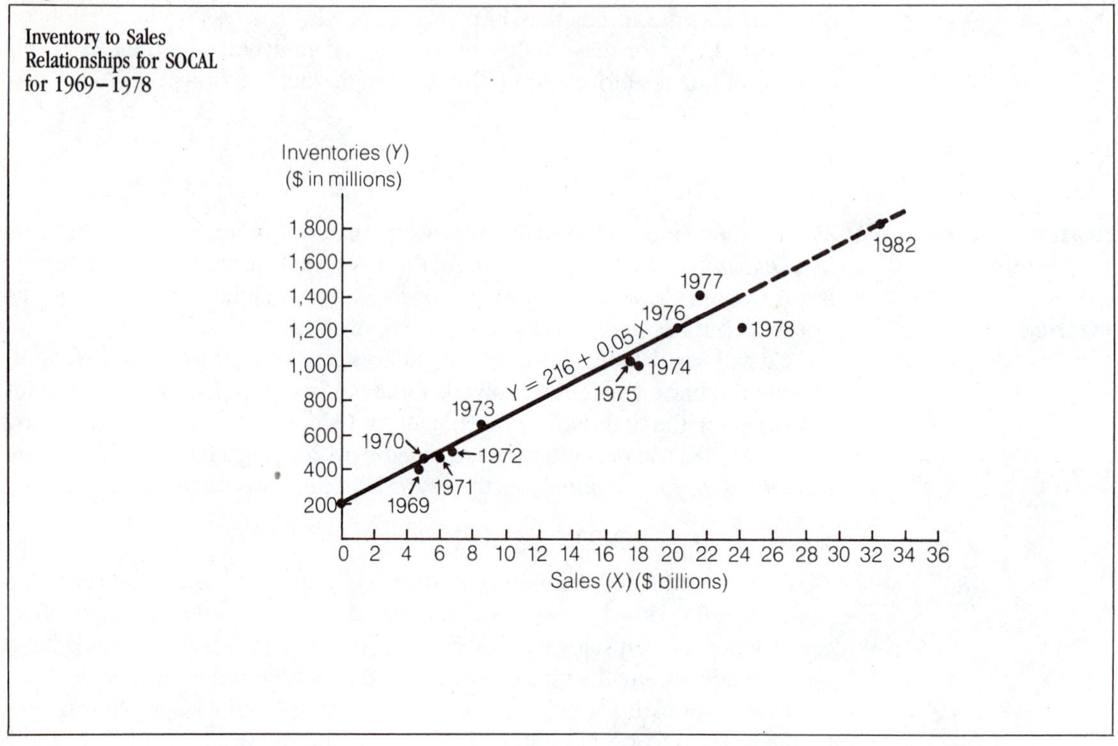

handling inventories such as improved transportation would also tend to cause the percentage of inventories to sales to decrease over time as sales increase. But the greater variety of products would cause inventories to rise as sales volume and product diversity increases. These influences appear to be counterbalancing, since the actual data for SOCAL indicate that the straight line calculated is a very good fit to the data.

Suppose that a sales forecast has been made for 1982 for SOCAL which projects that sales will increase at the same rate as between 1974 and 1978, a period when they increased by about 35 percent. This would result in sales of $32,543,000,000 for 1982. Given all of the uncertainties of the international oil market, a sales forecast for 1982 would require a very comprehensive study. But our interest is in developing the relations between sales and inventories. Taking the sales forecast as given, what projection for inventories would be appropriate? Table 8.3 shows that the ratio of inventories to sales has been in a downward trend for SOCAL, from over 9 percent in 1970 to 5 percent in 1978. But this result is mainly due to a mathematical relationship resulting from the positive amount of inventory as the intercept of the regression line. For example, consider the inventory to sales relationships for inventories forecast from the use of the regression line for the following sales levels (in millions of dollars):

Sales	Inventories	Ratio of Inventories to Sales
$ 5,000	$ 466	0.0932
10,000	716	0.0716
20,000	1,216	0.0608
30,000	1,716	0.0572

Note: These data are based on the use of the regression equation Inventories = $216 million + 0.05 sales.

As sales rise, the ratio of inventories to sales declines from 0.0932 to 0.0572. Use of the ratio of 0.0932 based on a sales level of $5,000,000,000 would have resulted in a forecast of inventories related to $30,000,000,000 sales of $2,796,000,000 instead of $1,716,000,000—an upside error of $1,080,000,000. This is due to the mathematical influence of the base stock inventory of $216 million in the regression equation. This constant has a greater influence when sales are small than when sales are large.

Thus if we had a sales forecast of sales for 1982 in the case of SOCAL of $32,543,000,000, the forecast of inventories, using the regression line, would be $1,843,000,000. Using the ratio of inventories to sales, we might use the average ratio of 0.0612 for 1974–1978 to get an inventory projection of $1,992,000,000, which is greater by $149 million than the forecast using the regression method. If we used the low ratio for 1978, which was 5 percent, we would be $216 million lower than with the projection by use of the regression method.

The percentage of sales method of projecting financing requirements will be unstable if the regression line for the data does not go through the origin. The regression method is thus seen to be superior to the percentage of sales method of forecasting financial requirements, particularly for longer term forecasts. When a firm is likely to have a base stock of inventory or fixed assets, the ratio of that item to sales declines as sales increase. In such cases, using historical relations between inventory and sales, for example, would set too high a norm, or control standard, as compared with the use of the regression method. This is an important difference between the two forecasting methods, and it is illustrated more completely in the following section.

Comparison of Forecasting Methods

Percent of Sales

The percent of sales method of financial forecasting assumes that certain balance sheet items vary directly with sales; that is, that the ratio of a given balance sheet item to sales remains constant. The postulated relationship is shown in Figure 8.3. *Notice that the percent of sales method implicitly assumes a linear relationship that passes through the origin.* The slope of the line representing the relationship may vary, but the line always passes through the origin. Implicitly, the relationship is established by finding one

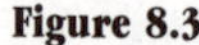

Figure 8.3

Percent of Sales

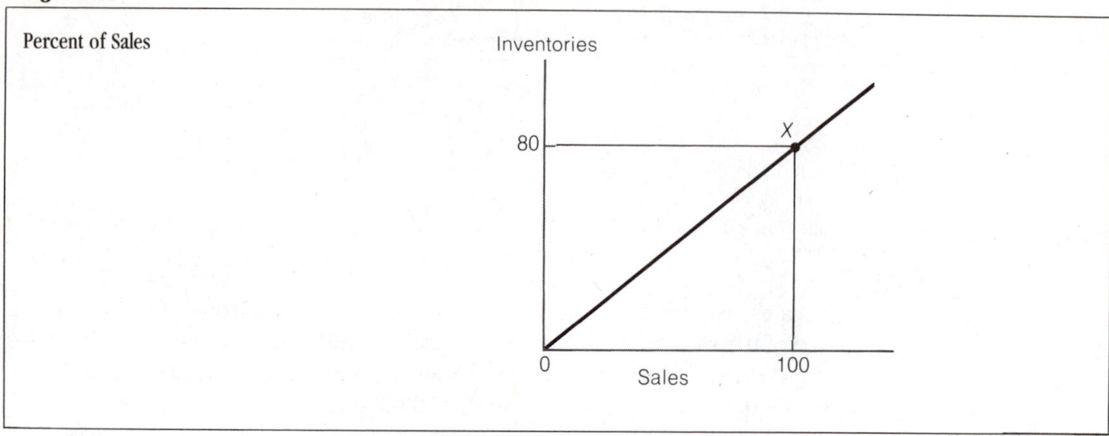

point, or ratio, such as that designated as *X* in Figure 8.3, and then connecting this point with the origin. Then, for any projected level of sales, the forecasted level of the particular balance sheet item can be determined.

Scatter Diagram, or Simple Linear Regression

The scatter diagram method differs from the percent of sales method principally in that it does not assume that the line of relationship passes through the origin. In its simplest form, the scatter diagram method calls for calculating the ratio between sales and the relevant balance sheet item at two points in time, extending a line through these two points, and using the line to describe the relationship between sales and the balance sheet item. The accuracy of the regression is improved if more points are plotted, and the regression line can be fitted mathematically (by a technique known as the method of least squares) as well as drawn in by eye.

The scatter diagram method is illustrated in Figure 8.4, where the percent of sales relationship is also shown for comparison. The error induced by the use of the percent of sales method is represented by the gap between the two lines. At a sales level of 125, the percent of sales method would call for an inventory of 100 versus an inventory of only 90 using a scatter diagram forecast. *Notice that the error is very small if sales continue to run at approximately the current level, but the gap widens and the error increases as sales deviate in either direction from current levels, as they probably would if a long-run forecast were being made.*

Curvilinear Simple Regression

Linear scatter diagrams, or linear regressions, assume that the slope of the regression line is constant. Although this condition does frequently exist, it is not a universal rule. Figure 8.5 illustrates the application of curvilinear simple regression to forecasting financial relationships. We have drawn this hypothetical illustration to show a flattening curve, which implies a decreasing relationship between sales and inventory beyond Point X, the current level of

Figure 8.4

Scatter Diagram, or Simple Linear Regression

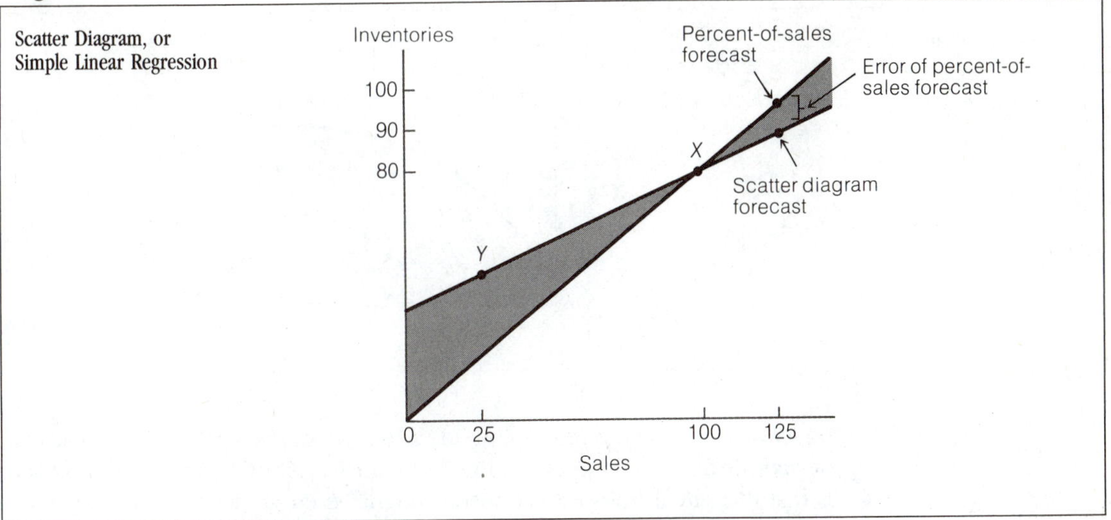

operations. In this case, the forecast of inventory requirements at a sales level of 125 would be too high if the linear regression method was used (but too low if sales declined from 100 to 50).

Multiple Regression

In our illustrations to this point, we have been assuming that the observations fell exactly on the relationship line. This implies perfect correlation, something that, in fact, seldom occurs. In practice, the actual observations would

Figure 8.5

Curvilinear Simple Regression

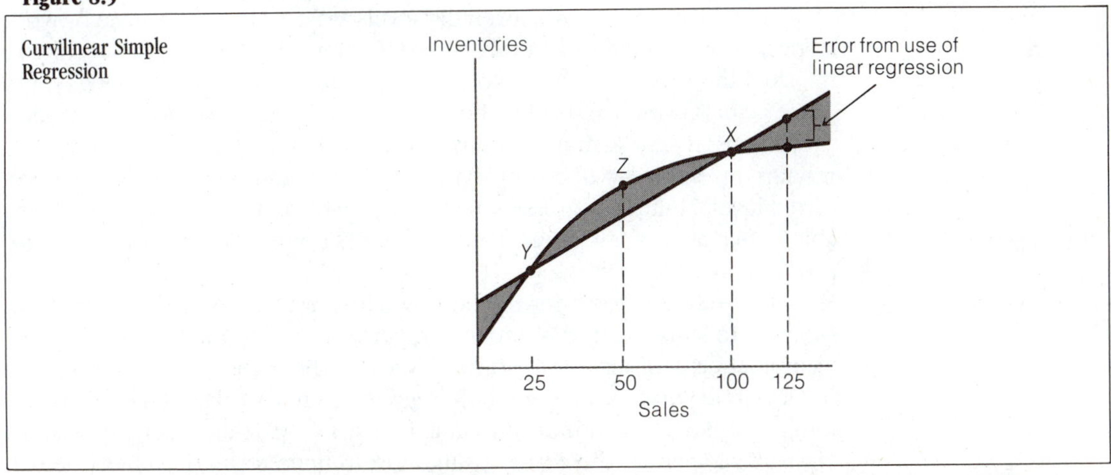

Figure 8.6

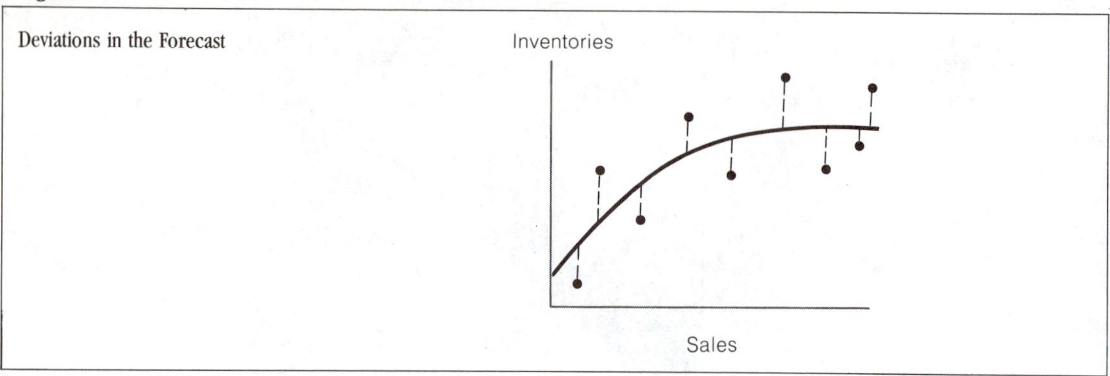

Deviations in the Forecast

be scattered about the regression line as shown in Figure 8.6. What causes the deviations from the regression line? One answer, if linear regression is used, is that the actual line of relationship might be curvilinear. But if curvilinear regression is used and deviations still occur, we must seek other explanations for the scatter around the regression line. The most obvious answer is that inventories are determined by factors in addition to sales.

A more sophisticated approach to forecasting a firm's assets calls for the use of *multiple regression analysis.* In simple regression, sales are assumed to be a function of only one variable; in multiple regression, sales are recognized to depend upon a number of variables. For example, in simple regression, we might state that sales are strictly a function of GNP. With multiple regression, we might state that sales depend on both GNP and a set of additional variables. For example, sales of ski equipment depend upon (1) the general level of prosperity as measured by GNP, personal disposable income, or other indicators of aggregate economic activity; (2) population increases; (3) number of lifts operating; (4) weather conditions; (5) advertising; and so forth.

In the illustration above, inventory levels are certainly influenced by work stoppages at the plants of suppliers. A steel fabricator anticipating a strike in the steel industry will stock up on steel products. Such hedge buying would cause actual inventories to be above the level forecast on the basis of sales projections. Then, assuming a strike does occur and continues for many months, inventories will be drawn down and may end up well below the predicted level. Multiple regression techniques, which introduce additional variables (such as work stoppages) into the analysis, are employed to further improve financial forecasting.

The need to employ more complicated forecasting techniques varies from situation to situation. For example, the percent of sales method may be perfectly adequate for making short-run forecasts where conditions are relatively stable, while curvilinear or multiple regression may be deemed essential for longer run forecasts in more dynamic industries. As in all other applications of financial analysis, the cost of using more refined techniques must be balanced against the benefits of increased accuracy. Most computer installations now have canned regression programs incorporated into their systems, making it extremely easy to use multiple regression techniques. At least in the larger corporations, multiple regression is widely used.

Statement of Changes in Financial Position

Financial forecasting is used to plan for financing requirements. The analysis of changes in the firm's financial position, called sources and uses of funds analysis, performs an important role here. If a firm requests a loan, the bank's loan officer will doubtless pose three questions: What has the firm done with the money it has? What will it do with the new funds? How will it repay the loan? The statement of changes in financial position, or sources and uses statement, helps provide answers to these questions and to others that interested parties may have about the firm. The information can indicate whether the firm is making progress or whether problems are arising. The nature of the statement typically involved is conveyed by Table 8.4, an actual illustration for the Standard Oil Company of California for 1978.

The main sources of funds were net income and depreciation. The main uses of funds were additions to properties, plant, and equipment. The excess of the sources of funds is related to the increase in working capital. One way to look at this is to recognize that the investment in current assets (a use of funds) exceeded the net increase in current liabilities (a source of funds) by the $97 million, which just balanced the excess of sources over uses of funds from other sources of $97 million. Thus in practice, the sources and uses of funds are divided between those that do not affect current assets and current liabilities and those that do. However, for ease of presentation we will not make this distinction in the procedures we describe. But the format is perfectly general so that it can be modified as desired.

The Nature of Depreciation

Before constructing a sources and uses of funds statement, we shall discuss the nature of depreciation. *Depreciation* is an annual charge against income that reflects the cost of the equipment used in the production process. For example, suppose a machine with an expected useful life of ten years and no expected salvage value was purchased in 1978 for $100,000. This cost must be charged against production during the machine's ten-year life; otherwise, profits will be overstated. If the machine is depreciated by the straight line method, the annual charge is $10,000. To determine income, this amount is deducted from sales revenues, along with such other costs as labor and raw materials. However, depreciation is not a cash outlay. Funds were expended back in 1978, so the depreciation charged against income each year is not a cash outlay. In this way it differs from labor or raw materials payments.

To illustrate the significance of depreciation in cash flow analysis, con-

Table 8.4

Standard Oil Company of California Consolidated Statement of Changes in Financial Position for the Year Ended December 31, 1978

	1978
Sources of Funds:	
Net income	$1,105,881,000
Depreciation, depletion and amortization	621,533,000
Deferred income taxes	79,353,000
Undistributed income of unconsolidated companies	(37,073,000)
Funds Provided by Operations	$1,769,694,000
Increases in long-term debt	27,724,000
Net book value of properties, plant and equipment sold or retired	59,360,000
	$1,856,778,000
Uses of Funds:	
Additions to properties, plant and equipment	$1,049,673,000
Cash dividends	434,581,000
Reductions in long-term debt	264,458,000
Other net increase in investments and advances	7,589,000
Other—net	3,674,000
	$1,759,975,000
Increase in Working Capital	$ 96,803,000
Analysis of Changes in Working Capital:	
Increase (decrease) in current assets:	
Cash and marketable securities	$ 535,639,000
Receivables	614,143,000
Inventories	(221,310,000)
	$ 928,472,000
(Increase) decrease in current liabilities:	
Accounts payable	$ (402,180,000)
Notes and loans payable	7,000,000
Current maturities of long-term debt	(208,239,000)
Federal and other taxes on income	(207,098,000)
Other	(21,152,000)
	$ (831,669,000)
Increase in Working Capital	$ 96,803,000

sider the Dallas Fertilizer and Chemical Company, which has the following income statement for 1981:

Sales	$300,000,000
Costs excluding depreciation	$270,000,000
Depreciation	10,000,000
Net income before taxes	$ 20,000,000
Taxes	8,000,000
Net income after taxes	$ 12,000,000

Assuming that sales are for cash and that all costs except depreciation are paid by cash during 1981, how much cash is available from operations to pay dividends, retire debt, or make investments in fixed or current assets (or both)? The answer is $22 million, the sum of after-tax profit plus depreciation. The sales are all for cash, so the firm took in $300 million in cash. Its costs other than depreciation were $270 million, and these were paid in cash, leaving $30 million. *Depreciation is not a cash charge*—the firm does not pay out the $10 million of depreciation expenses—so $30 million of funds remains after depreciation. Taxes, on the other hand, are paid in cash, so $8 million for taxes must be deducted from the $30 million gross operating cash flow, leaving a net cash flow from operations of $22 million. Since $300,000,000 flows in and $278,000,000 flows out, $22,000,000 *must* remain. This $22 million is, of course, exactly equal to net income after taxes plus depreciation: $12 million plus $10 million equals $22 million. As shown in the SOCAL example, depreciation is a non-cash charge which is added back to net income to arrive at *funds* (cash or working capital) *generated by operations.*

Sources and Uses Statement

Constructing a sources and uses of funds statement requires several steps. The changes in balance sheet items from one year to the next must be tabulated and then classified as either sources or uses of funds, according to the following pattern:

1. *Source of funds* means either a decrease in asset items or an increase in liability items.
2. *Use of funds* means either an increase in asset items or a decrease in liability items.

Table 8.5 gives Dallas Chemical's comparative balance sheets for 1980 and 1981 along with net changes in each item, classified as to source or use.

Table 8.5

Dallas Fertilizer and Chemical Company Comparative Balance Sheets and Sources and Uses of Funds (Millions of Dollars)

	Dec. 31, 1980		Dec. 31, 1981		Source	Use
Assets						
Cash		$ 10		$ 5	$ 5	
Marketable securities		25		15	10	
Net receivables		15		20		$ 5
Inventories		25		35		10
Gross fixed assets	$150		$175			25
(Less accumulated depreciation)[a]	−40		−50		10	
Net fixed assets		110		125		
Total assets		$185		$200		
Liabilities						
Accounts payable		$ 10		$ 6		$ 4
Notes payable		15		10		5
Other current liabilities		10		14	4	
Long-term debt		60		70	10	
Preferred stock		10		10	—	—
Common stock		50		50	—	—
Retained earnings		30		40	10	
Total claims on assets		$185		$200		

a. The accumulated depreciation is actually a "liability" account (a contra-asset) that appears on the left side of the balance sheet. Note that it is deducted, not added, when totaling the column.

Table 8.6

Dallas Fertilizer and Chemical Company, Statement of Changes in Financial Position, 1981 (Millions of Dollars)

	Amount		Percent	
Sources of Funds				
Net Income		$12	23.5	
Depreciation		10	19.6	
Decreases in working capital:				43.1
Reduction in cash	$ 5		9.8	
Sale of marketable securities	10		19.6	
Increase in other liabilities	4		7.9	
Total decrease in working capital		19		37.3
Increase in long-term debt		10		19.6
Total sources of funds		$51		100.0
Uses of Funds				
Increases in working capital:				
Inventory investment	$10		19.6	
Increase in receivables	5		9.8	
Reduction in notes payable	5		9.8	
Reduction in accounts payable	4		7.9	
Total increase in working capital		$24		47.1
Gross fixed assets expansion		25	49.0	
Dividends to stockholders		2	3.9	52.9
Total uses of funds		$51		100.0

The next step in constructing a sources and uses statement involves (1) making adjustments to reflect net income and dividends and (2) isolating changes in working capital (current assets and current liabilities). These changes are reflected in the statement shown in Table 8.6. Net income in 1981 amounted to $12 million, and dividends of $2 million were paid. The $12 million is treated as a source, the $2 million as a use. The $10 million in retained earnings shown in Table 8.5 is deleted from Table 8.6 to avoid double counting. This statement of sources and uses of funds tells the financial manager that plant size was expanded, that fixed assets amounting to $25 million were acquired, that inventories and net receivables increased as sales increased, and that the firm needed funds to meet working capital and fixed assets demands.

Previously, Dallas had been financing its growth through bank credit (notes payable). In the present period of growth, management decided to obtain some financing from permanent sources—long-term debt. It obtained enough long-term debt to finance some of the asset growth and also pay back some of its bank credit, thereby reducing accounts payable. In addition to the long-term debt, it obtained funds from earnings and from depreciation charges. Moreover, the firm had been accumulating marketable securities in anticipation of this expansion program, and some were sold to pay for new buildings and equipment. Finally, cash that had been accumulated in excess of the firm's needs was also worked down. In summary, the example illustrates how the sources and uses of funds statement can provide both a fairly complete picture of recent operations and a good perspective on the flow of funds within the company.

Pro Forma Sources and Uses of Funds

A pro forma, or projected, sources and uses of funds statement can also be constructed to show how a firm plans to acquire and employ funds during some future period. Earlier in the chapter we discussed financial forecasting, which involves the determination of future sales, the level of assets necessary to generate these sales (the left side of the projected balance sheet), and the manner in which the assets will be financed (the right side of the projected balance sheet). Given the projected balance sheet and supplementary projected data on earnings, dividends, and depreciation, the financial manager can construct a pro forma sources and uses of funds statement to summarize the firm's projected operations over the planning horizon. Such a statement is obviously of much interest to lenders as well as to the firm's own management.

Summary

Firms need assets to make sales; if sales are to be increased, assets must also be expanded. The first section of this chapter illustrates the relationship between sales and assets and shows how even a growing, profitable firm can have a cash flow problem.

The most important causal variable in determining financial requirements is a firm's projected dollar volume of sales; a good sales forecast is an essential foundation for forecasting financial requirements. The two principal methods used for making financial forecasts are (1) the percent of sales method and (2) the regression method. The first has the virtue of simplicity—the forecaster computes past relationships between asset and liability items and sales, assumes these same relationships will continue, and then applies the new sales forecast to get an estimate of the financial requirements.

However, since the percent of sales method assumes that the balance sheet-to-sales relationships will remain constant, it is only useful for relatively short-run forecasting. When longer range forecasts are being made, the regression method is preferable, as it allows for changing balance sheet-to-sales relationships. Linear regression can be expanded to curvilinear regression, and simple regression to multiple regression. These more complex methods are useful in certain circumstances, but their increased accuracy must be balanced against the increased costs of using them.

The tools and techniques we have discussed in this chapter are generally used in the following manner: As a first step, one of the long-range forecasting techniques is used to make a long-run forecast of the firm's financial requirements over a three- to five-year period. This forecast is then used to make the strategic financing plans during the planning period. Long lead times are necessary when companies sell bonds or stocks; otherwise financial managers might be forced to go into the market for funds during unfavorable periods. In addition to the long-run strategic forecasting, the financial manager must also make accurate short-run forecasts to be sure that funds will be available to meet seasonal and other short-run requirements.

A statement of changes in financial position, commonly called the sources and uses of funds statement, indicates where cash came from and how it was used. When a firm is negotiating for a loan, the first area of analysis is the determination of how funds have been used in the past, what funds will be generated in the future, and how they will be used. The sources and uses of funds statement on a historical basis provides necessary background for determining the pattern of funds flows. The pattern of funds flows and the effects on the firm's working capital position can indicate that the firm is making progress or that problems are developing. Particularly important is the formulation of sources and uses data on a pro forma, or projected, basis to provide a projection for analyzing what is likely to develop in future periods. Of particular interest is how the future funds flows will enable the firm to meet its interest and other payments schedules under alternative financing plans.

Questions

8.1 What should be the approximate point of intersection between the sales-to-asset regression line and the vertical axis (Y-axis intercept) for the following: inventory, accounts receivable, fixed assets? State your answer in terms of positive, zero, or negative intercept. Can you think of any accounts that might have a negative intercept?

8.2 How does forecasting financial requirements in advance of needs help financial managers perform their responsibilities more effectively?

8.3 Explain how a downturn in the business cycle could either cause a cash shortage for a firm or generate excess cash.

8.4 Explain this statement: To a considerable extent, current assets represent permanent assets.

8.5 What advantages might a multiple regression technique have over a simple regression technique in forecasting sales? What might be some drawbacks in the actual use of this technique?

Problems

8.1 The Blume Company's 1980 balance sheet is on page 217. Sales in 1980 totaled \$2 million. The ratio of net profit to sales was 5 percent, with a dividend payout ratio of 40 percent of net income. Sales are expected to increase by 30 percent during 1981. No long-term debt will be retired. Using the percentage of sales method, determine how much outside financing is required.

Blume Company
Balance Sheet
as of December 31, 1980

Assets		**Liabilities**	
Cash	$ 75,000	Accounts payable	$ 40,000
Accounts receivable	150,000	Accruals	25,000
Inventory	240,000	Notes payable	85,000
Current assets	$ 465,000	Total current liabilities	150,000
Net fixed assets	735,000	Long-term debt	250,000
		Total debt	$ 400,000
		Capital stock	450,000
		Retained earnings	350,000
Total assets	$1,200,000	Total liabilities and net worth	$1,200,000

8.2 Given the following data on the Hanes Corporation, predict next year's balance sheet:

This year's sales: $80,000,000

Next year's sales: $100,000,000

After-tax profits: 6% of sales

Dividend payout: 40%

This year's retained earnings: $21,500,000

Cash as percent of sales: 3%

Receivables as percent of sales: 12%

Inventory as percent of sales: 25%

Net fixed assets as percent of sales: 40%

Accounts payable as percent of sales: 8%

Accruals as percent of sales: 20%

Next year's common stock: $20,000,000

Hanes Corporation
Balance Sheet
as of December 31, 1980

Assets		**Liabilities**	
Cash	______	Accounts payable	______
Accounts receivable	______	Notes payable	______
Inventory	______	Accruals	______
Total current assets	______	Total current liabilities	______
Fixed assets	______	Common stock	______
		Retained earnings	______
Total assets	______	Total liabilities	______

8.3 The Kamberg Supply Company is a wholesale steel distributor. It purchases steel in carload lots from more than twenty producing mills and sells to several thousand steel users. The items carried include sheets, plates, wire products, bolts, windows, pipe, and tubing.

The company owns two warehouses of 25,000 square feet each and is contemplating the erection of another warehouse of 30,000 square feet. The nature of a steel supply business requires that the company maintain large inventories to take care of customer requirements in the event of mill strikes or other delays.

In examining patterns from 1974 through 1979, the company found consistent relationships among the following accounts as a percent of sales.

Current assets: 65%

Net fixed assets: 25%

Accounts payable: 10%

Other current liabilities, including accruals and provision for income taxes but not bank loans: 12%

Net profit after taxes: 5%

The company's sales for 1980 were $10 million, and its balance sheet on December 31, 1980, is shown below. The company expects its sales to increase by $1,000,000 each year. If this level is achieved, what will the company's financial requirements be at the end of the five-year period? Assume that accounts not tied directly to sales (for example, notes payable) remain constant and that the company pays no dividends.

a. Construct a pro forma balance sheet for the end of 1985, using "additional financing needed" as the balancing item.
b. What are the crucial assumptions you made in your projection method?

Kamberg Supply Company Balance Sheet as of December 31, 1980

Assets		**Liabilities**	
Current assets	$6,500,000	Accounts payable	$1,000,000
Fixed assets	2,500,000	Notes payable	1,200,000
		Other current liabilities	1,200,000
		Total current liabilities	$3,400,000
		Mortgage loan	1,000,000
		Common stock	2,000,000
		Retained earnings	2,600,000
Total assets	$9,000,000	Total liabilities and net worth	$9,000,000

8.4 One useful method of evaluating a firm's financial structure in relation to its industry is to compare it with financial ratio composites for the industry. A new firm, or an established firm contemplating entry into a new industry, may use such composites as a guide to its likely approximate financial position after the initial settling-down period.

The following data represent ratios for the publishing and printing industry for 1980.

Sales to net worth: 2.2 times

Current debt to net worth: 45%

Total debt to net worth: 80%

Current ratio: 2.4 times

Net sales to inventory: 5.1 times

Average collection period: 60 days

Net fixed assets to net worth: 72%

a. Complete the pro forma balance sheet (round to nearest thousand) for Original Printers, whose 1980 sales are $5 million.
b. What does the use of the financial ratio composites accomplish?
c. What other factors will influence the financial structure of the firm?

Original Printers, Inc.
Pro Forma Balance Sheet
as of December 31, 1980

Assets		**Liabilities**	
Cash	______	Current debt	______
Accounts receivable	______	Long-term debt	______
Inventory	______	Total debt	______
Current assets	______	Net worth	______
Fixed assets	______		
Total assets	______	Total liabilities and net worth	______

8.5 The 1980 sales of Ultrasonics, Inc., were $12 million. Common stock and notes payable are constant. The dividend payout ratio is 40 percent. Retained earnings shown on the December 31, 1979, balance sheet were $80,000. The percent of sales in each balance sheet item that varies directly with sales is expected to be:

	Percent
Cash	5
Receivables	15
Inventories	20
Net fixed assets	40
Accounts payable	10
Accruals	5
Profit rate (after taxes) on sales	4

---

a. Complete the balance sheet given below.
b. Suppose that in 1981 sales will increase by 20 percent over 1980 sales. How much additional (external) capital will be required?
c. Construct the year-end 1981 balance sheet. Set up an account for "financing needed" or "funds available."
d. What would happen to capital requirements under each of the following conditions?
   1. The profit margin went from 4 percent to 6 percent? from 4 percent to 2 percent? Set up an equation to illustrate your answers.

2. The dividend payout rate was raised from 40 percent to 80 percent? was lowered from 40 percent to 20 percent? Set up an equation to illustrate your answers.
3. Slower collections caused receivables to rise to 72 days of sales?

Ultrasonics, Inc.
Balance Sheet
as of December 31, 1980

Assets		**Liabilities**	
Cash	______	Accounts payable	______
Receivables	______	Notes payable	$ 900,000
Inventory	______	Accruals	______
Total current assets	______	Total current liabilities	______
Fixed assets	______	Common stock	$6,532,000
		Retained earnings	______
Total assets	______	Total liabilities and net worth	______

8.6 A firm has the following relationships. The ratio of assets to sales is 55 percent. Liabilities that increase spontaneously with sales are 15 percent. The profit margin on sales after taxes is 6 percent. The firm's dividend payout ratio is 40 percent.

a. If the firm's growth rate on sales is 15 percent per annum, what percentage of the sales increase in any year must be financed externally?
b. If the firm's growth rate on sales increases to 25 percent per annum, what percentage of the sales increase in any year must be financed externally?
c. How will your answer to Part a change if the profit margin increases to 8 percent?
d. How will your answer to Part b change if the firm's dividend payout is reduced to 10 percent?
e. If the profit margin increases from 6 percent to 8 percent and the dividend payout ratio is 20 percent, at what growth rate in sales will the external financing requirement percentage be exactly zero?

8.7 You are starting a new business. You know only two things: (1) the business you are planning to enter and (2) an estimated volume of sales. With the use of industry financial composites, you can project the balance sheet and income statement you are likely to have. Departures from this projection will provide a basis for analyzing causes of the deviations.

To illustrate: You plan to enter the manufacturing of industrial electrical instruments. Sales in your first full year of operation are expected to be $14,000,000. Based on the following industry composites for 1979, write the pro forma balance sheet and income statement for your company for 1980.

Current ratio: 2.4 times

Net income to sales: 5 percent

Sales to net worth: 3.5 times

Average collection period: 50 days

Sales to inventory: 5.5 times

Fixed assets to net worth: 60 percent

Current debt to net worth: 50 percent

Total debt to net worth: 80 percent

Cost of sales to sales: 60 percent

Operating expenses to sales: 30 percent

Profit before taxes to sales: 10 percent

8.8 The consolidated balance sheets for the Norton Corporation at the beginning and end of 1980 are shown below.

Norton Corporation
Balance Sheet,
Beginning and End, 1980
(Millions of Dollars)

	Jan. 1	Dec. 31	Source	Use
Assets				
Cash	$ 45	$ 21	_____	_____
Marketable securities	33	0	_____	_____
Net receivables	66	90	_____	_____
Inventories	159	225	_____	_____
Total current assets	$303	$336	_____	_____
Gross fixed assets	$225	$450		
Less: reserve for depreciation	(78)	(123)	_____	_____
Net fixed assets	147	327	_____	_____
Total assets	$450	$663		

	Jan. 1	Dec. 31	Source	Use
Liabilities				
Accounts payable	$ 45	$ 54	_____	_____
Notes payable	45	9	_____	_____
Other current liabilities	21	45	_____	_____
Long-term debt	24	78	_____	_____
Common stock	114	192	_____	_____
Retained earnings	201	285	_____	_____
Total claims on assets	$450	$663	_____	_____

The company bought $225 million worth of fixed assets. The charge for current depreciation was $45 million. Earnings after taxes were $114 million, and the company paid out $30 million in dividends.

a. Fill in the amount of source or use in the appropriate column.
b. Prepare a percentage statement of sources and uses of funds.
c. Briefly summarize your findings.

8.9 Listed below are the Consolidated Changes in Financial Position of Eli Lilly and Company for the year ended December 31, 1978, under the three main headings "Source of Working Capital," "Use of Working Capital," and "Changes in the Components of Working Capital."

Eli Lilly and Company and Subsidiaries
Consolidated Statements of Changes in Financial Position
(Year Ended December 31, 1978)
(Millions of Dollars)

Source of Working Capital	
Net income	$277
Charges to income not involving working capital	
Depreciation and amortization	45
Deferred income taxes	12
Total from operations	$334
Proceeds from sales of common stock under option plans	$ 1
Issuance of common stock in satisfaction of performance awards	2
Disposals of property and equipment	6
Additions to long-term debt	1
Other credits to additional paid-in capital	1
	$345
Use of Working Capital	
Cash dividends	$116
Additions to property and equipment	90
Increase in other assets—additional investment in Puerto Rico	147
Reductions of long-term debt	1
Purchase of common stock for treasury	4
	$358
Increase (decrease) in working capital	$ (13)
Changes in Components of Working Capital	
Increases (decreases) in current assets:	
Cash and securities	$ (51)
Receivables	50
Inventories	72
Prepaid expenses	14
	$ 85
Increases (decreases) in current liabilities:	
Loan payable	$ (26)
Accounts payable	42
Employee compensation and payroll taxes	27
Other liabilities	27
Federal and foreign income taxes	28
Increase (decrease) in working capital	$ 98
	$ (13)

a. List assets, claims on assets, and income statement items and show whether the change in each item was a source or use of funds.
b. For the five largest sources and uses, calculate the percentage to total sources or uses.
c. Comment on the pattern of sources and uses for Eli Lilly for 1978.

Selected References

Ansoff, H. Igor. "Planning as a Practical Management Tool." *Financial Executive* 32 (June 1964), pp. 34–37.

Carleton, Willard T. "An Analytical Model for Long-Range Financial Planning." *Journal of Finance* 25 (May 1970), pp. 291–315.

Carleton, Willard T.; Dick, Charles L., Jr.; and Downes, David H. "Financial Policy Models: Theory and Practice." *Journal of Financial and Quantitative Analysis* 8 (December 1973), pp. 691–709.

Chambers, John C.; Mullick, Satinder K.; and Smith, Donald D. "How to Choose the Right Forecasting Technique." *Harvard Business Review* 49 (July–August 1971), pp. 45–74.

Crum, Roy L.; Klingman, Darwin D.; and Tavis, Lee A. "Implementations of Large-Scale Financial Planning Models: Solution Efficient Transformations." *Journal of Financial and Quantitative Analysis* 14 (March 1979), pp. 137–152.

Francis, Jack Clark, and Rowell, Dexter R. "A Simultaneous Equation Model of the Firm for Financial Analysis and Planning." *Financial Management* 7 (Spring 1978), pp. 29–44.

Gentry, James A., and Pyhhr, Stephen A. "Simulating an EPS Growth Model." *Financial Management* 2 (Summer 1973), pp. 68–75.

Gershefski, George W. "Building a Corporate Financial Model." *Harvard Business Review* 47 (July–August 1969), pp. 61–72.

Gordon, Myron J., and Shillinglaw, Gordon. *Accounting: A Management Approach.* 4th ed. Homewood, Ill.: Irwin, 1969, Chapter 16.

Higgins, Robert C. "How Much Growth Can a Firm Afford?" *Financial Management* 6 (Fall 1977), pp. 7–16.

Merville, L. J., and Tavis, L. A. "Financial Planning in a Decentralized Firm under Conditions of Competitive Capital Markets." *Financial Management* 6 (Fall 1977), pp. 17–23.

Myers, Stewart C., and Pogue, Gerald A. "A Programming Approach to Corporate Financial Management." *Journal of Finance* 29 (May 1974), pp. 579–599.

Pappas, James L., and Huber, George P. "Probabilistic Short-Term Financial Planning." *Financial Management* 2 (Autumn 1973), pp. 36–44.

Parker, George G. C., and Segura, Edilberto L. "How to Get a Better Forecast." *Harvard Business Review* 49 (March–April 1973), pp. 99–109.

Smith, Gary, and Brainard, William. "The Value of A Priori Information in Estimating a Financial Model." *Journal of Finance* 31 (December 1976), pp. 1299–1322.

Wagle, B. "The Use of Models for Environmental Forecasting and Corporate Planning." *Operational Research Quarterly* 22, no. 3, (September 1971), pp. 327–336.

Warren, James M., and Shelton, John P. "A Simultaneous Equation Approach to Financial Planning." *Journal of Finance* 26 (December 1971), pp. 1123–1142.

Weston, J. Fred. "Forecasting Financial Requirements." *Accounting Review* 33 (July 1958), pp. 427–440.

9
Financial Planning and Control

The preceding chapter on financial forecasting emphasized relating the level and rate of growth of sales to the firm's required investment in assets to support those sales. Investments in assets, in turn, give rise to financing requirements. In the present chapter we continue to expand this planning framework. Here the emphasis is on profitability analysis, both in a broad long-term framework and also in connection with the shorter term forecasting that is the emphasis of the budgeting process. From a financial manager's standpoint, especially important in short-term budgeting is cash forecasting, or cash budgeting. But since the cash budget is a part of the firm's overall budgeting process, cash budgeting can best be understood within the general framework of budgeting. Our treatment of budgeting is to use it primarily for financial planning and control purposes; this contrasts with the procedural emphasis when budgeting is considered in the context of accounting. Four major topics are covered in this chapter:

1. *Breakeven analysis, or profit planning, as it is sometimes called.*
2. *Operating leverage—the sensitivity of operating income to changes in the volume of operations.*
3. *Budgeting in a planning and control framework.*
4. *Divisional control in a decentralized firm.*

These four topics are tied together by the framework of the planning and control process.

Investment, Volume, and Returns Analysis

The relationship between the size of investment outlays and the required volume to achieve profitability is generally referred to as *breakeven analysis.* If a firm's costs were all variable, the problem of breakeven volume would not arise. But since the level of total costs may be greatly influenced by the size of fixed investments that the firm makes, the resulting fixed costs will put the firm in a loss position until a sufficient volume of sales is achieved.

Table 9.1

Fixed and Variable Costs

Fixed Costs[a]	Direct (Variable) Costs
Depreciation on plant and equipment	Factory labor
Rentals	Materials
Salaries of research staff	Sales commissions
Salaries of executive staff	
General office expenses	

a. Some of these costs—for example, salaries and office expenses—can be varied to some degree; however, firms are reluctant to reduce these expenditures in response to temporary fluctuations in sales. Such costs are often called *semivariable* costs.

Breakeven analysis is, therefore, a formal planning approach based on relationships between sales or total revenues and total costs. If a firm is to avoid accounting losses, its sales must cover all costs—those that vary directly with production and those that do not change as production levels change. Table 9.1 lists costs that fall into each of these categories.

The nature of breakeven analysis is depicted in Figure 9.1, the basic breakeven chart. The chart works on a unit basis, with units produced shown on the horizontal axis and income and costs measured on the vertical axis. Fixed costs of $40,000 are represented by a horizontal line; they are the same—fixed—regardless of the number of units produced. Variable costs are assumed to be $1.20 a unit. Units are assumed to be sold at $2 apiece, so the total income is pictured as a straight line, which must increase with production. The slope, or rate of ascent, of the total revenue line is steeper than that of the total cost line. This must be true, because the firm is gaining $2 of revenue for every $1.20 paid out for labor and materials—the variable costs.

Up to the breakeven point, at the intersection of the total income and total cost lines, the firm suffers losses. After that point, it begins to make profits. Figure 9.1 indicates a breakeven point at a sales and cost level of $100,000, which is here a production level of 50,000 units.

Calculations of the breakeven point can also be carried out algebraically. We define:

S^* = Breakeven sales
Q^* = Breakeven quantity of units sold
P = Sales price per unit
v = Variable cost per unit
c = Contribution margin per unit
CR = Contribution ratio $= 1 - \frac{V}{PQ}$.

The firm's total revenues or sales function can be derived from the data given.

$$S = \$2Q.$$

The total cost function is:

$$TC = \$40{,}000 + \$1.20Q.$$

Figure 9.1

Breakeven Chart

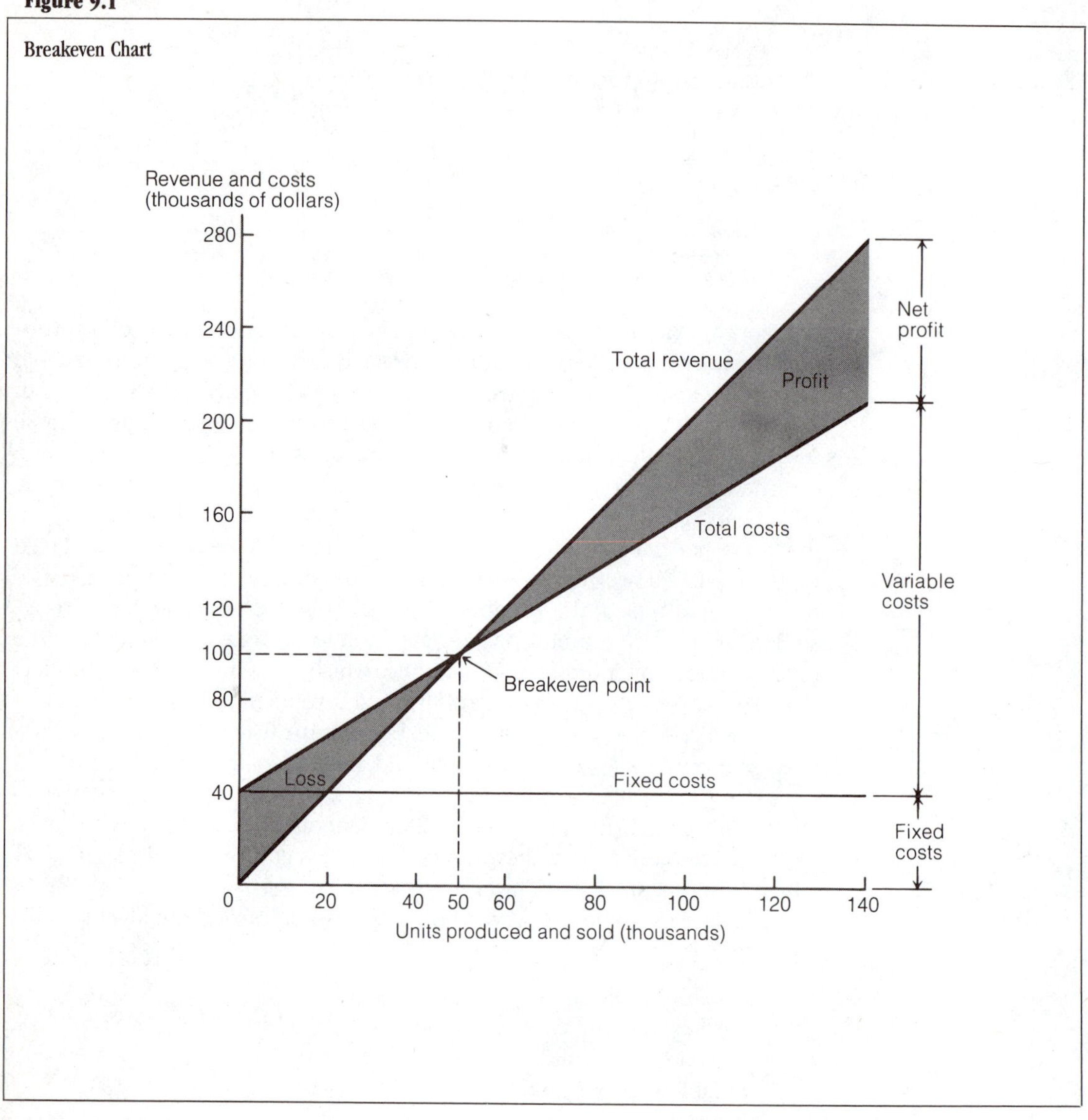

At the breakeven quantity, total revenues and total costs are equal. Therefore equating the sales and total cost functions:

$$\$2Q = \$40{,}000 + \$1.20Q$$

$$Q^* = 50{,}000.$$

The relationships are clarified further by use of a contribution income statement for various levels of units sold, as shown by Table 9.2.

Table 9.2

Contribution Income Statement at Various Quantities of Units Sold

Units sold *(Q)*	20,000	40,000	50,000	80,000	100,000	200,000
Sales *(S)*	\$40,000	\$80,000	\$100,000	\$160,000	\$200,000	\$400,000
Total variable expenses *(V)*	24,000	48,000	60,000	96,000	120,000	240,000
Contribution margin *(C)*	\$16,000	\$32,000	\$ 40,000	\$ 64,000	\$ 80,000	\$160,000
Fixed operating expenses *(F)*	40,000	40,000	40,000	40,000	40,000	40,000
Net operating income *(X)*	(\$24,000)	(\$ 8,000)	—	\$ 24,000	\$ 40,000	\$120,000

Note: $C = cQ$ and $X = cQ - F = C - F$.

$$CR = \left(1 - \frac{V}{PQ}\right).$$

Table 9.3

Derivations of Breakeven Quantity and Breakeven Sales

Breakeven Quantity = Q^*

$$P \cdot Q^* = vQ^* + F$$
$$P \cdot Q^* - vQ^* = F$$
$$Q^* = \frac{F}{P - v}$$
$$Q^* = \frac{F}{c} \tag{9.1A}$$

Breakeven Sales = S^*

$$S^* = F + V$$
$$= F + \frac{V \cdot S^*}{S^*}$$
$$S^* = PQ$$
$$S^* - \frac{V}{PQ}S^* = F$$
$$S^* = \frac{F}{1 - \frac{V}{PQ}}$$
$$S^* = \frac{F}{CR} \tag{9.1B}$$

We can illustrate the calculation of both Q^* and S^* from the data of our numerical example.

$$Q^* = \frac{F}{c}$$
$$Q^* = \frac{\$40{,}000}{\$.80}$$
$$Q^* = 50{,}000 \text{ units.}$$

$$S^* = \frac{F}{CR}$$
$$\frac{V}{PQ} = 0.6 \text{ at all quantities sold.}$$

Therefore,

$$CR = \left(1 - \frac{V}{PQ}\right) = 0.4.$$

Hence,

$$S^* = \frac{\$40{,}000}{0.4} = \$100{,}000.$$

From Table 9.2 and Figure 9.1, we can readily observe that the breakeven quantity is 50,000 units sold. The breakeven level of sales is $100,000. We can also derive the expressions for the breakeven quantity and the breakeven dollar volume of sales by beginning with the relationship that total revenues or sales equals total costs at breakeven. We then have the equations given in Table 9.3. Thus the breakeven quantity or breakeven sales volume can readily be calculated by use of the total fixed costs and a contribution margin relationship.

Nonlinear Breakeven Analysis

In breakeven analysis, linear (straight line) relationships are generally assumed. Although introducing nonlinear relationships complicates matters slightly, it is easy enough to extend the analysis in this manner. For example, it is reasonable to think that increased sales can be obtained only if prices are reduced. Similarly, empirical studies suggest that the average variable cost per unit falls over some range of output and then begins to rise. These assumptions are illustrated in Figure 9.2, where we see a loss region when sales are low, then a profit region (and a maximum profit), and finally another loss region at very high output levels.

Figure 9.2

Nonlinear Breakeven Chart

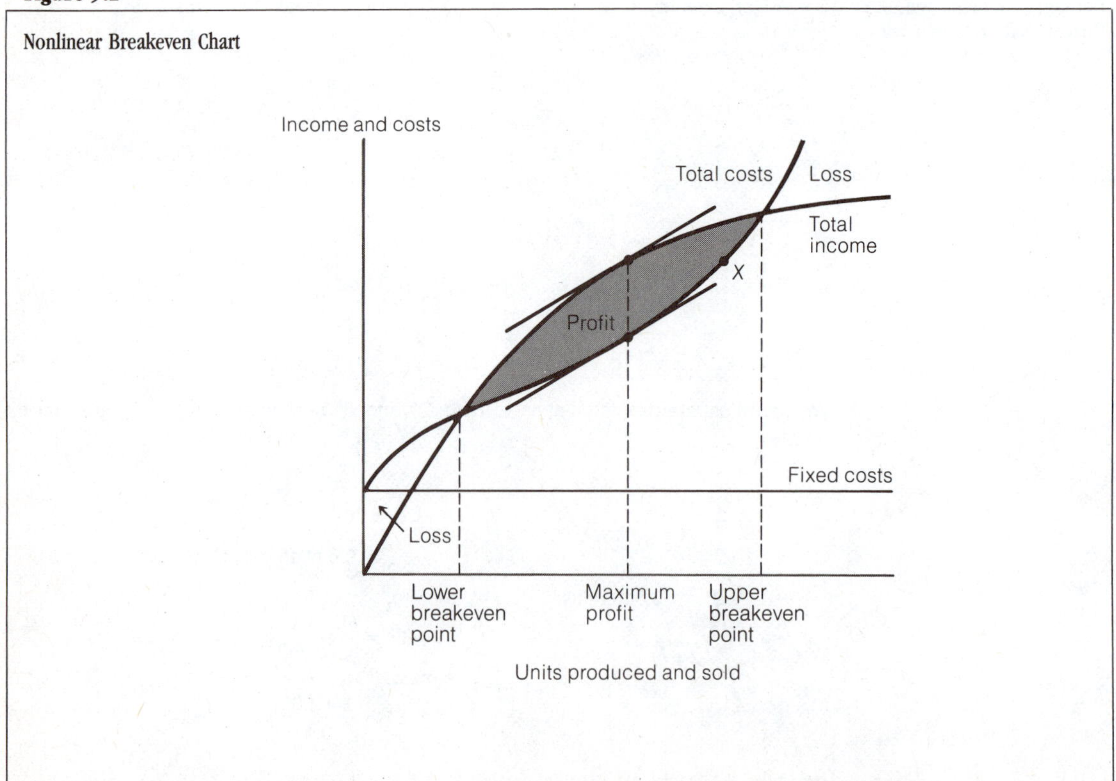

Applications of Breakeven Analysis

Used appropriately, breakeven analysis can shed light on a number of important business decisions by firms. In new product decisions, breakeven analysis helps determine the required sales volume for profitability. Breakeven analysis also provides a broad framework for studying the effects of a general expansion in the level of operations. Finally, in analyzing programs to modernize and automate, where the firm would be substituting fixed costs for variable costs, breakeven analysis helps analyze the consequences of shifting from variable costs to fixed costs. The key factor involved is the influence of volume changes on profitability changes when firms have a different relationship between fixed, variable, and total costs. The analysis of these relationships involves the analysis of operating leverage.

Operating Leverage

Operating leverage is defined as the extent to which a firm's operations involve fixed operating expenses (fixed manufacturing, selling, and administrative expense). The key factor that should be considered by management in determining operating leverage is a trade-off between automated equipment (large depreciation charges or fixed manufacturing expense) and labor (the absence of this expense). In the first case, where management has chosen fixed expense (automation) instead of variable expense (labor) to produce its product, the firm is said to be *highly levered.* Being highly levered means that a relatively small change in sales results in a large change in net operating income. This magnification of income (loss) is why leverage is significant. During a good year, leverage works to increase income relative to what it otherwise would be. During a bad year, it works to increase losses for the firm. Thus, leverage is a two-edged sword, working for or against the company.

The significance of the degree of operating leverage is illustrated by Figure 9.3, which contrasts the differing degrees of leverage of Firms A, B, and C. Firm A has a relatively small amount of fixed charges, and it does not have much automated equipment; so its depreciation cost is low. However, its variable cost line has a relatively steep slope, denoting that its variable costs per unit are higher than those of the other firms.

Firm B is considered to have a normal amount of fixed costs in its operations. It uses automated equipment (with which one operator can turn out a few or many units at the same labor cost) to about the same extent as the average firm in the industry. Firm B breaks even at a higher level of operations than does Firm A. At a production level of 40,000 units, B loses $8,000 but A breaks even.

Firm C has the highest fixed costs. It is highly automated, using expensive, high-speed machines that require very little labor per unit produced. With such an operation, its variable costs rise slowly. Because of the high overhead resulting from charges associated with the expensive machinery, Firm

Figure 9.3

Operating Leverage

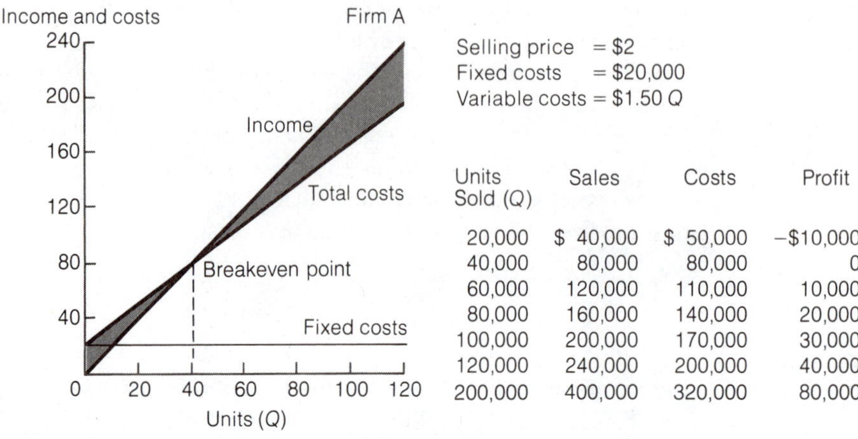

Selling price = \$2
Fixed costs = \$20,000
Variable costs = \$1.50 Q

Units Sold (Q)	Sales	Costs	Profit
20,000	\$ 40,000	\$ 50,000	−\$10,000
40,000	80,000	80,000	0
60,000	120,000	110,000	10,000
80,000	160,000	140,000	20,000
100,000	200,000	170,000	30,000
120,000	240,000	200,000	40,000
200,000	400,000	320,000	80,000

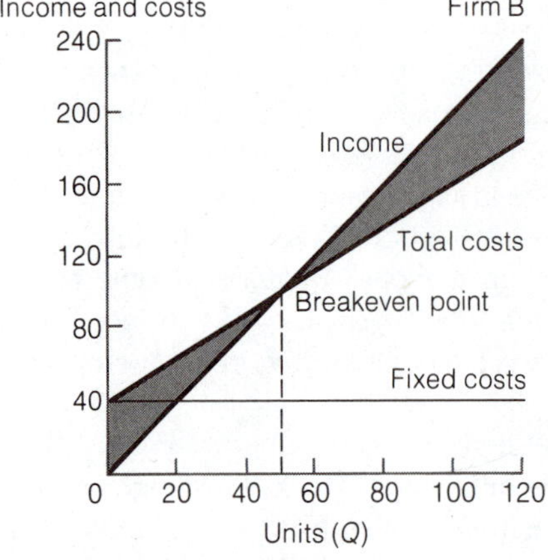

Selling price = \$2
Fixed costs = \$40,000
Variable costs = \$1.20 Q

Units Sold (Q)	Sales	Costs	Profit
20,000	\$ 40,000	\$ 64,000	−\$24,000
40,000	80,000	88,000	− 8,000
60,000	120,000	112,000	8,000
80,000	160,000	136,000	24,000
100,000	200,000	160,000	40,000
120,000	240,000	184,000	56,000
200,000	400,000	280,000	120,000

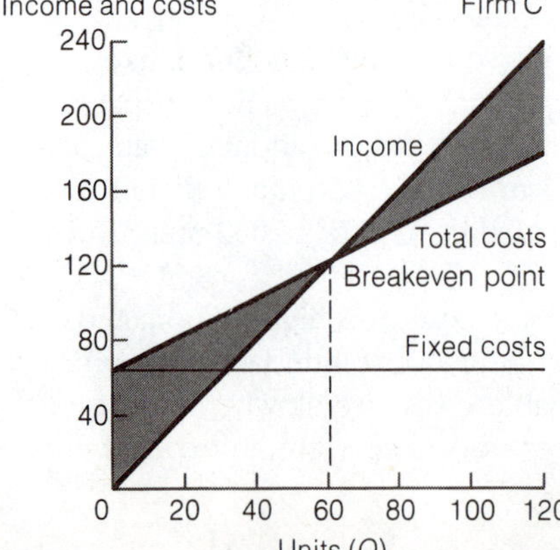

Selling price = \$2
Fixed costs = \$60,000
Variable costs = \$1Q

Units Sold (Q)	Sales	Costs	Profit
20,000	\$ 40,000	\$ 80,000	−\$40,000
40,000	80,000	100,000	− 20,000
60,000	120,000	120,000	0
80,000	160,000	140,000	20,000
100,000	200,000	160,000	40,000
120,000	240,000	180,000	60,000
200,000	400,000	260,000	140,000

C's breakeven point is higher than that for either Firm A or Firm B. Once Firm C reaches its breakeven point, however, its profits rise faster than do those of the other firms.

Alternative operating leverage decisions can have a great impact on the unit cost positions of the individual firms. Consider the relationships when 200,000 units are sold. We can calculate the average per unit costs of production for each firm, dividing total costs by the 200,000 units sold, to obtain:

	Costs per Unit
Firm A	$1.60
Firm B	$1.40
Firm C	$1.30

These results have important implications. At a high volume of operations of 200,000 units per period, Firm C has a substantial cost superiority over the other two firms and particularly over Firm A. Firm C could cut the price of its product to $1.50 per unit, which represents a level that would be unprofitable for Firm A, and still have more than a 13 percent ($.20/$1.50) return on sales. (The average pre-tax margin on sales for manufacturing firms is about 9 to 11 percent.) Another illustration of this idea is the difference in unit costs for Japanese versus U.S. steel companies. Japanese steel companies added capacity to produce 10 million tons or more per year, while only one or two U.S. steel companies added capacity to produce as much as 5 million tons per year. Operating with high fixed costs, but lower average unit costs, the Japanese companies have been able to sell steel in the United States at prices below the costs of the U.S. steel companies. While the total story is complex, the firms' operating leverage factor is an important influence on their relative costs per unit.

Degree of Operating Leverage

Operating leverage can be defined more precisely in terms of the way a given change in volume affects net operating income. For this purpose we use the following definition: The degree of operating leverage is the percentage change in operating income that results from a percentage change in units sold. Algebraically:

$$\begin{matrix}\text{Degree of} \\ \text{operating leverage}\end{matrix} = \frac{\text{Percentage change in operating income}}{\text{Percentage change in units sold}}.$$

For Firm B in Figure 9.3, the degree of operating leverage (OL_b) for a change in units of output from 100,000 to 120,000 is:

$$OL_b = \frac{\dfrac{\Delta\ \text{Income}}{\text{Income}}}{\dfrac{\Delta Q}{Q}} = \frac{\dfrac{\Delta X}{X}}{\dfrac{\Delta Q}{Q}}$$

$$= \frac{\frac{\$56{,}000 - \$40{,}000}{\$40{,}000}}{\frac{120{,}000 - 100{,}000}{100{,}000}} = \frac{\frac{\$16{,}000}{\$40{,}000}}{\frac{20{,}000}{100{,}000}}$$

$$= \frac{40\%}{20\%} = 2.0.$$

Here ΔX is the increase in net operating income. Q is the quantity of output in units, and ΔQ is the increase in output.

For linear breakeven, a formula has been developed to aid in calculating the degree of operating leverage at any level of output, Q:

$$\text{OL} = \frac{\frac{\Delta X}{X}}{\frac{\Delta Q}{Q}} = \frac{\frac{c\,\Delta Q}{cQ - F}}{\frac{\Delta Q}{Q}} = \frac{Qc\,\Delta Q}{\Delta Q(cQ - F)} = \frac{cQ}{X} = \frac{C}{X}. \tag{9.2}$$

We can apply the result in Equation 9.2 to the data for the three firms. Each has the same total revenue function TR = S = 2Q$. Their total costs functions and related measures are:

		V	$P - V = c$
Firm A	TC = $20,000 + $1.5Q	$1.5	$ .50
Firm B	TC = $40,000 + $1.2Q	$1.2	$ .80
Firm C	TC = $60,000 + $1.0Q	$1.0	$1.00

To calculate the degree of operating leverage at a sales volume of 100,000 units, for example, we can make use of the following pattern of income.

	$C = cQ$	$X = cQ - F$
Firm A	$ 50,000	$30,000
Firm B	80,000	40,000
Firm C	100,000	40,000

We now have the data needed to calculate the degree of operating leverage for each firm.

$$\text{OL} = \frac{C}{X} \quad \text{OL}_a = \frac{50{,}000}{30{,}000} = 1.67. \quad \text{OL}_b = \frac{80{,}000}{40{,}000} = 2. \quad \text{OL}_c = \frac{100{,}000}{40{,}000} = 2.5.$$

Thus, for a 100 percent increase in volume, Firm C, the company with the most operating leverage, will experience a profit increase of 250 percent; for the same 100 percent volume gain, Firm A, the one with the least leverage, will have only a 167 percent profit gain.

In summary, the calculation of the degree of operating leverage shows algebraically the same pattern that Figure 9.3 shows graphically—that the profits of Firm C, the company with the most operating leverage, are most sensitive to changes in sales volume, while those of Firm A, which has only a small amount of operating leverage, are relatively insensitive to volume changes. Firm B, with an intermediate degree of leverage, lies between the two extremes.[1]

The degree of operating leverage measures the effect on profitability of a change in either direction in the volume of output sold—that is, an increase or decrease in quantity sold. The measure has important implications for a number of areas of business and financial policy. Firm C's high degree of operating leverage suggests gains from increasing volume. Suppose Firm C could increase its quantity sold from 100,000 units to 120,000 units by cutting the price per unit to $1.90. The equation for net operating income is

$$\begin{aligned}\text{Net Operating Income } (X) &= PQ - vQ - F \\ &= \$1.90(120{,}000) - 120{,}000(\$1) - \$60{,}000 \\ &= \$228{,}000 - \$120{,}000 - \$60{,}000 \\ &= \$48{,}000.\end{aligned}$$

The equation shows that Firm C could increase its profits from $40,000 at a volume of 100,000 to $48,000 at a volume of 120,000. Thus a high degree of operating leverage suggests that an aggressive price policy may increase profits, particularly if the market is responsive to small price cuts.

On the other hand, Firm C's high degree of operating leverage tells us that the company is subject to large swings in profits as its volume fluctuates. Thus, if Firm C's industry is one whose sales are greatly affected by changes in the overall level of economic activity (as are, for example, the durable goods industries, such as machine tools, steel, and autos), its profits are subject to large fluctuations. Hence, the degree of financial leverage appropriate for Firm C to take on is lower than that for a firm with a lower degree of operating leverage and for industries whose sales are less sensitive to fluctuations in the level of the economy. (Financial leverage is discussed in Chapters 15 and 16.)

Cash Breakeven Analysis

Some of the firm's fixed costs are noncash outlays, and, for a period, some of its revenues may be in receivables. The cash breakeven chart for Firm B, constructed on the assumption that $30,000 of the fixed costs from the previous illustration are depreciation charges and, therefore, a noncash outlay, is shown in Figure 9.4. Because fixed cash outlays are only $10,000, the cash

1. The degree of operating leverage is a form of *elasticity concept* and thus is akin to the familiar price elasticity developed in economics. Since operating leverage is an elasticity, it varies, depending on the particular part of the breakeven graph that is being considered. For example, in terms of our illustrative firms, the degree of operating leverage is greatest close to the breakeven point, where a very small change in volume can produce a very large percentage increase in profits simply because the base profits are close to zero near the breakeven point.

Figure 9.4

Cash Breakeven Analysis

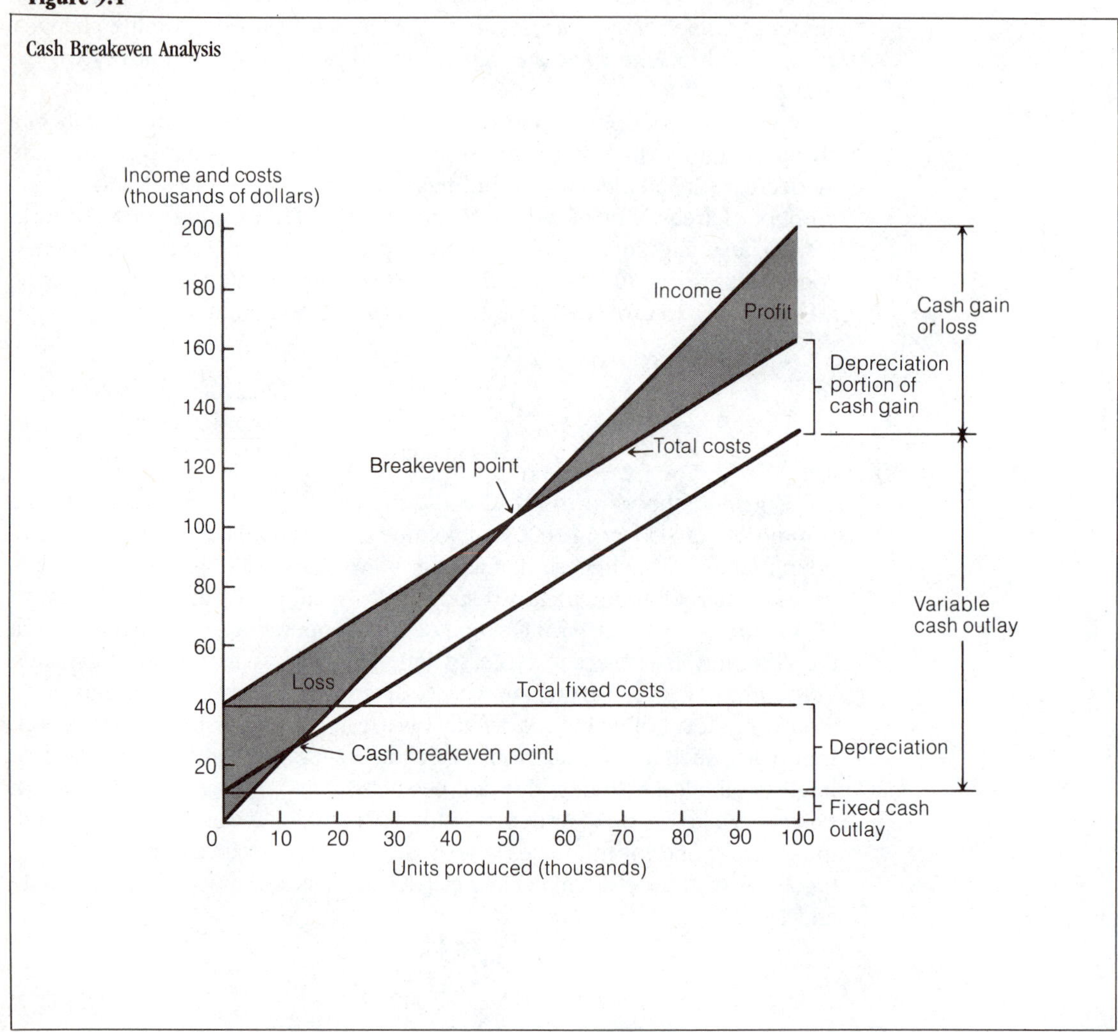

breakeven point is at 12,500 units rather than 50,000 units, which is the profit breakeven point.

An equation for the cash breakeven point based on sales dollars can be derived from the equation for the profit breakeven point (see Table 9.3). The only change is to reduce fixed costs by the amount of noncash outlays:

$$S^* = \frac{F - \text{Noncash outlays}}{\text{CR}}.$$

If noncash outlays are very close to total fixed costs, the cash breakeven point approaches zero. The cash breakeven point based on units of output is comparable to the profit breakeven quantity, except that fixed costs must be adjusted for noncash outlays:

$$Q^* = \frac{F - \text{Noncash outlays}}{c}.$$

Here again, if noncash outlays are very large, the cash breakeven point may be low, despite a large amount of fixed charges.

Cash breakeven analysis does not fully represent cash flows; for this a cash budget is required. But cash breakeven analysis is useful because it provides a picture of the flow of funds from operations. A firm may incur a level of fixed costs that will result in losses during business downswings but large profits during upswings. If cash outlays are small, the firm may be able to operate above the cash breakeven point even during periods of loss. Thus, the risk of insolvency (in the sense of inability to meet cash obligations) is small. This allows a firm to reach out for higher profits through automation and operating leverage.

Limitations of Breakeven Analysis

Breakeven analysis is useful in studying the relations among volume, prices, and costs; it is thus helpful in pricing, cost control, and decisions about expansion programs. It has limitations, however, as a guide to managerial actions.

Linear breakeven analysis is especially weak in what it implies about the sales possibilities for the firm. Any linear breakeven chart is based on a constant sales price. Therefore, in order to study profit possibilities under different prices, a whole series of charts is necessary—one for each price. Alternatively, nonlinear breakeven analysis can be used.

Breakeven analysis is also deficient with regard to costs; the relations indicated by the chart do not hold at all outputs. If sales increase to levels at which the existing plant and equipment are worked to capacity, additional workers are hired, and overtime pay increases; all this causes variable costs to rise sharply. Additional equipment and plant are required, thereby increasing fixed costs. Finally, over a period, the products sold by the firm change in quality and quantity. Such changes in product mix influence the level and slope of the cost function. Linear breakeven analysis is useful as a first step in developing the basic data required for pricing and for financial decisions. But more detailed analysis is required before final judgments can be made.

Planning and Control: Budgeting

Our orientation is toward financial planning and control, with the determination of investment requirements as a prime planning goal. In turn, we need to analyze how investment requirements give rise to financing needs. But the relationship between sales, investments, and financing requirements is not the total story. As our previous discussion of breakeven analysis and operating leverage emphasized, proper planning and control of the relationship between revenues and costs provide an overall framework. To help achieve the targeted profitability patterns, budgets provide a detailed analysis of revenues and outlays for the important categories of a firm's activity.

Nature of the Budgeting Process

A budget is a part of a broader financial planning and control process. Budgeting includes a plan that details revenues and how funds will be spent on labor, raw materials, capital goods, and so on, as well as periodic reviews of actual versus budgeted amounts. Budgeting is thus a management tool used both for planning and control. Depending on the nature of the business, detailed plans may be formulated for the next few months, the next year, the next five years, or even longer. A company engaged in, say, heavy construction must constantly extend bids that may or may not be accepted; it cannot, and indeed need not, plan as far ahead as an electric utility company. The electric utility can base its projections on population growth, which is predictable for five- to ten-year periods, and it *must* plan asset acquisitions years ahead because of the long lead times involved in constructing dams, nuclear power plants, and the like.

Fundamentally, the budgeting process is a method to improve operations —a continuous effort to specify what should be done to get the job completed in the best possible way. Corporate budgeting should not be thought of as a device for limiting expenditures; instead, it should be seen as a tool for obtaining the most productive and profitable use of the company's resources. The budget requires a set of performance standards, or targets, that can be compared to actual results. This process, called *controlling to plan,* is a continuous monitoring procedure that reviews and evaluates performance with reference to previously established standards.

The establishment of standards requires a realistic understanding of the activities carried on by the firm. Arbitrary standards, set without a basic understanding of the minimum costs as determined by the nature of the firm's operations, can do more harm than good. Budgets imposed in an arbitrary fashion may represent impossible targets at the one extreme or standards that are too lax at the other. If standards are unrealistically high, frustrations and resentment will develop. If they are unduly low, costs will swing out of control, profits will suffer, and morale will deteriorate. However, a set of budgets based on a clear understanding and careful analysis of operations can play an important positive role for the firm.[2]

2. The authors are familiar with one case where an unrealistic budget ruined a major national corporation. Top management set impossible performance and growth goals for the various divisions. The divisions, in an effort to meet the sales and profit projections, expanded into high-risk product lines (especially real estate development ventures), employed questionable accounting practices that tended to overstate profits, and the like. Debt financing was emphasized in order to leverage earnings. Things looked good for several years, but eventually the true situation became apparent. Top management brought in a team of consultants in an attempt to correct the problems, but it was too late; the firm was beyond help. To us, the most interesting point is that the consultants traced the firm's difficulties *directly* back to the unrealistic targets established by top management without adequate consultation with the division managers.

Budgets represent planning and control devices that enable management to anticipate change and adapt to it. Business operations in today's economic environment are complex and subject to heavy competitive pressures and many kinds of changes. The rate of growth of the economy as a whole fluctuates, and these fluctuations affect different industries in a number of different ways. If a firm plans ahead, the budget and control process can provide management with a good basis for understanding the firm's operations in relation to the general environment. This understanding can enable the firm to react quickly to developing events, thereby increasing its ability to perform effectively.

In summary, the budgeting process improves internal coordination. Decisions for each product at each stage and level—research, engineering, production, marketing, personnel, and finance—have an impact on the firm's profits. Coordination and control are the essence of profit planning, and the budget system provides an integrated picture of the firm's operations as a whole. It thus enables division managers to see the relationship of their part of the enterprise to the totality of the firm. For example, a production decision to alter the level of work-in-process inventories or a marketing decision to change the terms under which a particular product is sold can be traced through the entire budget system to show its effects on the firm's overall profitability. The budgeting system is thus a most important financial tool.

Budgeting and Planning

The relationship between budgeting and planning is outlined in Figure 9.5. Budgeting is part of the total planning activity in the firm, so we must begin with a statement of corporate goals or objectives. The statement of goals (shown in the box at the top of the figure) determines the second section of the figure, the corporate long-range plan. Moving down the figure, a segment of the corporate long-range plan includes a long-range sales forecast. This forecast requires a determination of the number and types of products that will be manufactured both at present and in the future years encompassed by the long-range plan—the product mix strategy.

Short-term forecasts and budgets are formulated within the framework of the long-range plan. For example, one might begin with a sales forecast covering six months or one year. This forecast provides a basis for, and is dependent on, the broad range of policies indicated in the lower portion of Figure 9.5. First, the manufacturing policies that cover the choice of types of equipment, plant layout, and production-line arrangements must be chosen. In addition, the kind of durability built into the products and their associated costs must be considered. Second, a broad set of marketing policies must be formulated. These policies relate to the development of the firm's own sales organization versus the use of outside sales organizations; the number of salespeople and the method by which they will be compensated; the forms of, types of, and amounts spent on advertising; and other factors. Third, the research and general management policies must be determined. Research

Figure 9.5

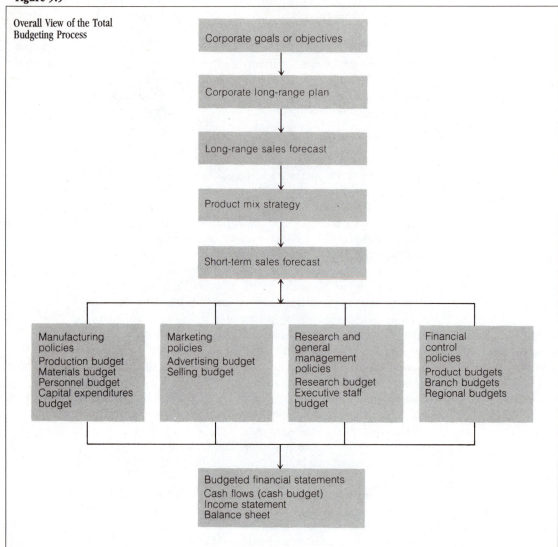

Overall View of the Total Budgeting Process

policies deal with the relative emphasis on basic versus applied research and the product areas emphasized by both types of research. Fourth, the financial policies (the subject of this chapter) must be set. The four major policies must be established simultaneously, since each affects the others. We shall concentrate on financial control policies, but it is important to realize the interdependence of financial and other policies.

Financial Control Policies

Financial control policies encompass the organization and content of various kinds of financial control budgets, including budgets for individual products and for every significant activity of the firm. Additional budgets, formulated to control operations at individual branch offices, are grouped and modified to control regional operations as well.

In a similar manner, policies established at the manufacturing, marketing, research, and general management levels give rise to another series of budgets. For example, the production budget reflects the use of materials, parts, labor, and facilities; and each of its major elements is likely to have its own budget program. There is usually a materials budget, a labor or personnel requirements budget, and a facilities or long-run capital expenditures budget. After the good is produced, the next step in the process is the creation of a marketing budget. Related to the overall process are the general office and executive requirements, which are reflected in the general and administrative budget system.

The results of projecting all these elements of cost are reflected in the budgeted (also called *pro forma* or *projected*) income statement. Anticipated sales give rise to contemplation of the various types of investments needed to produce the products; these investments, plus the beginning balance sheet, provide the necessary data for developing the assets side of the balance sheet.

Assets must be financed, but first a cash flow analysis (the cash budget) is needed. The cash budget indicates the combined effects of the budgeted operations on the firm's cash flows. A positive net cash flow indicates that the firm has ample financing. However, if an increase in the volume of operations leads to a negative cash flow, additional financing is required. This leads directly to choices of financing, which is the subject of a considerable portion of the remainder of the book.

Since the structures of the income statement and the balance sheet have already been covered in Chapter 7, the rest of this part of the text will deal with the two remaining aspects of the budgeting process—the cash budget and the concept of variable, or flexible, budgets.

Cash Budgeting

The cash budget indicates not only the total amount of financing required but its timing as well. It shows the amount of funds needed month by month, week by week, or even day by day; and it is one of the financial manager's most important tools. Because a clear understanding of the nature of cash budgeting is important, the process is described by means of an example that makes the elements of the cash budget explicit.

Marvel Toy is a medium-sized toy manufacturer. Sales are highly seasonal, the peak occurring in September, when retailers stock up for the Christmas season. All sales are on terms that allow a cash discount for payments made within thirty days; if the discount is not taken, the full amount must be paid in sixty days. However, Marvel, like most other companies, finds that some of its customers delay payment up to ninety days. Experience has shown that that on 20 percent of the sales, payment is made within thirty days; on 70 percent it is made within sixty days, and on 10 percent it is made within ninety days.

Marvel's production is geared to future sales. Purchased materials and parts, which amount to 70 percent of sales, are bought the month before the company expects to sell the finished product. Its own purchase terms permit Marvel to delay payment on its purchases for one month. Thus, if August sales are forecast at $30,000, Marvel's purchases during July will amount to $21,000, which it will pay in August.

Wages and salaries, rent, and other cash expenses for Marvel are given in Table 9.4. The company also has a tax payment of $8,000 coming due in August. Its capital budgeting plans call for the purchase in July of a new machine tool costing $10,000, payment to be made in September. Assuming the company needs to keep a $5,000 cash balance at all times and has $6,000 on July 1, what are Marvel's financial requirements for the period July through December?

The cash requirements are worked out in the cash budget shown in Table 9.4. The top half of the table provides a worksheet for calculating collections on sales and payments on purchases. The first line in the worksheet gives the sales forecast for the period May through January (May and June sales are necessary to determine collections for July and August). The second line shows cash collections. The first line under this heading shows that 20 percent of the sales during any given month are collected that month. The second line shows the collections on the prior month's sales—70 percent of sales in the preceding month. The third line gives collections from sales two months earlier—10 percent of sales in that month. The collections are summed to find the total cash receipts from sales during each month under consideration.

With the worksheet completed, the cash budget itself can be considered. Receipts from collections are given on the top line. Next, payments during each month are summarized. The difference between cash receipts and cash payments is the net cash gain or loss during the month; for July, there is a net cash loss of $4,200. The initial cash on hand at the beginning of the month is added to the net cash gain or loss during the month to yield the cumulative cash that will be on hand if no financing is done; at the end of July, Marvel Toy will have cumulative cash equal to $1,800. The desired cash balance, $5,000, is subtracted from the cumulative cash balance to determine the amount of financing the firm needs if it is to maintain the desired level of cash. At the end of July, Marvel will need $3,200; thus loans outstanding will total $3,200 at that time.

The same procedure is used in the following months. Sales will expand seasonally in August; with increased sales will come increased payments for purchases, wages, and other items. Moreover, the $8,000 tax bill is due in August. Receipts from sales will go up too, but the firm will still be left with a

Table 9.4

Marvel Toy Company
Worksheet and Cash Budget

Worksheet	May	June	July	Aug.	Sept.	Oct.	Nov.	Dec.	Jan.
Sales (net of cash discounts)	$10,000	$10,000	$20,000	$30,000	$40,000	$20,000	$20,000	$10,000	$10,000
Collections:									
First month (at 20%)	2,000	2,000	4,000	6,000	8,000	4,000	4,000	2,000	2,000
Second month (at 70%)		7,000	7,000	14,000	21,000	28,000	14,000	14,000	7,000
Third month (at 10%)			1,000	1,000	2,000	3,000	4,000	2,000	2,000
Total	$ 2,000	$ 9,000	$12,000	$21,000	$31,000	$35,000	$22,000	$18,000	$11,000
Purchases (70% of next month's sales)	$ 7,000	$14,000	$21,000	$28,000	$14,000	$14,000	$ 7,000	$ 7,000	
Payments (one month lag)		$ 7,000	$14,000	$21,000	$28,000	$14,000	$14,000	$ 7,000	$ 7,000
Cash Budget									
Receipts:									
Collections			$12,000	$21,000	$31,000	$35,000	$22,000	$18,000	$11,000
Payments:									
Purchases			$14,000	$21,000	$28,000	$14,000	$14,000	$ 7,000	
Wages and salaries			1,500	2,000	2,500	1,500	1,500	1,000	
Rent			500	500	500	500	500	500	
Other expenses			200	300	400	200	200	100	
Taxes			—	8,000	—	—	—	—	
Payment on machine			—	—	10,000	—	—	—	
Total payments			$16,200	$31,800	$41,400	$16,200	$16,200	$ 8,600	
Net cash gain (loss) during month			−$4,200	−$10,800	−$10,400	$18,800	$ 5,800	$ 9,400	
Cash at start of month if no borrowing is done			6,000	1,800	−9,000	−19,400	−600	5,200	
Cumulative cash (cash at start plus gains or minus losses)			$ 1,800	−$ 9,000	−$19,400	−$ 600	$ 5,200	$14,600	
Less: Desired level of cash			−5,000	−5,000	−5,000	−5,000	−5,000	−5,000	
Total loans outstanding to maintain $5,000 cash balance			$ 3,200	$14,000	$24,400	$ 5,600	—	—	
Surplus cash			—	—	—	—	$ 200	$ 9,600	

$10,800 cash deficit during the month. The total financial requirements at the end of August will be $14,000—the $3,200 needed at the end of July plus the $10,800 cash deficit for August. Loans outstanding at the end of August will thus total $14,000.

Sales peak in September, and the cash deficit during this month will amount to another $10,400. The total need for funds through September will increase to $24,400. Sales, purchases, and payments for past purchases will fall markedly in October; collections will be the highest of any month because they will reflect the high September sales. As a result, Marvel Toy will enjoy a healthy $18,800 cash surplus during October. This surplus can be used to pay off borrowings, so the need for financing will decline by $18,800 to $5,600.

Marvel will have another cash surplus in November, and this extra cash will permit the company to eliminate completely the need for financing. In fact, the company is expected to have $200 in surplus cash by the month's end, while another cash surplus in December will swell the amount of extra cash to $9,600. With such a large amount of unneeded funds, Marvel's treasurer will doubtless want to make investments in some interest-bearing securities or put the funds to use in some other way. (Types of investments for excess funds are discussed in Chapter 11.)

Variable, or Flexible, Budgets

Budgets are planned allocations of a firm's resources, based on forecasts for the future. Two important elements influence actual performance. One is the impact of external influences over which the firm has little or no control—developments in the economy as a whole and competitive developments in the firm's own industry. The other is the firm's level of efficiency at a given volume of sales, which is controllable. It is necessary to separate these two elements in evaluating individual performances.

Table 9.5

Hubler Department Store: Relationship between Sales and Employees

Month	Sales (in Millions of Dollars)	Number of Employees
January	$ 4	45
February	5	56
March	6	50
April	7	62
May	10	100
June	9	98
July	11	105
August	8	85

The essence of the variable budget system is its introduction of flexibility into budgets by its recognition that certain types of expenditures vary at different levels of output. Thus a firm may have alternative levels of outlay budgeted for different volumes of operations—high, low, medium. One of management's responsibilities is to determine which of the alternative budgets should be in effect for the planning period under consideration.

The regression method, described in the preceding chapter in connection with financial forecasting, can also be used to establish the basis for flexible budgeting. To illustrate: Suppose that a retail store, the Hubler Department Store, has had the experience indicated by the historical data set forth in Table 9.5. It is apparent from the data that the number of employees the firm needs is dependent on the dollar volume of sales in each month. This is seen more easily from the scatter diagram of Figure 9.6. The regression line is sloped positively because the number of employees increases as the volume of sales increases. The independent variable, dollar volume of sales, is called the control variable. Variations in the control variable cause changes in total expenses. The volume of sales can be forecast and the need for employees

Figure 9.6

Scatter Diagram and Regression Line: Hubler Department Store

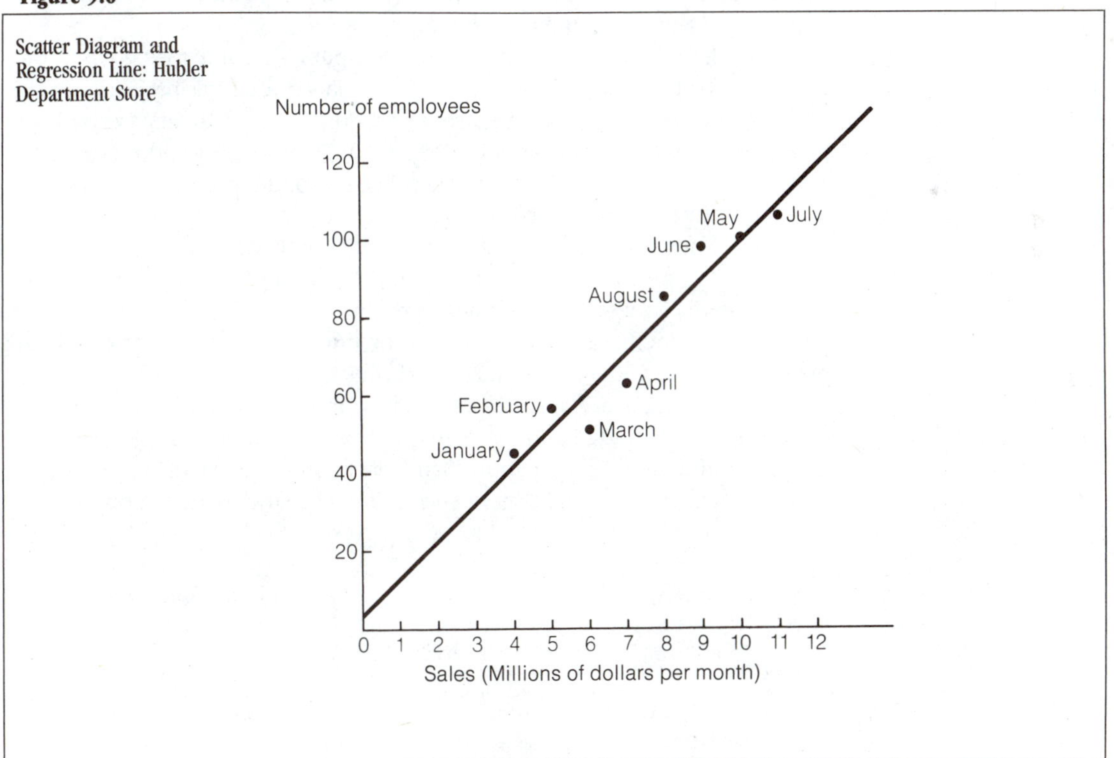

Table 9.6

Hubler Department Store Budget Allowance

Sales (in Millions of Dollars)	Number of Employees	Weekly Payroll Estimate (Average Wage $100)
$ 6	61	$ 6,100
7	70	7,000
8	80	8,000
9	89	8,900
10	99	9,900
11	109	10,900

read from the regression chart.[3] The relations are expressed in tabular form in Table 9.6. Given the forecast of sales, standards can be provided for the expected number of employees and the weekly payroll.[4]

Problems of Budgeting

The use of budget systems entails four major problems. First, budgetary programs can grow to be so detailed that they become cumbersome and unduly expensive. Overbudgeting can be inefficient.

Second, budgetary goals may come to supersede enterprise goals. A budget is a tool, not an end in itself. Enterprise goals by definition supersede subsidiary plans, of which budgets are a part. Moreover, budgets are based on future expectations that may not be realized. There is no good reason not to alter budgets as circumstances change. This reasoning is the core of the argument in favor of more flexible budgets.

Third, budgets can hide inefficiencies by continuing initial expenditures in succeeding periods without proper evaluation. Budgets growing from precedent usually contain undesirable expenditures. They should not be used as umbrellas for inefficient management. The budgetary process must contain a provision for periodic reexamination of standards.

Finally, budgets are sometimes used as pressure devices, defeating their basic objectives. Budgets that are instruments of tyranny cause resentment and frustration, feelings which in turn lead to inefficiency. In order to counteract this effect, top management should increase the participation of subordinates in preparing budgets.

3. The regression equation is $E = 3 + 9.6S$ where E is the number of employees and S equals sales in millions of dollars.
4. Regression analysis provides even more flexibility in budgeting than do the high, medium, and low levels mentioned earlier. Also, it is possible to include confidence levels when using the regression method. For example, Table 9.6 shows that when volume is at $8 million, Hubler expects to have 80 employees and a weekly payroll of $8,000. Assuming a standard error of 7, actual observations should be between 73 and 87 employees at this sales volume 95 percent of the time. Similar ranges can be determined for other volumes. As a matter of control policy, management may investigate whenever actual performances outside this expected range occur.

Use of Financial Plans and Budgets

Forecasts, or long-range plans, are necessary in all the firm's operations. The personnel department must have a good idea of the scale of future operations if it is to plan its hiring and training activities properly. The production department must be sure that productive capacity is available to meet the projected product demand. The finance department must be sure that funds are on hand to meet the firm's financial requirements.

The tools and techniques discussed in this and preceding chapters are used in several separate but related ways. First, the percent of sales method or, preferably, the regression method is used to make a long-range forecast of financial requirements over a projected three- to five-year period. This forecast is used to draw up the strategic financing plans during the planning period. The company might, for example, plan to meet its financial requirements with retained earnings and short-term bank debt during, say, 1980 and 1981, float a bond issue in 1982, use retained earnings in 1983, and finally sell an issue of common stock in 1984. Fairly long lead times are necessary when companies sell bonds or stocks; otherwise, they might be forced to go into the market during unfavorable periods.

In addition to long-run strategic planning, financial managers must also make accurate short-run forecasts to be sure that funds will be available to meet seasonal and other short-run requirements. They may, for example, meet with a bank loan officer to discuss their company's need for funds during the coming year. Prior to the meeting, the firm's accountants may prepare a detailed cash budget showing the maximum amount of money needed during the year, how much will be needed each month, and how cash surpluses will be generated at some point to enable the firm to repay the bank loan.

Financial managers will also have their firm's pro forma and most recent balance sheets and income statements, from which they will calculate the key financial ratios to show both actual and projected financial positions to the banker. If the firm's financial position is sound and its cash budget reasonable, the bank is more likely to make the required funds available. Even if the bank denies the loan request, the firm's financial managers will have time to seek other sources of funds. While it is not pleasant to have to look elsewhere for money, the firm needs to know ahead of time when a loan request will be refused.

Divisional Control in a Decentralized Firm

In our discussion of the Du Pont system of financial control in Chapter 7, we considered its use for the firm as a whole. However, the Du Pont system is mainly used to control the various parts of a multidivisional firm.

For organizational reasons, large firms are generally set up on a decentralized basis. For example, General Electric establishes separate divisions for heavy appliances, light appliances, power transformers, fossil fuel generating equipment, nuclear generating equipment, and so on. Each division is defined as a *profit center,* and each has its own investments—fixed and current assets, together with a share of such general corporate assets as research labs and headquarters buildings—and is expected to earn an appropriate return on them.

The corporate headquarters, or central staff, typically controls the various divisions by a form of the Du Pont system. When it is used for divisional control, the procedure is frequently referred to as ROI (return on investment) control. Here, profits are measured by operating earnings—income before taxes—as shown in Figure 9.7. Sometimes the earnings figure is calculated before depreciation, and total gross assets are measured before deduction of the depreciation reserve. Measurement on gross assets has the advantage of avoiding differences in ROI that are due to differences in the average age of the fixed assets. Older assets are more fully depreciated and have a higher depreciation reserve and lower net fixed asset amount. This causes the ROI on net total assets to be higher when fixed assets are older.

If a particular division's ROI falls below a target figure, then the centralized corporate staff helps the division's own financial staff trace back through the Du Pont system to determine the cause of the substandard ROI. Each division manager is judged by the division's ROI and rewarded or penalized accordingly. Division managers are thus motivated to keep their ROI up to the target level. Their individual actions should in turn maintain the firm's ROI at an appropriate level.

In addition to its use in managerial control, ROI can be used to allocate funds to the various divisions. The firm as a whole has financial resources—retained earnings, cash flow from depreciation, and the ability to obtain additional debt and equity funds from capital markets. These funds can be allocated on the basis of the divisional ROIs, in which instance divisions having high ROIs receive more funds than do those with low ones.[5]

A number of problems can arise if ROI control is used without proper safeguards. Since the divisional managers are rewarded on the basis of their ROI performance, it is absolutely essential for their morale that they feel their divisional ROI does indeed provide an accurate measure of relative performance. But ROI is dependent on a number of factors in addition to managerial competence, some of which are listed below.

1. *Depreciation.* ROI is very sensitive to depreciation policy. If one division is writing off assets at a relatively rapid rate, its annual profits—and hence its ROI—will be reduced.
2. *Book value of assets.* If an older division is using assets that have been largely written off, both its current depreciation charges and its investment base will be low. This will make its ROI high in relation to newer divisions.

5. The point of this procedure is to increase the firm's ROI. To maximize the overall ROI, marginal ROI among divisions should be equalized.

Figure 9.7

Du Pont Chart for Divisional Control

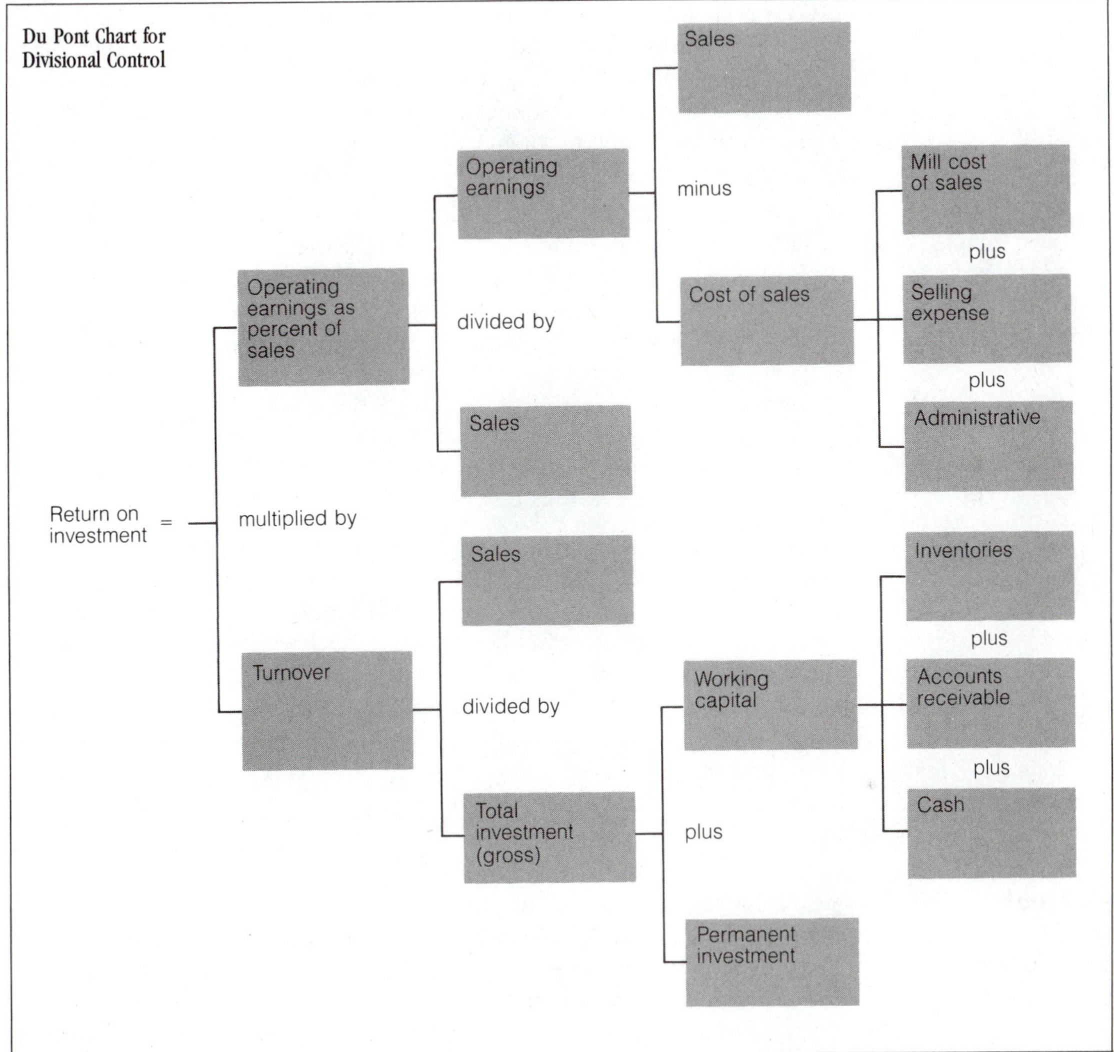

3. *Transfer pricing.* In most corporations some divisions sell to other divisions. At General Motors, for example, the Fisher Body Division sells to the Chevrolet Division. In such cases the price at which goods are transferred between divisions has a fundamental effect on divisional profits. If the transfer price of auto bodies is set relatively high, then Fisher Body will have a relatively high ROI and Chevrolet a relatively low one.
4. *Time periods.* Many projects have long gestation periods, during which expenditures must be made for research and development, plant construc-

tion, market development, and the like. Such expenditures add to the investment base without a commensurate increase in profits for several years. During this period, a division's ROI can be seriously reduced; and without proper constraints, its manager may be improperly penalized. Given the frequency of personnel transfers in larger corporations, it is easy to see how the timing problem can keep managers from making long-term investments that are in the best interests of the firm.

5. *Industry conditions.* If one division is operating in an industry where conditions are favorable and rates of return are high, while another is in an industry suffering from excessive competition, the environmental differences may cause the favored division to look good and the unfavored one to look bad, quite apart from any differences in their managers. Signal Companies' aerospace division, for example, could hardly have been expected to show up as well as their truck division in a year like 1973, when the entire aerospace industry was suffering severe problems and truck sales were booming. External conditions must be taken into account when appraising ROI performance.

Because of these factors, divisional ROIs must be supplemented with other criteria for evaluating performance. For example, a division's growth rate in sales, profits, and market share (as well as its ROI) in comparison with other firms in its own industry has been used in such evaluations. Although ROI control has been used with great success in U.S. industry, the system should not be employed mechanically. As with most other tools, it is helpful if used properly but destructive if misused.

External Uses of Financial Forecasts and Budgets

We have stressed the use of planning and budgeting for internal purposes—that is, to increase the efficiency of a firm's operations. With relatively minor modifications, the same tools and techniques can be used in both credit and security analysis. For example, outside security analysts can forecast a given firm's sales and, through the income statement and balance sheet relationships, can prepare pro forma (projected) balance sheets and income statements. Credit analysts can make similar projections to help estimate their customers' needs for funds and the likelihood that borrowers can make prompt repayment.

These kinds of analysis have actually been conducted on a large scale in recent years. Very complete financial data going back some twenty years on several thousand large, publicly owned corporations are now available on magnetic tapes (Standard & Poor's Compustat tapes). These tapes are being used in highly sophisticated ways by security analysts. From what we have seen, such analyses offer large potential benefits. The same tapes, frequently supplemented with additional data, are being used by the major lending institutions—banks and insurance companies—to forecast their customers' needs for funds and to plan their own financial requirements.

Summary

The general subject of this chapter is the financial planning and control process. A number of analytical approaches to help implement financial planning and control are set forth. Breakeven analysis investigates the relationship between investment outlays and the volume required to achieve profitability. Breakeven analysis focuses on the pattern of relations between total revenues and total costs. It is a method of relating fixed costs, variable costs, and total revenues to show the level of sales that must be attained if the firm is to operate at a profit. The analysis can be based on the number of units produced or on total dollar sales. It can be used for the entire company or for a particular product or division. With minor modifications, it can be put on a cash basis instead of a profit basis. Ordinarily, breakeven analysis is conducted on a linear, or straight line, basis. However, this is not necessary; nonlinear breakeven analysis is feasible and at times desirable.

Operating leverage is defined as the extent to which fixed costs are used in operations. The degree of operating leverage, defined as the percentage change in operating income that results from a specific percentage change in units sold, provides a precise measure of how much operating leverage a particular firm is employing. Breakeven analysis presents a graphic view of the effects on profits of changes in sales; the degree of operating leverage presents the same picture in algebraic terms. Breakeven analysis emphasizes the volume of sales required by the firm to achieve profitability. The degree of operating leverage measures the sensitivity of the firm's operating profitability to changes in the volume of sales. Both concepts measure the effects of the relative size of fixed costs in the total cost function of the firm.

The budgeting process provides more detailed analysis for the control of revenues and costs. The firm's budget is a detailed plan of how funds will be spent. A budget is a plan stated in terms of specific expenditures for specific purposes; it is used for both planning and control. Its overall purpose is to improve internal operations, thereby reducing costs and raising profitability. A budgeting system starts with a set of performance standards, or targets. The targets constitute, in effect, the firm's financial plan. The budgeted figures are compared with actual results; this is the control phase of the budget system, and it is a critical step in well-operated companies.

Although the entire budget system is vital to corporate management, one aspect of the system is especially important to the financial manager—the cash budget. The cash budget is, in fact, the principal tool for making short-run financial forecasts. If used properly, it can pinpoint the funds that will be needed, when they will be needed, and when cash flows will be sufficient to retire any necessary loans.

A good budget system recognizes that some factors lie outside the firm's control. Especially important here is the state of the economy and its effects on sales. Flexible budgets, assuming different levels of sales, are set up as targets for the different departments. A good system also ensures that those responsible for carrying out a plan are involved in its preparation; this procedure helps guard against the establishment of unrealistic targets and unattainable goals.

As a firm becomes larger, it must to some extent decentralize operations. But decentralized operations still require some centralized control. The principal tool used for such control is the return on investment (ROI) method. There are problems with ROI control; but if budgeting and ROI control are viewed as a communication system that aids the flow of information among managers of the firm, a dynamic interaction among managers can be developed. If the emphasis is on an informed interaction process, the results of operations as measured by ROI will be improved. Communication and motivation, the behavioral aspects of the budgeting process, cannot be overemphasized.

Questions

9.1 What benefits can be derived from breakeven analysis?

9.2 What is operating leverage? Explain how profits or losses can be magnified in a firm with high operating leverage as opposed to a firm without this characteristic.

9.3 What data are necessary to construct a breakeven chart?

9.4 What is the general effect of each of the following changes on a firm's breakeven point?

a. An increase in selling price with no change in units sold.

b. A change from the leasing of a machine for $5,000 a year to the purchase of the machine for $100,000. The useful life of this machine will be twenty years, with no salvage value. Assume straight line depreciation.

c. A reduction in variable labor costs.

9.5 In what sense can depreciation be considered a source of funds?

9.6 What use might a confidence interval scheme have in variable budgeting?

9.7 Why is a cash budget important even when there is plenty of cash in the bank?

9.8 What is the difference between the long-range financial forecasting concept (for example, the percent of sales method) and the budgeting concept? How might they be used together?

9.9 Assume that a firm is making up its long-run financial budget. What period should this budget cover—one month, six months, one year, three years, five years, or some other period? Justify your answer.

9.10 Is a detailed budget more important to a large, multidivisional firm than to a small, single-product firm?

9.11 Assume that your uncle is a major stockholder in a multidivisional firm that uses a naive ROI criterion for evaluating divisional managers and that bases managers' salaries in large part on this evaluation. You can have the job of division manager in any division you choose. If you are a salary maximizer, what divisional characteristics will you seek? If, because of your good performance, you become president of the firm, what changes will you make?

Problems

9.1 The Drake Corporation produces blenders, which it sells for $18. Fixed costs are $110,000 for up to 24,000 units of output. Variable cost is $10 per unit.

a. Make a contribution statement for Drake at sales of 12,000 units and at sales of 18,000 units.

b. What is the breakeven quantity? Illustrate by means of a chart.

c. What is Drake's degree of operating leverage at sales of 12,000 and 18,000 units?

d. What happens to the breakeven point if selling price falls to $16? What is the significance of the change to financial management? Illustrate by means of a chart.

e. How does the breakeven point change when the selling price falls to $16 but variable cost falls to $8 a unit? Illustrate by means of a chart.

9.2 For Benson Industries the following relations exist: Each unit of output is sold for $75; for output up to 25,000 units the fixed costs are $240,000; variable costs are $35 a unit.

a. Make a contribution statement for Benson at sales of 5,000 units and at sales of 8,000 units.

b. What is the breakeven quantity? Illustrate by means of a chart.

c. What is Benson's degree of operating leverage at sales of 5,000 and 8,000 units?

d. What happens to the breakeven point if the selling price rises to $85? What is the significance of the change to financial management? Illustrate by means of a chart.

e. What occurs to the breakeven point if the selling price rises to $85 but variable costs rise to $45 a unit? Illustrate by means of a chart.

9.3 The Kennington Tire Company is currently considering two possible mutually exclusive plant modernizations. Under the first, newer and more efficient machinery would be added; this would tend to reduce labor costs and, because of much less waste, raw material usage. The other alternative would involve a more extensive plant changeover to an entirely new process for forming and curing rubber. The second procedure would involve a more extensive investment in both plant and equipment, but it would result in larger savings in labor and materials costs.

The current sales level is about 76,500 units a year at a price of $40 each, but volume has fluctuated from year to year with changes in general economic conditions. The firm's management is primarily concerned with the extent to which profitability will be affected by each alternative project in relation to risk. (For current purposes, riskiness may be considered to be a function of the probability of not reaching the breakeven point.) A breakdown of costs for the current sales volume follows, together with estimates of what each item would be after each of the modernization proposals.

Estimated costs	Currently	Modernization I	Modernization II
Depreciation on plant and equipment	$513,000	$630,000	$787,500
Depreciation on building	288,000	360,000	468,000
Property taxes	36,000	45,000	63,000
Salary expense	639,000	693,000	778,500
Other fixed expenses	54,000	72,000	99,000
Factory labor	672,000	498,000	316,500
Raw materials	480,000	424,500	300,000
Variable selling expenses	72,000	72,000	72,000

a. Determine the breakeven point in units for the firm, assuming (1) no modernization is undertaken, (2) the first program is undertaken, and (3) the second program is undertaken.
b. Compute the degree of operating leverage at the current volume (76,500 units) for each of the three possibilities.
c. Compute profits for each alternative, assuming future sales of 76,500 units. Profits for each alternative at other sales levels have been calculated (to save you work) and are given below:

Unit Sales	Profits
No modernization	
65,000	$ 30,000
90,000	630,000
100,000	870,000
Modernization I	
65,000	$ (45,000)
90,000	630,000
100,000	900,000
Modernization II	
65,000	$(181,000)
90,000	594,000
100,000	904,000

d. Rank the alternatives in terms of potential riskiness.
e. How would the decision as to whether and how to modernize be affected by the expectation of large fluctuations in future sales?
f. (To be worked at the option of the instructor.) Suppose we have estimated the following probability distribution for sales:

Probability	Sales (in Units)
0.1	65,000
0.3	76,500
0.3	90,000
0.3	100,000

Use this information to determine the expected values of the three alternative courses of action.
g. Which project is best? What factors would influence your decision?

9.4 Gibson Electronics is considering developing a new miniature calculator. The quantity (Q) sold is a function of the price (P) where

$$Q = 2{,}000 - 10P.$$

Fixed costs are $24,000 and variable cost per unit is $60.

a. Graphically determine the breakeven points for the calculator in units and dollars.
b. What is the company's price at an output of 700 units?
c. What is its profit at that output?
d. What happens to the price and profits if the company sells 1,000 units?

9.5 The Samford Company is preparing its cash budget for the first six months of 1981. The sales data for 1980 and sales forecasts for January through July of 1981 are:

Actual Sales, 1980		Sales Forecast, 1981	
November	$350	January	$450
December	400	February	500
		March	700
		April	800
		May	600
		June	450
		July	300

All sales are made on credit, with 70 percent collected in the first month following the sale and 30 percent in the second month. Purchases are 60 percent of the following month's sales and are paid in the following month. Monthly expenses equal to 30 percent of the current month's sales are paid currently each month. Beginning cash is $100 and should not be permitted to fall below $100 in any of the following months. Bank borrowing is used to bring cash back to the $100 level. Whenever cash exceeds $100, the excess is used to pay off any bank loans outstanding. Formulate the cash budget for January through June 1981.

9.6 The Grady Company is planning to request a line of credit from its bank. The following sales forecasts have been made for 1981 and 1982:

November 1981	$300,000	April	$340,000
December	480,000	May	400,000
January 1982	350,000	June	550,000
February	270,000	July	320,000
March	180,000		

The expected credit sales collections are estimated as follows: collected within the month of sale, 20 percent; collected the month following the sale, 70 percent; collected the second month following the sale, 10 percent. Payments for labor and raw material costs are typically made during the month following the month in which these costs are incurred. Total labor and raw material costs for each month are estimated as follows:

November 1981	$200,000	April	$210,000
December	350,000	May	300,000
January 1982	280,000	June	200,000
February	220,000	July	250,000
March	175,000		

General and administrative salaries will amount to approximately $30,000 a month; lease payments under long-term lease contracts will be $20,000 a month; depreciation charges are $20,000 a month; miscellaneous expenses will be $1,500 a month; income tax payments of $75,000 will be due in both March and June. Cash on hand on January 1, 1982, will amount to $50,000, and a minimum cash balance of $80,000 should be maintained throughout the cash budget period.

a. Prepare a monthly cash budget for the first six months of 1982.

b. For each month during the period, prepare an estimate of required financing (or excess funds) which the Grady Company will need to borrow (or will have available to invest).

c. Suppose receipts from sales come in uniformly during the month; that is, one-thirtieth of the cash payments come each day. All outflows, however, are paid on the tenth of the month. Would this cash flow have an effect on the cash budget; that is, would the cash budget you have prepared be valid under these assumptions? If not, what would be done to make a valid estimation of financing requirements?

9.7 Gulf and Eastern, Inc., is a diversified multinational corporation that produces a wide variety of goods and services, including chemicals, soaps, tobacco products, toys, plastics, pollution control equipment, canned food, sugar, motion pictures, and computer software. The corporation's major divisions were brought together in the early 1960s under a decentralized form of management; each division was evaluated in terms of its profitability, efficiency, and return on investments. This decentralized organization persisted through most of the decade, during which Gulf and Eastern experienced a high average growth rate in total assets, earnings, and stock prices.

Toward the end of 1975, however, those trends were reversed. The organization was faced with declining earnings, unstable stock prices, and a generally uncertain future. This situation persisted into 1976, but during that year a new president, Lynn Thompson, was appointed by the board of directors. Thompson, who had served for a time on the financial staff of I. E. Du Pont, used the Du Pont system to evaluate the various divisions. All showed definite weaknesses.

Thompson reported to the board that a principal reason for the poor overall performance was a lack of control by central management over each division's activities. The consistently poor results of the corporation's budgeting procedures were particularly disturbing. Under that system, each division manager drew up a projected budget for the next quarter, along with estimated sales, revenue, and profit; funds were then allocated to the divisions, basically in proportion to their budget requests. However, actual budgets seldom matched the projections; wide discrepancies occurred; and this, of course, resulted in a highly inefficient use of capital.

In an attempt to correct the situation, Thompson asked the firm's chief financial officer to draw up a plan to improve the budgeting, planning, and control processes. When the plan was submitted, its basic provisions included the following:

1. To improve the quality of the divisional budgets, the division managers should be informed that the continuance of wide variation between their projected and actual budgets would result in dismissal.
2. A system should be instituted under which funds would be allocated to divisions on the basis of their average return on investment (ROI) during the last four quarters. Since funds were short, divisions with high ROIs would get most of the available money.
3. Only about half of each division manager's present compensation should be received as salary; the rest should be in the form of a bonus related to the division's average ROI for the quarter.
4. Each division should submit to the central office for approval all capital expenditure requests, production schedules, and price changes. Thus the company would be recentralized.

a. 1. Is it reasonable to expect the new procedures to improve the accuracy of budget forecasts?
   2. Should all divisions be expected to maintain the same degree of accuracy?
   3. In what other ways might the budgets be made?

b. 1. What problems would be associated with the use of the ROI criterion in allocating funds among the divisions?
   2. What effect would the period used in computing ROI (that is, four quarters, one quarter, two years, and so on) have on the effectiveness of this method?
   3. What problems might occur in evaluating the ROI in the crude rubber and auto tires divisions? between the sugar products and pollution control equipment divisions?

c. What problems would be associated with rewarding each manager on the basis of the division's ROI?

d. How well would Thompson's policy of recentralization work in this highly diversified corporation, particularly in light of the financial officer's three other proposals?

Selected References

Bacon, Jeremy. *Managing the Budget Function.* Studies in Business Policy, Report No. 131. New York: National Industrial Conference Board, 1970.

Barrett, M. Edgar, and Fraser, LeRoy B. III. "Conflicting Roles in Budgeting for Operations." *Harvard Business Review* 55 (July–August 1977), pp. 137–146.

Dearden, John. "The Case against ROI Control." *Harvard Business Review* 47 (May–June 1969), pp. 124–135.

Dhavale, Dileep, G., and Wilson, Hoyt G. "Breakeven Analysis with Inflationary Cost and Prices." *Engineering Economist* 25 (Winter 1980), pp. 107–121.

Grinold, R. D.; Hopkins, D. S. P.; and Massy, W. F. "A Model for Long-Range University Budget Planning under Uncertainty." *Bell Journal of Economics* 9 (Autumn 1978), pp. 396–420.

Gritta, Richard. "The Effect of Financial Leverage of Air Carrier Earnings: A Breakeven Analysis." *Financial Management* 8 (Summer 1979), pp. 53–60.

Hamermesh, Richard G. "Responding to Divisional Profit Crises." *Harvard Business Review* 55 (March–April 1977), pp. 124–130.

Helfert, Erich A. *Techniques of Financial Analysis.* 3d ed. Homewood, Ill.: Richard D. Irwin, 1972, Chapter 2.

Henning, Dale A. *Non-Financial Controls in Smaller Enterprises.* Seattle: University of Washington, College of Business Administration, 1964.

Hunt, Pearson. "Funds Position: Keystone in Financial Planning." *Harvard Business Review* 53 (May–June 1975), pp. 106–115.

Jaedicke, Robert K., and Robichek, Alexander A. "Cost-Volume-Profit Analysis under Conditions of Uncertainty." *Accounting Review* 39 (October 1964), pp. 917–926.

Jaedicke, Robert K., and Sprouse, Robert T. *Accounting Flows: Income, Funds, and Cash.* Englewood Cliffs, N.J.: Prentice-Hall, 1965.

Knight, W. D., and Weinwurn, E. H. *Managerial Budgeting.* New York: Macmillan, 1964.

Rappaport, Alfred. "Measuring Company Growth Capacity during Inflation." *Harvard Business Review* 57 (January–February 1979), pp. 91–100.

———. "A Capital Budgeting Approach to Divisional Planning and Control." *Financial Executive* 36 (October 1968), pp. 47–63.

Raun, D. L. "The Limitations of Profit Graphs, Breakeven Analysis, and Budgets." *Accounting Review* 39 (October 1964), pp. 927–945.

Reinhardt, U. E. "Breakeven Analysis for Lockheed's Tri Star: An Application of Financial Theory." *Journal of Finance* 28 (September 1973), pp. 821–838.

Searby, Frederick W. "Return to Return on Investment." *Harvard Business Review* 53 (March–April 1975), pp. 113–119.

Soldofsky, R. M. "Accountant's versus Economist's Concepts of Breakeven Analysis." *N.A.A. Bulletin* 41 (December 1959), pp. 5–18.

Stone, Bernell K.; Downes, David H.; and Magee, Robert P. "Computer-Assisted Financial Planning: The Planner-Model Interface." *Journal of Business Research* 5 (September 1977), pp. 215–233.

Appendix A to Chapter 9

Illustrative Budget System

Financial planning and control processes perform a central role in implementing the general planning activities of the firm. The financial planning and control manager analyzes the sales growth of the firm, the investment requirements to support planned growth, and the relations between revenues and costs, seeking to improve efficiency in the utilization of funds for investment outlays and to maintain cost control as well. The budgeting processes represent a part of the broader financial planning and control system. The illustrative budget system that is next presented provides an integrative approach to the relationship between financial planning and control and the budgetary process that most companies experience. A complete budget system includes (1) a production budget; (2) a materials purchases budget; (3) a budgeted, or pro forma, income statement; (4) a budgeted, or pro forma, balance sheet; and (5) a capital expenditure budget. Since capital expenditures are related directly to problems of the firm's growth, they have been considered separately in Chapters 13, 14, and 17.[1]

Tables 9A.1 through 9A.7 show a hypothetical budget system in process. In Tables 9A.2 through 9A.7 the lines are numbered consecutively from 1 to 54, so that it is easy to see the relations among the various budgets.

Table 9A.1 outlines the highly summarized cost accounting system, which is based on the standard costs of goods sold per unit. Standard costs include direct material, direct labor, and variable and fixed manufacturing expense. Standard costs are the costs of goods produced when the firm is operating at a high level of efficiency and when operations are near a level that may be regarded as "normal."[2]

1. Outlays for capital equipment do, of course, affect the cash budget, the income statement, and the balance sheet.
2. The terminology in this chapter follows accounting usage, but anyone familiar with economics can readily translate it into economic terms. For instance, "$6 per unit at standard output" is "average total (production) cost"; "marginal production cost" is $5 per unit; and so on.

Table 9A.1

Standard Costs Based on Volume of 1,000 Units per Month

	Per Unit
Direct material: 2 pieces at $1 per piece	$2
Direct labor: 1 hour at $2 per hour	2
Variable manufacturing expense: $1 per unit	1
Fixed manufacturing expense: $1,000 per month[a]	1
Cost of goods produced per unit	$6

a. Includes $200 depreciation charges.

Production Budget

The illustrative production budget (Table 9A.2) is based directly on the sales forecast and the estimated unit cost of production. It is assumed that the firm maintains its finished goods inventory at 50 percent of the following month's sales. In any month, the firm must produce the unit sales plus ending inventory less the beginning inventory level.

This example illustrates the financial consequences of a rise in sales from a $10,000-per-month level to a new plateau of $12,000. As production rises in

Table 9A.2

Production Budget

Estimated 1981, First Quarter

Item	Monthly Average, 1980	First Month	Second Month	Third Month	Source of Data
1. Sales at $10 per unit	$10,000	$10,000	$12,000	$12,000	Assumed
2. Unit sales	1,000	1,000	1,200	1,200	Line 1 divided by $10
3. Beginning inventory (units)	500	500	600	600	One-half of current month's sales
4. Difference (units)	500	500	600	600	Line 2 minus line 3
5. Ending inventory (units)	500	600	600	600	One-half of next month's sales
6. Production in units	1,000	1,100	1,200	1,200	Line 4 plus line 5
7. Estimated cost of goods produced	$ 6,000	$ 6,600	$ 7,200	$ 7,200	Line 6 times $6
8. Burden absorption, under or (over)	0	(100)	(200)	(200)	Line 6 times $1 less $1,000 fixed manufacturing expense
9. Adjusted cost of goods produced	$ 6,000	$ 6,500	$ 7,000	$ 7,000	Line 7 less line 8
9a. Adjusted cost per unit	$ 6	$ 5.91	$ 5.83	$ 5.83	Line 9 divided by line 6
10. Value of ending inventory (finished goods)	$ 3,000	$ 3,545	$ 3,500	$ 3,500	Line 5 multiplied by line 9a (rounded)

response to increased sales, the (standard) cost of goods produced also rises. But the standard cost of goods produced increases faster than actual costs increase because the unit cost of $6 includes fixed charges of $1 per unit. An increase of one unit of production actually raises total costs by only $5. The estimated total cost, however, increases by $6. Estimates of the cost of goods produced are made and then adjusted by the amount of under- or overabsorbed burden. Of course, the same result for calculating the adjusted cost of goods produced (Table 9A.2, line 9) is obtained by multiplying $5 by the number of units produced to get total variable costs and adding $1,000 in fixed costs to reach total adjusted cost of goods produced.

The per unit adjusted costs of goods produced ($5.91 for the first month) is required to calculate the ending inventory. The first-in, first-out method of inventory costing is employed. The calculation of the ending inventory value is required for the worksheet (Table 9A.6) used in developing the budgeted balance sheet (Table 9A.7).

Materials Purchases Budget

The level of operations indicated by the production budget in Table 9A.2 is based on the sales forecast and inventory requirements. The materials purchases budget (Table 9A.3) contains estimates of materials purchases that will be needed to carry out the production plans. Raw materials purchases depend in turn upon materials actually used in production, material costs (Table 9A.1), size of beginning inventories, and requirements for ending inventory.

The example in Table 9A.3 does not take into account economical ordering quantities (EOQs), as discussed in Chapter 11. EOQs are not integrated, primarily because they assume a uniform usage rate for raw materials, an assumption that is not met in the example. Also, the EOQ analysis assumes a

Table 9A.3

Materials Purchases Budget

Item	Monthly Average, 1980	First Month	Second Month	Third Month	Source of Data
		Estimated 1981, First Quarter			
11. Production in units	1,000	1,100	1,200	1,200	Line 6
12. Materials used (units)	2,000	2,200	2,400	2,400	Line 11 times 2
13. Raw materials, ending inventory	2,200	2,400	2,400	2,400	Raw materials requirements next month
14. Total	4,200	4,600	4,800	4,800	Line 12 plus line 13
15. Raw materials, beginning inventory	2,000	2,200	2,400	2,400	Raw materials requirements this month
16. Raw materials purchases	$2,200	$2,400	$2,400	$2,400	(Line 14 less line 15) times $1

constant minimum inventory, but the desired minimum inventory (Table 9A.3, line 13) shifts with production levels. In a practical situation, these assumptions might be approximated. EOQs could then be used to determine optimum purchase quantities, or more sophisticated operations research techniques might be used.

Cash Budget

The cash budget shown in Table 9A.4 is generated from information developed in the production and materials purchases budgets. In addition, estimates for other expense categories are required.[3] In Table 9A.4, only cash receipts from operations are considered, in order to emphasize the logic of the budget system. No account is taken of receipts or expenditures for capital

Table 9A.4

Cash Budget

Item	Monthly Average, 1980	Estimated 1981, First Quarter First Month	Second Month	Third Month	Source of Data
Receipts					
17. Accounts receivable collected	$10,000	$10,000	$10,000	$12,000	Sales of previous month
Disbursements					
18. Accounts payable paid	$ 2,000	$ 2,200	$ 2,400	$ 2,400	Raw materials purchases of previous month
19. Direct labor	2,000	2,200	2,400	2,400	Line 6 times $2
20. Indirect labor	700	700	700	700	Assumed
21. Variable manufacturing expenses	1,000	1,100	1,200	1,200	Line 6 times $1
22. Insurance and taxes	100	100	100	100	Assumed
23. General and administrative expenses	2,500	2,500	2,500	2,500	Assumed
24. Selling expense	500	500	600	600	5% of line 1
25. Total disbursements	$ 8,800	$ 9,300	$ 9,900	$ 9,900	Sum of lines 18 through 24
26. Cash from operations	$ 1,200	$ 700	$ 100	$ 2,100	Line 17 less line 25
26a. Initial cash	5,000	6,200	6,900	7,000	Preceding month, line 26b
26b. Cumulative cash	6,200	6,900	7,000	9,100	Line 26 plus line 26a
27. Desired level of cash	5,000	5,000	6,000	6,000	50% of current month's sales; approximately 4.2% of annual sales
27a. Cash available (needed) cumulative	$ 1,200	$ 1,900	$ 1,000	$ 3,100	Line 26b less line 27

3. These are assumed to be paid in the months the expenses are incurred, in order to reduce the volume of explanatory information.

items. This is because of the emphasis in this illustration on budgeting consequences of short-term fluctuations in the sales volume of the firm, although in practical situations it is a simple matter to incorporate capital expenditures into the cash budget. However, the fact that capital expenditures are ignored does not diminish their impact on cash flows. Capital expenditures occur sporadically and in amounts that sometimes overwhelm operating transactions.

Cash Budget Period

The three-month period used in the cash budget, Table 9A.4, is not necessarily the length of time for which a firm will predict cash flows. Although this period does coincide with the length of traditional ninety-day bank loans, the firm is more likely to utilize a six-month or one-year period. Normally, a six-month forecast is prepared on a monthly basis. Briefly, the cash budget period will vary with the line of business, credit needs, the ability to forecast the firm's cash flows for the distant future, and requirements of suppliers of funds.

Illustrative Cash Budget

The cash flow for a given period is the difference between receipts and expenditures for that period. In Table 9A.4, for the 1980 monthly averages, cash from operations ($1,200) is the difference between accounts receivable collected ($10,000) and total disbursements ($8,800). Note that collections from accounts receivable and accounts payable paid depend upon sales and purchases from the preceding months rather than on current sales.

The significant figure for the manager is cash available (or needed). Cash from operations in the first month of 1981, plus the initial cash balance at the beginning of the month, totals $6,900. The financial manager has previously determined that only $5,000 is needed to handle this level of sales. Consequently, the firm will have surplus cash of $1,900 by the end of the month, and $3,100 by the end of the third month. In the pro forma balance sheet (Table 9A.7), it is assumed that these cash surpluses are used to pay off notes payable.

Cash Budget Use

As mentioned earlier in the chapter, the financial manager uses the cash budget to anticipate fluctuations in the level of cash. Normally, a growing firm will be faced with continuous cash drains. The cash budget tells the manager the magnitude of the outflow. If necessary, he can plan to arrange for additional funds. The cash budget is the primary document presented to a lender to indicate the need for funds and the feasibility of repayment.

In Table 9A.4 the opposite situation is illustrated. The firm will have excess cash of at least $1,000 during each of the three months under consideration. The excess can be invested, or it can be used to reduce outstanding liabilities. In this example, the firm retires notes payable (Table 9A.7, line 49).

Such a small amount as $1,000 might be held as cash or as a demand deposit, but the alert financial manager will not allow substantial amounts of cash to remain idle.

Budgeted Income Statement

After a cash budget has been developed, two additional financial statements can be formulated—the budgeted income statement (Table 9A.5) and the budgeted balance sheet (Table 9A.7). They are prepared on an accrual rather than a cash basis. For example, the income statement accounts for depreciation charges. Expenses recognized on an accrual basis are included in total expenses (Table 9A.5, line 32); thus, calculated net income is lowered. The only accrual item assumed in this exhibit is depreciation, and this is assumed to be $200 monthly. The before-tax profit figure in the third month in the budgeted income statement (line 33) differs from line 26 in the cash budget only by the amount of depreciation.[4] This illustration makes clear the effect of noncash expenses on the income statement.

The preparation of the budgeted income statement follows standard accounting procedures. The major calculation involved is adjusted cost of sales, explained in Table 9A.6.

The budgeted income statement shows the impact of future events on the firm's net income. Comparison of future income with that of past periods indicates the difficulties that will be encountered in maintaining or exceeding

Table 9A.5

Budgeted Income Statement

Estimated 1981, First Quarter

Item	Monthly Average, 1980	First Month	Second Month	Third Month	Source of Data
28. Sales	$10,000	$10,000	$12,000	$12,000	Line 1
29. Adjusted cost of sales	6,000	5,955	7,045	7,000	Line 40
30. Gross income	$ 4,000	$ 4,045	$ 4,955	$ 5,000	Line 28 less line 29
31a. General and administrative expenses	2,500	2,500	2,500	2,500	Line 23
31b. Selling expenses	500	500	600	600	5% of line 1
32. Total expenses	$ 3,000	$ 3,000	$ 3,100	$ 3,100	Line 31a plus 31b
33. Net income before taxes	1,000	1,045	1,855	1,900	Line 30 less line 32
34. Federal taxes	500	522	928	950	50% of line 33
35. Net income after taxes	$ 500	$ 523	$ 927	$ 950	Line 33 less line 34

4. This close correspondence holds only in what is called a *steady state,* that is, when inventories and receivables are not being raised or lowered. Prior to the third month this condition does not hold.

Table 9A.6

Worksheet

Adjusted Cost of Sales
Estimated 1981, First Quarter

Item	Monthly Average, 1980	First Month	Second Month	Third Month	Source of Data
36. Adjusted cost of goods produced	$6,000	$6,500	$ 7,000	$ 7,000	Line 9
37. *Add:* Beginning inventory	3,000	3,000	3,545	3,500	Line 10, lagged one month
38. Sum	$9,000	$9,500	$10,545	$10,500	
39. *Less:* Ending inventory	3,000	3,545	3,500	3,500	Line 10
40. Adjusted cost of goods sold[a]	$6,000	$5,955	$ 7,045	$ 7,000	Line 38 less line 39

a. Note difference from line 9, adjusted cost of goods produced.

past performance. A forecast indicating low net income should cause management to increase sales efforts as well as to make efforts to reduce costs. Anticipation and prevention of difficulties can be achieved by a sound budgeting system.

Budgeted Balance Sheet

Lenders are interested in the projected balance sheet to see what the future financial position of the firm will be. Balance sheet projections discussed in the body of Chapter 9 were focused on year-to-year forecasts, and they assumed stable underlying relations. The budget technique deals with shorter term projections but is based on the same fundamental kinds of stable relations between the volume of sales and the associated asset requirements. Either method can be used, and each can operate as a check on the other. The budgeted balance sheet presented in Table 9A.7, however, is the result of a more detailed and analytical forecast of future operations. It is the logical culmination of the budget system and provides a complete reconciliation between the initial balance sheet, the cash budget, and the income statement.

The required information is readily available from past balance sheets or is contained in other elements of the budget system. For example, the initial balance of notes payable is $3,200. An increase in cash available (Table 9A.4, line 27a) is used to repay notes payable; a decrease is met by additional borrowing from a commercial bank. Other new items, such as long-term debt and common stock (Table 9A.7, lines 51 and 52), are taken from previous balance sheets.

The tables in this appendix present a simplified yet complete budget system that contains all the elements found in a voluminous and complex actual budget system of a firm. A person who understands the logic and flow of this budget system can approach an actual budget with perspective, looking for

Table 9A.7

Budgeted Balance Sheet

Estimated 1981, First Quarter

Item	Monthly Average, 1980	First Month	Second Month	Third Month	Source of Data
Assets					
41. Cash	$ 5,000	$ 5,000	$ 6,000	$ 6,000	Line 27
42. Government securities					
43. Net receivables	10,000	10,000	12,000	12,000	Sales of current month
44. Inventories:					
Raw materials	2,200	2,400	2,400	2,400	Line 13
Finished goods	3,000	3,545	3,500	3,500	Line 10
45. Current assets	$ 20,200	$ 20,945	$ 23,900	$ 23,900	Total lines 41 through 44
46. Net fixed assets	80,000	79,800	79,600	79, 400	$80,000 less $200 per month depreciation
47. Total assets	$100,200	$100,745	$103,500	$103,300	Total lines 45 and 46
Liabilities					
48. Accounts payable	$ 2,200	$ 2,400	$ 2,400	$ 2,400	Raw materials purchases this month (line 16)
49. Notes payable, $3,200	2,000	1,300	2,200	100	$3,200 less line 27a
50. Provisions for federal income tax	500	1,022	1,950	2,900	Cumulation of line 34
51. Long-term debt	25,000	25,000	25,000	25,000	Assumed
52. Common stock, $50,000	50,000	50,000	50,000	50,000	Assumed
53. Retained earnings, $20,000	$ 20,500	$ 21,023	$ 21,950	$ 22,900	Cumulation of line 35 plus $20,000
54. Total claims	$100,200	100,745	103,500	103,300	Sum of lines 48 through 53

the fundamental relations involved and then applying the patterns to actual budget systems of any degree of complexity.

Problem

9A.1 Examine carefully the budget system set forth in this appendix, then answer the following questions:

a. What advantages can you see to having a budget system such as the one described? Would such a system be more valuable (assuming a whole series of budgets where necessary) for a firm with ten employees or for one with 10,000 employees?

b. What would happen to the system if the sales forecast was far off the mark? How could variable sales be incorporated into the system?

c. Would a budget system such as this one be more useful for a firm whose sales were highly predictable or one whose sales were not very predictable?

d. How might a firm's budget system be computerized? Would such computerization be more useful for a firm with predictable or unpredictable sales?

e. Would such a budget system be more valuable for planning or for control purposes?

Part Three
Working Capital Management

In Part 2, we analyzed the firm's operations in an overall, aggregate manner. Now we must examine the various aspects of the firm's financial picture in more detail. In Part 3, we focus on the top half of the balance sheet, studying current assets, current liabilities, and the interrelationship between these two sets of accounts. This type of analysis is commonly called working capital management.

In Chapter 10, we examine some general principles of overall working capital management. In Chapter 11, we consider the determinants of current assets: cash, marketable securities, accounts receivable, and inventories. Finally, in Chapter 12 we discuss current liabilities, considering in some detail the principal sources and forms of short-term funds.

10
Working Capital Policy

Working capital *is a firm's investments in short-term assets—cash, short-term securities, accounts receivable, and inventories.* Gross working capital *is the firm's total current assets.* Net working capital *is current assets minus current liabilities.* Working capital management, *which encompasses all aspects of the administration of both current assets and current liabilities, has two main functions:*

1. *To adjust to changes in the firm's level of sales activity caused by seasonal, cyclical, and random factors. This function is important because a firm with favorable long-run prospects may experience severe difficulties and losses caused by adverse short-run developments.*
2. *To contribute to maximizing the value of the firm. Current asset holdings, for example, should be expanded to the point where marginal returns on increases in such assets are just equal to the cost of capital required to finance the increases. Current liabilities should be used in place of long-term debt whenever their use lowers the cost of capital.*

Chapter 10 discusses the nature of working capital management. The use of short-term debt versus long-term debt is considered after some necessary background is laid in a discussion of the term structure of interest rates. The risk-return trade-off of policies with regard to investments in current assets will then be analyzed. This is the framework for the following two chapters, which treat decisions on investments in individual current asset items and evaluation of alternative sources of short-term financing.

Importance of Working Capital Management

Working capital management includes a number of aspects that make it an important topic for study:

1. Surveys indicate that the largest portion of a financial manager's time is devoted to the day-by-day internal operations of the firm, which can appro-

priately be subsumed under the heading of working capital management.

2. Characteristically, current assets represent more than half the total assets of a business firm. Because they represent such a large investment and because this investment tends to be relatively volatile, current assets are worthy of the financial manager's careful attention.
3. Working capital management is particularly important for small firms. Although such firms can minimize their investment in fixed assets by renting or leasing plant and equipment, they cannot avoid investment in cash, receivables, and inventories. Therefore, current assets are particularly significant for the financial manager of a small firm. Further, because a small firm has relatively limited access to the long-term capital markets, it must necessarily rely heavily on trade credit and short-term bank loans, both of which affect net working capital by increasing current liabilities.
4. The relationship between sales growth and the need to finance current assets is close and direct. For example, if the firm's average collection period is forty days and its credit sales are $1,000 a day, it has an investment of $40,000 in accounts receivable. If sales rise to $2,000 a day, the investment in accounts receivable rises to $80,000. Sales increases produce similar immediate needs for additional inventories and, perhaps, for cash balances. All such needs must be financed; and since they are so closely related to sales volume, it is imperative that the financial manager keep aware of developments in the working capital segment of the firm. Of course, continued sales increases require additional long-term assets, which must also be financed. However, fixed asset investments, while critically important to the firm in a strategic, long-run sense, generally have more lead time in financing than do current asset investments.

Original Concept of Working Capital

The term *working capital* originated at a time when most industries were closely related to agriculture. Processors would buy crops in the fall, process them, sell the finished product, and end up just before the next harvest with relatively low inventories. Bank loans with maximum maturities of one year were used to finance both the purchase and the processing costs, and these loans were retired with the proceeds from the sale of the finished products.

This situation is depicted in Figure 10.1, where fixed assets are shown to be growing steadily over time, while current assets jump at harvest season and then decline during the year, ending at zero just before the next crop is harvested. Current assets are financed with short-term credit, and fixed assets are financed with long-term funds. Thus, the top segment of the graph deals with working capital.

The figure represents, of course, an ideal situation. Current assets build up gradually as crops are purchased and processed, inventories are drawn down less regularly, and ending inventory balances do not decline to zero. Nevertheless, the example does illustrate the general nature of the production and financing process. Working capital management consists of decisions relating to the top section of the graph—managing current assets and arranging the short-term credit used to finance them.

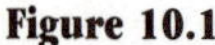

Figure 10.1

Fixed and Current Asset Patterns in Agriculture

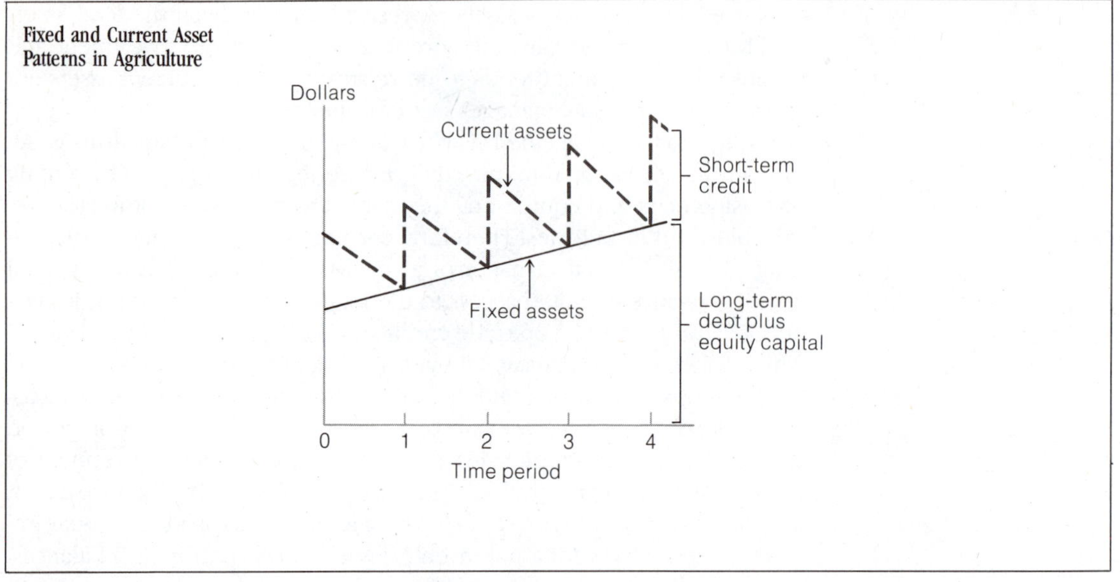

Extending the Working Capital Concept

As the economy became less oriented toward agriculture, the production and financing cycles of typical businesses changed. Although seasonal patterns still existed and business cycles caused asset requirements to fluctuate, it became apparent that current assets rarely, if ever, dropped to zero. This realization led to the development of the idea of permanent current assets, diagrammed in Figure 10.2. As the figure is drawn, it maintains the traditional notion that permanent assets should be financed with long-term capital and temporary assets with short-term credit.

The pattern shown in Figures 10.1 and 10.2 was considered desirable because it minimized the risk of the firm being unable to pay off its maturing obligations. To illustrate: Suppose a firm borrows on a one-year basis and uses the funds obtained to build and equip a plant. Cash flows from the plant (profits plus depreciation) are not sufficient to pay off the loan at the end of the year, so the loan has to be renewed. If the lender refuses to renew the loan, the firm has problems. If the plant had been financed with long-term debt, however, cash flows would have been sufficient to service the loan, and the problem of renewal would not have arisen. Thus, if a firm finances permanent assets with long-term capital and temporary assets with short-term capital, its financial risk is lower than if permanent assets are financed with short-term debt.

At the limit, a firm can attempt to exactly match the maturity structure of its assets and liabilities. A machine expected to last for five years could be financed by a five-year loan, a twenty-year building could be financed by a twenty-year mortgage bond, inventory expected to be sold in twenty days

Figure 10.2

Matching Financing to Asset Permanence

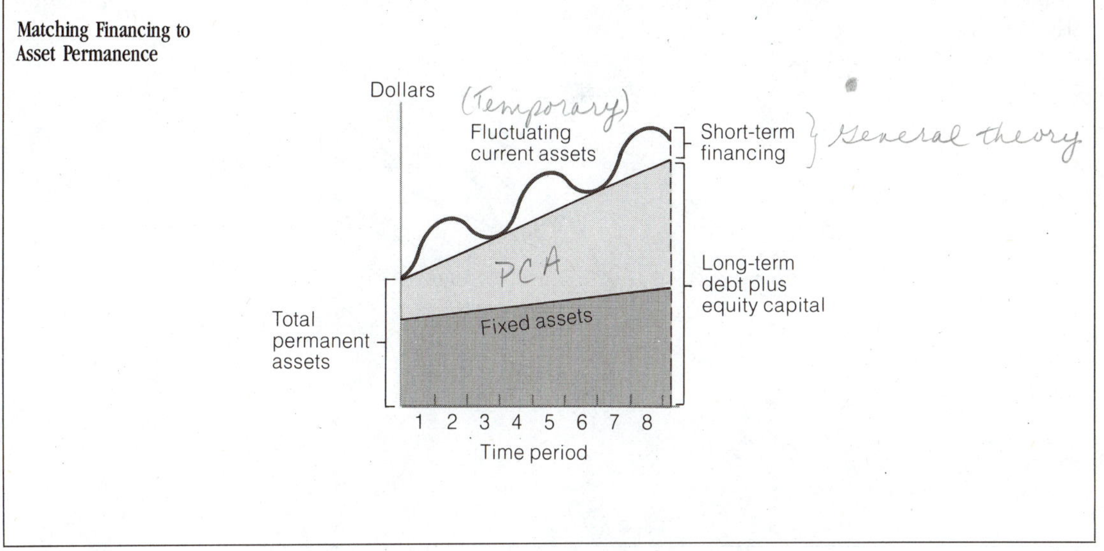

could be financed by a twenty-day bank loan, and so on. Actually, of course, uncertainty about the lives of assets prevents this exact maturity matching—a point that will be examined in the following sections.

Figure 10.2 shows the situation for a firm that attempts to match asset and liability maturities exactly. Although this policy can be followed, firms can choose other maturity-matching policies if they so desire. Figure 10.3, for example, illustrates the situation for a firm that finances all its fixed assets with long-term capital but part of its permanent current assets with short-term credit.[1]

The dashed line could even have been drawn *below* the line designating fixed assets, indicating that all the current assets and part of the fixed assets are financed with short-term credit; this would be a highly aggressive, nonconservative position, and the firm would certainly be subject to loan renewal problems and high risk.

Alternatively, as in Figure 10.4, the dashed line could be drawn *above* the line designating permanent current assets, indicating that long-term capital is being used to meet seasonal demands. In this case, the firm uses a small amount of short-term credit to meet its peak seasonal requirements, but it also meets part of its seasonal needs by "storing liquidity" in the form of marketable securities during the off-season. The humps above the dashed line represent short-term financing; the troughs below it represent short-term security holdings.

1. Firms generally have some short-term credit in the form of *spontaneous funds*—accounts payable and accruals (see Chapter 8). We could modify the graphs to take this into account, but nothing is lost by simply abstracting from spontaneous funds, as we do in the present analysis.

Figure 10.3

Short-Term Financing of Some Permanent Assets

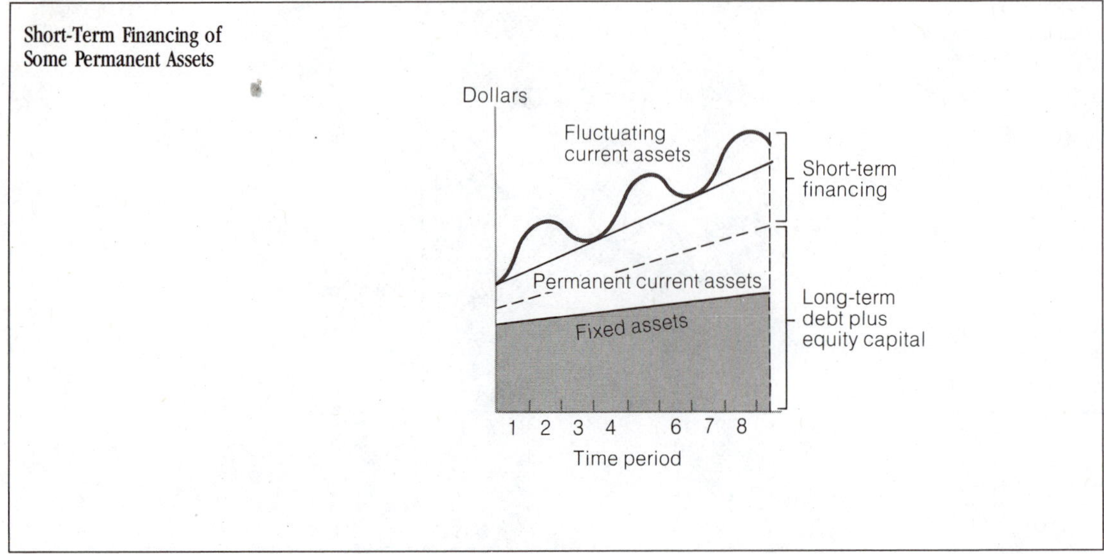

Figure 10.4

Fluctuating versus Permanent Assets and Liabilities

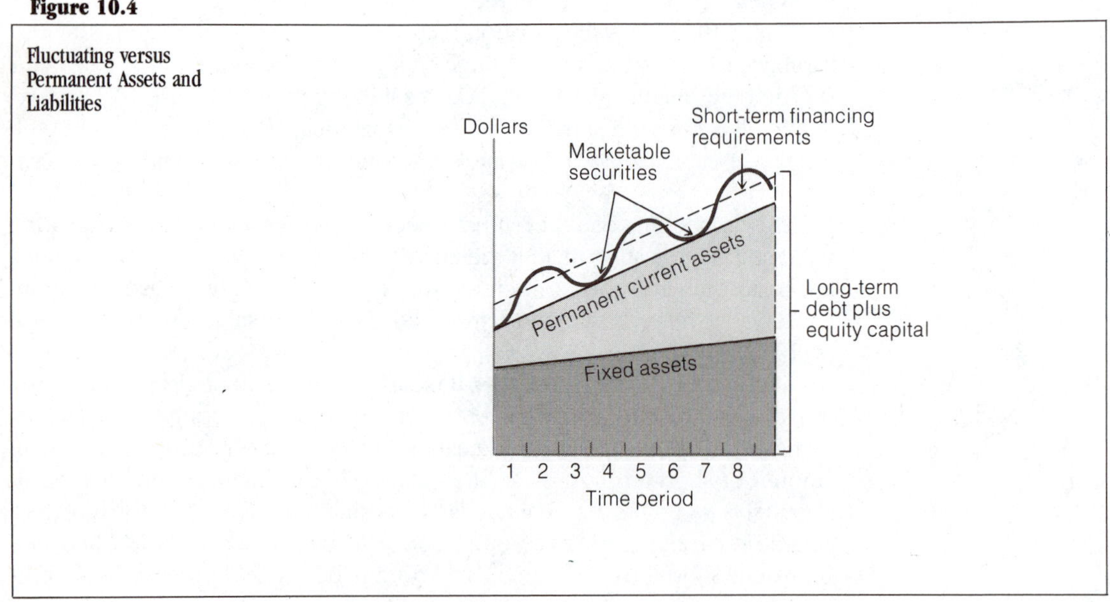

The Term Structure of Interest Rates

A basic consideration in the choice between the use of short-term versus long-term debt is relative costs and risks. Materials on the term structure of interest rates are set forth to provide background on the choices between the use of short-term versus long-term debt.

The *term structure of interest rates* describes the relationship between interest rates and loan maturity. When measuring the term structure, we generally use yields on United States government securities. The term structure on other instruments, however, varies similarly.

Figure 10.5 shows the term structure of rates in two years, 1976 and 1980. In the lower curve, for 1976, we see a pattern of rising yields. The shorter term maturities carry lower rates of interest than the longer term maturities. This rising yield structure has been characteristic of most years since 1930. The higher curve for 1980 shows a pattern which starts high and then declines until the fifth year, becoming relatively flat thereafter. By May 1980, the yield curve had dropped and its slope became positive, rising from 10 percent on short-term issues to about 11 percent on thirty-year maturities.

Figure 10.5

Term Structure of Rates on U.S. Government Securities, 1976 and 1980

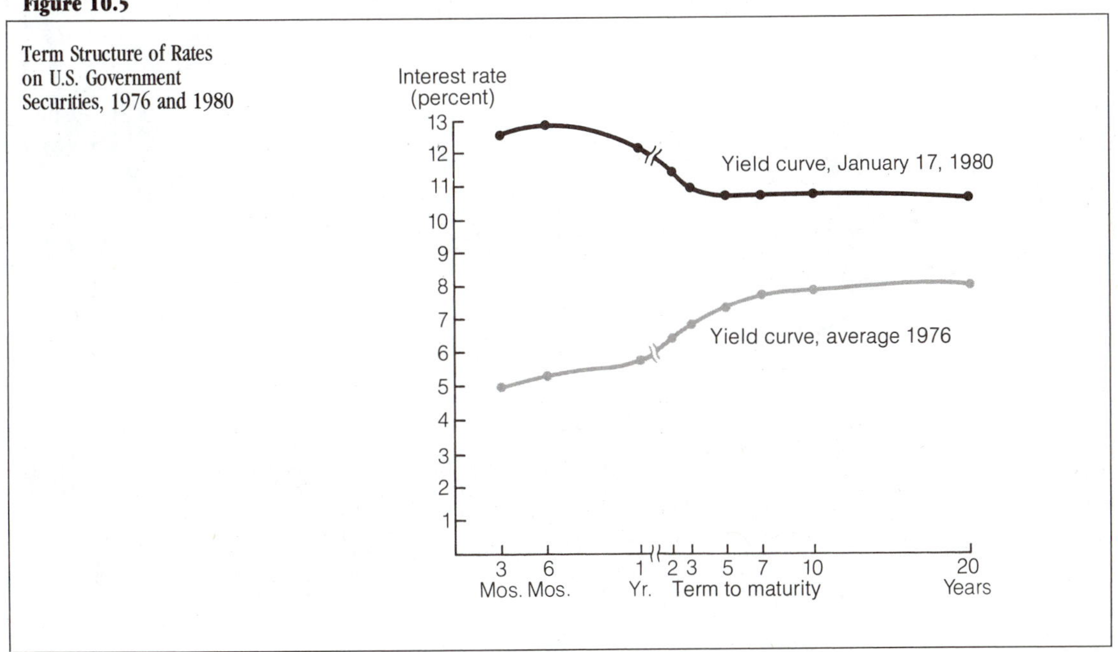

Sources: Curve for January 17, 1980, is from Salomon Brothers, *Bond Market Roundup*, Week Ending January 18, 1980, and curve for 1976 is from *Federal Reserve Bulletin*, February 1978, p. A27.

In addition to illustrating the changing term structure of interest rates, Figure 10.5 also reveals a shift in the *level of rates.* Between 1976 and 1980, the interest rate on all government securities—long-term and short-term—increased. Such movements represent changes in the general level of interest rates.[2] The historical pattern of the relationship between long- and short-term interest rates is shown for the period 1910 through 1979 in Figure 10.6. The long-term rate is represented by the Aaa bond rate—the rate on high-grade,

Figure 10.6

Long- and Short-Term Interest Rates

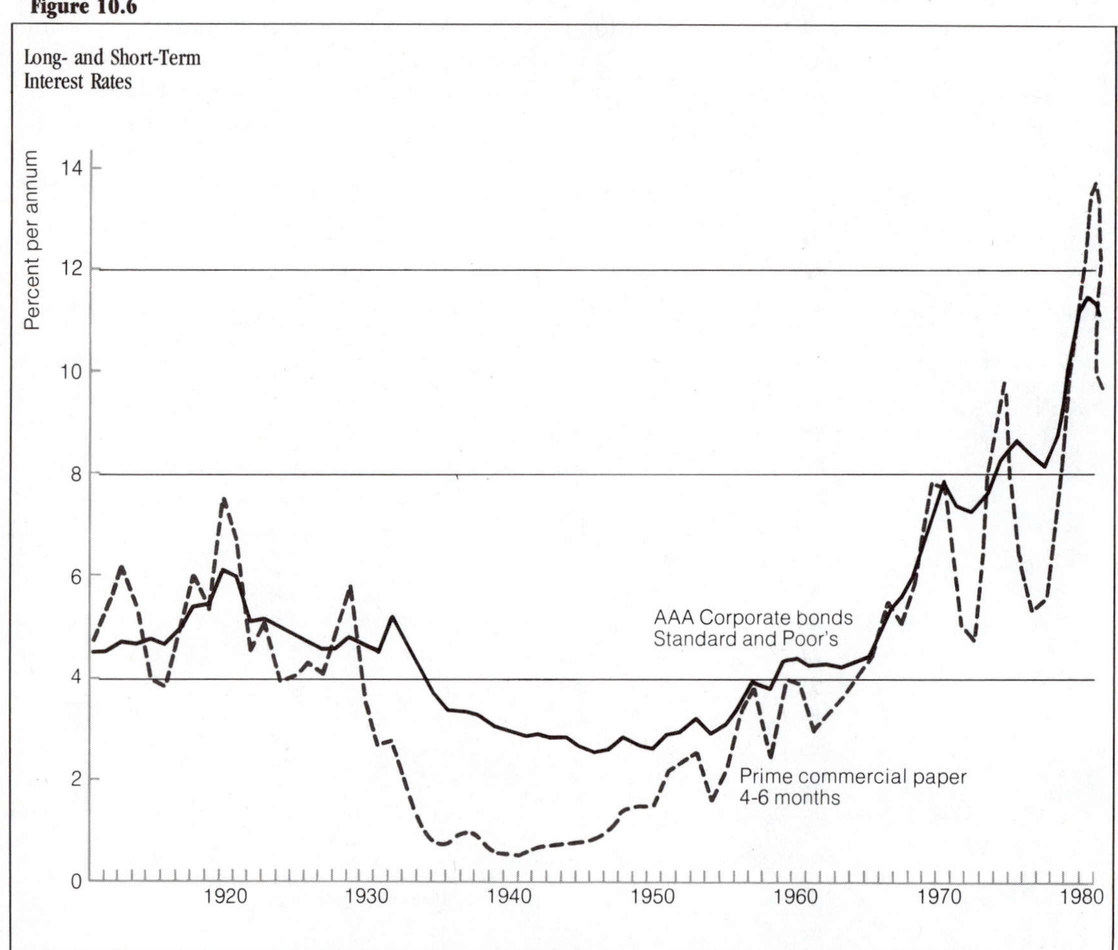

Source: Board of Governors of the Federal Reserve System, *1979 Historical Chart Book,* p. 96, and *Chart Book,* August 1980, pp. 72–73.

2. In addition to the level and term structure of rates on a given class of securities—in this case, government securities—there is also the pattern of relationships among different classes of securities—for example, mortgages, government bonds, corporates, and bank business loans. The relationship among classes of securities is not discussed here. In general, movements in the term structure and level of rates are similar for most classes of securities.

long-term (twenty-five years or more) corporate bonds. The short-term rate is represented by the rate on prime commercial paper—the four-to-six-month debt of top-quality firms.

Three points should be made about the graph: (1) both long-term and short-term rates generally rose over the period; (2) short-term rates were more volatile than long-term rates; and (3) long-term rates were generally above short-term rates.

Except for a few months in the mid-1950s the long-term rate was consistently above the short-term rate in all years from 1929 to 1966. However, in recent years short-term rates have more often been above long-term rates. This change occurred during 1966 and during parts of 1969, 1970, 1973, and again in late 1978, continuing persistently through at least the early part of 1980. In early 1980 the prime bank loan rate was 20 percent, prime commercial paper was yielding 17 percent, and the yield on corporate Aaa bonds was 13 percent.[3] But by midsummer 1980, the bank prime rate was down to 11.5 percent, the yield on prime commercial paper had declined to below 8.5 percent, and the yield on Aaa corporate bonds was slightly under 11 percent. By Autumn 1980, short-term rates had risen by over 200 basis points and long-term rates by about 130 basis points.

Theoretical Explanations for the Term Structure of Interest Rates

Three theories have been advanced to explain the term structure—the relationship between short-term and long-term interest rates: *the expectations theory, the liquidity preference theory, and the market segmentation theory.* We will consider each in turn.

Expectations Theory

The unbiased expectations theory asserts that, in equilibrium, the long-term rate is a geometric average of today's short-term rate and expected short-term rates in the future. To illustrate, let us consider an investor whose planning horizon is two years. Let r be the short-term interest rate and R be the long-term interest rate. Suppose he has \$100 and is considering two alternative investment strategies: (1) purchasing a two-year bond with a yield of 9 percent per year, or (2) purchasing a one-year bond that yields 8 percent, then reinvesting the \$108 he will have at the end of the year in another one-year bond. If he chooses Strategy 1, at the end of two years he will have

$$\text{Ending value} = \$100\,(1.09)\,(1.09) = \$118.81.$$

If he follows Strategy 2, his value at the end of two years will depend upon the yield on the one-year bond during the second year, r_2:

$$\text{Ending value} = \$100\,(1.08)\,(1 + r_2) = \$108\,(1 + r_2).$$

Under the expectations theory, the value of r_2 will be 10.01 percent, found as follows:

3. Federal Reserve Bank of St. Louis, *U.S. Financial Data* for the week ending January 16, 1980, pp. 6–7.

$$\begin{aligned} \$118.81 &= \$108\,(1 + r_2) \\ 1 + r_2 &= 1.1001 \\ r_2 &= 0.1001 = 10.01\% \end{aligned}$$

Suppose r_2 was greater than 10.01 percent, say 10.5 percent. In that case, our investor (and others) would be better off investing short-term, because he would end up with \$119.34, which is greater than \$118.81. Just the reverse would hold if $r_2 < 10.01$ percent. Thus, according to the expectations theory, capital market competition forces long-term rates to be equal to the (geometric) average of short-term rates over the holding period.

In more formal terminology, let the prefix t represent the year in which a given rate holds, and the postscript t represent the maturity associated with a given rate. Applying this terminology to our previous example, ${}_tR_{t+1} = {}_1R_2 = 9\%$ = the rate today on two-year bonds; ${}_tr_t = {}_1r_1 = 8\%$ = the rate today on one-year bonds; and ${}_{t+1}r_t = {}_2r_1 = 10.01\%$ = the rate expected to prevail next year on one-year bonds. In equilibrium, the expected returns on the two alternatives over the two-year holding period must be equal:

$$(1 + {}_tR_2)^2 = (1 + {}_tr_1)(1 + {}_{t+1}r_1),$$

or

$$(1 + {}_tR_2) = [(1 + {}_tr_1)(1 + {}_{t+1}r_1)]^{1/2}.$$

In general,

$$(1 + {}_tR_N) = [(1 + {}_tr_1)(1 + {}_{t+1}r_1) \cdots (1 + {}_{t+N-1}r_1)]^{1/N}.$$

Thus, if short-term rates are expected to rise in the future, the current long-term rate, ${}_tR_N$, will be higher than the current short-term rate, and vice versa if rates are expected to decline.

Richard Roll has demonstrated that for continuous compounding the yield to maturity over N periods is the simple arithmetic average of the N 1-period yields.[4] This simplifies the calculations for showing the relationship between short-term and long-term interest rates.

The unbiased expectations theory is illustrated in Table 10.1, where *long-term* is defined as five years. In Situation A, the expected trend in short-term rates is upward—from 6 percent to 10 percent over five years. The long-term rate is thus 8 percent, the mean of that series.[5] A lender could obtain an average yield of 8 percent on an investment either by lending long at 8 percent or by lending for one-year periods at increasing rates over the five years.

A reversal is illustrated in Situation B. There the trend in short-term rates is expected to be downward. Again, however, the mean of the short-term rates is 8 percent, so 8 percent is the effective long-term rate.

4. Richard Roll, *The Behavior of Interest Rates* (New York: Basic Books, 1970), p. 16.
5. The arithmetic mean is used for ease of exposition here, but the geometric mean will be used in later calculations and discussion.

Table 10.1

Hypothetical Relationship between Short-Term and Long-Term Interest Rates

	Situation A Expect Rising Rates			Situation B Expect Falling Rates		
Year	Long-Term[a] (5-Year Note)	Short-Term (1-Year Note)	Intermediate-Term (3-Year Note)	Long-Term[a] (5-Year Note)	Short-Term (1-Year Note)	Intermediate-Term (3-Year Note)
1	8	6	7	8	10	9
2		7			9	
3		8			8	
4		9			7	
5		10			6	

a. If the geometric average were used, for Situation A we would compute the current five-year long-term rate as:

$$\sqrt[5]{(1.06)(1.07)(1.08)(1.09)(1.10)} = \sqrt[5]{1.468698} = 1.079907,$$

representing virtually an 8 percent long-term rate. This approximates the result under continuous compounding, or the simple average.

The term structure of rates in Year 1 under Situations A and B is graphed in Figure 10.7. With expectations of rising rates, the yield curve is upward sloping. With expectations of falling rates, the yield curve slopes down.

Liquidity Preference Theory

The future is inherently uncertain, and when uncertainty is considered, the pure expectations theory must be modified. To illustrate, let us consider a situation where short-term rates are expected to remain unchanged in the future. In this case, the pure expectations theory predicts that short- and long-term bonds sell at equal yields. The liquidity preference theory, on the other hand, holds that long-term bonds must yield more than short-term bonds for two reasons. *First,* in a world of uncertainty, investors will, in general, prefer to hold short-term securities because they are more liquid; they can be converted to cash without danger of loss of principal. Investors will, therefore, accept lower yields on short-term securities. *Second,* borrowers react in exactly the opposite way from investors—business borrowers generally prefer long-term debt because short-term debt subjects a firm to greater dangers of having to refund debt under adverse conditions. Accordingly, firms are willing to pay a higher rate, other things held constant, for long-term than for short-term funds.

We see, then, that pressures on both the supply and demand sides—caused by liquidity preferences of both lenders and borrowers—will tend to make the yield curve slope upward. Figure 10.8 illustrates this effect.

Figure 10.7

Term Structure of Rates under Two Hypothetical Situations

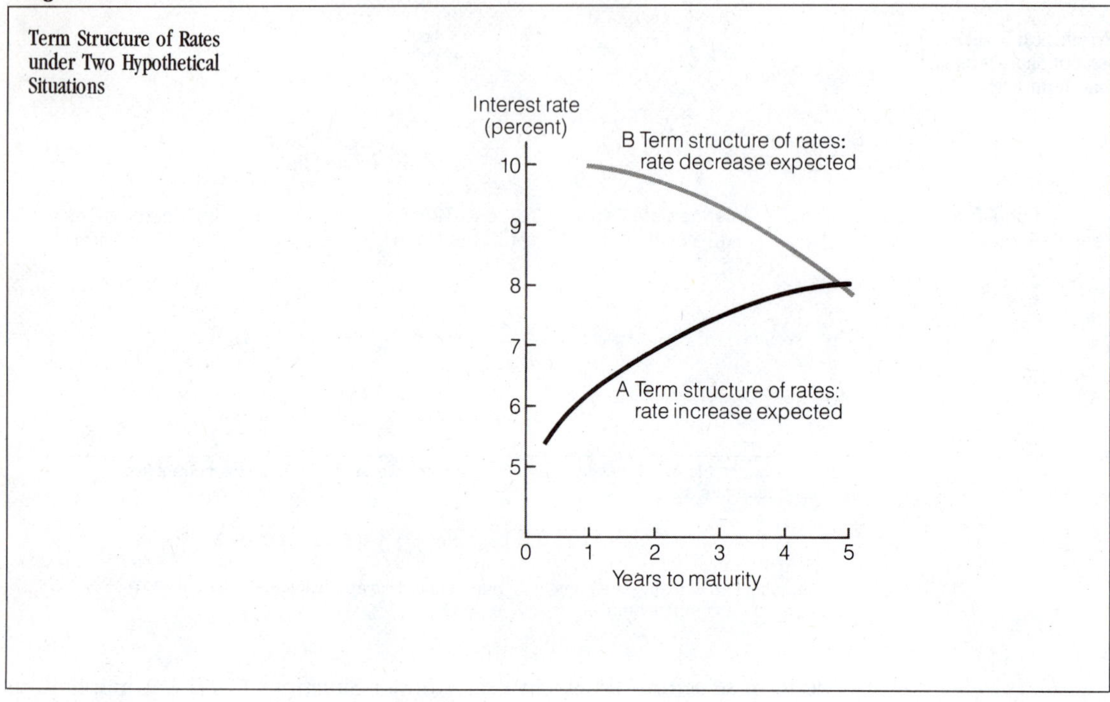

Figure 10.8

Term Structure with Liquidity Preference

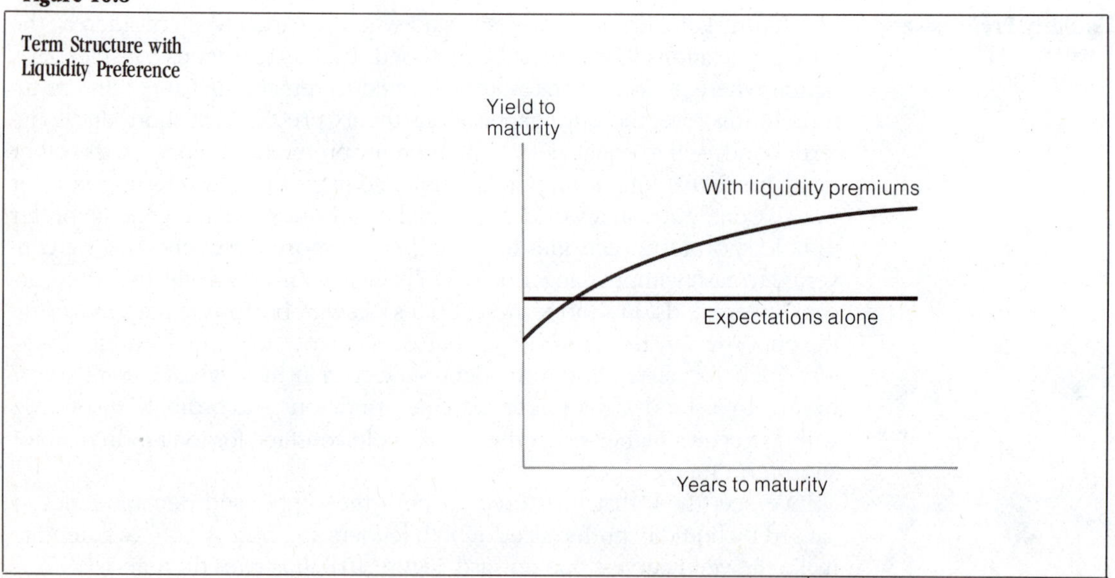

Market Segmentation, or Hedging-Pressure, Theory

The expectations theory assumes that, in the aggregate, lenders and borrowers are indifferent between long- and short-term investments except for any expected yield differentials between the types of securities.[6] The liquidity preference theory states that an upward bias exists—the yield curve slopes upward to a greater extent than is justified by expectations about future rates because investors prefer to lend short while borrowers prefer to borrow long.

The market segmentation, institutional, or hedging-pressure theory admits the liquidity preference argument as a good description of the behavior of investors with short horizons, such as commercial banks, which regard certainty of principal as more important than certainty of income because of the nature of their deposit liabilities. However, certain other investors with long-term liabilities, such as insurance companies, might prefer to buy long-term bonds because, given the nature of their liabilities, they find certainty of income highly desirable. On the other hand, borrowers relate the maturity of their debt to the maturity of their assets. Thus, the hedging-pressure theory characterizes market participants as having strong maturity preferences, then argues that interest rates are determined by supply and demand in each segmented market, with each maturity constituting a segment. In the strictest version of this theory, expectations play no role—bonds with different maturities are not substitutes for one another because of different demand preferences or the preferred habitat of both lenders and borrowers.

Empirical Evidence

Empirical studies suggest that there is some validity to each of these theories. Specifically, the recent work indicates that if lenders and borrowers have no reason for expecting a change in the general level of interest rates, the yield curve will be upward sloping because of liquidity preferences. (Under the expectations theory, the term structure of interest rates would be flat if there were no expectations of a change in the level of short-term rates.) However, it is a fact that during periods of extremely high interest rates, the yield curve is downward sloping; this proves that the expectations theory also operates. At still other times, when supply and demand conditions in particular maturity sectors change, the term structure seems to be modified, thus confirming the market segmentation theory. In summary, each theory has an element of truth, and each must be taken into account in seeking to understand the changing patterns observed in the term structure of interest rates.

6. In discussing the term structure of interest rates, we are holding constant the risk of default. This is done by using government securities, which presumably have no default risk.

The Use of Short-Term versus Long-Term Debt

With background on the patterns of the relative costs of short-term versus long-term debt, we can now consider decisions with regard to the relative use of each. The choice involves an analysis of relative flexibility, relative costs, and relative risks.

Flexibility of Short-Term Debt

If the need for funds is seasonal or cyclical, the firm may not want to commit itself to long-term debt. Such debt can be refunded, provided the loan agreement includes a call or prepayment provision; but even so, prepayment penalties can be expensive. Accordingly, if a firm expects its needs for funds to diminish in the near future, or if it thinks there is a good chance that such a reduction will occur, it may choose short-term debt for flexibility.

A cash budget can be used to analyze the flexibility aspect of the maturity structure of debt. To illustrate: Suppose a firm invests in a major new project by buying equipment with a ten-year life. The equipment will provide cash flows—depreciation plus profit—over its ten-year life. If the firm uses debt to finance the equipment purchase, it may schedule the debt's retirement to the expected cash flows from the project.

The Relative Cost of Short-Term versus Long-Term Debt

Until the late 1960s, the cost of short-term debt was generally below the cost of long-term debt. Recall also from the expectations theory that for an extended time period, long-term borrowing can be no worse than a succession of short-term borrowings. If long-term rates reflect an average of future short-term rates, the use of long-term borrowing already reflects the short-term rates that are expected to be experienced in the future.

Some might argue that short-term borrowing rates may actually be lower in the future than the rates reflected in current long-term borrowings. This is possible, of course; but if it happens, it will be an unexpected, essentially random, occurrence. As such, the unanticipated changes could go in either direction with equal probability, so no average gain or loss from unexpected changes in short-term rates can reasonably be argued.

However, to the extent that the liquidity preference theory of the term structure of interest rates dominates, short-term rates would be below long-term rates. From the standpoint of lenders, there is less risk on a short-term loan because of the opportunity to reevaluate the loan more frequently as it matures. From the standpoint of borrowers, longer term debt avoids the uncertainty of fluctuating short-term rates and the possibility of having to renew or refund debt under adverse money and capital market conditions.

The Risk-Return Trade-off

Even if the cost of short-term debt were lower than long-term debt, its use is likely to entail greater risk. Thus we are again faced with a trade-off between risk and rate of return. An example will clarify the nature of the risk-rate of return trade-off. The relationships are illustrated in Parts A and B of Table 10.2.

We assume that the firm has $100 million of assets, half held as fixed assets

Table 10.2

The Effect of Maturity Structure of Debt on Return on Equity (Millions of Dollars)

Part A

	Conservative	Average	Aggressive
Current assets	$ 50.00	$ 50.00	$ 50.00
Fixed assets	50.00	50.00	50.00
Total assets	$100.00	$100.00	$100.00
Short-term credit (at 7%)	$ —	$ 25.00	$ 50.00
Long-term debt (at 9%)	50.00	25.00	$ —
Total debt (Debt/Assets = 50%)	$ 50.00	$ 50.00	$ 50.00
Equity	50.00	50.00	50.00
Total liabilities and net worth	$100.00	$100.00	$100.00
Earnings before interest and taxes (EBIT)	$ 15.00	$ 15.00	$ 15.00
Less interest	−4.50	−4.00	−3.50
Taxable income	$ 10.50	$ 11.00	$ 11.50
Less taxes (at 50%)	−5.25	−5.50	−5.75
Earnings on common stock	$ 5.25	$ 5.50	$ 5.75
Rate of return on equity	10.5%	11.0%	11.5%
Current ratio	∞	2:1	1:1

Part B

	Conservative	Average	Aggressive
Current assets	$ 50.00	$ 50.00	$ 50.00
Fixed assets	50.00	50.00	50.00
Total assets	$100.00	$100.00	$100.00
Short-term credit (at 15%)	$ —	$ 25.00	$ 50.00
Long-term debt (at 10%)	50.00	25.00	—
Total debt (Debt/Assets = 50%)	$ 50.00	$ 50.00	$ 50.00
Equity	50.00	50.00	50.00
Total liabilities and net worth	$100.00	$100.00	$100.00
Earnings before interest and taxes (EBIT)	$ 15.00	$ 15.00	$ 15.00
Less interest	−5.00	−6.25	−7.50
Taxable income	$ 10.00	$ 8.75	$ 7.50
Less taxes (at 50%)	−5.00	−4.375	−3.75
Earnings on common stock	$ 5.00	$ 4.375	$ 3.75
Rate of return on equity	10.0%	8.75%	7.5%
Current ratio	∞	2:1	1:1

and half as current assets, and that it will earn 15 percent before interest and taxes on these assets. The debt ratio has been set at 50 percent, but the policy issue of whether to use short- or long-term debt has not been determined.

In Part A of Table 10.2, short-term debt is assumed to cost 7 percent, while long-term debt costs 9 percent. It is obvious that the greater the use of short-term debt, the higher the return on equity, because short-term debt is assumed to have lower costs.

On the other hand, in Part B of this table, the situation similar to the early part of 1980 is illustrated. Short-term credit cost 15 percent or more, while long-term debt was carrying about an 11 percent yield. But if the long-term debt had been obtained at an earlier period of time, it might be carrying only an 8 to 10 percent cost. Again, as predictable from the differential costs between short- and long-term debt, the return on equity would be highest for the greatest use of long-term debt. Since short-term interest rates are subject to greater swings and greater volatility than the cost of long-term debt, the rate of return on equity fluctuates most widely for the aggressive policy under which short-term debt is used to the greatest degree.

The firm employing a high proportion of short-term debt takes on additional risks. When the time comes to renew its debt, general money and capital market conditions may be relatively tight. Hence, not only might short-term funds cost more, but even worse, they may be unavailable. Furthermore, a succession of short-term borrowings while short-term interest rates are high will aggravate this problem.

Let us consider other risks of using a high proportion of short-term debt. For convenience, let us refer to the firm using a high proportion of short-term debt as Firm S and the firm using the higher proportion of long-term debt, Firm L. In addition to the risk of fluctuating interest charges, Firm S faces another risk as contrasted with Firm L. It may run into temporary difficulties that prevent it from being able to refund its debt. Remember that when Firm S's debt matures each year, the firm must negotiate new loans with its creditors, paying the going short-term rate. But suppose the loan comes up for renewal at a time when the firm is facing labor problems, a recession in demand for its products, extreme competitive pressures, or some other set of difficulties that has reduced its earnings.

The creditors will look at Firm S's ratios, especially the times interest earned and current ratios, to judge its creditworthiness. Firm S's current ratio is, of course, always lower than that of Firm L, but in good times this is overlooked. If earnings are high, the interest will be well covered and lenders will tolerate a low current ratio. If, however, earnings decline, pulling down the interest coverage ratio, creditors will certainly reevaluate Firm S's creditworthiness. At the very least, because of the perceived increased riskiness of the company, creditors will raise the interest rate charged; at the extreme, they will refuse to renew the loan. In the latter event, the firm will be forced to raise the funds needed to pay off the loan by selling assets at bargain basement prices, borrowing from other sources at exorbitant interest rates, or, in the extreme, going bankrupt.

Notice that if the firm follows a conservative policy of using all long-term debt, it need not worry about short-term temporary changes in either the term structure of interest rates or its own EBIT. Its only concern is with its long-run performance, and its conservative financial structure may permit it to survive in the short run to enjoy better times in the long run.

Relationship of Current Assets to Fixed Assets

In the chapters that deal with capital budgeting, we will see that capital budgeting decisions involve estimating the stream of benefits expected from a given project and then discounting the expected cash flows back to the present to find the present value of the project. Although current asset investment analysis is similar to fixed asset analysis in the sense that it also requires estimates of the effects of such investments on profits, it is different in two key respects:

1. Increasing the firm's current assets—especially cash and marketable securities—while holding constant expected production and sales reduces the riskiness of the firm, but it also reduces the overall return on assets.
2. Although both fixed and current asset holdings are functions of *expected* sales, only current assets can be adjusted to *actual* sales in the short run; hence, adjustments to short-run fluctuations in demand lie in the domain of working capital management.

Some of these ideas are illustrated in Figure 10.9, which shows the short-run relationship between the firm's current assets and output. The firm's fixed as-

Figure 10.9

Relationship between Current Assets and Output

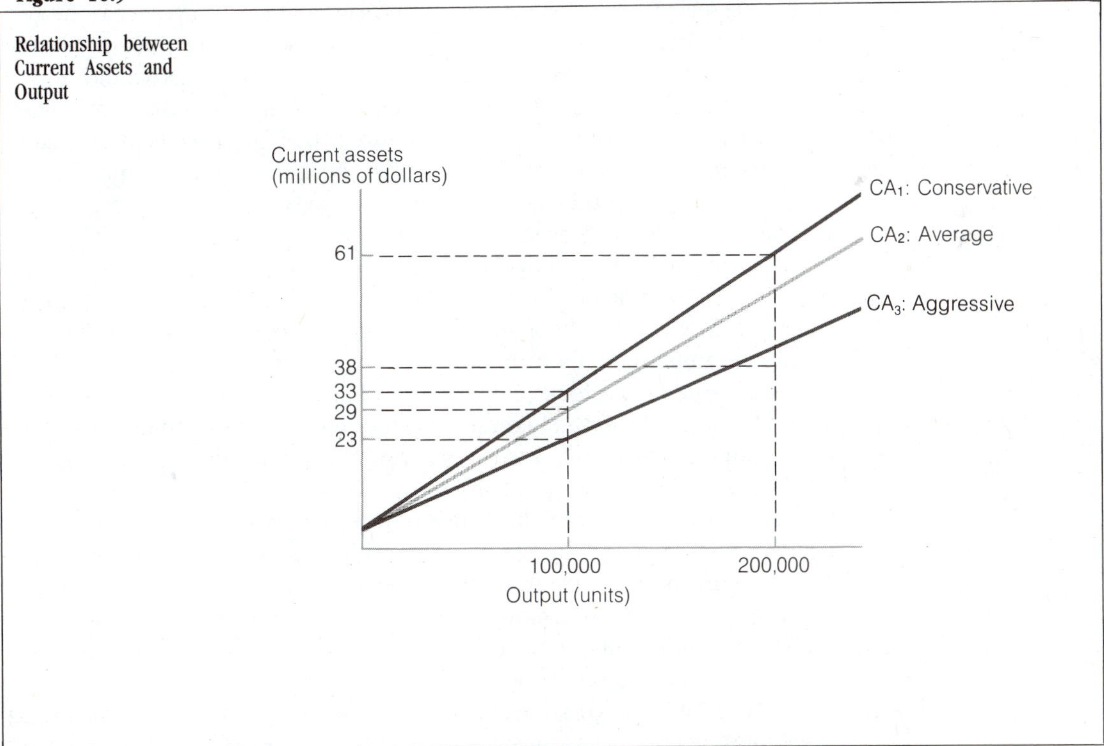

sets, assumed to be $50 million, cannot be altered in response to short-run fluctuations in output. Three possible current asset policies are depicted. CA_1 represents a conservative policy; relatively large balances of cash and marketable securities are maintained, large safety stocks of inventories are kept on hand, and sales are maximized by adoption of a credit policy that causes a high level of accounts receivable. CA_2 is somewhat less conservative than CA_1, and CA_3 represents a risky, aggressive policy.

Current asset holdings are highest at any output level under policy CA_1 and lowest under CA_3. For example, at an output of 100,000 units, CA_1 calls for $33 million of current assets, versus only $23 million for CA_3. If demand strengthens and short-run plans call for production to increase from 100,000 to 200,000 units, current asset holdings will likewise increase. Under CA_1 current assets rise to $61 million, but under CA_3 they rise to only $38 million. As we shall see in the following section, the more aggressive policy leads to a higher expected rate of return; it also entails greater risk.

Risk-Return Trade-off for Current Asset Holdings

If it could forecast perfectly, a firm would hold exactly enough cash to make disbursements as required, exactly enough inventories to meet production and sales requirements, exactly the accounts receivable called for by an optimal credit policy, and no marketable securities unless the interest returns on such assets exceeded the cost of capital (an unlikely occurrence). The current asset holdings under the perfect foresight case would be the theoretical minimum for a profit-maximizing firm. Any larger holdings would, in the sense of the Du Pont chart we described earlier, increase the firm's assets without a proportionate increase in its returns, thus lowering its rate of return on investment. Any smaller holdings would mean the inability to pay bills on time, lost sales and production stoppages because of inventory shortages, and lost sales because of an overly restrictive credit policy.

When uncertainty is introduced into the picture, current asset management involves (1) determination of the minimum required balances of each type of asset and (2) addition of a safety stock to account for the fact that forecasters are imperfect. If a firm follows policy CA_1 in Figure 10.9, it is adding relatively large safety stocks; if it follows CA_3, its safety stocks are minimal. In general, CA_3 produces the highest expected returns on investment, but it also involves the greatest risk; that is, following this policy may actually result in the *lowest* rate of return.

The effect of the three alternative policies on expected profitability is illustrated in Table 10.3. In Part A of this table it is assumed that the less aggressive current asset investment policies stimulate sales to a slight degree by having more variety in inventory, fewer stock-out problems, and so on. But still the indicated rate of return on assets is highest for the current asset policy of greatest aggressiveness, CA_3.

In Part B of Table 10.3, the assumption is made that the aggressive current asset investment policy results in a larger adverse sales effect and even lowers the earning rate. As a consequence, the most aggressive firm now has the low-

Table 10.3

Effects of Alternative Current Asset Policies on Rates of Return

Part A	CA_1	CA_2	CA_3
Sales	$110,000,000	$105,000,000	$100,000,000
EBIT at 15%	16,500,000	15,750,000	15,000,000
Current assets	70,000,000	55,000,000	40,000,000
Fixed assets	50,000,000	50,000,000	50,000,000
Total assets	$120,000,000	$105,000,000	$ 90,000,000
Rate of return on assets (EBIT/assets)	13.75%	15%	16.7%
Part B			
Sales	$115,000,000	$105,000,000	$ 80,000,000
EBIT rate	15%	15%	12%
EBIT amount	$ 17,250,000	$ 15,750,000	$ 9,600,000
Total assets	$120,000,000	$105,000,000	$ 90,000,000
Rate of return on assets (EBIT/assets)	14.4%	15%	10.7%

est indicated rate of return on assets. The situation of CA_2 does not change while the situation of CA_1 improves somewhat. The rate of return for the most conservative current asset policy is still somewhat below that of CA_2, which follows a middle of the road policy.

Again, the data in Table 10.3 illustrate the assumptions that produce the particular numbers. However, the table illustrates the general idea that the kind of current asset policy followed by a firm can result either in a stimulus to sales and profitability or in negative effects on both the volume of sales and profitability.

In the real world, things are considerably more complex than this simple example suggests. For one thing, different types of current assets affect both risk and returns differently. Increased holdings of cash do more to improve the firm's risk posture than a similar dollar increase in receivables or inventories; idle cash penalizes earnings more severely than does the same investment in marketable securities. Generalizations are difficult when we consider accounts receivable and inventories, because it is difficult to measure either the earnings penalty or the risk reduction that results from increasing the balances of these items beyond their theoretical minimums.

Can we resolve this risk-return trade-off to determine *precisely* the firm's optimal working capital policy—the policy that will maximize the value of existing common stock? In theory the answer is yes, but in practice it is not so. Determining the optimal policy would require detailed information on a complex set of variables—information that is unobtainable today. Progress is being made in the development of computer simulation models designed to help determine the effects of alternative financial policy choices, including working capital decisions; but no one using such models suggests that *optimal* solutions are now obtainable. We can, however, establish guidelines, or ranges of values, for each type of current asset; and we do have ways of examining the various types of short-term financing and their effects on the cost of capital. Because such information, used with good judgment, can be helpful to the financial manager, we shall consider these topics in the remaining chapters of Part 3.

Summary

Working capital is a firm's investments in short-term assets. *Gross working capital* is the firm's total current assets, and *net working capital* is current assets minus current liabilities. *Working capital management* involves all aspects of the administration of current assets and current liabilities.

Working capital policy is concerned with two sets of relationships among balance sheet items. The first policy question concerns the relationships among types of assets and the way these assets are financed. One policy calls for matching asset and liability maturities and financing current assets with short-term debt and fixed assets with long-term debt or equity; but this policy is unsound, because current assets represent levels of investments that increase as sales grow. If the policy is followed, the maturity structure of the debt is determined by the level of fixed versus current assets. Since short-term debt is frequently less expensive than long-term debt, the expected rate of return may be higher if more short-term debt is used. However, large amounts of short-term credit increase the risks of having to renew this debt at times of higher interest rates and of being unable to renew the debt at all if the firm experiences difficulties.

The second policy question deals with the determination of the level of total current assets to be held. Current assets vary with sales, but the ratio of current assets to sales is a policy matter. A firm that elects to operate aggressively will hold relatively small stocks of current assets, a policy that will reduce the required level of investment and increase the expected rate of return on investment. However, an aggressive policy also increases the likelihood of running out of inventories or losing sales because of an excessively tough credit policy. Both aspects of working capital policy involve risk-return trade-offs.

Questions

10.1 How does the seasonal nature of a firm's sales influence the decision about the amount of short-term credit in the financial structure?

10.2 Give your reaction to this statement: Merely increasing the level of current asset holdings does not necessarily reduce the riskiness of the firm. Rather, the composition of the current assets, whether highly liquid or highly illiquid, is the important factor to consider.

10.3 What is the advantage of matching the maturities of assets and liabilities? What are the disadvantages?

10.4 There have been times when the term structure of interest rates has been such that short-term rates were higher than long-term rates. Does this necessarily imply that the best financial policy for a firm is to use all long-term debt and no short-term debt? Explain.

10.5 Assuming a firm's volume of business remained constant, would you expect it to have higher cash balances (demand deposits) during a tight-money period or an easy-money period? Does this situation have any ramifications for federal monetary policy?

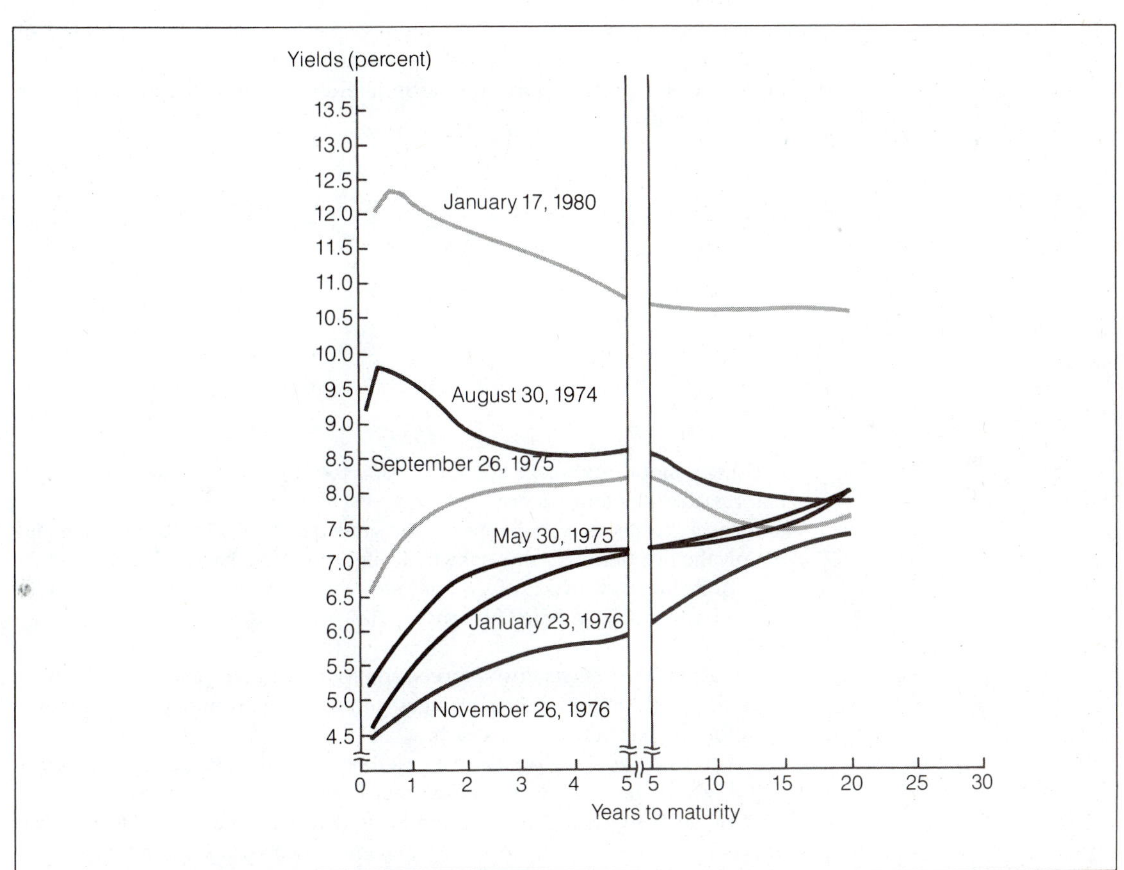

Problems

10.1 From the group of yield curves presented in the preceding figure, what generalizations can be made on the behavior of financial markets between 1974 and 1976? between 1976 and 1980?

10.2 From a recent issue of the *Federal Reserve Bulletin* or from another convenient source:

a. Construct a yield curve for the most complete 1979 data for U.S. government securities, using market yields for maturities of one year or less and the capital market rates for constant maturities for the maturities from two to twenty years.

b. Construct yield curves for the 1977 and 1978 average rates. Comment on any shifts you observe.

c. Next, add to the graph you developed in Part b the yield curve for the latest week available in the source you are using. Comment on any shifts in relation to 1978.

d. Why does the yield curve show only U.S. government security yields instead of including yields on commercial paper and corporate bonds?

10.3 Suppose that expected future short-term interest rates have the following alternative patterns:

Year	A	B	C	D
1	4%	8%	4%	8%
2	5	7	6	7
3	6	6	15	5
4	7	5	6	7
5	8	4	4	8

a. Using a simple arithmetic average, what is the current rate on a five-year note for each of the four patterns?

b. Using a geometric average, answer the same question as for Part a. (Hint: Multiply the five numbers, then take their fifth root. On a hand calculator use the y^x or x^x button with 0.2, which equals $\frac{1}{5}$. For example, for Interest Rate A the product is 6,720, and the fifth root is 5.827 percent.)

c. Optional:

1. Calculate the current two-, three-, and four-year note yields using both the arithmetic and geometric averages, and graph the resulting yield curves in four graphs of two curves each.
2. Is the height of the yield curve based on the arithmetic averages higher or lower than that based on the geometric averages?

10.4 The Morgan Tile Corporation is attempting to determine the optimal level of current assets for the coming year. Management expects sales potential to be approximately $1.5 million as a result of asset expansion presently being undertaken. Fixed assets total $500,000, and the firm wishes to maintain a 50 percent debt ratio. Morgan's interest cost is currently 10 percent on both short-term debt and longer-term debt. Three alternatives regarding the projected current asset level are available to the firm: (1) an aggressive policy requiring current assets of $500,000; (2) an average policy of $600,000 current assets; and (3) a conservative policy requiring current assets of $700,000. Under the three alternative current asset policies, Sales and EBIT/Sales would be:

	Aggressive	Average	Conservative
Sales	$1.0 million	$1.2 million	$1.5 million
EBIT/Sales	10%	10%	14%

a. What is the expected return on equity under each current asset level? (Assume a 40 percent tax rate.)
b. How would the overall riskiness of the firm vary under each policy? Discuss specifically the effect of current asset management on demand, expenses, fixed charges, risk of insolvency, and so on.

10.5 Three companies—Aggressive, Between, and Conservative—have different working capital management policies, as implied by their names. For example, Aggressive employs only minimal current assets and finances almost entirely with current liabilities and equity. This tight ship approach has a dual effect. It keeps total assets low, and thus tends to increase return on assets. But for reasons such as stock-outs, total sales are reduced; and since inventory is ordered more frequently and in smaller quantities, variable costs are increased. Condensed balance sheets for the three companies are presented below.

Balance Sheets

	Aggressive	Between	Conservative
Current assets	$150,000	$200,000	$300,000
Fixed assets	200,000	200,000	200,000
Total assets	$350,000	$400,000	$500,000
Current liabilities (at 12%)	$200,000	$100,000	$ 50,000
Long-term debt (at 10%)	0	100,000	200,000
Total debt	$200,000	$200,000	$250,000
Equity	150,000	200,000	250,000
Total claims on assets	$350,000	$400,000	$500,000
Current ratio	0.75:1	2:1	6:1

The cost of goods sold functions for the three firms are as follows:

Cost of goods sold = Fixed costs + Variable costs

Aggressive: Cost of goods sold = $200,000 + 0.70 (sales)

Between: Cost of goods sold = $290,000 + 0.65 (sales)

Conservative: Cost of goods sold = $390,000 + 0.60 (sales)

Sales for the three firms under different economic conditions are expected to be:

	Aggressive	Between	Conservative
Strong economy	$1,200,000	$1,200,000	$1,200,000
Average economy	900,000	1,000,000	1,150,000
Weak economy	700,000	900,000	1,050,000

	Total Current Assets	Net Working Capital[a]	Current Ratio	Net Profit
1. Cash is acquired through issuance of additional common stock.	_____	_____	_____	_____
2. Merchandise is sold for cash.	_____	_____	_____	_____
3. Federal income tax due for the previous year is paid.	_____	_____	_____	_____
4. A fixed asset is sold for less than book value.	_____	_____	_____	_____
5. A fixed asset is sold for more than book value.	_____	_____	_____	_____
6. Merchandise is sold on credit.	_____	_____	_____	_____
7. Payment is made to trade creditors for previous purchases.	_____	_____	_____	_____
8. A cash dividend is declared and paid.	_____	_____	_____	_____
9. Cash is obtained through short-term bank loans.	_____	_____	_____	_____
10. Short-term notes receivable are sold at a discount.	_____	_____	_____	_____
11. A profitable firm increases its fixed assets depreciation allowance account.	_____	_____	_____	_____
12. Marketable securities are sold below cost.	_____	_____	_____	_____

a. *Net working capital* is defined as current assets minus current liabilities.

a. Make out income statements for each company for strong, average, and weak economies using the following pattern:

Sales

Less cost of goods sold

Earnings before interest and taxes (EBIT)

Less interest expense

Taxable income

Less taxes (at 40%)

Net income

b. Compare the rates of return (EBIT/Assets and return on equity). Which company is best in a strong economy? in an average economy? in a weak economy?

c. What considerations for management of working capital are indicated by this problem?

10.6 Indicate the effects of the transactions listed above on each of the following: total current assets, working capital, current ratio, and net profit. Use + to indicate an increase, − to indicate a decrease, and 0 to indicate no effect. State necessary assumptions and assume an initial current ratio of more than 1 to 1.

continued from 288

	Total Current Assets	Net Working Capital[a]	Current Ratio	Net Profit
13. Uncollectable accounts are written off against the allowance account.	_____	_____	_____	_____
14. Advances are made to employees.	_____	_____	_____	_____
15. Current operating expenses are paid.	_____	_____	_____	_____
16. Short-term promissory notes are issued to trade creditors for prior purchases.	_____	_____	_____	_____
17. Ten-year notes are issued to pay off accounts payable.	_____	_____	_____	_____
18. A wholly depreciated asset is retired.	_____	_____	_____	_____
19. Accounts receivable are collected.	_____	_____	_____	_____
20. A stock dividend is declared and paid.	_____	_____	_____	_____
21. Equipment is purchased with short-term notes.	_____	_____	_____	_____
22. The allowance for doubtful accounts is increased.	_____	_____	_____	_____
23. Merchandise is purchased on credit.	_____	_____	_____	_____
24. The estimated taxes payable are increased.	_____	_____	_____	_____

a. *Net working capital* is defined as current assets minus current liabilities.

Selected References

Bean, Virginia L., and Griffith, Reynolds. "Risk and Return in Working Capital Management." *Mississippi Valley Journal of Business and Economics* 1 (Fall 1966), pp. 28–48.

Beranek, William. *Working Capital Management.* Belmont, Calif.: Wadsworth, 1968.

Cargill, Thomas F. "The Term Structure of Interest Rates: A Test of the Expectations Hypothesis." *Journal of Finance* 30 (June 1975), pp. 761–771.

Carleton, Willard T., and Cooper, Ian A. "Estimation and Uses of the Term Structure of Interest Rates." *Journal of Finance* 31 (September 1976), pp. 1067–1083.

Chervany, Norman L. "A Simulation Analysis of Causal Relationships within the Cash Flow Process." *Journal of Financial and Quantitative Analysis* 5 (December 1970), pp. 445–468.

Cossaboom, Roger A. "Let's Reassess the Profitability-Liquidity Trade-off." *Financial Executive* 39 (May 1971), pp. 46–51.

Dobson, Steven W.; Sutch, Richard C.; and Vanderford, David F. "An Evaluation of Alternative Empirical Models of the Term Structure of Interest Rates." *Journal of Finance* 31 (September 1976), pp. 1035–1065.

Echols, Michael E., and Elliott, Jan Walter. "A Quantitative Yield Curve Model for Estimating the Term Structure of Interest Rates." *Journal of Financial and Quantitative Analysis* 11 (March 1976), pp. 87–114.

Glautier, M. W. E. "Towards a Reformulation of the Theory of Working Capital." *Journal of Business Finance* 3 (Spring 1971), pp. 37–42.

Knight, W. D. "Working Capital Management: Satisficing versus Optimization." *Financial Management* 1 (Spring 1972), pp. 33–40.

Lambrix, R. J., and Singhvi, S. S. "Managing the Working Capital Cycle." *Financial Executive* 47 (June 1979), pp. 32–41.

Long, J. B. "Stock Prices, Inflation and the Term Structure of Interest Rates." *Journal of Financial Economics* 1 (July 1974), pp. 131–170.

Maier, Steven F., and Vander Weide, James H. "A Practical Approach to Short-Run Financial Planning." *Financial Management* 7 (Winter 1978), pp. 10–16.

Merville, L. J., and Tavis, L. A. "Optimal Working Capital Policies: A Chance-Constrained Programming Approach." *Journal of Financial and Quantitative Analysis* 8 (January 1973), pp. 47–60.

Modigliani, Franco, and Sutch, Richard. "Debt Management and the Term Structure of Interest Rates: An Empirical Analysis." *Journal of Political Economy* 75 (August 1967), pp. 569–589.

Nelson, Robert E., Jr. "The Practice of Business Liquidity Improvement: A Management Approach." *Business Horizons* 20 (October 1977), pp. 54–60.

Pesando, James E. "Determinants of Term Premiums in the Market for United States Treasury Bills." *Journal of Finance* 30 (December 1975), pp. 1317–1327.

Smith, Keith V. *Guide to Working Capital Management.* New York: McGraw-Hill, 1975.

———. *Management of Working Capital: A Reader.* New York: West, 1974.

———. "State of the Art of Working Capital Management." *Financial Management* 2 (Autumn 1973), pp. 50–55.

Stancill, James M. *The Management of Working Capital.* Scranton, Pa.: Intext Educational Publishers, 1971.

Tinsley, P. A. "Capital Structure, Precautionary Balances, and Valuation of the Firm: The Problem of Financial Risk." *Journal of Financial and Quantitative Analysis* 5 (March 1970), pp. 33–62.

Van Horne, James C. "A Risk-Return Analysis of a Firm's Working-Capital Position." *Engineering Economist* 14 (Winter 1969), pp. 71–89.

Vasicek, Oldrich. "An Equilibrium Characterization of the Term Structure." *Journal of Financial Economics* 5 (November 1977), pp. 177–188.

Walker, Ernest W. "Towards a Theory of Working Capital." *Engineering Economist* 9 (January–February 1964), pp. 21–35.

Walter, James E. "Determination of Technical Solvency." *Journal of Business* 30 (January 1959), pp. 30–43.

Yardini, Edward E. "A Portfolio-Balance Model of Corporate Working Capital." *Journal of Finance* 33 (May 1978), pp. 535–552.

Appendix A to Chapter 10

Interest Rate Futures and Riding the Yield Curve

Forward Rates and Futures Rates

If the term structure of interest rates conforms to the unbiased expectations theory, the current long-term rate is a simple average of the present and expected future short-term rates for continuous compounding. In symbols, the five-year rate today would be a simple average of the short-term rates over the same time period as shown in Equation 10A.1:

$$_1R_5 = (_1r_1 + {_2r_1} + {_3r_1} + {_4r_1} + {_5r_1})/5. \qquad (10A.1)$$

Table 10A.1 shows the long-term rates implied by an assumed sequence of expected future short-term rates. Table 10A.1 illustrates that the current long-term rate, with continuous compounding and under unbiased expectations, is a simple arithmetic average of the expected future one-year rates.

The one-period yield that is expected in the future has also been described as the *forward rate.* Under continuous compounding, the expected forward rates can be inferred simply and directly from the term structure of interest rates. An illustrative term structure of interest rates is set forth in Table 10A.2, and the data from Table 10A.2 are graphed in Figure 10A.1.

With continuous compounding, forward rates can be calculated from successive yields to maturity over different terms.[1] Formally, the relationship is as shown in Equation 10A.2:

$$_Nr_1 = N_tR_N - (N - 1)_tR_{N-1} \qquad (10A.2)$$

Table 10A.1

Long-Term Rates Implied by Short-Term Rates

Year	One-Year Rates (Percent)	Implied Current Long-Term Rates
1	6	5-year, 8%; 4-year, 7.5%; 3-year, 7%; 2-year, 6.5%;
2	7	
3	8	
4	9	
5	10	

1. Richard Roll, *The Behavior of Interest Rates* (New York: Basic Books, 1970), p. 16, equation (3–3).

Table 10A.2

Illustrative Term Structure of Interest Rates

Term of the Instrument	Yield to Maturity (Percent)
1 year	6
2 years	6.5
3 years	7
4 years	7.5
5 years	8

Using the data in Table 10A.2, we can calculate the implied forward rate at the beginning of the fifth year. The result is shown in Equation 10A.2a:

$$\begin{aligned} {}_5r_1 &= 5(8) - 4(7.5) \\ &= 40 - 30 = 10. \end{aligned} \qquad (10A.2a)$$

Thus the implied forward rate for the fifth year is 10 percent. In a like manner we can calculate the implied forward rates for the other years as well. The results are shown in Table 10A.3. We have illustrated consistency in the relationships in the three tables.

Forward rates are of importance because of their economic nature. The forward rate is the marginal return gained from an investment by holding or committing the investment for one additional time period. Thus the forward rate represents a return that will be realized over a future time period if the expectations implied by the current term structure of interest rates are realized.

Another form of return from an investment held over a future time period

Figure 10A.1

A Graph of the Term Structure of Interest Rates

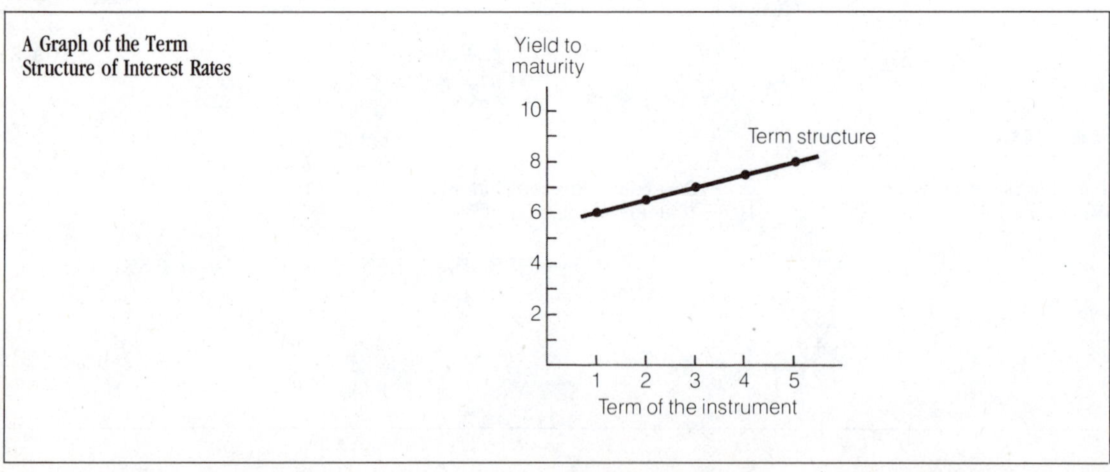

Table 10A.3

Forward Rates Implied by the Term Structure

Year	Implied Forward Rates (Percent)
1	6
2	7
3	8
4	9
5	10

is measured by the *futures rate.* Interest rate futures are contracts that call for transactions in specified financial instruments to take place on stated future dates. The yields on futures contracts for a series of years into the future would, in the absence of frictions or other types of market imperfections, be the same as the implied forward rates. The relationship between futures rates and implied forward rates is, in actuality, a matter of empirical testing. Divergences between the two sets of rates would offer possible profit-making opportunities. The relationship between futures and forward rates has become significant in recent years with the development of a market in interest rate futures.

The Establishment of an Interest Rate Futures Market

Interest rate futures are a relatively new development. In the fall of 1975 the Chicago Board of Trade established a contract for GNMA's (Government National Mortgage Association Securities). In early 1976 the International Monetary Market (IMM) of the Chicago Mercantile Exchange introduced a contract for ninety-day Treasury bills. In 1977 the Chicago Board of Trade extended trading to Treasury bond futures contracts. On August 7, 1980, the New York Stock Exchange, through its wholly owned subsidiary, the New York Futures Exchange, began trading in futures contracts for five major currencies plus twenty-year Treasury bonds. At the opening it was estimated that during 1979 the trading volume averaged about 50,000 contracts a day on the Chicago Board of Trade and on the IMM and that the New York Futures Exchange would reach between 15 percent and 20 percent of that volume in its first year.

The volume in these interest rate futures has grown substantially. For example, on an average day in 1979, futures contracts representing about $7\frac{1}{2}$ billion in three-month Treasury bills were traded on the International Monetary Market of the Chicago Mercantile Exchange. On an average day in 1979 at the Chicago Board of Trade (CBT), futures contracts representing almost $1 billion of long-term Treasury bonds were traded. Also, futures contracts representing over $$\frac{1}{2}$ billion of GNMA's changed hands on an average day in 1979.

The financial futures markets operate as do other futures markets. One of the most active futures markets is for three-month Treasury bills at the IMM. Through this exchange a customer might buy a contract to take delivery of and pay for $1 million of three-month Treasury bills on March 20, 1981. There are eight contract delivery months on the IMM extending at quarterly intervals for about two years into the future.

The contract price is quoted as the difference between $100 and the discount rate on the bill in question. Thus a contract fixing a bill rate at 8.5 percent would be quoted at $91.50. A clearinghouse places itself between the buyer and the seller so that the buyer's contract is not with the seller but with the clearinghouse. Also, the seller's contract is with the clearinghouse and not with the original buyer. For the financial liability of the clearinghouse, the clearing member firms must place margins on their contracts. For each purchase or sale of a three-month Treasury bill contract of $1 million on the IMM, the clearing member firm must post a margin of $1,200, which can be in the form of cash or a bank letter of credit. The clearing member firm in turn imposes an initial margin of at least $1,500 on the individual trader.

While the position is outstanding, the contract will be "marked-to-market" by the clearinghouse at the end of each business day. Either profits or losses are recorded, based on the position and price movements. Profits in the margin account may be withdrawn. If losses reduce the firm's margin below $1,200, the firm must make up the difference to the clearinghouse in cash before the clearinghouse opens the next day. The customer's margin account may fall below the initial $1,500; but if it falls below the $1,200 maintenance margin, the account must be brought back up to $1,500. There are also daily limits on the degree of price fluctuations. At the IMM, for example, no futures trades in Treasury bills can involve prices more than 50 basis points above or below the final settlement price of the previous day, though these margins may be temporarily increased if the daily limit restricts trading for a few days. (One hundred basis points equal 1 percent. The number of basis points is a convenient way to describe interest rate changes of fractions of a percent.)

The Relationship between the Forward and Futures Rates

In theory, in the absence of frictions and other market imperfections, a divergence between forward and futures rates could not persist. We shall illustrate how arbitrage operations under idealized conditions would prevent the persistence of a divergence. The basic data to be used in the analysis is set forth in Figure 10A.2.

Arbitrage operations simply imply that transactions can be made to obtain a sure profit without any risk. This will be illustrated by the pattern of data assumed in Figure 10A.2. In that figure, rates are presented for four cate-

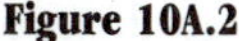

Figure 10A.2

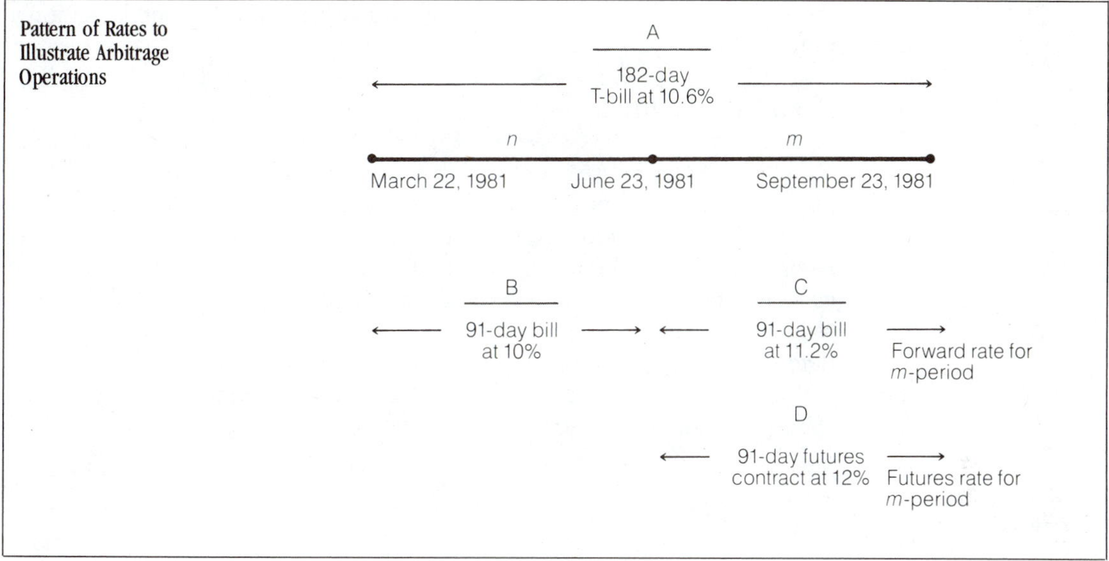

Pattern of Rates to Illustrate Arbitrage Operations

gories of Treasury bills. Treasury Bill A is a 182-day bill yielding 10.6 percent. T-Bill B is a 91-day bill starting immediately and carrying a yield of 10 percent. T-Bill C is a 91-day bill starting 91 days later and bearing a yield of 11.2 percent. Continuous compounding is assumed, so the yield on the 182-day bill is a simple average of the yields on the successive 91-day bills spanned by Bill A. Finally, Item D is a 91-day futures contract covering the second 91-day period and carrying a yield of 12 percent. The 12 percent yield for the T-Bill futures contract is chosen arbitrarily above Bill C to illustrate the arbitrage transactions that would be stimulated.

The patterns imply a positive term structure with the rate on the futures contract assumed to be above the rate on the forward contract. In the example the implied forward rate is the 11.2 percent on T-Bill C. Under the relationships assumed, the following actions would be taken.

1. Buying the 91-day T-bill futures contract to run for the m period after the elapse of the n period.
2. Taking a long position in the 91-day T-bill B for the n period.
3. Selling short the 182-day T-bill A for the $(n + m)$ period.

The second and third transactions are equivalent to shorting a 91-day T-bill for the m period.

Thus one earns 12 percent on the futures contract while paying only 11.2 percent in the short position in the 91-day T-bill for the m period. The results could also be expressed in terms of the lower price paid for the futures contract in which the buyer is taking a long position and the higher price on the forward contract that is sold short.

In expressing the results in the prices of the Treasury bills, we will follow the pattern laid out by Dennis R. Capozza and Bradford Cornell.[2] Although the T-bill futures contracts are denominated in units of $1 million, for ease of encompassing the numbers we will assume units of $1,000. The results are shown in Table 10A.4.

The net gain is thus $1.94 per $1,000 of bonds or $1,940 on the standard $1 million T-bill futures contract. In the illustration, the transactor is completely hedged, and no net investment is required to achieve the sure gain. The transactions would be expected to eliminate this arbitrage opportunity. Selling short the 182-day bill would tend to decrease its price, driving up its yield. Purchase of the futures contracts would tend to drive up their price and reduce their yield until profitable arbitrage opportunities no longer existed. Before reviewing the empirical studies on the relationship between forward and futures rates, we have laid the necessary foundation of discussing the concept of riding the yield curve.

Table 10A.4

Gain from Arbitraging When the Futures Rate Exceeds the Forward Rate

At time t:		
Inflow from shorting 182-day bill $(n + m)$	$= \exp[-0.106(0.5)](1,000)^{a}$	= $ 948.38
Outflow for investment in n-day bills (91 days)		$ 948.38
Net		= $ 0
At time $t + n$ (end of 91 days):		
Inflow from maturation of n-day bills	$= (948.38/975.31)(\$1,000)^{b}$	= $ 972.39
Outflow from taking delivery of bills on the futures contracts	$= \exp[-0.12(0.25)](\$1,000)$	= $ 970.45
Net gain		= $ 1.94 per bond
At time $t + n + m$:		
Inflow from maturation of the m-day bill bought through the futures market		= $1,000.00
Outflow from maturation of the shorted $(n + m)$-day bill		= $1,000.00
Net		= $ 0

a. Since continuous compounding of a discount bond is assumed, to have an annual yield of 10.6 percent requires that its price with six months to run is $e^{-0.106(0.5)}$ times the maturity value of the bond (here assumed to be $1,000). The "exp" is a generally used method of indicating the power to which e is raised.

b. $975.31 represents the price of the n-day bill at t, so the fraction represents the portion of the $1,000 maturity value purchased from the proceeds of shorting the $(n + m)$-day bill at time t.

2. Dennis R. Capozza and Bradford Cornell, "Treasury Bill Pricing in the Spot and Futures Markets," *Review of Economics and Statistics* 61 (November 1979), pp. 513–520.

Riding the Yield Curve

As interest rates have risen in recent years, cash managers have tried to avoid holding idle cash. Rather, they have sought to obtain a return by investing cash balances. A substantial amount of such funds has been placed in highly liquid, interest-earning marketable securities. U.S. Treasury bills have been used substantially as investment instruments. The Treasury bills futures market has enabled investments in Treasury bills to be made in a number of ways.

Suppose a cash manager has $1 million and will need it in 91 days to meet a commitment. During this time period, however, the cash manager wishes to earn interest on the $1 million and so invests in Treasury bills. There are at least three ways the cash manager can invest in the T-bills:

1. Invest for a maturity of less than 91 days, planning to roll over the investment into other, successive, bills maturing at the end of 91 days.
2. Buy a Treasury bill maturing in exactly 91 days.
3. Buy a Treasury bill of maturity longer than 91 days with a plan to sell the bill at the end of the 91 days.

The strategy of purchasing bills of maturities longer than the planned holding period and selling them prior to maturity is referred to as *riding the yield curve.*

If the term structure of interest rates is positive, the longer maturity the cash manager can get into, the higher will be the yield. But the term structure itself reflects expectations of future supply and demand relationships, and these are subject to change. Risks can come from a number of sources. Changes may take place in the term structure of interest rates. The relation between the spot, forward, and futures markets may change. Hence, among the alternatives that the cash manager may take to invest available funds are different kinds and degrees of risk in relation to potential movements and changes in the money and capital markets.

One alternative is to *match maturities.* This would represent simply buying, under our example, a 91-day Treasury bill. The funds earn whatever Treasury bills earn during that 91-day period of time. Another alternative would be to ride the yield curve on an unhedged basis. An illustration would be to buy 182-day Treasury bills with the intention of selling them at the end of 91 days.

A third alternative would be to ride the yield curve in a hedged position. To illustrate this concretely, we will use the data in Figure 10A.2, except that the rate on the futures contract for Period m will be assumed to be equal to the forward rate for the same time period (at 11.2 percent). With the positively sloped yield curve reflected in the data of Figure 10A.2, the transactions to ride the yield curve in a hedged position would be the following:

1. On March 22, 1981, buy the 182-day T-bill on a 10.6 percent basis at $948.38.
2. Sell a 91-day futures contract on an 11.2 percent basis at $972.39.

3. On June 23, 1981, deliver the T-bill with 91 days remaining to meet the futures contract requirement.

The treasurer has locked in the 10.6 percent yield on the 182-day bill as compared with the lower 10 percent yield on the 91-day bill available on March 22, 1981.

The differential gain from riding the yield curve in a hedged position results from the positive slope of the term structure curve and the relationship between short-term and long-term rates, which reflects the unbiased expectations theory. But compared with simply taking a position in the 91-day T-bill, riding the yield curve in a hedged position requires two transactions and commissions instead of one. So the results also depend on the commission levels in relation to the extent to which the yield curve is positively sloped. Also, of course, the higher demand for the 182-day bill as compared with the 91-day bill will tend to drive up the price (lower the yield) of the longer-term bill (as compared with the shorter term bill). The sale of the T-bill futures will tend to drive down their prices (raise the required yields). Thus the actions taken to benefit from the positively sloped term structure will tend to flatten the slope of the curve.

In the light of transactions of the types described above, it is not likely that opportunities for abnormal returns would persist. But the matter is best settled by empirical studies in the area.

Empirical Studies of Yields on Futures Contracts and the Behavior of Forward Rates

Empirical studies of opportunities for arbitrage profits in the relationship between forward and futures market rates have yielded different results through time. Both Donald J. Puglisi and Ben Branch found gains derived from hedged riding of the yield curve. Louis H. Ederington found the results to be less consistent. Dennis R. Capozza and Bradford Cornell observed a substantial differential of futures rates above implied forward rates for contracts whose maturities extended beyond seventeen to eighteen weeks. A study of a later time period by Marcelle Arak and Christopher J. McCurdy observed forward rates higher than futures rates on the June 1979 Treasury bills contracts over the period from November 1978 through April 1979. Arak and McCurdy also observed a substantial spread, with higher forward rates than futures rates in the September 1979 Treasury bill futures contracts traded on the International Monetary Market, particularly in June and July of 1979.

Most studies have found that the futures rates are below the forward rates near the maturity date of the futures contracts. The explanation generally given is the lower transactions costs in the futures contracts as compared with the spot or forward markets, in which transactions costs are generally greater.

For longer maturities, the persistently higher futures rates over forward rates that Capozza and Cornell observed are explained by the higher risk in futures contracts. Transactions in the Treasury bill cash and forward markets involve the creditworthiness of the instrument itself, and the T-bill presumably has no credit risk. The futures contracts, by contrast, involve the creditworthiness of the customers, of the trading firms, and of the clearinghouses. Therefore, futures contracts may involve some greater risks than do spot and forward contracts.

Conclusions on Opportunities in the Interest Rate Futures Markets

Like other futures markets, the interest rate futures markets perform socially useful economic functions. The futures markets rates themselves record expectations of future interest rate levels. And, as with other futures markets, the futures markets in interest rates can be used to reduce the risk of taking or holding a position in financial instruments.

Opportunities for arbitrage gains depend on the relationships among the spot, forward, and futures markets. The positive or negative yield curve structure also determines the kind of strategies that may be profitable and so, of course, the yield curve acts both as a stimulus and as a restraint. The cost of hedging will depend on the relative costs of using the forward and futures markets. In addition, transactions costs are important in determining the potential benefits of using the interest rate futures markets. If transactions costs are high, arbitrage opportunities are more limited. If transactions costs are low, periods can occur when arbitrage opportunities may exist.

Interest rate futures markets have been used in part to avoid taxes; the trader in this instance converts ordinary income into capital gains. However, Treasury rulings have greatly restricted the use of the interest rate futures markets in this way. One would expect different results from empirical studies done before and after these key rulings. One would also expect that competition would cause some of the tax avoidance benefits to be passed on to traders on the other side of the transactions.

It is also not surprising that speculators use the interest rate futures markets. To the extent that they do, the increased activity should be helpful to traders who have a need for hedging. This will be true only if the speculative activity does not introduce abnormal fluctuations and shifts in the underlying patterns of relationships.

In the long run, we would expect the interest rate futures markets to provide another alternative in the range of potential risk-return positions that a cash or a financial manager might employ. The interest rate futures markets can be viewed from three standpoints. First, the patterns between forward rates and interest rate futures provide opportunities for reducing risk by hedging and for bearing risk by taking speculative positions.

A second way to view the interest rate futures markets is in terms of the basic relations between spot and futures markets. If a commodity is storable, it can be bought today, stored, and sold at a future date. If the futures price were to exceed the spot price by more than the costs involved in storing, arbitrageurs would buy the commodity in the spot market—raising the price —and would sell it in the futures market, lowering the futures price. These activities would reduce the disparity between the futures price and the current price. Thus, a second benefit a futures market provides is to develop appropriate relationships between spot prices and futures prices.

A third way to view the interest rate futures markets is in a portfolio sense. Here we view the interest rate futures market as presenting another set of risk-return opportunities for financial managers and investors. The risk-return opportunities provided by the operation of the interest rate futures markets will fall on a curve representing risk-return relationships in various portfolio combinations. In the long run, the risk-return relationships offered by the operation of the interest rate futures markets will fall on the capital market line and provide additional alternative portfolio opportunities.

Selected References

Arak, Marcelle, and McCurdy, Christopher J. "Interest Rate Futures." *Quarterly Review, Federal Reserve Bank of New York* 4 (Winter 1979–1980), pp. 33–46.

Bacon, Peter W., and Williams, Richard. "Interest Rate Futures: New Tool for the Financial Manager." *Financial Management* 5 (Spring 1976), pp. 32–38.

Black, Fisher. "The Pricing of Commodity Contracts." *Journal of Financial Economics* 3 (March 1976), pp. 167–179.

Branch, Ben. "Testing the Unbiased Expectations Theory of Interest Rates." *Financial Review* (Fall 1978), pp. 51–66.

Burger, Albert E.; Lang, Richard W.; and Rasche, Robert H. "The Treasury Bill Futures Market and Market Expectations of Interest Rates." *Federal Reserve Bank of St. Louis Monthly Review* 59 (June 1977), pp. 1–9.

Capozza, Dennis R., and Cornell, Bradford. "Treasury Bill Pricing in the Spot and Futures Markets." *Review of Economics and Statistics* 61 (November 1979), pp. 513–520.

Cornell, Bradford. "Monetary Policy, Inflation Forecasting and the Term Structure of Interest Rates." *Journal of Finance* 33 (March 1978), pp. 117–127.

Dusak, K. "Futures Trading and Investor Returns: An Investigation of Commodity Market Risk Premiums." *Journal of Political Economy* 81 (November–December 1973), pp. 1387–1406.

Ederington, Louis H. "The Hedging Performance of the New Futures Market." *Journal of Finance* 34 (March 1979), pp. 157–170.

Elliott, J. W., and Baier, Jerome R. "Econometric Models and Current Interest Rates: How Well Do They Predict Future Fates?" *Journal of Finance* 34 (September 1979), pp. 975–986.

Fama, Eugene F. "Forward Rates as Predictors of Future Spot Rates." *Journal of Financial Economics* 3 (October 1976), pp. 361–378.

———. "Inflation Uncertainty and Expected Returns on Treasury Bills." *Journal of Political Economy* 84 (June 1976), pp. 427–448.

———. "Short-Term Interest Rates as Predictors of Inflation." *American Economic Review* 65 (June 1975), pp. 269–282.

Friedman, Benjamin M. "Interest Rate Expectations versus Forward Rates: Evidence from an Expectations Survey." *Journal of Finance* 34 (September 1979), pp. 965–973.

Grove, Myron A. "On 'Duration' and the Optimal Maturity Structure of the Balance Sheet." *Bell Journal of Economics and Management Science* 5 (Autumn 1974), pp. 696–709.

Hamburger, Michael J., and Platt, E. N. "The Expectations Hypothesis and the Efficiency of the Treasury Bill Market." *Review of Economics and Statistics* 57 (May 1975), pp. 190–199.

Holmes, Alexander B., and Kwast, Myron C. "Interest Rates and Inflationary Expectations: Tests for Structural Change 1952–1976." *Journal of Finance* 34 (June 1979), pp. 732–741.

Lang, Richard W., and Rasche, Robert H. "A Comparison of Yields on Futures Contracts and Implied Forward Rates." *Federal Reserve Bank of St. Louis Monthly Review* 60 (December 1978), pp. 21–30.

Levi, Maurice D. "Underutilization of Forward Markets or Rational Behavior." *Journal of Finance* 34 (September 1979), pp. 1013–1017.

Levi, Maurice D., and Makin, John H. "Fisher, Phillips, Friedman and the Measured Impact of Inflation on Interest." *Journal of Finance* 34 (March 1979), pp. 35–52.

Livingston, Miles. "A Theory of Humpbacked Bond Yield Curves." *Journal of Finance* 32 (December 1977), pp. 1747–1751.

McEnally, Richard W., and Rice, Michael L. "Hedging Possibilities in the Flotation of Debt Securities." *Financial Management* 8 (Winter 1979), pp. 12–18.

Nelson, Charles R. *The Term Structure of Interest Rates.* New York: Basic Books, 1971.

Osteryoung, Jerome S; Roberts, Gordon S.; and McCarty, Daniel E. "Ride the Yield Curve When Investing Idle Funds in Treasury Bills?" *Financial Executive* 47 (April 1979), pp. 10–15.

Puglisi, Donald, J. "Is the Futures Market for Treasury Bills Efficient?" *Journal of Portfolio Management* 4 (Winter 1978), pp. 64–67.

Rendleman, Richard J., Jr., and Carabini, Christopher E. "The Efficiency of the Treasury Bill Futures Market." *Journal of Finance* 34 (September 1979), pp. 895–914.

Roll, Richard. *The Behavior of Interest Rates.* New York: Basic Books, 1970.

Snyder, Linda. "How to Speculate in the World's Safest Investment." *Fortune,* July 1977, pp. 49–51.

11
Current Asset Management

In Chapter 10 we viewed working capital management in a general sense. Now we will focus our attention on the firm's investment in specific current assets, examining cash, marketable securities, accounts receivable, and inventories. According to Federal Trade Commission reports, current assets at the end of 1979 represented almost 50 percent of manufacturing companies' assets, so current asset management is clearly an important subject.

Cash Management

Controlling the investment in current assets begins with cash management. Cash consists of the firm's holdings of currency and demand deposits—the latter being by far the more important for most firms.

Why Hold Cash?

Businesses (and individuals) have three primary motives for holding cash: (1) the transactions motive, (2) the precautionary motive, and (3) the speculative motive.

Transactions Motive. The transactions motive for holding cash is to enable the firm to conduct its ordinary business—making purchases and sales. In lines of business where billings can be cycled throughout the month (such as the utilities) cash inflows can be scheduled and synchronized with the need for the cash outflows. We expect the cash to revenues ratio and cash to total assets ratio for such firms to be relatively low. In retail trade, by contrast, sales are more random, and a number of transactions may actually be conducted with physical currency. As a consequence, retail trade requires a higher ratio of cash to sales and of cash to total assets.

The seasonality of a business may give rise to a need for cash to purchase inventories. For example, raw materials may be available only during a harvest season and may be perishable, as in the food-canning business. Or sales may be seasonal, as they are in department stores (with the peaks around the Christmas and Easter holidays), giving rise to an increase in cash needs.

Precautionary Motive. The precautionary motive for holding cash relates primarily to the predictability of cash inflows and outflows. If the predictability is high, less cash need be held against an emergency or any other contingency. Another factor that strongly influences the precautionary motive is the ability to borrow additional cash on short notice. Borrowing flexibility is primarily a matter of the strength of the firm's relationships with banking institutions and other credit sources. The need for holding cash is satisfied in large part by having near-money assets such as short-term government securities.

Speculative Motive. The speculative motive for holding cash is to enable the firm to accept profit making opportunities that may arise. By and large, business accumulation of cash for speculative purposes is not widely found. Such accumulation is more common among individual investors. However, the firm's cash and marketable securities account may rise to rather sizable levels on a temporary basis as funds are accumulated to meet specific future needs. For example, at the end of 1977, IBM held $252 million in cash and $5.2 billion in marketable securities. Combined, these items represented 28.5 percent of IBM's year-end total assets of $14.0 billion. Whenever IBM introduces a new computer development, the cash requirements are quite substantial, since the total investment and production costs will be recovered over several years in monthly rental receipts.

Specific Advantages of Adequate Cash

In addition to these general motives, sound working capital management requires maintenance of an ample amount of cash for several other specific reasons:

1. It is essential that the firm have sufficient cash to take trade discounts. The payment schedule for purchases is referred to as the *term of the sale.* A commonly encountered billing procedure, or *term of trade,* is that of a 2 percent discount on a bill paid within ten days, with full payment required in thirty days, if the discount is not taken. (This is usually stated as 2/10, net 30.) Since the net amount is due in thirty days, failure to take the discount means paying the extra 2 percent for using the money an additional twenty days. The following equation can be used for calculating the cost, on an annual basis, of not taking discounts:[1]

1. To be more precise, we could use compound interest calculations with daily compounding. The basic formulation is to solve for the percentage cost, r, in the following:

$$(1.00 - 0.02)\left(1 + \frac{r}{365}\right)^{20} = 1$$

$$\left(1 + \frac{r}{365}\right)^{20} = 1/.98$$

$$\frac{r}{365} = (1/.98)^{1/20} - 1$$

$$r = 365(1/.98)^{1/20} - 365$$
$$r = 36.89\%.$$

$$\text{Cost} = \frac{\text{Discount percent}}{(100 - \text{Discount percent})} \times \frac{365}{(\text{Final due date} - \text{Discount period})}$$

The denominator in the first term (100 − Discount percent) equals the funds made available by not taking the discount. To illustrate, the cost of not taking a discount when the terms are 2/10, net 30 is computed:

$$\text{Cost} = \frac{2}{98} \times \frac{365}{20} = 0.0204 \times 18.25 = 37.23\%.$$

This represents an annual interest rate of over 37 percent. Most firms' cost of capital is substantially lower than 37 percent.

2. Since the current and acid test ratios are key items in credit analysis, it is essential that the firm, in order to maintain its credit standing, meet the standards of the line of business in which it is engaged. A strong credit standing enables the firm to purchase goods from trade suppliers on favorable terms and to maintain its line of credit with banks and other sources of credit.

3. Ample cash is useful for taking advantage of favorable business opportunities that may come along from time to time.

4. The firm should have sufficient liquidity to meet emergencies, such as strikes, fires, or marketing campaigns of competitors.

Using the knowledge about the general nature of cash flows presented in Chapter 8, financial managers may be able to improve the inflow-outflow pattern of cash. They can do so by better synchronization of flows and by reduction of float, explained in the following sections.

Synchronization of Cash Flows

With perfect synchronization of cash inflows and outflows and a high degree of predictability, cash balances could be held to low levels. An example of synchronization demonstrates how cash flows can be improved through more frequent requisitioning of funds by divisional offices from the firm's central office. Some Gulf Oil Corporation divisional field offices, for instance, formerly requisitioned funds once a week; now the treasurer's office insists on daily requisitions, thus keeping cash on tap as many as four days longer. On the basis of twenty offices, each requiring $1 million a week, the staggered requisitions make available the equivalent of $40 million for one day each week. At 6 percent interest, this earns better than $336,000 a year.

Moreover, effective forecasting can reduce the firm's investment in cash. The cash flow forecasting at CIT Credit Corporation illustrates this idea. An assistant treasurer forecasts planned purchases of automobiles by the dealers. This treasurer estimates daily the number of cars shipped to the 10,000 dealers who finance their purchases through CIT and then estimates how much money should be deposited in Detroit banks that day to pay automobile manufacturers. On one day the estimated required deposit was $6.4 million; the actual bill for the day was $6.397 million, a difference of 0.5 percent. Although such close forecasting cannot be achieved by every firm, the system enables CIT to economize on the amount of money it must borrow and thereby keeps interest expense to a minimum.

Expediting Collections and Check Clearing

One of the easiest ways to improve cash flow is to expedite the preparation of bills. A firm can control this process easily, and the cash free-up can be substantial. AT&T, for example, uses the computer to transmit billing information over telephone lines. Prompt mailing of bills also improves cash flow. Getting the bills out is one of the most efficient, yet most easily overlooked, methods of increasing receivables turnover and thereby improving cash flow.

Another important method of economizing on the amount of cash required is to hasten the process of clearing checks. Checks sent from customers in distant cities are subject to delays because of the time required for the check to travel in the mail and to be cleared through the banking system.

Even after a check has been received by a firm and deposited in its account, the funds cannot be spent until the check has been cleared. The bank in which the check is deposited presents the check to the bank on which it was drawn. Only when the latter bank transfers funds to the bank of deposit are they available for use by the depositor. Checks are generally cleared through the Federal Reserve System or through a clearinghouse set up by the banks in a particular city. Of course, if the check is drawn on the bank of deposit, that bank merely transfers funds from one depositor to another with bookkeeping entries. The length of time required for checks to clear is a function of the distance between the payer's and the payee's banks; in the case of clearinghouses, it can range from one day to three or four days. The maximum time for checks cleared through the Federal Reserve System is two days.

To reduce this delay, a *lockbox plan* can be used. If a firm makes a number of sales in distant cities, it can establish a lockbox in a post office located near its customers. It can then arrange for customers to send payments to that box and for a bank to pick up the checks and deposit them in a special checking account. The bank has the checks cleared in the local area and remits the money by wire to the firm's bank of deposit. If the distant customers are scattered, the firm can establish the lockbox in its own city and have the checks picked up by its own bank. The bank begins the clearing process and notifies the firm that a check has been received. In this way the clearing process starts before the firm processes the check. Using these methods reduces collection time by one to five days. Some firms have reported freeing funds in the amount of $5 million or more by these methods.

Slowing Disbursements

Just as expediting the collection process conserves cash, slowing disbursements accomplishes the same thing by keeping cash on hand for longer periods. An obvious way to do this is simply to delay payments, but this involves equally obvious difficulties. Firms have, in the past, devised rather ingenious methods for "legitimately" lengthening the collection period on their own checks, ranging from maintaining deposits in distant banks to using slow, awkward payment procedures. Since such practices are usually recognized for what they are, their use is severely limited.

The most widely publicized procedure in recent years has been the use of drafts. While a check is payable on demand, a draft must be transmitted to the issuer, who approves it and deposits funds to cover it, after which it can be collected. AT&T has used drafts in the following way:

> In handling its payrolls, for instance, AT&T can pay an employee by draft on Friday. The employee cashes the draft at his local bank, which sends it on to AT&T's New York bank. It may be Wednesday or Thursday before the draft arrives. The bank then sends it to the company's accounting department, which has until 3 P.M. that day to inspect and approve it. Not until then does AT&T deposit funds in its bank to pay the draft.[2]

Insurance companies also use drafts to pay claims.

Using Float

Checks written by firms (or individuals) are not deducted from bank records until they are actually received by the bank, possibly a matter of several days. The lag between the time the check is written until the time the bank receives it is known as *float.*

Some firms are able to exploit float to create what is effectively an interest-free loan. For example, a firm with only a moderate balance in its checking account and $100,000 in its savings account may write a check for $100,000, knowing that it will not clear for six or seven days. After six days it can move the $100,000 from the savings account to the checking account so the check will be covered. In the meantime, six days of interest ($100,000 at 6 percent) will have been earned on the savings account. This is the gain from float.

In reality, the problem is more complex. The check-writing firm in the illustration also receives checks, which it deposits in its savings account. Historically, banks have considered these deposits to be available to the company when they are deposited. If the firm is slow to deposit such checks, float is reduced.

Suppose a firm writes checks totaling about $5,000 each day. It takes about six or seven days for these checks to clear and to be deducted from the firm's bank account. Thus the firm's own checking records show a balance $30,000 less than that shown by the bank's records. If the firm receives checks in the amount of $5,000 daily and loses only four days while these checks are being deposited, its own books show a balance that is $20,000 larger than the bank's balance. Thus the firm's float—the difference between the $30,000 and the $20,000—is $10,000.

Clearly there are gains to be had from the skillful use of float. These gains are maximized by covering checks written at the last possible date and depos-

2. "More Firms Substitute Drafts for Checks to Pay, Collect Bills," *Wall Street Journal,* August 29, 1971.

iting checks received as quickly as possible. As previously noted, the effect is similar to an interest-free loan from the bank.

In the past, banks have compensated for funds lost through float by raising prices of other services, which are paid for by all customers. They have, for example, offset float costs by higher interest rates on loans or higher service charges. Thus other customers of the bank bore part of the cost if a firm used float successfully. Clearly, this was not desirable for either the bank or the other customers, and efforts to reduce the gains from using float have intensified in recent years.

One method banks would like to employ to reduce these gains is the electronic funds transfer system. EFTS, as it is called, would create a nationwide computer network that would substantially reduce float time. It presently takes several days to clear checks across the country. Under EFTS the time could be reduced to hours or even minutes. As yet no nationwide system exists, but developments in that direction are moving rapidly.

In addition to reducing the actual time it takes to clear a check, banks are attempting to more accurately match costs and revenues on individual accounts. One effect of this matching is a further reduction in the gains from using float. Table 11.1 depicts a typical commercial checking account service charge analysis. In the earnings credit section, the customer is credited for the average collected balance at the interest rate of 5 percent. The collected balance is the daily balance adjusted for the typical time it takes for the bank to collect on checks deposited. Thus, the estimated days of float will be low for a business dealing mostly with local customers and high for a business that receives payments from out-of-state customers. In this way the individual firm bears the cost of float directly. The expense part of the analysis is straightforward. In reality there are many more expense classifications than the few itemized here—among then lockbox charges, computer service billings, and required compensating balances.

In Table 11.1, the service charge to the firm is $10.98 after allowing for the

Table 11.1

State National Bank Commercial Service Charge Analysis Mail Order Supply Company, September 1981

Earnings Credit		
1 Days in month	31	
2 Less average days float	6	
3 Basis for earnings credit	25	
4 Average daily balance	$21,300.00	
5 Daily rate factor (at 5%)	0.000139	
6 Earnings credit (3 × 4 × 5)		$74.02
Service Debits		
7 20 deposits (at $.25 each)	$ 5.00	
8 3,200 checks deposited (at $.02 each)	64.00	
9 200 checks written (at $.08 each)	16.00	
10 Total service debits (7 + 8 + 9)		85.00
Service charge (10 − 6)		$10.98

earnings credit. In the event that the earnings credit exceeds the expenses, current regulations do not permit paying it to the depositor. But this regulation is under scrutiny and is likely to be changed in the near future.

The key point to remember is that the potential gains from using float are relative. Even though banks have taken steps to reduce the gains, the company that deposits checks from customers promptly and delays bank clearing of checks it writes for as long as possible will still have a relative advantage from float.

If a firm's own collection and clearing process is more efficient than that of the recipients of its checks—and this is often true of large, efficient firms—then the firm could show a negative balance on its own records and a positive balance on its bank's books. Some firms indicate that they *never* have true positive cash balances. One large manufacturer of construction equipment stated that, while its account according to its bank's records shows an average cash balance of about $2 million, its actual cash balance is *minus* $2 million; thus it has $4 million of float. Obviously the firm must be able to forecast its positive and negative clearings accurately in order to make such heavy use of float.

Cost of Cash Management[3]

We have just described a number of procedures that can be used to hold down cash balance requirements. Implementing these procedures, however, is not a costless operation. How far should a firm go in making its cash operations more efficient? As a general rule, a firm should incur these expenses so long as its marginal returns exceed its marginal expenses.

For example, suppose that by establishing a lockbox system and increasing the accuracy of cash inflow and outflow forecasts, a firm can reduce its investment in cash by $1.2 million. Further suppose that the firm borrows at an effective rate of 10 percent.[4] The steps taken release $1.2 million, and the cost of capital required to carry this $1.2 million investment in cash is $120,000. If the costs of the procedures necessary to release the $1.2 million are less than $120,000, the move is a good one; if the costs exceed $120,000, the greater efficiency is not worth the cost. It is clear that larger firms, with larger cash balances, can better afford to hire the personnel necessary to maintain tight control over their cash positions. Cash management is one element of business operations in which economies of scale are clearly present. In sum, the value of careful cash management depends on the cost of funds invested in cash, which in turn depends on the current rate of interest. In the 1970s, with interest rates at historic highs, firms began devoting more care than ever to cash management.

3. We are abstracting from the security aspects of cash management—the prevention of fraud and embezzlement. These topics are better covered in accounting than in finance courses.
4. The borrowing rate, 10 percent, is used rather than the firm's average cost of capital, because cash is a less risky investment than the firm's average assets. Notice also that before-tax figures are used here; the analysis can employ either before-tax or after-tax figures so long as consistency is maintained.

Determining the Minimum Cash Balance

Thus far we have seen that cash is held primarily for transactions purposes; the other traditional motives for holding cash—the speculative and precautionary motives—are today met largely by reserve borrowing and by holding short-term marketable securities. Some minimum cash balance (which can actually be negative if float is used effectively) is required for transactions, and an additional amount over and above this figure may be held as a safety stock. For many firms the total of transactions balances plus safety stock constitutes the minimum cash balance—the point at which the firm either borrows additional cash or sells part of its portfolio of marketable securities. For many other firms, however, banking relationships require still larger balances.

Compensating Balances

We have seen that banks provide services to firms. They clear checks, operate lockbox plans, supply credit information, and the like. These services cost the bank money, so the bank must be compensated for rendering them.

Banks earn most of their income by lending money at interest, and most of the funds they lend are obtained in the form of deposits. If a firm maintains a deposit account with an average balance of $100,000, and if the bank can lend these funds at a return of $8,000, then the account is, in a sense, worth $8,000 to the bank. Thus it is to the bank's advantage to provide services worth up to $8,000 to attract and hold the account.

Banks first determine the costs of the services rendered to their larger customers and then decide on the average account balances necessary to provide enough income to compensate for the costs. Firms often maintain these balances, called *compensating balances,* instead of paying cash service charges to the bank.[5]

Compensating balances are also required by some bank loan agreements. During periods when the supply of credit is restricted and interest rates are high, banks frequently insist that borrowers maintain accounts that average some percentage of the loan amount (15 percent is typical) as a condition for granting the loan. If the balance is larger than what the firm would otherwise maintain, then the effective cost of the loan is increased; the excess balance presumably compensates the bank for making the loan at a rate below what it could earn on the funds if they were invested elsewhere.[6]

Compensating balances can be established (1) as an absolute minimum, say $100,000, below which the actual balance must never fall, or (2) as a minimum average balance, perhaps $100,000 over a certain period, generally a month. The absolute minimum is a much more restrictive requirement, because the average amount of cash held during the month must be above $100,000 by the amount of transactions balances. The $100,000 in this case is "dead money" from the firm's standpoint. Under the minimum average, however, the balance can fall to zero one day provided it is $200,000 some other

5. Banks are compensated for services rendered either by compensating balances or by direct fees.

6. The interest rate effect of compensating balances is discussed further in Chapter 12.

day, with the average working out to $100,000. Thus the $100,000 in this case is available for transactions.

Statistics on compensating balance requirements are not available, but average balances are typical and absolute minimums are rare for business accounts. Discussions with bankers, however, indicate that absolute balance requirements are less rare during times of extremely tight money, such as the late 1960s and early 1970s.

The firm's minimum cash balance is set as the larger of (1) its transactions balances plus precautionary balances (that is, safety stocks) or (2) its required compensating balances. Statistics are not available on which factor is generally controlling, but in our experience compensating balance requirements generally dominate, except for firms subject to absolute minimum balances.[7]

Overdraft System

Most countries outside the United States use *overdraft systems.* In such systems a depositor can write checks in excess of the bank balance, and the bank automatically extends a loan to cover the shortage. The maximum amount of such loans must, of course, be established ahead of time. Statistics are not available on the usage of overdrafts in the United States, but a number of firms have worked out informal, and in some cases formal, overdraft arrangements; and the use of overdrafts has been increasing in recent years.

Cash Management

Several types of mathematical models have been developed to help determine optimal cash balances.[8] These models are interesting, and they are beginning to become practical. A wide range of methods to control the investment in cash has also been developed.

Recently, cash management has begun receiving increased emphasis, primarily in response to the high inflation rates that threaten to devalue any idle or unaccounted for cash. Corporations are tightening their cash controls to ensure that cash will not be forgotten in a dormant bank account or a distant subdivision. For example, Foremost-McKesson tightened internal controls and introduced an electronic funds transfer system, thereby gleaning an extra $30 million from operations. In order to protect its cash during an inflationary period, a firm must know exactly how much cash it has, and where it is. This explains the appearance of complicated cash management systems.

Interest in cash management is also being generated by the large number

7. This point is underscored by an incident that occurred at a professional finance meeting. A professor presented a scholarly paper that used operations research techniques to determine optimal cash balances for a sample of firms. He reported that actual cash balances of the firms greatly exceeded optimal balances, suggesting inefficiency and the need for more refined techniques. The discussant of the paper reported that she had written to the sample firms, asking why they were holding so much cash. The firms uniformly replied that their cash holdings were set by compensating balance requirements. The model thus was useful to determine the optimal cash balance in the absence of compensating balance requirements, but it was precisely those requirements that determined actual balances. Since the model did not include compensating balances as a determinant of cash balances, its usefulness is questionable.
8. Examples of cash management models are presented in Appendix A to this chapter.

of firms expanding overseas. Floating exchange rates compel firms to develop worldwide cash control systems. A centralized cash management system is necessary to prevent large currency exchange losses. Even if a firm wishes to avoid currency speculation, it still must carefully monitor exposure to rate changes and develop an appropriate system of hedges and other means for reducing risk. In many firms, the cash manager takes full responsibility for covering exposure, determining daily or weekly exchange rates for use by all divisions and subsidiaries.

Marketable Securities

Firms sometimes report sizable amounts of short-term marketable securities such as Treasury bills or bank certificates of deposit among their current assets. Why are marketable securities held? The two primary reasons—the need for a substitute for cash and the need for a temporary investment—are considered in this section.

Substitute for Cash

Some firms hold portfolios of marketable securities in lieu of large cash balances, liquidating part of the portfolio to increase the cash account when cash outflows exceed inflows. Data are not available to indicate the extent of this practice, but our impression is that it is not common. Most firms prefer to let their banks maintain such liquid reserves, and they borrow to meet temporary cash shortages.

Temporary Investment

In addition to using marketable securities as a buffer against cash shortages, firms also hold them on a strictly temporary basis. Firms engaged in seasonal operations, for example, frequently have surplus cash flows during part of the year and deficit cash flows the rest of the time. (See the illustrative cash budget in Table 9.4.) Such firms may purchase marketable securities during their surplus periods, then liquidate them when cash deficits occur. Other firms, particularly those in capital goods industries, where fluctuations are violent, attempt to accumulate cash or near-cash securities during a downturn in volume in order to be ready to finance an upturn.

Firms also accumulate liquid assets to meet predictable financial requirements. For example, if a major modernization program is planned for the near future, or if a bond issue is about to mature, the marketable securities portfolio may be increased to provide the required funds. Marketable securities holdings are also frequently increased immediately before quarterly corporate tax payments are due.

Some firms accumulate resources as a protection against a number of contingencies. When they make uninsurable product warranties, for example, companies must be ready to meet any claims that may arise. Firms in highly competitive industries must have resources to carry them through substantial shifts in the market structure. And firms in an industry in which new markets are emerging—for example, foreign markets—need to have resources to meet developments. These funds may be on hand for fairly long periods.

Criteria for Selecting Securities

Different types of securities, varying in risk of default, marketability, and length of maturity, are available. We will discuss some of the characteristics of these securities and the criteria that are applied in choosing among them.

Risk of Default. The firm's liquidity portfolio is generally held for a specific, known need; if it depreciates in value, the firm will be financially embarrassed. Most nonfinancial corporations do not have investment departments specializing in appraising securities and determining the probability of their going into default. Accordingly, the marketable securities portfolio is generally confined to securities with a minimal risk of default. However, the lowest risk securities also provide the lowest returns, so safety is bought at the expense of yield.

Marketability. The securities portfolio is usually held to provide liquid reserves or to meet known needs at a specific time. In either case, the firm must be able to sell its holdings and realize cash on short notice. Accordingly, the securities held in the portfolio must be readily marketable.

Maturity. We shall see in Chapter 20 that at interest rate levels below 8 percent, the price of a long-term bond (other than deep-discount bonds) fluctuates more with changes in interest rates than does the price of a similar short-term security. Further, as we saw in the last chapter, interest rates fluctuate widely over time. These two factors combine to make long-term bonds riskier than short-term securities for a firm's marketable securities portfolio. However, partly because of this risk differential, higher yields are more frequently available on long-term than on short-term securities; so again risk-return trade-offs must be recognized.

Given the motives most firms have for holding marketable securities portfolios, it is generally not feasible for them to be exposed to a high degree of risk from interest rate fluctuations. Accordingly, firms generally confine their portfolios to securities with short maturities. Only if the securities are expected to be held for a long period and not be subject to forced liquidation on short notice will long-term securities be chosen.

Investment Alternatives

The main investment alternatives open to business firms are given in Table 11.2. Returns are lower on the lower-risk government securities and on shorter maturities. Average rate levels vary with the general level of interest rates. Late 1974 was a period of relatively high interest rate levels. After dropping to substantially lower levels by mid-1977, interest rates began to firm up in 1978. By mid-1978, long-term rates had exceeded their high levels of 1974. However, short-term rates were still somewhat below the 1974 peaks.

Table 11.2

Alternative Marketable Securities for Investment[a]

	Approximate Maturities[b]	Approximate Yields[c] April 1977	May 1978	March 1980
U.S. Treasury bills	91–182 days	4.81%	6.52%	15.18%
U.S. Treasury certificates	9–12 months	5.20	7.78	16.07
U.S. Treasury notes	1–5 years	6.41	8.03	13.76
U.S. Treasury bonds	Over 5 years	7.45	8.33	12.79
Federal agencies	Over 5 years	7.71	8.60	13.21
Negotiable certificates of deposit with U.S. and foreign banks	Varies, up to 3 years	5.35	8.00	18.00
Prime commercial paper	Varies, up to 270 days	4.70	7.00	17.00
Bankers acceptances	90 days	4.74	7.19	17.30
Eurodollar bank time deposits	Varies, up to 1 year	5.18	7.82	19.25
Bonds of other domestic and foreign corporations (Aaa)	Varies, up to 30 years	8.53	9.02	14.20

a. The marketable securities listed in this table are only illustrative of a much larger range of available alternatives. For a more complete listing, including prices and yields, see Salomon Brothers, "Bond Market Roundup" and "International Bond Market Roundup," each published weekly.

b. The maturities are those at issue date. For outstanding securities, maturities varying almost by day or week are available.

c. Estimated yields for median maturities in the class.

The financial manager decides on a suitable maturity pattern for the holdings on the basis of how long the funds are to be held. The numerous alternatives can be selected and balanced in such a way that maturities and risks appropriate to the financial situation of the firm are obtained. Commercial bankers, investment bankers, and brokers provide the financial manager with detailed information on each of the listed forms of investment. Because the characteristics of investment outlets change with shifts in financial market conditions, it would be misleading to attempt to give detailed descriptions of them here. The financial manager should keep up to date on these characteristics and follow the principle of making investment selections that offer maturities, yields, and risks appropriate to the firm.

A policy that has been followed in recent years is riding the yield curve, discussed in Appendix A to Chapter 10. When the yield curve has a positive slope, buy longer term securities and sell prior to maturity to take advantage of the higher long-term interest rates. Also lengthen the average maturity of the marketable securities portfolio if the yield curve is expected to fall. Conversely, if the interest rate structure is expected to move upward, shorten the average maturity of the portfolio to take advantage of the higher yields that can be obtained later.

Effects of Inflation

Inflation devalues money very rapidly, making the careful investment of cash essential to the health of the firm. An improved cash management system keeps track of idle cash; but once this cash has been found, it can act as a hedge against inflation only if it is invested appropriately. During periods of tight money, neither small nor large firms can be confident of receiving bank loans to meet cash shortages. Therefore, it is imperative for them to keep cash reserves for future contingencies.

To protect these cash reserves against inflation, companies have begun to invest the funds aggressively, seeking higher yields. Idle cash is no longer merely kept in the bank or invested exclusively in Treasury bills. Certificates of deposit, municipal securities, and commercial paper offer higher rates of return and are therefore gaining in popularity. Firms are even using foreign instruments. For example, NCR invests in commercial paper, the Euromarket, and both domestic and Japanese certificates of deposit to increase pre-tax earnings by about $1 million per year. Litton Industries invests part of its portfolio in Swiss franc and German mark denominated time deposits and in foreign certificates of deposit. Even AT&T is liberalizing its liquid asset investment policies. It trades Treasury bills, looking for the best yield, rather than holding them to maturity. Its other investments include commercial paper, bankers acceptances, certificates of deposit, and overnight repurchase agreements. (Overnight repurchase agreements—repos—have a very short maturity, frequently no longer than one day. Therefore, they are especially appropriate for investing money that will be needed immediately.)

Management of Accounts Receivable: Credit Policy

The level of accounts receivable is determined by the volume of credit sales and the average period between sales and collections. The average collection period is dependent partly on economic conditions (during a recession or a period of extremely tight money, for example, customers may be forced to delay payment) and partly on a set of controllable factors—*credit policy variables.* The major policy variables include (1) credit standards—the maximum riskiness of acceptable credit accounts; (2) credit period—the length of time for which credit is granted; (3) discounts given for early payment; and (4) the firm's collection policy. We will discuss each policy variable separately and in qualitative rather than quantitative terms; then we will illustrate the interaction of these elements and discuss the actual establishment of a firm's credit policy.

Credit Standards

If a firm makes credit sales to only the strongest of customers, it will experience only small amounts of bad debt losses. On the other hand, it will probably lose sales, and the profit it foregoes on these lost sales may be greater than the costs it avoids. To determine the optimal credit standard, the firm relates the marginal costs of credit to the marginal profits on the increased sales.

Marginal costs include production and selling costs; but abstracting from them at this point, we will consider only those costs associated with the quality of the marginal accounts, or *credit quality costs.* These costs include (1) default, or bad debt losses; (2) higher investigation and collection costs; and (3) higher amounts tied up in receivables, resulting in higher costs of capital, due to less credit-worthy customers who delay payment longer than stronger customers.

Since credit costs and credit quality are correlated, it is important to be able to judge the quality of an account, and perhaps the best way to do this is in terms of the probability of default. Probability estimates are for the most part subjective; but credit rating is a well established practice, and a good credit manager can make reasonably accurate judgments of the probability of default by different classes of customers.

Five C's of Credit. To evaluate the credit risk, credit managers consider the five C's of credit: character, capacity, capital, collateral, and conditions. *Character* has to do with the probability that a customer will try to honor obligations. This factor is of considerable importance, because every credit transaction implies a promise to pay. Will the creditor make an honest effort to pay the debts, or is this credit applicant likely to try to get away with something? Experienced credit managers frequently insist that character is the most important issue in a credit evaluation.

Capacity describes a subjective judgment of the customer's ability to pay. It is gauged by the customer's past business performance record, supplemented by physical observation of the plant or store and business methods.

Capital is measured by the general financial position of the firm as indicated by a financial ratio analysis, with special emphasis on the tangible net worth of the enterprise.

Collateral is represented by assets offered by the customer as a pledge for security of the credit extended.

The fifth C, *conditions,* has to do with the impact of general economic trends on the firm or special developments in certain areas of the economy that may affect the customer's ability to meet the obligation.

The five C's of credit represent the factors by which the credit risk is judged. Information on these items is obtained from the firm's previous experience with the customer, supplemented by a well developed system of information-gathering. Two major sources of external information are available. The first is the credit associations. By periodic meetings of local groups and by correspondence, information on experience with debtors is exchanged. More formally, Credit Interchange, a system developed by the National Association of Credit Management for assembling and distributing information on debtors' past performance, is provided. The interchange reports show the paying record of the debtor, the industries from which he or she is buying, and the trading areas in which the purchases are being made.[9]

The second source of external information is the credit-reporting agencies, the best known of which is Dun & Bradstreet. Agencies that specialize in coverage of a limited number of industries also provide information. Representative of these are the National Credit Office and Lyon Furniture Mercantile Agency. These agencies provide data that can be used by the credit manager in the credit analysis; they also provide ratings similar to those available on corporate bonds.

An individual firm can translate its credit information into risk classes, grouped according to the probability of loss associated with sales to a customer. The combination of rating and supplementary information might lead to the following groupings of probable loss experience.

Risk Class Number	Probable Loss Ratio (in Percentages)
1	None
2	0–1/2
3	Over 1/2–1
4	Over 1–2
5	Over 2–5
6	Over 5–10
7	Over 10–20
8	Over 20

If the selling firm has a 20 percent margin over the sum of direct operating costs and all delivery and selling costs, and if it is producing at less than full capacity, it may adopt the following credit policies: selling on customary credit terms to Groups 1 through 5; selling to groups 6 and 7 under more stringent credit terms, such as cash on delivery; and requiring advance payment from Group 8. As long as the bad debt loss ratios are less than 20 percent, the additional sales are contributing something to overhead. However, the opportunity costs of the increased investment in receivables also must be taken into account in the analysis, as will be shown in the examples later in the chapter.

Statistical techniques, especially regression analysis and discriminant analysis, have been used with some success in judging creditworthiness.[10]

9. For additional information, see a publication of the National Association of Credit Management, *Credit Management Handbook,* 2d ed. (Homewood, Ill.: Richard D. Irwin, 1965).

10. Discriminant analysis, discussed in Appendix B to Chapter 7, partitions a sample into two or more components on the basis of a set of characteristics. The sample, for instance, might be loan applicants at a consumer loan company. The components into which they are classified might be those likely to make prompt repayment and those likely to default. The characteristics might be whether the applicant owns a home, how long the person has been with the current employer, level of income, and so on.

These methods work best when individual credits are relatively small and a large number of borrowers are involved, as in retail credit, consumer loans, mortgage lending, and the like. As the increase in credit card use and similar procedures builds up, as computers are used more frequently, and as credit records on individuals and small firms are developed, statistical techniques promise to become much more important than they are today.[11]

Terms of Credit

The terms of credit specify the period for which credit is extended and the discount, if any, for early payment. For example, as we saw earlier, if a firm's credit terms to all approved customers are stated as 2/10, net 30, then a 2 percent discount from the stated sales price is granted if payment is made within ten days, and the entire amount is due thirty days from the invoice date if the discount is not taken. If the terms are stated "net 60," this indicates that no discount is offered and that the bill is due and payable sixty days after the invoice date.

If sales are seasonal a firm may use seasonal dating. Jensen, Inc., a bathing suit manufacturer, sells on terms of 2/10, net 30, May 1 dating. This means that the effective invoice date is May 1, so the discount can be taken until May 10, or the full amount must be paid on May 30, regardless of when the sale was made. Jensen produces output throughout the year, but retail sales of bathing suits are concentrated in the spring and early summer. Because of its practice of offering seasonal datings, Jensen induces some customers to stock up early, saving Jensen storage costs and also nailing down sales.

Credit Period. Lengthening the credit period stimulates sales, but there is a cost to tying up funds in receivables. For example, if a firm changes its terms from net 30 to net 60, the average receivables for the year may rise from $100,000 to $300,000—the increase caused partly by the longer credit terms and partly by the larger volume of sales. The optimal credit period is determined by the point where marginal profits on increased sales are exactly offset by the costs of carrying the higher amounts of accounts receivable.

Cash Discounts. The effect of granting cash discounts can be analyzed similarly to the credit period. For example, if a firm changes its terms from net 30 to 2/10, net 30, it may well attract customers who want to take discounts, thereby increasing gross sales. Also, the average collection period will be shortened, as some old customers pay more promptly to take advantage of the discount. Offsetting these benefits is the cost of the discounts taken. The optimal discount is established at the point where costs and benefits are exactly offsetting.

11. It has been said that the biggest single deterrent to the increased automation of credit processes is George Orwell's classic book, *1984*, in which he described the social dangers of centralized files of information on individuals. Orwell's omnipresent watcher, Big Brother, is mentioned frequently in congressional sessions discussing mass storage of information relevant to credit analysis.

Collection Policy

Collection policy refers to the procedures the firm follows to obtain payment of past-due accounts. For example, it may send a letter to such accounts when they are ten days past due; it may use a more threatening letter, followed by a telephone call, if payment is not received within thirty days; and it may turn the account over to a collection agency after ninety days.

The collection process can be expensive in terms of both out-of-pocket expenditures and lost goodwill, but at least some firmness is needed to prevent an undue lengthening in the collection period and to minimize outright losses. Again, a balance must be struck between the costs and benefits of different collection policies.

Accounts Receivable versus Accounts Payable

Whenever goods are sold on credit, two accounts are created. An asset item called an *account receivable* appears on the books of the selling firm, and a liability item called an *account payable* appears on the books of the purchaser. At this point we are analyzing the transaction from the viewpoint of the seller, so we have concentrated on the type of variables under the seller's control. (In Chapter 12 we will examine the transaction from the viewpoint of the purchaser, discussing accounts payable as a source of funds and considering the cost of these funds vis-à-vis funds obtained from other sources.)

Evaluating Changes in Credit Policy[12]

Table 11.3 and following examples show the implementation of the relationship between marginal returns and the marginal costs of changing credit policies. The Wales firm at present has total credit sales of $10,000,000 per year. Its average collection period is 60 days. The current bad debt loss ratio on these sales is 2 percent. Wales is considering a change in credit standards that

Table 11.3

Evaluating the Effects of a Change in Credit Standards

Part A. Incremental Investment	
1. Additional sales per day $500,000/365	$1,369.86
2. Multiplied by average collection period on new sales × 90	123,287
3. Variable costs of investment in receivables 0.70(123,287)	86,301
4. Other working capital requirements for the incremental sales $500,000(0.3)	150,000
5. Total incremental investment from lowering credit standards (3 + 4)	236,301
Part B. Incremental Profitability	
6. Contribution margin on incremental sales 0.3($500,000)	$150,000
7. Less increase in bad debt losses 0.04(500,000)	−20,000
8. Less cost of funds in incremental investment 0.15(236,301)	−35,445
9. Increase in net cash flows (6 − 7 − 8)	$ 94,555

12. Appendix C to this chapter summarizes some recent literature dealing with conceptual issues in connection with the measurement of the effect of changes in credit policies.

would result in an increase in sales of $500,000 and a bad debt loss ratio on these incremental sales of 4 percent, and an average collection period of 90 days. Wales's ratio of variable costs to sales is 70 percent, and it can accommodate the incremental sales with existing capacity; for incremental sales, the other net working capital investment requirements are 30 percent of sales; the required rate of return on investment in receivables is 15 percent.

There are several reasons for the procedures used in Table 11.3. The first relates to the measurement of the investment in receivables. If the sales were not made, the variable costs of producing the receivables would not be incurred. Hence, the variable cost ratio is multiplied times the invoice value of the receivables to measure the opportunity costs of investment in receivables. In a subsequent example, in which the incremental receivables result from a longer collection period on existing sales, the incremental investment is measured at the full invoice value of the receivables.

Line 4 takes into account other working capital requirements related to the incremental sales. Chapter 8 fully developed the basis for relating incremental investments to incremental sales. Following the methodology of that chapter, the increment in sales would produce an increment in other current assets as well as in receivables. Fixed assets would not be affected because we have assumed that the firm can handle the incremental sales with existing capacity. From the investment requirements for the other current assets, we deduct the spontaneous financing provided from current liabilities. We have used the estimate that the other net working capital investment requirements are 30 percent of sales.

In Part B, which deals with incremental profitability, we use the contribution margin on incremental sales rather than the net profit ratio. We are measuring here the contribution to cash flows from the incremental sales, so we do not take fixed costs into account.

Under the assumptions of this example, it is profitable to relax the credit standards as described. This result, of course, depends on the data of the case and does not represent a general result.

In considering a change in credit terms, we return to the facts at the beginning of the preceding example, when the Wales firm had total credit sales of $10 million per year, an average collection period of 60 days, and a bad debt loss ratio of 2 percent. Wales is now considering a change in credit terms. The average collection period would increase to 70 days, and the new bad debt loss ratio which applies to all sales—old and incremental—would be 3 percent. Table 11.4 analyzes this change in credit terms.

The analysis for a change in credit policy is similar to that for a change in credit terms. The effect on cash flows might be an item of expense change in connection with increasing or decreasing collection efforts. For example, if collection efforts were reduced, we could have the same effects as shown in Table 11.4 plus a reduction of collection expenses by 1 percent of the old sales. This would reduce cash outflows by $100,000. The net increase in cash

Table 11.4

Analysis of Changes in Credit Terms

Part A. Incremental Investment		
1. Old sales per day $10 million/365		$ 27,397.26
2. Multiplied by increase in average collection period on old sales × 10		273,973
3. Additional sales per day $500,000/365		1,369.86
4. Multiplied by average collection period on new sales × 70		95,890
5. Variable costs of investment in receivables 0.7(95,890)		67,123
6. Other working capital requirements for the incremental sales $500,000(0.3)		150,000
7. Total incremental investment from lengthening credit terms (2 + 5 + 6)		491,096
Part B. Incremental Profitability		
8. Contribution margin on incremental sales 0.3 ($500,000)		$150,000
9. Bad debt losses on new total sales 0.03($10,500,000)	$315,000	
Bad debt losses on old total sales 0.02($10,000,000)	200,000	
Increase in bad debt losses		−115,000
10. Cost of funds in the incremental investment 0.15($491,096)		− 73,664
11. Increase in net cash flows (8 − 9 − 10)		($ 38,664)

inflows would become positive by $100,000 − $38,664, which is $61,336. So the methodology for analyzing the effects of changes in collection policy or collection efforts is the same as for a change in credit terms plus a change in collection expenses in the incremental cash flows analysis.

The results yielded by Table 11.4 indicate that the lengthening of credit terms would be unprofitable. Again, the results reflect the particular assumptions embedded in the case example. In Table 11.4 the measurement of the increase in receivables due to the change in collection period on the old sales was carried at invoice value and not adjusted by the variable cost ratio. The reason is that the alternative is not to make the sales, in which case total cash flows would be decreased by the total amount of the sales. In lines 3 through 5, however, the opportunity cost of the investment in receivables created by the new sales includes only the variable costs, which would not otherwise have been incurred if the new sales had not been made. This is in contrast to the treatment of the old sales, for which the adjustment takes into account that the average collection period has been increased by ten days. Hence the receipt of the revenues based on sales has been delayed by ten days. The logic of the other calculations in Table 11.4 is the same as for those in Table 11.3.

The foregoing examples illustrate the basic concepts involved and the appropriate methodology to employ. The actual implementation of changes in credit policy requires that some very difficult judgments be made, since estimating the changes in sales and costs associated with changes in credit policy involves some uncertainty.

For these reasons, firms usually move slowly toward optimal credit policies. One or two credit variables are changed slightly, the effect of the changes is observed, and a decision is made to change these variables even more or to retract them. Further, different credit policies are appropriate at different times, depending on economic conditions. Thus, credit policy is not a static, once-for-all-time decision. Rather, it is fluid, dynamic, and ever changing in its effort to reach a continually moving optimal target.

Inventory

Manufacturing firms generally have three kinds of inventories: (1) raw materials, (2) work in process, and (3) finished goods. The level of *raw materials inventories* is influenced by anticipated production, seasonality of production, reliability of sources of supply, and efficiency of scheduling purchases and production operations. *Work-in-process inventory* is strongly influenced by the length of the production period, which is the time between placing raw material in production and completing the finished product. Inventory turnover can be increased by decreasing the production period. One means of accomplishing this is to perfect engineering techniques, thereby speeding up the manufacturing process. Another means is to buy items rather than make them.

The level of *finished goods inventories* is a matter of coordinating production and sales. The financial manager can stimulate sales by changing credit terms or by granting credit to marginal risks. Whether the goods remain on the books as inventories or as receivables, the financial manager has to finance them. Many times, firms find it desirable to make the sale, so they are one step nearer to realizing cash. The potential profits can outweigh the additional collection risk.

Our primary focus in this section is control of investment in inventories. Inventory models, developed as an aid in this task, have proved extremely useful in minimizing inventory requirements. As our examination of the Du Pont system in Chapter 7 showed, any procedure that can reduce the investment required to generate a given sales volume may have a beneficial effect on the firm's rate of return and hence on the value of the firm.

Determinants of the Size of Inventories

Although wide variations occur, inventory to sales ratios are generally concentrated in the 12 to 20 percent range, and inventory to total assets ratios are concentrated in the 16 to 30 percent range.

The major determinants of investment in inventory are (1) level of sales, (2) length and technical nature of the production processes, and (3) durability versus perishability (the style factors) in the end product. Inventories in the tobacco industry, for example, are large because of the long curing process. Similarly, in the machinery manufacturing industries, inventories are large because of the long work-in-process period. However, inventories in oil and gas production are low, because raw materials and goods in process are small in relation to sales. In the canning industry, average inventories are large because of the seasonality of the raw materials.

With respect to durability and style factors, large inventories are found in the hardware and the precious metals industries because durability is great and the style factor is small. Inventories are small in baking because of the perishability of the final product and in printing because the items are manufactured to order.

Within limits set by the economics of a firm's industry, there exists a potential for improvement in inventory control from the use of computers and operations research. Although the techniques are far too diverse and complicated for a complete treatment in this text, the financial manager should be prepared to use the contributions of specialists who have developed effective procedures for minimizing the investment in inventory.

An illustration of the techniques at the practical level is Harris Electronic's inventory system, which works like this: Tabulator cards are inserted in each package of five electronic tubes leaving Harris's warehouse. They are identified by account number, type of merchandise, and price of the units ordered. As the merchandise is sold, the distributor collects the cards and files the replacement order with no paperwork, simply by sending in the cards.

Western Union Telegraph Company equipment accepts the punched cards and transmits information on them to the warehouse, where it is duplicated on other punched cards. A typical order of 5,000 tubes of varying types can be received in about seventeen minutes, assembled in about ninety minutes, and delivered to Boston's Logan Airport in an additional forty-five minutes. Orders from 3,000 miles away can be delivered within twenty-four hours, a savings of thirteen days in some cases.

Information on the order also goes into a computer, which keeps track of stock-on-hand data for each item. When an order draws the stock down below the *order point,* this triggers action in the production department, where additional units of the item are then manufactured for stock. In the next section, we will examine both the optimal order point and the number of units that should be manufactured—called the *economic ordering quantity (EOQ).*

Generality of Inventory Analysis

Managing assets of all kinds is basically an inventory problem; the same method of analysis applies to cash and fixed assets as to inventories themselves. First, a basic stock must be on hand to balance inflows and outflows of the items, the size of the stock depending on the patterns of flows, whether regular or irregular. Second, because the unexpected may always occur, it is necessary to have safety stocks on hand, representing the little extra to avoid the costs of not having enough to meet current needs. Third, additional amounts may be required to meet future growth needs; these are called *anticipation stocks.* Related to anticipation stocks is the recognition that there are optimum purchase sizes, defined as *economic ordering quantities.* In borrowing money, in buying raw materials for production, or in purchasing plants and equipment, it is cheaper to buy more than just enough to meet immediate needs.

With the foregoing as a basic foundation, we can develop the theoretical basis for determining the optimal investment in inventory, illustrated in Figure 11.1. Some costs rise with larger inventories; among these are warehousing costs, interest on funds tied up in inventories, insurance, and obsolescence. Other costs decline with larger inventories; these include the loss of profits resulting from sales lost because of lack of stock, costs of production interruptions caused by inadequate inventories, and possible purchase discounts.

The costs that decline with higher inventories are designated by the declining curve in Figure 11.1; those that rise with larger inventories are designated by the rising curve. The total costs curve is the total of the rising and declining curves, and it represents the total cost of ordering and holding inventories. At the point where the absolute value of the slope of the rising curve is equal to the absolute value of the slope of the declining curve (that is, where marginal rising costs are equal to marginal declining costs), the total costs curve is at a minimum. This represents the optimum size of investment in inventory.

Inventory Decision Models

The generalized statements in the preceding section can be made more specific. In fact, it is usually possible to specify the curves shown in Figure 11.1, at least to a reasonable approximation, and actually to find the minimum point on the total costs curve. Since entire courses in operations research programs are devoted to inventory control techniques, and since a number of books have been written on the subject, we obviously cannot deal with inventory decision models in a very complete fashion. The model we illustrate, however, is probably the most widely used, even by quite sophisticated firms, and it can be readily expanded to encompass any desired refinements.

Looking at Figure 11.1, we find (1) that some costs associated with inventories decline as inventory holdings increase, (2) that other costs rise, and (3) that the total inventory-associated cost curve has a minimum point. The purpose of the basic inventory model is to locate this minimum and the economic order quantity (EOQ) which will lead to minimum costs. We will assume that the Emerson Company expects to achieve a sales volume of 3,600 widgets during 1980 and that Emerson is quite confident of hitting this target. Further, these sales are expected to be evenly distributed over the year, so inventories will decline smoothly and gradually. The widgets are purchased for $40 each. No inventory is on hand at the beginning of the year, and none will be held at year-end.

Figure 11.1

Determination of Optimal Investment in Inventory[a]

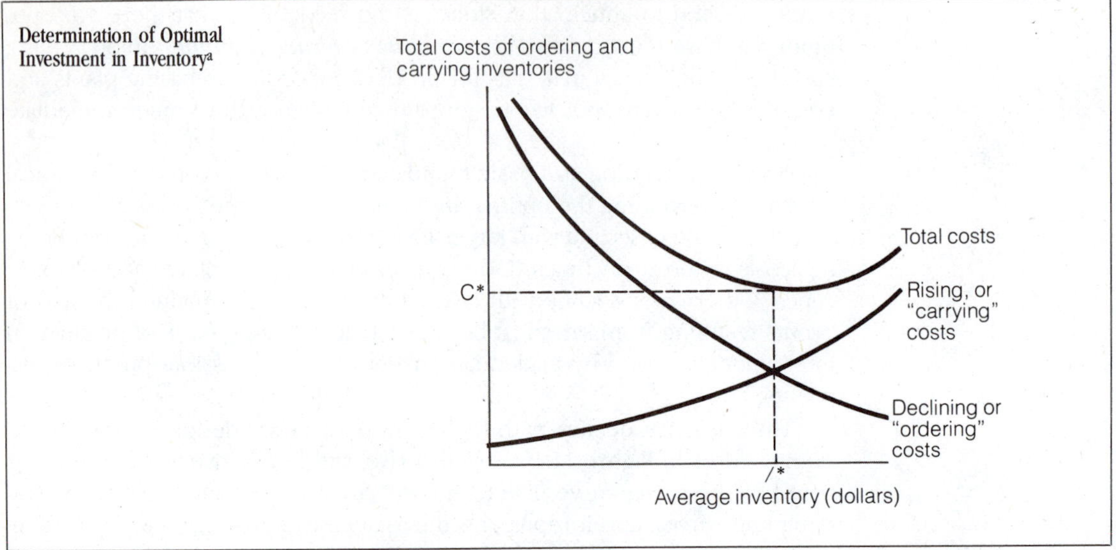

a. The asterisks at C and I indicate the total costs and average inventory associated with the optimal order quantity.

The notation and illustrative numerical amounts that we shall use in the analysis are:

A = Average inventory = $Q/2$

C = Carrying cost expressed as a percentage of inventory purchase price = 25%

CP = Carrying cost expressed in dollars per unit of inventory = \$10

EOQ = Economic order quantity

F = Fixed costs of placing and receiving orders = \$5,400

K = Total carrying costs = CPA

N = Number of orders placed per year = U/Q

P = Purchase price per unit of inventory = \$40

Q = Order quantity

R = Total ordering costs = $F + VN$

S = Safety stock

T = Total inventory costs = $K + R = CPA + F + VN$

U = Annual usage in units = 3,600

V = Variable cost per order of ordering, shipping, and receiving = \$125

These notations are independent of symbols used elsewhere in the book.

The Emerson Company could place one order for $Q = 3{,}600$ units at the start of the year. If it did, the average inventory for the year, A, would be equal to

$$A = \frac{Q}{2} = \frac{U}{2} = \frac{3{,}600}{2} = 1{,}800 \text{ units.} \tag{11.1}$$

Since widgets cost \$40 each, the average investment in inventories is \$72,000.

Alternatively, Emerson could place two orders for 1,800 each, in which case average inventories would be

$$A = \frac{1{,}800}{2} = 900,$$

or four orders of 900 each for an average inventory of 450, and so on. Inventory investment declines correspondingly.

We can see that average inventories are a function of the number of orders placed per year, N. Specifically, when the number of orders placed is incorporated into the calculation, Equation 11.1 becomes

$$A = \frac{U/2}{N} = \frac{U}{2N} = \frac{Q}{2}. \tag{11.1a}$$

By ordering more frequently (increasing N), Emerson can reduce its average inventory further and further.

How far should inventory reductions be carried? Smaller inventories involve lower *carrying costs*—cost of capital tied up in inventories, storage costs, insurance, and so on—but, since smaller average inventories imply more frequent orders, they involve higher *ordering costs.*

Classification of Costs

The first step in the process of building an inventory model is to specify those costs that rise and those that decline with higher levels of inventory. Table 11.5 lists some typical costs associated with carrying inventories. In the table, we have broken the costs down into three categories: those associated with holding inventories, those associated with running short of inventory, and those associated with ordering, receiving, and paying for inventories.

Although they may well be the most important element, we shall disregard the second category of costs—the costs of running short—at this point. These costs will be considered at a later stage, when we add safety stocks to the inventory model. Further, we shall disregard quantity discounts, although it is easy enough to adjust the basic model to include discounts.[13] The costs

13. See John F. Magee and Harlan C. Meal, "Inventory Management and Standards," in *The Treasurer's Handbook*, ed. J. Fred Weston and Maurice B. Goudzwaard (Homewood, Ill.: Dow Jones–Irwin, 1976).

Table 11.5

Costs Associated with Inventories

Carrying Costs
1. Cost of capital tied up
2. Storage costs
3. Insurance
4. Property taxes
5. Depreciation and obsolescence

Costs of Running Short
1. Loss of sales
2. Loss of customer goodwill
3. Disruption of production schedules

Shipping, Receiving, and Ordering Costs
1. Cost of placing order, including production setup costs
2. Shipping and handling costs
3. Quantity discounts lost

that remain for consideration at this stage, then, are carrying costs and ordering costs.

Carrying Costs

Carrying costs generally rise in direct proportion to the average amount of inventory carried. For example, Emerson's cost of capital is 10 percent, and depreciation is estimated to amount to 5 percent per year. Lumping together these and Emerson's other costs of carrying inventory produces a total cost of 25 percent of the investment in inventory. Defining the percentage cost as *C,* we can, in general, find the total carrying costs as the percentage carrying cost *(C)* times the price per unit *(P)* times the average number of units *(A):*

$$\begin{aligned} K &= \text{total carrying costs} \\ &= (C)(P)(A). \end{aligned} \tag{11.2}$$

If Emerson elects to order only once a year, average inventories will be 3,600/2 = 1,800 units; the cost of carrying the inventory will be 0.25 × \$40 × 1,800 = \$18,000. If the company orders twice a year and, hence, has average inventories that are half as large, total carrying costs will decline to \$9,000, and so on.

In an unpublished study, the U.S. Department of Commerce estimated that, on the average, manufacturing firms have an annual cost of carrying inventories that equals 25 percent of original inventory cost. This percentage was broken down as follows:

Obsolescence	9.00%
Physical depreciation	5.00
Interest	7.00
Handling	2.50
Property taxes	0.50
Insurance	0.25
Storage	0.75
Total	25.00%

These costs obviously vary from situation to situation, but, with carrying costs of this order of magnitude, inventories deserve careful attention.

Shipping, Receiving, and Ordering Costs

Although carrying costs are entirely variable and rise in direct proportion to the average size of inventories, ordering costs consist of both a fixed and a variable component. The costs of a purchasing and receiving department are both fixed and variable. The personnel and space assigned to purchasing and receiving functions involve costs that are relatively fixed in total amount *(F).* In our example, this total is estimated to be $5,400. On the other hand, the cost of *placing* an order—interoffice memos, long-distance telephone calls, setting up a production run, and so on—are costs per order. Their total is the cost of placing an order *(V)* times the number of orders placed *(N).* The company's cost of ordering, shipping, and receiving, which we define as *V,* is $125 per order.

Combining these components of ordering costs, we obtain the following equation for *R,* the total cost of placing and receiving orders:

$$R = (F) + (V)N \tag{11.3}$$

where

F = Fixed ordering costs
V = Cost per order
N = Number of orders placed

To illustrate, if $V = \$125$, $U = 3{,}600$ and $A = 100$, $A = Q/2$, so $Q = 2A$ or 200 and $N = U/Q$ or $3{,}600/200 = 18$. Then *R,* the total ordering cost, is

$$R = \$5{,}400 + \$125(18) = \$7{,}650.$$

Total Inventory Costs

Inventory carrying costs *(K),* as defined in Equation 11.2, and ordering costs *(R),* as defined in Equation 11.3, may be combined to find total inventory costs *(T)* as follows:

$$\begin{aligned} T &= K + R \\ &= (C)(P)(A) + F + (V)(N). \end{aligned} \tag{11.4}$$

Recognizing that $A = Q/2$ and $N = U/Q$, Equation 11.4 may be rewritten as an explicit function of *Q:*

$$T = CP\left(\frac{Q}{2}\right) + V\left(\frac{U}{Q}\right) + (F) \tag{11.5}$$

$$= CP\left(\frac{Q}{2}\right) + VUQ^{-1} + F \tag{11.6}$$

The pattern of carrying costs and ordering costs related to the above data is set forth in Table 11.6. The data are graphed in Figure 11.2.

Table 11.6

Costs Associated with Inventory Decisions

Q (1)	Safety Stock (S) (2)	Average Inventory (A) $\left(\frac{Q}{2} + S\right)$ (3)	Total Carrying Cost $(K) = (CPA)$ (4)	Fixed Ordering Cost (F) (5)	Variable Ordering Cost (VN) (6)	Total Ordering Cost (5) + (6) (7)	Total Inventory Cost (4) + (7) (8)
100	0	50	$ 500	$5,400	$4,500	$9,900	$10,400
200	0	100	1,000	5,400	2,250	7,650	8,650
300	0	150	1,500	5,400	1,500	6,900	8,400
400	0	200	2,000	5,400	1,125	6,525	8,525
500	0	250	2,500	5,400	900	6,300	8,800
600	0	300	3,000	5,400	750	6,150	9,150

From both Table 11.6 and Figure 11.2, we can determine the EOQ. We observe that the lowest total cost occurs at a quantity of 300 in Table 11.6. This is also the point at which total costs are a minimum in Figure 11.2. The EOQ is at the intersection of the total carrying costs and the variable ordering costs.

We can also determine the optimal order quantity algebraically. This is the value of Q that minimizes T. We find this optimal quantity, the EOQ, by

Figure 11.2

Determination of the Optimal Order Size

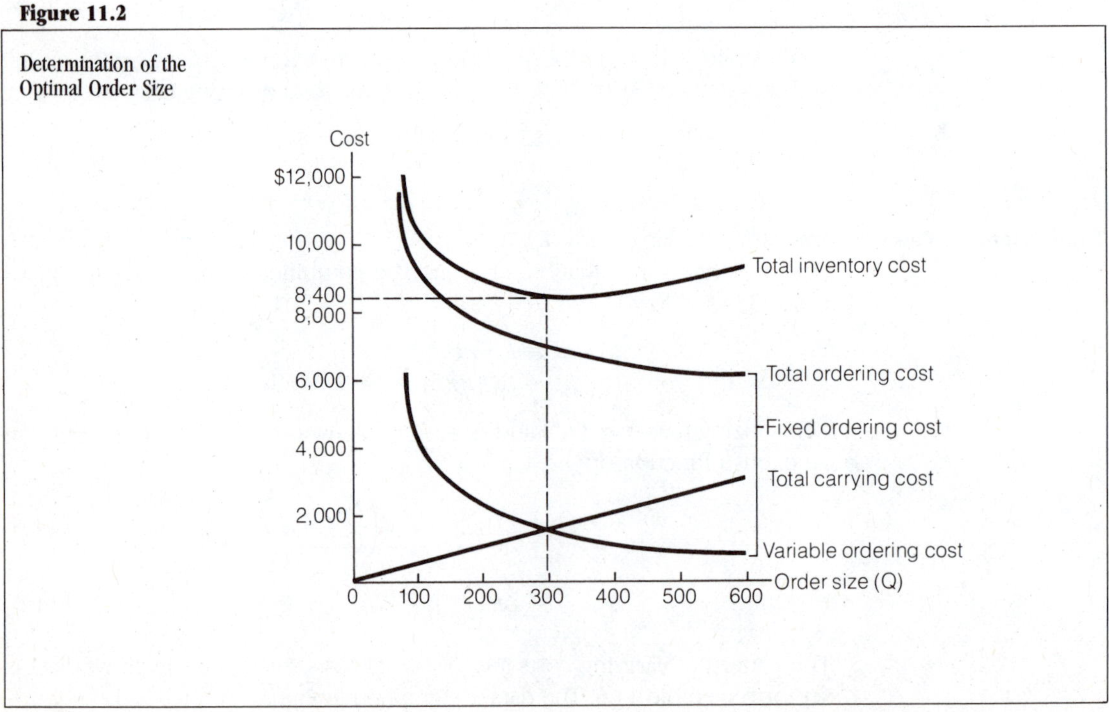

differentiating Equation 11.6 with respect to Q, setting the derivative equal to zero, and obtaining[14]

$$\text{EOQ} = \sqrt{\frac{2VU}{CP}}. \tag{11.7}$$

In the Emerson case, we find

$$\begin{aligned}\text{EOQ} &= \sqrt{\frac{2(\$125)(3{,}600)}{(0.25)(\$40)}} \\ &= \sqrt{\frac{\$900{,}000}{\$10}} \\ &= \sqrt{\$90{,}000} \\ &= 300 \text{ units.}\end{aligned}$$

If this quantity is ordered twelve times a year (3,600/300 = 12), or every thirty days, the total costs of ordering and carrying inventories, calculated from Equation 11.6, will be:

$$\begin{aligned}T &= CP\left(\frac{Q}{2}\right) + \frac{VU}{Q} + F \\ &= \$10\left(\frac{300}{2}\right) + \frac{(\$125)(3{,}600)}{300} + \$5{,}400 \\ &= \$1{,}500 + \$1{,}500 + \$5{,}400 \\ &= \$8{,}400.\end{aligned}$$

That is the lowest possible cost of ordering and carrying the required amount of inventories.

Equation 11.7 gives us the optimum, or cost minimizing, order quantity for given levels of usage *(U)*, inventory carrying cost *(C)*, and fixed order costs *(F)*. Knowing the EOQ and continuing our assumption of zero beginning and ending inventory balances, we find the optimal average inventory as

14. Proof: Differentiate Equation 11.6 with respect to Q and set equal to zero, then solve for Q:

$$\frac{\delta T}{\delta Q} = \frac{CP}{2} - \frac{VU}{Q^2} = 0$$

$$\frac{CP}{2} = \frac{VU}{Q^2}$$

$$Q^2 = \frac{2VU}{CP}$$

$$Q = \sqrt{\frac{2VU}{CP}}$$

$$A = \frac{\text{EOQ}}{2} = \frac{300}{2} = 150.$$

Emerson will thus have an average inventory investment of 150 units at $40 each, or $6,000.

Relationship between Sales and Inventories

Intuitively, we would suppose that the higher the ordering or processing costs, the less frequently orders should be placed. However, the higher the carrying costs of inventory, the more frequently stocks should be ordered. These two features are incorporated in the EOQ formula. Notice also that if Emerson's sales had been estimated at 900 units, the EOQ would have been 150, while the average inventory would have been 75 units instead of the 150 called for with sales of 3,600 units. Thus, a quadrupling of sales leads to only a doubling of inventories. The general rule is that the EOQ increases with the *square root* of sales, so any increase in sales results in a less than proportionate increase in inventories. The financial manager should keep this in mind in establishing standards for inventory control.

Extending the EOQ Model to Include Safety Stocks

The basic EOQ model assumes a predictable sales activity, a constant usage over the year, and an immediate replenishment of the inventory stocks. For the Emerson Company, with an annual demand of 3,600 units, and an EOQ of 300 units, there is a need to order twelve times each year, once every thirty days. If the beginning and ending inventory balances are zero, the maximum inventory would be 300 units with an average of 150 units. The slope of the daily usage line is ten units.

Order Point

We can relax the assumption of instantaneous order and delivery. Let us assume Emerson requires eight days to place an order and receive the delivery. In order not to interrupt its sales activities, Emerson must keep an eight-day stock, or eighty units, on hand whenever it places an order (Daily usage × Lead time = 10 × 8 = 80). The stock that must be on hand at the time of ordering is defined as the order point; whenever inventory falls below this point, a new order will be placed. If Emerson's inventory control process is automated, the computer will generate an order when the stock on hand falls to eighty units.[15] These conditions are reflected in Figure 11.3.

15. If a new order must be placed before a subsequent order is received—that is, if the normal delivery lead time is longer than the time between orders—then what might be called a goods in transit inventory builds up. This complicates matters somewhat, but the simplest solution to the problem is to deduct goods in transit when calculating the order point. In other words, the order point would be calculated as Order point = Lead time × Daily usage − Goods in transit.

Figure 11.3

Demand Forecast with Certainty

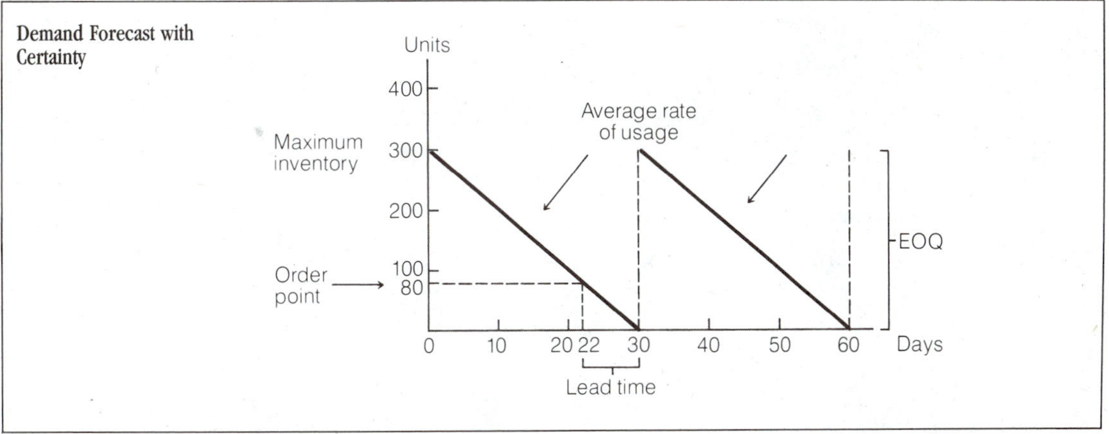

EOQ Model with Uncertainty

To this point we have assumed that usage (demand) is known with certainty and is uniform throughout time and that the order lead time never varies. Either or both of these assumptions could be incorrect, so it is necessary to modify the EOQ model to allow for this possibility. This modification generally takes the form of adding a *safety stock* to average inventories.

An optimal safety stock should be at a point where the increased carrying cost is equal to the opportunity cost of a possible stock-out. The increased carrying cost is *CP* times the safety stock, *S*. The stock-out cost reflects four factors:

Stock-out cost = Inventory cycles per year × Stock-out units
× Probability of a possible stock-out × Unit stock-out cost.

Inventory cycles per year is, of course, $N = U/Q = 3{,}600/300 = 12$.

The stock-out units would be the difference between the maximum daily usage (15 units) during the lead time (8 days) and the order point without a safety stock. In this case, the stock-out units are: $(15 \times 8) - 80 = 40$.

Let us assume that Emerson Company expects the following probability distribution for its daily usage.

Daily Usage	Probability
15	0.2
10	0.5
8	0.2
4	0.1

The maximum stock-out probability the company is willing to take is 0.2. The unit stock-out cost is $5.21.

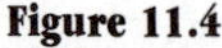

Figure 11.4

Demand Forecast with Safety Stock to Account for Uncertainty

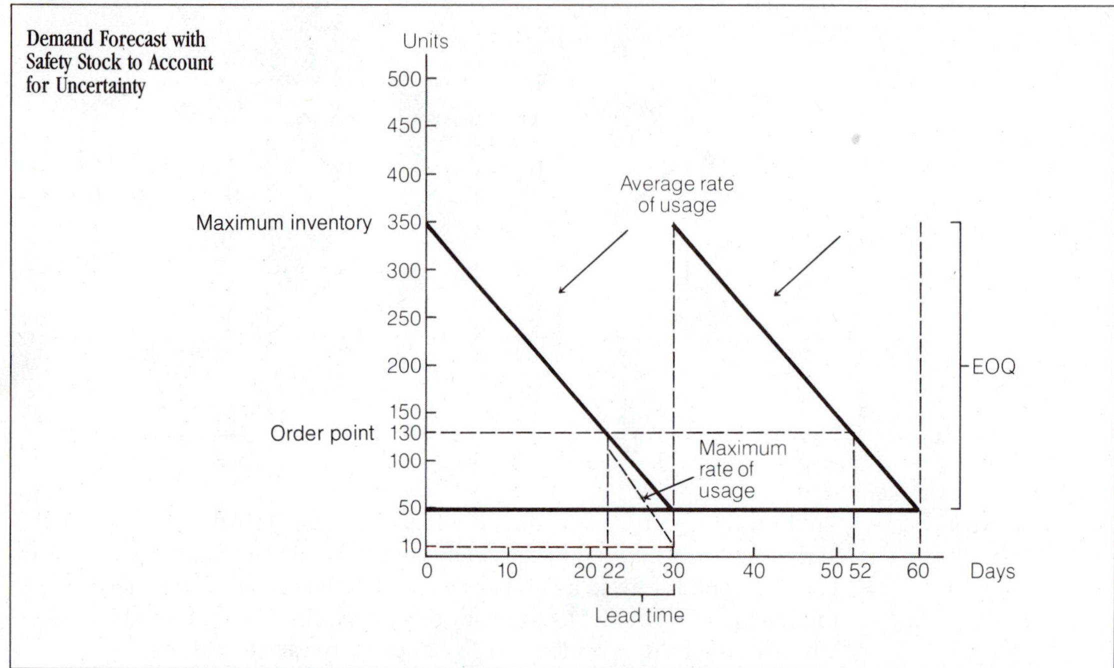

We now have all the data required to calculate the required safety stock.

$$\begin{aligned} \text{Stock-out cost} &= \text{Carrying cost of safety stock} \\ (12)(40)(0.2)(\$5.21) &= \$10X \\ X &= 50 \text{ units.} \end{aligned}$$

With fifty units of safety stock, the patterns of usage and order point are shown in Figure 11.4.

The initial order would be 350 units instead of 300 units, and the subsequent orders would be for 300 units each. The new order point will be: (Safety stock) + (Usage × Lead time) = 50 + 10(8) = 130. When the inventory level hits 130 units, Emerson should reorder. With a lead time of 8 days, Emerson can experience the high usage rate of 15 units per day over the 8-day delivery period without a stockout. The 15 units rate of use is shown by the steeper line in Figure 11.4.

The analysis of the EOQ can be illustrated by use of the data in Table 11.7 and depicted in Figure 11.5.

Both Table 11.7 and Figure 11.5 show that the EOQ remains at 300 units. The increase in total carrying costs resulting from an addition of a fixed amount for carrying the safety stocks of 50 units at $10 per unit does not affect the cost minimizing quantity. But as shown in Figure 11.5, the low point of the total inventory cost is no longer at the intersection of the variable ordering

Table 11.7

Analysis of Inventory Costs Including Safety Stocks

Q	Safety Stock (S)	Average Inventory (A) $\left(\frac{Q}{2} + S\right)$	Total Carrying Cost (K) (CPA)	Fixed Ordering Cost (F)	Variable Ordering Cost (VN)	Total Ordering Cost (5) + (6)	Total Inventory Cost (4) + (7)
(1)	(2)	(3)	(4)	(5)	(6)	(7)	(8)
100	50	100	$1,000	$5,400	4,500	$9,900	10,900
200	50	150	1,500	5,400	2,250	7,650	9,150
300	50	200	2,000	5,400	1,500	6,900	8,900
400	50	250	2,500	5,400	1,125	6,525	9,025
500	50	300	3,000	5,400	900	6,300	9,300
600	50	350	3,500	5,400	750	6,150	9,650

costs and the total carrying costs. When total carrying costs include the costs of the safety stock, those costs lie above the total carrying costs without safety stock. Thus, the intersection point between the variable ordering costs and the total carrying costs is now to the left of the low point of the total inventory costs.

Effects of Inflation on EOQ

During inflation, formal models such as the EOQ must be adjusted. As freight costs rise, the cost of placing an order may increase rapidly. Purchase prices may also rise abruptly and repeatedly. Therefore, the values used in the EOQ equation may not remain constant for any appreciable length of time. If so,

Figure 11.5

Analysis of Inventory Costs with Safety Stocks

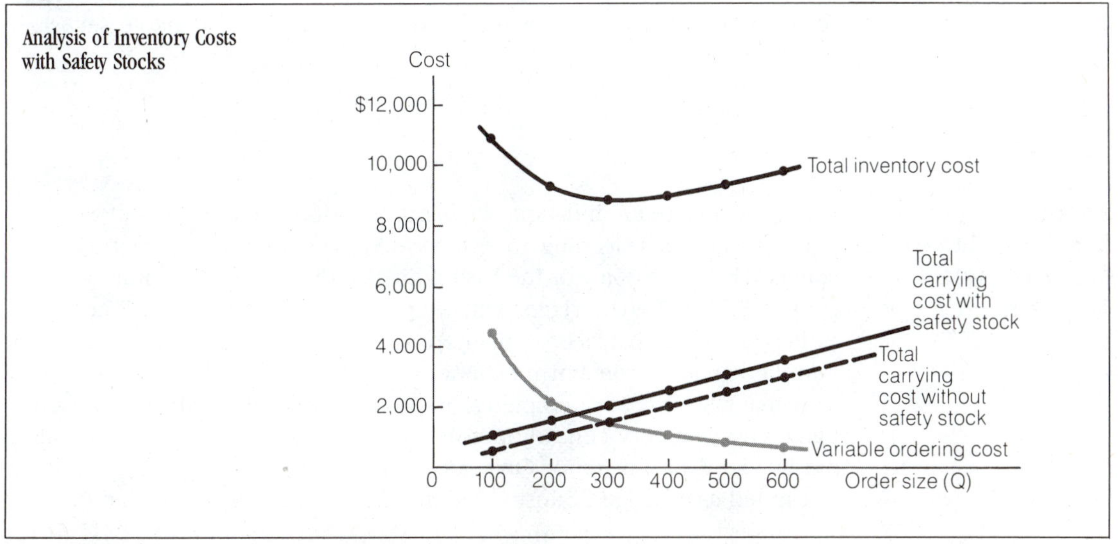

the optimal order quantity will not remain fixed. Some companies will need greater flexibility in the timing of their orders than that afforded by the automatic order point because they may be able to buy marginal production at reduced prices. Also, certain companies may stockpile inventories, taking advantage of the opportunity to purchase supplies before major price increases and gaining protection against shortages. Therefore, during periods of inflation and tight money, a firm may need more flexible inventory management as it attempts to take advantage of bargains and provide for future contingencies. The basic logic of the inventory model remains intact: Some costs will rise with larger inventories, and others will fall. Although an optimum is still there to be found, it may change and require repeated findings.

Cash Management as an Inventory Problem

In our cash budgeting discussion in Chapter 9, we indicated that firms generally have minimum desired cash balances. Then, in discussing cash management, we considered the various factors that influence cash holdings. We did not, however, attempt to specify optimum cash balances, which can be found by the use of inventory models such as those just discussed. Cash management, together with inventory controls, is the area of financial management where mathematical tools have proved most useful.

Sophisticated cash management models recognize the uncertainty inherent in forecasting both cash inflows and cash outflows. Inflows are represented, in effect, by the orders in our inventory model; they come principally from receipts, borrowing, and sales of securities. The primary carrying cost of cash is the opportunity cost of having funds tied up in nonearning assets (or in low-yielding near-cash items); the principal ordering costs are brokerage costs associated with borrowing funds or converting marketable securities into cash.

Recent Restructuring of Current Asset Management

During recent years, inflation has exerted serious pressure on most firms' liquidity positions, leading to extensive restructuring of current asset accounts. The bankruptcy of the cash-poor Penn Central Transportation Company in 1970 helped to trigger a growing concern about liquidity. When money becomes tight, banks become more selective in granting loans and cannot be relied on to rescue a firm experiencing a sudden shortage of cash. Therefore, many firms have attempted to improve their liquidity positions through tightening inventory control, increasing receivables turnover, and reducing the dividend payout ratio. One good target is inventories that have been stockpiled as a hedge against inflation and shortages, in what is an obvious trade-off between liquidity and inventory level. In the early 1970s, Texas Instruments quadrupled its cash to assets ratio by liquidating inventory, decreasing receivables, and retaining earnings. A growing tendency is for firms to retain earnings to build cash balances.

IBM is an example of how the liquidity position of a firm may change in a short period of time. IBM's cash and marketable securities at year-end 1977 were $5.4 billion, representing 28.5 percent of the $19 billion total assets. One year later, cash and marketable securities had declined to $4 billion, a decrease of 26 percent. A further decline to $3.77 took place by the end of 1979. A shift from buying to leasing by users of IBM equipment required an investment by IBM of $2.7 billion in rental machines during 1978 and of $4.21 billion in 1979. During 1979, IBM raised $1.5 billion in debt financing, the proceeds of which were to be used for investments in manufacturing facilities and in rental equipment. IBM made a $1 billion debt offering in October 1979 and later in the year borrowed $300 million from Saudi Arabia; the remaining $200 million came from other sources.

Summary

This chapter focused attention on four types of current assets—cash, marketable securities, accounts receivable, and inventories. It examined the motives for holding cash and ways of minimizing the investment in cash. Then the minimum cash balance a firm is likely to hold was considered. This minimum is the higher (1) of compensating balance requirements or (2) of transactions balances plus a safety stock.

Marketable securities are held as a substitute for cash safety stocks and as temporary investments while the firm is awaiting permanent investment of funds. Safety stocks are almost always held in low-risk, short-maturity securities; temporary investments are held in securities whose maturity depends on the length of time before the funds are permanently employed.

The investment in accounts receivable is dependent on sales and on the firm's credit policy. The credit policy, in turn, involves four controllable variables: credit standards, the length of the credit period, cash discounts, and the collection policy. The significant aspect of credit policy is its effect on sales. An easy credit policy stimulates sales but involves costs of capital tied up in receivables, bad debts, discounts, and higher collection costs. The optimal credit policy is one for which the difference between these costs and the cash inflows generated by the credit policy change makes the maximum contribution to the value of the firm.

Inventories—raw materials, work in process, and finished goods—are necessary in most businesses. Rather elaborate systems for controlling the level of inventories have been designed. These systems frequently use computers for keeping records of all the items in stock. An inventory control model that considers anticipated sales, ordering costs, and carrying costs can be used to determine EOQs for each item.

The basic inventory model recognizes that certain costs (carrying costs) rise as average inventory holdings increase but that certain other costs (ordering costs and stock-out costs) fall as these holdings increase. The two sets of costs make up the total cost of ordering and carrying inventories, and the EOQ model is designed to locate an optimal order size that will minimize total inventory costs.

Questions

11.1 How can better methods of communication reduce the necessity for firms to hold large cash balances?

11.2 Discuss this statement: The highly developed financial system of the United States, with its myriad of different near-cash assets, has greatly reduced cash balance requirements by reducing the need for transactions balances.

11.3 Would you expect a firm with a high growth rate to hold more or fewer precautionary and speculative cash balances than a firm with a low growth rate? Explain.

11.4 Many firms that find themselves with temporary surplus cash invest these funds in Treasury bills. Since Treasury bills frequently have the lowest yield of any investment security, why are they chosen as investments?

11.5 Assume that a firm sells on terms of net 30 and that its accounts are, on the average, thirty days overdue. What will its investment in receivables be if its annual credit sales are approximately $720,000?

11.6 Evaluate this statement: It is difficult to judge the performance of many of our employees but not that of the credit manager. If the credit manager is performing perfectly, credit losses are zero; the higher our losses (as a percent of sales), the worse the performance.

11.7 Explain how a firm can reduce its investment in inventory by having its supplier hold raw materials inventories and its customers hold finished goods inventories. What are the limitations of such a policy?

11.8 What factors are likely to reduce the holdings of inventory in relation to sales in the future? What factors will tend to increase the ratio? What, in your judgment, is the net effect?

11.9 What are the probable effects of the following on inventory holdings?

a. Manufacture of a part formerly purchased from an outside supplier.
b. Greater use of air freight.
c. Increase, from 7 to 17, in the number of styles produced.
d. Large price reductions to your firm from a manufacturer of bathing suits if the suits are purchased in December and January.

11.10 Inventory decision models are designed to help minimize the cost of obtaining and carrying inventory. Describe the basic nature of the fundamental inventory control model, discussing specifically the nature of increasing costs, decreasing costs, and total costs. Illustrate your discussion with a graph.

Problems

11.1 Hayes Associates is short on cash and is attempting to determine whether it would be advantageous to forego the discount on this month's purchases or to borrow funds to take advantage of the discount. The discount terms are 2/10, net 45.

a. What is the maximum annual interest rate that Hayes Associates should pay on borrowed funds? Why?

b. What are some of the intangible disadvantages associated with foregoing the discount?

11.2 Scott, Inc., currently has a centralized billing system located in New York City. However, over the years its customers gradually have become less concentrated on the East Coast and now cover the entire United States. On average, it requires five days from the time customers mail payments until Scott is able to receive, process, and deposit their payments. To shorten this time, Scott is considering the installation of a lockbox collection system. It estimates that the system will reduce the time lag from customer mailing to deposit by three and one-half days. Scott has a daily average collection of $700,000.

a. What reduction in cash balances can Scott achieve by initiating the lockbox system?

b. If Scott has an opportunity cost of 8 percent, how much is the lockbox system worth on an annual basis?

c. What is the maximum monthly charge Scott can pay for the lockbox system?

11.3 A firm issues checks in the amount of $1 million each day and deducts them from its own records at the close of business on the day they are written. On average, the bank receives and clears the checks (deducts them from the firm's bank balance) the evening of the fourth day after they are written; for example, a check written on Monday will be cleared on Friday afternoon. The firm's loan agreement with the bank requires it to maintain a $750,000 minimum average compensating balance; this is $250,000 greater than the cash safety stock the firm would otherwise have on deposit.

a. Assuming that the firm makes its deposit in the late afternoon (and the bank includes the deposit in the day's transactions), how much must the firm deposit each day to maintain a sufficient balance once it reaches a steady state?

b. How many days of float does the firm carry?

c. What ending daily balance should the firm try to maintain at the bank and on its own records?

d. Explain how float can help increase the value of the firm's common stock. Use a partial balance sheet and the Du Pont system concept in your answer.

11.4 The Fulton Company has been reviewing its credit policies. The credit standards it has been applying have resulted in annual credit sales of $5,000,000. Its average collection period is 30 days, with a bad debt loss ratio of 1 percent. Because persistent inflation has caused deterioration in the financial position of many of its customers, Fulton is considering a reduction in its credit standards. As a result, it expects incremental credit sales of $400,000 on which the average collection period (ACP) would be 60 days and on which the bad debt loss (BDL) ratio would be 3 percent. The variable cost ratio (VCR) to sales for Fulton is 70 percent. The ratio of other net working capital requirements to sales is 0.25. The required return on investment in receivables is 15 percent.

Evaluate the relaxation in credit standards that Fulton is considering.

11.5 Instead of relaxing credit standards, Fulton is considering simply lengthening credit terms from net 20 to net 50, a procedure that would increase the average collection period from 30 days to 60 days. Under the new policy, Fulton expects incremental sales to be $500,000 and the new bad debt loss ratio to rise to 2 percent on *all* sales. Assume all other returns hold. Evaluate the lengthening in credit terms that Fulton is considering.

11.6 Gulf Distributors makes all sales on a credit basis; once each year it routinely evaluates the creditworthiness of all its customers. The evaluation procedure ranks customers from 1 to 5, in order of increasing risk. Results of the ranking are as follows:

Category	Percentage Bad Debts	Average Collection Period (Days)	Credit Decision	Annual Sales Lost through Credit Restrictions
1	None	10	Unlimited credit	None
2	1.0	12	Unlimited credit	None
3	3.0	20	Limited credit	$360,000
4	9.0	60	Limited credit	$180,000
5	16.0	90	No credit	$720,000

The variable cost ratio is 75 percent. The ratio of other net working capital investment to sales is 40 percent. The opportunity cost of investment in receivables is 15 percent.

What will be the effect on profitability of extending full credit to category 3? to category 4? to category 5?

11.7 The following relationships for inventory purchase and storage costs have been established for the Norman Corporation.

1. Orders must be placed in multiples of 100 units.
2. Requirements for the year are 180,000 units *(U)*. (Use fifty weeks in a year for calculations.)
3. The purchase price per unit *(P)* is $2.
4. The carrying cost *(C)* is 50 percent of the purchase price of goods.
5. The cost per order placed *(V)* is $400.
6. Desired safety stock *(S)* is 10,000 units (on hand initially).
7. One week is required for delivery.
   a. What is the most economical order quantity?
   b. What is the optimal number of orders to be placed?
   c. At what inventory level should a reorder be made?

11.8 The following relationships for inventory purchase and storage costs have been established for the Lomer Fabricating Corporation.

1. Orders must be placed in multiples of 100 units.
2. Requirements for the year are 400,000 units *(U)*. (Use fifty weeks in a year for calculations.)
3. The purchase price per unit *(P)* is $2.
4. The carrying cost *(C)* is 20 percent of the purchase price of goods.
5. The cost per order placed *(V)* is $50.
6. Desired safety stock *(S)* is 10,000 units (on hand initially).
7. One week is required for delivery.

a. What is the most economical order quantity?
b. What is the optimal number of orders to be placed?
c. At what inventory level should a reorder be made?

11.9 The following relationships for inventory purchases and storage costs have been established for the Milton Processing Corporation.
1. Orders must be placed in multiples of 100 units.
2. Requirements for the year are 500,000 units. (Use fifty weeks in a year for calculations.)
3. The purchase price per unit is $5.
4. The carrying cost is 20 percent of the purchase price of goods.
5. The cost per order placed is $25.
6. Desired safety stock is 10,000 units (on hand initially).
7. Two weeks are required for delivery.
   a. What is the most economical order quantity? (Round to hundreds.)
   b. What is the optimal number of orders to be placed?
   c. At what inventory level should a reorder be made?
   d. If annual unit sales double, what is the percent increase in the EOQ? What is the elasticity of EOQ with respect to sales (percent change in EOQ/percent change in sales)?
   e. If the cost per order placed doubles, what is the percent increase in EOQ? What is the elasticity of EOQ with respect to cost per order?

Selected References

Andrews, Victor L. "Captive Finance Companies." *Harvard Business Review* 42 (July–August 1964), pp. 80–92.

Benishay, Haskel. "A Stochastic Model of Credit Sales Debt." *Journal of the American Statistical Association* 61 (December 1966), pp. 1010–1028.

———. "Managerial Controls of Accounts Receivable: A Deterministic Approach." *Journal of Accounting Research* 3 (Spring 1965), pp. 114–133.

Beranek, William. "Financial Implications of Lot-Size Inventory Models." *Management Science* 13 (April 1967), pp. 401–408.

———. *Analysis for Financial Decisions.* Homewood, Ill.: Irwin, 1963, Chapter 10.

Brosky, John J. *The Implicit Cost of Trade Credit and Theory of Optimal Terms of Sale.* New York: Credit Research Foundation, 1969.

Frost, Peter A. "Banking Services, Minimum Cash Balances and the Firm's Demand for Money." *Journal of Finance* 25 (December 1970), pp. 1029–1039.

Gitman, Lawrence J., and Goodwin, Mark D. "An Assessment of Marketable Securities Management Practices." *Journal of Financial Research* 2 (Fall 1979), pp. 161–169.

Gitman, Lawrence J.; Moses, Edward A.; and White, I. Thomas. "An Assessment of Corporate Cash Management Practices." *Financial Management* 8 (Spring 1979), pp. 32–42.

Greer, Carl C. "The Optimal Credit Acceptance Policy." *Journal of Financial and Quantitative Analysis* 2 (December 1967), pp. 399–415.

Hadley, G., and Whitin, T. M. *Analysis of Inventory Systems.* Englewood Cliffs, N.J.: Prentice-Hall, 1963.

Lane, Sylvia. "Submarginal Credit Risk Classification." *Journal of Financial and Quantitative Analysis* 7 (January 1972), pp. 1379–1385.

Lewellen, Wilbur G. "Finance Subsidiaries and Corporate Borrowing Capacity." *Financial Management* 1 (Spring 1972), pp. 21–32.

Long, Michael S. "Credit Screening System Selection." *Journal of Financial and Quantitative Analysis* 11 (June 1976), pp. 313–328.

Magee, John F. "Guides to Inventory Policy, I." *Harvard Business Review* 34 (January–February 1956), pp. 34, 49–60.

———. "Guides to Inventory Policy, II." *Harvard Business Review* 34 (March–April 1956), pp. 49–60.

———. "Guides to Inventory Policy, III." *Harvard Business Review* 34 (May–June 1956), pp. 57–70.

Magee, John F., and Meal, Harlan C. "Inventory Management and Standards." In *The Treasurer's Handbook.* Edited by J. Fred Weston and Maurice B. Goudzwaard. Homewood, Ill.: Dow Jones–Irwin, 1976, pp. 496–542.

Mehta, Dileep. "Optimal Credit Policy Selection: A Dynamic Approach." *Journal of Financial and Quantitative Analysis* 5 (December 1970), pp. 421–444.

———. "The Formulation of Credit Policy Models." *Management Science* 15 (October 1968), pp. 30–50.

Schwartz, Robert A. "An Economic Model of Trade Credit." *Journal of Financial and Quantitative Analysis* 9 (September 1974), pp. 643–657.

Scott, James H., Jr. "The Tax Effects of Investment in Marketable Securities on Firm Valuation." *Journal of Finance* 34 (May 1979), pp. 307–324.

Searby, Frederick W. "Cash Management: Helping Meet the Capital Crisis." In *The Treasurer's Handbook.* Edited by J. Fred Weston and Maurice Goudzwaard. Homewood, Ill.: Dow Jones–Irwin, 1976, pp. 440–456.

Snyder, Arthur. "Principles of Inventory Management." *Financial Executive* 32 (April 1964), pp. 13–21.

Starr, Martin K., and Miller, David W. *Inventory Control: Theory and Practice.* Englewood Cliffs, N.J.: Prentice-Hall, 1962.

Wagner, Harvey M. *Principles of Operations Research—With Applications to Managerial Decisions.* Englewood Cliffs, N.J.: Prentice Hall, 1969, Chapters 9 and 19 and Appendix 2.

Wrightsman, Dwayne. "Optimal Credit Terms for Accounts Receivable." *Quarterly Review of Economics and Business* 9 (Summer 1969), pp. 59–66.

Appendix A to Chapter 11

The Payment Pattern Approach to Receivables Management

The management of accounts receivable is an important aspect of working capital management for a firm that sells on credit. The rate at which credit sales are converted into cash measures the efficiency of a firm's collection policy and the performance of its collection efforts. Two key issues facing the financial executive in accounts receivable management are the forecasting and the control of accounts receivable. We first examine two methods widely used by corporations, namely, the Days' Sales Outstanding (DSO) and the Aging Schedule (AS). We then focus our attention on the payment pattern approach, which offers a better means of monitoring accounts receivable.

Corporate Practice

According to a survey by B. K. Stone in 1976, out of the companies which reported the use of some systematic procedures to project accounts receivable, a great majority used either a pro forma projection of DSO or some other ratio of receivables to a measure of sales. In the control of receivables, AS is reportedly the popular method.

Days' Sales Outstanding

The Average Days' Sales Outstanding (DSO) at a given time t is usually calculated as the ratio of receivables to a measure of daily sales:

$$DSO_t = \frac{\text{Total AR}_t}{\text{Daily Sales}}.$$

The daily sales figure is obtained by averaging sales over a recent time period. The averaging period may be thirty days, sixty days, ninety days, or another relevant period. Clearly, DSO is affected by both the level of sales and the averaging period used.

The Aging Schedule

The Aging Schedule (AS) is the percentage of end-of-quarter accounts receivable in different age groups. Here, the phrase *age group* refers to the period of time that receivables have been outstanding from the time of sales. A strong AS shows only a small percentage of end-of-quarter receivables based on old sales, with the highest percentage based on the most recent month's sales.

Table 11A.1

DSO with Varying Sales Pattern and Varying Averaging Periods ($ Figures in Thousands)

			Daily Sales If Averaging Period Is the Most Recent:			End-of-Quarter DSO (In Days) If Averaging Period Is:		
Month	Sales	Receivables at End of Quarter	30 Days	60 Days	90 Days	30 Days	60 Days	90 Days
January	$60	$ 12						
February	60	36						
March	60	54						
		$102	$2	$2	$2	51	51	51
April	$30	$ 6						
May	60	36						
June	90	81						
		$123	$3	$2.50	$2	41	49	62
July	$90	$ 18						
August	60	36						
September	30	27						
		$ 81	$1	$1.50	$2	81	54	41

Problems with These Approaches

Both the DSO and the AS are affected by the pattern of sales within a quarter. Table 11A.1 shows the end-of-quarter DSO for three different sales patterns. Total sales for the three quarters are identical at $180,000; only the monthly distributions differ from quarter to quarter. The payment pattern is assumed to be constant, with collections of 10 percent of sales during the month that sales are made and 30 percent, 40 percent, and 20 percent in the three

Table 11A.2

Aging Schedules ($ Figures in Thousands)

Month	Sales	Total Receivables at End of Quarter	Age Group (in Days)	Percent of Total
January	$60	$ 12	61–90	12%
February	60	36	31–60	35
March	60	54	0–30	53
		$102		100%
April	$30	$ 6	61–90	5%
May	60	36	31–60	29
June	90	81	0–30	66
		$123		100%
July	$90	$ 18	61–90	22%
August	60	36	31–60	45
September	30	27	0–30	33
		$ 81		100%

months that follow. As a result, end-of-quarter receivables are 20 percent of the first month's sales, 60 percent of the second, and 90 percent of the third. If sales were level at $60,000 per month, the DSO would be constant at 51 days, as shown for the first quarter in Table 11A.1 (look in the 30 days column under End-of-Quarter DSO). With changing sales patterns the DSO varies, changing to 41 for the second quarter and 81 for the third.

Table 11A.2 shows the aging schedule for the same sales and collections data. If sales were level at $60,000 monthly, the AS would be constant, with 53 percent in the 0 to 30 days group, 35 percent in the 31 to 60 days group, and 12 percent in the 61 to 90 days group (shown for the first quarter in the Percent of Total column). But with a changing sales pattern, the AS becomes erratic. If sales are rising, as in the second quarter, the uncollected receivables from the first two months make up a relatively small portion (34 percent) of end-of-quarter receivables. Consequently, the payment experience appears to be improving. When sales are falling, as in the third quarter, uncollected receivables based on heavy sales for the first two months make up 67 percent of end-of-quarter receivables, and the payment experience appears to be worsening. Thus seasonal variations in sales can send false signals to the credit manager, even though the true collection experience is unchanged.

Other factors can also cause DSO and AS figures to shift. The DSO figures can be further distorted when alternative averaging periods are used to calculate daily sales. For the data in Table 11A.1, third quarter daily sales rise from $1,000 based on a 30-day average to $2,000 based on a 90-day average. The corresponding end-of-quarter DSO falls from an alarming 81 days to a healthy 41 days. The way the credit manager perceives the collection experience as measured by the DSO will depend on which averaging period is chosen.

The AS figures can be further distorted if payments on the most recent month's sales are unusually high or low. A high proportion of payments on the most recent month's sales means that receivables for the previous two months will make up a higher percentage of end-of-quarter receivables, even though the old receivables may be normal in relation to the sales for those months. For instance, if receivables from September sales were $10,000 (instead of the $27,000 shown in Table 11A.2) because customers paid $20,000 during September instead of the normal $3,000, the proportion of receivables in the three age groups would have been:

Month	Receivables	Age Groups	Percent of Total
July	$18	61–90	28%
August	36	31–60	56
September	10	0–30	16
	$64		100%

In this example, the exceptionally high collections on September sales—a condition favorable to the firm—distorts the percentages to create the impression that the aging schedule has deteriorated.

Payment Pattern Approach

We have seen that the DSO and AS procedures can be unreliable in the forecasting and control of accounts receivable. The major deficiency of both methods lies in their aggregation of sales and accounts receivable over a particular time period, a quarter in the above example. The payment pattern approach, suggested by W. G. Lewellen and R. W. Johnson in 1972 and by B. K. Stone in 1976, overcomes this difficulty to produce an analysis of payment behavior which is, of course, the real issue of interest to management.

The Payment Pattern

A (monthly) payment pattern is characterized by the proportions of credit sales in a given month that are paid in that month and a number of subsequent months. Table 11A.3 gives the monthly cash flows and accounts receivable arising from $60,000 of credit sales in January. The payment pattern is reflected in the last column: We see that 90% of payment for January sales remains outstanding at the end of that month, 60% at the end of February, and 20% at the end of March. A graphical representation of the payment pattern is given in Figure 11A.1; the dotted and shaded rectangles represent, respectively, the accounts receivable proportions and the accumulated paid proportions of January sales at different points in time.

Mathematically, a payment pattern can be expressed as a sequence of numbers (P_0, P_1, P_2, $\cdots$, P_H), where P_i, called the payment proportion, denotes the proportion of credit sales paid i months after the month of sale and $P_0 + P_1 + \cdots + P_H = 1$. H is the payment horizon, that is, the number of months required for a given month's credit sales to be completely collected.

Table 11A.3

Payment Pattern of $60,000 of Credit Sales in January

	Collections from January Sales during Month		Receivables from January Sales Outstanding at End of Month	
Month	(Percent)	(in Thousands)	(in Thousands)	(Percent)
January	10	$ 6	$54	90
February	30	18	36	60
March	40	24	12	20
April	20	12	0	0

Figure 11A.1

Graph of Payment Pattern of $60,000 of Credit Sales in January

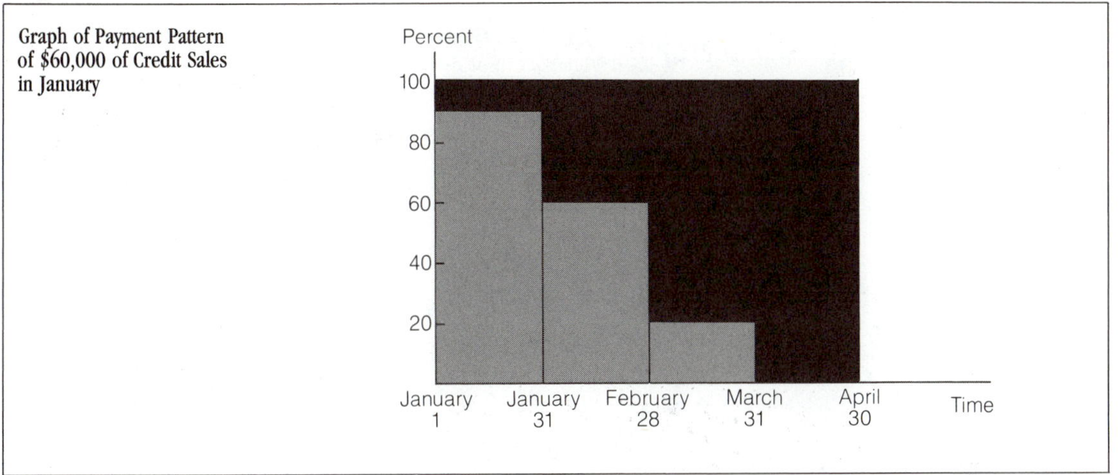

Once a payment pattern is known, we can easily derive the accounts receivable pattern to be the sequence of numbers

$$(F_0, F_1, \cdots, F_{H-1})$$

where F_i, called the balance fraction, is the remaining accounts receivable i months after the month of sale and $F_i = 1 - (P_0 + P_1 + \cdots + P_i)$. At the end of the payment horizon, the credit sales in any particular month are fully paid so that $F_H = 1 - (P_0 + P_1 + \cdots + P_H) = 0$. In the above numerical example, $H = 3$, $P_0 = 0.1$, $P_1 = 0.3$, $P_2 = 0.4$, $P_3 = 0.2$, and $F_0 = 1 - 0.1 = 0.9$, $F_1 = 1 - (0.1 + 0.3) = 0.6$, and $F_2 = 1 - (0.1 + 0.3 + 0.4) = 0.2$.

When the payment pattern remains the same, that is, the numbers $P_0, P_1, \cdots, P_H$ remain unchanged from month to month, it is said to be constant. For example, using the same data as in Table 11A.1, we observe a constant payment pattern (0.1, 0.3, 0.4, 0.2) and consequently a constant accounts receivable pattern (0.9, 0.6, 0.2) as exhibited in Table 11A.4.

The major deficiency of the DSO and AS methods is due to the aggregation of sales and accounts receivable over a number of time periods. This aggregation makes it difficult to detect changes in the payment behavior. In the payment pattern approach, the problem is overcome by matching accounts receivable to sales in the month of origin. As a consequence, the payment pattern approach, in contrast to the DSO and AS, is not sales-level dependent. No matter what the sales pattern may be, the last column in Table 11A.4 remains unchanged, provided the payment pattern is constant. Conversely, any change in payment behavior would be immediately reflected and recognized. Thus, the payment proportions P_i and the balance proportions F_i provide efficient means of control for the credit manager. For example, assume that a firm's historical accounts receivable pattern was (0.9, 0.6, 0.2). In early March,

Table 11A.4

Accounts Receivable as Percentages of Original Sales

Month of Origin	Sales during That Month (in Thousands)	Receivables at End of Quarter (in Thousands)	Percentage Outstanding (Receivables/Sales in Month of Origin)
January	$60	$ 12	20%
February	60	36	60
March	60	54	90
		$102	
April	$30	$ 6	20%
May	60	36	60
June	90	81	90
		$123	
July	$90	$ 18	20%
August	60	36	60
September	30	27	90
		$ 81	

assume that the report on actual payments for January and February credit sales showed a current balance fraction for January sales of $F_1 = 0.70$ versus the pro forma value of 0.60 and a balance fraction for February sales of $F_0 =$ 0.95 versus the pro forma value of 0.90. A problem, created by two consecutive adverse and large deviations from the normal pattern, is indicated.

The procedures proposed by Michael D. Carpenter and Jack E. Miller in 1979 build on the payments pattern framework. For brevity, their study will be referred to by the initials CM. Their methodology can be explained by the use of Table 11A.5. Column 1 sets forth the twelve months for a given year. Column 2 is the sales pattern by month for the four quarters of the year. The sales patterns shown are constant at $60 per month for the first quarter, then rise from $30 to $90 during the second quarter, fall from $90 to $30 during the third quarter, and return to the constant $60 per month for the fourth quarter.

The next three columns express receivables at the end of the month and quarter in three forms: Column 3 shows dollar amount; Column 4, percent of sales of the given month, and Column 5, a weighted days' sales outstanding (WDSO). We shall explain the amounts for each of these columns starting with Column 4, the percent of sales. Recall the following payments and receivables pattern:

Month of Sales	Payments Pattern	Receivables Pattern
t	10%	90%
$t + 1$	30	60
$t + 2$	40	20
$t + 3$	20	0

Table 11A.5

Changes in Receivables Due to Collections or Sales Volume

		Receivables Outstanding at End of Period			Comparison to Previous Period				Comparison to Standard Period			
						Change in Receivables Due to Change in:				Change in Receivables Due to Change in:		
Month (1)	Sales (2)	Dollar Amount (3)	Percent of Sales (4)	Weighted DSO (Days) (5)	Change in WDSO (Days) (6)	Collection Experience (7)	Sales Pattern (8)	Total (9)	Change in WDSO (Days) (10)	Collection Experience (11)	Sales Pattern (12)	Total (13)
January	$60	$ 12	20%	6	—	—	—		—	—	—	
February	60	36	60	18	—	—	—		—	—	—	
March	60	54	90	27	—	—	—		—	—	—	
		$102		51								
April	$30	$ 15	50%	15	9	9	($ 6)	3	9	$ 9	($ 6)	3
May	60	36	60	18	—	—	—	—	—	—	—	—
June	90	72	80	24	(3)	(9)	27	18	(3)	(9)	27	18
		$123		57	6	$0	$21	$21	6	$ 0	$21	$21
July	$90	$ 36	40%	12	(3)	($9)	$30	21	6	$18	6	24
August	60	36	60	18	—	—	—	—	—	—	—	—
September	30	24	80	24	—	—	(48)	(48)	(3)	(3)	(27)	(30)
		$ 96		54	(3)	($9)	($18)	($27)	3	$15	($21)	(6)
October	$60	$ 24	40%	12	—	—	($12)	(12)	6	$12	—	12
November	60	30	50	15	(3)	(6)	—	(6)	(3)	(6)	—	(6)
December	60	54	90	27	3	6	24	30	—	—	—	—
		$108		54	$0	$0	$12	$12	3	$ 6	—	6

For the first two quarters of the year, therefore, the payments and receivables percentages shown in Table 11A.6 would be expected. For example, in Table 11A.6 in the first column, headed Month of Payment, we take March, the month in which the first quarter ends. Under Receivables, the second section of the table data, we find 20 percent underlined for March in the January column. Under Payments, the first section of the table data, the January column shows payments of 10 percent of January sales paid in January, 30 percent paid in February, and 40 percent in March. These percentages total to 80 percent, thus explaining the 20 percent receivables shown for March as related to January sales. The receivables at the end of March for sales made in February are shown as 60 percent and for sales made in March, 90 percent. These percentages correspond to the percentages shown in Column 4 of Table 11A.5. Note that the heading for this section of data is Receivables Outstanding at End of Period. These percentages represent the receivables outstanding at the end of March expressed as percentages of sales made in each of the three months of the quarter.

When these percents are applied to the sales for the corresponding months as set forth in Column 2 of Table 11A.5, we obtain the dollar amounts of receivables outstanding at the end of the period related to the sales for each month as shown in Column 3. Summing the dollar amounts of outstanding receivables generated by each month's sales, we obtain the total dollar amount of receivables outstanding at the end of the quarter, which is $102 for the first quarter.

Column 5 of Table 11A.5 is the weighted DSO (WDSO). The WDSO is simply the percentages from Column 4 multiplied by 30 (for days per month). For the first three months and for the first quarter we have:

	Weighted DSO
January	$0.2 \times 30 = 6$
February	$0.6 \times 30 = 18$
March	$0.9 \times 30 = 27$
First Quarter	$1.7 \times 30 = 51$

The resulting WDSOs correspond to the numbers in the first four rows of Column 5.

The remaining eight columns represent two methods of making comparisons between the experience of the current month and a reference month. First, a comparison with the previous quarter is made. Second, a comparison is made with the standard (first quarter) period. The analysis separates the change in receivables from the reference period into "efficiency" and "volume" variances.

First, let us describe the comparisons with the previous period. The change in the weighted DSO (WDSO) is $\text{WDSO}_t - \text{WDSO}_{t-1}$. For an example, we compare the WDSO for April with that of January; this is 15 less 6, or a

Table 11A.6

Payments and Receivables Percentages

	Payments			Receivables		
	Month of Sales			Month of Sales		
Month of Payment	January	February	March	January	February	March
January	10%			90%		
February	30	10%		60%	90%	
March	40	30	10%	20	60	90%
April	20	40	30	—	20%	60%
May	—	20	40		—	20
June	—	—	20			—

change in WDSO of 9 days. The remaining figures in Column 6 are calculated by comparing the WDSOs for corresponding months of the previous quarter. May of 18 less February of 18 is zero. June of 24 less March of 27 is −3.

We next compute the change in receivables due to collection experience (efficiency) and sales patterns (volume). The change in receivables due to changes in collections is: $(S_t/30)$ times ΔWDSO. For April this would be ($30/30) × 9 = $9. The change in receivables due to changes in the sales pattern (where ADS is average daily sales for the period and $\Delta ADS = ADS_t - ADS_{t-1}$) is: $(\Delta ADS)WDSO_{t-1}$. For April this would be ($30/30 − $60/30) × 6 = −$6. For each of the four quarters, we sum the numbers for the three months. Column 9 is the sum of Columns 7 and 8.

In Columns 10 through 13, the reference month in the comparison is a standard period. For the example, the reference is to the months of the first quarter. Thus, while their comparison to the *previous* period relates April to January, July to April, and October to July, their comparison to the *standard* period relates April, July, and October to January. We have modified the Carpenter-Miller analysis to make it correspond exactly to the procedures used above in making comparisons to the previous period. For July, for example, the change in receivables due to the change in collections is ($90/30) × 6 = $18. For July, the change in receivables due to changes in the sales pattern is: ($90/30 − $60/30) × 6 = $6.

The example shows that collection experience deteriorated in June, July, and November when related to the corresponding months in the immediately preceding quarter. When compared to the first, second, and third months of the first quarter, collection experience deteriorated in June,[1] September, and November.

1. This would be the same comparison as for the previous period, where the second quarter is related to the first quarter and, hence, the first quarter is both the previous and the standard period for the second quarter.

When comparisons are made to corresponding months of the previous quarter, sales volume variances are negative for April, September, and October. When compared to the standard period, the sales volume variances are negative for April and September only, since the fourth quarter sales pattern duplicates the first quarter sales pattern.

The emphasis on the sales pattern approach presented by Lewellen and Johnson and by B. K. Stone was to relate receivables to the percent of sales of the given month. Control standards are developed from the percentages based on the payment pattern and corresponding receivables pattern. CM built upon the payment pattern concept to develop some additional evaluation relations. The key measure is the weighted DSO (WDSO). The changes in the WDSO, or changes in the ADS with the WDSO of the previous reference period, enable them to calculate efficiency and volume variances in receivables. The resulting data enable the credit executive to separate the changes in collection experience from changes in the sales patterns. The executive is thus better able to evaluate the current state of collections and receivables investment. Since it is now possible to distinguish between changes in credit experience and in sales volume, the credit executive can plan to work on changing collection performance or to alter the credit-related variables that influence the volume of sales. Or the changes in receivables may guide the credit executive to communicate the need for changes in the levels of financing in response to the changing investment levels in receivables.

Selected References

Carpenter, Michael D., and Miller, Jack E. "A Reliable Framework for Monitoring Accounts Receivable." *Financial Management* 8 (Winter 1979), pp. 37–40.

Lewellen, W. G., and Edmister, R. O. "A General Model for Accounts Receivable Analysis and Control." *Journal of Financial and Quantitative Analysis* 8 (March 1973), pp. 195–206.

Lewellen, W. G., and Johnson, R. W. "Better Way to Monitor Accounts Receivable." *Harvard Business Review* 50 (May–June 1972), pp. 101–109.

Stone, B. K. "Payments-Pattern Approach to Forecasting and Control of Accounts Receivable." *Financial Management* 5 (1976), pp. 65–82.

Appendix B to Chapter 11

Cash Management Models

Inventory-like models have been constructed to aid the financial manager in determining the firm's optimum cash balances. Four such models—those developed by William J. Baumol, Merton H. Miller and Daniel Orr, William Beranek, and D. J. White and J. M. Norman—are presented in this appendix.

Baumol Model

The classic article on cash management by William J. Baumol applies the EOQ model to the cash management problem.[1] Although Baumol's article emphasized the macroeconomic implications for monetary theory, he recognized the implications for business finance and set the stage for further work in this area. In essence, Baumol recognized the fundamental similarities of inventories and cash from a financial viewpoint. In the case of inventories, ordering and stock-out costs make it expensive to keep inventories at a zero level by placing orders for immediate requirements only. But costs are also involved with *holding* inventories, and an optimal policy balances the opposing costs of ordering and holding inventory.

With cash and securities the situation is very similar. Order costs come in the form of clerical work and brokerage fees in the making of transfers between the cash account and an investment portfolio. On the other side of the coin, there are holding costs, such as interest foregone when large cash balances are held to avoid the costs of making transfers. Further, costs are associated with running out of cash, just as in the case of inventories. As with inventories, the optimal cash balance minimizes these costs.

In its most operational form, the Baumol model assumes that a firm's cash balances behave, over time, in a sawtooth manner, as shown in Figure 11B.1. Receipts come in at periodic intervals, such as Time 0, 1, 2, 3, and so forth; expenditures occur continuously throughout the periods. Since the model as-

We would like to acknowledge the assistance of Richard A. Samuelson in the preparation of this appendix.

1. William J. Baumol, "The Transactions Demand for Cash: An Inventory Theoretic Approach," *Quarterly Journal of Economics* 66 (November 1952), pp. 545–556.

Figure 11B.1

Baumol's Pattern of Receipts and Expenditures

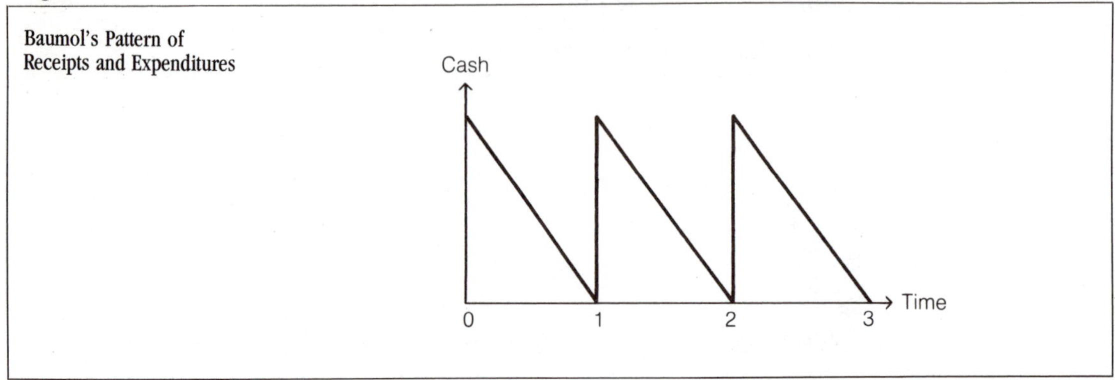

sumes certainty, the firm can adopt an optimal policy that calls for investing I dollars in a short-term investment portfolio at the beginning of each period, then withdrawing C dollars from the portfolio and placing them in the cash account at regular intervals during the period. The model must, of course, take into account both the costs of investment transactions and the costs of holding cash balances.

The decision variables facing the financial manager for a single period are illustrated in Figure 11B.2. The manager has an amount of cash equal to T for the period's transactions. A portion of the initial cash, $R = T - I$, is retained in the form of cash, and the balance, I, is invested in a portfolio of

Figure 11B.2

Baumol's Transfers from Securities to Cash

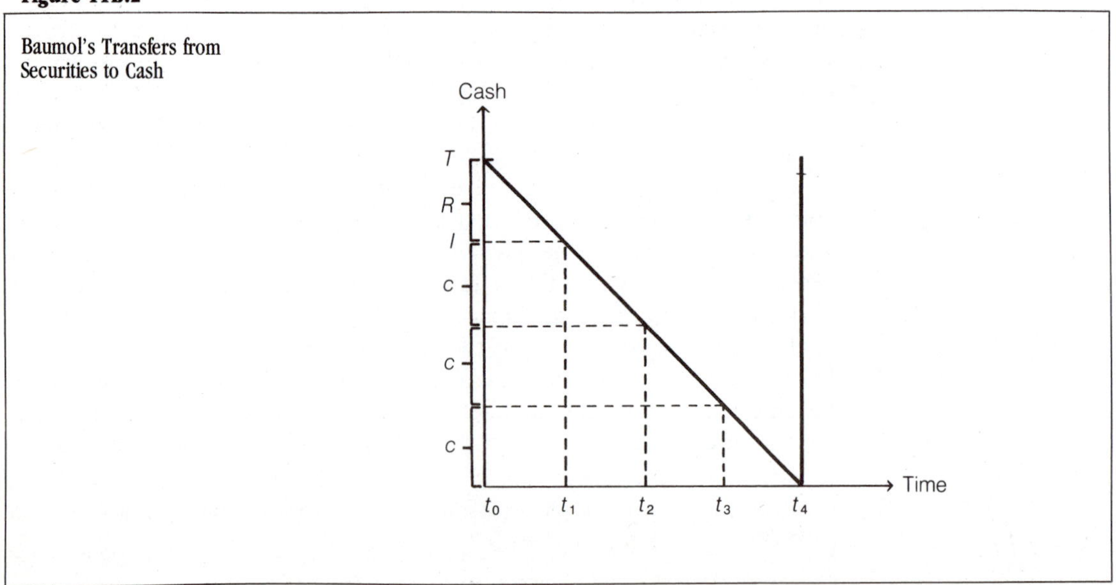

short-term liquid assets that earns a rate of return, i. The retained cash, R, is sufficient to meet expenditures during the period from t_0 to t_1. An additional C dollars will be transferred from the investment portfolio to the cash account at time t_1 to cover expenditures for the period from t_1 to t_2; C dollars will again be withdrawn at time t_2 and t_3. Receipts of T dollars flow into the cash account again at t_4, and the same process is repeated during the following period.

If the disbursements are assumed to be continuous, then $R = T - I$ dollars withheld from the initial cash receipt will serve to meet payments during a fraction of the period between receipts equal to $(T - I)/T$ times the length of the period. Further, since the average cash holding for that time will be $(T - I)/2$, the interest cost (opportunity cost) of withholding that money will be

$$\left(\frac{T-I}{2}\right) i \left(\frac{T-I}{T}\right),$$

where i is the interest rate on invested funds. A brokerage fee is required to invest the I dollars, and this fee is equal to $b_d + k_d I$, where b_d and k_d are the fixed and variable costs, respectively, of making deposits (investments). Similarly, b_w and k_w are the fixed and variable costs of making withdrawals.

The cost of obtaining cash for the remainder of the period is found, similarly, to be

$$\left(\frac{C}{2}\right) i \left(\frac{I}{T}\right) + (b_w + k_w C)\frac{I}{C}.$$

The first term is the interest (opportunity) cost of holding the average amount $(C/2)$ of cash over the subperiod, and the second term is the brokerage cost of making withdrawals from the investment account.

Combining these component costs, the total cost function is given by

$$Z = \left(\frac{T-I}{2}\right) i \left(\frac{T-I}{T}\right) + b_d + k_d I + \left(\frac{C}{2}\right) i \left(\frac{I}{T}\right) + (b_w + k_w C)\frac{I}{C}. \quad (11B.1)$$

The optimal value for C is found by differentiating Equation 11B.1 with respect to C and setting the derivative equal to zero. This gives

$$C = \sqrt{\frac{2b_w T}{i}}. \quad (11B.2)$$

R, the optimum cash balance to withhold from the initial receipt, is found by differentiating Equation 11B.1 with respect to I, which gives

$$R = T - I = C + T\left(\frac{k_w + k_d}{i}\right). \quad (11B.3)$$

In order to minimize costs, the financial manager will then withhold R dollars from the initial receipts to cover expenditures for the beginning of the period and will withdraw C dollars from his or her investment portfolio I/C times per period.

To illustrate the Baumol model, let T = \$1,200,000 per year, b_d = \$10, k_d = 0, i = 10%, b_w = \$26, and k_w = 0. Using Equation 11B.2, solve for C:

$$C = \sqrt{\frac{2(\$26)(\$1{,}200{,}000)}{0.10}} \approx \$25{,}000.$$

With T = \$1,200,000 (or \$100,000 per month), C = \$25,000, or an optimum of four cash withdrawals from investments per month. Using Equation 11B.3:

$$R = \$25{,}000 + \$100{,}000\left(\frac{0+0}{0.10}\right) = \$25{,}000.$$

These results illustrate the pattern depicted by Figure 11B.2. Then, using Equation 11B.1:

$$\begin{aligned} Z = &\left(\frac{\$25{,}000}{2}\right)\left(\frac{0.10}{12}\right)\left(\frac{\$25{,}000}{\$100{,}000}\right) + \$10 \\ &+ \left(\frac{\$25{,}000}{2}\right)\left(\frac{0.10}{12}\right)\left(\frac{\$75{,}000}{\$100{,}000}\right) + \$26\left(\frac{\$75{,}000}{\$25{,}000}\right) \\ = &\ (\$12{,}500)(0.00833)(0.25) + \$10 \\ &+ (\$12{,}500)(0.00833)(0.75) + (\$26)(3) \\ = &\ \$26.03 + \$10 + \$78.09 + \$78 \\ = &\ \$192.12. \end{aligned}$$

The financial manager knows all of the items listed as input information but does not know C, R, I, or Z. Using Equation 11B.2, the manager obtains C. Using Equation 11B.3, the manager calculates R, from which I can also be obtained. The manager then has all the information required to calculate Equation 11B.1, which represents Z, the total cost function for cash management when the size of the cash withdrawals, C, from investments is optimal. (R and I will also be optimal.)

While the Baumol model captures the essential elements of the problem,

Figure 11B.3

Realistic Pattern of Receipts and Expenditures for a Firm

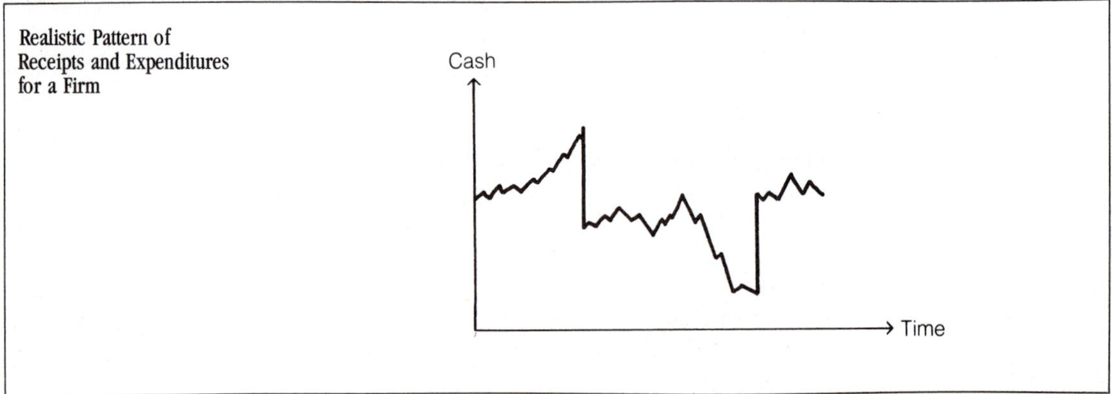

its restrictive assumptions about the behavior of cash inflows and outflows are probably more applicable to an individual than to a business firm. For the firm, inflows are likely to be less lumpy, and outflows are likely to be less smooth. Instead, the behavior of cash balances might resemble the pattern of Figure 11B.3. Daily changes in the cash balance may be up or down, following an irregular and somewhat unpredictable pattern. When the balance drifts upward for some length of time, a point is reached at which the financial officer orders a transfer of cash to the investment portfolio, and the cash balance is returned to some lower level. When disbursements exceed receipts for some period of time, investments are sold and a transfer is made to the cash account to restore the cash balance to a higher level. If this particular behavior is typical, then the certainty assumptions of the Baumol model are too restrictive to make it operational.

Miller-Orr Model

Merton Miller and Daniel Orr expanded the Baumol model by incorporating a stochastic generating process for periodic changes in cash balances so that the cash pattern resembles that shown in Figure 11B.3.[2] In contrast to the completely deterministic assumptions of the Baumol model, Miller and Orr assume that net cash flows behave as if they were generated by a "stationary random walk." This means that changes in the cash balance over a given period are random in both size and direction and that they form a normal distribution as the number of periods observed increases. The model allows for a priori knowledge, however, that changes at a certain time have a greater probability of being either positive or negative.

The Miller-Orr model is designed to determine the time and size of transfers between an investment account and the cash account according to a decision process illustrated in Figure 11B.4. Changes in cash balances are allowed to go up until they reach some level h at time t_1; they are then reduced to level z, the *return point,* by investing h $-$ z dollars in the investment portfolio. Next, the cash balance wanders aimlessly until it reaches the minimum balance point, r, at t_2. At this time, enough earning assets are sold to return the cash balance to its return point, z. Miller and Orr define t so that $1/t$ is "some small fraction of a working day such as $1/8$," or, equivalently, "the number of operating cash transactions per day." We suppose that during any such hour the cash balance will either increase by m dollars with probability p or decrease by m dollars with probability $q = 1 - p$. Most of their analysis is based on the "special symmetric or zero-drift case in which $p = q = 1/2$." For this special case, the variance of daily changes in the cash balance is equal to m^2t.[3] The model is based on a cost function similar to Baumol's, and it in-

2. Merton H. Miller and Daniel Orr, "A Model for the Demand for Money by Firms," *Quarterly Journal of Economics* 80 (August 1966), pp. 413–435.
3. Ibid., pp. 418, 419, 422.

Figure 11B.4

Miller-Orr Cash Management Model

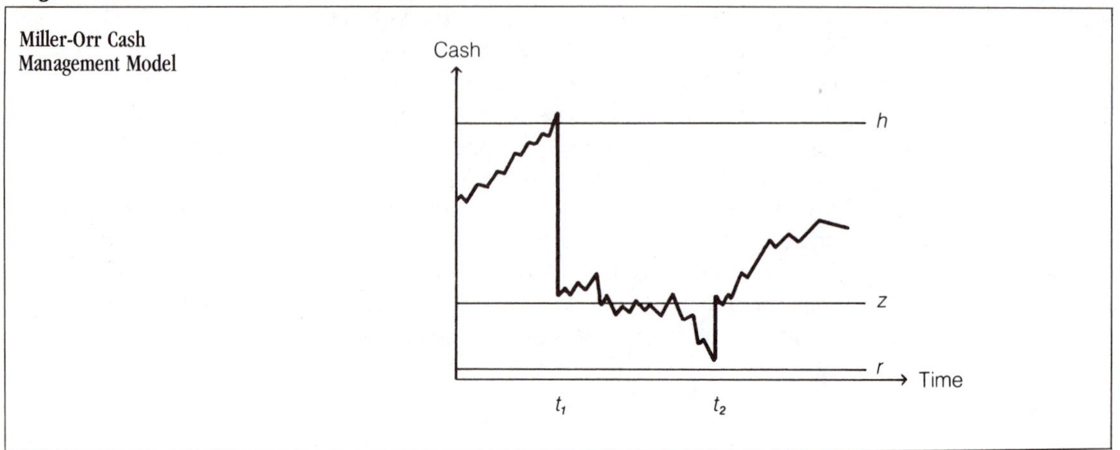

cludes elements for the cost of making transfers to and from cash and for the opportunity cost of holding cash. The upper limit, h, which cash balances should not be allowed to surpass, and the return point, z, to which the balance is returned after every transfer either to or from the cash account, are computed so as to minimize the cost function. The lower limit is assumed to be given, and it could be the minimum balance required by the banks in which the cash is deposited.

The cost function for the Miller-Orr model can be stated as $E(c) = bE(N)/T + iE(m)$, where $E(N)$ = the expected number of transfers between cash and the investment portfolio during the planning period; b = the cost per transfer; T = the number of days in the planning period; $E(m)$ = the expected average daily balance; and i = the daily rate of interest earned on the investments. The objective is to minimize $E(c)$ by choice of the variables h and z, the upper control limit and the return point, respectively.

The solution as derived by Miller and Orr becomes

$$z^* = \left(\frac{3b\sigma^2}{4i}\right)^{1/3}. \tag{11B.4}$$

The variance of the daily changes in the cash balance is represented by σ^2. As would be expected, a higher transfer cost, b, or variance, σ^2, would imply a greater spread between the upper and lower control limits. For the special case where p (the probability that cash balances will increase) equals 0.5, and q (the probability that cash balances will decrease) equals 0.5, the upper control limit will always be three times greater than the return point, z:

$$h^* = 3z^* \tag{11B.4a}$$

To illustrate the Miller-Orr model, let b = \$25, m = \$10, $t = 8$, i = 20%, r = 0, and $\sigma^2 = m^2t = 800$. Given Equation 11B.4:

$$z^* = \left[\frac{3(\$25)(800)}{4(0.20/365)}\right]^{1/3} = \left(\frac{\$60{,}000}{0.0021917808}\right)^{1/3}$$
$$= (\$27{,}375{,}000)^{1/3}$$
$$= \$301.38 \approx \$300$$
$$h^* = 3(\$301.38) = \$904.14 \approx \$900$$
$$\text{For } r = 100, \text{h* would be \$1,000 and } Z \text{ would be \$400.}$$

Miller and Orr tested their model by applying it to nine months of data on the daily cash balances and purchases and sales of short-term securities of a large industrial company. When the decisions of the model were compared to those actually made by the treasurer of the company, the model was found to produce an average daily cash balance that was about 40 percent *lower* ($160,000 for the model and $275,000 for the treasurer). Looking at it from another side, the model would have been able to match the $275,000 average daily balance with only 80 transactions, as compared to the treasurer's 112 actual transactions.

As with most inventory control models, the Miller-Orr model's performance depends not only on how well the conditional predictions (in this case the expected number of transfers and the expected average cash balance) conform to actuality but also on how well the parameters are estimated. In this model, b, the transfer cost, is sometimes difficult to estimate. In Miller and Orr's study, the order costs included such components as "(a) making two or more long-distance phone calls plus 15 minutes to a half-hour of the assistant treasurer's time, (b) typing up and carefully checking an authorization letter with four copies, (c) carrying the original of the letter to be signed by the treasurer, and (d) carrying the copies to the controller's office where special accounts are opened, the entries are posted and further checks of the arithmetic are made."[4] These clerical procedures were thought to be in the magnitude of $20 to $50 per order. In the application of their model, however, Miller and Orr did not rely on their estimate for order costs; instead, they tested the model through the use of a series of "assumed" order costs until the model used the same number of transactions as did the treasurer. They could then determine the order cost implied by the treasurer's own action. The results were then used to evaluate the treasurer's performance in managing the cash balances and so provided valuable information to the treasurer.

The treasurer found, for example, that his action in purchasing securities was often inconsistent. Too often he made small-lot purchases well below the minimum of $h - z$ computed by the model, while at other times he allowed cash balances to drift to as much as double the upper control limit before

4. Merton H. Miller and Daniel Orr, "An Application of Control-Limit Models to the Management of Corporate Cash Balances," in *Financial Research and Management Decisions*, ed. A. A. Robichek (New York: Wiley, 1967), pp. 133–151.

making a purchase. If it did no more than give the treasurer some perspective about his buying and selling activities, the model was used successfully.[5]

Beranek Model

William Beranek has devoted a chapter in his text, *Analysis for Financial Decisions,* to the problem of determining the optimal allocation of available funds between the cash balance and marketable securities.[6] His approach differs from Baumol's in that he includes a probability distribution for expected cash flows and a cost function for the loss of cash discounts and deterioration of credit rating when the firm is caught short of cash. The decision variable in Beranek's model is the allocation of funds between cash and investments at the beginning of the period. Withdrawals from investment are assumed to be possible only at the end of each planning period.

According to Beranek, it is more helpful for the analysis of cash management problems to regard cash *disbursements* as being directly controllable by management and relatively lumpy and to regard *receipts* as being uncontrollable and continuous. In the certainty case, this pattern of cash balance behavior would be the reverse of the sawtooth pattern assumed by Baumol, and it would look like the pattern illustrated in Figure 11B.5. In explaining this approach, one can argue that institutional customs and arrangements might cause cash outflows to be concentrated at periodic intervals. Wages and salaries are ordinarily paid weekly or monthly, credit terms for merchandise purchases may allow payment on the tenth and final days of the month, and other significant outflows, such as tax and dividend payments, will be concentrated at regular intervals. Insofar as cash outflows are controllable and recur in a cyclical manner, the financial manager can predict cash needs over a planning period and can invest a portion of the funds that are not expected to be needed during the planning period.

In Beranek's model, the financial manager is regarded as having total resources of k dollars available at the beginning of a planning period. The manager expects the net cash drain (receipts less disbursements) at the end of the period to be y dollars (either positive or negative), with a probability distribution $g(y)$. The financial manager's objective of maximizing returns by investment in securities is constrained by transactions costs and the risk of being short of cash when funds are needed for expenditures. Beranek considers that *short costs* consist of cash discounts forgone and the deterioration of the firm's credit rating when it is unable to meet payments in time. It might be more realistic, however, to think of short costs as the cost of borrowing on a line of credit, since the company would undoubtedly prefer short-term bor-

5. For a cash planning approach related to credit decisions by the use of a financial simulation model, see Bernell K. Stone, "Cash Planning and Credit-Line Determination with a Financial Statement Simulator: A Cash Report on Short-Term Financial Planning," *Journal of Financial and Quantitative Analysis* 8 (November 1973), pp. 711–730.

6. William Beranek, *Analysis for Financial Decisions* (Homewood, Ill.: Irwin, 1963), pp. 345–387.

Figure 11B.5

Beranek's Pattern of Receipts and Expenditures

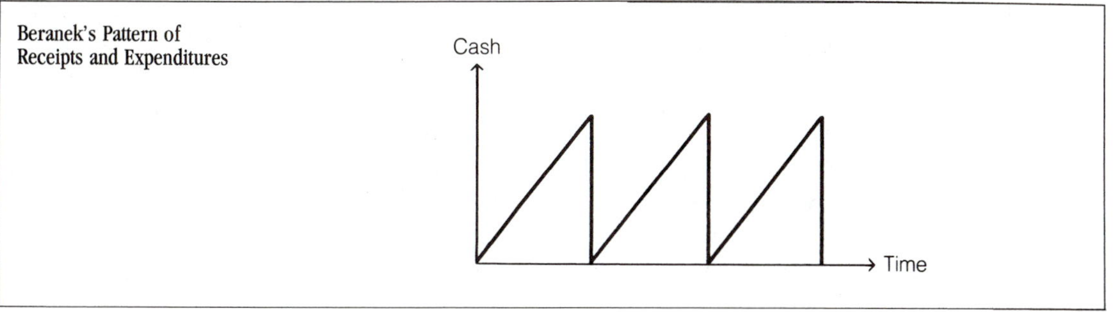

rowing to forgoing cash discounts or allowing its credit rating to deteriorate.

Given the probability distribution of net cash flows, the costs of running short of cash, and the opportunity cost of holding cash balances, Beranek develops a cost function and differentiates it to find the optimal initial cash balance, which is the amount of cash that should be on hand at the start of the period. His solution calls for setting the cash balance at a level such that, once the critical level is set, the cumulative probability of running short of cash is equal to the ratio d/a, where d = net return on the investment portfolio and a = incremental cost of being short $1 of cash. This means that the financial manager should continue shifting resources from the opening cash balance to securities until the expectation that the ending cash balance will be below the critical minimum is equal to the ratio of the incremental net return per dollar of investment to the incremental short cost per dollar.

White and Norman Model

D. J. White and J. M. Norman developed a model for an English insurance company similar in spirit to the Beranek model.[7] Investment decisions are assumed to be considered periodically, and cash inflows from premiums and outflows for claims and expenses are assumed to fluctuate randomly according to some known distribution. In addition, another cash outflow for "call-offs" by the stockbrokers is assumed to have an independent distribution function. A penalty rate on overdrafts (borrowings), analogous to Beranek's short-cost function, is also included in the model, while transactions costs are ignored (or implicitly considered in the net rate of return on investments). The opening cash balance that maximizes expected wealth at the end of the period is the relevant decision variable. The optimal solution is a function of Beranek's d, the incremental return per dollar of investment, and the interest rate on overdrafts.

7. D. J. White and J. M. Norman, "Control of Cash Reserves," *Operational Research Quarterly* 16 (September 1965), pp. 309–328.

A Comparison of the Models

The models described in this appendix differ primarily in the emphasis given to various costs affecting their solutions. The Baumol and the Miller-Orr models give critical emphasis to the costs arising from transfers between the cash account and the investment portfolio. They ignore the alternative of borrowing and concentrate on the liquidation of investments to meet the needs for cash outflows. The Beranek and the White-Norman models, on the other hand, give critical emphasis to the costs arising from the shortage of cash (the cost of borrowing, from one viewpoint), while transactions costs are only indirectly considered. The latter models ignore the alternatives of liquidating investments to meet cash needs. A model that directly incorporates both the possibility of borrowing and the possibility of holding a portfolio of liquid assets would be desirable, since it is not clear that liquidation of investments would always be preferable to borrowing or vice versa.

Of all the models, the Miller-Orr version appears to be the easiest to implement, if for no other reason than the simplicity of its decision rules. Decision models are more likely to be used when management can easily understand their application. In addition, the Miller-Orr decision model's planning period covers a longer period of time, so it does not have to be revised as often as the Beranek and White-Norman models. The financial manager who uses a Beranek or a White-Norman model must feed information into the model and derive a decision each time a transfer between cash and securities is being considered. While this must be counted as a disadvantage of these models, it could result in better decisions by making the models more responsive to conditions existing at the time decisions are made.

The Miller-Orr model has an element of flexibility, however, that should not be overlooked. Expectations that cash balances are more likely to either increase or decrease over a given period can be incorporated into the calculation of the optimal values for the decision variables. Thus, if a business is subject to seasonal trends, the optimal control limits can be adjusted for each season by using different values for p and q, the respective probabilities that cash will increase and decrease.

The Miller-Orr model is built on the assumption that cash balances behave as if they were generated by a random walk. To the extent that this assumption is erroneous, management will find the model of little use. If management can significantly control the timing of cash outflows (and perhaps even cash inflows), then a model of the Beranek or White-Norman type may be more suitable. In this case, management should not have too much difficulty forming the subjective probability distributions that are needed for these models. In reality, it would probably be true that cash flows are partly random and partly controllable, so the applicability of any of the models can be determined only by testing them with actual data.

It should be remembered that decision models of the type discussed in this appendix are not intended to be applied blindly. There are difficulties in estimating parameters and probabilities. But even more important, the financial manager often has available information that is not directly incorporated into the model. Thus a model, acting ignorantly and unaware of other relevant information, might provide completely erroneous advice. On the other hand, despite their restrictive assumptions and errors, decision models perform effectively if they capture the essential elements in a decision problem. Cash management models should be used as a guide to intelligent decision making, tempered with the manager's own good judgment.

Selected References

Archer, Stephen H. "A Model for the Determination of Firm Cash Balance." *Journal of Financial and Quantitative Analysis* 1 (March 1966), pp. 1–11.

Baumol, William J. "The Transactions Demand for Cash: An Inventory Theoretic Approach." *Quarterly Journal of Economics* 65 (November 1952), pp. 545–556.

Budin, Morris, and Van Handel, Robert J. "A Rule-of-Thumb Theory of Cash Holdings by Firm." *Journal of Financial and Quantitative Analysis* 10 (March 1975), pp. 85–108.

Calman, Robert F. *Linear Programming and Cash Management/CASH ALPHA.* Cambridge, Mass.: M.I.T. Press, 1968.

Constantinides, George M. "Stochastic Cash Management with Fixed and Proportional Transaction Costs." *Management Science* 22 (August 1976), pp. 1320–1331.

Daellenbach, Hans G. "Are Cash Management Optimization Models Worthwhile?" *Journal of Financial and Quantitative Analysis* 9 (September 1974), pp. 607–626.

Eppen, Gary D., and Fama, Eugene F. "Cash Balance and Simple Dynamic Portfolio Problems with Proportional Costs." *International Economic Review* 10 (June 1969), pp. 110–133.

Mao, James C. T., and Sarndal, Carl E. "Cash Management: Theory and Practice." *Journal of Business Finance & Accounting* 5 (Autumn 1978), pp. 329–338.

Miller, Merton H., and Orr, Daniel. "The Demand for Money by Firms: Extension of Analytic Results." *Journal of Finance* 23 (December 1968), pp. 735–759.

———. "A Model of the Demand for Money by Firms." *Quarterly Journal of Economics* 80 (August 1966), pp. 413–435.

Orgler, Yair E. *Cash Management.* Belmont, Calif.: Wadsworth, 1970.

Sethi, Suresh P., and Thompson, Gerald L. "Application of Mathematical Control Theory to Finance: Modeling Simple Dynamic Cash Balance Problems." *Journal of Financial and Quantitative Analysis* 5 (December 1970), pp. 381–394.

Appendix C to Chapter 11

Credit Policy Decisions

The formulations used in the analysis of credit policy decisions in Chapter 11 represent an approximation for purposes of simplification. The theoretically correct methodology requires that the time value of money be taken into account, as proposed by Kim-Atkins and Hill-Riener. In this appendix, we shall (1) present two alternative formulations for analyzing cash discount rate decisions and work through numerical illustrations of each methodology, (2) develop the basis for the approximation method, and (3) demonstrate the equivalence of the two methodologies analytically.

Credit Policy Analysis Using Two Alternative Formulations

The application of compound interest relations in the analysis of credit policy decisions will be shown in connection with decisions on the size of cash discount rates for early payment. Hill and Riener formulate a decision model for cash discount rate policy by the use of Equation 11C.1.

$$\text{NPV} = p(1-\delta)\text{S}\left(1+\frac{k}{365}\right)^{-M} + (1-p)\text{S}\left(1+\frac{k}{365}\right)^{-N} - \text{S}\left(1+\frac{k}{365}\right)^{-C}. \quad \textbf{(11C.1)}$$

The meanings of the symbols and the illustrative numerical input values to be used are as follows:

NPV = Net gain (loss) from the change in cash discount policy

p = Proportion of sales with the discount = 0.4

$(1-p)$ = Proportion of sales without the discount = 0.6

δ = Percentage discount for early payment = 2% = 0.02

S = Initial level of sales = \$10 million

k = Applicable cost of capital, measuring the time value of funds = 10% = 0.10

M = Average collection period on sales with the discount = 10

N = Average collection period on sales without the discount = 70

C = Overall average collection period before the cash discount rate change = 60

In this example it is assumed that initially the firm offers no cash discount for early payment and its average collection period is sixty days. The firm then offers a 2 percent discount if payment is made in ten days, with the payment due at the end of sixty days otherwise. Under these circumstances, it is expected that 40 percent of credit sales will be paid in ten days, with the remaining 60 percent having an average collection period of seventy days. To keep the illustration as simple as possible, it is assumed that neither the volume of sales nor the bad debt loss experience will be affected; only the timing of the payments on credit sales will be changed.

Using the data of the example in the Hill-Riener formulation, the calculation of the net benefit of providing a 2 percent discount for early payment is shown in Equation 11C.1a.

$$\begin{aligned} \text{NPV} &= 0.4(0.98)(10{,}000{,}000)(1.000274)^{-10} \\ &\quad + 0.6(10{,}000{,}000)(1.000274)^{-70} - 10{,}000{,}000(1.000274)^{-60} \\ &= 3{,}909{,}275 + 5{,}886{,}032 - 9{,}836{,}966 \\ &= -\$41{,}659. \end{aligned} \tag{11C.1a}$$

We find that the net benefit is a negative \$41,659. Under the assumptions of this illustration, it would be better not to offer the 2 percent cash discount. Next we analyze this decision using the simplified procedure explained in the chapter. This methodology employs Equation 11C.2.

$$\Delta \text{P} = -\frac{k\text{S}}{365}[pM(1-\delta) + (1-p)N - C] - p\,\delta\text{S}. \tag{11C.2}$$

The only new symbol is ΔP, which represents the change in "profit," or net income. Using the same input values as before, we perform the calculations as shown in Equation 11C.2a.

$$\begin{aligned} \Delta \text{P} &= -\frac{0.1(10{,}000{,}000)}{365}\{[0.4(10)(0.98) + 0.6(70)] - 60\} \\ &\quad - 0.4(0.02)10{,}000{,}000 \\ &= -2{,}739.726[(3.92 + 42) - 60] - 80{,}000 \\ &= -2{,}739.726(-14.08) - 80{,}000 \\ &= 38{,}575.342 - 80{,}000 \\ &= -\$41{,}425. \end{aligned} \tag{11C.2a}$$

The result we obtain is a negative \$41,425. This result differs from the compound interest formulation result by 0.005617, or slightly over one-half of 1 percent. Thus the two methodologies give approximately the same result. Let us next see why this is so.

Basis for the Approximation Methodology

The simplified approximation method used in the chapter comes from the logic of the expansion of a binomial series. The general expression for the expansion of a binomial series is shown in Equation 11C.3.

$$(a + b)^n = a^n + na^{n-1}b + \frac{n(n-1)}{2}a^{n-2}b^2 + \cdots + b^n \quad (11C.3)$$

In Equation 11C.1 the compound interest factor corresponds in form to the binomial expression which is expanded in Equation 11C.3, where:

$$a = 1$$

$$b = \frac{k}{365} = \frac{0.10}{365} = 0.000274$$

$n = -M$ or $-N$ or $-C = -10$ or -70 or -60, respectively.

Next, insert the numerical values into the first three terms of the binomial expansion of Equation 11C.3, as shown in Equation 11C.3a, for the exponent value of -60. Recall that $(a + b)^{-n}$ is equal to $1/(a + b)^n$.

$$\begin{aligned} 1/(1 + 0.000274)^{60} &= 1/[1^{60} + (60)(1^{59})(0.000274) \\ &\quad + \frac{(60)(59)}{2}(1^{58})(0.000274)^2] \\ &= 1/[1 + 0.01644 + 1{,}770(0.0000000751)] \\ &= 1/(1 + 0.01644 + 0.0001329) \\ 0.9836966 &\cong 0.9836973. \end{aligned} \quad (11C.3a)$$

We observe in the final result for the computations in Equation 11C.3a that the exact value of the compound interest relationship on the left-hand side of the equation does not differ from the summation of the first three terms of the binomial expansion until we get to the sixth decimal place. The third term of the binomial expansion does not influence the result until the fourth decimal place, and then by only a very small magnitude. Because the binomial expansion approximates the compound interest calculation very quickly, the first two terms of the expansion are often used in place of the compound interest calculation for convenience.[1] Using this approximation, we have the relationship shown in Equation 11C.4.

$$[1 + (k/365)]^n = 1 + n(k/365). \quad (11C.4)$$

From the numerical illustration in Equation 11C.3a we can see that the approximation illustrated in Equation 11C.4 does not differ from the exact compound interest calculation until the fourth decimal place: 0.9836966 = 1 −

1. Miller and Modigliani employed the same type of approximation. See M. H. Miller and F. Modigliani, "Dividend Policy, Growth, and the Valuation of Shares," *Journal of Business* 34 (October 1961), p. 423, Equations 22a and 22b of n. 15.

0.01644 ≅ 0.98356. If rounding took place at the fourth decimal place, the difference would be only 0.0001. If rounding is at the third decimal place, the result for both the exact compound interest calculation and the two-term binomial expansion is 0.984.

The Analytic Equivalence of the Two Formulations

In Table 11C.1, we demonstrate the equivalence between the compound interest formulation in Equation 11C.1 and its approximation in Equation 11C.2. We rewrite Equation 11C.1 using the relationship set forth in Equation 11C.4, which is the two-term binomial expansion approximation to the compound interest calculation. After some algebraic steps, explained in the table, we arrive at Equation 11C.2. Thus both approaches are theoretically correct. The compound interest formulation is more precise, but the simplification retains the analytical spirit of the compound interest formulation expressed in Equation 11C.1. The simplified formulation has the convenience of avoiding the need to use compound interest tables, while obtaining essentially the same results.

In analyzing prospective credit policy changes, it is necessary to make a forecast of what the effects will be. For example, we do not know in advance what percentage of our credit customers will take the discounts and what percentage will not. For those who do not take the discount, the average collection period also has to be projected. So an additional argument for the simpli-

Table 11C.1

Reconciliation of Two Formulations for Analyzing Credit Policy Decisions

$$\text{NPV} = p(1-\delta)S\left(1+\frac{k}{365}\right)^{-M} + (1-p)S\left(1+\frac{k}{365}\right)^{-N} - S\left(1+\frac{k}{365}\right)^{-C}. \quad \textbf{(11C.1)}$$

$$\text{Rewrite (11C.1) using} \quad \left(1+\frac{k}{365}\right)^{n} = \left(1+\frac{nk}{365}\right). \quad \textbf{(11C.4)}$$

$$\text{NPV} = p(1-\delta)S\left(1-\frac{kM}{365}\right) + (1-p)S\left(1-\frac{kN}{365}\right) - S\left(1-\frac{kC}{365}\right) \text{ Factor out } S/365.$$

$$= \frac{S}{365}[p(1-\delta)(365-kM) + (1-p)(365-kN) - (365-kC)] \text{ Multiply through.}$$

$$= \frac{S}{365}[p365 - p\delta365 + p\delta kM - pkM + 365 - p365 + pkN - kN - 365 + kC]$$

Cancel terms and regroup.

$$= \frac{S}{365}[kp\,\delta\,M - p\,\delta365 + pk(N-M) + k(C-N)] \text{ Factor out } k.$$

$$= \frac{kS}{365}\left[p\,\delta M - \frac{p\,\delta365}{k} + pN - pM + C - N\right] \text{ Regroup.}$$

$$\text{NPV} = \Delta P = -\frac{kS}{365}[pM(1-\delta) + (1-p)N - C] - p\delta S. \text{ This is Equation 11C.2.}$$

fied approach is that the parameters used in the analysis are subject to a far larger margin of error than the small approximations employed in the simplified formulation. Even if a computerized analysis of credit policy changes were employed, the simplified approach would achieve substantial savings in computer processing time by avoiding the necessity of the compound interest calculations. However, we are not arguing for the superiority of either approach. We simply observe that they both have the same theoretical basis and give approximately the same results.

Selected References

Atkins, Joseph C, and Kim, Yong H. "Comment and Correction: Opportunity Cost in the Evaluation of Investment in Accounts Receivable." *Financial Management* 6 (Winter 1977), pp. 71–74.

Dyl, Edward A. "Another Look at the Evaluation of Investments in Accounts Receivable." *Financial Management* 6 (Winter 1977), pp. 67–70.

Hill, Ned C., and Riener, Kenneth D. "Determining the Cash Discount in the Firm's Credit Policy." *Financial Management* 8 (Spring 1979), pp. 68–73.

Kim, Yong H., and Atkins, Joseph C. "Evaluating Investments in Accounts Receivable: A Maximizing Framework." *Journal of Finance* 33 (May 1978), pp. 403–412.

Oh, John S. "Opportunity Cost in the Evaluation of Investment in Accounts Receivable." *Financial Management* 5 (Summer 1976), pp. 32–36.

Walia, Tirlochan S. "Explicit and Implicit Cost of Changes in the Level of Accounts Receivable and the Credit Policy Decision of the Firm," *Financial Management* 6 (Winter 1977), pp. 75–78.

12

Major Sources and Forms of Short-Term Financing

In Chapter 10 we discussed the maturity structure of the firm's debt and showed how this structure can affect both risk and expected returns. However, a variety of short-term credits are available to the firm, and the financial manager must know the advantages and disadvantages of each. Accordingly, in this chapter we take up the main forms of short-term credit, considering both the characteristics and the sources of this credit.

Short-term credit *is defined as debt originally scheduled for repayment within one year. The three major sources of funds with short maturities, ranked in descending order by volume of credit supplied, are (1) trade credit among firms, (2) loans from commercial banks, and (3) commercial paper.*

Trade Credit

In the ordinary course of events, a firm buys its supplies and materials on credit from other firms, recording the debt as an *account payable.* Accounts payable, or *trade credit,* is the largest single category of short-term credit, representing about 40 percent of the current liabilities of nonfinancial corporations.[1] This percentage is somewhat larger for small firms. Because these firms may not qualify for financing from other sources, they rely rather heavily on trade credit.

Trade credit is a spontaneous source of financing in that it arises from ordinary business transactions. For example, suppose a firm makes average purchases of $2,000 a day on terms of net 30. On the average, it will owe 30 times $2,000, or $60,000, to its suppliers. If its sales and, consequently, its purchases double, accounts payable will also double—to $120,000. The firm will have spontaneously generated an additional $60,000 of financing. Similarly, if the terms of credit are extended from 30 to 40 days, accounts payable

1. In Chapter 11, we discussed trade credit from the viewpoint of minimizing investment in current assets. In the present chapter we look at the other side of the coin—trade credit as a source, rather than a use, of financing. In Chapter 11, the use of trade credit by customers resulted in an asset investment called *accounts receivable.* In the present chapter, the use of trade credit gives rise to short-term obligations, generally called *accounts payable.*

will expand from $60,000 to $80,000; thus, lengthening the credit period, as well as expanding sales and purchases, generates additional financing.

Credit Terms

The terms of sales, or *credit terms,* describe the payment obligation of the buyer. The following discussion outlines the four main factors that influence the length of credit terms: the economic nature of the product, the seller's circumstances, the buyer's circumstances, and cash discounts.

Economic Nature of the Product. Commodities with high sales turnover are sold on relatively short credit terms; buyers resell the products rapidly, generating cash that enables them to pay the suppliers. Groceries have a high turnover, but perishability also plays a role. The credit extended for fresh fruits and vegetables might run from five to ten days, whereas the credit extended on canned fruits and vegetables would more likely be fifteen to thirty days. Terms for items that have a slow retail turnover, such as jewelry, may run six months or longer.

Seller Circumstances. Financially weak sellers must require cash or exceptionally short credit terms. For example, farmers sell livestock to meatpacking companies on a cash basis. In many industries, variations in credit terms can be used as a sales promotion device. Although the use of credit as a selling device could endanger sound credit management, the practice does occur, especially when the seller's industry has excess capacity. Also, large sellers can use their position to impose relatively short credit terms. However, the reverse appears more often in practice; that is, financially strong sellers are suppliers of funds to small firms.

Buyer Circumstances. In general, financially sound retailers who sell on credit may, in turn, receive slightly longer terms. Some classes of retailers regarded as selling in particularly risky areas (such as clothing) receive extended credit terms but are offered large discounts to encourage early payment.

Cash Discounts. A cash discount is a reduction in price based on payment within a specified period. The costs of not taking cash discounts often exceed the rate of interest at which the buyer can borrow, so it is important that a firm be cautious in its use of trade credit as a source of financing; it could be quite expensive. If the firm borrows and takes the cash discount, the period during which accounts payable remain on the books is reduced. The effective length of credit is thus influenced by the size of discounts offered. Credit terms typically express the amount of the cash discount and the date of its expiration, as well as the final due date. We noted earlier that one of the most frequently encountered terms is 2/10, net 30. (If payment is made within ten days of the invoice date, a 2 percent cash discount is allowed. If the cash discount is not taken, payment is due thirty days after the date of invoicing.) The cost of not taking cash discounts can be substantial, as shown here.[2]

	Cost of Credit If the Cash Discount Is Not Taken	
Credit Terms	Simple Interest (Percent)	Compound Interest with Daily Compounding (Percent)
1/10, net 20	36.87	36.70
1/10, net 30	18.43	18.35
2/10, net 20	74.49	73.81
2/10, net 30	37.24	36.89

Concept of Net Credit

Trade credit has double-edged significance for the firm. It is a source of credit for financing purchases, and it is a use of funds to the extent that the firm finances credit sales to customers. For example, if, on the average, a firm sells $3,000 worth of goods a day and has an average collection period of forty days, at any balance sheet date it will have accounts receivable of approximately $120,000.

If the same firm buys $2,000 worth of materials a day and the balance is outstanding for twenty days, accounts payable will average $40,000. The firm is thus extending net credit of $80,000—the difference between accounts receivable and accounts payable.

Large firms and well-financed firms of all sizes tend to be net suppliers of trade credit; small firms and undercapitalized firms of all sizes tend to be net users of trade credit. It is impossible to generalize about whether it is better to be a net supplier or a net user; the choice depends on the firm's circumstances and on the various costs and benefits of receiving and using trade credit.

Advantages of Trade Credit as a Source of Financing

Trade credit, a customary part of doing business in most industries, is convenient and informal. A firm that does not qualify for credit from a financial institution may receive trade credit because previous experience has familiarized the seller with the creditworthiness of the customer. The seller knows the merchandising practices of the industry and is usually in a good position

2. Simple interest uses: $(1 - d)(1 + tr/365) = 1$, where d = Cash discount, t = Number of days earlier money is paid when the cash discount is taken, and r = Effective interest rate. Solving for r, we have

$$r = \frac{d}{1-d} \cdot \frac{365}{t}.$$

The daily compounding formulation is

$$(1 - d)(1 + r/365)^t = 1.$$

Solving for r, we have

$$r = 365\,[1/(1 - d)]^{1/t} - 365.$$

to judge the capacity of the customer and the risk of selling on credit. The amount of trade credit fluctuates with the buyer's purchases, subject to any credit limits that may be operative.

Whether trade credit costs more or less than other forms of financing is a moot question. The buyer often has no alternative form of financing available, and the costs may be commensurate with the risks to the seller. But in some instances, trade credit is used simply because the buyer does not realize how expensive it is. In such circumstances, careful financial analysis may lead to the substitution of alternative forms of financing.

At the other extreme, trade credit may represent a virtual subsidy or sales promotion device offered by the seller. The authors know, for example, of cases where manufacturers quite literally supplied *all* the financing for new firms by selling on credit terms substantially longer than those of the new company. In one instance a manufacturer, eager to obtain a dealership in a particular area, made a loan to the new company to cover operating expenses during the initial phases and geared the payment of accounts payable to cash receipts. Even in such instances, however, the buying firm must be careful that it is not really paying a hidden financing cost in the form of higher product prices than could be obtained elsewhere. Extending credit involves a cost to the selling firm, and this firm may well be raising its own prices to offset the apparently free credit it extends.

Importance of Good Supplier Relations during Inflation

During the recent period of inflation and tight money, firms have raised their standards for extending trade credit to their customers. Since cleaning up accounts receivable is one way to obtain a more favorable liquidity position, suppliers are becoming more selective when extending trade credit. Therefore, it is important for a firm to earn the confidence of its suppliers. Showing good financial ratios and paying promptly are excellent ways to achieve this goal. But even if these indicators are unfavorable, a firm may still be able to obtain trade credit by offering realistic plans for improving its situation. The experience of W. T. Grant Company is illustrative. For the fiscal year ended January 31, 1975, W. T. Grant showed an operating loss of $177 million. Top management announced policy changes, replaced key personnel, and offered security through an inventory lien. Grant's suppliers continued to extend trade credit, some in amounts greater than $1 million. W. T. Grant lost another $111 million in the next six months and went bankrupt. But its experience shows that it is possible, even in adversity, to achieve continuity in the supply of trade credit by managing the credit relationship well.

Short-Term Financing by Commercial Banks

Commercial bank lending, which appears on the balance sheet as *notes payable,* is second in importance to trade credit as a source of short-term financing. Banks occupy a pivotal position in the short-term and intermediate-term money markets. Their influence is greater than it appears to be from the dollar amounts they lend, because the banks provide nonspontaneous funds. As a firm's financing needs increase, it requests additional funds from banks. If the request is denied, often the alternative is to slow down the rate of growth or to cut back operations.

Characteristics of Loans from Commercial Banks

In the following sections, the main characteristics of lending patterns of commercial banks are briefly described.

Forms of Loans. A single loan obtained from a bank by a business firm is not different in principle from a loan obtained by an individual. In fact, it is often difficult to distinguish a bank loan to a small business from a personal loan. The loan is obtained by signing a conventional promissory note. Repayment is made in a lump sum at maturity (when the note is due) or in installments throughout the life of the loan.

A *line of credit* is a formal or informal understanding between the bank and the borrower concerning the maximum loan balance the bank will allow the borrower. For example, a bank loan officer may indicate to a financial manager that the bank regards the firm as "good" for up to $80,000 for the forthcoming year. Subsequently, the manager signs a promissory note for $15,000 for 90 days—thereby "taking down" $15,000 of the total line of $80,000 in credit. This amount is credited to the firm's checking account at the bank. At maturity, the checking account is charged for the amount of the loan. Interest may be deducted in advance or may be paid at maturity. Before repayment of the $15,000, the firm may borrow additional amounts up to the total of $80,000.

A more formal procedure may be followed. To illustrate, Chrysler Corporation arranged a line of credit for over $100 million with a group of banks. The banks were formally committed to lend Chrysler the funds if they were needed. Chrysler, in turn, paid a commitment fee of approximately one-quarter of 1 percent of the unused balance of the commitment to compensate the banks for making the funds available.

Size of Customers. Banks make loans to firms of all sizes. By dollar amount, the bulk of loans from commercial banks is obtained by firms with total assets of $5 million and more. But by number of loans, firms with total assets of $50,000 and less account for about 40 percent of bank loans.

Maturity. Commercial banks concentrate on the short-term lending market. Short-term loans make up about two-thirds of bank loans by dollar amount, whereas term loans (loans with maturities longer than one year) make up only one-third.

Security. If a potential borrower is a questionable credit risk, or if the firm's financing needs exceed the amount that the loan officer of the bank considers to be prudent on an unsecured basis, some form of security is required. More than half the dollar value of bank loans is secured. (The forms of security are described later in this chapter.) In terms of the number of bank loans, two-thirds are secured through the endorsement of a third party who guarantees payment of the loan in the event the borrower defaults.

Compensating Balances. Banks typically require that a regular borrower maintain an average checking account balance equal to 15 or 20 percent of the outstanding loan. These balances, commonly called *compensating balances,* are a method of raising the effective interest rate. For example, if a firm needs $80,000 to pay off outstanding obligations but must maintain a 20 percent compensating balance, it must borrow $100,000 in order to obtain the required $80,000. If the stated interest rate is 5 percent, the effective cost is actually 6¼ percent ($5,000 divided by $80,000).[3] These *loan* compensating balances are, of course, added to any *service* compensating balances (discussed in Chapter 11) that the firm's bank may require.

Repayment of Bank Loans. Because most bank deposits are subject to withdrawal on demand, commercial banks seek to prevent firms from using bank credit for permanent financing. A bank may therefore require its borrowers to "clean up" their short-term bank loans for at least one month each year. If a firm is unable to become free of bank debt at least part of each year, it is using bank financing for permanent needs and should develop additional sources of long-term or permanent financing.

Cost of Commercial Bank Loans. Most loans from commercial banks have recently cost from 10 to 20 percent, with the effective rate depending on the characteristics of the firm and the level of interest rates in the economy. If the firm can qualify as a prime risk because of its size and financial strength, the rate of interest will be one-half to three-quarters of a percent above the rediscount rate charged by federal reserve banks to commercial banks. On the other hand, a small firm with below-average financial ratios may be required to provide collateral security and to pay an effective rate of interest of 2 to 3 points above the prime rate.

"Regular" Interest. Determination of the effective, or true, rate of interest on a loan depends on the stated rate of interest and the lender's method of charging interest. If the interest is paid at the maturity of the loan, the stated rate of interest is the effective rate of interest. For example, on a $20,000 loan for one year at 10 percent, the interest is $2,000.

3. Note, however, that the compensating balance is generally set as a minimum monthly average; if the firm maintains this average anyway, the compensating balance requirement does not entail higher effective rates.

$$\text{“Regular” loan, interest paid at maturity} = \frac{\text{Interest}}{\text{Borrowed amount}}$$
$$= \frac{\$2{,}000}{\$20{,}000} = 10\%.$$

Discounted Interest. If the bank deducts the interest in advance (discounts the loan), the effective rate of interest is increased. On the $20,000 loan for one year at 10 percent, the discount is $2,000, and the borrower obtains the use of only $18,000. The effective rate of interest is 11.1 percent (versus 10 percent on a "regular" loan):

$$\text{Discounted loan} = \frac{\text{Interest}}{\text{Borrowed amount} - \text{Interest}} = \frac{\$2{,}000}{\$18{,}000} = 11.1\%.$$

Installment Loan. If the loan is repaid in twelve monthly installments but the interest is calculated on the original balance, then the effective rate of interest is even higher. The borrower has the full amount of the money only during the first month and by the last month has already paid eleven-twelfths of the loan. Thus the borrower of $20,000 pays $2,000 for the use of about half the amount received ($20,000 or $18,000, depending on the method of charging interest), since the *average* amount outstanding during the year is only $10,000 or $9,000. If interest is paid at maturity, the approximate effective rate on an installment loan is calculated as follows:

$$\text{Interest rate on average amount of installment loan} = \frac{\$2{,}000}{\$10{,}000} = 20\%.$$

Under the discounting method, the effective cost of the installment loan is approximately 22 percent:

$$\text{Interest rate on discounted installment loan} = \frac{\$2{,}000}{\$9{,}000} = 22.2\%.$$

Here we see that interest is calculated on the *original* amount of the loan, not on the amount actually outstanding (the declining balance), and this causes the effective interest rate to be approximately double the stated rate. Interest is calculated by the installment method on most consumer loans (for example, automobile loans), but the installment method is not often used for business loans larger than about $15,000.

Choice of Banks

Banks have direct relationships with their borrowers. There is much personal association over the years, and the business problems of the borrower are frequently discussed. Thus banks often provide informal management counseling services. A potential borrower seeking such a relationship should recognize the important differences among banks considered in the following discussion.

1. Banks have different basic policies toward risk. Some are inclined to follow relatively conservative lending practices; others engage in what are

properly termed creative banking practices. The policies reflect partly the personalities of the bank officers and partly the characteristics of the bank's deposit liabilities. Thus a bank with fluctuating deposit liabilities in a static community tends to be a conservative lender. A bank whose deposits are growing with little interruption may follow liberal credit policies. A large bank with diversification over broad geographical regions or among several industries can obtain the benefit of combining and averaging risks. Thus marginal credit risks that may be unacceptable to a small bank or to a specialized unit bank can be pooled by a branch banking system to reduce the overall risks of a group of marginal accounts.

2. Some bank loan officers are active in providing counsel and in stimulating development loans to firms in their early and formative years. Certain banks even have specialized departments to make loans to firms expected to become growth firms. Bankers in such departments can provide much counseling to customers.

3. Banks differ in the extent to which they support a borrower's activities in bad times. This characteristic is referred to as the bank's degree of loyalty. Some banks put great pressure on a business to liquidate its loans when the firm's outlook becomes clouded, whereas others stand by the firm and work diligently to help it attain a more favorable condition.

4. Another characteristic by which banks differ is the degree of deposit stability. Instability arises not only from fluctuations in the level of deposits but also from the composition of deposits. Deposits can take the form of *demand deposits* (checking accounts) or *time deposits* (savings accounts, certificates of deposit, Christmas clubs). Total deposits tend to be more stable when time deposits are substantial. Differences in deposit stability go a long way toward explaining differences in the extent to which banks are willing or able to help borrowers work their way out of difficulties or even crises.

5. Banks differ greatly in the degree of loan specialization. Larger banks have separate departments specializing in different kinds of loans, such as real estate, installment, and commercial loans. Within these broad categories they may specialize by line of business, such as steel, machinery, or textiles. Smaller banks are likely to reflect the nature of the business and economic environment in which they operate. They tend to become specialists in specific lines, such as oil, construction, or agriculture. The borrower can obtain more creative cooperation and more active support at the bank that has the greatest experience and familiarity with the borrower's particular type of business. The financial manager should therefore choose a bank with care. The bank that is excellent for one firm may be unsatisfactory for another.

6. The size of a bank can be an important characteristic. Since the maximum loan a bank can make to any customer is generally limited to 10 percent

of the bank's capital accounts (capital stock plus retained earnings), it generally is not appropriate for large firms to develop borrowing relationships with small banks.

7. With the heightened competition among commercial banks and other financial institutions, the aggressiveness of banks has increased. Modern commercial banks now offer a wide range of financial and business services. Most large banks have business development departments that provide counseling to firms and serve as intermediaries on a wide variety of their requirements.

Commercial Paper

Commercial paper, which consists of promissory notes of large firms, is sold primarily to other business firms, insurance companies, pension funds, and banks. Although the amounts of commercial paper outstanding are much smaller than bank loans outstanding, this form of financing has grown rapidly in recent years.

Maturity and Cost

Maturities of commercial paper generally vary from two months to one year, with an average of about five months. The rates on prime commercial paper vary, but they are generally about half a percent below those on prime business loans. And since compensating balances are not required for commercial paper, the *effective* cost differential is still wider.[4]

Use

The use of the open market for commercial paper is restricted to a comparatively small number of concerns that are exceptionally good credit risks. Dealers prefer to handle the paper of concerns whose net worth is $10 million or more and whose annual borrowing exceeds $1 million.

Advantages and Disadvantages

The commercial paper market has some significant advantages:

1. It permits the broadest and the most advantageous distribution of paper.
2. It provides more funds at lower rates than do other methods.
3. The borrower avoids the inconvenience and expense of financing arrangements with a number of institutions, each of which requires a compensating balance.
4. Publicity and prestige accrue to the borrower as its product and paper become more widely known.
5. The commercial paper dealer frequently offers valuable advice to clients.

A basic limitation of the commercial paper market is that the size of the funds available is limited to the excess liquidity that corporations (the main sup-

4. However, this factor is offset to some extent by the fact that firms issuing commercial paper are sometimes required by commercial paper dealers to have unused bank lines of credit to back up their outstanding commercial paper, and fees must be paid on these lines.

pliers of funds) have at any particular time. Another disadvantage is that a debtor who is in temporary financial difficulty receives little help because commercial paper dealings are impersonal. Banks are much more personal and much more likely to help a good customer weather a temporary storm.[5]

Effects of Inflation

During periods of inflation and tight money, many commercial paper sellers are pushed out of the market. Ryder System, a Florida trucking company, was forced to turn to bank loans for $10 million of financing during 1974 because they were able to find buyers for only $15 million of their commercial paper. Thus, during inflationary periods, firms may be forced to seek the more expensive bank loans since they can no longer sell the cheaper commercial paper.

Bankers Acceptances during Inflation

Bankers acceptances gain popularity during inflationary periods. A bankers acceptance is a draft drawn by an individual and accepted by a bank; it orders the bank to pay a specific sum to a third party at a particular time. Bankers acceptances are an effective method of short-term financing since the drawer gains time before funds are due. The appeal of bankers acceptances, which are traded in an active secondary market, results from two basic characteristics. First, they are safe. Since they usually finance the shipment and storage of goods, the inventory can be pledged as collateral. Return to investors is usually comparable to the return on a good certificate of deposit. During periods of inflation, when investors become increasingly selective, a bankers acceptance may look safer than commercial paper or even the certificates of deposit of some banks. Second, when an acceptance is backed by readily marketable goods and a warehouse receipt has been issued, the acceptance is eligible for rediscount with the Federal Reserve.

Use of Security in Short-Term Financing

Given a choice, it is ordinarily better to borrow on an unsecured basis, since the bookkeeping costs of secured loans are often high. However, it frequently happens that a potential borrower's credit rating is not sufficiently strong to justify the loan. If the loan can be secured by some form of collateral to be

5. This point was emphasized dramatically in the aftermath of the Penn Central bankruptcy. Penn Central had a large amount of commercial paper that went into default and embarrassed corporate treasurers who had been holding the paper as part of their liquidity reserves. Immediately after the bankruptcy, the commercial paper market dried up to a large extent, and some companies that had relied heavily on this market found themselves under severe liquidity pressure as their commercial paper matured and could not be refunded. Chrysler, for example, had to seek bank loans of over $500 million because it could not sell commercial paper for a time. Without adequate bank lines, Chrysler might well have been forced into bankruptcy itself, even though it was then basically sound, because of the Penn Central panic. Incidentally, the Federal Reserve Board recognized that many other firms would be in the same position as Chrysler and so expanded bank reserves in order to enable the banking system to take up the slack caused by the withdrawal of funds from the commercial paper market.

claimed by the lender in the event of default, then the lender may extend credit to an otherwise unacceptable firm. Similarly, a firm that can borrow on an unsecured basis may elect to use security if it finds that this will induce lenders to quote a lower interest rate.

Several different kinds of collateral can be employed—marketable stocks or bonds, land or buildings, equipment, inventory, and accounts receivable. Marketable securities make excellent collateral, but few firms hold portfolios of stocks and bonds. Similarly, real property (land and buildings) and equipment are good forms of collateral, but they are generally used as security for long-term loans. The bulk of secured short-term business borrowing involves the pledge of short-term assets—accounts receivable or inventories.

In the past, state laws varied greatly with regard to the use of security in financing. By the late 1960s, however, most states had adopted the *Uniform Commercial Code* (UCC), which standardized and simplified the procedure for establishing loan security.

The heart of the UCC is the *security agreement,* a standardized document, or form, on which are stated the specific pledged assets. The assets can be items of equipment, accounts receivable, or inventories. Procedures for financing under the UCC are described in the following sections.

Financing Accounts Receivable

Accounts receivable financing involves either the assigning of receivables or the selling of receivables (factoring). Assigning, or pledging, of accounts receivable is characterized by the fact that the lender not only has a lien on the receivables but also has recourse to the borrower (seller); if the person or firm that bought the goods does not pay, the selling firm must take the loss. In other words, the risk of default on the accounts receivable pledged remains with the borrower. Also, the buyer of the goods is not ordinarily notified about the pledging of the receivables. The financial institution that lends on the security of accounts receivable is generally either a commercial bank or one of the large industrial finance companies.

Factoring, or selling accounts receivable, involves the purchase of accounts receivable by the lender without recourse to the borrower (seller). The buyer of the goods is notified of the transfer and makes payment directly to the lender. Since the factoring firm assumes the risk of default on bad accounts, it must do the credit checking. Accordingly, factors provide not only money but also a credit department for the borrower. Incidentally, the same financial institutions that make loans against pledged receivables also serve as factors. Thus, depending on the circumstances and the wishes of the borrower, a financial institution will provide either form of receivables financing.

Procedure for Pledging Accounts Receivable

The financing of accounts receivable is initiated by a legally binding agreement between the seller of the goods and the financing institution. The agreement sets forth in detail the procedure to be followed and the legal obligations of both parties. Once the working relationship has been established, the seller periodically takes a batch of invoices to the financing institution. The lender reviews the invoices and makes an appraisal of the buyers. Invoices of companies that do not meet the lender's credit standards are not accepted for pledging. The financial institution seeks to protect itself at every phase of the operation. Selection of sound invoices is the essential first step. If the buyer of the goods does not pay the invoice, the lender still has recourse against the seller of the goods. However, if many buyers default, the seller may be unable to meet the obligation to the financial institution.

Additional protection afforded the lender is that the loan is generally for less than 100 percent of the pledged receivables; for example, the lender may advance the selling firm 75 percent of the amount of the pledged receivables.

Procedure for Factoring Accounts Receivable

The procedure for factoring is somewhat different from that for pledging. Again, an agreement between the seller and the factor is made to specify legal obligations and procedural arrangements. When the seller receives an order from a buyer, a credit approval slip is written and immediately sent to the factoring company for a credit check. If the factor does not approve the sale, the seller generally refuses to fill the order. This procedure informs the seller, prior to the sale, about the buyer's creditworthiness and acceptability to the factor. If the sale is approved, shipment is made and the invoice is stamped to notify the buyer to make payment directly to the factoring company.

The factor performs three functions in carrying out the procedure outlined above: (1) credit checking, (2) lending, and (3) risk bearing. The seller can select various combinations of these functions by changing provisions in the factoring agreement. For example, a small- or medium-sized firm can avoid establishing a credit department. The factor's service may well be less costly than a department that has a capacity in excess of the firm's credit volume. Also, if the firm uses a part-time noncredit specialist to perform credit checking, the person's lack of education, training, and experience may result in excessive losses.

The seller may, for example, have the factor perform the credit-checking and risk-taking functions but not the lending function. In this situation, the following procedure is carried out on receipt of a $10,000 order. The factor checks and approves the invoices, and the goods are shipped on terms of net 30. Payment is made to the factor, who remits to the seller. But if the factor has received only $8,500 by the end of the credit period, it must still remit $10,000 to the seller (less the factor's fees, of course).

Now consider the more typical situation, where the factor performs a lending function by making payment in advance of collection. The goods are shipped, and even though payment is not due for thirty days, the factor immediately makes funds available to the seller. Suppose $10,000 worth of goods is shipped; the factoring commission for credit checking is 1½ percent of the invoice price, or $150; and the interest expense is computed at the prime rate plus two percent—for example, 15 percent annual rate on the invoice balance, or $125.[6] The seller's accounting entry is as follows:

Cash	$8,725	
Interest expense	125	
Factoring commission	150	
Reserve: Due from factor on collection of account	1,000	
Accounts receivable		$10,000

The $1,000 due from the factor on collection of the account is a 10 percent reserve established by the factor to cover disputes between sellers and buyers on damaged goods, goods returned by the buyer to the seller, and failure to make an outright sale of the goods. The amount is paid to the seller when the factor collects on the account.

Factoring is normally a continuous process rather than the single cycle described above. The seller of the goods receives orders and transmits the purchase orders to the factor for approval; on approval, the goods are shipped; the factor advances the money to the seller; the buyers pay the factor when payment is due; and the factor periodically remits any excess reserve to the seller of the goods. Once a routine is established, a continuous circular flow of goods and funds takes place among the seller, the buyers, and the factor. Thus, once the factoring agreement is in force, funds from this source are *spontaneous*.

Cost of Receivables Financing

Accounts receivable pledging and factoring services are convenient and advantageous, but they can be costly. The credit checking commission is 1 to 3 percent of the amount of invoices accepted by the factor, and the cost of money is reflected in the interest rate (somewhat above the prevailing prime rate) charged on the unpaid balance of the funds advanced by the factor. Where the risk to the factor is excessive, the factor purchases the invoices (with or without recourse) at discounts from face value.

Evaluation of Receivables Financing

It cannot be said categorically that accounts receivable financing is always either a good or a bad method of raising funds for an individual business. Among the advantages is, first, the flexibility of this source of financing. As the firm's sales expand and more financing is needed, a larger volume of invoices is generated automatically. Because the dollar amounts of invoices

6. Since the interest is for only one month, we take one-twelfth of the stated rate, 15 percent, and multiply this by the $10,000 invoice price:

$$1/12 \times 0.15 \times \$10,000 = \$125.$$

Note that the effective rate of interest is really more than 15 percent, because a discounting procedure is used and the borrower does not get the full $10,000. In many instances, however, the factoring contract calls for interest to be computed on the invoice price *less* the factoring commission and the reserve account.

vary directly with sales, the amount of readily available financing increases. Second, receivables or invoices provide security for a loan that a firm might otherwise be unable to obtain. Third, factoring provides the services of a credit department that might otherwise be available to the firm only under much more expensive conditions.

Accounts receivable financing also has disadvantages. First, when invoices are numerous and relatively small in dollar amount, the administrative costs involved may render this method of financing inconvenient and expensive Second, the firm is using a highly liquid asset as security. For a long time, accounts receivable financing was frowned on by most trade creditors; it was regarded as confession of a firm's unsound financial position. It is no longer regarded in this light, however, and many sound firms engage in receivables pledging or factoring. Still, the traditional attitude causes some trade creditors to refuse to sell on credit to a firm that is factoring or pledging its receivables, on the ground that this practice removes one of the most liquid of the firm's assets and, accordingly, weakens the position of other creditors.

Future Use of Receivables Financing

We will make a prediction at this point. In the future, accounts receivable financing will increase in relative importance. Computer technology is rapidly advancing toward the point where credit records of individuals and firms can be kept in computer memory units. Systems already have been devised whereby a retailer can insert an individual's magnetic credit card into a box and receive a signal showing whether the person's credit is good and whether a bank is willing to buy the receivable created when the store completes the sale. The cost of handling invoices will be greatly reduced from present-day costs because the new systems will be so highly automated. This will make it possible to use accounts receivable financing for very small sales, and it will reduce the cost of all receivables financing. The net result will be a marked expansion of accounts receivable financing.

Inventory Financing

A rather large volume of credit is secured by business inventories. If a firm is a relatively good credit risk, the mere existence of the inventory may be a sufficient basis for receiving an unsecured loan. If the firm is a relatively poor risk, the lending institution may insist on security, which often takes the form of a blanket lien against the inventory. Alternatively, trust receipts, field warehouse financing, or collateral certificates can be used to secure loans. These methods of using inventories as security are discussed below.

Blanket Inventory Lien

The blanket inventory lien gives the lending institution a lien against all inventories of the borrower. However, the borrower is free to sell the inventories; thus the value of the collateral can be reduced.

Trust Receipts

Because of the weaknesses of the blanket lien for inventory financing, another kind of security is often used—the trust receipt. A trust receipt is an instrument acknowledging that the borrower holds the goods in trust for the lender. On receiving funds from the lender, the borrowing firm conveys a trust receipt for the goods. The goods can be stored in a public warehouse or held on the borrower's premises. The trust receipt provides that the goods are held in trust for the lender or are segregated on the borrower's premises on behalf of the lender and that proceeds from the sale of such goods are transmitted to the lender at the end of each day. Automobile dealer financing is the best example of trust receipt financing.

One defect of this form of financing is the requirement that a trust receipt must be issued for specific goods. For example, if the security is bags of coffee beans, the trust receipts must indicate the bags by number. In order to validate its trust receipts, the lending institution must send someone to the borrower's premises to see that the bag numbers are correctly listed. Furthermore, complex legal requirements for trust receipts require the attention of a bank officer. Problems are compounded if borrowers are widely separated geographically from the lender. To offset these inconveniences, warehousing is coming into wide use as a method of securing loans with inventory.

Field Warehouse Financing

Like trust receipts, field warehouse financing uses inventory as security. A public warehouse represents an independent third party engaged in the business of storing goods. Sometimes the warehouse is not practical because of the bulkiness of goods and the expense of transporting them to and from the borrower's premises. Field warehouse financing represents an economical method of inventory financing in which the "warehouse" is established on the borrower's premises. To provide inventory supervision, the lending institution employs a third party in the arrangement, the field warehousing company. This company acts as the control (or supervisory) agent for the lending institution.

Field warehousing is illustrated by a simple example. Suppose a potential borrower has stacked iron in an open yard on its premises. A field warehouse can be established if, say, a field warehousing concern places a temporary fence around the iron and erects a sign stating: "This is a field warehouse supervised and conducted by the Smith Field Warehousing Corporation.

The example illustrates the two elements in the establishment of a warehouse: (1) public notification of the field warehouse arrangement and (2) supervision of the warehouse by a custodian of the field warehouse concern. When the field warehousing operation is relatively small, the second condition is sometimes violated by hiring an employee of the borrower to supervise the inventory. This practice is viewed as undesirable by the lending institution because there is no control over the collateral by a person independent of the borrowing concern.[7]

The field warehouse financing operation is described best by a specific illustration. Assume that a tomato canner is interested in financing operations by bank borrowing. The canner has funds sufficient to finance 15 to 20 percent of operations during the canning season. These funds are adequate to purchase and process an initial batch of tomatoes. As the cans are put into boxes and rolled into the storerooms, the canner needs additional funds for both raw materials and labor.

Because of the canner's poor credit rating, the bank decides that a field warehousing operation is necessary to secure its loans. The field warehouse is established, and the custodian notifies the lending institution of the description, by number, of the boxes of canned tomatoes in storage and under his control. Thereupon the lending institution establishes for the canner a deposit on which it can draw. From this point on, the bank finances the operations. The canner needs only enough cash to initiate the cycle. The farmers bring more tomatoes; the canner processes them; the cans are boxed and the boxes put into the field warehouse; field warehouse receipts are drawn up and sent to the bank; the bank establishes further deposits for the canner on the basis of the receipts; and the canner can draw on the deposits to continue the cycle.

Of course, the canner's ultimate objective is to sell the canned tomatoes. As the canner receives purchase orders, it transmits them to the bank, and the bank directs the custodian to release the inventories. It is agreed that, as remittances are received by the canner, they will be turned over to the bank. These remittances pay off the loans made by the bank.

Typically, a seasonal pattern exists. At the beginning of the tomato harvesting and canning season, the canner's cash needs and loan requirements begin to rise, and they reach a maximum by the end of the canning season. It is hoped that, just before the new canning season begins, the canner has sold a sufficient volume to have paid off the loan completely. If for some reason the canner has had a bad year, the bank may carry the company over another year to enable it to sell off its inventory.

Acceptable Products. In addition to canned foods, which account for about 17 percent of all field warehouse loans, many other product inventories provide a basis for field warehouse financing. Some of these are miscellaneous gro-

7. This absence of independent control was the main cause of the breakdown that resulted in the huge losses connected with loans to the Allied Crude Vegetable Oil Company headed by Anthony (Tino) DeAngelis. American Express Field Warehousing Company hired men from Allied's staff as custodians. Their dishonesty was not discovered because of another breakdown—the fact that the American Express touring inspector did not actually take a physical inventory of the warehouses. As a consequence, the swindle was not discovered until losses running into the hundreds of millions of dollars had been suffered. See Norman C. Miller, *The Great Salad Oil Swindle* (Baltimore, Md.: Penguin Books, 1965), pp. 72–77.

ceries, which represent about 13 percent; lumber products, about 10 percent; and coal and coke, about 6 percent.

These products are relatively nonperishable and are sold in well developed, organized markets. Nonperishability protects the lender who has to take over the security. For this reason a bank will not make a field warehousing loan on perishables such as fresh fish. However, frozen fish, which can be stored for a long time, can be field warehoused. An organized market also aids the lender in disposing of inventory that it takes over. Banks are not interested in going into the canning or the fish business. They want to be able to dispose of an inventory quickly and with the expenditure of a minimum amount of their own time.

Cost of Financing. The fixed costs of a field warehousing arrangement are relatively high; such financing is therefore not suitable for a very small firm. If a field warehouse company sets up the warehouse itself, it typically sets a minimum fixed charge, plus about 1 or 2 percent of the amount of credit extended to the borrower. Furthermore, the financing institution charges interest at a rate somewhat above the prevailing prime rate. The minimum size of an efficient warehousing operation requires an inventory of about $100,000.

Appraisal. The use of field warehouse financing as a source of funds for business firms has many advantages. First, the amount of funds available is flexible because the financing is tied to the growth of inventories, which in turn is related directly to financing needs. Second, the arrangement increases the acceptability of inventories as loan collateral. Some inventories are not accepted by a bank as a security without a field warehousing arrangement. Third, the necessity for inventory control, safekeeping, and the use of specialists in warehousing has resulted in improved warehouse practices. The services of the field warehouse companies have often saved money for the firm, in spite of the financing costs mentioned above. The field warehouse company may suggest inventory practices that reduce both the number of people the firm has to employ and inventory damage and loss as well.

The major disadvantage of a field warehousing operation is the fixed cost element, which reduces the feasibility of this form of financing for small firms.

Collateral Certificates

A collateral certificate guarantees the existence of the amount of inventory pledged as loan collateral. It is a statement issued periodically to the lender by a third party, who certifies that the inventory exists and that it will be available if needed.

This method of bank financing is becoming increasingly popular, primarily because of its flexibility. First, there is no need for physical segregation or possession of inventories. Therefore, collateral certificates can even be used to cover work-in-process inventories, facilitating more freedom in the movement of goods. Second, the collateral certificate can provide for a receivables financing plan, allowing financing to continue smoothly as inventories are converted into receivables. Third, the certificate issuer usually provides a number of services to simplify loan administration for both the borrower and the lender.

Summary

Short-term credit is debt originally scheduled for repayment within one year. The three major sources of short-term credit are trade credit among firms, loans from commercial banks, and commercial paper.

Trade credit (represented by accounts payable) is the largest single category of short-term credit; it is especially important for smaller firms. Trade credit is a *spontaneous source of financing* in that it arises from ordinary business transactions; as sales increase, so does the supply of financing from accounts payable.

Bank credit occupies a pivotal position in the short-term money market. Banks provide the marginal credit that allows firms to expand more rapidly than is possible through retained earnings and trade credit. A denial of bank credit often means that a firm must slow its rate of growth.

Bank interest rates are quoted in three ways—regular compound interest, discount interest, and installment interest. Regular interest needs no adjustment; it is correct as stated. Discount interest requires a small upward adjustment to make it comparable to regular compound interest rates. Installment interest rates require a large adjustment, and frequently the true interest rate is double the quoted rate for an installment loan.

Bank loans are personal in the sense that the financial manager meets with the banker, discusses the terms of the loan, and reaches an agreement that requires direct and personal negotiation. Commercial paper, however, although it is physically similar to a bank loan, is sold in a broad, impersonal market. A California firm might, for example, sell commercial paper to a manufacturer in the Midwest.

Only the very strongest firms are able to use the commercial paper markets. The nature of these markets is such that the firm selling the paper must have a reputation so good that buyers of the paper are willing to buy it without any sort of credit check. Interest rates in the commercial paper market are the lowest available to business borrowers.

The most common forms of collateral used for short-term credit are inventories and accounts receivable. Accounts receivable financing can be done either by pledging the receivables or by selling them outright (often called factoring). When the receivables are pledged, the borrower retains the risk that the person or firm owing the receivables will not pay; in factoring, this risk is typically passed on to the lender. Because factors take the risk of default, they investigate the purchaser's credit; therefore, factors can perform three functions: lending, risk bearing, and credit checking. When receivables are pledged, the lender typically performs only the first of these functions.

Loans secured by inventories are not satisfactory under many circumstances. For certain kinds of inventory, however, the technique known as field warehousing is used to provide adequate security to the lender. Under a field warehousing arrangement, the inventory is physically controlled by a warehouse company, which releases the inventory only on order from the lending institution. Canned goods, lumber, steel, coal, and other standardized products are goods usually covered in field warehouse arrangements.

Questions

12.1 It is inevitable that firms will obtain a certain amount of their financing in the form of trade credit, which is (to some extent) a free source of funds. What are some other reasons for firms to use trade credit?

12.2 Discuss the statement: Commercial paper interest rates are always lower than bank loan rates to a given borrower. Nevertheless, many firms perfectly capable of selling commercial paper employ higher-cost bank credit. Indicate (a) why commercial paper rates are lower than bank rates and (b) why firms might use bank credit in spite of its higher cost.

12.3 Discuss the statement: Trade credit has an explicit interest rate cost if discounts are available but not taken. There are also some intangible costs associated with the failure to take discounts.

12.4 A large manufacturing firm that had been selling its products on a 3/10, net 30 basis changed its credit terms to 1/20, net 90. What changes might be anticipated on the balance sheets of the manufacturer and of its customers?

12.5 The availability of bank credit is more important to small firms than to large ones. Why?

12.6 What factors should a firm consider in selecting its primary bank? Would it be feasible for a firm to have a primary deposit bank (the bank where most of its funds are deposited) and a different primary loan bank (the bank where it does most of its borrowing)?

12.7 Indicate whether each of the following changes will raise or lower the cost of a firm's accounts receivable financing, and explain why this occurs:

a. The firm eases up on its credit standards in order to increase sales.
b. The firm institutes a policy of refusing to make credit sales if the amount of the purchase (invoice) is below $100. Previously, about 40 percent of all invoices were below $100.
c. The firm agrees to give recourse to the finance company for all defaults.
d. A firm that already has a recourse arrangement is merged into a larger, stronger company.
e. A firm without a recourse arrangement changes its terms of trade from net 30 to net 90.

12.8 Would a firm that manufactures specialized machinery for a few large customers be more likely to use a form of inventory financing or a form of accounts receivable financing? Why?

12.9 Discuss the statement: A firm that factors its accounts receivable will look better in a ratio analysis than one that discounts its receivables.

12.10 Why would it not be practical for a typical retailer to use field warehouse financing?

12.11 Describe an industry that might be expected to use each of the following forms of credit, and explain your reasons for choosing each one:
a. Field warehouse financing
b. Factoring
c. Accounts receivable discounting
d. Trust receipts
e. None of these

Problems

12.1 What is the equivalent annual interest rate that would be lost if a firm failed to take the cash discount under each of the following terms?
a. 1/15, net 30
b. 2/10, net 60
c. 3/10, net 60
d. 2/10, net 40
e. 1/10, net 40

12.2 Wilber Corp. is negotiating with the Citizen's Bank for a $500,000 one-year loan. Citizen has offered Wilber the following three alternatives:
1. A 15 percent interest rate, no compensating balance, and interest due at the end of the year.
2. A 13 percent interest rate, a 20 percent compensating balance, and interest due at the end of the year.
3. An 11 percent interest rate, a 15 percent compensating balance, and the loan discounted.

If Wilber wishes to minimize the effective interest rate, which alternative will it choose?

12.3 Mark Industries is having difficulty paying its bills and is considering foregoing its trade discounts on $300,000 of accounts payable. As an alternative, Mark can obtain a sixty-day note with a 14 percent annual interest rate. The note will be discounted, and the trade credit terms are 2/10, net 60.
a. Which alternative has the lower effective cost?
b. If Mark does not take its trade discounts, what conclusions may outsiders draw?

12.4 Best Catsup Company is considering the following two alternatives for financing next year's canning operations:
1. Establishing a $1 million line of credit with a 12 percent annual interest rate on the used portion and a 1 percent commitment fee rate on the unused portion. A $150,000 compensating balance will be required at all times on the entire $1 million line.
2. Using field warehousing to finance $850,000 of inventory. Financing charges will be a flat fee of $500, plus 2 percent of the maximum amount of credit extended, plus a 10 percent annual interest rate on all outstanding credit.

Best has $150,000 of funds available for inventory financing, so financing requirements will be equal to the expected inventory level minus $150,000.

All financing is done on the first of the month and is sufficient to cover the value of the expected inventory at the end of the month. Expected inventory levels are as follows:

Month	Amount	Month	Amount
July 19X0	$ 150,000	January 19X1	$600,000
August	400,000	February	450,000
September	600,000	March	350,000
October	800,000	April	225,000
November	1,000,000	May	100,000
December	750,000	June	0

Which financing plan has the lowest cost? (Hints: Under the bank loan plan, borrowings in July are $150,000 and in December $750,000; under the field warehousing plan, July borrowings are zero and December borrowings are $600,000.)

12.5 The balance sheet of the Atlantic Credit Corporation is shown here.

a. Calculate commercial paper as a percentage of short-term financing, as a percentage of total-debt financing, and as a percentage of all financing.

b. Why do finance companies such as Atlantic Credit use commercial paper to such a great extent?

c. Why do they use both bank loans and commercial paper?

Atlantic Credit Corporation Balance Sheet (in Millions of Dollars)

Assets		Liabilities	
Cash	$ 75	Bank loans	$ 250
Net receivables	2,400	Commercial paper	825
Marketable securities	150	Other current	375
Repossessions	5	Total due within a year	$1,450
Total current assets	$2,630	Long-term debt	1,000
Other assets	170	Total shareholders' equity	350
Total assets	$2,800	Total claims	$2,800

12.6 The Shelby Saw Corporation had sales of $4 million last year and earned a 3 percent after-tax return on total assets. Although its terms of purchase are thirty days, accounts payable represent sixty days' purchases. The company is seeking to increase bank borrowings in order to become current in meeting its trade obligations (that is, reduce them to thirty days). The company's balance sheet follows.

a. How much bank financing is needed to eliminate past-due accounts payable?

b. As a bank loan officer, would you make the loan? Explain.

Shelby Saw Corporation
Balance Sheet

Assets		Liabilities	
Cash	$ 100,000	Accounts payable	$ 600,000
Accounts receivable	300,000	Bank loans	500,000
Inventory	1,400,000	Accruals	400,000
Current assets	$1,800,000	Current liabilities	$1,500,000
Land and buildings	700,000	Mortgage or real estate	600,000
Equipment	500,000	Net worth	900,000
Total assets	$3,000,000	Claims on assets	$3,000,000

12.7 Fair Deal Co. estimates that the seasonal nature of its business will create the need for an additional $200,000 of cash for the month of November. Fair Deal has three options available to provide the needed funds. It can:

1. Establish a one-year line of credit for $200,000 with a commercial bank. The commitment fee will be 0.5 percent, and the interest charge on the used funds will be 15 percent per annum. The minimum time the funds can be used is thirty days.
2. Forego the November trade discount of 2/10, net 40 on $200,000 of accounts payable.
3. Issue $200,000 of sixty-day commercial paper at a 14 percent per annum interest rate. Since the funds are required for only thirty days, the excess funds ($200,000) can be invested in 13 percent per annum marketable securities for the month of December. The total transaction fee on purchasing and selling the marketable securities is 0.5 percent of the fair value.

Which financing arrangement results in the lowest cost?

12.8 Collins Manufacturing needs an additional $100,000. The financial manager is considering two methods of obtaining this money: a loan from a commercial bank or a factoring arrangement. The bank charges 12 percent per annum interest, discount basis. It also requires a 15 percent compensating balance. The factor is willing to purchase Collins's accounts receivable and to advance the invoice amount less a 3 percent factoring commission on the invoices purchased each month. (All sales are on thirty-day terms.) A 10 percent annual interest rate will be charged on the total invoice price and deducted in advance. Also, under the factoring agreement, Collins can eliminate its credit department and reduce credit expenses by $2,000 per month. Bad debt losses of 10 percent on the factored amount can also be avoided.

a. How much should the bank loan be in order to net $100,000? How much accounts receivable should be factored to net $100,000?
b. What are the effective interest rates and the annual total dollar costs, including credit department expenses and bad debt losses, associated with each financing arrangement?
c. Discuss some considerations other than cost that may influence management's choice between factoring and a commercial bank loan.

12.9 The Shandow Insulation Company has been growing rapidly, but because of insufficient working capital, it has now become slow in paying bills. Of its total accounts payable, $96,000 is overdue. This threatens Shandow's relationship with its main supplier of powders used in the manufacture of various kinds of insulation materials for aircraft and missiles. Over 75 percent of its sales are to six large, financially strong defense contractors. The company's balance sheet, sales, and net profit for the past year are shown below:

Shandow Corporation Balance Sheet

Cash	$ 28,800	Trade credit[a]	$240,000
Receivables	320,000	Bank loans	192,000
Inventories		Accruals[a]	48,000
Raw material	38,400		
Work in process	192,000	Total current debt	$480,000
Finished goods	57,600	Mortgages on equipment	288,000
		Capital stock	96,000
Total current assets	636,800	Retained earnings	96,000
Equipment	323,200		
Total assets	$ 960,000	Total liabilities and net worth	$960,000
Sales	$1,920,000		
Profit after taxes	96,000		

[a]Increases spontaneously with sales increases.

Shandow is considering two altèrnative methods to solve its payments problem: factoring and receivables financing.
Additional information:

Receivables turn over six times a year. (Sales/receivables = 6.)

All sales are made on credit.

The factor requires a 15 percent reserve for returns on disputed items.

The factor also requires a 1.5 percent commission on average receivables outstanding, payable at the time the receivable is purchased, to cover the costs of credit checking.

There is an interest charge by the factor at the prime rate (12 percent) plus 3 percent based on receivables *less* any reserve requirements and commissions. This payment is made at the beginning of the period and is deducted from the advance.

Receivables financing would involve the same costs as factoring except the factoring commission and a 20 percent reserve rather than 15 percent under factoring.

a. When sales are $1,920,000, on average, what is the total amount of receivables outstanding?
b. What is the average duration of advances, on the basis of 360 days a year?
c. How much cash does the firm actually receive under factoring as compared with receivables financing?
d. What is the total annual dollar cost of financing under factoring as compared with receivables financing?

e. What is the annual effective percentage financing cost paid on the money received under factoring as compared with receivables financing?
f. Which method of financing should Shandow utilize?

12.10 The Morton Plastics Company manufactures plastic toys. It buys raw materials, manufactures the toys in the spring and summer, and ships them to a large number of department stores and toy stores by late summer or early fall. The company factors its receivables. If it did not, Morton's balance sheet would have appeared as follows:

Morton Company
Pro Forma Balance Sheet as of October 31, 19X0

Cash	$ 40,000	Accounts payable	$1,200,000
Receivables	1,200,000	Notes payable	800,000
Inventory	800,000	Accruals	80,000
Total current assets	$2,040,000	Total current debt	$2,080,000
		Mortgages	200,000
		Common stock	400,000
Fixed assets	800,000	Retained earnings	160,000
Total assets	$2,840,000	Total claims	$2,840,000

Morton provides advanced dating on its sales; thus its receivables are not due for payment until January 31, 19X1. Also, the company would have been overdue on some $800,000 of its accounts payable if the above situation actually existed.

Morton has an agreement with a finance company to factor the receivables for the period October 31 through January 31 of each selling season. The factoring company charges a flat commission of 1.5 percent, plus interest at 3 points over the prime rate (15 percent) on the outstanding balance. It deducts a reserve of 15 percent for returned and damaged materials. Interest and commission are paid in advance. No interest is charged on the reserved funds or on the commission.

a. Show the balance sheet of Morton on October 31, 19X0, giving effect to the purchase of all the receivables by the factoring company and the use of the funds to pay accounts payable.
b. If the $1.2 million is the average level of outstanding receivables and if they turn over four times a year (hence the commission is paid four times a year), what are the total dollar costs of financing and the effective annual interest rate?
c. What are the advantages to Morton Plastics of using factoring, as opposed to discounting its receivables?

Selected References

Abraham, Alfred B. "Factoring: The New Frontier for Commercial Banks." *Journal of Commercial Bank Lending* 53 (April 1971), pp. 32–43.

Baxter, Nevins D. *The Commercial Paper Market.* Princeton, N.J.: Princeton University Press, 1964.

Baxter, Nevins D., and Shapiro, Harold T. "Compensating Balance Requirements: The Results of a Survey." *Journal of Finance* 19 (September 1964), pp. 483–496.

Brosky, John J. *The Implicit Cost of Trade Credit and Theory of Optimal Terms of Sale.* New York: Credit Research Foundation, 1969.

Crane, Dwight B., and White, William L. "Who Benefits from a Floating Prime Rate?" *Harvard Business Review* 50 (January–February 1972), pp. 121–129.

Denonn, Lester E. "The Security Agreement." *Journal of Commercial Bank Lending* 50 (February 1968), pp. 32–40.

Hayes, Douglas A. *Bank Lending Policies: Domestic and International.* Ann Arbor, Mich.: University of Michigan Press, 1971.

Nadler, Paul S. "Compensating Balances and the Prime at Twilight." *Harvard Business Review* 50 (January–February 1972), pp. 112–120.

Robinson, Roland I. *The Management of Bank Funds,* Parts III and IV. New York: McGraw-Hill, 1962.

Schadrack, Frederick C., Jr. "Demand and Supply in the Commercial Paper Market." *Journal of Finance* 25 (September 1970), pp. 837–852.

Shay, Robert P., and Greer, Carl C. "Banks Move into High-Risk Commercial Financing." *Harvard Business Review* 46 (November–December 1968), pp. 149–153, 156–161.

Stone, Bernell K. "The Cost of Bank Loans." *Journal of Financial and Quantitative Analysis* 7 (December 1972), pp. 2077–2086.

Part Four
Investment Decisions

In Part 3, we dealt with the top portion of the firm's balance sheet—the current assets and liabilities. Now, in Part 4, we move down to the lower left side of the statement, focusing on the decisions involved in fixed asset acquisitions.

Capital budgeting—the planning of expenditures whose returns will extend beyond one year—is covered in Chapter 13. Uncertainty about both the costs and the returns associated with a project is introduced in Chapter 14. Since projects differ in riskiness, that chapter develops methods of analysis which can be used to incorporate risk into the decision-making process.

13
Capital Budgeting Techniques

Capital budgeting involves the entire process of planning expenditures whose returns are expected to extend beyond one year. The choice of one year is arbitrary, of course, but it is a convenient cutoff point for distinguishing between kinds of expenditures. Obvious examples of capital outlays are expenditures for land, buildings, and equipment, and for permanent additions to working capital associated with plant expansion. An advertising or promotion campaign or a research and development program is also likely to have an impact beyond one year, so they too can be classified as capital budgeting expenditures.

Capital budgeting is important for the future well-being of the firm; it is also a complex, conceptually difficult topic. As we shall see later in this chapter, the optimum capital budget—the level of investment that maximizes the present value of the firm—is simultaneously determined by the interaction of supply and demand forces under conditions of uncertainty. Supply forces refer to the supply of capital to the firm, or its cost of capital schedule. Demand forces relate to the investment opportunities open to the firm, as measured by the stream of revenues that will result from an investment decision. Uncertainty enters the decision because it is impossible to know exactly either the cost of capital or the stream of revenues that will be derived from a project.

To facilitate an exposition of the investment decision process, we have broken the topic down into its major components. In this chapter, we consider the capital budgeting process and the techniques generally employed by reasonably sophisticated business firms. Here our focus is on the time factor, and the compound interest concepts covered in the preceding chapters are used extensively. Uncertainty is explicitly and formally considered in Chapter 14, and the cost of capital concept is developed and related to capital budgeting in Chapters 15 through 17.

Significance of Capital Budgeting

A number of factors combine to make capital budgeting perhaps the most important decision with which financial management is involved. Further, all departments of a firm—production, marketing, and so on—are vitally affected by the capital budgeting decisions; so all executives, no matter what their primary responsibility, must be aware of how capital budgeting decisions are made. These points are discussed in this section.

Long-Term Effects

First and foremost, the fact that the results continue over an extended period means that the decision maker loses some flexibility. The firm must make a commitment into the future. For example, the purchase of an asset with an economic life of ten years requires a long period of waiting before the final results of the action can be known.

Asset expansion is fundamentally related to expected future sales. A decision to buy or to construct a fixed asset that is expected to last five years involves an implicit five-year sales forecast. Indeed, the economic life of a purchased asset represents an implicit forecast for the duration of the economic life of the asset. Hence, failure to forecast accurately will result in overinvestment or underinvestment in fixed assets.

An erroneous forecast of asset requirements can result in serious consequences. If the firm has invested too much in assets, it will incur unnecessarily heavy expenses. If it has not spent enough on fixed assets, two serious problems may arise. First, the firm's equipment may not be sufficiently modern to enable it to produce competitively. Second, if it has inadequate capacity, it may lose a portion of its share of the market to rival firms. To regain lost customers typically requires heavy selling expenses, price reduction, product improvements, and so forth.

Timing the Availability of Capital Assets

Another problem is to phase properly the availability of capital assets in order to have them come "on stream" at the correct time. For example, the executive vice-president of a decorative tile company gave the authors an illustration of the importance of capital budgeting. His firm tried to operate near capacity most of the time. For about four years there had been intermittent spurts in the demand for its product; when these spurts occurred, the firm had to turn away orders. After a sharp increase in demand, the firm would add capacity by renting an additional building, then purchasing and installing the appropriate equipment. It would take six to eight months to have the additional capacity ready. At this point the company frequently found that there was no demand for its increased output—other firms had already expanded their operations and had taken an increased share of the market, with the result that demand for this firm had leveled off. If the firm had properly forecast demand and had planned its increase in capacity six months or one year in advance, it would have been able to maintain its market—indeed, to obtain a larger share of the market.

Good capital budgeting will improve the timing of asset acquisitions and the quality of assets purchased. This result follows from the nature of capital goods and their producers. Capital goods are not ordered by firms until they see that sales are beginning to press on capacity. Such occasions occur simultaneously for many firms. When the heavy orders come in, the producers of capital goods go from a situation of idle capacity to one where they cannot meet all the orders that have been placed. Consequently, large backlogs accumulate. Since the production of capital goods involves a relatively long work-in-process period, a year or more of waiting may be involved before the additional modern capital goods are available. Furthermore, the quality of the capital goods, produced on rush order, may deteriorate. These factors have obvious implications for purchasing agents and plant managers.

Raising Funds

Another reason for the importance of capital budgeting is that asset expansion typically involves substantial expenditures. Before a firm spends a large amount of money, it must make the proper plans—large amounts of funds are not available automatically. A firm contemplating a major capital expenditure program may need to arrange its financing several years in advance to be sure of having the funds required for the expansion.

An Overview of Capital Budgeting

Capital budgeting is, in essence, an application of a classic proposition from the economic theory of the firm: Namely, a firm should operate at the point where its marginal revenue is just equal to its marginal cost. When this rule is applied to the capital budgeting decision, marginal revenue is taken to be the percentage rate of return on investments, while marginal cost is the firm's marginal cost of capital.

A simplified version of the concept is depicted in Figure 13.1a. Here the horizontal axis measures the dollars of investment during a year, while the vertical axis shows both the percentage cost of capital and the rate of return on projects. The projects are denoted by boxes—Project A, for example, calls for an outlay of $3 million and promises a 17 percent rate of return; Project B requires $1 million and yields about 16 percent; and so on. The last investment, Project G, simply involves buying 4 percent government bonds, which may be purchased in unlimited quantities. In Figure 13.1b the concept is generalized to show smoothed investment opportunity schedules *(IRR),* and three alternative schedules are presented.[1]

The curve *MCC* designates the marginal cost of capital, or the cost of each additional dollar acquired for purposes of making capital expenditures. As it

1. The investment opportunity schedules measure the rate of return on each project. The rate of return on a project is generally called the *internal rate of return (IRR).* This is why we label the investment opportunity schedules *IRR.* The process of calculating the *IRR* is explained later in this chapter.

Figure 13.1

Illustrative Capital Budgeting Decision Process

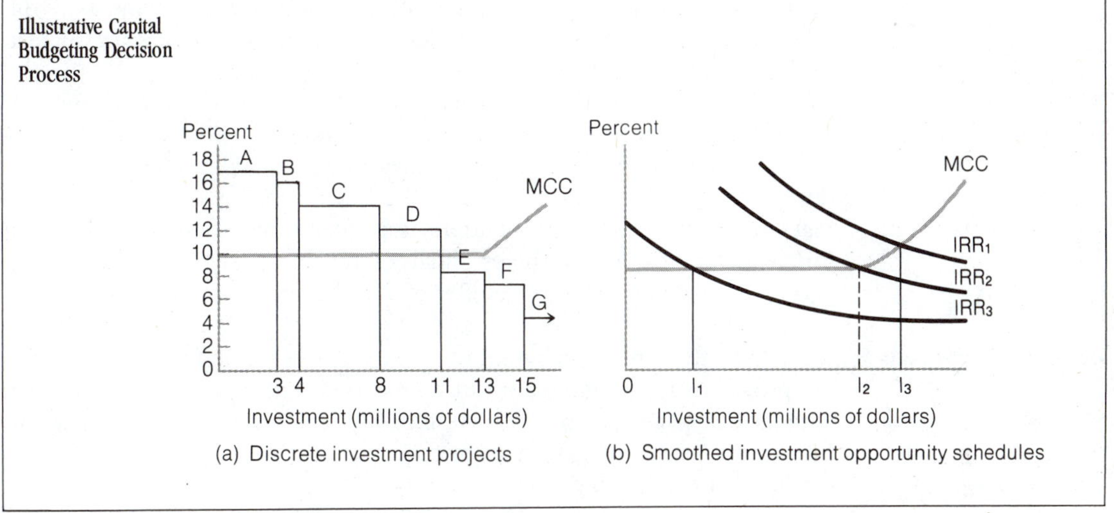

is drawn in Figure 13.1a, the marginal cost of capital is constant at 10 percent until the firm has raised \$13 million, after which the marginal cost of capital curve turns up.[2] To maximize profits, the firm should accept Projects A through D, obtaining and investing \$11 million, and reject E, F, and G.

Notice that three alternative investment opportunity schedules are shown in Figure 13.1b. IRR_1 designates relatively many good investment opportunities, while IRR_3 designates relatively few good projects. The three different curves could be interpreted as applying either to three different firms or to one firm at three different times. As long as the *IRR* curve cuts the *MCC* curve to the left of I_2—for example, at I_1—the marginal cost of capital is constant. To the right of I_2—for example, at I_3—the cost of capital is rising. Therefore, if investment opportunities are such that the *IRR* curve cuts the *MCC* curve to the right of I_2, the *actual* marginal cost of capital (a single point) varies, depending on the *IRR* curve. In this chapter we generally *assume* that the *IRR* curve cuts the *MCC* curve to the left of I_2. This permits us to assume that the cost of capital is constant. The assumption is relaxed in Chapter 16, where we show how the *MCC* varies with the amount of funds raised during a given year.

At the applied level, the capital budgeting process is much more complex than the preceding example suggests. Projects do not just appear; a continuing stream of good investment opportunities results from hard thinking, careful planning, and, often, large outlays for research and development. Moreover, some very difficult measurement problems are involved: The sales and

2. The reasons for assuming this particular shape for the marginal cost of capital curve are explained in Chapter 16.

costs associated with particular projects must be estimated, frequently for many years into the future, in the face of great uncertainty. Finally, some difficult conceptual and empirical problems arise over the methods of calculating rates of return and the cost of capital.

Business is required to take action, however, even in the face of the kinds of problems described; this requirement has led to the development of procedures that assist in making optimal investment decisions. One such procedure, forecasting, was discussed in Chapter 8; uncertainty is discussed in formal terms in the next chapter; and the important subject of the cost of capital is deferred to Chapter 16. The essentials of the other elements of capital budgeting are taken up in the remainder of this chapter.

Investment Proposals

Aside from the actual generation of ideas, the first step in the capital budgeting process is to assemble a list of the proposed new investments, together with the data necessary to appraise them. Although practices vary from firm to firm, proposals dealing with asset acquisitions are frequently grouped according to the following four categories:

1. Replacements.
2. Expansion: additional capacity in existing product lines.
3. Expansion: new product lines.
4. Other (for example, pollution control equipment).

These groupings are somewhat arbitrary, and it is frequently difficult to decide the appropriate category for a particular investment. In spite of such problems, the scheme is used quite widely and, as we shall see, with good reason.

Ordinarily, replacement decisions are the simplest to make. Assets wear out or become obsolete, and they must be replaced if production efficiency is to be maintained. The firm has a very good idea of the cost savings to be obtained by replacing an old asset, and it knows the consequences of nonreplacement. All in all, the outcomes of most replacement decisions can be predicted with a high degree of confidence.

Examples of the second investment classification are proposals for adding more machines of the type already in use or the opening of new branches in a city-wide chain of food stores. Expansion investments are frequently incorporated in replacement decisions. To illustrate, an old, efficient machine may be replaced by a larger and more efficient one.

A degree of uncertainty—sometimes extremely high—is clearly involved in expansion, but the firm at least has the advantage of examining past production and sales experience with similar machines or stores. When it considers an investment of the third kind, expansion into new product lines, little, if any, experience is available on which to base decisions. To illustrate, when Union Carbide decided to develop the laser for commercial application, it had very little idea of either the development costs or the specific applications to which lasers could be put. Under such circumstances, any estimates must at best be treated as very crude approximations.

The "other" category is a catchall and includes intangibles; an example is a proposal to boost employee morale and productivity by installing a music system. Mandatory pollution control devices, which must be undertaken even though they produce no revenues, are another example of the "other" category. Major strategic decisions such as plans for overseas expansion, or mergers, might also be included here, but more frequently they are treated separately from the regular capital budget.

Administrative Aspects

Other important aspects of capital budgeting involve administrative matters. Approvals are typically required at higher levels within the organization as we move away from replacement decisions and as the sums involved increase. One of the most important functions of the board of directors is to approve the major outlays in a capital budgeting program. Such decisions are crucial for the future well-being of the firm.

The planning horizon for capital budgeting programs varies with the nature of the industry. When sales can be forecast with a high degree of reliability for ten to twenty years, the planning period is likely to be correspondingly long; electric utilities are an example of such an industry. Also, when the product-technology developments in the industry require an eight-to-ten-year cycle to develop a new major product, as in certain segments of the aerospace industry, a correspondingly long planning period is necessary.

After a capital budget has been adopted, payments must be scheduled. Characteristically, the finance department is responsible for scheduling payments and for acquiring funds to meet payment schedule requirements. The finance department is also primarily responsible for cooperating with the members of operating divisions to compile systematic records on the uses of funds and the uses of equipment purchased in capital budgeting programs. Effective capital budgeting programs require such information as the basis for periodic review and evaluation of capital expenditure decisions—the feedback and control phase of capital budgeting, often called the *post audit review.*

The foregoing represents a brief overview of the administrative aspects of capital budgeting; the analytical problems involved are considered next.

Choosing among Alternative Proposals

In most firms there are more proposals for projects than the firm is able or willing to finance. Some proposals are good, others are poor, and methods must be developed for distinguishing between the good and the poor. Essentially, the end product is a ranking of the proposals and a cutoff point for determining how far down the ranked list to go.

In part, proposals are eliminated because they are *mutually exclusive.* Mutually exclusive proposals are alternative methods of doing the same job. If one piece of equipment is chosen to do the job, the others will not be required. Thus, if there is a need to improve the materials handling system in a chemical plant, the job may be done either by conveyer belts or by fork-lift trucks. The selection of one method of doing the job makes it unnecessary to use the others: They are mutually exclusive items.

Independent items are pieces of capital equipment that are being considered for different kinds of projects or tasks that need to be accomplished. For example, in addition to the materials handling system, the chemical firm may need equipment to package the end product. The work would require a packaging machine, and the purchase of equipment for this purpose would be independent of the equipment purchased for materials handling.

To distinguish among the many items that compete for the allocation of the firm's capital funds, a ranking procedure must be developed. This procedure requires calculating the estimated benefits from the use of equipment and then translating the estimated benefits into a measure of the advantage of the purchase of the equipment. Thus, an estimate of benefits is required, and a method for converting the benefits into a ranking measure must be developed.

Measures of Cash Flows

It is especially important to use the correct concept of expected returns representing the future net cash flows. An illustration will help clarify some important relationships. A firm has the income statement shown in Table 13.1.

Expected net cash flows or expected future returns are equal to net operating income before deduction of payments to the financing sources—but after the deduction of applicable taxes and with depreciation added back.

$$\text{Expected returns} = X(1 - T) + \text{Dep} = \$30{,}000(0.6) + \$15{,}000 = \$33{,}000. \tag{13.1}$$

Thus net operating income after taxes is before deduction of financial payments such as interest on debt and dividends to shareholders. Since interest costs are included in the net operating income, they are included in the fu-

Table 13.1

Illustrative Income Statement

Sales	$145,000
Operating costs	100,000
Earnings before depreciation, interest and taxes (EBDIT)	45,000
Depreciation expense (Dep)	15,000
Net operating income *(X)*; (NOI); (EBIT)	30,000
Interest expense (Int)	5,000
Income before taxes	25,000
Taxes (T) at 40 percent	10,000
Net income (NI)	$ 15,000

ture returns from investments. We should note also that future returns can be defined on the most inclusive measure of income (EBDIT) or on the measure net of prior deductions.

$$\begin{aligned}\text{Expected returns} &= (\text{EBDIT})(1 - \text{T}) + \text{TDep} \\ &= \$45{,}000(0.6) + 0.4(\$15{,}000) = \$33{,}000.\end{aligned} \tag{13.2}$$

When we express EBDIT in terms of its components, we can readily demonstrate the equivalence of expected returns defined on EBDIT in Equation 13.2 with expected returns defined on EBIT, or X, in Equation 13.1. EBDIT is equal to X plus Dep, so we can write for Equation 13.2:

$$\text{Expected returns} = X(1 - \text{T}) + \text{Dep}\,(1 - \text{T}) + \text{TDep} = \text{X}(1 - \text{T}) + \text{Dep}. \tag{13.2a}$$

The last formulation of 13.2a is, of course, exactly Equation 13.1. Similarly, we can start with a net income formulation of expected returns.

$$\begin{aligned}\text{Expected returns} &= \text{NI} + (\text{Int})(1 - \text{T}) + \text{Dep} \\ &= \$15{,}000 + \$5{,}000(0.6) + \$15{,}000 = \$33{,}000.\end{aligned} \tag{13.3}$$

Again we obtain the same numerical result as we did using Equation 13.1, and the logical equivalence is also readily established. We add back to NI what is required to reach X as follows:

$$\text{NI} + \text{T}(X - \text{Int}) + \text{Int} = X.$$

We then change the combination of terms.

$$\begin{aligned}\text{NI} + \text{T}X - \text{T}(\text{Int}) + \text{Int} &= X \\ \text{NI} + \text{Int}\,(1 - \text{T}) &= X - \text{T}X \\ \text{NI} + \text{Int}\,(1 - \text{T}) &= X(1 - \text{T}).\end{aligned} \tag{13.3a}$$

Thus when Dep is added to both sides of 13.3a, we will have future returns defined on both net operating income *(X)* and on net income (NI).

If a firm is not using debt as a part of its financing, it would not have interest expense, so its income statement would appear as in Table 13.2. The equivalent measures of future returns in Table 13.2 follow.

Table 13.2

Cash Flows with No Debt Interest

Sales	$145,000
Operating costs (except depreciation)	100,000
Earnings before depreciation, interest and taxes (EBDIT)	45,000
Depreciation expense (Dep)	15,000
Net operating income (NOI); also (EBIT), *(X)*	30,000
Taxes (T) at 40 percent	12,000
Net income (NI); *X* (1 − T)	$ 18,000

Expected cash flows: $X(1 - \text{T}) + \text{Dep} = \$30{,}000(0.6) + \$15{,}000 = \$33{,}000.$

$$\text{Expected cash flows: EBDIT}(1 - \text{T}) + \text{TDep} = \$45{,}000(0.6) + 0.4(\$15{,}000) = \$33{,}000.$$

Expected cash flows: $\text{NI} + \text{Dep} = \$18{,}000 + \$15{,}000 = \$33{,}000.$

Again the expected returns defined on EBIT, EBDIT, or NI give the same result. Finally, in a number of theoretical studies, it is assumed that the firm is adding to its gross fixed assets an amount each year exactly equal to its depreciation expense. In the resulting models, the cash flows from the investment in new assets and the deduction for depreciation cancel out. We would then go back to the income statement in Table 13.1, starting with EBIT. The relationships would be:

$$\begin{aligned}\text{Expected cash flows} &= X(1 - \text{T}) - \text{Investment} + \text{Dep} = X(1 - \text{T}) \\ &= \$30{,}000(0.6) = \$18{,}000. \\ \text{Expected cash flows} &= \text{NI} + \text{Int}\ (1 - \text{T}) - \text{Investment} + \text{Dep.} \\ &= \text{NI} + \text{Int}\ (1 - \text{T}) = \$15{,}000 + 0.6(\$5{,}000) = \$18{,}000.\end{aligned}$$

The central point is that all costs of financing are already included in the measurement of expected future returns. Accordingly, when we discount future returns by the firm's cost of capital, the costs of all forms of financing utilized by the firm are already included in the cost of capital.[3]

Importance of Good Data

Most discussions of measuring the cash flows associated with capital projects are relatively brief, but it is important to emphasize this: *In the entire capital budgeting procedure, probably nothing is of greater importance than a reliable estimate of the cost savings or revenue increases that will be achieved from the prospective outlay of capital funds.* The increased output and sales revenue resulting from expansion programs are obvious benefits. Cost reduction benefits include changes in quality and quantity of direct labor; in amount and cost of scrap and rework time; in fuel costs; and in maintenance expenses, down time, safety, flexibility, and so on. So many variables are involved that it is obviously impossible to make neat generalizations. However, this should not minimize the crucial importance of the required analysis of the benefits derived from capital expenditures. Each capital equipment expenditure must be examined in detail for possible additional costs and savings.

All the subsequent procedures for ranking projects are no better than the data input—the old saying, "garbage in, garbage out," is certainly applicable to capital budgeting analysis. Thus, the data assembly process is not a routine clerical task to be performed on a mechanical basis. It requires continuous monitoring and evaluation of estimates by those competent to make such

3. The discussion of the cost of capital presented in Chapter 16 will demonstrate this concept.

evaluations—engineers, accountants, economists, cost analysts, and other qualified persons.

After costs and benefits have been estimated, they are utilized for ranking alternative investment proposals. How this ranking is accomplished is our next topic.

Ranking Investment Proposals

The point of capital budgeting—indeed, the point of all financial analysis—is to make decisions that will maximize the value of the firm. The capital budgeting process is designed to answer two questions: (1) Which of several mutually exclusive investments should be selected? (2) How many projects, in total, should be accepted?

Among the many methods used for ranking investment proposals, three are discussed here.[4]

1. *Payback method (or payback period):* Number of years required to return the original investment.
2. *Net present value (NPV) method:* Present value of future returns discounted at the appropriate cost of capital, minus the cost of the investment.
3. *Internal rate of return (IRR) method:* Interest rate which equates the present value of future returns to the investment outlay.

In the next sections of this chapter, the nature and characteristics of the three methods are illustrated and explained. To make the explanations more meaningful, the same data set is used to illustrate each procedure.

Payback Method

Assume that a firm is considering two projects. Each requires an investment of $1,000. The firm's marginal cost of capital is 10 percent.[5] The net cash flows (net operating income after taxes plus depreciation) from Investments A and B are shown in Table 13.3.

The *payback period* is the number of years it takes a firm to recover its original investment from net cash flows. Since the cost is $1,000, the payback period is two and one-third years for Project A and four years for Project B. If the firm were employing a three-year payback period, Project A would be accepted, but Project B would be rejected.

4. A number of "average rate of return" methods have been discussed in the literature and used in practice. These methods are generally unsound and, with the widespread use of computers, completely unnecessary. We discussed them in earlier editions, but they are deleted from this edition. We also note that a "benefit/cost" or "profitability index" method is sometimes used; this method is taken up in Appendix A to this chapter.
5. A discussion of how the cost of capital is calculated is presented in Chapter 16. For now, the cost of capital should be considered as the firm's opportunity cost of making a particular investment. That is, if the firm does not make a particular investment, it saves the cost of this investment; and if it can invest these funds in another project that provides a return of 10 percent, then its opportunity cost of making the first investment is 10 percent.

Table 13.3

Net Cash Flows

Year	A	B
1	$500	$100
2	400	200
3	300	300
4	100	400
5	10	500
6	10	600

Although the payback period is very easy to calculate, it can lead to the wrong decisions. As the illustration demonstrates, it ignores income beyond the payback period. If the project is one that matures in later years, the use of the payback period can lead to the selection of less desirable investments. Projects with longer payback periods are characteristically those involved in long-range planning—developing a new product or tapping a new market. These are the major strategic decisions that determine a firm's fundamental position, but they also involve investments that do not yield their highest returns for a number of years. This means that the payback method may be biased against the very investments that are most important to a firm's long-run success.

When we recognize the longer period over which an investment is likely to yield savings, we identify another weakness in the use of the payback method for ranking investment proposals: its failure to take into account the time value of money. To illustrate, consider two assets, X and Y, each costing $300 and each having the following cash flows:

Year	X	Y
1	$200	$100
2	100	200
3	100	100

Each project has a two-year payback; hence, each would appear equally desirable. However, we know that a dollar today is worth more than a dollar next year, so Project X, with its faster cash flow, is certainly more desirable.

The use of the payback period is sometimes defended on the grounds that returns beyond three or four years are fraught with such great uncertainty that it is best to disregard them altogether in a planning decision. However, this is clearly an unsound procedure. Some investments with the highest returns are those which may not come to fruition for eight to ten years. The new product cycle in industries involving advanced technologies may not have a payoff for eight or nine years. Furthermore, even though returns that occur after three, four, or five years may be highly uncertain, it is important to make a judgment about the likelihood of their occurring. To ignore them is to assign a zero probability to these distant receipts, a procedure that can hardly produce the best results.

Another defense of the payback method is that a firm that is short of cash must necessarily give great emphasis to a quick return of its funds so that they may be put to use in other places or in meeting other needs. However, this does not relieve the payback method of its many shortcomings, and there are better methods for handling the cash shortage situation.[6]

A third reason for using payback is that projects with faster paybacks typically have more favorable short-run effects on earnings per share. Firms that use payback for this reason are sacrificing future growth for current accounting income, and in general such a practice will not maximize the value of the firm. The discounted cash flow techniques discussed in the next section, if used properly, automatically give consideration to the present earnings versus future growth trade-off and strike the balance that will maximize the firm's value.

The payback method is also used sometimes simply because it is so easy to apply. If a firm is making many small capital expenditure decisions, the costs of using more complex methods may outweigh the benefits of possibly "better" choices among competing projects. Thus, many electric utility companies with very sophisticated capital budgeting procedures use discounted cash flow techniques for larger projects, while using payback on certain small, routine replacement decisions. When these sophisticated companies do use the payback method, however, they generally do so only after special studies have indicated that the payback method will provide sufficiently accurate answers for the decisions at hand.

Finally, many firms use payback in combination with one of the discounted cash flow procedures described below. The NPV or IRR method is used to appraise a project's profitability, while the payback is used to show how long the initial investment will be at risk; that is, payback is used as a risk indicator. Recent surveys have shown that when larger firms use payback in connection with major projects, it is almost always used in this manner.

Net Present Value Method

As the flaws in the payback method were recognized, people began to search for methods of evaluating projects that would recognize that a dollar received immediately is preferable to a dollar received at some future date. This recognition led to the development of *discounted cash flow (DCF) techniques* to take account of the time value of money. One such discounted cash flow technique is called the net present value method, or sometimes simply the present value method. *To implement this approach, find the present value of the expected net cash flows of an investment, discounted at the cost of capital,*

6. We interpret a cash shortage to mean that the firm has a high opportunity cost for its funds and a high cost of capital. We would consider this high cost of capital in the internal rate of return method or the net present value method, thus taking account of the cash shortage.

and subtract from it the initial cost outlay of the project.[7] If the net present value is positive, the project should be accepted; if negative, it should be rejected. If the two projects are mutually exclusive, the one with the higher net present value should be chosen.

The equation for the net present value (NPV) is[8]

$$NPV = \left[\frac{F_1}{(1+k)^1} + \frac{F_2}{(1+k)^2} + \cdots + \frac{F_N}{(1+k)^N}\right] - I$$

$$= \sum_{t=1}^{N} \frac{F_t}{(1+k)^t} - I. \quad (13.4)$$

Here F_1, F_2, and so forth, represent the net cash flows; k is the marginal cost of capital; I is the initial cost of the project; and N is the project's expected life.

The net present values of Projects A and B are calculated in Table 13.4. Project A has an NPV of \$91, while B's NPV is \$403. On this basis, both should be accepted if they are independent, but B should be the one chosen if they are mutually exclusive.

Table 13.4

Calculating the Net Present Value (NPV) of Projects with \$1,000 Cost

	Project A			Project B		
Year	Net Cash Flow	PVIF (10%)	PV of Cash Flow	Net Cash Flow	PVIF (10%)	PV of Cash Flow
1	\$500	0.9091	\$ 455	\$100	0.9091	\$ 91
2	400	0.8264	331	200	0.8264	165
3	300	0.7513	225	300	0.7513	225
4	100	0.6830	68	400	0.6830	273
5	10	0.6209	6	500	0.6209	310
6	10	0.5645	6	600	0.5645	339
		PV of inflows	\$1,091			\$1,403
		Less: cost	− 1,000			− 1,000
		NPV	\$ 91			\$ 403

7. If costs are spread over several years, this must be taken into account. Suppose, for example, that a firm bought land in 1978, erected a building in 1979, installed equipment in 1980, and started production in 1981. One could treat 1978 as the base year, comparing the present value of the costs as of 1978 to the present value of the benefit stream as of that same date.
8. The second equation is simply a shorthand expression in which sigma (Σ) signifies "sum up" or add the present values of N profit terms. If $t = 1$, then $F_t = F_1$ and $1/(1 + k)^t = 1/(1 + k)^1$; if $t = 2$, then $F_t = F_2$ and $1/(1 + k)^t = 1/(1 + k)^2$; and so on until $t = N$, the last year the project provides any profits. The symbol $\sum_{t=1}^{N}$ simply says "Go through the following process: Let $t = 1$ and find the PV of F_1; then let $t = 2$ and find the PV of F_2. Continue until the PV of each individual profit has been found; then add the PVs of these individual profits to find the PV of the asset."

When a firm takes on a project with a positive NPV, the value of the firm increases by the amount of the NPV. In our example, the value of the firm increases by $403 if it takes on Project B, but by only $91 if it takes on Project A. Viewing the alternatives in this manner, it is easy to see why B is preferred to A, and it is also easy to see the logic of the NPV approach.

Internal Rate of Return Method

The internal rate of return (IRR) is defined as the *interest rate that equates the present value of the expected future cash flows, or receipts, to the initial cost outlay.* The equation for calculating the internal rate of return is

$$\frac{F_1}{(1+R)^1} + \frac{F_2}{(1+R)^2} + \cdots + \frac{F_N}{(1+R)^N} - I = 0$$

$$\sum_{t=1}^{N} \frac{F_t}{(1+R)^t} - I = 0. \qquad (13.5)$$

Here we know the value of I and also the values of $F_1, F_2, \cdots, F_N$, but we do not know the value of R. Thus, we have an equation with one unknown, and we can solve for the value of R. Some value of R will cause the sum of the discounted receipts to equal the initial cost of the project, making the equation equal to zero, and that value of R is defined as the internal rate of return; that is, the solution value of R is the IRR.

Notice that the internal rate of return formula, Equation 13.5, is simply the NPV formula, Equation 13.4, solved for that particular value of k that causes the NPV to equal zero. In other words, the same basic equation is used for both methods, but in the NPV method the discount rate (k) is specified and the NPV is found, while in the IRR method the NPV is specified to equal zero and the value of R that forces the NPV to equal zero is found.

The internal rate of return may be found by trial and error. First, compute the present value of the cash flows from an investment, using an arbitrarily selected interest rate. (Since the cost of capital for most firms has been in the range of 10 to 15 percent, projects will hopefully promise a return of at least 10 percent. Therefore, 10 percent is a good starting point for most problems.) Then compare the present value so obtained with the investment's cost. If the present value is higher than the cost figure, try a higher interest rate and go through the procedure again. Conversely, if the present value is lower than the cost, lower the interest rate and repeat the process. Continue until the present value of the flows from the investment is approximately equal to its cost. *The interest rate that brings about this equality is defined as the internal rate of return.*[9]

9. In order to reduce the number of trials required to find the internal rate of return, it is important to minimize the error at each iteration. One reasonable approach is to make as good a first approximation as possible, then to "straddle" the internal rate of return by making fairly large changes in the interest rate early in the iterative process. In practice, if many projects are to be evaluated or if many years are involved, relatively inexpensive hand calculators can be used to solve for the internal rate of return.

This calculation process is illustrated in Table 13.5 for Projects A and B. First, the 10 percent interest factors are obtained from Table A.2 at the end of the book. These factors are then multiplied by the cash flows for the corresponding years, and the present values of the annual cash flows are placed in the appropriate columns. For example, the PVIF of 0.9091 is multiplied by $500, and the product, $455, is placed in the first row of Column A.

The present values of the yearly cash flows are then summed to get the investment's total present value. Subtracting the cost of the project from this figure gives the net present value. As the net present values of both investments are positive at the 10 percent rate, increase the rate to 15 percent and try again. *At this point the net present value of Investment A is zero, which indicates that its internal rate of return is 15 percent. Continuing, B is found to have an internal rate of return of approximately 20 percent.*[10]

Table 13.5

Finding the Internal Rate of Return

	Cash Flows (F_t Values)		
	Year	F_A	F_B
I = Investment = $1,000	1: F_1 =	$500	$100
	2: F_2 =	400	200
	3: F_3 =	300	300
	4: F_4 =	100	400
	5: F_5 =	10	500
	6: F_6 =	10	600

	10 Percent			15 Percent			20 Percent		
		Present Value			Present Value			Present Value	
Year	PVIF	A	B	PVIF	A	B	PVIF	A	B
1	0.9091	455	91	0.8696	435	87	0.8333	417	83
2	0.8264	331	165	0.7561	302	151	0.6944	278	139
3	0.7513	225	225	0.6575	197	197	0.5787	174	174
4	0.6830	68	273	0.5718	57	229	0.4823	48	193
5	0.6209	6	310	0.4972	5	249	0.4019	4	201
6	0.5645	6	339	0.4323	4	259	0.3349	3	201
Present value		1,091	1,403		1,000	1,172		924	991
Net present value = PV − I									
		91	403		0	172		(76)	(9)

10. The IRR can also be estimated graphically. First, calculate the NPV at two or three discount rates as in Table 13.5. Next, plot these NPV's against the discount rates—see Figure 13.2 in the next section for an example. The horizontal axis intercept is the IRR.

Table 13.6

The Prospective Projects Schedule

Nature of Proposal	Amount of Funds Required	Cumulative Total	IRR
1. Purchase of leased space	$2,000,000	$ 2,000,000	23%
2. Mechanization of accounting system	1,200,000	3,200,000	19
3. Modernization of office building	1,500,000	4,700,000	17
4. Addition of power facilities	900,000	5,600,000	16
5. Purchase of affiliate	3,600,000	9,200,000	13
6. Purchase of loading docks	300,000	9,500,000	12
7. Purchase of tank trucks	500,000	10,000,000	11
			10% cutoff
8. Installation of conveyor system	200,000	10,200,000	9
9. Construction of new plant	2,300,000	12,500,000	8
10. Purchase of executive aircraft	200,000	12,700,000	7

What is so special about the particular discount rate that equates the cost of a project with the present value of its expected cash flows? Suppose that the weighted cost of all of the funds obtained by the firm is 10 percent. If the internal rate of return on a particular project is 10 percent, the same as the cost of capital, the firm would be able to use the cash flow generated by the investment to repay the funds obtained, including the costs of the funds. If the internal rate of return exceeds 10 percent, the value of the firm increases. If the internal rate of return is less than 10 percent, taking on the project would cause a decline in the value of the firm. It is this breakeven characteristic that increases or decreases the value of the firm and makes the internal rate of return of particular significance.

Assuming that the firm uses a cost of capital of 10 percent, the internal rate of return criterion states that, if the two projects are independent, both should be accepted—they both do better than break even. If they are mutually exclusive, B ranks higher and should be accepted, while A should be rejected.

A more complete illustration of how the internal rate of return would be used in practice is given in Table 13.6. Assuming a 10 percent cost of capital, the firm should accept Projects 1 through 7, reject Projects 8 through 10, and have a total capital budget of $10 million.

IRR for Level Cash Flows

If the cash flows from a project are level, or equal in each year, then the project's internal rate of return can be found by a relatively simple process. In essence, such a project is an annuity: The firm makes an outlay, *I,* and receives a stream of cash flow benefits, *F,* for a given number of years. The IRR for the project is found by applying Equation 4.6, presented in Chapter 4.

To illustrate, suppose a project has a cost of $10,000 and is expected to produce cash flows of $1,627 a year for ten years. The cost of the project,

\$10,000, is the present value of an annuity of \$1,627 a year for ten years, so, applying Equation 4.6, we obtain

$$\frac{I}{F} = \frac{\$10{,}000}{\$1{,}627} = 6.1463 = \text{PVIFA}.$$

Looking up PVIFA in Table A.4, across the ten-year row, we find it (approximately) under the 10 percent column. Accordingly, 10 percent is the IRR on the project. In other words, 10 percent is the value of R that would force Equation 13.5 to zero when F is constant at \$1,627 for ten years and I is \$10,000. This procedure works only if the project has constant annual cash flows; if it does not, the IRR must be found by trial and error or by using a calculator.

Basic Differences between the NPV and IRR Methods[11]

As noted above, the NPV method (1) accepts all independent projects whose NPV is greater than zero and (2) ranks mutually exclusive projects by their NPV's, selecting the project with the higher NPV according to Equation 13.4:

$$\text{NPV} = \sum_{t=1}^{N} \frac{F_t}{(1+k)^t} - I. \tag{13.4}$$

The IRR method, on the other hand, finds the value of R that forces Equation 13.4 to equal zero:

$$\text{NPV} = \sum_{t=1}^{N} \frac{F_t}{(1+R)^t} - I = 0. \tag{13.5}$$

The IRR method calls for accepting independent projects where R, the internal rate of return, is greater than k, the cost of capital, and for selecting among mutually exclusive projects depending on which has the higher IRR.

It is apparent that the only structural difference between the NPV and IRR methods lies in the discount rates used in the two equations—all the values in the equations are identical except for R and k. Further, we can see that if $R > k$, then NPV > 0.[12] *Accordingly, the two methods give the same accept-reject decisions for specific projects—if a project is acceptable under the* NPV *criterion, it is also acceptable if the* IRR *method is used.*

11. This section is relatively technical and may be omitted on a first reading without loss of continuity.
12. This can be seen by noting that NPV = 0 only when $R = k$:

$$\text{NPV} = \sum_{t=1}^{N} \frac{F_t}{(1+k)^t} - I = \sum_{t=1}^{N} \frac{F_t}{(1+R)^t} - I = 0,$$

if and only if $R = k$. If $R > k$, then NPV > 0, and if $R < k$, then NPV < 0. We should also note that, under certain conditions, there may be more than one root to Equation 13.5; hence multiple IRR's are found. See Appendix A to this chapter for a more detailed discussion of the multiple root problem.

However, under certain conditions the NPV and IRR methods can *rank* projects differently, and if mutually exclusive projects are involved or if capital is limited, then rankings can be important. The conditions under which different rankings can occur are as follows:

1. The cost of one project is larger than that of the other.
2. The timing of the projects' cash flows differs. For example, the cash flows of one project may increase over time, while those of the other decrease, or the projects may have different expected lives.

The first point can be seen by considering two mutually exclusive projects, L and S, of greatly differing sizes. Project S calls for the investment of $1.00 and yields $1.50 at the end of one year. Its IRR is 50 percent, and at a 10 percent cost of capital its NPV is $0.36. Project L costs $1 million and yields $1.25 million at the end of the year. Its IRR is only 25 percent, but its NPV at 10 percent is $136,375. The two methods rank the projects differently: $IRR_s > IRR_l$, but $NPV_l > NPV_s$. This is, of course, an extreme case, but whenever projects differ in size, the NPV and the IRR can give different rankings.[13]

The effect of differential cash flows is somewhat more difficult to understand, but it can be illustrated by an example. Consider two projects, A and B, whose cash flows over their three-year lives are given below:

Cash Flow from Project		
Year	A	B
1	$1,000	$ 100
2	500	600
3	100	1,100

Project A's cash flows are higher in the early years, but B's cash flows increase over time and exceed those of A in later years. Each project costs $1,200, and their NPV's discounted at the specified rates, are shown below:

	NPV	
Discount Rate	A	B
0%	$ 400	$ 600
5	292	390
10	197	213
15	113	64
20	38	(63)
24	(16)	(152)
32	(112)	(302)

13. Projects of different size *could* be ranked the same by the NPV and IRR methods; that is, different sizes do not necessarily mean different rankings.

At a zero discount rate, the NPV of each project is simply the sum of its receipts less its cost. Thus, the NPV of Project A at 0 percent is \$1,000 + \$500 + \$100 − \$1,200 = \$400; that of Project B is \$100 + \$600 + \$1,100 − \$1,200 = \$600. As the discount rate rises from zero, the NPV's of the two projects fall from these values.

The NPV's are plotted against the appropriate discount rates in Figure 13.2, a graph defined as a *present value profile.* Notice that the vertical axis intercepts are the NPV's when the discount rate is zero, while the horizontal axis intercepts show each project's IRR. The internal rate of return is defined as that point where NPV is zero; therefore, A's IRR is approximately 23 percent, while B's is approximately 17 percent. Because its largest cash flows come late in the project's life, when the discounting effects of time are most significant, B's NPV falls rapidly as the discount rate rises. However, since A's cash flows come early, when the impact of higher discount rates is not so severe, its NPV falls less rapidly as interest rates increase.

Notice that if the cost of capital is below 10 percent, B has the higher NPV but the lower IRR, while at a cost of capital above 10 percent A has both the higher NPV and the higher IRR. We can generalize these results: *Whenever the* NPV *profiles of two projects cross one another, a conflict will exist if the cost of capital is below the crossover rate.* For our illustrative projects, no conflict would exist if the firm's cost of capital exceeded 10 percent, but the two methods would rank A and B differently if k were less than 10 percent.

Figure 13.2

Present Value Profile

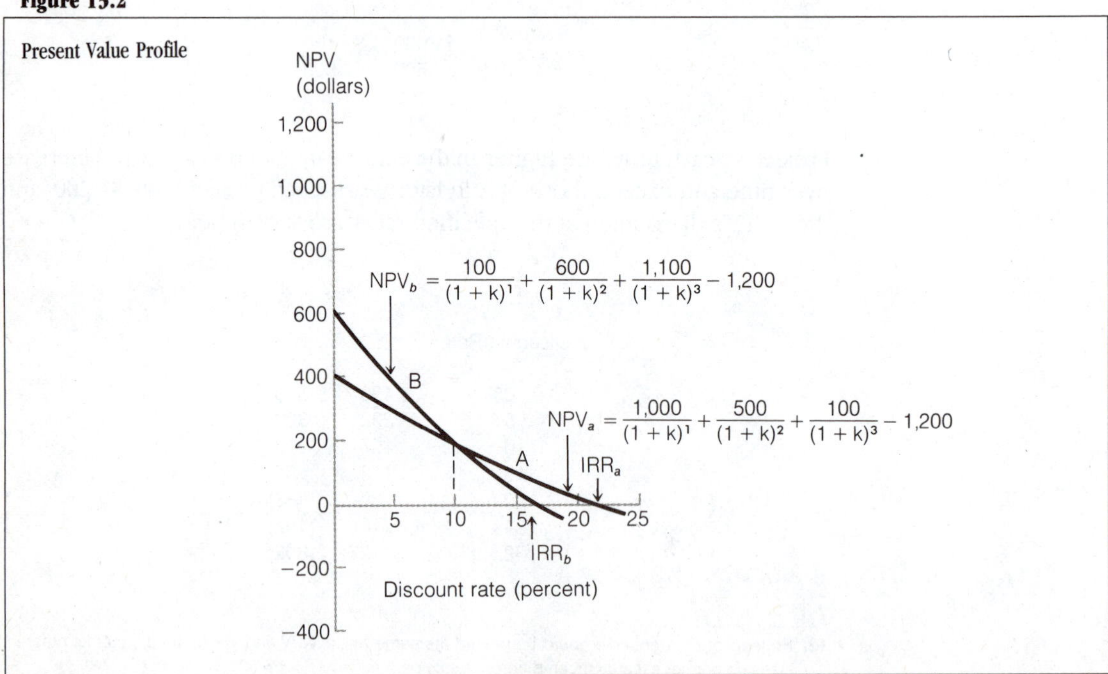

How should such conflicts be resolved? For example, when the NPV and IRR methods yield conflicting rankings, which of two mutually exclusive projects should be selected? Assuming that management is seeking to maximize the value of the firm, the correct decision is to select the project with the higher NPV. After all, the NPV's measure the projects' contributions to the value of the firm, so the one with the higher NPV must be contributing more to the firm's value. *This line of reasoning leads to the conclusion that firms should, in general, use the* NPV *method for evaluating capital investment proposals.*[14] Recognizing this point, sophisticated firms generally rely on the NPV method. These firms often calculate (by computer) both the NPV and the IRR, but they rely on the NPV when conflicts arise among mutually exclusive projects.

Capital Budgeting Project Evaluation

Thus far the problem of measuring cash flows—the benefits used in the present value calculations above—has not been dealt with directly. This matter will now be discussed, and a few simple examples given. The procedures developed here can be used both for expansion and for replacement decisions.

Simplified Model for Determining Cash Flows[15]

One way of considering the cash flows attributable to a particular investment is to think of them in terms of comparative income statements. This is illustrated in the following example.

The Widget Division of the Culver Company, a profitable, diversified manufacturing firm, purchased a machine five years ago at a cost of $7,500. The machine had an expected life of fifteen years at time of purchase and a zero estimated salvage value at the end of the fifteen years. It is being depreciated on a straight line basis and has a book value of $5,000 at present. The division manager reports that, for $12,000 (including installation), a new machine can be bought which, over its ten-year life, will expand sales from $10,000 to $11,000 a year. Further, it will reduce labor and raw materials usage suffi-

14. The question of *why* the conflict arises is an interesting one. Basically, it has to do with the reinvestment of cash flows—the NPV method implicitly assumes reinvestment at the marginal cost of capital (MCC), while the IRR method implicitly assumes reinvestment at the internal rate of return. For a value-maximizing firm, reinvestment at the MCC is the better assumption. The rationale is as follows: A value-maximizing firm will expand to the point where it accepts all projects yielding more than the MCC (these projects will have NPV > 0). How these projects are financed is irrelevant—the point is that they will be financed and accepted. Now consider the question of the cash flows from a particular project. If these cash flows are reinvested, at what rate will reinvestment occur? All projects that yield more than the cost of capital have already been accepted; thus, these cash flows can only be invested in physical assets yielding *less than* the MCC or be used in lieu of other capital with a cost of MCC. A rational firm will take the second alternative, so reinvested cash flows will save the firm the cost of capital. The effect of this is that cash flows are reinvested to yield the cost of capital, the assumption implicit in the NPV method. For a detailed discussion, see Appendix A to this chapter.

15. The procedure described in this section facilitates understanding of the capital investment analysis process, but the alternative worksheet illustrated in the next section is preferred for repeated calculations.

ciently to cut operating costs from $7,000 to $5,000. The new machine has an estimated salvage value of $2,000 at the end of ten years. The old machine's current market value is $1,000. Taxes are at a 40 percent rate and are paid quarterly, and the firm's cost of capital is 10 percent. Should Culver buy the new machine?

The decision calls for five steps: (1) estimating the actual cash outlay attributable to the new investment, (2) determining the incremental cash flows, (3) finding the present value of the incremental cash flows, (4) adding the present value of the expected salvage value to the present value of the total cash flows, and (5) seeing whether the NPV is positive or whether the IRR exceeds the cost of capital. These steps are explained further in the following sections.

Estimated Cash Outlay. The net initial cash outlay consists of these items: (1) payment to the manufacturer, (2) tax effects, and (3) proceeds from the sale of the old machine. Culver must make a $12,000 payment to the manufacturer of the machine, but its next quarterly tax bill will be reduced because of the loss it will incur when it sells the old machine: Tax saving = (Loss) (Tax rate) = ($4,000) (0.4) = $1,600. The tax reduction will occur because the old machine, which is carried at $5,000, will be written down by $4,000 ($5,000 less $1,000 salvage value) immediately upon the purchase of the new one.

To illustrate, suppose the Culver Company's taxable income in the quarter in which the new machine is to be purchased would have been $100,000 without the purchase of the new machine and the consequent write-off of the old machine. With a 40 percent tax rate, Culver would have had to write a check for $40,000 to pay its tax bill. However, if it bought the new machine and sold the old one, it would take an operating loss of $4,000—the $5,000 book value on the old machine less the salvage value. (The loss is an operating loss, not a capital loss, because it is in reality simply recognizing that depreciation charges, an operating cost, were too low during the old machine's five-year life.[16] With this $4,000 additional operating cost, the next quarter's taxable income would be reduced from $100,000 to $96,000, and the tax bill from $40,000 to $38,400. This means, of course, that the firm's cash outflow for taxes would be $1,600 less *because* of the purchase of the new machine.

In addition, there would be a cash inflow of $1,000 from the sale of the old machine. The net result is that the purchase of the new machine would involve an immediate net cash outlay of $9,400, the cost used for capital budgeting purposes:

16. If Culver traded in the old machine as partial payment for the new one, the loss would be added to the depreciable cost of the new machine, and there would be no immediate tax saving.

Invoice price of new machine	$12,000
Less: Tax savings	−1,600
Salvage of old machine	−1,000
Net cash outflow (cost)	$ 9,400

If additional working capital is required as a result of a capital budgeting decision, as would generally be true for expansion investments (as opposed to cost-reducing replacement investments), this factor must be taken into account. The amount of *net* working capital (additional current assets required as a result of the expansion minus any spontaneous funds generated by the expansion) is estimated and added to the initial cash outlay. We assume that Culver will not need any additional working capital, so this factor is ignored in the example.

Annual Benefits. Column 1 in Table 13.7 shows the Widget Division's estimated income statement as it would be without the new machine; Column 2 shows the statement as it would look if the new investment were made. (It is assumed that these figures are applicable for each of the next ten years; if this is not the case, then cash flow estimates must be made for each year.) Column 3 shows the differences between the first two columns.

For capital budgeting analysis, the cash flows that are discounted are the net after-tax operating cash flows. The data in Table 13.7 represent accounting income and must be adjusted in order to be on a cash rather than accrual basis and also to exclude all payments to the sources of financing. In Table 13.7 depreciation is a noncash charge; interest charges and dividends paid are cash flows to the financing sources.

While depreciation is a noncash charge, it is deductible for computing in-

Table 13.7

Comparative Accounting Income Statement Framework for Considering Cash Flows

	Without New Investment (1)		With New Investment (2)		Difference: (2) − (1) (3)	
Sales		$10,000		$11,000		$1,000
Operating costs	$7,000		$5,000		($2,000)	
Depreciation	500		1,000		500	
Interest charges	500		1,000		500	
Income before taxes		$ 2,000		$ 4,000		$2,000
Taxes (T = 0.4)		800		1,600		800
Income after taxes		$ 1,200		$ 2,400		$1,200
Dividends paid		600		1,200		600
Additions to retained earnings		$ 600		$ 1,200		$ 600

Table 13.8

Net Operating Cash Flow Statement

	Without New Investment (1)	With New Investment (2)	Difference or Incremental Flows: (2) − (1) (3)
Sales	\$10,000	\$11,000	\$1,000
Operating cash costs (O)[a]	7,000	5,000	(2,000)
Net operating cash income (NOI)[a]	\$ 3,000	\$ 6,000	\$3,000
Taxes (T = 0.4)	1,200	2,400	1,200
After-tax operating income: NOI (1 − T)	\$ 1,800	\$ 3,600	\$1,800
Depreciation tax benefit (T × Dep)	200	400	200
Net cash flows (*F*)	\$ 2,000	\$ 4,000	\$2,000

a. Does not include depreciation as a cash cost since this is a cash flow statement and depreciation is not a cash cost.

come tax, and income tax payments are cash flows. The cash flows must include the depreciation tax benefits.

Table 13.8 shows the operating cash flows without the new investment, with the new investment, and the difference, or incremental flows.

The incremental cash flows can also be calculated using the following equation. Let ΔSales be the change in sales, ΔO the change in operating costs, ΔNOI the change in operating cash income, ΔDep the change in depreciation, and T the marginal corporate income tax rate. Then

$$\begin{aligned}\Delta\text{Cash flow} &= \text{Change in after-tax operating cash income} \\ &\quad + \text{Change in depreciation tax benefit} \\ \Delta F &= \Delta\text{NOI}\,(1 - \text{T}) + \text{T}\Delta\text{Dep} \\ \Delta F &= (\Delta\text{Sales} - \Delta\text{O})(1 - \text{T}) + \text{T}\Delta\text{Dep} \qquad (13.6) \\ \Delta F &= [(\text{Sales}_2 - \text{Sales}_1) - (\text{O}_2 - \text{O}_1)](1 - \text{T}) + \text{T}(\text{Dep}_2 - \text{Dep}_1) \\ \text{or } \Delta F &= [(\text{Sales}_2 - \text{Sales}_1) - (\text{O}_2 - \text{O}_1) - (\text{Dep}_2 - \text{Dep}_1)](1 - \text{T}) \\ &\quad + (\text{Dep}_2 - \text{Dep}_1). \qquad (13.7)\end{aligned}$$

For the Widget Division analysis:

$$\begin{aligned}\Delta\text{Cash flow} &= [(\$11{,}000 - \$10{,}000) - (\$5{,}000 - \$7{,}000)](1 - 0.4) \\ &\quad + (0.4)(\$1{,}000 - \$500) \\ &= [\$1{,}000 - (-\$2{,}000)](0.6) + (0.4)(\$500) \\ \Delta F &= \$1{,}800 + \$200 = \$2{,}000\end{aligned}$$

or

$$\Delta F = (\$1{,}000 + \$2{,}000 - \$500)(0.6) + \$500 = \$2{,}000.$$

This \$2,000 result checks out with the bottom line figure in the last column of Table 13.8. What happens if there is no change in sales? The equation is still valid, but ΔSales = 0. In this case, the problem is a simple replacement decision, with a new machine replacing an old one to reduce costs. The sales levels are the same with and without the investment and do not show up in the incremental column.

Finding the PV of the Benefits. We have explained in detail how to measure the annual benefits. The next step is to determine the present value of the benefit stream. The interest factor for a ten-year, 10 percent annuity is found to be 6.1446 from Table A.4. This factor, when multiplied by the $2,000 incremental cash flow, results in a present value of $12,289.

Salvage Value. The new machine has an estimated salvage value of $2,000; that is, Culver expects to be able to sell the machine for $2,000 after ten years of use. The present value of an inflow of $2,000 due in ten years is $771, found as $2,000 × 0.3855. If additional working capital had been required and included in the initial cash outlay, this amount would be added to the salvage value of the machine because the working capital would be recovered if and when the project is abandoned.

Notice that the salvage value is a return of capital, not taxable income, so it is *not* subject to income taxes. Of course, when the new machine is actually retired ten years hence, it might be sold for more or less than the expected $2,000, so either taxable income or a deductible operating loss could arise, but $2,000 is the best present estimate of the new machine's salvage value.

Determining the Net Present Value. The project's net present value is found as the sum of the present values of the inflows, or benefits, less the outflows, or costs:

Inflows: PV of annual benefits	$12,289
PV of salvage value, new machine	771
Less: Net cash outflow, or cost	(9,400)
Net present value (NPV)	$ 3,660

Since the NPV is positive, the project should be accepted.

Worksheet for Determining Cash Flows

Table 13.9 summarizes the five-step capital budgeting decision process described above. Using the Culver Company investment problem as an example, we first calculate the total outflows for the proposed project by subtracting from the cost of the new machine the sum of the funds received from the sale of the old machine plus the tax savings resulting from that sale. Recall that a $4,000 operating loss will occur if the old machine with a book value of $5,000 is sold for $1,000. Since the old machine is sold at a loss, the $1,000 received from the sale is not taxed. Only the *gain* on the sale of any asset is taxed. Further, the $4,000 loss is a tax deduction for next quarter's tax payment, and it results in a tax saving of $1,600.

Table 13.9

Worksheet for Capital Budgeting Project Evaluation

1. *Project Cost, or Initial Outflows Required to Undertake the Project*[a]	
Investment in new equipment	$12,000
Receipt from sale of old machine	(1,000)
Add (or subtract) the taxes (or tax savings) resulting from the gain (or loss) on the old machine: tax rate (T) times gain or loss	(1,600)
Total project cost	$ 9,400
2. *Calculation of Annual Benefits*[b]	
ΔSales	$ 1,000
Less: ΔO	(2,000)[c]
ΔDep	500
ΔTaxable income	$ 2,500
Less: Δtax at 40%	1,000
ΔAfter-tax profits	$ 1,500
Plus: ΔDep	500
ΔCash flow	$ 2,000
3. *Present Value of Benefits*	
Δ*F* × Interest factor	
$2,000 × 6.1446 =	$12,289
4. *Present Value of Expected Salvage*	
Expected salvage value × Interest factor $2,000 × 0.3855 =	$ 771
5. *Net Present Value*	
PV of inflows: Annual benefits	$12,289
Salvage	771
	$13,060
Less: Project cost	9,400
NPV	$ 3,660

a. If project costs are incurred over a number of years, then the present value of project costs must be calculated.
b. It should be noted that if the annual cash flows are not level, the annuity format cannot be used. Also note that if accelerated depreciation is used, the annuity format can almost never be used; in this case, cash flows are unlikely to be uniform from year to year. These restrictions might appear to present serious problems to practical applications in capital budgeting, but they seldom do. Most corporations have either computer facilities or time-sharing arrangements with computer service facilities that handle these nonannuity cases without difficulty.
c. Refer to Equation 13.6. We are subtracting the change in cost from the change in sales: ΔO = $5,000 − $7,000 = −$2,000. Therefore, ΔSales − ΔO = $1,000 − (−$2,000) = $3,000.

Next, we calculate the net annual benefits, then find the present value of this benefit stream, which is $12,289, and we find the present value of the expected salvage value of the new machine, $771. Since salvage value is a *return of capital,* not taxable income, no taxes are deducted from the salvage value.

Finally, we sum up the PV of the inflows and then deduct the project cost to determine the NPV, $3,660 in this example. Since the NPV is positive, the project should be accepted.[17]

17. Alternatively, the internal rate of return on the project could have been computed and found to be 18 percent. Because this is substantially in excess of the 10 percent cost of capital, the internal rate of

Alternative Capital Budgeting Worksheet

Table 13.10 presents an alternative worksheet for evaluating capital projects. The top section shows net cash flows at the time of investment; since all these flows occur immediately, no discounting is required and the interest factor is 1.0. The lower section of the table shows future cash flows—benefits from increased sales and/or reduced costs, depreciation, and salvage value. These flows occur over time, so it is necessary to convert them to present values. The NPV as determined in the alternative format, $3,660, agrees with the figure as calculated in Table 13.9.

Table 13.10

Alternative Worksheet for Capital Budgeting Project Evaluation

	Amount before Tax	Amount after Tax[a]	Year Event Occurs	PV Factor at 10%	PV
Outflows at time investment is made					
Investment in new equipment	$12,000	$12,000	0	1.0000	$12,000
Salvage value of old	(1,000)	(1,000)	0	1.0000	(1,000)
Tax effect of the sale[b]	(4,000)	(1,600)	0	1.0000	(1,600)
Increased working capital (if necessary)	c	—	0	1.0000	—
Total initial outflows (PV of costs)					$ 9,400
Inflows, or annual returns					
Benefits[d]	$ 3,000	$ 1,800	1–10	6.1446	$11,060
Depreciation on new (annual)[b]	1,000	400	1–10	6.1446	2,458
Depreciation on old (annual)[b]	(500)	(200)	1–10	6.1446	(1,229)
Salvage value on new	2,000	2,000	10	0.3855	771
Return of working capital (if necessary)	c	—	10	0.3855	—
Total periodic inflows (PV of benefits)					$13,060

NPV = PV of benefits less PV of cost = $13,060 − $9,400 = $3,660.

a. Amount after tax equals amount before tax times T or (1 − T), where T = Tax rate.
b. Deductions (tax loss and depreciation) are multiplied by T.
c. Not applicable.
d. Benefits are multiplied by (1 − T).

return method also indicates that the investment should be undertaken. In this case, the R is found as follows:

PV of benefit stream + PV of salvage − Cost = 0.

$$\sum_{t=1}^{10} \frac{\$2{,}000}{(1+R)^t} + \frac{\$2{,}000}{(1+R)^{10}} - \$9{,}400 = 0.$$

$2,000 (IF for PV of 10-year annuity) + $2,000 (PV of $1 in 10 years) − $9,400 = 0.

Try IFs for 18 percent:

$2,000(4.4941) + $2,000(0.1911) − $9,400 = $8,988 + $382 − $9,400 = $−30,

which is very close to zero, indicating that the internal rate of return is approximately equal to 18 percent.

Accelerated Depreciation

Thus far in our illustrations of capital budgeting, it has been assumed that straight line depreciation was used, thus enabling us to derive uniform cash flows over the life of the investment. Realistically, however, firms usually employ *accelerated depreciation* methods; when such is the case, it is necessary to modify the procedures outlined thus far. With accelerated depreciation, the deduction for depreciation expense is no longer a constant amount. It is, rather, larger in the earlier years and then declining. But for the entire period of a capital budgeting analysis, the present value of all of the accelerated depreciation tax deductions can be calculated.

Appendix C contains present value factors for accelerated depreciation. The factors in the table are developed as shown in the example in Table 13.11. In this example, we are interested in the factor for depreciation by the sum-of-years'-digits method over a five-year period with a 10 percent cost of capital. We first find the fraction of $1 that is received in each year, then discount that amount at 10 percent. The sum of the present values of the amounts received during the five years, shown in the product column, equals the accelerated depreciation factor (0.805 in this example).

To find the present value of the depreciation tax savings when an investment is depreciated by an accelerated method, we multiply the tax rate by the accelerated depreciation factor by the amount of the investment. For a $20,000 investment:

$$\begin{aligned} PV &= T(\text{accelerated depreciation PV factor})I \\ &= 0.4(0.805)(\$20{,}000) = \$6{,}440. \end{aligned}$$

Appendix C gives factors for both the sum-of-years'-digits and double declining balance depreciation methods, for various asset lives, and for different discount rates. The factor of 0.805 calculated in Table 13.11 can also be found in Appendix C—in the 10 percent column at Period 5.

We may utilize these accelerated depreciation factors to recalculate the Culver example, using the alternative, and somewhat streamlined, decision

Table 13.11

Calculation of the Accelerated Depreciation Factor

Year	Depreciation Fraction Applied to Asset Cost	Amount of Depreciation	10% Discount Factor	Product
1	5/15	0.33333	0.9091	0.303
2	4/15	0.26667	0.8264	0.220
3	3/15	0.20000	0.7513	0.150
4	2/15	0.13333	0.6830	0.091
5	1/15	0.06667	0.6209	0.041
Totals	1.00	1.00000	Factor =	0.805

Table 13.12

Calculations for Replacement Decision: Accelerated Depreciation

	Amount before Tax	Amount after Tax[a]	Year Event Occurs	Present Value Factor at 10%	Present Value
Outflows at time investment is made					
Investment in new equipment	$12,000	$12,000	0	1.0000	$12,000
Salvage value of old	(1,000)	(1,000)	0	1.0000	(1,000)
Tax loss on sale	(4,000)	(1,600)	0	1.0000	(1,600)
Total outflows (Present value of costs)					$ 9,400
Inflows, or annual returns					
Benefits	3,000	1,800	1–10	6.1446	$11,060
Depreciation on new (total)	10,000	4,000	1–10	0.6850	2,740
Depreciation on old (annual)	(500)	(200)	1–10	6.1446	(1,229)
Salvage value on new	2,000	2,000	10	0.3855	771
Total inflows (Present value of benefits)					$13,342
Present value of inflows less present value of outflows = $3,942.					

a. The "tax loss on sale" and depreciation figures are multiplied by T, the tax rate, to obtain the after-tax figures, while the benefits are multiplied by (1 – T).

format shown in Table 13.12. The top section of the table presents the cash outflows at the time the investment is made. All these flows occur immediately, so no discounting is required, and the present value factor is 1.0. No tax adjustment is necessary on the invoice price of the new machine, but, as we saw above, the $4,000 loss on the old machine creates a $1,600 tax reduction, which is deducted from the price of the new machine. Also, the $1,000 salvage value on the old machine is treated as a reduction in cash outflows necessary to acquire the new machine. Notice that since the $1,000 is a recovery of capital investment, it is not considered to be taxable income; hence, no tax adjustment is made for the salvage value.

In the lower section of the table we see that net income before tax increases by $3,000 a year—a sales increase of $1,000 plus a cost reduction of $2,000. However, this amount is taxable, so with a 40 percent tax, the after-tax benefits are reduced to $1,800. This $1,800 is received each year for ten years, so it is an annuity. The present value of the annuity, discounted at the 10 percent cost of capital, is $11,060.

Cash inflows also come from the depreciation on the new machine—depreciation on the new machine totals $10,000, and the tax saving totals $4,000. In Table 13.12, we assume that the new investment is depreciated by the double declining balance (DDB) method over a ten-year period; hence a factor of 0.685, taken from Appendix C, is applied to the after-tax depreciation figure of $4,000 to obtain a present value of $2,740 for the depreciation tax shelter.[18]

The old machine was being depreciated by the straight line method; hence it provides a cash flow of $500 before taxes and $200 after taxes for ten years. Observe that the depreciation on the old machine is *subtracted* from the inflows section. The logic here is that, had the replacement *not* been made, the company would have had the benefit of the $500 depreciation each year for the next ten years. With the replacement, however, all this depreciation is taken as an operating loss immediately and is shown as the tax loss on the sale in the upper section of the table.

When the present values of the inflows and outflows are summed, we obtain the project's NPV. In this example, the NPV is $3,942 versus $3,660 for the straight line text example. In general, NPV's are higher when accelerated depreciation is used, as the PV of the depreciation benefit is higher than it would be under straight line.

Capital Rationing

Ordinarily, firms operate as illustrated in Figure 13.1; that is, they take on investments to the point where the marginal returns from investment are just equal to their estimated marginal cost of capital. For firms operating in this way, the decision process is as described above—they make those investments having positive net present values, reject those whose net present values are negative, and choose between mutually exclusive investments on the basis of the higher net present value. However, a firm will occasionally set an absolute limit on the size of its capital budget for any one year that is less than the level of investment it would undertake on the basis of the criteria described above.

The principal reason for such action is that some firms are reluctant to engage in external financing (borrowing or selling stock). One management, recalling the plight of firms with substantial amounts of debt in the 1930s, may simply refuse to use debt. Another management, which has no objection to selling debt, may not want to sell equity capital for fear of losing some measure of voting control. Still others may refuse to use any form of outside financing, considering safety and control to be more important than additional profits. These are all cases of capital rationing, and they result in limiting the rate of expansion to a slower pace than would be dictated by "purely rational profit-maximizing behavior."[19]

18. The terms *tax shelter* or *tax shield* are frequently used to denote the value of depreciation and other items which shelter or shield income from taxes.

19. We should make three points here. First, we *do not* necessarily consider a decision to hold back on expansion irrational. If the owners of a firm have what they consider to be plenty of income and wealth, then it might be quite rational for them to "trim their sails," relax, and concentrate on enjoying what they have already earned rather than on earning still more. Such behavior would not, however, be appropriate for a publicly owned firm.

Project Selection under Capital Rationing

How should projects be selected under conditions of capital rationing? First, note that under conditions of true capital rationing, the firm's value is not being maximized—if management were maximizing, then it would move to the point where the marginal project's NPV was zero, and capital rationing as defined would not exist. So, if a firm uses capital rationing, it has ruled out value maximization. The firm may, however, want to maximize value *subject to the constraint that the capital ceiling is not exceeded.* Following constrained maximization behavior will, in general, result in a lower value than following unconstrained maximization, but some type of constrained maximization may produce reasonably satisfactory results. Linear programming is one method of constrained maximization that has been applied to capital rationing. To our knowledge, this method has not been widely applied, but much work is going on in the area, and linear programming may, in the future, prove useful in capital budgeting.[20]

If a financial manager does face capital rationing and cannot get the constraint lifted, the manager's objective should be to select projects, subject to the capital rationing constraint, such that the sum of the projects' NPV's is maximized. Linear programming can be used, but there is really no practical alternative that will approximate the true maximum. Reasonably satisfactory results may be obtained by ranking projects by their internal rates of return and then, starting at the top of this list of projects, by taking investments of successively lower rank until the available funds have been exhausted. However, no investment with a negative NPV (or an internal rate of return below the cost of capital) should be undertaken.

A firm might, for example, have the investment opportunities shown in Table 13.13 and only $6 million available for investment. In this situation, the firm would probably accept Projects 1 through 4 and Project 6, ending with a capital budget of $5.9 million and a cumulative NPV of $2.6 million. Under no circumstances should it accept Project 8, 9, or 10, as they all have internal rates of return of less than 10 percent (and also net present values less than zero).

The second point is that it is not correct to interpret as capital rationing a situation where the firm is willing to sell additional securities at the going market price but finds that it cannot because the market will simply not absorb more of its issues. Rather, such a situation indicates that the cost-of-capital curve is rising. If more acceptable investments are indicated than can be financed, then the cost of capital being used is too low and should be raised.

Third, firms sometimes set a limit on capital expenditures, not because of a shortage of funds, but because of limitations on other resources, especially managerial talent. A firm might, for example, feel that its personnel development program is sufficient to handle an expansion of no more than 10 percent a year, then set a limit on the capital budget to insure that expansion is held to that rate. This is not *capital* rationing—rather, it involves a downward reevaluation of project returns if growth exceeds some limit; that is, expected rates of return are, after some point, a decreasing function of the level of expenditures.

20. For a further discussion of programming approaches to capital budgeting, see Appendix A to this chapter.

Table 13.13

The Prospective Projects Schedule

Nature of Proposal	Project's Cost	Cumulative Total of Costs	Internal Rate of Return	PV of Benefits	Project's NPV
1. Purchase of leased space	$2,000,000	$ 2,000,000	23%	$3,200,000	$1,200,000
2. Mechanization of accounting system	1,200,000	3,200,000	19	1,740,000	540,000
3. Modernization of office building	1,500,000	4,700,000	17	2,070,000	570,000
4. Addition of power facilities	900,000	5,600,000	16	1,125,000	225,000
5. Purchase of affiliate	3,600,000	9,200,000	13	4,248,000	648,000
6. Purchase of loading docks	300,000	9,500,000	12	342,000	42,000
7. Purchase of tank trucks	500,000	10,000,000	11	540,000	40,000
		cutoff			
8. Installation of conveyor system	200,000	10,200,000	9	186,000	(14,000)
9. Construction of new plant	2,300,000	12,500,000	8	2,093,000	(207,000)
10. Purchase of executive aircraft	200,000	12,700,000	7	128,000	(72,000)

Summary

Capital budgeting, which involves commitments for large outlays whose benefits (or drawbacks) extend well into the future, is of the greatest significance to a firm. Decisions in these areas will therefore have a major impact on the future well-being of the firm. This chapter focused on how capital budgeting decisions can be made more effective in contributing to the health and growth of a firm. The discussion stressed the development of systematic procedures and rules for preparing a list of investment proposals, for evaluating them, and for selecting a cutoff point.

The chapter emphasized that one of the most crucial phases in the process of evaluating capital budget proposals is obtaining a dependable estimate of the benefits that will be obtained from undertaking the project. It cannot be overemphasized that the firm must allocate to competent and experienced personnel the making of these judgments.

Determining Cash Flows. The cash inflows from an investment are the incremental change in after-tax net operating cash income plus the incremental depreciation tax benefit; the cash outflow is the cost of the investment less the salvage value received on an old machine plus any tax loss (or less any tax savings) when the machine is sold.

Ranking Investment Proposals. Three commonly used procedures for ranking investment proposals were discussed in the chapter: payback, net present value, and internal rate of return.

Payback is defined as the number of years required to return the original investment. Although the payback method is used frequently, it has serious conceptual weaknesses, because it ignores the facts (1) that some receipts come in beyond the payback period and (2) that a dollar received today is more valuable than a dollar received in the future.

Net present value is defined as the present value of future returns, discounted at the cost of capital, minus the cost of the investment. The NPV method overcomes the conceptual flaws noted in the use of the payback method.

Internal rate of return is defined as the interest rate that equates the present value of future returns to the investment outlay. The internal rate of return method, like the NPV method, meets the objections to the payback approach.

In most cases, the two discounted cash flow methods give identical answers to these questions: Which of two mutually exclusive projects should be selected? How large should the total capital budget be? However, under certain circumstances conflicts may arise. Such conflicts are caused by the fact that the NPV and IRR methods make different assumptions about the rate at which cash flows may be reinvested, or the opportunity cost of cash flows. In general, the assumption of the NPV method (that the opportunity cost is the cost of capital) is the correct one. Accordingly, our preference is for using the NPV method to make capital budgeting decisions.

Questions

13.1 A firm has $100 million available for capital expenditures. Suppose Project A involves purchasing $100 million of grain, shipping it overseas, and selling it within a year at a profit of $20 million. The project has an IRR of 20 percent and an NPV of $20 million, and it will cause earnings per share (EPS) to rise within one year. Project B calls for the use of the $100 million to develop a new process, acquire land, build a plant, and begin processing. Project B, which if chosen cannot be postponed, has an NPV of $50 million and an IRR of 30 percent. But the fact that some of the plant costs will be written off immediately, combined with the fact that no revenues will be generated for several years, means that accepting Project B will reduce short-run EPS.

a. Should the short-run effects on EPS influence the choice between the two projects?

b. How might situations such as the one described here influence a firm's decision to use payback as a screening criterion?

13.2 Are there conditions under which a firm might be better off if it chose a machine with a rapid payback rather than one with the largest rate of return?

13.3 Company X uses the payback method in evaluating investment proposals and is considering new equipment whose additional net after-tax earnings will be $150 a year. The equipment costs $500, and its expected life is ten years (straight line depreciation). The company uses a three-year payback as its criterion. Should the equipment be purchased under the above assumptions?

13.4 What are the most critical problems that arise in calculating a rate of return for a prospective investment?

13.5 What other factors in addition to rate of return analysis should be considered in determining capital expenditures?

13.6 Would it be beneficial for a firm to review its past capital expenditures and capital budgeting procedures? Explain.

13.7 Fiscal and monetary policies are tools used by the government to stimulate the economy. Using the analytical devices developed in this chapter, explain how each of the following might be expected to stimulate the economy by encouraging investment:

a. A speedup of tax-allowable depreciation (for example, the accelerated methods permitted in 1954 or the guideline depreciable life revisions of 1962).
b. An easing of interest rates.
c. Passage of a new federal program giving more aid to the poor.
d. An investment tax credit.

Problems

13.1 A firm has an opportunity to invest in a machine at a cost of $656,670. The net cash flows after taxes from the machine would be $210,000 per year and would continue for 5 years. The applicable cost of capital for this project is 12 percent.

a. Calculate the net present value for the investment.
b. What is the internal rate of return for the investment?
c. Should the investment be made?

13.2 The following facts are presented on an opportunity to invest in Machine A: Cost of equipment is $120,000. The life is 10 years. The estimated after-tax salvage value at the end of 10 years would be $20,000. The additional investment in working capital required would be $30,000. The applicable tax rate is 40 percent. The cost savings per year are estimated to be cash flows of $40,000 per year for 10 years. The applicable cost of capital is 12 percent. The pro forma income statement for this activity would be:

Sales	$140,000
Operating costs	100,000
Earnings before depreciation, interest and taxes (EBDIT)	40,000
Depreciation	10,000
Earnings before interest and taxes = (EBIT) = (NOI) = (X)	30,000
Taxes at 40 percent	12,000
Net income $X(1 - T)$	$ 18,000

a. Use the worksheet method to calculate the NPV from the project.
b. Present two formulations of the tax-adjusted net cash flows.
c. Should the investment be made?

13.3 After using Machine A for 5 years, the firm has an opportunity to invest in Machine B, which would replace Machine A. Machine B would have a 5-year life, cost $80,000, have a salvage value of $20,000, generate sales of $150,000 per year, and reduce operating expenses by $10,000 per year. If the replacement were made by investing in Machine B, the amount realized on the sale of Machine A would be $30,000.

a. Present the comparative income statements and cash flows for Machines A and B and for the change created by adding Machine B.
b. Calculate the NPV for the investment in Machine B.
c. Compare your results for the NPV of Machine B to the NPV for Machine A previously calculated. Should the investment in Machine B be made?

13.4 The Farlow Company is considering the replacement of a riveting machine with a new one that will increase the earnings before depreciation from $20,000 per year to $51,000 per year. The new machine will cost $100,000 and have an estimated life of eight years with no salvage value. The applicable corporate tax rate is 40 percent, and the firm's cost of capital is 12 percent. The old machine has been fully depreciated and has no salvage value.

a. Evaluate the replacement decision, using straight line depreciation.
b. Evaluate the replacement decision, using sum-of-years'-digits accelerated depreciation.

13.5 Assume that the Farlow Company will be able to realize an investment tax credit of 10 percent on the purchase of the new machine for $100,000; the machine will have a salvage value of $12,000. Assume further that the old machine has a book value of $40,000 and a remaining life of eight years. If replaced, the old machine can be sold now for $15,000. Use straight line depreciation. Evaluate the investment decision.

13.6 Natural Beverages is contemplating the replacement of one of its bottling machines with a newer and more efficient one. The old machine has a book value of $500,000 and a remaining useful life of five years. The firm does not expect to realize any return from scrapping the old machine in five years, but it can sell the machine now to another firm in the industry for $300,000.

The new machine has a purchase price of $1.1 million, an estimated useful life of five years, and an estimated salvage value of $200,000. It is expected to economize on electric power usage, labor, and repair costs and to reduce the number of defective bottles. In total, an annual saving of $250,000 will be realized if the new machine is installed. The company is in the 40 percent tax bracket, has a 10 percent cost of capital, and uses straight line depreciation. (Note: To calculate depreciation, assume that the salvage value is deducted from initial cost to get the depreciable cost.)

a. What is the initial cash outlay required for the new machine?
b. What are the cash flows in Years 1 to 5?
c. What is the cash flow from the salvage value in Year 5?
d. Should Natural Beverages purchase the new machine? Support your answer.

13.7 The FM Company has cash inflows of $275,000 and cash outflows of $210,000 per year on Project A. The investment outlay is $144,000; its life is 8 years; the tax rate is 40 percent. The applicable cost of capital is 14 percent.

a. Calculate the net cash flows and the net present value for Project A, using straight line depreciation for tax purposes.
b. If the earnings before depreciation, interest, and taxes are $40,000 per year, what is the net present value for Project A, using straight line depreciation?
c. Recalculate your answer under Part b, using sum-of-years'-digits depreciation.

13.8 The Starbuck Company is considering the purchase of a new machine tool to replace an obsolete one. The machine being used for the operation has both a tax book value and a market value of zero; it is in good working order and will last, physically, for at least an additional fifteen years. The proposed machine will perform the operation so much more efficiently that Starbuck engineers estimate that labor, material, and other direct costs of the operation will be reduced $4,500 a year if it is installed. The proposed machine costs $24,000 delivered and installed, and its economic life is estimated to be fifteen years, with zero salvage value. The company expects to earn 12 percent on its investment after taxes (12 percent is the firm's cost of capital). The tax rate is 40 percent, and the firm uses straight line depreciation.
a. Should Starbuck buy the new machine?
b. Assume that the tax book value of the old machine is $6,000, that the annual depreciation charge is $400, and that the machine has no market value. How do these assumptions affect your answer?
c. Answer Part b, assuming that the old machine has a market value of $4,000.
d. Answer Part b, assuming that the annual saving will be $6,000.
e. Answer Part a, assuming that the relevant cost of capital is now 6 percent. What is the significance of this change? What can be said about Parts b, c, and d under this assumption?
f. In general, how would each of the following factors affect the investment decision, and how should each be treated?
   1. The expected life of the existing machine decreases.
   2. Capital rationing is imposed on the firm.
   3. The cost of capital is not constant but is rising.
   4. Improvements in the equipment to be purchased are expected to occur each year, and the result will be to increase the returns or expected savings from the new machine over the savings expected with this year's model for every year in the foreseeable future.

13.9 Each of two mutually exclusive projects involves an investment of $120,000. Cash flows (after-tax profits plus depreciation) for the two projects have a different time pattern, although the totals are approximately the same. Project M will yield high returns early and lower returns in later years. (It is a mining type of investment, and the expense of removing the ore is lower at the entrance to the mine, where there is easier access.) Project O yields low returns in the early years and higher returns in the later years. (It is an orchard type of investment, and it takes a number of years for trees to mature and be fully bearing.) The cash flows from the two investments are as follows:

Year	Project M	Project O
1	$70,000	$10,000
2	40,000	20,000
3	30,000	30,000
4	10,000	50,000
5	10,000	80,000

a. Compute the present value of each project when the firm's cost of capital is 0 percent, 6 percent, 10 percent, and 20 percent.
b. Compute the internal rate of return (IRR) for each project.
c. Graph the present value of the two projects, putting net present value (NPV) on the Y-axis and the cost of capital on the X-axis.
d. Can you determine the IRR of the projects from your graph? Explain.
e. Which project would you select, assuming no capital rationing and a constant cost of capital of 8 percent? of 10 percent? of 12 percent? Explain.
f. If capital were severely rationed, which project would you select?

13.10 Because of increasing energy prices, David Bradshaw, the Chief Financial Officer of General Tools Company, is quite concerned about the gas bill of his firm.

Also, Bradshaw is interested in the new tax benefits from installing energy conservation equipment. To encourage energy conservation and to promote industrial and agricultural conversions from oil and gas to alternative forms of energy, the Energy Tax Act of 1978 provided a 10 percent credit in addition to the regular investment credit for "alternative energy property"—such as equipment that uses fuel other than oil or natural gas—and for "specially defined energy property" intended to reduce energy waste in existing facilities. The credit is not refundable, but it can be used to offset 100 percent of tax liability.

Bradshaw is considering the installation of new energy-saving solar equipment to replace the conventional boiler, which uses gas as the only energy source and which can be used for another 15 years. The new solar system is estimated to have a lifetime of 15 years and requires a capital investment of $24,000. The net book value of the old boiler is $10,000. There is no salvage value for either equipment. However, the new system is expected to have an energy saving of one billion BTUs per year. The firm will have a combined 20 percent tax credit on the investment in the new solar system.

The current price is $2.04 for 1,000 cubic feet of natural gas, which contains a million BTUs. The required rate of return on investment is 15 percent after tax; the annual operating and maintenance expenses for the new solar system are estimated to be $400 less than for the conventional boiler; and the old boiler has a current market value of $8,000. The corporate tax rate is 40 percent, and the firm uses straight line depreciation.

a. As a financial analyst, what is your recommendation to Bradshaw?
b. Suppose the annual growth rate of gas prices is expected to be 15 percent. How will this affect your evaluation?

13.11 The Grant Corporation is considering a project which has a five-year life and costs $2,500. It would save $410 per year in operating costs and increase revenue by $300 per year. It would be financed with a five-year loan with the following payment schedule (the annual rate of interest is 8 percent). No salvage value for the new purchased equipment is assumed at the end of the project.

Payment	Interest	Repayment of Principal	Balance
$626.14	$200.00	$426.14	$2,073.86
626.14	165.91	460.23	1,613.63
626.14	129.09	497.05	1,116.58
626.14	89.33	536.81	579.77
626.14	46.37	579.77	0
	$630.70	$2,500.00	

If the company has a 12 percent after-tax cost of capital and a 40 percent tax rate, what is the net present value of the project if the company uses

a. straight line depreciation?
b. double declining balance depreciation (DDB) for the first four years of the project, then straight line depreciation in the fifth year?

13.12 You are considering the economic value of an MBA. Assuming that you can and do enroll in a business school immediately, expenses are $8,000 per year and foregone income is $12,000 per year for the required two years. Your expected yearly income for the following eighteen years is increased by $12,919.

a. What is the return on investment earned? (Hint: It is more than 10 percent.)
b. What are some of the major complicating factors ignored in the information presented?

Selected References

Ang, James S. "A Graphical Presentation of an Integrated Capital Budgeting Model." *Engineering Economist* 23 (Winter 1978), pp. 101–116.

Baumol, William J., and Quandt, Richard E. "Investment and Discount Rates under Capital Rationing—A Programming Approach." *Economic Journal* 75 (June 1965), pp. 317–329.

Beenhakker, Henri L. "Sensitivity Analysis of the Present Value of a Project." *Engineering Economist* 20 (Winter 1975), pp. 123–149.

Bernhard, Richard H. "Mathematical Programming Models for Capital Budgeting—A Survey, Generalization, and Critique." *Journal of Financial and Quantitative Analysis* 4 (June 1969), pp. 111–158.

Bierman, Harold, Jr., and Smidt, Seymour. *The Capital Budgeting Decision.* 3d ed. New York: Macmillan, 1971.

Brick, John R., and Thompson, Howard E. "The Economic Life of an Investment and the Appropriate Discount Rate." *Journal of Financial and Quantitative Analysis* 13 (December 1978), pp. 831–846.

Brigham, Eugene F. "Hurdle Rates for Screening Capital Expenditure Proposals." *Financial Management* 4 (Autumn 1975), pp. 17–26.

Brigham, Eugene R., and Pettway, Richard H. "Capital Budgeting by Utilities." *Financial Management* 2 (Autumn 1973), pp. 11–22.

Ciccolo, John, and Fromm, Gary. " 'Q' and the Theory of Investment." *Journal of Finance* 34 (May 1979), pp. 535–547.

Cooley, Philip L.; Roenfeldt, Rodney L.; and Chew, It-Keong. "Capital Budgeting Procedures under Inflation." *Financial Management* 4 (Winter 1975), pp. 18–27.

Dean, Joel. *Capital Budgeting.* New York: Columbia University Press, 1951.

Donaldson, Gordon. "Strategic Hurdle Rates for Capital Investment." *Harvard Business Review* 50 (March–April 1972), pp. 50–58.

Elton, Edwin J. "Capital Rationing and External Discount Rates." *Journal of Finance* 25 (June 1970), pp. 573–584.

Fama, Eugene F., and Schwert, G. William. "Asset Returns and Inflation." *Journal of Financial Economics* 5 (November 1977), pp. 115–146.

Fogler, H. Russell. "Ranking Techniques and Capital Rationing." *Accounting Review* 47 (January 1972), pp. 134–143.

Fowler, J., and Rorke, C. Harvey. "Capital Budgeting, Capital Asset Pricing and Externalities." *Journal of Business Finance and Accounting* 6 (Summer 1979), pp. 145–155.

Gitman, Lawrence J., and Forrester, John R., Jr. "A Survey of Capital Budgeting Techniques Used by Major U.S. Firms." *Financial Management* 6 (Fall 1977), pp. 66–71.

Grinyer, J. R. "Relevant Criterion Rates in Capital Budgeting." *Journal of Business Finance and Accounting* 1 (Autumn 1974), pp. 357–374.

Grossman, Elliott S. *A Guide to the Determinants of Capital Investment.* Conference Board Report No. 721. New York: Conference Board, 1977, pp. 1–41.

Hastie, Larry K. "One Businessman's View of Capital Budgeting." *Financial Management* 3 (Winter 1974), pp. 36–44.

Hawkins, Clark A., and Adams, Richard A. "A Goal Programming Model for Capital Budgeting." *Financial Management* 3 (Spring 1974), pp. 52–57.

Hoskins, Colin G., and Mumey, Glen A. "Payback: A Maligned Method of Asset Ranking." *Engineering Economist* 25 (Fall 1979), pp. 53–65.

Ignizio, James P. "An Approach to the Capital Budgeting Problem with Multiple Objectives." *Engineering Economist* 21 (Summer 1976), pp. 259–272.

Jean, William H. "Terminal Value or Present Value in Capital Budgeting Programs." *Journal of Financial and Quantitative Analysis* 6 (January 1971), pp. 649–652.

———. *Capital Budgeting.* Scranton, N.J.: International Textbook, 1969.

———. "On Multiple Rates of Return." *Journal of Finance* 23 (March 1968), pp. 187–192.

Jeynes, Paul H. "The Significance of Reinvestment Rate." *Engineering Economist* 9 (Fall 1965), pp. 1–9.

Johnson, Robert W. *Capital Budgeting.* Belmont, Calif.: Wadsworth, 1970.

Klammer, Thomas. "Empirical Evidence of the Adoption of Sophisticated Capital Budgeting Techniques." *Journal of Business* 45 (July 1972), pp. 387–397.

Krasker, William S. "The Rate of Return to Storing Wines." *Journal of Political Economy* 87 (December 1979), pp. 1363–1367.

Lerner, Eugene M., and Rappaport, Alfred. "Limit DCF in Capital Budgeting." *Harvard Business Review* 46 (July–August 1968), pp. 133–139.

Lewellen, Wilbur G.; Lanser, Howard P.; and McConnell, John J. "Payback Substitutes for Discounted Cash Flow." *Financial Management* 2 (Summer 1973), pp. 17–23.

Mao, James C. T. "Survey of Capital Budgeting: Theory and Practice." *Journal of Finance* 25 (May 1970), pp. 349–360.

Martin, John D., and Scott, David F., Jr. "Debt Capacity and the Capital Budgeting Decision." *Financial Management* 5 (Summer 1976), pp. 7–14.

Merrett, A. J., and Sykes, Allen. *Capital Budgeting and Company Finance.* London: Longmans, Green & Company, 1966.

Merville, L. J., and Tavis, L. A. "A Generalized Model for Capital Investment." *Journal of Finance* 28 (March 1973), pp. 109–118.

Meyer, Richard L. "A Note on Capital Budgeting Techniques and the Reinvestment Rate." *Journal of Finance* 34 (December 1979), pp. 1251–1254.

Meyers, Stephen L. "Avoiding Depreciation Influences on Investment Decisions." *Financial Management* 1 (Winter 1972), pp. 17–24.

Nelson, Charles R. "Inflation and Capital Budgeting." *Journal of Finance* 31 (June 1976), pp. 923–931.

Pappas, James L. "The Role of Abandonment Value in Capital Asset Management." *Engineering Economist* 22 (Fall 1976), pp. 53–61.

Petry, Glenn H. "Effective Use of Capital Budgeting Tools." *Business Horizons* 19 (October 1975), pp. 57–65.

Petty, J. William; Scott, David F., Jr.; and Bird, Monroe M. "The Capital Expenditure Decision-Making Process of Large Corporations." *Engineering Economist* 20 (Fall 1966), pp. 53–61.

Pratt, John W., and Hammond, John S. III. "Evaluating and Comparing Projects: Simple Detection of False Alarms." *Journal of Finance* 34 (December 1979), pp. 1231–1242.

Quirin, G. David. *The Capital Expenditure Decision.* Homewood, Ill.: Richard D. Irwin, 1967.

Robichek, Alexander A.; Ogilvie, Donald G.; and Roach, John D. C. "Capital Budgeting: A Pragmatic Approach." *Financial Executive* 37 (April 1969), pp. 26–38.

Robichek, Alexander A., and Van Horne, James C. "Abandonment Value and Capital Budgeting." *Journal of Finance* 22 (December 1967), pp. 577–590.

Sarnat, Marshall, and Levy, Haim. "The Relationship of Rules of Thumb to the Internal Rate of Return: A Restatement and Generalization." *Journal of Finance* 24 (June 1969), pp. 479–489.

Schall, Lawrence D.; Sundem, Gary L.; and Geijsbeek, William R. "Survey and Analysis of Capital Budgeting Methods." *Journal of Finance* 33 (March 1978), pp. 281–292.

Schwab, Bernhard, and Lusztig, Peter. "A Note on Abandonment Value and Capital Budgeting." *Journal of Financial and Quantitative Analysis* 5 (September 1970), pp. 377–380.

———. "A Comparative Analysis of the Net Present Value and the Benefit-Cost Ratios as Measures of the Economic Desirability of Investments." *Journal of Finance* 24 (June 1969), pp. 507–516.

Solomon, Ezra. *The Theory of Financial Management.* New York: Columbia University Press, 1963.

———. *The Management of Corporate Capital.* New York: Free Press of Glencoe, 1959.

Stephen, Frank. "On Deriving the Internal Rate of Return from the Accountant's Rate of Return." *Journal of Business Finance and Accounting* 3 (Summer 1976), pp. 147–150.

Taggart, Robert A., Jr. "Capital Budgeting and the Financing Decision: An Exposition." *Financial Management* 6 (Summer 1977), pp. 59–64.

Van Horne, James C. "A Note on Biases in Capital Budgeting Introduced by Inflation." *Journal of Financial and Quantitative Analysis* 6 (January 1971), pp. 653–658.

Waters, Robert C., and Bullock, Richard L. "Inflation and Replacement Decisions." *Engineering Economist* 21 (Summer 1976), pp. 249–257.

Weingartner, H. Martin. "Some New Views on the Payback Period and Capital Budgeting Decisions." *Management Science* 15 (August 1969), pp. 594–607.

———. "The Generalized Rate of Return." *Journal of Financial and Quantitative Analysis* 1 (September 1966), pp. 1–29.

———. "Capital Budgeting of Interrelated Projects: Survey and Synthesis." *Management Science* 12 (March 1966), pp. 485–516.

———. *Mathematical Programming and the Analysis of Capital Budgeting Problems.* Englewood Cliffs, N.J.: Prentice-Hall, 1963.

Williams, John Daniel, and Rakich, Jonathan S. "Investment Evaluation in Hospitals." *Financial Management* 2 (Summer 1973), pp. 30–35.

Appendix A to Chapter 13

Additional Issues in Capital Budgeting Analysis

Several related issues are covered in this supplement to the basic capital budgeting processes described in Chapter 13. These topics include: (1) analyzing projects of different scale, (2) projects of different lives, (3) reinvestment rate considerations, (4) capital budgeting under inflation, (5) multiple IRR solutions, and (6) capital rationing.

Projects of Different Scale

Considerations involved in projects of different scale are illustrated by the following example. Suppose that we are comparing Project A, which calls for a $1 million investment in a conveyor belt system for handling goods in a storage warehouse, with Project B, which calls for an expenditure of $300,000 to do the same thing using forklift trucks. Cash savings from the use of the equipment are $200,000 per year for the conveyor belt system and $71,560 per year for the forklift trucks, each for ten years. At a 12 percent cost of capital, the gross present value and net present values are shown in Table 13A.1, along with their respective IRR's.

The conveyor system and the forklift trucks are alternative methods of handling materials in the warehouse and are mutually exclusive investments. Hence their ranking determines which will be selected. By the NPV method, Project A is preferred. But the IRR method gives B a higher rank. To aid in the evaluation of the two alternative projects, we have also calculated another measure of investment worth, the profitability index (PI), which has been proposed to deal with the issue of unequal scale of investment.

Table 13A.1

Data on Mutually Exclusive Investments of Different Scale

Project	Equipment	Investment Costs	Cash Flows	GPV at 12%	NPV	IRR	PI
A	Conveyor belt	$1,000,000	$200,000	$1,130,040	$130,040	15%	1.13
B	Forklift trucks	300,000	71,560	404,328	104,328	20%	1.35

The Profitability Index

The profitability index (PI), or the benefit/cost ratio as it is sometimes called, is defined as

$$PI = \frac{\text{PV Benefits}}{\text{Cost}} = \frac{\sum_{t=1}^{N} \frac{F_t}{(1+k)^t}}{\text{Cost}}. \quad (13A.1)$$

The PI shows the *relative* profitability of any project, or the PV of benefits per dollar of cost.[1]

As was true in the NPV versus IRR comparison, the NPV and PI always make the same accept-reject decisions, but NPV and PI can give different project rankings, which presents problems when mutually exclusive projects are compared. When we calculate the ratio of the present value of the returns on each project to its cost, we find A's ratio to be 1.13 and B's ratio to be 1.35. Thus, using the PI for our ranking, we would select Project B because it produces higher net returns for each dollar invested.

Given this conflict, which project should be accepted? Alternatively stated: Is it better to use the net present value approach on an absolute basis (NPV) or on a relative basis (PI)? We can be guided to the correct answer by use of an incremental approach. The differential between the initial outlays of the two projects ($700,000) can be looked upon as an investment itself, Project C. That is, Project A can be broken down into two components, one identically equal to Project B and one a residual project equal to the hypothetical Project C. The hypothetical investment has a net present value equal to the differential between the NPV of the first two projects, or $25,712. This is shown below:

Project	Cost	NPV
A	$1,000,000	$130,040
B	−300,000	−104,328
C	$ 700,000	$ 25,712

Since the hypothetical Project C has a positive net present value, it should be accepted. This amounts to accepting Project A.

To put it another way, Project A can be split into two components, one costing $300,000 and having a net present value of $104,328, the other costing $700,000 and having a net present value of $25,712. As each of the two components has a positive net present value, both should be accepted; but if Project B is accepted, the effect is to reject the second component of Project A, the hypothetical Project C. As the PI method selects Project B while the NPV method selects Project A, we conclude that the NPV method is preferable.

Alternatively, we can make an adjustment to make the projects of equal

1. If costs are incurred in more than one year, they should be netted against cash inflows in the corresponding years; if costs exceed cash inflows in some years, the denominator must be the PV of the costs.

scale or size. We can calculate the NPV*, the NPV based on terminal values, by assuming an additional investment of $700,000 for Project B, earning at the project's cost of capital. If the project cost of capital is 12 percent, for example, the extra investment earns and is discounted at 12 percent rates. The present value of the inflows must therefore be $700,000. We have added $700,000 to both the gross present value and the investment cost, so the NPV* of Project B is $104,328, the same as its NPV. The PI method would now take into account the additional $700,000 investment and its present value of $700,000. The original PV of benefits was $404,328, to which is added the PV of $700,000, for total PV benefits equal to $1,104,328. Next we divide by the cost of $1,000,000 to obtain a PI of 1.10, which is less than the 1.13 PI calculated for Project A. Thus when the PI is adjusted for differences in scale or size of investments, it will give the same rankings as the NPV.

An extreme example is often cited to argue for the superiority of the PI method. Suppose that Project L costs $1 million and has a net present value of $100,000, while Project S costs $100,000 and has a net present value of $99,000. It may be argued that the benefits from Project S are almost as great as for Project L, but the amount of funds invested is much smaller. However, if we perform an NPV* analysis by assuming an investment of an additional $900,000 in Project S at the applicable cost of capital to make its cost equal with Project L's, we find that the NPV* of Project S will be $1,000 less than NPV* for Project L. It may be argued that Project S without the additional investment is less risky because of the smaller investment outlay. But as we will see in Chapter 14, riskiness should be evaluated directly. A small project may be subject to greater variation in returns than a larger one. It is not valid to assume that riskiness is proportional to the size of the project. While we have emphasized that, in finance, mechanical rules should not be substituted for judgment, the NPV* generally provides the correct result, which should be set aside only for compelling reasons and after all important facets of the evidence have been included in the analysis.

Projects of Unequal Lives

To simplify the analysis, the previous capital budgeting examples assumed that alternative investments had equal lives. Suppose, however, that we must choose between two mutually exclusive investments that have different lives. For example, Investment 1 has a life of five years while Investment 2 has a life of seven years. An illustration would be a wooden bridge that would have a shorter life and lower initial cost than a steel bridge. Both provide about the same quantity of services per year, but the wooden bridge would require more maintenance and more frequent replacement. But since the lives of the two alternative investments are different, the net present value of the cash flows cannot be compared directly. The problem is pictured in Figure 13A.1 for a five- and a seven-year alternative.

A computationally easy and theoretically sound method for handling this

Figure 13A.1

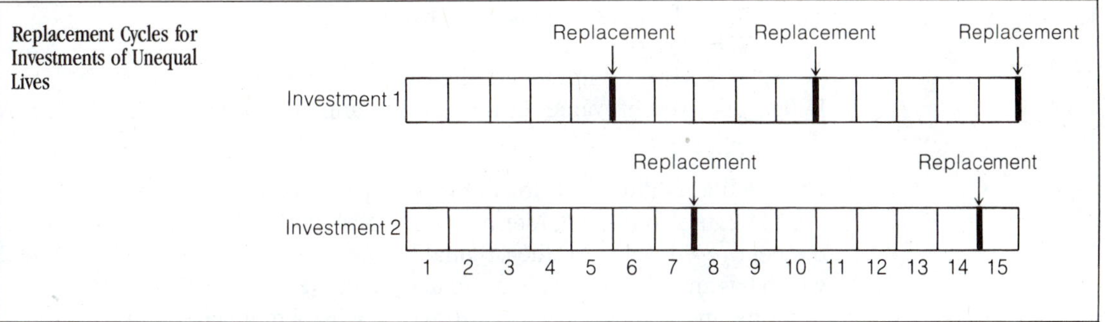

Replacement Cycles for Investments of Unequal Lives

different length of lives problem is to replace each alternative as it wears out and find the total net present value of each infinitely replaced alternative.[2] Then the net present value of each infinite-lived alternative can be compared. To find the net present value of each extended alternative, which we shall call NPV_∞:

1. Find the net present value NPV_N of the cash flows for each alternative for the original life and for the applicable cost of capital, k.
2. Divide NPV_N by the present value interest factor for an annuity for N years at rate k. This gives an equivalent level annuity amount (a) that will give the same present value NPV_N if invested at rate k for N years.
3. Divide the annuity (a) by the applicable cost of capital (k) to obtain NPV_∞. (The present value of an amount received to infinity is the amount divided by the discount factor.)

Procedures 1 and 2 have the effect of normalizing, both by the amount of the investment and by the number of years that the cash flows from the investment are received. This makes it possible to compare directly the two streams of normalized annual cash flows.

The third step takes the level annual flows normalized by the amount of investment and discounts them to infinity. Even when the discount rates are different, we have an NPV evaluation over infinite lives, so that again direct comparisons can appropriately be made.

The three steps above are summarized and expressed in symbols in Equation 13A.2.

$$NPV_\infty = \frac{[NPV_N/PVIFA_{k,N}]}{k} = \frac{a}{k} \tag{13A.2}$$

where

NPV_∞ = Present value of the infinite-lived alternative

2. An alternative method is to equate lives by assuming a reinvestment rate for the shorter-lived project for the additional years required to equate lives.

a = Equivalent level annuity
N = Life of the original alternative
k = Cost of capital
NPV_N = Net present value of the cash flows for the original life, N
$PVIFA_{k,N}$ = Present value factor for an annuity of \$1 at rate k for N years.

The method is illustrated for the mutually exclusive Projects 1 and 2 in Table 13A.2. In Table 13A.2, Alternative 1 is preferable. Note that comparison of the net present value for the original lives would have selected Alternative 2, which has an NPV of \$129.20, compared to the NPV of \$99.08 for Alternative 1.

Some methods for evaluating unequally-lived mutually exclusive alternatives compare the annuities a in the above analysis. Since NPV_∞ is the quotient of a divided by k, this method can lead to the wrong choice if the risk classes of the alternatives differ so that the cost of capital, k, is different. In the Table 13A.2 example a comparison of annuities would have selected the \$28.31 for Alternative 2 versus \$26.14 for Alternative 1. In most replacement decisions, however, k will be the same and the two methods will give the same decision. The method used in the table assumes that the projects can be repeated in perpetual replacement chains. If this assumption is not appropriate, an alternative method is to assume a reinvestment rate for the project of shorter duration, thus equalizing its life with the project of longer duration.

Table 13A.2

Evaluating Projects of Unequal Lives

Project	Initial Cost *(I)*	Life *(N)*	Cost of Capital *(k)*	Annual Net Cash Flow *(F)*
1	\$280	5 years	10%	\$100
2	\$350	7 years	12%	\$105

For Alternative 1,

$$NPV_N = (PVIFA_{k,N})\ F - I$$
$$= (PVIFA_{10\%,\ 5\ yrs.})\ \$100 - \$280$$
$$= (3.7908)(\$100) - \$280 = \$99.08,$$
$$a = \frac{NPV_N}{(PVIFA_{k,N})} = \frac{\$99.08}{3.7908} = \$26.137,$$

and

$$NPV_\infty = \frac{\$26.137}{0.10} = \$261.37.$$

Similarly, for Alternative 2,

$$NPV_N = (4.5638)\$105 - \$350 = \$129.20,$$
$$a = \frac{\$129.20}{4.5638} = \$28.310,$$

and

$$NPV_\infty = \frac{\$28.310}{0.12} = \$235.92.$$

Reinvestment Rate Assumptions

For projects of different scale and of different lives, different ranking criteria give different results. Comparing the NPV and IRR methods, we find different reinvestment rate assumptions to be the cause of the different rankings. The NPV method assumes that the opportunity exists to reinvest the cash flows from a project at the cost of capital, while the IRR method assumes reinvestment at the IRR. This point is presented in the following steps:

Step 1. Notice that both the NPV and IRR methods employ the compounding and discounting relationships introduced in Chapter 4. For example, to determine the NPV of a project, we discount the series of cash flows at the appropriate rate and then subtract the initial project cost.

Step 2. Recall that the present value of any future sum is defined as the beginning amount, which, when compounded at a specified and constant interest rate, will grow to equal the future amount over the stated time period. We can see in Tables A.1 and A.2 at the end of the book, for instance, that the present value of $1,217, due in five years and discounted at 4 percent, is $1,000, because $1,000 compounded at 4 percent for five years will grow to $1,217. Thus, compounding and discounting are reciprocal processes.

Step 3. Compounding requires reinvestment of all interest earned. In any period, the amount that earns interest is the original invested amount plus the sum of all interest earned in prior periods. Therefore, compounding and its reciprocal, discounting, both assume the reinvestment of all earnings.

Step 4. The NPV method implicitly assumes that all cash flows are reinvested at the cost of capital, k; the implicitly assumed reinvestment rate in the IRR method is R, which is the IRR in the solution process.

Step 5. Suppose the cash flows from a project are not reinvested but are used for current consumption. No reinvestment is involved; yet an IRR for the project could still be calculated. Does this show that the reinvestment assumption is not *always* implied in the IRR calculation? The answer is no; reinvestment itself is not necessarily assumed, but the *opportunity* of reinvestment is assumed. Because that assumption is made in the very construction of the PV equations and because calculation of both NPV and IRR is based on those equations, we simply could not define or interpret the concepts of NPV and IRR without assuming reinvestment.

Terminal Value

These concepts and the impact of actual reinvestment rates on the choice of capital budgeting methods can be made clear through the use of an example involving both *terminal value* (the value of an asset at a future time) and present value. First note that the value of any asset or collection of assets, such as a firm, can be estimated at any point in time. We are primarily interested in the value of the asset at the present time—its present value—because this figure represents the contribution of that asset to the value of the firm, which is what management seeks to maximize. However, the terminal value is useful for examining the difference between the NPV and the IRR.

Table 13A.3

Project Data for Analyzing Reinvestment Rate Assumptions

Project	Cost	Year 1	Year 2	Year 3	Cost of Capital
Project X	$10,000	$5,000	$5,000	$ 5,000	10%
Project Y	$10,000	$ 0	$ 0	$17,280	10%

A firm is considering two alternative projects, X and Y, whose salient features are presented in Table 13A.3. Both projects cost $10,000, but Project X provides cash flows every year, while Project Y has no cash flows until Year 3.

The usual NPV and IRR measures are presented in Table 13A.4. Project X has an IRR of 23.4 percent, which is higher than the 20 percent IRR of Project Y. But at the 10 percent cost of capital, the NPV of Project Y is $2,982, which is higher than Project X's NPV of $2,435. Which of the two projects should be selected?

The assumptions with regard to reinvestment rates become critical. Project Y has no intermediate cash flows, so it is not affected by reinvestment rate assumptions. However, the terminal values of Project X will be affected by the reinvestment rate assumption for cash flows during Years 2 and 3. The calculation of terminal values for different reinvestment rate assumptions are presented in Table 13A.5.

The terminal values of Project X, as shown in Table 13A.5, range from $15,918 to $19,063, depending on the reinvestment rate assumptions for cash flows during Years 2 and 3. The value to the firm is the present value of the terminal value, discounted at the 10 percent cost of capital. This value is $12,982 if Project Y is chosen. But it will range from $11,959 to $14,322, depending upon reinvestment opportunities, if Project X is selected. At a reinvestment rate of somewhat under 15 percent, the adjusted net present values

Table 13A.4

Calculation of NPV and IRR

	Alternative Discount Rates	Present Value at Alternative Discount Rates	NPV	IRR
Project X	6.0%	$13,365	$3,365	
	10.0	12,435	2,435	
	20.0	10,533	533	
	23.4	9,996	(4)	23.4%
Project Y	6.0	$14,508	$4,508	
	10.0	12,982	$2,982	
	20.0	10,000	0	20.0%
	23.4	9,196	(804)	

Table 13A.5

Effect of Reinvestment Rate Assumptions on NPV* and IRR*

	Alternative Reinvestment Rates	Resulting Terminal Values	Present Value of Terminal Value at 10 Percent	NPV*	IRR*
Project X	6%	$15,918	$11,959	$1,959	16.76%
	10	16,550	12,434	2,434	18.29
	15	17,363	13,045	3,045	20.19
	20	18,200	13,674	3,674	22.09
	25	19,063	14,322	4,322	23.99
Project Y	6%	$17,280	$12,982	$2,982	20.00%
	10	17,280	12,982	2,982	20.00
	15	17,280	12,982	2,982	20.00
	20	17,280	12,982	2,982	20.00
	25	17,280	12,982	2,982	20.00

and IRR's of the projects are approximately equal. If the expected reinvestment rates are 15 percent or higher, Project X should be chosen. If the expected reinvestment rate is well under 15 percent, Project Y is preferable. Thus 15 percent corresponds to a crossover point in the evaluation of the two projects.

Measurement of Adjusted NPV and IRR

We can use the terminal value concept to reformulate an adjusted NPV and an adjusted IRR as follows:

$$\text{NPV}^* = \frac{\text{Terminal value}}{(1 + k)^N} - \text{Cost}. \tag{13A.3}$$

$$\text{IRR}^* = \text{Solution value of } R \text{ in the equation}$$

$$\frac{\text{Terminal value}}{(1 + R)^N} - \text{Cost} = 0. \tag{13A.4}$$

NPV* is based on a terminal value obtained by compounding at a rate different from the cost of capital. IRR* is an internal rate of return based on a terminal value obtained by compounding at a rate different from the project's unadjusted internal rate of return.

To calculate these modified NPV's and IRR's, we need the relevant terminal values. In order to calculate terminal values, we need reinvestment rates. If the pattern of reinvestment rates can be estimated, we *should* calculate NPV* and IRR*. They provide measures of project profitability based on assumptions different from the unmodified versions.

For example, for Projects X and Y, let us assume that both the reinvestment rate and the cost of capital, *k,* are 10 percent. The present value of the terminal value of Project X is $12,434, which is less than the present value of the terminal value of Project Y ($12,982). At the 10 percent cost of capital, the value of the IRR* or the solution value of R in Equation 13A.4 is 18.29 percent for Project X, which is less than the 20 percent for Project Y. Note that the NPV* and the IRR* give the same rankings. This will always be the case when the reinvestment rate and the cost of capital are equal. For the data in Table 13A.5 the IRR* for Project X would be greater than the IRR* for Project Y at reinvestment rates greater than 14.8 percent. But the NPV* will also be greater for Project X than for Project Y at reinvestment rates greater than 14.8 percent. The NPV* and IRR* may appear to give different rankings only if the analyst fails to make the proper adjustment for differences in project scale or size of the initial investment outlay.

Comparing Projects with Unequal Lives by Use of NPV* and IRR*

The use of reinvestment rate assumptions made in calculating NPV* and IRR* provides another method for comparing projects with unequal lives. For example, let us compare Projects A and B, with the same scale but unequal lives. Each has an investment cost of $10,000 and an applicable cost of capital of 10 percent. Project A provides cash flows of $5,000 per year for three years, while Project B provides cash flows of $2,200 for ten years. The NPV for each is:

$$\begin{aligned} NPV_a &= \$5{,}000(2.4869) - \$10{,}000 = \$2{,}435. \\ NPV_b &= \$2{,}200(6.1446) - \$10{,}000 = \$3{,}518. \end{aligned}$$

The IRR for each is:

$$\begin{aligned} IRR_a &= 10{,}000/5{,}000 = 2.0000 \text{ interest factor for 3 years} = 23.38\%. \\ IRR_b &= 10{,}000/2{,}200 = 4.5455 \text{ interest factor for 10 years} = 17.68\%. \end{aligned}$$

We observe that Project A has a lower NPV and a higher IRR. But the project lives are different, so the comparison is not complete. We can make use of reinvestment rate assumptions for the shorter-lived project to the last year of the longer project and calculate the NPV* and/or IRR*. Since the adjusted measures give the same rankings, it is necessary to calculate only one of them. We shall calculate both for illustrative purposes. First we calculate the terminal values:

$$\begin{aligned} GTV_a &= \$5{,}000(CVIFA_{10\%,\ 3\ yrs.})(CVIF_{10\%,\ 7\ yrs.}) \\ &= \$5{,}000\,(3.3100)(1.9487) = \$32{,}251, \text{ and} \\ GTV_b &= \$2{,}200\,(CVIFA_{10\%,\ 10\ yrs.}) \\ &= \$2{,}200(15.937) = \$35{,}061, \end{aligned}$$

where GTV is gross terminal value.

We can now calculate the adjusted NPV*:

$$\begin{aligned} NPV^*_a &= \$32{,}251(PVIF_{10\%,\ 10\ yrs.}) - \$10{,}000 \\ &= \$32{,}251(0.3855) - \$10{,}000 \\ &= \$12{,}433 - \$10{,}000 = \$2{,}433, \text{ and} \\ NPV^*_b &= \$35{,}061(PVIF_{10\%,\ 10\ yrs.}) - \$10{,}000 \\ &= \$35{,}061(0.3855) - \$10{,}000 \\ &= \$13{,}516 - \$10{,}000 = \$3{,}516. \end{aligned}$$

Next, we calculate the adjusted IRR*.

$$IRR^*_a = GTV/Cost = CVIF_{X\%,\ 10\ yrs.} = 32{,}251/10{,}000 = 3.2251 = 12.42\%.$$
$$IRR^*_b = GTV/Cost = CVIF_{X\%,\ 10\ yrs.} = 35{,}061/10{,}000 = 3.5061 = 13.37\%.$$

We observe that Project B has a higher ranking under both the NPV* and the IRR* measures. Project B also has the higher unadjusted NPV. The results for the adjusted measures reflect the reinvestment rate assumption made. We assumed reinvestment at the cost of capital. It requires only a slight increase in the reinvestment rate assumed for Project A for the seven additional years to match the ten-year life of Project B, at which point Project A becomes equal in merit to Project B.

$$\begin{aligned} 35{,}061 &= 16{,}550(CVIF_{X\%,\ 7\ yrs.}) \\ 2.118489 &= CVIF_{X\%,\ 7\ yrs.} \\ X &= 11.32\%. \end{aligned}$$

Thus the reinvestment rate assumption is crucial for the outcome in ranking alternative projects. But it may also be useful for financial managers to think about reinvestment opportunities and the related rates for a more complete evaluation of projects. It is necessary to look into the future and make forecasts for individual projects even when ranking is not involved—for example, to determine an unadjusted NPV. This is because of the continuing impact of a high rate of inflation in the U.S. economy. We therefore next consider how inflation needs to be taken into account in capital budgeting analysis.

Capital Budgeting Procedures under Inflation

Since 1966 the United States has experienced persistent inflation at levels exceeding the moderate price level changes of previous peacetime periods. What effects does this have on the results of capital budgeting analysis?[3] We can analyze the impacts of inflation by using an illustrative example to clarify the new influences introduced.

Let us begin with the standard capital budgeting case in which inflation is absent. The expression for calculating the net present value of the investment is shown in Equation 13A.5.

$$\overline{NPV} = \sum_{t=1}^{N} \frac{\bar{F}_t}{(1 + k)^t} - I. \qquad (13A.5)$$

The symbols used have the following meanings and values:

$\overline{NPV}$ = Expected net present value of the project

3. For articles on this subject see J. C. Van Horne, "A Note on Biases in Capital Budgeting Introduced by Inflation," *Journal of Financial and Quantitative Analysis* 6 (January 1971), pp. 653–658; and P. L. Cooley, R. L. Roenfeldt, and It-Keong Chew, "Capital Budgeting Procedures under Inflation," *Financial Management* 4 (Winter 1975), pp. 18–27. Also see Cooley, Roenfeldt, and Chew's exchange with M. C. Findlay and A. W. Frankle in *Financial Management* 5 (Autumn 1976), pp. 83–90.

$\bar{F}_t$ = Expected net cash flows per year from the project = \$20,000
k = Cost of capital applicable to the risk of the project = 9 percent
N = Number of years the net cash flows are received = 5
I = Required investment outlay for the project = \$75,000

With the data provided, we can utilize Equation 13A.5 as follows:

$$\begin{aligned}\overline{\text{NPV}}_0 &= \sum_{t=1}^{N} \frac{\$20{,}000}{(1.09)^t} - \$75{,}000 \\ &= \$20{,}000(3.8897) - \$75{,}000 \\ &= \$77{,}794 - \$75{,}000 \\ &= \$2{,}794.\end{aligned}$$

We find that the project has an expected net present value of \$2,794; under the simple conditions assumed, we would accept the project. Now let us consider the effects of inflation. Suppose that inflation at an annual rate of 6 percent is expected to take place during the five years of the project. Since investment and security returns are based on expected future returns, the anticipated inflation rate will be reflected in the required rate of return on the project or the applicable cost of capital for the project. This relationship has long been recognized in financial economics and is known as the *Fisher effect.* In formal terms we have:

$$(1 + k_j)(1 + n) = (1 + K_j), \tag{13A.6}$$

where K_j is the required rate of return in nominal terms and n is the anticipated annual inflation rate over the life of the project. For our example, Equation 13A.6 would be:

$$(1 + 0.09)(1 + 0.06) = (1 + 0.09 + 0.06 + 0.0054).$$

If the cross product term 0.0054 is included in the addition, we would have 0.1554 as the required rate of return in nominal terms. However, since the cross product term is generally small and since both k_j, the required rate of return in real terms, and n, the anticipated inflation rate, are estimates, it is customary practice to make a simple addition of the real rate and the inflation rate. The required nominal rate of return K_j that would be used in the calculation would therefore be 15 percent.

It is at this point that some biases in capital budgeting under inflationary conditions may be introduced. The market data utilized in the estimated current capital costs will include the premium for anticipated inflation. But while the market remembers to include an adjustment for inflation in the capitalization factor, in the capital budgeting analysis the cash-flow estimates may fail to include an element to reflect future inflation. As a consequence, the analysis would appear as in the calculations below for $\overline{\text{NPV}}_1$.

$$\overline{\text{NPV}}_1 = \sum_{t=1}^{N} \frac{\$20{,}000}{(1.09)^t(1.06)^t} - \$75{,}000 \doteq \sum_{t=1}^{N} \frac{\$20{,}000}{(1.15)^t} - \$75{,}000$$

$$\doteq \$20{,}000(3.3522) - \$75{,}000$$
$$\doteq \$67{,}044 - \$75{,}000 \doteq (\$7{,}956).$$

It now appears that the project will have a negative net present value of almost \$8,000. With a negative net present value of substantial magnitude, the project would be rejected. However, a sound analysis requires that the anticipated inflation rate also be taken into account in the cash flow estimates as well. Initially, for simplicity, let us assume that the same inflation rate of 6 percent is applicable to the net cash flows. We take this step in setting forth the expression for $\overline{\text{NPV}}_2$ as follows:

$$\overline{\text{NPV}}_2 = \sum_{t=1}^{N} \frac{\$20{,}000(1.06)^t}{(1.09)^t(1.06)^t} - \$75{,}000 = \sum_{t=1}^{N} \frac{\$20{,}000}{(1.09)^t} - \$75{,}000.$$

Since the inflation factors are now in both the numerator and the denominator and are the same, they can be cancelled. The result for the calculation of $\overline{\text{NPV}}_2$ will therefore be the same as for $\overline{\text{NPV}}_0$ (a positive \$2,794). Thus when anticipated inflation is properly reflected in both the cash flow estimates in the numerator and the required rate of return from market data in the denominator, the resulting $\overline{\text{NPV}}$ calculation will be both in real and nominal terms. This was noted by M. Chapman Findlay III as follows: "Any properly measured, market-determined wealth concept is, simultaneously, *both nominal and real.* . . . Hence, $\overline{\text{NPV}}$, or any other wealth measure, gives the amount for which one can 'cash out' now (nominal) and also the amount of today's goods that can be consumed at today's prices (real)."[4] Thus if inflation is reflected in both the cash flow estimates and the required rate of return, the resulting $\overline{\text{NPV}}$ estimate will be free of inflation bias.

To this point we have purposely kept the analysis simple in order to focus on the basic principles involved, since controversy has erupted over certain issues. In applying these concepts, the anticipated inflation might be expected to affect the required rate of return and the cash flow estimates differently. Indeed, the components of the net cash flows, the cash outflows and the cash inflows, may themselves be influenced by the anticipated inflation to different magnitudes. These complications will not, however, change the basic method of analysis, only the specifics of the calculations. The nature of the more complex case is indicated by Equation 13A.7.

$$\overline{\text{NPV}}_0 = \sum_{t=1}^{N} \frac{[(\overline{\text{Inflows}})_t(1 + n_i)^t - (\overline{\text{Outflows}})_t(1 + n_o)^t](1 - T)}{(1 + K)^t} + \frac{(\overline{\text{Depr}})_t(T)}{(1 + K)^t}. \quad \textbf{(13A.7)}$$

The cash inflows may be subject to a different rate of inflation from the rate of inflation in the cash outflows, and both may differ from the anticipated rate of

4. M. C. Findlay, "Reply," *Financial Management* 5 (Autumn 1976), pp. 83–90.

Table 13A.6

Expected Net Cash Flows without Inflation Effects

	1	2	3	4	5
Expected cash inflows	$40,000	$50,000	$60,000	$70,000	$80,000
Expected cash outflows	15,000	25,000	35,000	45,000	55,000
	25,000	25,000	25,000	25,000	25,000
Times (1 − Tax rate)	0.50	0.50	0.50	0.50	0.50
	12,500	12,500	12,500	12,500	12,500
Depreciation (tax rate)	7,500	7,500	7,500	7,500	7,500
Expected net cash flows ($\bar{F}_t$)	$20,000	$20,000	$20,000	$20,000	$20,000

inflation reflected in the required rate of return in the denominator. Some illustrative data will demonstrate the application of Equation 13A.7.

Table 13A.6 sets forth data for expected cash flows without inflation effects. The pattern is a constant $20,000 per year for five years as in the original example. In Table 13A.7 the estimates of expected net cash flows include inflation effects. The cash inflows are subject to a 7 percent inflation rate, while the cash outflows are subject to an 8 percent inflation rate. The resulting expected net cash flows are shown in the bottom line of the table. The required rate of return of 15 percent is assumed as before to reflect a 6 percent inflation rate.

The calculation of the expected net present value ($\overline{NPV}_3$) is shown in Table 13A.8. Taking all the inflation influences into account, $\overline{NPV}_3$ is a negative $1,447. The project would be rejected. In this example, the inflationary forces on the cash outflows were greater than for the cash inflows. Some have suggested that this influence has been sufficiently widespread and that it accounts for the sluggish rate of capital investment in the United States since the early 1970s.

In the situation we illustrated initially, failure to take inflation into account in the expected cash flows resulted in an erroneous capital budgeting analysis. A project was rejected that, measured correctly, produced a return exceeding the required rate of return. There would be an unsound allocation

Table 13A.7

Expected Net Cash Flows Including Inflation Effects

	1	2	3	4	5
Expected cash inflows (η = 7%)	$42,800	$57,250	$73,500	$91,770	$112,240
Expected cash outflows (η = 8%)	16,200	29,150	44,100	61,200	80,795
	26,600	28,100	29,400	30,570	31,445
Times (1 − Tax rate)	0.50	0.50	0.50	0.50	0.50
	13,300	14,050	14,700	15,285	15,723
Depreciation (tax rate)	7,500	7,500	7,500	7,500	7,500
Expected net cash flows ($\bar{F}_t$)	$20,800	$21,550	$22,200	$22,785	$ 23,223

Table 13A.8

Calculation of $\overline{NPV}_3$

Year	Cash Flow (1)	Discount Factor (15%) (2)	Present Value (1) × (2)
1	$20,800	0.8696	$18,088
2	21,550	0.7561	16,294
3	22,200	0.6575	14,597
4	22,785	0.5718	13,028
5	23,223	0.4972	11,546
		$\overline{NPV}_3$ =	$73,553 − $75,000
			= ($1,447)

of capital if the inflation-caused bias in the analysis had not been taken into account. In our second, and more complex, example, inflation caused the cash outflows to grow at a higher rate than the cash inflows. As a consequence, the expected net present value of the project was negative. Making the inflation adjustment does not always necessarily result in a positive net present value for the project—it simply results in a more accurate estimate of the net benefits from the project, positive or negative.

Multiple Solutions in Calculating IRR

A totally different problem, unrelated to anything discussed thus far, can arise when the IRR is used to rank projects: Under certain circumstances, several different values of r can be used to solve Equation 13A.8:

$$I = \frac{F_1}{(1+r)^1} + \frac{F_2}{(1+r)^2} + \cdots + \frac{F_N}{(1+r)^N}. \quad (13A.8)$$

Notice that this equation is a polynomial of degree N. Therefore, there are N different roots, or solutions, to the equation. All except one of the roots either are imaginary numbers or are negative when investments are normal—a normal investment being one that has one or more outflows (costs) followed by a series of inflows (receipts)—so in the normal case only one positive value of r appears. If, however, a project calls for a large outflow either sometime during or at the end of its life, then it is a nonnormal project, and the possibility of multiple real roots arises.

To illustrate this problem, suppose the project calls for an expenditure of $1,600 for a pump that will enable the firm to recover $10,000 of oil from a field at the end of one year.[5] If the new pump is not installed, the firm will recover the same $10,000 of oil at the end of two years. Obviously, if the pump

5. This example is drawn from J. H. Lorie and L. J. Savage, "Three Problems in Capital Rationing," *Journal of Business* 28 (October 1955), pp. 236–237.

Figure 13A.2

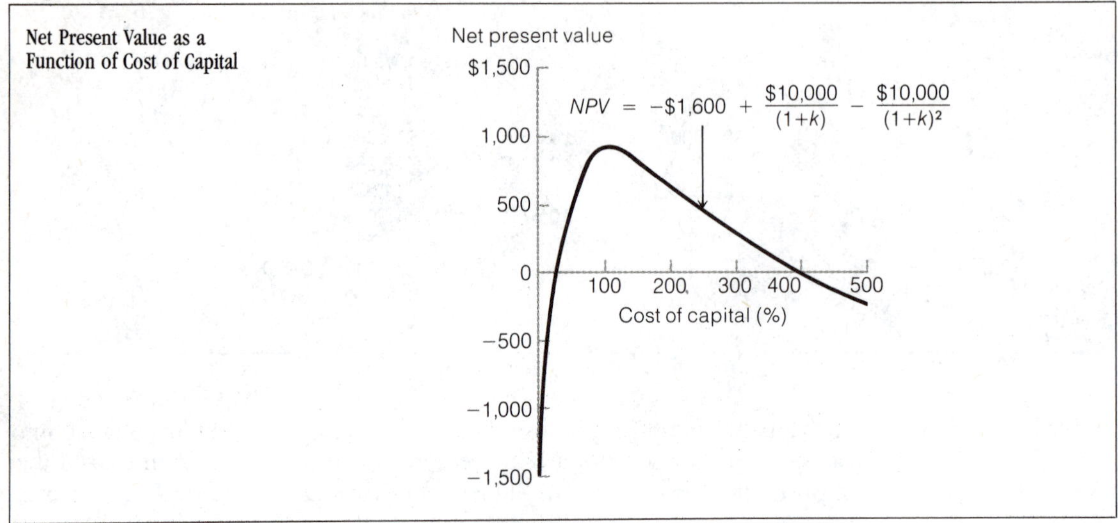

Net Present Value as a Function of Cost of Capital

is installed and the oil is recovered at the end of Year 1, there will be no oil at the end of Year 2. Therefore, the project's cash flows are as follows:

Year end	0	1	2
Cash flow	−$1,600	+$10,000	−$10,000

These values can be substituted into Equation 13A.8 to derive the NPV for the investment:

$$\text{NPV} = -\$1{,}600 + \frac{\$10{,}000}{(1+r)} - \frac{\$10{,}000}{(1+r)^2}.$$

NPV = 0 when r = 25 percent *and* when r = 400 percent, so the IRR of the investment is *both* 25 percent and 400 percent. This relationship is graphically depicted in Figure 13A.2. Note that no dilemma would arise if the NPV method were used—we would simply replace r with k in the equation above, find the NPV, and use this for ranking.[6]

Programming Approaches to Capital Rationing

The problems encountered in capital budgeting that cause conflicts in making decisions are summarized in Table 13A.9. If none of the problems listed in the table apply, then the NPV, IRR, and PI methods always provide identical answers to the critical capital budgeting question: What projects should be ac-

6. For additional insights into the multiple root problem, see James C. T. Mao, *Quantitative Analysis of Financial Decisions* (New York: Macmillan, 1969), Chapter 6.

Table 13A.9

Conditions under which NPV, IRR, and PI May Rank Conflicting Projects Differently

Part A: Project Characteristics

1. The cash flow of one project increases over time, while that of the other decreases.
2. The projects have different expected lives.
3. The cost of one project is larger than that of the other.

Part B: Firm Characteristics

4. Investment opportunities in the future are expected to be different than they are this year, and the direction of change (better or worse) is known.
5. The cost of capital is expected to change in the future, and the direction of change is known.
6. Capital rationing is being imposed upon the firm.

cepted in the capital budget? However, if any of the project characteristics shown in Part A of Table 13A.9 apply, then the three methods can give different rankings to mutually exclusive projects. If none of the firm characteristics in Part B of the table apply, these conflicts really present no problem, as all conflicts should be resolved in favor of the NPV method because it selects the set of projects that maximizes the firm's value.

Very serious difficulties can arise when any of the firm characteristics in Table 13A.9 exist, because then future investment opportunities cease to be constant. In that case, *neither the standard* NPV, IRR, *nor* PI *methods will necessarily select a set of projects that maximizes the firm's value.* However, the NPV concept can be expanded to take account of both firm and project characteristics through the programming approach outlined below.

The programming approach is, in essence, a methodology that seeks to determine the value of the "modified NPV" (NPV*) discussed previously. Initially, consider a procedure that can, at least conceptually, improve our decision. Figure 13A.3 gives a matrix of investments in, and cash flows from, alternative projects. The values in the cells of the matrix are the net cash flows attributable to Projects A, B, . . . over Years 1, 2, . . . , *N*. The rows of the matrix thus represent the investment opportunities available during the relevant time horizon, while the columns of the matrix represent the net cash flows from all projects during a given year. The cash flows in a particular cell can be either positive or negative; a negative cash flow represents an investment, while a positive cash flow represents the benefits resulting from the investment.

Figure 13A.3 simply describes the investment opportunities open to the firm—the capital projects it can undertake. If no capital rationing is imposed, the firm will be able to take on all of the projects that have positive NPV's. If we make the further assumption that the cost of capital is constant, then the straightforward NPV method can be used to determine which of the available projects should be accepted.

Capital Rationing

Suppose, however, that the firm is subject to capital rationing. Specifically, assume that it has an initial amount of money available for investment at the be-

Figure 13A.3

Matrix of Future Investment Opportunities

Years (t)

Projects (j)	1	2	3	4	5	6	7	8	9	10	11	12	13	14	15	···N
A	F_{a1}	F_{a2}	F_{a3}													
B	F_{b1}	F_{b2}	F_{b3}	F_{b4}												
C	F_{c1}	F_{c2}	F_{c3}	F_{c4}	F_{c5}	F_{c6}	F_{c7}									
D		F_{d2}	F_{d3}	F_{d4}	F_{d5}	→										
E		F_{e2}	F_{e3}	···												
F		F_{f2}	F_{f3}	···												
G		F_{g2}	F_{g3}	···												
H			F_{h3}	···												
I			F_{i3}	···												
J			F_{j3}	···												
K				F_{k4}												
L				F_{l4}												
M				F_{m4}												
N					F_{n5}	···										
O					F_{o5}	···										
P					F_{p5}	···										
⋮					⋮											

ginning of Year 1. It can invest this amount but no more. Further, assume that the funds available for investment in future years must come from cash generated from these same investments. Therefore, the funds available for investment in Year 2 will depend on the profitability of the set of investments chosen in Year 1; investment funds available in Year 3 will depend upon cash throw-off from investments in Years 1 and 2, and so forth.[7]

If the projects available for investment in Year 2 are more profitable than those available in Year 1—that is, if they have higher internal rates of return—the firm should perhaps select investments in Year 1 that will have fast paybacks. This will make funds available for the profitable investment opportunities in Year 2. This is, however, only an approximation. Conceptually, the firm should select its investment in each year (subject to the capital rationing con-

7. The concept could also be extended to include any specific amount of external funds during each year. In this case, the capital constraint would be the internally generated funds plus the allowed external funds.

straint) so as to maximize the net present value of future cash flows. These cash flows should, of course, be discounted at the firm's cost of capital. If the investment opportunities were infinitely divisible—for example, if they were securities such as stocks or bonds that could be purchased in larger or smaller quantities—then the firm could use a technique known as *linear programming* to determine the optimal set of investment opportunities. If such opportunities are not infinitely divisible—and in capital budgeting they typically are not—then a more complex procedure known as *integer programming* must be used to find the optimal investment strategy.[8] Regardless of the computational process used to solve the problem, the firm should seek the set of investment opportunities that maximizes the NPV of the firm without exceeding the capital rationing constraint.

Changing Cost of Capital

Assuming that the cost of capital is constant, linear or integer programming offers a conceptual solution to the problem of capital budgeting under capital rationing. These methods do not, however, offer a solution to the general case of a changing cost of capital. For example, if the cost of capital is rising at the point where the IRR curve cuts the MCC curve, the wealth-maximizing set of projects—with regard both to the total budget and to the choices among competing projects—can be determined only by an iterative, or trial-and-error, process. With linear or integer programming, the cost of capital must be given as an input. If, however, the cost of capital *depends* upon the size of the capital budget, then the cost of capital obviously cannot be *assumed* when determining the capital budget. What is required is a dynamic programming model that, through an iterative process, simultaneously determines the capital budget and the marginal cost of capital. Such models are quite complex, but they do have practical applications in capital budgeting; these formal aspects may be pursued further in courses in management science or in operations research.

Problems

13A.1 The Waterford Company is considering two mutually exclusive machine purchases. Machine A costs $6,210 and will produce a return of $1,750 per year. Machine B costs $5,130 and will produce a return of $1,375 per year. Both machines have a six-year life and no salvage value.

a. Compute the present value and net present value of each project if the firm's cost of capital is zero percent, 6 percent, 10 percent, and 20 percent.

b. Compute the internal rate of return for each project.

c. Graph the present values of the two projects, putting net present value (NPV) on the Y-axis and the cost of capital on the X-axis.

8. H. Martin Weingartner, in *Mathematical Programming and the Analysis of Capital Budgeting Problems* (Englewood Cliffs, N.J.: Prentice-Hall, 1963), has shown how integer programming can be used in capital budgeting decisions.

d. Could you determine the IRR of the projects from your graph? Explain.
e. Treat the differential cost of Machine A as an investment and its differential cash flows as the return from the investment. Calculate the internal rate of return on the $1,080 investment.

13A.2 The Harris Company is analyzing two mutually exclusive machine purchases. One is an electric-powered materials handling unit that costs $10,000 and will produce a return of $3,650 per year for five years. A gas-powered materials handling unit costs $7,000 and produces a return of $2,350 per year, also for five years. If the firm's cost of capital is 12 percent, which of the two machines should be purchased?

13A.3 A firm is comparing the purchase of two mutually exclusive machine investments. Machine F involves an investment of $40,000 and would produce annual net cash flows after taxes of $12,000 for five years. Machine H would require an investment of $100,000 and would produce annual cash flows after taxes of $30,000 for seven years. Machine H is somewhat more risky and requires a cost of capital of 12 percent, compared to 10 percent for Machine F. Which machine should be selected?

13A.4 The Norfolk Company is considering two investment projects, each costing $20,000. Project A will provide cash flows of $5,432 per year during its ten-year life. Project B has the same lifetime but will have cash flows of $104,675 at the end of Year 10 only. Norfolk has a cost of capital of 12 percent.
a. First, use the present value method to calculate the NPV and IRR for each project. Which project should be accepted?
b. Calculate the terminal values at different reinvestment rates: 6%, 10%, 12%, 14%, 15%, 20%, and 25%. Based on the calculated terminal values, what will be the NPV* and IRR* for each project? How will this affect the investment decision?

13A.5 The Longdon Company has two alternative investment projects, E and F. As a result of a capital rationing policy, the management is contemplating which project they should accept. The following table provides the management with all the related financial information:

	Project E	Project F
Cost	$15,000	$15,000
Cash flow per year (F_t)	$ 5,500	$ 3,200
Life	4 years	8 years
Cost of capital	12%	12%

a. Calculate the NPV and IRR for each project and make your recommendation.
b. Calculate the NPV*'s and IRR*'s at reinvestment rates of 10%, 12%, 16%, and 20%. How would these calculations affect the management's decision?

13A.6 If the opportunity cost of capital is 15 percent, which of the following three projects has the highest PI? Which will increase shareholders' wealth the most?

Year	Project A	Project B	Project C
0	$-300	$-1,000	$-600
1	320	750	1,100
2	320	750	—
3		750	—

13A.7 The R&R Company is asking your opinion about an investment opportunity of $60,000 which is expected to yield benefits over a four-year period. Annual cash inflows of $150,000 and annual cash outflows of $125,000 are expected, excluding taxes and the depreciation tax shelter. The tax rate is 45 percent, and cost of capital is 9 percent. R&R uses straight line depreciation.

a. What is your suggestion?
b. After a careful evaluation, you discover that no adjustments have been made for inflation or price level changes. The data for the first year are correct, but after that inflows are expected to increase at 3 percent per year and outflows at 4 percent per year; the annual rate of inflation is expected to be about 5 percent. Taking these additional items into account, what is your recommendation?

13A.8 The Comex Company is considering investing in a machine that produces Frisbees. The cost of the machine is $40,000. Production by year during the four-year life of the machine is expected to be as follows: 12,000 units, 16,000 units, 20,000 units, 18,000 units. The market for Frisbees is increasing; hence management believes that the price of Frisbees will increase at about 10 percent annually, compared to the general rate of inflation of 9 percent. The price of Frisbees in the first year will be $2, but plastic used to produce Frisbees is rapidly becoming more expensive. Because of this, production cash outflows are expected to grow at 15 percent per year. First-year production cost will be $1 per unit.

The company will use sum-of-years'-digits depreciation on the new machine. There will be no salvage value at the end of the fourth year. The company's tax rate is 40 percent, and its cost of capital is 18 percent, based on the existing rate of inflation. Should the project be undertaken?

13A.9 Your firm is considering an investment in a machine that produces bowling balls. The cost of the machine is $100,000 with zero expected salvage value. Annual production in units during the five-year life of the machine is expected to be 5,000, 8,000, 12,000, 10,000, and 6,000.

The price of bowling balls is expected to rise from $20 during Year 1 at a rate of 2 percent per year for the following four years. Production cash outflows are expected to grow at 10 percent per year from the first-year production costs of $10 per unit.

Depreciation of the machine will be on a straight line basis. The applicable tax rate is 40 percent, and the applicable cost of capital is 15 percent. Should the investment in the machine be made?

13A.10 You are given the following information about an investment of $40,000: It is expected to yield benefits over a five-year period. It is also expected that there will be annual cash inflows of $90,000 and annual cash outflows of $75,000, excluding taxes and the depreciation tax shelter. There will be no salvage value;

straight line depreciation is used. The tax rate is 40 percent, and the cost of capital is 8 percent.

a. Compute the net present value of the investment.
b. On investigation, you discover that no adjustments have been made for inflation or price level changes. Year 1 data are correct, but after that inflows are expected to increase at 4 percent per year and outflows at 6 percent per year. The general rate of inflation is expected to be about 6 percent, causing the cost of capital to rise to 14 percent. Reevaluate the net present value of the project in light of this information.

13A.11 The investors who set up a firm have a 10 percent cost of capital. Two projects, A and B, are available; each costs $20,000 and provides cash flows as follows:

Year	Project A	Project B
1	$10,000	$ 0
2	10,000	0
3	10,000	35,000

a. Calculate IRR* and NPV* for each project. Assume that cash flows from Project A are reinvested at 14 percent.
b. Which project should be accepted?
c. Is there a reinvestment rate at which the firm should be indifferent between the two projects? If so, what is it?

13A.12 A coal mining firm is considering opening a strip mine, the cost of which is $4.4 million. Cash flows will be $27.7 million, all coming at the end of one year. The land must be returned to its natural state at a cost of $25 million, payable after two years. The IRR is found to be either 9.2 percent or 420 percent. Should the project be accepted (a) if k = 8 percent, or (b) if k = 14 percent? Explain your reasoning.

Selected References

Bailey, Andrew D., Jr., and Jensen, Daniel L. "General Price Level Adjustments in the Capital Budgeting Decision." *Financial Management* 6 (Spring 1977), pp. 26–31.

Beranek, William. "Some New Capital Budgeting Theorems." *Journal of Financial and Quantitative Analysis* 13 (December 1978), pp. 809–829.

Bernhard, Richard H. " 'Modified' Rates of Return for Investment Project Evaluation—A Comparison and Critique." *Engineering Economist* 24 (Spring 1979), pp. 161–167.

———. "Some New Capital Budgeting Theorems: Comment." *Journal of Financial and Quantitative Analysis* 13 (December 1978), pp. 825–829.

———. "Mathematical Programming Models for Capital Budgeting—A Survey, Generalization, and Critique." *Journal of Financial and Quantitative Analysis* 4 (June 1969), pp. 111–158.

Bradley, Stephen, and Frey, Sherwood C., Jr. "Equivalent Mathematical Programming Models of Pure Capital Rationing." *Journal of Financial and Quantitative Analysis* 13 (June 1978), pp. 345–361.

Burton, R. M., and Damon, W. W. "On the Existence of a Cost of Capital under Pure Capital Rationing." *Journal of Finance* 26 (September 1974), pp. 1165–1173.

Findlay, M. Chapman, III, and Williams, Edward E. "Capital Allocation and the Nature of Ownership Equities." *Financial Management* 1 (Summer 1972), pp. 68–76.

Hawkins, Clark A., and Adams, Richard A. "A Goal Programming Model for Capital Budgeting." *Financial Management* 3 (Spring 1974), pp. 52–57.

Lee, Sang M., and Lerro, A. J. "Capital Budgeting for Multiple Objectives." *Financial Management* 3 (Spring 1974), pp. 58–66.

Lockett, A. Geoffrey, and Tomkins, Cyril. "The Discount Rate Problem in Capital Rationing Situations: Comment." *Journal of Financial and Quantitative Analysis* 5 (June 1970), pp. 245–260.

Lorie, James H., and Savage, Leonard J. "Three Problems in Rationing Capital." *Journal of Business* 28 (October 1955), pp. 227–239.

McEnroe, John E., and Nikolai, Loren A. "Information: The Impact upon Investment Criteria." *Journal of Business Research* 7 (December 1979), pp. 315–330.

Myers, Stewart C. "A Note on Linear Programming and Capital Budgeting." *Journal of Finance* 27 (March 1972), pp. 89–92.

Sartoris, William L., and Spruill, M. Lynn. "Goal Programming and Working Capital Management." *Financial Management* 3 (Spring 1974), pp. 67–74.

Schwab, Bernhard, and Lusztig, Peter. "A Comparative Analysis of the Net Present Value and the Benefit Cost Ratios as Measures of the Economic Desirability of Investments." *Journal of Finance* 24 (June 1969), pp. 507–516.

Weingartner, H. Martin. "Capital Rationing: n Authors in Search of a Plot." *Journal of Finance* 32 (December 1977), p. 1403.

———. *Mathematical Programming and the Analysis of Capital Budgeting Problems.* Englewood Cliffs, N.J.: Prentice-Hall, 1963.

———. "The Excess Present Value Index—A Theoretical Basis and Critique." *Journal of Accounting Research* 1 (Autumn 1963), pp. 213–224.

14
Investment Decisions under Uncertainty

In Chapter 5, some basic risk and return relationships were set forth for subsequent use with related topics. In this chapter, we develop the foundation for these risk-return relationships to provide a more complete understanding of the uses and limitations of the concepts and then cover some further applications in the evaluation of investment projects. The two approaches of analyzing projects in isolation and in a portfolio context are utilized throughout, with emphasis on the latter.

The traditional measures of risk have been applied to individual projects in isolation. Newer approaches have recognized that individual projects can be combined with others into groups of projects, or portfolios. Viewing an individual project in its broader portfolio context changes the appropriate measure of risk to be applied. The derivation of the portfolio approach will be emphasized in this chapter, starting with a discussion of the traditional risk measures applied to individual projects so that the relationships between the different approaches can be seen.

The traditional measures of risk for projects in isolation are stated in terms of probability distributions. The tighter the probability distribution of expected future returns, the smaller the risk of a given project. The measure of tightness it utilizes is the standard deviation. The tighter the probability distribution, the smaller the standard deviation. However, the standard deviation must also be related to the expected return. The coefficient of variation is a measure of risk in which the standard deviation is normalized by dividing by the expected value, or mean.

Portfolio Risk

When considering the riskiness of a particular investment, it is frequently useful to consider the relationship between the investment in question and other existing assets or potential investment opportunities. To illustrate, a steel company may decide to diversify into residential construction materials. It knows that when the economy is booming, the demand for steel is high, and the returns from the steel mill are large. Residential construction, on the other hand, tends to be countercyclical: When the economy as a whole is in a recession, the demand for construction materials is high.[1] Because of these divergent cyclical patterns, a diversified firm with investments in both steel and construction could expect to have a more stable pattern of revenues than would a firm engaged exclusively in either steel or residential construction. In other words, the deviations of the returns on the *portfolio of assets,* σ, may be less than the sum of the deviations of the returns from the individual assets.[2]

This point is illustrated in Figure 14.1. Part a of the figure shows the rate of return variations for the steel plant, while Part b shows the fluctuations for the residential construction material division and Part c shows the rate of return for the combined company. When the returns from steel are large, those from residential construction are small, and vice versa. As a consequence, the combined rate of return is relatively stable.

If we calculate the correlation between the rates of return on the steel and construction divisions, we find the correlation coefficient to be negative. If Projects A and B have a high degree of *negative correlation,* then taking on the two investments reduces the firm's overall risk. This risk reduction is defined as a *portfolio effect.*

On the other hand, if there had been a high *positive correlation* between Projects A and B—that is, if returns on A were high at the same time those on

Figure 14.1

Relationship of Returns on Two Hypothetical Investments

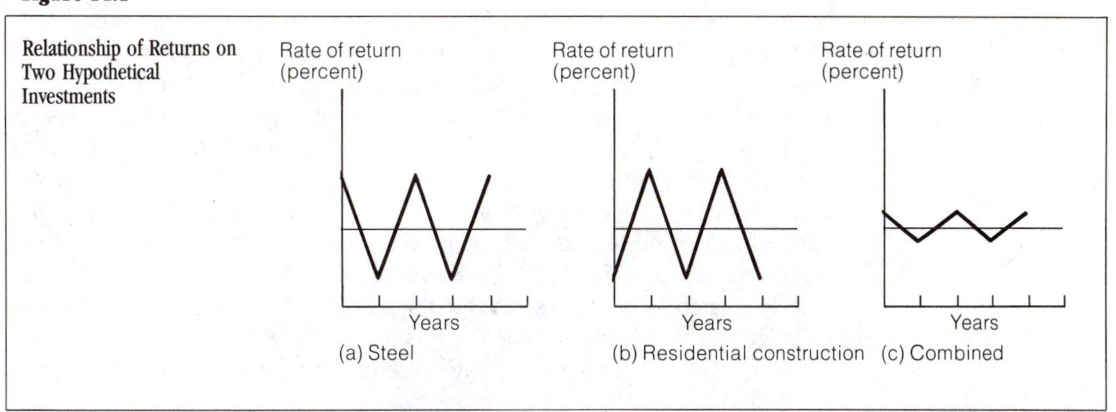

1. The reason for the countercyclical behavior of the residential construction industry has to do with the availability of credit. When the economy is booming, interest rates are high. High interest rates seem to discourage potential home buyers more than they do other demanders of credit. As a result, the residential construction industry has historically shown marked countercyclical tendencies.
2. These conclusions obviously hold also for portfolios of financial assets—stocks and bonds. In fact, the basic concepts of portfolio theory were developed specifically for common stocks by Harry Markowitz and were first presented in his article, "Portfolio Selection," *Journal of Finance* 7 (March 1952), pp. 77–91. The logical extension of portfolio theory to capital budgeting calls for considering firms as having "portfolios of tangible assets."

B were high—overall risk could not have been reduced significantly by diversification. If the correlation between A and B had been +1.0, the risk reduction would have been zero, so no portfolio effects would have been obtained.

If the returns from the two projects were completely uncorrelated—that is, if the correlation coefficient between them was zero—then diversification would benefit the firm to at least some extent. The larger the number of uncorrelated, or independent, projects the firm takes on, the smaller will be the variation in its overall rate of return.[3] Uncorrelated projects are not as useful for reducing risk as are negatively correlated ones, but they are better than positively correlated projects.

Correlation coefficients range from +1.0, indicating perfect positive correlation, to −1.0, indicating perfect negative correlation. If the correlation coefficient is zero, then the projects are independent, or uncorrelated.

We can summarize the arguments on portfolio risk that have been presented thus far:

1. If *perfectly negatively correlated* projects are available in sufficient number, then diversification can completely eliminate risk. Perfect negative correlation is, however, almost never found in the real world.
2. If *uncorrelated* projects are available in sufficient number, then diversification can reduce risk significantly—to zero at the limit.
3. If all alternative projects are *perfectly positively correlated,* then diversification does not reduce risk at all.

In fact, most projects are *positively* correlated but not *perfectly* correlated. The degree of intercorrelation among projects depends upon economic factors, and these factors are usually amenable to analysis. Returns on investments in projects closely related to the firm's basic products and markets will ordinarily be highly correlated with returns on the remainder of the firm's assets, and such investments will not generally reduce the firm's risk. However, investments in other product lines and in other geographic markets may have a low degree of correlation with other components of the firm and may therefore reduce overall risk. Accordingly, if an asset's returns are not too closely related to the firm's other major assets (or, better still, are negatively correlated with other investments), this asset is more valuable to a risk-averting firm than is a similar asset whose returns are positively correlated with the bulk of the assets.

Expected Return on a Portfolio

A portfolio is defined as a combination of assets, and portfolio theory deals with the selection of optimal portfolios; that is, portfolios that provide the highest possible return for any specified degree of risk, or the lowest pos-

3. The principle involved here is the so-called *law of large numbers.* As the number of independent projects is increased, the standard deviation of the returns on the portfolio of projects will decrease with the square root of the number of projects taken on.

sible risk for any specified rate of return. Since portfolio theory has been developed most thoroughly for *financial assets*—stocks and bonds—we shall, for the most part, restrict our discussion to these assets.[4] However, extensions of financial asset portfolio theory to physical assets are readily made, and certainly the concepts are relevant in capital budgeting.

The rate of return on a portfolio is always a linear function—simply a weighted average of the returns of the individual securities in the portfolio. For example, if 50 percent of the portfolio is invested in a security with a 6 percent expected return (Security L), and 50 percent in one with a 10 percent expected return (Security M), the expected rate of return on the portfolio is

$$\begin{aligned} E(R_p) &= w(6\%) + (1 - w)(10\%) \\ &= 0.5(6\%) + 0.5(10\%) = 8\%. \end{aligned}$$

Here, $E(R_p)$ is the expected return on the portfolio, w is the percent of the portfolio invested in Security L and $(1 - w)$ is the percent invested in Security M. If all of the portfolio is invested in L, the expected return is 6 percent. If all is invested in M, the expected return is 10 percent. If the portfolio contains some of each, the expected portfolio return is a linear combination of the two securities' expected returns—for example, 8 percent in our present case. Therefore, given the expected returns on the individual securities, the expected return on the portfolio depends upon the amount of funds invested in each security.

Figure 14.2 illustrates the possible returns for our two-asset portfolio. Line LM represents all possible expected returns when Securities L and M are combined in different proportions. Note that when 50 percent of the portfolio is

Figure 14.2

Rates of Return on a Two-Asset Portfolio

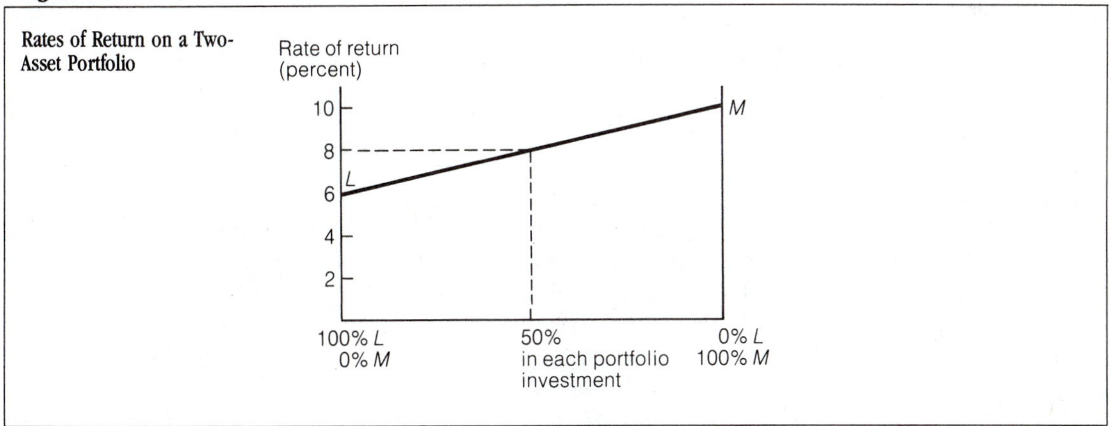

4. Financial assets are highly divisible and available in large numbers, and a great deal of data is available on such assets. Capital assets such as plant and equipment, on the other hand, are "lumpy," and the data needed to apply portfolio theory to such assets are not readily available.

invested in each asset, the expected return on the portfolio is seen to be 8 percent, just as we calculated above.

In general, the expected return on an n-asset portfolio is defined by Equation 14.1:

$$E(R_p) = \sum_{j=1}^{N} w_j R_j. \tag{14.1}$$

Here w_j is the percent of the portfolio invested in the jth asset, and R_j is the expected return on the jth asset. To illustrate, if the portfolio consists of five securities, whose individual returns are shown in the parentheses, then the expected return would be computed as follows:

$$\begin{aligned} E(R_p) &= w_1R_1 + w_2R_2 + w_3R_3 + w_4R_4 + w_5R_5 \\ &= 0.05(20\%) + 0.10(15\%) + 0.20(5\%) + 0.25(10\%) + 0.40(25\%) \\ &= 16\%. \end{aligned}$$

Thus, the portfolio's expected return is a weighted average of the returns on each included asset, with the weights being the proportion of funds invested in each security. Of course, the sum of the weights is always equal to 1; for example,

$$\sum_{j=1}^{N} w_j = 0.05 + 0.10 + 0.20 + 0.25 + 0.40 = 1.$$

Riskiness of a Portfolio

The riskiness of a portfolio is measured by the standard deviation, a normalized index of dispersion. Visually, we can see in Figure 14.3 that the probability distribution for Portfolio X has a wider spread—a greater dispersion of expected returns—than Portfolio Y. Thus Portfolio X has greater risk than Portfolio Y. The numerical values of such differences can also be calculated. Equation 14.2 is used to calculate any standard deviation:

$$\sigma_p = \sqrt{\sum_{s=1}^{N} (R_{ps} - \bar{R}_p)^2 P_s}. \tag{14.2}$$

Here σ_p is the standard deviation of the portfolio's expected returns; R_{ps} is the expected portfolio return given the sth state of the economy; $\bar{R}_p$ is the mean value of the n possible returns; and P_s is the probability of occurrence of the sth state of the economy.[5]

A fundamental aspect of portfolio theory is the idea that the riskiness inherent in any single asset held in a portfolio is different from the riskiness of that asset held in isolation. As we shall see, it is possible for a given asset to be

5. Equation 14.2 is derived from the general definition of the standard deviation, and it may be interpreted similarly; that is, the actual returns earned on a portfolio should lie within $\pm 1\sigma_p$ approximately 68 percent of the time.

Figure 14.3

Distributions of Portfolio Returns

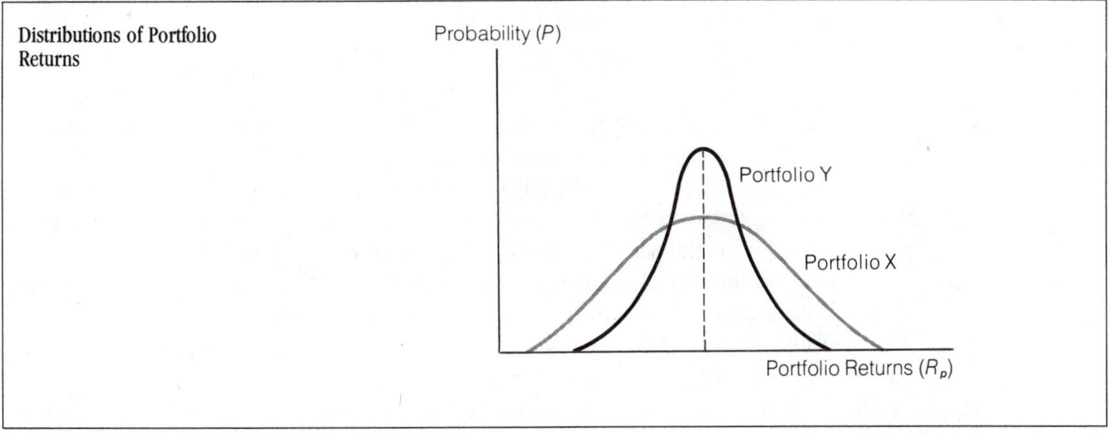

quite risky when held in isolation, but not very risky if held in a portfolio. The impact of a single asset on a portfolio's riskiness—which is the riskiness of the asset when it is held in a portfolio—is discussed later in this chapter.

Measuring the Riskiness of a Portfolio: The Two-Asset Case

Equation 14.2 could be used to calculate the riskiness of a portfolio, but, under the assumption that the distributions of returns on the individual securities are normal, a complicated looking but operationally simple equation can be used to determine the risk of a two-asset portfolio.[6] We are working with Securities A and B:

$$\sigma_p = \sqrt{w^2\sigma_a{}^2 + (1 - w)^2\sigma_b{}^2 + 2w(1 - w)\text{Cov}_{ab}}. \quad (14.3)$$

The *covariance* (Cov) between two securities depends upon (1) the *correlation* between the two securities, and (2) the *standard deviation* of each security's returns; it is calculated as follows:

$$\text{Cov}_{ab} = \rho_{ab}\sigma_a\sigma_b. \quad (14.4)$$

Here Cov_{ab} is the covariance between Securities A and B; ρ_{ab} is the correlation coefficient between A and B; and σ_a and σ_b are the standard deviations of the securities' returns.

6. Equation 14.3 is derived from 14.2 in the standard statistics books. Notice that if $w = 1$, all of the portfolio is invested in Project A and Equation 14.3 reduces to

$$\sigma_p = \sqrt{\sigma_a{}^2} = \sigma_a.$$

The portfolio contains but a single asset, so the risk of the portfolio and that of the asset are identical. It may also be noted that Equations 14.2 and 14.3 can be expanded to include any number of assets by adding additional variance and covariance terms.

Substituting Equation 14.4 for Cov_{ab} in Equation 14.3, we may rewrite Equation 14.3 as Equation 14.5:

$$\sigma_p = \sqrt{w^2\sigma_a{}^2 + (1-w)^2\sigma_b{}^2 + 2w(1-w)\rho_{ab}\sigma_a\sigma_b}. \tag{14.5}$$

Here w is the percentage of the total portfolio value invested in Security A; $(1 - w)$ is the percentage of the portfolio invested in Security B; σ_a is the standard deviation of Security A; σ_b is the standard deviation of Security B; and ρ_{ab} is the correlation coefficient between the securities. Stated another way, if σ_a is the standard deviation of Security A and σ_b is the standard deviation of Security B, then σ_p, the standard deviation of a *portfolio* containing both A and B, is a function of σ_a, σ_b, ρ_{ab}, and w; the specific functional relationship is given as Equation 14.3 or 14.5. Examples of the use of Equation 14.5 are given in a later section.

If $\rho_{ab} = +1.0$, then Equation 14.5 may be simplified to the following linear expression: $\sigma_p = w\sigma_a + (1 - w)\sigma_b$; otherwise, 14.5 is a quadratic equation, and some value of w causes σ_p to be minimized. If we differentiate Equation 14.5 with respect to w, set this derivative equal to zero, and solve for w, we obtain:

$$w_a = \frac{\sigma_b(\sigma_b - \rho_{ab}\sigma_a)}{\sigma_a{}^2 + \sigma_b{}^2 - 2\rho_{ab}\sigma_a\sigma_b}. \tag{14.6}$$

A usual condition assumed in using the equation is that $0 \leq w \leq 1.0$; that is, no more than 100 percent of the portfolio can be in any one asset, and negative positions (short positions) cannot be maintained in any asset.

Two special cases of Equation 14.6 are worthy to note. First, notice that when the returns of Securities A and B are negatively correlated, that is, $\rho_{ab} = -1.0$, then substituting $\rho_{ab} = -1.0$ in Equation 14.6 yields Equation 14.6a, *which can be used only if* $\rho_{ab} = -1.0$.

$$w_a = \frac{\sigma_b}{\sigma_a + \sigma_b}. \tag{14.6a}$$

To illustrate the use of Equation 14.6a, suppose the returns of Securities A and B are perfectly negatively correlated, that is, $\rho_{ab} = -1.0$, $\sigma_a = 2.0$, and $\sigma_b = 4.0$. The riskiness of the portfolio (σ_p) consisting of Securities A and B will be completely eliminated, or equal to zero, if, and only if, 67 percent of the portfolio is invested in Security A:

$$w_a = \frac{4}{2+4} = \frac{4}{6} = 0.67 = 67\%.$$

The second special case is when the returns of Securities A and B are independent ($\rho_{ab} = 0$); substituting $\rho_{ab} = 0$ in Equation 14.6 now yields Equation 14.6b, *which can be used only if* $\rho_{ab} = 0$.

$$w_a = \frac{\sigma_b{}^2}{\sigma_a{}^2 + \sigma_b{}^2}. \tag{14.6b}$$

To illustrate the use of Equation 14.6b, suppose $\rho_{ab} = 0$, $\sigma_a = 8$, and $\sigma_b = 6$. The riskiness of the portfolio (σ_p) is minimized if, and only if, the percentage of the portfolio invested in Security A is equal to 36 percent, computed as follows:

$$w_a = \frac{36}{64 + 36} = \frac{36}{100} = 0.36 = 36\%.$$

Measuring the Riskiness of a Portfolio: The N-Asset Case

An expanded form of Equation 14.3 has been developed to compute the standard deviation of a portfolio consisting of any number of securities:

$$\sigma_p = \sqrt{\sum_{i=1}^{N} w_i^2 \sigma_i^2 + 2\sum_{i=1}^{N-1} \sum_{j=i+1}^{N} w_i w_j \rho_{ij} \sigma_i \sigma_j}. \qquad (14.7)$$

Here w_i is the proportion of the investment allocated to Security *i*, w_j is the proportion allocated to Security *j*, ρ_{ij} is the correlation coefficient between Security *i* and Security *j*, and *N* is the number of securities contained in the portfolio.

Since Equation 14.7 has *N* securities, there are *N* variance terms (that is, $w_i^2 \sigma_i^2$) and $N^2 - N$ covariance terms (that is, $w_i w_j \rho_{ij} \sigma_i \sigma_j$). Since the covariance terms increase quadratically as the number of assets increases, the expanded equation becomes quite complex if *N* is large. For example, if *N* is 500, Equation 14.7 will have 250,000 terms under the radical! The index model utilized by W. F. Sharpe reduces the computational requirements substantially.[7]

Portfolio Opportunities

Suppose we are considering *N* assets, with *N* being any number greater than one. These assets can be combined into an almost limitless number of portfolios, and each possible portfolio will have an expected rate of return, $E(R_p)$, and risk, σ_p. The hypothetical set of all possible portfolios—defined as the *attainable set*—is graphed as the shaded area in Figure 14.4.

Given the full set of potential portfolios that can be constructed from the available assets, which portfolio should *actually* be constructed? This choice involves two separate decisions: (1) determining the *efficient set of portfolios* and (2) choosing from the efficient set the single portfolio that is best for the individual investor. In the remainder of this section we discuss the concept of the efficient set of portfolios; in the next section we consider choices among efficient portfolios.

An *efficient portfolio* is a portfolio that provides the highest possible expected return for any degree of risk, or the lowest possible degree of risk for any expected return. In Figure 14.4 the boundary BCDE defines the *efficient*

7. W. F. Sharpe, *Portfolio Theory and Capital Markets* (New York: McGraw-Hill, 1970), Chapter 7, "Index Models," pp. 117–140.

Figure 14.4

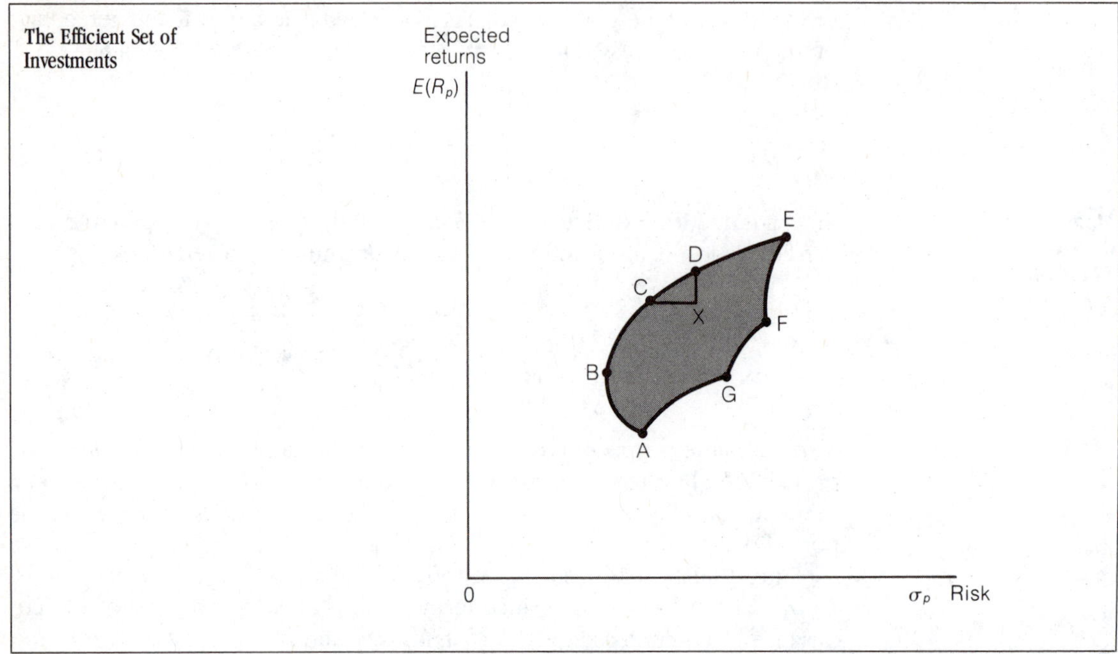

The Efficient Set of Investments

set of portfolios.[8] Portfolios to the left of the efficient set are not possible, because they lie outside the attainable set; that is, there is no set of R_i values that will yield a portfolio with an expected rate of return $E(R_p)$ and risk (σ_p) represented by a point to the left of BCDE. Portfolios to the right of the efficient set are inefficient because some other portfolio could provide either a higher return with the same degree of risk or a lower risk for the same rate of return. To illustrate, consider Point X. Portfolio C provides the same rate of return as does Portfolio X, but C is less risky. At the same time, Portfolio D is as risky as Portfolio X, but D provides a higher expected rate of return. Points C and D (and other points on the boundary of the efficient set between C and D) are said to *dominate* Point X.

Utility Theory and Portfolio Choices

The assumption of risk aversion is basic to many decision models used in finance. Since this assumption is so important, it is appropriate to discuss why risk aversion generally holds.

In theory, we can identify three possible attitudes toward risk: a desire for

8. A computational procedure for determining the efficient set of portfolios was developed by Harry Markowitz and first reported in his article, "Portfolio Selection," *Journal of Finance* 7 (March 1952), pp. 77–91.

risk, an aversion to risk, and an indifference to risk. A *risk seeker* is one who prefers risk; given a choice between more and less risky investments with identical expected monetary returns, this person would prefer the riskier investment. Faced with the same choice, the *risk averter* would select the less risky investment. The person who is indifferent to risk would not care which investment he or she received. *There undoubtedly are individuals who prefer risk and others who are indifferent to it, but both logic and observation suggest that business managers and stockholders are predominantly risk averters.*

Why does risk aversion generally hold? Given two investments, each with the same expected dollar returns, why would most investors prefer the less risky one? Several theories have been advanced in answer to this question, but perhaps the most logically satisfying one involves *utility theory.*

At the heart of utility theory is the notion of *diminishing marginal utility for money.* If, for example, you had no money and then received $100, you could satisfy your most immediate needs. If you then received a second $100, you could utilize it, but the second $100 would not be quite as necessary to you as the first $100. Thus, the "utility" of the second, or *marginal,* $100 is less than that of the first $100, and so on for additional increments of money. Therefore, we say that the marginal utility of money is diminishing.

Figure 14.5 graphs the relationship between income or wealth and its utility, where utility is measured in units called *utils.* Curve A, the one of primary interest, is for someone with a diminishing marginal utility for money. An individual with $5,000 would have 10 utils of "happiness" or satisfaction. With

Figure 14.5

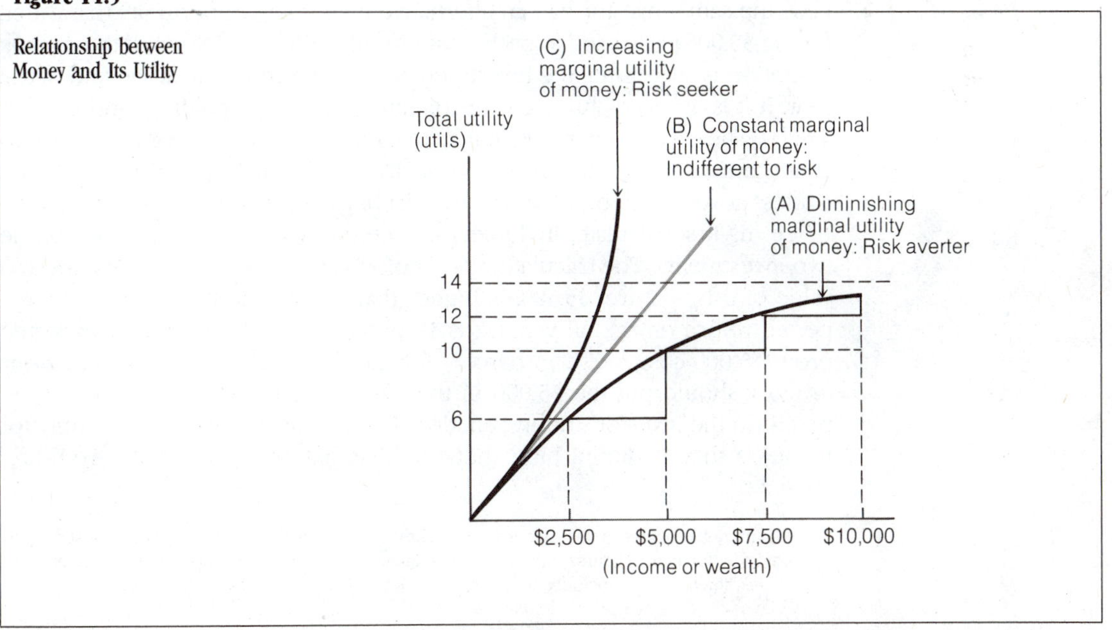

Relationship between Money and Its Utility

an additional $2,500, the individual's satisfaction would rise to 12 utils, an increase of two units. But with a loss of $2,500, the individual's satisfaction would fall to six utils, a loss of four units.

Most investors (as opposed to people who go to Las Vegas) appear to have a declining marginal utility for money, and this directly affects their attitudes toward risk. Our measures of risk estimate the likelihood that a given return will turn out to be above or below the expected return. Someone who has a constant marginal utility for money will value each dollar of "extra" returns just as highly as each dollar of "lost" returns. On the other hand, someone with a diminishing marginal utility for money will get more "pain" from a dollar lost than "pleasure" from a dollar gained. Because of the diminishing utility of money function, the second individual will be very much opposed to risk and will require a very high return on any investment that is subject to much risk. In Curve A of Figure 14.5, for example, a gain of $2,500 from a base of $5,000 would bring two utils of additional satisfaction, but a $2,500 loss would cause a four-util satisfaction loss. Therefore, a person with this utility function and $5,000 would be unwilling to make a bet with a 50–50 chance of winning or losing $2,500. However, the risk-indifferent individual with Curve B would be indifferent to the bet, and the risk lover would be eager to make it.

Diminishing marginal utility leads directly to risk aversion, and this risk aversion is reflected in the capitalization rate investors apply when determining the value of a firm. To make this clear, let us assume that government bonds are riskless securities and that such bonds currently offer a 5 percent rate of return.[9] Thus, someone who bought a $5,000 United States Treasury bond and held it for one year would end up with $5,250, a profit of $250. Suppose the same investor had an alternative investment opportunity that called for the $5,000 to be used to back a wildcat oil-drilling operation. If the drilling operation is successful, the investment will be worth $7,500 at the end of the year. If it is unsuccessful, the investor can liquidate the holdings and recover $2,500. There is a 60 percent chance that oil will be discovered and a 40 percent chance of a dry hole. If our investor has only $5,000 to invest, would the riskless government bond or the risky drilling operation be the wiser choice?

Let us first calculate, in Table 14.1, the expected monetary values of the two investments. The calculation for the oil venture shows that the expected value of this venture, $5,500, is higher than that of the bond. (Also, the expected return on the oil venture is 10 percent [calculated as $500 expected profit/$5,000 cost] versus 5 percent for the bond.) Does this mean that our investor should put the $5,000 in the wildcat well? Not necessarily—it depends on the investor's utility function. If this individual's marginal utility for money is sharply diminishing, then the potential loss of utility that would re-

9. We shall not consider in this discussion any risk of price declines in bond prices caused by increases in the level of interest rates. Thus, the risk with which we are concerned at this point is *default risk,* the risk that principal and interest payments will not be made as scheduled.

Table 14.1

Expected Returns from Two Projects

	Drilling Operation			Government Bond		
States of Nature	Probability (1)	Outcome (2)	(1) × (2) (3)	Probability (1)	Outcome (2)	(1) × (2) (3)
Oil	0.6	$7,500	$4,500	1.0	$5,250	$5,250
No oil	0.4	2,500	1,000			
		Expected value =	$5,500			$5,250

sult from a dry hole, or no oil, might not be fully offset by the potential gain in utility that would result from the development of a producing well. If the utility function that is shown in Curve A of Figure 14.5 is applicable, this is exactly the case. To show this, we modify the expected monetary value calculation to reflect utility considerations. Reading from Figure 14.5, Curve A, we see that this particular risk-averse investor would have approximately 12 utils if he or she invests in the wildcat venture and oil is found, 6 utils if this investment is made and no oil is found, and 10.5 utils with certainty if the investor chooses the government bond. This information is used in Table 14.2 to calculate the *expected utility* for the oil investment. No calculation is needed for the government bond; we know its utility is 10.5 regardless of the outcome of the oil venture.

Since the *expected utility* from the wildcat venture is only 9.6 utils versus 10.5 from the government bond, we see that for this investor the government bond is the preferred investment. Thus, even though the *expected monetary value* for the oil venture is higher, *expected utility* is higher for the bond; risk considerations therefore lead us to choose the safer government bond.

Risk-Return Indifference Curves

Given the efficient set of portfolio combinations, which specific portfolio should an investor choose? To determine the optimal portfolio for a particular investor, we must know the person's attitude toward risk, what is called the risk-return trade-off function.

Table 14.2

Expected Utility of Oil Drilling Project

States of Nature	Probability (1)	Monetary Outcome (2)	Associated Utility (3)	(1) × (3) (4)
Oil	0.6	$7,500	12.0	7.2
No oil	0.4	2,500	6.0	2.4
			Expected utility =	9.6 utils

Figure 14.6

Indifference Curves for Risk and Expected Rate of Return

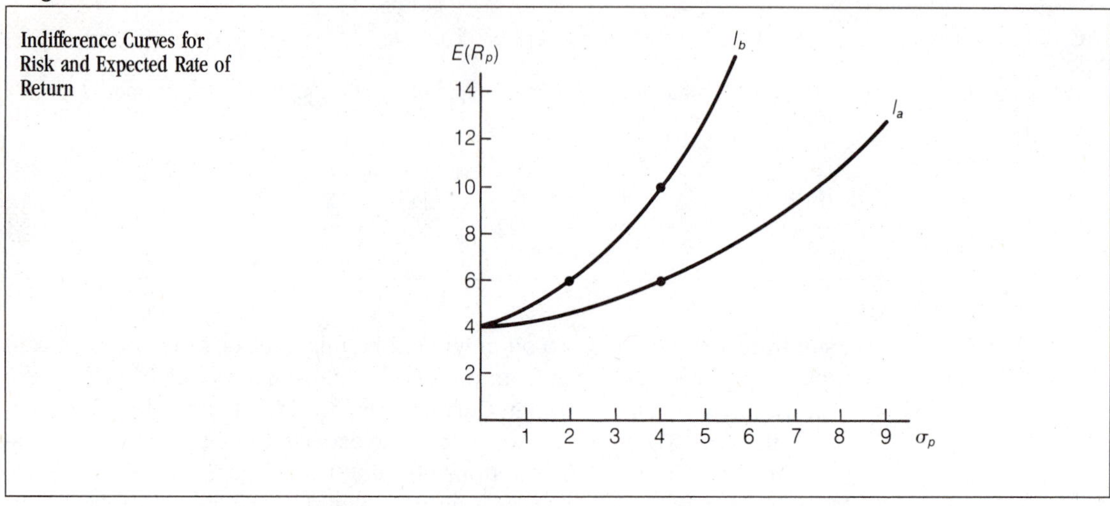

An investor's risk-return preference function is based on the standard economic concept of indifference curves illustrated in Figure 14.6. The curves labelled I_a and I_b represent the indifference curves of individuals A and B. A is equally well satisfied with a riskless 4 percent return, an expected 6 percent return with risk of $\sigma_p = 4$ percent, and so on. B is indifferent between the riskless 4 percent portfolio, a portfolio with an expected return of 6 percent but with a risk of $\sigma_p = 2$ percent, and so on.

Notice that B requires a higher expected rate of return to compensate for a given increase in risk than does A; thus, B is more *risk averse* than A. For example, if $\sigma_p = 4$ percent, B requires a return of 10 percent, while A has a required return of only 6 percent. In other words, B requires a *risk premium* —defined as the difference between the riskless return (4 percent) and the required return—of 6 percentage points to compensate for a risk of $\sigma_p = 4$ percent, while A's risk premium for this degree of risk is only 2 percentage points.

An infinite number of utility curves (like those in Figure 14.7) could be drawn for each individual representing the risk-return trade-off for different levels of satisfaction. For a given level of σ_p, a greater $E(R_p)$ is received as the curves move farther out to the left. Each point on curve I_{a2} represents a higher level of satisfaction, or greater utility, than any point on I_{a1}, and I_{a3} represents more utility than I_{a2}. Also, different individuals are likely to have different sets of curves or different risk-return trade-offs. Since the curves of B start from the same point and have a greater slope in the risk-return plane than the curves of A, this indicates that investor B requires a higher return for the same amount of risk. Then, similarly for Investor B, as the curves move to the left, they represent higher levels of satisfaction.

Figure 14.7

Family of Indifference Curves for Individuals A and B

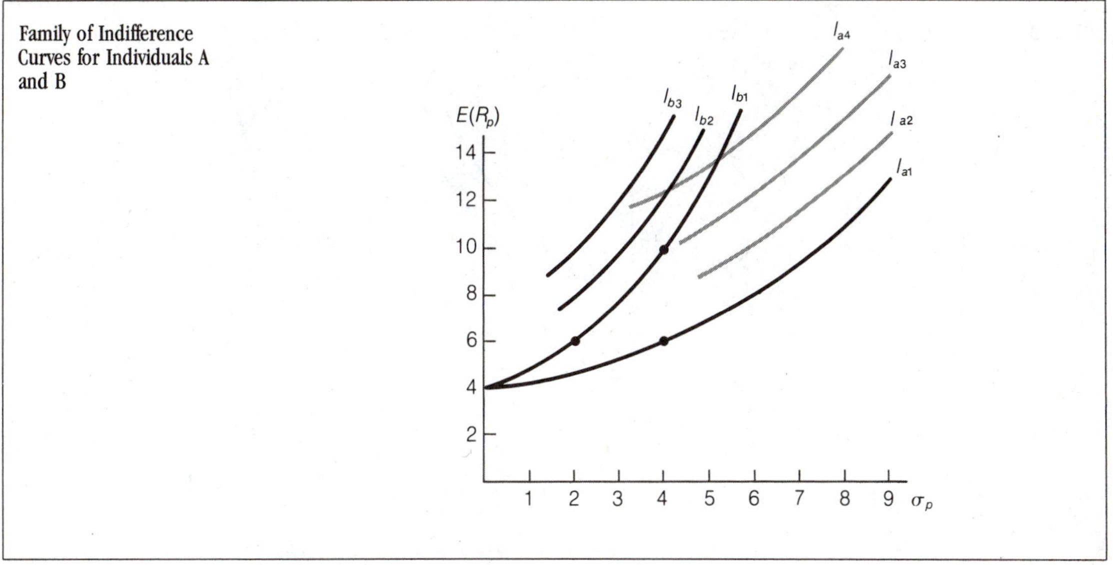

The Optimal Portfolio for an Investor

We can now combine the efficient set of portfolios with indifference curves to determine an individual investor's optimal portfolio. In Figure 14.8 we see that the optimal portfolio is found at the tangency point between the efficient set of portfolios and an indifference curve—this tangency point marks the highest level of satisfaction the investor can attain. Investor A picks a combination of securities (a portfolio) that provides an expected return of about 13 percent and has a risk of about $\sigma_p = 5$ percent. Investor B, who is more risk averse than A, picks a portfolio with a lower expected return (about 11 percent) but a riskiness of only $\sigma_p = 3.7$ percent.

To complete the analysis, we note that A's portfolio contains a larger amount of the more risky securities, while our risk averter, B, selects a portfolio more heavily weighted with low-risk securities.

Investment Decisions under Uncertainty in the CAPM Framework

In Figure 14.8 we graphed a set of portfolio opportunities provided by the market and illustrated a method for selecting the optimal portfolio. In Figure 14.9 the relationships are developed still further to convey the underlying logic of the *capital asset pricing model* (CAPM). Figure 14.9 shows a feasible set of portfolios of risky assets and a set of utility indifference curves (I_1, I_2, I_3), which represent the trade-off between risk and return for an investor. Point *N,* where the utility curve is tangent to the portfolio opportunities curve, *ANMB,* represents an equilibrium: It is the point where the investor

Figure 14.8

Optimal Portfolio Selection

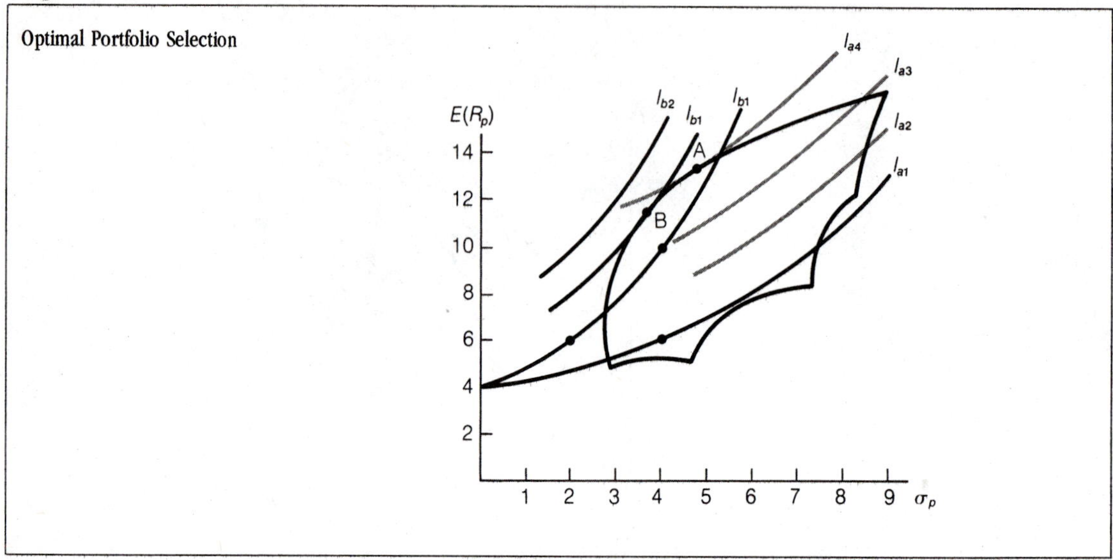

obtains the highest return for a given amount of risk (σ_N) or the smallest risk while obtaining a given expected return, $E(R_N)$.[10]

However, the investor can do better than Portfolio N by reaching a higher indifference curve. In addition to the risky securities represented in the feasible set of portfolios, there is a risk-free asset that yields R_F; this is also shown in Figure 14.9. With the additional alternative of investing in the risk-free asset, the investor can create a new portfolio that combines the risk-free asset with a portfolio of risky assets. This enables the individual to achieve any combination of risk and return lying along a straight line connecting R_F and the point of tangency of the straight line at M on the portfolio opportunities curve. All portfolios on the line R_FMZ are preferred to the other risky portfolio opportunities on Curve *ANMB* (except for Portfolio M, which they have in common); the points on the line R_FMZ represent the highest attainable combinations of risk and return.

Given the new opportunity set R_FMZ, our investor will move to point P, on a higher risk-return indifference curve. Note that line R_FMZ dominates the opportunities that could have been achieved from the portfolio opportunities curve *ANMB* alone. In general, if investors can include both the risk-free security and a fraction of the risky portfolio, M, in their own portfolios, they will have the opportunity to move to a point such as P. In addition, if they can borrow as well as lend (lending is equivalent to buying risk-free securities) at the riskless rate R_F, they can move out onto line segment MZ and will do so if their utility indifference curves are tangent to R_FMZ in that section.

10. To economize on notation we shall usually write σ_p for $\sigma_{(R_p)}$ and σ_m for $\sigma_{(R_m)}$, and so on.

Figure 14.9

Investor Equilibrium Combining the Risk-Free Asset with the Market Portfolio

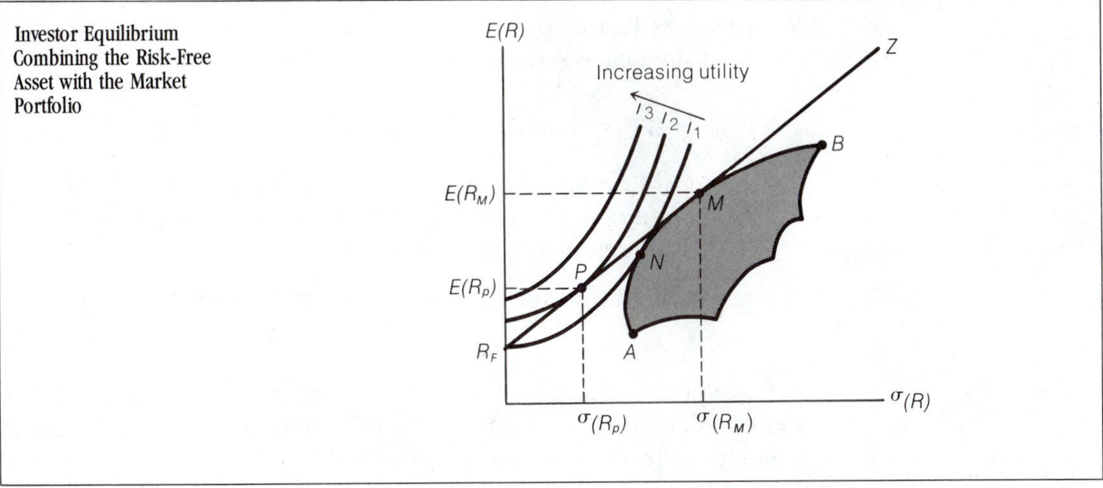

Under the conditions set forth in Figure 14.9, all investors would hold portfolios lying on the line $R_F MZ$; this implies that they would hold only efficient portfolios, which are linear combinations of the risk-free security and the risky Portfolio *M*. For the capital market to be in equilibrium, *M* must be a portfolio that contains every asset in exact proportion to that asset's fraction of the total market value of all assets; that is, if Security J is *w* percent of the total market value of all securities, *w* percent of the market Portfolio *M* will consist of Security J. In effect, *M* represents "the market." Thus, in equilibrium, all investors will hold efficient portfolios with standard deviation-return combinations along the line $R_F MZ$. The particular location of a given individual on the line will be determined by the point at which that person's indifference curve is tangent to the line, and this in turn reflects the person's attitude toward risk, or degree of risk aversion.

The line $R_F MZ$ in Figure 14.9 (using the "rise over run" concept) is stated by Equation 14.8:

$$E(R_p) = R_F + \frac{E(R_M) - R_F}{\sigma_{(R_M)}}\sigma_{(R_p)}. \tag{14.8}$$

Thus, the expected return on any portfolio is equal to the riskless rate plus a risk premium equal to $[E(R_M) - R_F]/\sigma(R_M)$ times the portfolio's standard deviation. Therefore, the *capital market line* (CML) for efficient portfolios bears a linear relationship between expected return and risk, and it may be rewritten as follows:

$$E(R_p) = R_F + \lambda^* \sigma_p. \tag{14.8a}$$

Here:

$E(R_p)$ = Expected return on an efficient portfolio

R_F = Risk-free interest rate

λ^* = Market price of risk; $\lambda^* = \dfrac{E(R_M) - R_F}{\sigma_M}$

σ_p = Standard deviation of returns on an efficient portfolio

$E(R_M)$ = Expected return on the market portfolio

σ_M = Standard deviation of returns on the market portfolio.

All efficient portfolios, including the market portfolio, lie on the CML. Hence:

$$E(R_M) = R_F + \lambda^* \sigma_M. \qquad (14.8b)$$

Both Equations 14.8a and 14.8b state that the expected return on an efficient portfolio in equilibrium is equal to a risk-free return plus the market price of risk multiplied by the standard deviation of the portfolio returns. This relationship is graphed in Figure 14.10. The CML is drawn as a straight line with an intercept at R_F, the risk-free return, and a slope equal to the market price of risk (λ^*), which is the market risk premium $[E(R_M) - R_F]$ divided by σ_M. Thus, the market price of risk, λ^*, is a normalized risk premium. The market price of risk reflects the attitudes of individuals in the aggregate (that is, all individuals) toward risk; thus, it reflects a composite of the utility functions of all individuals.

The Security Market Line (SML)

Thus far we have developed the market model with respect to *portfolios.* Our next step is to relate the model to individual securities. First, note that the expected returns for an individual security or investment can be represented as points on the following *security market line:*[11]

Figure 14.10

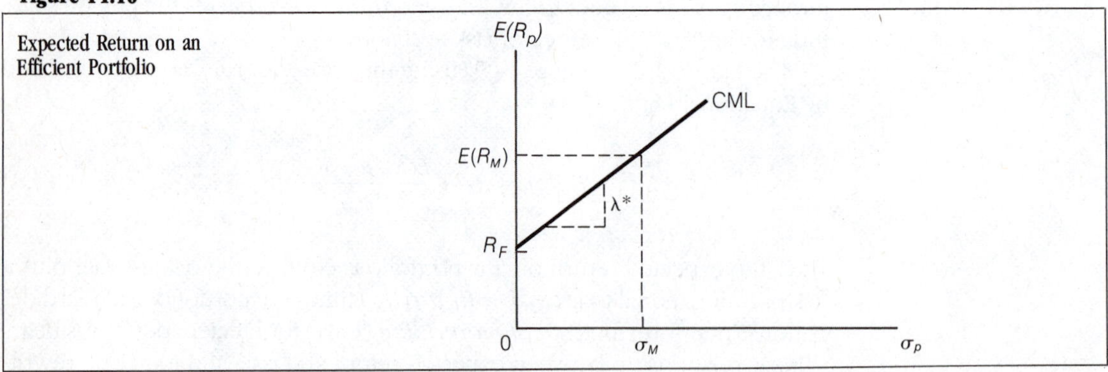

Expected Return on an Efficient Portfolio

11. M. C. Jensen, "Capital Markets: Theory and Evidence," *Bell Journal of Economics and Management Science* 3 (Autumn 1972), pp. 357–398.

$$E(R_j) = R_F + \lambda \, \mathrm{Cov}(R_j,R_M). \tag{14.9}$$

Here:

λ = Price of risk for securities = $[E(R_M) - R_F]/\sigma^2_M$

$\mathrm{Cov}(R_j,R_M)$ = Covariance of the returns of Security J with returns on the market

$E(R_j)$ = Expected return on an individual Security J.

Equation 14.9 for the security market line (SML) is graphed in Figure 14.11, which relates the covariance of the returns on the individual security to the expected return on the individual security.[12] We have now developed the

Figure 14.11

The SML for Individual Securities

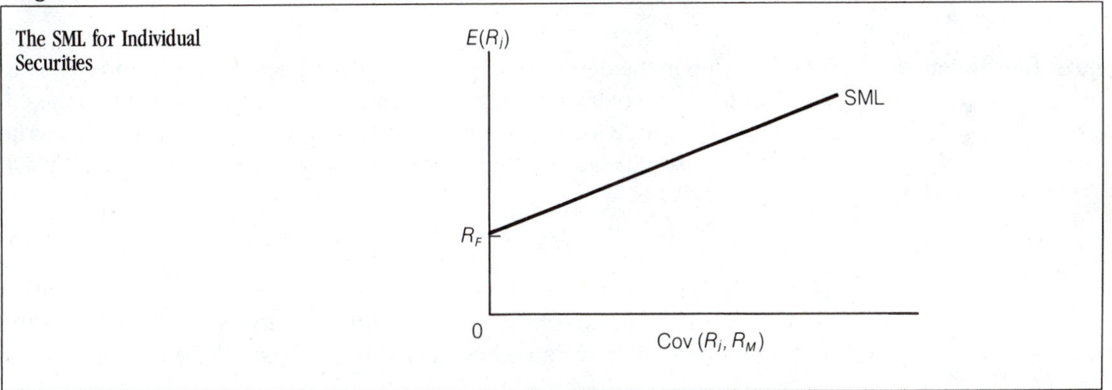

12. The relationship between SML and CML can be shown as follows:

$$\text{(SML): } E(R_j) = R_F + \frac{[E(R_M) - R_F]}{\sigma^2_M}\mathrm{Cov}(R_j,R_M)$$

$$\mathrm{Cov}(R_j,R_M) = \rho(R_j,R_M)\sigma_j\sigma_M,$$

where

$\rho(R_j,R_M)$ = Correlation coefficient between the return of Security J and the market portfolio

σ_j = Standard deviation of the return of Security J

σ_M = As defined before.

Therefore,

$$E(R_j) = R_F + \frac{[E(R_M) - R_F]}{\sigma^2_M}\rho(R_j,R_M)\sigma_j\sigma_M$$

$$= R_F + \frac{[E(R_M) - R_F]}{\sigma_M}\rho(R_j,R_M)\sigma_j.$$

If J is an efficient portfolio, $\rho(R_j,R_M) = 1$. Then SML reduces to CML.

$$E(R_j) = R_F + \frac{[E(R_M) - R_F]}{\sigma_M}\sigma_j$$

$$= R_F + \lambda^*\sigma_j.$$

background for understanding how the SML presented in Chapter 5 is derived.

The SML differs from the CML in two respects. First, for the individual securities or individual firms, the risk measure is the covariance instead of the standard deviation. This is an important conceptual difference because it conveys the recognition that the risk of an individual security or firm is measured in terms of its contribution to the risk of the portfolio into which it is placed. Second, the price of risk is shown as the excess market return normalized by the *variance* of market returns in the denominator instead of the standard deviation. The effect is to change the dimensionality, or scale, of the security market line as compared with the capital market line.

Beta Coefficients

The final step in the development of the CAPM framework is to express risk in terms of the beta coefficient. Rearrange Equation 14.9 by first dividing the covariance of the individual securities by σ^2_M to obtain β_j. We can then write Equation 14.10, which is another version of the security market line in which the return $E(R_j)$ is:

$$E(R_j) = R_F + [E(R_M) - R_F]\beta_j. \tag{14.10}$$

Here β_j is the volatility of the individual security's returns relative to market returns. In this form, we see that the individual security's risk premium is the market risk premium weighted by the relative risk or volatility of the individual security.

Required Return on an Investment

Equation 14.10 states that the expected return on an individual security or real investment is represented by a risk-free rate of interest plus a risk premium. Earlier literature did not provide a theory for the determination of the risk premium. Capital market theory shows the risk premium to be equal to the market risk premium weighted by the index of the systematic risk of the individual security or real investment.

The β for an individual security reflects industry characteristics and management policies that determine how returns fluctuate in relation to variations in overall market returns. If the general economic environment is stable, if industry characteristics remain unchanged, and if management policies have continuity, the measure of β will be relatively stable when calculated for different time periods. However, if these conditions of stability do not exist, the value of β will vary.

The great advantage of Equation 14.10 is that all its factors other than β are market-wide constants. If β's are stable, the measurement of expected returns is straightforward. For example, the returns on the market for long periods have been shown by the studies of L. Fisher and J. Lorie to be at the 9 to 11 percent level.[13] The level of R_F has been characteristically at the 4 to 6 percent level. Thus the expected return on an individual investment, using the lower of each of the two numbers and a β of 1.2, would be:

$$E(R_j) = 4\% + (9\% - 4\%)1.2 = 10\%. \qquad (14.10a)$$

The higher of each of the two figures gives an $E(R_j)$ of 12%:

$$E(R_j) = 6\% + (11\% - 6\%)1.2 = 12\%. \qquad (14.10b)$$

Thus we have numerical measures of the amount of the risk premium that is added to the risk-free return to obtain a risk-adjusted discount rate. The risk-free rate and the market risk premium (the excess of the market return over the risk-free rate) are economy-wide measures. They vary for different time periods, but provide a basis for measurements that can be used in making judgmental decisions. In the numerical illustrations above, if a firm has a beta of 1.2, we would expect its required return according to the security market line to be between 10 and 12 percent, depending on general interest levels. This provides us with a relatively narrow boundary of returns within which managerial judgments may be exercised.

Risk-Adjusted Investment Hurdle Rates

The capital asset pricing model permits the criteria for asset expansion decisions under uncertainty to be set out unambiguously and compactly. The basic relation expressed in Equation 14.10 can also be used to formulate a criterion for capital budgeting decisions;[14] that is, the relationship in Equation 14.10 can be extended to apply to the expected return $E(R_j^\circ)$ on an individual project and its volatility measure, β_j°, as set forth in Inequality 14.11.[15]

$$E(R_j^\circ) > R_F + [E(R_M) - R_F]\beta_j^\circ. \qquad (14.11)$$

In Inequality 14.11 the market constants remain the same. However, the variables for the individual firm now become variables for the individual project by addition of an appropriate superscript. Inequality 14.11 expresses the condition that must hold if the project is to be acceptable. The expected return on the new project must exceed the pure rate of interest plus the market risk premium weighted by β_j°, the measure of the individual project's systematic risk.

The general relationships have been illustrated in Figure 14.12. The criterion in graphical terms is to accept all projects that plot above the market line

13. L. Fisher and J. Lorie, "Rates of Return on Investments in Common Stocks," *Journal of Business* 37 (January 1964), pp. 1–21; L. Fisher, "Some New Stock-Market Indexes," *Journal of Business* 39 (January 1966), pp. 191–218.

14. M. E. Rubinstein, "A Synthesis of Corporate Financial Theory," *Journal of Finance* 28 (March 1973), p. 167.

15. The superscript ° indicates an individual investment project.

Figure 14.12

Illustration of the Use of Investment Hurdle Rates

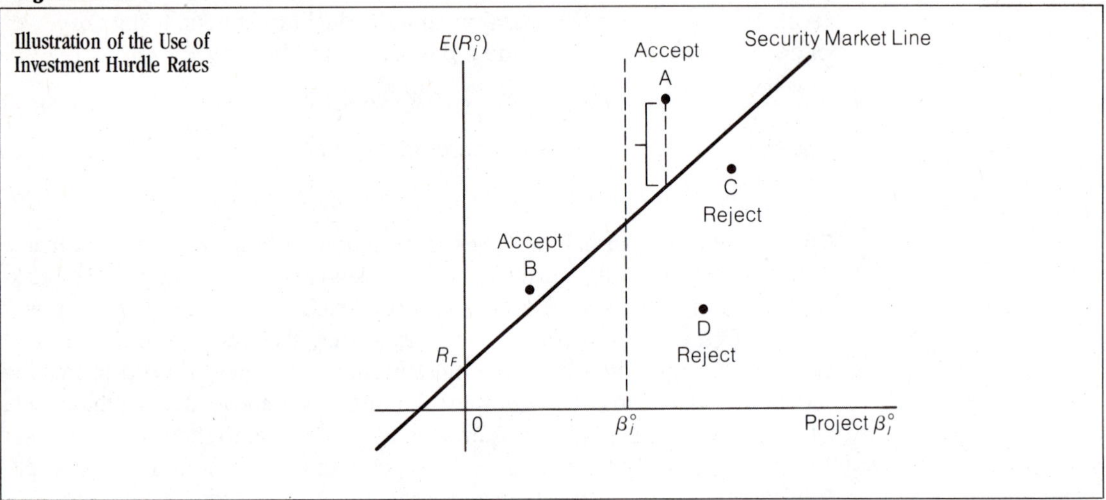

and reject all those that plot below the market line. Managers seek to find new projects such as A and B in Figure 14.12 with returns in excess of the levels required by the risk-return market equilibrium relation illustrated in the figure. When such projects are added to the firm's operations, the expected returns on the firm's common stock (at its previous existing price) will be higher than required by the market line. These "excess returns" induce a rise in price until the return on the stock $E(R_j)$ is at an equilibrium level represented by the security market line in Figure 14.12. These general concepts may now be illustrated more concretely in a numerical example.

The Morton Company Case. In the case that follows, four states-of-the-world are considered with respect to future prospects for real growth in Gross National Product. State 1 represents a relatively serious recession, State 2 is a mild recession, State 3 is a mild recovery, and State 4 is a strong recovery. The probabilities of these alternative future states-of-the-world are set forth in Column 2 of Table 14.3. Estimates of market returns and project rates of return are set forth in the remaining columns.

The Morton Company is considering four projects in a capital expansion program. The economics staff projected the future course of the market portfolio over the estimated life span of the projects under each of the four states-of-the-world (first three columns in Table 14.3); it recommended the use of a risk-free rate of return of 5 percent. The company's finance department provided the estimates of project returns conditional on the state-of-the-world (Columns 4 through 7 in Table 14.3). Each project involves the same investment.

Table 14.3

Summary of Information—Morton Case

State of World (s) (1)	Subjective Probability (P_s) (2)	Market Return (R_{Ms}) (3)	Project Rates of Return: Project 1 (4)	Project 2 (5)	Project 3 (6)	Project 4 (7)
1	0.1	−0.15	−0.30	−0.30	−0.09	−0.05
2	0.3	0.05	0.10	−0.10	0.01	0.05
3	0.4	0.15	0.30	0.30	0.05	0.10
4	0.2	0.20	0.40	0.40	0.08	0.15

Assuming that the projects are independent and that the firm can raise sufficient funds to finance all four projects, which projects would be accepted using the market price of risk (MPR) criterion?

Solution Procedure. In Table 14.4 the data provided by market relationships are utilized to calculate the expected return on the market along with its variance and standard deviation. The probabilities of the future states-of-the-world are multiplied by the associated market returns and their products are summed to obtain the expected market return $E(R_M)$ of 10 percent.

The expected market return $E(R_M)$ is used in calculating the variance and standard deviation of the market returns. This is shown in Columns 4 through 6 of Table 14.4. The expected return is deducted from the return under each state, and deviations from $E(R_M)$ in Column 4 are squared in Column 5. In Column 6 the squared deviations are multiplied by the probabilities of each expected future state (which appear in Column 1). These products are summed to give the variance of the market return. The square root of the variance is its standard deviation.

A similar procedure is followed in Table 14.5 for calculating the expected return and the covariance for each of the four individual projects. The expected return is obtained by multiplying the probability of each state times

Table 14.4

Calculation of Market Parameters

s	P_s (1)	R_M (2)	P_sR_M (3)	$(R_M - \bar{R}_M)$ (4)	$(R_M - \bar{R}_M)^2$ (5)	$P_s(R_M - \bar{R}_M)^2$ (6)
1	0.1	−0.15	−0.015	−0.25	0.0625	0.00625
2	0.3	0.05	0.015	−0.05	0.0025	0.00075
3	0.4	0.15	0.060	0.05	0.0025	0.00100
4	0.2	0.20	0.040	0.10	0.0100	0.00200
			$\bar{R}_M = 0.10$			$\text{Var}(R_M) = 0.01$
						$\sigma_{R_M} = 0.1$

Table 14.5

Calculation of Expected Returns and Covariances for the Four Hypothetical Projects

s	P_s (1)	R_j (2)	P_sR_j (3)	$(R_j - \overline{R}_j)$ (4) $(R_M - \overline{R}_M)$ (5) (6)	$P_s(R_j - \overline{R}_j)(R_M - \overline{R}_M)$ (7)
1	0.1	−0.30	−0.03	(−0.50)(−0.25) = 0.125	0.0125
2	0.3	0.10	0.03	(−0.10)(−0.05) = 0.005	0.0015
3	0.4	0.30	0.12	(+0.10)(+0.05) = 0.005	0.0020
4	0.2	0.40	0.08	(+0.20)(+0.10) = 0.020	0.0040
		$\overline{R}_1$ =	0.20		$Cov(R_1,R_M)$ = 0.0200
1	0.1	−0.30	−0.03	(−0.44)(−0.25) = 0.110	0.0110
2	0.3	−0.10	−0.03	(−0.24)(−0.05) = 0.012	0.0036
3	0.4	0.30	0.12	(+0.16)(+0.05) = 0.008	0.0032
4	0.2	0.40	0.08	(+0.26)(+0.10) = 0.026	0.0052
		$\overline{R}_2$ =	0.14		$Cov(R_2,R_M)$ = 0.0230
1	0.1	−0.09	−0.009	(−0.12)(−0.25) = 0.030	0.0030
2	0.3	0.01	0.003	(−0.02)(−0.05) = 0.001	0.0003
3	0.4	0.05	0.020	(+0.02)(+0.05) = 0.001	0.0004
4	0.2	0.08	0.016	(+0.05)(+0.10) = 0.005	0.0010
		$\overline{R}_3$ =	0.030		$Cov(R_3,R_M)$ = 0.0047
1	0.1	−0.05	−0.005	(−0.13)(−0.25) = 0.0325	0.00325
2	0.3	0.05	0.015	(−0.03)(−0.05) = 0.0015	0.00045
3	0.4	0.10	0.040	(+0.02)(+0.05) = 0.0010	0.00040
4	0.2	0.15	0.030	(+0.07)(+0.10) = 0.0070	0.00140
		$\overline{R}_4$ =	0.080		$Cov(R_4,R_M)$ = 0.00550

the associated forecasted return. The deviations of the return under each state from the expected return are next calculated in Column 4; the deviations of the market returns from their mean are repeated for convenience in Column 5, and the products of these two are calculated in Column 6. Finally, these products are multiplied by the probability factors and summed to determine the covariance for each of the four projects (Column 7).

In Table 14.6, the beta for each project is calculated as the ratio of its covariance to the variance of the market return, and they are employed in Table 14.7 to estimate the required return on each project in terms of the market line relationship. The risk-free rate of return is assumed to be 5 percent, with a market risk premium of 5 percent.

Table 14.6

Calculation of the Betas

$$\beta_1^\circ = 0.0200/0.01 = 2.00$$
$$\beta_2^\circ = 0.0230/0.01 = 2.30$$
$$\beta_3^\circ = 0.0047/0.01 = 0.47$$
$$\beta_4^\circ = 0.0055/0.01 = 0.55$$

Table 14.7

Calculation of Excess Returns

Project Number (1)	Measurement of Required Return (2)	Estimated Return (3)	Excess Return (Percent) (4)
P1	$E(R_1) = 0.05 + 0.05(2.0) = 0.150$	0.200	5.00
P2	$E(R_2) = 0.05 + 0.05(2.3) = 0.165$	0.140	−2.50
P3	$E(R_3) = 0.05 + 0.05(0.47) = 0.0735$	0.030	−4.35
P4	$E(R_4) = 0.05 + 0.05(0.55) = 0.0775$	0.080	0.25

Required returns, as shown in Column 2 of Table 14.7, are deducted from the estimated returns for each individual project to derive the "excess returns." These relations are depicted graphically in Figure 14.13. The MPR criterion accepts the projects with positive excess returns, which appear above the MPR line. It rejects those with negative excess returns (plotted below the MPR line).

Risk and the Timing of Returns

By its nature, the discount rate serves both to allow for the time value of money *and* to provide an allowance for the relative riskiness of a project's returns. In other words, both *time* and *risk* are accounted for by one adjustment process. Since time and risk are really separate variables, this combination value must be carefully chosen if it is to be appropriate for its intended purpose.

A firm using the risk-adjusted discount rate approach for its capital budgeting decisions will have an overall rate that generally reflects its overall, market-determined riskiness. This rate will be used for "average" projects.

Figure 14.13

Application of the CAPM Investment Criterion

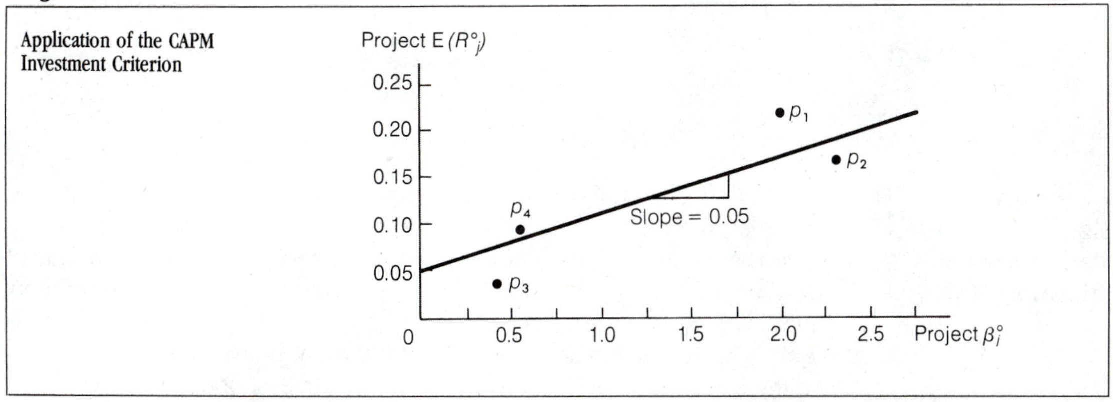

Lower rates will be used for less risky projects, and higher rates will be used for riskier projects. To facilitate the decision process, corporate headquarters may prescribe rates for different divisions and for different classes of investments (for example, replacement, expansion of existing lines, expansion into new lines). Then, investments of a given class within a given division are analyzed in terms of the prescribed rate. For example, replacement decisions in the retailing division of an oil company might all be evaluated with an 8 percent cost of capital, while exploration and production investments might require a 20 percent return.

Notice what such a procedure implies about risk: Risk increases with time, and it imposes a relatively severe burden on long-term projects. This means that short-payoff alternatives will be selected over those with longer payoffs when, for example, there are alternative ways of performing a given task. It also means that less capital-intensive methods of performing given tasks will be employed.

However, there are a substantial number of projects for which distant returns are *not* more difficult to estimate than near-term returns. For example, the estimated returns on a water pipeline serving a developing community may be quite uncertain in the short run, because the rate of growth of the community is uncertain. However, the water company may be quite sure that in time the community will be fully developed and will utilize the full capacity of the pipeline. Similar situations could exist in many public projects—water projects, highway programs, schools, and so forth; in public utility investment decisions; and when industrial firms are building plants to serve specified geographic markets.

To the extent that this implicit assumption of rising risk over time reflects the facts, then a constant discount rate, k, may be appropriate. In the vast majority of business situations, risk actually is an increasing function of time, so a constant risk-adjusted discount rate is reasonable. There are, however, situations for which this is not true; one should be aware of the relationships described in this chapter and avoid the pitfall of unwittingly penalizing long-term projects when they are not, in fact, more risky than shorter-term projects.

Certainty Equivalent and Risk-Adjusted Discount Rates

Since both the certainty equivalent approach and risk-adjusted discount rates may be employed, we shall present materials on each and on their relationships. The certainty equivalent method follows directly from the concepts of utility theory presented earlier in this chapter. Under the subjective certainty equivalent approach, the decision maker must specify how much money is required with certainty in order to be indifferent between this certain sum and the expected value of a risky sum. To illustrate, suppose a rich eccentric offered you the following two choices.

1. Flip a fair coin. If a head comes up, you receive \$1 million, but if a tail comes up you get nothing. The expected value of the gamble is \$500,000 (= 0.5 × \$1,000,000 + 0.5 × 0).
2. You do not flip a coin; you simply pocket \$300,000 cash.

If you find yourself indifferent between the two alternatives, then \$300,000 is your certainty equivalent for the risky \$500,000 expected return. In other words, the certain or riskless amount provides exactly the same utility as the risky alternative. Any certainty equivalent less than \$500,000 indicates a risk aversion.

The certainty equivalent concept is illustrated in Figure 14.14. The curve shows a series of risk-return combinations to which the decision maker is indifferent. For example, Point A represents an investment with a perceived degree of risk as measured by its beta value, β_A, and with an expected dollar return of \$2,000. The individual whose risk-return trade-off function, or indifference curve, is shown here is indifferent between a sure \$1,000, an expected \$2,000 with risk β_A, and an expected \$3,000 with risk β_B.

Given the risk-return indifference curve of investors in general, the firm could adjust the NPV equation as follows:

1. Substitute R_F for k in the denominator of the equation

$$\text{NPV} = \sum_{t=1}^{N} \frac{F_t}{(1 + R_F)^t} - I,$$

where R_F is the discount rate applicable for riskless investments such as United States government bonds.

Figure 14.14

Certainty Equivalent Returns

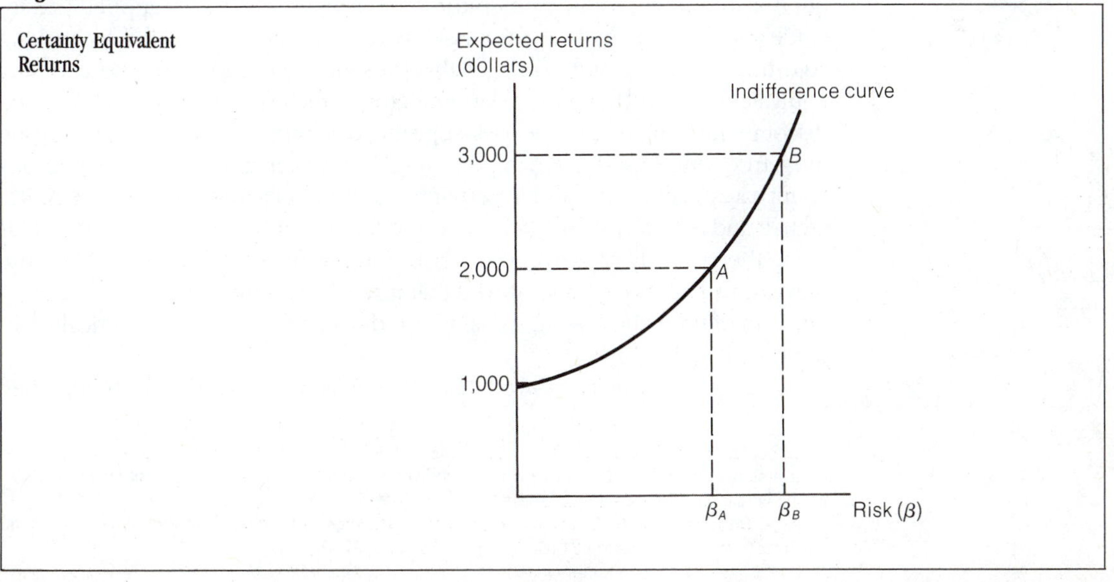

2. Divide the certainty equivalent of a risky return by the risky return to obtain a *certainty equivalent adjustment factor,*

$$\phi_A = \frac{\text{Certain return}}{\text{Risky return}} = \frac{\$1,000}{\$2,000} = 0.50 \text{ for } \beta_A$$

and

$$\phi_B = \frac{\$1,000}{\$3,000} = 0.33 \text{ for } \beta_B .$$

3. Conceptually, ϕ values could be developed for all possible values of β. The range of ϕ would be from 1.0 for $\beta = 0$ to a value close to zero for large values of β, assuming risk aversion.[16]

4. The risk-aversion functions of all individuals could, conceptually, be averaged to form a "market risk-aversion function." An example of such a function is shown in Figure 14.15.

5. Given the market risk-aversion function and the degree of risk inherent in any risky return, the risky return could be replaced by its certainty equivalent:

$$\text{Certainty equivalent of } F_t = \phi_t F_t .$$

6. The basic NPV equation could then be converted to Equation 14.12.

$$\text{NPV} = \sum_{t=1}^{N} \frac{F_t}{(1+k)^t} - I = \sum_{t=1}^{N} \frac{\phi_t F_t}{(1+R_F)^t} - I. \qquad (14.12)$$

The numerator of the equation has been converted into a certainty equivalent amount, to which the risk-free return is applied as the discount factor. Without the adjustment to the numerator, the discount factor, *k,* is applied and includes an adjustment factor for risk. Thus, risk can be handled by making adjustments to the numerator of the present value equation (the certainty equivalent method) or to the denominator of the equation (the risk-adjusted discount rate method). The risk-adjusted discount rate method is the one most frequently used, probably because it is easier to estimate suitable discount rates than it is to derive certainty equivalent factors. However, A. A. Robichek and S. C. Myers in 1966 advocated the certainty equivalent approach as being theoretically superior to the risk-adjusted discount rate method.[17] Still, they, as well as H. Y. Chen, showed that if risk is perceived to be an increasing function of time, then using a risk-adjusted discount rate is a theoretically valid procedure.[18]

Robichek and Myers showed that risk-adjusted rates tend to lump together

16. Of course, different individuals may have different ϕ functions, depending on their degrees of risk aversion. Further, an individual's own ϕ function might shift over time as personal situations, including wealth and family status, change.

17. A. A. Robichek and S. C. Myers, "Conceptual Problems in the Use of Risk-Adjusted Discount Rates," *Journal of Finance* 21 (December 1966), pp. 727–730.

18. H. Y. Chen, "Valuation under Uncertainty," *Journal of Financial and Quantitative Analysis* 2 (September 1967), pp. 313–326.

Figure 14.15

Changes in Perceived Risk over Time

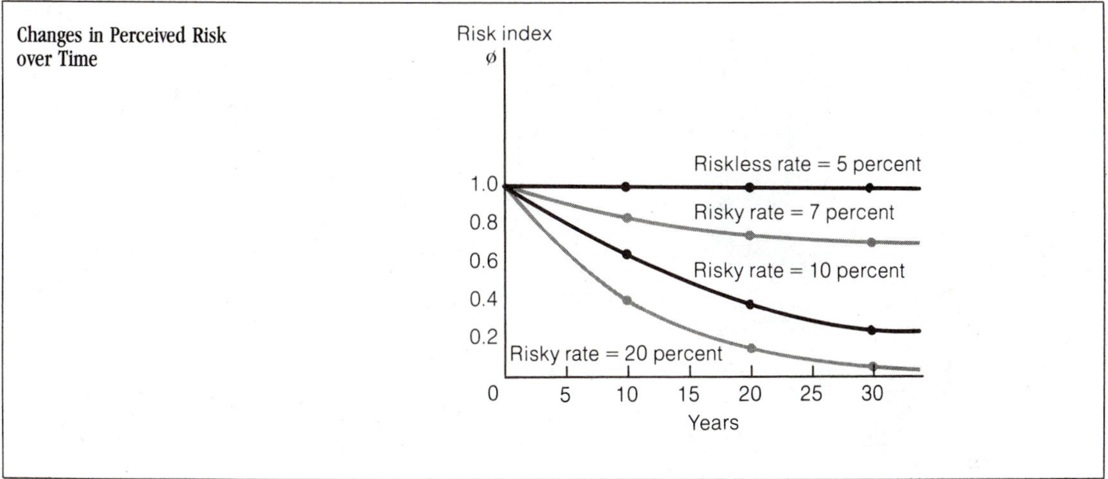

Notes

1. The smaller the value of ϕ, the index of risk, the greater the perceived risk.
2. For a given riskless rate (for example, 5 percent) and risky rate (for example, 10 percent), the value of ϕ_t declines over time; that is, with a constant risk premium (5 percent = 10 percent − 5 percent), the declining curve indicates that perceived risk increases with time. Therefore, a constant risk premium (and risk-adjusted discount rate) implies that risk of an individual cash flow is perceived to be higher and higher the further into the future the cash flow is due.
3. At any given point in time (other than $t = 0$), ϕ, the index of perceived risk, is lower as the risk premium becomes higher. At the point 10 years, for example, the ϕ for the 7 percent risky rate, with a 2 percent risk premium, is 0.828; it is 0.628 for the 10 percent rate; and it is 0.403 for the 15 percent rate.

the pure rate of interest, a risk premium, and time (through the compounding process), while the certainty equivalent approach keeps risk and the pure rate of interest separate. This separation gives an advantage to certainty equivalents. However, financial managers are more familiar with the concept of risk-adjusted discounts, and it is easier to use market data to develop adjusted discount rates. Still, the certainty equivalent method may be applicable for project returns that are not characterized by increasing risk with time.

If the risk-adjusted discount rate method is to be used, it is important to choose the values of these rates carefully. We will now consider the particular assumptions that are implicit in the choice of a constant risk-adjusted discount rate over time. Here the "risk index" (ϕ) is calculated as the ratio of the present value interest factor for a risky cash flow divided by the present value interest factor of a riskless asset.[19]

$$\text{Index of risk} = \phi_t = \frac{\text{PVIF}_{\text{Risky asset}}}{\text{PVIF}_{\text{Riskless asset}}} = \frac{(1 + \text{Risky rate})^{-t}}{(1 + \text{Riskless rate})^{-t}}. \quad (14.13)$$

To illustrate, suppose we are calculating ϕ, the risk index, for a cash flow expected after ten years when the riskless rate is 5 percent and the risky rate is

19. This discussion parallels that of Robichek and Myers, "Conceptual Problems in the Use of Risk-Adjusted Discount Rates."

Table 14.8

Calculation of Certainty Equivalents

Discount Rate—Years	Riskless Project 5%	Risky Project 10%	*RI*
0	1.0000	1.0000	1.000
1	0.9524	0.9091	0.955
10	0.6139	0.3855	0.628
20	0.3769	0.1486	0.394
30	0.2314	0.0573	0.248

Note: The $RI = 1.0$ when $t = 0$ because

$$\frac{\text{PVIF}_{\text{Risky rate}}}{\text{PVIF}_{\text{Riskless rate}}} = \frac{(1 + k)^0}{(1 + R_F)^0} = \frac{1}{1} = 1.0$$

where
R_F = Riskless rate and k = Risky rate.

10 percent. The interest factors are found in Table A.2 at the end of the book to be 0.6139 and 0.3855 for the riskless and risky assets, respectively, so the certainty equivalent risk index is found as follows:

$$\text{Risk index} = \phi_{10} = \frac{0.3855}{0.6139} = 0.628.$$

Equation 14.13 is used to work out a range of values in Table 14.8 for a pair of interest rates over time and in Figure 14.15 these values (and others) are plotted. Risk, as measured by ϕ_t, is an increasing function of both *time* and the *differential between the riskless and risky discount rates.* In other words, a given risk premium has a larger and larger impact on the risk index as the time horizon is lengthened. This phenomenon occurs, of course, because of the compounding effect.

Certainty Equivalent Formulations Using the CAPM

The use of the capital asset pricing model is sufficiently flexible that if one prefers to use a certainty equivalent formulation, a risk adjustment term can be added to the numerator and the risk-free rate employed as the discount factor. We shall demonstrate both the development of a risk-adjusted rate and the use of the certainty equivalent method.

Recall the general form of the security market line, which was first given in Equation 5.9:

$$E(R_j) = R_F + \lambda\,\text{Cov}(R_j,R_M). \tag{5.9}$$

Suppose that we are given the economy-wide parameters of a value of R_F equal to 5 percent and a λ of 4. The risk characteristics of the investment, security, firm, or other capital assets are defined by the value of the covariance term. Some illustrative values of the covariance term and the associated expected returns are shown in Table 14.9.

Table 14.9

Returns Related to Risk

	Expressed as Decimals		Expressed as Percents	
	$Cov(R_j,R_M)$	$E(R_j)$	$Cov(R_j,R_M)$	$E(R_j)$
A	0	0.05	0	5
B	0.0050	0.07	0.50	7
C	0.0150	0.11	1.50	11
D	0.0175	0.12	1.75	12
E	0.0250	0.15	2.50	15

The relationships shown in Table 14.9 can also be graphed, as in Figure 14.16. The security market line depicted in Figure 14.16 is a risk-return trade-off function. The average investor is indifferent to a riskless asset with a certain 5 percent return, a moderately risky asset with an 11 percent return, or a very risky asset with a 15 percent expected return. As risk increases, higher and higher returns on investment are required to compensate investors for the additional risk.

The difference between the required rate of return on a particular risky asset and the rate of return on a riskless asset is defined as the risk premium on the risky asset. For the security market line depicted in Figure 14.16, the riskless rate is 5 percent; a 2 percent risk premium is required to compensate for a covariance of 0.5 percent, and a 10 percent risk premium is attached to

Figure 14.16

Illustrative Risk-Return Relationships

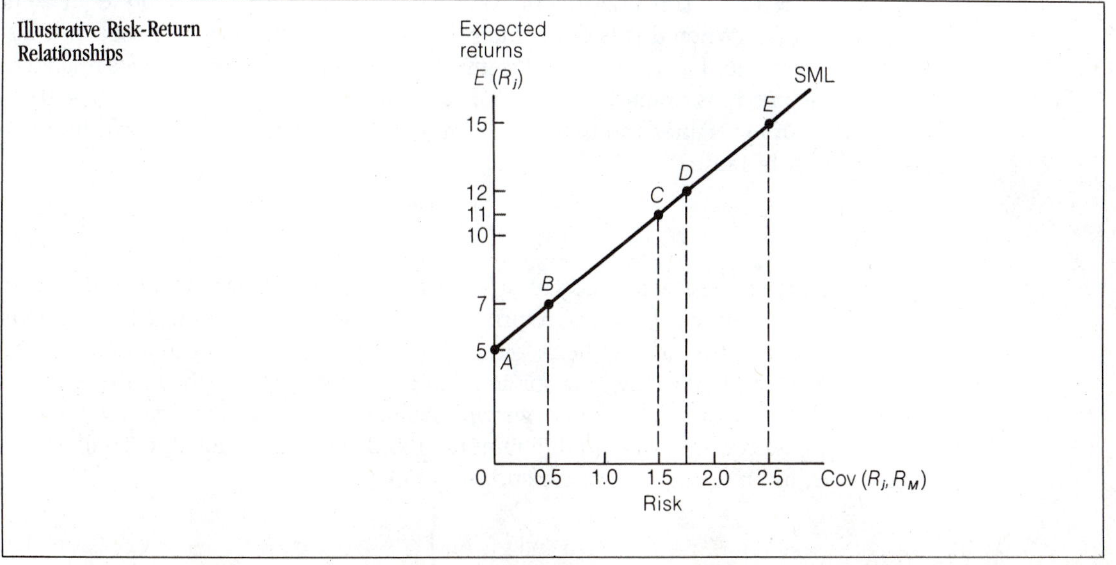

an investment with a covariance of 2.5 percent. The average investor is indifferent between risky investments B, C, D, and E and the riskless asset A.

If a particular firm's stock is located at Point D on the security market line, investors expect the rate of return on the stock to be 12 percent. If the firm changes the nature of its investment projects so that it takes on projects that reduce the covariance of its returns with the market, then a lower required rate of return results; it may move down to Point C on the security market line. Conversely, if the firm changes its investment program so that its covariance moves up to 2.5 percent, the return required by investors will be 15 percent.

Because compounding over time has a compounding effect on the risk premium, it is sometimes desirable to be able to use a certainty equivalent discount rate. The security market line expression lends itself to this reformulation. To do this, we first make use of the following definition:

$$E(R_j) = \frac{E(X_j)}{V_j}.$$

This enables us to rewrite the security market line relationship as shown in Equation 14.14, which, after we rearrange terms, becomes Equation 14.14a.

$$\frac{E(X_j)}{V_j} = R_F + \lambda \operatorname{Cov}\left(\frac{X_j}{V_j}, R_M\right) \tag{14.14}$$

$$\frac{1}{V_j}[E(X_j) - \lambda \operatorname{Cov}(X_j, R_M)] = R_F.$$

$$V_j = \frac{E(X_j) - \lambda \operatorname{Cov}(X_j, R_M)}{R_F}. \tag{14.14a}$$

Equation 14.14a makes an adjustment to the numerator representing the asset returns. This adjustment converts the returns to a certainty equivalent amount. When this is done, the risk-free rate of return can be used as a discount rate. To illustrate what is involved, let us assume some values related to the previous example. Let: $X_j = \$120$; $\lambda = 4$; $\operatorname{Cov}(X_j, R_M) = 17.5$; $R_F = 0.05$.

These values can then be utilized in Equation 14.14a as shown in Equation 14.14a′:

$$V_j = \frac{120 - 4(17.5)}{0.05} = \frac{120 - 70}{0.05} = \frac{50}{0.05} = \$1{,}000. \tag{14.14a′}$$

Thus we see that the risky returns are \$120. The risk adjustment is \$70. Hence, the certainty equivalent returns are \$50. When we discount the certainty equivalent returns at the risk-free rate of 5 percent, we obtain a value for the asset of \$1,000. However, for a one-period model such as the CAPM reflected in the security market line, we will obtain the same results if we use the risk-adjusted values both in the numerator and in the denominator. To illustrate, let us first recognize the relationship in Equation 14.15.

$$\operatorname{Cov}\left(\frac{X_j}{V_j}, R_M\right) = \operatorname{Cov}(R_j, R_M). \tag{14.15}$$

Rearranging terms and inserting values known to this point we obtain:

$$\mathrm{Cov}(X_j, R_M) = V_j\,\mathrm{Cov}(R_j, R_M). \tag{14.15a}$$
$$17.5 = 1{,}000\,\mathrm{Cov}(R_j, R_M). \tag{14.15b}$$
$$\mathrm{Cov}(R_j, R_M) = 17.5/1{,}000 = 0.0175. \tag{14.15c}$$

In developing the expression for the value of the asset in risk-adjusted terms, we express the security market line in the form of Equation 14.16.

$$\frac{E(X_j)}{V_j} = R_F + \lambda\,\mathrm{Cov}(R_j, R_M). \tag{14.16}$$

Solving for the value of the asset, we obtain Equation 14.16a:

$$V_j = \frac{E(X_j)}{R_F + \lambda\,\mathrm{Cov}(R_j, R_M)}. \tag{14.16a}$$

We can now use Equation 14.16a to obtain the value of the firm, using a risk-adjusted discount rate.

$$V_j = \frac{120}{0.05 + 4(0.0175)}$$

$$V_j = \frac{120}{0.05 + 0.07} = \frac{120}{0.12} = \$1{,}000.$$

Thus we obtain the same value whether we use the certainty equivalent formulation and the risk-free return or the risk-adjusted values in both the numerator and the denominator.

It has been customary to convert the risky return to a certainty equivalent return by applying a certainty equivalent factor, ϕ. In the informal approaches to the treatment of risk the value of ϕ was formulated on a judgmental basis. However, with the use of the security market line we were able to develop a data-based estimate of ϕ. Using the information from the example above, we found that the certainty equivalent return was $50, while the risky return was $120. The ratio between the two was 0.4167. Hence, we can take Equation 14.14a and, instead of subtracting the risk adjustment factor, multiply by the certainty equivalent factor, ϕ, as shown in Equation 14.17.

$$V_j = \frac{\phi E(X_j)}{R_F}. \tag{14.17}$$

When we insert the appropriate values, we again obtain a value of $1,000 for the asset:

$$V_j = \frac{0.4167(120)}{0.05} = \frac{50}{0.05} = \$1{,}000.$$

Thus the use of the security market line enables us to express valuation relationships in either the risk-adjusted form or in their certainty equivalent form.

The methodology provided by the CAPM framework can also be applied to projects as discussed in this chapter. For projects:

$$V_j^\circ = \frac{E(X_j^\circ) - \lambda \mathrm{Cov}(X_j^\circ, R_M)}{R_F}. \tag{14.18}$$

$$\mathrm{NPV}_j^\circ = (V_j^\circ - \mathrm{Cost}_j^\circ). \tag{14.19}$$

Thus the use of the market price of risk criterion provides us with a very flexible tool for making an adjustment for risk in analyzing investment projects of differing risks. To illustrate the application of the last two equations, we will use the data for Project 4 in the Morton Company Case discussed previously. The required rate of return was:

$$E(R_4^\circ) = R_F + [E(R_M) - R_F]\beta_4^\circ.$$

Inserting values:

$$7.75\% = 5\% + [10\% - 5\%]0.55.$$

The $E(R_4^\circ)$ value of 7.75 percent represents a risk-adjusted required rate of return on the project based on the beta risk measure equal to 0.55. We can also express this equation with covariance, using the relationship

$$\begin{aligned}\mathrm{Cov}(R_4^\circ, R_M) &= \beta_4^\circ \mathrm{Var}(R_M)\\ &= 0.55(0.01)\\ &= 0.0055.\end{aligned}$$

The returns from the project that we actually observe are the dollar returns indicated by the X_4° values. Suppose that the cost of the project (Cost_4°) or investment outlay is \$1,000. We can then calculate $\mathrm{Cov}(X_4^\circ, R_M)$:

$$\mathrm{Cov}(R_4^\circ, R_M) = \mathrm{Cov}\left(\frac{X_4^\circ}{\mathrm{Cost}_4^\circ}, R_M\right) = \frac{1}{\mathrm{Cost}_4^\circ}\mathrm{Cov}(X_4^\circ, R_M).$$

Hence

$$\begin{aligned}\mathrm{Cov}(X_4^\circ, R_M) &= \mathrm{Cost}_4^\circ \mathrm{Cov}(R_4^\circ, R_M)\\ &= 1{,}000(0.0055)\\ &= 5.5.\end{aligned}$$

We now have the information to utilize Equation 14.18 for Project 4:[20]

$$\begin{aligned}V_4^\circ &= \frac{E(X_4^\circ) - \lambda \mathrm{Cov}(X_4^\circ, R_M)}{R_F}\\ &= \frac{80 - 5(5.5)}{0.05} = \frac{80 - 27.5}{0.05}\\ &= \$1{,}050.\end{aligned}$$

Since the cost of Project 4 is \$1,000 and its value is \$1,050, the net gain or the net present value for the investment in Project 4 (NPV°) is \$50. Note that the

20. Recall that $\lambda = [E(R_M - R_F)]/\sigma_M^2$. From Table 14.4 we have $E(R_M) = 0.10$ and $\sigma_M^2 = 0.01$. With $R_F = 0.05$, $\lambda = 5$.

risk adjustment factor is 27.5, or 0.344 times the expected dollar returns from the project. The certainty equivalent adjustment factor (ϕ) would be (1 − 0.344), which equals 0.656. This illustrates how the CAPM can provide a measure of the risk adjustment factor to calculate a certainty equivalent amount in the numerator to which the risk-free return in the denominator can be applied.

We recognize that the computations of beta for individual assets are sometimes not statistically significant and often not stable over time. Nevertheless, the methodology described provides a starting point. In addition, a risk adjustment factor, taking other dimensions of risk into account as well as judgmental factors, may be used in estimating a project's net present value.

The Use of Risk-Adjusted Discount Rates: An Example

Along with the SML, the coefficient of variation can aid in the analysis of investment decisions under uncertainty. In addition, the use of these two alternative approaches to measuring the risk adjustment factor does not necessarily give conflicting results. This is the case even when one investment has a greater CV but a smaller beta. Assume that the risk-free rate is 6 percent and the expected market return is 11 percent. Consider two investments, I and J, for which the measures in Table 14.10 have been calculated.

If the financial manager uses the SML, the required returns for the two investments are:

$$R_I^* = 0.06 + (0.11 - 0.06)\,1.5 = 0.135.$$
$$R_J^* = 0.06 + (0.11 - 0.06)\,2.0 = 0.16.$$

Using the CAPM, Investment I has a required return of 13.5 percent but an expected return of 20 percent; Investment J has a required return of 16 percent but an expected return of 14 percent. For Investment I the expected return exceeds the required return by 6.5 percentage points; for Investment J the expected return falls short of the required return by 2 percentage points.

But the coefficient of variation of Investment I is greater than the coefficient of variation of Investment J. Suppose the decision maker formulates a risk adjustment relationship based on the coefficient of variation, such as:

$$R^* = \text{Risk-free return} + 0.03\ \text{CV}.$$

Table 14.10

Return and Risk Estimates for Two Investment Projects

	Investment I	Investment J
Expected return (R)	0.20	0.14
Standard deviation (σ)	0.80	0.42
Coefficient of variation (CV)	4.00	3.00
Beta (β)	1.50	2.00

The required return for Investment I is 18 percent, while the required return for Investment J is 15 percent. Investment I still exceeds its required return, and Investment J still falls somewhat short of its required return. However, the decision is closer, because the expected return on Investment I is only 2 percentage points above its required return, while the expected return for Investment J is only 1 percentage point below its required return.

If the investments are mutually exclusive (for example, a gas-powered versus an electric-powered forklift truck for handling materials in a factory), Investment I will probably be preferred to Investment J. But with the results so close, the financial manager may request that estimates of revenues, investment costs, maintenance costs, and all other factors that might affect the measures in Table 14.10 be re-examined and reworked. A sensitivity analysis of the critical factors affecting the level and variability of returns would be useful to estimate their influence on the measures in Table 14.10. Thus the use of both the CV and β approaches might result in better insights and decisions by the financial manager.

Summary

Two facts of life in finance are (1) that investors are averse to risk and (2) that at least some risk is inherent in most business decisions. Given investor aversion to risk and differing degrees of risk in different financial alternatives, it is necessary to consider risk in financial analysis.

Our first task is to define what we mean by risk; our second task is to measure it. The concept of *probability* is a fundamental element in both the definition and the measurement of risk. A *probability distribution* shows the probability of occurrence of each possible outcome, assuming a given investment is undertaken. The mean, or weighted average, of the distribution is defined as the *expected value* of the investment. The *coefficient of variation* of the distribution or, sometimes, the *standard deviation,* both of which measure the extent to which actual outcomes are likely to vary from the expected value, are used as measures of risk.

In appraising the riskiness of an individual capital investment, not only the variability of the expected returns of the project itself but also the correlation between expected returns on this project and the remainder of the firm's assets must be taken into account. This relationship is called the *portfolio effect* of the particular project. Favorable portfolio effects are strongest when a project is negatively correlated with the firm's other assets and weakest when positive correlation exists. Portfolio effects lie at the heart of the firm's efforts to diversify into product lines not closely related to the firm's main line of business.

The riskiness of a portfolio is measured by the standard deviation of expected returns. From any group of risky assets it is possible to develop an investment portfolio opportunity set in terms of risk and expected returns. Within the opportunity set, there will be a smaller group of alternative portfolios that provide the maximum return for a given level of risk (and the minimum risk for a given level of return). This is the efficient set of portfolios. Given equal expected returns, a risk-averse investor would choose the one that minimizes investor risk.

The trade-off between risk and expected return is expressed graphically as indifference curves. For any individual there is a unique set of indifference curves that can be used to determine the individual's optimum portfolio, including the fraction that should be invested in risk-free assets. The availability of a risk-free asset enables the investor to combine the risk-free asset with a portfolio of risky assets. A straight line drawn from the return on the risk-free asset to a point through a point of tangency with the portfolio opportunities curve defines the risk-return relations for the market, and the line is the capital market line (CML). The highest utility level is achieved for the investor by the point of tangency of the individual's indifference curve for risk and returns with the capital market line. If this point is to the left of the market portfolio tangency, the investor holds risk-free assets as well as risky assets and so has both less risk and less return on his or her total portfolio. If the investor is less risk averse, the point of tangency with the CML is to the right of the market portfolio. This investor borrows to invest more in risky assets and accordingly has more risk and higher expected returns.

The risk-return relationships for individual securities (imperfect portfolios) use the covariance of individual security returns with the market returns as the measure of risk. The relation between returns and the covariance for individual securities defines the security market line (SML).

Another way to describe the return-risk relationship is in terms of beta coefficients. β is simply the covariance standardized by the market variance. With risk expressed in this way, expected return can be stated as a β multiple of the market risk premium (expected return on the market less the risk-free rate) plus the risk-free rate. All factors except β are market-wide constants.

The capital asset pricing model provides a means for determining a market adjusted discount rate that is project specific and appropriate for determining the NPV of risky capital budgeting projects. The CAPM can be used with either the certainty equivalent or the risk adjusted discount rate formulation of the NPV equation.

The SML is useful in quantifying the relationship between return and risk. However, its estimates are subject to change over time and have not been measured with precision. SML measures must be combined with judgmental estimates to arrive at financial decisions. In formulating judgments, the earlier measures of risk—the standard deviation and the coefficient of variation—will also aid in the analysis.

Thus we have two useful formal approaches to investment decisions under uncertainty. In addition, the formal approaches should be supplemented by techniques such as decision tree formulations, sensitivity analysis, and simulation of the consequences of alternative estimates of critical variables in the calculations. Simulation of possible outcomes enables us to determine the variations in the measures used in the formal approaches resulting from alternative estimates of critical input variables. Formal approaches, simulation with sensitivity analysis, and judgmental methods are all required in the effort to make sound investment decisions in a world in which outcomes are uncertain.

Questions

14.1 Define the following terms, using graphs to illustrate your answers wherever feasible:
a. risk
b. uncertainty
c. probability distribution
d. expected value
e. standard deviation
f. coefficient of variation
g. portfolio effects

14.2 The probability distribution of a less risky expected return is more peaked than that of a risky return. What shape would the probability distribution have for
a. completely certain returns?
b. completely uncertain returns?

14.3 Project A has an expected return of $500 and a standard deviation of $100. Project B also has a standard deviation of $100, but it has an expected return of $300. Which project is riskier? Why?

14.4 Assume that residential construction and industries related to it are countercyclical to the economy in general and to steel in particular. Does this negative correlation between steel and construction-related industries necessarily mean that a savings and loan association, whose profitability tends to vary with construction levels, would be less risky if it diversified by acquiring a steel distributor?

14.5 What is the value of decision trees in managerial decision making? (See Appendix 14B.)

14.6 In computer simulation, the computer makes a large number of trials to show what the various outcomes of a particular decision might be if the decision could be made many times under the same conditions. In practice, the decision will be made only once, so how can simulation results be useful to the decision maker?

14.7 Suppose that inflation causes the nominal risk-free return and the market return to rise by an equal amount. Will the market risk premium be affected?

Problems

14.1 An investment proposal has been analyzed, and the following information has been established:

Cash Flow	
Probability	Amount
0.3	$15,000
0.5	20,000
0.2	25,000

The outlay is $100,000, the expected life is ten years, and the cost of capital is 12 percent. Assume zero salvage value.

a. Calculate the expected NPV and expected IRR.
b. Calculate the probability that the investment will be a good one (that is, have NPV > 0).

14.2 The Rowan Company is faced with two mutually exclusive investment projects. Each project costs $4,500, and each has an expected life of three years. Annual net cash flows from each project begin one year after the initial investment is made and have the following probability distributions:

Project A		Project B	
Probability	Cash Flow	Probability	Cash Flow
0.2	$4,000	0.2	$ 0
0.6	4,500	0.6	4,500
0.2	5,000	0.2	12,000

Rowan has decided to evaluate the riskier project at a 12 percent rate and the less risky project at a 10 percent rate.

a. What is the expected value of the annual net cash flows from each project?
b. What is the risk-adjusted NPV of each project?
c. If it were known that Project B was negatively correlated with other cash flows of the firm, while Project A was positively correlated, how should this knowledge affect the decision?

14.3 Your firm is considering the purchase of a tractor. It has been established that this tractor will cost $32,000, will produce revenues in the neighborhood of $10,000 (before tax), and will be depreciated via straight line to zero in eight years. The board of directors, however, is having a heated debate as to whether the tractor can be expected to last eight years. Specifically, Wayne Brown insists that he knows of some that have lasted only five years. Tom Miller agrees with Brown but argues that it is more likely that the tractor will give eight years of service. Brown agrees. Finally, Laura Evans says she has seen some last as long as ten years. Given this discussion, the board asks you to prepare a sensitivity analysis to ascertain how important the uncertainty about the life of the tractor is. Assume a 40 percent tax rate on both income and capital loss, zero salvage value, and a cost of capital of 10 percent. (See Appendix 14B.)

14.4 You have an investment opportunity for which the outlay and cash flows are uncertain. Analysis has produced the following subjective probability assessments:

Outlay		Annual Cash Flow	
Probability	Amount	Probability	Amount
0.4	$ 80,000	0.2	$14,000
0.3	100,000	0.5	16,000
0.2	120,000	0.3	18,000
0.1	140,000		

Let the cost of capital be 12 percent, life expectancy be ten years, and salvage value be zero.

a. Construct a decision tree for this investment to show probabilities, payoffs, and expected NPV. (See discussion in Appendix 14B.)
b. Calculate the expected NPV, again using expected cash flow and expected outlay.
c. What is the probability of and the NPV of the worst possible outcome?
d. What is the probability of and the NPV of the best possible outcome?
e. Compute the probability that this will be a good investment.

14.5 Your firm is considering two mutually exclusive investment projects—Project A at a cost of $110,000 and Project B at a cost of $140,000. The planning division of your firm has estimated the following probability distribution of cash flows to be generated by each project in each of the next five years:

Project A		Project B	
Probability	Cash Flow	Probability	Cash Flow
0.2	$15,000	0.2	$10,000
0.6	30,000	0.6	40,000
0.2	35,000	0.2	60,000

a. Which of the projects is the riskier if the coefficient of variation is used as a measure of risk?
b. Each project's risk is different from that of the firm as a whole. The firm's management adjusts for risk by means of the formula:

$$R_j = R_F + 10\text{CV}$$

where:

R_j = Required rate of return on the jth project
R_F = Risk-free rate = 6 percent
CV = Coefficient of variation of the project's cash flows.

What are the required rates of return on Projects A and B?

c. Which of the projects, if either, should be accepted by the firm? Explain and support your answer. In calculating the NPVs, round the cost of capital figures calculated in Part b to the nearest whole number.

14.6 The risk-free rate is 4 percent, and the market risk premium is 5 percent. Under consideration for investment outlays are Projects A, B, and C, with estimated betas of 0.8, 1.2, and 2, respectively. What will be the required rates of return on these projects based on the security market line approach?

14.7 The risk-free rate of return is 6 percent, and the market risk premium is 5 percent. The beta of the project under analysis is 1.8, with expected net cash flows after taxes estimated at $600 for five years. The required investment outlay on the project is $1,800.

a. What is the required risk-adjusted return on the project?
b. Should the project be accepted?

14.8 The McWilliams Company is considering two investment projects, A and B, for which the following measures have been calculated:

	Investment A	Investment B
Investment outlay required (*I*)	\$20,000	\$20,000
Expected return (*R*)	0.20	0.20
Standard deviation of returns (σ)	0.40	0.60
Coefficient of variation of returns (CV)	2.0	3.0
Beta of returns (β)	1.8	1.2

The vice-president of finance has formulated a risk adjustment relationship based on the coefficient of variation:

$$\text{Required return on a project} = \text{Risk-free return} + 0.04\text{CV}.$$

He also takes into consideration the security market line relationship, using 6 percent as the estimate of the risk-free return and 5 percent as the market risk premium.

a. What is the required return on each project, using alternative methods of calculating the risk adjustment factor?
b. If the two projects are independent, should they both be accepted?
c. If the projects are mutually exclusive, which one should be accepted?
d. Depending upon the approach to risk measurement used, why might the two investments have different risks?
e. What additional analysis might be performed before a final decision is made?

14.9 You are given the following information for an investment project: P = \$3 per unit; vc = \$2 per unit; FC = \$300. The risk-free rate is 5 percent = R_F. (Use Var $R_M = 0.01$.)
Also:

P_s	R_M	Q
0.2	−0.05	0
0.5	0.10	600
0.3	0.20	1,000

where:
P = Selling price per unit sold
vc = Variable costs per unit sold
$c = (P - vc)$ = Contribution margin per unit
Q = Units of output sold
FC = Total fixed costs

a. What is lambda, or the market risk measure?
b. What is the value of the investment project?
c. What is the required return on the investment project?

14.10 Given the following facts (the investment cost of each project is equal):

S	P_s	R_{Ms}	Return to Project 1	Return to Project 2
1	0.1	−0.3	−0.4	−0.4
2	0.2	−0.1	−0.2	−0.2
3	0.3	0.1	0	0.6
4	0.4	0.3	0.7	0

Calculate:

a. The three means, the variances, the standard deviations, and the covariance of Project 1 with the market, covariance of Project 2 with the market, covariance of Project 1 with Project 2, the correlation coefficients ρ_{1M}, ρ_{2M}, and the correlation coefficient of Project 1 with Project 2.

b. If Projects 1 and 2 were to be combined into a portfolio, what would be the weights of each project, w_1 and w_2, in the portfolio to minimize the portfolio standard deviation?
   Calculate the expected return on that portfolio and its standard deviation.

c. $R_F = 0.04$. Calculate the security market line.
   On a graph:
   1. Plot the security market line.
   2. Plot points for Project 1 and for Project 2.

d. If you had to choose between the two projects, which would you select?

14.11 Consider two projects with different risk. The risky project has a risky rate of 12 percent. The riskless project has a riskless rate of 6 percent.

a. Calculate the risk index (RI) for each project for years 0, 1, 5, 10, 20, and 30.

b. What are the implications of your results?

14.12 We have the following data on market parameters: The risk-free rate is 6 percent, the expected return on the market is 11 percent, and the variance on the market is 1 percent. The covariance of the net operating income of the firm with the market returns is $40. The expected net operating income of the firm *(X)* is $320.

a. Calculate the value of the firm, using a certainty equivalent amount in the numerator and the risk-free rate in the denominator.

b. Calculate the value of the firm using risk-adjusted measures.

c. How do your results compare?

14.13 The Pierson Company is considering two mutually exclusive investment projects, P and Q. The risk and return estimates for these two investment projects are as follows:

	Project P	Project Q
Expected return *(R)*	0.15	0.18
Standard deviation (σ)	0.50	0.75
Coefficient of variation (CV)	2.50	3.00
Beta (β)	1.80	1.40

Assume that the risk-free rate is 10 percent and the expected market return is 14 percent.

a. What would be the firm's decision if the SML analysis is used?

b. Suppose the firm has formulated a risk adjustment equation based on the coefficient of variation, such as:

$$\text{Required rate of return } (R^*) = R_F + 0.02\text{CV}.$$

How would this adjustment equation affect the management's decision?

Selected References

Adler, Michael. "On Risk-Adjusted Capitalization Rates and Valuation by Individuals." *Journal of Finance* 25 (September 1970), pp. 819–836.

Aggarwal, Raj. "Corporate Use of Sophisticated Capital Budgeting Techniques: A Strategic Perspective and a Critique of Survey Results." *Interfaces* 10 (April 1980), pp. 31–34.

Ashton, D. J., and Atkins, D. R. "Interactions in Corporate Financing and Investment Decisions—Implications for Capital Budgeting: A Further Comment." *Journal of Finance* 33 (December 1978), pp. 1447–1453.

Bar-Yosef, Sasson, and Mesnick, Roger. "On Some Definitional Problems with the Method of Certainty Equivalents." *Journal of Finance* 32 (December 1977), 1729–1737.

Bierman, Harold, Jr., and Hass, Jerome E. "Capital Budgeting under Uncertainty: A Reformulation." *Journal of Finance* 28 (March 1973), pp. 119–130.

Bierman, Harold, Jr., and Hausman, Warren H. "The Resolution of Investment Uncertainty through Time." *Management Science* 18 (August 1972), pp. 654–662.

Bogue, Marcus C., and Roll, Richard. "Capital Budgeting of Risky Projects with 'Imperfect' Markets for Physical Capital." *Journal of Finance* 29 (May 1974), pp. 601–613.

Bower, Richard S., and Jenks, Jeffrey M. "Divisional Screening Rates." *Financial Management* 4 (Autumn 1975), pp. 42–49.

Chen, Houng-Yhi. "Valuation under Uncertainty." *Journal of Financial and Quantitative Analysis* 2 (September 1967), pp. 313–325.

Cooley, Philip L.; Roenfeldt, Rodney L.; and Chew, It-Keong. "Clarification of Three Capital Budgeting Criteria." *Financial Review* (Spring 1977), pp. 20–27.

Fama, Eugene F. "Risk-Adjusted Discount Rates and Capital Budgeting under Uncertainty." *Journal of Financial Economics* 5 (August 1977), pp. 3–24.

Grayson, C. Jackson, Jr. *Decisions under Uncertainty: Drilling Decisions by Oil and Gas Operators.* Boston: Division of Research, Harvard Business School, 1960.

Greer, Willis R., Jr. "Capital Budgeting Analysis with the Timing of Events Uncertain." *Accounting Review* 45 (January 1970), pp. 103–114.

Hayes, Robert H. "Incorporating Risk Aversion into Risk Analysis." *Engineering Economist* 20 (Winter 1975), pp. 99–121.

Hertz, David B. "Investment Policies That Pay Off." *Harvard Business Review* 46 (January–February 1968), pp. 96–108.

———. "Risk Analysis in Capital Investment." *Harvard Business Review* 42 (January–February 1964), pp. 95–106.

Hong, Hai, and Rappaport, Alfred. "Debt Capacity, Optimal Capital Structure, and Capital Budgeting." *Financial Management* 7 (Autumn 1978), pp. 7–11.

Latane, H. A., and Tuttle, Donald L. "Decision Theory and Financial Management." *Journal of Finance* 21 (May 1966), pp. 228–244.

Lintner, John. "Security Prices, Risk and Maximal Gains from Diversification." *Journal of Finance* 20 (December 1965), pp. 587–616.

Litzenberger, Robert H., and Budd, Alan P. "Corporate Investment Criteria and the Valuation of Risk Assets." *Journal of Financial and Quantitative Analysis* 5 (December 1970), pp. 395–420.

Litzenberger, Robert H., and Joy, O. M. "Decentralized Capital Budgeting Decisions and Shareholder Wealth Maximization." *Journal of Finance* 30 (June 1975), pp. 993–1002.

———. "Target Rates of Return and Corporate Asset and Liability Structure under Uncertainty." *Journal of Financial and Quantitative Analysis* 10 (March 1971), pp. 21–36.

Lockett, A. Geoffrey, and Gear, Anthony E. "Multistage Capital Budgeting under Uncertainty." *Journal of Financial and Quantitative Analysis* 10 (March 1975), pp. 21–36.

Magee, J. F. "How to Use Decision Trees in Capital Investment." *Harvard Business Review* 42 (September–October 1964), pp. 79–96.

Maier, Steven F., and Vander Weide, James H. "Capital Budgeting in the Decentralized Firm." *Management Science* 23 (December 1976), pp. 433–443.

Mao, James C. T. "Survey of Capital Budgeting: Theory and Practice." *Journal of Finance* 25 (May 1970), pp. 349–360.

Mao, James C. T., and Helliwell, John F. "Investment Decisions under Uncertainty: Theory and Practice." *Journal of Finance* 24 (May 1969), pp. 323–338.

Martin, John D., and Scott, David F. "Debt Capacity and the Capital Budgeting Decision: A Revisitation." *Financial Management* 9 (Spring 1980), pp. 23–26.

Merrow, Edward W.; Chapel, Stephen W.; and Worthing, Christopher. "A Review of Cost Estimation in New Technologies: Implications for Energy Process Plants." Prepared for the Department of Energy by the RAND Corp., Santa Monica, Calif. (July 1979), pp. 1–117.

Miller, Edward M. "Uncertainty Induced Bias in Capital Budgeting." *Financial Management* 7 (Autumn 1978), pp. 12–18.

Moag, Joseph S., and Lerner, Eugene M. "Capital Budgeting Decisions under Imperfect Market Conditions—A Systems Framework." *Journal of Finance* 24 (September 1969), pp. 613–621.

Myers, Stewart C. "Procedures for Capital Budgeting under Uncertainty." *Industrial Management Review* 9 (Spring 1968), pp. 1–15.

Myers, Stewart C., and Turnbull, Stuart M. "Capital Budgeting and the Capital Asset Pricing Model: Good News and Bad News." *Journal of Finance* 32 (May 1977), pp. 321–336.

Osteryoung, Jerome S.; Scott, Elton; and Roberts, Gordon S. "Selecting Capital Projects with the Coefficient of Variation." *Financial Management* 6 (Summer 1977), pp. 59–64.

Perrakis, Stylianos. "Certainty Equivalents and Timing Uncertainty." *Journal of Financial and Quantitative Analysis* 10 (March 1975), pp. 109–118.

Peterson, D. E., and Laughhunn, D. J. "Capital Expenditure Programming and Some Alternative Approaches to Risk." *Management Science* 17 (January 1971), pp. 320–336.

Quirin, G. David. *The Capital Expenditure Decision.* Homewood, Ill.: Irwin, 1967.

Rendleman, Richard J., Jr. "Ranking Errors in CAPM Capital Budgeting Applications." *Financial Management* 40 (Winter 1978), pp. 40–44.

Robichek, Alexander A. "Interpreting the Results of Risk Analysis." *Journal of Finance* 30 (December 1975), pp. 1384–1386.

Robichek, A., and Myers, S. "Risk-Adjusted Discount Rates." *Journal of Finance* 21 (December 1966), pp. 727–730.

———. *Optimal Financing Decisions.* Englewood Cliffs, N.J.: Prentice-Hall, 1965, Chapter 5.

Schall, Lawrence D., and Sundem, Gary L. "Capital Budgeting Methods and Risk: A Further Analysis." *Financial Management* 9 (Spring 1980), pp. 7–11.

Stapleton, Richard C. "Portfolio Analysis, Stock Valuation and Capital Budgeting Rules for Risky Projects." *Journal of Finance* 26 (March 1971), pp. 95–118.

Swalm, Ralph O. "Utility Theory—Insights into Risk Taking." *Harvard Business Review* 44 (November–December 1966), pp. 123–136.

Thompson, Howard E. "Mathematical Programming, the Capital Asset Pricing Model and Capital Budgeting of Inter-Relating Projects." *Journal of Finance* 31 (March 1976), pp. 125–131.

Turnbull, S. M. "Market Imperfections and the Capital Asset Pricing Model." *Journal of Business Finance and Accounting* 4 (Autumn 1977), pp. 327–337.

Tuttle, Donald L., and Litzenberger, Robert H. "Leverage, Diversification and Capital Market Effects on a Risk-Adjusted Capital Budgeting Framework." *Journal of Finance* 23 (June 1968), pp. 427–444.

U.S. Congress, Subcommittee on Economy in Government of the Joint Economic Committee. *Economic Analysis of Public Investment Decisions: Interest Rate Policy and Discounting Analysis.* Washington, D.C.: Government Printing Office, 1968.

Van Horne, James C. "An Application of the CAPM to Divisional Required Returns." *Financial Management* 9 (Spring 1980), pp. 14–19.

———. "The Variation of Project Life as a Means for Adjusting for Risk." *Engineering Economist* 21 (Spring 1976), pp. 151–158.

———. "The Analysis of Uncertainty Resolution in Capital Budgeting for New Products." *Management Science* 15 (April 1969), pp. 376–386.

———. "Capital Budgeting Decisions Involving Combinations of Risky Investments." *Management Science* 13 (October 1966), pp. 84–92.

Wallingford, B. A. "A Survey and Comparison of Portfolio Selection Models." *Journal of Financial and Quantitative Analysis* 3 (June 1967), pp. 85–106.

Weston, J. Fred. "Investment Decisions Using the Capital Asset Pricing Model." *Financial Management* 2 (Spring 1973), pp. 25–33.

Weston, J. Fred, and Chen, Nai-fu. "A Note on Capital Budgeting and the Three Rs." *Financial Management* 9 (Spring 1980), pp. 12–13.

Woods, Donald H. "Improving Estimates That Involve Uncertainty." *Harvard Business Review* 45 (July–August 1966), pp. 91–98.

Appendix A to Chapter 14

Comparing the Riskiness of Investment Projects

One of the assumptions made in the development of asset pricing models is that the distribution of returns is approximately normal. The mean and variance (or standard deviation) can then be used to compare the entire probability distributions, thus facilitating risk measurement and comparisons of the risks of different projects. We first illustrate the applicable procedures.

Suppose that we have the continuous probability distribution shown in Figure 14A.1. This is a normal curve with a mean of 20 and a standard deviation of 5; x could be dollars, percentage rates of return, or any other units. If we want to know the probability that an outcome will fall between 15 and 30, we must calculate the area beneath the curve between these points, the shaded area in the diagram.

The area under the curve between 15 and 30 can be determined by integrating the curve over this interval, or, since the distribution is normal, by reference to statistical tables of the area under the normal curve, such as Appendix D.[1] To use these tables, it is necessary only to know the mean and standard deviation of the distribution.[2] The distribution to be investigated must first be standardized by using the following formula:

$$z = \frac{x - \mu}{\sigma}, \tag{14A.1}$$

where z is the standardized variable, or the number of standard deviations from the mean;[3] x is the outcome of interest; and μ and σ are the mean and

1. The equation for the normal curve is tedious to integrate, thus making the use of tables much more convenient. The equation for the normal curve is

$$f(x) = \frac{1}{\sqrt{2\pi\sigma^2}} e^{-(x - \mu)^2/2\sigma^2},$$

where π and e are mathematical constants; μ and σ denote the mean and standard deviation of the probability distribution, and x is any possible outcome.

2. The calculating procedure for means and standard deviations is illustrated in Chapter 14, Table 14.4.
3. Note that if the point of interest is 1σ away from the mean, then $x - \mu = \sigma$, so $z = \sigma/\sigma = 1.0$. Thus, when $z = 1.0$, the point of interest is 1σ away from the mean; when $z = 2$ the value is 2σ, and so forth.

Figure 14A.1

Continuous Probability Distribution

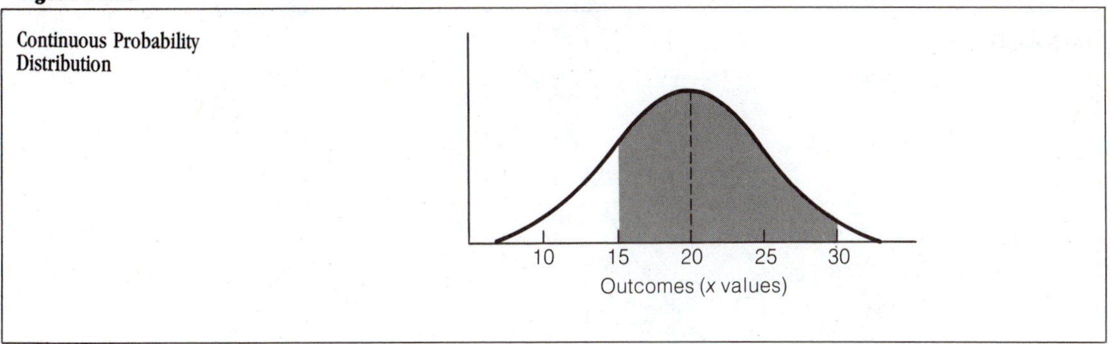

standard deviation of the distribution, respectively. For our example, where we are interested in the probability that an outcome will fall between 15 and 30, we first normalize these points of interest using Equation 14A.1:

$$z_1 = \frac{15 - 20}{5} = -1.0; z_2 = \frac{30 - 20}{5} = 2.0.$$

The areas associated with these z values are found in Table 14A.1 to be 0.3413 and 0.4773.[4] This means that the probability is 0.3413 that the actual outcome will fall between 15 and 20, and 0.4773 that it will fall between 20 and 30. Summing these probabilities shows that the probability of an outcome falling between 15 and 30 is 0.8186, or 81.86 percent.

Suppose we had been interested in determining the probability that the actual outcome would be greater than 15. Here we would first note that the

Table 14A.1

Area under the Normal Curve of Error

z	Area from the Mean to the Point of Interest	Ordinate
0.0	0.0000	0.3989
0.5	0.1915	0.3521
1.0	0.3413	0.2420
1.5	0.4332	0.1295
2.0	0.4773	0.0540
2.5	0.4938	0.0175
3.0	0.4987	0.0044

z = number of standard deviations from the mean. Some area tables are set up to indicate the area to the left or right of the point of interest; in this book we indicate the area between the mean and the point of interest.

4. Note that the negative sign on z_1 is ignored, since the normal curve is symmetrical around the mean; the minus sign merely indicates that the point lies to the left of the mean.

Figure 14A.2

The Normal Curve

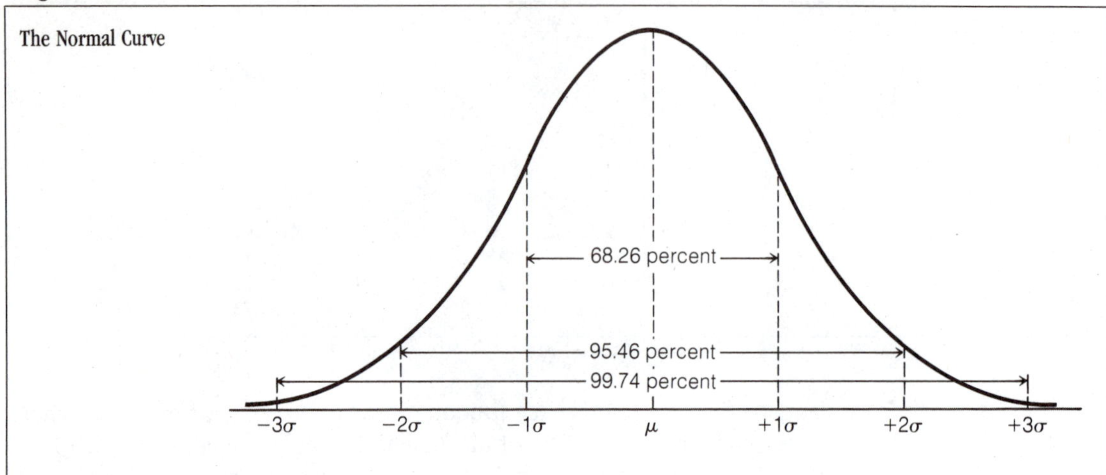

probability that the outcome will be between 15 and 20 is 0.3413. Then we would observe that the probability of an outcome greater than the mean, 20, is 0.5000. Thus, the probability is 0.3413 + 0.5000 = 0.8413, or 84.13 percent, that the outcome will exceed 15.

Some interesting properties of normal probability distributions can be seen by examining Table 14A.1 and Figure 14A.2, which is a graph of the normal curve. For any normal distribution, the probability of an outcome falling within plus or minus one standard deviation from the mean is 0.6826, or 68.26 percent: 0.3413 percent × 2.0. If we take the range within two standard deviations of the mean, the probability of an occurrence within this range is 95.46 percent; and 99.74 percent of all outcomes will fall within three standard deviations of the mean. Although the distribution theoretically runs from minus infinity to plus infinity, the probability of occurrences beyond about three standard deviations is very near zero.

Illustrating the Use of Probability Concepts

The concepts discussed both in Chapter 14 and in the preceding section of this appendix can be clarified by a numerical example. Consider three states of the economy: boom, normal, and recession. Next, assume that we can attach a probability of occurrence to each state of the economy, and, further, that we can estimate the dollar returns that will occur on each of two projects under each possible state. With this information, we construct Table 14A.2.

The expected values of Projects A and B are calculated by Equation 14A.2,

$$\bar{F}_j = \sum_{s=1}^{N} F_{js}P_s, \tag{14A.2}$$

Table 14A.2

Means and Standard Deviations of Projects A and B

State of the Economy	Probability of Its Occurring, P_s	Return F_{js}	$F_{js}P_s$
Project A			
Recession	0.2	$400	$ 80
Normal	0.6	500	300
Boom	0.2	600	120
	1.0	Expected value =	$500
Standard deviation = σ_A = $63.25.			
Project B			
Recession	0.2	$300	$ 60
Normal	0.6	500	300
Boom	0.2	700	140
	1.0	Expected value =	$500
Standard deviation = σ_B = $126.49.			

and the standard deviations of their respective returns are found by Equation 14A.3.

$$\sigma_j = \sqrt{\sum_{s=1}^{N} (F_{js} - \bar{F}_j)^2 P_s}. \tag{14A.3}$$

Figure 14A.3

Probability Distributions for Projects A and B

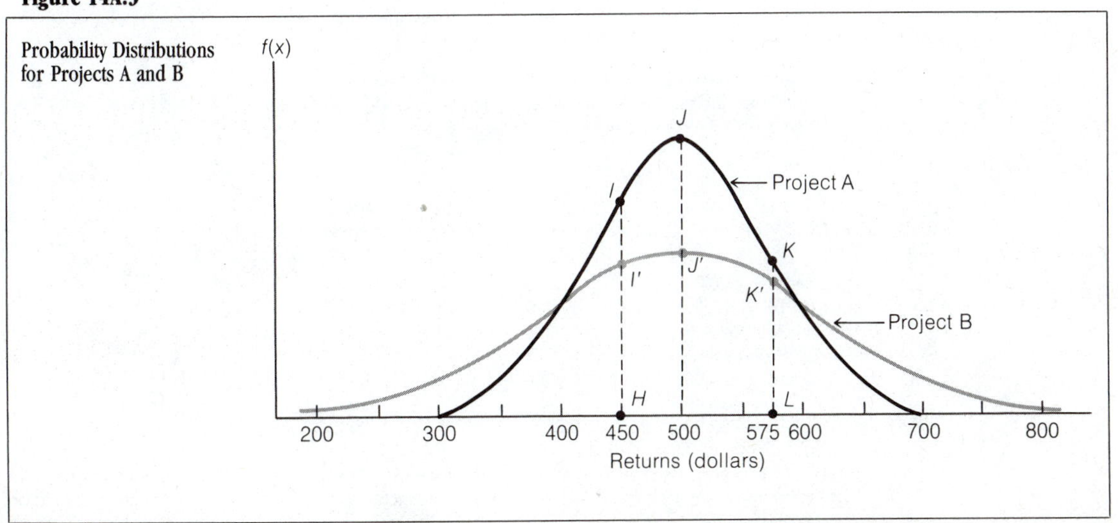

On the assumption that the returns from Projects A and B are normally distributed, knowing the mean and the standard deviation as calculated in Table 14A.2 permits us to graph probability distributions for Projects A and B; these distributions are shown in Figure 14A.3.[5] The expected value of each project's cash flow is seen to be \$500; however, the flatter graph of B indicates that this is the riskier project.

Suppose we want to determine the probabilities that the actual returns of Projects A and B will be in the interval \$450 to \$575. Using Equation 14A.1 and Figure 14A.3, we can calculate the respective probability distributions. The first step is to calculate the z values of the interval limits for the two projects:

Project A

$$\text{lower } z_1 = \frac{\$450 - \$500}{\$63.25} = -0.79.$$

$$\text{upper } z_2 = \frac{\$575 - \$500}{\$63.25} = 1.19.$$

Project B

$$\text{lower } z_1 = \frac{\$450 - \$500}{\$126.49} = -0.40.$$

$$\text{upper } z_2 = \frac{\$575 - \$500}{\$126.49} = 0.59.$$

In Appendix D at the end of the book, which is a more complete table of z values, we find the areas under a normal curve for each of these four z values:

5. Normal probability distributions can be constructed once the mean and standard deviation are known, using a table of *ordinates* of the normal curve. (See Column 3 of Table 14A.1.) This table is similar to the table of areas used above, except that the ordinate table gives relative *heights* of probability curve *f(x)* at various *z* values rather than areas beneath the curve. Figure 14A.3 was constructed by plotting points at various *z* values according to the following formula:

$$f(x) = \frac{1}{\sigma} \times (\text{Ordinate for } z \text{ value}),$$

where the ordinate value is read from a table of ordinates.

For example, the points corresponding to the mean and +1 and +2 standard deviations for Projects A and B were calculated as follows:

Project A (1)	z (2)	Ordinate at z (3)	$1/\sigma$ (4)	*f(x)*: (3) × (4) (5)
Mean = 500.00	0	0.3989	1/63.3	0.0063
$+1\sigma$ = 563.25	1	0.2420	1/63.3	0.0038
$+2\sigma$ = 626.50	2	0.0540	1/63.3	0.0009
Project B				
Mean = 500.00	0	0.3989	1/126.49	0.0032
$+1\sigma$ = 626.49	1	0.2420	1/126.49	0.0019
$+2\sigma$ = 752.98	2	0.0540	1/126.49	0.0004

Column 5 above gives the relative heights of the two distributions: Thus, if we decide (for pictorial convenience) to let the curve for Project B be 3.2 inches high at the mean, then the curve should be 1.9 inches high at $\mu \pm 1\sigma$, and the curve for Project A should be 6.3 inches at the mean and 3.8 inches at $\pm 1\sigma$. Other points in Figure 14A.3 were determined in like manner.

Project A	*z* Value	Area
lower *z*:	− .79	0.2852
upper *z*:	1.19	0.3830
	Total area =	0.6682, or 66.82 percent

Project B	*z* Value	Area
lower *z*:	−0.40	0.1554
upper *z*:	0.59	0.2224
	Total area =	0.3778, or 37.78 percent

Thus, there is about a 67 percent chance that the actual cash flow from Project A will lie in the interval $450 to $575, and about a 38 percent probability that B's cash flow will fall in this interval.

Now look back at Figure 14A.3 and observe the two areas that were just calculated. For Project A, the area bounded by *HIJKL* represents about 67 percent of the area under A's curve. For Project B, that area bounded by *HI'J'K'L* includes about 38 percent of the total area.

Cumulative Probability

Suppose we ask these questions: What is the probability that the cash flows from Project A will be at least $100? $150? $200? and so on. Obviously, there is a higher probability of their being at least $100 rather than $150, at least $150 rather than $200, and so on. In general, the most convenient way of expressing the answer to such "at least" questions is through the use of *cumulative probability distributions;* these distributions for Projects A and B are calculated in Table 14A.3 and are plotted in Figure 14A.4.

Suppose Projects A and B each cost $450; then, if each project returns at least $450, they will both break even. What is the probability of breaking even on each project? From Figure 14A.4 we see that the probability is 78 percent that Project A will break even, while the breakeven probability is only 65 percent for the riskier Project B. However, there is virtually no chance that A will yield more than $650, while B has a 5 percent chance of returning $700 or more.

Other Distributions

Thus far we have assumed that project returns fit a probability distribution that is approximately normal. Many distributions do fit this pattern, and normal distributions are relatively easy to work with. Therefore, much of the work done on risk measurement assumes a normal distribution. However, other distributions are certainly possible; Figure 14A.5 shows distributions skewed to the right and left, respectively. For two possible investments with equal expected returns, *F,* would an investor prefer a normal, a left-skewed, or a right-skewed distribution? A distribution skewed to the right, such as the

Table 14A.3

Cumulative Probability Distributions for Projects A and B

Expected Return	z Value	Cumulative Probability
Project A		
300	−3.16	0.9992[a]
400	−1.58	0.9429[b]
450	−0.79	0.7852
500	0.00	0.5000[c]
575	1.19	0.1170[d]
600	1.58	0.0571
700	3.16	0.0008[a]
Project B		
200	−2.37	0.9911[b]
300	−1.58	0.9429
400	−0.79	0.7852
450	−0.40	0.6554
500	0.00	0.5000[c]
575	0.59	0.2776[d]
600	0.79	0.2148
700	1.58	0.0571
800	2.37	0.0089

a. Not shown in Appendix D.
b. 0.5000 plus area under left tail of the normal curve; for example, for Project A, 0.5000 + 0.4429 = 0.9429 = 94.3 percent for $z = -1.58$.
c. The mean has a cumulative probability of 0.5000 = 50 percent.
d. 0.5000 less area under right tail of the normal curve; for example, for Project A, 0.5000 − 0.3830 = 0.1170 = 11.7 percent for $z = 1.19$.

one in Figure 14A.5a, would probably be chosen because the odds on a very low return are small, while there is some chance of very high returns. For the left-skewed distributions, there is little likelihood of large gains but a large cumulative probability of losses. Skewness is in the direction of the "long tail" of the probability distribution.

Problems

14A.1 The sales of the Cleveland Company for next year have the following probability distribution:

Probability	Sales (Millions of Dollars)
0.1	$10
0.2	12
0.4	15
0.2	18
0.1	20

Figure 14A.4

Cumulative Probability Distributions for Projects A and B

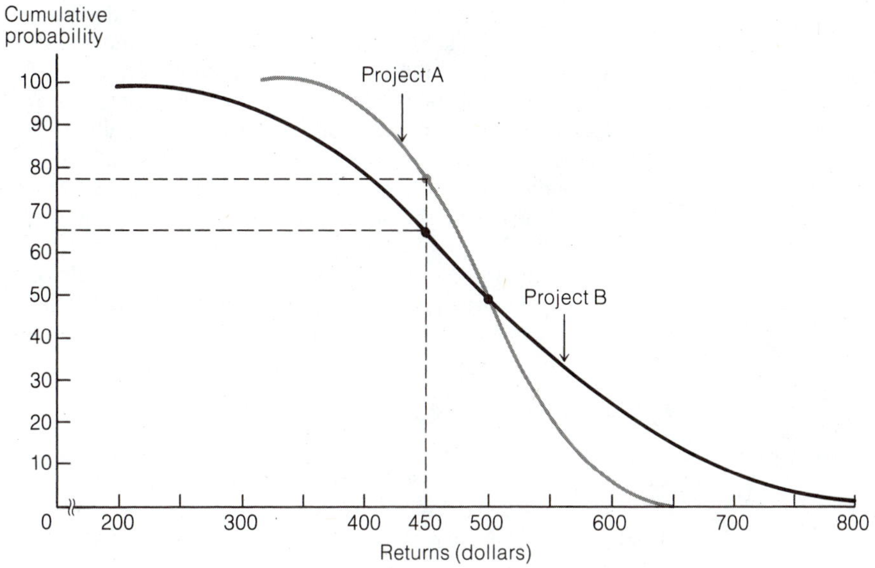

Figure 14A.5

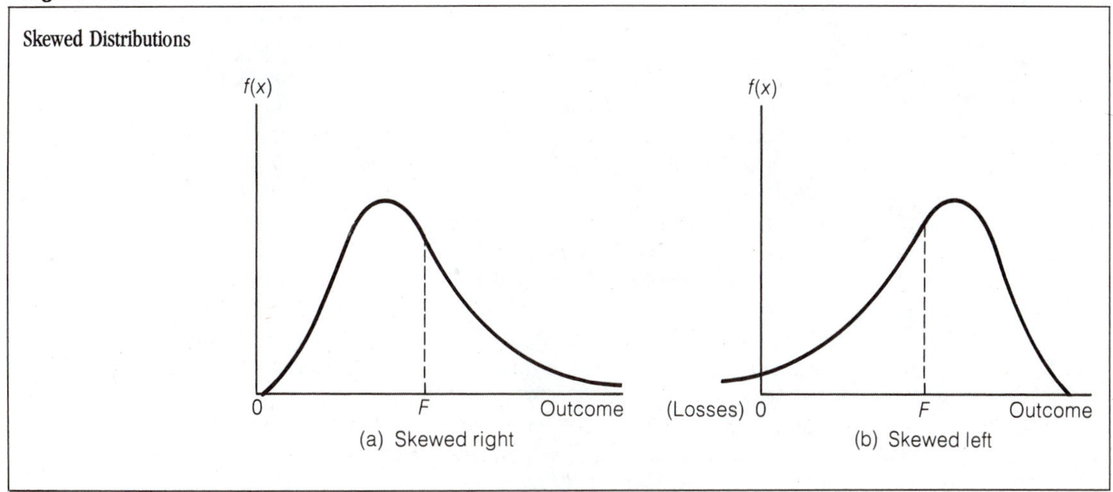

Skewed Distributions

a. On graph paper, plot sales on the horizontal axis and probability of sales on the vertical axis, using the points given above. Draw a smooth curve connecting your plotted points. What can you say about this curve?
b. Compute the mean of the probability distribution.
c. Compute the standard deviation of the probability distribution.
d. Compute the coefficient of variation of the probability distribution.
e. What is the probability that sales will exceed $16 million?
f. What is the probability that sales will fall below $13 million?
g. What is the probability that sales will be between $13 and $16 million?
h. What is the probability that sales will exceed $17 million?

14A.2 Mutual of Poughkeepsie offers to sell your firm a $1 million one-year term insurance policy on your corporate jet for a premium of $7,500. The probability that the plane will be lost or incur damages in that amount in any 12-month period is 0.001.
a. What is the insurance company's expected gain from sale of the policy?
b. What is the insurance company's expected gain or loss if the probability of a $1 million fire loss is 0.01? Would the insurance company still offer your firm the same policy for the same premium? Explain.

Selected References

Baesel, Jerome B. "On the Assessment of Risk: Some Further Considerations." *Journal of Finance* 29 (December 1974), pp. 1491–1494.

Blume, Marshall E. "On the Assessment of Risk." *Journal of Finance* 26 (March 1971), pp. 1–10.

Byrne, R.; Charnes, A.; Cooper, W.; and Kortanek, K. "Some New Approaches to Risk." *Accounting Review* 63 (January 1968), pp. 18–37.

Hertz, David B. "Risk Analysis in Capital Investment." *Harvard Business Review* 57 (September–October 1979), pp. 169–181.

Hespos, Richard F., and Strassmann, Paul A. "Stochastic Decision Trees for the Analysis of Investment Decisions." *Management Science* 11 (August 1965), pp. 244–259.

Keeley, Robert, and Westerfield, Randolph. "A Problem in Probability Distribution Techniques for Capital Budgeting." *Journal of Finance* 27 (June 1972), pp. 703–709.

Lessard, Donald R., and Bower, Richard S. "An Operational Approach to Risk Screening." *Journal of Finance* 28 (May 1973), pp. 321–338.

Lewellen, Wilbur G., and Long, Michael S. "Simulation versus Single-Value Estimates in Capital Expenditure Analysis." *Decision Sciences* 3 (1973), pp. 19–33.

Miller, Edward M. "Risk, Uncertainty, and Divergence of Opinion." *Journal of Finance* 32 (September 1977), pp. 1151–1168.

Robinson, Lindon, and Barry, Peter J. "Risk Efficiency Using Stochastic Dominance and Expected Gain-Confidence Limits." *Journal of Finance* 33 (September 1978), pp. 1244–1249.

Rubenstein, Albert H., and Schroder, Hans-Horst. "Managerial Differences in Assessing Probabilities of Technical Success for R&D Projects." *Management Science* 24 (October 1977), pp. 137–148.

Schwendiman, Carl J., and Pinches, George E. "An Analysis of Alternative Measures of Investment Risk." *Journal of Finance* 30 (March 1975), pp. 193–200.

Appendix B to Chapter 14

Evaluating Uncertain Cash Flows over Time

In Appendix A to Chapter 14, we presented some of the statistical theory upon which risk analysis is based. In this appendix, we deal with the problem of uncertain returns over time. Our discussion is divided into two cases: (1) where expected returns are normally distributed and are independent from one period to another, and (2) where normality and intertemporal independence do not hold.

Independent Returns over Time

In Appendix A to Chapter 14 we calculated an investment's one-year expected return, and the standard deviation of that return, as follows:
Expected return for year *t:*

$$\bar{F}_t = \sum_{s=1}^{N} (F_{ts}P_{ts}). \qquad (14B.1)$$

Standard deviation of expected return for year *t:*

$$\sigma_t = \left[\sum_{s=1}^{N} (F_{ts} - \bar{F}_t)^2 P_{ts}\right]^{1/2} \qquad (14B.2)$$

If the probability distribution P_{ts} is normal, and if the expected cash flow in year t, $\bar{F}_t$ is independent of the cash flow in year $(t - 1)$, then we can find the present value of an uncertain stream of returns by use of Equation 14B.3 and the standard deviation of this PV by use of Equation 14B.4:
Expected present value of investment:

$$\text{PV} = \sum_{t=1}^{N} \left[\frac{\bar{F}_t}{(1 + k)^t}\right] \qquad (14B.3)$$

Standard deviation of expected present value of the investment:

$$\sigma_{\text{PV}} = \left[\sum_{t=1}^{N} \frac{\sigma_t^2}{(1 + k)^{2t}}\right]^{1/2} \qquad (14B.4)$$

Here

F_{ts} = Cash flow return associated with the *s*th probability in year *t*
P_{ts} = Probability of the *s*th return in year *t*
$\overline{F}_t$ = Expected cash flow return from the investment in the *t*th year, an average weighted by probabilities
σ_t = Standard deviation of the expected returns in the *t*th year
PV = Present value of all expected returns over the *N*-year life of the investment
k = Appropriate rate of discount for the future returns
σ_{PV} = Standard deviation of the present value of expected returns.[1]

Equation 14B.1 calculates the expected returns of an investment for a given year, *t,* as a weighted average, the items to be averaged being the possible outcomes and the weights being the probabilities associated with each possible outcome for the year. Equation 14B.2 calculates the standard deviation of the expected return in year *t.* Equation 14B.3 discounts the expected returns over each year of the project's life to find the present value of the project, and Equation 14B.4 calculates the standard deviation of the expected PV of the project. The first two equations deal with the returns and risk for individual years, while the last two equations deal with returns and risk of the project as a whole.

Comparison of Two Investments with Uncertain Returns over Future Time Periods

The application and significance of the basic formulas can best be conveyed by illustrative examples. The relevant data and calculations are set forth in Tables 14B.1 for Project A and 14B.2 for Project B. Project A's cash investment is \$100. Returns are expected over three periods. Five "states of the world" are possible; that is, $s = 1 \ldots 5$, and the outcomes for each of these states are given in the columns headed F_{1s}, F_{2s}, F_{3s}. Note that the range of possible returns widens in the later periods.

The associated probabilities are in the columns headed P_{1s}, P_{2s}, and P_{3s}. It should be noted that in Period 2 the probability distribution is somewhat flatter than in Period 1, and that in Period 3 the probability distribution is even more flat and is also skewed somewhat to the left, or toward the possibility of lower returns. Thus, the combination of a wider range of outcomes and flatter probability distribution for Periods 2 and 3 indicates that greater uncertainty is associated with returns expected in the more distant future.

Given these data, the expected returns for Project A for each period are calculated and found to be \$70, \$60, and \$50, respectively. The standard deviation of each of these returns is then calculated, using Equation 14B.2. Next, Equation 14B.3 is used to calculate Project A's expected present value, \$161.40, using a 6 percent discount rate. Finally, Equation 14B.4 is used to find the standard deviation of that present value, \$43.27.

1. For a proof of Equation 14B.4, see Frederick S. Hillier, "The Derivation of Probabilistic Information for the Evaluation of Risky Investments," *Management Science* 9 (April 1963), pp. 443–457.

Table 14B.1

Probable Returns from Risky Investment A

Investment A = $100 (Cash Outflow in Period 0)

(1) Calculation of Expected Returns

State (s)	F_{1s}	P_{1s}	$F_{1s}P_{1s}$	F_{2s}	P_{2s}	$F_{2s}P_{2s}$	F_{3s}	P_{3s}	$F_{3s}P_{3s}$
	Period 1			Period 2			Period 3		
1	50	0.10	5	20	0.10	2	−40	0.10	−4
2	60	0.20	12	40	0.25	10	30	0.30	9
3	70	0.40	28	60	0.30	18	50	0.30	15
4	80	0.20	16	80	0.25	20	80	0.20	16
5	90	0.10	9	100	0.10	10	140	0.10	14
			$\sum_{s=1}^{5}(F_{1s}P_{1s}) = \bar{F}_1 = 70$			$\bar{F}_2 = 60$			$\bar{F}_3 = 50$

(2) Calculation of Standard Deviation

State (s)	$(F_{1s}-\bar{F}_1)^2$	P_{1s}	$(F_{1s}-\bar{F}_1)^2P_{1s}$	$(F_{2s}-\bar{F}_2)^2$	P_{2s}	$(F_{2s}-\bar{F}_2)^2P_{2s}$	$(F_{3s}-\bar{F}_3)^2$	P_{3s}	$(F_{3s}-\bar{F}_3)^2P_{3s}$
	Period 1			Period 2			Period 3		
1	400	0.10	40	1600	0.10	160	8100	0.10	810
2	100	0.20	20	400	0.25	100	400	0.30	120
3	0	0.40	0	0	0.30	0	0	0.30	0
4	100	0.20	20	400	0.25	100	900	0.20	180
5	400	0.10	40	1600	0.10	160	8100	0.10	810
			$\sigma_1^2 = \sum_{s=1}^{5}(F_{1s}-\bar{F}_1)^2P_{1s} = 120$			$\sigma_2^2 = 520$			$\sigma_3^2 = 1920$
			$\sigma_1 = \sqrt{120} = \$10.95$			$\sigma_2 = \sqrt{520} = \$22.80$			$\sigma_3 = \sqrt{1920} = \$43.82$

(3) $PV_a = \frac{70}{1.06} + \frac{60}{(1.06)^2} + \frac{50}{(1.06)^3} = \frac{70}{1.060} + \frac{60}{1.124} + \frac{50}{1.191} = \$161.40$

(4) $\sigma_{PV} = \left[\frac{120}{(1.06)^2} + \frac{520}{(1.06)^4} + \frac{1920}{(1.06)^6}\right]^{1/2} = \left[\frac{120}{1.124} + \frac{520}{1.262} + \frac{1920}{1.419}\right]^{1/2}$

$= [106.76 + 412.04 + 1,353.07]^{1/2} = [1,871,87]^{1/2} = \$43.27$

In Table 14B.2, similar calculations are performed for Project B, which also involves an outlay of $100. To simplify the calculations, we assume that the indicated probabilities are the same for each of the three periods, but note that the expected returns drop with each successive year. Thus, the standard deviation of expected returns, $\sigma_t = \$10.95$, is the same for each of the three periods, but the coefficient of variation, which is the standard deviation divided by the mean return, is lower for the earlier returns, because expected returns are declining. Thus, the riskiness of Project B is also increasing over

Table 14B.2

Probable Returns from Risky Investment B

Investment B = $100

(1) Cash Inflows

P_{1S}	F_{1S}	F_{2S}	F_{3S}
0.10	40	30	20
0.20	50	40	30
0.40	60	50	40
0.20	70	60	50
0.10	80	70	60
$\bar{F}_t$ =	60	50	40

(2) $\sigma_t = [0.10(-20)^2 + 0.20\,(-10)^2 + 0.20(10)^2 + 0.10(20)^2]^{1/2} = [120]^{1/2} = \$10.95$

(3) $$\text{PV}_b = \frac{60}{1.060} + \frac{50}{1.124} + \frac{40}{1.191} = 56.60 + 44.48 + 33.59 = \$134.67$$

(4) $$\sigma_{\text{PV}} = \left[\frac{120}{1.124} + \frac{120}{1.262} + \frac{120}{1.419}\right]^{1/2} = [106.76 + 95.09 + 84.57]^{1/2} = [286.42]^{1/2}$$

$$= \$16.92$$

time. Equations 14B.3 and 14B.4 are again used to calculate the present value of the expected returns, $134.67, and the standard deviation of the expected value, $16.92.

Knowing the mean (PV) and the standard deviation (σ_{PV}) as calculated in Tables 14B.1 and 14B.2, and assuming that the returns from Projects A and B are normally distributed, we can construct probability distribution graphs for the two projects; these distributions are shown in Figure 14B.1. The expected

Figure 14B.1

Probability Distributions of PV for Projects A and B

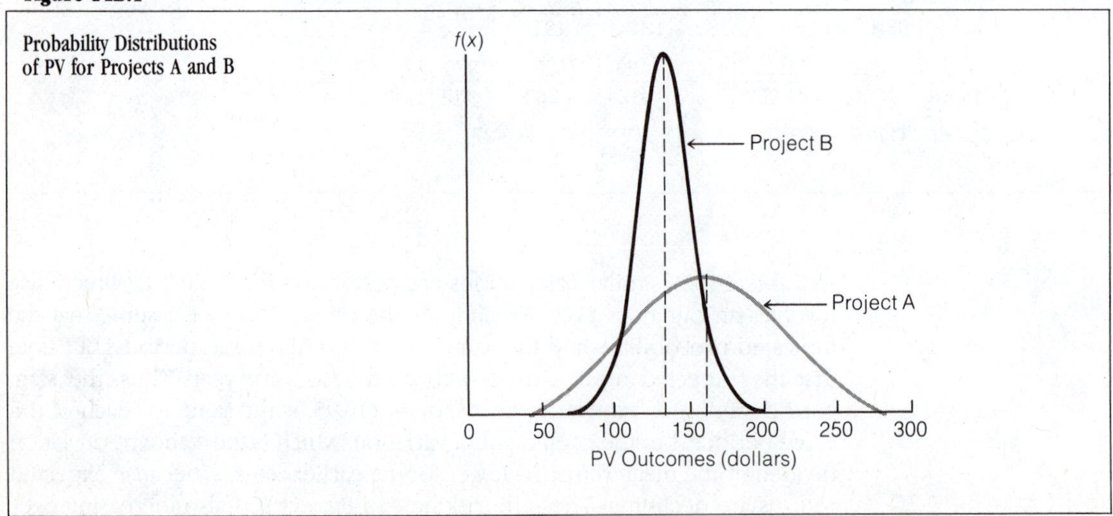

PV of Project A is seen to be $161, while that of B is $135. However, the larger standard deviation and flatter graph of A indicate that A is the riskier project.

The decision maker must still choose between the riskier but probably more profitable project, A, and the less risky but probably less profitable project, B. How is this choice made? Conceptually, the information on relative project riskiness could be used to establish risk-adjusted discount rates, which could then be used to calculate risk-adjusted NPV's, using the market price of risk theory described in Chapter 14. This would require the calculation of the systematic risk measures, covariance or beta, over multiple time periods.[2] Further discussion of the relationship between risk and the cost of capital will be deferred to Chapter 17.

Cumulative Probability

A useful and practical way of expressing the distributions of Projects A and B is in terms of cumulative probabilities (discussed in detail in Appendix A to Chapter 14). We know that Projects A and B each have a cost of $100. What is the probability that the present value of the cash flows from each of these projects will be *at least* $100, that is, that the NPV will be zero or greater? Cumulative probabilities are used to answer this question.

Cumulative probabilities are developed from the data on the area under the normal curve given in Appendix D. In Table 14B.3, the data on Projects A and B are combined with the information on the area under the normal curve. The various entries in Columns 1 and 2 of this table represent possible outcomes for the PV of Projects A and B. Since the investment outlay for each project is $100, this sum can be subtracted from the PV figures in Columns 1 and 2 to obtain the NPV values in Columns 3 and 4. The z values in Column 5 simply denote the number of standard deviations each entry is from the mean, and Column 6 gives the probability of realizing PV's and NPV's *at least* as large as those shown in Columns 1 through 4. From Appendix D, we see that for the first line of Table 14B.3, the probability of an outcome's lying to the left of -3σ is 0.0013, or 0.13 percent, so the probability of the outcome's lying to the right of -3σ, that is, the probability of NPV_a being at least $-\$68.35$ or NPV_b being at least $-\$16.07$ is 100.00 percent $-$ 0.13 percent $=$ 99.87 percent $\approx$ 99.9 percent. The other values in Table 14B.3 are developed similarly. Note that the last two rows of the table indicate that the probability of at least breaking even is 92.2 percent for Project A and 98.0 percent for Project B.

Figure 14B.2 shows these data on cumulative probabilities in graph form. Here it is easy to see that Project B has only a small chance of not breaking even, but it also has virtually no chance of earning an NPV of over about $60.

2. See Marcus Bogue and Richard Roll, "Capital Budgeting of Risky Projects with 'Imperfect' Markets for Physical Capital," *Journal of Finance* 29 (May 1974), pp. 601–613.

Table 14B.3

Cumulative Probabilities of Expected Present Values of Investments A and B

Expected PV of at Least		Expected NPV of at Least		z Value[a]	Cumulative Probability
A	B	A	B		
(1)	(2)	(3)	(4)	(5)	(6)
$ 31.59	$ 83.91	$ (68.41)	$ (16.09)	−3z	99.9%[b]
74.86	100.83	(25.14)	0.83	−2z	97.7
118.13	117.75	18.13	17.75	−1z	84.1
161.40	134.67	61.40	34.67	—	50.0
204.67	151.59	104.67	51.59	+1z	15.9[c]
247.94	168.51	147.94	68.51	2z	2.3
291.21	185.43	191.21	85.43	3z	.1
$100.00		0.00		−1.42	92.2%[d]
	$100.00		0.00	−2.05	98.0[e]

a. z = Number of standard deviations from mean PV.
b. 0.5000 *plus* area under *left* tail of normal curve; for example, 0.5000 + 0.4987 = 99.9 percent for $z = -3$.
c. 0.5000 *less* area under *right* tail of normal curve; for example, 0.5000 − 0.4772 = 2.3 percent for $z = 2$.
d. NPV = PV − Cost.

$$z = \frac{PV}{\sigma NPV} \text{ where NPV} = 0.$$

Since the PV differs from the NPV by a constant, $\sigma_{NPV} = \sigma_{PV}$,

$$z = \frac{61.40}{43.27} = 1.42 \text{ for Project A.}$$

The area under the right tail of the normal curve associated with $z = 1.42$ is 0.4222, so Area = 0.5000 + 0.4222 = 0.9222, and the probability of NPV ≥ 0 is 92.2 percent.

e. For Project B,

$$z = \frac{34.67}{16.92} = 2.05 \text{ where NPV} = 0,$$

and the associated area = 0.5000 + 0.4798 = 0.9798, so the probability of NPV ≥ 0 is 98 percent for Project B.

Project A, on the other hand, has a higher probability of losing money, but it also has a fairly high probability of achieving an NPV of over $100.

It is clear that Investment A has a higher expected return than Investment B. However, disregarding portfolio effects, Investment B is less risky. Selection between A and B would depend upon the decision maker's attitude toward risk, as well as upon how the two investments might fit in with the firm's other assets.

Interdependent Returns over Time: The Hillier and Hertz Approaches

The foregoing presentation represents a general method for dealing with risk when the returns of one period do not depend upon outcomes in other years; that is, when the returns are *independent* and when the expected returns for a given year are normally distributed. When these conditions of independence and normality do not hold, the calculations become more complicated. The models for which expected net cash flows between periods are correlated (the expected returns between time periods are dependent) and

Figure 14B.2

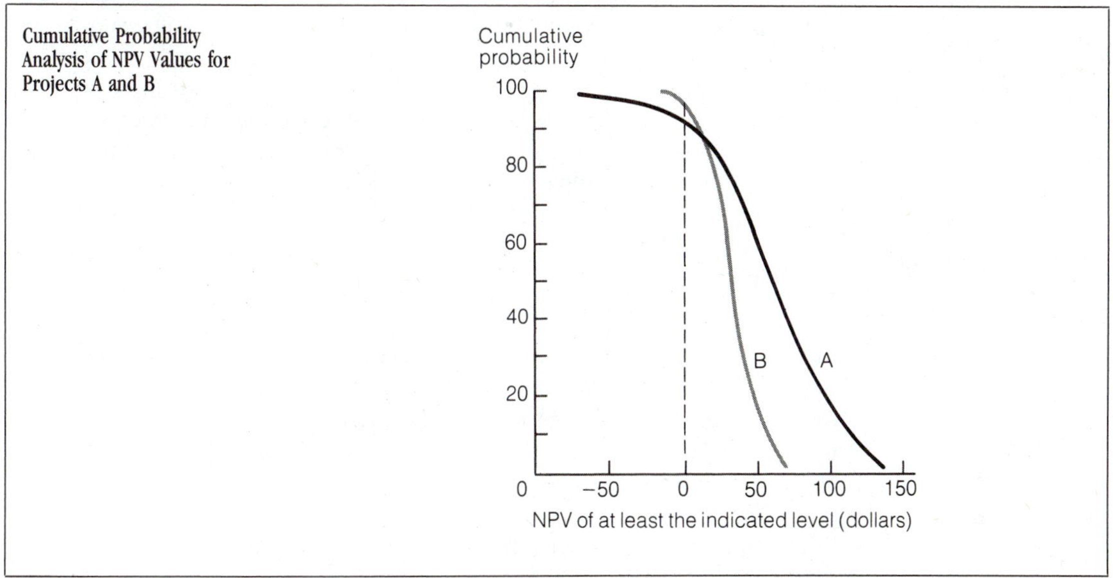

Cumulative Probability Analysis of NPV Values for Projects A and B

those for which only some of the returns of an investment are correlated and some are independent have been treated by Frederick Hillier.[3] Mathematical techniques are also available for dealing with nonnormal probability distributions. We shall not go into the technical methodology involved, but Hillier's approach has proved to be a useful way of dealing with uncertainty in at least some practical situations.

Another approach to capital budgeting under uncertainty has been presented in an article by David Hertz.[4] He is particularly persuasive in indicating that, taking probabilities into account, the expected rate of return may be quite different from the conventional best-single-estimate approach. Hertz illustrates the use of the probability information in an approach that requires only a range of high and low values around expected values of such key variables as sales, profit margins, and so forth. Under his method, the decision maker is not required to assign probabilities to the variables, but must choose only (1) the expected value, (2) an upper estimate, and (3) a lower estimate. The Monte Carlo method, which involves using a table of random numbers to generate the possible probabilities, is used to generate the required probability distributions.[5]

3. See Frederick S. Hillier, "The Derivation of Probabilistic Information for the Evaluation of Risk Investments," *Management Science* 9 (April 1963), pp. 44–57; and Frederick S. Hillier and David V. Heebink, "Evaluating Risky Capital Investments," *California Management Review* 8 (Winter 1965), pp. 71–80.

4. David B. Hertz, "Uncertainty and Investment Selection," in *The Treasurer's Handbook,* ed. J. F. Weston and M. B. Goudzwaard (Homewood, Ill.: Dow Jones–Irwin, 1976), Chapter 18, pp. 376–420.

5. For a discussion of the nature of the Monte Carlo method and some applications, see C. McMillan and R. F. Gonzalez, *Systems Analysis* (Homewood, Ill.: Irwin, 1965), pp. 76–121.

The Monte Carlo method also permits assignment of values that reflect differing degrees of dependence between some events and some subsequent events. For example, the expected sales for the firm, as well as its selling prices, might be determined by the intensity of competition in conjunction with the total size of market demand and its growth rate. A further advantage of the Hertz technique is that, by separating the individual factors that determine profitability, the separate effects of each factor can be estimated and the sensitivity of profitability to each factor can be determined. If the effects of a particular factor on the final results are negligible, it is not necessary for management to analyze that particular factor in any great detail.

Sensitivity Analysis

The NPV of a project will, in the final analysis, depend upon such factors as quantity of sales, sales prices, input costs, and the like. If these values turn out to be favorable—that is, output and sales prices are high, and costs are low—then profits, the realized rate of return, and the actual NPV will be high, and the converse if these values are unfavorable. Recognizing these causal relationships, managers often calculate project NPV's under alternative assumptions, then see just how sensitive NPV is to changing conditions. One example that recently came to the authors' attention involves a fertilizer company that was comparing two alternative types of phosphate plants. Fuel represented a major cost, and one plant used coal, which may be obtained under a long-term, fixed-cost contract, while the other used oil, which must be purchased at current market prices. Considering present and projected future prices, the oil-fired plant looked better—it had a considerably higher NPV. However, oil prices are volatile, and if prices rose by more than the expected rate, this plant would have been unprofitable. The coal-fired plant, on the other hand, had a lower NPV under the expected conditions, but this NPV was not sensitive to changing conditions in the energy market. The company finally selected the coal plant because the sensitivity analysis indicated it to be less risky.

Monte Carlo Simulation Analysis

Sensitivity analysis as practiced by the fertilizer company described above is informal in the sense that no probabilities are attached to the likelihood of various outcomes. *Monte Carlo simulation analysis* represents a refinement that does employ probability estimates. In this section we first describe how *decision trees* can be used to attach probabilities to different outcomes, and then we illustrate how full-scale computer simulation can be employed to analyze major projects.

Decision Trees. Most important decisions are not made once and for all at one point in time. Rather, decisions are made in stages. For example, a petroleum firm considering the possibility of expanding into agricultural chemicals might take the following steps:

1. Spend $100,000 for a survey of supply-demand conditions in the agricultural chemical industry.

2. If the survey results are favorable, spend \$500,000 on a pilot plant to investigate production methods.
3. Depending on the costs estimated from the pilot study and the demand potential from the market study, either abandon the project, build a large plant, or build a small one.

Thus, the final decision actually is made in stages, with subsequent decisions depending on the results of previous decisions.

The sequence of events can be mapped out like the branches of a tree, hence the name *decision tree.* As an example, consider Figure 14B.3. There it is assumed that the petroleum company has completed its industry supply-demand analysis and pilot plant study, and has determined that it should proceed to develop a full-scale production facility. The firm must decide whether to build a large plant or a small one. The estimated probabilities of demand levels for the plant's products are 50 percent for high demand, 30 percent for medium demand, and 20 percent for low demand. Depending on demand, net cash flows (sales revenues minus operating costs, all discounted to the present) will range from \$8.8 million to \$1.4 million if a large plant is built and from \$2.6 million to \$1.4 million if a small plant is built.

The initial costs of the large and small plants are shown in Column 5 of the figure; when these investment outlays are subtracted from the PV of cash

Figure 14B.3

Illustrative Decision Tree

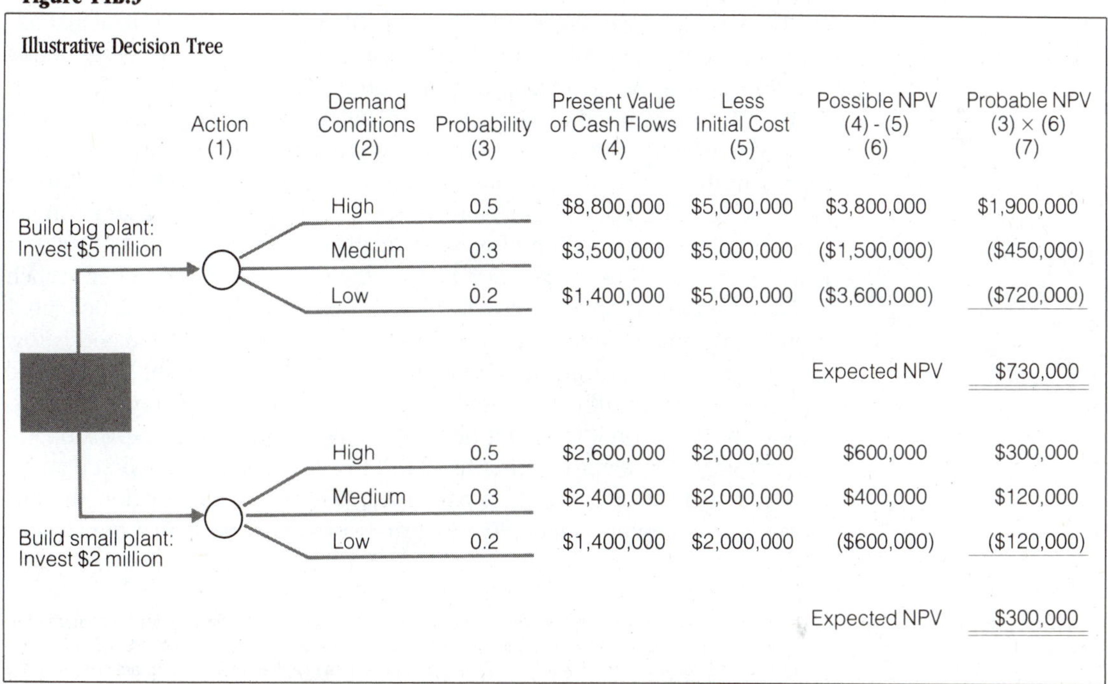

Action (1)	Demand Conditions (2)	Probability (3)	Present Value of Cash Flows (4)	Less Initial Cost (5)	Possible NPV (4) - (5) (6)	Probable NPV (3) × (6) (7)
Build big plant: Invest \$5 million	High	0.5	\$8,800,000	\$5,000,000	\$3,800,000	\$1,900,000
	Medium	0.3	\$3,500,000	\$5,000,000	(\$1,500,000)	(\$450,000)
	Low	0.2	\$1,400,000	\$5,000,000	(\$3,600,000)	(\$720,000)
					Expected NPV	\$730,000
Build small plant: Invest \$2 million	High	0.5	\$2,600,000	\$2,000,000	\$600,000	\$300,000
	Medium	0.3	\$2,400,000	\$2,000,000	\$400,000	\$120,000
	Low	0.2	\$1,400,000	\$2,000,000	(\$600,000)	(\$120,000)
					Expected NPV	\$300,000

Note: The figures in Column 4 are the annual cash flows from operations—sales revenues minus cash operating costs—discounted at an appropriate rate.

flows, the result is the set of possible NPV's shown in Column 6. One, but only one, of these NPV's will actually occur. Finally, we multiply Column 6 by Column 3 to obtain Column 7, and the sums in Column 7 give the expected NPV's of the large and small plants.

Because the expected NPV of the larger plant ($730,000) is larger than that of the small plant ($300,000), should the decision be to build the large plant? Perhaps, but not necessarily. Notice that the range of outcomes is greater if the large plant is built, with the actual NPV's (Column 6 in Figure 14B.3) varying from $3.8 million to *minus* $3.6 million. However, a range of only $600,000 to minus $600,000 exists for the small plant. Since the required investments for the two plants are not the same, we must examine the coefficients of variation of the net present value possibilities in order to determine which alternative actually entails the greater risk. The coefficient of variation for the large plant's present value is 4.3, while that for the small plant is only 1.5.[6] Thus, risk is greater if the decision is to build the large plant.

The decision maker could take account of the risk differentials in a variety of ways. Utility values could be assigned to the cash flows given in Column 4 of Figure 14B.3, thus stating Column 7 in terms of expected utility. The decision maker would then choose the plant size that provided the greatest utility. Alternatively, the certainty equivalent or risk-adjusted discount rate methods could be used in calculating the present values given in Column 4. The plant that offered the larger risk-adjusted net present value would then be the optimal choice.

The decision tree illustrated in Figure 14B.3 is quite simple; in actual use, the trees are frequently far more complex and involve a number of sequential decision points. As an example of a more complex tree, consider Figure 14B.4. The boxes numbered 1, 2, and so on, are *decision points,* that is, instances when the firm must choose between alternatives, while the circles represent the possible actual outcomes, one of which will follow these decisions. At Decision Point 1, the firm has three choices: to invest $3 million in a large plant, to invest $1.3 million in a small plant, or to spend $100,000 on market research. If the large plant is built, the firm follows the upper branch, and its position has been fixed—it can only hope that demand will be high. If it builds the small plant, then it follows the lower branch. If demand is low, no further action is required. If demand is high, Decision Point 2 is reached, and the firm must either do nothing or else expand the plant at a cost of another $2.2 million. (Thus, if it obtains a large plant through expansion, the cost is $500,000 greater than if it had built the large plant in the first place.)

If the decision at Point 1 is to pay $100,000 for more information, the firm moves to the center branch. The research modifies the firm's information

6. Using Equation 14.2 and the data on possible returns in Figure 14B.3, the standard deviation of returns for the larger plant is found to be $3.155 million and that for the smaller one is $458,260. Dividing each of these standard deviations by the expected returns for their respective plant size gives the coefficients of variation.

Figure 14B.4

Decision Tree with Multiple Decision Points

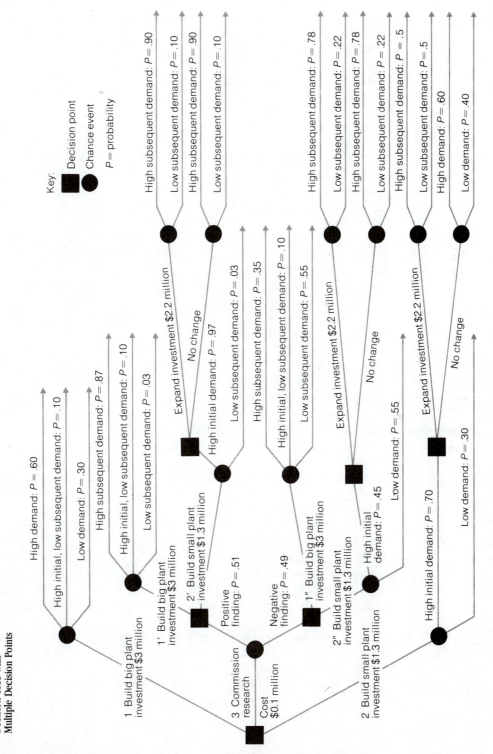

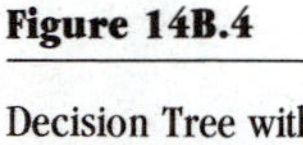

about potential demand. Initially, the probabilities were 70 percent for high demand and 30 percent for low demand. The research survey will show either favorable (positive) or unfavorable (negative) demand prospects. If they are positive, we assume that the probability for high final demand will be 87 percent and that for low demand will be 13 percent; if the research yields negative results, the odds on high final demand are only 35 percent and those for low demand are 65 percent. These results will, of course, influence the firm's decision as to whether to build a large or a small plant.

If the firm builds a large plant and demand is high, then sales and profits will be large. However, if it builds a large plant and demand is weak, sales will be low and losses, rather than profits, will be incurred. On the other hand, if it builds a small plant and demand is high, sales and profits will be lower than they could have been had a large plant been built, but the chances of losses in the event of low demand will be eliminated. Thus, the decision to build the large plant is riskier than the one to build the small plant. The decision to commission the research is, in effect, an expenditure to reduce the degree of uncertainty in the decision on which plant to build; the research provides additional information on the probability of high versus low demand, thus lowering the level of uncertainty.

The decision tree in Figure 14B.4 is incomplete in that no dollar outcomes (or utility values) are assigned to the various situations. If this step were taken, along the lines shown in the last two columns of Figure 14B.3, then expected values could be obtained for each of the alternative actions. These expected values could then be used to aid the decision maker in choosing among the alternatives.

Computer Simulation

The concepts embodied in decision tree analysis can be extended to computer simulation. To illustrate the technique, let us consider a proposal to build a new textile plant. The cost of the plant is not known for certain, although it is expected to run about $150 million. If no problems are encountered, the cost can be as low as $125 million, while an unfortunate series of events—strikes, unprojected increases in materials costs, technical problems, and the like—could result in the investment outlay running as high as $225 million.

Revenues from the new facility, which will operate for many years, will depend on population growth and income in the region, competition, developments in synthetic fabrics research, and textile import quotas. Operating costs will depend on production efficiency, materials and labor cost trends, and the like. Since both sales revenues and operating costs are uncertain, annual profits are also uncertain.

Assuming that probability distributions can be assigned to each of the major cost and revenue determinants, a computer program can be constructed to simulate what is likely to happen. In effect, the computer selects one value at random from each of the relevant distributions, combines it with other values selected from the other distributions, and produces an estimated profit

Figure 14B.5

Simulation for Investment Planning

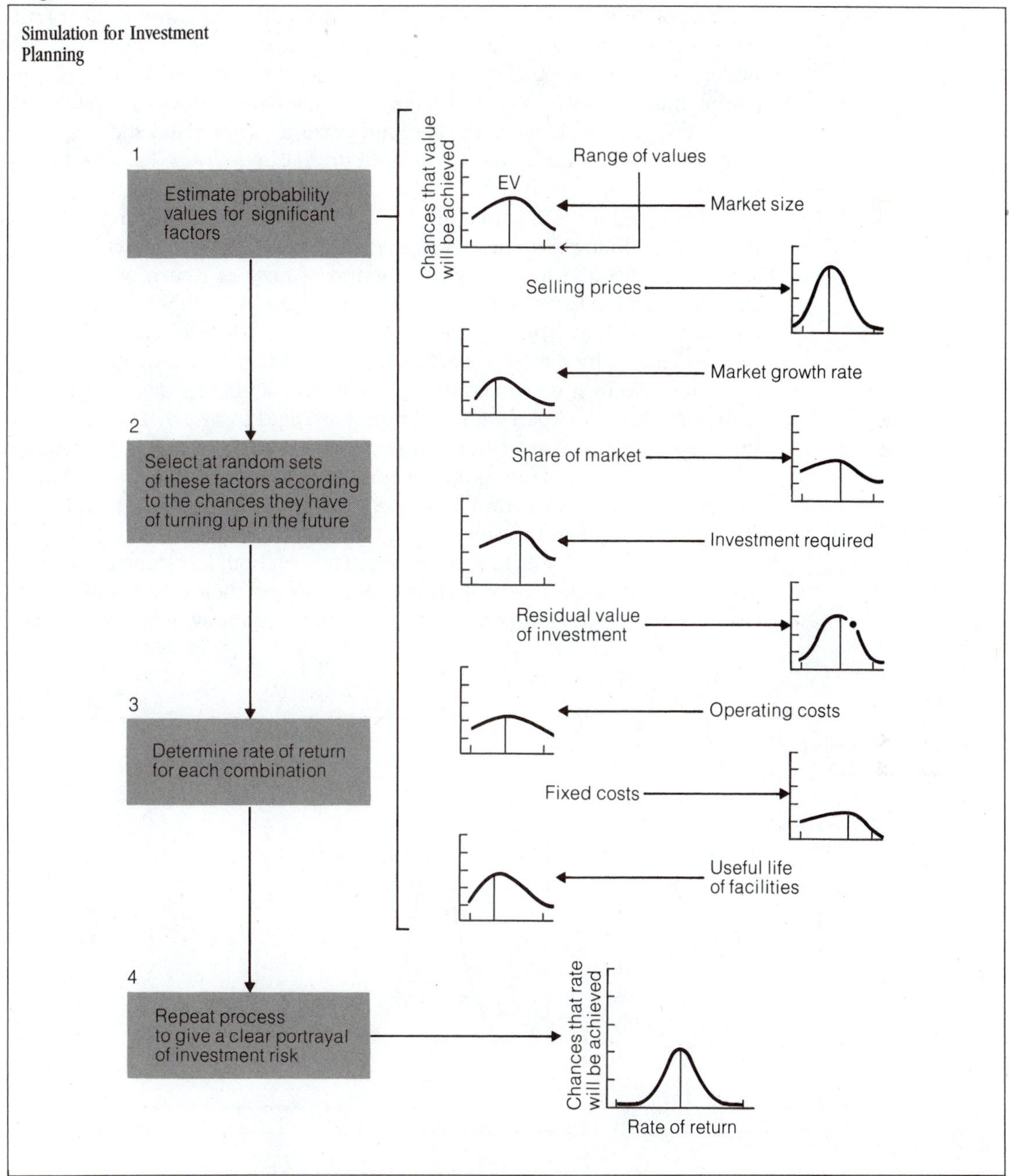

Source: Adapted from David B. Hertz, "Uncertainty and Investment Selection," in J. Fred Weston and Maurice Goudzwaard, eds., *The Treasurer's Handbook* (Homewood, Ill.: Dow Jones-Irwin, 1976), p. 408. © 1976 by Dow Jones-Irwin.

and net present value or rate of return on investment.[7] This particular profit and rate of return occur, of course, only for the particular combination of values selected during this trial. The computer goes on to select other sets of values and to compute other profits and rates of return repeatedly, for perhaps several hundred trials. A count is kept of the number of times each rate of return is computed, and when the computer runs are completed, the frequency with which the various rates of return occurred can be plotted as a frequency distribution.

The procedure is illustrated in Figures 14B.5 and 14B.6. Figure 14B.5 is a flowchart outlining the simulation procedure described above, while Figure 14B.6 illustrates the frequency distribution of rates of return generated by such a simulation for two alternative projects, X and Y, each with an expected cost of $20 million. The expected rate of return on Investment X is 15 percent, and that of Investment Y is 20 percent. However, these are only the *average* rates of return generated by the computer; simulated rates range from −10 percent to +45 percent for Investment Y and from 5 to 25 percent for Investment X. The standard deviation generated for X is only 4 percentage points—68 percent of the computer runs had rates of return between 11 and 19 percent—while that for Y is 12 percentage points. Clearly, then, Investment Y is riskier than Investment X.

The computer simulation has provided us with both an estimate of the expected returns on the two projects and an estimate of their relative risks. A decision about which alternative should be chosen can now be made, perhaps

Figure 14B.6

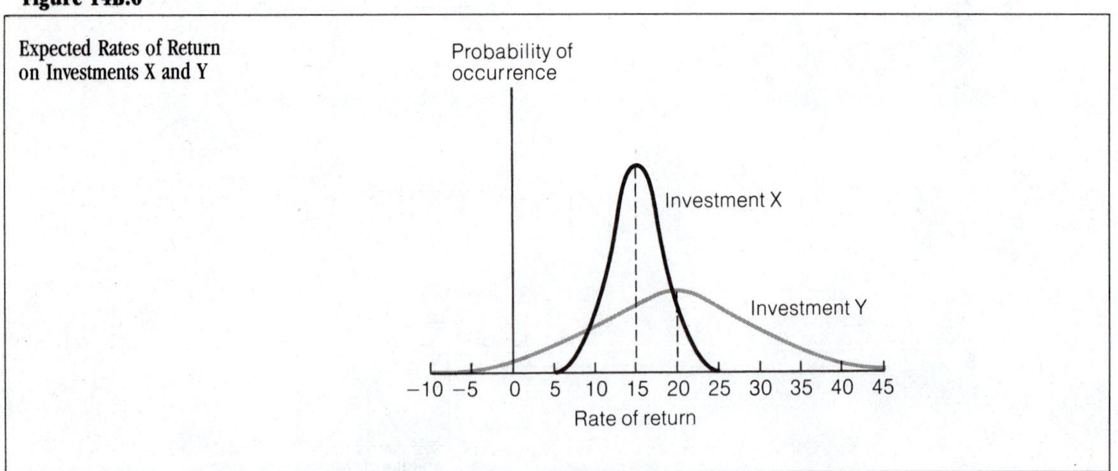

7. If the variables are not independent, then conditional probabilities must be employed. For example, if demand is weak, then both sales in units and sales prices are likely to be low, and these interrelationships must be taken into account in the simulation.

by using the risk-adjusted discount rate method or perhaps in a judgmental, informal manner by the decision maker.

However, computer simulation is not always feasible for risk analysis. The technique involves obtaining probability distributions about a number of variables—investment outlays, unit sales, product prices, input prices, asset lives, and so on—and a fair amount of programming and machine-time costs. Therefore, full-scale simulation is not generally worthwhile except for large and expensive projects, such as major plant expansions or new-product decisions. In those cases, however, when a firm is deciding whether to accept a major undertaking involving millions of dollars, computer simulation can provide valuable insights into the relative merits of alternative strategies.

Problems

14B.1 The financial vice-president for the Atkins Manufacturing Company is analyzing the potential of a $1,500 investment in a new machine. His estimate of the cash-flow distribution for the three-year life of the machine is shown below:

Period 1		Period 2		Period 3	
Probability	Cash Flow	Probability	Cash Flow	Probability	Cash Flow
0.10	$800	0.10	$800	0.20	$1,200
0.20	600	0.30	700	0.50	900
0.40	400	0.40	600	0.20	600
0.30	200	0.20	500	0.10	300

Probability distributions are assumed to be independent. Treasury bills are yielding 10 percent. To evaluate the investment, the vice-president has asked you to make the following calculations:

a. The expected net present value of the project.
b. The standard deviation about the expected value.
c. The probability that the net present value will be zero or less (assume the distribution is normal and continuous).
d. The probability that the net present value will be greater than zero.
e. The probability that the net present value will at least equal the mean.
f. The profitability index of the expected value.
g. The probability that the profitability index will be less than 1; greater than 2.

14B.2 The Eastern Tool and Die Company is considering an investment in a project that requires an initial outlay of $3,000 with an expected net cash flow generated over three periods as follows:

Period 1		Period 2		Period 3	
Probability	Cash Flow	Probability	Cash Flow	Probability	Cash Flow
0.10	$ 800	0.10	$ 800	0.20	$ 800
0.20	1,000	0.30	1,000	0.50	1,000
0.40	1,500	0.40	1,500	0.20	1,500
0.30	2,000	0.20	2,000	0.10	2,000

a. What is the expected net present value of this project? (Assume that the probability distributions are independent and that Treasury bills are yielding 10 percent.)
b. Calculate the standard deviation about the expected value.
c. Find the probability that the net present value will be zero or less. (Assume that the distribution is normal and continuous.) What is the probability that the NPV will be greater than zero?
d. Calculate the profitability index of the expected value. What is the probability that the index will be less than 1? greater than 2?

14B.3 The Parker Company has the following probability distributions for net cash flows during the first year for a potential project:

Probability	Cash Flow
0.50	$100
0.30	200
0.20	300

Performance of similar projects in the past has indicated that the net cash flow distributions are not independent. The level of demand and the related net cash flow returns experienced in Period 1 influence the achievements in Period 2 in the following way:

If Year 1 = $100, the distribution for Year 2 is:

0.70	$100
0.20	200
0.10	300

If Year 1 = $200, the distribution for Year 2 is:

0.10	$100
0.60	200
0.30	300

If Year 1 = $300, the distribution for Year 2 is:

0.10	$100
0.20	200
0.50	300
0.20	400

a. If $200 is earned in Year 1, what is the probability that the second year's earnings will be $200 or less?
b. What is the probability that earnings will be $100 for Year 1 and $200 for Year 2?
c. What is the probability that the Parker Company will earn more than $300 on this project in the second year?

d. If earnings for the first year are $300, what is the probability that $200 or more will be earned the second year?
e. What is the probability that Parker will earn at least $600 over the life of the project?

Selected References

Baron, David P. "Investment Policy, Optimality, and the Mean-Variance Model." *Journal of Finance* 34 (March 1979), pp. 207–232.

Ben-Shahar, Haim, and Werner, Frank M. "Multiperiod Capital Budgeting under Uncertainty: A Suggested Application." *Journal of Financial and Quantitative Analysis* 12 (December 1977), pp. 859–877.

Bernardo, John J., and Lanser, Howard P. "A Capital Budgeting Decision Model with Subjective Criteria." *Journal of Financial and Quantitative Analysis* 12 (June 1977), pp. 261–275.

Brumelle, Shelby L., and Schwab, Bernhard. "Capital Budgeting with Uncertain Future Opportunities: A Markovian Approach." *Journal of Financial and Quantitative Analysis* 7 (January 1973), pp. 111–122.

Celec, Stephen E., and Pettway, Richard H. "Some Observations on Risk-Adjusted Discount Rates: A Comment." *Journal of Finance* 34 (September 1979), pp. 1061–1063.

Edelman, Franz, and Greenberg, Joel S. "Venture Analysis: The Assessment of Uncertainty and Risk." *Financial Executive* 37 (August 1969), pp. 56–62.

Elton, Edwin J., and Gruber, Martin J. "On the Maximization of the Geometric Mean with Lognormal Return Distribution." *Management Science* 21 (December 1974), pp. 483–488.

Hillier, Frederick S. "The Derivation of Probabilistic Information for the Evaluation of Risky Investments." *Management Science* 9 (April 1963), pp. 443–457.

Hillier, Frederick S., and Heebink, David V. "Evaluation of Risky Capital Investments." *California Management Review* 8 (Winter 1965), pp. 71–80.

Hsaio, Frank S. T., and Smith, James W. "An Analytical Approach to Sensitivity Analysis of the Internal Rate of Return Model." *Journal of Finance* 33 (May 1978), pp. 645–649.

Kryzanowski, Lawrence; Lusztig, Peter; and Schwab, Bernhard. "Monte Carlo Simulation and Capital Expenditure Decisions—A Case Study." *Engineering Economist* 18 (Fall 1972), pp. 31–48.

Lewellen, Wilber G. "Reply to Pettway and Celec." *Journal of Finance* 34 (September 1979), pp. 1065–1066.

Smidt, Seymour. "A Bayesian Analysis of Project Selection and of Post Audit Evaluations." *Journal of Finance* 34 (June 1979), pp. 675–688.

Appendix C to Chapter 14

Abandonment Value

At some future time, usually because of unforeseen problems, it may become more profitable to abandon a project, even though its economic life has not yet ended, than to continue its operation. Taking this possibility into consideration in the capital budgeting process may increase the project's expected net present value and reduce its standard deviation of returns. In this discussion we first show how to include *abandonment value* in the analysis when making accept-reject decisions, and then we look at criteria for actually abandoning a project after it has been accepted.[1]

The analysis required for taking abandonment value into account in evaluating an investment project involves no principles beyond those already set forth. However, because it does represent an important aspect of the decision process, it is useful to have a decision model that includes abandonment value in its framework. The principles involved may best be conveyed through a specific example illustrating the role of abandonment value in evaluating projects under uncertainty.

The Palmer Corporation has invested $300 in new machinery with expected cash flows over two years. This is shown in Table 14C.1.

There are two sets of probabilities associated with the project. The initial probabilities should be interpreted as probabilities of particular cash flows from the first year only; the conditional probabilities are the probabilities of particular cash flows in the second year, given that a specific outcome has occurred in the first year. Thus, the results in the second year are *conditional* upon the results of the first year. If high profits occur in the first year, chances are that the second year will also bring high profits. To obtain the probability that a particular first-year outcome and a particular second-year outcome will both occur, we must multiply the initial probability by the conditional probability to obtain what is termed the *joint probability*.

These concepts are applied to the data of Table 14C.1 to construct Table 14C.2. The project is not expected to have any returns after the second year. The firm's cost of capital is 12 percent. To indicate the role of abandonment

1. For an early treatment of abandonment value, see Alexander A. Robichek and James C. Van Horne, "Abandonment Value and Capital Budgeting," *Journal of Finance* 22 (December 1967), pp. 577–590.

Table 14C.1

Expected Cash Flows

Year 1		Year 2	
Cash Flow	Initial Probability P (1)	Cash Flow	Conditional Probability P (2|1)
$200	(0.3)	$100	(0.3)
		200	(0.5)
		300	(0.2)
300	(0.4)	200	(0.3)
		300	(0.5)
		400	(0.2)
400	(0.3)	300	(0.3)
		400	(0.4)
		500	(0.3)

Table 14C.2

Calculation of Expected Net Present Value

Year 1			Year 2			Probability Analysis				
Cash Flow (1)	PV Factor (2)	Present Value: (1) × (2) (3)	Cash Flow (4)	PV Factor (5)	Present Value: (4) × (5) (6)	Present Value of Total Cash Flow: (3) + (6) (7)	Initial Probability (8)	Conditional Probability (9)	Joint Probability: (8) × (9) (10)	Expected Value: (7) × (10) (11)
			$100	0.7972	80	$259		0.3	0.09	$ 23
$200	0.8929	179	200	0.7972	159	338	0.3	0.5	0.15	51
			300	0.7972	239	418		0.2	0.06	25
			200	0.7972	159	427		0.3	0.12	51
300	0.8929	268	300	0.7972	239	507	0.4	0.5	0.20	101
			400	0.7972	319	587		0.2	0.08	47
			300	0.7972	239	596		0.3	0.09	54
400	0.8929	357	400	0.7972	319	676	0.3	0.4	0.12	81
			500	0.7972	399	756		0.3	0.09	68
									1.00	$501

Expected present value = $501
Expected net present value = $201

Table 14C.3

Calculation of Standard Deviation

NPV^a –	Exp. NPV =	Deviation	Squared Deviation ×	Joint Probability =	Amount
(41)	201	(242)	58,564	0.09	5,271
38	201	(163)	26,569	0.15	3,985
118	201	(83)	6,889	0.06	413
127	201	(74)	5,476	0.12	657
207	201	6	36	0.20	7
287	201	86	7,396	0.08	592
296	201	95	9,025	0.09	812
376	201	175	30,625	0.12	3,675
456	201	255	65,025	0.09	5,852
				1.00	21,264

Expected standard deviation = $\sigma = (21{,}264)^{1/2} =$ \$146

a. Value from Column 7, Table 14C.2, minus \$300 cost.

value, we first calculate the expected net present value of the investment and its expected standard deviation without considering abandonment value. In the calculation made in Table 14C.2, we find the expected NPV to be \$201.

Next, in Table 14C.3, we calculate the standard deviation of the future cash flows, finding $\sigma =$ \$146. The decision maker can expand this analysis to take abandonment value into account. Suppose the abandonment value of the project at the end of the first year is estimated to be \$250. This is the amount that can be obtained by liquidating the project after the first year, and the \$250 is independent of actual first-year results. If the project is abandoned after one year, then the \$250 will replace any second-year returns. In other words, if the project is abandoned at the end of Year 1, then Year 1 returns will increase by \$250 and Year 2 returns will be zero. The present value of this estimated \$250 abandonment value is, therefore, compared with the expected present values of the cash flows that would occur during the second year if abandonment did not take place. But to make the comparison valid, we must use the second year flows based on the conditional probabilities only, rather than the joint probabilities that were used in the preceding analysis. This calculation is shown in Table 14C.4.

We next compare the present value of the \$250 abandonment value, \$250 × 0.8929 = \$223, with the branch expected present values for each of the three possible cash flow patterns (branches) depicted in Table 14C.4. If the \$223 present value of abandonment exceeds one or more of the expected present values of the possible branches of cash flows, taking abandonment value into account will improve the indicated returns from the project. The \$223 does exceed the \$152 expected PV shown in Table 14C.4 for second year cash flows when the first year cash flow is \$200. In Table 14C.5, therefore, abandonment after Year 1 is assumed for the \$200 case and the new

Table 14C.4

Expected Present Values of Cash Flow during the Second Year

Cash Flow	PV Factor	PV	Conditional Probability		Expected Present Value
$100	0.7972	80	0.3		$ 24
200	0.7972	159	0.5		80
300	0.7972	239	0.2		48
				Branch total	$152
200	0.7972	159	0.3		$ 48
300	0.7972	239	0.5		120
400	0.7972	319	0.2		64
				Branch total	$232
300	0.7972	239	0.3		$ 72
400	0.7972	319	0.4		128
500	0.7972	399	0.3		120
				Branch total	$320

NPV is calculated; the $250 abandonment value is added to the $200 cash flow to obtain a $450 Year 1 cash flow, and the Year 2 cash flow becomes $0. The new calculation of the standard deviation is shown in Table 14C.6.

We may now compare the results when abandonment value is taken into account with the results when it is not considered. Including abandonment value in the calculations increases the expected net present value from $201 to $223, or by about 10 percent; it reduces the expected standard deviation of returns from $146 to $119 and the coefficient of variation from 0.73 to 0.53.

Table 14C.5

Expected Net Present Value with Abandonment Value Included

Year 1 Cash Flow ×	PV Factor =	PV	Year 2 Cash Flow ×	PV Factor =	PV	Present Value of Total Cash Flow ×	Joint Proba-bility =	Expected Value
(1)	(2)	(3)	(4)	(5)	(6)	(7)	(8)	(9)
$450	0.8929	$402	$ 0	0.7972	$ 0	$402	0.30	$121
			200	0.7972	159	427	0.12	51
300	0.8929	268	300	0.7972	239	507	0.20	101
			400	0.7972	319	587	0.08	47
			300	0.7972	239	596	0.09	54
400	0.8929	357	400	0.7972	319	676	0.12	81
			500	0.7972	399	756	0.09	68
							1.00	

Expected present value = $523

Expected net present value = $223

Table 14C.6

Calculation of Standard Deviation for Net Cash Flow with Abandonment Value Included

NPV[a] −	Exp. NPV =	Deviation	Deviation² ×	Joint Probability =	Amount
102	223	(121)	14,641	0.30	4,392
127	223	(96)	9,216	0.12	1,106
207	223	(16)	256	0.20	51
287	223	64	4,096	0.08	328
296	223	73	5,329	0.09	480
376	223	153	23,409	0.12	2,809
456	223	233	54,289	0.09	4,886
					14,052
				Expected standard deviation = $(14{,}052)^{1/2}$ =	119

a. Value from Column 7, Table 14C.5, minus $300 cost.

Thus, for this problem, abandonment value improves the attractiveness of the investment.

Abandonment value is important in another aspect of financial decision making: the reevaluation of projects in succeeding years after they have been undertaken. The decision to continue the project or to abandon it sometime during its life depends on which branch occurs during each time period. For example, suppose that during Year 1 the cash flow actually obtained was $200. Then the three possibilities associated with Year 2 are the three that were conditionally dependent upon a $200 outcome in Year 1. The other six probabilities for Year 2, which were considered in the initial evaluation, were conditional upon other first year outcomes and are thus no longer relevant. A calculation (Table 14C.7) is then made of the second year net cash flows, discounted back one year.

At the end of the first year the abandonment value is $250. This is compared with the expected present value of the second year net cash flow series, discounted one year. This value is determined to be $171, so the abandonment value of $250 exceeds the net present value of returns for the second year. Therefore, the project should be abandoned at the end of the first year.

Table 14C.7

Calculation of Expected Net Cash Flow for Second Period when $200 Was Earned during the First Year

Cash Flow ×	PV Factor =	PV ×	Probability Factor =	Discounted Expected Cash Flow
$100	0.8929	$ 89	0.3	$ 27
200	0.8929	179	0.5	90
300	0.8929	268	0.2	54
			Expected present value =	$171

Note that it is not necessary to compare the standard deviations, because with abandonment the standard deviation of returns is zero, which is certainly lower than the standard deviation of any set of uncertain second year cash flows.

In summary, it is sometimes advantageous to abandon a project even though the net present value of continued operation is positive. The basic reason is that the present value of abandonment after a shorter time may actually be greater than the present value of continued operation. For example, consider a truck with two years of remaining useful life. The present value of continued use is, say, \$900, but the current market value of the truck is \$1,000. Clearly, if the proceeds from the sale can be invested to earn at least the applicable cost of capital, the better decision would be to sell the truck.

Further Developments in Abandonment Decision Rules

The traditional abandonment decision rule is that the project should be abandoned in the first year that abandonment value exceeds the present value of remaining expected cash flows from continued operation. More recently it has become evident that this decision rule may not result in the optimal abandonment decision.[2] Abandonment at a later date may result in an even greater net present value. Returning to our example of the truck, there is one option that has not been considered, which is to operate the truck for another year with a present value of \$500 and then abandon it, with the present value of abandonment in a year being \$600. Thus, the present value of this alternative is \$1,100. The truck should be used for one year and then sold.

The optimal abandonment decision rule is to determine the combination of remaining operating cash flows and future abandonment that has the maximum expected net present value. This decision rule is, unfortunately, difficult to implement, especially when the project life is long and there are numerous opportunities for abandonment over time. If a piece of equipment can be used for twenty years or abandoned at the end of any year, then twenty different net present value calculations would be required to determine the optimum pattern that will result in maximum expected net present value.

It is argued that this approach is too cumbersome and that all that is required is to find that there is at least one pattern of cash flows that yields an expected net present value greater than the value of abandonment. Thus the rule becomes an accept-reject decision: Continue to operate the project so long as expected present value of continued operation and abandonment at any later period is greater than the value of abandonment now. Under this system, there is no need ever to determine the maximum expected net pres-

2. See E. A. Dyl and H. W. Long, "Abandonment Value and Capital Budgeting: Comment," *Journal of Finance* (March 1969), pp. 88–95; A. A. Robichek and J. C. Van Horne, "Reply," *Journal of Finance* 24 (March 1969), pp. 96–97; O. Maurice Joy, "Abandonment Values and Abandonment Decisions: A Clarification," *Journal of Finance* 31 (September 1976), pp. 1225–1228.

ent value. Furthermore, since it is impossible to predict accurately future abandonment value, whatever the expected net present value is, it will surely be inaccurate.

The accept-reject decision has one shortcoming, however; it does not provide a means of selecting between mutually exclusive investments or of making capital rationing decisions. To return to our truck example a final time, we have shown that the present value is $1,100 when the truck is operated for another year. Using the accept-reject rule, we would continue to operate the truck. But suppose a truck could be leased for $1,000 for one year and would produce cash flows worth $1,200 at net present value. If only one truck is required (mutually exclusive choice decision), or if the only source of the $1,000 to lease the truck is the sale of the old truck (capital rationing), then the value to the firm is maximized if the truck is sold and the new truck leased.

It is evident that both rules (the maximum net present value rule, and the accept-reject rule) have merit. Maximum net present value should be employed whenever capital rationing or mutually exclusive choices are involved. Accept-reject can be used to reduce the cumbersomeness of the problem whenever one decision is independent of all others. (Problem 14C.3 provides an opportunity to explore both of these approaches.)

Problems

14C.1 In its first year of operation at Delta Steel Corporation, a new electric furnace employed in the scrap steel division produced a savings of $400 a month over the basic oxygen furnace. The scrap steel division at Delta Steel is quite old and inefficient. Before the new electric furnace was installed, management estimated that the company could save $4,980 a year if the scrap-melting division was eliminated. Management must decide what action to take for the second year. The new furnace has no scrap value. The required rate of return for the firm is 6 percent.

a. If the savings in the second year are equal to those obtained in the first year, should the scrap division be abandoned?

b. What decision would be reached if the cost analysis of savings per month with the electric furnace for the second year is:

Probability	Amount
0.05	$200
0.15	300
0.50	400
0.20	500
0.10	600

14C.2 A firm has invested $4,000 in automated machinery, with probable net cash flows over two years as follows:

Year 1		Year 2	
Net Cash Flow	Initial Probability P (1)	Net Cash Flow	Conditional Probability P (2|1)
		$2,500	(0.3)
$3,000	(0.3)	3,000	(0.5)
		3,500	(0.2)
		3,000	(0.3)
4,000	(0.4)	4,000	(0.5)
		5,000	(0.2)
		4,000	(0.3)
5,000	(0.3)	5,000	(0.4)
		6,000	(0.3)

The firm's cost of capital is 12 percent.

a. Calculate the expected net present value and standard deviation of the investment without considering abandonment value.
b. If the abandonment value at the end of Year 1 is $2,800, calculate the new expected net present value and standard deviation of the project.
c. During Period 1, the cash flow actually experienced was $3,000. Should the project now be abandoned, or should it be continued through Period 2?

14C.3 The following investment decision is being considered by Citrus Farms. For $7,000 the company can acquire ownership of ten acres of fifteen-year-old orange trees and a fifteen-year lease on the land. The productive life of an orange tree is divided into stages, as follows:

Stage	Age of Trees	Expected Annual Profit from 10 Acres
Peak	16–20 years	$1,000
Adult	21–25 years	900
Mature	26–30 years	800

There is a market for decorative orange trees. Suppliers will buy trees and remove them according to a schedule based on age of the tree. Expected prices that could be obtained for the ten-acre total are: $9,000 at end of age 20, $12,000 at age 25, and $8,000 at age 30.

a. Citrus Farms has a 10 percent cost of capital. What is the present value of each alternative? Since the land and anything on it will belong to the lessor in fifteen years, assume that once the trees are harvested, the land will not be replanted by Citrus.
b. As an alternative to this investment, Citrus can use the $7,000 to buy a new orange sorting machine. The machine would reduce sorting expense by $1,300 a year for fifteen years. Which investment would you make? Why? Assume all other investment opportunities for the next fifteen years will earn the cost of capital.

c. In the tenth year you discover that everyone else with twenty-five-year-old trees has sold them. As a consequence, the price you can get for your trees is only $8,000. Since so many trees have been sold for decoration, small orange crops are expected for the next five years. As a result, the price will be higher. Your acreage will yield $1,200 a year. The selling price of your trees in another five years is expected to still be depressed to $6,000. What should you do?
d. What was the net present value of your actual investment over the fifteen-year period given the developments in Part c?
e. What would have been the outcome if you had sold the trees in the tenth year for $8,000?

Appendix D to Chapter 14

Some Further Implications of Portfolio Theory

Effects of Diversification: Some Illustrations with a Two-Asset Portfolio

The concepts of portfolio diversification discussed in Chapter 14 are here further clarified by some additional illustrations. Assume that two investment securities, A and B, are available and that we have a specific amount of money to invest in these securities. We can allocate our funds between the securities in any proportion. Security A has an expected rate of return $E(R_a) = 5$ percent and a standard deviation of expected returns $\sigma_a = 4$ percent; for Security B, the expected return $E(R_b) = 8$ percent and the standard deviation $\sigma_b = 10$ percent.

Our ultimate task is to determine the optimal portfolio, that is, the optimal percentage of our available funds to invest in each security. Intermediate steps include (1) determining the attainable set of portfolios, (2) determining the efficient set from among the attainable set, and (3) selecting the best portfolio from the efficient set.

There is not yet sufficient information to select the best portfolio—we need data on the degree of correlation between the two securities' returns (ρ_{ab}) in order to construct the attainable and efficient portfolios. Let us assume three different degrees of correlation: $\rho_{ab} = +1.0$, $\rho_{ab} = 0$, and $\rho_{ab} = -1.0$, and then develop the portfolios' expected returns $E(R_p)$ and standard deviations of returns σ_p for each case.

To calculate $E(R_p)$ and σ_p, we use Equations 14D.1 and 14D.2:

$$E(R_p) = w\, E(R_a) + (1 - w)\, E(R_b), \qquad (14D.1)$$

and

$$\sigma_p = \sqrt{w^2\sigma_a{}^2 + (1 - w)^2\sigma_b{}^2 + 2w(1 - w)\rho_{ab}\,\sigma_a\,\sigma_b}. \qquad (14D.2)$$

We may now substitute in the given values for R_a and R_b and then solve Equation 14D.1 for $E(R_p)$ at different values of w. For example, when w equals 0.75, then

$$E(R_p) = 0.75\,(5\%) + 0.25(8\%) = 5.75 \text{ percent.}$$

Similarly, we can substitute the given values for σ_a, σ_b, and ρ_{ab}, then solve Equation 14D.2 for σ_p at different values of w. For example, when $\rho_{ab} = 0$ and $w = 75$ percent, then

$$\sigma_p = \sqrt{(0.5625)(16) + (0.0625)(100) + 2(0.75)(0.25)(0)(4)(10)}$$
$$= \sqrt{9 + 6.25} = \sqrt{15.25} = 3.9\%.$$

The equations can be solved for other values for w and for the three cases, $\rho_{ab} = +1.0$, 0, and -1.0; Table 14D.1 gives the solution values for $w = 100$ percent, 75 percent, 50 percent, 25 percent, and 0 percent, and Figure 14D.1

Figure 14D.1

Illustrations of Portfolio Returns, Risk, and the Attainable Set of Portfolios

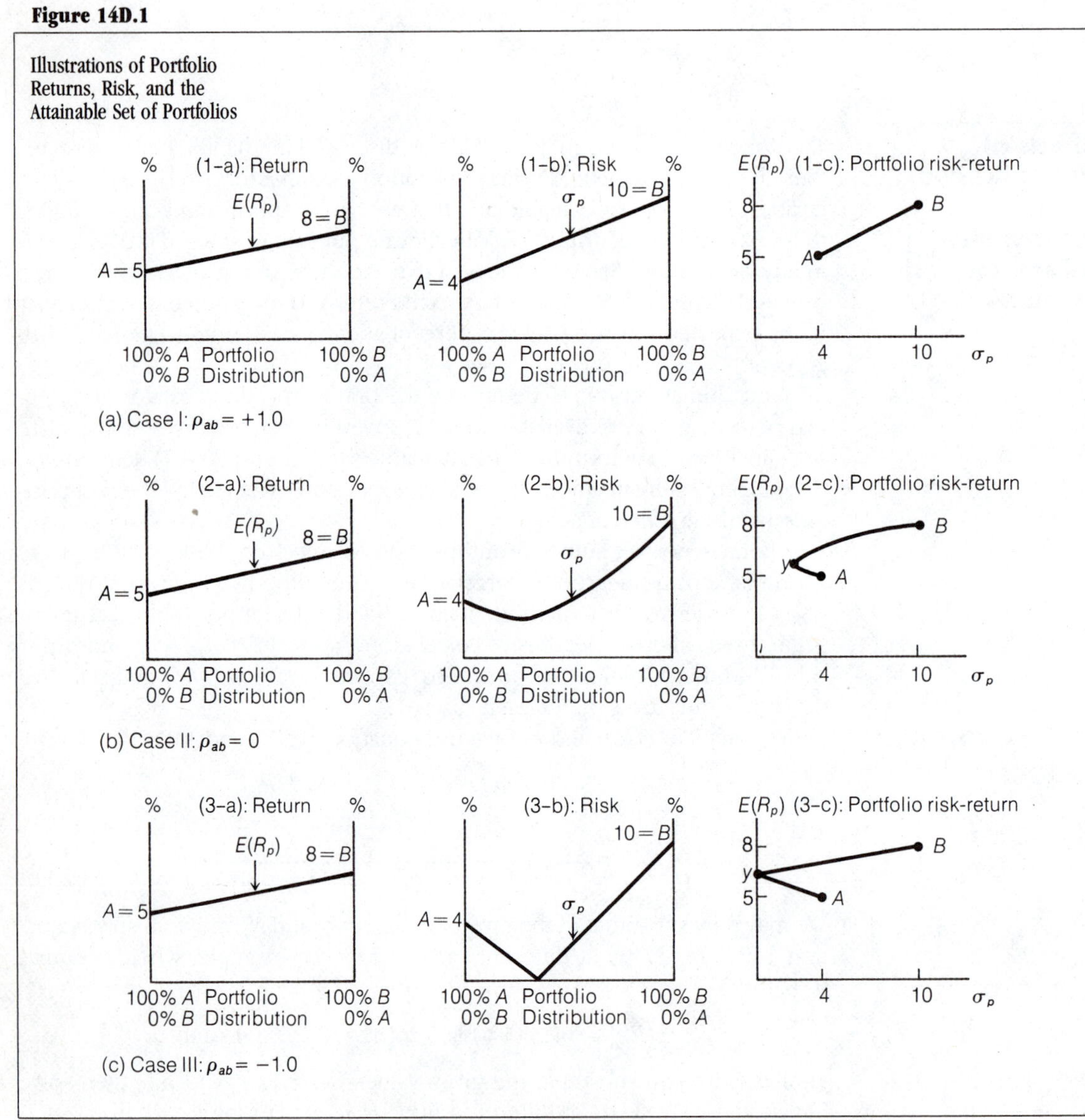

Table 14D.1

$E(R_p)$ and σ_p under Various Assumptions

Percent of Portfolio in Security A (Value of w)	Percent of Portfolio in Security B (Value of $1 - w$)	$\rho_{ab} = +1.0$		$\rho_{ab} = 0$		$\rho_{ab} = -1.0$	
		$E(R_p)$	σ_p	$E(R_p)$	σ_p	$E(R_p)$	σ_p
100	0	5.00	4.0	5.00	4.0	5.00	4.0
75	25	5.75	5.5	5.75	3.9	5.75	0.5
50	50	6.50	7.0	6.50	5.4	6.50	3.0
25	75	7.25	8.5	7.25	7.6	7.25	6.5
0	100	8.00	10.0	8.00	10.0	8.00	10.0

gives plots of $E(R_p)$, σ_p, and the attainable set of portfolios for each case. In both the table and the graphs, note the following points:

1. $E(R_p)$ is a linear function of w, and the graphs of $E(R_p)$ are identical in the three cases because $E(R_p)$ is independent of the correlation between Securities A and B.
2. σ_p is linear in Case I, where $\rho_{ab} = +1.0$; it is nonlinear in Case II; and Case III of the figure shows that risk can be completely diversified away when $\rho_{ab} = -1.0$.[1]
3. Panels 1-c, 2-c, and 3-c give the attainable set of portfolios consisting of Securities A and B. With only two securities, the attainable set is a curve or line rather than an area. If more securities were added, then the shaded area shown in Figure 14.4 would develop.
4. That part of the attainable set from Y to B in Cases II and III is efficient; that part from A to Y is inefficient. In Case I, all parts of the attainable set are efficient.

Figure 14D.2 consolidates the attainable sets for the three cases to facilitate comparison. The most interesting aspect of the graph is the clear demonstration that the lower the value of ρ_{ab}, the better the portfolios that can be constructed. For any specified rate of return as shown on the vertical axis, σ_p is lowest for $\rho_{ab} = -1$ and highest for $\rho_{ab} = +1$, while the rate of return that can be achieved at any specified degree of risk is highest for $\rho_{ab} = -1$ and lowest for $\rho_{ab} = +1$ (except for Point B, at which all the curves converge since the total investment is 100 percent in B).

Obviously, only one correlation coefficient can exist between Securities A and B; assume that the actual ρ_{ab} is 0. It now remains to select the best portfolio (that is, the percentage of the total funds to be invested in each security). This decision depends upon individual investors' risk aversion as represented by their risk-return indifference curves. In Figure 14D.3 we show the attainable set of portfolios for $\rho_{ab} = 0$ from Figure 14D.2 and the indifference

1. The minimum points for Figure 14D.1b were found by using Equation 14.6 in the chapter.

Figure 14D.2

Attainable Sets of Portfolios for the Three Cases

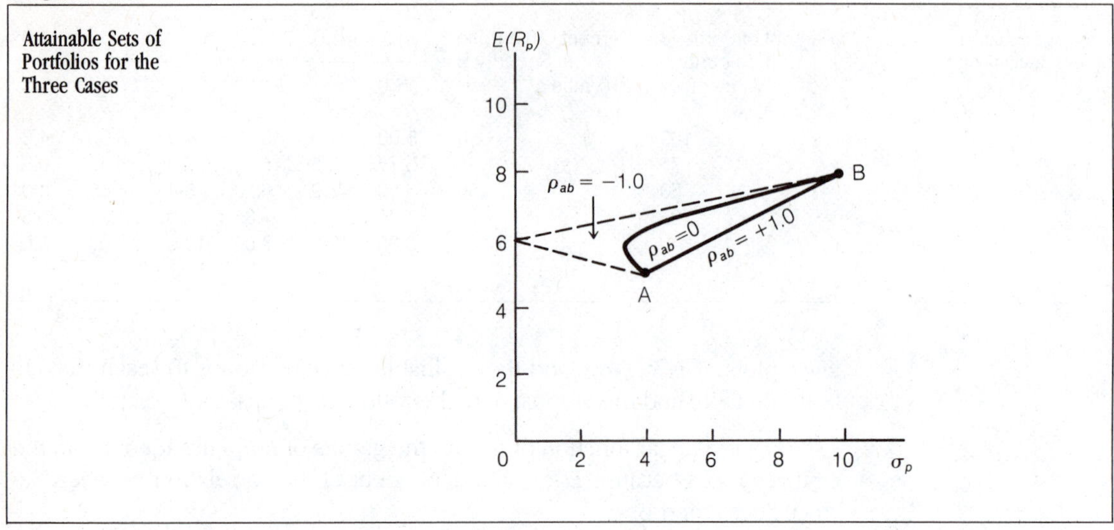

Figure 14D.3

Selecting the Optimal Portfolio

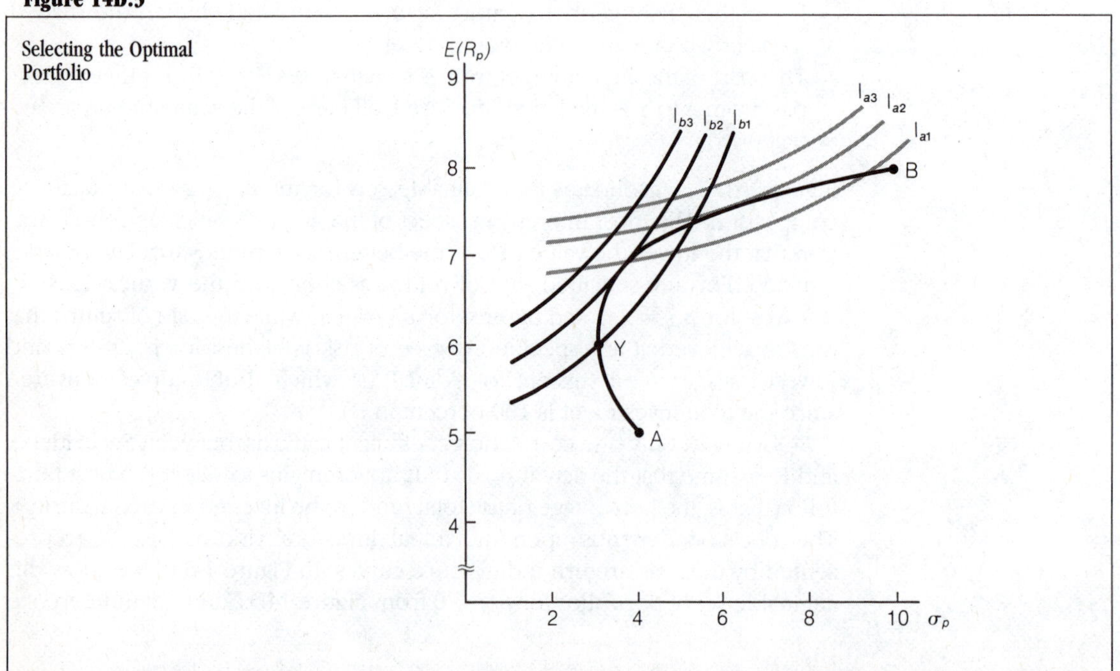

curves for Investors A and B taken from Figure 14.7 in Chapter 14. Given these possibilities, Investor A would choose a portfolio providing an expected rate of return of 7.2 percent with $\sigma_p = 7.4$, while Investor B would choose a portfolio with $E(R_p) = 6.2$ and $\sigma_p = 4.7$. A's portfolio would consist of 27 percent Security A and 73 percent Security B, while B's portfolio would contain 60 percent Security A and 40 percent Security B.[2]

Relationship between Correlation and Expected Rates of Return

If a security or other asset has returns that are less than perfectly positively correlated with the returns on other assets, then combining this new asset with other assets will produce favorable portfolio effects. Further, the lower the degree of correlation, the larger the portfolio effects. Now suppose you hold a portfolio of securities with an expected return $E(R_p) = 8$ percent and $\sigma_p = 6$ percent. You learn of a new security, Z, that has an expected return of 8 percent, $\sigma_z = 6$ percent, and the correlation of Z's returns with those on your present portfolio is -0.5.

If you sell off part of your present portfolio and use the proceeds to purchase Security Z, your expected rate of return will remain at 8 percent, but your portfolio's risk will decline, so you would make this shift. If others have favorable portfolio effects from Security Z, they too will seek to buy it, and the collective action will tend to drive Z's price up and its expected yield down. We see, then, that a security's degree of correlation with other securities influences the rate of return on the security in the marketplace. This aspect of portfolio theory is vitally important in analyzing the riskiness of a firm's securities and hence its cost of capital.

Security Risk versus Portfolio Risk

An empirical study by W. H. Wagner and S. C. Lau can be used to demonstrate the effects of diversification.[3] They divided a sample of 200 NYSE stocks into six subgroups based on the Standard and Poor's quality ratings as of June 1960. Then they constructed portfolios from each of the subgroups, using one to twenty randomly selected securities and applying equal weights to each security. Table 14D.2 can be used to summarize some effects of diversification for the first subgroup (A+ quality stocks). As the number of securities in the portfolio increases, the standard deviation of portfolio returns decreases, but at a decreasing rate, with further reductions in risk being relatively small after

2. These percentages can be determined by Equation 14D.1 simply by seeing what percentage of the two securities is consistent with $E(R_p) = 7.2\%$ and 6.2%.
3. W. H. Wagner and S. C. Lau, "The Effect of Diversification on Risk," *Financial Analysts' Journal* 27 (November–December 1971), pp. 48–53.

Table 14D.2

Reduction in Portfolio Risk through Diversification

Number of Securities in Portfolio	Standard Deviation of Portfolio Returns (σ_p) (% per Month)	Correlation with Return on Market Index[a]
1	7.0	0.54
2	5.0	0.63
3	4.8	0.75
4	4.6	0.77
5	4.6	0.79
10	4.2	0.85
15	4.0	0.88
20	3.9	0.89

a. The "market" here refers to an unweighted index of all NYSE stocks.

about ten securities are included in the portfolio. More will be said about the third column of the table, correlation with the market, shortly.

These data indicate that even well diversified portfolios possess some level of risk that cannot be diversified away. Indeed, this is exactly the case, and the general situation is illustrated graphically in Figure 14D.4. The risk of the portfolio, σ_p, has been divided into two parts. The part that can be reduced through diversification is defined as *unsystematic* risk, while the part that cannot be eliminated is defined as *systematic,* or market-related, risk.[4]

Figure 14D.4

Reduction of Risk through Diversification

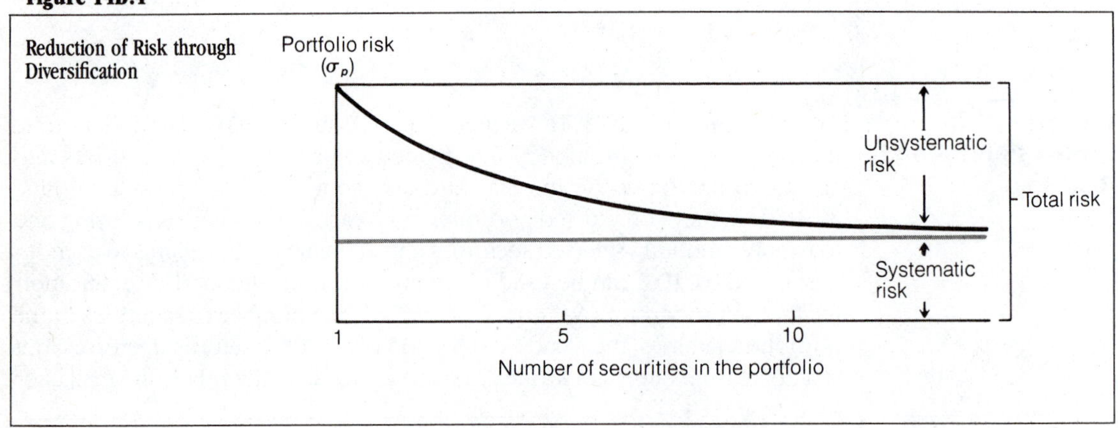

4. In the real world, it is extremely difficult to find stocks with zero or negative correlations; hence, some risk is inherent in any stock portfolio.

Now refer back to the third column of Table 14D.2. Notice that as the number of securities in each portfolio increases, and as the standard deviation decreases, the correlation between the return on the portfolio and the return on the market index increases. Thus, a broadly diversified portfolio is highly correlated with the market, and its risk (1) is largely systematic and (2) arises because of general market movements.

We can summarize our analysis of risk to this point as follows:

1. The risk of a portfolio can be measured by the standard deviation of its rate of return, σ_p.
2. The risk of an individual security is its contribution to the portfolio's risk.
3. The standard deviation of a stock's return, σ_i, is the relevant measure of risk for an undiversified investor who holds only one security.
4. A stock's standard deviation reflects both unsystematic risk that can be eliminated by diversification and systematic or market-related risk; only the systematic component of security risk is relevant for the well diversified investor, so only this element is reflected in the risk premium.
5. A stock's systematic risk is measured by its volatility in relation to the general market. This factor is analyzed next.

Efficient versus Inefficient Portfolios

William F. Sharpe derived the following relationship between total risk and its components, unsystematic (diversifiable) and systematic risk:

$$(\sigma_j)^2 = (\sigma_j^s)^2 + (\sigma_j^u)^2 \qquad (14D.3)$$

where σ_j = Standard deviation of R_j
σ_j^s = Security J's systematic risk ($=\beta_j \sigma_M$)
σ_j^u = Security J's unsystematic risk.[5]

These relationships apply to portfolios as well:

$$(\sigma_p)^2 = (\sigma_p^s)^2 + (\sigma_p^u)^2 \qquad (14D.4)$$

where σ_p = Standard deviation of rate of return on portfolio
σ_p^s = Portfolio's systematic risk
σ_p^u = Portfolio's unsystematic risk.

The relationship between systematic risk and volatility is the same for securities and portfolios. Thus,

$$\sigma_p^s = \beta_p \, \sigma_M. \qquad (14D.5)$$

Efficient portfolios have no unsystematic risk. Thus a portfolio with some unsystematic risk that has not been diversified away is inefficient. Individual se-

5. William F. Sharpe, *Portfolio Theory and Capital Markets* (New York: McGraw-Hill, 1970), pp. 96–97.

curities are likely to include some unsystematic risk, so they are inefficient portfolios.

Equation 14D.3 divides the variance of Security J's return into two parts, (1) the systematic risk component, $(\sigma^s)^2$, which is $(\beta_j \sigma_M)^2$—that is, its beta coefficient times the standard deviation of market returns—and (2) the unsystematic residual risk component, $(\sigma_j^u)^2$. The unsystematic component can be eliminated through diversification, but the systematic component can only be reduced by altering the firm's correlation with the market—that is, by attempting to change its beta coefficient through a change in investment or financial policy.

The logical conclusion of all this is that if investors think in portfolio terms, then they should not worry about the unsystematic risk because it can be diversified away. Thus, investors should consider only systematic risk in Equation 14D.3. Since the variance of the market is a given, the determinant of relative riskiness among stocks is the beta coefficient.

This type of analysis provides the foundations for the development of the capital asset pricing model (CAPM) summarized in the chapter. In this appendix we shall now set forth other aspects of the capital asset pricing model. The riskiness of a portfolio of assets as measured by its standard deviation of returns is generally less than the average of the risks of the individual assets as measured by their standard deviations. Since investors generally hold portfolios of securities, not just one security, it is reasonable to consider the riskiness of a security in terms of its contribution to the riskiness of the portfolio rather than in terms of its riskiness if held in isolation. *The significant contribution of the capital asset pricing model (CAPM) is that it provides a measure of the risk of a security in the portfolio sense.*

The Trade-off between Risk and Return

Since investors as a group are averse to risk, the higher the risk of a stock, the higher its required rate of return. Figure 14D.5 illustrates this concept. Here, the required rate of return is plotted on the vertical axis, and risk is shown on the horizontal axis. The line showing the relationship between risk and rate of return is defined as the *security market line* (SML). The intercept of the security market line, R_F, is the riskless rate of return, generally taken as the return on U.S. Treasury securities. Riskless securities have beta coefficients equal to zero; since returns on riskless securities are fixed and constant, they do not move at all with changes in the market. An "average" stock has a beta of 1.0, and such a stock has a required rate of return, R_M, equal to the market average return. A relatively low-risk stock might have a beta of 0.6 and a required rate of return equal to R_L, while a relatively high-risk stock might have a beta of 1.4 and a required return equal to R_H.

Betas of Portfolios

It should be noted that a portfolio made up of low beta securities will itself have a low beta, as the beta of any set of securities is a weighted average of the betas of the individual securities:

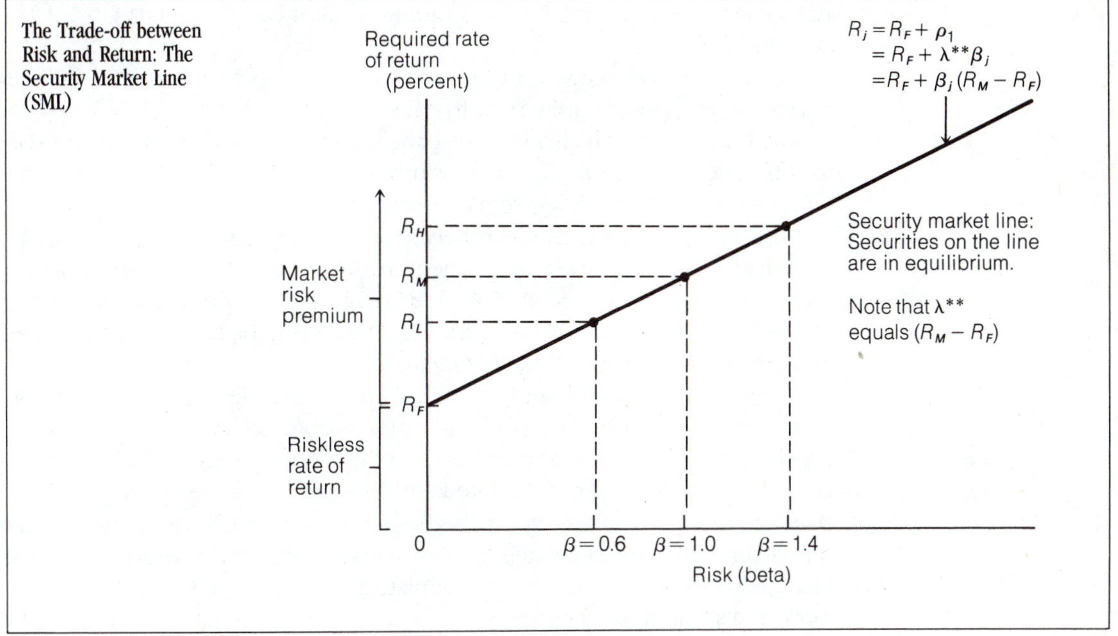

Figure 14D.5

The Trade-off between Risk and Return: The Security Market Line (SML)

$$\beta_p = \sum_{i=1}^{N} w_i \beta_j . \tag{14D.6}$$

Here β_p is the beta of the portfolio, which reflects how volatile the portfolio is in relation to the market index; w_i is the percentage of the portfolio invested in the ith stock; and β_j is the beta coefficient of the jth stock.

The beta coefficients of mutual funds, pension funds, and other large portfolios are presently being calculated and used to judge the riskiness of these portfolios, and funds are actually being constructed to provide investors with specified degrees of riskiness. It is too early to judge how well betas will work as a measure of long-term risk, but the financial community is actually using these concepts in security selection and portfolio construction.

Cost of Capital Dynamics

The expected return on any stock is equal to the riskless rate of return plus a risk premium. Since the risk premium for the entire market is equal to $R_M - R_F$, we can develop the following relation, which is one form of the security market line equation introduced in Chapter 5.

$$\bar{R}_j = R_F + (\bar{R}_M - R_F)\beta_j . \tag{5.10}$$

Stated in words, the expected return on any stock is equal to the sum of the riskless rate of return plus the product of the stock's beta coefficient times the risk premium on the market as a whole. If beta is less than 1.0, then the stock has a smaller than average risk premium, while if beta is larger than 1.0, the converse holds.

Interest rates change over time, and when they do, the change in R_F is reflected in the cost of equity both for the "average" stock R_M, and for any individual stock, R_i. Such changes cause the security market line in Figure 14D.5 to shift. The intercept term, R_F, goes up or down, while the slope of the line could increase, decrease, or remain constant.[6]

Risk premiums, which are reflected in the slope of the security market line, may also change over time. When investors are pessimistic and worried, the market line of Figure 14D.5 will tend to be steep, implying a high "price of risk," whereas when investors are less risk averse, the price of risk declines and the market line is less steeply inclined.

A number of careful studies confirm that rates of return rise with risk. However, the empirical tests do not show stable relationships; rather, depending on the test period analyzed and the methodology used, many security market lines could be generated. This instability is to be expected for two reasons: First, we would expect the empirical market line measured for different time periods to change as both interest rates and investors' outlooks change. Second, we are forced to estimate the market line on the basis of imperfect data, and where errors in the data exist, estimating problems are bound to arise.[7]

Problems

14D.1 We have two assets with the following characteristics:

$$E(R_i) = 12\% \quad \sigma_i = 5\%$$
$$E(R_j) = 15\% \quad \sigma_j = 10\%$$

a. Use the two assets to form a portfolio with minimum variance for correlation coefficient values of 0, −1, −0.5, and +0.5.
b. For each minimum variance portfolio, calculate (1) the expected return on the portfolio and (2) the standard deviation of the portfolio.
c. Comment on your results.

14D.2 You are planning to invest $100,000. Two securities, A and B, are available. The expected return for A is 9 percent and $\sigma_a = 4$ percent; the expected return for B is 10 percent and $\sigma_b = 5$ percent; $\rho_{ab} = 0.5$.

a. Construct a table similar to Table 14D.1, giving $E(R_p)$ and σ_p for 100 percent, 75 percent, 50 percent, 25 percent, and 0 percent investment in Stock A.
b. Use your calculated $E(R_p)$ and σ_p values to graph the attainable set of portfolios and indicate which part of the attainable set is efficient.

6. R. H. Litzenberger and A. P. Budd, "Secular Trends in Risk Premiums," *Journal of Finance* 27 (September 1972), pp. 857–864.

7. However, these problems are probably less severe in the capital asset pricing model than are the problems encountered using alternative approaches.

c. Using hypothetical indifference curves, show how an investor might choose a portfolio consisting of Stocks A and B.

14D.3 You are planning to invest $100,000. Two securities, I and J, are available, and you can invest in either of them or in a portfolio with some of each. You estimate that the following probability distributions of returns are applicable:

Security I		Security J	
0.1	−5%	0.1	0%
0.2	0	0.2	5
0.4	11.25	0.4	8.75
0.2	15	0.2	10
0.1	20	0.1	15

The expected returns are 9 percent and 8 percent for I and J, respectively; that is, $E(R_i)$ = 9 percent and $E(R_j)$ 8 percent. σ_i = 7.56 percent and σ_j = 3.75 percent.

a. Assume $\rho_{ij} = -0.5$. What percentage of your portfolio should be invested in each security in order to minimize your investment risk?

b. Calculate σ_p and $E(R_p)$ for portfolios consisting of 100 percent I and 0 percent J; 100 percent J and 0 percent I; and the minimum risk portfolio as calculated in Part a. (Hint: Notice that some of these data are given above.)

c. Graph the *feasible* set of portfolios, and identify the *efficient* section of the feasible set.

d. Suppose your risk-return trade-off function, or indifference curve, is a linear family of lines with a slope of 0.15. Use this information, plus the graph constructed in Part c, to locate (approximately) your optimal portfolio. Give the percentage of your funds invested in each security, and the optimal portfolio's σ_p and $E(R_p)$. (Hint: Estimate σ_p and $E(R_p)$ graphically, then use the equation for $E(R_p)$ to determine w.) What is the probability that your optimal portfolio will, in fact, yield less than 4.15 percent?

e. Demonstrate why a graph of the efficient set such as the one you constructed in Part c above is always linear if portfolios are formed between a riskless security (a bond) and a risky asset (a stock or perhaps a portfolio of stocks).

14D.4 You are planning to invest $200,000. Two securities, C and D, are available, and you can invest in either of them or in a portfolio with some of each. You estimate that the following probability distributions of returns are applicable:

Security C		Security D	
0.2	−4%	0.2	2%
0.3	0	0.3	4
0.3	12	0.3	8
0.2	26	0.2	10

The expected returns are 8 percent and 6 percent for C and D respectively; that is, $E(R_c)$ = 8 percent and $E(R_d)$ = 6 percent, σ_c = 10.84 percent and σ_d = 2.97 percent.

a. Assume $\rho_{cd} = -0.5$. What percentage of your portfolio should be invested in each security in order to minimize your investment risk?
b. Calculate σ_p and $E(R_p)$ for portfolios consisting of 100 percent C and 0 percent D; 100 percent D and 0 percent C; and the minimum risk portfolio as calculated in Part a. (Hint: Notice that some of these data are given above.)
c. Graph the *feasible* set of portfolios, and identify the *efficient* section of the feasible set.
d. Suppose your risk-return trade-off function, or indifference curve, is a linear family of lines with a slope of 0.25. Use this information, plus the graph constructed in Part c, to locate (approximately) your optimal portfolio. Give the percentage of your funds invested in each security and the optimal portfolio's σ_p and $E(R_p)$. (Hint: Estimate σ_p and $E(R_p)$ graphically, then use the equation for $E(R_p)$ to determine w.)
e. What is the probability that your optimal portfolio will, in fact, yield less than 1.15 percent?
f. Demonstrate *why* a graph of the efficient set such as the one you constructed in Part c above is always linear if portfolios are formed between a riskless security (a bond) and a risky asset (a stock or perhaps a portfolio of stocks).

Selected References

Bowman, Robert G. "The Theoretical Relationship between Systematic Risk and Financial (Accounting) Variables." *Journal of Finance* 34 (June 1979), pp. 617–630.

Brenner, Menachem, and Smidt, Seymour. "A Simple Model of Non-Stationarity of Systematic Risk." *Journal of Finance* 32 (September 1977), pp. 1081–1092.

Chen, Elaine T. "Uncertain Inflation and Capital Asset Prices." *Southern Economic Journal* 46 (January 1980), pp. 763–776.

Elton, Edwin J., and Gruber, Martin J. "Taxes and Portfolio Composition." *Journal of Financial Economics* 6 (December 1978), pp. 399–410.

Elton, Edwin J.; Gruber, Martin J.; and Urich, Thomas J. "Are Betas Best?" *Journal of Finance* 33 (December 1978), pp. 1375–1384.

Friend, Irwin; Westerfield, Randolph; and Granito, Michael. "New Evidence on the Capital Asset Pricing Model." *Journal of Finance* 33 (June 1978), pp. 903–920.

Gentry, James, and Pike, John. "An Empirical Study of the Risk-Return Hypothesis Using Common Stock Portfolios of Life Insurance Companies." *Journal of Financial and Quantitative Analysis* 5 (June 1970), pp. 179–186.

Gooding, Arthur E. "Perceived Risk and Capital Asset Pricing." *Journal of Finance* 33 (December 1978), pp. 1401–1424.

Holthausen, Duncan M., and Hughes, John S. "Commodity Returns and Capital Asset Pricing." *Financial Management* 7 (Summer 1978), pp. 37–52.

Litzenberger, Robert H., and Ramaswamy, Krishna. "The Effect of Personal Taxes and Dividends on Capital Asset Prices: Theory and Empirical Evidence." *Journal of Financial Economics* 7 (June 1979), pp. 163–195.

Mayers, David, and Rice, Edward M. "Measuring Portfolio Performance and the Empirical Content of Asset Pricing Models." *Journal of Financial Economics* 7 (March 1979), pp. 3–28.

Roll, Richard. "Ambiguity When Performance Is Measured by the Securities Market Line." *Journal of Finance* 33 (September 1978), pp. 1051–1069.

———. "A Critique of the Asset Pricing Theory's Tests, Part 1: On Past and Potential Testability of the Theory." *Journal of Financial Economics* 4 (March 1977), pp. 129–176.

Ross, Stephen. "The Current Status of the Capital Asset Pricing Model." *Journal of Finance* 33 (June 1978), pp. 885–901.

Senbet, Lemma W., and Thompson, Howard E. "The Equivalence of Alternative Mean-Variance Capital Budgeting Models." *Journal of Finance* 32 (May 1978), pp. 395–401.

Sharpe, William F. *Portfolio Analysis and Capital Markets.* New York: McGraw-Hill, 1970.

———. "Capital Asset Prices: A Theory of Market Equilibrium." *Journal of Finance* 19 (September 1964), pp. 425–442.

———. "A Simplified Model for Portfolio Analysis." *Management Science* 10 (January 1963), pp. 277–293.

Siegel, Jeremy J., and Warner, Jerold B. "Indexation, the Risk-Free Asset, and Capital Market Equilibrium." *Journal of Finance* 32 (September 1977), pp. 1101–1107.

Singer, Ronald F. "Market Prices vs. Equilibrium Prices: Returns Variance, Serial Correlation, and the Role of the Specialist." *Journal of Finance* 34 (June 1979), pp. 609–616.

Smith, Keith V. "The Effect of Intervaling on Estimating Parameters of the Capital Asset Pricing Model." *Journal of Financial and Quantitative Analysis* 13 (June 1978), pp. 313–332.

Stoll, Hans R. "Commodity Futures and Spot Price Determination and Hedging in Capital Market Equilibrium." *Journal of Financial and Quantitative Analysis* 14 (November 1979), pp. 873–894.

Tobin, James. "Liquidity Preference as Behavior towards Risk." *Review of Economic Studies* 25 (February 1958), pp. 65–86.

Trauring, Mitchell. "A Capital Asset Pricing Model with Investors' Taxes and Three Categories of Investment Income." *Journal of Financial and Quantitative Analysis* 14 (September 1979), pp. 537–545.

Wagner, W. H., and Lau, S. C. "The Effect of Diversification on Risk." *Financial Analysts' Journal* 27 (November–December 1971), pp. 48–53.

Part Five
Cost of Capital and Valuation

Part 4 developed the concepts needed for making investment decisions; in a number of places it made use of cost of capital. Part 5 provides the basis for determining what the relevent cost of capital is and how it is influenced by financial decisions. It also examines financing decisions in the broad categories of debt versus equity. It attempts to determine the optimal financial structure—the financial structure that simultaneously minimizes the firm's cost of capital and maximizes its market value. Financing decisions and investment decisions are interdependent—the optimal financing plan and the optimal level of investment must be determined simultaneously—so Part 5 also serves the important function of integrating the theory of capital budgeting with the theory of capital structure. In Part 5, we come to the very heart of managerial finance. We analyze the factors affecting the firm's cost of capital and value. In Chapters 5 and 6, risk, return, and valuation were discussed without consideration of two major areas of financial policies of the firm: capital structure and dividend policy. Chapter 15 analyzes the influence of capital structure decisions on the riskiness of the returns of a firm and hence on its required return and value. Chapter 16 discusses how the firm may move toward its goals of minimizing its cost of capital and maximizing its value. Chapter 17 discusses the role of dividend policy and its possible influences on the value of the firm.

15
Financial Structure and the Use of Leverage

Previous chapters have shown that risk, return, and value are interrelated. One of the financial manager's principal goals is to maximize the value of the firm's securities. While there are a number of aspects of value, a central influence on valuation is the required capitalization factor, whose magnitude is influenced by risk. Hence this chapter starts with a summary discussion of value and required return as an introduction to the remainder of the chapter, which analyzes how the firm's financial structure affects the riskiness of returns. The extent to which debt is used in a firm's financial structure is a measure of the degree of financial leverage used by the firm. The relationships between operating leverage (discussed in Chapter 9) and financial leverage are also analyzed in the present chapter.

Definitions of Value

While it may be difficult to ascribe monetary returns to certain kinds of assets —works of art, for instance—the fundamental characteristic of business assets is that they give rise to income flows. Sometimes these flows are easy to determine and measure—the interest return on a bond is an example. At other times, the cash flows attributable to the asset must be estimated, as was done in Chapters 13 and 14, in the evaluation of projects. Regardless of the difficulties of measuring income flows, it is the prospective return from assets that gives them value.

Liquidating Value versus Going-concern Value

Several different definitions of *value* exist in the literature and are used in practice, with different ones being appropriate at different times. The first distinction that must be made is that between liquidating value and going-concern value. *Liquidating value* is defined as the amount that could be realized if an asset or a group of assets (the entire assets of a firm, for example) is sold separately from the organization that has been using them. If the owners of a machine shop decide to retire, they might auction off their inventory and equipment, collect their accounts receivable, and then sell their land and buildings to a grocery wholesaler for use as a warehouse. The sum of the proceeds from each category of assets would be the liquidating value of the assets. If their debts are subtracted from this amount, the difference would represent the liquidating value of their ownership in the business.

On the other hand, if the firm is sold as an operating business to a corporation or to an individual, the purchaser would pay an amount equal to the *going-concern value* of the company. If the going-concern value exceeds the liquidating value, the difference represents the value of the organization as distinct from the value of the assets.[1]

Book Value versus Market Value

We must also distinguish between *book value,* or the accounting value at which an asset is carried, and *market value,* the price at which the asset can be sold. If the asset in question is a firm, it actually has two market values—a liquidating value and a going-concern value. Only the higher of the two is generally referred to as *the* market value.

For stocks, an item of primary concern in this chapter, book value per share is the firm's total common equity—common stock, capital or paid-in surplus, and accumulated retained earnings—divided by shares outstanding. For a given firm, book value per share might be $50. The market value, which is what people will actually pay for a share of the stock, could be above or below the book value. Nuclear Research, for example, has a book value per share of $8.27 and a market value of $25.50; West Virginia Railroad, on the other hand, has a book value of $112.80 versus a market value of only $6.75. Nuclear Research's assets produce a high and rapidly growing earnings stream; West Virginia Railroad's assets are far less productive. Since market value is dependent upon earnings while book value reflects historical cost, it is not surprising to find deviations between book and market values in a dynamic, uncertain world.

Market Value versus "Fair" or "Reasonable" Value

The concept of a fair or reasonable value (sometimes called the *intrinsic* value) is widespread in the literature on stock market investments. Although the market value of a security is known at any given time, the security's fair value as viewed by different investors could differ. B. Graham, D. L. Dodd, and S. Cottle, in a leading investments text, define fair value as "that value which is justified by the facts; e.g., assets, earnings, dividends. . . . The computed [fair] value is likely to change at least from year to year, as the factors governing that value are modified."[2]

Although Graham, Dodd, and Cottle develop this concept for security (that is, stock and bond) valuation, the idea is applicable to all business assets. What it involves, basically, is estimating the future net cash flows attributable to an asset; determining an appropriate capitalization, or discount, rate; and then finding the present value of the cash flows. This, of course, is exactly what was done in Chapters 13 and 14, where the concept of reasonable value

1. Accountants have termed this difference "goodwill," but "organization value" would be a more appropriate description.
2. B. Graham; D. L. Dodd; and S. Cottle, *Security Analysis* (New York: McGraw-Hill, 1961), p. 28.

was developed for application in finding the present value of investment opportunities.

The procedure for determining an asset's value is known as the *capitalization-of-income method of valuation.* This is simply a fancy name for the present value of a stream of earnings, discussed at length in Chapter 4. *In going through the present chapter, keep in mind that value, or the price of securities, is exactly analogous to the present value of assets as determined in Chapters 13 and 14.* From this point on, whenever the word *value* is used, we mean the *present value* found by capitalizing expected future cash flows.

The Required Rate of Return[3]

The first step in using the capitalization of income procedure is to establish the proper capitalization rate, or discount rate, for the security. *This rate is defined as the required rate of return, and it is the minimum rate of return necessary to induce investors to buy or hold the security.* For any given risky security, J, the expected rate of return, $\overline{R}_j$, is equal to the riskless rate of interest, R_F, plus a risk premium—in other words, the security market line (SML) relation introduced in Chapter 5.

$$\overline{R}_j = R_F + (\overline{R}_M - R_F)\beta_j. \tag{5.11}$$

The SML specifies the relationship between risk and the expected rate of return.[4] One advantage of the use of the SML is that the components of risk can be identified and estimated from readily available published data. The risk premium is composed of two parts: the risk premium on the market as a whole and a risk measure for the individual security. The risk premium for the market as a whole is the amount by which the return on a broad market index such as the Standard & Poor's 500 stock index exceeds a risk-free return measured by the current yield on U.S. government securities, which are free of default risk. The expected return on the market may be referred to as $\overline{R}_M$ so that the risk premium on the market is: $(\overline{R}_M - R_F)$.

$$\text{Market risk premium} = (\overline{R}_M - R_F). \tag{15.1}$$

It can be demonstrated that the securities market pays a premium only for that part of the risk of a security that cannot be eliminated by diversification. Risk that cannot be diversified away is called systematic risk and is measured by the covariance of the returns on the individual security with the returns on

3. In Chapter 14 the application of the capital asset pricing model to analyzing investment decisions under uncertainty was set forth. Here the application of the CAPM to the determination of the required rate of return on different types of securities and therefore to valuation questions is set forth.

4. Although not necessary to our use and application of the SML concepts in this chapter, a formal development of the SML relationships was presented in Chapter 14. These SML relationships are now standard in finance literature and in general use among financial firms such as Merrill Lynch, the Wells Fargo Bank, and Value Line. The terms are now used in advertisements and discussions in the financial press such as the *Wall Street Journal.*

the market portfolio. The systematic risk of a security, when normalized by the variance of the market returns, is referred to as the beta of the security. From Chapter 5 we have:

$$\beta_j = \frac{\text{Cov}(R_j, \overline{R}_M)}{\text{Var}(R_M)}$$

where:

β_j = Risk of an individual security, J

$\text{Cov}(R_j, \overline{R}_M)$ = Covariance of the returns on the individual security with the returns on the market

$\text{Var}(R_M)$ = Variance of the returns on the market

To illustrate the application of these concepts, we shall use some specific magnitudes for each of the terms involved. The return on the market $(\overline{R}_M)$ has ranged from 9 percent to 13 percent; the variance of the returns on the market [$\text{Var}(R_M)$] is about 1 percent; the risk-free rate (R_F) has ranged from about 5 percent to 7 percent. Using the mid-point of the ranges of values for the market returns and the risk-free rate we have:

$$(\overline{R}_M - R_F) = (0.11 - 0.06) = 0.05 = 5\%. \qquad \textbf{(15.1a)}$$

The risk premium, ρ_j, is the product of the market risk premium times the risk of the individual security, β_j, which varies somewhat above and below 1.[5] Hence for a β_j of 1.2 the value of the risk premium, ρ_j, on the individual Security J is:

$$\rho_j = (\overline{R}_M - R_F)\beta_j = (0.11 - 0.06)1.2 = 0.06 = 6\%.$$

This indicates that 6 percent would be added to the risk-free return, R_F, to obtain an expected return of 12 percent on an individual security, J. Note that the two measures, the risk-free return, R_F, and the market risk premium $(\overline{R}_M - R_F)$, are economy-wide parameters. Thus we can use them with the beta of any security to obtain its expected return. This can be demonstrated by the use of the graph of the SML.

Figure 15.1 presents a graph of the SML. The expected rate of return is shown on the vertical axis, while risk, measured here as the beta of the security, is shown on the horizontal axis.

Since a riskless asset, by definition, has no risk, R_F lies on the vertical axis. As risk increases, the expected rate of return also increases. A relatively low-risk security, such as that of Firm A, might have a risk index of $\beta_a = 0.4$ and an expected rate of return $\overline{R}_a = 8$ percent. A more risky security, such as that of Firm B, might have a risk index of $\beta_b = 1.4$ and an expected rate of return of $\overline{R}_b = 13$ percent.

5. The covariance of the market returns with the market returns is its variance, so the beta of the market is $\text{Var}(R_M)/\text{Var}(R_M)$, which equals 1. Normal values of the betas of individual securities would be from about 0.5 to 1.5.

Figure 15.1

The Relationship between Risk and the Expected Rate of Return: The Security Market Line (SML)

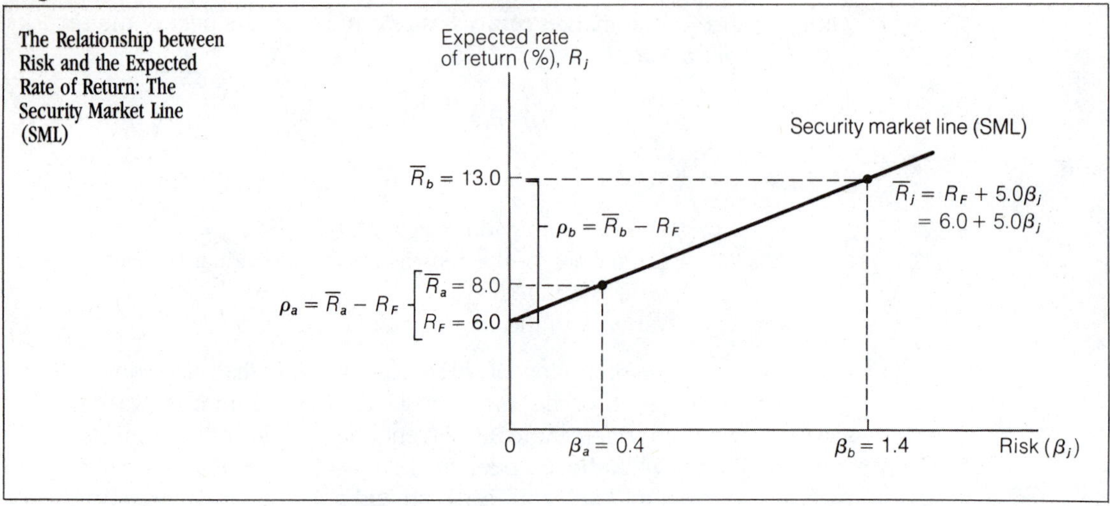

In the illustrative case, the slope of the SML is 5.0, indicating that the expected rate of return rises by one percent for each 0.2 increase in the security's beta. The beta is 0.4 for Firm A, so the risk premium on that security is 2 percent (5.0 × 0.4 = 2 percent), while the beta on Security B is 1.4, making its risk premium 7 percent (5.0 × 1.4 = 7 percent). When these two risk premiums are added to the riskless rate, R_F, we obtain the expected rates of return:

$$\overline{R}_a = 6\% + 2\% = 8\%.$$
$$\overline{R}_b = 6\% + 7\% = 13\%.$$

Notice that the graph can also be used to analyze the securities of a single firm. Since a company's bonds have a smaller standard deviation of expected returns than its common stock, $\overline{R}_a$ might be the expected rate of return on the firm's bonds, while $\overline{R}_b$ might refer to its common stock. The company's preferred stock and convertibles would lie on the SML between $\overline{R}_a$ and $\overline{R}_b$.

Since the SML is a market-wide relationship, the "expected" return on a security is "required" for market equilibrium relationships. In the subsequent section on common stock valuation, the return on stock equity *required* by equilibrium relationships will be designated as R^* in contrast to $\overline{R}_s$, a return *expected* from individual security earnings and price relationships. Thus each security has a required rate of return, R^*, and an expected rate of return, $\overline{R}$. The required rate of return is determined in part by the level of interest rates (the risk-free rate) in the economy and in part by the riskiness of the individual security. The expected rate of return on a bond or a share of preferred stock is determined primarily by interest or preferred dividends, while the expected rate of return on common stock depends on earnings available for distribution as cash dividends and on growth. Risk, required returns, and expected returns are all affected by financial leverage, as we will see in the following materials.

Financial Leverage, Holding Investment Constant

Basic Definitions

Business risk is measured by the variability of the *operating income* (EBIT) produced by the firm's portfolio of assets and product-market activities. One influence on the degree of variability in EBIT is the extent to which the firm has fixed operating expenses (operating leverage), such as depreciation on fixed assets. *Financial leverage* is measured by the extent to which the assets of the firm are financed with debt. Financial leverage shows up as interest expense, causing additional variability in net income over and above the variability in operating income caused by operating leverage. The increased variability in net income reflects *financial risk.*

Financial structure refers to the way the firm's assets are financed; it is the entire right-hand side of the balance sheet. *Capital structure* is the permanent financing of the firm, represented primarily by long-term debt, preferred stock, and common equity, but excluding all short-term credit. Thus a firm's capital structure is only a part of its financial structure. *Common equity* includes common stock, capital surplus, and accumulated retained earnings.

The key concept for this chapter is *financial leverage,* or the *leverage factor,* defined as the ratio of total debt (B) to total assets (TA) or total value (V) of the firm. For example, a firm having a total value of $100 million and a total debt of $50 million would have a leverage factor of 50 percent.[6] Thus $B/V =$ 50 percent. The B/V ratio implies a debt to common stock (B/S) ratio. B/S is equal to $B/V \div (1 - B/V)$. Thus, if $B/V = 0.5$, then $B/S = 1$.

Finally, we should distinguish at the outset between business risk and financial risk. *Business risk* is the inherent uncertainty or variability of expected pre-tax returns on the firm's portfolio of assets. This kind of risk was examined in Chapter 14, where it was defined in terms of the probability distribution of returns on the firm's assets. *Financial risk* is the additional risk induced by the use of financial leverage.

Impact of Financial Leverage

Perhaps the best way to understand the proper use of financial leverage is to analyze its impact on profitability and fluctuations in profitability under a range of leverage conditions.[7] As an example, consider four alternative finan-

6. The present discussion will consider variations in financial leverage in the context of a debt-equity trade-off. No distinction will be made between long- and short-term debt. Also, V is the market value of the firm, while TA is the book value of total assets.

7. We shall initially hold the level of investment constant, considering only different financial structures for a firm of the same size. Since firms also face decisions that require a choice between debt and equity for financing an increase in investment, this second type of decision will next be analyzed with the benefit of the perspective provided by the more general analysis of the financial structure decision in its pure form.

Table 15.1

Four Alternative Financial Structures, Universal Machine Company, Based on Book Values (Thousands of Dollars)

Structure 1 (B/S = 0%; B/TA = 0%)			
		Total debt	$ 0
		Common stock ($10 par)	10,000
Total assets	$10,000	Total claims	$10,000
Structure 2 (B/S = 25%; B/TA = 20%)			
		Total debt (10%)	$ 2,000
		Common stock ($10 par)	8,000
Total assets	$10,000	Total claims	$10,000
Structure 3 (B/S = 100%; B/TA = 50%)			
		Total debt (10%)	$ 5,000
		Common stock ($10 par)	5,000
Total assets	$10,000	Total claims	$10,000
Structure 4 (B/S = 400%; B/TA = 80%)			
		Total debt (10%)	$ 8,000
		Common stock ($10 par)	2,000
Total assets	$10,000	Total claims	$10,000

cial structures for the Universal Machine Company, a manufacturer of equipment used by industrial firms. The alternative balance sheets are displayed in Table 15.1.

Structure 1 uses no debt and consequently has a leverage factor of zero; Structure 2 has a leverage factor of 20 percent; Structure 3 has a leverage factor of 50 percent; and Structure 4 has a leverage factor of 80 percent. How do these different financial patterns affect stockholder returns? As can be seen from Table 15.2, the answer depends partly on Universal's level of sales and partly on the probability assessments associated with its alternative potential sales levels. The probability distribution for future sales, constructed by Universal's marketing department in cooperation with representatives from the general staff group of top management, was based on their knowledge of present supply and demand conditions along with estimates for future economic conditions and sales. The probable conditions range from very poor (zero sales due to a labor strike resulting from some very difficult labor negotiations currently underway) to very good under an optimistic assessment of the future outlook. It is assumed that the firm has total assets of $10,000,000.[8] The rate of interest on debt is 10 percent, and the assumed tax rate is 50 percent. Variable costs are estimated to be 40 percent of sales, and fixed costs equal $2,000,000.

Table 15.2 lays out the pattern of the analysis. It begins by listing the probability of sales at levels indicated by the next line. The fixed costs as shown remain the same for each level of sales. The total amount of variable costs in-

8. The numbers are rounded for convenience; in most tables and calculations the analysis will be made in thousands of dollars, and the last three zeros will be explicitly omitted.

Table 15.2

Stockholders' Returns and Earnings per Share under Various Leverage and Economic Conditions, Universal Machine Company (Thousands of Dollars)

Probability of indicated sales	0.1	0.3	0.4	0.2
Sales in dollars	$ 0	$6,000	$10,000	$20,000
Costs:				
Fixed costs	2,000	2,000	2,000	2,000
Variable costs (40% of sales)	—	2,400	4,000	8,000
Total costs (except interest)	$2,000	$4,400	$ 6,000	$10,000
Earnings before interest and taxes (EBIT)	−$2,000	$1,600	$ 4,000	$10,000
Capital Structure 1				
EBIT	−$2,000	$1,600	$ 4,000	$10,000
Less: Interest	0	0	0	0
Less: Income taxes (50%)[a]	−1,000	800	2,000	5,000
Net profit after taxes	−$1,000	$ 800	$2,000	$ 5,000
Earnings per share on 1,000 shares	−$1.00	$.80	$2.00	$5.00
Return on stockholders' equity	−10%	8%	20%	50%
Capital Structure 2				
EBIT	−$2,000	$1,600	$ 4,000	$10,000
Less: Interest (10% × $2,000)	200	200	200	200
Earnings before taxes	−2,200	1,400	3,800	9,800
Less: Income taxes (50%)[a]	−1,100	700	1,900	4,900
Net profit after taxes	−$1,100	$ 700	$ 1,900	$ 4,900
Earnings per share on 800 shares	−$1.38	$.88	$2.38	$6.13
Return on stockholders' equity	−13.8%	8.8%	23.8%	61.3%
Capital Structure 3				
EBIT	−$2,000	$1,600	$ 4,000	$10,000
Less: Interest (10% × $5,000)	500	500	500	500
Earnings before taxes	−2,500	1,100	3,500	9,500
Less: Income taxes (50%)[a]	−1,250	550	1,750	4,750
Net profit after taxes	−$1,250	$ 550	$ 1,750	$ 4,750
Earnings per share on 500 shares	−$2.50	$1.10	$3.50	$9.50
Return on stockholders' equity	−25%	11%	35%	95%
Capital Structure 4				
EBIT	−$2,000	$1,600	$ 4,000	$10,000
Less: Interest (10% × $8,000)	800	800	800	800
Earnings before taxes	−2,800	800	3,200	9,200
Less: Income taxes (50%)[a]	−1,400	400	1,600	4,600
Net profit after taxes	−$1,400	$ 400	$ 1,600	$ 4,600
Earnings per share on 200 shares	−$7.00	$2.00	$8.00	$23.00
Return on stockholders' equity	−70%	20%	80%	230%

a. The tax calculation assumes that losses are carried back and result in tax credits.

creases with the level of sales, since variable costs are 40 percent of sales. The fixed costs and variable costs are added to obtain total costs. Sales minus total costs equal earnings before interest and taxes (EBIT). Based on the indicated level of earnings before interest and taxes for the four sales levels associated with probabilities ranging from 0.1 to 0.4, the effects of the four alternative capital structures are analyzed.

Capital Structure 1 is considered first. Since it employs no leverage, the interest expense is zero. EBIT divided by the 1 million shares of common stock gives earnings per share associated with each of the probability factors and with each of the alternative levels of sales. The rate of return on common stock is EBIT minus taxes divided by stockholders' equity.

When debt is introduced into the capital structure (starting with Structure 2), interest on the debt is deducted from EBIT before the tax rate is applied and the net profit after taxes is calculated. Then, earnings per share on the indicated number of shares and the return on stockholders' equity are calculated as before. Capital Structure 1 (the one with no debt) is now compared with Capital Structure 3 (the one with the 50 percent leverage factor), since Structure 3's leverage factor approximates that for all manufacturing industries in the United States in recent years. For Capital Structure 1, earnings per share range from a loss of $1 per share to a profit of $5 a share—a range of $6. Under Capital Structure 3, the range in earnings per share is from a loss of $2.50 to a profit of $9.50. This is a range of $12, double the range in earnings per share of Structure 1. Similarly, the return on shareholders' equity for Structure 1 has a range of 60 percentage points, while the return for Structure 3 has a range of 120 percentage points.

Table 15.2 shows the two return relationships—earnings per share and return on stockholders' equity—associated with leverage. Under any given financial structure, earnings per share and the return on stockholders' equity increase with improved sales levels. Also, these earnings are magnified as leverage is increased. Thus increased leverage increases the degree of fluctuation in earnings per share and in returns on equity for any given degree of fluctuation in sales and its related return on total assets. If used successfully, leverage increases the returns to the owners of the firm; but if unsuccessful, it

Figure 15.2

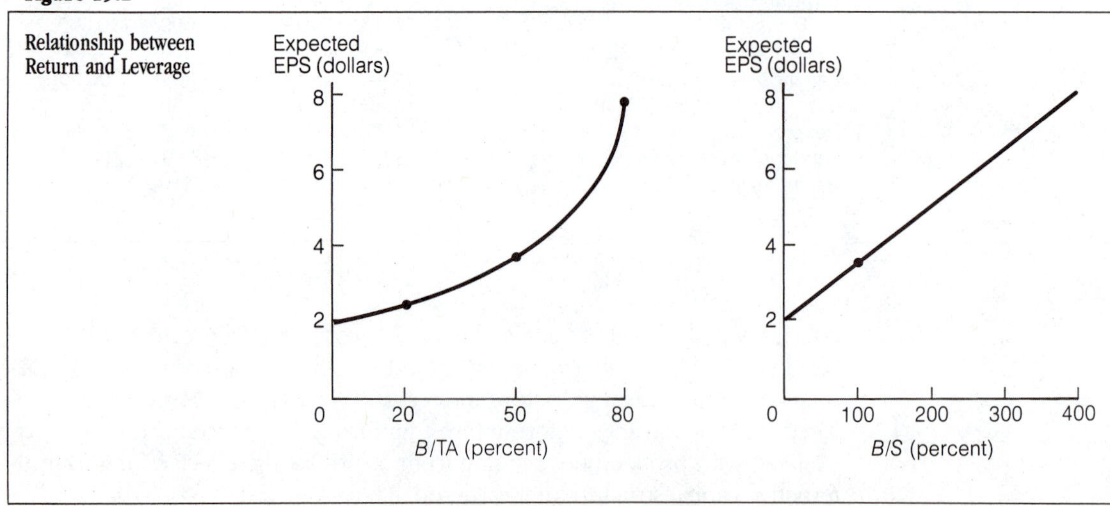

can result in inability to pay fixed charge obligations and, ultimately, in financial difficulties leading to financial reorganization or bankruptcy.[9]

Table 15.3 performs a return-risk analysis of the four financial structures. Applying the probability factors to each of the associated earnings per share results, the table calculates the expected earnings per share and the associated variance and standard deviation for each financial structure. Then it divides the standard deviation by the expected earnings per share to obtain the coefficient of variation. Figure 15.2 provides a graph of the expected earnings

Table 15.3

Return-Risk Analysis of the Four Financial Structure Alternatives

	s	p_s	EPS	p_sEPS	EPS − E(EPS)	[EPS − E(EPS)]²	p_s[EPS − E(EPS)]²
Structure 1	1	0.1	−$1.00	−0.10	−2.94	8.6436	0.8644
	2	0.3	0.80	0.24	−1.14	1.2996	0.3899
	3	0.4	2.00	0.80	0.06	0.0036	0.0014
	4	0.2	5.00	1.00	3.06	9.3636	1.8727
			E(EPS) =	$1.94			σ^2 = 3.1284
							σ = 1.7687
				CV = σ/E(EPS) = 0.912			
Structure 2	1	0.1	−$1.38	−0.138	−3.68	13.5424	1.3542
	2	0.3	0.88	0.264	−1.42	2.0164	0.6049
	3	0.4	2.38	0.952	0.08	0.0064	0.0026
	4	0.2	6.13	1.226	3.83	14.6689	2.9338
			E(EPS) =	$2.30			σ^2 = 4.8955
							σ = 2.2126
					CV = 0.962		
Structure 3	1	0.1	−$2.50	−0.25	−5.88	34.5744	3.4574
	2	0.3	1.10	0.33	−2.28	5.1984	1.5595
	3	0.4	3.50	1.40	0.12	0.0144	0.0058
	4	0.2	9.50	1.90	6.12	37.4544	7.4909
			E(EPS) =	$3.38			σ^2 = 12.5136
							σ = 3.5375
					CV = 1.05		
Structure 4	1	0.1	−$7.00	−0.70	−14.70	216.09	21.6090
	2	0.3	2.00	0.60	−5.70	32.49	9.7470
	3	0.4	8.00	3.20	0.30	0.09	0.0360
	4	0.2	23.00	4.60	15.30	234.09	46.8180
			E(EPS) =	$7.70			σ^2 = 78.2100
							σ = 8.8436
					CV = 1.149		

9. See Chapter 24 for an explanation of the nature of financial reorganization and bankruptcy.

per share as calculated in Table 15.3 in relation to the four alternative debt to equity and debt to total asset ratios. The figure shows that the expected earnings per share increase linearly with the debt to equity ratio and increase at an increasing rate when the leverage factor is measured by the debt to total asset ratio.

We now turn to a consideration of measures of the riskiness of the expected returns in relation to the alternative levels of sales and the alternative financial structures employed. We have noted how leverage increases the variability of earnings per share and the variability of returns to stockholders. For example, using no leverage, earnings per share range from a loss of $1 to a gain of $5. With a leverage of 80 percent the range is from a loss of $7 to a gain of $23.

There are three measures of this variability in earnings induced by leverage; each is, in some sense, a measure of risk. The three measures of risk are the standard deviation, the coefficient of variation, and the beta coefficient. The standard deviation and coefficient of variation of expected earnings per share are calculated in Table 15.3. In each case the coefficient of variation is calculated by dividing the standard deviation by the average earnings per share. The coefficient of variation rises from 0.912 in Structure 1 to 1.149 in Structure 4. Clearly, both these measures of risk rise with increased leverage.

The third measure of risk is the beta coefficient (β) for the various leverage factors illustrated. First, the market return parameters must be estimated. The basic estimates of the market return are shown for the four probability factors in Table 15.4. Applying the probability factors to the four alternative estimates of the return on the market, the expected or average return on the market is shown to be 10 percent. The deviations of the market returns from their mean are calculated in Column 5. In Column 6 these deviations are squared. In Column 7 the probability factors are applied; then the items are summed to obtain the variance of the market, which is approximately 1 percent. The standard deviation of the market returns would, therefore, be 0.1.

With the use of the parameters calculated in Table 15.4, we can calculate the betas for each level of leverage of the Universal Machine Company. (Assume a risk-free rate of 5 percent.) First we obtain $E(X)$ and $Cov(X,R_M)$ for

Table 15.4

Estimation of Market Parameters

s (1)	p_S (2)	R_M (3)	$p_S R_M$ (4)	$[R_M - E(R_M)]$ (5)	$[R_M - E(R_M)]^2$ (6)	$p_S[R_M - E(R_M)]^2$ (7)
1	0.1	(0.15)	(0.015)	(0.25)	0.0625	0.00625
2	0.3	0.05	0.015	(0.05)	0.0025	0.00075
3	0.4	0.15	0.060	0.05	0.0025	0.00100
4	0.2	0.20	0.040	0.10	0.0100	0.00200
		$E(R_M) =$	0.10		Var R_M =	0.01000
					$\sigma(R_M)$ =	0.10

Structure 1, the unlevered firm. Note that X is after taxes, and recall that $(R_M - \bar{R}_M)$ is in Column 5 of Table 15.4.

s	p_s	X	p_sX	$(X - \bar{X})(R_M - \bar{R}_M)P_s$	
1	0.1	−$1,000	−$ 100	(−$2,940)(−0.25)0.1 =	$ 73.5
2	0.3	800	240	(−1,140)(−0.05)0.3 =	17.1
3	0.4	2,000	800	(60)(0.05)0.4 =	1.2
4	0.2	5,000	1,000	(3,060)(0.10)0.2 =	61.2
			$\bar{X}$ = $1,940	Cov(X,R_M) =	$153.0

Next we find Cov(R_j,R_M), which is equal to Cov$(X_j,R_M)/V_u$, where V_u is the market value of the unlevered firm. In Chapter 14, we saw that

$$V_u = \frac{E(X) - \lambda \text{Cov}(X,R_M)}{R_F}. \tag{14.14b}$$

From above, we have $E(X)$ = $1,940 and Cov$(X,R_M)$ = $153. Recall that

$$\lambda = \frac{E(R_M) - R_F}{\sigma_M^2}.$$

In this case

$$\lambda = \frac{0.10 - 0.05}{0.01} = 5.$$

Therefore:

$$V_u = \frac{\$1{,}940 - 5(\$153)}{0.05} = \$23{,}500.$$

We can now find Cov(R_j,R_M) = $153/$23,500 = 0.0065.

To calculate the betas for the four alternative leverage ratios, we first find β_u, the beta for the unlevered firm. Recall that $\beta_j = \text{Cov}(R_j,R_M)/\text{Var}(R_M)$; therefore $\beta_u = 0.0065/0.01 = 0.65$. The betas for the levered alternatives are calculated in Table 15.5. In Columns 2 through 4 we find V_L, the market value of the levered firm, using the relation $V_L = V_u + TB$. The debt to total market value ratio is calculated in Column 5. In Columns 6 and 7 we find the debt to equity ratio, using the relation $S = V_L - B$ to find the market value of equity. Columns 7 through 10 calculate the levered betas using the relation $\beta_L = \beta_u + \beta_u(B/S)(1 - T)$.

Table 15.5

Calculation of the Beta Coefficients for Four Alternative Leverage Ratios Universal Machine Company (Based on Market Values)

Financial Structure (1)	B (2)	TB (3)	V_L (4)	B/V_L: (2) ÷ (4) (5)	S: (4) − (2) (6)	B/S: (2) ÷ (6) (7)	$B/S(1-T)$: (7) × 0.5 (8)	$B/S(1-T)\beta_u$: (8) × 0.65 (9)	β_j: 0.65 + (9) (10)
1	0	0	—	—	—	—	—	—	0.65
2	$2,000	$1,000	$24,500	8.16%	$22,500	8.89%	0.0445	0.0289	0.68
3	5,000	2,500	26,000	19.23	21,000	23.81	0.1191	0.0774	0.73
4	8,000	4,000	27,500	29.09	19,500	41.03	0.2052	0.1334	0.78

Finally we calculate the required rate of return using the SML:

$$R_j^* = R_F + (\bar{R}_M - R_F)\beta_j$$

Financial Structure (1)	β_j (2)	R_j^* (3)
1	0.65	8.25
2	0.68	8.40
3	0.73	8.65
4	0.78	8.90

In Table 15.5, one risk measure, the beta coefficient, is exhibited in relationship to the leverage ratios of debt to the total market value of the firm (Column 5) and the debt to the total market value of the equity (Column 7). Since the leverage ratios are measured in market values in Table 15.5, as is required by the theoretical relationship between β and leverage, they differ from the leverage ratios measured at book, which were first set forth in Table 15.1.

Table 15.6 summarizes the behavior of two other risk measures—the

Table 15.6

Risk-Return Trade-off for Various Leverage Ratios, Universal Machine Company (Based on Book Values)

Debt/Assets	Debt/Equity	Expected EPS	Standard Deviation	Coefficient of Variation
0%	0%	$1.94	1.77	0.912
20	25	2.30	2.21	0.962
50	100	3.38	3.54	1.050
80	400	7.70	8.84	1.150

Figure 15.3

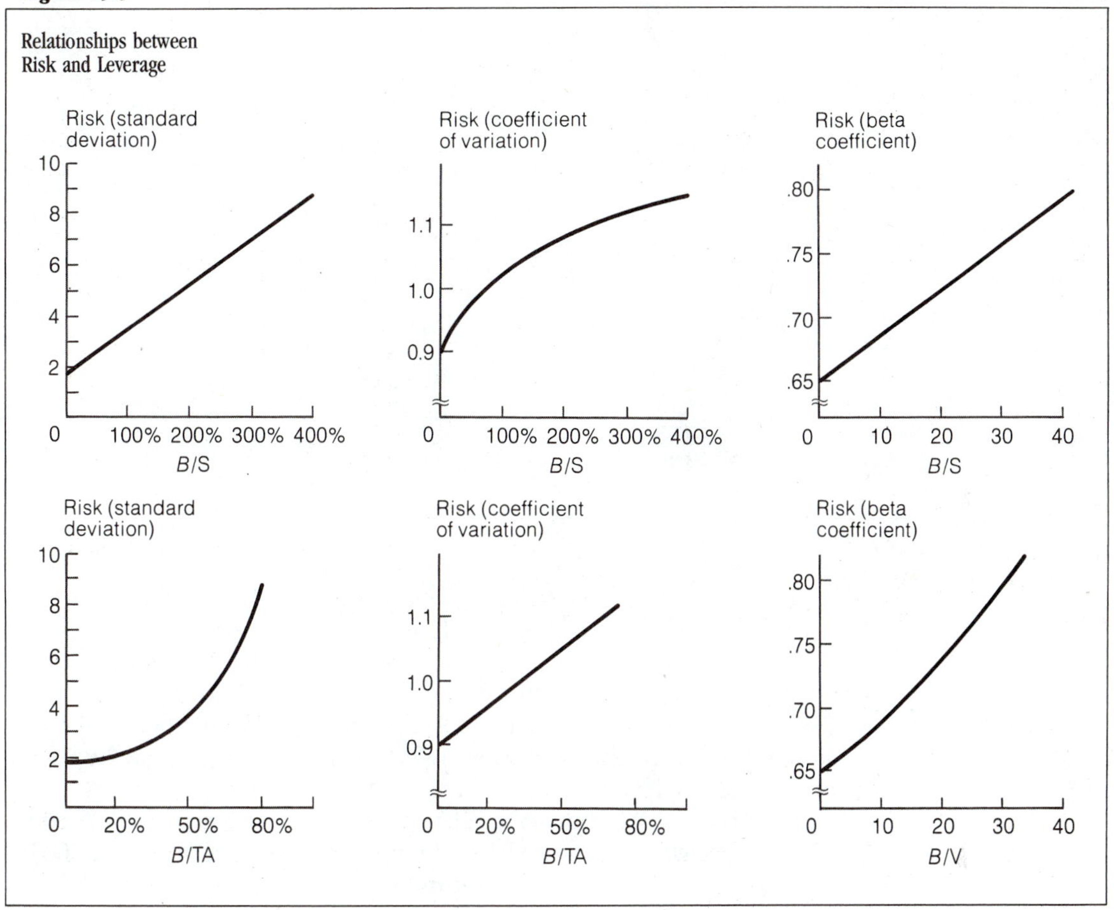

standard deviation and coefficient of variation—that were developed in Table 15.3 for the four alternative leverage ratios shown here at book.

These numerical relationships between leverage and the three risk measures are summarized in Figure 15.3. Risk, as measured by the standard deviation, has a linear relationship to the debt to equity ratio measured at book value but an upward curvilinear relationship to the debt to total assets ratio at book value. Conversely, when risk is measured by the coefficient of variation, the relationship to the book debt to equity ratio is curvilinear downward, and the relationship to the book debt to total assets ratio is linear. Because of the theoretical relationship between beta and leverage, the relevant leverage ratios for comparison with beta are at market values. At market values, the relationship between beta and the debt to equity ratio is linear, and between beta and the ratio of debt to the total value of the firm is curvilinear upward. The different shapes of the relationship stem from the basic underlying theory of

Table 15.7

Leverage, Return and Risk Relationships

Part A	Leverage Ratio *B/TA*	Expected EPS	Coefficient of Variation
	0%	1.94	0.912
	20	2.30	0.962
	50	3.38	1.050
	80	7.70	1.150

Part B	Leverage Ratio *B/V*	Required Return on Equity	Beta Coefficient
	0%	8.25	0.65
	$8.1\dot{6}$	8.40	0.68
	19.23	8.65	0.73
	29.09	8.90	0.78

the computations involved. But what is common to all of the six portrayals of the relationship between risk and leverage is that to obtain the higher expected earnings (whether measured by earnings per share or return on stockholders' equity) that go with increased leverage, the firm must incur more risk. As previously indicated, there is a positive relationship between return and risk, and there is also a positive relationship between risk and the degree of leverage employed.

Thus far we have shown the relation between leverage and risk. Next we depict the relation between risk and return. This will provide a specific example of the trade-off between risk and return.

In Table 15.7 we present two illustrative measures of the leverage, return, and risk relationships. In Part A of the table, the leverage ratio, as measured by debt to total assets at book values, is related to expected earnings per share and the coefficient of variation. In Part B, the leverage, as measured by debt to equity at market values, is related to the expected return on equity and the beta measure of risk.

The nature of these relationships is depicted graphically in Figure 15.4. There is an upward curvilinear relationship between the coefficient of variation and earnings per share when the leverage ratio is measured by debt to total assets at book value. There is a linear relationship between beta and the return on equity when leverage is measured by the debt to value ratio at market values. But regardless of whether the relationship is linear or nonlinear, there is agreement that in order to obtain the higher expected earnings that go with increased leverage, the firm must accept more risk.

Another dimension of the return-leverage-risk relationship is exhibited by Figure 15.5, which sets forth a relationship between rates of return on assets and rates of return on net worth under different leverage conditions. For zero

Figure 15.4

EPS and Coefficient of Variation; Return on Equity and Beta

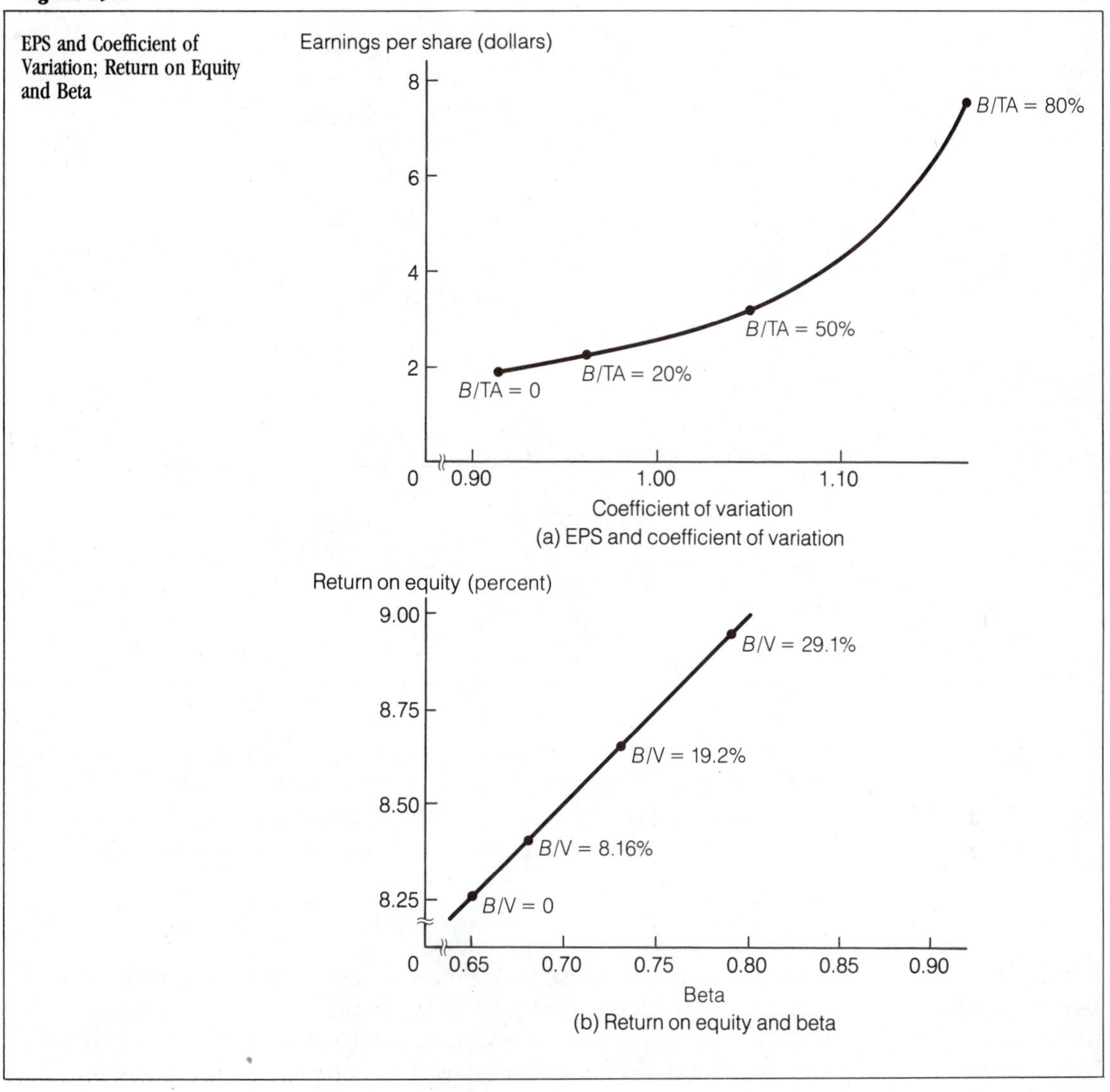

leverage, the line of relationship begins at the origin and has a slope that is less steep than the slope of the relationship when leverage is employed. With leverage, the intercept of the line is negative, indicating that at low rates of return on total assets, the return on net worth is negative (representing a loss). The intersection of the three lines is at the 10 percent rate of return on total assets, which is equal to the before-tax interest cost of debt. At this intersection point the return on net worth is 5 percent. The 50 percent tax rate reduces the 10 percent return on total assets to a return of 5 percent on net worth regardless of the degree of leverage. When returns on assets are higher than 10 percent, debt-financed assets can cover interest cost and still leave

Figure 15.5

Relationship between Rates of Return on Assets and Rates of Return on Net Worth under Different Leverage Conditions

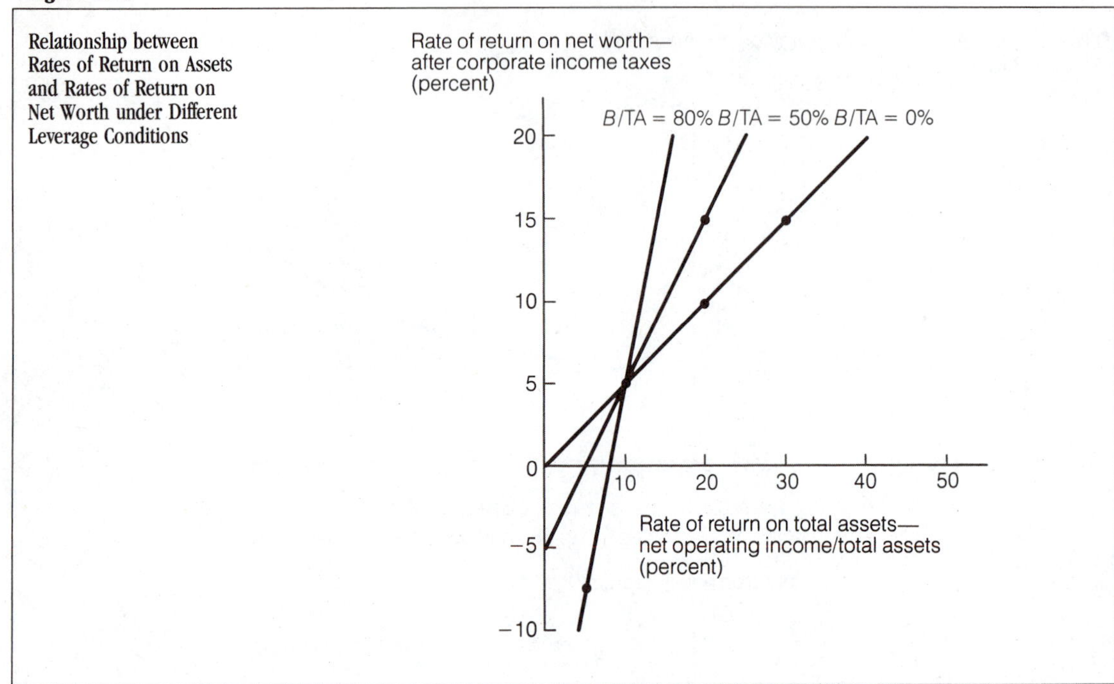

something over for the stockholders. But the reverse holds if assets earn less than 10 percent. Figure 15.5 illustrates a general proposition: Whenever the return on assets exceeds the cost of debt, leverage is favorable; and the higher the leverage factor, the higher the rate of return on common equity.

Financial Leverage with Additional Investment

Thus far in the analysis we have simply varied leverage, holding constant the total amount of investment by the firm. In real world decision making, it is often necessary to perform an analysis in which alternative leverage structures are considered along with financing that increases the firm's amount of investment and size of total assets. This aspect of combining the financing and leverage decisions will be developed by a continuation of the Universal Machine Company example. Universal's latest balance sheet is set forth in Table 15.8. Universal manufactures equipment used in industrial manufacturing. Its major product is a lathe used to trim the rough edges off sheets of fabricated steel. The lathes sell for $100,000 each. As is typically the case for producers of durable capital assets, the company's sales fluctuate widely, far more than does the overall economy. For example, during nine of the preceding twenty-five years, the company's sales have been below the breakeven point, so losses have been relatively frequent.

Table 15.8

Universal Machine Company Balance Sheet for Year Ended December 31, 1980 (Thousands of Dollars)

Cash	$ 300	Total liabilities having an average cost of 10%	$ 5,000
Receivables (net)	1,200		
Inventories	1,400		
Plant (net)	3,000	Common stock ($10 par)	5,000
Equipment (net)	4,100		
Total assets	$10,000	Total claims on assets	$10,000

Although future sales are uncertain, current demand is high and appears to be headed higher. Thus, if Universal is to continue its sales growth, it will have to increase capacity. A capacity increase involving $2 million of new capital is under consideration. James Watson, the financial vice-president, learns that he can raise the $2 million by selling bonds with a 10 percent coupon or by selling 100,000 shares of common stock at a market price of $20 per share. Fixed costs after the planned expansion will be $2 million a year. Variable costs excluding interest on the debt will be 40 percent of sales.[10] The probability distribution for future sales possibilities is the same as was set forth in the previous section analyzing the pure leverage decision for Universal.

Although Watson's recommendation will be given much weight, the final decision for the method of financing rests with the company's board of directors. Procedurally, the financial vice-president analyzes the situation, evaluates all reasonable alternatives, comes to a conclusion, and then presents the alternatives with his recommendations to the board. For his own analysis, as well as for presentation to the board, Watson prepares the materials shown in Table 15.9.

The top third of the table calculates earnings before interest and taxes (EBIT) for different levels of sales ranging from $0 to $20 million. The firm suffers an operating loss until sales are $3.3 million, but beyond that point it enjoys a rapid rise in gross profit.

The middle third of the table shows the financial results that will occur at the various sales levels if bonds are used. First, the $700,000 annual interest charges ($500,000 on existing debt plus $200,000 on the new bonds) are deducted from the earnings before interest and taxes. Next, taxes are taken out; and if the sales level is so low that losses are incurred, the firm receives a tax credit. Then, net profits after taxes are divided by the 500,000 shares outstanding to obtain earnings per share (EPS) of common stock.[11] The various EPS figures are multiplied by the corresponding probability estimates to obtain an expected EPS of $3.18.

10. The assumption that variable costs will be a constant percentage of sales over the entire range of output is not valid, but variable costs are relatively constant over the output range likely to occur.
11. The number of shares initially outstanding can be calculated by dividing the $5 million common stock figure given on the balance sheet by the $10 par value.

Table 15.9

Profit Calculations at Various Sales Levels, Universal Machine Company (Thousands of Dollars)

Probability of indicated sales	0.1	0.3	0.4	0.2
Sales in units	0	60	100	200
Sales in dollars	$ 0	$6,000	$10,000	$20,000
Costs:				
Fixed costs	2,000	2,000	2,000	2,000
Variable costs (40% of sales)	0	2,400	4,000	8,000
Total costs (except interest)	$2,000	$4,400	$ 6,000	$10,000
Earnings before interest and taxes (EBIT)	−$2,000	$1,600	$ 4,000	$10,000
Financing with bonds (*B*/TA = 58.3%; *B*/*S* = 140%)				
Less: Interest (10% × $7,000)	$ 700	$ 700	$ 700	$ 700
Earnings before taxes	−2,700	900	3,300	9,300
Less: Income taxes (50%)	−1,350	450	1,650	4,650
Net profit after taxes	−$1,350	$ 450	$ 1,650	$ 4,650
EPS on 500,000 shares[a]	−$2.70	$.90	$3.30	$9.30
Expected EPS $3.18				
Financing with stock (*B*/TA = 41.7%; *B*/*S* = 71.4%)				
Less: Interest (10% × $5,000)	$ 500	$ 500	$ 500	$ 500
Earnings before taxes	−2,500	1,100	3,500	9,500
Less: Income taxes (50%)	−1,250	550	1,750	4,750
Net profit after taxes	−$1,250	$ 550	$ 1,750	$ 4,750
EPS on 600,000 shares[a]	−$2.08	$.92	$2.92	$7.92
Expected EPS $2.82				

a. The EPS figures can also be obtained using the following formula:

$$\text{EPS} = \frac{(\text{Sales} - \text{Fixed costs} - \text{Variable costs} - \text{Interest})(1 - \text{Tax rate})}{\text{Shares outstanding}}$$

For example, at sales = $10 million:

$$\text{EPS}_{\text{bonds}} = \frac{(10 - 2 - 4 - 0.7)(0.5)}{0.5} = \$3.30.$$

$$\text{EPS}_{\text{stock}} = \frac{(10 - 2 - 4 - 0.5)(0.5)}{0.6} = \$2.92.$$

The bottom third of the table calculates the financial results that will occur with stock financing. Net profit after interest and taxes is divided by 600,000—the original 500,000 plus the new 100,000 shares ($20 × 100,000 = $2 million)—to find earnings per share. Expected EPS is computed in the same way as for the bond financing.

Figure 15.6 shows the probability distribution of earnings per share. Stock financing has the tighter, more peaked distribution. We know from Table 15.3 that it will also have a smaller coefficient of variation than bond financing. Hence, stock financing is less risky than bond financing. However, the expected earnings per share are lower for stock than for bonds, so we are again faced with the kind of risk-return trade-off that characterizes most financial decisions.

Figure 15.6

Probability Curves for Stock and Bond Financing

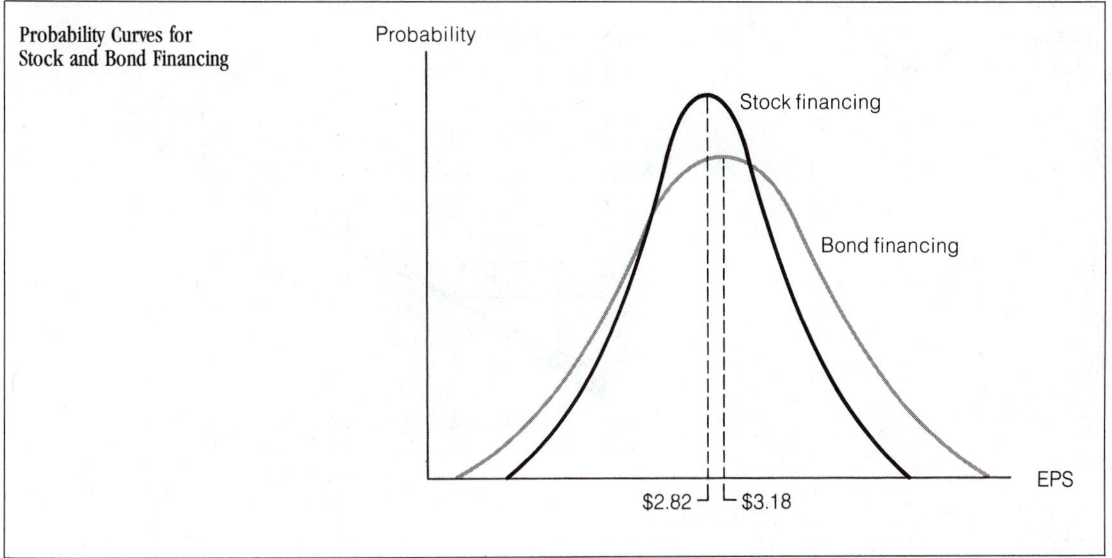

What choice should Watson recommend to the board? How much leverage should Universal Machine use? These questions cannot be answered at this point; the answers must be deferred until some additional concepts have been covered and the effects of leverage on the cost of both debt and equity capital have been examined.

Breakeven Analysis

Another way of presenting the data on Universal's two financing methods is shown in Figure 15.7, a breakeven chart similar to the charts used in Chapter 9. If sales are depressed to zero, the debt financing line cuts the y-axis at −$2.70, below the −$2.08 intercept of the common stock financing line. The debt line has a steeper slope and rises faster, however, showing that earnings per share will go up faster with increases in sales if debt is used. The two lines cross at sales of $6.2 million. Below that sales volume, the firm will be better off issuing common stock; above that level, debt financing will produce higher earnings per share.[12]

12. Since the equation in this case is linear, the breakeven or indifference level of sales $(P \cdot Q)$ can be found as follows:

$$EPS_S = \frac{(P \cdot Q - 2.0 - 0.4P \cdot Q - 0.5)(0.5)}{0.6} = \frac{(P \cdot Q - 2.0 - 0.4P \cdot Q - 0.7)(0.5)}{0.5} = EPS_B$$

$$P \cdot Q = \$6.2 \text{ million, and EPS} = \$1.02.$$

Figure 15.7

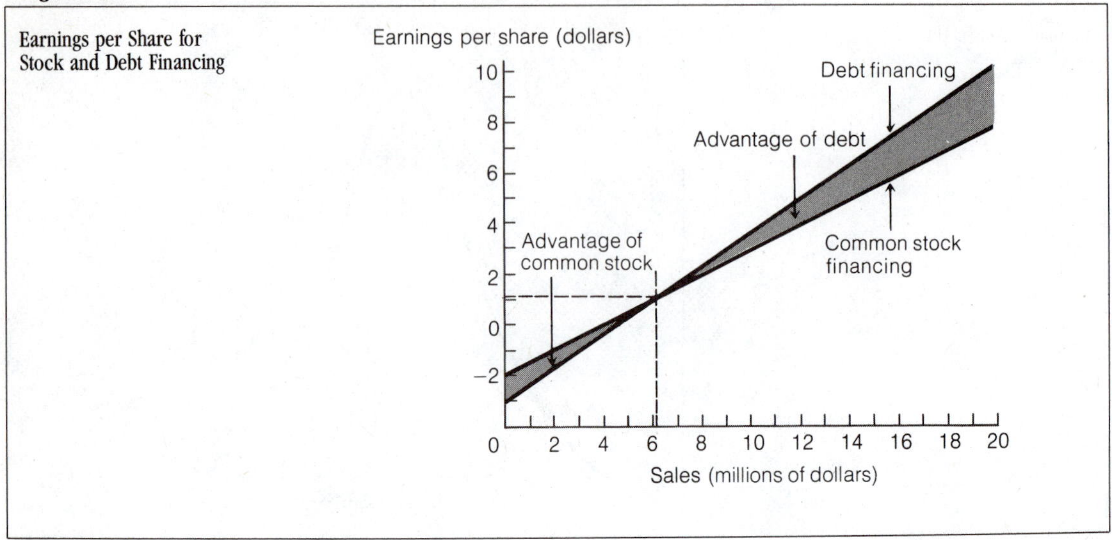

Earnings per Share for Stock and Debt Financing

If Watson and his board of directors *know with certainty* that sales will never again fall below $6.2 million, bonds are the preferred method of financing the asset increase. But they cannot know this for certain. In fact, they know that in previous years, sales have fallen below this critical level. Further, if any detrimental long-run events occur, future sales may again fall well below $6.2 million. If sales continue to expand, however, there will be higher earnings per share from using bonds; and no officer or director will want to forego these substantial advantages.

Watson's recommendation and the directors' decision will depend on (1) each person's appraisal of the future and (2) each person's psychological attitude toward risk.[13] The pessimists, or risk averters, will prefer to employ common stock, while the optimists, or those less sensitive to risk, will favor bonds. This example, which is typical of many real world situations, suggests that the major disagreements over the choice of forms of financing are likely to reflect uncertainty about the future levels of the firm's sales. The uncertainty in turn reflects the characteristics of the firm's environment—general business conditions, industry trends, and quality and aggressiveness of management.

13. Theory suggests that the decision should be based on stockholders' utility preferences, or the market risk-return trade-off function discussed in Chapter 14. In practice, it is difficult to obtain such information as *data,* so decisions of this sort are generally based on the subjective judgment of the decision maker. A knowledge of the theory, even if it cannot be applied directly, is extremely useful in making good judgmental decisions. Further, knowing the theory permits the firm to structure research programs and data-collecting systems that will make direct application of the theory increasingly feasible in future years.

Relationship of Financial Leverage to Operating Leverage

Chapter 9 showed that a firm has some degree of control over its production processes; it can, within limits, use either a highly automated production process with high fixed costs but low variable costs or a less automated process with lower fixed costs but higher variable costs. If a firm uses a high degree of operating leverage, its breakeven point is at a relatively high sales level, and changes in the sales level have a magnified (or "leveraged") impact on profits. Notice that financial leverage has exactly the same kind of effect on profits; the higher the leverage factor, the higher the breakeven sales volume and the greater the impact on profits from a given change in sales volume.

In Chapter 9 the *degree of operating leverage* was defined as the percentage change in operating profits associated with a given percentage change in sales volume, and Equation 15.2 (a form of Equation 9.2) was developed for calculating operating leverage:

$$\text{Degree of operating leverage at Point } Q = \frac{Q(P-v)}{Q(P-v)-F} = \frac{C}{X} \qquad (15.2)$$

$$= \frac{P \cdot Q - V}{P \cdot Q - V - F} \qquad (15.2a)$$

where:

Q = Units of output
P = Average sales price per unit of output
v = Variable cost per unit
F = Total fixed operating costs
PQ = Sales in dollars
V = Total variable costs

Applying the formula to Universal Machine at a sales level of \$10,000 (see Table 15.2) and assuming that one machine sells for \$100, operating leverage is 1.50; thus a 100 percent increase in volume produces a 150 percent increase in profit:

$$\text{Degree of operating leverage} = \frac{100(\$100-\$40)}{100(\$100-\$40)-\$2{,}000}$$

$$= \frac{\$10{,}000-\$4{,}000}{\$10{,}000-\$4{,}000-\$2{,}000}$$

$$= \frac{\$6{,}000}{\$4{,}000} = 1.50 \text{ or } 150\%.$$

Operating leverage affects earnings before interest and taxes (EBIT), while financial leverage affects earnings after interest and taxes, the earnings available to common stockholders. In terms of Table 15.2, operating leverage affects the top section of the table and financial leverage the lower sections. Thus, if Universal had more operating leverage, its fixed costs would be higher than \$2,000, its variable cost ratio would be lower than 40 percent of sales, and earnings before interest and taxes would vary with sales to a greater extent. Financial leverage takes over where operating leverage leaves off, further magnifying the effect on earnings per share of a change in the level of sales. For this reason, operating leverage is sometimes referred to as first-stage leverage and financial leverage as second-stage leverage.

Degree of Financial Leverage

The *degree of financial leverage* is defined as the percentage change in earnings available to common stockholders that is associated with a given percentage change in earnings before interest and taxes (EBIT). An equation has been developed as an aid in calculating the degree of financial leverage for any given level of EBIT and interest charges *(rB)*.[14]

$$\text{Degree of financial leverage} = \frac{\text{EBIT}}{\text{EBIT} - rB} = \frac{X}{X - rB}. \quad (15.3)$$

For Universal Machine at an output of 100 units and an EBIT of \$4,000, the degree of financial leverage with bond financing is:

$$\text{Financial leverage for bonds} = \frac{\$4{,}000}{\$4{,}000 - \$700} = 1.21.$$

14. The equation is developed as follows:
a. Notice that EBIT = $Q(P - v) - F$.

b. $$\text{Earnings per share (EPS)} = \frac{(EBIT - rB)(1 - T)}{N},$$

where:
EBIT = Earnings before interest and taxes.
rB = Interest paid.
T = Corporate tax rate.
N = Number of shares outstanding.

c. The expression rB is a constant, so ΔEPS, the change in EPS, is:

$$\Delta\text{EPS} = \frac{\Delta\text{EBIT}(1 - T)}{N}.$$

d. The percentage increase in EPS is the change in EPS over the original EPS, or

$$\frac{\dfrac{\Delta\text{EBIT}(1 - T)}{N}}{\dfrac{(\text{EBIT} - rB)(1 - T)}{N}} = \frac{\Delta\text{EBIT}}{\text{EBIT} - rB}.$$

e. The degree of financial leverage is the percentage change in EPS over the percentage change in EBIT, so:

$$\text{Financial leverage} = \frac{\dfrac{\Delta\text{EBIT}}{\text{EBIT} - rB}}{\dfrac{\Delta\text{EBIT}}{\text{EBIT}}} = \frac{\text{EBIT}}{\text{EBIT} - rB} = \frac{X}{X - rB}.$$

Therefore, a 100 percent increase in EBIT results in a 121 percent increase in earnings per share. If stock financing is used, the degree of financial leverage can be calculated and found to be 1.14; thus a 100 percent increase in EBIT produces a 114 percent increase in EPS.

Combining Operating and Financial Leverage

Operating leverage causes a change in sales volume to have a magnified effect on EBIT; and if financial leverage is superimposed on operating leverage, changes in EBIT have a magnified effect on earnings per share. Therefore, if a firm uses a considerable amount of both operating leverage and financial leverage, even small changes in the level of sales will produce wide fluctuations in EPS.

Equation 15.2 for the degree of operating leverage can be combined with Equation 15.3 for financial leverage to show the total leveraging effect of a given change in sales on earnings per share.[15]

$$\text{Combined leverage effect} = \frac{Q(P - v)}{Q(P - v) - F - rB}. \tag{15.4}$$

For Universal Machine at an output of 100 units (or $10 million of sales) the combined leverage effect, using debt financing, is:

$$\begin{aligned}\text{Combined leverage effect} &= \frac{100(\$100 - \$40)}{100(\$100 - \$40) - \$2{,}000 - \$700}\\ &= \frac{\$6{,}000}{\$6{,}000 - \$2{,}000 - \$700}\\ &= 181.8 \text{ percent.}\end{aligned}$$

A 100 percent increase in sales from 100 units to 200 units will cause EPS to increase by 181.8 percent, so the new EPS figure will be 1.818 times the original EPS:

15. Equation 15.4 is developed as follows:
   a. Recognize that EBIT = $Q(P - v) - F$; then rewrite Equation 15.3 as:

$$\frac{\text{EBIT}}{\text{EBIT} - rB} = \frac{Q(P - v) - F}{Q(P - v) - F - rB}. \tag{15.3a}$$

   b. The total leverage effect is equal to the degree of operating leverage times the degree of financial leverage:

$$\begin{aligned}\text{Combined leverage effect} &= \text{Equation 15.2} \times \text{Equation 15.3a}\\ &= \frac{Q(P - v)}{Q(P - v) - F} \cdot \frac{Q(P - v) - F}{Q(P - v) - F - rB}\\ &= \frac{Q(P - v)}{Q(P - v) - F - rB}.\end{aligned} \tag{15.4}$$

$$\begin{aligned} EPS_{200\ units} &= EPS_{100\ units} + (EPS_{100\ units}) \times 1.818 \\ &= EPS_{100\ units} \times (1 + 1.818) \\ &= \$3.30 \times 2.818 = \$9.30. \end{aligned}$$

These figures agree, of course, with those worked out in Table 15.8.

Financial and operating leverage can be employed in various combinations. In the Universal Machine example, the combined leverage factor of 1.818 was obtained by using a degree of operating leverage of 1.50 and a degree of financial leverage of 1.21, but many other combinations of financial and operating leverage would have produced the same combined leverage factor. Within limits, firms can and do make trade-offs between financial and operating leverage.

The usefulness of the degree of leverage concept lies in the facts that (1) it enables firms to specify the precise effect of a change in sales volume on earnings available to common stock, and (2) it permits firms to show the interrelationship between operating and financial leverage. The concept can, for example, be used to show a business person that a decision to automate and to finance new equipment with bonds will result in a situation where a 10 percent decline in sales will produce a 50 percent decline in earnings, whereas a different operating and financial leverage package will be such that a 10 percent sales decline will cause earnings to decline by only 20 percent. In our experience, having the alternatives stated in this manner gives decision makers a better idea of the ramifications of their actions.[16]

Financial Structures in Practice

An overview of financial structures in a wide range of industries is set forth in Table 15.10. Financial structure is measured in the table by the ratio of common stockholders' equity to total capitalization, where total capitalization represents long-term financing. The ratio of shareholders' equity to total capitalization is used because some of the financing items that are not equity are not pure debt either—for example, preferred stock and deferred credits. Preferred stock usually has a limited, but not legally required, return and so is a form of leveraging common stock, but without risk of default. Deferred credits are mostly deferred tax obligations which pay no interest and generally increase in amount if a firm continues to grow and make investments in fixed assets.

The data in Table 15.10 show that, in general, manufacturing companies have lower leverage (a higher equity base) than do most utilities. Among the nonfinancials, air transport has the lowest ratio of equity to total capitaliza-

16. The concept is also useful for investors. If firms in an industry are classified as to their degrees of total leverage, an investor who is optimistic about prospects for the industry may favor those firms with high leverage, and one who is pessimistic may favor those with low leverage.

Table 15.10

Ratio of Common Stock Shareholders' Equity to Total Capitalization, All Manufacturing and Selected Utilities, 1978

	Percent
All manufacturing[a]	51.8
Electric utilities	37.2
Gas utilities	47.5
AT&T	44.4
Air transport	61.8
Railroads	34.6
Banking[a]	4.0
Savings & loans[a]	7.0
Finance companies[a]	20.0

a. Ratio of equity to total assets.
Sources: *Industry Surveys* (New York: Standard & Poor's, 1979, 1980). Used by permission. Also Federal Trade Commission, *Quarterly Financial Reports,* (Washington, D.C.: Government Printing Office, 1979).

tion. Banking firms operate with a very low ratio of equity to total assets. For finance companies, the ratio of debt to equity is about 400 percent. (Equity to total assets = 0.2, so debt is 0.8 of total assets; debt to equity is 0.8/0.2, which equals 400 percent).

Within all manufacturing, the amount of leverage employed depends upon how narrowly or broadly the industry is defined. Using the Federal Trade Commission's relatively broad classification of industries, we find that most industries fall within 4 to 5 percentage points of the all-manufacturing average. For the fourth quarter of 1979, when the all-manufacturing ratio of debt to total assets was 50 percent, the ratio for drugs and for instruments was about 40 percent. At the other end of the scale the total debt to total asset ratio for the aircraft and guided missiles industry was 66 percent. But with these three exceptions, most of the other industries were close to the all-manufacturing average.

However, when industries are defined more narrowly, as in the Dun & Bradstreet studies, much more variation is observed, as illustrated by Table 15.11, which presents the ratio of total debt to tangible net worth for a sample of manufacturing industries in 1978. A wide range of debt to worth ratios is exhibited, the lowest being 50 percent, for book publishing, and the highest 185 percent, for household appliances. But within these wide variations most of the debt to tangible net worth ratios fall in the range of 90 to 100 percent. This corresponds to the 50 percent debt to total asset ratio for all manufacturing from the Federal Trade Commission data, which is equivalent to a debt to net worth ratio of 100 percent. Similarly, the Dun & Bradstreet data indicate that for most wholesaling industries the ratio of total debt to tangible net worth is in the 90 to 110 percent range. For retailing industries, the ratio is lower, falling mostly in the 50 to 70 percent range.

Leverage ratios vary among individual firms even more than among indus-

Table 15.11

Ratio of Total Debt to Tangible Net Worth, Manufacturing, 1978

	Percent
Book publishing	50
Soap and other detergents	56
Mattresses and bedsprings	63
Malt liquors	65
Sawmills and planing mills	66
Sporting and athletic goods	69
Plumbing, heating, and air conditioning	76
Soft drinks: Bottled and canned	76
Engineering and scientific instruments	77
Airplane parts and accessories	80
Paints and allied products	80
Concrete block and brick	80
Motor vehicle parts and accessories	80
Chemicals: Alkalies and chlorine	85
Plastics materials and resins	90
Meat packing plants	90
Electric lamps	92
Office, computing, and accounting machines	93
Farm machinery and equipment	93
Metal stampings	93
Electric transformers	94
Work clothing: Men's and boys'	95
Textile machinery	96
Grain mill products: Flour	97
Suits and coats: Men's and boys'	97
Agricultural chemicals, nitrogenous	105
Paperboard boxes: Folding	107
Blast furnaces and steel mills	109
Dairy products: Milk, fluid	110
Canned fruits and vegetables	111
Knit outerwear mills	112
Dresses: Women's, misses', and juniors'	114
Paper mills, except building paper	118
Women's and misses' suits and coats	128
Petroleum refining	138
Household appliances	185

Source: "The Ratios," *Dun's Review,* October 1979. Reprinted by permission of Dun & Bradstreet.

tries. In Table 15.12 the equity to total capitalization ratios for selected electric utility companies are presented. Even within this small sample a range of from 29.5 percent to over 40 percent is observed.

Among industrial companies, variations in leverage ratios are even wider. Table 15.13 presents the ratios of debt to total capitalization for the aerospace industry in 1978. Of course, the aerospace industry itself is highly diverse, encompassing airframe companies, general aviation firms, shipbuilding, propul-

Table 15.12

Equity to Total Capitalization Ratios, Selected Electric Utility Companies, December 31, 1978

Company	Common Stock and Surplus to Total Capitalization (Percent)
Central Illinois Public Service	32.3
Detroit Edison Company	31.2
Consolidated Edison of New York	40.6
Montana Power Company	38.7
Dayton Power & Light	37.0
Middle South Utilities	29.5
American Electric Power	34.1

Source: *Moody's Handbook of Common Stocks* (New York: Moody's Investors Service, Spring 1980). Used by permission.

sion, subcontractors, and diversified companies with some capabilities in electrical and electronics manufacturing. But even within a subgroup, one observes a range of debt to total capitalization as low as 3.7 percent for King Radio and as high as 79.9 percent for Aeronca Inc. Among the large airframe companies, debt-to-total-capitalization ratios of 5 percent are observed for Boeing and McDonnell Douglas. The ratio moves up toward 50 percent for Grumman and Lockheed, with Rockwell International in between.

Thus, wide ranges in leverage ratios are observed among individual companies. The large differences in turn reflect a wide range of influences on financial leverage decisions. The kinds of variables and factors that can influence financial leverage decisions are surveyed in the following section.

Factors Influencing Financial Structure

Thus far the discussion has touched on the factors that are generally considered when a firm formulates basic policies relating to its financial structure. The more important of these financial structure determinants will now be briefly discussed. They are: (1) growth rate of future sales, (2) stability of future sales, (3) competitive structure of the industry, (4) asset structure of the firm, (5) control position and attitudes toward risk of owners and management, and (6) lenders' attitudes toward the firm and the industry.

Growth Rate of Sales

The future growth rate of sales is a measure of the extent to which the earnings per share of a firm are likely to be magnified by leverage. If sales and earnings grow at a rate of 8 to 10 percent a year, for example, financing by debt with limited fixed charges should magnify the returns to owners of the stock.[17] This can be seen from Figure 15.7 earlier in the chapter.

17. Such a growth rate is also often associated with a high profit rate.

Table 15.13

Debt to Total Capitalization, Aerospace Industry, 1978

Company	Percent
Diversified	
EG&G Inc.	14.8
Martin Marietta	13.3
Raytheon Co.	9.0
Signal Cos.	30.3
TRW Inc.	28.1
Teledyne Inc.	22.0
Subcontractors, Systems	
Aeronca Inc.	79.9
CCI Corp.	45.1
E-Systems	20.8
Fairchild Industries	16.5
Hazeltine Corp.	10.3
Heath Tecna Corp.	53.4
Hexcel Corp.	28.3
King Radio	3.7
Northrop Corp.	7.6
Pneumo Corp.	40.4
Rohr Industries	68.2
Sierracin Corp.	10.2
Simmonds Precision Prods.	25.9
TRE Corp.	17.6
VSI Corp.	10.6
Airframe	
Boeing Co.	5.3
Grumman Corp.	45.5
Lockheed Corp.	51.3
McDonnell Douglas	5.9
Rockwell Intl.	24.4
Propulsion, Engines	
Thiokol Corp.	9.1
United Technologies	28.9
General Aviation	
Bangor Punta	43.2
Cessna Aircraft	15.1
Gates Learjet	15.8
Shipbuilding	
Amer. Ship Building	31.1
General Dynamics	7.4
Todd Shipyards	69.3

Source: *Industry Surveys, Aerospace, Basic Analysis* (New York: Standard & Poor's, April 3, 1980), p. A35. Used by permission.

However, the common stock of a firm whose sales and earnings are growing at a favorable rate commands a high price; thus it sometimes appears that equity financing is desirable. The firm must weigh the benefits of using leverage against the opportunity of broadening its equity base when it chooses between future financing alternatives. Such firms are expected to have a moderate to high level of debt financing.

Sales Stability

Sales stability and debt ratios are directly related. With greater stability in sales and earnings, a firm can incur the fixed charges of debt with less risk than when its sales and earnings are subject to periodic declines; in the latter instance it will have difficulty meeting its obligations. The stability of the utility industry, combined with relatively favorable growth prospects, has resulted in high leverage ratios in that industry.

Competitive Structure

Debt-servicing ability is dependent on the profitability, as well as the volume, of sales. Hence, the stability of profit margins is as important as the stability of sales. The ease with which new firms can enter the industry and the ability of competing firms to expand capacity both influence profit margins. A growth industry promises higher profit margins, but such margins are likely to narrow if the industry is one in which the number of firms can be easily increased through additional entry. For example, the franchised fast-service food companies were a very profitable industry in the early 1960s, but it was relatively easy for new firms to enter this business and compete with the older firms. As the industry matured during the late 1960s and early 1970s, the capacity of the old and the new firms grew at an increased rate. As a consequence, profit margins declined.

Asset Structure

Asset structure influences the sources of financing in several ways. Firms with long-lived fixed assets, especially when demand for their output is relatively assured (for example, utilities), use long-term mortgage debt extensively. Firms that have their assets mostly in receivables and in inventory whose value is dependent on the continued profitability of the individual firm (for example, those in wholesale and retail trade) rely less on long-term debt financing and more on short-term financing.

Management Attitudes

The management attitudes that most directly influence the choice of financing are those concerning control of the enterprise and risk. Large corporations whose stock is widely owned may choose additional sales of common stock because such sales will have little influence on the control of the company.

In contrast, the owners of small firms may prefer to avoid issuing common stock in order to be assured of continued control. Because they generally have confidence in the prospects of their companies and because they can see the large potential gains to themselves resulting from leverage, managers of such firms are often willing to incur high debt ratios.

The converse can, of course, also hold; the owner-manager of a small firm may be *more* conservative than the manager of a large company. If the net worth of the small firm is, say, $1 million, and if it all belongs to the owner-manager, that individual may well decide that he or she is already prosperous enough and may elect not to risk using leverage in an effort to become still more wealthy.

Lender Attitudes

Regardless of managements' analyses of the proper leverage factors for their firms, there is no question but that lenders' attitudes are frequently important —sometimes the most important—determinants of financial structures. In the majority of cases, the corporation discusses its financial structure with lenders and gives much weight to their advice. But when management is so confident of the future that it seeks to use leverage beyond norms for the industry, lenders may be unwilling to accept such debt increases. They emphasize that excessive debt reduces the credit standing of the borrower and the credit rating of the securities previously issued. The lenders' point of view has been expressed by a borrower (a financial vice-president), who stated, "Our policy is to determine how much debt we can carry and still maintain an Aa bond rating, then use that amount less a small margin for safety."

In the following chapter the concepts developed to this point in the book will be extended to the formal theory of the cost of capital. The way investors appraise the relative desirability of increased returns versus higher risks is a most important consideration—one that, in general, invalidates the theory that firms should strive for maximum earnings per share regardless of the risks involved.

Summary

Financial leverage, which means using debt to boost rates of return on net worth over the returns available on assets, is the primary topic covered in this chapter. Whenever the return on assets exceeds the cost of debt, leverage is favorable, and the return on equity is raised by using it. However, leverage is a two-edged sword, and if the returns on assets are less than the cost of debt, then leverage reduces the returns on equity. The more leverage a firm employs, the greater this reduction. As a result, leverage may be used to boost stockholder returns, but it is used at the risk of increasing losses if the firm's economic fortunes decline. Thus gains and losses are magnified by leverage; and the higher the leverage employed by a firm, the greater will be the volatility of its returns.

Whenever available, probability data can be used to make the risk-return trade-off involved in the use of financial leverage more precise. The expected earnings per share (EPS) and coefficient of variation (CV) of these earnings can be calculated under alternative financial plans, and these EPS versus CV comparisons aid in making choices among plans.

Financial leverage is similar to operating leverage—a concept discussed in Chapter 9. As is true for operating leverage, financial leverage can be defined rigorously and measured in terms of the *degree of financial leverage.* In addition, the effects of financial and operating leverage can be combined, with the combined leverage factor showing the percentage changes in earnings per share that will result from a given percentage change in sales.

Questions

15.1 How will each of the occurrences listed below affect a firm's financial structure, capital structure, and net worth?
  a. The firm retains earnings of $100 during the year.
  b. A preferred stock issue is refinanced with bonds.
  c. Bonds are sold for cash.
  d. The firm repurchases 10 percent of its outstanding common stock with excess cash.
  e. An issue of convertible bonds is converted.

15.2 From an economic and social standpoint, is the use of financial leverage justifiable? Explain by listing some advantages and disadvantages.

15.3 Financial leverage and operating leverage are similar in one very important respect. What is this similarity, and why is it important?

15.4 How does the use of financial leverage affect the breakeven point?

15.5 Would you expect risk to increase proportionately, more than proportionately, or less than proportionately with added financial leverage? Explain.

15.6 What are some reasons for variations of debt ratios among the firms in a given industry?

15.7 Why is the following statement true? Other things being the same, firms with relatively stable sales are able to incur relatively high debt ratios.

15.8 Why do public utility companies usually pursue a different financial policy from that of trade firms?

15.9 The use of financial ratios and industry averages in the financial planning and analysis of a firm should be approached with caution. Why?

Problems

15.1 The Layton Company has total assets of $10 million. Earnings before interest and taxes were $2 million in 1980, and the tax rate was 40 percent. Given the following leverage ratios and corresponding interest rates, calculate Layton's rate of return on equity (net income/equity) for each amount of debt.

Leverage (Debt/Total Assets)	Interest Rate on Debt
0%	—
10	10%
30	10
50	12
60	15

15.2 The Roland Company wishes to calculate next year's return on equity under different leverage ratios. Roland's total assets are \$10 million, and its tax rate is 40 percent. The company is able to estimate next year's earnings for three possible states of the world. It estimates that 1981 earnings before interest and taxes will be \$3 million with a 0.2 probability, \$2 million with a 0.5 probability, and \$500,000 with a 0.3 probability. Calculate Roland's expected return on equity, the standard deviation, and the coefficient of variation for each of the following leverage ratios:

Leverage (Debt/Total Assets)	Interest Rate
0%	—
10	10%
30	10
50	12
60	15

15.3 Bernard Company has 1 million shares of common stock outstanding, with a \$10 par value. The tax rate is 40 percent, and earnings before interest and taxes are \$2 million. Calculate earnings per share, price per share, and the leverage ratio, using both book and market values of equity, for the following information:

Debt (B)	Interest Rate (R_b)	Return on Equity (R_s)
\$ 0	—	12%
1,000,000	10%	12
3,000,000	10	13
5,000,000	11	16
6,000,000	14	20

Calculate price per share by dividing EPS by R_s. Next, calculate the number of shares of equity retired by dividing each amount of increase in debt by the share price resulting from the previous level of debt. (The number of equity shares retired is subtracted from the previous number of equity shares to obtain the number of shares of stock remaining for each level of debt.)

15.4 The tax rate for the Grayson Company is 40 percent and its beta is 0.8 if it employs no leverage. The financial manager of Grayson uses the following expression to calculate the influence of leverage on beta:

$$\beta_j = \beta_u[1 + (B/S)(1 - T)].$$

a. Several alternative target leverage ratios are being considered. What will be the beta on the common stock of Grayson Company if the following alternative leverage ratios are employed—that is, B/S = 0.4? 0.8? 1.0? 1.2? 1.6?

b. If the financial manager of Grayson uses the SML to estimate the required return on equity, what are the required rates of return on equity at each of the above leverage ratios? (The estimated risk-free return is 6 percent, and the market risk premium is 5 percent.)

15.5 The Swensen Company plans to raise a net amount of \$240 million for new equipment financing and working capital. Two alternatives are being considered. Common stock may be sold at a market price of \$42 a share to net \$40, or debentures yielding 9 percent may be issued with a 2 percent flotation cost. The balance sheet and income statement of the Swensen Company prior to financing are given below:

The Swensen Company Balance Sheet as of December 31, 1980 (Millions of Dollars)

Current assets	$ 800	Accounts payable	$ 150
Net fixed assets	400	Notes payable to bank	250
		Other current liabilities	200
		Total current liabilities	$ 600
		Long-term debt	250
		Common stock, $2 par	50
		Retained earnings	300
Total assets	$1,200	Total claims	$1,200

The Swensen Company Income Statement for Year Ended December 31, 1980 (Millions of Dollars)

Sales	$2,200
Net income before taxes (10%)	$ 220
Interest on debt	40
Net income subject to tax	$ 180
Tax (50%)	90
Net income after tax	$ 90

Annual sales are expected to be distributed according to the following probabilities:

Annual Sales	Probability
$1,400	0.20
2,000	0.30
2,500	0.40
3,200	0.10

a. Assuming that net income before interest and taxes remains at 10 percent of sales, calculate earnings per share under both the stock financing and the debt financing alternatives at each possible level of sales.

b. Calculate expected earnings per share under both debt and stock financing.

15.6 United Battery Corporation produces one product, a long-life rechargeable battery for use in small calculators. Last year 50,000 batteries were sold at $20 each. United Battery's income statement is shown below:

United Battery Corporation Income Statement for Year Ended December 31, 1980

Sales		$1,000,000
Less: Variable costs	$400,000	
Fixed costs	200,000	600,000
EBIT		$ 400,000
Less: Interest		125,000
Net income before tax		$ 275,000
Less: Income tax (T = 0.40)		110,000
Net income		$ 165,000
EPS (100,000 shares)		$1.65

a. Calculate the following for United Battery's 1980 level of sales:
   1. Degree of operating leverage
   2. Degree of financial leverage
   3. Combined leverage effect

b. United Battery is considering changing to a new production process for manufacturing the batteries. Highly automated and capital intensive, the new process will double fixed costs to $400,000 but will decrease variable costs to $4 a unit. If the new equipment is financed with bonds, interest will increase by $70,000; if it is financed by common stock, total stock outstanding will increase by 20,000 shares. Assuming that sales remain constant, calculate for each financing method:
   1. Earnings per share
   2. Combined leverage

c. Under what conditions would you expect United Battery to want to change its operations to the more automated process?

d. If sales are expected to increase, which alternative will have the greatest impact on EPS? Illustrate with an example.

15.7 The Hunter Corporation plans to expand assets by 50 percent. To finance the expansion, it is choosing between a straight debt issue and common stock. Its current balance sheet and income statement are shown below:

Hunter Corporation Balance Sheet as of December 31, 1980

		Debt (at 8%)	$140,000
		Common stock, $10 par	350,000
		Retained earnings	210,000
Total assets	$700,000	Total claims	$700,000

Hunter Corporation Income Statement for Year Ended December 31, 1980

Sales	$2,100,000	Earnings per share:	$\frac{\$103,600}{35,000} = \$2.96$
Total costs (excluding interest)	1,881,600		
Net operating income	$ 218,400	Price-earnings ratio:	10 X[a]
Debt interest	11,200		
Income before taxes	$ 207,200	Market price:	10 × $2.96 = $29.60
Taxes (at 50%)	103,600		
Net income	$ 103,600		

a. The price-earnings ratio is the market price per share divided by earnings per share. It represents the amount of money an investor is willing to pay for $1 of current earnings. The higher the riskiness of a stock, the lower its P-E ratio, other things held constant. The concept of price-earnings ratio is discussed at some length in Chapter 7.

If Hunter Corporation finances the $350,000 expansion with debt, the rate on the incremental debt will be 11 percent, and the price-earnings ratio of the common stock will be 8 times. If the expansion is financed by equity, the new stock can be sold at $25, the required yield to maturity on debt will be 10 percent, and the price-earnings ratio of all the outstanding common stock will remain at 10 times.

a. Assuming that net income before interest and taxes (EBIT) is 10 percent of sales, what are the earnings per share at sales levels of $0, $700,000, $1,400,000, $2,100,000, $2,800,000, $3,500,000, and $4,200,000, when financing is with common stock? when financing is with debt? (Assume no fixed costs of production.)

b. Make a chart for EPS, indicating the crossover point in sales (where EPS using bonds = EPS using stock).
c. Using the price-earnings ratio, calculate the market value per share of common stock for each sales level for both the debt and the equity financing.
d. Using data from Part c, make a chart of market value per share for the company, and indicate the crossover point (where market value per share using bonds equals market value per share using stocks).
e. Which form of financing should be used if the firm follows the policy of seeking to maximize
   1. EPS?
   2. market price per share?
f. Now assume that the following probability estimates of future sales have been made: 5 percent chance of $0, 7.5 percent chance of $700,000, 20 percent chance of $1,400,000, 35 percent chance of $2,100,000, 20 percent chance of $2,800,000, 7.5 percent chance of $3,500,000, and 5 percent chance of $4,200,000. Calculate expected values for EPS and market price per share under each financing alternative.
g. What other factors should be taken into account in choosing between the two forms of financing?
h. Would it matter if the presently outstanding stock were all owned by the final decision maker (the president) and represented his entire net worth? Would it matter if he were compensated entirely by a fixed salary? If he had a substantial number of stock options?

Selected References

Altman, Edward I. "Corporate Bankruptcy Potential, Stockholder Returns, and Share Valuation." *Journal of Finance* 24 (December 1969), pp. 887–900.

Arditti, Fred D. "Risk and the Required Return on Equity." *Journal of Finance* 22 (March 1967), pp. 19–36.

Carleton, Willard T., and Silberman, Irwin H. "Joint Determination of Rate of Return and Capital Structure: An Econometric Analysis." *Journal of Finance* 32 (June 1977), pp. 811–821.

Chen, Andrew H., and Kim, E. Han. "Theories of Corporate Debt Policy: A Synthesis." *Journal of Finance* 34 (May 1979), pp. 371–384.

Donaldson, Gordon. "Strategy for Financial Emergencies." *Harvard Business Review* 47 (November–December 1969), pp. 67–79.

———. "New Framework for Corporate Debt Capacity." *Harvard Business Review* 40 (March–April 1962), pp. 117–131.

———. *Corporate Debt Capacity.* Boston: Division of Research, Harvard Business School, 1961.

Ferri, Michael G., and Jones, Wesley H. "Determinants of Financial Structure: A New Methodological Approach." *Journal of Finance* 34 (June 1979), pp. 631–644.

Ghandhi, J. K. S. "On the Measurement of Leverage." *Journal of Finance* 21 (December 1966), pp. 715–726.

Haslem, John A. "Leverage Effects on Corporate Earnings." *Arizona Review* 19 (March 1970), pp. 7–11.

Hong, Hai. "Inflation and the Market Value of the Firm: Theory and Tests." *Journal of Finance* 32 (September 1977), pp. 1031–1048.

Hunt, Pearson. "A Proposal for Precise Definitions of 'Trading on the Equity' and 'Leverage.'" *Journal of Finance* 16 (September 1961), pp. 377–386.

Johnson, W. Bruce. "The Cross-sectional Stability of Financial Patterns." *Journal of Business Finance and Accounting* 5 (Summer 1978), pp. 207–214.

Kim, E. Han. "A Mean-Variance Theory of Optimal Capital Structure and Corporate Debt Capacity." *Journal of Finance* 33 (March 1978), pp. 45–63.

Kim, E. Han; Lewellen, Wilbur G.; and McConnell, John J. "Financial Leverage Clienteles: Theory and Evidence." *Journal of Financial Economics* 7 (March 1979), pp. 83–109.

Kim, E. Han; McConnell, John J.; and Greenwood, Paul R. "Capital Structure Rearrangements and Me-First Rules in an Efficient Capital Market." *Journal of Finance* 32 (June 1977), pp. 789–810.

Krainer, Robert E. "Interest Rates, Leverage, and Investor Rationality." *Journal of Financial and Quantitative Analysis* 12 (March 1977), pp. 1–16.

Kraus, Alan, and Litzenberger, Robert. "A State-Preference Model of Optimal Financial Leverage." *Journal of Finance* 28 (September 1973), pp. 911–922.

Lev, Baruch, and Pekelman, Dov. "A Multiperiod Adjustment Model for the Firm's Capital Structure." *Journal of Finance* 30 (March 1975), pp. 75–91.

Litzenberger, Robert H., and Sosin, Howard B. "A Comparison of Capital Structure Decisions of Regulated and Non-regulated Firms." *Financial Management* 8 (Autumn 1979), pp. 17–21.

———. "The Theory of Recapitalizations and the Evidence of Dual Purpose Funds." *Journal of Finance* 32 (December 1977), pp. 1433–1455.

Lloyd-Davies, Peter R. "Optimal Financial Policy in Imperfect Markets." *Journal of Financial and Quantitative Analysis* 10 (September 1975), pp. 457–481.

Myers, Stewart C. "Determinants of Corporate Borrowing." *Journal of Financial Economics* 5 (November 1977), pp. 147–175.

Phillips, Paul D.; Groth, John C.; and Richards, R. Malcolm. "Financing the Alaskan Project: The Experience at Sohio." *Financial Management* 8 (Autumn 1979), pp. 7–16.

Ross, S. A. "The Determination of Financial Structure: The Incentive-Signalling Approach." *Bell Journal of Economics* 8 (Spring 1977), pp. 23–40.

Scott, David F., and Martin, John D. "Industry Influence on Financial Structure." *Financial Management* 4 (Spring 1975), pp. 67–73.

Taggart, Robert A., Jr. "A Model of Corporate Financing Decisions." *Journal of Finance* 32 (December 1977), pp. 1467–1484.

Tepper, Irwin, and Affleck, A. R. P. "Pension Plan Liabilities and Corporate Financial Strategies." *Journal of Finance* 29 (December 1974), pp. 1549–1564.

Toy, Norman, et al. "A Comparative International Study of Growth, Profitability, and Risk as Determinants of Corporate Debt Ratios in the Manufacturing Sector." *Journal of Financial and Quantitative Analysis* 9 (November 1974), pp. 875–886.

Turnbull, Stuart M. "Debt Capacity." *Journal of Finance* 34 (September 1979), pp. 931–940.

Vickers, Douglas. "Disequilibrium Structures and Financing Decisions in the Firm." *Journal of Business Finance and Accounting* 1 (Autumn 1974), pp. 375–388.

Wippern, Ronald F. "Financial Structure and the Value of the Firm." *Journal of Finance* 21 (December 1966), pp. 615–634.

Wrightsman, Dwayne. "Tax Shield Valuation and the Capital Structure Decision." *Journal of Finance* 33 (May 1978), pp. 650–656.

16
The Cost of Capital

The cost of capital is a critically important topic for three reasons. First, as we saw in Chapters 13 and 14, capital budgeting decisions have a major impact on the firm, and proper capital budgeting requires an estimate of the cost of capital. Second, as we saw in Chapter 15, financial structure can affect both the size and the riskiness of the firm's earnings stream and hence the value of the firm. A knowledge of the cost of capital and how it is influenced by financial leverage is useful in making capital structure decisions. Finally, a number of other decisions—including those related to leasing, to bond refunding, and to working capital policy—require estimates of the cost of capital.[1]

This chapter first establishes that the cost of capital, calculated as a weighted average, is the rate of return which must be earned so that the value of the firm and the market price of its common stock does not decline. Second, it considers the cost of the individual components of the capital structure—debt, preferred stock, and equity. Because investors perceive different classes of securities as having different degrees of risk, there are variations in cost of the different types of securities. Third, it brings the individual component costs together to form a weighted cost of capital. Fourth, it illustrates the concepts developed in the earlier sections with an example of the cost of capital calculation for an actual company. Finally, it develops the interrelationship between the cost of capital and the investment opportunity schedule and discusses the simultaneous determination of the marginal cost of capital and the marginal return on investment.

1. The cost of capital is also vitally important in regulated industries, including electric, gas, telephone, and transportation. In essence, regulatory commissions seek to measure a utility's cost of capital, then set prices so the company will just earn this rate of return. If the estimate is too low, the company will not be able to attract sufficient capital to meet long-run demands for service, and the public will suffer. If the estimate is too high, customers will pay too much for service.

Composite, or Overall, Cost of Capital

Suppose a particular firm's cost of debt is estimated to be 8 percent, its cost of equity is estimated to be 12 percent, and the decision has been made to finance next year's projects by selling debt. The argument is sometimes advanced that the cost of these projects is 8 percent because debt is being used to finance them. However, this position contains a basic fallacy. To finance a particular set of projects with debt implies that the firm is also using up some of its potential for obtaining new low-cost debt. As expansion occurs in subsequent years, the firm will find it necessary at some point to use additional equity financing to keep the debt ratio from becoming too large.

To illustrate: The firm in our example has an 8 percent cost of debt and a 12 percent cost of equity. In the first year it borrows heavily, using up its debt capacity in the process, to finance projects yielding 9 percent. In the second year it has projects available that yield 11 percent (well above the return on first-year projects), but it cannot accept them because they will have to be financed with 12 percent equity money. To avoid this problem, the firm should view itself as an ongoing concern, and its cost of capital should be calculated as a weighted average, or composite, of the various types of funds it uses: debt, preferred stock, and common equity.

Basic Definitions

Both students and financial managers are often confused about how to calculate and use the cost of capital. To a large extent, this confusion results from imprecise, ambiguous definitions; but a careful study of the following definitions will eliminate the confusion.

Capital (or financial) *components* are the items on the right-hand side of the balance sheet; they include various types of debt, preferred stock, and common equity. Any net increase in assets must be financed by an increase in one or more capital components.

Capital is a necessary factor of production; like any other factor, it has a cost. The cost of each component is defined as its *component cost.* For example, if a firm can borrow money at 8 percent, by definition, its component cost of debt is 8 percent.[2] This chapter will concentrate primarily on debt, preferred stock, retained earnings, and new issues of common stock. These are the capital structure components, and their component costs are identified by the following symbols:

k_b = Interest rate on firm's new debt = Component cost of debt, before tax

$k_b(1 - T)$ = Component cost of debt, after tax, where T = Marginal tax rate; $k_b(1 - T)$ = debt cost used to calculate the marginal cost of capital

2. We will see later that there is an after-tax cost of debt; for now it is sufficient to know that 8 percent is the before-tax component cost of debt. (The effects of debt on the cost of equity will also be considered later.)

k_{ps} = Component cost of preferred stock

k_r = Component cost of retained earnings (or internal equity)

k_e = Component cost of new issues of common stock (or external equity)

k_s = Required rate of return on common equity in general when no distinction is made between k_e and k_r, or when k_s represents a weighted average of incremental funds raised from retained earnings and from external equity

k = Weighted or composite cost of capital. If a firm raises new capital to finance asset expansion, and if it is to keep its capital structure in balance (that is, if it is to keep the same percentage of debt, preferred stock, and common equity funds), then it will raise part of new funds as debt, part as preferred stock, and part as common equity (with equity coming either from retained earnings or from the sale of new common stock).[3] Also, k is a marginal cost; it is the ratio of incremental financing costs to incremental funds raised per time period to finance an investment program[4]

These definitions and concepts are explained in detail in the remainder of the chapter, which seeks to accomplish two goals: (1) to develop a marginal cost of capital schedule (k = MCC) that can be used in capital budgeting, and (2) to determine the mix of types of capital that will minimize the MCC schedule. If the firm finances so as to minimize its MCC, uses this MCC to calculate NPV's, and makes capital budgeting decisions on the basis of the NPV method, these actions will lead to a maximization of the prices of its securities.

Before-Tax Component Cost of Debt (k_b)

If a firm borrows \$100,000 for one year at 10 percent interest, it must pay the investors who purchase the debt a total of \$10,000 annual interest on their investment:

$$k_b = \text{Before-tax cost of debt} = \frac{\text{Interest}}{\text{Principal}} = \frac{\$10{,}000}{\$100{,}000} = 10\%. \quad (16.1)$$

For now, assume that the firm pays no corporate income tax (the effect of income taxes on the analysis of cost of capital is treated in a later section of the chapter). Under this assumption, the firm's dollar interest cost is \$10,000, and its percentage cost of debt is 10 percent. As a first approximation, the compo-

3. Firms do try to keep their debt, preferred stock, and common equity in balance; they do not try to maintain any proportional relationship between the common stock and retained earnings accounts as shown on the balance sheet.

4. As discussed in Chapter 14, k also reflects the riskiness of the firm's various assets. If a firm uses risk-adjusted discount rates for different capital projects, the average of these rates weighted by the sizes of the various investments should equal k.

nent cost of debt is equal to the rate of return earned by investors, or the interest rate on debt.[5] If the firm borrows and invests the borrowed funds to earn a return just equal to the interest rate, then the earnings available to common stock remain unchanged.[6] This is demonstrated below.

The ABC Company has sales of $1 million, operating costs of $900,000, and no debt. Its income statement is shown in the Before column of Table 16.1. The firm borrows $100,000 at 10 percent and invests the funds in assets whose use causes sales to rise by $14,000 and operating costs to rise by $4,000. Hence, profits before interest rise by $10,000. The new situation is shown in the After column. Earnings are unchanged, since the investment just earns its component cost of capital. Note that the cost of debt applies to new debt, not to the interest of any previously outstanding debt. In other words,

5. The cost of convertible debt is slightly more complicated, but it can be calculated using the following formula:

$$M = \sum_{t=1}^{N} \frac{c}{(1 + k_c)^t} + \frac{tv}{(1 + k_c)^N},$$

where:
M = Price of the convertible bond
c = Annual interest in dollars
tv = Expected terminal value of the bond in Year N
N = Expected number of years the bond will be outstanding
k_c = Required rate of return on the convertible

The risk to an investor holding a convertible is somewhat higher than that on a straight bond but somewhat less than that on common stock. Accordingly, the cost of convertibles is generally between that on bonds and that on stock. (This concept is discussed in detail in Chapter 22.) Note also that the after-tax cost of a convertible can be found as k_c in the equation, but in that case c would be multiplied by $(1 - T)$, where T is the marginal corporate tax rate.

6. Note that this definition is a *first approximation;* it is modified later to take account of the deductibility of interest payments for income tax purposes. Note also that here the cost of debt is considered in isolation. The impact of debt on the cost of equity, as well as on future increments of debt, is treated when the weighted cost of a combination of debt and equity is derived. Finally, flotation costs, or the costs of selling the debt, are ignored. Flotation costs for debt issues are generally quite low; in fact, most debt is placed directly with banks, insurance companies, pension funds, and the like and involves no flotation costs. If flotation costs are not involved, the cost of debt can be approximated by the following equation:

$$k_b = \frac{c_t + \dfrac{M - p_b}{N}}{\dfrac{M + p_b}{2}},$$

where:
c_t = Periodic interest payment in dollars
M = Par or maturity value of the bond
p_b = Bond's issue price (Hence $M - p_b$ is the premium or discount)
N = Life of the bond

The equation is an approximation, as it does not consider compounding effects. However, the approximation is quite close; for example, with a 5 percent, twenty-five-year, $1,000 par value bond sold at $980, the formula gives k_b = 5.13 versus 5.15 as found from a bond table.

Table 16.1

Income Statement for the ABC Company

	Before	After
Sales	$1,000,000	$1,014,000
Operating costs	900,000	904,000
Earnings before interest	$ 100,000	$ 110,000
Interest	—	10,000
Earnings	$ 100,000	$ 100,000

we are interested in the cost of new debt, or the marginal cost of debt. The primary concern with the cost of capital is its use in a decision-making process—the decision whether to obtain capital to make new investments. Whether the firm borrowed at high or low rates in the past is irrelevant.[7]

Thus far we have used debt with a maturity of one year to focus on the basic concepts. But for multiple years, the yield to maturity is the basis for calculating the relevant cost of debt. As a practical matter, we could look in the financial section of a newspaper to obtain the coupon, maturity, and current price for a bond. For example, on February 5, 1980, Dow Chemical's 7.75% coupon bonds with a maturity date in 1999 closed at 72⅞. The yield to maturity (with compounding semiannually) would be:

$$\$728.75 = \sum_{t=1}^{38} \frac{\$38.75}{(1 + k_b)^t} + \frac{\$1,000}{(1 + k_b)^{38}}$$

$$= \sum_{t=1}^{38} \frac{\$38.75}{(1.05615)^t} + \frac{\$1,000}{(1.05615)^{38}}$$

$$= 603.55 + 125.44$$

$$\$728.75 \cong \$728.99.$$

The 5.615 percent was obtained by trial and error as the half-year interest rate that equates the present value of the coupons plus the maturity value to the current price of the bond. Thus the cost of nineteen-year maturity debt of Dow Chemical in early 1980 was 11.23 percent (that is, 5.615 percent times 2). An average over all long-term maturities would be the cost of long-term debt. Since Dow's long-term debt is rated mostly Aa quality, its cost of short-term debt would be based on the bank prime rate (at 15¼ percent on February 5, 1980) or the yield on four-month prime commercial paper (at 13.03 on February 1, 1980).

7. Whether the firm borrowed at high or low rates in the past is, of course, important in terms of the effect of the interest charges on current profits, but it is not relevant for current decisions. For current financial decisions, only current interest rates are relevant.

Preferred Stock

Preferred stock, described in detail in Chapter 20, is a hybrid between debt and common stock. Like debt, preferred stock carries a fixed commitment on the part of the corporation to make periodic payments; and in liquidation the claims of the preferred stockholders take precedence over those of the common stockholders. Failure to make the preferred dividend payments does not result in bankruptcy, however, as does nonpayment of interest on bonds. Thus, to the firm, preferred stock is somewhat more risky than common stock but less risky than bonds. Just the reverse holds for investors. To the investor, preferred is less risky than common but more risky than bonds. Thus an investor who is willing to buy the firm's bonds on the basis of a 10 percent interest return might, because of risk aversion, be unwilling to purchase the firm's preferred stock at a yield of less than 11 percent.[8] Assuming the preferred issue is a perpetuity that sells for $75 a share and pays an $8 annual dividend, its yield is calculated as follows:

$$\text{Preferred yield} = \frac{\text{Preferred dividend}}{\text{Price of preferred stock}} = \frac{d_{ps}}{p_{ps}} = \frac{\$8}{\$75} = 10.67\%. \quad (16.2)$$

Assuming the firm can sell additional preferred stock on the same yield basis, the cost of preferred is also 10.67 percent. In other words, as a first approximation, the component cost of preferred stock *(k_{ps})* is equal to the return investors receive on the shares as calculated in Equation 16.2.

If the firm receives less than the market price of preferred stock when it sells new preferred, p_{ps} in the denominator of Equation 16.2 should be the net price received by the firm. Suppose, for example, the firm must incur a selling, or *flotation,* cost of $3 a share. In other words, buyers of the preferred issue pay $75 a share, but brokers charge a selling commission of $3 a share, so the firm nets $72 a share. The cost of new preferred to the firm is calculated in Equation 16.2a:

$$k_{ps} = \text{Cost of preferred} = \frac{d_{ps}}{p_{ps}} = \frac{\$8}{\$72} = 11.11\%. \quad (16.2a)$$

Using the net proceeds percentage, calculated by deducting the ratio of flotation costs to gross proceeds, the same result is obtained.

$$k_{ps} = \text{Cost of preferred} = \frac{\text{Preferred yield}}{(1 - \text{Flotation cost})}$$

$$= \frac{10.67\%}{(1 - 0.04)} = 11.11\%. \quad (16.2b)$$

8. The 85 percent dividend credit (discussed in Chapter 3) makes preferred stock an attractive investment to other corporations, such as commercial banks and stock insurance companies. This pushes the yield down close to yields on bonds of similar companies.

Most preferred stocks entitle their owners to regular, fixed dividend payments similar to bond interest. Although some preferred issues are eventually retired, most are perpetuities whose value is found as follows:

$$p_{ps} = \frac{d_{ps}}{k_{ps}}.$$

In this case, d_{ps} is the dividend on the preferred stock, and k_{ps} is the appropriate capitalization rate for investments of this degree of risk. For example, General Motors has a preferred stock outstanding that pays a \$3.75 annual dividend. The average annual yield on preferred stock in late 1946, when the stock was issued, was 3.79 percent. The GM preferred stock was a no par stock that sold at 100 to yield 3.75 percent at the issue date. Preferred stock yields during March 1977 averaged 7.14 percent. On April 21, 1977, the \$3.75 preferred stock of General Motors closed at \$52. The yield on a preferred stock is similar to that on a perpetual bond and is found by solving for k_{ps}. For the GM issue, the price of the stock for February 5, 1980, in newspaper market quotations was \$37.25, and its annual dividend is seen to be \$3.75. Thus the yield is 10.0671 percent, calculated as follows:

$$k_{ps} = \frac{d_{ps}}{p_{ps}} = \frac{\$3.75}{\$37.25} = 10.0671\%.$$

The valuation relationship expressed for k_{ps} is also implied. If we know the promised dividend payment on the preferred stock and its current yield, we can determine its value:

$$p_{ps} = \frac{\$3.75}{0.100671} = \$37.25.$$

Tax Adjustment

As they stand, the definitions of the *component costs of debt* and of *preferred stock* are incompatible when taxes are introduced into the analysis, because interest payments are a deductible expense, whereas preferred dividends are not. The following example illustrates the point.

The ABC Company can borrow \$100,000 at 10 percent, or it can sell 1,000 shares of \$10 preferred stock to net \$100 a share. Assuming a 46 percent tax rate, its before-investment situation is given in the Before column of Table 16.2. At what rate of return must the company invest the proceeds from the new financing to keep the earnings available to common shareholders from changing?

As can be seen from the tabulations in Table 16.2, if the funds are invested to yield 10 percent before taxes, earnings available to common stockholders are constant if debt is used, but they decline if the financing is with preferred stock. To maintain the \$54,000 net earnings requires that funds generated

Table 16.2

Tax Adjustment for Cost of Debt

		Invest in Assets Yielding:		
		10%	10%	18.519%
	Before	Debt	Preferred	Preferred
Earnings before interest and taxes (EBIT)	\$100,000	\$110,000	\$110,000	\$118,519
Interest	—	−10,000	—	—
Earnings before taxes (EBT)	\$100,000	\$100,000	\$110,000	\$118,519
Taxes (at 46%) *(T)*	−46,000	−46,000	−50,600	−54,519
Preferred dividends	—	—	−10,000	−10,000
Available for common dividends	\$ 54,000	\$ 54,000	\$ 49,400	\$ 54,000

from the sale of preferred stock be invested to yield 18.519 percent before taxes or 10 percent after taxes.[9]

Since stockholders are concerned with after-tax rather than before-tax earnings, only the cost of capital *after* corporate taxes should be used. The cost of preferred stock is already on an after-tax basis as defined, but a simple adjustment is needed to arrive at the after-tax cost of debt. It is recognized that interest payments are tax deductible. In effect, the federal government pays part of a firm's interest charges. Therefore, the cost of debt capital is calculated as follows:

$$\begin{aligned} k_b(1 - T) &= \text{After-tax cost of debt} \\ &= \text{Before-tax cost} \times (1.0 - \text{Tax rate}). \end{aligned} \tag{16.3}$$

Whenever the weighted cost of capital *(k)* is calculated, $k_b\ (1 - T)$—not k_b—is used.

Example. Before-tax cost of debt = 10 percent; tax rate = 46 percent. $k_b(1 - T)$ = after-tax cost = $(0.10)(1 - 0.46) = (0.10)(0.54) = 5.40$ percent.

Common Stock Returns and Valuation

While the same principles apply to the valuation of common stocks as to bonds or preferred stocks, two features make their analysis more difficult. First is the degree of certainty with which receipts can be forecast. For bonds and preferred stocks, this forecast presents little difficulty, since the interest payments or preferred dividends are known with relative certainty. However, in the case of common stocks, forecasting future earnings, dividends, and stock prices can be difficult. The second complicating feature is that, unlike interest and preferred dividends, common stock earnings and dividends are generally expected to grow, not remain constant. Hence, while standard an-

9. The 18.519 percent is found as follows: 10%/(1 − Tax rate) = 10%/0.54.

nuity formulas can be applied, more difficult conceptual schemes must also be used.

The price today of a share of common stock, p_0, depends on the return investors expect to receive if they buy the stock and the riskiness of these expected cash flows. The expected returns consist of two elements: (1) the dividend expected in each year *t*, defined as d_t, and (2) the price investors expect to receive when they sell the stock at the end of Year *N*, defined as p_n. The price includes the return of the original investment plus a capital gain (or minus a capital loss). If investors expect to hold the stock for one year, and if the stock price is expected to grow at the rate *g*, the valuation equation is:

$$p_0 = \frac{\text{Expected dividend} + \text{Expected price (Both at end of Year 1)}}{1.0 + \text{Required rate of return}}$$

$$= \frac{d_1 + p_1}{(1 + k_s)} = \frac{d_1 + p_0(1 + g)}{(1 + k_s)}, \qquad (16.4)$$

which results in Equation 16.5 after simplification.[10]

$$p_0 = \frac{d_1}{k_s - g}. \qquad (16.5)$$

Equations 16.4 and 16.5 represent the present value of the expected dividends and the year-end stock price, discounted at the required rate of return. Solving Equation 16.5 gives the expected or intrinsic price for the stock. To illustrate: Suppose you are thinking of buying a share of United Rubber common stock and holding it for one year. You note that United Rubber earned \$2.86 per share last year and paid a dividend of \$1.90. Earnings and dividends have been rising at about 5 percent a year, on the average, over the last ten to fifteen years, and you expect this growth to continue. Further, if earnings and dividends grow at the expected rate, you think the stock price will likewise grow by 5 percent a year.

The next step is to determine the required rate of return on United Rubber stock. The current rate of interest on U.S. Treasury securities, R_F, is about 9 percent. But United Rubber is clearly more risky than government securities. Competitors can erode the company's market; labor problems can disrupt operations; an economic recession can cause sales to fall below the breakeven point; auto sales can decline, pulling down United Rubber's own

10.

$$p_0 = \frac{d_1 + p_0(1 + g)}{(1 + k_s)}. \qquad (16.4)$$

$$p_0(1 + k_s) = d_1 + p_0(1 + g)$$

$$p_0(1 + k_s - 1 - g) = d_1$$

$$p_0(k_s - g) = d_1$$

$$p_0 = \frac{d_1}{k_s - g}. \qquad (16.5)$$

Notice that this equation is developed for a one-year holding period. In a later section, we will show that it is also valid for longer periods, provided the expected growth rate is constant.

sales and profits; and so on. Further, even if sales, earnings, and dividends meet projections, the stock price can still fall as a result of a generally weak market.

Given all these risk factors, you conclude that a 7 percent risk premium is justified, so you calculate your required rate of return on United Rubber's stock, k_s^*, as follows:

$$k_s^* = R_F + \rho = 9\% + 7\% = 16\%.$$

Next, you estimate the dividend for the coming year, d_1, as follows:

$$d_1 = d_0(1 + g) = \$1.90\ (1.05) = \$2.$$

Now you have the necessary information to estimate the fair value of the stock by the use of Equation 16.6:

$$p_0 = \frac{d_1}{k_s^* - g} \qquad (16.6)$$

$$= \frac{\$2}{0.16 - 0.05} = \$18.18.$$

To you, \$18.18 represents a reasonable price for United Rubber's stock. If the actual market price is less, you will buy it; if the actual price is higher, you will not buy it, or you will sell if you own it.[11]

Estimating the Rate of Return on a Stock

In the preceding section we calculated the expected price of United Rubber's stock to a given investor. Let us now change the procedure somewhat and calculate the rate of return you can expect if you purchase the stock at the current market price per share. The expected rate of return, defined as $\bar{k}_s$, is analogous to the internal rate of return on a capital project: $\bar{k}_s$ is the discount rate that equates the present value of the expected dividends, d_1, and the final stock price, p_1, to the present stock price, p_0:

$$p_0 = \frac{d_1 + p_1}{(1 + \bar{k}_s)} = \frac{d_1 + p_0(1 + g)}{(1 + \bar{k}_s)}.$$

If United Rubber is selling for \$20 per share, you can calculate $\bar{k}_s$ as follows:

$$\$20 = \frac{\$2 + \$20(1.05)}{(1 + \bar{k}_s)} = \frac{\$2 + \$21}{(1 + \bar{k}_s)}$$

11. Notice the similarity between this process and the NPV method of capital budgeting described in Chapter 13. In the earlier chapter, we (1) estimated a cost of capital for the firm, which compares with estimating k_s^*, our required rate of return; (2) discounted expected future cash flows, which are analogous to dividends plus the future stock price; (3) found the present value of future cash flows, which corresponds to the fair value of the stock; (4) determined the initial outlay for the project, which compares with finding the actual price of the stock; and (5) accepted the project if the PV of future cash flows exceeded the initial cost of the project, which is similar to comparing the fair value of the stock to its market price.

$$\$20(1+\bar{k}_s) = \$23$$
$$1+\bar{k}_s = 1.15$$
$$\bar{k}_s = 0.15 \text{ or } 15\%.$$

Thus, if you expect to receive a $2 dividend and a year-end price of $21, your expected rate of return on the investment is 15 percent.

Notice that the expected rate of return, $\bar{k}_s$, consists of two components, an expected dividend yield and an expected capital gains yield:

$$\bar{k}_s = \frac{\text{Expected dividend}}{\text{Present price}} + \frac{\text{Expected increase in price}}{\text{Present price}} = \frac{d_1}{p_0} + g. \tag{16.7}$$

For United Rubber bought at a price of $20:

$$\bar{k}_s = \frac{\$2}{\$20} + \frac{\$1}{\$20} = 10\% + 5\% = 15\%.$$

Given an expected rate of return of 15 percent, should you make the purchase? This depends on how the expected return compares with the required return. If $\bar{k}_s$ exceeds k_s^*, buy; if $\bar{k}_s$ is less than k_s^*, sell; and if $\bar{k}_s$ equals k_s^*, the stock price is in equilibrium and you should be indifferent. In this case, your 16 percent required rate of return for United Rubber exceeds the 15 percent expected return, so you should not buy the stock.[12] This decision was already evident in the $18.18 value you calculated for the stock, which is less than the $20 market price.

Cost of Retained Earnings (k_r)[13]

The cost of preferred stock is based on the return that investors require if they are to purchase the preferred stock; the cost of debt is based on the interest rate investors require on debt issues, adjusted for taxes. The cost of equity obtained by retained earnings can be defined similarly. It is k_r, the rate

12. Notice the similarity between this process and the IRR method of capital budgeting. The expected rate of return, $\bar{k}_S$, corresponds to the IRR on a project, and the required rate of return, k_S^*, corresponds to the cost-of-capital cutoff rate used in capital budgeting.

13. The term *retained earnings* can be interpreted to mean the balance sheet item "retained earnings," consisting of all the earnings retained in the business throughout its history; or it can mean the income statement item "additions to retained earnings." The latter definition is used in this chapter. For our purpose, *retained earnings* refers to that part of current earnings not paid out in dividends but retained and reinvested in the business.

Equity is defined in this chapter to *exclude* preferred stock. Equity is the sum of capital stock, capital surplus, and accumulated retained earnings. Note that our treatment of the cost of retained earnings does not consider certain complications caused by personal income taxes on dividend income and by brokerage costs incurred in reinvesting dividend income. Similarly, we do not explicitly treat the cost of depreciation generated funds in the chapter. These topics are, however, treated in Appendix A to this chapter.

of return stockholders require on the firm's common stock. Why? The answer is that if the funds are invested at a lesser rate, the market price of the firm's stock will decline. We therefore substitute k_r into Equation 16.6, which becomes 16.6a.

$$p_0 = \frac{d_1}{k_r - g}. \tag{16.6a}$$

In equilibrium, the expected and required rates of return must be equal, so we can solve for k_r to obtain the required rate of return on common equity financed from retained earnings:

$$k_r = \frac{d_1}{p_0} + \text{Expected } g. \tag{16.7a}$$

To illustrate, we return to the United Rubber (UR) example, a firm expected to earn \$3 a share and to pay a \$2 dividend during the coming year. The company's earnings, dividends, and stock price have all been growing at about 5 percent a year, and this growth rate is expected to continue indefinitely. The stock is in equilibrium and currently sells for \$20 a share. Using this information, the required rate of return on the stock in equilibrium can be computed using Equation 16.7a.

$$k_r = \frac{\$2}{\$20} + 5\% = 15\%.$$

The expected growth rate for the price of the shares is 5 percent, which, on the \$20 initial price, should lead to a \$1 increase in the value of the stock, to \$21. Barring changes in the general level of stock prices, this price increase will be attained if UR invests the \$1 of retained earnings to yield 15 percent. However, if the \$1 is invested to yield only 10 percent, then earnings will grow by only 10 cents a share during the year, not by the expected 15 cents a share. The new earnings will be \$3.10, a growth of only 3.33 percent, rather than the expected \$3.15, or 5 percent increase. If investors believe that the firm will earn only 10 percent on retained earnings in the future and attain only a 3.33 percent growth rate, they will reappraise the value of the stock downward according to Equation 16.5:

$$p_0 = \frac{d_1}{k_r - g} = \frac{\$2}{0.15 - 0.0333} = \frac{\$2}{0.1167} = \$17.14.$$

Hence, UR will suffer a price decline if it invests equity funds—retained earnings—at less than its component cost of capital.

If UR refrains from making new investments and pays all its earnings in dividends, it will cut its growth rate to zero. However, the price of the stock will not fall because investors will still get the required 15 percent rate of return on their shares:

$$k_r = \frac{d_1}{p_0} + g = \frac{\$3}{\$20} + 0 = 15\%,$$

or

$$p_0 = \frac{\$3}{0.15 - 0} = \$20.$$

All the return would come in the form of dividends, but the actual rate of return would match the required 15 percent.

This example demonstrates a fundamentally important fact. If a firm earns its required rate of return, k_r, then when it retains earnings and invests them in its operations, its current stock price will not change as a result of this financing and investment. However, if it earns less than k_r, the stock price will fall; and if it earns more, the stock price will rise.

Cost of New Common Stock, or External Equity Capital (k_e)

The cost of new common stock, or *external* equity capital, k_e, is higher than the cost of retained earnings, k_r, because of flotation costs involved in selling new common stock. What rate of return must be earned on funds raised by selling stock to make the action worthwhile? To put it another way, what is the cost of new common stock? The answer is found by applying the following formula:

$$k_e = \frac{d_1}{p_0(1-f)} + g = \frac{d_1}{p_n} + g \qquad (16.8)$$

$$= \frac{\text{Dividend yield}}{1 - \text{Flotation percentage}} + \text{Growth.}^{14}$$

14. The equation is derived as follows:

Step 1. The old stockholders expect the firm to pay a stream of dividends, d_t; this income stream is derived from existing assets. New investors likewise expect to receive the same stream of dividends, d_t. For new investors to obtain this stream without impairing that of the old investors, the new funds obtained from the sale of stock must be invested at a return high enough to provide a dividend stream whose present value is equal to the price the firm receives:

$$p_n = \sum_{t=1}^{\infty} \frac{d_t}{(1 + k_e)^t}, \qquad (16.8a)$$

where:

p_n = Net price to the firm
d_t = Dividend stream to new stockholders
k_e = Cost of new outside equity

Step 2. If flotation costs are expressed as a percentage, f, of the gross price of the stock, p_0, we can express p_n as follows:

$$p_n = p_0(1 - f).$$

Step 3. When growth is a constant, Equation 16.8a reduces to

$$p_n = p_0(1 - f) = \frac{d_1}{k_e - g}. \qquad (16.8b)$$

Step 4. Equation 16.8b can be solved for k_e:

$$k_e = \frac{d_1}{p_0(1 - f)} + g. \qquad (16.8)$$

Here f is the percentage cost of selling the issue, so $p_0(1-f) = p_n$ is the net price received by the firm. For example, if p_0 is \$10 and f is 10 percent, then the firm receives \$9 for each new share sold; hence p_n is \$9. (Equations 16.7 and 16.8 are strictly applicable only if future growth is expected to be constant.)

For United Rubber, the cost of new outside equity is computed as follows:

$$k_e = \frac{\$2}{\$20(1-0.10)} + 5\% = 16.11\%.$$

Investors require a return of $k_r = 15$ percent on UR's stock. However, because of flotation costs, UR must earn *more* than 15 percent on external stock-financed investments to provide this 15 percent. Specifically, if UR earns 16.11 percent on investments financed by new common stock issues, then earnings per share will not fall below previously expected earnings, the expected dividend can be maintained, the growth rate for earnings and dividends will be maintained, and (as a result of all this) the price per share will not decline. If UR earns less than 16.11 percent, then earnings, dividends, and growth will fall below expectations, causing the price of the stock to decline. Since the cost of capital is *defined* as the rate of return that must be earned to prevent the price of the stock from falling, we see that the company's cost of external equity, k_e, is 16.11 percent.[15]

Finding the Basic Required Rate of Return on Common Equity

The basic rate of return investors require on a firm's common equity, k_s, is a key quantity. This required rate of return is the cost of retained earnings, and it forms the basis for the cost of capital obtained from new stock issues. How is it estimated?

Although complicated procedures for making this estimation can be used, satisfactory estimates can be obtained in any of three ways:

1. Estimate the security market line (SML). Estimate the relative riskiness of the firm in question; then use the estimate to obtain the required rate of return on the firm's stock:

$$k_s^* = R_F + \rho.$$

Under this procedure, the estimated cost of equity (k_s) will move up or down with changes in interest rates and in investor psychology.[16]

15. The cost of external equity is sometimes defined as:

$$k_e = \frac{k_r}{1-f}.$$

This equation is correct if the firm's expected growth rate is zero (see Equation 16.8). In other cases it tends to overstate k_e.

16. See Appendix C to this chapter for illustrations of the use of the capital asset pricing model in calculating the cost of capital for firms.

2. An alternative procedure, which should be used in conjunction with the one described above, is to estimate the basic required rate of return as follows:
   a. Assume that investors expect the past realized rate of return on the stock to be earned in the future, so the expected return is equal to $\bar{k}_s$.
   b. Assume that the stock is in equilibrium, with $k_s^* = \bar{k}_s$.
   c. Under these assumptions, the required rate of return can be estimated as equal to the past realized rate of return:

$$k_s^* = \bar{k}_s = \frac{d_1}{p_0} + \text{Past growth rate.}$$

   Stockholder returns are derived from dividends and capital gains, and the total of the dividend yield plus the average growth rate over the past five to ten years can give an estimate of the total returns that stockholders expect in the future from a particular share of stock.

3. For "normal" companies in "normal" times, past growth rates can be projected into the future, and the second method will give satisfactory results. However, if the company's growth has been abnormally high or low, either because of its own unique situation or because of general economic conditions, then investors will not project the past growth rate into the future, so Method 2 will not yield a good estimate of k_s^*. In this case, g must be estimated in some other manner. Security analysts regularly make earnings growth forecasts, looking at such factors as projected sales, profit margins, and competitive factors. Someone making a cost of capital estimate can obtain such analysts' forecasts and use them as a proxy for the growth expectations of investors in general, combine this g with the current dividend yield, and estimate $\bar{k}_s$ as

$$k_s^* = \frac{d_1}{p_0} + \text{Growth rate as projected by security analysts.}$$

   Again, note that this estimate of k_s^* is based on the assumption that g is expected to remain constant in the future.

Based on our own experience in estimating equity capital costs, we recognize that both careful analysis and very fine judgments are required in this process. It would be nice to pretend that these judgments are unnecessary and to specify an easy, precise way of determining the exact cost of equity capital. Unfortunately, this is not possible. Finance is in large part a matter of judgment, and we simply must face this fact. Also, because the total world market portfolio has not been identified and used in CAPM measurements, R. W. Roll cautions that precise return-risk relationships have not been established. See R. W. Roll, "A Critique of the Asset Pricing Theory's Tests," *Journal of Financial Economics,* 4 (March 1977), pp. 129–176.

The Effects of Leverage–the MM Propositions

Under a number of assumptions, Franco Modigliani and M. H. Miller (MM) have formulated some relationships between the cost of capital and capital structure.[17] The key assumptions are homemade leverage and no bankruptcy costs. Homemade leverage implies that personal and corporate leverage are perfect substitutes and that individuals can offset corporate leverage by personal leverage to eliminate any advantages (except corporate tax effects) of corporate leverage by arbitrage transactions. With no bankruptcy costs, firms can be formed, go bankrupt and be liquidated, be formed again, and so on, with very small transactions costs. Hence by diversification, investors can eliminate unsystematic risk, so that required returns will reflect only the systematic risk measured by covariance or the beta of the individual asset. A number of MM propositions then follow.[18]

Proposition I states that the cost of capital of an unlevered firm is the after-tax net operating income divided by the value of the unlevered firm.

$$k_u = \frac{\overline{X}(1 - T)}{V_u}. \tag{I}$$

It can also be shown that in the MM world, the following relationships hold.

$$V_L = V_u + TB \text{ and } S = V_L - B,$$

where B is the market value of the firm's debt.

It follows then, that the weighted cost of capital for a levered firm would be:

$$k = \frac{\overline{X}(1 - T)}{V_L}. \tag{Ia}$$

This is the same as Proposition I, except that the denominator is the value of the leveraged firm and the result is the weighted cost of capital. Proposition II, which can be derived from the foregoing, provides a measure of the cost of equity capital.

$$k_s = k_u + (k_u - k_b)(1 - T)B/S. \tag{II}$$

Proposition II states that the cost of equity rises with leverage in a linear fashion, with the slope of the line equal to $(k_u - k_b)(1 - T)$, as shown in Figure 16.1.

Finally, it can also be demonstrated that three formulations for measuring the weighted cost of capital give the same results. These are:

17. See F. Modigliani and M. H. Miller, "The Cost of Capital, Corporation Finance and the Theory of Investment," *American Economic Review* 48 (June 1958), pp. 261–297; and "The Cost of Capital, Corporation Finance and the Theory of Investment: Reply," *American Economic Review* 49 (September 1958), pp. 655–669; "Taxes and the Cost of Capital: A Correction," *American Economic Review* 53 (June 1963), pp. 433–443; and "Reply," *American Economic Review* 55 (June 1965), pp. 524–527.
18. Formal proofs of these propositions are presented in Appendix B to this chapter.

Figure 16.1

Cost of Equity Capital as a Function of Leverage

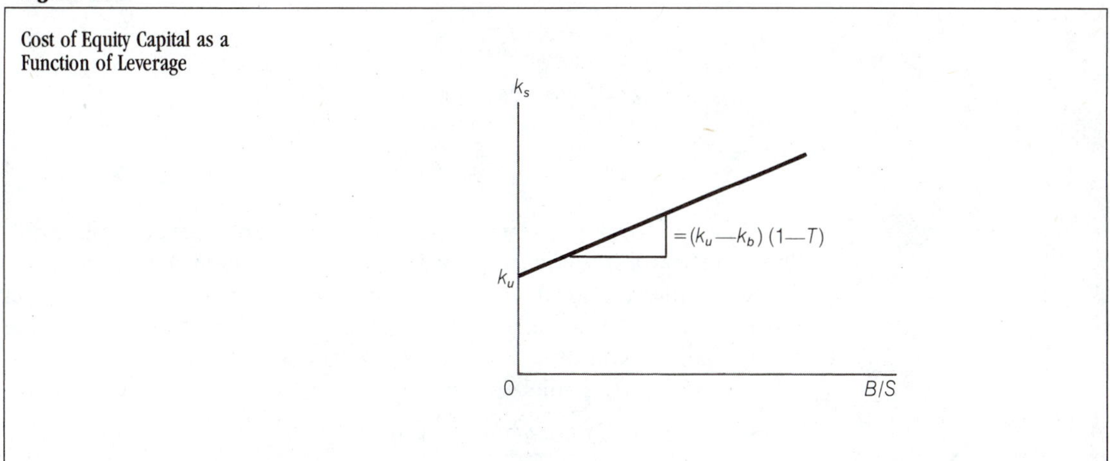

1. $k = k_b(1 - T)(B/V) + k_s(S/V)$
2. $k = \dfrac{\overline{X}(1 - T)}{V}$.
3. $k = k_u(1 - TL)$ where $L = B/V$.

(Note: From this point on, V is understood to be V_L, and the value of an unlevered firm will be designated V_u.)

We can give content to these relationships by an illustrative example. We consider two alternative capital structures for the Stevens Company:

Stevens Company, Balance Sheet, Unlevered

Total assets $1,000,000	Stockholders' equity $1,000,000

Stevens Company, Balance Sheet, Levered

Total assets $1,000,000	Debt at 10%	$ 500,000
	Stockholders' equity	500,000
	Total claims	$1,000,000

The applicable corporate tax rate is 40 percent. The income statements for Stevens would reflect the two different capital structures.

Stevens Company Income Statements

	Unlevered	Levered
Net operating income *(X)*	$200,000	$200,000
Interest on debt $(k_b B)$	—	50,000
Income before taxes $(X - k_b B)$	$200,000	$150,000
Taxes at 40% $T(X - k_b B)$	80,000	60,000
Net income $(X - k_b B)(1 - T)$	$120,000	$ 90,000

With the above accounting information, which represents data generally available in financial reports and financial manuals, we can apply the MM propositions. For an unlevered firm of similar characteristics to Stevens, we obtain a measure of the cost of capital for an unlevered firm, k_u, which we will assume to be 12 percent. All other relationships can now be computed.

Stevens' value as an unlevered firm would be:

$$V_u = \frac{\overline{X}(1 - T)}{k_u} = \frac{(\$200{,}000)0.6}{0.12} = \$1{,}000{,}000.$$

We find that without leverage, market value of Stevens is equal to the book value of its total assets. Next, consider Stevens as a levered firm. Its new value becomes:

$$V_L = V_u + TB = \$1{,}000{,}000 + 0.4(\$500{,}000) = \$1{,}200{,}000.$$

Now the market value of Stevens exceeds the book value of its total assets. The market value of the equity, *S*, is:

$$S = V_L - B = \$1{,}200{,}000 - \$500{,}000 = \$700{,}000.$$

The cost of equity capital of Stevens, unlevered, is equal to k_u, or 12 percent. As a levered firm, the cost of equity capital for Stevens can be calculated by two relationships:

$$k_s = k_u + (k_u - k_b)(1 - T)B/S \text{ or } k_s = \text{NI}/S.$$

The first formulation is MM's Proposition II. The second is a conventional accounting relationship. We illustrate both:

$$\begin{aligned} k_s &= 0.12 + (0.12 - 0.10)(0.6)(5/7) \\ &= 0.12 + 0.008571 \\ &= 12.8571\%. \end{aligned} \qquad \begin{aligned} k_s &= 90{,}000/700{,}000 \\ k_s &= 12.8571\%. \end{aligned}$$

The SML formulation of the cost of equity capital is:

$$k_s = R_F + (R_M - R_F)\beta_u[1 + (B/S)(1 - T)].$$

(Recall from Chapter 15 that $\beta_u[1 + (B/S)(1 - T)] = \beta_L$.)

For the Stevens example, let

$$R_F = 0.10, R_M = 0.115, \text{ and } \beta_u = 1.3333.$$

We then have:

$$k_s = 0.10 + (0.115 - 0.10)1.3333[1 + (5/7)(0.6)] = 0.128571 = 12.8571\%.$$

With leverage, the cost of equity capital has risen from 12 percent to 12.86 percent. What happens to the weighted cost of capital? We can employ all three formulations:

1. $k = k_b(1 - T)(B/V) + k_s(S/V)$ $\quad k = 0.10(0.6)(5/12) + 0.128571(7/12)$
$\quad k = 0.025 + 0.075 = 10\%.$

2. $k = \dfrac{\overline{X}(1 - T)}{V_L}$ $\quad k = \dfrac{120{,}000}{1{,}200{,}000} = 10\%.$

3. $k = k_u(1 - TL)$ $\quad k = 0.12[1 - 0.4(5/12)] = 0.12(5/6)$
$\quad k = 10\%.$

Each formulation gives a weighted cost of capital of 10 percent. The example illustrates that the use of leverage has increased the value of the firm from \$1,000,000 to \$1,200,000. The weighted cost of capital has been reduced from 12 percent to 10 percent. Thus under the MM propositions, the influence of the tax subsidy on debt is to increase the value of the firm and decrease its weighted cost of capital.

We believe that these kinds of results are applicable to the real world for companies like Kellogg and IBM, which until recent years had virtually no debt in their capital structures. With the relatively small fraction of total assets now represented by debt, this is still relatively non-risky debt. For the amount of debt financing that they have employed to date, the effects predicted by the MM propositions could be expected to hold. But when companies have leverage ratios with debt of one-half or more of total market value, the possibilities of bankruptcy costs are likely to result in some increase in the cost of debt and a rise in the cost of equity that is not linear but curved upward—increasing at an increasing rate as leverage is perceived to add to risks of bankruptcy costs and losses.

The Nature of Bankruptcy Costs

Bankruptcy costs take several forms. The most obvious are the legal, accounting, and other administrative costs associated with financial readjustments and legal proceedings. In addition to these direct costs, some costs of bankruptcy arise before the actual legal procedures of bankruptcy take place. As the operating performance of the firm deteriorates in relation to its fixed contractual obligations, or as the amount of debt increases in relation to the firm's equity for a given level of operating performance, the financial markets may become increasingly reluctant to provide additional financing. While these conditions deteriorate, a number of costs arise as a result of different degrees of financial inadequacy or failure on the part of the firm. These costs, in order of seriousness, include the following:

1. Financing under increasingly onerous terms, conditions, and rates, representing increased costs.
2. Loss of key employees. If the firm's prospects are unfavorable, able employees and executives will seek alternative employment.
3. Loss of suppliers of the most salable types of goods. The suppliers may fear that they will not be paid or that the customer will not achieve sales growth in the future.
4. Loss of sales that comes from lack of confidence on the part of customers that the firm will be around to stand behind the product.
5. Lack of financing under any terms, conditions, and rates to carry out favorable but risky investments because the overall prospects of the firm are not favorable in relation to its existing obligations.
6. Need to liquidate fixed assets to meet working capital requirements (forced reduction in the scale of operations).
7. Formal bankruptcy proceedings, with the incurrence of legal and administrative costs. In addition, a receiver will be appointed to conduct the firm's operations, and this may involve a disruption of operations.

It is therefore clear that when indirect as well as direct bankruptcy costs are taken into account, they may be substantial. The costs of building up new organizations after old ones have been broken up represent substantial transactions costs in the creation and destruction of organizations.

Thus, we believe that the MM world applies for moderate amounts of leverage. However, we shall indicate how increased leverage is likely to cause departures from the MM relations. We present a further basis for this view in the following section.

Effects of Risky Leverage with Bankruptcy Costs

Effect of Leverage on the Cost of Equity

In Chapter 15, we used the Universal Machine Company case to demonstrate that for any given degree of business risk, the higher the debt ratio, the larger the measures of variability in earnings per share and return on equity. The higher the level of debt, the higher the fixed charges and the higher the probability of not being able to cover them. The inability to meet fixed charges may trigger a number of penalty clauses in the debt indentures (agreements) and lead to reorganization or bankruptcy (see Chapter 24), with attendant costs of attorneys and court proceedings. Even before such legal difficulties, the increasing risk of financial difficulties may result in the loss of key employees (who find positions with firms whose financial outlook is safer), in the reduced availability of goods from key suppliers, and in reduced financing.

The existence of substantial bankruptcy costs causes the relationship between leverage and the related risks of equity and debt to become curvilinear upward, thereby increasing the required returns on equity and debt. In this section we will analyze the effect of required returns on equity. Accordingly,

Table 16.3

Leverage, Risk Indexes, and the Required Rates of Return on Equity for Universal Machine Company

Leverage: (Debt/Equity) B/S	Without Bankruptcy Penalties[a] ρ_1^*	ρ_2^*	With Bankruptcy Penalties[b] ρ_1	ρ_2	Required Return on Equity Without Bankruptcy Penalties[c]	With Bankruptcy Penalties[d]
0	6%	0%	6%	0%	12.00	12.00
0.25	6	0.75	6	0.75	12.75	12.75
0.43	6	1.29	6	1.29	13.29	13.29
0.67	6	2.01	6	3.51	14.01	15.51
1.00	6	3.00	6	6.00	15.00	18.00
1.50	6	4.50	6	11.86	16.50	23.86
4.00	6	12.00	6	33.54	24.00	45.54

a. The columns are calculated as follows:

$R_F = 0.06$; $(R_M - R_F) = 0.05$; $\beta_u = 1.2$; $T = 0.5$; $\rho_1^* = \beta_u(R_M - R_F)$; $\rho_2^* = (B/S)(1 - T)\rho_1^*$.

b. Calculations: This procedure involves modifying on a judgmental basis the basic equation for the relationship between the levered beta and the unlevered beta:

$$\rho_1 = \beta_u(R_M - R_F).$$

For ρ_2 we have:
- $B/S \leq 0.43$ $\quad \rho_2 = (B/S)(1 - T)\,\rho_1$.
- $B/S = 0.67$ $\quad \rho_2 = (0.5 + B/S)(1 - T)\,\rho_1$.
- $B/S = 1.00$ $\quad \rho_2 = (1 + B/S)(1 - T)\,\rho_1$.
- $B/S = 1.50$ $\quad \rho_2 = (1 + B/S)^{1.5}(1 - T)\,\rho_1$.
- $B/S = 4.00$ $\quad \rho_2 = (1 + B/S)^{1.5}(1 - T)\,\rho_1$.

c. Calculations: $6\% + \rho_1^* + \rho_2^*$.

d. Calculations: $6\% + \rho_1 + \rho_2$.

the relationship between leverage and the required rates of return can be as set forth in Table 16.3.

In Chapter 15 we indicated that the required rate of return consisted of the riskless rate plus a risk premium: $k_s = R_F + \rho$. Here we divide ρ into two components, ρ_1, a premium for business risk, and ρ_2, a premium required to compensate equity investors for the additional risk brought on by financial leverage. Expressed as an equation:

$$k_s = R_F + \rho_1 + \rho_2. \tag{16.9}$$

The riskless rate of return, R_F, is a function of general economic conditions, Federal Reserve policy, and the like. The premium for business risk, ρ_1, is a function of the nature of the firm's industry, its degree of operating leverage, its diversification, and so on. Financial risk, ρ_2, depends on the degree of financial leverage employed.[19]

In Table 16.3 we illustrate how the magnitudes of business and financial risk can be measured in relation to leverage and then indicate their plausible impact on the required rates of return on equity.[20] The calculations of ρ_1^* and

19. The value of ρ_2 increases at an increasing rate with leverage because bankruptcy, as opposed to lower earnings, becomes an increasing threat as the debt ratio rises; and bankruptcy may have high costs of its own (see Chapter 24).

20. Keep in mind that throughout this analysis we are holding constant the firm's assets and the EBIT on these assets. We wish to consider the effect of leverage on the cost of capital *holding other things constant.*

ρ_2^* are based on the assumptions of no substantial bankruptcy costs. The expression ρ_1^* is simply the beta of an unlevered firm multiplied by the market risk premium, and ρ_2^* is ρ_1^* multiplied by *B/S,* as measured in Chapter 15 times $(1 - T)$.

With bankruptcy costs, however, the indexes of financial risk are likely to increase at an increasing rate when leverage passes some critical point and become curvilinear upward as measured in Table 16.3, which is also graphed in Figure 16.2. The required rate of return on equity is 12 percent if the company uses no debt, but k_s^* increases after debt passes some critical level and is 23.86 percent if the debt to value ratio is as high as 60 percent.[21] With leverage beyond 60 percent, it is likely that the required cost of equity is so high that the funds for all practical purposes are not available.

Figure 16.2

Illustrative Relationship between the Cost of Equity and Financial Leverage

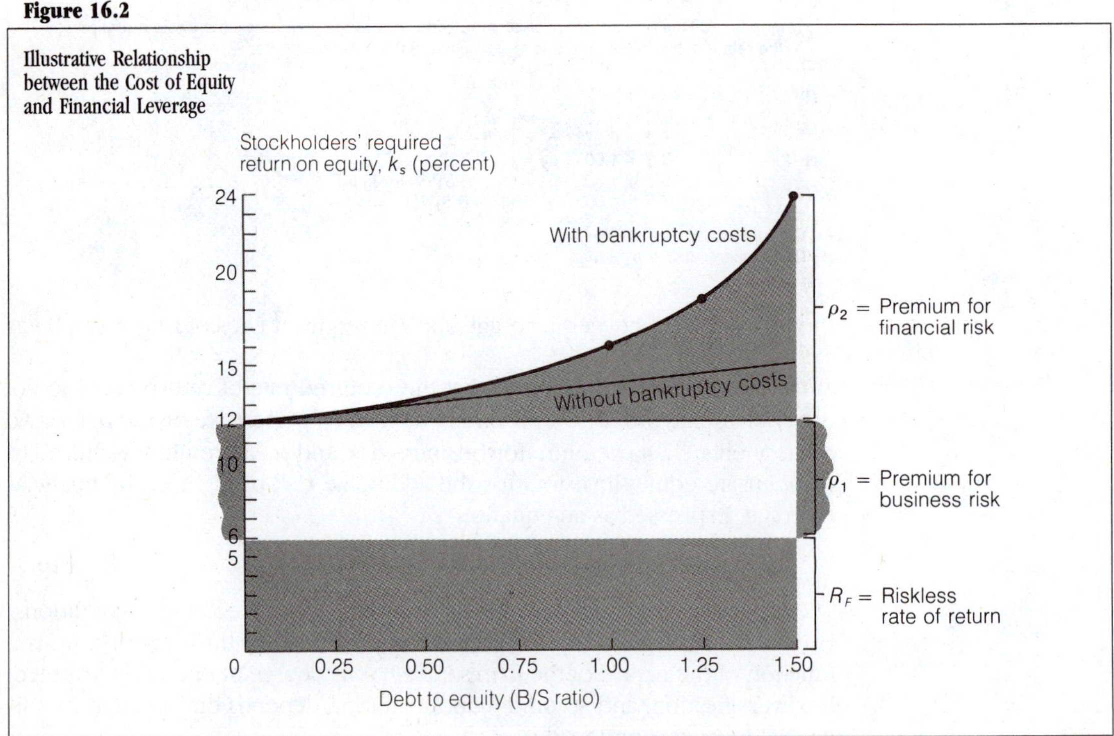

21. This corresponds to a debt to equity ratio of 150 percent. In this example we assume that the risk-return trade-off function has been estimated, perhaps in a subjective manner, by the financial manager. The precise specification of such risk-return functions is one of the more controversial areas of finance, and having attempted to measure them empirically ourselves, we can attest to the difficulties involved. However, even though the precise shape of the function is open to question, it is generally agreed (1) that the curve is upward sloping and (2) that some estimate, be it better or worse, is necessary if we are to obtain a cost of capital for use in capital budgeting. In this chapter our main concern is that the broad concepts be grasped.

Effect of Leverage on the Component Cost of Debt

The component cost of debt is also affected by leverage. The higher the leverage ratio, the higher the cost of debt. Further, the cost of debt can be expected to rise at an increasing rate with leverage. To see why this is so, we can again consider the Universal Machine Company example. The more debt the firm has, the higher the interest requirements; and the higher the interest charges, the greater the probability that earnings (EBIT) will not be sufficient to meet these charges. Creditors will perceive this increasing risk as the debt ratio rises, and they will begin charging a higher risk premium above the riskless rate, causing the firm's interest rate to rise. (Since creditors are risk averters and are assumed to have a diminishing marginal utility for money, they will demand that interest rates be increased to compensate for the increased risk.)

One other effect that may operate to raise interest rates at an increasing rate is the fact that a firm may need to use a variety of sources in order to borrow large amounts of funds in relation to its equity base. For example, a firm may be able to borrow from banks only up to some limit set by bank policy or bank examiner regulations. In order to increase its borrowings, the firm will have to seek other institutions, such as insurance companies and finance companies, that may demand higher interest rates than those charged by banks. Such an effect may tend to cause interest rates to jump whenever the firm is forced to find new lenders.

Table 16.4 shows the estimated relationships among leverage, the interest rate, and the after-tax cost of debt for Universal Machine Company. Assuming a 50 percent tax rate, the after-tax cost of debt is half the interest rate; these figures are also shown in Figure 16.3, where they are plotted against the debt ratio. In the example, Universal's cost of debt is constant until the debt to assets ratio passes 20 percent or $2 million; then it begins to climb.

Table 16.4

Effect of Leverage on the Cost of Debt for Universal Machine Company

Leverage (Debt/Assets)	Interest Rate (k_b)	After-Tax Cost of Debt $k_b(1-T)$
0%	10.0%	5.0%
10	10.0	5.0
20	10.0	5.0
30	10.8	5.4
35	11.0	5.5
40	13.0	6.5
50	16.0	8.0
60	27.0	13.5

Figure 16.3

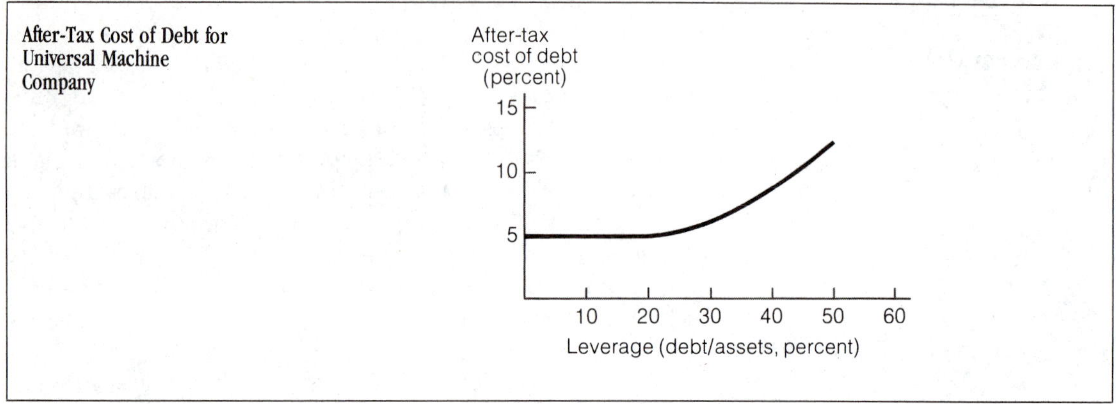

After-Tax Cost of Debt for Universal Machine Company

Combining Debt and Equity: Weighted Average, or Composite, Cost of Capital

Debt and equity can be combined to determine Universal Machine's average, or composite, cost of capital; Table 16.5 shows the calculations used to determine the weighted average cost. We shall assume conditions under which the cost of equity rises curvilinearly with leverage and the cost of debt is not constant. The average cost, together with the component cost of debt and equity, is plotted against the debt ratio at market value in Figure 16.4. Here the composite cost of capital is minimized when its debt ratio is approximately 35 percent, so Universal's optimal capital structure calls for about 35 percent debt and 65 percent equity.

Note that the average cost of capital curve is relatively flat over a fairly broad range. If Universal Machine's debt ratio is in the range of 20 to 40 percent, the average cost of capital cannot be lowered very much by moving to the optimal point. This appears to be a fairly typical situation, since almost any "reasonable" schedule for the component costs of debt and equity will produce a saucer-shaped average cost of capital schedule similar to that shown in Figure 16.4. This gives financial managers a large degree of flexibility in planning their financing programs, permitting them to sell debt one year and equity the next in order to take advantage of capital market conditions and to avoid high flotation costs associated with small security issues.

Table 16.5 and Figure 16.4 are based on the assumption that the firm is planning to raise a given amount of new capital during the year. For a larger or smaller amount of new capital, some other cost figures may be applicable; the optimal capital structure may call for a different debt ratio, and the minimum average cost of capital *(k)* may be higher or lower.

Since interest on debt is deductible for tax purposes, the use of debt provides a tax shelter for some of the firm's cash flows. Hence the value of a firm

Table 16.5

Calculation of Points on Average Cost of Capital Curve (Percent), or the Composite Cost of Capital for Different Capital Structures for Universal Machine Company

	Percent of Total (1)	Component Costs (2)	Weighted, or Composite, Cost: $k = (1) \times (2) \div 100$ (3)[a]
Debt	0	5.00	0.0
Equity	100	12.00	12.0
	100		12.0
Debt	10	5.00	0.5
Equity	90	12.30	11.1
	100		11.6
Debt	20	5.00	1.0
Equity	80	12.75	10.2
	100		11.2
Debt	30	5.40	1.6
Equity	70	13.29	9.3
	100		10.9
Debt	35	5.50	1.9
Equity	65	13.50	8.8
	100		10.7
Debt	40	6.50	2.6
Equity	60	15.51	9.3
	100		11.9
Debt	50	8.00	4.0
Equity	50	18.00	9.0
	100		13.0
Debt	60	13.50	8.1
Equity	40	23.86	9.5
	100		17.6

a. We divide by 100 to obtain percentages; figures are rounded to the nearest tenth.

increases with increases in debt if the only influence operating is the tax shelter effect of increased debt. But risks of rising bankruptcy costs will cause the value of a firm to fall at some level of increased leverage.

The existence of both tax shelter benefits of corporate debt and increased risks of rising bankruptcy costs with increased leverage will cause the value of the firm to behave as depicted in Figure 16.5. As the amount of debt in the financial structure increases, the present value of tax savings will initially cause the market value of the firm to rise. (The slope of the line will be equal to the corporate tax rate.) However, at some point, bankruptcy costs will cause the market value of the firm to be less than what it would have been if the only in-

Figure 16.4

Cost of Capital Curves for Universal Machine Company

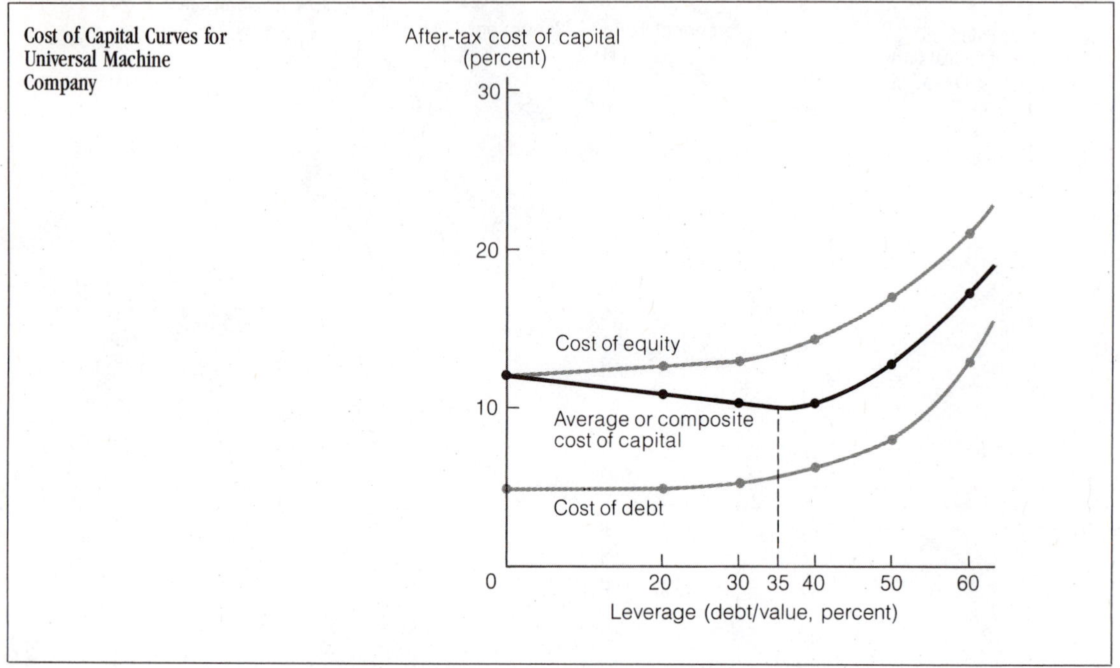

fluence were corporate income taxes. Possible bankruptcy costs may become so large that the indicated market value of the firm actually begins to turn down (Point C in Figure 16.5.). This point represents the target leverage ratio at which the market value of the firm is maximized—the optimal financial structure.

We emphasize an important distinction in the circumstances postulated for the analysis. In one analysis, we hold the total amount of capital or of financing constant, changing only the mix of financing. We seek the optimal or target debt (leverage) ratio at which the (weighted) average cost of capital is at a minimum. This is the leverage ratio which maximizes the value of the firm. In a second framework for analysis, discussed in Chapter 15, we focus on related investment decisions, determining the size of the total capital budget in relation to the levels of the (weighted) marginal cost of capital. In this second context, the value of the firm is maximized when the size of the total capital budget is determined by the level of investment at which the marginal returns from investment are equal to the marginal cost of funds. After discussing the use of book versus market values, we shall discuss the measurement of the cost of capital in a specific case that illustrates the distinctions and appropriate applications of the concepts of the average cost of capital and the marginal cost of capital.

Figure 16.5

Influence of Debt on Market Value of the Firm

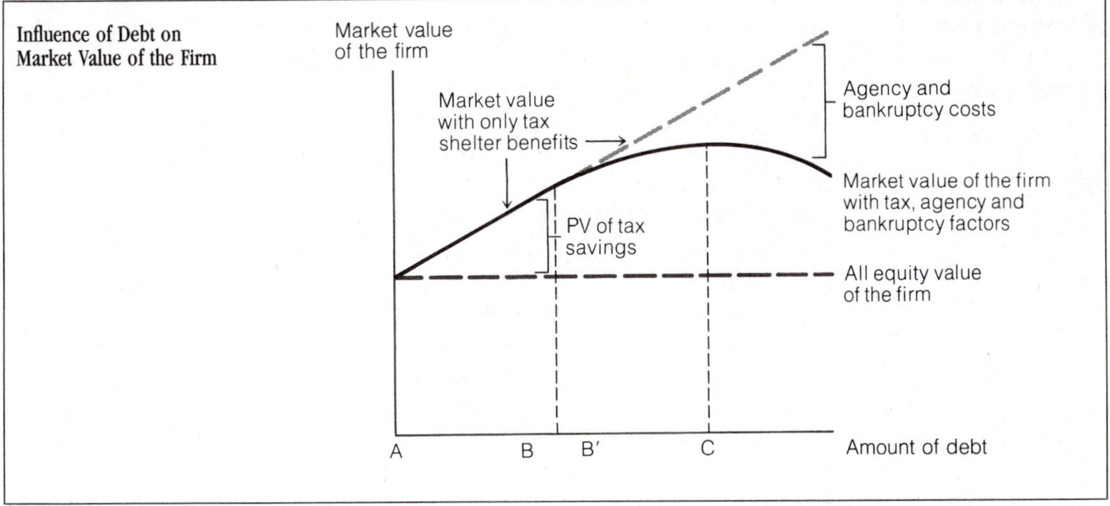

Book Rates and Market Weights

The correct principles to apply are now summarized. The basic issues are whether to use the actual historical financing costs of the firm and whether to use book or market values in calculating the proportions or weights of each source of financing. Financing costs must represent current opportunity costs, so the actual historical financing costs (reflected in the books) are not relevant. By the same reasoning, an average of past costs or an estimate of average expected future costs does not provide a correct measure of the current opportunity costs of funds.

With regard to weights or proportions of each source of financing, theory calls for the use of equilibrium market values. However, current market values may not be equilibrium values, so we do not necessarily apply the market values that we observe at a particular time. We should use those proportions or weights that represent the debt capacity of the firm appropriate for use in formulating the firm's target leverage proportions. A wide range of factors would have to be taken into consideration by the management of a firm in formulating its target leverage ratio. (Finance theory does not provide a precise theory for specifying a target leverage ratio.)

The future prospects of the firm represent an important factor to take into account—as well as the extent to which the future performance of the firm is subject to variability. These and other factors are reflected in the market value of the firm's equity shares and in the ratio of the market value of equity to its book value. In the example that follows we shall emphasize this principle: When the market to book ratio is greater than 1, the firm's prospects are viewed as relatively favorable, and higher target leverage ratio is appropriate. When the market to book ratio is less than 1, the target leverage ratio will be relatively lower.

Calculating the Marginal Cost of Capital for an Actual Company

The concepts and procedures discussed above can be tied together by applying them to an actual company—the Continental Container Company. Continental Container is a large firm with assets of $950 million and sales of $1.5 billion in 1979. The analysis was made in late 1979 for use in planning for 1980 and for the three-year period 1980–1982. Dividends have been paid since 1923, even during the depression of the 1930s. On the basis of an indicated dividend rate of $2 and a current price of $20.00 a share, the dividend yield at the time of analysis is 10 percent.[22] Over the past ten years, earnings, dividends, and the price of the stock have grown at a rate of about 5 percent; all indications are that the same rate of growth will be maintained in the foreseeable future.[23] Since internally generated funds provide sufficient equity, only the costs of internal equity (found in this case to be the 10 percent dividend yield plus the 5 percent growth rate, or a total of 15 percent) need be considered.

The average interest rate on Continental Container's outstanding debt is 7.5 percent, but much of this debt was issued in earlier years, when interest rates were much lower than they are now. Current market yields (in the second half of 1980) on both long-term and short-term debt are about 11 percent, and approximately this rate will be associated with new debt issues. After a 46 percent income tax, the cost of debt is estimated to be 5.94 percent. The cost of preferred stock is stated to be 6.75 percent, but it was also issued when rates were low. On the basis of current market yields, the estimated cost of new preferred stock is 11 percent.

The right-hand side of Continental Container's balance sheet is given in Table 16.6. A large portion (24 percent) of the firm's funds are "free" in the sense that no interest is charged for them; accounts payable and accruals are in this class. Some argue that "free" capital should be included in the calculation of the overall cost of capital. Under certain circumstances this procedure is valid; usually, however, only "nonfree" capital need be considered.[24] Of this remaining capital structure, 33 percent is debt, 2 percent is preferred

22. Dividend yields on other companies at about the same time were: Ford Motor Company, 12%; Portland General Electric, 13%; Continental Group, 8.1%; American Can, 8.5%; and Safeway, 7.4%.

23. Earnings per share for 1968 were $2.25, while EPS for 1978 were $3.65. Dividing $3.65 by $2.25 gives 1.62, which is the CVIF for ten years at 5 percent from Table A.1 at the end of the text. Thus EPS grew at a 5 percent rate over the ten-year period from 1968 through 1978. Dividends grew similarly, and security analysts are projecting a continuation of these rates.

24. The primary justification for ignoring "free" capital is that in the capital budgeting process these spontaneously generated funds are netted out against the required investment outlay, then ignored in the cost of capital calculation. To illustrate: Consider a retail firm thinking of opening a new store. According to customary practice, the firm should (1) estimate the required outlay, (2) estimate the net receipts (additions to profits) from the new store, (3) discount the estimated receipts at the cost of capital, and (4) accept the decision to open the new store only if the net present value of the expected revenue stream exceeds the investment outlay. The estimated accruals, trade payables, and other costless forms of credit are deducted from the investment to determine the "required outlay" before making the calculation. Alternatively, "free" capital could be costed in, and working capital associated with specific projects could be added in when determining the investment outlay. In most instances, the two procedures will result in similar decisions.

Table 16.6

Continental Container Company Right-Hand Side of Balance Sheet (Millions of Dollars)

	Amount	Percent	Nonfree Funds Only	
Payables and accruals	$186	19.6%		
Tax accruals	44	4.6		
Total "free" current funds	$230	24.2%		
Interest bearing debt	$238	25.0%	$238	33.1%
Preferred stock	14	1.5	14	1.9
Common equity	468	49.3	468	65.0
Nonfree funds	$720	75.8%	$720	100.0%
Total financing	$950	100.0%		

stock, and 65 percent is common equity. The financing proportions at market value have also been calculated. In connection with FASB Statement No. 33 requirements (discussed in Appendix A to Chapter 7), Continental has estimated the current value of its debt. In addition, market values of its preferred stock and common stock are readily available. The resulting proportions at market value were calculated as shown in Table 16.7. The current value of debt is 80 percent of its book value because interest rates have risen substantially above the average coupon rates on its debt. The even larger rise in preferred stock yields resulted in a market value of preferred at half the book value. Because of the moderate growth rate that Continental has experienced,

Table 16.7

Continental Container Company Financing Proportions at Two Market/Book Ratios

	Market Value of Equity Less than Book #1 Market Value		Market Value of Equity Greater than Book #2 Market Value	
	Amount	Percent	Amount	Percent
Interest bearing debt	$190	31	$190	24
Preferred stock	7	1	7	1
Common equity	421	68	608	75
	$618	100	$805	100

#1 Debt = 0.8 book debt
Preferred stock = 0.5 book preferred
Common equity = 0.9 book equity
#2 Common equity = 1.3 book equity

the ratio of the market value of its stock to its book value is 0.9 to 1. At an earlier period, the ratio was 1.3 to 1, so the impact of that ratio is shown as the #2 percentages.

A member of the finance committee at Continental argued that a lower ratio of market value of equity to total capital should support a lower leverage ratio and a higher ratio of market would call for a higher target leverage ratio. His reasoning was that a market to book ratio of more than one for equity reflected profitable investment performance and opportunities. A low ratio of market to book reflected unfavorable investment opportunities. He argued further that from practical considerations, a firm whose market to book value of equity is 1.3 will be able to borrow more than a firm whose book value of equity is the same size, but whose market to book ratio is below 1. The market to book ratio is an index of the past and potential performance of the firm. These general performance capabilities of the firm should be reflected in its debt capacity and therefore the capital structure target formulated. Accordingly, he proposed that target capital structure proportions follow the pattern set forth in Table 16.8. He proposed that when the market value of equity was below book value, the target leverage ratio measured by market values should be lower. This reflected the greater risk attached to a firm whose performance resulted in a ratio of the market value of equity to book value of less than one. Conversely, when the ratio of market to book was greater than one, the firm should employ a higher ratio of leverage. The practical effect was to raise the proportion of higher-cost equity for the firm when market to book value is less than one and lower it when market to book is more than one.

The effects of these different approaches are illustrated in Table 16.9. Part A applies the actual book value proportions to the current market costs of each component of financing. The resulting weighted cost of capital is approximately 12 percent. The condition when the market to book ratio exceeds one is shown in Part B. The target leverage ratio is higher and the weighted cost of capital declines below 11.5 percent. Part C of Table 16.9 reflects Continental's current situation. A lower target leverage ratio is formulated with a resulting weighted cost of capital of 12.33 percent. These costs of capital results may seem high, but recall that we are making the calculations for a period of time during which the bank prime rate on short-term loans has been in the 11 to 20 percent range.

Table 16.8

Target Capital Structure Proportions Related to Market/Book Ratios

	#1 Target Proportions	#2 Target Proportions
Interest bearing debt	29	39
Preferred stock	1	1
Common equity	70	60

Table 16.9

Calculation of the Weighted Cost of Capital with Different Leverage Targets

	Proportion (1)	Component Cost (2)	Product: (1) × (2) (3)
Part A			
Actual Book			
Interest bearing debt	0.33	5.94	1.96
Preferred stock	0.02	11.00	0.22
Common equity	0.65	15.00	9.75
			k = 11.93
Part B			
Market Equity to Book above 1			
Interest bearing debt	0.39	5.94	2.32
Preferred stock	0.01	11.00	0.11
Common equity	0.60	15.00	9.00
			k = 11.43
Part C			
Market Equity to Book below 1			
Interest bearing debt	0.29	5.94	1.72
Preferred stock	0.01	11.00	0.11
Common equity	0.70	15.00	10.50
			k = 12.33

Marginal Cost of Capital When New Common Stock Is Used

In the preceding example we assumed that the company would finance only with debt, preferred stock, and *internally generated equity*. On this basis we found the weighted average cost of new capital (or the marginal cost of capital) to be 12.33 percent. What would have occurred, however, if the firm's need for funds had been so great that it was forced to sell new common stock? The answer is that its marginal cost of new capital would be increased. To show why this is so, we shall extend the Continental Container example.

First, suppose that during 1979 Continental Container had total earnings of \$59 million available for common stockholders, paid \$27 million in dividends, and retained \$32 million. We know that to keep the capital structure in balance, the retained earnings should equal 70 percent of the net addition to capital (the other 30 percent being debt and preferred stock). Therefore, the total amount of new capital that can be obtained on the basis of the retained earnings is

$$\text{Retained earnings} = \text{Percent equity} \times \text{New capital}$$

$$\text{New capital} = \frac{\text{Retained earnings}}{\text{Percent equity}}$$

$$= \frac{\$32 \text{ million}}{0.70} = \$45.7 \text{ million.}$$

Next, we note that 1 percent of the new capital, or about \$450,000, should be preferred stock and that 29 percent, or \$13.3 million, should be debt. In other words, Continental Container can raise a total of $45.7 million—$32 million from retained earnings, $13.3 million in the form of debt, and $450,000 in the form of preferred stock—in its target capital structure proportions.

If all financing up to $45.7 million is in the prescribed proportions, the composite cost of new capital *up to $45.7 million* is still 12.33 percent, the previously computed weighted average cost of capital.

When the total of the required funds exceeds $45.7 million, however, Continental must begin relying on more expensive new common stock. Therefore, beyond this amount we must compute a new marginal cost of capital. Assuming Continental will incur a flotation cost on new equity issues equal to 10 percent, we can compute the cost of capital for funds over $45.7 million as shown in Table 16.10. According to Table 16.9, as long as the company raises no more than $45.7 million, its weighted average and marginal cost of new or incremental capital is 12.33 percent. But as shown in Table 16.10, amounts over $45.7 million have a cost of 13.11 percent. Thus the marginal cost of capital beyond $45.7 million is 13.11 percent.

Other Breaks in the MCC Schedule

The marginal cost of capital schedule shows the relationship between the weighted average cost of each dollar raised *(k)* and the total amount of capital raised during the year, other things (such as the riskiness of the assets acquired) held constant. In the preceding section, we saw that Continental Container's MCC schedule increases at the point where the company's retained earnings are exhausted and it begins to use more expensive new common stock.

Actually, any time a component cost rises, a similar break will occur. For

Table 16.10

Calculation of Continental Container's Marginal Cost of Capital Using External Common Stock

1. Find the cost of new equity:

$$\text{Cost of new common stock} = \frac{\text{Dividend yield}}{1 - \text{Flotation percentage}} + \text{Growth}$$

$$k_e = \frac{0.10}{0.90} + 5\% = 16.1\%.$$

2. Find a new weighted or composite cost of each dollar of new capital in excess of $45.7 million, using only new common stock for the equity component:

	Proportion	× Component cost	= Product
External Equity Financing:			
Interest bearing debt	0.29	5.94%	1.723
Preferred stock	0.01	11.00	0.110
Common equity	0.70	16.11	11.277
			k = 13.110

example, if Continental could obtain only \$15 million of debt at 11 percent, with additional debt costing 12 percent, then this rise in k_b would produce a higher $k_b(1 - T)$, which in turn would lead to a higher k. Under the assumptions made thus far, the break would occur at \$51.7 million, found as:

$$\frac{\text{Break in MCC schedule caused}}{\text{by rising debt cost}} = \frac{\text{Amount of lower-cost debt}}{\text{Debt as percentage of capital raised}}$$

$$= \frac{\$15 \text{ million}}{0.29} = \$51.7 \text{ million.}$$

Suppose that only an additional \$5 million over and above the first \$15 million can be borrowed at 12 percent, after which the before-tax component cost of new debt rises to 13 percent. A new break will occur, this one at \$69.0 million.

$$\frac{\text{Amount of lower-cost debt}}{\text{Debt/Total capital}} = \frac{\$15 \text{ million} + \$5 \text{ million}}{0.29} = \$69.0 \text{ million.}$$

Similar breaks could be caused by increases in the cost of preferred stock, higher common stock flotation costs as more stock is sold, and perhaps even a change in k_s, the basic required rate of return on the firm's common equity (as discussed in Chapter 15).[25]

In general, breaks in the MCC schedule occur whenever any component cost increases as a result of the volume of capital raised, and the breaking points can be calculated by the use of Equation 16.10:

$$\text{Break in MCC} = \frac{\begin{array}{c}\text{Total amount of lower-cost capital}\\ \text{for a given component}\end{array}}{\begin{array}{c}\text{Percentage of total capital}\\ \text{represented by the component}\end{array}}. \quad (16.10)$$

Continental Container will experience higher component costs for debt at \$15 million and at \$20 million, for preferred at \$5 million (12%), and for common equity at \$32 million (when retained earnings are exhausted) and at \$45 million (at 18 percent with 10 percent flotation costs). Equation 16.10 can be used to compute breaks in the company's MCC schedule. It is necessary to calculate a different MCC = k for the interval between each of the breaks in the MCC schedule. For example, we have already calculated the MCC from zero to \$45.7 million as 12.33 percent and that from \$45.7 to \$51.7 million as 13.11 percent. The calculations for the other breakpoints are:

25. It has been argued that as a company sells more and more stock or other types of securities, it must attract investors who are less and less familiar with and impressed by the company and that the securities must thus be sold at lower prices and higher yields. This pressure can affect all securities, new and old. If the sale of additional stock permanently lowers the price of old stock, then the reduction in value must be assessed as a marginal cost of the new stock. This situation is said to exist for the utilities, whose huge recurrent issues of securities in recent years have been depressing the prices of their outstanding securities.

Component Weight	At $51.7 million		At $64.3 million		At $69.0 million		At $500.0 million	
0.29	6.48	1.88	6.48	1.88	7.02	2.04	7.02	2.04
0.01	11.00	0.11	11.00	0.11	11.00	0.11	12.00	0.12
0.70	16.11	11.28	19.44	13.61	19.44	13.61	19.44	13.61
		k = 13.27		k = 15.60		k = 15.76		k = 15.77

(The 19.44% cost of new equity is calculated as follows: If 18% is the stated cost of equity and the growth rate is 5%, then the dividend yield, or d_1/p_0, must be 13%, since $18\% = d_1/p_0 + g$. It follows that the actual cost to Continental of the new equity is

$$\frac{\text{Dividend yield}}{1 - \text{Flotation cost}} + g = \frac{13\%}{1 - 0.10} + 5\% = 19.44\%.)$$

We can then observe the following schedule:

Point Where Break Occurs	Cause of Break	k in Interval before Break
$ 45.7 million	Shift from k_r to k_e	13.11%
51.7	Rising k_b	13.27
64.3	Rising k_e	15.60
69.0	Rising k_b	15.76
500.0	Rising k_{ps}	15.77

The values of k for each interval shown above are plotted as the step-function MCC schedule in Figure 16.6a. This graph is highly idealized; in fact, the actual MCC curve looks much more like the one shown in Figure 16.6b. Here the curve is flat until it reaches the vicinity of $45.7 million; it then turns up gradually and continues rising. It will go up gradually rather than suddenly because the firm will probably make small adjustments to its target debt ratio, its dividend payout ratio, the actual types of securities its uses, and so on. And the curve will continue to rise because, as more and more of its securities are put on the market during a fairly short period, it will experience more and more difficulty in getting the market to absorb the new securities.

Ordinarily, a firm will calculate its MCC schedule as a step-function similar to the one shown in Figure 16.6a, then smooth it out by connecting the values of k shown in the middle of each interval. Recognition of the types of estimates and approximations that go into the step-function curve makes the smoothing process appear less arbitrary than it does at first.

In the earlier analysis, associated with Figure 16.4, we were investigating the influence of the financing mix or financial structure on the firm's cost of capital. The financing mix was varied, but the total amount of capital raised was not. Since a marginal cost is the increment in cost as the total amount of financing is increased, varying the financing mix while holding the total amount of financing constant means that the relevant cost of capital is the

Figure 16.6

Relationship between Marginal Cost of Capital and Amount of Funds Raised

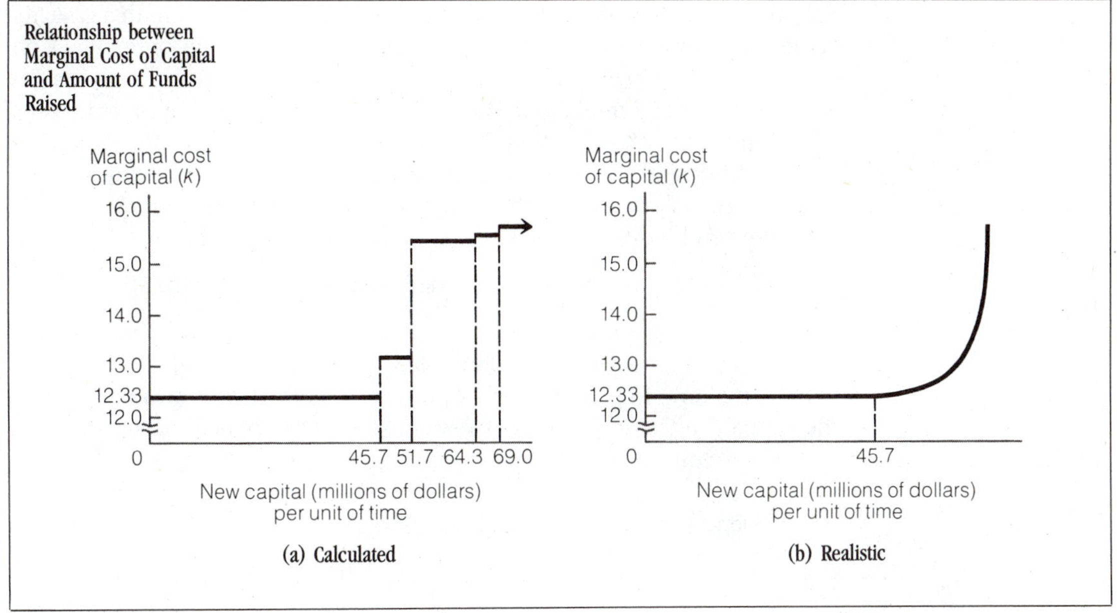

weighted average cost of capital (WACC). We can say either that no marginal cost of capital is involved or that the marginal cost of capital is equal to the WACC (symbolized by k).

In the present analysis, Figure 16.6 portrays the effects of increasing the total amount of new financing while holding the financing mix fixed at the target proportions. Over the flat segment of the MCC curve, the average cost of capital is equal to the marginal cost of capital. When the marginal cost of capital begins to rise, the curve that is an average cost in relation to the MCC lies below the MCC. (If nine people who are all six feet tall come into a room in sequence, the average and marginal height will be 6 feet. If the tenth person entering is 7 feet tall, the marginal height will be 7 feet, but the average height will be 6.1 feet.) We exhibit only the MCC in Figure 16.6 because we are analyzing the determination of the total capital budget for a firm; hence the MCC is relevant as the investment hurdle rate. But recall that we are holding the financing mix at its optimal proportions, so the MCC for each amount of new financing is also the WACC for the optimal mix of financing that minimizes the level of the MCC curve. For these reasons, we again use k as the symbol for the cost of capital along the MCC curve.

Combining the MCC and the Investment Opportunity Schedules

Having developed the firm's MCC schedule and planned its financing mix so as to minimize the schedule, the financial manager's next task is to utilize the MCC in the capital budgeting process. How is this done? First, suppose that the k value in the flat part of the MCC schedule is used as the discount rate for calculating the NPV and that the total cost of all projects with NPV > 0 is less than the dollar amount at which the MCC schedule turns up. In this case, the value of *k* that was used is the correct one. For example, if Continental Container uses 12.33 percent as its cost of capital and finds that the acceptable projects total $45.7 million or less, then 12.33 percent is the appropriate cost of capital for capital budgeting.[26]

But suppose the acceptable projects total more than $45.7 million with a 12.33 percent discount rate. What do we do now? The most efficient procedure is given below.

Step 1. Calculate and plot the MCC schedule as shown in Figure 16.6.

Step 2. Ask the operating personnel to estimate the dollar volume of acceptable projects at a range of discount rates, say 17 percent, 16 percent, 15 percent, 14 percent, 13 percent, and 12 percent. There will thus be an estimate of the capital budget at a series of *k* values. For Continental Container, these values were estimated as follows:

Capital Budget (in Millions)	$30	$40	$50	$60	$70	$80
k	17%	16%	15%	14%	13%	12%

Step 3. Plot the capital budget points *(k)* as determined in Step 2 on the same graph as the MCC; this plot is labeled IRR in Figure 16.7.[27]

Step 4. The correct MCC for use in capital budgeting—assuming both the MCC and IRR curves are developed correctly—is the value at the intersection of the two curves, 13.4 percent. If this value of *k* is used to calculate NPV's, then projects totaling $66 million will have NPV's greater than zero. This is the capital budget that will maximize the value of the firm.

Dynamic Considerations

Conditions change over time; and when they do, the firm must make adjustments. First, the firm's individual situation may change. For example, as it grows and matures, its business risk may decline; this may in turn lead to an optimal capital structure that includes more debt. Second, capital market con-

26. We are, of course, not considering project risk; here we assume that the average riskiness of all projects undertaken is equal to the average riskiness of the firm's existing plant. Some projects may be more risky than average and therefore call for a risk-adjusted cost of capital greater than 12.33 percent, while others may be less risky than average and call for a cost of capital less than 12.33 percent.

27. To see why the capital budget line, *k*, is a type of IRR curve, consider the following:
    1. The NPV of a project is zero if the project's IRR is equal to *k*.
    2. If no projects have NPV $\geq$ 0 at $k = 15\%$, then no projects have IRR $\geq$ 15%.
    3. If $20 million of projects have NPV $\geq$ 0 at $k = 14\%$, then these projects all have $14\% \leq \text{IRR} \leq 15\%$.
    4. If the projects are completely divisible and if we examine very small changes in *k*, then we will have a continuous IRR curve. As it is, the curve labeled IRR in Figure 16.7 is an approximation. But the example does illustrate how an IRR curve can be developed even though a company uses the NPV capital budgeting method.

Figure 16.7

Interfacing the MCC and IRR Curves to Determine the Total Capital Budget for a Given Time Period

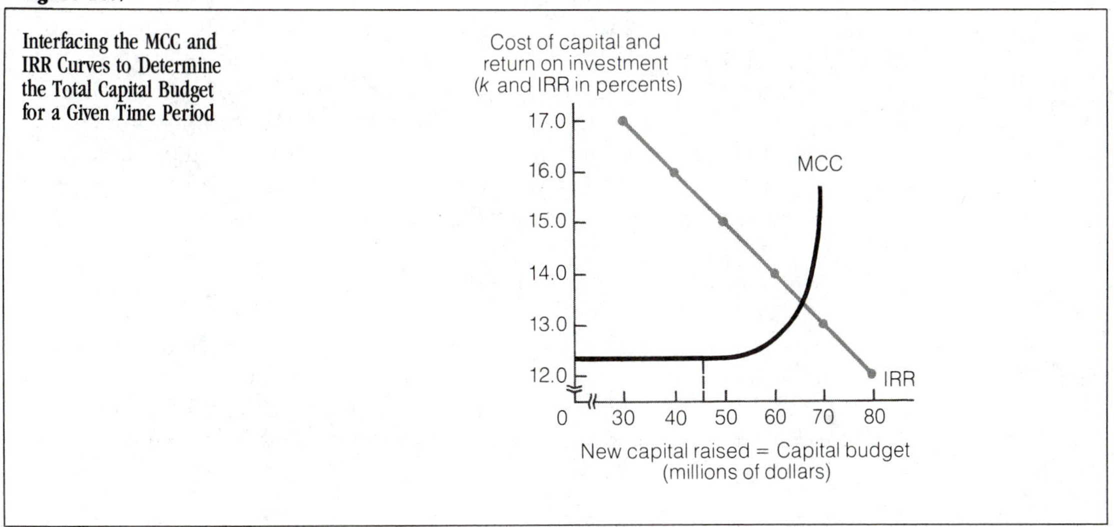

ditions may undergo a pronounced long-run change, making either debt or equity relatively favorable. This too may lead to a new optimal capital structure. Third, even though the long-run optimal structure remains unchanged, temporary shifts in the capital markets may suggest that the firm use either debt or equity, departing somewhat from the optimal capital structure, then adjust back to the long-run optimum in subsequent years. Fourth, the supply and demand for funds varies from time to time, causing shifts in the cost of both debt and equity and, of course, in the marginal cost of capital.

The inflation rate in the United States during 1979 was at the 13 percent level. With the continuing wide range of international and domestic economic uncertainties, many are concerned that it will be difficult to reduce the inflation rate substantially within the next several years. During the first half of 1977, the bank prime rate was around 6 percent. By April 1980, the prime rate reached 20 percent, but by May 22, it had declined to 15.5 percent. By the end of May, it had fallen to 14 percent. In March 1980, corporate Aaa bond yields were in the 13 percent range. By the end of May, the Aaa bond rate was slightly below 11 percent. The cost of common stock equity must be higher than the cost of the more senior Aaa bonds. Hence, if a high inflation rate persists, the cost of capital for even large, strong companies is likely to be in the 12 to 14 percent range. Because the financial markets have fluctuated so widely in recent years, it is necessary for firms to periodically re-examine their cost of capital.

Marketability and Rates of Return

So far, whenever we have discussed the required rate of return on securities, we have concentrated on two factors—the riskless rate of interest and the risk inherent in the security in question. However, we should note that investors also value flexibility, or maneuverability. An investor who becomes disenchanted with a particular investment or who needs funds for consumption or other investments finds it highly desirable to be able to liquidate current holdings. Other things being equal, the higher the liquidity, or marketability, the lower the investment's required rate of return. Accordingly, we expect to find listed stocks selling on a lower yield basis than over-the-counter stocks and widely traded stocks selling at lower yields than stocks with no established market. Since investments in small firms are generally less liquid than those in large companies, we have another reason for expecting to find higher required returns among smaller companies.

Large Firms versus Small Firms

Other significant differences in capital costs exist between large and small firms. These differences are especially pronounced for privately owned small firms. The same concepts are involved, and the methods of calculating the average and marginal cost of capital are similar; but some points of difference arise:

1. It may be difficult to obtain reasonable estimates of equity capital costs for small, privately owned firms.
2. Tax considerations are generally quite important for privately owned companies, since owner-managers may be in the top personal tax brackets. This factor can cause the effective after-tax cost of retained earnings to be considerably lower than the after-tax cost of new outside equity.
3. Flotation costs for new security issues, especially new stock issues, are much higher for small than for large firms (see Chapter 18).

Points 2 and 3 both cause the marginal cost curves for small firms to rise rapidly once retained earnings are exhausted, and these relationships have implications for the growth and development of large versus small firms.

Summary

The required rate of return on any security, k_j^*, is the minimum rate of return necessary to induce investors to buy or to hold the security; it is a function of the riskless rate of interest and the investment's risk characteristics:

$$\overline{k}_j = R_F + \rho_j = R_F + (\overline{R}_M - R_F)\beta_j .$$

When graphed, this equation is called the security market line (SML), from which the required return, k_j^*, is specified. Because investors generally dislike risk, the required rate of return is higher on riskier securities. As a class, bonds are less risky than preferred stocks; and preferred stocks, in turn, are less risky than common stocks. The result is that the required rate of return is lowest for bonds, higher for preferred stocks, and highest for common stocks. Within each of these security classes, there are variations among the issuing firms' risks; hence, required rates of return vary among firms.

The *cost of debt*, $k_b(1 - T)$, is defined as the required yield to maturity on new increments of debt capital multiplied by (1 − Tax rate). The *preferred stock cost* to the company is the effective yield and is found as the annual preferred dividend divided by the net price the company receives when it sells new preferred stock. In equation form:

$$\text{Cost of preferred stock} = k_{ps} = \frac{\text{Preferred dividend}}{\text{Net price of preferred}}.$$

The *cost of common equity* is defined as the minimum rate of return that must be earned on equity-financed investments to keep the value of the existing common equity unchanged. This required rate of return is the rate of return that investors expect to receive on the company's common stock—the dividend yield plus the capital gains yield. Sometimes, we assume that investors expect to receive about the same rates of return in the future that they have received in the past; in this case, we can estimate the required rate of return on the basis of actual historical returns.

Equity capital comes from two sources—retained earnings and the sale of new issues of common stock. The basic required rate of return *(k_r)* is used for the cost of retained earnings. However, new stock has a higher cost because of flotation costs associated with the sale of stock. The cost of new common stock issues is computed as follows:

$$\text{Cost of new stock} = k_e = \frac{\text{Dividend yield}}{1 - \text{Flotation percentage}} + \text{Growth}.$$

New common stock is therefore more expensive than retained earnings.

If a firm has a high leverage ratio, increasing the proportion of debt will make the debt riskier because it increases the probability of bankruptcy. If bankruptcy costs are substantial, the value of the firm will rise, reach a peak, and then fall. The maximum point on this curve indicates a target debt ratio.

The first step in calculating the weighted average cost of capital, *k,* is to determine the cost of the individual capital components. The next step is to establish the proper set of weights to be used in the averaging process. The optimal capital structure varies from industry to industry, with more stable industries having optimal capital structures that call for the use of more debt than unstable industries. The market to book relation of a firm's common equity may also influence the target leverage ratio.

The *marginal cost of capital schedule,* defined as the cost of incremental funds raised during a period of time, is of interest for two reasons. First, the firm should finance in a manner that minimizes the MCC schedule; therefore, it must measure the MCC. Second, the MCC is the rate that should be used in the capital budgeting process. The firm should take on new capital projects only if the net present values are positive when evaluated at the marginal cost of capital.

The marginal cost of capital is constant over a range, then begins to rise. The rise is probably gradual rather than abrupt because firms make small adjustments in their target debt ratios, begin to use an assortment of securities, retain more of their earnings, and so on, as they reach the limit of internally generated equity funds:

Questions

16.1 Suppose that basic business risks to all firms in any given industry are similar.
   a. Would you expect all firms in each industry to have approximately the same cost of capital?
   b. How would the averages differ among industries of unequal business risks?

16.2 Why are internally generated retained earnings less expensive than equity raised by selling stock?

16.3 Prior to the 1930s the corporate income tax was not very important, since the rates were fairly low. Also, prior to the 1930s preferred stock was much more important than it has been since that period. Is there a relationship between the rise of corporate income taxes and the decline in importance of preferred stock?

16.4 Describe how each of the following situations will affect the cost of capital to corporations in general.
   a. The federal government solves the problem of business cycles (that is, cyclical stability is increased).
   b. The Federal Reserve Board takes action to lower interest rates.
   c. The cost of floating new stock issues rises.

16.5 The firm's covariance is 0.014, the risk-free rate is 10 percent, the market risk premium $(\bar{R}_M - R_F)$ is 5 percent, and the variance of the market returns is 1 percent.
   a. With no bankruptcy costs, what is the cost of capital, k, for an unlevered firm?
   b. What is the beta of the firm?

16.6 Assume that the information in Question 16.5 is all on an after-tax basis, that the corporate tax rate is 50 percent, and that the firm has a debt to equity ratio of 100 percent, with a debt cost of 10 percent.
   a. What is the new beta of the firm?
   b. What is its return on equity?
   c. What is the cost of capital for the levered firm?

16.7 An unlevered firm has a beta of 0.8. How much leverage can it employ if its corporate tax rate is 50 percent and it aims to have a beta of 1.2?

16.8 The formula $k_r = (d_1/p_0) + g$, where d_1 = expected dividend, p_0 = the current price of a stock, and g = the past rate of growth in dividends, is sometimes used to estimate k_r, the cost of equity capital from retained earnings. Explain the implications of the formula.

16.9 What factors operate to cause the cost of debt to increase with financial leverage?

16.10 Explain the relationship between the required rate of return on common equity (k_s^*) and the debt ratio.

16.11 How will the various component costs of capital and the average cost of capital be likely to change if a firm expands its operations into a new, more risky industry?

16.12 The stock of XYZ Company is currently selling at its low for the year, but management feels that the stock price is only temporarily depressed because of investor pessimism. The firm's capital budget this year is so large that XYZ is contemplating the use of new outside equity. However, management does not want to sell new stock at the current low price and is therefore considering a departure from its "optimal" capital structure by borrowing the funds it would otherwise have raised in the equity markets. Does this seem to be a wise move? Explain.

16.13 Explain the following statement: The marginal cost of capital is an average in some sense.

Problems

16.1 The Allen Company is expected to grow at 9 percent per year. Allen's common stock sells for $30 per share, and the company pays a dividend of $2.40 per share. What is its cost of equity capital?

16.2 The Haley Company has a beta of 1.5. It has no debt in its capital structure.
   a. The expected market rate of return is 14 percent and the risk-free rate is 6 percent. What is the cost of equity capital for Haley?
   b. Should Haley accept a project that earns a rate of return of 15 percent and has a beta of 0.9?

16.3 The Young Company's financing plans for next year include the sale of long-term bonds with a 9 percent coupon. The company believes it can sell the bonds at a price that will give a yield to maturity of 10 percent. If the tax rate is 40 percent, what is Young's after-tax cost of debt?

16.4 The Weber Company plans to issue twenty-year bonds which have a 10 percent coupon. The bonds have a par value of $1,000 and can be sold for $920. Interest is paid semiannually.
   a. What is the yield to maturity on the new bond issue?
   b. If this were a perpetual bond issue, what would be its yield to maturity?

16.5 Consider the following perpetual preferred stock issue. The preferred stock carries a dividend yield of 10 percent and has a par value of $100. The market price of the preferred stock is $96.17. The flotation costs on this preferred stock issue are 6 percent of its market price. What is the yield to maturity?

16.6 The Dome Company earns $5 per share. The expected year-end dividend is $1.60, and price per share is $40. Dome's earnings, dividends, and stock price have been growing at 8 percent per year, and this growth rate is expected to continue indefinitely. New common stock can be sold to net $38. What is Dome's cost of retained earnings (required rate of return on internally financed equity)?

16.7 The Canes Company is expected to pay a year-end dividend of $4.40. Canes earns $7.70 per share, and its stock sells at $55 per share. Stock price, earnings, and dividends are expected to grow 6 percent per year indefinitely.
   a. Calculate the stockholders' rate of return.
   b. Assume that Canes's additional retained earnings are reinvested at 9 percent rather than at the cost of capital. Also assume that this new growth rate is permanent, that dividends remain constant, and that the firm continues to earn the same rate of return on its original capital as it has in previous years. What will the price of the common stock be at the end of one year?
   c. If the firm has a zero growth rate and pays out all its earnings as dividends,

what is the stockholder's rate of return? (Use the original stock price in your calculations).

16.8 The DOT Company has $200 million total net assets at the end of 1980. It plans to increase its production machinery in 1981 by $50 million. Bond financing, at an 11 percent rate, will sell at par. Preferred will have an 11.5 percent interest payment and will be sold at a par value of $100. Common stock currently sells for $50 per share and can be sold to net $45 after flotation costs. There is $10 million of internal funding available from retained earnings. Over the past few years, dividend yield has been 6 percent and the firm's growth rate 8 percent. The tax rate is 40 percent. The present capital structure shown below is considered optimal:

Debt: 8% coupon bonds	$40,000,000	
9% coupon bonds	40,000,000	$ 80,000,000
Preferred stock		20,000,000
Common stock ($10 par)	$40,000,000	
Retained earnings	60,000,000	
Equity		100,000,000
		$200,000,000

a. How much of the $50 million must be financed by equity capital if the present capital structure is to be maintained?
b. How much of the equity funding must come from the sale of new common stock?
c. What is DOT's cost of new equity?
d. What is DOT's incremental cost of capital?

16.9 The Bolan Company's cost of equity is 18 percent. Bolan's before-tax cost of debt is 12 percent, and its tax rate is 40 percent. Using the following balance sheet, calculate Bolan's after-tax weighted average cost of capital:

Assets		Liabilities	
Cash	$ 100	Accounts payable	$ 200
Accounts receivable	200	Accrued taxes due	200
Inventories	300	Long-term debt	400
Plant and equipment, net	1,800	Equity	1,600
Total assets	$2,400	Total liabilities	$2,400

16.10 Faber Company is considering payment of a $1 per share dividend. Stockholders can invest dividends to earn 18 percent; investors are taxed at 30 percent, and the brokerage costs on reinvestment are 3.5 percent. What rate of return must Faber earn on retained earnings to equate incremental internal earnings to what stockholders would receive externally?

16.11 You are planning to form a new company, and you can use several different capital structures. Investment bankers indicate that debt and equity capital will cost the following under different debt ratios (debt/total assets):

Debt Ratio	20% and Below	21 to 40%	41 to 50%	51 to 65%
Before-tax cost of debt	8%	9%	11%	14%
Cost of equity capital	12	13	18	25

a. Assuming a 40 percent tax rate, what is the after-tax weighted cost of capital for the following capital structures?

	(1)	(2)	(3)	(4)	(5)	(6)	(7)	(8)
Debt	0%	20%	21%	40%	41%	50%	51%	65%
Equity	100	80	79	60	59	50	49	35

b. Which capital structure minimizes the weighted average cost of capital?

16.12 On January 1, 1981, the total assets of the Stone Company were $60 million. By the end of the year total assets are expected to be $90 million. (Assume there is no short-term debt.) The firm's capital structure, shown below, is considered to be optimal:

Debt (10% coupon bonds)	$24,000,000
Preferred stock (at 10.5%)	6,000,000
Common equity	30,000,000
	$60,000,000

New bonds will have an 11 percent coupon rate and will be sold at par. Preferred stock will have an 11.5 percent rate and will also be sold at par. Common stock, currently selling at $30 a share, can be sold to net the company $27 a share. Stockholders' required rate of return, estimated to be 12 percent, consists of a dividend yield of 4 percent and an expected growth of 8 percent. Retained earnings are estimated to be $3 million (ignoring depreciation). The marginal corporate tax rate is 40 percent.

a. Assuming all asset expansion (gross expenditures for fixed assets plus related working capital) is included in the capital budget, what is the dollar amount of the capital budget (ignoring depreciation)?
b. To maintain the present capital structure, how much of the capital budget must be financed by equity?
c. How much of the new equity funds needed must be generated internally? How much externally?
d. Calculate the cost of each of the equity components.
e. At what level of capital expenditures will there be a break in the MCC schedule?
f. Calculate the MCC both below and above the break in the schedule.
g. Plot the MCC schedule. Also, draw in an IRR schedule that is consistent with the MCC schedule and the projected capital budget.

16.13 The Adair Company forecasts the following capital structure as of December 31, 1981:

Debt (at 6.5%)		$12,000,000
Preferred (at 6.5%)		4,000,000
Common stock	$ 4,000,000	
Retained earnings	12,000,000	
Common equity		16,000,000
Total capitalization		$32,000,000

Earnings per share have grown steadily from $0.93 in 1973 to $2 estimated for 1981. Expecting this growth to continue, the investment community has applied a price/earnings ratio of 10 to yield a current market price of $20. Adair's last annual dividend was $1.25, and the company expects the dividend to grow at the same rate as earnings. The addition to retained earnings for 1981 is projected at $4 million; these funds will be available during the next budget year. The corporate tax rate is 40 percent.

Assuming that the capital structure relations set out above are maintained, new securities can be sold at the following costs:

Bonds:
Up to and including $3 million of new bonds, 10 percent yield to investor on all new bonds
From $3.01 million to $6 million of new bonds, 10.5 percent yield to investor on this increment of bonds
Over $6 million of new bonds, 12 percent yield to investor on this increment of bonds
Preferred:
Up to and including $1 million of preferred stock, 10 percent yield to investor on all new preferred stock
From $1.01 million to $2 million of preferred stock, 10.5 percent yield to investor on this increment of preferred stock
Over $2 million of preferred stock, 12.5 percent yield to investor on this increment of preferred stock
Common:
Up to $4 million of new outside common stock, $20 a share less $2.50 a share flotation cost
Over $4 million of new outside common stock, $20 a share less $5 a share flotation cost on this increment of new common

a. At what dollar amounts of new capital will breaks occur in the MCC?
b. Calculate the MCC in the interval between each of these breaks; then plot the MCC schedule.
c. Discuss the breaking points in the marginal cost curve. What factors in the real world would tend to make the marginal cost curve smooth?
d. Assume now that Adair has the following investment opportunities:
   1. It can invest any amount up to $4 million at a 15 percent rate of return.
   2. It can invest an additional $8 million at a 13.7 percent rate of return.
   3. It can invest still another $12 million at an 11.8 percent rate of return.

   Thus Adair's total potential capital budget is $24 million. Determine the size of the company's optimal capital budget for the year.

Selected References

Adler, Michael. "On the Risk-Return Trade-Off in the Valuation of Assets." *Journal of Financial and Quantitative Analysis* 4 (December 1969), pp. 493–512.

Aivazian, Varouj, and Callen, Jeffrey L. "Investment, Market Structure, and the Cost of Capital." *Journal of Finance* 34 (March 1979), pp. 85–92.

Alberts, W. W., and Archer, S. H. "Some Evidence on the Effect of Company Size on the Cost of Equity Capital." *Journal of Financial and Quantitative Analysis* 8 (March 1973), pp. 229–245.

Archer, Stephen H., and Faerber, LeRoy G. "Firm Size and the Cost of Equity Capital." *Journal of Finance* 21 (March 1966), pp. 69–84.

Arditti, Fred. D. "The Weighted Average Cost of Capital: Some Questions on Its Definition, Interpretation and Use." *Journal of Finance* 28 (September 1973), pp. 1001–1007.

———. "Risk and the Required Return on Equity." *Journal of Finance* 22 (March 1967), pp. 19–36.

Arditti, Fred D., and Pinkerton, John M. "The Valuation and the Cost of Capital of the Levered Firm with Growth Opportunities." *Journal of Finance* 33 (March 1978), pp. 65–73.

Arditti, Fred D., and Tysseland, Milford S. "Three Ways to Present the Marginal Cost of Capital." *Financial Management* 2 (Summer 1973), pp. 63–67.

Auerbach, Alan J. "Wealth Maximization and the Cost of Capital." *Quarterly Journal of Economics* 43 (August 1979), pp. 433–446.

Barges, Alexander. *The Effect of Capital Structure on the Cost of Capital.* Englewood Cliffs, N.J.: Prentice-Hall, 1963.

Baron, David P. "Firm Valuation, Corporate Taxes, and Default Risk." *Journal of Finance* 30 (December 1975), pp. 1251–1264.

Baxter, Nevins D. "Leverage, Risk of Ruin, and the Cost of Capital." *Journal of Finance* 22 (September 1967), pp. 395–404.

Ben-Shahar, Haim, and Ascher, Abraham. "Capital Budgeting and Stock Valuation: Comment." *American Economic Review* 57 (March 1967), pp. 209–214.

Beranek, William. "The Weighted Average Cost of Capital and Shareholder Wealth Maximization." *Journal of Financial and Quantitative Analysis* 12 (March 1977), pp. 17–32.

———. "A Little More on the Weighted Average Cost of Capital." *Journal of Financial and Quantitative Analysis* 10 (December 1975), pp. 892–896.

———. "The Cost of Capital, Capital Budgeting, and the Maximization of Shareholder Wealth." *Journal of Financial and Quantitative Analysis* 10 (March 1975), pp. 1–20.

———. *The Effects of Leverage on the Market Value of Common Stocks.* Madison, Wisc.: Bureau of Business Research and Service, University of Wisconsin, 1964.

Bierman, Harold, Jr., and Oldfield, George S., Jr. "Corporate Debt and Corporate Taxes." *Journal of Finance* 34 (September 1979), pp. 951–956.

Bodenhorn, Diran. "A Cash Flow Concept of Profit." *Journal of Finance* 19 (March 1964), pp. 16–31.

Boness, A. James. "A Pedagogic Note on the Cost of Capital." *Journal of Finance* 19 (March 1964), pp. 99–106.

Boness, A. James, and Frankfurter, George M. "Evidence of Non-homogeneity of Capital Costs within 'Risk-Classes.'" *Journal of Finance* 32 (June 1977), pp. 775–787.

Bower, Richard S., and Bower, Dorothy H. "Risk and Valuation of Common Stock." *Journal of Political Economy* 77 (May–June 1969), pp. 349–362.

Brennan, M. J., and Schwartz, E. S. "Corporate Income Taxes, Valuation, and the Problem of Optimal Capital Structure." *Journal of Business* 51 (January 1978), pp. 103–114.

Brewer, D. E., and Michaelson, J. "The Cost of Capital, Corporation Finance, and the Theory of Investment: Comment." *American Economic Review* 55 (June 1965), pp. 516–524.

Chen, Andrew. "Recent Developments in the Cost of Debt Capital." *Journal of Finance* 33 (June 1978), pp. 863–883.

Cooper, Ian A., and Carleton, Willard T. "Dynamics of Borrower-Lender Interaction: Partitioning Final Payoff in Venture Capital Finance." *Journal of Finance* 34 (May 1979), pp. 517–529.

Copeland, Basil L., Jr. "Estimates of the Cost of Equity for Public Utilities." *Journal of Business Research* 7, no. 1 (1979), pp. 9–24.

Davis, E. W., and Yeomans, K. A. "Market Discount on New Issues of Equity: The Influence of Firm Size, Method of Issue and Market Volatility." *Journal of Business Finance & Accounting* 3 (Winter 1976), pp. 27–42.

Ezzell, John R., and Porter, R. Burr. "Flotation Costs and the Weighted Average Cost of Capital." *Journal of Financial and Quantitative Analysis* 11 (September 1976), pp. 403–414.

Fama, Eugene F. "Risk, Return, and Equilibrium: Some Clarifying Comments." *Journal of Finance* 23 (March 1968), pp. 29–40.

Fama, Eugene F., and Miller, Merton H. *The Theory of Finance.* New York: Holt, Rinehart and Winston, 1972.

Feldstein, Martin; Green, Jerry; and Sheshinski, Eytan. "Corporate Financial Policy and Taxation in a Growing Economy." *Quarterly Journal of Economics* 43 (August 1979), pp. 411–431.

———. "Inflation and Taxes in a Growing Economy with Debt and Equity Finance." *Journal of Political Economy* 86 (April 1978), pp. S53–S70.

Glenn, David W. "Super Premium Security Prices and Optimal Corporate Financing Decisions." *Journal of Finance* 31 (May 1976), pp. 507–524.

Gordon, Myron. *The Investment, Financing, and Valuation of the Corporation.* Homewood, Ill.: Richard D. Irwin, 1962.

Gordon, Myron J., and Gould, Lawrence I. "The Cost of Equity Capital with Personal Income Taxes and Flotation Costs." *Journal of Finance* 33 (September 1978), pp. 1201–1212.

———. "The Cost of Equity Capital: A Reconsideration." *Journal of Finance* 33 (June 1978), pp. 849–861.

Gordon, Myron J., and Kwan, Clarence C. Y. "Debt Maturity, Default Risk, and Capital Structure." *Journal of Banking and Finance* 3 (December 1979), pp. 313–329.

Haley, Charles W., and Schall, Lawrence D. "Problems with the Concept of the Cost of Capital." *Journal of Financial and Quantitative Analysis* 13 (December 1978), pp. 847–870.

Hamada, Robert S. "Financial Theory and Taxation in an Inflationary World: Some Public Policy Issues." *Journal of Finance* 34 (May 1979), pp. 347–369.

———. "Portfolio Analysis, Market Equilibrium and Corporation Finance." *Journal of Finance* 24 (March 1969), pp. 13–32.

Haugen, Robert A., and Kumar, Prem. "The Traditional Approach to Valuing Levered-

Growth Stocks: A Clarification." *Journal of Financial and Quantitative Analysis* 9 (December 1974), pp. 1031–1044.

Haugen, Robert A., and Pappas, James L. "Equilibrium in the Pricing of Capital Assets, Risk-Bearing Debt Instruments, and the Question of Optimal Capital Structure." *Journal of Financial and Quantitative Analysis* 6 (June 1971), pp. 943–954.

Haugen, Robert A., and Senbet, Lemma W. "The Insignificance of Bankruptcy Costs to the Theory of Optimal Capital Structure." *Journal of Finance* 32 (May 1978), pp. 383–393.

Haugen, Robert A., and Wichern, Dean W. "The Intricate Relationship between Financial Leverage and the Stability of Stock Prices." *Journal of Finance* 30 (December 1975), pp. 1283–1292.

Hawkins, David F. "Toward an Old Theory of Equity Valuation." *Financial Analysts Journal* 33 (November–December 1977), pp. 48–53.

Higgins, Robert C. "Growth, Dividend Policy and Capital Costs in the Electric Utility Industry." *Journal of Finance* 29 (September 1974), pp. 1189–1201.

Hirshleifer, Jack. "Investment Decisions under Uncertainty: Applications of the State-Preference Approach." *Quarterly Journal of Economics* 83 (May 1966), pp. 252–277.

Hite, Gailen L. "Leverage, Output Effects, and the M-M Theorems." *Journal of Financial Economics* 4 (March 1977), pp. 177–202.

Jensen, Michael C. "Risk, the Pricing of Capital Assets, and the Evaluation of Investment Portfolios." *Journal of Business* 42 (April 1969), pp. 167–247.

Keenan, Michael. "Models of Equity Valuation: The Great Serm Bubble." *Journal of Finance* 25 (May 1970), pp. 243–273.

Keenan, Michael, and Maldonado, Rita M. "The Redundancy of Earnings Leverage in a Cost of Capital Decision Framework." *Journal of Business Finance and Accounting* 3 (Summer 1976), pp. 43–56.

Krouse, Clement G. "Optimal Financing and Capital Structure Programs for the Firm." *Journal of Finance* 27 (December 1972), pp. 1057–1072.

Kumar, Prem. "Growth Stocks and Corporate Capital Structure Theory." *Journal of Finance* 30 (May 1975), pp. 532–547.

Lee, Wayne Y., and Barker, Henry H. "Bankruptcy Costs and the Firm's Optimal Debt Capacity: A Positive Theory of Capital Structure." *Southern Economic Journal* 43 (April 1977), pp. 1453–1465.

Lerner, Eugene M., and Carleton, Willard T. "Reply." *American Economic Review* 57 (March 1967), pp. 220–222.

———. *A Theory of Financial Analysis.* New York: Harcourt, Brace & World, 1966.

———. "Financing Decisions of the Firm." *Journal of Finance* 21 (May 1966), pp. 202–214.

———. "The Integration of Capital Budgeting and Stock Valuation." *American Economic Review* 54 (September 1964), pp. 683–702.

Lewellen, Wilbur G. "A Conceptual Reappraisal of Cost of Capital." *Financial Management* 3 (Winter 1974), pp. 63–70.

———. *The Cost of Capital.* Belmont, Calif.: Wadsworth, 1969, Chapters 3–4.

Lewellen, Wilbur G., and McConnell, John J. "Utility Rate Regulation." *Journal of Business Research* 7, no. 2 (1979), pp. 117–138.

Lintner, John. "The Aggregation of Investors' Judgments and Preferences in Purely Competitive Security Markets." *Journal of Financial and Quantitative Analysis* 4 (December 1969), pp. 347–400.

———. "Security Prices, Risk, and Maximal Gains from Diversification." *Journal of Finance* 20 (December 1965), pp. 587–616.

———. "The Cost of Capital and Optimal Financing of Corporate Growth." *Journal of Finance* 18 (May 1963), pp. 292–310.

———. "Dividends, Earnings, Leverage, Stock Prices and the Supply of Capital to Corporations." *Review of Economics and Statistics* 44 (August 1962), pp. 243–269.

Long, Michael S., and Racette, George A. "Stochastic Demand, Output and the Cost of Capital." *Journal of Finance* 29 (May 1974), pp. 499–506.

Merton, Robert C. "On the Pricing of Contingent Claims and the Modigliani-Miller Theorem." *Journal of Financial Economics* 5 (November 1977), pp. 241–249.

Mossin, Jan. "Security Pricing and Investment Criteria in Competitive Markets." *American Economic Review* 59 (December 1969), pp. 749–756.

Mumey, Glen A. *Theory of Financial Structure.* New York: Holt, Rinehart and Winston, 1969.

Myers, Stewart C. "Interactions of Corporate Financing and Investment Decisions—Implications for Capital Budgeting." *Journal of Finance* 29 (March 1974), pp. 1–25.

Nantell, Timothy J., and Carlson, C. Robert. "The Cost of Capital as a Weighted Average." *Journal of Finance* 30 (December 1975), pp. 1343–1355.

Petry, Glenn H. "Empirical Evidence on Cost of Capital Weights." *Financial Management* 4 (Winter 1975), pp. 58–65.

Pettit, R. Richardson, and Westerfield, Randolph. "Using the Capital Asset Pricing Model and the Market Model to Predict Security Returns." *Journal of Financial and Quantitative Analysis* 9 (September 1974), pp. 579–605.

Porterfield, James T. S. *Investment Decisions and Capital Costs.* Englewood Cliffs, N.J.: Prentice-Hall, 1965.

Reilly, Raymond R., and Wecker, William E. "On the Weighted Average Cost of Capital." *Journal of Financial and Quantitative Analysis* 8 (January 1973), pp. 123–126.

Robichek, Alexander A. "Risk and the Value of Securities." *Journal of Financial and Quantitative Analysis* 4 (December 1969), pp. 513–538.

Robichek, Alexander A., and McDonald, John G. "The Cost of Capital Concept: Potential Use and Misuse." *Financial Executive* 33 (June 1965), pp. 2–8.

Robichek, Alexander A., and Myers, Stewart C. *Optimal Financial Decisions.* Englewood Cliffs, N.J.: Prentice-Hall, 1965.

Schall, L. D., and Kerr, H. S. "The Validity of Existing Capitalization Methods." *Engineering Economist* 24 (Fall 1978), pp. 29–35.

Schwartz, Eli. "Theory of the Capital Structure of the Firm." *Journal of Finance* 14 (March 1959), pp. 18–39.

Schwartz, Eli, and Aronson, J. Richard. "Some Surrogate Evidence in Support of the Concept of Optimal Capital Structure." *Journal of Finance* 22 (March 1967), pp. 10–18.

Scott, David F., Jr. "Evidence on the Importance of Financial Structure." *Financial Management* 1 (Summer 1972), pp. 45–50.

Scott, J. H. "Bankruptcy, Secured Debt, and Optimal Capital Structure." *Journal of Finance* 32 (March 1977), pp. 1–19.

———. "A Theory of Optimal Capital Structure." *Bell Journal of Economics* 7 (Spring 1976), pp. 33–54.

Shiller, Robert J., and Modigliani, Franco. "Coupon and Tax Effects on New and Seasoned Bond Yields and the Measurement of the Cost of Debt Capital." *Journal of Financial Economics* 7 (September 1979), pp. 297–318.

Solomon, Ezra. "Measuring a Company's Cost of Capital." *Journal of Business* 28 (October 1955), pp. 240–252.

Sosin, Howard B. "Neutral Recapitalizations: Predictions and Tests Concerning Valuation and Welfare." *Journal of Finance* 33 (September 1978), pp. 1228–1234.

Stapleton, R. C., and Subrahmanyam, M. G. "Market Imperfections, Capital Market Equilibrium, and Corporation Finance." *Journal of Finance* 32 (May 1977), pp. 307–319.

Sullivan, Timothy G. "The Cost of Capital and the Market Power of Firms." *Review of Economics and Statistics* 60 (May 1968), pp. 209–217.

Thompson, H. "Estimating the Cost of Equity Capital for Electric Utilities: 1958–1976." *Bell Journal of Economics* 10 (Autumn 1979), pp. 619–635.

Trout, Robert R. "Comment: Regulatory Procedures, Investment Opportunities, Stock Valuation." *Journal of Business Research* 7, no. 3 (1979), pp. 259–266.

Vickers, Douglas. "The Cost of Capital and the Structure of the Firm." *Journal of Finance* 25 (March 1970), pp. 35–46.

———. *The Theory of the Firm: Production, Capital and Finance.* New York: McGraw-Hill, 1968.

———. "Profitability and Reinvestment Rates: A Note on the Gordon Paradox." *Journal of Business* 39 (July 1966), pp. 366–370.

Weston, J. Fred. "A Test of Cost of Capital Propositions." *Southern Economic Journal* 30 (October 1963), pp. 105–112.

Weston, J. Fred, and Lee, Wayne Y. "Cost of Capital for a Division of a Firm: Comment." *Journal of Finance* 32 (December 1977), pp. 1779–1780.

Wippern, Ronald F. "Financial Structure and the Value of the Firm." *Journal of Finance* 21 (December 1966), pp. 615–634.

Appendix A to Chapter 16

Two Additional Issues on the Cost of Capital

Cost of Retained Earnings

Whenever Firm A retains a portion of its net income instead of paying it out in dividends, there is an opportunity cost to stockholders. The *opportunity cost* to shareholders is what they could have earned with the funds. If the shareholders could have earned 12 percent with the funds on investments of equivalent risk, then the required return on the common stock of Firm A is 12 percent. The alternative opportunities of shareholders determines the required return on the common stock of Firm A.

But how do we determine the alternative opportunities available to the shareholders of Firm A? One approach has been to argue that differential taxes are applicable to receiving cash dividends as compared with receiving the income in the form of capital gains. Under this approach, some hold that the differential tax rates on ordinary income versus capital gains result in a lower required return on retained earnings. For example, if the required return on equity of Firm A is 12 percent and the effective personal income tax rate of its shareholders is 40 percent, the cost of retained earnings might be argued to be:

$$k_r = k_s\left(\frac{1 - T_p}{1 - T_g}\right)$$

$$= 0.12\left(\frac{0.60}{0.84}\right) = 0.12(0.7143) = 0.0857 = 8.57\%.$$

Here T_p is the applicable personal income tax rate on ordinary personal income and T_g is the capital gains tax rate at 40 percent of the personal income tax rate. Based on these relationships, if the cost of equity capital is 12 percent, the cost of retained earnings is about 8.6 percent. But there are two broad reasons for not accepting this result. One is the external yield criterion set forth by Ezra Solomon.[1] The other is the M. H. Miller and M. S. Scholes analysis which describes how cash dividends can be shielded from ordinary personal income rates.[2]

1. Ezra Solomon, *The Theory of Financial Management,* (New York: Columbia University Press, 1963), pp. 53–55.
2. M. H. Miller and M. S. Scholes, "Dividends and Taxes," *Journal of Financial Economics* 6 (1978), pp. 333–364.

The *external yield criterion* is what the firm can earn on the direct investment of its funds. The basic idea is that the required return for the retained earnings for a firm is what the firm itself could earn on external investment opportunities. Essentially, this approach argues that the opportunity foregone by the retention of earnings is represented by investments Firm A could make in another business firm. Market equilibrium relationships suggest that the external opportunities will make k_s and k_r approximately equal.

Even more fundamental is the analysis by Miller and Scholes (MS). The wealth accumulator can borrow to obtain interest deductions that offset the personal income taxes on dividend income. Ultimately, the wealth accumulators are borrowing from low tax bracket taxpayers. In addition, the risk levels of the borrowers can be restored to their previous levels by investment in insurance or pension funds, as well as a variety of other markets. These permit tax-free accumulations of wealth at before-tax interest rates on investment. They conclude that tax laws and various forms of financial institutions have produced opportunities which make "taxable investors indifferent to dividends despite tax differentials in favor of capital gains."[3]

The nature of the Miller and Scholes position can be illustrated by an example. Firm A earns 10 percent on its investments. The applicable personal income tax rate for Firm A's investors is 40 percent, and the applicable tax rate on capital gains is 16 percent. In addition, it is possible for these investors to borrow at 6 percent, and they can buy life insurance policies to provide an annual yield of 6 percent, which is not taxed. We shall consider a number of alternative patterns of returns for investors in Firm A.

Situation 1. Assume that the stock of Firm A sells for $10 a share and pays no dividends. Consider an investment in 1,000 shares of stock of Firm A. What is the present value of the investment if cashed out at the end of 10 years?

The stock of Firm A has a value which grows at 10 percent compounded. Hence, the present value of the initial $10,000 investment in the common stock of Firm A would be:

$10,000(CVIF 10%,10) = $10,000(2.5937) =	$25,937
Cost of stock	10,000
Capital gain	$15,937
Capital gain tax (16%)	2,550
Capital gain after tax	$13,387
Original value of stock	10,000
Net proceeds, end of 10 years	$23,387
PV factor = PVIF(6%,10)	×0.5584
PV of net proceeds	$13,059

The net present value of this investment is $3,059. It is an investment which earns 10 percent, pays a tax rate of 16 percent, and has a cost of capital of 6

3. Ibid., p. 333.

percent. How would this return be affected by the payment of cash dividends by the firm?

Situation 2. In the second case, Firm A pays out all of its earnings as dividends. The investors receive $1,000 per year in cash dividends. Since these dividends are subject to the ordinary personal income tax rate, the after-tax income that they yield is $600 per year. This annuity is worth $4,416. The present value of the sale of the stock at $10,000 would be obtained by using the 0.5584 present value factor to obtain $5,584. The sum of the two returns is exactly $10,000. This is to be expected: The earning rate of Firm A is 10 percent, but the receipts of the investors are after a 40 percent tax. Therefore, the investors net only 6 percent. Hence the cash dividends are disadvantageous to the investors if they take no offsetting actions.

Situation 3. Firm A pays out its earnings as dividends, but the investors borrow an amount whose interest cost exactly balances the dividends received. In addition, the proceeds of the borrowing are used to unlever the investors by the purchase of insurance.[4] Since the debt interest should be $1,000 and the interest rate paid is 6 percent, the borrowing must be $16,667. This amount is invested in insurance. The present value of the proceeds after 10 years would be calculated as follows:

Cash in the insurance policy

$16,667 × (CVIF 6%,10) =	
$16,667 × (1.7908) =	$29,847
Investment	16,667
Gain on insurance	$13,180
Repay borrowing from $16,667 of insurance proceeds	

Total cash flow at ten-year end

Net from insurance	$13,180
Sale of stock	10,000
Total	$23,180
PVIF (6%,10)	0.5584
Present value	$12,944

The NPV of the investment is approximately the same as in Situation 1, in which Firm A paid no cash dividends. Two offsetting factors are operating. The firm earns at a 10 percent rate, but the opportunity returns to the investors is 6 percent. On the other hand, the insurance accumulation is tax free. MS comment that a practical method of avoiding a tax on the interest earned on the insurance contract is to borrow up to the cash surrender value of the policy. These influences need not be perfectly offsetting, but

4. Note the comment by MS on the unlevering role of insurance: "The role of insurance in offsetting leverage involves more, of course, than merely the marginal adjustments to changes in dividends in our examples. Insurance, by eliminating one of the risks attaching to the human capital, permits accumulators to take a more aggressive, levered position in their investment portfolios." Ibid., p. 343, n. 13.

they operate in opposite directions.[5] The investors are not subject to higher personal income tax rates on the cash dividends, so this does not influence the results.

Thus, to the extent that cash dividends can be shielded by debt interest and borrowing can be unlevered by insurance, the risk-return position of the investors is essentially unchanged. Their return from the investment is approximately the same whether the firm pays cash dividends or retains the earnings, given appropriate assumptions about the earnings rate on retentions. The Miller-Scholes analysis indicates that the cost of retained earnings is not likely to be lower than the cost of external equity financing except for flotation costs, as discussed in the chapter.

Cost of Depreciation-Generated Funds

The first increment of cash flow used to finance any year's capital budget is depreciation-generated funds. In their statements of changes in financial position, corporations generally show depreciation charges to be a very substantial noncash charge. For capital budgeting purposes, should depreciation be considered free capital, should it be ignored completely, or should a charge be assessed against it? The answer is that a charge should be assessed against these funds, and that this cost is the weighted cost of capital before outside equity is used.

The reasoning here is that the firm could, if it so desired, distribute the depreciation-generated funds to its creditors and stockholders, the parties who financed the assets in the first place. For example, if $10 million of depreciation-generated funds were available, the firm could either reinvest them or distribute them. If they are to be distributed, the distribution must be to both bondholders and stockholders in proportion to their shares of the capital structure; otherwise, the capital structure will change. Obviously, this distribution should take place if the funds cannot be invested to yield the cost of capital, but retention should occur if the internal rate of return exceeds the cost of capital. Since the cost of depreciation-generated funds is equal to the weighted cost of capital, depreciation does not enter the calculation of the weighted cost of capital.

Depreciation may, however, affect the cost of capital *schedule.* If we are concerned with gross capital expenditures—including replacement as well as expansion investments—then the cost of capital schedule that includes de-

5. Limitations on interest deductions are required to prevent complete tax avoidance. MS observe: "The role of insurance as a vehicle for accumulation at the before-tax rate should also make clear why limits on deductions for interest were necessary for the proof of the strong invariance proposition and are less arbitrary than may appear at first sight. Were it not for the assumed interest limitation, the income tax could in principle be gutted completely. Taxpayers would borrow until the tax shield on the interest payments had reduced their tax liabilities to zero. Since the proceeds of the borrowing are held in insurance, no risks are incurred by either the taxpayer-borrowers or their creditors." Ibid., p. 344.

preciation is the relevant one. The flat part of the marginal cost of capital curve, before it is increased by using external equity funds at higher rates, would be extended by the inclusion of depreciation. But if we are concerned with the effects of *net increases* in assets, then the schedule without depreciation is appropriate.

Problems

16A.1 Assume that the personal income tax rate on ordinary income is 40 percent and on capital gains the rate is 16 percent. In addition, it is possible to borrow at 10 percent, and life insurance policies can be bought to provide an annual untaxed yield of 10 percent.

Compare the following alternative investment policies with respect to their present value if each is cashed out at the end of 10 years.

a. Buy 1,000 shares of stock in a firm that earns 15 percent and pays no dividends. The shares sell for $10 each.

b. Buy 1,000 shares of a firm that earns 15 percent per year and pays it all out in dividends. The shares sell for $10.

c. Invest as in Part b, but also borrow an amount such that the before-tax dividends received are exactly equaled by the interest payments on debt. Invest the proceeds of the loan in the insurance program described.

16A.2 Assume that the personal income tax rate on ordinary income is 35 percent and on capital gains the rate is 14 percent. In addition, it is possible to borrow at 10 percent, and life insurance policies can be bought to provide an annual untaxed yield of 6 percent.

Compare the following alternative investment policies with respect to their present value if each is cashed out at the end of 10 years.

a. Buy 1,000 shares of stock in a firm that earns 15 percent and pays no dividends. The shares sell for $10 each.

b. Buy 1,000 shares of a firm that earns 15 percent per year and pays it all out in dividends. The shares sell for $10.

c. Invest as in Part b, but also borrow an amount such that the before-tax dividends received are exactly equaled by the interest payments on debt. Invest the proceeds of the loan in the insurance program described.

d. Assume the same conditions as in Part c except the borrowing rate is 6 percent.

e. Assume the same conditions as in Part c except the borrowing rate is 8 percent.

Appendix B to Chapter 16

The Modigliani-Miller Propositions on the Cost of Capital

The classic 1958 Modigliani-Miller article on the cost of capital has generated much theoretical and empirical work. Their work is central to modern finance theory, and we believe their propositions are well illustrated by the financial policies of many large successful U.S. corporations that employ only moderate amounts of debt. At a minimum, the MM propositions are a reference framework for any alternative theories of the cost of capital. We shall therefore compactly derive their propositions so that their implications may be more fully understood and used. Some proposed modifications are also evaluated.

If we begin by accepting a fundamental relationship—that the value of an unlevered firm in a given risk class is net operating income after tax divided by the cost of capital of an unlevered firm—everything else in MM can be derived. So we begin with Proposition I, as set forth in Equation 16B.1.

$$V_u = \frac{\overline{X}(1-T)}{k_u}. \qquad (16B.1)$$

A simple rearrangement gives us the cost of capital of an unlevered firm in Equation 16B.1a.

$$k_u = \frac{\overline{X}(1-T)}{V_u}. \qquad (16B.1a)$$

The next relation follows from a simple arbitrage process. Based on two decision alternatives described below, some associated investment and returns patterns follow:

Decision	Investment	Return
A. Buy α of Firm L	αS_L	$\alpha(X - k_bB)(1-T)$
B. Buy α of Firm U; Borrow $\alpha(1-T)B$	$\alpha S_u - \alpha(1-T)B$	$\alpha(X)(1-T) - \alpha(1-T)k_bB = \alpha(X - k_bB)(1-T)$

Decision A is to buy a fraction of the common equity of a levered firm. Decision B is to buy the same fraction of the common equity of an unlevered firm and to create an amount of homemade leverage equivalent to that represented by the investment decision in the equity of the levered firm by selling $\alpha(1 - T)$ amount of debt. The amount of each investment reflects the two alternative decisions. The return from the investment in the equity of the levered firms is the α fraction of its income after deduction of debt, interest, and taxes. For Decision B, the return is given as a fraction of the after-tax income of the unlevered firm less the interest (after taxes) paid on the homemade borrowings. The returns from the two investments are seen to be equal. Since the returns are equal, their investment market values will also be equal. It follows that:

$\alpha S_L = \alpha S_u - \alpha(1 - T)B$	Divide through by α.
$S_L = S_u - (1 - T)B$	Multiply by $(1 - T)$.
$S_L = S_u - B + TB$	Regroup terms.
$S_L + B = S_u + TB.$	Since $S_L + B = V_L$ and $S_u = V_u$,

then

$$V_L = V_u + TB. \tag{16B.2}$$

Also,

$$V_u = V_L - TB.^{1} \tag{16B.2a}$$

Equations 16B.2 and 16B.2a represent an important implication of the MM relations. Because of the tax subsidy represented by the tax deductibility of interest on debt, the value of a levered firm will be greater than the value of the

$$k_s = \frac{\text{NI}}{S}. \tag{16B.4a}$$

1. For later use, note that

$$k_u = \frac{\overline{X}(1 - T)}{V_L - TB}.$$

Hence,

$$\overline{X}(1 - T) = k_u V_L - k_u TB \tag{16B.3}$$

MM with Taxes

$\text{NI} = (X - k_b B) - (X - k_b B)T$	This is NOI after debt, interest, and taxes. We multiply by T.
$= X - k_b B - XT + k_b BT$	We then regroup terms.
$= X(1 - T) - k_b B(1 - T)$	Use Equation 16B.3 to substitute for $X(1 - T)$.
$= k_u V_L - k_u BT - k_b B(1 - T).$	Divide by S.

$$\frac{\text{NI}}{S} = k_s = \frac{k_u S}{S} + \frac{k_u B}{S} - \frac{k_u BT}{S} - \frac{k_b B}{S}(1 - T) \quad \text{Regroup terms.}$$

$$= k_u + k_u \frac{B}{S}(1 - T) - k_b \frac{B}{S}(1 - T) \quad \text{Factor } B/S(1 - T) \text{ from last two terms.}$$

$$k_s = k_u + (k_u - k_b)(1 - T)(B/S). \tag{16B.4}$$

unlevered firm by the amount of debt multiplied by the applicable corporate tax rate. Since the value of the common equity, S, is equal to the value of the levered firm less the value of debt, the effects of leverage decisions on the market behavior of the common equity are predictable on the basis of the Equation 16B.2 relations.

We next develop MM's Proposition II, which deals with the cost of equity capital. We start with the accounting definition of net income.
This is MM's Proposition II, which states that the cost of equity is equal to the cost of capital of an unlevered firm plus the after-tax difference between the cost of capital of an unlevered firm and the cost of debt, weighted by the leverage ratio. The cost of equity will therefore rise linearly with increased leverage. The cost of equity can also be measured by the accounting ratio of net income to the value of equity to obtain the same result as in Equation 16B.4. Next the weighted cost of capital (WCC) can be formulated in three versions. We start with the descriptive buildup of the cost of capital as the weighted costs of debt and equity. In symbols, that is:

$$1.\ \ k = \text{WCC} = k_b(1-T)\frac{B}{V_L} + k_s\frac{S}{V_L}. \qquad \textbf{(16B.5)}$$

We then substitute Equation 16B.4 for k_s in Equation 16B.5 and multiply through.

$$k = k_b(1-T)\frac{B}{V_L} + \left[k_u + (k_u - k_b)\frac{B}{S}(1-T)\right]\frac{S}{V_L}$$

$$= k_b(1-T)\frac{B}{V_L} + k_u\frac{S}{V_L} + k_u\frac{B}{V_L}(1-T) - k_b\frac{B}{V_L}(1-T).$$

The first and last terms cancel.

$$= \frac{k_u S}{V_L} + \frac{k_u B}{V_L} - \frac{k_u TB}{V_L}.$$

The first two terms can be written as $k_u V_L/V_L$.

$$k = \frac{k_u V_L - k_u TB}{V_L}.$$

Use Equation 16B.3 to substitute in the numerator.

$$2.\ \ k = \frac{\overline{X}(1-T)}{V_L}. \qquad \textbf{(16B.6)}$$

This is the second formulation of WCC and is the levered firm's valuation counterpart to MM's Proposition I in Equation 16B.1 for unlevered firms.

The third formulation starts with Equation 16B.2:

$$V_L = V_u + TB.$$

Rewrite V_u from Equation 16B.1.

$$V_L = \frac{\overline{X}(1 - T)}{k_u} + TB.$$

Multiply TB by k_u/k_u.

$$V_L = \frac{\overline{X}(1 - T) + k_u TB}{k_u}.$$

Solve for k_u.

$$k_u = \frac{\overline{X}(1 - T)}{V_L} + \frac{k_u TB}{V_L}.$$

Use Equation 16B.6 for k.

$$k_u = k + \frac{k_u TB}{V_L}.$$

Let L = B/V_L and solve for k.

$$k = k_u - k_u TL.$$

Factor k_u from the right-hand terms.

$$3.\ k = k_u(1 - TL). \qquad (16B.7)$$

The three formulations of the WCC have been shown in this appendix to be mathematically equivalent. In the example in Chapter 16, we showed how the numerical results are obtained by all three equations, and that, along with this section of the appendix, completes the main relationships developed by MM. We shall next review two criticisms of their propositions, since they call for alternative operational procedures which some financial managers have adopted.

The MM Propositions with Depreciable Assets

Haim Levy and F. D. Arditti (LA) presented an analysis which argued that MM propositions must be modified to recognize a reduction in the value of the firm when assets are depreciable.[2] The issue of leverage is not involved, so we will focus on their unlevered firm case. In the basic LA equation for the unlevered firm, the firm's annual post-tax cash flows are:

$$X^t = (1 - T)X + K - K, \qquad (16B.8)$$

where $-K$ is the annual investment and $+K$ the depreciation charge, assumed to be equal in their model.

LA then state, "We claim that one cannot cancel the +K and −K terms and then apply the appropriate discount rates to the expected value of the result-

2. H. Levy and F. D. Arditti, "Valuation, Leverage, and the Cost of Capital in the Case of Depreciable Assets," *Journal of Finance* 28 (June 1973), pp. 687–693.

ing cash flow expression. The reason is that while the replacement outlay (−K) is a certain amount, only a part of the +K term is certain."[3] They reformulate Equation 16B.8 as:

$$X^t = (1 - T)C + TK - K, \tag{16B.9}$$

where C is the annual pre-tax flow before depreciation and interest.

They observe:

Thus X^t is separated into two distinct components: (a) an uncertain stream equal to (1 − T)C; and (b) a certain stream equal to . . . TK − K in the unlevered case. . . . So TK is a certain stream and should be capitalized by the riskless rate r. The annual investment flow, −K, must also be treated as a certain amount, since our model requires the firm to invest an amount equal to its depreciation expense in order to assure perpetual asset lives. Hence TK − K may be treated as a certain stream.[4]

Their resulting valuation relationship is:

$$V_u = \frac{(1 - T)\overline{C}}{\rho^t} - \frac{(1 - T)K}{r}, \tag{16B.10}$$

where "C denotes the expected cash flow . . . and ρ^t denotes . . . the required rate of return on a pure equity stream." They point out that their resulting valuation expression is smaller than the MM values by

$$\frac{1}{r} - \frac{1}{\rho^t}(1 - T)K$$

and that the MM valuation expressions must be correspondingly reduced for the case of depreciable assets.

R. S. Paul commented that the LA results assume that their ρ^t is the same ρ^t used by MM to discount the unlevered firm's EBIT.[5] All of LA's modifications assume that the same rate would be used to discount both the expected pretax operating cash flow $(\overline{C})$ and the expected EBIT $(\overline{X})$. Paul demonstrates the basic LA assumption cannot be made, consistent with the underlying nature of the models under analysis. The example she presents is reproduced in Table 16B.1.

Since the two firms have the same EBIT, they must have the same value. But if 10 percent is the applicable discount rate for Firm A, it has a value of \$1,500. Using LA Equation 3, reproduced above as 16B.10, not changing ρ^t and using a 5 percent riskless rate gives a value of \$1,050 for Firm B. This suggests that the discount rate for discounting $\overline{C}$ is not the same discount rate applicable to $\overline{X}$. Paul then demonstrates this analytically, using the symbol $\hat{\rho}^t$

3. Ibid., p. 688.
4. Ibid., pp. 688–689.
5. R. S. Paul, "Comment," *Journal of Finance* 30 (March 1975), pp. 211–213.

Table 16B.1

Comparisons of Two Firms with Equal EBIT

Distribution of Annual Flows for Firm A with No Depreciable Assets

P	C = Pre-Tax Operating Cash Flow	K = Depreciation	X = EBIT	Y[a] = Net Cash Flow
0.2	150	0	150	90
0.5	200	0	200	120
0.3	400	0	400	240
1.0	$\overline{C} = 250$	$K = 0$	$\overline{X} = 250$	$\overline{Y} = 150$

Distribution of Annual Flows for Firm B with Depreciable Assets

P	C = Pre-Tax Operating Cash Flow	K = Depreciation	X = EBIT	Y[a] = Net Cash Flow
0.2	225	75	150	90
0.5	275	75	200	120
0.3	475	75	400	240
1.0	$\overline{C} = 325$	$K = 75$	$\overline{X} = 250$	$\overline{Y} = 150$

a. $Y = [X(1 - T) + K] - K$, where the bracketed term represents after-tax operating cash flow and the $-K$ represents the capital outflow necesssary to maintain the operating cash flow at its present level.

Source: R. S. Paul, "Comment," *Journal of Finance* 30 (March 1975), p. 212. Used by permission.

(rho with a hat) to indicate the appropriate capitalization rate for $\overline{C}$. For the firms to have the same value, it follows that:

$$\frac{(1 - T)\overline{C}_b}{\hat{\rho}^t} = \frac{(1 - T)\overline{C}_a}{\rho^t} + \frac{(1 - T)K}{r}. \qquad (16B.11)$$

But C_a is the same as X_b with the same probability distributions, so with substitution we have the following relation for any Firm B with depreciable assets:

$$\frac{(1 - T)C_b}{\hat{\rho}^t} = \frac{(1 - T)\overline{X}_b}{\rho^t} + \frac{(1 - T)K}{r}. \qquad (16B.12)$$

When we solve Equation 16B.12 for the first term on the right-hand side, we have the following result:

$$V_u = \frac{(1 - T)\overline{X}_b}{\rho^t} = \frac{(1 - T)\overline{C}_b}{\hat{\rho}^t} - \frac{(1 - T)K}{r}. \qquad (16B.13)$$

The first equality is MM's original Proposition I. The second equality is LA's Equation 3 for depreciable assets, shown to be the same as MM's expression if $\hat{\rho}^t$ is changed appropriately. The basic point is that once $\overline{C}_b$ contains both the uncertain and certain cash flow stream components, it would be capitalized by a lower discount rate than $\overline{X}_b$, which contains only the uncertain cash flow streams. In their reply LA acknowledged that $\hat{\rho}^t$ had to be 0.081 (below 0.10) for the equality to hold.[6] In so doing, they acknowledged the validity of the clarification presented by Paul. It appears that LA misinterpreted Paul's analysis since they concluded their reply to her as follows: "It appears that Paul believes that the discount rate (in her example, 10%) is independent of the probability distribution of returns. Why else would she apply the same discount rate of 10% to stream C_a as well as stream C_b?"[7] But Paul did this only to emphasize that it resulted in unequal values for the two firms, which could not be the case, given the underlying facts and assumptions. In doing so, she established that $\hat{\rho}^t$ has to be lower than ρ^t. When this is recognized, MM's Proposition I applies as fully to the valuations of firms with depreciable assets as to firms with nondepreciable assets.

The Weighted Average Cost of Capital as a Cutoff Rate

Another criticism is that the application of the weighted average cost of capital as derived in the MM propositions is incorrectly specified as an investment hurdle rate or for deriving the value of the firm. The expression we developed from the MM materials and now generally referred to as the "traditional textbook theory" is:

$$V_L = \frac{\overline{X}(1 - T)}{k_s(S/V) + (1 - T)r(B/V)}. \qquad (16B.14)$$

Here we use r for k_b. But in developing other relationships, MM also have:

$$V = \frac{\overline{X}(1 - T)}{k_u} + TB = \frac{\overline{X}(1 - T)}{k_u} + \frac{TrB}{r}. \qquad (16B.15)$$

Building on the Equation 16B.15 relationship, Arditti and Levy (AL)[8] proposed that the true valuation formula is:

$$V_L^* = \frac{(\overline{X} - rB)(1 - T) + rB}{k(S/V) + r(B/V)} = \frac{\overline{X}(1 - T) + rBT}{k^*}. \qquad (16B.16)$$

In the AL expression, the capitalization factor uses the before-tax cost of debt rather than the after-tax cost of debt and adds the interest tax shelter to the cash flows in the numerator to be capitalized. We shall demonstrate that the AL formulation is actually the same as the "traditional textbook" formulation and that when appropriately applied to projects give the same results.[9]

We shall develop a proof that

$$V_L^* = V_L.$$

6. H. Levy and F. D. Arditti, "Reply," *Journal of Finance* 30 (March 1975), pp. 221–223.
7. Ibid., p. 222.
8. F. D. Arditti and H. Levy, "The Weighted Average Cost of Capital as a Cutoff Rate: A Critical Analysis of the Classical Textbook Weighted Average," *Financial Management* 6 (Fall 1977), pp. 24–34.
9. See similar demonstrations in the group of articles on the "Weighted Average Cost of Capital" in *Financial Management* 8 (Summer 1979) by K. J. Boudreaux and H. W. Long; J. R. Ezzell and R. B. Porter; M. Ben-Horim, and A. C. Shapiro.

As before, let

$$L = B/V_L.$$

Then

$$\begin{aligned} k &= rL(1 - T) + k_s(1 - L) \\ &= rL - rLT + k_s(1 - L). \end{aligned}$$

AL define k^* as

$$k^* = rL + k_s(1 - L).$$

Thus,

$$k^* = k + TrL$$

$$V_L^* = \frac{\overline{X}(1 - T) + rTLV_L^*}{K + rTL} \tag{16B.17}$$

Multiply by the denominator of the right-hand side of Equation 16B.17:

$$\begin{aligned} V_L^*(k + rTL) &= \overline{X}(1 - T) + rTLV_L^* \\ kV_L^* + rTLV_L^* &= kV_L + rTLV_L^*. \end{aligned} \tag{16B.18}$$

Cancel common terms on each side of Equation 16B.18:

$$V_L^* = V_L.$$

It has therefore been established that the AL expression in Equation 16B.16 is identical to the MM formulation.

A numerical illustration can be provided from the example in Chapter 16 where:

$\overline{X} = \$200{,}000$
$T = 40\%$
$k_s = 12.8571\%$
$k_b = r = 10\%$
$B = \$500{,}000$
$S = \$700{,}000$
$V_L = B + S = \$1{,}200{,}000$
$k_u = 12\%$
$k = 10\%$

For k^* we would have:

$$\begin{aligned} k^* &= k + \frac{rBT}{V_L} = 0.10 + \frac{0.10(500{,}000)0.4}{1{,}200{,}000} = 0.10 + \frac{20{,}000}{1{,}200{,}000} \\ &= 0.10 + 0.01667 = 0.11667 = 11.667\%. \end{aligned}$$

Using the AL expression for V_L:

$$V_L^* = \frac{\overline{X}(1-T) + rBT}{k^*} = \frac{120{,}000 + 0.10(500{,}000)0.4}{0.11667}$$

$$= \frac{120{,}000 + 20{,}000}{0.11667} = \frac{140{,}000}{0.11667} = \$1{,}200{,}000$$

This is, of course, the same as the V_L we obtained before.

Project Evaluation

AL next evaluate a project with an investment cost, I, and an earnings annuity of $\overline{Y}$ in perpetuity. The standard NPV approach states:

$$\text{NPV} = \frac{\overline{Y}(1-T)}{k} - \text{I}. \quad (16B.19)$$

AL state that the actual net present value is NPV* defined as:

$$\text{NPV}^* = \frac{\overline{Y}(1-T) + Tr(B/V)\text{I}}{k^*} - \text{I}. \quad (16B.20)$$

But this NPV* formulation is inconsistent in shifting to a book (investment) basis for leverage, while the market value of the firm increases by (I + NPV*). To maintain a constant leverage ratio, the firm must increase debt by an amount equal to (I + NPV*)(B/V). When we make the necessary adjustment to the NPV* formulations, we obtain Equation 16B.20a.

$$\text{NPV}^* = \frac{\overline{Y}(1-T) + Tr(B/V)(\text{I} + \text{NPV}^*)}{k^*} - \text{I}. \quad (16B.20a)$$

Multiply through numerator:

$$\text{NPV}^* = \frac{\overline{Y}(1-T)}{k^*} + \frac{rT(B/V)\text{I}}{k^*} + \frac{rT(B/V)(\text{NPV}^*)}{k^*} - \text{I}.$$

Move NPV* term to left side of equation and factor out NPV*.

$$\text{NPV}^*\left(1 - \frac{rTB}{k^*V}\right) = \frac{\overline{Y}(1-T) + rT(B/V)\text{I}}{k^*} - \text{I}.$$

Multiply both sides by k^*.

$$\text{NPV}^*\left(k^* - \frac{rTB}{V}\right) = \overline{Y}(1-T) + rT(B/V)\text{I} - k^*\text{I}.$$

But $-k^*\text{I} + rT(B/V)\text{I}$ can be written as $[k^* - rT(B/V)]\text{I} = k\text{I}$, since $[k^* - rT(B/V)] = k$. Then we have

$$k\text{NPV}^* = \overline{Y}(1-T) - k\text{I}.$$

Next divide by k to obtain

$$\text{NPV}^* = \frac{\bar{Y}(1 - T)}{k} - \text{I} = \text{NPV}.$$

Thus when the target leverage ratio is maintained by applying it to the increase in the market value of the firm instead of to the book value of the new investment, NPV* is equal to the traditional NPV.

We can continue our previous numerical example to illustrate the formal proof. Let I be \$10,000 and $\bar{Y}$ = \$2,500. Using the traditional measure of NPV, we have:

$$\text{NPV} = \frac{\$2{,}500(0.6)}{0.10} - \$10{,}000 = \frac{1{,}500}{0.10} - \$10{,}000 = \$5{,}000.$$

The same data can be applied to the NPV* formulation as corrected in Equation 16B.20a. The value of NPV* that satisfies the corrected equation is \$5,000:

$$\begin{aligned}\text{NPV}^* &= \frac{\$1{,}500 + 0.4(0.10)(5/12)(15{,}000)}{0.116667} - \$10{,}000 \\ &= \$12{,}857 + \frac{5/12(600)}{0.116667} - \$10{,}000 \\ &= \$12{,}857 + \frac{250}{0.116667} - \$10{,}000 \\ &= \$5{,}000 = \text{NPV}.\end{aligned}$$

Again, the proposed reformulation actually reinforces the MM relationships when used in a manner consistent with the underlying theory.

Problems

16B.1 Companies U and L are identical in every respect except that U is unlevered while L has \$10 million of 5 percent bonds outstanding. Assume (1) that all of the MM assumptions are met, (2) that the tax rate is 40 percent, (3) that EBIT is \$2 million, and (4) that the equity capitalization rate for Company U is 10 percent.

a. What value would MM estimate for each firm?

b. Suppose V_u = \$8 million and V_L = \$18 million. According to MM, do these represent equilibrium values? If not, explain the process by which equilibrium will be restored. No calculations are necessary.

16B.2 You are provided the following information: The firm's expected net operating income (X) is \$600. Its value as an unlevered firm (V_u) is \$2,000. The tax rate is 40 percent. The cost of debt is 10 percent. The ratio of debt to equity for the levered firm, when it is levered, is 1. Use the MM propositions to:

a. Calculate the after-tax cost of equity capital for both the levered and the unlevered firm.

b. Calculate the after-tax weighted average cost of capital for each.

c. Why is the cost of equity capital higher for the levered firm, but the weighted average cost of capital lower?

16B.3 Company A and Company B are in the same risk class and are identical in every respect except that Company A is levered, while Company B is not. Company A has $3 million in 5 percent bonds outstanding. Both firms earn 10 percent *before interest and taxes* on their $5 million of total assets. Assume perfect capital markets, rational investors, a tax rate of 40 percent, and a capitalization rate of 10 percent for an all equity company. Use the MM propositions for the following:

a. Compute the values of Firms A and B.
b. Calculate the after-tax weighted cost of capital for Firms A and B. Which is lower and why?
c. Company B (the wholly equity-financed firm) wants to change its capital structure by introducing debt. Management believes that the cost of equity to the firm will take the form

$$k_s = R_F + \rho_1 + \rho_2,$$

where

k_s = Cost of equity

R_F = After-tax riskless interest rate, currently at about 6 percent

ρ_1 = Premium demanded of the firm as a result of its particular business activity, currently estimated to be 4 percent

ρ_2 = Premium demanded as a result of the firm's financial leverage

Management believes that the premium, ρ_2, can be approximated by taking the firm's *debt-assets* ratio, squaring it, and multiplying by 0.10 to give the additional percentage points of premium required by the market. Management also feels that the firm's cost of debt is a function of the debt ratio, and estimates that this function is approximately equal to the following schedule:

Debt/Assets Ratio	After-Tax Cost of Debt
0%	0.05
20%	0.05
30%	0.06
40%	0.07
60%	0.12

Under these assumptions, is there an optimal capital structure for Firm B? If so, what is this optimal debt-equity ratio?

16B.4 The cost of debt before taxes is 10 percent. The cost of equity for a levered firm is 14 percent. The debt to total value of the levered firm is 50 percent. The corporate tax rate is 40 percent. Using the MM propositions,

a. What is the cost of capital of the levered firm?
b. What would be the cost of capital of the firm if it were unlevered?

Selected References

Boudreaux, K. J., et al. "The Weighted Average Cost of Capital: A Discussion." *Financial Management* 8 (Summer 1979), pp. 7–14.

Hite, Gailen L. "Leverage, Output Effects, and the M-M Theorems." *Journal of Financial Economics* 4 (March 1977), pp. 177–202.

Martin, John D.; Scott, David F., Jr.; and Vandell, Robert F. "Equivalent Risk Classes: A Multidimensional Examination." *Journal of Financial and Quantitative Analysis* 14 (March 1979), pp. 101–118.

Miller, Merton H. "Debt and Taxes." *Journal of Finance* 32 (May 1977), pp. 261–275.

Miller, Merton H., and Modigliani, Franco. "Cost of Capital to Electric Utility Industry." *American Economic Review* 56 (June 1966), pp. 333–391.

Modigliani, Franco, and Miller, Merton H. "Reply." *American Economic Review* 55 (June 1965), pp. 524–527.

———. "Taxes and the Cost of Capital: A Correction." *American Economic Review* 53 (June 1963), pp. 433–443.

———. "The Cost of Capital, Corporation Finance and the Theory of Investment: Reply." *American Economic Review* 48 (September 1958), pp. 655–669.

———. "The Cost of Capital, Corporation Finance and the Theory of Investment." *American Economic Review* 48 (June 1958), pp. 261–297.

Nielsen, Niels Christian. "On the Financing and Investment Decisions of the Firm." *Journal of Banking and Finance* 2 (June 1978), pp. 79–101.

Resek, Robert W. "Multidimensional Risk and the Modigliani-Miller Hypothesis." *Journal of Finance* 25 (March 1970), pp. 47–52.

Robichek, Alexander A.; McDonald, J. G.; and Higgins, R. C. "Some Estimates of the Cost of Capital to Electric Utilities, 1954–1957: Comment." *American Economic Review* 57 (December 1967), pp. 1278–1288.

Stapleton, R. C. "A Note on Default Risk, Leverage and the MM Theorem." *Journal of Financial Economics* 2 (December 1975), pp. 377–382.

Stiglitz, Joseph E. "A Re-examination of the Modigliani-Miller Theorem." *American Economic Review* 59 (December 1969), pp. 784–793.

Appendix C to Chapter 16

Using the CAPM to Estimate a Firm's Cost of Capital

Three steps are required in using the capital asset pricing model (CAPM) to estimate a firm's cost of equity capital:

1. *Estimate the market parameters in order to estimate the security market line.*
2. *Estimate the firm's beta coefficient.*
3. *Utilize the estimates to formulate a judgment of the firm's cost of equity capital.*

Each of these steps will be covered, first explaining the formal methodology involved and then indicating the kinds of judgments required to arrive at a number or range of numbers for the firm's cost of equity capital.

Estimating the Market Parameters

The key market parameters to estimate are the risk-free rate of return, the expected return on the market, and the variance of the market return. With these we have estimates of the key market-determined variables of the security market line. For example, suppose that we estimated the risk-free return to be 6 percent, the return on the market to be 10 percent, and the variance of the market to be 1 percent. The security market line could then be expressed as shown in Equations 16C.1 and 16C.2:

$$\bar{k}_j = R_F + \lambda \, \mathrm{Cov}(R_j, R_M) \tag{16C.1}$$

where

$$\lambda = \frac{R_M - R_F}{\mathrm{Var}(R_M)}.$$

$$\bar{k}_j = R_F + (R_M - R_F)\beta_j. \tag{16C.2}$$

When we fill in the illustrative market parameters, we obtain Equations 16C.1a and 16C.2a:

$$\bar{k}_j = 0.06 + \frac{(0.10 - 0.06)}{0.01} \mathrm{Cov}(R_j, R_M) \tag{16C.1a}$$

$$= 0.06 + 4 \, \mathrm{Cov}(R_j, R_M).$$

$$\bar{k}_j = 0.06 + 0.04(\beta_j) \qquad (16C.2a)$$

where $$\beta_j = \frac{\text{Cov}(R_j,R_M)}{\text{Var}(R_M)}.$$

Thus if we knew that the beta for the firm under analysis was 1.5, using Equation 16C.2a we would have:

$$\bar{k}_j = 0.06 + 0.04(1.5). \qquad \text{Cov}(R_j,R_M) = \beta_j \text{Var}(R_M).$$
$$\bar{k}_j = 0.12. \qquad \text{Cov}(R_j,R_M) = 1.5(0.01) = 0.015.$$

Thus the cost of equity capital for the firm would be 12 percent.

This brief overview indicates the power of the CAPM approach. Once we have good estimates of the market parameters, all we need to know is the systematic risk measure for the firm or project to obtain an estimate of the required return on that investment. Much empirical work has been performed on the estimates of the market parameters. Some of these represent formal scholarly studies analyzing the empirical validity of the capital asset pricing model.[1] Other estimates of market parameters are available from various financial firms and services such as Merrill Lynch, Pierce, Fenner and Smith, Wells Fargo Bank, and the Value Line. The sophisticated methodologies utilized include analysis over a number of periods typically using intervals of one month; some services use intervals as short as one week or one day.

The nature of the sophisticated procedures for estimating the market parameters can be conveyed by Table 16C.1, which provides data for calculating the market parameters. The percent returns listed in Column 5 are obtained by adding the dividend yield in Column 4 plus the capital gain calculated in Column 3 from the information on the Standard & Poor 500 stock price index data listed in Column 2. Taking the mean value of the data in Column 5, we can obtain the mean market return over the period, 10 percent.

In Column 6 the deviations from the market return are listed. In Column 7 the deviations are squared, then summed and divided by 19 to obtain the 0.0124 estimate of market variance.[2]

The risk-free return is estimated by use of the six-month treasury bill rate. The average for the years indicated are listed in Column 8. These average annual values are summed and divided by 20 to obtain an estimate of the risk-free return for the time period covered, which is 6 percent.

1. F. Black; M. C. Jensen; and M. Scholes, "The Capital Asset Pricing Model: Some Empirical Tests," in *Studies in the Theory of Capital Markets,* ed. M. C. Jensen (New York: Praeger, 1972), pp. 79–121; M. H. Miller and M. Scholes, "Rates of Return in Relation to Risk: A Re-Examination of Some Recent Findings," in *Studies in the Theory of Capital Markets,* pp. 47–78; E. F. Fama and James D. MacBeth, "Risk, Return and Equilibrium: Empirical Tests," *Journal of Political Economy* 81 (May–June 1973), pp. 607–636; I. Friend and M. E. Blume, "Measurement of Portfolio Performance under Uncertainty," *American Economic Review* 60 (September 1970), pp. 561–575; Nancy L. Jacob, "The Measurement of Systematic Risk for Securities and Portfolios: Some Empirical Results," *Journal of Financial and Quantitative Analysis* 6 (March 1971), pp. 815–834.
2. We divide by 19 rather than 20 since one degree of freedom has been lost in that the calculation of the variance involves the use of the mean return on the market, which has already been calculated.

The estimates we have obtained reflect the characteristics of the market with the turbulence introduced by unsettled economic conditions following 1966. The returns of individual firms have not generally succeeded in rising to include an inflation premium. When aggregated, the market returns are also low. Thus our 10 percent estimate dominated by the weak securities market in recent years does not adequately reflect a required inflation premium in returns. Most previous studies of market parameters utilize at least sixty months of returns and so have at least sixty observations as compared with the twenty in Table 16C.1. Of course, a larger number of observations will re-

Table 16C.1

Estimate of Market Parameters

Year	S&P 500 Price Index	Change in Price (Percent)	Dividend Yield	Percent Return	Return Deviation	Market Variance	Risk-Free Return
(t)	p_t	$\frac{p_t}{P_{t-1}} - 1$	$\frac{d_t}{p_t}$	R_{Mt} (3) + (4)	$(R_{Mt} - \overline{R}_M)$ $(5 - \overline{R}_M)$	$(R_{Mt} - \overline{R}_M)^2$ $(6)^2$	R_F
(1)	(2)	(3)	(4)	(5)	(6)	(7)	(8)
0	55.85						
1	66.27	0.1866	0.0298	0.2164	0.1164	0.013549	0.03
2	62.38	(0.0587)	0.0337	(0.0250)	(0.1250)	0.015625	0.03
3	69.87	0.1201	0.0317	0.1518	0.0518	0.002683	0.03
4	81.37	0.1646	0.0301	0.1947	0.0947	0.008968	0.04
5	88.17	0.0836	0.0300	0.1126	0.0136	0.000185	0.04
6	85.26	(0.0330)	0.0340	0.0010	(0.0990)	0.009801	0.04
7	91.93	0.0782	0.0320	0.1102	0.0102	0.000104	0.05
8	87.70	0.0736	0.0307	0.1043	0.0043	0.000018	0.05
9	97.84	(0.0087)	0.0324	0.0237	(0.0763)	0.005822	0.07
10	83.22	(0.1494)	0.0383	(0.1111)	(0.2111)	0.044563	0.06
11	98.29	0.1811	0.0314	0.2125	0.1125	0.012656	0.05
12	109.20	0.1110	0.0284	0.1394	0.0394	0.001552	0.05
13	107.43	(0.0162)	0.0306	0.0144	(0.0856)	0.007327	0.07
14	82.85	(0.2288)	0.0447	(0.1841)	(0.2841)	0.080713	0.08
15	85.17	0.0280	0.0431	0.0711	(0.0289)	0.000835	0.06
16	102.01	0.1977	0.0376	0.2353	0.1353	0.018306	0.06
17	114.74	0.1248	0.0432	0.1680	0.0680	0.004624	0.08
18	125.24	0.0915	0.0435	0.1350	0.0350	0.001225	0.09
19	139.61	0.1147	0.0440	0.1587	0.0587	0.003446	0.05
20	150.64	0.0790	0.0450	0.1240	0.0240	0.000576	0.07
21	165.72	0.1001	0.1460	0.2461	0.1461	0.021345	0.16
				2.100		0.253923	1.26
				$\overline{R}_M = \frac{2.100}{21} = 0.10$		$\text{Var}(R_M) = \frac{0.253923}{20} = 0.0127$	$\overline{R}_F = \frac{1.26}{21} = 0.06$

duce the variance measured, so that the longer term studies suggest that 1 percent is a good estimate of market variance on the average. Inspection of Column 8 containing the risk-free return measures indicates a range of from 3 percent to 16 percent. The higher values of R_F have predominated in the later years.

Thus to reflect an anticipated inflation premium in the market returns, it would be appropriate to use 7 to 10 percent for the risk-free return and 13 to 16 percent for the market returns. For our illustrative computation procedures, we shall use the following as the market parameters:

$$R_M = 12\%; \text{Var}(R_M) = 1\%; R_F = 7\%.$$

Next we seek to calculate the cost of capital for individual firms. Suppose that we have calculated the beta of two firms under analysis—International and the Jordan Corporation—as 1.2 and 1.6 respectively. An estimate of the required return on equity for each would be:

$$k_i^* = 0.07 + 0.05(1.2) = 0.13.$$
$$k_j^* = 0.07 + 0.05(1.6) = 0.15.$$

Without a careful analysis of the economics of the industry in which International and Jordon operate, we could not defend any particular estimates of the costs of equity for the two companies. An industry and financial analysis would be likely to demonstrate that the performance of Jordan is more volatile than for International and to support the direction of the result that the cost of equity capital was higher for Jordan than for International. This suggests further analysis of the components of the beta measures for the two companies.

Measuring Business and Financial Risks

The capital asset pricing model enables us to separate the components of business and financial risks. Proposition II of MM in their original (partial equilibrium) formulation can be expressed both without and with taxes:

No taxes $k_s = k_u + (k_u - k_b)\frac{B}{S}.$

With taxes $k_s = k_u + (k_u - k_b)\frac{B(1-T)}{S}.$

From a paper by Robert S. Hamada,[3] the corresponding formulations in the CAPM framework are:

No taxes $\overline{k}_s = R_F + \lambda\text{Cov}(R_u, R_M)\left[1 + \frac{B}{S}\right].$

3. Robert S. Hamada, "Portfolio Analysis, Market Equilibrium and Corporation Finance," *Journal of Finance* 24 (March 1969), pp. 13–31.

With taxes $\overline{k}_s = R_F + \lambda\text{Cov}(R_u, R_M)\left[1 + \frac{B(1-T)}{S}\right].$

Under both:

$$k_u = \frac{E(X)(1-T)}{V_u} \qquad k = \frac{E(X)(1-T)}{V_L}.$$

Recall that:

k_u = Cost of capital of an unlevered firm

k_s = Cost of equity capital of a levered firm

k = Weighted average cost of capital of a levered firm

The CAPM formulations can also be expressed in the form that utilizes beta as the measure of risk as follows:

$$\overline{k} = R_F + [\overline{R}_M - R_F]\beta_u\left[1 + \frac{B(1-T)}{S}\right], \qquad (16C.3)$$

where β_u is for an unlevered firm. When we multiply the terms we have the expression as shown in Equation 16C.3a:

$$\overline{k}_s = R_F + [\overline{R}_M - R_F]\beta_u + [\overline{R}_M - R_F]\beta_u\frac{B(1-T)}{S}. \qquad (16C.3a)$$

The beta that we observe is thus composed of the elements shown in Equation 16C.4:

$$\beta_j = \beta_u\left[1 + \frac{B(1-T)}{S}\right]. \qquad (16C.4)$$

We can thus separate the elements of business risk and financial risk as shown in Equation 16C.4a.

$$\beta_j = \beta_u + \beta_u\left[\frac{B(1-T)}{S}\right]. \qquad (16C.4a)$$

Then, solving Equation 16C.4 for the business risk term from the observed data, we have the relationship shown in Equation 16C.4b:

$$\beta_u = \frac{\beta_j}{\left[1 + \frac{B(1-T)}{S}\right]}. \qquad (16C.4b)$$

We can now apply these relationships using the data for International and Jordan. Based on an analysis of the capital structure of International and Jordan, we estimate the debt to equity ratio at market values of 50 percent and 100 percent respectively. The effective corporate tax rate for both companies is 40 percent. We can, therefore, proceed to calculate the business risk for each company, as shown in Equation 16C.4c:

Table 16C.2

Components of a Firm's Cost of Capital

	After-Tax Cost of Equity Capital: k_S (1)	= Risk-Free Element: R_F (2)	+ Premium for Business Risk: $(R_M - R_F)\beta_u$ (3)	+ Premium for Financial Risk: $(R_M - R_F)\beta_u(B/S)(1 - T)$ (4)
International	12.98%	7%	5%(0.92) = 4.6%	5%(0.92)(0.5)(0.6) = 1.38%
Jordan	15.00%	7%	5%(1.00) = 5%	5%(1.00)(1.0)(0.6) = 3.00%

$$\text{International: } \beta_u = \frac{1.2}{1 + 0.5(0.6)} = \frac{1.2}{1.3} = 0.92.$$

$$\text{Jordan: } \beta_u = \frac{1.6}{1 + 1(0.6)} = 1.00. \qquad (16C.4c)$$

As shown, we obtain a β_u for International of 0.92 and for Jordan of 1.0. This enables us to set forth the relationships that isolate the components of the risk premium in the cost of equity for each company as shown in Table 16C.2.

In Table 16C.2 we see that the risk-free element in the cost of equity capital for both International and Jordon is 7 percent. This is a market parameter. The premium for business risk is the market risk premium multiplied times each firm's beta as an unlevered firm. This component is 4.6 percent for International as compared with 5.0 percent for Jordan.

The third element in the cost of equity capital for each firm is the premium for business risk multiplied by the leverage element. This adds 1.38 percent to the cost of equity for International because of its lower leverage ratio. Jordan, which has a debt to equity ratio of 1, adds a premium for financial risk of 3.00 percent. Thus the lower cost of equity capital for International reflects its lower premium for business risk and—more significantly—its lower premium for financial risk.

In this appendix we have illustrated the application of some of the central concepts of the capital asset pricing model. In actual use, much more sophisticated computations of each of the elements would be employed. However, one way of checking the results from the use of more complex methods is to make rough estimates, utilizing the procedures here described.

Estimates of the Firm's Cost of Capital

We can now calculate the cost of capital for each of the two companies. After a careful analysis of the current yields to maturity of the outstanding debt of the two companies, we estimate International's market cost of debt at 10 percent and Jordan's at 14 percent. Recall that the debt to equity ratio at market for International is 50 percent and for Jordan, 100 percent.

We utilize the standard expression for the cost of capital.

$$k = k_b(1 - T)\frac{B}{V} + k_s\frac{S}{V}.$$

We can then calculate the cost of capital for each company:

International

$$k = 0.10(0.6)(1/3) + 0.1298(2/3)$$
$$= 0.02 + 0.08653$$
$$= 0.1065 = 10.65\%.$$

Jordan

$$k = 0.14(0.6)(0.5) + 0.1500(0.5)$$
$$= 0.042 + 0.075$$
$$= 0.117 = 11.70\%.$$

Although Jordan has a much higher cost of debt and a higher cost of equity as compared with International, its weighted cost of capital is only slightly more than one percentage point higher than International's cost of capital. Since Jordan uses a higher proportion of debt, its financial risk compounds its greater business risk. But the tax advantage of debt offsets to a substantial degree its higher financial costs. Jordan's differentially higher cost of capital, while small in absolute terms, is still significant, since the valuation of a firm is highly sensitive to the cost of capital employed.

Problems

16C.1 The following data have been developed for the Bradford Company.

State	Probability	Market Return R_M	Return for the Firm k_j
1	0.1	−0.15	−0.30
2	0.3	0.05	0.00
3	0.4	0.15	0.20
4	0.2	0.20	0.50

The risk-free rate is 6 percent. Calculate the following:

a. The market return.
b. The variance of the market.
c. The equation of the security market line.
d. The covariance of the returns of Bradford with the returns on the market.
e. The expected return for the Bradford Company.
f. The required return for Bradford.

16C.2 The following data have been developed for the Stell Company.

Year	Return on the Market	Company Returns
19X8	0.27	0.25
19X7	0.12	0.05
19X6	(0.03)	(0.05)
19X5	0.12	0.15
19X4	(0.03)	(0.10)
19X3	0.27	0.30

The yield to maturity on Treasury bills is 0.066, and it is expected to remain at this point for the foreseeable future. (Assume 5 degrees of freedom for the covariance and variance calculations and 6 degrees for the means.) Make calculations of the following:

a. The market return.
b. The variance of the market.
c. The equation of the security market line.
d. The expected return for Stell.
e. The covariance of Stell returns with the returns on the market.
f. The required return for Stell.

16C.3 The chief financial officer of the Starch Company seeks to determine the value of the division and the cost of capital for the Adhesive Division (without any leverage). He has gathered the following data. (Ignore taxes).

Year	Return on the Market	Earnings before Interest and Taxes
19X1	0.27	$ 25
19X2	0.12	5
19X3	(0.03)	(5)
19X4	0.12	15
19X5	(0.03)	(10)
19X6	0.27	30

The yield to maturity on Treasury bills is 0.066, and it is expected to remain at this level in the foreseeable future. For the unlevered division, compute (a) the value of the division and (b) the cost of capital. Assume 5 degrees of freedom for the covariance and variance calculations and 6 degrees for the means.

16C.4 The Myers Corporation has a total investment of $200 million in five divisions.

Division	Divisional Investment	Divisional Beta Coefficient (estimated)
A	$60	0.5
B	50	2.0
C	30	4.0
D	40	1.0
E	20	3.0

Management believes that there is a systematic relationship between each division's return and market returns as described by the beta coefficients, and these relationships are assumed to be stable over time.

The current risk-free rate is 5 percent, while expected market returns have the following probability distribution for the next period:

Probability	Market Return
0.1	6%
0.2	8
0.4	10
0.2	12
0.1	14

a. What is the estimated equation for the security market line (SML)?
b. Compute the expected return on the Myers Corporation for the next period.
c. Suppose management receives a proposal for a new division. The investment needed to create the new division is $50 million; it will have an expected return of 15 percent, and its estimated beta coefficient is 2.5. Should the new division be created? At what expected rate of return would management be indifferent to starting the new division?

16C.5 You are given the following data on market returns (R_M) and the returns on Stocks A and B.

	Returns by Year					
Return	19X3	19X4	19X5	19X6	19X7	19X8
R_M	0.20	0.10	−0.05	0.15	0.30	−0.10
R_A	0.25	0.05	−0.15	0.15	0.55	−0.25
R_B	−0.20	0.30	0.70	−0.10	0.50	−0.60

a. The risk-free rate of return is 6 percent. Determine the market return and variance.
b. For Stocks A and B determine the following:
Expected return ($\overline{R}_i$)
Covariance with the market [Cov(R_i,R_M)]
Beta (β_i)
Required return (R_i^*)
Variance of historic returns (σ_i^2)
c. What percent of the risk of Stocks A and B is systematic? Explain.
d. Graph the security market line and the returns of the two stocks.
e. Assuming no changes in variance or covariance of returns, what would you expect to happen to the prices of the two stocks? Why?
f. If both stocks were priced on the SML, which would have the higher yield? Which has the higher variance? Explain this apparent paradox.

16C.6 Before taking leverage into account, the Elgin Company has developed the following data with respect to a new project.

State	Probability	Market Return R_M	Project Return R_j
1	0.1	−0.15	−0.20
2	0.3	0.05	0.00
3	0.4	0.15	0.20
4	0.2	0.20	0.30

The risk of the project makes a leverage ratio (debt to value) of 0.5 appropriate. The Elgin Company's effective corporate tax rate is 40 percent. The risk-free rate is 6 percent. Should the project be undertaken?

Selected References

Gordon, Myron J., and Halpern, Paul J. "Cost of Capital for a Division of a Firm: Reply." *Journal of Finance* 32 (December 1977), pp. 1781–1782.

———. "Cost of Capital for a Division of a Firm." *Journal of Finance* 29 (September 1974), pp. 1153–1163.

Jarrett, Jeffrey E. "Estimating the Cost of Capital for a Division of a Firm, and the Allocation Problem in Accounting." *Journal of Business Finance and Accounting* 5 (Spring 1978), pp. 39–48.

Myers, Stewart C. "The Application of Finance Theory to Public Utility Rate Cases." *Bell Journal of Economics and Management Science* 3 (Spring 1972), pp. 58–97.

Pettway, R. H. "On the Use of β in Regulatory Proceedings: An Empirical Examination." *Bell Journal of Economics* 9 (Spring 1978), pp. 239–248.

Appendix D to Chapter 16

The State-Preference Model

Three important recent developments in finance are the Capital Asset Pricing Model (CAPM), the State-Preference Model (SPM), and the Option Pricing Model (OPM). The Capital Asset Pricing Model has been presented in Chapter 5. The Option Pricing Model will be set forth in Appendix A to Chapter 22. In this appendix we describe the State-Preference Model to wrap up the discussion of financial leverage.

Alternative Future States-of-the-World

The State-Preference Model provides a useful way of looking at the world and the nature of securities. One way of describing uncertainty about the future is to say that one of a set of possible states-of-the-world will occur. Definition of a set of states provides a means of describing characteristics of securities, since any security can be regarded as a contract to pay an amount that depends on the state that actually occurs.

For example, the decision to invest in the securities of a machinery manufacturer or of a machinery manufacturer to issue securities under a favorable set of conditions will depend on the potential future states of the economy. Will the economy be sufficiently strong that the demand for capital goods will provide favorable demand factors for a machinery manufacturer? Similarly, in the production plans of an automobile manufacturer or in an investor's decision to buy securities of an automobile company, will the future state of the economy be sufficiently strong to stimulate consumer optimism, resulting in a high volume of automobile purchases? Some of the main factors influencing the future states-of-the-world that will influence the sales of a firm or the prospects for investments in a firm are set forth in Table 16D.1.

As a practical matter a person will explicitly consider only a small number of factors in making a decision. Hence, individual decision makers are likely to select those variables judged to be most critical for influencing the payoff possibilities of securities in which a position or investment is contemplated. For practical reasons, therefore, alternative future states-of-the-world might be summarized into forecasts of alternative levels or rates of growth in the

This section was written with the valuable counsel of Professor Harry DeAngelo.

Table 16D.1

Central Factors Influencing Estimates of Future States-of-the-World for Use in Forecasting the Sales of the Firm

A. Economy
1. Growth rate of GNP—real terms
2. Growth rate of GNP—inflation
3. Growth rate of monetary base (availability)
4. Long-term interest rates
5. Short-term interest rates

B. Competition
1. Prices of rival products
2. New products by rivals
3. Changes in products by rivals
4. New advertising campaigns by rivals
5. Salesperson and other selling efforts by rivals
6. Prices of industry-substitute products
7. Quality of industry-substitute products

C. Cultural and political factors
1. Externalities and their influences on sales of our products
2. Product liabilities

gross national product. Ultimately, a wide variety of the factors listed in Table 16D.1 is likely to be reflected in levels of gross national product. Furthermore, the rate of growth and the performance of most individual industries in the economy are greatly influenced by movements in gross national product. Thus alternative future states-of-the-world may be characterized in terms of four possibilities with respect to gross national product. These might be a strong rate of growth, a moderate rate of growth, a moderate decline, or a substantial decline.

While for practical problems we might limit the number of alternative future states-of-the-world, from another standpoint—that of personal portfolio construction—we would like to provide for all possible future states-of-the-world. If we could always find a security that provided some payoff under one of the many possible future states-of-the-world, we could hedge by combining a large number of securities so that regardless of the future state-of-the-world that occurs, we would receive some payoff. The securities we encounter in the real world are complex securities in the sense that their payoffs are positive, but generally different, amounts under alternative states-of-the-world. If actual securities could provide some payoff for every possible future state-of-the-world by appropriately combining long and short positions in securities, we could create a pure, or primitive, security.

The Concept of a Pure Security

A pure or primitive security is one that pays off $1 if one particular future state-of-the-world occurs and pays off nothing if any other state-of-the-world occurs. This seems like an abstract concept, so let us develop the idea further

Table 16D.2

Payoffs in Relation to Prices of Baskets of Fruit

	Bananas	Apples	Prices
Basket #1	10	20	\$8
Basket #2	30	10	\$9

by means of an example. We shall take the case of the Mistinback Company, which sells baskets of fruit. This particular company limits its sales to only two types of baskets. Basket 1 is composed of 10 bananas and 20 apples and sells for \$8. Basket 2 is composed of 30 bananas and 10 apples and sells for \$9. The question is posed: What is the price of one banana or one apple only? The situation may be summarized by the payoffs set forth in Table 16D.2.

To calculate the value of a banana or an apple, we set up two equations:

$$10\ V_b + 20\ V_a = \$8.$$

$$30\ V_b + 10\ V_a = \$9.$$

Solving simultaneously, we obtain

$$V_a = \$.30.$$

$$V_b = \$.20.$$

We may now apply this same analysis to securities. Any individual security is similar to a mixed basket of goods with regard to alternative future states-of-the-world. Recall that a pure security is a security that pays \$1 if a specified state occurs and nothing if any other state occurs.[1]

We may proceed to determine the price of a pure security in a manner analogous to that employed for the fruit baskets. Consider Security j, which pays \$10 if State 1 occurs and \$20 if State 2 occurs. The current price of Security j is \$8. Security k pays \$30 if State 1 occurs and \$10 if State 2 occurs. Its current price is \$9. Note that State 1 might be a GNP growth during the year of 8 percent in real terms, while State 2 might represent a growth in real national product of only 1 percent. In Table 16D.3 the payoff for the two securities is set forth. Here, F_{j1} is the payoff in State 1 to Security j, F_{k1} is the payoff in State 1 to Security k, and so on. The equations for determining the prices for the two pure securities related to the situation described are:

$$p_1F_{j1} + p_2F_{j2} = p_j.$$

$$p_1F_{k1} + p_2F_{k2} = p_k.$$

1. Observe that this is a clear form of nondiversification. It represents putting all of one's financial resources into one state-basket.

Table 16D.3

Payoff Table for Securities 1 and 2

	State 1	State 2	
Security j	F_{j1} = \$10	F_{j2} = \$20	p_j = \$8
Security k	F_{k1} = \$30	F_{k2} = \$10	p_k = \$9

Proceeding analogously to the situation for the fruit baskets, we insert the value of security payoffs into the two equations to obtain the price of Pure Security 1 as \$.20 and the price of Pure Security 2 as \$.30.

$$10p_1 + 20p_2 = \$8$$
$$30p_1 + 10p_2 = \$9$$
$$p_1 = \$.20$$
$$p_2 = \$.30$$

It should be emphasized that the p_1 of \$.20 and the p_2 of \$.30 are not assigned to Securities j and k.

In sum, Securities j and k represent bundles of returns under alternative future states. Any actual security provides different payoffs for different future states. But under appropriately defined conditions, the prices of pure securities can be determined from the prices of actual securities. The concept of a pure security is useful for analytical purposes as well as for providing a useful point of view in financial analysis as illustrated in the following section, which provides an application of the State-Preference Model to leverage decisions.

Use of the SPM to Determine the Optimal Financial Leverage

The State-Preference Model has been used to analyze the question of optimal financial leverage.[2] The ideas will be conveyed by a specific example. It is assumed that there are four possible states-of-the-world and that the capital markets are complete in that there exists at least one security for every possible state-of-the-world such that there is a full set of primitive securities. The symbols that will be utilized are listed in Table 16D.4, and the data that will be analyzed in this example are summarized in Table 16D.5.

In Table 16D.5 we have ordered the states by the size of the EBIT that the firm will achieve under alternative states. Column 3 of the table lists the prices of primitive securities for each of the four states. In Column 4 we list the failure or bankruptcy costs associated with the inability to meet debt obligations.

In this state-preference framework, let us analyze the position of debt holders and equity holders. Table 16D.6 analyzes the amounts received under alternative conditions. Under Condition 1 the EBIT is equal to or exceeds the

2. Alan Kraus and Robert Litzenburger, "A State-Preference Model of Optimal Financial Leverage," *Journal of Finance* 28 (September 1973), pp. 911–922.

Table 16D.4

Symbols Used in the SPM Analysis of Optimal Financial Leverage

p_s = Market price of the primitive security that represents a claim on one dollar in State *s* and zero dollars in all other states
X_s = Earnings before interest and taxes that the firm will achieve in State *s* (EBIT)
B = Nominal payment to debt, representing a promise to pay Fixed Amount B, irrespective of the state that occurs
$S(B)$ = Market value of the firm's equity as a function of the amount of debt issued by the firm
$V(B)$ = Market value of the firm as a function of the amount of debt issued
f_s = Costs of failure in State *s*; $0 < f_s \leq X_s$
T = Corporate tax rate = 50%.

Table 16D.5

Data for SPM Analysis of Optimal Financial Leverage

s (1)	X_s (2)	p_s (3)	f_s (4)
1	$ 100	$0.30	$ 100
2	500	0.50	400
3	1,000	0.20	500
4	2,000	0.10	1,200

Table 16D.6

Amounts Received under Alternative Conditions

Condition	Amount of X_s in Relation to B (1)	Debt Holders Receive (2)	Equity Holders Receive (3)
1	$X_s \geq B$	B	$(X_s - B)(1 - T)$
2	$0 \leq X_s < B$	$(X_s - f_s)$	0
3	$X_s < 0$	0	0

debt obligation. Under that condition, debt holders will receive B and equity holders will receive the income remaining after deduction of B and of taxes. Under Condition 2, the EBIT is positive but less than the amount of the debt obligation, B. The debt holders will receive whatever EBIT remains after payment of the failure or bankruptcy costs. Equity holders will receive nothing. If the EBIT is negative, neither the debt holders nor equity holders receive anything. These relationships are quite logical and straightforward.

The amounts received under alternative conditions as outlined in Table 16D.7 are multiplied by the prices of the primitive securities to obtain the value of debt holders' receipts and of equity holders' receipts as well as the value of the firm under alternative conditions. The value of debt holders' re-

Table 16D.7

Formulas for the Value of the Firm under Alternative Conditions

Condition	Amount of X_s in Relation to B (1)	Debt Holders Receive (2)	Value of Debt Holders' Receipts in State s (3)	Equity Holders Receive (4)	Value of Equity Holders' Receipts in State s (5)	Value of the Firm in State s (6)
1	$X_s \geq B$	B	Bp_s	$(X_s - B)(1 - T)$	$(X_s - B)(1 - T)p_s$	$Bp_s + (X_s - B)(1 - T)p_s$
2	$0 \leq X_s < B$	$(X_s - f_s)$	$(X_s - f_s)p_s$	0	0	$(X_s - f_s)p_s$
3	$X_s < 0$	0	0	0	0	0

ceipts is obtained by simply multiplying what the debt holders receive by p_s and similarly for the value of equity holders' receipts. The value of the firm is obtained by adding the value of the debt holders' receipts to the value of the equity holders' receipts.

In Table 16D.8 we utilize the preceding information to calculate the value of the firm under alternative debt levels. On the left-hand side of the table we begin by specifying the amount of debt and the resulting relationships between X_s, the EBIT under alternative states, and the promised debt payment. The subsequent lines on the left then set forth the applicable formulas for calculating the state contingent value of the firm depending upon the level of debt utilized. For example, when the firm is unlevered, its value is equal to EBIT times (1 minus the tax rate) times the price of the primitive security for each state summed over all the states. Using the illustrative data from Table 16D.5, we obtain the amounts on the right-hand column of Table 16D.8.

When debt is 100, EBIT is equal to or greater than debt for all states-of-the-world. The formula employed, therefore, is set forth in Table 16D.7 under Condition 1 and shown in Column 6. Again, the numbers from 16D.5 are inserted to obtain a current market value of the firm, $V(100)$, of \$395 for Debt Level 2 in Table 16D.8.

We shall discuss the pattern for debt of \$1,000 as illustrative of the remaining sections of Table 16D.8. When B is equal to \$1,000 the EBIT is less than the promised debt payment for States 1 and 2 and equal to or greater than debt for States 3 and 4. As Table 16D.7 indicates, Condition 2, therefore, obtains for States 1 and 2, while Condition 1 obtains for States 3 and 4. The applicable formulas are therefore utilized to obtain a $V(1{,}000)$ of \$400, as shown in Table 16D.8.

An analysis of Table 16D.8 shows that the highest value of the firm is obtained when debt leverage of \$500 is employed by the firm. For any other lev-

Table 16D.8

Calculations of the Value of the Firm under Alternative Debt Levels

Condition	State	Value of Firm's State s Payoff
1. $B = 0,\ X_s > B$ for all s	1	100(0.5)0.3 = 15
$V_s(0) = \sum_{s=1}^{4} X_s(1 - T)p_s$	2	500(0.5)0.5 = 125
	3	1,000(0.5)0.2 = 100
	4	2,000(0.5)0.1 = 100
		$V(0)$ = $340
2. $B = 100,\ X_s \geq B$ for all s	1	100(0.3) + (100 − 100)(0.5)0.3 = 30
$V_s(100) = \sum_{s=1}^{4} Bp_s + \sum_{s=1}^{4} (X_s - B)(1 - T)p_s$	2	100(0.5) + (500 − 100)(0.5)0.5 = 150
	3	100(0.2) + (1,000 − 100)(0.5)0.2 = 110
	4	100(0.1) + (2,000 − 100)(0.5)0.1 = 105
		$V(100)$ = $395
3. $B = 500,\ X_s < B$ for $s = 1$; $X_s \geq B$ for $s = 2, 3, 4$	1	(100 − 100)0.3 = 0
$V_s(500) = (X_s - f_s)p_s$ for $s = 1$	2	500(0.5) + (500 − 500)(0.5)0.5 = 250
$V_s(500) = \sum_{s=2}^{4} Bp_s + \sum_{s=2}^{4} (X_s - B)(1 - T)p_s$	3	500(0.2) + (1,000 − 500)(0.5)0.2 = 150
	4	500(0.1) + (2,000 − 500)(0.5)0.1 = 125
		$V(500)$ = $525
4. $B = 1{,}000,\ X_s < B$ for $s = 1, 2$; $X_s \geq B$ for $s = 3, 4$	1	(100 − 100)0.3 = 0
$V_s(1{,}000) = \sum_{s=1}^{2} (X_s - f_s)p_s$	2	(500 − 400)0.5 = 50
$V_s(1{,}000) = \sum_{s=3}^{4} Bp_s + \sum_{s=3}^{4} (X_s - B)(1 - T)p_s$	3	1,000(0.2) + (1,000 − 1,000)(0.5)0.2 = 200
	4	1,000(0.1) + (2,000 − 1,000)(0.5)0.1 = 150
		$V(1{,}000)$ = $400
5. $B = 2{,}000,\ X_s < B$ for $s = 1, 2, 3$; $X_s \geq B$ for $s = 4$	1	(100 − 100)0.3 = 0
$V_s(2{,}000) = \sum_{s=1}^{3} (X_s - f_s)p_s$	2	(500 − 400)0.5 = 50
$V_s(2{,}000) = Bp_s + (X_s - B)(1 - T)p_s$ for $s = 4$	3	(1,000 − 500)0.2 = 100
	4	2,000(0.1) + (2,000 − 2,000)(0.5)0.1 = 200
		$V(2{,}000)$ = $350

el of debt obligations the value of the firm is lower. This example illustrates that with taxes and bankruptcy costs, there exists an optimal amount of leverage.[3]

Implications for Leverage Decisions

Our use of the State-Preference Model has enabled us to analyze some conditions under which an optimal capital leverage exists.[4] This result is, of course, not perfectly general since it was based on a specific illustration. Some more general relationships will now be set forth. First we need to introduce the concept of complete capital markets. *Complete capital markets* are those in which a security exists for every possible state-of-the-world, so that it is possible to create a full set of primitive securities. In complete capital markets, in the absence of such imperfections as taxes, agency costs, and bankruptcy costs, capital structure would not matter (the Modigliani-Miller propositions would obtain).

The leverage policy of a firm consists of repackaging the claims on its EBIT. The only reason why repackaging of claims on the firm's EBIT would have an effect on the value of the firm would be that the firm had thereby provided investors with a new set of market opportunities for forming portfolios or taking a position with regard to future states-of-the-world. But if the capital markets are already complete, the firm has added nothing by a repackaging of claims on EBIT since no new independent investment opportunities can be provided. All possible future states-of-the-world have already been covered by existing securities.

The proof of the Modigliani-Miller independence thesis does not depend on the assumption that the firm will always meet its debt obligations. For some debt levels the firm may not meet its debt obligations in some states-of-the-world and would be bankrupt. If there are no bankruptcy penalties or bankruptcy costs (the situation in a perfect market), the *nature* of the claims on the firm's EBIT have been fundamentally unaltered. Thus the value of the firm remains unchanged.

Thus complete and perfect capital markets constitute sufficient conditions for the Modigliani-Miller propositions to hold. But as the foregoing example illustrated, the taxation of corporate profits and the existence of bankruptcy-

3. Kraus and Litzenburger conclude with regard to their analysis as follows: "Contrary to the traditional net income approach to valuation, if the firm's debt obligation exceeds its earnings in some states the firm's market value is *not* necessarily a concave (from below) function of its debt obligation." Ibid., p. 918. However, this result follows only from their formulation of the problem in discontinuous terms. The problem could equally well be formulated with continuous functions in such a way that the resulting value of the firm would be a continuous and concave (from below) function of *B*.
4. Problems 16D.4 and 16D.5 illustrate that the production decisions and capital structure decisions of the firm can be interdependent, given the presence of imperfections.

agency penalties represent market imperfections under which the capital structure choice will affect the value of the firm. We conclude that Modigliani and Miller are correct under properly specified conditions.

Furthermore, it is the absence of complete and perfect capital markets that makes capital structure matter. It is not clear whether the actual number of securities approximates the condition of completeness of the capital markets. However, without question there are corporate income taxes as well as agency and bankruptcy costs. The extent to which agency and bankruptcy costs significantly affect capital structure is an empirical matter.

Problems

16D.1 Security A pays \$30 if State 1 occurs and \$10 if State 2 occurs. Security B pays \$20 if State 1 occurs and \$40 if State 2 occurs. The price of Security A is \$5 and the price of Security B is \$10.

a. Set up the payoff table for Securities A and B.

b. Determine the prices of pure Securities 1 and 2.

16D.2 The common stock of GM will pay \$70 if State 1 occurs, in which the U.S. economy is in an upswing and GM's production volume of small cars causes the volume of imports to decline. In State 2 the U.S. economy experiences stagflation, with real growth at 1 percent per year and inflation near the two-digit rate. In State 2, the common stock of GM pays \$35. In State 2, Control Data pays \$68. In State 1, Control Data pays \$55. The current price of GM is \$53, and the current price of Control Data is \$60.

a. Set up the payoff tables for GM and Control Data.

b. Determine the prices of the two pure securities.

16D.3 The Sand Corporation is evaluating alternatives for financing its production. There are essentially three possible levels of production, depending on which state-of-the-world occurs. Cost of failure and earnings before interest and taxes are different for each state. The company is considering use of debt in the amount of \$0, \$1,000, \$3,000, or \$6,000 and would like to know which alternative will maximize the expected value of the firm, given the primitive security prices associated with each state. The tax rate is 40 percent.

State (s)	Planned Production EBIT (X_s)	Price of Primitive Security (p_s)	Cost of Failure (f_s)
1	2,000	0.30	500
2	4,000	0.50	1,500
3	8,000	0.20	4,000

16D.4 The Kendrick Company is evaluating three alternative production plans (X_s, Y_s, and Z_s), as follows. Cost of failure is the same for each plan. Prices of primitive securities for the four possible states are as indicated.

State (s)	Price of Primitive Security (p_s)	Cost of Failure (f_s)	Planned Production EBIT (X_s)	(Y_s)	(Z_s)
1	0.10	100	200	600	100
2	0.40	600	1,200	1,500	800
3	0.30	1,500	3,000	2,800	3,200
4	0.20	2,000	3,500	3,000	3,800

Assuming the production will be financed with funds including $3,000 of debt, which of the three production plans would maximize the value of the firm? The tax rate is 40 percent.

16D.5 Under production Plan A the EBIT of the firm for alternative states-of-the-world is indicated by the X_s column. The price of the primitive pure securities in State s is p_s. The failure or bankruptcy costs are f_s. Under production Plan B, the EBIT of the firm is indicated by X'_s. Production Plan B involves giving up $300 in State 3 to add $300 in State 2. Since the prices of pure securities and bankruptcy costs are given by the market, they remain unchanged under production Plan B. The tax rate is 40 percent.

s	X_s	p_s	f_s	X'_s
1	$ 500	0.20	100	$ 500
2	600	0.40	300	900
3	1,400	0.30	500	1,100
4	2,000	0.10	800	2,000

a. What is the optimal financial leverage for production Plan A by the criterion of maximizing the value of the firm? Calculate the value for debt levels of $0, $500, $600, $1,400, and $2,000.

b. Is the optimal financial leverage changed by new production Plan B? Answer for debt levels of $0, $500, $900, $1,100, and $2,000.

c. What implications do the results under Plans A and B have for the interdependence between production plans and financial structure?

Selected References

Arrow, K. J. "The Role of Securities in the Optimal Allocation of Risk-Bearing." *Review of Economic Studies* 31 (April 1964), pp. 91–96.

Dyl, Edward A. "A State Preference Model of Capital Gains Taxation." *Journal of Financial and Quantitative Analysis* 14 (September 1979), pp. 529–535.

Hirshleifer, J. "Investment Decisions under Uncertainty: Application of the State-Preference Approach." *Quarterly Journal of Economics* 80 (May 1966), pp. 262–277.

Kraus, Alan, and Litzenberger, Robert. "A State-Preference Model of Optimal Financial Leverage." *Journal of Finance* 28 (September 1973), pp. 911–922.

Myers, S. C. "A Time-State Preference Model of Security Valuation." *Journal of Financial and Quantitative Analysis* 3 (March 1968), pp. 1–33.

Sharpe, W. F. "State-Preference Theory." In *Portfolio Theory and Capital Markets.* New York: McGraw-Hill, 1970, Chapter 10.

17
Dividend Policy and Valuation

Dividend policy determines the division of earnings between payments to stockholders and reinvestment in the firm. Retained earnings are one of the most significant sources of funds for financing corporate growth, but dividends constitute the cash flows that accrue to stockholders. The factors that influence the allocation of earnings to dividends or retained earnings are the subject of this chapter.

Dividend Payments

Dividends are normally paid quarterly. For example, Liggett Group pays annual dividends of $2.50. In financial parlance we say that Liggett Group's regular quarterly dividend is 62.5 cents or that its regular annual dividend is $2.50. The management of a company such as Liggett Group conveys to stockholders, sometimes by an explicit statement in the annual report and sometimes by implication, an expectation that the regular dividend will be maintained if at all possible. Further, management conveys its belief that earnings will be sufficient to maintain the dividend.

Under other conditions, a firm's cash flows and investment needs may be too volatile for it to set a very high regular dividend. On the average, however, it needs a high dividend payout to dispose of funds not necessary for reinvestment. In such a case, the directors can set a relatively low regular dividend—low enough that it can be maintained even in low profit years or in years when a considerable amount of reinvestment is needed—and supplement it with an extra dividend in years when excess funds are available. General Motors, whose earnings fluctuate widely from year to year, has long followed the practice of supplementing its regular dividend with an extra dividend paid in addition to the regular fourth quarter dividend.

Payment Procedure

The actual payment procedure is of some importance, and the following is an outline of the payment sequence.

1. *Declaration date.* The directors meet, say, on November 15 and declare the regular dividend. On this date, they issue a statement similar to the following: "On November 15, 1980, the directors of the XYZ Company met

and declared the regular quarterly dividend of 50 cents a share, plus an extra dividend of 75 cents a share, to holders of record on December 15, payment to be made on January 2, 1981."

2. *Holder-of-record date.* On December 15, the *holder-of-record-date,* the company closes its stock transfer books and makes up a list of the shareholders as of that date. If XYZ Company is notified of the sale and transfer of some stock before December 16, the new owner receives the dividend. If notification is received on or after December 16, the old stockholder gets the dividend.
3. *Ex dividend date.* Suppose Irma Jones buys 100 shares of stock from Robert Noble on December 13. Will the company be notified of the transfer in time to list her as the new owner and thus pay her the dividend? To avoid conflict, the brokerage business has set up a convention of declaring that the right to the dividend remains with the stock until four days prior to the holder-of-record date; on the fourth day before the record date, the right to the dividend no longer goes with the shares. The date when the right to the dividend leaves the stock is called the *ex dividend date.* In this case, the ex dividend date is four days prior to December 15, or December 11. Therefore, if Jones is to receive the dividend, she must buy the stock by December 10. If she buys it on December 11 or later, Noble will receive the dividend. The total dividend, regular plus extra, amounts to $1.25, so the ex dividend date is important. Barring fluctuations in the stock market, we would normally expect the price of a stock to drop by approximately the amount of the dividend on the ex dividend date.
4. *Payment date.* The company actually mails the checks to the holders of record on January 2, the payment date.

Factors Influencing Dividend Policy

What factors determine the extent to which a firm will pay out dividends instead of retaining earnings? As a first step toward answering this question, we shall consider some of the factors that influence dividend policy.

Legal Rules

Although state statutes and court decisions governing dividend policy are complicated, their essential nature can be stated briefly. The legal rules provide that dividends must be paid from earnings—either from the current year's earnings or from past years' earnings as reflected in the balance sheet account "retained earnings."

State laws emphasize three rules: (1) the net profits rule, (2) the capital impairment rule, and (3) the insolvency rule. The *net profits rule* provides that dividends can be paid from past and present earnings. The *capital impairment rule* protects creditors by forbidding the payment of dividends from capital. (Paying dividends from capital would be distributing the investment in a company rather than its earnings.)[1] The *insolvency rule* provides that corporations cannot pay dividends while insolvent. (*Insolvency* is here defined, in the bankruptcy sense, as liabilities exceeding assets; and to pay dividends under such conditions would mean giving stockholders funds that rightfully belong to the creditors.)

Legal rules are significant in that they provide the framework within which dividend policies can be formulated. Within their boundaries, however, financial and economic factors have a major influence on policy.

Liquidity Position

Profits held as retained earnings (which show up on the right-hand side of the balance sheet) are generally invested in assets required for the conduct of the business. Retained earnings from preceding years are already invested in plant and equipment, inventories, and other assets; they are not held as cash. Thus, even if a firm has a record of earnings, it may not be able to pay cash dividends because of its liquidity position. Indeed, a growing firm, even a very profitable one, typically has a pressing need for funds. In such a situation the firm may elect not to pay cash dividends.

If this point is not clear, refer again to Table 7.1—the Walker-Wilson Company's balance sheet. The retained earnings account shows $400,000, but the cash account shows only $50,000. Since some cash must be retained to pay bills, it is clear that Walker-Wilson's cash position precludes a dividend of even $50,000.

Need to Repay Debt

When a firm has sold debt to finance expansion or to substitute for other forms of financing, it is faced with two alternatives. It can refund the debt at maturity by replacing it with another form of security, or it can make provisions for paying off the debt. If the decision is to retire the debt, this will generally require the retention of earnings.

Restrictions in Debt Contracts

Debt contracts, particularly when long-term debt is involved, frequently restrict a firm's ability to pay cash dividends. Such restrictions, which are designed to protect the position of the lender, usually state that (1) future dividends can be paid only out of earnings generated *after* the signing of the loan agreement (that is, they cannot be paid out of past retained earnings) and (2) that dividends cannot be paid when net working capital (current assets minus current liabilities) is below a specified amount. Similarly, preferred stock agreements generally state that no cash dividends can be paid on the common stock until all accrued preferred dividends have been paid.

Rate of Asset Expansion

The more rapid the rate at which the firm is growing, the greater its needs for financing asset expansion. The greater the future need for funds, the more likely the firm is to retain earnings rather than pay them out. If a firm seeks to

1. It is possible, of course, to return stockholders' capital; when this is done, however, the procedure must be clearly stated as such. A dividend paid out of capital is called a *liquidating* dividend.

raise funds externally, natural sources are the present shareholders, who already know the company. But if earnings are paid out as dividends and are subjected to high personal income tax rates, only a portion of them will be available for reinvestment.

Profit Rate

The rate of return on assets determines the relative attractiveness of paying out earnings in the form of dividends to stockholders (who will use them elsewhere) or using them in the present enterprise.

Stability of Earnings

A firm that has relatively stable earnings is often able to predict approximately what its future earnings will be. Such a firm is therefore more likely to pay out a higher percentage of its earnings than is a firm with fluctuating earnings. The unstable firm is not certain that in subsequent years the hoped-for earnings will be realized, so it is likely to retain a high proportion of current earnings. A lower dividend will be easier to maintain if earnings fall off in the future.

Access to the Capital Markets

A large, well-established firm with a record of profitability and stability of earnings has easy access to capital markets and other forms of external financing. A small, new, or venturesome firm, however, is riskier for potential investors. Its ability to raise equity or debt funds from capital markets is restricted, and it must retain more earnings to finance its operations. A well-established firm is thus likely to have a higher dividend payout rate than is a new or small firm.

Control

Another important variable is the effect of alternative sources of financing on the control situation in the firm. As a matter of policy, some corporations expand only to the extent of their internal earnings. This policy is defended on the ground that raising funds by selling additional common stock dilutes the control of the dominant group in that company. At the same time, selling debt increases the risks of fluctuating earnings to the present owners of the company. Reliance on internal financing in order to maintain control reduces the dividend payout.

Tax Position of Stockholders

The tax position of the corporation's owners greatly influences the desire for dividends. For example, a corporation closely held by a few taxpayers in high income tax brackets is likely to pay a relatively low dividend. The owners are interested in taking their income in the form of capital gains rather than as dividends, which are subject to higher personal income tax rates. However, the stockholders of a large, widely held corporation may be interested in a high dividend payout.

At times there is a conflict of interest in large corporations between stockholders in high income tax brackets and those in low tax brackets. The former may prefer to see a low dividend payout and a high rate of earnings retention in the hope of an appreciation in the capital stock of the company. The latter may prefer a relatively high dividend payout. The dividend policy in such firms may be a compromise between a low and a high payout—an intermediate payout ratio. If one group comes to dominate the company and sets, say, a low payout policy, those stockholders who seek income are likely to sell their shares over time and shift into higher-yielding stocks. Thus, to at least some extent, a firm's payout policy determines the type of stockholders it has—and vice versa. This has been called the "clientele influence" on dividend policy.

Tax on Improperly Accumulated Earnings

In order to prevent wealthy stockholders from using the corporation as an "incorporated pocketbook" by which they can avoid high personal income tax rates, tax regulations applicable to corporations provide for a special surtax on improperly accumulated income. However, Section 531 of the Revenue Act of 1954 places the burden of proof on the Internal Revenue Service to justify penalty rates for accumulation of earnings. That is, earnings retention is justified unless the IRS can prove otherwise.

General Dividend Patterns in the Economy

Table 17.1 presents after-tax profits, dividends, and the dividend payouts for the postwar years 1946 to 1979. Payouts for selected time periods are also calculated. During 1947 to 1955, the postwar adjustment and the time of the Korean conflict, the payout was about 50 percent. It remained at this 50 percent rate during the 1955 to 1966 period of price stability. During the first part of the inflationary period that started in 1966, the dividend payout remained stable at 50 percent. However, during the period of continued inflation and the rise in oil prices from 1973 on, the dividend payout has risen to 61 percent.

Another perspective is obtained by examining growth rate patterns for selected time periods, as shown in Table 17.2. The postwar period, 1948 to 1966, was characterized by relative price stability in which the consumers' price index (CPI) increased by less than 2 percent per annum. The GNP, after-tax profits, and dividends all grew at about a 6 percent rate. From 1966 to 1972, the CPI increased at a 4.32 percent per year rate, and GNP in nominal terms was growing at a 7.64 percent rate. After-tax profits were virtually flat, while dividends did not quite keep up with the inflation rate—the real dividend growth rate was slightly negative.

For the period 1972 to 1979, the CPI has increased over 8 percent per year. The GNP in nominal terms has grown at a rate of 10.55 percent per year but at less than 2.5 percent per year in real terms. After-tax profit growth did not keep up with the inflation rate, while dividend growth was 11.5 percent per annum, representing a margin of 3.31 percent over the inflation rate. Hence the dividend payout rate increased from 49 percent to 61 percent.

Table 17.1

Dividend Payout Patterns, 1946–1979 (Billions of Dollars)

	After-Tax Profits	Dividends	Dividend Payout
1946	$ 7.5	$ 5.6	0.75%
1947	10.9	6.3	0.58
1948	16.7	7.0	0.42
1949	16.7	7.2	0.43
1950	15.7	8.8	0.56
1951	15.5	8.5	0.55
1952	16.0	8.5	0.53
1953	15.2	8.8	0.58
1954	17.0	9.1	0.54
1955	22.6	10.3	0.46
1956	20.9	11.1	0.53
1957	20.6	11.5	0.56
1958	18.5	11.3	0.61
1959	24.6	12.2	0.50
1960	23.9	12.9	0.54
1961	24.1	13.3	0.55
1962	30.9	14.4	0.47
1963	33.4	15.5	0.46
1964	39.0	17.3	0.44
1965	46.2	19.1	0.41
1966	48.9	19.4	0.40
1967	46.8	20.1	0.43
1968	46.4	21.9	0.47
1969	41.8	22.6	0.54
1970	33.4	22.9	0.69
1971	39.5	23.0	0.58
1972	50.5	24.6	0.49
1973	50.4	27.8	0.55
1974	31.2	31.0	0.99
1975	46.1	31.9	0.69
1976	63.0	37.5	0.60
1977	77.3	42.1	0.54
1978	83.2	47.2	0.57
1979	85.8	52.7	0.61
Dividend payout			
1947–1955	146.3	74.5	0.51
1955–1966	353.6	168.3	0.48
1966–1972	307.3	154.5	0.50
1972–1979	487.5	294.8	0.61

Note that the second column shows corporate profits with inventory valuation and capital consumption adjustments.
Sources: President's Council of Economic Advisers, *Economic Report of the President* (Washington, D.C.: Government Printing Office, January 1980), Table B–79; and U.S. Department of Commerce, Bureau of Economic Analysis, *Survey of Current Business* (Washington, D.C.: Government Printing Office, December 1979), Table 7.

Table 17.2

Compound Annual Growth Rates in Selected Series, 1948–1979

	1948–1966	1966–1972	1972–1979
GNP	6.11%	7.64%	10.55%
After-tax profits	6.15	0.54	6.81
Dividends	5.83	4.04	11.50
CPI	1.67	4.32	8.19

Source: President's Council of Economic Advisers, *Economic Report of the President* (Washington, D.C.: Government Printing Office, 1980).

Because of the impact of inflation since 1966, it is useful to deflate both after-tax profits and dividends by the CPI. We find that deflated dividends increased at a 1.3 percent rate from 1966 to 1979, while deflated after-tax profits were decreasing at a rate of 2 percent per year for the same time period. In spite of declining real profits, real dividends have been relatively stable. This is also shown by Figure 17.1, which presents deflated after-tax profits and deflated dividends for the 1946 to 1979 period. Deflated dividends remained at about $20 billion from 1965 through 1975. Dividends moved up to about $24 billion for 1978 and 1979. But considerable stability in deflated dividends is exhibited for most of the 1966 to 1979 period. With the background of dividend patterns for the economy as a whole, we next turn to an examination of dividend policy at the level of the individual firm.

Dividend Policy Decisions

Most corporations seek to maintain a target dividend per share. However, dividends increase with a lag after earnings rise. That is, they are increased only after an increase in earnings appears clearly sustainable and relatively permanent. When dividends have been increased, strenuous efforts are made to maintain them at the new level. If earnings decline, the existing dividend generally is maintained until it is clear that an earnings recovery will not take place.

Figure 17.2 illustrates these ideas by showing the earnings and dividend patterns for the Walter Watch Company over a thirty-year period. Initially, earnings are $2 and dividends $1 a share, providing a 50 percent payout ratio. Earnings rise for four years, while dividends remain constant; thus the payout ratio falls during this period. During 1955 and 1956, earnings fall substantially; however, the dividend is maintained, and the payout ratio rises above the 50 percent target. During the period between 1956 and 1960, earnings experience a sustained rise. Dividends are held constant for a time, while management seeks to determine whether the earnings increase is permanent. By 1961, the earnings gains seem permanent, and dividends are raised in three steps to reestablish the 50 percent target payout. During 1965 a strike causes earnings to fall below the regular dividend; expecting the earnings decline to be temporary, management maintains the dividend. Earnings fluctuate on a

Figure 17.1

Corporate Earnings after Taxes and Dividends (CPI Deflated), 1946–1979

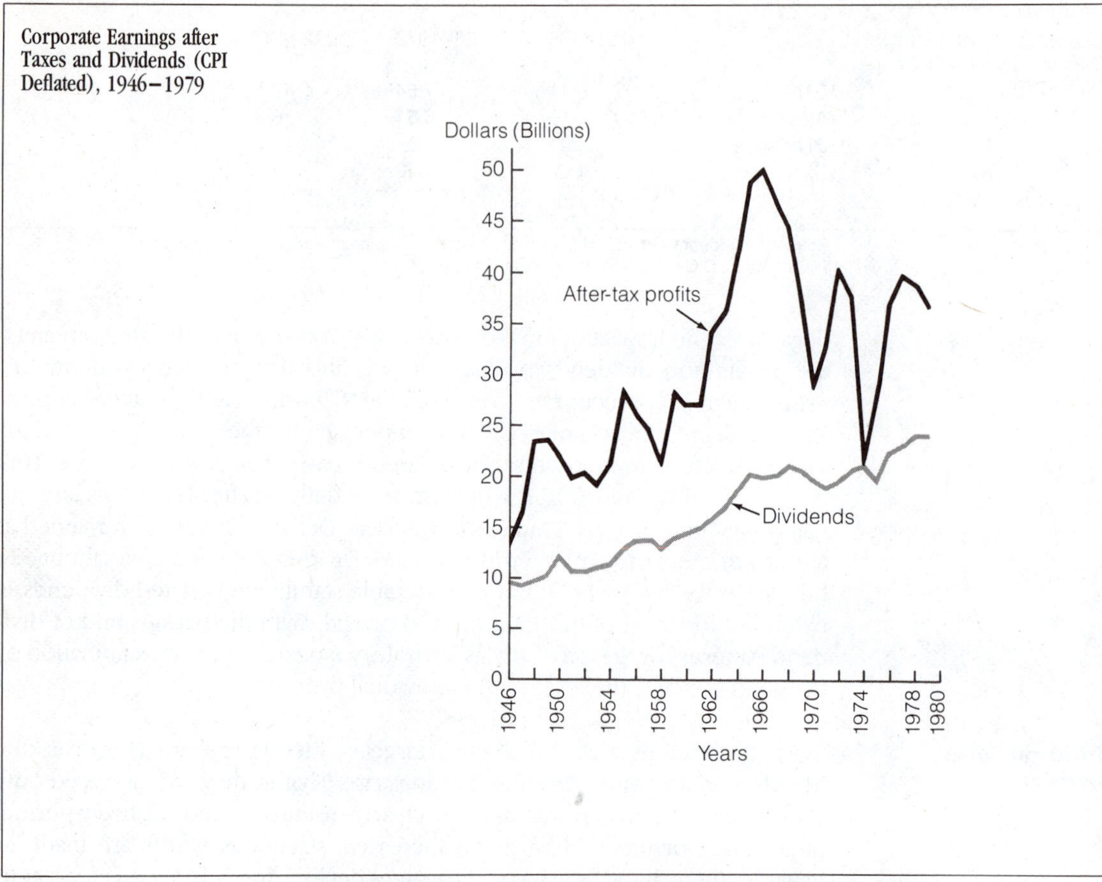

Source: President's Council of Economic Advisers, *Economic Report of the President* (Washington, D.C.: Government Printing Office, 1980).

fairly high plateau from 1966 through 1972, during which time dividends remain constant. A new increase in earnings induces management to raise the dividend in 1973 to reestablish the 50 percent payout ratio.

Rationale for Stable Dividends

Like the great majority of firms, Walter Watch keeps its dividend at a relatively steady dollar amount but allows its payout ratio to fluctuate. Why does it follow such a policy?

Consider the stable dividend policy from the standpoint of the stockholders as owners of the company. Their acquiescence with the general practice must imply that stable dividend policies lead to higher stock prices on the average than do alternative dividend policies. Is this a fact? Does a stable divi-

Figure 17.2

Dividends and Earnings Patterns for the Walter Watch Company

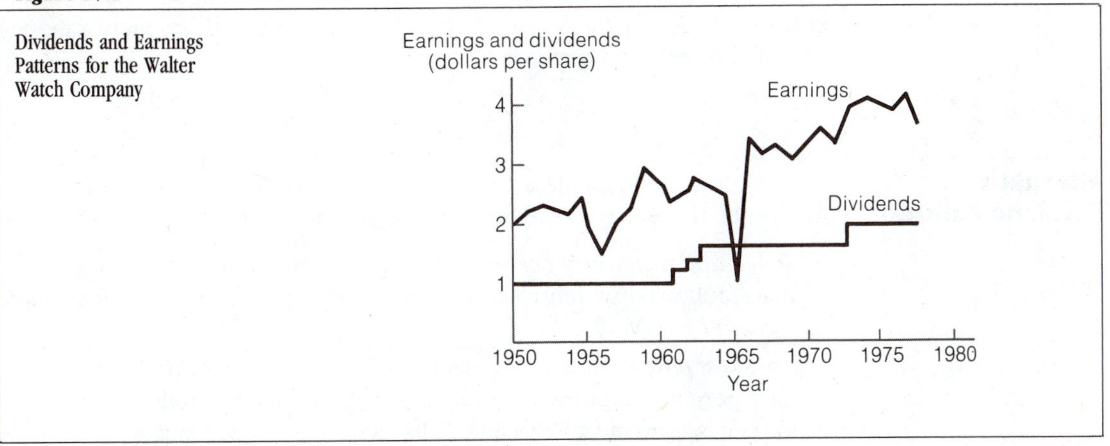

dend policy maximize equity values for a corporation? There has been no truly conclusive empirical study of dividend policy, so any answer to the question must be regarded as tentative. On logical grounds, however, there is reason to believe that a stable dividend policy does lead to higher stock prices. First, investors can be expected to value more highly dividends they are more sure of receiving, since fluctuating dividends are riskier than stable ones. Accordingly, the same average amount of dividends received under a fluctuating dividend policy is likely to have a higher discount factor applied to it than is applied to dividends under a stable dividend policy. In the terms used in Chapter 16, this means that a firm with a stable dividend will have a lower required rate of return—or cost of equity capital—than one whose dividends fluctuate.

Second, many stockholders live on income received in the form of dividends. These stockholders are greatly inconvenienced by fluctuating dividends, and they will likely pay a premium for a stock with a relatively assured minimum dollar dividend.

A third advantage of a stable dividend from the standpoint of both the corporation and its stockholders is the requirement of legal listing. *Legal lists* are lists of securities in which mutual savings banks, pension funds, insurance companies, and other fiduciary institutions are permitted to invest. One of the criteria for placing a stock on the legal list is that dividend payments are maintained. Thus legal listing encourages pursuance of a stable dividend policy.

On the other hand, if a firm's investment opportunities fluctuate from year to year, should it not retain more earnings during some years in order to take advantage of opportunities when they appear and increase dividends when good internal investment opportunities are scarce? This line of reasoning leads to a recommendation for a fluctuating payout for companies whose investment opportunities are unstable. However, the logic of the argument is diminished by recognizing that it is possible to maintain a reasonably stable dividend by using outside financing, including debt, to smooth out the differences between the funds needed for investment and the amount of money provided by retained earnings.

Alternative Dividend Policies

Before considering dividend policy at a theoretical level, it is useful to summarize the three major types of dividend policies:

1. *Stable dollar amount per share.* The policy of a stable dollar amount per share, followed by most firms, is the policy implied by the words *stable dividend policy.*
2. *Constant payout ratio.* Very few firms follow a policy of paying out a constant percentage of earnings. Since earnings fluctuate, following this policy necessarily means that the dollar amount of dividends will fluctuate. For reasons discussed in the preceding section, this policy is not likely to maximize the value of a firm's stock. Before its bankruptcy, Penn Central Railroad followed the policy of paying out half its earnings—"A dollar for the stockholders and a dollar for the company," as one director put it.
3. *Low regular dividend plus extras.* The low regular dividend plus extras policy is a compromise between the first two. It gives the firm flexibility, but it leaves investors somewhat uncertain about what their dividend income will be. If a firm's earnings are quite volatile, however, this policy may well be its best choice.

The relative merits of these three policies can be evaluated better after a discussion of the residual theory of dividends, the topic covered in the next section.

Residual Theory of Dividends

The preceding chapters on capital budgeting and the cost of capital indicated that the cost of capital schedule and the investment opportunity schedule generally must be combined before the cost of capital can be established. In other words, the optimum capital budget, the marginal cost of capital, and the marginal rate of return on investment are determined *simultaneously.* This section examines the simultaneous solution in the framework of what is called the *residual theory of dividends.*[2] The theory draws on materials developed earlier in the book—capital budgeting and the cost of capital—and serves to provide a bridge between these key concepts.

The starting point in the theory is that investors prefer to have the firm retain and reinvest earnings rather than pay them out in dividends if the return

2. "Residual" connotes *left over.* The residual theory of dividend policy implies that dividends are paid after internal investment opportunities have been exhausted.

on reinvested earnings exceeds the rate of return the investors can obtain on other investments of comparable risk. If the corporation can reinvest retained earnings at a 20 percent rate of return, while the best rate stockholders can obtain if they receive earnings in the form of dividends is 10 percent, then stockholders prefer to have the firm retain the profits.

Chapter 16 showed that the cost of equity capital obtained from retained earnings is an *opportunity cost* that reflects rates of return open to equity investors. If a firm's stockholders can buy other stocks of equal risk and obtain a 10 percent dividend plus capital gains yield, then 10 percent is the firm's cost of retained earnings. The cost of new outside equity raised by selling common stock is higher because of the costs of floating the issue.

Most firms have an optimum debt ratio that calls for at least some debt, so new financing is done partly with debt and partly with equity. Debt has a different, and generally lower, cost than equity, so the two forms of capital must be combined to find the *weighted average cost of capital.* As long as the firm finances at the optimum point (using an optimum amount of debt and equity) and uses only internally generated equity (retained earnings), its marginal cost of each new dollar of capital is minimized.

Internally generated equity is available for financing a certain amount of new investment; beyond this amount, the firm must turn to more expensive new common stock. At the point where new stock must be sold, the cost of equity and, consequently, the marginal cost of capital rise.

These concepts, which were developed in Chapter 16, are illustrated in Figure 17.3. The firm has a marginal cost of capital of 10 percent so long as retained earnings are available; the marginal cost of capital begins to rise when new stock must be sold.

The hypothetical firm has $50 million of earnings and a 50 percent optimum debt ratio. It can make net investments (investments in addition to asset replacements financed from depreciation) up to $100 million—$50 mil-

Figure 17.3

The Marginal Cost of Capital

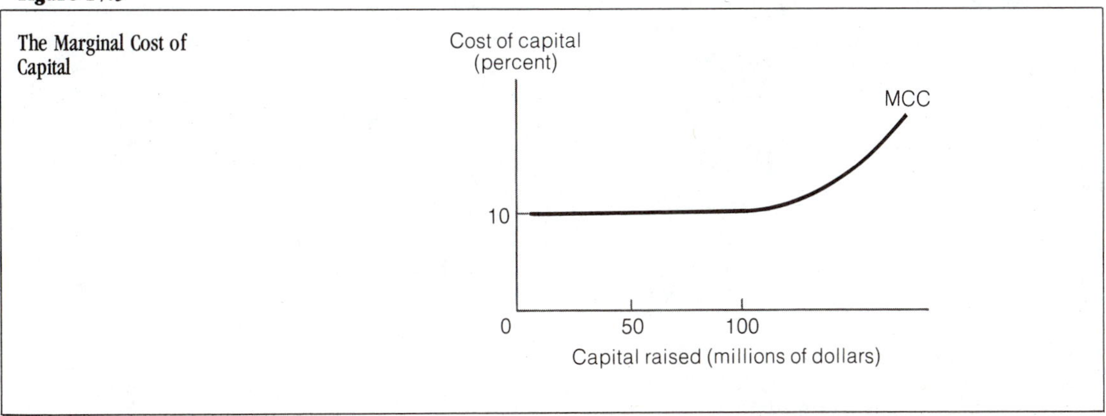

lion from retained earnings plus $50 million new debt supported by the retained earnings if it does not pay dividends. Therefore, its marginal cost of capital is constant at 10 percent for up to $100 million of capital. Beyond $100 million, the marginal cost of capital begins rising as the firm begins to use more expensive new common stock.

Suppose the firm's capital budgeting department draws up a list of investment opportunities, ranked in the order of each project's IRR, and plots them on a graph. The investment opportunity curves of three different years—one for a good year (IRR_1), one for a normal year (IRR_2), and one for a bad year (IRR_3)—are shown in Figure 17.4. The IRR_1 curve shows that the firm can invest more money, and at higher rates of return, than it can when the investment opportunities are those given by IRR_2 and IRR_3.

The investment opportunity schedule is now combined with the cost of capital schedule in Figure 17.5. The point where the investment opportunity curve cuts the cost of capital curve defines the proper level of new investment. When investment opportunities are relatively poor, the optimum level of investment is $25 million; when opportunities are about normal, it is $75 million; and when opportunities are relatively good, it is $125 million.

Consider the situation where IRR_1 is the appropriate schedule. Suppose the firm has $50 million in earnings and a 50 percent target debt ratio, so it can finance $100 million ($50 million earnings plus $50 million new debt) *if it retains all its earnings.* If it pays out part of the earnings in dividends, then it will have to begin using expensive new common stock sooner, so the cost of capital curve will rise sooner. This suggests that under the conditions of IRR_1 the firm should retain all its earnings and actually sell some new common stock in order to take advantage of its investment opportunities. Its payout ratio would thus be zero percent.

Under the conditions of IRR_2, however, the firm should invest only $75

Figure 17.4

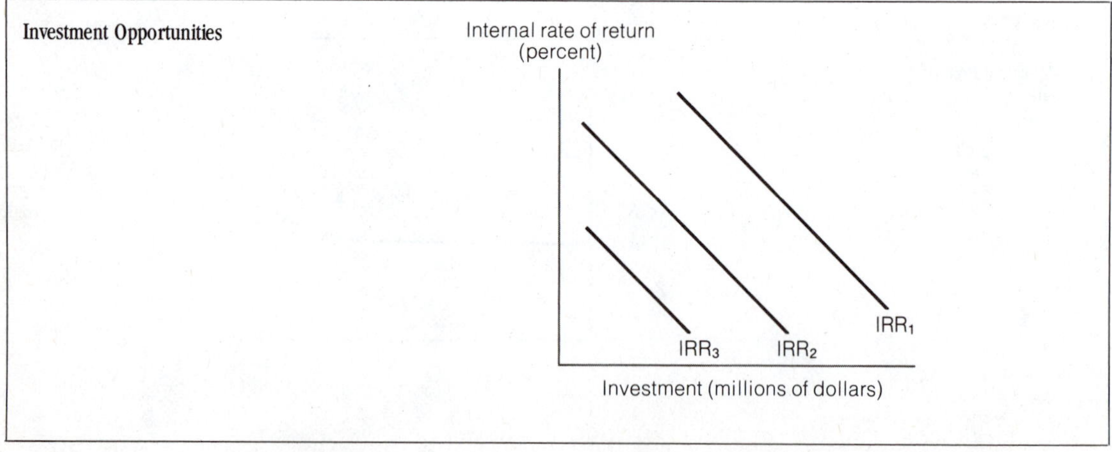

Figure 17.5

Interrelationships among Cost of Capital, Investment Opportunities, and New Investment

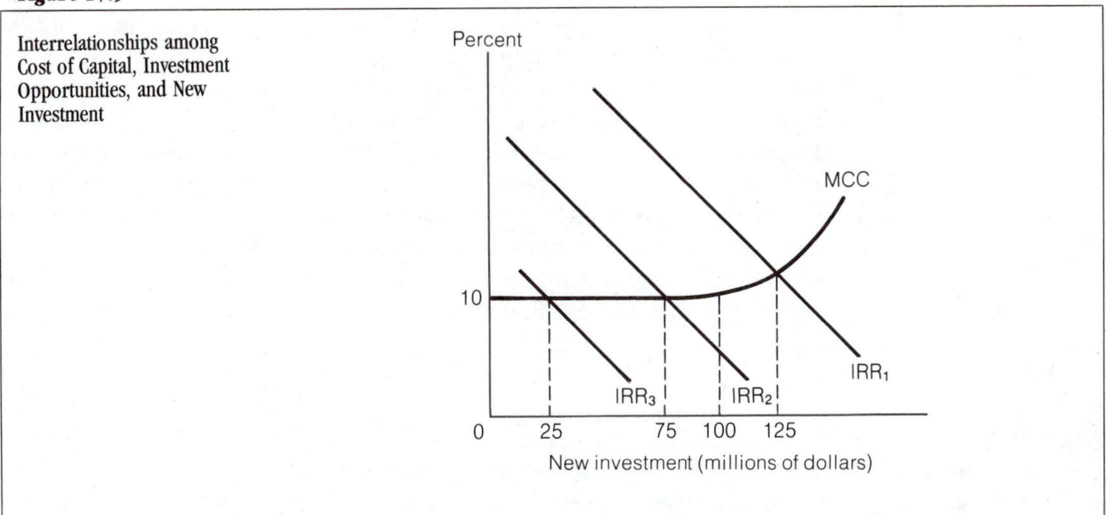

million. How should this investment be financed? First, notice that if it retains the full amount of its earnings, $50 million, it will need to sell only $25 million of new debt. However, by doing this, the firm will move away from its target capital structure. To stay on target, the firm must finance the required $75 million half by equity (retained earnings) and half by debt—that is, $37.5 million by retained earnings and $37.5 million by debt. If the firm has $50 million in total earnings and decides to retain and reinvest $37.5 million, it must distribute the residual $12.5 million to its stockholders. In this case, the payout ratio is 25 percent ($12.5 million divided by $50 million).

Finally, under the bad conditions of IRR_3, the firm should invest only $25 million. Because it has $50 million in earnings, it could finance the entire $25 million out of retained earnings and still have $25 million available for dividends. Should this be done? Under the assumptions, this would not be a good decision, because it would move the firm away from its target debt ratio. To stay in the 50-50 debt/equity position, the firm must retain $12.5 million and sell $12.5 million of debt. When the $12.5 million of retained earnings is subtracted from the $50 million of earnings, the firm is left with a residual of $37.5 million—the amount that should be paid out in dividends. In this case the payout ratio is 75 percent.

Long-Run Viewpoint

A conflict apparently exists between the residual theory and the statement made in an earlier section that firms should and do maintain reasonably stable cash dividends. How can this conflict be reconciled?

A firm may have a target capital structure without being at that target at all times. In other words, it need not adjust its dividend each and every year. Firms do have target debt ratios, but they also have a certain amount of flexibility; they can be moderately above or below the target debt position in any year with no serious adverse consequences. This means that if an unusually large number of good investments are available in a particular year, the firm does not necessarily have to cut its dividend to take advantage of them; it can borrow somewhat more heavily than usual in that particular year without getting its debt ratio too far out of line. Obviously, however, this excessive reliance on debt cannot continue for too many years without seriously affecting the debt ratio, necessitating either a sale of new stock or a cut in dividends and an attendant increase in the level of retained earnings.

High and Low Dividend Payout Industries

Some industries are experiencing rapid growth in the demand for their products, a condition which obviously affords firms in the industries many good investment opportunities. Electronics, office equipment, and entertainment are examples of such industries in recent years. Other industries have experienced much slower growth and even declines. Examples of slow-growth industries are cigarette manufacturing and textiles. Still other industries are growing at about the same rate as the general economy; oil, autos, and banking are representative.

The theory suggests that firms in rapidly growing industries should generally have IRR curves that are relatively far to the right on graphs such as Figure 17.5; for example, Xerox, Polaroid, and IBM might have investment schedules similar to IRR_1. The tobacco companies, on the other hand, could be expected to have investment schedules similar to IRR_3.

Each of these firms would, of course, experience shifts in investment opportunities from year to year, but the curves would *tend* to be in about the same part of the graph. In other words, firms such as Xerox would tend to have more investment opportunities than money, so we would expect them to have zero (or very low) payout ratios. Reynolds Tobacco, on the other hand, would tend to have more money than good investments, so we would expect it to pay out a relatively high percentage of earnings in dividends. These companies do, in fact, conform with our expectations.

Conflicting Theories on Dividends

Two basic schools of thought on dividend policy have been expressed in the theoretical literature of finance. One school, associated with Myron Gordon and John Lintner, among others, holds that the capital gains expected to result from earnings retention are riskier than are dividend expectations. Accordingly, these theorists suggest that the earnings of a firm with a low payout ratio are typically capitalized at higher rates than the earnings of a high payout firm, other things held constant.

The other school, associated with Merton Miller and Franco Modigliani, holds that investors are basically indifferent to returns in the form of dividends or capital gains. When firms raise or lower their dividends, if their stock prices tend to rise or fall in like manner, does this prove that investors prefer dividends? Miller and Modigliani argue that it does not, that any effect a change in dividends has on the price of a firm's stock is related primarily to information about expected future earnings conveyed by a change in dividends. Recalling that corporate managements dislike cutting dividends, Miller and Modigliani argue that increases in cash dividends raise expectations about the level of future earnings—that they have favorable *information content.* In terms of Figure 17.2, Miller and Modigliani would say that Walter Watch's dividend increases in 1961, 1962, 1963, and 1973 had information content about future earnings—that they signaled to stockholders that management expected the recent earnings increases to be permanent.

Dividends are probably subject to less uncertainty than capital gains, but they are taxed at a higher rate. How do these two forces balance out? Some argue that the uncertainty factor dominates; others feel that the differential tax rate is the stronger force and causes investors to favor corporate retention of earnings; still others, like Miller and Scholes, reason that investors have opportunities for altering the tax effects of dividends. Nor do systematic empirical studies settle the matter.[3]

Expected Dividends as the Basis for Stock Values

Another issue is the role of dividends in stock valuation models. According to generally accepted theory, stock prices are determined as the present value of a stream of cash flows. In other words, the capitalization of income procedure applies to stocks as well as to bonds and other assets. What are the cash flows that corporations provide to their stockholders? What flows do the markets in fact capitalize? A number of different models have been formulated. At least four different categories of flows have been capitalized in alternative formulations: (1) the stream of dividends, (2) the stream of earnings, (3) the current earnings plus flows resulting from future investment opportunities, and (4) the discounting of cash flows as in capital budgeting models. Merton Miller and Franco Modigliani have demonstrated that these different approaches are equivalent and yield the same valuations.[4]

In Chapter 6 we presented a very general multiperiod stock valuation model. The "free cash flows" (the cash flows adjusted by the need to provide

3. For contrasting findings see F. Black and M. Scholes, "The Effects of Dividend Yield and Dividend Policy on Common Stock Prices and Returns," *Journal of Financial Economics* 1 (May 1974), pp. 1–22, versus R. H. Litzenberger and K. Ramaswamy, "The Effect of Personal Taxes and Dividends on Capital Asset Prices: Theory and Evidence," *Journal of Financial Economics* 7 (June 1979), pp. 163–196.
4. See Merton H. Miller and Franco Modigliani, "Dividend Policy, Growth, and the Valuation of Shares," *Journal of Business* 34 (October 1961), pp. 411–433.

funds for investment) of the firm represented the stream of receipts that are capitalized. Since the stream of dividends model is also widely employed, we shall describe its use here.

The dividend valuation model gives results similar to those provided by the more general free cash flow model presented in Chapter 6. However, unless the firm uses internal financing completely, some of the relationships such as $g = bR$ are no longer valid for the dividend stream capitalization model. (Recall that b = net investment/earnings and R = internal profitability rate.) If the firm uses external financing, either debt or equity, the growth rate of dividends per share can no longer be predicted from the b times R relationship. The determinants of g become more complicated.[5] However, one way to deal with this is simply to measure the historical behavior of g and use such values of g measured over historical time periods (plus possible adjustments for future expectations) in the dividend valuation formula.[6]

In the dividend formulation, a share of common stock may be regarded as similar to a perpetual bond or share of perpetual preferred stock, and its value may be established as the present value of its stream of dividends:

$$\begin{aligned} \text{Value of stock} = p_0 &= \text{PV of expected future dividends} \\ &= \frac{d_1}{(1+k_s)^1} + \frac{d_2}{(1+k_s)^2} + \cdots \\ &= \sum_{t=1}^{\infty} \frac{d_t}{(1+k_s)^t}. \end{aligned} \tag{17.1}$$

Unlike bond interest and preferred dividends, common stock dividends are not generally expected to remain constant in the future; hence we cannot work with the convenient annuity formulas. This fact, combined with the much greater uncertainty about common stock dividends than about bond interest or preferred dividends, makes common stock valuation a more complex task than bond or preferred stock valuation.

Equation 17.1 is general in the sense that the time pattern of d_t can be anything; d_t can be rising, falling, constant, or it can even fluctuate randomly, and Equation 17.1 will still hold. For many purposes, however, it is useful to estimate a particular time pattern for d_t and then develop a simplified, easier to evaluate, version of the stock valuation model expressed in Equation 17.1. We

5. Ibid. The following becomes the expression for g:

$$g = bR\frac{1-b_r}{1-b} - b_e k\frac{1}{1-b},$$

where b_r is internal financing per dollar of earnings, b_e is external financing per dollar of earnings, and b is total financing per dollar of earnings. When all financing is internal, $b_e = 0$ and $b_r = b$; so $g = bR$. When all financing is external, $b_r = 0$ and $b_e = b$; so $g = [b/(1-b)](R-k)$. See MM, p. 423, Equation 25.

6. At the end of this chapter, Problems 17.14/15 and 17.16/17 illustrate the use of the dividend stream formula and of the free cash flow formula, respectively.

shall consider the special cases of zero growth, constant growth, and supernormal growth.

Stock Values with Zero Growth

Suppose the rate of growth is measured by the rate at which dividends are expected to increase. If future growth is expected to be zero, the value of the stock reduces to the same formula as was developed for a perpetual bond:

$$\text{Price} = \frac{\text{Dividend}}{\text{Capitalization rate}}$$

$$p_0 = \frac{d_1}{k_s}. \tag{17.2}$$

Solving for k_s, we obtain

$$k_s = \frac{d_1}{p_0}, \tag{17.2a}$$

which states that the required rate of return on a share of stock that has no growth prospects is simply the dividend yield.

"Normal," or Constant, Growth

Year after year, the earnings and dividends of most companies have been increasing. In general, this growth is expected to continue in the foreseeable future at about the same rate as the GNP. Without inflation, an average, or "normal," company would grow at a rate of from 3 to 5 percent a year. With inflation, the inflation rate would be added to the "real" growth to obtain growth in nominal terms. The rate of nominal growth will depend on the inflation rate and on the ability of the firm to achieve growth in relation to the nominal growth of the economy. Thus, if a company's previous dividend, which has already been paid, was d_0, its dividend in any future year *(t)* may be forecast as $d_t = d_0(1 + g)^t$, where g = the expected rate of growth. For example, if United Rubber just paid a dividend of $1.90 (that is, d_0 = $1.90), and investors expect a 5 percent growth rate, the estimated dividend one year hence will be d_1 = ($1.90)(1.05) = $2; d_2 will be $2.09; and the estimated dividend five years hence will be

$$\begin{aligned} d_t &= d_0(1 + g)^t \\ d_5 &= \$1.90(1.05)^5 \\ &= \$2.42. \end{aligned}$$

Using this method of estimating future dividends, the current price, p_0, is determined as follows:

$$\begin{aligned} p_0 &= \frac{d_1}{(1 + k_s)^1} + \frac{d_2}{(1 + k_s)^2} + \frac{d_3}{(1 + k_s)^3} + \cdots \\ &= \frac{d_0(1 + g)^1}{(1 + k_s)^1} + \frac{d_0(1 + g)^2}{(1 + k_s)^2} + \frac{d_0(1 + g)^3}{(1 + k_s)^3} + \cdots \\ &= \sum_{t=1}^{\infty} \frac{d_0(1 + g)^t}{(1 + k_s)^t}. \end{aligned} \tag{17.3}$$

If g is constant, Equation 17.3 may be simplified as follows:[7]

$$p_0 = \frac{d_1}{k_s - g}. \tag{17.4}$$

A necessary condition for the constant growth model is that k_s be greater than g; otherwise, Equation 17.4 gives nonsense answers. If k_s equals g, the equation blows up, yielding an infinite price; if k_s is less than g, a *negative* price results. Since neither infinite nor negative stock prices make sense, it is clear that in equilibrium k_s must be greater than g.

Note that Equation 17.4 is sufficiently general to encompass the no-growth case described above. If growth is zero, this is simply a special case, and Equation 17.4 is equal to Equation 17.2.[8]

"Supernormal" Growth

Firms typically go through life cycles during part of which their growth is much faster than that of the economy as a whole. Automobile manufacturers in the 1920s and computer and office equipment manufacturers in the 1960s are examples. Figure 17.6 illustrates such supernormal growth and compares it with normal growth, zero growth, and negative growth.[9]

The illustrative supernormal growth firm is expected to grow at a 20 percent rate for ten years, then to have its growth rate fall to 4 percent, the norm

7. The proof of Equation 17.4 is as follows. Rewrite Equation 17.3 as

$$p_0 = d_0\left[\frac{(1+g)}{(1+k_s)} + \frac{(1+g)^2}{(1+k_s)^2} + \frac{(1+g)^3}{(1+k_s)^3} + \cdots + \frac{(1+g)^N}{(1+k_s)^N}\right]. \tag{1}$$

Multiply both sides of Equation 1 by $(1 + k_s)/(1 + g)$:

$$\left[\frac{(1+k_s)}{(1+g)}\right]p_0 = d_0\left[1 + \frac{(1+g)}{(1+k_s)} + \frac{(1+g)^2}{(1+k_s)^2} + \cdots + \frac{(1+g)^{N-1}}{(1+k_s)^{N-1}}\right]. \tag{2}$$

Subtract Equation (1) from Equation (2) to obtain

$$\left[\frac{(1+k_s)}{(1+g)} - 1\right]p_0 = d_0\left[1 - \frac{(1+g)^N}{(1+k_s)^N}\right].$$

$$\left[\frac{(1+k_s)-(1+g)}{(1+g)}\right]p_0 = d_0\left[1 - \frac{(1+g)^N}{(1+k_s)^N}\right].$$

Assuming $k_s > g$, as $N \rightarrow \infty$ the term in brackets on the right side of the equation $\rightarrow$ 1.0, leaving

$$\left[\frac{(1+k_s)-(1+g)}{(1+g)}\right]p_0 = d_0,$$

which simplifies to

$$(k_s - g)p_0 = d_0(1+g) = d_1$$

$$p_0 = \frac{d_1}{k_s - g}. \tag{17.4}$$

8. The logic underlying this analysis implicitly assumes that investors are indifferent to dividend yield or capital gains.

9. A *negative growth rate* represents a declining company. A mining company whose profits are falling because of a declining ore body is an example.

for the economy. The value of a firm with such a growth pattern is determined by the following equation:

Present price = PV of dividends during supernormal growth period + Value of stock price at end of supernormal growth period discounted back to present.

$$p_0 = \sum_{t=1}^{N} \frac{d_0(1+g_s)^t}{(1+k_s)^t} + \left(\frac{d_{N+1}}{k_s - g_n}\right)\left(\frac{1}{(1+k_s)^N}\right). \qquad (17.5)$$

Here g_s is the supernormal growth rate, g_n is the normal growth rate, and N is the period of supernormal growth.

Working through an example will help make this clear. Consider a supernormal growth firm whose previous dividend was \$1.92 (that is, d_0 = \$1.92), with the dividend expected to increase by 20 percent a year for ten years and thereafter at 4 percent a year indefinitely. If stockholders' required rate of return is 9 percent on an investment with this degree of risk, what is the value of the stock? On the basis of the calculations in Table 17.3, the value is found to be \$138.29, the present value of the dividends during the first ten years plus the present value of the stock at the end of the tenth year.

Comparing Companies with Different Expected Growth Rates

It is useful to summarize this section by comparing the four illustrative firms whose dividend trends are graphed in Figure 17.6. Using the valuation equations developed above, the conditions assumed in the preceding examples, and the additional assumptions that each firm had earnings per share during the preceding reporting period of \$3.60 (that is, EPS_0 = \$3.60) and paid out 53.3 percent of its reported earnings (therefore dividends per share

Figure 17.6

Illustrative Dividend Growth Rates

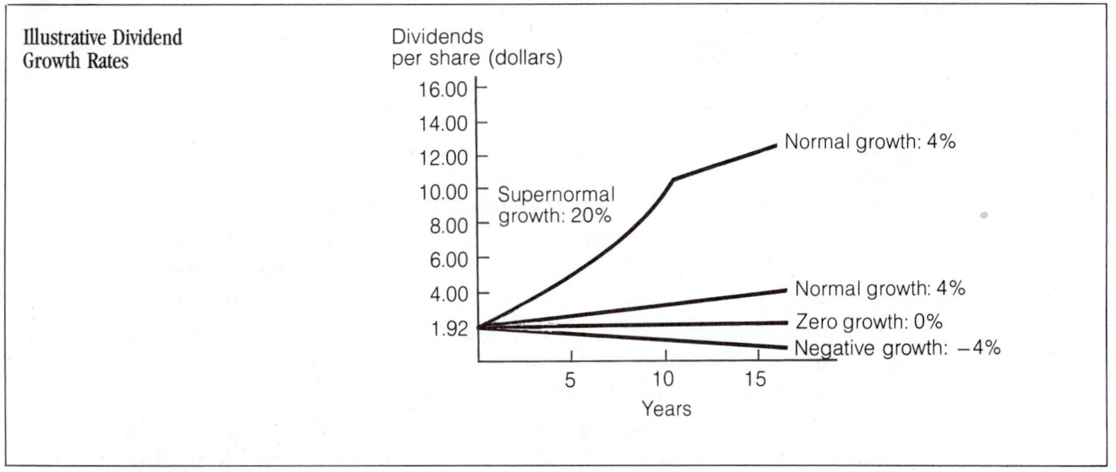

Table 17.3

Method of Calculating the Value of a Stock with Supernormal Growth

Assumptions:

a. Stockholders' capitalization rate is 9 percent; that is, $k_s = 9\%$.

b. Growth rate is 20 percent for ten years, 4 percent thereafter; that is, $g_s = 20\%$, $g_n = 4\%$, and $N = 10$.

c. Last year's dividend was $1.92; that is, $d_0 = \$1.92$.

Step 1. Find present value of dividends during rapid growth period:

End of Year	Dividend $\$1.92(1.20)^t$	PVIF = $1/(1.09)^t$	Present Value
1	$ 2.30	0.9174	$ 2.11
2	2.76	0.8417	2.32
3	3.32	0.7722	2.56
4	3.98	0.7084	2.82
5	4.78	0.6499	3.11
6	5.73	0.5963	3.42
7	6.88	0.5470	3.76
8	8.26	0.5019	4.15
9	9.91	0.4604	4.56
10	11.89	0.4224	5.02

$$\text{PV of first ten years' dividends} = \sum_{t=1}^{10} \frac{d_0(1+g_s)^t}{(1+k_s)^t} = \$33.83$$

Step 2. Find present value of Year 10 stock price:

a. Find value of stock at end of Year 10:

$$p_{10} = \frac{d_{11}}{k_s - g_n} = \frac{\$11.89(1.04)}{0.05} = \$247.31.$$

b. Discount p_{10} back to present:

$$PV = p_{10}\left(\frac{1}{1+k_s}\right)^{10} = \$247.31(0.4224) = \$104.46.$$

Step 3. Sum to find total value of stock today:

$$p_0 = \$33.83 + \$104.46 = \$138.29.$$

last year, d_0, were $1.92 for each company), we show prices, dividend yields, and price-earnings ratios (hereafter written P-E) in Table 17.4.

Investors require and expect a return of 9 percent on each of the stocks. For the declining firm, this return consists of a relatively high current dividend yield combined with a capital *loss* amounting to 4 percent a year. For the no-growth firm, there is neither a capital gain nor a capital loss expectation, so the 9 percent return must be obtained entirely from the dividend yield. The normal growth firm provides a relatively low current dividend yield but a 4 percent a year capital gain expectation. Finally, the supernormal growth firm has the lowest current dividend yield but the highest capital gain expectation.

What is expected to happen to the prices of the four illustrative firms' stocks over time? Three of the four cases are straightforward: The zero growth firm's price is expected to be constant (that is, $p_t = p_{t+1}$); the declining firm is expected to have a falling stock price; and the constant growth firm's stock is expected to grow at a constant rate, 4 percent. The supernormal growth case is more complex, but what is expected can be seen from the data in Table 17.3.

It can readily be shown that

$$\sum_{t=1}^{10} \frac{(1+g_s)^t}{(1+k_s)^t} = (1+\text{h})\left[\frac{(1+\text{h})^{10}-1}{\text{h}}\right]$$

where $\frac{(1+g_s)}{(1+k_s)} = (1+\text{h})$ for ease of expression.[10] For the example in Table 17.3, we have:

$$1+\text{h} = \frac{(1+g_s)}{(1+k_s)} = \frac{1.20}{1.09} = 1.1009174, \quad \text{h} = 0.1009174.$$

$$(1+\text{h})^{10} = (1.1009174)^{10} = 2.615456.$$

$$(1+\text{h})^{10} - 1 = 1.615456.$$

$$(1+\text{h})\left[\frac{(1+\text{h})^{10}-1}{\text{h}}\right] = (1.1009174)\left[\frac{2.615456-1}{0.1009174}\right] = 17.623.$$

$$d_0(17.623) = 1.92(17.623) = 33.836.$$

The PV of the first ten years' dividends shown in Table 17.3 is \$33.83, approximately the same. Note that the present price, p_0, is \$138.29 and that the expected price in Year 10, p_{10}, is \$247.31. This represents an average growth rate of 6 percent.[11] We do not show, though we could, that the expected growth rate of the stock's price is higher than 6 percent in the early part of the ten-

10. Numerical calculation procedure for a summation expression.

Let $\left(\frac{1+g_S}{1+k_S}\right) = (1+h)$

and write out the summation expression.

$$\sum_{t=1}^{10}\left(\frac{1+g_S}{1+k_S}\right)^t = \sum_{t=1}^{10}(1+h)^t = (1+h)+(1+h)^2+(1+h)^3\ldots(1+h)^{10}$$

$$= (1+h)[1+(1+h)+(1+h)^2\ldots(1+h)^9]$$

The terms in the brackets represent the sum of an annuity.

$$= (1+h)\left[\frac{(1+h)^N-1}{(1+h)-1}\right] = (1+h)\left[\frac{(1+h)^N-1}{h}\right].$$

The expression in brackets is the sum of an annuity formula.

11. Found from Table 17.3; \$247.31/\$138.29 = \$1.79, and this is approximately the CVIF for a 6 percent growth rate.

Table 17.4

Prices, Dividend Yields, and Price-Earnings Ratios for 9 Percent Returns under Different Growth Assumptions

		Price	Current Dividend Yield	P-E Ratio[a]
Declining firm:	$p_0 = \frac{d_1}{k_s - g} = \frac{\$1.84}{0.09 - (-0.04)}$	\$ 14.15	13%	3.9
No-growth firm:	$p_0 = \frac{d_1}{k_s} = \frac{\$1.92}{0.09}$	\$ 21.33	9%	5.9
Normal growth firm:	$p_0 = \frac{d_1}{k_s - g} = \frac{\$2.00}{0.09 - 0.04}$	\$ 40.00	5%	11.1
Supernormal growth firm:	$p_0 =$ (See Table 17.3.)	\$138.29	1.7%	38.4

a. It was assumed at the beginning of this example that each company is earning \$3.60 initially. This \$3.60, divided into the various prices, gives the indicated P-E ratios.

We might also note that as the supernormal growth rate declines toward the normal rate (or as the time when this decline will occur becomes more imminent), the high P-E ratio must approach the normal P-E ratio; that is, the P-E of 38.4 will decline year by year and equal 11.1, that of the normal growth company, in the tenth year. See A. A. Robichek and M. C. Bogue, "A Note on the Behavior of Expected Price/Earnings Ratios over Time," *Journal of Finance* 26 (June 1971), pp. 731–736.

Note also that d_1 differs for each firm, being calculated as follows:

$$d_1 = EPS_0(1 + g)(\text{Payout}) = \$3.60(1 + g)(0.533).$$

year supernormal growth period and less than 6 percent toward the end of the period, as investors perceive the approaching end of the supernormal period. From Year 11 on, the company's stock price and dividend are expected to grow at the normal rate, 4 percent.

The relationships among the P-E ratios, shown in the last column of Table 17.4, are similar to what one would intuitively expect—the higher the expected growth (all other things the same), the higher the P-E ratio.[12]

Stock Dividends and Stock Splits

Another aspect of dividend policy is stock dividends and stock splits. A *stock dividend* is paid in additional shares of stock instead of in cash and simply involves a bookkeeping transfer from retained earnings to the capital stock account.[13] In a *stock split* there is no change in the capital accounts; instead, a

12. Differences in P-E ratios among firms can also arise from differences in the rates of return, k_s, which investors use in capitalizing the future dividend streams. If one company has a higher P-E than another, this could be caused by a higher g, a lower k, or a combination of these two factors.
13. The transfer from retained earnings to the capital stock account must be based on market value. In other words, if a firm's shares are selling for \$100 and it has 1 million shares outstanding, a 10 percent stock dividend requires the transfer of \$10 million (100,000 × \$100) from retained earnings to capital stock. Stock dividends are thus limited by the size of retained earnings. The rule was put into effect to prevent the declaration of stock dividends unless the firm has had earnings.

larger number of shares of common stock is issued. In a two-for-one split, stockholders receive two shares for each one previously held. The book value per share is cut in half; and the par, or stated, value per share of stock is similarly changed.

From a practical standpoint there is little difference between a stock dividend and a stock split. The New York Stock Exchange considers any distribution of stock totaling less than 25 percent of outstanding stock to be a stock dividend and any distribution of 25 percent or more a stock split.

Since the two are similar, the issues outlined below are discussed in connection with both stock dividends and stock splits.

Price Effects

The results of a careful empirical study of the effects of stock dividends are available and can be used as a basis for observations on their price effects.[14] (The findings of the study are presented in Table 17.5.) When stock dividends were associated with a cash dividend increase, the value of the company's stock six months after the ex dividend date had risen by 8 percent. When stock dividends were not accompanied by cash dividend increases, stock values fell by 12 percent during the subsequent six-month period.

The data in Table 17.5 seem to suggest that stock dividends are seen for what they are—simply additional pieces of paper—and that they are not perceived as representing true income. When they are accompanied by higher earnings and cash dividends, investors bid up the value of the stock. However, when they are not accompanied by such increases, the dilution of earnings and dividends per share causes the price of the stock to drop. The fundamental determinant is underlying earnings and dividend trends.

Similar results were developed more rigorously in the pioneering study by Eugene Fama, Lawrence Fisher, Michael Jensen, and Richard Roll using residual analysis, which measures differences from returns predicted by the

Table 17.5

Price Effects of Stock Dividends

	Prices at Selected Dates (in Percentages)		
	Six Months prior to Ex Dividend Date	At Ex Dividend Date	Six Months after Ex Dividend Date
Cash dividend increase	100	109	108
No cash dividend increase	100	99	88

14. C. Austin Barker, "Evaluation of Stock Dividends," *Harvard Business Review* 36 (July–August 1958), pp. 199–214. Barker's study has been replicated several times in recent years, and his results are still valid.

Table 17.6

Effect of Stock Dividends on Stock Ownership

	Percentage Increase in Ownership 1950–1953
Stock dividend, 25% and over	30
Stock dividend, 5–25%	17
All stock dividends	30
No stock dividends or splits	5

Source: C. Austin Barker, "Evaluation of Stock Dividends," *Harvard Business Review* 36 (July–August 1958), pp. 99–114.

security market line.[15] Positive abnormal returns were observed before the split. When the sample was divided between splits with dividend increases and those with decreases, a difference in post-split performance was observed. The dividend increase group showed slightly positive returns following the split. The poor dividend performance group experienced declines in cumulative average residuals until about a year after the split. The hypothesis suggested is that the splits and associated dividend experience convey a message about future changes in the firms' expected cash flows.

Effects on Extent of Ownership

Table 17.6 shows the effect of stock dividends on common stock ownership during a four-year period. Large stock dividends resulted in the largest percentage increases in stock ownership. The use of stock dividends increased share ownership by 25 percent on the average. For companies and industries that did not offer stock splits or stock dividends, the increase was only 5 percent. Furthermore, the degree of increase itself increased with the size of the stock dividend. This evidence suggests that regardless of the effect on the total market value of the firm, the use of stock dividends and stock splits effectively increases stock ownership by lowering the price at which shares are traded to a more popular range.

Stock Repurchases as an Alternative to Dividends

Treasury stock is the name given to common stock that has been repurchased by the issuing firm, and the acquisition of treasury stock represents an alternative to the payment of dividends. If some of the outstanding stock is repurchased, fewer shares will remain outstanding; and assuming that the repurchase does not adversely affect the firm's earnings, the earnings per share of the remaining shares will increase. This increase in earnings per share may

15. Eugene Fama, Lawrence Fisher, Michael Jensen, and Richard Roll, "The Adjustment of Stock Prices to New Information," *International Economic Review* 10 (February 1969), pp. 1–21.

result in a higher market price per share, so capital gains will have been substituted for dividends. These effects can be seen from the following example.

The National Development Corporation (NDC) earned \$4.4 million in 1980; of this amount, 50 percent, or \$2.2 million, has been allocated for distribution to common shareholders. There are currently 1.1 million shares outstanding, and the market value is \$20 a share. NDC can use the \$2.2 million to repurchase 100,000 of its shares through a tender offer for \$22 a share, or it can pay a cash dividend of \$2 a share.[16]

The effect of the repurchase on the EPS and market price per share of the remaining stock can be determined in the following way:

$$\text{Current EPS} = \frac{\text{Total earnings}}{\text{Number of shares}} = \frac{\$4.4 \text{ million}}{1.1 \text{ million}}$$

$$= \$4 \text{ per share.}$$

$$\text{Current P-E ratio} = \frac{\$20}{\$4} = 5 \text{ times.}$$

$$\begin{matrix}\text{EPS after repurchase} \\ \text{of 100,000 shares}\end{matrix} = \frac{\$4.4 \text{ million}}{1 \text{ million}} = \$4.40 \text{ per share.}$$

$$\begin{matrix}\text{Expected market price} \\ \text{after repurchase}\end{matrix} = (\text{P-E})(\text{EPS}) = (5)(\$4.40) = \$22 \text{ per share.}$$

It can be seen from this example that investors will receive benefits of \$2 a share in any case, in the form of either a \$2 dividend or a \$2 increase in stock price. The result occurs because of the assumptions that (1) shares can be repurchased at \$22 a share, (2) total earnings will remain unchanged, and (3) the P-E ratio will remain constant. If shares could be bought for less than \$22, the operation would be even better for *remaining* stockholders, but the reverse would hold if NDC paid more than \$22 a share. Furthermore, the P-E ratio might change as a result of the repurchase operation—rising if investors viewed it favorably, falling if they viewed it unfavorably. Some factors that might affect P-E ratios are considered next.

Advantages of Repurchases from the Stockholder's Viewpoint

A number of possible advantages to stockholders may accrue from share repurchases. Gains earned on share repurchase are taxed at the long-term capital gains rate, assuming the investor has held the stock for at least the minimum one-year holding period and does not come under some special rules

16. Stock repurchases are commonly made in three ways. First, a publicly owned firm can simply buy its own stock through a broker on the open market. Second, it can issue a *tender*, under which it permits stockholders to send in ("tender") their shares to the firm in exchange for a specified price per share. When tender offers are made, the firm generally indicates that it will buy up to a specified number of shares within a specified time period (usually about two weeks); if more shares are tendered than the company wishes to purchase, then purchases are made on a pro rata basis. Finally, the firm can purchase a block of shares from one large holder on a negotiated basis. If the latter procedure is employed, care must be taken to ensure that the single stockholder does not receive preferential treatment.

for large holders. Otherwise, the profits on share repurchase are taxed at the rates on ordinary personal income. Since the capital gains tax rates are in general only about one-half of the ordinary tax rates, this is clearly a benefit.

By reducing the equity base through share repurchase, while holding the level of debt the same, the debt to equity ratio of the firm has been increased. Tax shelter benefits and other advantages of increased leverage may therefore also benefit shareholders.

The stockholder has a choice: sell or not sell. The person who receives a dividend has to accept the payment and pay the tax.

A qualitative advantage advanced by market practitioners is that repurchase can often remove a large block of stock overhanging the market.

Advantages of Repurchases from Management's Viewpoint

Advantages to management of repurchases include the following: Studies have shown that dividends are sticky in the short run because managements are reluctant to raise them if the new dividend cannot be maintained in the future. Hence, if the excess cash flow is thought to be only temporary, management may prefer to "conceal" the distribution in the form of share repurchases rather than to declare a cash dividend that they believe cannot be maintained.

Repurchased stock can be used for acquisitions or released when stock options are exercised. Discussions with financial managers indicate that it is frequently more convenient and less expensive to use repurchased stock rather than newly issued stock for these purposes and when convertibles are converted or warrants exercised.

If directors have large holdings themselves, they may have especially strong preferences for repurchases rather than dividend payments because of the tax factor.

One interesting use of stock repurchases was Standard Products' strategy of repurchasing its own stock to thwart an attempted takeover. Defiance Industries attempted to acquire a controlling interest in Standard Products through a tender offer of $15 a share. Standard's management countered with a tender offer of its own at $17.25 a share, financed by $1.725 million in internal funds and by $3.525 million in long-term debt. This kept stockholders from accepting the outside tender offer and enabled Standard Products' management to retain control.

Repurchases can be used to effect large-scale changes in capital structure. For example, at one time American Standard had virtually no long-term debt outstanding. The company decided that its optimal capital structure called for the use of considerably more debt, but even if it financed *only* with debt it would have taken years to get the debt ratio up to the newly defined optimal level. So the company sold $22 million of long-term debt and used the proceeds to repurchase its common stock, thereby producing an instantaneous change in its capital structure.

Finally, treasury stock can be resold in the open market if the firm needs additional funds.

Disadvantages of Repurchases from the Stockholder's Viewpoint

Disadvantages to stockholders of repurchases include the following: Stockholders may not be indifferent to dividends and capital gains, and the price of the stock may benefit more from cash dividends than from repurchases. Cash dividends are generally thought of as being relatively dependable, and repurchases are not. Further, if a firm announces a regular, dependable repurchase program, the improper accumulation tax may become a threat.

The *selling* stockholders may not be fully aware of all the implications of a repurchase or may not have all pertinent information about the corporation's present and future activities. For this reason, firms generally announce a repurchase program before embarking on it.

The corporation may pay too high a price for the repurchased stock, to the disadvantage of remaining stockholders. If the shares are inactive, and if the firm seeks to acquire a relatively large amount of its stock, the price may be bid above a maintainable price and then fall after the firm ceases its repurchase operations.

By reducing the proportion of cash or marketable securities in the asset structure, the risk composition of the firm's assets and earnings may be increased. The P-E ratio may therefore drop.

Disadvantages of Repurchases from Management's Viewpoint

Disadvantages to management of repurchases include the following: Studies have shown that firms that repurchase substantial amounts of stock have poorer growth rates and investment opportunities than firms that do not. Thus some people feel that announcing a repurchase program is like announcing that management cannot locate good investment projects. One could argue that instituting a repurchase program should be regarded in the same manner as announcing a higher dividend payout, but if repurchases are regarded as indicating especially unfavorable growth opportunities, then they can have an adverse impact on the firm's image and on the price of its stock.

Repurchases may involve some risk from a legal standpoint. The SEC may raise serious questions if it appears that the firm is manipulating the price of its shares. Also, if the Internal Revenue Service can establish that the repurchases are primarily for the avoidance of taxes on dividends, then penalties may be imposed on the firm under the improper accumulation of earnings provision of the tax code. Actions have been brought against closely held companies under Section 531, but we know of no case where such an action has been brought against a publicly owned firm, even though some firms have retired over half their outstanding stock.

Conclusion on Stock Repurchases

When all the pros and the cons on stock repurchases are totaled, where do we stand? Our own conclusions can be summarized as follows: Repurchases on a regular, systematic, dependable basis (like quarterly dividends) are not feasible because of uncertainties about the tax treatment of such a program and about the market price of the shares, how many shares will be tendered, and so on. However, repurchases do offer some significant advantages over dividends, so the procedure should be given careful consideration on the basis of the firm's unique situation. They can be especially valuable to effect a significant shift in capital structure within a short period. Repurchases may increase the riskiness of the firm's assets and earnings. The latter two effects may represent a form of expropriation of bondholders.

Summary

Dividend policy determines the extent of internal financing by a firm. The financial manager decides whether to release corporate earnings from the control of the enterprise. Because dividend policy may affect such areas as the financial structure, the flow of funds, corporate liquidity, stock prices, and investor satisfaction, it is clearly an important aspect of financial management.

In theory, once the firm's debt policy and cost of capital have been determined, dividend policy should automatically follow. Under our theoretical model, dividends are simply a residual after investment needs have been met; if the residual policy is followed and if investors are indifferent to receiving their investment returns in the form of dividends or capital gains, stockholders are better off than they are under any other possible dividend policy. However, the financial manager simply does not have all the information assumed in the theory, and judgment must be exercised.

As a guide to financial managers responsible for dividend policy, the following is a summary of the major economic and financial factors influencing dividend policy: (1) rate of growth and profit level, (2) stability of earnings, (3) age and size of firm, (4) cash position, (5) need to repay debt, (6) control, (7) maintenance of a target dividend, (8) tax position of stockholders, (9) tax position of the corporation (including improper accumulation considerations).

Some of the factors listed lead to higher dividend payouts and some to lower payouts. It is not possible to provide a formula that can be used to establish the proper dividend payout for a given situation; this is a task requiring the exercise of judgment. But the considerations summarized above provide a checklist for guiding dividend decisions.

Empirical studies indicate a wide diversity of dividend payout ratios, not only among industries but also among firms in the same industry. Studies also show that dividends are more stable than earnings. Firms are reluctant to raise dividends in years of good earnings, and they resist dividend cuts as earnings decline. In view of investors' observed preference for stable dividends and of the probability that a cut in dividends is likely to be interpreted as forecasting a decline in earnings, stable dividends make good sense.

Stock values are determined as the present value of a stream of cash flows. Therefore, the time pattern of these expected cash flows is very important in valuation of stock. The earnings and dividends of most companies have been increasing at a rate of 3 to 5 percent a year—this is considered a normal growth rate. Some companies may have prospects for no growth at all; others may anticipate a period of supernormal growth before settling down to a normal growth rate; still others may grow in a random fashion.

Neither stock dividends nor stock splits alone exert a major influence on prices. The fundamental determinant of the price of the company's stock is the company's earning power compared with the earning power of other companies. However, both stock splits and stock dividends can be used as effective instruments of financial policy. They are useful devices for reducing the price at which stocks are traded, and studies indicate that they tend to broaden the ownership of a firm's shares.

Stock repurchases have been used as an alternative to cash dividends. Although repurchases have significant advantages over dividends, they also have disadvantages; in particular, they necessarily involve greater uncertainty than cash dividends. Generalizations about stock repurchases are difficult; each firm has its unique problems and conditions, and repurchase policy must be formulated within the context of the firm's characteristics and circumstances as a whole.

Questions

17.1 As an investor, would you rather invest in a firm with a policy of maintaining a constant payout ratio, a constant dollar dividend per share, or a constant regular quarterly dividend plus a year-end extra when earnings are sufficiently high or corporate investment needs are sufficiently low? Explain your answer.

17.2 How would each of the following changes probably affect aggregate payout ratios? Explain your answer.

a. An increase in the personal income tax rate
b. A liberalization in depreciation policies for federal income tax purposes
c. A rise in interest rates
d. An increase in corporate profits
e. A decline in investment opportunities

17.3 Discuss the pros and cons of having the directors formally announce what a firm's dividend policy will be in the future.

17.4 Most firms would like to have their stock selling at a high P-E ratio and have extensive public ownership (many different shareholders). Explain how stock dividends or stock splits may be compatible with these aims.

17.5 What is the difference between a stock dividend and a stock split? As a stockholder, would you prefer to see your company declare a 100 percent stock dividend or a two-for-one split?

17.6 In theory, if we had perfect capital markets, we would expect investors to be indifferent about whether cash dividends were issued or an equivalent repurchase of stock outstanding were made. What factors might in practice cause investors to value one over the other?

17.7 Discuss this statement: The cost of retained earnings is less than the cost of new outside equity capital. Consequently, it is totally irrational for a firm to sell a new issue of stock and to pay dividends during the same year.

17.8 Would it ever be rational for a firm to borrow money in order to pay dividends? Explain.

17.9 Unions have presented arguments similar to the following: "Corporations such as General Foods retain about half their profits for financing needs. If they financed by selling stock instead of by retaining earnings, they could cut prices substantially and still earn enough to pay the same dividend to their shareholders. Therefore, their profits are too high." Evaluate this statement.

17.10 If executive salaries are tied more to the size of the firm's sales or its total assets rather than to profitability, how might managers' policies be adverse to the interests of stockholders?

Problems

17.1 The Bane Engineering Company has $2 million of backlogged orders for its patented solar heating system. Management plans to expand production capacity by 30 percent with a $6 million investment in plant machinery. The firm wants to maintain a 45 percent debt to total asset ratio in its capital structure; it also wants to maintain its past dividend policy of distributing 20 percent of after-tax earnings. In 1980 earnings were $2.6 million. How much external equity must the firm seek at the beginning of 1981?

17.2 Lifton Company expects next year's after-tax income to be $5 million. The firm's current debt-equity ratio is 80 percent. If Lifton has $4 million of profitable investment opportunities and wishes to maintain its current debt-equity ratio, how much should it pay out in dividends next year?

17.3 After a 3 for 1 stock split, Novak Company paid a dividend of $4. This represents an 8 percent increase over last year's pre-split dividend. Novak Company's stock sold for $80 prior to the split. What was last year's dividend per share?

17.4 The following is an excerpt from a 1977 *Wall Street Journal* article:

> General Motors Corp., confident of its outlook for auto sales and profit, boosted its quarterly dividend to $1 a share from 85 cents and declared a special year-end dividend of $2.25 a share. Both the quarterly and the special are payable Dec. 10 to stock of record Nov. 17.
>
> The sizeable fourth quarter payout, totaling $3.25 a share, is a record for any GM dividend in the final quarter. Last year, the No. 1 auto maker, buoyed by strong sales and sharply improved earnings, paid $3 a share in the fourth quarter.
>
> The $3.25-a-share fourth quarter will bring GM's total cash dividend on common stock for 1977 to a record $6.80 (sic) a share, up from the previous record, set last year, of $5.55 a share.
>
> Yesterday's action by GM directors underscored the wave of higher profit that most of the auto makers have been riding for almost two years. Moreover, in raising its quarterly dividend to $1 a share, GM indicated that it expects strong sales and earnings to continue into 1978. In announcing the board's action, Thomas A. Murphy, chairman, and Elliott M. Estes, president, said the dividends "reflect GM's strong earnings and capital position and our confidence in the fundamental strength of the U.S. economy and the automotive market."
>
> The 85-cents-a-share quarterly dividend was instituted by GM in 1966; it was scaled back in 1974 when the auto industry entered a prolonged slump. The 85-cent rate was restored in the third quarter of 1976.[17]

17. "General Motors Boosts Payout to $1 a Share," *Wall Street Journal,* November 8, 1977. Reprinted by permission of The Wall Street Journal,

a. Did GM appear to be following a stable dividend payout ratio or a policy of a stable dollar amount of dividends per quarter? What role did the fourth-quarter year-end "extras" perform in this policy?
b. Some authors have suggested that dividends have "announcement effects," performing the role of signaling investors that a change in underlying earning power has taken place. Is there anything in the article relevant to the concept that dividend changes convey information to investors?

17.5 In 1979 the Odom Company paid dividends totaling $1,125,000. For the past ten years, earnings have grown at a constant rate of 10 percent. After-tax income was $3,750,000 for 1979. However, in 1980, earnings were $6,750,000 with investment of $5,000,000. It is predicted that Odom Company will not be able to maintain this higher level of earnings and will return to its previous 10 percent growth rate. Calculate dividends for 1980 if Odom Company follows each of the following policies:
a. Its dividend payment is stable and growing.
b. It continues the 1979 dividend payout ratio.
c. It uses a pure residual dividend policy (30 percent of the $5,000,000 investment was financed with debt).
d. The investment in 1980 is financed 90 percent with retained earnings and 10 percent with debt. Any earnings not invested are paid out as dividends.
e. The investment in 1980 is financed 30 percent with external equity, 35 percent with debt, and 40 percent with retained earnings. Any earnings not invested are paid out as dividends.

17.6 Raffer Company stock earns $7 per share, sells for $30, and pays a $4 dividend per share. After a 2 for 1 split, the dividend will be $2.70 per share. By what percentage has the payout increased?

17.7 Barnes Company has 500,000 shares of common stock outstanding. Its capital stock account is $500,000, and retained earnings are $2 million. Barnes is currently selling for $10 per share and has declared a 10 percent stock dividend. After distribution of the stock dividend, what balances will the retained earnings and capital stock accounts show?

17.8 The directors of Northwest Lumber Supply have been comparing the growth of their market price with that of one of their competitors, Parker Panels. Their findings are summarized in the following tables.

Northwest Lumber Supply

Year	Earnings	Dividend	Payout	Price	P-E
1978	$4.30	$2.58	60%	$68	15.8
1977	3.85	2.31	60	60	15.6
1976	3.29	1.97	60	50	15.2
1975	3.09	1.85	60	42	13.6
1974	3.05	1.83	60	38	12.5
1973	2.64	1.58	60	31	11.7
1972	1.98	1.19	60	26	13.1
1971	2.93	1.76	60	31	10.6
1970	3.48	2.09	60	35	10.1
1969	2.95	1.77	60	30	10.2

Parker Panels

Year	Earnings	Dividend	Payout	Price	P-E
1978	$3.24	$1.94	60%	$70	21.6
1977	2.75	1.79	65	56	20.4
1976	2.94	1.79	61	53	18.0
1975	2.93	1.73	59	48	16.4
1974	2.90	1.65	57	44	15.2
1973	2.86	1.57	55	41	14.3
1972	2.61	1.49	57	35	13.4
1971	1.55	1.50	97	20	12.9
1970	2.24	1.50	67	34	15.2
1969	2.19	1.49	68	30	13.7

Both companies are in the same markets, and both are similarly organized (approximately the same degree of operating and financial leverage). Northwest has been consistently earning more per share; yet for some reason, it has not been valued at as high a P-E ratio as Parker. What factors would you point out as possible causes for this lower market valuation of Northwest's stock?

17.9 Associated Engineers has experienced the following sales, profit, and balance sheet patterns. Identify the financial problem that has developed, and recommend a solution for it.

Associated Engineers Financial Data, 1970–1979 (Millions of Dollars)

Income Statements	1970	1971	1972	1973	1974	1975	1976	1977	1978	1979
Sales	$100	$140	$180	$200	$240	$400	$360	$440	$480	$680
Profits after tax	10	14	18	20	24	40	36	44	48	68
Dividends	8	10	12	12	14	20	20	28	36	48
Retained earnings	$ 2	$ 4	$ 6	$ 8	$ 10	$ 20	$ 16	$ 16	$ 12	$ 20
Cumulative retained earnings	$ 2	$ 6	$ 12	$ 20	$ 30	$ 50	$ 66	$ 82	$ 94	$114

Balance Sheets	1970	1971	1972	1973	1974	1975	1976	1977	1978	1979
Current assets	$ 20	$ 30	$ 40	$ 50	$ 60	$100	$ 80	$110	$120	$160
Net fixed assets	30	40	50	50	60	100	100	110	120	180
Total assets	$ 50	$ 70	$ 90	$100	$120	$200	$180	$220	$240	$340
Trade credit	$ 8	$ 12	$ 16	$ 18	$ 20	$ 36	$ 30	$ 40	$ 40	$120
Bank credit	8	12	20	20	26	58	28	40	40	40
Other	2	10	12	12	14	16	16	18	16	16
Total current liabilities	$ 18	$ 34	$ 48	$ 50	$ 60	$110	$ 74	$ 98	$ 96	$176
Long-term debt	0	0	0	0	0	10	10	10	20	20
Total debt	$ 18	$ 34	$ 48	$ 50	$ 60	$120	$ 84	$108	$116	$196
Common stock	30	30	30	30	30	30	30	30	30	30
Retained earnings	2	6	12	20	30	50	66	82	94	114
Net worth	$ 32	$ 36	$ 42	$ 50	$ 60	$ 80	$ 96	$112	$124	$144
Total claims on assets	$ 50	$ 70	$ 90	$100	$120	$200	$180	$220	$240	$340

17.10 Babco Industries has earnings this year of $16.5 million, 50 percent of which is required to take advantage of the firm's excellent investment opportunities. The firm has 206,250 shares outstanding, selling currently at $320 a share. Ralph Miller, a major stockholder (18,750 shares), has expressed displeasure with a great deal of managerial policy. Management has approached him with the prospect of selling his holdings back to the firm, and he has expressed a willingness to do this at a price of $320 a share. Assuming that the market uses a constant P-E ratio of 4 in valuing the stock, answer the following questions:

a. Should the firm buy Miller's shares? Assume that dividends will not be paid on them if they are repurchased.
b. How large a cash dividend should be declared?
c. What is the final value of Babco Industries' stock after all cash payments to shareholders?

17.11 Dundie Tobacco Company has for many years enjoyed a moderate but stable growth in sales and earnings. However, cigarette consumption and, consequently, Dundie's sales have been falling off recently, partly because of a national awareness of the dangers of smoking to health. Anticipating further declines in tobacco sales for the future, Dundie's management hopes eventually to move almost entirely out of the tobacco business and develop a new diversified product line in growth-oriented industries.

Dundie has been especially interested in the prospects for pollution control devices. (Its research department has already done much work on problems of filtering smoke.) Right now, the company estimates that an investment of $24 million is necessary to purchase new facilities and begin operations on developing these products, but the investment could return about 18 percent within a short time. Other investment opportunities total $9.6 million and are expected to return about 12 percent.

The company has been paying a $2.40 dividend on its 6 million shares outstanding. The announced dividend policy has been to maintain a stable dollar dividend, raising it only when it appears that earnings have reached a new, permanently higher level. The directors might, however, change this policy if reasons for doing so are compelling. Total earnings for the year are $22.8 million, common stock is currently selling for $45, and the firm's current leverage ratio (B/A) is 45 percent. Current costs of various forms of financing are:

New bonds: 7%

New common stock sold at $45 to yield the firm $41

Investors' required rate of return on equity: 9%

Tax rate: 40%

a. Calculate the marginal cost of capital above and below the point of exhaustion of retained earnings for Dundie.
b. How large should the company's capital budget for the year be?
c. What is an appropriate dividend policy for the firm? How should the capital budget be financed?
d. How might risk factors influence Dundie's cost of capital, capital structure, and dividend policy?
e. What assumptions, if any, do your answers to the above make about investors' preference for dividends versus capital gains—that is, regarding different d/p and g components of k?

17.12 Because of ill health and old age, Jane Ashby contemplates the sale of her shoe store. Her corporation has the following balance sheet:

Assets		**Liabilities and Net Worth**	
Cash	$ 6,000	Notes payable—bank	$ 2,000
Receivables, net	2,000	Accounts payable	4,000
Inventories	13,000	Accruals	1,000
Fixtures and equipment less			
$10,000 reserve for depreciation	14,000	Common stock plus surplus	28,000
Total assets	$35,000	Total liabilities and net worth	$35,000

Annual before-tax earnings (after rent, interest, and salaries) for the preceding three years have averaged $8,000.

Ashby has set a price of $40,000, which includes all the assets of the business except cash; the buyer is to assume all debts. The assets include a five-year lease on the building in which the store is located and the goodwill associated with the name of Ashby Shoes. Assume that both Ashby and the potential purchaser are in the 40 percent tax bracket.

a. Is the price of $40,000 a reasonable one? Explain.
b. What other factors should be taken into account in arriving at a selling price?
c. What is the significance, if any, of the five-year lease?

17.13 The Ellis Company is a small jewelry manufacturer. The company has been successful and has grown. Now, Ellis is planning to sell an issue of common stock to the public for the first time, and it faces the problem of setting an appropriate price on its common stock. The company feels that the proper procedure is to select firms similar to it, with publicly traded common stock, and to make relevant comparisons.

The company finds several jewelry manufacturers similar to it with respect to product mix, size, asset composition, and debt/equity proportions. Of these, Bonden and Seeger are most similar.

Relationships	Bonden	Seeger	(Ellis Totals)
Earnings per share, 1978	$ 5.00	$ 8.00	$ 1,500,000
Average, 1972–1978	4.00	5.00	1,000,000
Price per share, 1978	48.00	65.00	—
Dividends per share, 1978	3.00	4.00	700,000
Average, 1972–1978	2.50	3.25	500,000
Book value per share	45.00	70.00	12,000,000
Market-book ratio	107%	93%	—

a. How can these relationships be used to help Ellis arrive at a market value for its stock?
b. What price do you recommend if Ellis sells 500,000 shares?

17.14 An investor requires a 20 percent return on the common stock of the M Company. During its most recent complete year, the M Company stock earned $4 and paid $2 per share. Its earnings and dividends are expected to grow at a 32 percent rate for five years, after which they are expected to grow at 8 percent per year. At what value of the M Company stock would the investor earn a required 20 percent return?

17.15 The Rowe Company is contemplating the purchase of the Colima Company. During the most recent year, Colima had earnings of $2 million and paid dividends of $1 million. The earnings and dividends of Colima are expected to grow at an annual rate of 30 percent for five years, after which they will grow at an 8 percent rate per year. The required return on an investment with the risk characteristics of the Colima Company is 16 percent.

What is the maximum that the Rowe Company could pay for the Colima Company to earn at least a 16 percent return on its investment?

17.16 The Stoll Company has a beta of 1.2. The expected return on the market is 12 percent, the risk-free rate is 7 percent, and the market variance is 1 percent. The net operating income of the Stoll Company for the year just completed was $8 million, with an applicable corporate tax rate of 40 percent.

a. Assuming no growth in Stoll's NOI is expected, what would be the value of the firm?
b. Next assume that the internal profitability rate of Stoll is 15 percent and that the ratio of investment to net operating income averages 0.60. What would be the value of Stoll under these new assumptions?

17.17 The Porter Company has a required return of 15 percent. Its net operating income, now $6 million, is expected to grow at a rate of 28.8 percent for the next 6 years with a ratio of investment to net operating income of 0.40. The applicable tax rate is 40 percent.

a. If after the period of supernormal growth, the net operating income of Porter has zero growth, what is the value of the firm now?
b. If after the period of supernormal growth, the net operating income of Porter grows at 10 percent per year, what is the value of the firm now?

Selected References

Austin, Douglas V. "Treasury Stock Reacquisition by American Corporations: 1961–67." *Financial Executive* 37 (May 1969), pp. 41–49.

Barnea, Amir, and Logue, Dennis E. "Evaluating the Forecasts of a Security Analyst." *Financial Management* 2 (Summer 1973), pp. 38–45.

Bar-Yosef, Sasson, and Brown, Lawrence D. "A Reexamination of Stock Splits Using Moving Betas." *Journal of Finance* 32 (September 1977), pp. 1069–1080.

Bar-Yosef, Sasson, and Kolodny, Richard. "Dividend Policy and Capital Market Theory: A Reply." *Review of Economics and Statistics* 60 (August 1978), pp. 477–478.

Ben-Zion, Uri, and Kolodny, Richard. "Size, Leverage, and Dividend Record as Determinants of Equity Risk." *Journal of Finance* 30 (June 1975), pp. 1015–1026.

Bhattacharya, S. "Imperfect Information, Dividend Policy, and 'The Bird in the Hand' Fallacy." *Bell Journal of Economics* 10 (Spring 1979), pp. 259–270.

Bierman, Harold, Jr., and West, Richard. "The Acquisition of Common Stock by the Corporate Issuer." *Journal of Finance* 21 (December 1966), pp. 687–696.

Black, F., and Scholes, M. "The Effects of Dividend Yield and Dividend Policy on Common Stock Prices and Returns." *Journal of Financial Economics* 1 (May 1974), pp. 1–22.

Bower, Richard S.; Johnson, Keith B.; Lutz, Walter J.; and Tapley, T. Craig. "Investment

Opportunities and Stock Valuation." *Journal of Business Research* 5 (March 1977), pp. 39–61.

Brennan, Michael. "Note on Dividend Irrelevance and the Gordon Valuation Model." *Journal of Finance* 26 (December 1971), pp. 1115–1123.

Brigham, Eugene. "The Profitability of a Firm's Repurchase of Its Own Common Stock." *California Management Review* 7 (Winter 1964), pp. 69–75.

Brigham, Eugene, and Gordon, Myron J. "Leverage, Dividend Policy, and the Cost of Capital." *Journal of Finance* 23 (March 1968), pp. 85–104.

———. "A Reply to Leverage, Dividend Policy and the Cost of Capital: A Comment." *Journal of Finance* 25 (September 1970), pp. 904–908.

Charest, Guy. "Dividend Information, Stock Returns and Market Efficiency, I, II." *Journal of Financial Economics* 6 (June–September 1978), pp. 265–296, 297–330.

Copeland, Thomas E. "Liquidity Changes Following Stock Splits." *Journal of Finance* 34 (March 1979), pp. 115–141.

Davenport, Michael. "Leverage, Dividend Policy and the Cost of Capital: A Comment." *Journal of Finance* 25 (September 1970), pp. 893–897.

Elton, Edwin J., and Gruber, Martin J. "Marginal Stockholder Tax Rates and the Clientele Effect." *Review of Economics and Statistics* 52 (February 1970), pp. 68–74.

———. "The Cost of Retained Earnings—Implications of Share Repurchase." *Industrial Management Review* 9 (Spring 1968), pp. 68–74.

———. "The Effect of Share Repurchases on the Value of the Firm." *Journal of Finance* 23 (March 1968), pp. 135–150.

Fama, Eugene F. "The Empirical Relationships between the Dividend and Investment Decisions of Firms." *American Economic Review* 64 (June 1974), pp. 304–318.

Fama, Eugene F., and Babiak, Harvey. "Dividend Policy: An Empirical Analysis." *Journal of the American Statistical Association* 63 (December 1968), pp. 1132–1161.

Fama, Eugene F.; Fisher, Lawrence; Jensen, Michael; and Roll, Richard. "The Adjustment of Stock Prices to New Information." *International Economic Review* 10 (February 1969), pp. 1–21.

Fewings, David R. "The Impact of Growth on the Risk of Common Stocks." *Journal of Finance* 30 (May 1975), pp. 525–531.

Friend, Irwin, and Puckett, Marshall. "Dividends and Stock Prices." *American Economic Review* 54 (September 1964), pp. 656–682.

Frost, Peter A. "Dividend Policy and Capital Market Theory: A Comment." *Review of Economics and Statistics* 60 (August 1978), pp. 475–477.

Gentry, James A., and Pyhrr, Stephen A. "Simulating an EPS Growth Model." *Financial Management* 2 (Summer 1973), pp. 68–75.

Gordon, Myron J. "Optimal Investment and Financing Policy." *Journal of Finance* 18 (May 1963), pp. 264–272.

———. *The Investment, Financing and Valuation of the Corporation.* Homewood, Ill.: Irwin, 1962.

———. "Dividends, Earnings and Stock Prices." *Review of Economics and Statistics* 41 (May 1959), pp. 99–105.

Hakansson, Nils H. "On the Dividend Capitalization Model under Uncertainty." *Journal of Financial and Quantitative Analysis* 4 (March 1969), pp. 65–87.

Haugen, Robert A. "Expected Growth, Required Return, and the Variability of Stock Prices." *Journal of Financial and Quantitative Analysis* 5 (September 1970), pp. 297–308.

Hausman, W. H.; West, R. R.; and Largay, J. A. "Stock Splits, Price Changes, and Trading Profits: A Synthesis." *Journal of Business* 44 (January 1971), pp. 69–77.

Higgins, Robert C. "Growth, Dividend Policy and Capital Costs in the Electric Utility Industry." *Journal of Finance* 29 (September 1974), pp. 1189–1201.

———. "Dividend Policy and Increasing Discount Rate: A Clarification." *Journal of Financial and Quantitative Analysis* 7 (June 1972), pp. 1757–1762.

———. "The Corporate Dividend-Saving Decision." *Journal of Financial and Quantitative Analysis* 7 (March 1972), pp. 1527–1541.

Holt, Charles C. "The Influence of Growth Duration on Share Prices." *Journal of Finance* 17 (September 1962), pp. 465–475.

Johnson, Keith B. "Stock Splits and Price Changes." *Journal of Finance* 21 (December 1966), pp. 675–686.

Lee, Cheng F. "Functional Form and the Dividend Effect in the Electric Utility Industry." *Journal of Finance* 31 (December 1976), pp. 1481–1486.

Lewellen, Wilbur G.; Stanley, Kenneth L.; Lease, Ronald C.; and Schlarbaum, Gary G. "Some Direct Evidence on the Dividend Clientele Phenomenon." *Journal of Finance* 33 (December 1978), pp. 1385–1399.

Lintner, John. "Inflation and Security Returns." *Journal of Finance* 30 (May 1975), pp. 259–280.

———. "Optimal Dividends and Corporate Growth under Uncertainty." *Quarterly Journal of Economics* 88 (February 1964), pp. 49–95.

———. "Dividend Policy and Market Valuations: A Reply." *Journal of Business* 36 (January 1963), pp. 116–119.

———. "Dividends, Earnings, Leverage, Stock Prices and the Supply of Capital to Corporations." *Review of Economics and Statistics* 44 (August 1962), pp. 243–269.

———. "Distribution of Incomes of Corporations among Dividends, Retained Earnings, and Taxes." *American Economic Review* 46 (May 1956), pp. 97–113.

Litzenberger, Robert H., and Van Horne, James C. "Elimination of the Double Taxation of Dividends and Corporate Financial Policy." *Journal of Finance* 33 (June 1978), pp. 737–750.

Long, John B., Jr. "The Market Valuation of Cash Dividends: A Case to Consider." *Journal of Financial Economics* 6 (June–September 1978), pp. 235–264.

———. "Efficient Portfolio Choice with Differential Taxation of Dividends and Capital Gains." *Journal of Financial Economics* 5 (August 1977), pp. 25–53.

Malkiel, Burton G. "Equity Yields, Growth, and the Structure of Share Prices." *American Economic Review* 53 (December 1963), pp. 467–494.

Mao, James C. T. "The Valuation of Growth Stocks: The Investment Opportunities Approach." *Journal of Finance* 21 (March 1966), pp. 95–102.

Mehta, Dileep R. "The Impact of Outstanding Convertible Bonds on Corporate Dividend Policy." *Journal of Finance* 31 (May 1976), pp. 489–506.

Mendelson, Morris. "Leverage, Dividend Policy and the Cost of Capital: A Comment." *Journal of Finance* 25 (September 1970), pp. 898–903.

Michel, Allen. "Industry Influence on Dividend Policy." *Financial Management* 8 (Autumn 1973), pp. 35–45.

Millar, James A., and Fielitz, Bruce D. "Stock-Split and Stock-Dividend Decisions." *Financial Management* 2 (Winter 1973), pp. 35–45.

Miller, Merton H., and Modigliani, Franco. "Dividend Policy and Market Valuation: A Reply." *Journal of Business* 36 (January 1963), pp. 411–433.

———. "Dividend Policy, Growth, and the Valuation of Shares." *Journal of Business* 34 (October 1961), pp. 411–433.

Miller, Merton H., and Scholes, Myron S. "Dividends and Taxes." *Journal of Financial Economics* 6 (December 1978), pp. 333–364.

Norgaard, Richard, and Norgaard, Corine. "A Critical Examination of Share Repurchase." *Financial Management* 3 (Spring 1974), pp. 44–50.

Ofer, Aharon R. "Investors' Expectations of Earnings Growth, Their Accuracy and Effects on the Structure of Realized Rates of Return." *Journal of Finance* 30 (May 1975), pp. 509–523.

Pettit, R. Richardson. "Taxes, Transactions Costs and the Clientele Effect of Dividends." *Journal of Financial Economics* 5 (December 1977), pp. 419–436.

———. "The Impact of Dividend and Earnings Announcements: A Reconciliation." *Journal of Business* 49 (January 1976), pp. 86–96.

———. "Dividend Announcements, Security Performance, and Capital Market Efficiency." *Journal of Finance* 27 (December 1972), pp. 993–1007.

Pettway, Richard H., and Malone, R. Phil. "Automatic Dividend Reinvestment Plans of Nonfinancial Corporations." *Financial Management* 2 (Winter 1973), pp. 11–18.

Porterfield, James T. S. "Dividends, Dilution, and Delusion." *Harvard Business Review* 37 (November–December 1959), pp. 156–161.

Pringle, John J. "Price/Earnings Ratios, Earnings per Share, and Financial Management." *Financial Management* 2 (Spring 1973), pp. 34–40.

Silvers, J. B. "An Alternative to the Yield Spread as a Measure of Risk." *Journal of Finance* 28 (September 1973), pp. 933–955.

Soldofsky, Robert M., and Murphy, James T. *Growth Yields on Common Stock—Theory and Tables.* Iowa City, Iowa: State University of Iowa, 1963.

Soter, Dennis S. "The Dividend Controversy—What It Means for Corporate Policy." *Financial Executive* 47 (May 1979), pp. 38–43.

Stewart, Samuel S., Jr. "Should a Corporation Repurchase Its Own Stock?" *Journal of Finance* 31 (June 1976), pp. 911–921.

Stone, B. K. "The Conformity of Stock Values Based on Discounted Dividends to a Fair-Return Process." *Bell Journal of Economics* 6 (Autumn 1975), pp. 698–702.

Sussman, M. R. *The Stock Dividend.* Ann Arbor, Mich.: Bureau of Business Research, University of Michigan, 1962.

Thompson, Howard E. "A Note on the Value of Rights in Estimating the Investor Capitalization Rate." *Journal of Finance* 28 (March 1973), pp. 157–160.

Van Horne, James C., and Glassmire, William F., Jr. "The Impact of Unanticipated Changes in Inflation on the Value of Common Stocks." *Journal of Finance* 27 (December 1972), pp. 1081–1092.

Walter, James E. *Dividend Policy and Enterprise Valuation.* Belmont, Calif.: Wadsworth, 1967.

———. "Dividend Policy: Its Influence on the Value of the Enterprise." *Journal of Finance* 18 (May 1963), pp. 280–291.

———. "Dividend Policies and Common Stock Prices." *Journal of Finance* 11 (March 1956), pp. 29–41.

Warren, James M. "An Operational Model for Security Analysis and Valuation." *Journal of Financial and Quantitative Analysis* 9 (June 1974), pp. 395–422.

Watts, Ross. "The Information Content of Dividends." *Journal of Business* 46 (April 1973), pp. 191–211.

Wendt, Paul F. "Current Growth Stock Valuation Methods." *Financial Analysts' Journal* 33 (March–April 1965), pp. 3–15.

West, Richard R., and Bierman, Harold, Jr. "Corporate Dividend Policy and Preemptive Security Issues." *Journal of Business* 42 (January 1968), pp. 71–75.

West, Richard R., and Brouilette, Alan B. "Reverse Stock Splits." *Financial Executive* 38 (January 1970), pp. 12–17.

Whittington, G. "The Profitability of Retained Earnings." *Review of Economics and Statistics* 54 (May 1972), pp. 152–160.

Woods, Donald H., and Brigham, Eugene F. "Stockholder Distribution Decisions: Share Repurchase or Dividends." *Journal of Financial and Quantitative Analysis* 1 (March 1966), pp. 15–28.

Wrightsman, Dwayne, and Horrigan, James O. "Retention, Risk of Success, and the Price of Stock." *Journal of Finance* 30 (December 1975), pp. 1357–1359.

Young, Allan E. "Common Stock Repurchasing: Another Means of Reducing Corporate Size." *Journal of Accounting, Auditing and Finance* 3 (Spring 1980), pp. 244–250.

———. "Financial, Operating, and Security Market Parameters of Repurchasing." *Financial Analysts' Journal* 25 (July–August 1969), pp. 123–128.

Part Six
Long-Term Financing Decisions

In Part One, we covered the fundamental concepts of Managerial Finance. In Part Two, we developed materials for the analysis, planning, and control of the firm as a whole and for the control of decentralized divisions within the firm. In Part Three, we considered the top half of the balance sheet, analyzing current assets, current liabilities, and the interactions between the two. Then, in Part Four, we moved to the lower left side of the balance sheet, examining the process by which firms decide on investment in fixed assets. With the guidance of the concepts developed in Part Five on the cost of capital and valuation, we can now evaluate individual financing decisions.

In Part Six, we move to the lower right side of the balance sheet, to consider the various types of long-term funds available to the firm when it seeks long-term external capital. Within the framework of the relationship between financial structure and the cost of capital, decisions on individual financing episodes can be made to help the firm toward its objective of achieving an optimal mix of financing. Chapter 18 presents an overview of the capital markets, explaining institutional material essential to an understanding of the use of the financial markets by business firms. Chapter 19 analyzes the conditions under which common stock financing is used. Chapter 20 describes the nature of long-term debt and preferred stocks and their role in the financing of the firm. Chapter 21 analyzes leasing decisions. Chapter 22 discusses the nature and use of warrants, convertibles, and options.

18

Capital Markets: Institutions and Behavior

With a background of investment plans related to the value-maximizing cost of capital, we now turn to the objective of an optimal mix of financing that will result from individual financing decisions. The present chapter deals with a number of aspects of the institutions and behavior of the capital markets business firms use in financing. We begin with an overview of the main sources of funds used by business corporations. We examine the increasingly important practice of financing directly from such institutions as insurance companies and banks. We then turn to the investment banking mechanism by which the funds of individual investors are mobilized for use by business firms. We analyze the relative costs of different methods of sale of new issues with particular attention to competitive versus negotiated securities offerings. We summarize and discuss the implications of the securities laws for financing by business firms. The timing of financing decisions is analyzed in the light of theories of capital market efficiency.

Sources of Business Financing

An overview of the three broad sources of funds used by business corporations is presented in Table 18.1. The sources are internal cash flows, short-term external funds, and long-term external funds. The first two categories of financing were discussed in previous chapters. The third is the subject of this chapter, which provides an overview of the market mechanisms for raising long-term funds. The overview is intended as a framework for the discussion of individual forms of long-term financing, which are presented in the remaining chapters of this section.

The data in Table 18.1 show that internal financing provides over 60 percent of the sources of funds for business corporations. External financing averages 36.5 percent of total sources. Of the external financing, long-term financing is more than two-thirds of the total. Short-term external financing is a kind of balance wheel, increasing as a source of financing when the economy

Table 18.1

Sources of Funds for Business Corporations, 1972–1980 (Billions of Dollars)

	Internal Cash Flow		Short-Term External Funds		Long-Term External Funds		
	Amount	Percent	Amount	Percent	Amount	Percent	Total
1972	$ 87	60	$10	7	$47	33	144
1973	102	57	32	18	45	25	179
1974	116	57	37	18	51	25	204
1975	119	76	(14)	(9)	52	33	157
1976	140	67	22	10	48	23	210
1977	155	66	29	12	52	22	236
1978	174	63	37	13	65	24	276
1979	200	62	45	14	78	24	323
1980	195	65	25	8	79	27	299

Source: Data from Donald E. Woolley and Beverly Lowen, *Credit and Capital Markets, 1980* (New York: Bankers Trust Company, 1980), p. T26. Reprinted by permission. Woolley is senior vice president of Bankers Trust Company, and Lowen is senior economist of Bankers Trust Company.

is strong and decreasing during recessions. Long-term external financing now represents a market of over $80 billion per year of net funds raised.

In making decisions about where and how to raise long-term funds, one important choice is between private sources and the public markets. Private financing represents funds obtained directly from one or a few individuals or financial institutions, such as banks, insurance companies, or pension funds. Public financing uses investment bankers to sell securities to a large number of investors—both individuals and financial institutions. In the 1800s, before the development of broad financial markets, business firms were financed by a few wealthy individuals. One of the economic contributions of investment banking was to bring the general public into such financing by assembling smaller amounts of funds from larger numbers of sources and making the total available to business firms. By the 1930s, large pools of funds had been accumulated in insurance companies, pension funds, and commercial banks. This resulted in an increase in direct financing that bypassed to some degree the use of investment banking. Since direct financing is less complicated than public financing, it will be covered first in the chapter. Then the nature of investment banking will be discussed.

Direct Financing

Two major forms of direct long-term financing are term lending by commercial banks and insurance companies and the private placement of securities with insurance companies and pension funds. *Term loans* are direct business loans with a maturity of more than one year but less than fifteen years and with provisions for systematic repayment (amortization during the life of the loan). *Private placements* are direct business loans with a maturity of more than fifteen years.[1] Approximately half of such placements have been in the form of long-term promissory notes.[2] The distinction is, of course, arbitrary. Private placement differs from the term loan only in its arbitrary maturity length; this distinction becomes even fuzzier when we discover that some private placements call for repayment of a substantial portion of the principal within five to ten years.[3] Thus, term loans and private placements represent about the same kind of financing arrangements.

The total amount of bank term loans outstanding at the end of 1979 was $103 billion. The net amount of corporate debt sold on a private basis that remained outstanding at the end of 1979 was $145 billion. These two forms of direct financing sum to $248 billion. All corporate bonds outstanding at the end of 1979 totalled $431 billion. Hence direct financing was 58 percent of corporate bond funding.[4] These data establish that direct financing represents a major portion of long-term financing of business firms.

The central question of interest to financial managers is: What are the advantages and disadvantages of these two major sources of financing? The considerations that make direct financing of interest to borrowers can be shown under the heading of demand factors:

1. Term loans and private placements represent in part a shift by business firms from dependence on short-term bank borrowing to a greater utilization of longer term financing. This shift helps businesses avoid the problem of unavailability of short-term loans during tight money periods.
2. Term loans and private placements were stimulated after 1934 by the increased cost and time involved in public offerings. The Securities Acts of 1933 and 1934 required that new financing go through a registration process and a twenty-day waiting period. Developing data for the SEC registration statements increased the cost of public flotations, particularly for issues of less than $1 million, because the fixed costs were spread over small amounts.
3. A public offering takes time to prepare. There are registration statements to be written, underwriting agreements to be made, and a possible two-to-three-month waiting period before the offering can be made. A private placement or term loan can be taken care of in a matter of hours, especially where there is a continuing relationship between the insurance company or bank and the borrower.

1. This is the dividing line drawn by N. H. Jacoby and R. J. Saulnier, *Term Lending to Business* (New York: National Bureau of Economic Research, 1942), pp. 10–14 and Appendix B, pp. 143–147. See also the analysis in Avery B. Cohan, *Private Placements and Public Offerings* (Chapel Hill: School of Business Administration, University of North Carolina, 1961), pp. 2–5.
2. E. Raymond Corey, *Direct Placement of Corporate Securities* (Cambridge, Mass.: School of Business Administration, Harvard University, 1961), pp. 115–116.
3. Ibid., pp. 120–121.
4. Salomon Brothers, *1980 Prospects for the Credit Markets* (New York: Salomon Brothers, 1980), pp. 23–24.

4. If the securities of a public offering are widely held, it is more difficult to negotiate a modification in the indenture (loan agreement) provisions. If, for example, some of the terms of a direct loan have become onerous (not in the best interests of the borrower), the borrower can negotiate directly with the bank or the insurance company. It is much more difficult to contact thousands of bondholders to obtain agreement about modifying provisions of the bond issue.
5. The increased rates of corporate taxation in the 1930s made it more difficult for small and medium-sized firms to finance their growth with internal funds. It thus became necessary for them to turn to external sources, and direct longer term loans represented one of these available sources. One study observes that "the most important characteristic of the private placement market is that it serves as the major source of long-term debt financing for smaller, less financially secure companies."[5] The supply of long-term funds increased in the early 1930s for various reasons:

a. Inauguration in 1933 of deposit insurance by the Federal Deposit Insurance Corporation reduced the likelihood of widespread runs on banks by depositors. The result was greater stability of the deposits in small banks as well as greater stability of the banks' own deposits in the larger correspondent banks. This stability made it feasible for commercial banks to extend longer term loans.
b. Also, because of the slow recovery in business conditions after emerging from the severe recession of 1929–1933, the surviving commercial banks had excess reserves, and insurance companies were continuing to accumulate funds. Thus ample funds were available, and suppliers were looking for new ways of lending them.
c. The increase in pension funds and state and local retirement funds greatly augmented the money available for longer term financing.

Characteristics of Term Loans and Private Placements

Most term loans are repayable on an amortized basis. Because this repayment, or amortization, schedule is a particularly important feature of such loans, it is useful to describe how it is determined. The purpose of amortization, of course, is to have the loan repaid gradually over its life rather than fall due all at once; this protects both the lender and the borrower against the possibility that the borrower will not make adequate provisions for retirement of the loan during its life. Amortization is especially important where the loan is for the purpose of purchasing a specific item of equipment; here the schedule of repayment will be geared to the productive life of the equipment, and payments will be made from cash flows resulting from use of the equipment.

To illustrate how the amortization schedule is determined, assume that a

5. E. Shapiro and C. R. Wolf, *The Role of Private Placements in Corporate Finance* (Cambridge, Mass.: School of Business Administration, Harvard University, 1972), p. 2.

firm borrows $1,000 on a ten-year loan, that interest is computed at 8 percent on the declining balance, and that the principal and interest are to be paid in ten equal installments. What is the amount of each of the ten annual payments? To find this value we must use the present value concepts developed in Chapter 4.

First, notice that the lender advances $1,000 and receives in turn a ten-year annuity of a dollars each year. In Chapter 4 we saw that these receipts could be calculated as:

$$a = \frac{PV_{at}}{PVIFA},$$

where:

a = Annual receipt
PV_{at} = Present value of the annuity
PVIFA = Appropriate interest factor (found in Appendix Table A.3)

Substituting the $1,000 for PV_{at} and the interest factor for a ten-year, 8 percent annuity—6.7101—for PVIFA, we find:

$$a = \frac{\$1{,}000}{6.7101} = \$149.$$

Therefore, if the firm makes ten annual installments of $149 each, it will have retired the $1,000 loan and provided the lender an 8 percent return on the investment.

Table 18.2 breaks down the annual payments into interest and repayment components and proves in the process that level payments of $149 will, in fact, retire the $1,000 loan and give the lender an 8 percent return. This breakdown is important for tax purposes, because the interest payments are deductible expenses to the borrower and taxable income to the lender.

Table 18.2

Term Loan Schedule

Year	Total Payment	Interest[a]	Amortization Repayment	Remaining Balance
1	$149	$80	$ 69	$931
2	149	74	75	856
3	149	68	81	775
4	149	62	87	688
5	149	55	94	594
6	149	48	101	493
7	149	39	110	383
8	149	31	118	265
9	149	21	128	137
10	149	11	138	—

a. Interest for the first year is 0.08 × $1,000 = $80; for the second year, 0.08 × $931 = $74; and so on.

Other Characteristics

Maturity. For commercial banks, the term loan runs five years or less (typically three years). For insurance companies, typical maturities have been five to fifteen years. This difference reflects the fact that liabilities of commercial banks are shorter term than those of insurance companies. Banks and insurance companies occasionally cooperate in their term lending. For example, if a firm (usually a large one) seeks a fifteen-year term loan, a bank may take the loan for the first five years and an insurance company for the last ten years.

Collateral. Commercial banks require security on about 60 percent of the volume and 90 percent of the number of term loans made. They take as security mainly stocks, bonds, machinery, and equipment. Insurance companies also require security on nearly one-third of their loans, frequently using real estate as collateral on the longer term ones.

Options. In recent years institutional investors have increasingly taken compensation in addition to fixed interest payments on directly negotiated loans. The most popular form of additional compensation is an option to buy common stock, the option being in the form of detachable warrants permitting the purchase of the shares at stated prices over a designated period. (See Chapter 22 for more details on warrants.)

Terms of Loan Agreements

A major advantage of a term loan is that it assures the borrower of the use of the funds for an extended period. On a ninety-day loan, since the commercial bank has the option to renew or not renew, it has frequent opportunities to reexamine the borrower's situation. If it has deteriorated unduly, the loan officer simply does not renew the loan. On a term loan, however, the bank or insurance company has committed itself for a period of years. Because of this long-term commitment, restrictive provisions are incorporated into the loan agreement to protect the lender for the duration of the loan. The most important of these provisions (though by no means all of them) are listed below:

1. *Current ratio.* The current ratio must be maintained at some specified level—2½ to 1; 3 to 1; 3½ to 1—depending on the borrower's line of business. Net working capital must also be maintained at some minimum level.
2. *Additional long-term debt.* Typically, there are prohibitions against (a) incurring additional long-term indebtedness, except with the permission of the lender; (b) the pledging of assets; (c) the assumption of any contingent liabilities, such as guaranteeing the indebtedness of a subsidiary; and (d) the signing of long-term leases beyond specified amounts.
3. *Management.* The loan agreement may require (a) that any major changes in management personnel be approved by the lender; (b) that life insurance be taken out on the principals or key people in the business; and (c) that a voting trust be created or proxies be granted for a specified period to ensure that the management of the company will be under the control of the group on which the lender has relied in making the loan.

4. *Financial statements.* The lender will require the borrower to submit periodic financial statements for review.

Costs

Another major aspect of term loans is their cost. As with other forms of lending, the interest rate on these loans varies with the size of the loan and the quality of the borrower, reflecting also the fixed costs of making loans. Surveys show that on small term loans the effective interest rate may run up to as much as six to eight percentage points above the prime rate. On loans of $1 million and more, term loan rates have been close to the prime rate.

The interest rate may be fixed for the life of the loan, or it may vary. Often the loan agreement specifies that the interest rate will be based on the average of the rediscount rate in the borrower's Federal Reserve district during the previous three months—generally 1 or 2 percent above the rediscount rate.[6] It may also be geared to the published prime rate charged by New York City banks.

P. A. Hays, M. D. Joehnk, and R. W. Melicher analyzed risk premiums when corporate debt was issued in public offerings versus private placements during the 1970–1975 time period.[7] Risk premiums were measured for 376 public issues and 314 private placements by relating their yields to maturity to the yield to maturity on U.S. Treasury securities of comparable maturities. On public offerings, risk premiums were smaller when the issue size was large, the issue was secured, the EBIT trend was favorable, and the times interest earned ratio was favorable. Risk premiums were larger when the years to maturity were longer and the long-term debt to total asset ratio higher. For private placements, only the issue size and times interest earned ratio were significant and negatively related to risk premiums. Also, the years to maturity variable was negative rather than positive in determining the level of the required yield. For both public and private offerings, risk premiums were negatively related to the level of economic activity as measured by industrial production. They were also negatively related to market factors such as the level of free reserves. In addition, for private placements the risk premium was positively related to plant and equipment expenditure expectations and negatively related to the amount of life insurance funds available for direct placements.

While the model was able to explain approximately 50 percent of the variation in risk premiums, the variables that were important in doing so differed. Risk premiums for public offerings were largely explained by default risk measures in the form of issue and issuing firm characteristics. Risk premiums in the private market were explained more by economic and market-related factors. The authors conclude that investors in the public market used differ-

6. The rediscount rate is the rate of interest at which a bank can borrow from a Federal Reserve Bank.
7. P. A. Hays, M. D. Joehnk, and R. W. Melicher, "Differential Determinants of Risk Premiums in the Public and Private Corporate Bond Markets," *Journal of Financial Research* 2 (Fall 1979), pp. 143–152.

ent measures to assess investment attractiveness than did investors in the private placement market.

On private placements, the interest rate generally runs from about ten to fifty basis points higher than that on comparable public issues. In the Hays-Joehnk-Melicher study the yield to maturity on the private placements was forty-six basis points higher than on the public offerings. Thus, to some extent, the economies of using private placements are offset by their somewhat higher interest rates.

From the standpoint of the borrower, the advantages of direct financing are:

1. Much seasonal short-term borrowing can be dispensed with, thereby reducing the danger of nonrenewal of loans.
2. The borrower avoids the expenses of SEC registration and investment bankers' distribution.
3. Less time is required to complete arrangements for obtaining a loan than is involved in a bond issue.
4. Since only one lender is involved, rather than many bondholders, it is possible to modify the loan indenture.

The disadvantages to a borrower of direct financing are:

1. The interest rate may be higher on a term loan than on a short-term loan because the lender is tying up money for a longer period and therefore does not have the opportunity to review the borrower's status periodically (as is done with a short-term loan).
2. The cash drain is large. Since the loans provide for regular amortization or sinking fund payments, the company experiences a continuous cash drain. From this standpoint, direct loans are less advantageous than equity money (which never has to be repaid), a preferred stock without maturity, or even a bond issue without a sinking fund requirement.
3. Since the loan is a long-term commitment, the lender employs high credit standards, insisting that the borrower be in a strong financial position and have a good current ratio, a low debt-equity ratio, good activity ratios, and good profitability ratios.
4. The loan agreement has restrictions that are not found in a ninety-day note. (The reasons for the restrictions and their nature have already been explained.)
5. Investigation costs may be high. The lender stays with the company for a longer period. Therefore, the longer term outlook for the company must be looked into, and the lender makes a more elaborate investigation than would be done for a short-term note. For this reason the lender may set a minimum on any loan (for example, $50,000) in order to recover the costs of investigating the applicant.

In addition, there are some advantages to the public distribution of securities that are not achieved by term loans or private placement, including these considerations:

1. The firm establishes its credit and achieves publicity by having its securities publicly and widely distributed. Because of this, it will be able to engage in future financing at lower rates.
2. The wide distribution of debt or equity may enable its repurchase on favorable terms at some subsequent date if the market price of the securities falls.

Thus direct long-term financing has both advantages and limitations. While it has grown to represent a substantial volume of financing, public financing of long-term funds still predominates and is likely to continue doing so. Therefore, the institutions for long-term public financing are discussed next.

Investment Banking

In the U.S. economy, saving is done by one group of persons and investing by another. (*Investing* is used here in the sense of actually putting money into plant, equipment, and inventory, not in the sense of buying securities.) Savings are placed with financial intermediaries who, in turn, make the funds available to firms wishing to acquire plants and equipment and to hold inventories.

One of the major institutions performing this channeling role is the *investment banking* institution. The term *investment banker* is somewhat misleading, since investment bankers are neither investors nor bankers. That is, they do not invest their own funds permanently; nor are they repositories for individuals' funds, as are commercial banks or savings banks. What, then, is the nature of investment banking?

The many activities of investment bankers can be described first in general terms and then with respect to specific functions. The traditional function of the investment banker has been to act as the middleman in channeling driblets of individuals' savings and funds into the purchase of business securities. The investment banker does this by purchasing and distributing the new securities of individual companies while performing the functions of underwriting, distribution of securities, and advice and counsel.

Underwriting

Underwriting is the insurance function of bearing the risks of adverse price fluctuations during the period in which a new issue of securities is being distributed. The nature of the investment banker's underwriting function can best be conveyed by example: A business firm needs $10 million. It selects an investment banker, holds conferences, and decides to issue $10 million of bonds. An underwriting agreement is drawn up. On a specific day, the investment banker presents the company with a check for $10 million (less commission). In return, the investment banker receives bonds in denominations of $1,000 each to sell to the public.

The company receives the $10 million before the investment banker has sold the bonds. Between the time the firm is paid the $10 million and the time the bonds are sold, the investment banker bears all the risk of market price fluctuations in the bonds. Conceivably, it can take the investment banker days, months, or longer to sell bonds. If the bond market collapses in the interim, the investment banker carries the risk of loss on the sale of the bonds.

There have been dramatic instances of bond market collapses within one week after an investment banker has bought $50 million or $100 million of bonds. For example, in the spring of 1974 an issue of New Jersey Sporting Arena bonds dropped $140 per $1,000 bond during the underwriting period, costing the underwriters an estimated $8 million. The issuing firm, however, does not need to be concerned about the risk of market price fluctuations while the investment banker is selling the bonds, since it has received its money. One fundamental economic function of the investment banker, then, is to underwrite the risk of a decline in the market price between the time the money is transmitted to the firm and the time the bonds are placed in the hands of their ultimate buyers. For this reason, investment bankers are often called underwriters; they underwrite risk during the distribution period.

Distribution

The second function of the investment banker is marketing new issues of securities. The investment banker is a specialist with a staff and organization to distribute securities and, therefore, the capacity to perform the physical distribution function more efficiently and more economically than can an individual corporation. A corporation that wished to sell an issue of securities would find it necessary to establish a marketing or selling organization—a very expensive and ineffective method of selling securities. The investment banker has a permanent, trained staff and dealer organization available to distribute securities. In addition, the investment banker's reputation for selecting good companies and pricing securities fairly builds up a broad clientele over time, and this further increases the efficiency with which securities can be sold.

Advice and Counsel

The investment banker, engaged in the origination and sale of securities, through experience becomes an expert adviser about terms and characteristics of securities that will appeal to investors. This advice and guidance is valuable. Furthermore, the person's reputation as a seller of securities depends on the subsequent performance of the securities. Therefore, investment bankers often sit on the boards of firms whose securities they have sold. In this way they can provide continuing financial counsel and increase the firm's probability of success.

Investment Banking Operation

Probably the best way to gain a clear understanding of the investment banking function is to trace the history of a new issue of securities.[8] Accordingly, this section describes the steps necessary to issue new securities.

Preunderwriting Conferences

First, the members of the issuing firm and the investment banker hold preunderwriting conferences at which they discuss the amount of capital to be raised, the type of security to be issued, and the terms of the agreement. Memorandums are written by the treasurer of the issuing company to the firm's directors and other officers describing proposals suggested at the conferences. Meetings of the board of directors of the issuing company are held to discuss the alternatives and to attempt to reach a decision.

At some point, the issuer enters an agreement with the investment banker that a flotation will take place. The investment banker then begins to conduct an underwriting investigation. If the company is proposing to purchase additional assets, the underwriter's engineering staff may analyze the proposed acquisition. A public accounting firm is called upon to make an audit of the issuing firm's financial situation and also helps prepare the registration statements in connection with these issues for the SEC.

A firm of lawyers is called in to interpret and judge the legal aspects of the flotation. In addition, the originating underwriter (who is the manager of the subsequent underwriting syndicate) makes an exhaustive investigation of the company's prospects.

When the investigations are completed, but before registration with the SEC is made, an underwriting agreement is drawn up by the investment banker. Terms of the tentative agreement may be modified through discussions between the underwriter and the issuing company, but the final agreement will cover all underwriting terms except the price of the securities.

Registration Statement

A registration statement containing all relevant financial and business information on the firm then is filed with the SEC. The statutes set a twenty-day waiting period (which in practice may be shortened or lengthened by the SEC) during which the SEC staff analyzes the registration statement to determine whether there are any omissions or misrepresentations of fact. During the examination period, the SEC can file exceptions to the registration statement or can ask for additional information from the issuing company or the underwriters. Also during this period, the investment bankers are not per-

8. The process described here relates primarily to situations where the firm doing the financing picks an investment banker, then negotiates over the terms of the issue. An alternative procedure, used extensively only in the public utility industry, is for the selling firm to specify the terms of the new issue, then to have investment bankers bid for the entire new issue with *sealed bids*. The very high fixed costs that an investment banker must incur to thoroughly investigate the company and its new issue rule out sealed bids except for the largest issues. The operation described in this section is called *negotiated underwriting*. Competition is keen among underwriters, of course, to develop and maintain working relations with business firms.

mitted to offer the securities for sale, although they can print a preliminary prospectus with all the customary information except the offering price.

Pricing the Securities

The actual price the underwriter pays the issuer is not generally determined until the end of the registration period. There is no universally followed practice, but one common arrangement for a new issue of stock calls for the investment banker to buy the securities at a prescribed number of points below the closing price on the last day of registration. For example, in October 1977 the stock of Wilcox Chemical Company had a current price of $38 and had traded between $35 and $40 a share during the previous three months. The firm and the underwriter agreed that the investment banker would buy 200,000 new shares at $2.50 below the closing price on the last day of registration. The stock closed at $36 on the day the SEC released the issue, so the firm received $33.50 a share. Typically, such agreements have an escape clause that provides for the contract to be voided if the price of the securities falls below some predetermined figure. In the case of Wilcox, this *upset price* was set at $34 a share. Thus, if the closing price of the shares on the last day of registration had been $33.50, Wilcox would have had the option of withdrawing from the agreement.

This arrangement holds, of course, only for additional stock offerings of firms whose old stock was previously traded. When a company goes public for the first time, the investment banker and the firm negotiate a price in accordance with the valuation principles described in Chapters 16 and 17.

The investment banker has an easier job if the issue is priced relatively low, but the issuer of the securities naturally wants as high a price as possible. Some conflict on price therefore arises between the investment banker and the issuer. If the issuer is financially sophisticated and makes comparisons with similar security issues, the investment banker is forced to price close to the market.

Underwriting Syndicate

The investment banker with whom the issuing firm has conducted its discussions does not typically handle the purchase and distribution of the issue alone, unless the issue is a very small one. If the sums of money involved are large and the risks of price fluctuations are substantial, the investment banker forms a syndicate in an effort to minimize the amount of personal risk. A syndicate is a temporary association for the purpose of carrying out a specific objective. The nature of the arrangements for a syndicate in the underwriting and sale of a security through an investment banker can best be understood with the aid of Figure 18.1

The managing underwriter invites other investment bankers to participate in the transaction on the basis of their knowledge of the particular kind of offering to be made and their strength and dealer contacts in selling securities of this type. Each investment banker has business relationships with other investment bankers and dealers and thus has a selling group composed of these people.

Some firms combine all these characteristics. For example, Merrill Lynch, Pierce, Fenner & Smith underwrites some issues and manages the underwriting of others. On still other flotations, it is invited by the manager to join in the distribution of the issue. It also purchases securities as a dealer, carries an inventory of those securities, and publishes lists of securities it has for sale. In addition to being a dealer, Merrill Lynch, of course, carries on substantial activity as a broker. An individual investment firm may also carry on all these functions.

There are also firms with a narrower range of functions—specialty dealers, specialty brokers, and specialty investment counselors. Thus, in the financial field, there is often specialization of financial functions. A *dealer* purchases securities outright, holds them in inventory, and sells them at whatever price can be gotten. The dealer may benefit from price appreciation or may suffer a loss on declines, as any merchandiser does. A *broker,* on the other hand, takes orders for purchases and transmits them to the proper exchange; the gain is the commission charged for the service.

Syndicates are used in the distribution of securities for three reasons:

1. A single investment banker may be financially unable to handle a large issue alone.
2. The originating investment banker may desire to spread the risk even if it is financially able to handle the issue alone.
3. The utilization of several selling organizations (as well as other underwriters) permits an economy of selling effort and expense and encourages nationwide distribution.

Participating underwriters and dealers are provided with full information on all phases of these financing transactions, and they share in the underwriting commission. Suppose that an investment banker buys $10 million worth of bonds to be sold at par, or $1,000 each. If this banker receives a two-point spread, the logical course is to buy the bonds from the issuer at 98; that is, the banker must pay the issuer $9.8 million for the issue of $10 million. Typically, on a two-point spread, the managing underwriter receives the first one-quarter of one percent for originating and managing the syndicate. Next, the entire underwriting group receives about 0.75 percent. Members of the selling group receive about 1 percent as a sales commission.

The manager of the underwriting group who makes a sale to an ultimate purchaser of the securities receives the 0.25 percent as manager, 0.75 percent as underwriter, and 1 percent as seller—the full 2 percent. If the manager wholesales some of the securities to members of the selling group who make the ultimate sale, they receive the 1 percent selling commission and the manager receives the other 1 percent for managing and underwriting the issue. If the issue is managed by one firm, underwritten by a second, and sold by a third, the 2 percent commission is divided, with 1 percent going to the selling firm, 0.75 percent to the underwriter, and 0.25 percent to the manager of the underwriting group.

Figure 18.1

Diagram of Sales of $100 Million of Bonds through Investment Bankers

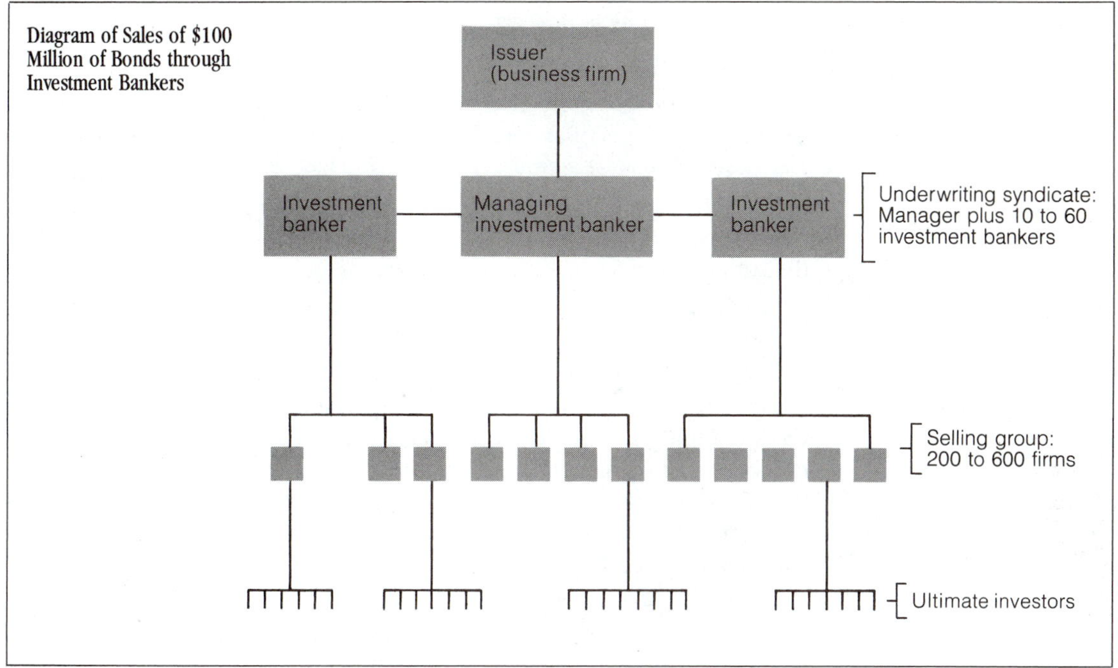

Variations take place around these patterns. In early October 1979, IBM sold $500 million in seven-year notes and $500 million in twenty-five-year debentures; the commissions on the debentures were higher than those on the notes. On the notes, the total fee was $6.25 per note, representing about five-eighths of one percent of the selling price to buyers. The management fee was $1.25 and the underwriter fee was also $1.25, with a selling commission of $3.75. The total fee on the debentures was seven-eighths of one percent, or $8.75, with $1.75 to the managers, $2 to the underwriters, and $5 to the sellers.[9]

Ordinarily, each underwriter's liability is limited to the agreed-upon commitment. For example, an investment banker who participates in a $20 million offering and agrees to see to it that $5 million of the securities are sold no longer is responsible after the $5 million of securities are sold.

Selling Group

The selling group is formed primarily for the purpose of distributing securities; it consists of dealers, who take relatively small participations from the members of the underwriting group. The underwriters act as wholesalers; members of the selling group act as retailers. The number of investment banking houses in a selling group depends partly on the size of the issue. A

9. W. Guzzardi, Jr., "The Bomb IBM Dropped on Wall Street," *Fortune*, November 19, 1979, p. 53.

selling group may have as many as three hundred to four hundred dealers. The operation of the selling group is controlled by the *selling group agreement,* which usually covers the following major points.

1. *Description of the issue.* The description is set forth in a report on the issue—the prospectus—which fully describes the issue and the issuer.
2. *Concession.* Members of the selling group subscribe to the new issue at a public offering price less the *concession* given to them as a commission for their selling service. The selling commission is generally greater than the sum of the managing and underwriting fees.
3. *Handling purchased securities.* The selling group agreement provides that no member of the selling group will be permitted to sell the securities below the public offering price. The syndicate manager invariably "pegs" the quotation in the market by placing continuous orders to buy at the public offering price. A careful record is kept of bond or stock certificate numbers so that repurchased securities can be identified with the member of the selling group who sold them. The general practice is to cancel the commission on such securities. Repurchased securities are then placed with other dealers for sale.[10]
4. *Duration of selling group.* The most common provision in selling group agreements is that the group has an existence of thirty days, subject to earlier termination by the manager. The agreement may be extended, however, for an additional eighty days by members representing 75 percent of the selling group.

Offering and Sale

After the selling group has been formed, the actual offering takes place. Publicity for the sale is given in advance of the offering date. Advertising material is prepared for release as soon as permitted. The actual day of the offering is chosen with a view to avoiding temporary congestion in the security market and other unfavorable events or circumstances.

The formal public offering is called *opening the books,* an archaic term reflecting ancient customs of the investment banking trade. When the books are opened, the manager accepts subscriptions to the issue from both selling group participants and outsiders who wish to buy. If the demand is great, the books may be closed immediately and an announcement made that the issue is oversubscribed; the issue is said to "fly out the window." If the reception is weak, the books may remain open for an extended period.

Market Stabilization

During the period of the offering and distribution of securities, the manager of the underwriting group typically stabilizes the price of the issue. The dura-

10. Without these repurchase arrangements, members of the selling group could sell their share of the securities on the market instead of soliciting new purchasers. Since the pegging operation is going on, there will be a ready market for the securities; consequently, a penalty is necessary to avoid thwarting the syndicate operation.

tion of the price-pegging operation is usually thirty days. The price is pegged by placing orders to buy at a specified price in the market. The pegging operation is designed to prevent a cumulative downward movement in the price, which would result in losses for all members of the underwriting group. Since the manager of the underwriting group has the major responsibility, that person assumes the task of pegging the price.

If the market deteriorates during the offering period, the investment banker carries a substantial risk. For this reason, the pegging operation may not be sufficient to protect the underwriters. In one Pure Oil Company issue of $44 million convertible preferred stock, only $1 million of shares were sold at the $100 offering price. At the conclusion of the underwriting agreement, initial trading took place at $74, incurring for the investment bankers a loss of over $11 million ($43 million × 26 percent). In the Textron issue of June 1967, the offering was reduced from $100 million to $50 million because of market congestion, and 5 percent of the bonds still were unsold after the initial offering. Other such cases can be cited.

It has been charged that pegging the price during the offering period constitutes a monopolistic price-fixing arrangement. Investment bankers reply, however, that not to peg the price would increase the risk and therefore the underwriting cost to the issuer. On balance, it appears that the pegging operation has a socially useful function. The danger of monopolistic pricing is avoided, or at least mitigated substantially, by competitive factors. If an underwriter attempts to set a monopolistic price on a particular issue of securities, the investor can turn to thousands of other securities that are not price pegged. The degree of control over the market by the underwriter in a price-pegging operation seems negligible.

IBM's October 1979 Debt Offering

The IBM debt offering of October 1979 provides an informative case study of the nature of modern investment banking and underwriting.[11] IBM's debt offering was called the largest in U.S. corporate history. It represented a combined offering by IBM of $500 million in seven-year notes and $500 million in twenty-five-year debentures (unsecured long-term debt) for a total of $1 billion. IBM's customary investment banker had been Morgan Stanley & Co. For this offering, IBM requested separate proposals from Morgan Stanley and from Salomon Brothers. It was reported that IBM's financial management was of the opinion that two managers would provide better execution of the sale and back it up with a larger amount of capital. John H. Gutfreund, Salomon Brother's managing partner, is quoted as stating, "A major corporation is best served by two sets of eyes and ears." Robert H. B. Baldwin, president of Morgan Stanley, is said to have responded, "You need only one brain sur-

11. This summary is based on contemporaneous accounts in the financial press and in the later article by Guzzardi, "The Bomb IBM Dropped on Wall Street," pp. 52–56. Our assessment of the financing differs from the views expressed in the latter account.

geon."[12] Morgan Stanley dropped out as manager and Merrill Lynch became the co-manager, with an underwriting group totaling 227 members.

The Salomon and Morgan Stanley proposals had been presented to IBM early in September 1979. The ensuing discussions during that month took place during a period when the prime rate was increased five times, reaching a level of 13.5 percent by September 28. The planned date for the offering was moved up from October 15 to the first week in October. A pricing meeting took place on October 3, 1979, with rapidly rising yields taking place in the money markets. Discussions centered around prices based on a yield of seven basis points above Treasury notes for the IBM notes and twelve basis points above Treasury bonds for the IBM debentures. Taking the small price discounts into account, IBM was paying 9.62 percent for the seven-year notes and 9.41 percent for the twenty-five-year debentures. The underwriting spread or commission on the notes was five-eighths of 1 percent, or $6.25 per note. The underwriter fee on the debentures was seven-eighths of 1 percent, or $8.75 per debenture.

October 3 was a Wednesday. After the pricing meeting, which ended at 12:40 p.m., the market yield of Treasury bonds moved up during the afternoon by five basis points. The IBM offering began on Thursday, October 4. Also on Thursday the Treasury auctioned $2.5 billion of four-year notes yielding 9.79 percent, higher than the 9.62 percent for the IBM seven-year notes.

On Saturday, October 6, the Federal Reserve System announced an increase in its discount rate from 11 percent to 12 percent. A number of other credit-tightening policies, called "Draconian" in their severity, were implemented. As a result of the Fed's actions, by Tuesday, October 9, an additional increase in the prime rate was announced, with a rise of one full percent—to 14.5 percent. On Wednesday morning, October 10, the underwriting syndicate was disbanded. The price of both the notes and the debentures fell by about $5 each, with yields rising to 10.65 percent per note and 10.09 percent for the debentures.

When the syndicate was disbanded, it was estimated that $600 to $700 million of the issue had been sold. Using the mid-figure of $650 and applying the underwriting fees indicated revenues of about $5 million. When the market quotations dropped after the syndicate was disbanded, the losses on the $350 million sold at lower prices were estimated at around $15 million. The potential losses to individual underwriters were substantial. The two managers, Salomon and Merrill Lynch, each underwrote over $124 million. Morgan Stanley took $40 million. First Boston and Goldman Sachs each took $20 million.

Underwriting exposure must also take the practice of *swapping* into account. To sell institutional buyers a new issue, the seller takes in exchange (swaps) some other bonds that the institutions already own. The value placed on the bonds taken in exchange may have a substantial effect on the actual

12. Guzzardi, "The Bomb IBM Dropped on Wall Street," p. 52.

price received. Another aspect is the practice of hedging. When in a long position on bonds while interest rates are rising, the underwriter can take self-protective action by selling other issues short.

A controversy remains over whether the IBM issue was priced "too tight." During the month of September preceding the actual offering, the Federal funds rate, the prime rate, and the discount rate had all been increasing. The financial markets during the week of October 3, when the pricing decision was made, were hectic if not chaotic. Undoubtedly, the severe measures taken by the Federal Reserve System on Saturday, October 6, 1979, were in the air during the week.[13] For example, the October 5 *Wall Street Journal* reported, "Another negative development was the apparent decision by the Federal Reserve System to tighten its credit reins further and to push key short-term interest rates still higher." Whether the underwriters should have given themselves more cushion to avoid a subsequent price decline is a matter of judgment. From one standpoint, the price decline of $4 to $5 after disbanding the underwriting syndicate was relatively modest, given the sharply rising interest rates during the period and the Fed announcement on Saturday, October 6. Differences in judgment on this matter are likely, but such differences in judgment are what make markets.

The IBM offering illustrates a number of basic characteristics of investment banking. One is that the risks are real. Two, competition between investment bankers continues to be vigorous and tough. Three, a corporate issue of a well managed, prestigious firm which is taking on debt for the first time (and in moderate quantity in relation to its total assets) will be rated Aaa and priced close to Treasury issues. Fourth, the turbulence of the financial markets during the week of the offering made the task of the underwriters and the company a supremely difficult one. It demonstrated the great risk-taking and judgment required to make decisions in the face of an extremely turbulent financial environment. Fifth, the episode illustrates the high drama, the considerable financial sophistication, and the continued great challenges that exist in the field of financial decision making.

Costs of Flotation

The cost of selling new issues of securities is put into perspective in Table 18.3. The table summarizes recent data on costs of flotation compiled by the SEC. Two important generalizations can be drawn from these data:

1. The cost of flotation for common stock is greater than for preferred stock, and the costs of both are greater than the cost of flotation for bonds.
2. The cost of flotation as a percentage of the gross proceeds is greater for small issues than for large ones.

13. "Prices Drop Further as Record IBM Offer Encounters Surprising Buyer Resistance," *Wall Street Journal*, October 5, 1979, p. 37.

Table 18.3

Costs of Flotation as a Percentage of Proceeds for Common Stock Issues, 1971–1975[a]

Size of Issue (Millions of Dollars)	Underwriting				Rights with Standby Underwriting				Rights	
	Number	Compensation as a Percentage of Proceeds	Other Expenses as a Percentage of Proceeds	Total Cost as a Percentage of Proceeds	Number	Compensation as a Percentage of Proceeds	Other Expenses as a Percentage of Proceeds	Total Cost as a Percentage of Proceeds	Number	Total Cost as a Percentage of Proceeds
Under 0.50	0	—	—	—	0	—	—	—	3	8.99
0.50–0.99	6	6.96	6.78	13.74	2	3.43	4.80	8.24	2	4.59
1.00–1.99	18	10.40	4.89	15.29	5	6.36	4.15	10.51	5	4.90
2.00–4.99	61	6.59	2.87	9.47	9	5.20	2.85	8.06	7	2.85
5.00–9.99	66	5.50	1.53	7.03	4	3.92	2.18	6.10	6	1.39
10.00–19.99	91	4.84	0.71	5.55	10	4.14	1.21	5.35	3	0.72
20.00–49.99	156	4.30	0.37	4.67	12	3.84	0.90	4.74	1	0.52
50.00–99.99	70	3.97	0.21	4.18	9	3.96	0.74	4.70	2	0.21
100.00–500.00	16	3.81	0.14	3.95	5	3.50	0.50	4.00	9	0.13
Total/Average	484	5.02	1.15	6.17	56	4.32	1.73	6.05	38	2.45

a. Issues are included only if the company's stock was listed on the NYSE, AMEX, or regional exchanges prior to the offering; any associated secondary distribution represents less than 10 percent of the total proceeds of the issue, and the offering contains no other types of securities.

Source: From Clifford W. Smith, Jr., "Substitute Methods for Raising Additional Capital: Rights Offerings versus Underwritten Issues," *Journal of Financial Economics,* December 1977, Vol. 5, No. 3. By permission of North-Holland Publishing Company, Amsterdam.

The explanations for these relationships are found in the amount of risk involved and in the job of physical distribution. Bonds are generally bought in large blocks by relatively few institutional investors, whereas stocks are bought by millions of individuals. For this reason the distribution job for common stock is harder and the expenses of marketing it are greater. Similarly, stocks are more volatile than bonds, so underwriting risks are larger for stock than for bond flotations.

Reasons for the variation in cost with the size of issue are also easily found. First, certain fixed expenses are associated with any distribution of securities: the underwriting investigation, the preparation of the registration statement, legal fees, and so on. Since these expenses are relatively large and fixed, their percentage of the total cost of flotation runs high on small issues. Second, small issues are typically those of relatively less well-known firms, so underwriting expenses may be larger than usual because the danger of omitting vital information is greater. Furthermore, the selling job is more difficult; salespeople must exert greater effort to sell the securities of less well-known firms. For these reasons the underwriting commission, as a percentage of the gross proceeds, is relatively high for small issues.

Flotation costs are also influenced by whether or not the issue is a rights offering, and if it is, by the extent of the underpricing.[14] If rights are used, and if the underpricing is substantial, then the investment banker bears little risk of being unable to sell the shares. Further, very little selling effort is required in such a situation. These two factors enable a company to float new securities to its own stockholders at a relatively low cost. However, rights offerings without use of underwriters accounted for only 38 of the 578 issues sold (less than 7 percent) during the 1971–1975 period covered in Table 18.3.

Flotation Costs on Negotiated versus Multiple-Bidding Underwritings

The general practice is for a long-term relationship to develop between a business firm and its investment banker. The investment banking firm builds up a cumulative background of knowledge and understanding through its continuous counseling with the firm over a period of years. On a particular financing, the firm's historical investment banker already has considerable background knowledge. It takes much more time and expense for another investment banking firm to develop a comparable fund of knowledge. The business firm is therefore likely to look to its traditional investment banker on any new financing requirement. The terms and arrangements on any particular issue will be worked out in direct negotiations between the firm and its investment banker. These are called negotiated underwritings.

14. Rights offerings involve the sale of stock to existing stockholders. The topic is discussed extensively in Chapter 19.

However, for public utility firms, more than one investment banker is likely to be competing for the business of underwriting a particular issue. The SEC Rule U-50 makes competitive bidding mandatory on new issues of securities by public utility holding companies. Whether required by law or not, it is more likely that competitive bidding will be used by public utilities than by industrial firms. The characteristics of public utilities are more uniform, with fewer special circumstances than for industrial firms in a wide variety of business activities. Also, as regulated industries, the utilities have long been required to provide substantial amounts of information on a relatively uniform basis. Hence the kinds of information that the historical investment banker develops for an industrial firm over a longer period of time are more easily developed for utility firms. The question of the relative costs of negotiated versus "competitive" underwritings has been raised.

The terms *negotiated* and *competitive* are sometimes misleading. Negotiated underwritings are as fully competitive as underwritings with bidding by more than one investment banker. The performance of the historical investment banker must assure the firm that no other investment banker could do the job better. Hence the potential competition from others waiting in the wings for the opportunity of displacing the historical investment banker assures that competition is as effective on single bids as on multiple bidding. Thus the empirical studies are measuring not only the effects of multiple bidding on the costs of underwriting but also the characteristics of the firms and the nature of the general financial market conditions that are likely to result in negotiated versus multiple bidding underwritings in particular cases.

Several recent articles have studied the relative costs of negotiated versus multiple-bidding underwritings. In their studies, Gary Tallman, David Rush, and Ronald Melicher (TRM) concluded that "competitive offerings appeared to be less costly during stable market conditions, but that negotiated offerings might be more advantageous during unstable markets." Their empirical results indicated that underwriter compensation was a positive function of "default risk" and a negative function of "market preference for utility bonds" in the case of competitive issues only.[15] In their paper on utility debt, Edward Dyl and Michael Joehnk found that competitive offerings result in lower underwriting charges, attempting to hold all other factors constant. But they also found a significant fixed cost element in the flotation charges for competitive issues.[16] With different data sets, Ederington reached conclusions similar to TRM: Competitive offerings might be more desirable during stable markets and negotiated offerings superior during troubled markets. Ederington found that the negotiated offering variable was significant in explaining yield

15. Gary Tallman, David Rush, and Ronald Melicher, "Competitive versus Negotiated Underwriting Costs for Regulated Industries," *Financial Management* 3 (Summer 1974), pp. 49–55.

16. Edward Dyl and Michael Joehnk, "Competitive versus Negotiated Underwriting of Public Utility Debt," *Bell Journal of Economics* 7 (Autumn 1976), pp. 680–689.

spreads and implied a yield eight basis points higher than a similar competitive issue. He came to the conclusion that some relaxation of SEC Rule U-50, at least during periods of great market uncertainty, might be appropriate.[17]

A more recent study was made by M. Chapman Findlay III, Keith B. Johnson, and T. Gregory Morton (FJM) in 1979.[18] The independent variables used in their study were: (1) issuer size, (2) type of utility, (3) seasoning, (4) maturity, (5) sinking fund, (6) type of offering, (7) issue size, (8) stock market ebullience, (9) bond market interest rate, (10) volume conditions, (11) AT&T ownership, and (12) S&P's rating class. The dependent variable employed is the ratio of total direct issuance cost (underwriter fees plus other direct expenses) to gross total dollar amount raised in the issue. Regressions were run on the total sample of 628 issues and on the subsamples of 135 communications and 493 electric, gas, and water issues.

The most significant variable was found to be the presence of a low (Bbb) bond rating. This should probably be considered in conjunction with the significance of the high (Aaa) rating variables as well. Together, these results would seem to be a proxy for selling effort and/or risk effect. The implication is that even after taking account of the yield differential, Aaa utility bonds were viewed as fast or easy sales, and Bbb bonds were seen as slow or hard sales. These results are consistent with earlier studies, which found default risk premium to be the most important explanatory variable.

The next variable to enter the regression was issuer size. This variable undoubtedly acts as a proxy for any economies of scale in the underwriting process. Besides that, issuer size may also proxy a repeat business effect from the underwriter's perspective. Finally, the level of interest rates, as depicted by the Aaa utility bond average, had a significantly positive influence on flotation costs.

The FJM study demonstrates that the traditional competitive-negotiated issue question is far more complex than it would appear. At least four reasons why high interest rates might lead to high flotation costs were discussed—higher inventory carrying costs, reduction in underwriter competition, higher interest rate risk, and negotiated offerings. Only the last is related to the mode of issue, and it had perhaps the least convincing economic rationale. Where the firm and its situation are standard, this facilitates a competitive bidding process. Where the situation is more complex, a negotiated transaction is more likely. As the previous studies indicate, even where competitive bids have been used, a shift may be made to a negotiated transaction when the markets themselves become unsettled. Apparently it is for this reason that the FJM study concludes that "the data and methodology employed in

17. Louis Ederington, "Negotiated versus Competitive Underwritings of Corporate Bonds," *Journal of Finance* 31 (March 1976), pp. 17–28.

18. M. Chapman Findlay III, Keith B. Johnson, and T. Gregory Morton, "An Analysis of the Flotation Cost of Utility Bonds, 1971–76," *Journal of Financial Research* 2 (Fall 1979), pp. 133–142.

all studies to date are simply too crude to determine whether an inefficiency exists with respect to mode of banker compensation which can be exploited by a purchaser of intermediation services."[19]

Regulation of Security Trading

The operations of investment bankers, exchanges, and over-the-counter markets described in the previous sections of this chapter are significantly influenced by a series of federal statutes enacted during and after 1933. The financial manager is affected by these laws for several reasons:

1. Corporate officers are subject to personal liabilities.
2. The laws affect the ease and costs of financing and the behavior of the money and capital markets in which the corporation's securities are sold and traded.
3. Investors' willingness to buy securities is influenced by the existence of safeguards provided by these laws.

Securities Act of 1933

The first of the securities acts, the Securities Act of 1933, followed congressional investigations of the stock market collapse of 1929–1932. Motivating the act were (1) the large losses to investors, (2) the failures of many corporations on which little information had been provided, and (3) the misrepresentations that had been made to investors.

The basic objective of the Securities Act of 1933 is to provide for both *full disclosure* of relevant information and a *record of representations.* The act seeks to achieve these objectives by the following means:

1. It applies to all interstate offerings to the public in amounts of $1,500,000 or more. (Some exemptions are government bonds and bank stocks.)
2. Securities must be registered at least twenty days before they are publicly offered. The registration statement provides financial, legal, and technical information about the company. A prospectus summarizes this information for use in selling the securities. If information is inadequate or misleading, the SEC will delay or stop the public offering. (Obtaining the information required to review the registration statement may result in a waiting period that exceeds twenty days.)
3. After the registration has become effective, the securities can be offered if accompanied by the prospectus. Preliminary, or "red herring," prospectuses can be distributed to potential buyers during the waiting period.
4. If the registration statement or prospectus contains misrepresentations or omissions of material facts, any purchaser who suffers a loss can sue for damages. Liabilities and severe penalties can be imposed on the issuer and

19. Ibid., p. 142.

its officers, directors, accountants, engineers, appraisers, and underwriters and on all others who participated in preparing the registration statement.

Securities Exchange Act of 1934

The Securities Exchange Act of 1934 extends the disclosure principle applied to new issues by the Securities Act of 1933 to trading in already issued securities (the secondhand securities market). It seeks to accomplish this by the following measures:

1. It establishes the Securities and Exchange Commission. (The Federal Trade Commission had been administering the Securities Act of 1933.)
2. It provides for registration and regulation of national securities exchanges. Companies whose securities are listed on an exchange must file reports similar to registration statements with both the SEC and the stock exchange and must provide periodic reports as well.
3. It establishes control over corporate "insiders." Officers, directors, and major stockholders of a corporation must file monthly reports of changes in holdings of the corporation's stock. Any short-term profits from such transactions are payable to the corporation.
4. It gives the SEC the power to prohibit manipulation by such devices as pools (aggregations of funds used to affect prices artificially), wash sales (sales among members of the same group to record artificial transaction prices), and pegging the market other than during stock flotations.
5. It gives the SEC control over the proxy machinery and practices.
6. It establishes control over the flow of credit into security transactions by giving the board of governors of the Federal Reserve System the power to control margin requirements.

Appraisal of Regulation of Security Trading

Why should security transactions be regulated? It can be argued that a great body of relevant knowledge is necessary to make an informed judgment of the value of a security. Moreover, security values are subject to many gyrations that influence stability and business conditions generally. Hence, social well-being requires that orderly markets be promoted. There are three primary objectives of regulation:

1. To protect investors from fraud and to provide them with a basis for informed judgments.
2. To control the volume of bank credit to finance security speculation.
3. To provide orderly markets in securities.

Progress has been made on all three counts. There has been some cost in the increased time and expense involved in new flotations by companies, although the benefits seem worth their costs. The regulations are powerless to prevent investors from investing in unsound ventures or to prevent stock prices from skyrocketing during booms and plummeting during periods of pessimism. Still, requirements for increased information have been of value in preventing fraud and gross misrepresentations.

From the standpoint of the financial manager, regulation has a twofold significance. It affects both the costs of issuing securities and the riskiness of securities—and hence the rate of return investors require when they purchase stocks and bonds. As previous chapters have shown, these two factors have an important bearing on the firm's cost of capital and, through the capital budgeting process, on its investment decisions. Further, since business investment is a key determinant of employment and production in the economy, efficient capital markets have an important impact on all of society.

Costs of Different Kinds of Financing over Time

As mentioned earlier, interest rates vary widely over time. In addition, the relative costs of debt, preferred stock, and equity fluctuate. Data on these relative costs are presented in Figure 18.2, which shows that earnings/price ratios have fluctuated from 16 percent to 7 percent.[20] During the 1960s, E/P ratios averaged about 6 percent, ranging from 4.7 to 6.7 percent. However, in the 1970s, the rising costs of capital associated with inflation drove stock prices down and E/P ratios up to over 11 percent in 1974 and 1978. Yields on bonds have fluctuated to a much lesser extent. Furthermore, since bonds and preferred stocks both provide a stable, fixed income to investors, they are close substitutes for each other and their yields closely parallel each other.[21]

Interest Rate Forecasts

Within the framework of general economic and financial patterns, short-term interest rate patterns and forecasts can be analyzed through the use of flow of funds accounts. These accounts, summarized in Table 18.4, depict the behavior of the major kinds of suppliers and demanders of funds. By projecting the

20. An earnings/price ratio, the reciprocal of a P-E ratio, does not measure exactly the cost of equity capital, but it does indicate *trends* in this cost. In other words, when earnings/price ratios are high, the cost of equity capital tends to be high, and vice versa.

21. Preferred stock yields are not shown in Figure 18.2 because they have been very close to Aaa corporate bond yields (lower by five to fifty basis points during the period covered by the figure). Historically, bond yields have tended to be lower than preferred stock yields, because bonds have priority over preferred stocks and, hence, are less risky. However, preferred stock dividends are largely tax-exempt to corporate owners, so after-tax yields (to corporations) are considerably higher than those on bonds. Of the dividends received by a corporate stockholder, 85 percent are tax-exempt to the receiver, whereas interest income is fully taxable. During the 1960s, certain corporations (insurance companies, savings and loans, mutual savings banks) that had previously paid very low taxes became subject to higher taxes. These firms bought preferred stocks, thereby pushing preferred stock before-tax yields below those of bonds in the late 1960s and early 1970s.

Figure 18.2

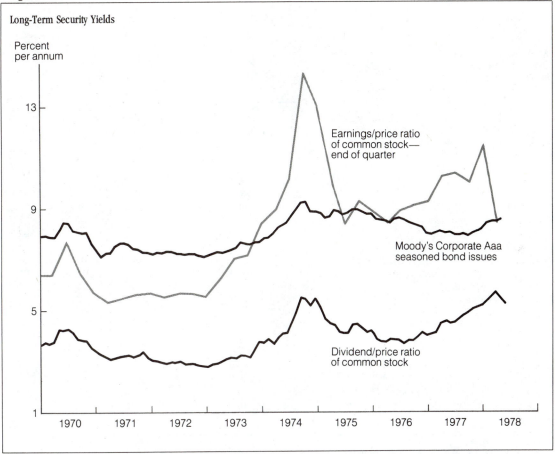

Long-Term Security Yields

Source: Board of Governors of the Federal Reserve System, *Federal Reserve Monthly Chart Book,* June 1978, p. 69.

sources and uses of funds in different categories, the direction of the pressure on interest rates can be estimated.[22]

Table 18.4 can be used in the following way. Historical patterns can be established to show uses and sources of funds in relation to the growth of the economy as a whole (as measured by GNP). In any particular year, if the demand for funds grows faster than the supply in relation to historical patterns, interest rates are likely to rise. The extra funds are supplied by the commercial banking system—the pivot in the financial mechanism. Whenever the demand for funds must be met by drawing on the commercial banking system to a greater than normal degree, interest rates rise.

22. Compilations of studies of this kind are facilitated by the flow of funds data developed by the Federal Reserve System and published monthly in the *Federal Reserve Bulletin.*

Table 18.4

Summary of Supply and Demand in U.S. Credit Markets (Annual Net Increases in Amounts Outstanding—Billions of Dollars)

	Annual Net Increases in Amounts Outstanding						
	1974	1975	1976	1977	1978	1979[a]	1980[a]
Net Demand							
Privately held mortgages	42.2	42.0	70.4	109.0	116.5	118.5	100.7
Corporate and foreign bonds	29.1	39.1	39.1	37.4	33.5	32.8	42.7
Short-term business borrowing	50.4	−16.0	9.8	47.0	78.5	112.9	81.5
Short-term other borrowing	16.3	14.4	40.7	49.6	66.0	62.3	43.9
Privately held federal debt	28.4	82.6	71.8	73.3	83.8	66.9	96.5
Tax-exempt notes and bonds	14.5	16.3	17.1	31.1	32.9	22.0	27.0
Total net demand for credit	180.9	178.4	248.9	347.4	411.2	415.4	392.3
Net Supply[b]							
Thrift institutions	25.8	53.7	70.0	81.8	80.2	66.7	58.8
Insurance, pensions, endowments	29.0	40.9	53.1	67.3	70.2	75.1	81.4
Investment companies	1.7	3.7	4.6	6.7	8.3	23.2	20.7
Other nonbank finance	3.9	−4.3	8.7	17.6	15.9	25.6	19.5
Subtotal nonbank finance	60.4	94.0	136.4	173.4	174.6	190.6	180.4
Commercial banks[c]	52.6	29.9	59.6	83.5	107.0	124.3	100.0
Business corporations	8.8	11.6	7.7	4.9	4.5	10.3	12.2
State and local government	1.1	2.4	4.9	11.3	14.7	5.2	3.0
Foreign[d]	18.5	7.1	19.6	44.1	57.4	21.7	34.6
Subtotal	141.4	145.0	228.2	317.2	358.2	352.1	330.2
Residual (mostly household direct)	39.5	33.4	20.7	30.2	53.0	63.3	62.1
Total net supply of credit	180.9	178.4	248.9	347.4	411.2	415.4	392.3

a. Preliminary figures.
b. Excludes funds for equities, cash, and miscellaneous demands not tabulated above.
c. Includes loans transferred to books of nonoperating holding and other bank-related companies.
d. Includes U.S. branches of foreign banks.
Source: Henry Kaufman, James McKeon, and David Foster, *1980 Prospects for Financial Markets* (New York: Salomon Brothers, 1979), Table 1. Reprinted by permission.

Another significant statistic in the table is the rise in the supply of funds from "Residual (mostly households direct)"; funds from this source increased in 1974. Because of restrictive Federal Reserve policies, the ability of the commercial banks and other financial institutions to supply funds was held back in relation to demand. This produced high interest rates, which induced individuals, businesses, and others to make their surplus funds available to borrowers. The supply of funds was thereby augmented from nonbanking sources but only at substantially higher interest rates. By this test, a firming of interest rates during 1978 and 1979 was also indicated.

Most longer term predictions for the financial market call for continued high interest rates with only moderate declines of short duration from time to time. The causes are diverse, but a major factor is the efforts of governments throughout the world to achieve full employment and high growth rates. A worldwide capital shortage has resulted.

Interest Rates as an Index of Availability of Funds

The data on fluctuations in short- and long-term interest rates demonstrate that the cost of capital is one of the most volatile inputs purchased by firms. While the cost variations associated with interest rate fluctuations are substantial, the greatest significance of interest rates is their role as an index of the availability of funds. A period of high interest rates reflects tight money, which in turn is associated with tight reserve positions at commercial banks. At such times interest rates rise. However, since there are conventional limits on interest rates, a larger quantity of funds is demanded by borrowers than banks are able to make available. Banks therefore begin to ration funds among prospective borrowers by continuing lines of credit to traditional customers and restricting loans to new borrowers.

Small firms characteristically have greater difficulty than large ones in obtaining financing during periods of tight money; and even among large borrowers, the bargaining position of the financial institutions is stronger. It is a lender's rather than a borrower's market. Consequently, the cost is higher and the conditions in all loan agreements are more restrictive when the demand for funds is high. For small- and medium-sized firms, a period of rising interest rates may mean difficulty in obtaining any financing at all.

Periods of tight money have a particularly strong impact on utilities and other heavy industries, state and local governments, and the housing and construction sectors. (The heavy long-term investments in these areas cause the impact of interest rates on profitability to be especially significant.) During the credit crunch of 1974, funds became virtually unavailable to these sectors. Utility companies were forced to reduce planned expansions, state and local financing became difficult, and housing and construction declined substantially. The tightness of monetary conditions in the late autumn of 1977 again affected these sectors.

Efficient Capital Markets

One of the central issues in connection with the timing and selection of alternative forms and sources of financing is whether financial managers can "beat the market" if the capital markets are efficient in some sense. There is considerable disagreement in both theory and practice with regard to the questions raised. First let us consider what is involved in the nature of efficient markets.[23]

23. A more complete treatment of efficient capital markets is presented in T. E. Copeland and J. F. Weston, *Financial Theory and Corporate Policy* (Reading, Mass.: Addison-Wesley, 1979), pp. 196–248.

Forms of Capital Market Efficiency

Capital market efficiency has been defined in three forms.[24] These are described as (1) weak-form efficiency, (2) semistrong-form efficiency, and (3) strong-form efficiency.

The weak form of capital market efficiency holds that excess or abnormal returns cannot be earned on the basis of historical price or returns information. This argues that the historical pattern of prices or returns on stocks will not provide a basis for superior forecasting of future prices or returns.

The predictions of the weak form of financial market efficiency are in direct contradiction to the activity of chartists or technical analysts. Chartists argue that by observing the pattern of price or returns behavior that some trading rules can be developed for achieving superior performance.

However, a number of academic studies have been made of historical patterns of prices or returns. These studies have indicated that stock price changes over time were essentially independent of one another.[25] Such findings of independence are consistent with weak-form efficiency, which argues that one cannot use past price or returns information to make superior predictions of future price or return patterns.

Semistrong-form efficient markets mean that investors cannot earn abnormal returns from trading rules based on publicly available information. Examples of public information include annual reports of companies, investment advisory data, ticker tape information, and articles and stories in newspapers and the financial press. Semistrong efficiency argues that existing prices reflect all public information, good or bad. All the information currently known to the market is already impounded in current market prices. Except for the predictable upward drift which constitutes part of the normal return on a security, prices change only when new information arrives.

Just as weak-form efficiency is associated with the activity of technical analysts, the implications of semistrong efficiency relate to the work of security analysts. Fundamental security analysis implies that the processing of public information will provide a basis for achieving superior performance. The semistrong efficiency theory, however, holds that the activity of fundamental analysis guarantees that security prices will in fact reflect processing of public information. This view argues that fundamental analysts will have returns commensurate with the ability with which they evaluate publicly available data. A highly able analyst will earn high returns; those of lesser ability will earn lower returns, as in most other fields of executive and managerial activity. The individual investor, unless trained to the same level as the professional

24. Eugene F. Fama, "The Behavior of Stock Prices," *Journal of Business* 38 (January 1965), pp. 34–105, "Efficient Capital Markets: A Review of Theory and Empirical Work," *Journal of Finance* 25 (May 1970), pp. 383–417; and *Foundations of Finance* (New York: Basic Books, 1976).

25. S. S. Alexander, "Price Movements in Speculative Markets: Trends or Random Walks," *Industrial Management Review* 2 (May 1961), pp. 7–26; B. Mandelbrot, "The Variation of Certain Speculative Prices," reprinted in *The Random Character of Stock Market Prices,* edited by Paul H. Cootner (Cambridge, Mass.: MIT Press, 1964), pp. 307–332; and Eugene F. Fama and Marshall S. Blume, "Filter Rules and Stock Market Trading Profits," *Journal of Finance* 25 (May 1970), pp. 226–241.

analyst and able to commit as much time and study as the professional analyst, is not likely to do as well. There is considerable evidence to support the predictions of semistrong-form market efficiency theories.[26]

Strong-form market efficiency holds that excess returns cannot be earned using any information source, regardless of whether or not it is publicly available. This implies that even corporate insiders will not, on average, be able to benefit from the information they receive ahead of the general public. The theory is that competition among those with inside information will very quickly result in equilibrium prices. The movements of the equilibrium prices will not provide opportunities for abnormal returns.

The empirical studies on the strong-form of market efficiency have found that exceptional returns have been earned.[27] They suggest that specialists on the major stock exchanges and officers and directors of firms may be accorded privileged information that can be used as a basis for earning above-average returns.

On balance, then, the evidence appears to be consistent with the achievement of both weak-form and semistrong-form market efficiency. However, empirical studies suggest that strong-form market efficiency is not achieved in practice.

Implications of Efficient Capital Markets

The evidence on the efficiency of financial markets has implications for investors, financial managers, and regulators. From the standpoint of investors, the evidence suggests that the appropriate strategy is deciding what risk level is preferred. A choice is made to invest in government bonds, savings accounts, common stocks, commodities, and so on. Market efficiency suggests that after a selection of the target level of risk, a well-diversified portfolio of investments will do as well as any other selection strategy.

From the standpoint of financial managers, efficient markets also have important implications. They mean, for example, that when investing in marketable securities, financial managers cannot expect to do better than the average. Prices largely reflect publicly available information, and the returns achieved should be consistent with the risks taken.

Particularly relevant for the kinds of financial policies with which we will be dealing in the remainder of the book are questions related to choosing be-

26. Eugene F. Fama, Lawrence Fisher, Maurice Jensen, and Richard Roll, "The Adjustment of Stock Prices to New Information," *International Economic Review* 10 (Feburary 1969), pp. 1–21; Maurice Jensen, "The Performance of Mutual Funds in the Period 1954–64," *Journal of Finance* 23 (May 1968), pp. 389–416; R. S. Kaplan and Richard Roll, "Investor Evaluation of Accounting Information; Some Empirical Evidence," *Journal of Business* 45 (April 1972), pp. 225–257; and Myron S. Scholes, "Market for Securities: Substitution versus Price Pressure and the Effects of Information on Share Prices," *Journal of Business* 45 (April 1972), pp. 179–211.

27. J. E. Finnerty, "Insiders and Market Efficiency," *Journal of Finance* 31 (September 1976), pp. 1141–1148; R. G. Ibbotson, "Price Performance of Common Stock New Issues," *Journal of Financial Economics* 2 (September 1975), pp. 235–272; and J. F. Jaffe, "The Effect of Regulation Changes on Insider Trading," *Bell Journal of Economics and Management Science* 5 (Spring 1974), pp. 93–121.

tween debt and equity financing and the timing of such financing. To gain from timing decisions requires the ability to make accurate predictions of the future. But the theory of efficient markets predicts that superior forecasting is not likely to be achieved. If prices and returns reflect all public information in an unbiased manner, current prices and returns represent a consensus about the future by the market as a whole. Of course, such consensus forecasts can be wrong, but since the error is as likely to be above as below the actual behavior of the market in the future, efforts to outjudge the market are as likely to be wrong as they are to be right.

Hence, those who support the efficient markets view argue that it is a waste of time for financial managers to try to outguess the market on interest rate trends and the relative cost of debt and equity funds. They recommend that financial managers focus on improving the operating efficiency and performance of their individual companies and forget about forecasting security prices.

Efficient markets also have important implications for regulators. Opportunities for taking advantage of privileged information are relatively limited and short-lived. The greater proportion of gains and losses occurs because of changes in the economic and financial outlook that were not generally anticipated. On a relative basis, the gains and losses from manipulative behavior are small and are exceptions to the general pattern of operations of the financial markets.

Financial Planning in Efficient Markets

There are many misconceptions about what the notion of efficient markets implies. Some confuse it with the idea of perfect markets, which implies no frictions, complete costless knowledge, and atomistic buyers and sellers with no influence on prices. Others are agnostics with respect to efficient markets on other grounds. While they concede that the markets do reflect and impound all currently available information, they argue that the information which the market incorporates changes over time. There are both long-run and cyclical developments taking place in the economy. In early 1980, for example, some argued that it was clearly impossible for the Federal Reserve authorities to continue the tight money policies which resulted in short-term interest rates rising above 20 percent by March 1980. They claimed that overall monetary-fiscal policy was subject to alternative degrees of tightness and ease and that it was likely that there would be a reversal of interest rate levels sometime during 1980. This did in fact occur. However, it occurred very rapidly and on an order of magnitude that had not been predicted. While general predictions about changes in interest rate levels and the state of the financial markets can be made, systematic evidence of timing forecasts and degree of change forecasts which would be necessary to earn abnormal returns is lacking.

Those who believe in efficient markets say that management should not try to outguess the market on interest rate trends. They hold that financial managers should focus on their own company's performance and let the market take care of itself. In addition, they recommend that business firms finance as needed.

Our position is pragmatic—that the financial markets are efficient in both the weak and the semistrong forms. As a practical matter, then, within the framework that the firms are not likely to beat the market on day-to-day movements, financial managers participate in the development of long-range investment and financing programs related to the long-range strategic planning of firms. Within these long-range plans, financial managers can make forecasts for investment programs and financial needs. Financing will be timed and related to the forms and sources that seem advantageous from a long-range planning perspective.

The literature on efficient markets, however, emphasizes that financial managers who feel that their judgment of security prices and returns is superior to that exhibited by the markets should have their decisions rooted in economic and financial analysis. The efficient markets literature admonishes that the likelihood of better than a 50-50 success rate in outguessing the market is difficult to achieve. This suggests further that financial managers keep careful records of what they do in trying to beat the market. It is important that their performance not be evaluated on a subjective basis. Instead it should be recorded carefully and objectively, if possible, to determine the results of efforts to "beat the market." It is important that managers' conclusions and evaluations be based on fact, not fantasy.

Summary

Longer term obligations are sold directly to investors or through the investment banking distribution systems. Two major forms of direct financing are term lending by commercial banks and the private placement of securities with insurance companies and pension funds. Term loans and private placements represent similar financing arrangements. Their advantages are avoidance of SEC registration procedures, flexibility in renegotiation of terms, and the assurance of availability of financing provided by long-term arrangements as compared with short-term bank borrowing.

Ordinarily, direct loans are retired by systematic repayments (amortization payments) over the life of the loan. Security, generally in the form of a chattel mortgage on equipment, is often employed, although the larger, stronger companies are usually able to borrow on an unsecured basis. Commercial banks typically make small short-term loans; life insurance companies and pension funds grant larger, longer-term loans.

Like rates on other credits, the cost of direct loans varies with the size of the loan and the strength of the borrower. For small loans to small companies, rates may be as high as 20 percent; for large loans to large firms, they will probably be close to the prime lending rate. Since these loans run for long periods, during which interest rates can change radically, many of them have variable interest rates, with the rate set at a certain level above the prime rate or above the Federal Reserve rediscount rate. Often, direct loans include a "kicker" in the form of warrants to purchase the borrower's equity securities near the price prevailing at the time of the loan transaction.

Another aspect of direct loans is the series of *protective covenants* contained in most loan agreements. The lender's funds are tied up for a long period, and during this time the borrower's situation can change markedly. For self-protection, the lender includes in the loan agreement stipulations that the borrower will maintain the current ratio at a specified level, limit acquisitions of additional fixed assets, keep the debt ratio below a stated amount, and so on. These provisions are necessary from the lender's point of view, but they restrict the borrower's actions.

The investment banker provides middleman services to both the seller and the buyer of new securities, helping plan the issue, underwriting it, and handling the job of selling the issue to the ultimate investor. The cost of this service to the issuer is related to the magnitude of the total job that must be performed to place the issue. The investment banker must also look to the interests of the brokerage customers; if these investors are not satisfied with the banker's products, they will deal elsewhere.

Flotation costs are lowest for bonds, higher for preferred stock, and highest for common stock. Larger companies have lower flotation costs than smaller ones for each type of security, and most companies can cut their stock flotation costs by issuing the new securities to stockholders through rights offerings. (These offerings are discussed in Chapter 19.)

The financial manager should be familiar with the federal laws regulating the issuance and trading of securities, because they influence liabilities and affect financing methods and costs. Regulation of securities trading seeks (1) to provide information that investors can utilize as a basis for judging the merits of securities, (2) to control the volume of credit used in securities trading, and (3) to provide orderly securities markets. The laws do not, however, prevent either purchase of unsound issues or wide price fluctuations. They raise the costs of flotation somewhat, but they also probably decrease the cost of capital by increasing public confidence in the securities markets.

Changes in the relative costs and availability of different forms and sources of financing raise questions as to the timing of decisions. The efficient markets theories are summarized to consider their implications for efforts by financial managers to "beat the market." Since the prices and returns prevailing at any point in the financial markets reflect all available historical and current public information, it is difficult for financial managers to achieve superior performance by judging that security market conditions may be better or worse in the future. However, government policies, which appear to overshoot at times and which do change, have great impact on the state of the financial markets. In addition, repetitive fluctuations are observed in financial market prices and returns. These patterns tempt financial managers to judge that some periods are more favorable for financing of particular types than others.

Questions

18.1 List several possible advantages to a firm that lists its stock on a major stock exchange.

18.2 Would you expect the cost of capital of a firm to be affected if it changed its status from one traded over the counter to one traded on the New York Stock Exchange? Explain.

18.3 Evaluate the following statement: Buying stocks is in the nature of true investment; stock is purchased in order to receive a dividend return on the invested capital. Short selling, on the other hand, is fundamentally a form of gambling; it is simply betting that a stock's price will decline. Consequently, if we do not wish to see Wall Street turned into an eastern Las Vegas, all short selling should be forbidden.

18.4 Evaluate the following statement: The fundamental purpose of the federal security laws dealing with new issues is to prevent investors, principally small ones, from sustaining losses on the purchase of stocks.

18.5 Suppose two similar firms are each selling $10 million of common stock. The firms are of the same size, are in the same industry, have the same leverage, and so on—except that one is publicly owned and the other is closely held.

a. Will their costs of flotation be the same?

b. If the issue were $10 million of bonds, would your answer be the same?

18.6 Define these terms: *brokerage firm, underwriting group, selling group,* and *investment banker.*

18.7 Each month the Securities and Exchange Commission publishes a report of the transactions made by the officers and directors of listed firms in their own companies' equity securities. Why do you suppose the SEC makes this report?

18.8 The SEC forbids officers and directors to sell short the shares of their own companies. Why do you suppose this rule is on the books?

18.9 Prior to 1933, investment banking and commercial banking were both carried on by the same firm. In that year, however, the Banking Act required that these functions be separated. On the basis of your knowledge of investment banking and commercial banking, discuss the pros and cons of this forced separation.

18.10 Before entering a formal agreement, investment bankers carefully investigate the companies whose securities they underwrite; this is especially true of the issues of firms going public for the first time.

a. Since the bankers do not themselves plan to hold the securities but intend to sell them to others as soon as possible, why are they so concerned about making careful investigations?

b. Does your answer to the question have any bearing on the fact that investment banking is a very difficult field to break into? Explain.

18.11 a. If competitive bidding were required on all security offerings, would flotation costs be higher or lower?

b. Would the size of the issuing firm be material in determining the effects of required competitive bidding?

18.12 Since investment bankers price new issues in relation to outstanding issues, should a spread exist between the yields on the new and the outstanding issues? Discuss this matter separately for stocks and bonds.

18.13 What issues are raised by the increasing purchase of equities by institutional investors?

18.14 Discuss the following statement: It makes good sense for a firm to fund its floating debt, because this relieves the possibility that it will be called upon to pay off debt at an awkward time. From the standpoint of cost, however, it is always cheaper to use short-term debt than long-term debt.

18.15 Historical data indicate that more than twice as much capital is raised yearly by selling bonds than by selling common stocks. Does this indicate that corporate capital structures are becoming overburdened with debt?

18.16 Is the Federal Reserve's tight money policy restraining the country's economic growth? Discuss the pros and cons from the corporation's viewpoint.

18.17 Why do interest rates on different types of securities vary widely?

18.18 What does GNP represent? Why are its levels and growth significant to the financial manager?

18.19 When are short-term interest rates higher than long-term rates? What is indicated if short-term rates are high in relation to long-term rates for a prolonged period of time (such as twenty years) in a given country?

18.20 During a period of ten years, the price level in a particular country doubled. But during the following ten years, the price level was relatively stable. Discuss the effects on interest rates during the two ten-year periods.

Problems

18.1 Your firm is planning to sell $1.5 million of bonds with a fifteen-year maturity. The going rate on debt of this quality and maturity is 10 percent. However, total costs of the underwriting have been estimated to be 10.5 percent of gross proceeds. Calculate the cost of this debt to your firm. (Hint: Let the coupon rate be 10 percent so that the bonds will sell at face value; then solve for the IRR, which will make the future payments on the bond equal to face value less 10.5 percent—that is, to $895 per bond.)

18.2 If your firm sells preferred stock in the amount of $1.5 million, the total flotation expense will be about 11.5 percent of gross proceeds. If the going rate on preferred stock of the same quality as your firm's is 12 percent, what is the effective cost of the preferred stock issue? (Assume the stock will remain outstanding in perpetuity.)

18.3 The Algonquin Table Company was planning to issue $5 million of new common stock. In reaching the decision as to the form of offering, the firm considered two alternatives:

—A rights offering, with out-of-pocket cost as a percentage of new capital at 1.4 percent.

—An underwriting, with out-of-pocket cost as a percentage of new capital at 7.0 percent.

Algonquin chose the second alternative. Given the difference in cost, this choice seems paradoxical.

a. From Table 18.3, what proportion of issues this size are made by rights offerings instead of by underwriters?

b. Discuss the influence of other factors (in addition to direct costs cited) that must be taken into account in choosing between the two alternative methods of offering. In your answer consider the following, as well as other factors that may occur to you:

   1. Timing of receipt of flows.
   2. Risk.
   3. Other internal benefits and costs.

4. Distribution.
5. Effect on stock price.

18.4 Each of three companies is considering a new offering:

—The Crown Company is in the paint manufacturing industry and has total assets of $30 million. It contemplates a new common stock issue of $1.5 million. It has determined that use of an underwriter will be desirable.

—The Apache Company is in the small aircraft industry and has assets of $1 billion. It intends a $40 million offering using rights with a standby underwriting.

—AT&T plans a $500 million common stock offering using rights and direct sale without use of an investment banker.

What will be the compensation costs as a percent of proceeds for each of the three companies? Explain the reasons for the differences in costs.

18.5 In March 1975, three executives of the Hughes Aircraft Company, one of the largest privately owned corporations in the world, decided to break away from Hughes and to set up a company of their own. The principal reason for this decision was capital gains; Hughes Aircraft stock was all privately owned, and the corporate structure made it impossible for executives to be granted stock purchase options. Hughes's executives received substantial salaries and bonuses, but that income was all taxable at normal tax rates, and no capital gains opportunities were available.

The three men, Jim Adcock, Robert Goddard, and Rick Aiken, located a medium-size electronics manufacturing company available for purchase. All the stock of this firm, Baynard Industries, was owned by the founder, Joseph Baynard. Although the company was in excellent shape, Baynard wanted to sell it because of his failing health. A price of $5.7 million had been established, based on a price-earnings ratio of 12 and annual earnings of $475,000. Baynard gave the three prospective purchasers an option to purchase the company for the agreed price; the option was to run for six months, during which time the three men were to arrange financing with which to buy the firm.

Adcock consulted with Jules Scott, a partner in the New York investment banking firm of Williams Brothers and an acquaintance of some years' standing, to seek his assistance in obtaining the funds necessary to complete the purchase. Adcock, Goddard, and Aiken each had some money available to put into the new enterprise, but they needed a substantial amount of outside capital. There was some possibility of borrowing part of the money, but Scott discouraged this idea. His reasoning was, first, that Baynard Industries was already highly leveraged, and if the purchasers were to borrow additional funds, there would be a very severe risk that they would be unable to service this debt in the event of a recession in the electronics industry. Although the firm was currently earning $475,000 a year, this figure could quickly turn into a loss in the event of a few canceled defense contracts or cost miscalculations.

Scott's second reason for discouraging a loan was that Adcock, Goddard, and Aiken planned not only to operate Baynard Industries and seek internal growth but also to use the corporation as a vehicle for making further acquisitions of electronics companies. This being the case, Scott believed that it would be wise for the company to keep any borrowing potential in reserve for use in later acquisitions. Scott proposed that the three partners obtain funds to purchase Baynard Industries in accordance with the figures shown in the following table.

Baynard Industries

Price paid to Joseph Baynard (12 × $475,000 earnings)			$5,700,000
Authorized shares		5,000,000	
Initially issued shares		1,125,000	
Initial distribution of shares:			
Adcock	100,000 shares at $1.00		$ 100,000
Goddard	100,000 shares at $1.00		100,000
Aiken	100,000 shares at $1.00		100,000
Williams Brothers	125,000 shares at $7.00		875,000
Public stockholders	700,000 shares at $7.00		4,900,000
	1,125,000		$6,075,000
Underwriting costs: 5% of $4,900,000		$ 245,000	
Legal fees, and so on, associated with issue		45,000	290,000
			$5,785,000
Payment to Joseph Baynard			5,700,000
Net funds to Baynard Industries			$ 85,000

Baynard Industries was to be reorganized with an authorized 5,000,000 shares, with 1,125,000 to be issued at the time the transfer took place and the other 3,875,000 to be held in reserve for possible issuance in connection with acquisitions. Adcock, Goddard, and Aiken were each to purchase 100,000 shares at a price of $1 a share, the par value. Williams Brothers was to purchase 125,000 shares at a price of $7. The remaining 700,000 shares were to be sold to the public at a price of $7 a share.

Williams Brothers' underwriting fee was proposed to be 5 percent of the shares sold to the public, or $245,000. Legal fees, accounting fees, and other charges associated with the issue were expected to amount to $45,000, for a total underwriting cost of $290,000. After deducting the underwriting charges and the payment to Baynard from the gross proceeds of the stock sale, the reorganized Baynard Industries would receive funds in the amount of $85,000, for use in internal expansion.

As a part of the initial agreement, Adcock, Goddard, and Aiken each were to be given options to purchase an additional 80,000 shares at a price of $7 a share for one year, while Williams Brothers would be given an option to purchase an additional 100,000 shares at $7 a share in one year.

a. What was the total underwriting charge, expressed as a percentage of the funds raised by the underwriter? Does this charge seem reasonable in the light of published statistics on the cost of floating new issues of common stock?
b. Suppose that the three men had estimated the following probabilities for the firm's stock price one year from purchase:

Price	Probability
$ 1	0.05
5	0.10
9	0.35
13	0.35
17	0.10
21	0.05

Assuming Williams Brothers exercises its options, calculate the following ratio (ignore time-discount effects):

$$\frac{\text{Gross profit to Williams Brothers}}{\text{Funds raised by underwriter}}.$$

Disregard Williams Brothers' profit on the 125,000 shares it bought outright at the initial offering. Comment on the ratio.

c. Would Adcock, Goddard, and Aiken be purchasing their stock at a "fair" price? Should the prospectus have disclosed the fact that they would buy their stock at $1 a share, whereas public stockholders would buy their stock at $7 a share?
d. Would it have been reasonable for Williams Brothers to purchase its initial 125,000 shares at a price of $1?
e. Do you see any problems of control for Adcock, Goddard, and Aiken?
f. Would the expectation of an exceptionally large need for investment funds next year be a relevant consideration in deciding on the amount of funds to be raised at the time being discussed?

Selected References

Andersen, Leonal C. "Is There a Capital Shortage: Theory and Recent Evidence." *Journal of Finance* 31 (May 1976), pp. 257–268.

Angermueller, Hans H., and Taylor, Michael A. "Commercial vs. Investment Bankers." *Harvard Business Review* 55 (September–October 1977), pp. 132–144.

Baumol, William J. *The Stock Market and Economic Efficiency.* New York: Fordham University Press, 1965.

Benston, George J., and Smith, Clifford W., Jr. "A Transactions Cost Approach to the Theory of Financial Intermediation." *Journal of Finance* 31 (May 1976), pp. 215–231.

Brown, J. Michael. "Post-Offering Experience of Companies Going Public." *Journal of Business* (January 1970), pp. 10–18.

Cohen, Kalman J.; Maier, Steven F.; Schwartz, Robert A.; and Whitcomb, David K. "Limit Orders, Market Structure, and the Returns Generation Process." *Journal of Finance* 33 (June 1978), pp. 723–736.

Copeland, Thomas E. "A Model of Asset Trading under the Assumption of Sequential Information Arrival." *Journal of Finance* 31 (September 1976), pp. 1149–1168.

Dann, Larry Y.; Mayers, David; and Raab, Robert J., Jr. "Trading Rules, Large Blocks and the Speed of Price Adjustment." *Journal of Financial Economics* 4 (January 1977), pp. 3–22.

Davey, Patrick J. "Private Placements: Practices and Prospects." *Conference Board Information Bulletin* (January 1979), pp. 1–14.

Dougall, Herbert E., and Gaumnitz, Jack E. *Capital Markets and Institutions.* 4th ed. Englewood Cliffs, N. J.: Prentice-Hall, 1980.

Draper, Dennis W., and Hoag, James W. "Financial Intermediation and the Theory of Agency." *Journal of Financial and Quantitative Analysis* 13 (November 1978), pp. 595–611.

Eiteman, David K. "The S.E.C. Special Study and the Exchange Markets." *Journal of Finance* 21 (May 1966), pp. 311–323.

Freund, William C. "The Dynamic Financial Markets." *Financial Executive* 33 (May 1965), pp. 11–26, 57–58.

Friend, Irwin, and Blume, Marshall. "Competitive Commissions on the New York Stock Exchange." *Journal of Finance* 28 (September 1973), pp. 795–819.

Friend, Irwin; Hoffman, G. W.; and Winn, W. J. *The Over-the-Counter Securities Market.* New York: McGraw-Hill, 1958.

Friend, Irwin; Longstreet, James R.; Mendelson, Morris; Miller, Ervin; and Hess, Arleigh R., Jr. *Investment Banking and the New Issue Market.* Cleveland: World Publishing, 1967.

Furst, Richard W. "Does Listing Increase the Market Price of Common Stocks?" *Journal of Business* 43 (April 1970), pp. 174–180.

Goldsmith, Raymond W. *The Flow of Capital Funds in the Postwar Economy.* New York: National Bureau of Economic Research, 1965.

Goulet, Waldemar M. "Price Changes, Managerial Actions and Insider Trading at the Time of Listing." *Financial Management* 3 (Spring 1974), pp. 30–36.

Hamilton, James L. "Marketplace Fragmentation, Competition, and the Efficiency of the Stock Exchange." *Journal of Finance* 34 (March 1979), pp. 171–187.

Hayes, Samuel L. III. "The Transformation of Investment Banking." *Harvard Business Review* 57 (January–February 1979), pp. 153–170.

Hays, Patrick A.; Joehnk, Michael D.; and Melicher, Ronald W. "Differential Determinants of Risk Premiums in the Public and Private Corporate Bond Markets." *Journal of Financial Research* 2 (Fall 1979), pp. 143–152.

Ibbotson, Roger G., and Jaffe, Jeffrey F. " 'Hot Issue' Markets." *Journal of Finance* 30 (June 1975), pp. 1027–1042.

Joehnk, Michael, and Kidwell, David S. "Comparative Costs of Competitive and Negotiated Underwritings in the State and Local Bond Market." *Journal of Finance* 34 (June 1979), pp. 725–731.

Johnson, Keith; Morton, T. Gregory; and Findlay, M. Chapman III. "An Analysis of the Flotation Cost of Utility Bonds." *Journal of Financial Research* 2 (Fall 1979), pp. 133–142.

———. "An Empirical Analysis of the Flotation Cost of Corporate Securities, 1971–1972." *Journal of Finance* 30 (June 1975), pp. 1129–1133.

Johnson, Ramon E. "Term Structures of Corporate Bond Yields as a Function of Risk of Default." *Journal of Finance* 22 (May 1967), pp. 313–345.

Karna, Adi S. "The Cost of Private Versus Public Debt Issues." *Financial Management* 1 (Summer 1972), pp. 65–67.

Kessel, Reuben A. *Cyclical Behavior of the Term Structure of Interest Rates.* New York: National Bureau of Economic Research, 1965.

Krainer, Robert E. "A Reexamination of the Theory of Monopsonistic Discrimination in the Capital Market." *Journal of Business* 47 (July 1974), pp. 429–439.

Logue, Dennis E., and Jarrow, Robert A. "Negotiation vs. Competitive Bidding in the Sale of Securities by Public Utilities." *Financial Management* 31 (Autumn 1978), pp. 31–39.

Logue, Dennis E., and Lindvall, John R. "The Behavior of Investment Bankers: An Econometric Investigation." *Journal of Finance* 29 (March 1974), pp. 203–215.

Malkiel, Burton G. "The Capital Formation Problem in the United States." *Journal of Finance* 34 (May 1979), pp. 291–306.

———. *The Term Structure of Interest Rates.* Princeton, N.J.: Princeton University Press, 1966.

Mandelker, Gershon, and Ravic, Artur. "Investment Banking: An Economic Analysis of Optimal Underwriting Contracts." *Journal of Finance* 32 (June 1977), pp. 683–694.

Massaro, Vincent G. "Corporate Capital Structures and Financing Patterns: 1977–1980." *Conference Board Report No. 734.* New York: Conference Board, 1977, pp. 1–37.

Moor, Roy E. "The Timing of Financial Policy." In *The Treasurer's Handbook,* edited by J. Fred Weston and Maurice B. Goudzwaard. Homewood, Ill.: Dow Jones–Irwin, 1976, pp. 43–67.

Morrison, Ann M. "The Venture Capitalist Who Tries to Win Them All." *Fortune,* January 28, 1980, pp. 96–99.

Parker, George G. C., and Cooperman, Daniel. "Competitive Bidding in the Underwriting of Public Utilities Securities." *Journal of Financial and Quantitative Analysis* 13 (December 1978), pp. 885–902.

Rhoades, Stephen A. "Nonbank Thrift Institutions as Determinants of Performance in Banking Markets." *Journal of Economics and Business* 32 (Fall 1979), pp. 66–72.

Robinson, Roland, and Bartell, H. Robert, Jr. "Uneasy Partnership: SEC/NYSE." *Harvard Business Review* 43 (January–February 1965), pp. 76–88.

Seligman, Daniel. "The Revolt of the Lenders." *Fortune,* March 24, 1980, pp. 57–59.

Sorensen, Eric H. "The Impact of Underwriting Method and Bidder Competition upon Corporate Bond Interest Cost." *Journal of Finance* 34 (September 1979), pp. 863–869.

Stapleton, R. C., and Subrahmanyam, M. G. "Marketability of Assets and the Price of Risk." *Journal of Financial and Quantitative Analysis* 14 (March 1979), pp. 1–10.

Stoll, Hans R. "The Supply of Dealer Services in Securities Markets." *Journal of Finance* 33 (September 1978), pp. 1133–1151.

Stoll, Hans R., and Curley, Anthony J. "Small Business and the New Issues Market for Equities." *Journal of Financial and Quantitative Analysis* 5 (September 1970), pp. 309–322.

Van Horne, James C. "New Listings and Their Price Behavior." *Journal of Finance* 25 (September 1970), pp. 783–794.

———. *Function and Analysis of Capital Market Rates.* Englewood Cliffs, N.J.: Prentice-Hall, 1970.

Wachtel, Paul; Sametz, Arnold; and Shuford, Harry. "Capital Shortages: Myth or Reality." *Journal of Finance* 31 (May 1976), pp. 269–286.

West, Richard R., and Tinic, Seha M. "Corporate Finance and the Changing Stock Market." *Financial Management* 3 (Autumn 1974), pp. 14–23.

19
Common Stock

Common equity or, if unincorporated firms are being considered, partnership or proprietorship interests constitute the first source of funds to a new business and the base of support for borrowing by existing firms. Accordingly, our discussion of specific forms of long-term financing will begin with an analysis of common stock.

Apportionment of Income, Control, and Risk

The nature of equity ownership depends on the form of the business or organization. The central problem of such ownership revolves around an apportionment of certain rights and responsibilities among those who have provided the funds necessary for the operation of the business. The rights and responsibilities attaching to equity consist of positive considerations—income potential and control of the firm—and negative considerations—loss potential, legal responsibility, and personal liability.

General Rights of Holders of Common Stock

The rights of holders of common stock in a business corporation are established by the laws of the state in which the corporation is chartered and by the terms of the charter granted by the state. Charters are relatively uniform on many matters, including collective and specific rights.

Collective Rights. Certain collective rights are usually given to the holders of common stock. Some of the more important rights allow stockholders (1) to amend the charter with the approval of the appropriate officials in the state of incorporation, (2) to adopt and amend bylaws, (3) to elect the directors of the corporation, (4) to authorize the sale of fixed assets, (5) to enter into mergers, (6) to change the amount of authorized common stock, and (7) to issue preferred stock, debentures, bonds, and other securities.

Specific Rights. Holders of common stock also have specific rights as individual owners: (1) the right to vote in the manner prescribed by the corporate charter, (2) the right to sell their stock certificates (their evidence of ownership) and in this way to transfer their ownership interest to other persons, (3) the right to inspect the corporate books,[1] and (4) the right to share residual assets of the corporation on dissolution. (However, the holders of common stock are last among the claimants to the assets of the corporation.)

Apportionment of Income

Two important positive considerations are involved in equity ownership: income and control. The right to income carries the risk of loss. Control also involves responsibility and liability. In an individual proprietorship that uses funds supplied only by the owner, the owner has a 100 percent right to income and control and to loss and responsibility. As soon as the proprietor incurs debt, however, he or she has entered into contracts that limit the freedom to control the firm and to apportion the firm's income. In a partnership, these rights are apportioned among the partners in an agreed upon manner. In the absence of a formal agreement, a division is made by state law. In a corporation, more significant issues arise concerning the rights of the owners.

Apportionment of Control

Through the right to vote, holders of common stock have legal control of the corporation. As a practical matter, however, in many corporations the principal officers constitute all, or a majority, of the members of the board of directors. In this circumstance the board may be controlled by the management rather than by the owners. However, numerous examples demonstrate that stockholders can reassert their control if they are dissatisfied with the corporation's policies. In recent years, proxy battles with the aim of altering corporate policies have occurred fairly often, and firms whose managers are unresponsive to stockholders' desires are subject to takeover bids by other firms.

As receivers of residual income, holders of common stock are frequently referred to as the ultimate entrepreneurs in the firm. They are the ultimate owners, and they have the ultimate control. Presumably, the firm is managed on behalf of the holders of common stock, but there has been much dispute about the actual situation. The point of view has been expressed that the corporation is an institution with an existence separate from that of its owners, that it exists to fulfill certain functions for stockholders as only one among other important groups, such as workers, consumers, and the economy as a whole. While this view has some validity, ordinarily the officers of a firm are also large stockholders. In addition, more and more firms are relating officers' compensation to the firm's profit performance, either by granting executives stock purchase options or by giving them bonuses. These actions are, of course, designed to make managers' personal goals more consistent with those of the stockholders—to increase the firm's earnings and stock price.

1. Obviously, a corporation cannot have its business affairs disturbed by allowing every stockholder to go through any records the stockholder wants to inspect. Furthermore, a corporation cannot wisely permit a competitor who buys shares of its common stock to look at all the corporation records. There must be, and there are, practical limitations to this right.

Table 19.1

Balance Sheets for Corporations A and B

Corporation A				Corporation B			
		Debt	$ 20			Debt	$ 60
		Equity	80			Equity	40
Total assets	$100	Total claims	$100	Total assets	$100	Total claims	$100

Apportionment of Risk

Another consideration involved in equity ownership is risk: On liquidation, holders of common stock are last in the priority of claims. Therefore, the portion of capital they contribute provides a cushion for creditors if losses occur on dissolution. The equity to total assets ratio indicates the percentage by which assets may shrink in value on liquidation before creditors will incur losses.

For example, compare two corporations, A and B, whose balance sheets are shown in Table 19.1. The ratio of equity to total assets in Corporation A is 80 percent. Total assets will therefore have to shrink by 80 percent before creditors will lose money. By contrast, in Corporation B the extent by which assets will have to shrink in value on liquidation before creditors lose money is only 40 percent.

Common Stock Financing

Before undertaking an evaluation of common stock financing, more of the important characteristics of such stock will be described: (1) the nature of voting rights, (2) the nature of the preemptive right, and (3) variations in the forms of common stock.

Nature of Voting Rights

For each share of common stock owned, the holder has the right to cast one vote at the annual meeting of stockholders or at such special meetings as may be called.

Proxy. Provision is made for the temporary transfer of the right to vote by an instrument known as a *proxy.* The transfer is limited in its duration; typically it applies only to a specific occasion such as the annual meeting of stockholders.

The SEC supervises the use of the proxy machinery and frequently issues rules and regulations to improve its administration. SEC supervision is justified for at least two reasons:

1. If the proxy machinery is left wholly in the hands of management, there is a danger that the incumbent management will be self-perpetuated.
2. If it is made easy for minority groups of stockholders and opposition stockholders to oust management, there is a danger that they will gain control

of the corporation for temporary advantages or to place themselves or their friends in management positions.

Cumulative Voting. A method of voting that has come into increased prominence is cumulative voting. Cumulative voting for directors is required in twenty-two states, including California, Illinois, Pennsylvania, Ohio, and Michigan. It is permissible in eighteen, including Delaware, New York, and New Jersey. Ten states make no provision for it.

Cumulative voting permits multiple votes for a single director. For example, suppose six directors are to be elected. The owner of 100 shares can cast 100 votes for each of the six openings. Cumulatively, then, the stockholder has 600 votes. When cumulative voting is permitted, the stockholder can accumulate the votes and cast all of them for *one* director, instead of 100 each for *six* directors. Cumulative voting is designed to enable a minority group of stockholders to obtain some voice in the control of the company by electing at least one director to the board.

The nature of cumulative voting is illustrated by the use of the following formula:

$$req. = \frac{des.(n)}{\# + 1} + 1, \tag{19.1}$$

where:

req. = Number of shares required to elect a desired number of directors
des. = Number of directors stockholder desires to elect
n = Total number of shares of common stock outstanding and entitled to be voted[2]
= Total number of directors to be elected

The formula can be made more meaningful by an example. The ABC company will elect six directors. There are fifteen candidates and 100,000 shares entitled to be voted. If a group desires to elect two directors, how many shares must it have?

$$req. = \frac{2 \times 100{,}000}{6 + 1} + 1 = 28{,}572.$$

Observe the significance of the formula. Here, a minority group wishes to elect one-third of the board of directors. It can achieve its goal by owning less than one-third the number of shares of stock.[3]

2. An alternative that may be agreed to by the contesting parties is to define n as the number of shares *voted,* not *authorized to be voted.* This procedure, which in effect gives each group seeking to elect directors the same percentage of directors as their percentage of the voted stock, is frequently followed. When it is used, a group that seeks to gain control with a minimum investment must estimate the percentage of shares that will be voted and then obtain control of more than 50 percent of that number.
3. Note also that at least 14,287 shares must be controlled to elect one director. Any number less than that constitutes a useless minority.

Alternatively, assuming that a group holds 40,000 shares of stock in the company, how many directors can it elect following the rigid assumptions of the formula? The formula can be used in its present form or can be solved for *des.* and expressed as:

$$des. = \frac{(req. - 1)(\# + 1)}{n}. \tag{19.2}$$

Inserting the figures, the calculation is:

$$des. = \frac{39{,}999 \times 7}{100{,}000} = 2.8.$$

The 40,000 shares can thus elect two and eight-tenths directors. Since directors cannot exist as fractions, the group can elect only two directors.

As a practical matter, suppose that in the above situation the total number of shares is 100,000; hence 60,000 shares remain in other hands. The voting of all 60,000 shares may not be concentrated. Suppose the 60,000 shares (cumulatively 360,000 votes) not held by the minority group are distributed equally among ten candidates—with 36,000 shares held by each candidate. If the minority group's 240,000 votes are distributed equally among each of six candidates, it can elect all six directors even though it does not have a majority of the stock.

Actually, it is difficult to make assumptions about how the opposition votes will be distributed. What is shown here is a good example of game theory. One rule in this theory is to assume that your opponents will do the worst they can do to you and to counter with actions to minimize the maximum loss. This is the kind of assumption followed in the formula. If the opposition concentrates its votes in the optimum manner, what is the best you can do to work in the direction of your goal? Other plausible assumptions can be substituted if there are sufficient facts to support alternative hypotheses about the opponents' behavior.

Preemptive Right

The preemptive right gives holders of common stock the first option to purchase additional issues of common stock. In some states, this right is made part of every corporate charter; in others, it is necessary to insert the right specifically in the charter.

The purpose of the preemptive right is twofold. First, it protects the power of control of present stockholders. If it were not for this safeguard, the management of a corporation under criticism from stockholders could prevent stockholders from removing it from office by issuing a large number of additional shares at a very low price and purchasing these shares itself. Management would thereby secure control of the corporation to frustrate the will of the current stockholders.

The second, and by far the more important, protection that the preemptive right affords stockholders concerns dilution of value. For example, assume that 1,000 shares of common stock, each with a price of $100, are outstanding—making the total market value of the firm $100,000. An additional

1,000 shares are sold at $50 a share—a total of $50,000—thereby raising the market value of the firm to $150,000. When the total market value is divided by the new total shares outstanding, a value of $75 a share is obtained. Thus selling common stock at below market value will dilute the price of the stock and will be detrimental to present stockholders and beneficial to those who purchase the new shares. The preemptive right prevents such occurrences. (This point is discussed at length later in the chapter.)

Forms of Common Stock[4]

Classified. Classified common stock was used extensively in the late 1920s, sometimes in ways that misled investors. During that period Class A common stock was usually nonvoting, and Class B was usually voting. Thus promoters could control companies by selling large amounts of Class A stock while retaining Class B stock.

In more recent years there has been a revival of Class B common stock for sound purposes. It is used by small, new companies seeking to acquire funds from outside sources. Class A common stock is sold to the public and typically pays dividends; its holders have full voting rights. Class B common stock is retained by the organizers of the company, but dividends are not paid on it until the company has established its earning power. By the use of this classified stock, the public can take a position in a conservatively financed growth company without sacrificing income.

Founders' Shares. Founders' shares are somewhat like Class B stock except that they carry *sole* voting rights and typically do not confer the right to dividends for a number of years. Thus the organizers of the firm are able to maintain complete control of the operations in the firm's crucial initial development. At the same time, other investors are protected against excessive withdrawals of funds by owners.

Evaluation of Common Stock as a Source of Funds

Thus far, the chapter has covered the main characteristics of common stock (frequently referred to as equity shares). Now it will appraise this type of financing from the viewpoint of the issuer and from a social viewpoint.

4. Besides *common stock,* accountants also use the term *par value* to designate an arbitrary value assigned when stock is sold. When a firm sells newly issued stock, it must record the transaction on its balance sheet. For example, suppose a newly created firm commences operations by selling 100,000 shares at $10 a share, raising a total of $1 million. This $1 million must appear on the balance sheet. But what will it be called? One choice is to assign the stock a "par value" of $10 and label the $1 million "common stock." Another choice is to assign a $1 par value and show $100,000 ($1 par value × 100,000 shares) as "common stock" and $900,000 as "paid-in surplus." Still another choice is to disregard the term *par value* entirely—that is, use no-par stock—and record the $1 million as "common stock." Since the choice is quite arbitrary for all practical purposes, more and more firms are adopting the last procedure and abolishing the term *par value.* Because there are quite enough useful concepts and terms in accounting and finance, we heartily applaud the demise of useless ones such as this.

From the Viewpoint of the Issuer

Advantages. There are several advantages to the issuer of financing with common stock:

1. Common stock does not entail fixed charges. If the company generates the earnings, it can pay common stock dividends. In contrast to bond interest, however, there is no legal obligation to pay dividends.
2. Common stock carries no fixed maturity date.
3. Since common stock provides a cushion against losses of creditors, the sale of common stock increases the creditworthiness of the firm.
4. Common stock can at times be sold more easily than debt. It appeals to certain investor groups because (a) it typically carries a higher expected return than does preferred stock or debt; and (b) since it represents the ownership of the firm, it provides the investor with a better hedge against inflation than does straight preferred stock or bonds. Ordinarily, common stock increases in value when the value of real assets rises during an inflationary period.[5]
5. Returns from common stock in the form of capital gains are subject to the lower personal income tax rates on capital gains. Hence the effective personal income tax rates on returns from common stock may be lower than the effective tax rates on the interest on debt.

Disadvantages. Disadvantages to the issuer of common stock are:

1. The sale of common stock extends voting rights or control to the additional stock owners who are brought into the company. For this reason, among others, additional equity financing is often avoided by small and new firms, whose owner-managers may be unwilling to share control of their companies with outsiders.
2. Common stock gives more owners the right to share in income. The use of debt may enable the firm to utilize funds at a fixed low cost, whereas common stock gives equal rights to new stockholders to share in the net profits of the firm.
3. As we saw in Chapter 18, the costs of underwriting and distributing common stock are usually higher than those for underwriting and distributing preferred stock or debt. Flotation costs for selling common stock are characteristically higher because (a) costs of investigating an equity security investment are higher than investigating the feasibility of a comparable debt security; and (b) stocks are more risky, which means equity holdings must be diversified, which in turn means that a given dollar amount of new stock must be sold to a greater number of purchasers than the same amount of debt.

5. During the inflation of the last decade, the lags of product price increases behind the rise of input costs have depressed corporate earnings and increased the uncertainty of earnings growth, causing price-earnings multiples to fall.

4. As we saw in Chapter 16, if the firm has more equity or less debt than is called for in the optimum capital structure, the average cost of capital will be higher than necessary.
5. Common stock dividends are not deductible as an expense for calculating the corporation's income subject to the federal income tax, but bond interest is deductible. The impact of this factor is reflected in the relative cost of equity capital vis-à-vis debt capital.

From a Social Viewpoint

From a social viewpoint, common stock is a desirable form of financing because it renders business firms (a major segment of the economy) less vulnerable to the consequences of declines in sales and earnings. Common stock financing involves no fixed charges, the payment of which might force a faltering firm into reorganization or bankruptcy.

However, another aspect of common stock financing may have less desirable social consequences. Common stock prices fall in recessions, a phenomenon that represents a rise in the cost of equity capital. The rising cost of equity raises the overall cost of capital, which in turn reduces investment. This reduction further aggravates the recession. However, an expanding economy is accompanied by rising stock prices, and with rising stock prices comes a drop in the cost of capital. This in turn stimulates investment, which may add to a developing inflationary boom. In summary, a consideration of its effect on the cost of capital suggests that stock financing may tend to amplify cyclical fluctuations. Just how these opposing forces combine to produce a net effect is unknown, but the authors believe that the first is the stronger—that stock financing tends to stabilize the economy.

Use of Rights in Financing

If the preemptive right is contained in a firm's charter, then the firm must offer any new common stock to existing stockholders. If the charter does not prescribe a preemptive right, the firm has a choice of making the sale to its existing stockholders or to an entirely new set of investors. If it sells to the existing stockholders, the stock flotation is called a *rights offering.* Each stockholder is issued an option to buy a certain number of the new shares, and the terms of the option are contained on a piece of paper called a *right.* Each stockholder receives one right for each share of stock owned. The advantages and disadvantages of rights offerings are described in the following section.

Theoretical Relationships of Rights Offerings

Several issues confront the financial manager who is deciding on the details of a rights offering. The various considerations can be shown by the use of illustrative data on the Southeast Company, whose balance sheet and income statement are given in Table 19.2.

Table 19.2

Southeast Company Financial Statements before Rights Offering

Partial Balance Sheet

		Total debt (at 5%)	$ 40,000,000
		Common stock	10,000,000
		Retained earnings	50,000,000
Total assets	$100,000,000	Total liabilities and capital	$100,000,000

Partial Income Statement

Total earnings	$10,000,000
Interest on debt	2,000,000
Income before taxes	$ 8,000,000
Taxes (50% assumed)	4,000,000
Earnings after taxes	$ 4,000,000
Earnings per share (1 million shares)	$4
Market price of stock (price-earnings ratio of 25 assumed)	$100

Southeast earns $4 million after taxes and has 1 million shares outstanding, so earnings per share are $4. The stock sells at 25 times earnings, or for $100 a share. The company plans to raise $10 million of new equity funds through a rights offering and decides to sell the new stock to shareholders for $80 a share. The questions now facing the financial manager are:

1. How many rights will be required to purchase a share of the newly issued stock?
2. What is the value of each right?
3. What effect will the rights offering have on the price of the existing stock?

Number of Rights Needed to Purchase a New Share

As, already mentioned, Southeast plans to raise $10 million in new equity funds and to sell the new stock at a price of $80 a share. Dividing the subscription price into the total funds to be raised gives the number of shares to be issued:

$$\text{Number of new shares} = \frac{\text{Funds to be raised}}{\text{Subscription price}} = \frac{\$10{,}000{,}000}{\$80} = 125{,}000 \text{ shares.}$$

The next step is to divide the number of new shares into the number of previously outstanding shares to get the number of rights required to subscribe to one share of the new stock. Note that stockholders always receive one right for each share of stock they own:

$$\frac{\text{Number of rights needed to}}{\text{buy a share of the stock}} = \frac{\text{Old shares}}{\text{New shares}} = \frac{1{,}000{,}000}{125{,}000} = 8 \text{ rights.}$$

Therefore, a stockholder will have to surrender eight rights plus $80 to receive one of the newly issued shares. If the subscription price had been set at $95 a share, 9.5 rights would have been required to subscribe to each new share; if the price had been set at $10 a share, only 1 right would have been needed. If the number of new shares exceeds the number of old shares, the number of rights required to subscribe to each new share would be a fraction of 1. For example, if the number of old shares is 1,000,000 and 1,600,000 new shares are to be issued, the number of rights required to subscribe to each new share would be ⅝ of 1 right. Trading in the rights would take place so that exact, not fractional, numbers of new shares could be purchased by the exercise of rights plus the required cash.

Value of a Right

It is clearly worth something to be able to pay less than $100 for a share of stock selling for $100. The right provides this privilege, so it must have a value. To see how the theoretical value of a right is established, we continue with the example of the Southeast Company, assuming that it will raise $10 million by selling 125,000 new shares at $80 a share.

Notice that the *market value* of the old stock was $100 million: $100 a share times 1 million shares. (The book value is irrelevant.) When the firm sells the new stock, it brings in an additional $10 million. As a first approximation, assume that the market value of the common stock increases by exactly this $10 million. Actually, the market value of all the common stock will go up by more than $10 million if investors think the company will be able to invest these funds at a yield substantially in excess of the cost of equity capital, but it will go up by less than $10 million if investors are doubtful of the company's ability to put the new funds to work profitably in the near future.

Under the assumption that market value exactly reflects the new funds brought in, the total market value of the common stock after the new issue will be $110 million. Dividing this new value by the new total number of shares outstanding, 1.125 million, gives a new market value of $97.78 a share. Therefore, after the financing has been completed, the price of the common stock will have fallen from $100 to $97.78.

Since the rights give the stockholders the privilege of paying only $80 for a share of stock that will end up being worth $97.78—thereby saving them $17.78—is $17.78 the value of each right? The answer is no, because eight rights are required to buy one new share. The $17.78 must be divided by 8 to get the value of each right. In the example, each one is worth $2.22.

Ex Rights

The Southeast Company's rights have a very definite value, and this value accrues to the holders of the common stock. But what happens if stock is traded during the offering period? Who will receive the rights—the old owners or the new? The standard procedure calls for the company to set a *holder of rec-*

ord date and for the stock to go *ex rights* after that date. If the stock is sold prior to the ex rights date, the new owner receives the rights; if it is sold on or after the ex rights date, the old owner receives them. For example, on October 15, Southeast Company announces the terms of the new financing; the company states that rights will be mailed out on December 1 to stockholders of record as of the close of business on November 15. Anyone buying the old stock on or before November 15 will receive the rights; anyone buying the stock on or after November 16 will *not* receive them. Thus November 16 is the *ex rights date;* before November 16 the stock sells *rights on.* In the case of Southeast Company, the rights-on price is $100, and the ex rights price is expected to be $97.78.

Formula Value of a Right

Rights on. Equations have been developed for determining the value of rights without going through all the procedures described above. While the stock is still selling rights on, the value at which the rights will sell when they are issued can be found by use of the following formula:

$$\text{Value of one right} = \frac{\text{Market value of stock, rights on} - \text{Subscription price}}{\text{Number of rights required to purchase 1 share} + 1}$$

$$v_r = \frac{p_0 - p^s}{\# + 1}, \tag{19.3}$$

where:

p_0 = Rights-on price of the stock
p^s = Subscription price
= Number of rights required to purchase a new share of stock
v_r = Value of one right

Substituting the appropriate values for the Southeast Company:

$$v_r = \frac{\$100 - \$80}{8 + 1} = \frac{\$20}{9} = \$2.22.$$

This agrees with the value of the rights found by the step-by-step analysis.

Ex Rights. Suppose you are a stockholder in the Southeast Company. When you return to the United States from a trip to Europe, you read about the rights offering in the newspaper. The stock is now selling ex rights for $97.78 a share. How can you calculate the theoretical value of a right? By using the following formula, which follows the logic described in preceding sections, you can determine the value of each right:

$$\text{Value of one right} = \frac{\text{Market value of stock, ex rights} - \text{Subscription price}}{\text{Number of rights required to purchase 1 share}}$$

$$v_r = \frac{p_e - p^s}{\#} \tag{19.4}$$

$$= \frac{\$97.78 - \$80}{8} = \frac{\$17.78}{8} = \$2.22.$$

Here, p_e is the ex rights price of the stock.[6]

Effects on Position of Stockholders

Stockholders have the choice of exercising their rights or selling them. If they have sufficient funds and want to buy more shares of the company's stock, they will exercise the rights. If they do not have the money or do not want to buy more stock, they will sell the rights. In either case, provided the formula value of the rights holds true, stockholders will neither benefit nor lose by the rights offering. This statement can be made clear by considering the position of an individual stockholder in the Southeast Company.

The stockholder has eight shares of stock before the rights offering. Each share has a market value of $100, so the stockholder has a total market value of $800 in the company's stock. If, after the rights offering, a shareholder exercises the rights, this individual will be able to purchase one additional share at $80—a new investment of $80. With a total investment of $880, the stockholder will own nine shares of the company's stock, which now has a value of $97.78 a share. The value of this stock will be $880, exactly what was invested in it.

Alternatively, by selling the eight rights, which have a value of $2.22 each, the holder will receive $17.76 and will thus have the original eight shares of stock plus $17.76 in cash. But the original eight shares of stock now have a

6. We developed Equation 19.4 directly from the verbal explanation given in the immediately preceding section. Equation 19.3 can thus be derived from Equation 19.4 as follows:

$$p_e = p_0 - v_r. \tag{19.5}$$

Substituting Equation 19.5 into Equation 19.4:

$$v_r = \frac{p_0 - v_r - p^s}{\#}. \tag{19.6}$$

Simplifying Equation 19.6:

$$v_r = \frac{p_0 - p^s}{\#} - \frac{v_r}{\#}$$

$$v_r + \frac{v_r}{\#} = \frac{p_0 - p^s}{\#}$$

$$v_r\left(\frac{\# + 1}{\#}\right) = \frac{p_0 - p^s}{\#}$$

$$v_r = \frac{p_0 - p^s}{\#} \cdot \frac{\#}{\# + 1}$$

$$v_r = \frac{p_0 - p^s}{\# + 1}.$$

The result is Equation 19.3.

market price of $97.78 a share. The $782.24 market value of this stock plus the $17.76 in cash is the same as the $800 market value of stock with which the investor began.

Oversubscription Privilege

Even though the rights are very valuable and should be exercised, some stockholders neglect to do so. Still, all the stock is sold because of the *oversubscription privilege* contained in most rights offerings. This privilege gives subscribing stockholders the right to buy, on a pro rata basis, all shares not taken in the initial offering. To illustrate: If Jane Doe owns 10 percent of the stock in Southeast Company, and if 20 percent of the rights offered by the company are not exercised (or sold) by the stockholders to whom they were originally given, then she can buy an additional 2.5 percent of the new stock.[7] Since this stock is a bargain—$80 for stock worth $97.78—Jane Doe and other stockholders will use the oversubscription privilege, thereby assuring the full sale of the new stock issue.

Relationship between Market Price and Subscription Price

We can now investigate the factors influencing the use of rights and, if they are used, the level at which the subscription price is set. The Southeast Company's articles of incorporation permit the firm to decide whether to use rights, depending on whether their use is advantageous to the firm and its stockholders. The financial vice-president of the company is considering three methods of raising the sum of $10 million:

1. The company could sell to the public, through investment bankers, additional shares at approximately $100 a share. The company would net approximately $96 a share; thus it would need to sell approximately 105,000 shares in order to cover the underwriting commission.
2. The company could sell additional shares through rights, using investment bankers and paying a commission of 1 percent on the total dollar amount of the stock sold plus an additional ¾ percent on all shares unsubscribed and taken over by the investment bankers. Allowing for the usual market pressure when common stock is sold, the new shares would be sold at a 20 percent discount, or at $80. Thus 125,000 additional shares would be offered through rights. With eight rights, an additional share could be purchased at $80. Since stockholders are given the right to subscribe to any unexercised rights on a pro rata basis, only those shares not subscribed to on the original or secondary level are sold to the underwriters and subjected to the ¾ percent additional commission.
3. The company could sell additional shares through rights, at $10 a share, and not use investment bankers. The number of additional shares of common stock to be sold would be 1 million. For each right held, existing

7. Eighty percent of the stock was subscribed. Since Jane Doe subscribed to 10/80, or 12.5 percent, of the stock that was taken, she can obtain 12.5 percent of the unsubscribed stock. Therefore, her oversubscription allocation is 12.5 percent × 20 = 2.5 percent of the new stock.

stockholders would be permitted to buy one share of the new common stock.

Method 1 uses investment bankers and no rights at all. In this circumstance the underwriting commission, or flotation cost, is approximately 4 percent. In Method 2, where rights are used with a small discount, the underwriting commission is reduced, because the discount removes much of the risk of not being able to sell the issue. The underwriting commission consists of two parts —1 percent on the original issue and an additional ¾ percent commission on all unsubscribed shares the investment bankers are required to take over and sell. Thus the actual commission ranges somewhere between 1 percent and 1¾ percent. Under Method 3, the subscription price is $10 a share. With such a large concession, the company does not need to use investment bankers at all, because the rights are certain to have value and to be either exercised or sold. Which of the three methods is superior?

Method 1 provides a wider distribution of the securities sold, thereby lessening any possible control problems. The investment bankers assure that the company will receive the $10 million involved in the new issue, and they give the firm ongoing financial counsel. The company pays for these services in the form of underwriting charges. After the issue, the stock price should be approximately $100.

Under Method 2, by utilizing rights, the company reduces its underwriting expenses and the unit price per share (from $100 to $97.78). Some stockholders may suffer a loss because they neither exercise nor sell their rights. Existing stockholders will buy some of the new shares, so the distribution is likely to be narrower than under Method 1. Because of the underwriting contract, the firm is assured of receiving the funds sought. Finally, investors often like the opportunity to purchase additional shares through rights offerings; thus their use may increase stockholder loyalty.

Method 3 involves no underwriting expense and results in a substantial decrease in the unit price of shares. Initially, however, the shares are less widely distributed than under either of the other two methods. Method 3 also has a large stock-split effect, which results in a much lower final stock price per share than under either of the other two methods.[8] Many people feel that there is an optimal stock price—one that will produce a maximum total market value of the shares—and that this price is generally in the range of $30 to $60 a share. If this is the feeling of Southeast's directors, they may believe that Method 3 will permit them to reach the more desirable price range while at the same time reducing flotation costs on the new issue. However, since the rights have a substantial value, any stockholder who fails either to exercise or to sell them will suffer a serious loss.

8. Stock splits were discussed in Chapter 17. Basically, a stock split is simply the issuance of additional shares to existing stockholders for *no* additional funds. Stock splits divide the "pie" into more pieces.

Table 19.3

Summary of Three Methods of Raising Additional Money

	Advantages	Disadvantages
Method 1	1. Wide distribution 2. Certainty of receiving funds	1. High underwriting costs
Method 2	1. Small underwriting costs 2. Lower unit price of shares 3. Certainty of receiving funds 4. Increased stockholder loyalty	1. Narrow distribution 2. Losses to forgetful stockholders
Method 3	1. No underwriting costs 2. Substantial decrease in unit price of shares 3. Increased stockholder loyalty	1. Narrow distribution 2. Severe losses to forgetful stockholders

The three methods are summarized in Table 19.3. The most advantageous method depends on the company's needs. For a company strongly interested in wide distribution of its securities, Method 1 is preferable. For a firm most interested in reducing the unit price of its shares and confident that the lower unit price will induce wide distribution, Method 3 is preferable. For a company whose needs are moderate in both directions, Method 2 may offer a satisfactory compromise. Whether rights will be used and the level of the subscription price both depend on the company's needs at a particular time.

Exercise of Rights

Interestingly enough, it is expected that a small percentage of stockholders will neglect to exercise or to sell their rights. In a recent offering, the holders of 1½ percent of General Motors common stock did not exercise their rights. The loss experienced by these stockholders was $1.5 million. In a recent AT&T issue, the loss to shareholders who neglected to exercise their rights was $960,000.

Market Price and Subscription Price

Measured from the registration date for the new issue of the security, the average percentage by which the subscription prices of new issues were below their market prices has been about 15 percent in recent years. Examples of price concessions of 40 percent or more can be observed in a small percentage of issues, but the most frequently encountered discounts are from 10 to 20 percent.

Effect on Subsequent Behavior of Market Price

It is often said that issuing new stock through rights will depress the price of the company's existing common stock. To the extent that a subscription price in connection with the rights offering is lower than the market price, there will be a "stock-split effect" on the market price of the common stock. With the prevailing market price of Southeast Company's stock at $100 and a $10 subscription price, the new market price will probably drop to about $55.

But whether, because of the rights offering, the actual new market price will be $55 or lower or higher is unknown. Again, empirical analysis of the movement in stock prices during rights offerings indicates that generalization is not practical. What happens to the market prices of the stock ex rights and after the rights trading period depends on the future earnings prospects of the issuing company.

Advantages of Use of Rights in New Financing

The preemptive right gives shareholders the protection of preserving their pro rata share in the earnings and control of the company. It also benefits the firm. By offering new issues of securities to existing stockholders, the firm increases the likelihood of a favorable reception for the stock. By their ownership of common stock in the company, investors have already evaluated the company favorably. They may therefore be receptive to the purchase of additional shares, particularly when the following information is taken into account.

The shares purchased with rights are subject to lower margin requirements. For example, margin requirements since January 1974 have been 50 percent; in other words, people buying listed stocks must put up at least $50 of their own funds for every $100 of securities purchased. However, if shares of new stock issues are purchased with rights, only $25 per $100 of common stock purchased must be furnished by investors; they are permitted by law to borrow up to 75 percent of the purchase price. Furthermore, the absence of a clear pattern in the price behavior of the adjusted market price of the stocks and rights before, during, and after the trading period may enhance interest in the investment possibilities of the instruments.

These factors can offset the tendency toward a downward pressure on the price of the common stock occurring at the time of a new issue.[9] With the increased interest in (and advantages afforded by) the rights offering, the "true" or "adjusted" downward price pressure may actually be avoided.

A related advantage is that the issuer's flotation costs associated with a rights offering are lower than the cost of a public flotation. The costs referred to here are cash costs. For example, the flotation costs of common stock issues during the period 1971 to 1975 were 6.17 percent on public issues compared with 2.45 percent on rights offerings.[10]

The financial manager can obtain positive benefits from underpricing. Since a rights offering is a stock split to a certain degree, it causes the market

9. The downward pressure develops because of an increase in the supply of securities without a necessarily equivalent increase in the demand. Generally it is a temporary phenomenon, and the stock tends to return to the theoretical price after a few months. Obviously, if the acquired funds are invested at a very high rate of return, the stock price benefits; if the investment does not turn out well, the stock price suffers.

10. C. W. Smith, Jr., "Substitute Methods for Raising Additional Capital: Rights Offerings versus Underwritten Issues," *Journal of Financial Economics* 5 (December 1977), pp. 273–307.

price of the stock to fall to a level lower than it otherwise would be. But stock splits can increase the number of shareholders in a company by bringing the price of a stock down to a more attractive trading level. Furthermore, a rights offering may be associated with increased dividends for the stock owners.[11]

In general, a rights offering can stimulate an enthusiastic response from stockholders and from the investment market as a whole, with the result that opportunities for financing become more attractive to the firm. Thus the financial manager may be able to engage in common stock financing at lower costs and under more favorable terms.

Choosing among Alternative Forms of Financing

A pattern of analysis can be formulated for choosing among alternative forms of financing. This framework applies to the decision choices involved in evaluating the other major forms of financing covered: various forms of debt, preferred stock, lease financing, and financing in international markets, among others. Thus the pattern of analysis has broad applications.

The framework set forth brings together a number of topics that have already been treated. Risk aspects were covered in Chapters 5 and 15. Relative costs were covered in Chapters 14 and 16. Control was discussed earlier in this chapter.

To make the application of the concepts more concrete, a case will be used to illustrate and exemplify the procedures involved. Stanton Chemicals, having estimated that it will need to raise $200 million for an expansion program, discusses with its investment bankers whether it should raise the $200 million through debt financing or through selling additional shares of common stock. The bankers are asked to make their recommendation to Stanton's board of directors using the information on industry financial ratios and the company's 1981 balance sheet and income statement found in Tables 19.4, 19.5, and 19.6, respectively.

Table 19.4

Chemical Industry Financial Ratios

Current ratio: 2.0 times
Sales to total assets: 1.6 times
Current debt to total assets: 30%
Long-term debt to net worth: 40%
Total debt to total assets: 50%
Coverage of fixed charges: 7 times
Net income to sales: 5%
Return on total assets: 9%
Net income to net worth: 13%

11. The increased dividends may convey information that the prospective earnings of the firm have improved and may result in a higher market price for the firm's stock.

Table 19.5

Stanton Chemicals Company Balance Sheet as of December 31, 1981 (Millions of Dollars)

Assets		Liabilities		
Total current assets	$1,000	Notes payable (at 10%)	$300	
Net fixed assets	800	Other current liabilities	400	
		Total current liabilities		$ 700
		Long-term debt (at 10%)		300
		Total debt		$1,000
		Common stock, par value $1		100
		Paid-in capital		300
		Retained earnings		400
Total assets	$1,800	Total claims on assets		$1,800

Stanton's dividend payout has averaged about 30 percent of net income. At present, its cost of debt is 10 percent and its cost of equity 14 percent. If the additional funds are raised by debt, the cost of debt will be 12 percent, and the cost of equity will rise to 16 percent. If the funds are raised by equity, the cost of debt will remain at 10 percent, and the cost of equity will fall to 12 percent; new equity will initially be sold at $9 per share.

Stanton's common stock is widely held; there is no strong control group. The market parameters are a risk-free rate of 6 percent and an expected return on the market of 11 percent. The debt will carry a maturity of ten years and will require a sinking fund of $20 million per year in addition to the present $20 million annual sinking fund requirement.

In their analysis of which form of financing should be chosen, the investment bankers consider the following factors:

A. Risk

1. Financial structure
2. Fixed charge coverage
3. Coverage of cash flow requirements
4. Level of beta

Table 19.6

Stanton Chemicals Company Income Statement for Year Ended December 31, 1981 (Millions of Dollars)

	1981	Pro Forma after Financing
Total revenues	$3,000	$3,400
Depreciation expense	200	220
Other costs	2,484	2,820
Net operating income	$ 316	$ 360
Interest expense	60	
Net income before taxes	$ 256	
Income taxes (at 50%)	128	
Net income	$ 128	

Table 19.7

Stanton Financial Structure (Millions of Dollars)

	Present		Pro Forma				Industry Standard
			Debt		Equity		
	Amount	Percent	Amount	Percent	Amount	Percent	Percent
Current debt	$ 700	39	$ 700	35	$ 700	35	30
Long-term debt	300	17	500	25	300	15	20
Total debt	$1,000	56	$1,200	60	$1,000	50	50
Equity	800	44	800	40	1,000	50	
Total assets	$1,800	100	$2,000	100	$2,000	100	
Long-term debt to net worth		38		63		30	40

B. Relative costs

1. Effects on market value per share of common stock
2. Effects on cost of capital

C. Effects on control

The solution process proceeds as follows. First, the two forms of financing are examined with reference to the firm's risk as measured by its financial structure (see Table 19.7). Stanton fails to meet the industry standards on both the short-term and total debt ratios. If it finances with debt, its financial structure ratios will be further deficient. If it finances with equity, its long-term debt to net worth ratio will be strengthened, and it will meet the industry standard for the total debt to total assets ratio. Stanton should therefore seek to fund some short-term debt into longer term debt in the future, and it should try to build up its equity base further from retained earnings.

Stanton's fixed charge coverage is analyzed next, in Table 19.8. The table shows that the company's fixed charge coverage is below the industry standard. The use of debt financing will further aggravate the weakness in this area. The use of equity financing will move the company toward the industry standard.

Table 19.8

Fixed Charge Coverage (Millions of Dollars)

	Present	Pro Forma		Industry Standard
		Debt	Equity	
Net operating income	$316	$360	$360	
Interest expenses	60	90	60	
Coverage ratio	5.27	4.00	6.00	7.00

Table 19.9

Stanton's Cash Flow Coverage (Millions of Dollars)

	Present	Pro Forma Debt	Pro Forma Equity	Industry Standard
Net operating income	$316	$360	$360	
Depreciation expense	200	220	220	
Cash inflow	$516	$580	$580	
Interest expenses	60	84	60	
Sinking fund payments	20	40	20	
Before-tax sinking fund payments	40	80	40	
Cash outflow requirements	$100	$164	$100	
Cash flow coverage ratio	5.16	3.54	5.80	3.00

Stanton's cash flow coverage is analyzed in Table 19.9. To obtain the cash inflow, depreciation expense is added to net operating income. To obtain the cash outflow requirements, the before-tax sinking fund payment is added to the interest expenses. The sinking fund payments must be placed on a before-tax basis because they are not a tax-deductible expense.

The resulting cash flow coverage ratios appear satisfactory when measured against the industry standard of 3.00. However, this result has to be qualified by the recognition that a full analysis of cash flow coverage must consider other cash outflow requirements. These will include scheduled principal repayments on debt obligations, preferred stock dividends, payments under lease obligations, and probably some capital expenditures that are regarded as essential for the continuity of the firm. Within the broader definition of cash outflow requirements, Stanton's cash flow coverage would undoubtedly be lowered.

The next consideration is the effect of the various forms of financing on the level of the firm's beta. As indicated earlier, Stanton's cost of equity is at present 14 percent. Using the security market line and additional data on the market parameters already provided, Stanton's present level of beta can be determined as follows:

$$k_s = R_F + (\bar{R}_M - R_F)\beta$$
$$0.14 = 0.06 + (0.11 - 0.06)\beta$$
$$\beta = 1.6 \text{ at present.}$$

Stanton's present level of beta is 1.6. As stated earlier, if the additional funds are raised by debt, the cost of equity will rise to 16 percent. The implied new beta will therefore be:

$$0.16 = 0.06 + (0.05)\beta$$
$$\beta = 2.0.$$

Stanton's beta will rise to 2 with debt financing. With equity financing, the cost of equity will fall to 12 percent. The implied new beta will thus be 1.2.

Table 19.10

Calculation of the Amount of Debt Interest for Stanton (Millions of Dollars)

	No Expansion		Expansion with Debt		Expansion with Equity	
Form of Debt	Amount	Rate	Amount	Rate	Amount	Rate
$300 million short-term notes payable	$30	10%	$36	12%	$30	10%
$300 million existing long-term debt	30	10	30	10	30	10
$200 million new long-term debt	—		24	12	—	
Total interest expense	$60		$90		$60	

Four measures of risk have been used to assess the effect of choosing between equity financing and debt financing. Each measure has covered different aspects of risk, and the results for Stanton have all pointed in the same direction. If debt financing is used, the financial structure ratios will be above the industry standards, the deficiency in the fixed charge coverage ratio will be further aggravated, and the cash flow coverage will move toward the industry standard (and by a broader measure may even fall below it). The existing 1.6 beta level is relatively high. The use of debt financing will push the beta level to 2, which is high for an industrial firm. The use of equity financing will move the beta level toward the average beta level of the market, which is 1. Clearly, therefore, from the standpoint of the four different measures of risk, equity financing is the more favorable.

The next consideration is the relative costs of the different forms of financing. Relative costs are measured by the effects of each form of financing on the market value per share of common stock and by the effects on the firm's cost of capital. To apply these two criteria it is first necessary to calculate the amount of interest expense (in Table 19.10) for use in the income statements (Table 19.11).

Table 19.11

Stanton's Income Statements (Millions of Dollars)

	No Expansion	Expansion with Debt	Expansion with Equity
Net operating income	$316	$360	$360
Interest expense	60	90	60
Net income before taxes	$256	$270	$300
Income taxes (at 50%)	128	135	150
Net income	$128	$135	$150

The total amount of interest expense without expansion is $60 million. Interest expense will remain unchanged if the expansion is financed by equity funds. If the expansion is financed by long-term debt, the facts of the problem state that the cost of debt will rise to 12 percent. The opportunity cost of all debt funds is therefore 12 percent, and an argument can be made that all forms of debt should bear the higher 12 percent rate. However, the actual rate paid on the long-term debt will remain at 10 percent, while the short-term notes payable must be renewed periodically at the higher 12 percent rate (as shown in Table 19.10). If the expansion is financed by debt, the total interest expense will be $90 million. The total interest expense amounts needed for the income statements in Table 19.11 are now available. With the information developed in the income statements, the market value of equity can be calculated (see Table 19.12).

The net income under each alternative is capitalized by the applicable cost of equity to obtain the total market value of equity. The price per share can also be determined. The total number of shares of common stock outstanding remains unchanged with no expansion or with expansion financed by debt. The facts of the case stated that if equity were sold, the price would be $9 per share; the $200 of new financing divided by the $9 equals 22.2 million shares. Thus the total number of shares is 122.2 million (the original 100 million plus the additional 22.2 million). The indicated new price per share of common stock is obtained by dividing the total value of equity by the total number of shares of common stock outstanding. The resulting new price per share declines with expansion by debt financing and increases with expansion by equity financing—which means that equity financing is more favorable than debt financing. If debt financing were used, the criterion of maximizing share price would recommend that the expansion program not be adopted.

This result can be checked further by calculating the total market value of the firm (see Table 19.13). The total market value is obtained by adding the amount of debt to the market value of equity. It is increased by expansion with either debt or equity. However, as shown in Table 19.12, the market price per share of common stock is decreased by expansion with debt.

Table 19.12

Stanton's Market Value of Equity (Millions of Dollars)

	No Expansion	Expansion with Debt	Expansion with Equity
Net income (NI)	$128	$135	$150
Cost of equity (k_s)	0.14	0.16	0.12
Value of equity (S)	$914	$844	$1,250
Number of shares	100	100	122.2
Price per share	$9.14	$8.44	$10.23

Table 19.13

Stanton's Market Value (Millions of Dollars)

	No Expansion	Expansion with Debt	Expansion with Equity
Market value of equity	\$ 914	\$ 844	\$1,250
Amount of debt	600	800	600
Value of the firm	\$1,514	\$1,644	\$1,850

The main reason for calculating the total market value of the firm is to determine the firm's capital structure proportions for use in the cost of capital calculations. The leverage ratios are calculated in Table 19.14.

Table 19.14

Calculation of Stanton's Leverage Ratios

	No Expansion	Expansion with Debt	Expansion with Equity
Total debt	\$ 600	\$ 800	\$ 600
Market value of the firm	\$1,514	\$1,644	\$1,850
Debt to value ratio	0.40	0.49	0.32

The leverage ratio is increased if debt is employed but decreased if equity financing is employed. Using the capital structure proportions from Table 19.14, the weighted average cost of capital can be calculated:

	$k_b(1-T)(B/V) + k_s(S/V) = k$
No expansion	$0.10(0.5)(0.40) + 0.14(0.60) = 0.020 + 0.084 = 10.4\%$
Expansion with debt	$0.12(0.5)(0.49) + 0.16(0.51) = 0.029 + 0.082 = 11.1\%$
Expansion with equity	$0.10(0.5)(0.32) + 0.12(0.68) = 0.016 + 0.082 = 9.8\%$

Expansion with debt will raise Stanton's cost of capital from 10.4 percent to 11.1 percent. Expansion with equity will lower the company's cost of capital from 10.4 percent to 9.8 percent. These results are consistent with the findings for the market value per share of common stock, where debt financing caused a decrease and equity financing an increase. Thus the cost of capital and market price per share of common stock criteria provide consistent findings. For example, we could also obtain the value of the firm using

$$V_L = \frac{X(1-T)}{k_u} + TB.$$

For the no expansion case, we have

$$\begin{aligned} k &= k_b(1-T)(L) + k_s(1-L), \text{ where } L = B/V. \\ &= 0.10(0.5)(0.4) + 0.14(0.6) \\ &= 0.02 + 0.084 = 0.104. \end{aligned}$$

Since $k = k_u(1 - TL)$,

$$0.104 = k_u(1 - 0.2),$$

and

$$k_u = 0.13.$$

Hence,

$$V_L = \frac{\$316(0.5)}{0.13} + 0.5(600)$$

$$= \$1{,}515.$$

The final item on the checklist of factors for evaluating alternative forms of financing is "effects on control." The problem states that the common stock is already widely held so that there is no control problem to militate against the use of equity financing.

The investment bankers summarize the evidence with respect to the two forms of financing as follows. Risks are already high and will be further increased if debt financing is used. As a result of this substantial increase in risk, the costs of both debt and equity funds will rise. With equity financing, the value per share of common stock is increased and the cost of capital reduced. There is no control issue. On the basis of all the factors considered, the common stock financing is recommended.

The Stanton case illustrates the application of a checklist of key factors to evaluate alternative forms of financing. Four measures of risk and several measures of costs to the firm (returns to investors) are employed. Relative costs of financing can be evaluated by reference to effects on market value per share of common stock, on the cost of capital, and on control of the firm. Thus the analysis is essentially a risk-return evaluation and reflects a basic theme that runs through all of the chapters of this book.

Summary

The explanations of common stock financing and of the advantages and disadvantages of external equity financing compared with the use of preferred stock and debt provide a basis for making sound decisions when common stock financing is being considered by a firm.

Rights offerings can be used effectively by financial managers. If the new financing associated with the rights represents a sound decision—one likely to result in improved earnings for the firm—a rise in stock values will probably result. The use of rights will permit shareholders to preserve their positions or improve them. However, if investors feel that the new financing is not well advised, the rights offering may cause the price of the stock to decline by more than the value of the rights. Because rights offerings are directed to existing shareholders, their use can reduce the costs of floating the new issue.

A major decision for financial managers in a rights offering is where to set the subscription price, or the amount of the concession from the existing market price of the stock. Formulas reflecting the static effects of a rights offering indicate that neither the company nor the stockholders gain or lose from the price changes. The rights offering has the effect of a stock split; that is, the level set for the subscription price reflects to a great degree the objectives and effects of a stock split.

The subsequent price behavior of the rights and the common stock in the associated new offering reflects the earnings and dividends prospects of the company as well as underlying developments in the securities markets. The new financing associated with the rights offering can be an indicator of prospective growth in the company's sales and earnings. The stock-split effects of the rights offering can be used to alter the company's dividend payments. The effects of these developments on the market behavior of the rights and the securities before, during, and after the rights trading period reflect the expectations of investors toward the outlook for the earnings of the firm.

A framework for decisions on choosing among various forms of financing is applied to the evaluation of common stock financing and can also be applied to the other forms of financing discussed in subsequent chapters.

Questions

19.1 By what percentage could total assets shrink in value on liquidation before creditors incur losses in each of the following cases?
   a. Equity to total assets ratio of 50 percent
   b. Debt to equity ratio of 50 percent
   c. Debt to total assets ratio of 40 percent

19.2 How many shares must a minority group own in order to assure election of two directors if nine new directors will be elected and 200,000 shares are outstanding? Assume cumulative voting exists.

19.3 Should the preemptive right entitle stockholders to purchase convertible bonds before they are offered to outsiders?

19.4 What are the reasons for not letting officers and directors of a corporation make short sales in their company's stock?

19.5 It is frequently stated that the primary purpose of the preemptive right is to allow individuals to maintain their proportionate share of the ownership and control of a corporation.
   a. Just how important do you suppose this consideration is for the average stockholder of a firm whose shares are traded on the New York or the American stock exchange?
   b. Is the preemptive right likely to be of more importance to stockholders of closely held firms? Explain.

19.6 How would the success of a rights offering be affected by a declining stock market?

19.7 What are some of the advantages and disadvantages of setting the subscription price on a rights offering substantially below the current market price of the stock?

19.8 a. Is a firm likely to get wider distribution of shares if it sells new stock through a rights offering or directly to underwriters?

b. Why would a company be interested in getting a wider distribution of shares?

19.9 Explain why a share of no-growth common stock is similar to a share of preferred stock.

19.10 Explain the importance in common stock valuation of:

a. Current dividends
b. Current market price
c. Expected future growth rate
d. Market capitalization rate

Problems

19.1 The common stock of Arlington Development Company is selling for $32 a share on the market. Stockholders are offered one new share at a subscription price of $20 for every three shares held. What is the value of each right?

19.2 United Appliance Company common stock is priced at $40 a share on the market. Notice is given that stockholders can purchase one new share at a price of $27.50 for every four shares held.

a. At approximately what market price will each right sell?
b. Why will this be the approximate price?
c. What effect will the issuance of rights have on the original market price?

19.3 Eileen Johnson has 600 shares of Fisher Industries. The market price per share is $81. The company now offers stockholders one new share at a price of $45 for every five shares held.

a. Determine the value of each right.
b. Assume (1) that Johnson uses 160 rights and sells the other 440, and (2) that she sells 600 rights at the market price you have calculated. Prepare a statement showing the changes in her position under each of the two assumptions.

19.4 As a shareholder of Younger Corporation, you are notified that for each seven shares you own, you have the right to purchase one additional share at a price of $15. The current market price of Younger Stock is $63 per share.

a. Determine the value of each right.
b. At the time of the offering your total assets consist of 490 shares of Younger stock and $1,500 in cash. Prepare a statement to show total assets before the offering and total assets after the offering if you exercise all the rights.
c. Prepare a statement to show total assets after the offering if you sell all the rights.

19.5 The Northridge Company has the following balance sheet and income statement:

The Northridge Company Balance Sheet before Rights Offering

		Total debt (6%)	$ 7,000,000
		Common stock (100,000 shares)	3,000,000
		Retained earnings	4,000,000
Total assets	$14,000,000	Total liabilities and capital	$14,000,000

The Northridge Company Income Statement

Earning rate: 10.5% on total assets	
Earnings before interest and taxes	$1,470,000
Interest on debt	420,000
Income before taxes	$1,050,000
Taxes (40% rate)	420,000
Earnings after taxes	$ 630,000
Earnings per share	$6.30
Dividends per share (56% of earnings)	$3.53
Price-earnings ratio	15 times
Market price per share	$94.50

The company plans to raise an additional $5 million through a rights offering; the additional funds will continue to earn 10.5 percent. The price-earnings ratio is assumed to remain at 15 times, the dividend payout will continue to be 56 percent, and the 40 percent tax rate will remain in effect. (Do not attempt to use the formula given in the chapter. Additional information is given here that violates the "other things constant" assumption inherent in the formula.)

a. Assuming subscription prices of $25, $50, and $80 a share:
   1. How many additional shares of stock will have to be sold?
   2. How many rights will be required to purchase one new share?
   3. What will be the new earnings per share?
   4. What will be the new market price per share?
   5. What will be the new dividend per share if the dividend payout ratio is maintained?

b. Suppose you held 100 shares of Northridge before the rights offering. After you exercise your rights, what is the net value of your position?

19.6 As one of the minority shareholders of the Belmont Corporation, you are dissatisfied with the current operations of the company. You feel that if you could gain membership on the company's board of directors, you could persuade the company to make improvements. The problem is that current management controls 75 percent of the stock, you control only 7 percent, and the balance is held by other minority shareholders. There is a total of 500,000 voting shares. Ten directors will be elected at the next annual stockholder meeting.

a. If voting is noncumulative, can you elect yourself director?
b. Suppose you are able to persuade all the minority shareholders that you should be elected. If voting is noncumulative, can they elect you?
c. If voting is cumulative, can you elect yourself director?
d. What percent of the minority shares other than your own will you need to have voted for you to be certain of election?
e. What is the number of directors the minority shareholders can elect with certainty?

19.7 The Frost Crop Food Company is engaged principally in the business of growing, processing, and marketing a variety of frozen vegetables. A major company in this field, it produces and markets high quality food at premium prices.

During each of the past several years the company's sales have increased and the needed inventories have been financed from short-term sources. The officers have discussed the idea of refinancing their bank loans with long-term debt or common stock. A common stock issue of 310,000 shares sold at this time (present market price $72 a share) will yield $21 million after expenses. The same sum can be raised by selling twelve-year bonds with an interest rate of 8 percent and a sinking fund to retire the bonds over their twelve-year life. (See financial ratios and statements below.)

a. Should Frost Crop Food refinance the short-term loans? Why?
b. If the bank loans should be refinanced, what factors should be considered in determining which form of financing to use?

Food Processing Industry Financial Ratios

Current ratio: 2.2 times
Sales to total assets: 2.0 times
Sales to inventory: 5.6 times
Average collection period: 22.0 days
Current debt/total assets: 25–30%
Long-term debt/total assets: 10–15%
Preferred/total assets: 0.5%
Net worth/total assets: 60–65%
Profits to sales: 2.3%
Net profits to total assets: 4.0%
Profits to net worth: 8.4%
Expected growth rate of earnings and dividends: 6.5%

Frost Crop Food Company Consolidated Balance Sheet as of March 31, 1980 (Millions of Dollars)[a]

Current assets	$141	Accounts payable	$12	
Fixed plant and equipment	57	Notes payable	36	
Other assets	12	Accruals	15	
		Total current liabilities		$ 63
		Long-term debt (at 5%)		63
		Preferred stock		9
		Common stock (par $6)	$12	
		Retained earnings	63	
		Stockholders' equity		75
Total assets	$210	Total claims on assets		$210

a. The majority of harvesting activities do not begin until late April or May.

Frost Crop Food Company Consolidated Income Statement for Year Ended March 31, 1980 (Millions of Dollars)

	1977	1978	1979	1980
Net sales	$225.0	$234.6	$292.8	$347.1
Cost of goods sold	146.1	156.6	195.3	230.4
Gross profit	$ 78.9	$ 78.0	$ 97.5	$116.7
Other expenses	61.8	66.0	81.0	88.5
Operating income	$ 17.1	$ 12.0	$ 16.5	$ 28.2
Other income (net)	−3.3	−4.2	−5.7	−9.3
Earnings before tax	$ 13.8	$ 7.8	$ 10.8	$ 18.9
Taxes	7.2	3.3	5.4	9.6
Net profit	$ 6.6	$ 4.5	$ 5.4	$ 9.3
Preferred dividend	0.3	0.3	0.3	0.3
Earnings available to common stock	$ 6.3	$ 4.2	$ 5.1	$ 9.0
Earnings per share	$3.15	$2.10	$2.55	$4.50
Cash dividends per share	$1.29	$1.44	$1.59	$1.80
Price range for common stock:				
High	$66.00	$69.00	$66.00	$81.00
Low	$30.00	$42.00	$51.00	$63.00

19.8 In 1976 Inland Steel was planning an expansion program. It estimated that it would need to raise an additional $200 million. Inland Steel discussed with its investment banker the alternatives of raising the $200 million by the use of debt financing or by selling additional shares of common stock. Assume that you were asked to make the recommendation to Inland Steel's board of directors, based on the additional background information that follows.

Steel Industry Standards

1. Long term debt to shareholders' equity	30 percent
2. Shareholders' equity to total assets	55 percent
3. Fixed charges coverage	7X
4. Current ratio	2.1X
5. Return on net worth	11 percent

Inland Steel Balance Sheet as of December 31, 1975 (Millions of Dollars)

Total current assets	$ 600	Notes payable, 10%	$100	
Net fixed assets	1,200	Other current liabilities	100	
		Total current liabilities		$ 200
		Long-term debt, 10%		500
		Other liabilities		300
		Total debt		$1,000
		Common stock, par value $1		100
		Paid-in capital		300
		Retained earnings		400
Total assets	$1,800	Total claims on assets		$1,800

Inland Steel Income Statement for Year Ended December 31, 1975 (Millions of Dollars)

	Current Year	With Expansion, Pro Forma
Total revenues	$2,000	$2,400
Net operating income	231	260
Interest expense	60	
Net income before taxes	171	
Income taxes at 25%	43	
Net income	$ 128	

The dividend payout had averaged about 50 percent of net income. Inland Steel's cost of debt was 10 percent at the time. The cost of equity was 14 percent. If the additional funds were raised by debt, the cost of debt would have been 12 percent, and the cost of equity would have risen to 16 percent. If the additional funds were raised by equity, the cost of debt would have remained at 10 percent and the cost of equity would have fallen to 12 percent. Equity would have been sold at $9 per share.

a. Make a financial risk analysis using financial structure ratios.
b. Complete the pro forma income statements under the two alternative forms of financing.
c. Calculate the fixed charge coverage ratio.
d. Calculate the market value of equity and the indicated market price per share before and after financing by the two alternative methods.
e. Calculate the value of the firm and the *B/S, B/V,* and *S/V* percentages.
f. Calculate the weighted cost of capital at present and under the two financing alternatives.
g. Make a recommendation for a decision between the two alternative methods of financing.

Selected References

Bacon, Peter W. "The Subscription Price in Rights Offerings." *Financial Management* 1 (Summer 1972), pp. 59–64.

Bear, Robert M., and Curley, Anthony J. "Unseasoned Equity Financing." *Journal of Financial and Quantitative Analysis* 10 (June 1975), pp. 311–325.

Donaldson, Gordon. "Financial Goals: Management vs. Stockholders." *Harvard Business Review* 41 (May–June 1963), pp. 116–129.

Duvall, Richard M., and Austin, Douglas V. "Predicting the Results of Proxy Contests." *Journal of Finance* 20 (September 1965), pp. 467–471.

Fruhan, William E., Jr. "Lessons from Levitz: Creating Share Value." *Financial Analysts Journal* 36 (March–April 1980), pp. 25–32, 34–40, 42–45.

Ibbotson, R. R. "Price Performance of Common Stock New Issues." *Journal of Financial Economics* 2 (September 1975), pp. 235–272.

Keane, Simon M. "The Significance of the Issue Price in Rights Issues." *Journal of Business Finance* 4, (1972), pp. 40–45.

Lee, Steven James. "Going Private." *Financial Executive* 42 (December 1974), pp. 10–15.

Logue, Dennis E. "On the Pricing of Unseasoned Equity Issues: 1965–1969." *Journal of Financial and Quantitative Analysis* 8 (January 1973), pp. 91–104.

McDonald, J. G., and Fisher, A. K. "New Issue Stock Price Behavior." *Journal of Finance* 27 (March 1972), pp. 97–102.

Nelson, J. Russell. "Price Effects in Rights Offerings." *Journal of Finance* 20 (December 1965), pp. 647–650.

Smith, Clifford W., Jr. "Alternative Methods for Raising Capital: Rights versus Underwritten Offerings." *Journal of Financial Economics* 5 (December 1977), pp. 273–307.

Stevenson, Harold W. *Common Stock Financing.* Ann Arbor, Mich.: University of Michigan, 1957.

Stoll, Hans R., and Curley, Anthony J. "Small Business and the New Issues Market for Equities." *Journal of Financial and Quantitative Analysis* 5 (September 1970), pp. 309–322.

Thompson, Howard E. "A Note on the Value of Rights in Estimating the Investor Capitalization Rate." *Journal of Finance* 28 (March 1973), pp. 157–160.

Van Horne, James C. "New Listings and their Price Behavior." *Journal of Finance* 25 (September 1970), pp. 783–794.

Young, Alan, and Marshall, Wayne. "Controlling Shareholder Servicing Cost." *Harvard Business Review* 49 (January–February 1971), pp. 71–78.

20
Debt and Preferred Stock

There are many classes of fixed income securities: long-term and short-term, secured and unsecured, marketable and nonmarketable, participating and nonparticipating, senior and junior, and so on. Financial managers, with the counsel of investment bankers and other financial advisers, seek to package securities with characteristics that will make them attractive to the widest range of different types of investors. By relating the design of securities effectively to the tastes and needs of potential investors, financial managers can hold the firm's costs of financing to the lowest possible levels. This chapter deals with the two most important types of long-term, fixed-income securities —bonds and preferred stocks.

Instruments of Long-Term Debt Financing

An understanding of long-term forms of financing requires some familiarity with technical terminology. The discussion of long-term debt therefore begins with an explanation of several important instruments and terms.

Bond

Most people have had some experience with short-term promissory notes. A *bond* is simply a long-term promissory note.

Mortgage

A *mortgage* represents a pledge of designated property for a loan. Under a *mortgage bond,* a corporation pledges certain real assets as security for the bond. A mortgage bond is therefore secured by real property.[1] The pledge is a condition of the loan.

Debenture

A *debenture* is a long-term bond that is *not* secured by a pledge of any specific property. However, like other general creditor claims, it is secured by any property not otherwise pledged.

1. There is also the *chattel mortgage,* which is secured by personal property; but this is generally an intermediate-term instrument. *Real property* is defined as real estate—land and buildings. *Personal property* is defined as any other kind of property, including equipment, inventories, and furniture.

Indenture

The long-term relationship between the borrower and the lender of a long-term promissory note is established in a document called an *indenture.* In the case of an ordinary sixty- or ninety-day promissory note, few developments are likely to occur in the life or affairs of the borrower that will endanger repayment. The lender looks closely at the borrower's current position, because current assets are the main source of repayment. A bond, however, is a long-term contractual relationship between the bond issuer and the bondholder; over this extended period the bondholder has cause to worry that the issuing firm's position may change materially.

In the ordinary common stock or preferred stock certificate or agreement, the details of the contractual relationship can be summarized in a few paragraphs. The bond indenture, however, can be a document of several hundred pages that discusses a large number of factors important to the contracting parties, such as: (1) the form of the bond and the instrument; (2) a complete description of property pledged; (3) the authorized amount of the bond issue; (4) detailed protective clauses, or *covenants,* which usually include limits on indebtedness, restrictions on dividends, and a sinking fund provision; (5) a minimum current ratio requirement; and (6) provisions for redemption or call privileges.

Trustee

Bonds are not only of long duration but also, usually, of substantial size. Before the rise of large aggregations of savings through insurance companies or pension funds, no single buyer was able to buy an issue of such size. Bonds were therefore issued in denominations of $1,000 each and were sold to a large number of purchasers. To facilitate communication between the issuer and the numerous bondholders, a trustee was appointed to represent the bondholders. The trustee is still presumed to act at all times for the protection of the bondholders and on their behalf.

Any legal person, including a corporation, is considered competent to act as a trustee. Typically, however, the duties of the trustee are handled by a department of a commercial bank.

Trustees have three main responsibilities:

1. They certify the issue of bonds. This duty involves making certain that all the legal requirements for drawing up the bond contract and the indenture have been carried out.
2. They police the behavior of the corporation in its performance of the responsibilities set forth in the indenture provisions.
3. They are responsible for taking appropriate action on behalf of the bondholders if the corporation defaults on payment of interest or principal.

It is said that in many corporate bond defaults in the early 1930s, trustees did not act in the best interests of the bondholders. They did not conserve the assets of the corporation effectively, and often they did not take early action, thereby allowing corporation executives to continue their salaries and to dispose of assets under conditions favorable to themselves but detrimental to the bondholders. In some cases, assets pledged as security for the bonds were sold, and specific security was thus no longer available. The result in many instances was that holders of mortgage bonds found themselves more in the position of general creditors than of secured bondholders.

As a consequence of such practices, Congress passed the Trust Indenture Act of 1939 in order to give more protection to bondholders. The act provides (1) that trustees must be given sufficient power to act on behalf of bondholders; (2) that the indenture must fully disclose rights and responsibilities and must not be deceptive; (3) that bondholders can make changes in the indenture; (4) that prompt, protective action be taken by the trustees for bondholders if default occurs; (5) that an arm's-length relationship exist between the issuing corporation and the trustee; and (6) that the corporation must make periodic reports to its trustee to enable that person to carry out the protective responsibilities.

Call Provision

A *call provision* gives the issuing corporation the right to call in the bond for redemption. The provision generally states that the company must pay an amount greater than the par value of the bond; this additional sum is defined as the *call premium.* The call premium is typically equal to one year's interest if the bond is called during the first year, and it declines at a constant rate each year thereafter. For example, the call premium on a $1,000 par value, twenty-year, 6 percent bond is generally $60 if called during the first year, $57 if called during the second year (calculated by reducing the $60, or 6 percent, premium by one-twentieth), and so on.

The call privilege is valuable to the firm but potentially detrimental to the investor, especially if the bond is issued in a period when interest rates are thought to be cyclically high. The problem for investors is that the call privilege enables the issuing corporation to substitute bonds paying lower interest rates for bonds paying higher ones. Consider a simple example of consols (bonds with no maturity). Suppose consols are sold to yield 10 percent when interest rates are high. If interest rates drop so that the consols yield 8 percent, the value of the bond theoretically could rise to $1,250. Suppose the issuing firm can call the bond by paying a $100 premium. The investor receives $1,100 for a bond whose market value will otherwise be $1,250. The callability of the bond will probably prevent its rising to the full $1,250 in the marketplace.

This disadvantage of the call privilege to the investor is supported by empirical data. Studies indicate that when interest rate levels are high, new issues of callable bonds must bear yields from one-quarter to one-half of 1 percent higher than the yields of noncallable bonds. If callability is deferred for five years (that is, if the issuer cannot exercise the call privilege until the bond has been outstanding for at least five years), in periods of relatively high interest rates, the yields for long-term bonds with five years of call deferment are about 0.13 percent lower than the yields for similar bonds that can be called immediately. During periods of relatively low interest rates, the discount for five years of deferment drops to about 0.04 percent from yields on fully callable bonds.[2] (The procedures for calculating when it is advantageous for the corporation to call or refund a bond or preferred stock issue are presented later in the chapter.)

Sinking Fund

A *sinking fund* is a provision that facilitates the orderly retirement of a bond issue (or, in some cases, preferred stock issue). Typically, it requires the firm to buy and retire a portion of the bond issue each year. Sometimes the stipulated sinking fund payment is tied to the current year's sales or earnings, but usually it is a mandatory fixed amount. If it is mandatory, a failure to meet the payment causes the bond issue to be thrown into default and can lead the company into bankruptcy. Obviously, then, a sinking fund can constitute a dangerous cash drain on the firm.

In most cases the firm (the bond trustee) is given the right to handle the sinking fund in either of two ways:

1. It can call a certain percentage of the bonds at a stipulated price each year (for example, 2 percent of the original amount at a price of $1,050). The serial numbers of the actual bonds to be called are determined by a lottery.
2. To retire the required face amount of the bonds, it can buy the bonds on the open market.

The firm will do whichever results in the required reduction of outstanding bonds for the smallest outlay. Therefore, if interest rates have risen (and the price of the bonds has fallen), the firm will choose the open market alternative. If interest rates have fallen (and bond prices have risen), it will elect the option of calling bonds.

The call provision of the sinking fund at times works to the detriment of bondholders. If, for example, the bond carries a 7 percent interest rate, and if yields on similar securities are 4 percent, the bond will sell for well above par. A sinking fund call at par thus greatly disadvantages some bondholders.

On balance, securities that provide for a sinking fund and continuing redemption are likely to be offered initially on a lower yield basis than are securities without such a fund. Since sinking funds provide additional protection to investors, sinking fund bonds are likely to sell initially at higher prices; hence, they have a lower cost of capital to the issuer.

Funded Debt

Funded debt is simply long-term debt. A firm planning to "fund" its floating debt will replace short-term securities by long-term securities. *Funding* does not imply placing money with a trustee or other repository; part of the jargon of finance, it simply means long-term.[3]

2. See F. C. Jen and J. E. Wert, "The Effects of Call Risk on Corporate Bond Yields," *Journal of Finance* 22 (December 1967), pp. 637–651; and G. Pye, "The Value of Call Deferment on a Bond: Some Empirical Results," *Journal of Finance* 22 (December 1967), pp. 623–636.

3. Tampa Electric Company provides a good example of funding. This company has a continuous construction program. Typically, it uses short-term debt to finance construction expenditures. However, once short-term debt has built up to about $75 million, the company sells a stock or bond issue, uses the proceeds to pay off its bank loans, and starts the cycle again. The high flotation costs of small security issues make this process desirable.

Secured Bonds

Secured long-term debt can be classified according to (1) the priority of claims, (2) the right to issue additional securities, and (3) the scope of the lien.

Priority of Claims

A senior mortgage has prior claims on assets and earnings. Senior railroad mortgages, for example, have been called the "mortgages next to the rail," implying that they have the first claim on the land and assets of the railroad corporations. A junior mortgage is a subordinate lien, such as a second or third mortgage. It is a lien or claim junior to others.

Right to Issue Additional Securities

Mortgage bonds can also be classified with respect to the right to issue additional obligations pledging already encumbered property.

In the case of a *closed-end mortgage,* a company cannot sell additional bonds (beyond those already issued) secured by the property specified in the mortgage. For example, assume that a corporation with plant and land worth $5 million has a $2 million mortgage on these properties. If the mortgage is closed-end, no more bonds having first liens on this property can be issued. Thus a closed-end mortgage provides security to the bond buyer. The ratio of the amount of the senior bonds to the value of the property is not increased by subsequent issues.

If the bond indenture is silent on this point, it is called an *open-end mortgage.* Its nature can be illustrated by referring to the example cited above. Against property worth $5 million, bonds of $2 million are sold. If an additional first mortgage bond of $1 million is subsequently sold, the property has been pledged for a total of $3 million of bonds. If, on liquidation, the property sells for $2 million, the original bondholders will receive 67 cents on the dollar. If the mortgage had been closed-end, they would have been fully paid.

Most characteristic is the *limited open-end mortgage.* Its nature can be indicated by continuing the example. A first mortgage bond issue of $2 million, secured by the property worth $5 million, is sold. The indenture provides that an additional $1 million worth of bonds—or an additional amount of bonds to bring the total to 60 percent of the original cost of the property—can be sold. Thus the mortgage is open only to a certain point.

Scope of the Lien

Bonds can also be classified with respect to the scope of their lien. A lien is granted on certain specified property. When a *specific lien* exists, the security for a first or second mortgage is a specifically designated property. On the other hand, a *blanket mortgage* pledges all real property currently owned by the company. Real property includes only land and those things affixed thereto; thus a blanket mortgage is not a mortgage on cash, accounts receivables, or inventories, which are items of personal property. A blanket mortgage gives more protection to the bondholder than does a specific mortgage because it provides a claim on all real property owned by the company.

Unsecured Bonds

Debentures

The reasons for a firm's use of unsecured debt are diverse. Paradoxically, the extremes of financial strength and weakness may give rise to its use. Also, tax considerations and great uncertainty about the level of the firm's future earnings have given rise to special forms of unsecured financing. A *debenture* is an unsecured bond and, as such, provides no lien on specific property as security for the obligation. Debenture holders are therefore general creditors whose claim is protected by property not otherwise pledged. The advantage of debentures from the issuer's standpoint is that the property is left unencumbered for subsequent financing. However, in practice, the use of debentures depends on the nature of the firm's assets and its general credit strength.

A firm whose credit position is exceptionally strong can issue debentures; it simply does not need specific security. However, the credit position of a company may be so weak that it has no alternative to the use of debentures; all its property may already be encumbered. The debt portion of American Telephone & Telegraph's vast financing program since the end of World War II has been mainly through debentures. AT&T is such a strong institution that it does not have to provide security for its debt issues.

Debentures are also issued by companies in industries where it is not practical to provide a lien through a mortgage on fixed assets. Examples of such companies are large mail order houses and finance companies, which characteristically do not have large fixed assets in relation to their total assets. The bulk of their assets is in the form of inventory or receivables, neither of which is satisfactory security for a mortgage lien.

Subordinated Debentures

The term *subordinate* means below or inferior. Thus *subordinated debt* has claims on assets after unsubordinated debt in the event of liquidation. Debentures can be subordinated to designated notes payable—usually bank loans—or to any or all other debt. In the event of liquidation or reorganization, the debentures cannot be paid until senior debt *as named in the indenture* has been paid. Senior debt typically does not include trade accounts payable. How the subordination provision strengthens the position of senior debt holders is shown in Table 20.1.

In Table 20.1, where $200 is available for distribution, the subordinated debt has a claim on 25 percent of $200, or $50. However, this claim is subordinated only to the bank debt (the only senior debt) and is added to the $100 claim of the bank. As a consequence, 75 percent of the bank's original claim is satisfied.

Where $300 is available for distribution, the $75 allocated to the subordinated debt is divided into two parts; $50 goes to the bank, and the other $25 remains for the subordinated debt holders. In this situation, the senior bank debt holders are fully paid off, 75 percent of other debt is paid, and only 25 percent of subordinated debt is paid.

Subordination is frequently required. Alert credit managers of firms supplying trade credit or commercial bank loan officers typically insist on subor-

Table 20.1

Illustration of Bankruptcy Payments to Senior Debt, Other Debt, and Subordinated Debt

Financial Structure	Book Value (1)	Percent of Total Debt (2)	Initial Allocation (3)	Actual Payment (4)	Percent of Original Claim Satisfied (5)
$200 available for claims on liquidation					
Bank debt	$200	50%	$100	$150	75%
Other debt	100	25	50	50	50
Subordinated debt	100	25	50	0	0
Total debt	$400	100%	$200	$200	50%
Net worth	300				0
Total	$700				29%
$300 available for claims on liquidation					
Bank debt	$200	50%	$150	$200	100%
Other debt	100	25	75	75	75
Subordinated debt	100	25	75	25	25
Total debt	$400	100%	$300	$300	75%
Net worth	300				0
Total	$700				43%

Steps:

1. Express each type of debt as a percentage of total debt (Column 2).
2. Multiply the debt percentages (Column 2) by the amount available to obtain the initial allocations (Column 3).
3. The subordinated debt is subordinate to bank debt. Therefore, the initial allocation to subordinate debt is added to the bank debt allocation until it has been exhausted or until the bank debt is finally paid off (Column 4).

dination, particularly where debt is owed to the principal stockholders or officers of a company. Often, subordinated debentures are also convertible into the common stock of the issuing company.

In comparison to subordinated debt, preferred stock suffers from the disadvantage that its dividends are not deductible as an expense for tax purposes. Subordinated debentures have been referred to as being like a special kind of preferred stock, the dividends of which *are* deductible as an expense for tax purposes. Subordinated debt has therefore become an increasingly important source of corporate capital.

The reasons for the use of subordinated debentures are clear. They offer a great tax advantage over preferred stock; yet they do not restrict the borrower's ability to obtain senior debt, as would be the case if all debt sources were on an equal basis.

The use of subordinated debentures is further stimulated by periods of tight money, when commercial banks tend to require a greater equity base for short-term financing. These debentures provide a greater equity cushion for loans from commercial banks or other forms of senior debt. Their use also illustrates the development of hybrid securities that emerge to meet the changing situations that develop in the capital market.

Income Bonds

Income bonds provide that interest must be paid only if the earnings of the firm are sufficient to meet the interest obligations. The principal, however, must be paid when due. Thus the interest itself is not a fixed charge. Income bonds historically have been issued because a firm has been in financial difficulties and its history suggests that it may be unable to meet a substantial level of fixed charges in the future. More generally, however, income bonds simply provide flexibility to the firm in the event that earnings do not cover the amount of interest that would otherwise have to be paid. Income bonds are like preferred stock in that the firm will not be in default if current payments on the obligations are not made. They have an additional advantage over preferred stock in that the interest is a deductible expense for corporate income tax computations, while the dividends on preferred stock are not.

The main characteristic and distinct advantage of the income bond is that interest is payable only if the company achieves earnings. Since earnings calculations are subject to differing interpretations, the indenture of the income bond carefully defines income and expenses. If it did not, litigation might result. Some income bonds are cumulative indefinitely (if interest is not paid, it accumulates, and it must be paid at some future date); others are cumulative for the first three to five years, after which they become noncumulative.

Income bonds usually contain sinking fund provisions to provide for their retirement. The annual payments to the sinking funds range between ½ and 1 percent of the face amount of the original issue. Because the sinking fund payment requirements are typically contingent on earnings, a fixed cash drain on the company is avoided. Typically, income bondholders do not have voting rights when the bonds are issued. Sometimes bondholders are given the right to elect some specified number of directors if interest is not paid for a certain number of years.

Sometimes income bonds are convertible; there are sound reasons for convertibility if the bonds arise out of a reorganization. Creditors who receive income bonds in exchange for defaulted obligations have a less desirable position than they had previously. Since they have received something based on an adverse and problematical forecast of the company's future, it is appropriate that if the company does prosper, income bondholders are entitled to participate. When income bonds are issued in situations other than reorganization, the convertibility feature is likely to make the issue more attractive to prospective bond buyers.

Bond Values and Their Fluctuations

In Chapter 16, we presented materials on the cost of capital for both long-term debt and short-term debt. In analyzing the characteristics of bonds, we here treat bond values and their fluctuations. This is one aspect of the risk of bond investments and therefore affects the ability of the issuing firm to sell bonds to potential buyers. The cost of debt is, of course, implicit in the bond valuation formulas.

Bond values are relatively easy to determine. The expected cash flows are the annual interest payments plus the principal due when the bond matures. Depending on differences in the risk of default on interest or principal, the appropriate capitalization (or discount) rate applied to different bonds varies. A U.S. Treasury security, for example, has less risk than a security issued by a corporation; consequently, a lower discount (or capitalization) rate is applied to its interest payments. The actual calculating procedures employed in bond valuation are illustrated by the following examples.

Perpetual Bond

After the Napoleonic Wars (1814), England sold a huge bond issue, which it used to pay off many smaller issues that had been floated in prior years to pay for the war. Since the purpose of the new issue was to consolidate past debts, the individual bonds were called consols. Suppose the bonds paid $50 interest annually to perpetuity. (Actually, interest was stated in British pounds.) What would the bonds be worth under current market conditions?

First, note that the value v_b of any perpetuity is computed as follows:[4]

$$\begin{aligned} v_b &= \frac{c}{(1+k_b)^1} + \frac{c}{(1+k_b)^2} + \cdots \\ &= \frac{c}{k_b}. \end{aligned} \tag{20.1}$$

Here c is the constant annual interest in dollars and k_b the appropriate interest rate (or required rate of return) for the bond issue. In this chapter, we use k_b, k_{ps}, and k_s to designate the required rates of return on debt, preferred stock, and common stock, respectively. Equation 20.1 is an infinite series of

4. A perpetuity is a bond that never matures, that pays interest indefinitely. Equation 20.1 is simply the present value of an infinite series; its proof is demonstrated below. Rewrite Equation 20.1 as follows:

$$v_b = c\left[\frac{1}{(1+k_b)^1} + \frac{1}{(1+k_b)^2} + \cdots + \frac{1}{(1+k_b)^N}\right]. \tag{1}$$

Multiply both sides of Equation 1 by $(1 + k_b)$:

$$v_b(1+k_b) = c\left[1 + \frac{1}{(1+k_b)^1} + \frac{1}{(1+k_b)^2} + \cdots + \frac{1}{(1+k_b)^{N-1}}\right]. \tag{2}$$

Subtract Equation 1 from Equation 2, obtaining:

$$v_b(1+k_b-1) = c\left[1 - \frac{1}{(1+k_b)^N}\right]. \tag{3}$$

As $N \rightarrow \infty$, $\frac{1}{(1+k_b)^N} \rightarrow 0$, so Equation 3 approaches

$$v_b k_b = c.$$

and

$$v_b = \frac{c}{k_b}. \tag{20.1}$$

$\$c$ a year, and the value of the bond is the discounted sum of the infinite series.

We know that the consol's annual interest payment is \$50; therefore, the only other thing we need in order to find its value is the appropriate interest rate. This is commonly taken as the going interest rate, or yield, on bonds of similar risk. Suppose we find such bonds to be paying 4 percent under current market conditions. Then the consol's value is determined as follows:

$$v_b = \frac{c}{k_b} = \frac{\$50}{0.04} = \$1{,}250.$$

If the going rate of interest rises to 5 percent, the value of the bond falls to \$1,000(\$50/0.05). If interest rates continue rising, when the rate goes as high as 6 percent, the value of the consol will be only \$833.33. Values of this perpetual bond for a range of interest rates are given in the following table:

Current Market Interest Rate	Current Market Value
2%	\$2,500.00
3	1,666.67
4	1,250.00
5	1,000.00
6	833.33
7	714.29
8	625.00

Short-Term Bond

Suppose the British government issues bonds with the same risk of default as the consols but with a three-year maturity. The new bonds also pay \$50 interest and have a \$1,000 maturity value. What will the value of these new bonds be at the time of issue if the going rate of interest is 4 percent? To find this value, we must solve Equation 20.2:

$$v_b = \frac{c_1}{(1 + k_b)^1} + \frac{c_2}{(1 + k_b)^2} + \frac{c_3 + M}{(1 + k_b)^3}. \qquad (20.2)$$

Here M is the maturity value of the bond. The solution is given in the following tabulation.[5]

Year	Receipt	4 Percent Discount Factors	Present Value
1	\$50	0.9615	\$ 48.08
2	\$50	0.9246	46.23
3	\$50 + \$1,000	0.8890	933.45
		Bond value =	\$1,027.76

5. If the bond has a long maturity, twenty years for example, we would certainly want to calculate its present value by finding the present value of a twenty-year annuity and adding to it the present value of the \$1,000 principal received at maturity. Special bond tables have been devised to simplify the calculation procedure. Note also that k_b frequently differs for the long- and short-term bonds; as we saw in Chapter 10, unless the yield to maturity curve is flat, long- and short-term rates differ.

At the various rates of interest used in the perpetuity example, this three-year bond will have the following values:

Current Market Interest Rate	Current Market Value
2%	$1,086.50
3	1,056.54
4	1,027.76
5	1,000.00
6	973.25
7	947.52
8	922.66

Interest-Rate Risk

Figure 20.1 shows how the values of the long-term bond (the consol) and the short-term bond change in response to changes in the going market rate of interest. Note how much less sensitive the short-term bond is to changes in interest rates. At a 5 percent interest rate, both the perpetuity and the short-term bonds are valued at $1,000. When rates rise to 8 percent, the long-term bond falls to $625, while the short-term bond falls only to $923. A similar situation occurs when rates fall below 5 percent. *This differential responsiveness to changes in interest rates depends on the required yield levels.* At the lower yields depicted in Figure 20.1, the longer the maturity of a security, the great-

Figure 20.1

Values of Long-Term and Short-Term Bonds, 5 Percent Coupon Rate, at Different Market Interest Rates

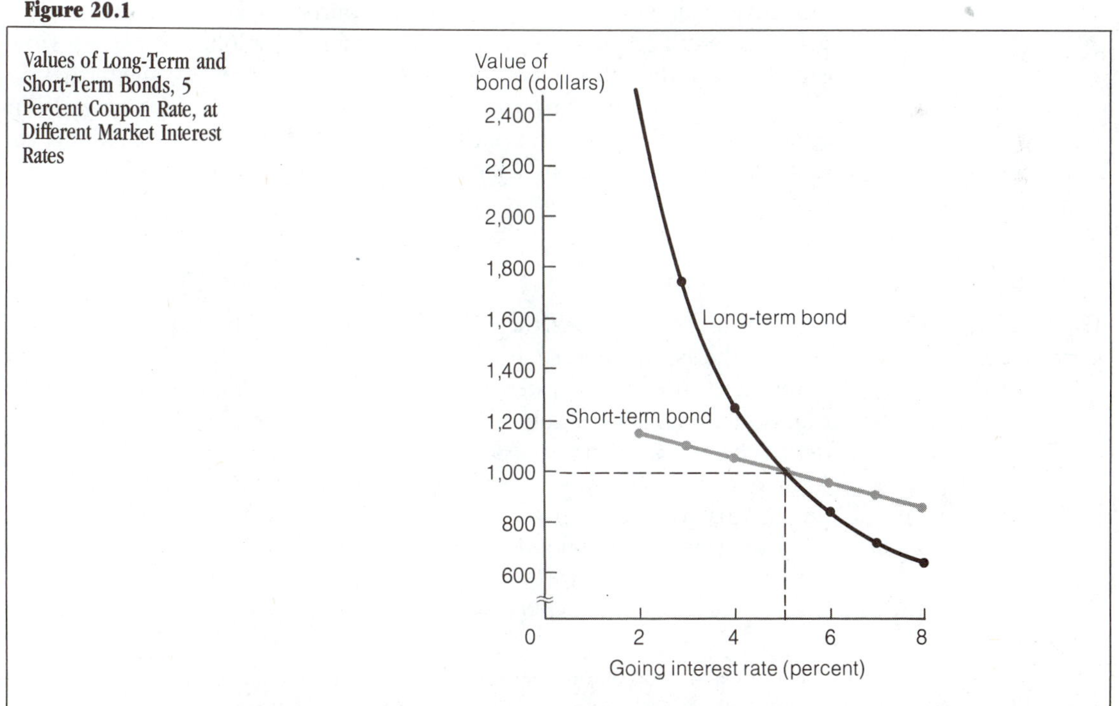

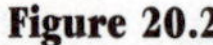

Figure 20.2

Values of 20-Year and 30-Year Bonds at Required Yields of 10 to 25 Percent

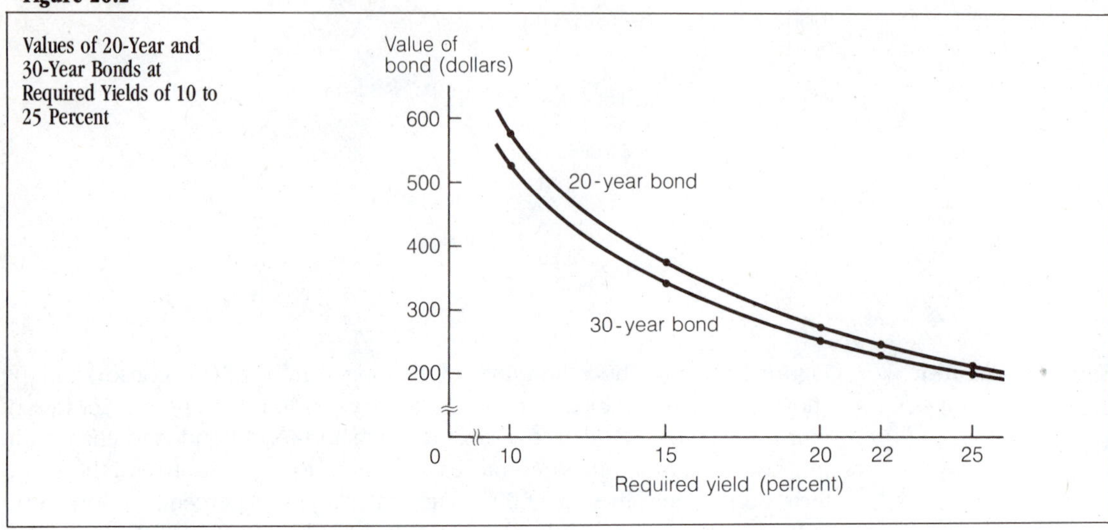

er its price change in response to a given change in interest rates. This helps explain why corporate treasurers are reluctant to hold their near-cash reserves in the form of long-term debt instruments. These reserves are held at moderate interest levels for precautionary purposes, and treasurers are unwilling to sacrifice safety for a little higher yield on a long-term bond. However, for deep discount bonds at yields of 10 percent or more, the further decline in price with higher required yields is at a lesser rate for longer term bonds than for shorter term bonds. This is depicted in Figure 20.2, where the value of the thirty-year bond falls less rapidly than the value of the twenty-year bond as required yields rise from 10 to 25 percent.[6]

The Cost of Long-Term Debt

In calculating bond values, the discount rate we use is the required rate of return on the bond, representing the cost of long-term debt. If we have the bond value—that is, what we are required to pay to purchase the bond—we can solve for the bond's yield to maturity as a measure of the cost of long-term debt. For example, suppose a perpetuity has a stated par value of $1,000 and a 5 percent coupon (that is, it pays 5 percent, or $50 annually, on this stated value) and that it is currently selling for $625. We can solve Equation 20.1 for k_b to find the yield on the bond:

$$\text{Yield on a perpetuity} = k_b = \frac{c}{v_b} = \frac{\$50}{\$625} = 8\%.$$

6. We are indebted to Professor Charles Higgins of the University of Redlands for pointing out this switchover.

If the bond sells for $1,250, the formula shows that the yield is 4 percent. For the three-year bond paying $50 interest a year, if the price of the bond is $922.66, the yield to maturity is found by solving for k_b in Equation 20.2. The solution PVIF is the one for 8 percent:[7]

$$\begin{aligned}\$922.66 &= \$50(\text{PVIF}) + \$50(\text{PVIF}) + \$1{,}050(\text{PVIF})\\ &= \$50(0.9259) + \$50(0.8573) + \$1{,}050(0.7938)\\ &= \$46.30 + \$42.87 + \$833.49 = \$922.66.\end{aligned}$$

The interest factors are taken from the 8 percent column of Table A.2 in Appendix A at the end of the book. The solution procedure is exactly like that for finding the internal rate of return in capital budgeting.

Characteristics of Long-Term Debt

From the viewpoint of long-term debt holders, debt is good in regard to risk, has limited advantages in regard to income, and is weak in regard to control. To elaborate:

1. In the area of risk, debt is favorable because it gives the holder priority both in earnings and in liquidation. Debt also has a definite maturity and is protected by the covenants of the indenture.
2. In the area of income, the bondholder has a fixed return; except in the case of income bonds, interest payments are not contingent on the company's level of earnings. However, debt does not participate in any superior earnings of the company, and gains are limited in magnitude. Bondholders actually suffer during inflationary periods. A twenty-year, 6 percent bond pays $60 of interest each year. Under inflation, the purchasing power of this $60 is eroded, causing a loss in real value to the bondholder.[8] Frequently, long-term debt is callable. If bonds are called, the investor receives funds that must be reinvested to be kept active.
3. In the area of control, the bondholder usually does not have the right to vote. However, if the bonds go into default, then bondholders in effect take control of the company.

From the viewpoint of long-term debt issuers, there are several advantages and disadvantages to bonds. The advantages are:

1. The cost of debt is definitely limited. Bondholders do not participate in superior profits (if earned).

7. We first tried the PVIF's for 6 percent, found that the equation did not work, then raised the PVIF to 8 percent, where the equation did work. This indicated that 8 percent was the yield to maturity on the bond. In practice, specialized interest tables (called *bond tables*) generated by a computer are available to facilitate determination of the yield to maturity on bonds with different stated interest rates, and on bonds selling for various discounts below or premiums above their maturity values. The results can also be obtained directly on a programmable hand calculator.
8. Recognizing this fact, investors demand higher interest rates during inflationary periods.

2. Not only is the cost limited, but typically the expected yield is lower than that of common stock.
3. The owners of the corporation do not share their control when debt financing is used.
4. The interest payment on debt is deductible as a tax expense.
5. Flexibility in the financial structure of the corporation can be achieved by inserting a call provision in the bond indenture.

The disadvantages are:

1. Debt is a fixed charge; if the earnings of the company fluctuate, it may be unable to meet the charge.
2. As seen in Chapter 15, higher risk brings higher capitalization rates on equity earnings. Thus, even though leverage is favorable and raises earnings per share, the higher capitalization rates attributable to leverage may drive the common stock value down.
3. Debt usually has a fixed maturity date, and the financial officer must make provision for repayment of the debt.
4. Since long-term debt is a commitment for a long period, it involves risk. The expectations and plans on which the debt was issued may change, and the debt may prove to be a burden. For example, if income, employment, the price level, and interest rates all fall greatly, the prior assumption of a large amount of long-term debt may have been an unwise financial policy. The railroads are always given as an example in this regard. They were able to meet their ordinary operating expenses during the 1930s but were unable to meet the heavy financial charges they had undertaken earlier, when their prospects looked more favorable than they turned out to be.
5. In a long-term contractual relationship, the indenture provisions are likely to be much more stringent than they are in a short-term credit agreement. Hence the firm may be subject to much more disturbing and crippling restrictions than if it had borrowed on a short-term basis or had issued common stock.
6. There is a limit on the extent to which funds can be raised through long-term debt. Generally accepted standards of financial policy dictate that the debt ratio shall not exceed certain limits. When debt goes beyond these limits, its cost rises rapidly.

Decisions on the Use of Long-Term Debt

When a number of methods of long-term financing are being considered, the following conditions favor the use of long-term debt:

1. Sales and earnings are relatively stable, or a large increase in future sales and earnings is expected to provide a substantial benefit from the use of leverage.

2. A substantial rise in the price level is expected in the future, making it advantageous for the firm to incur debt that will be repaid with cheaper dollars.
3. The existing debt ratio is relatively low for the line of business.
4. Management thinks the price of the common stock in relation to that of bonds is temporarily depressed.
5. Sale of common stock would involve problems of maintaining the existing control pattern in the company.

Decisions about the use of debt can also be considered in terms of the average cost of capital curve, as developed in Chapter 16: Firms have optimal capital structures, or perhaps optimal ranges, and the average cost of capital is higher than it need be if the firm uses other than an optimal amount of debt. The factors listed above all relate to the optimal debt ratio; some cause the optimal ratio to increase, and others cause it to decrease.

Whenever the firm contemplates raising new outside capital and chooses between debt and equity, it implicitly makes a judgment about its actual debt ratio in relation to the optimal ratio. For example, consider Figure 20.3, which shows the assumed shape of the Longstreet Company's average cost of capital schedule. If Longstreet plans to raise outside capital, it must make a judgment about whether it is presently at Point A or Point B. If it decides that it is at A, it should issue debt; if it believes that it is at B, it should sell new common stock. This, of course, is a judgment decision; but all the factors discussed in this chapter must be considered in a qualitative way as well as on the basis of the formal analysis presented in Chapter 16.

Nature of Preferred Stock

Preferred stock has claims and rights ahead of common stock but behind all bonds. The preference may be a prior claim on earnings, a prior claim on as-

Figure 20.3

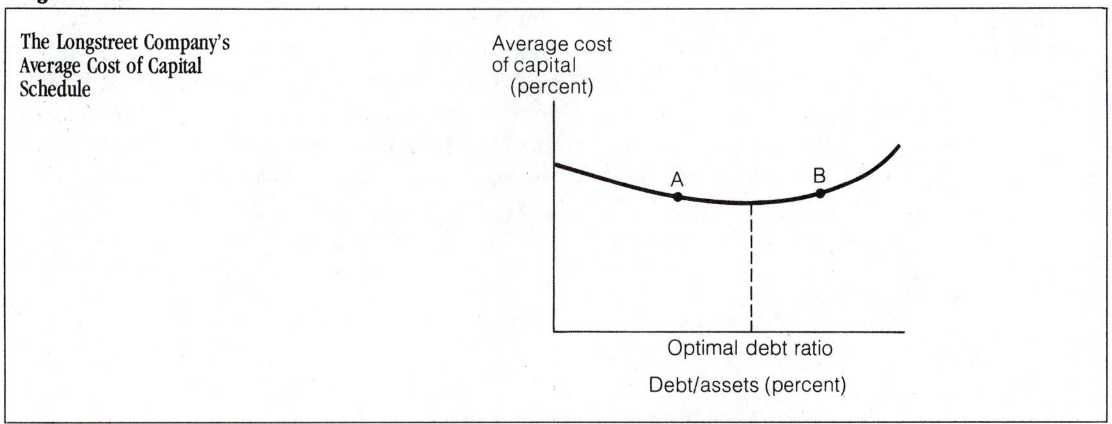

The Longstreet Company's Average Cost of Capital Schedule

sets in the event of liquidation, or a preferential position with regard to both earnings and assets.

The hybrid nature of preferred stock becomes apparent when we try to classify it in relation to bonds and common stock. The priority feature and the (generally) fixed dividend indicate that preferred stock is similar to bonds. Payments to preferred stockholders are limited in amount, so that common stockholders receive the advantages (or disadvantages) of leverage. However, if the preferred dividends are not earned, the company can forego paying them without danger of bankruptcy. In this characteristic, preferred stock is similar to common stock. Moreover, failure to pay the stipulated dividend does not cause default of the obligation, as does failure to pay bond interest.

In some types of analysis, preferred stock is treated as debt. This occurs, for example, when the analysis is being made by a *potential stockholder* considering the earnings fluctuations induced by fixed charge securities. Suppose, however, that the analysis is by a *bondholder* studying the firm's vulnerability to failure brought on by declines in sales or income. Since the dividends on preferred stock are not a fixed charge (in the sense that failure to pay them represents a default of an obligation), preferred stock represents a cushion; it provides an additional equity base. For *stockholders,* it is a leverage-inducing instrument much like debt. For *creditors,* it constitutes additional net worth. Preferred stock can therefore be treated as either debt or equity, depending on the nature of the problem under consideration.[9]

The dividends on preferred stock represent a perpetuity. Therefore, the valuation and cost of preferred stock measures are based on the perpetuity formulation.

$$k_{ps} = \frac{d_{ps}}{p_{ps}}. \tag{20.3}$$

Major Provisions of Preferred Stock Issues

Because the possible characteristics, rights, and obligations of any specific security vary so widely, a point of diminishing returns is quickly reached in a descriptive discussion of the different kinds of securities. As economic circumstances change, new kinds of securities are manufactured. Their number and variety are limited chiefly by the imagination and ingenuity of the managers formulating the terms of the issues. It is not surprising, then, that preferred stock can be found in many forms. The following sections will look at the main terms and characteristics in each case and examine the possible variations in relation to the circumstances in which they could occur.[10]

9. Accountants generally include preferred stock in the equity portion of the capital structure. But preferred is very different from common equity.

10. Much of the data in this section is taken from a study by Donald E. Fischer and Glenn A. Wilt, Jr., "Non-convertible Preferred Stocks as a Financing Instrument, 1950–1965," *Journal of Finance* 23 (September 1968), pp. 611–624.

Priority in Assets and Earnings

Many provisions in a preferred stock certificate are designed to reduce the purchaser's risk in relation to the risk carried by the holder of common stock. Preferred stock usually has priority with regard to earnings and assets. Two provisions designed to prevent undermining this priority are often found. The first states that, without the consent of the preferred stockholders, there can be no subsequent sale of securities having a prior or equal claim on earnings. The second seeks to keep earnings in the firm. It requires a minimum level of retained earnings before common stock dividends are permitted. In order to assure the availability of liquid assets that can be converted into cash for the payment of dividends, the maintenance of a minimum current ratio may also be required.

Par Value

Unlike common stock, preferred stock usually has a par value; this value is a meaningful quantity. First, the par value establishes the amount due the preferred stockholders in the event of liquidation. Second, the preferred dividend is frequently stated as a percentage of the par value. For example, J. I. Case's preferred stock outstanding has a par value of $100 and a stated dividend of 7 percent of par. (It would, of course, be just as appropriate for the Case preferred stock to state simply that the annual dividend is $7; on many preferred stocks the dividends are stated in this manner rather than as a percentage of par value.)

Cumulative Dividends

A high percentage of preferred stock issues provides for cumulative dividends—that is, all past preferred dividends must be paid before common dividends can be paid. The cumulative feature is therefore a protective device. If the preferred stock were not cumulative, preferred and common stock dividends could be passed by for a number of years. The company could then vote a large common stock dividend but only the stipulated payment to preferred stock. Suppose that preferred stock with a par value of $100 carried a 7 percent dividend and that the company did not pay dividends for several years, thereby accumulating funds that would enable it to pay in total about $50 in dividends. It could pay a single $7 dividend to the preferred stockholders and a $43 dividend to the common stockholders. Obviously, this device could be used to evade the preferred position that the holders of preferred stock have tried to obtain. The cumulative feature prevents such evasion.[11]

Large arrearages on preferred stock make it difficult to resume dividend payments on common stock. To avoid delays in beginning common stock dividend payments again, a compromise arrangement with the holders of common stock is likely to be worked out. A package offer is one possibility; for example, a recapitalization plan may provide for an exchange of shares. The arrearage will be wiped out by the donation of common stock with a value

11. Note, however, that compounding is absent in most cumulative plans. In other words, the arrearages themselves earn no return.

equal to the amount of the preferred dividend arrearage, and the holders of preferred stock will thus be given an ownership share in the corporation. In addition, resumption of current dividends on the preferred may be promised. Whether these provisions are worth anything depends on the future earnings prospects of the company.

The advantage to the company of substituting common stock for dividends in arrears is that it can start again with a clear balance sheet. If earnings recover, dividends can be paid to the holders of common stock without making up arrearages to the holders of preferred stock. The original common stockholders, of course, will have given up a portion of their ownership of the corporation.

Convertibility

Approximately 40 percent of the preferred stock that has been issued in recent years is convertible into common stock. For example, 1 share of a particular preferred stock could be convertible into 2.5 shares of the firm's common stock at the option of the preferred shareholder. (The nature of convertibility will be discussed in Chapter 22.)

Some Infrequent Provisions

Some of the other provisions occasionally encountered in preferred stocks include the following:

1. *Voting rights.* Sometimes preferred stockholders are given the right to vote for directors. When this feature is present, it generally permits the preferred stockholders to elect a *minority* of the board, say three out of nine directors. The voting privilege becomes operative only if the company has not paid the preferred dividend for a specified period, say six, eight, or ten quarters.
2. *Participating.* A rare type of preferred stock is one that participates with the common stock in sharing the firm's earnings. The following factors generally relate to participating preferred stocks: (a) the stated preferred dividend is paid first—for example, $5 a share; (b) next, income is allocated to common stock dividends up to an amount equal to the preferred dividend—in this case, $5; and (c) any remaining income is shared equally between the common and preferred stockholders.
3. *Sinking fund.* Some preferred issues have a sinking fund requirement. When they do, the sinking fund ordinarily calls for the purchase and retirement of a given percentage of the preferred stock each year.
4. *Maturity.* Preferred stocks almost never have maturity dates on which they must be retired. However, if the issue has a sinking fund, this effectively creates a maturity date.
5. *Call provision.* A call provision gives the issuing corporation the right to call in the preferred stock for redemption, as for bonds. If it is used, the call provision generally states that the company must pay an amount great-

er than the par value of the preferred stock, the additional sum being defined as the *call premium.* For example, a $100 par value preferred stock might be callable at the option of the corporation at $108 a share.

Evaluation of Preferred Stock

There are both advantages and disadvantages to selling preferred stock. Among the advantages are:

1. In contrast to bonds, the obligation to make fixed interest payments is avoided.
2. A firm wishing to expand because its earning power is high can obtain higher earnings for the original owners by selling preferred stock with a limited return rather than by selling common stock.
3. By selling preferred stock, the financial manager avoids the provision of equal participation in earnings that the sale of additional common stock would require.
4. Preferred stock also permits a company to avoid sharing control through participation in voting.
5. In contrast to bonds, it enables the firm to conserve mortgageable assets.
6. Since preferred stock typically has no maturity and no sinking fund, it is more flexible than bonds.

Among the disadvantages are:

1. Characteristically, preferred stock must be sold on a higher yield basis than that for bonds.[12]
2. Preferred stock dividends are not deductible as a tax expense, a characteristic that makes their cost differential very great in comparison with that of bonds.
3. As shown in Chapter 16, the after-tax cost of debt is approximately half the stated coupon rate for profitable firms. The cost of preferred, however, is the full percentage amount of the preferred dividend.[13]

In fashioning securities, the financial manager needs to consider the investor's point of view. Frequently it is asserted that preferred stocks have so

12. Historically, a given firm's preferred stock generally carried higher rates than its bonds because of the preferred's greater risk from the holder's viewpoint. However, as is noted below, the fact that preferred dividends are largely exempt from the corporate income tax has made preferred stock attractive to corporate investors. In recent years, high-grade preferreds on average have sold on a lower yield basis than high-grade bonds. As an example, on March 27, 1973, AT&T sold a preferred issue that yielded 7.28 percent to an investor. On that same date, AT&T bonds yielded 7.55 percent, or 0.27 percent more than the preferred. The tax treatment accounted for this differential; the *after-tax* yield was greater on the preferred stock than on the bonds.
13. By far the most important issuers of nonconvertible preferred stocks are the utility companies. For these firms, taxes are an expense for rate-making purposes—that is, higher taxes are passed on to the customers in the form of higher prices—so tax deductibility is not an important issue. This explains why utilities issue about 85 percent of all nonconvertible preferreds.

many disadvantages to both the issuer and the investor that they should never be issued. Nevertheless, preferred stock is issued in substantial amounts. Preferred stock provides the following advantages to the investor:

1. It provides reasonably steady income.
2. Preferred stockholders have a preference over common stockholders in liquidation; numerous examples can be cited where the preference position of holders of preferred stock saved them from losses incurred by holders of common stock.
3. Many corporations (for example, insurance companies) like to hold preferred stocks as investments because 85 percent of the dividends received on these shares is not taxable.

Preferred stock also has some disadvantages to investors:

1. Although the holders of preferred stock bear a substantial portion of ownership risk, their returns are limited.
2. Price fluctuations in preferred stock are far greater than those in bonds; yet yields on bonds are frequently higher than those on preferred stock.
3. The stockholders have no legally enforceable right to dividends.
4. Accrued dividend arrearages are seldom settled in cash comparable to the amount of the obligation that has been incurred.

Recent Trends

Because of the nondeductibility of preferred stock dividends as a tax expense, many companies have retired their preferred stock. Often debentures or subordinated debentures are offered to preferred stockholders in exchange, since the interest on the debentures is deductible as a tax expense.

When the preferred stock is not callable, the company must offer terms of exchange sufficiently attractive to induce the preferred stockholders to agree to the exchange. Characteristically, bonds or other securities in an amount somewhat above the recent value of the preferred stock are issued in exchange. Sometimes bonds equal in market value to the preferred stock are issued along with additional cash or common stock to provide an extra inducement to the preferred stockholders. At other times the offer is bonds equal to only a portion of the current market value of the preferred with an additional amount represented by cash or common stock that will bring the total offered the preferred stockholder to something over the preferred market value as of a recent date.

U.S. Steel's replacement of its 7 percent preferred stock in 1965 is a classic illustration of these exchange patterns. U.S. Steel proposed that its 7 percent preferred stock be changed into 4⅝ percent thirty-year bonds at a rate of $175 principal amount of bonds for each preferred share. On August 17, 1965, when the plan was announced, the preferred stock was selling at $150. U.S. Steel also announced that the conversion would increase earnings available to common stock by $10 million yearly, or 18 cents a share at 1965 federal income tax rates; this was sufficient inducement to persuade the company to give the preferred stockholders the added $25 a share.

Decision Making on the Use of Preferred Stock

As a hybrid security, preferred stock is favored by conditions that fall between those favoring common stock and those favoring debt. When a firm's profit margin is high enough to more than cover preferred stock dividends, it is advantageous to employ leverage. However, if the firm's sales and profits are subject to considerable fluctuation, the use of debt with fixed interest charges may be unduly risky. Preferred stock can offer a happy compromise. Its use is strongly favored if the firm already has a debt ratio that is high in relation to the reference level maximum for the line of business.

Relative costs of alternative sources of financing are always important considerations. When the market prices of common stocks are relatively low, the costs of common stock financing are relatively high.

The costs of preferred stock financing follow interest rate levels more than common stock prices; in other words, when interest rates are low, the cost of preferred stock is also likely to be low. When the cost of fixed income instruments, such as preferred stock, are low and the costs of variable value securities, such as common stock, are high, the use of preferred stock is favored. Preferred stock may also be the desired form of financing whenever the use of debt will involve excessive risk, but the issuance of common stock will result in problems of control for the dominant ownership group in the company.

Rationale for Different Classes of Securities

At this point the following questions are likely to come to mind: Why are there so many different forms of long-term securities? Why is anybody ever willing to purchase subordinated bonds or income bonds? The answers to both questions can be made clear by reference to Figure 20.4: The now familiar trade-off function is drawn to show the risk and expected returns for the various securities of the Longstreet Company. Longstreet's first mortgage bonds are slightly more risky than U.S. Treasury bonds and sell at a slightly higher expected return. The second mortgage bonds are yet more risky and have a still higher expected return. Subordinated debentures, income bonds, and preferred stocks all are increasingly risky and have increasingly higher expected returns. Longstreet's common stock, the riskiest security the firm issues, has the highest expected return of any of its offerings.

Why does Longstreet issue so many different classes of securities? Why not just offer one type of bond plus common stock? The answer lies in the fact that different investors have different risk-return trade-off preferences, so if the company's securities are to appeal to the broadest possible market, Long-

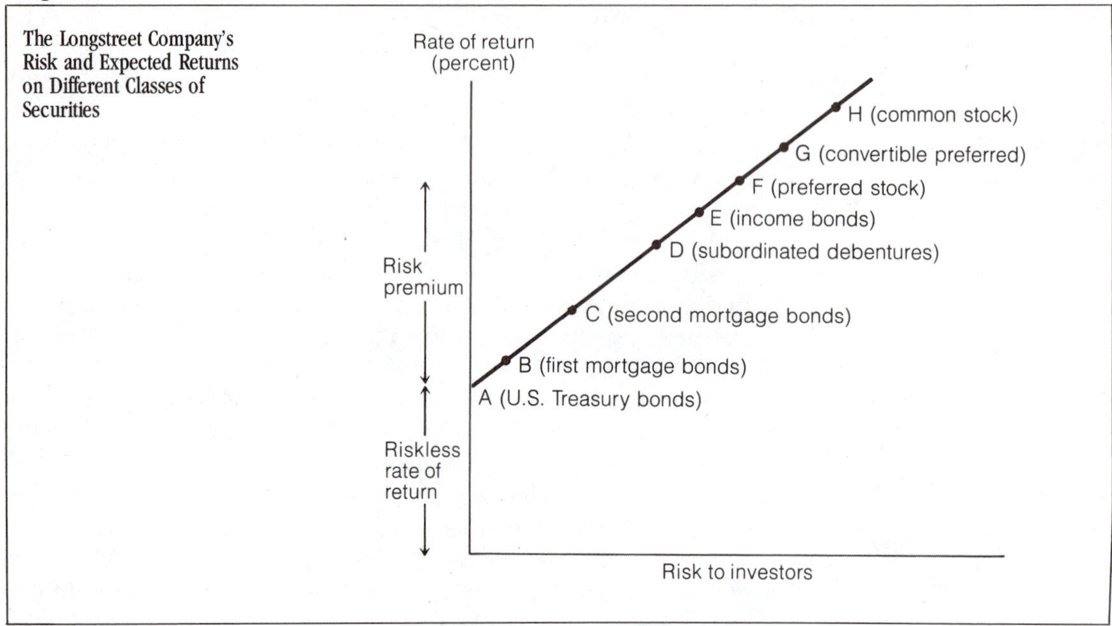

Figure 20.4 The Longstreet Company's Risk and Expected Returns on Different Classes of Securities

street must offer as many as investors seem to want. Used wisely, a policy of selling differentiated securities can lower a firm's overall cost of capital below what it would be if it issued only one class of debt and common stock.

Refunding a Bond or a Preferred Stock Issue

Suppose a company sells bonds or preferred stock at a time when interest rates are relatively high. Provided the issue is callable, as many are, the company can sell a new issue of low-yielding securities if and when interest rates drop and use the proceeds to retire the high-rate issue. This is called a *refunding operation.*

The decision to refund a security issue is analyzed in much the same manner as a capital budgeting expenditure. The costs of refunding—the investment outlay—are (1) the call premium paid for the privilege of calling the old issue and (2) the flotation costs incurred in selling the new issue. The annual receipts, in the capital budgeting sense, are the interest payments saved each year; for example, if interest expense on the old issue is $1 million while that on the new issue is $700,000, the $300,000 saving constitutes the annual benefit.

In analyzing the advantages of refunding, the recommended procedure is the net present value method—discounting the future interest savings back to the present and comparing the discounted value with the cash outlays associated with the refunding. In the discounting process, the after-tax cost of the new debt, not the average cost of capital, is used as the discount factor. The reason for this is that there is relatively little risk to the savings; their value is known with relative certainty (which is quite unlike most capital budgeting decisions). The following case illustrates the calculations needed in a refunding decision.

As discussed in Chapters 10 and 18, interest rate levels peaked cyclically in the autumn of 1974, when the rates on new issues of Aaa corporate bonds exceeded 10 percent. By December 1976 these yields had declined almost to 8 percent, representing a swing of approximately 200 basis points. The last half of 1976 was characterized by a substantial activity in refunding of bond and preferred stock issues at lower interest rates. A moderate increase in interest rates occurred during the early part of January 1977, but refundings continued to be attractive. Cyclical swings from higher interest rates to lower interest rates, coupled with call provisions enabling firms to redeem bonds or preferred stock at prices below their prevailing market prices have given rise to periodic opportunities for firms to engage in refunding operations. A framework for analyzing refunding decisions is therefore presented.[14]

To provide a focus for the analysis, the presentation will make use of a case to exemplify the basic ideas. The Becker Company has a $50,000,000 long-term bond issue outstanding which has an additional ten years to maturity and bears a coupon interest rate of 12 percent. The interest payments are made semiannually. Financial market conditions have given the firm the opportunity of refinancing the debt with another ten-year bond but at the lower rate of 10 percent. The firm plans to use all debt financing for the proposed bond refunding project. The firm's applicable corporate tax rate is 40 percent. The relevant data on the old issue and on the new refunding issues are summarized below:

	Old Issue	New Issue
Face amount	$50,000,000	$51,716,000
Interest rate	r = 12%	r_1 = 10%
Life of bond	25 years	10 years
Maturity date	August 16, 1988	August 16, 1988
Flotation costs[a]	$750,000	$775,740
Net proceeds of sale	$49,250,000	$50,940,260
Date issued	August 16, 1963	August 16, 1978
Redemption date	August 16, 1978	—
Call price	$104	—

a. Flotation costs on both the old and new issue are 1.5% of gross proceeds.

14. A considerable amount of literature on refunding has appeared in recent years. That literature is summarized and critiqued in Appendix A to this chapter.

This is fundamentally a capital budgeting decision, so we shall present our analysis through a capital budgeting worksheet approach. A summary capital budgeting worksheet is presented in Table 20.2. We shall discuss the reasoning behind the calculation of each item, keying the discussion to the numbered lines in Table 20.2.

Part A. After-Tax Refunding Costs

What is the investment required to refund the issue? There are four components to the required investment outlay: the call premium on the old issue, flotation costs on the new issue, tax savings on flotation costs on the new issue, and tax savings on flotation costs on the old issue.

1. Call Premium. The call premium is 4 percent of face value as given by the bond indenture on the old issue. Since this is a tax-deductible expense, the actual cost is reduced by the company's tax rate of 40 percent.

$$\text{Before-tax call premium} = \text{Call rate} \times \text{Face amount}$$
$$\$2{,}000{,}000 = 0.04 \times \$50{,}000{,}000.$$

$$\text{After-tax call premium} = \text{Before-tax call premium} \times (1 - \text{Tax rate})$$
$$\$1{,}200{,}000 = \$2{,}000{,}000 \times (1 - 0.40).$$

Although the Becker Company must expend $2 million on the call premium, this is a deductible expense. Since the company is in a 40 percent tax bracket, it saved $800,000 in taxes. The after-tax cost of the call is therefore only $1,200,000.

2. Flotation Costs on the New Issue. At 1.5 percent of $51,716,000 we obtain $775,740. This is the amount subject to tax deductions.

Table 20.2

Capital Budgeting Worksheet Analysis of Bond Refunding

	Amount before Tax	Amount after Tax	Timing of Event	Present Value Factor	Present Value
Part A. After-Tax Refunding Costs					
1. Call premium	$2,000,000	$1,200,000	0	1.0	$1,200,000
2. Flotation costs on new issue	775,740	775,740	0	1.0	775,740
3. Tax savings on flotation costs of new issue	77,574	31,030	1 – 10	7.3601	(228,384)
4. Tax savings on flotation costs on old	300,000	120,000	0	1.0	(120,000)
issue	30,000	12,000	1 – 10	7.3601	88,321
Present value of after-tax refunding costs					$1,715,677
Part B. Interest Savings					
5. Interest savings on new issue	$1,000,000	$600,000/2	1 – 20	14.8775	$4,463,250

3. Tax Savings on Flotation Costs of New Issue. For tax purposes, costs are amortized over the life of the new bond, or ten years. Assuming straight line amortization, the annual tax deduction is given by:

$$\text{Annual tax deduction} = \frac{\text{Flotation costs}}{\text{Life of bond (new issue)}}$$

$$\$77{,}574 = \frac{\$775{,}740}{10}.$$

Since Becker Company is in the 40 percent tax bracket, it has a tax savings of \$31,030 a year (\$77,574 × 0.40) for ten years. This is an annuity of \$31,030 for ten years. The present value of the annuity is found by discounting at the after-tax cost of the new debt issue. The after-tax cost of debt is the before-tax interest rate times (one minus the tax rate), that is, 10.0 × 0.60, or 6 percent.

$$\begin{aligned}\text{PV of tax savings} &= \text{Annual after-tax savings} \times \text{PVIFA (6\%, 10 years)}\\ &= \$31{,}030(7.3601)\\ &= \$228{,}384.\end{aligned}$$

The after-tax amount of new flotation costs is:

New flotation costs	\$775,740
Less: PV of tax savings	228,384
PV of the new flotation costs, net of tax	\$547,356

4. Tax Savings on Flotation on Old Issue. The old issue has an unamortized flotation cost of \$750,000(10/25) = \$300,000. This can be recognized immediately as an expense, thus creating an after-tax savings of 0.4(\$300,000) = \$120,000. The firm will, however, lose a deduction of \$30,000 a year for ten years, or an after-tax benefit of \$12,000 a year. The present value of this lost benefit, discounted at 6 percent is:

$$\begin{aligned}\text{PV of lost benefit} &= \$12{,}000 \times \text{PVIFA(6\%, 10 years)}\\ &= \$12{,}000 \times 7.3601\\ &= \$88{,}321.\end{aligned}$$

The net after-tax effect of old flotation costs is:

Tax savings on old flotation costs	\$120,000
Less: PV of lost benefits	88,321
Net after-tax effect of old flotation costs	\$ 31,679

The total of the four items is:

1. Call premium	$1,200,000
2. Flotation costs on new issue	775,740
3. Tax savings on flotation cost on new issue	(228,384)
4. Tax savings on flotation costs on old issue	(31,679)
Present value of after-tax refunding costs	$1,715,677

In a capital budgeting sense, the $1,715,677 represents the investment outlay to obtain the interest savings on the new issue. These are covered in Part B of Table 20.2.

5. Interest Savings on the New Issue. The interest rate on the old issue was 12 percent. On the new issue, the interest rate will be 10 percent. Hence there is a savings of 2 percent on the $50,000,000 issue outstanding. The after-tax interest savings therefore are:

Interest savings

$$\$50{,}000{,}000(0.02)(1 - 0.4) = \$600{,}000.$$

Present value of interest savings

$$\$600{,}000/2 \times \text{PVIFA}(3\%, 20 \text{ periods}) = \$300{,}000(14.8775) = \$4{,}463{,}250.$$

Since semiannual compounding is used, the annual savings and the 6 percent interest factor are divided by 2. The number of periods are multiplied by 2. The result is a total present value of interest savings of $4,463,250.

We can now make a net present value analysis of the refunding decision. The basic capital budgeting relationship is:

$$\text{Present value of investment} = \text{Gross present value of benefits} - \text{Present value of costs.}$$

For the refunding problem under analysis we have:

$$\$2{,}747{,}573 = \$4{,}463{,}250 - \$1{,}715{,}677.$$

Since the present value of the interest savings exceeds the after-tax refunding costs by a substantial amount, it will be profitable to refund the old bond issue. While we have placed the analysis in a capital budgeting worksheet framework, we can also express the relations in a more formal capital budgeting model. Most generally, the NPV from refunding can be expressed as in Equation 20.4.

$$\text{NPV} = \overset{(1)}{\sum_{t=1}^{N} \frac{(1-T)(r-r_1)B}{[1+(1-T)r_1]^t}} - \overset{(2)}{\sum_{t=1}^{N} \frac{(1-T)r_1\Delta B}{[1+(1-T)r_1]^t}} - \overset{(3)}{\frac{\Delta B}{[1+(1-T)r_1]^N}}$$

$$- \overset{(4)}{[(1-T)\text{RC} - \Delta B]}, \tag{20.4}$$

where r and B without subscripts are the interest rate and debt amount, respectively, for the old issue.

There are four terms on the right-hand side of the equation. Term 1 is the present value of the interest savings for refunding the old issue—the $4,463,250 that we have calculated. Term 2 is the present value of the interest on the incremental debt. This amount is $765,894 for our problem:

Interest on incremental debt

$$\$1{,}716{,}000(0.10)(1 - 0.4) = \$171{,}600(0.6) = \$102{,}960.$$

$$\$102{,}960 \div 2 = \$51{,}480(14.8775) = \$765{,}894.$$

Term 3 is the present value of the incremental debt to be repaid at maturity. For our problem this would be: $1,716,000 × PVIF(3%, 20 periods) = $1,716,000(0.5537) = $950,149. Term 4 is the amount of equity financing; it is the refunding costs less the portion of refunding costs financed by the incremental debt. In the Becker refunding, all financing was by the incremental debt, so this term of equity financing is zero. The NPV calculation is:

Interest saving[a]		$4,463,250
Less: interest on incremental debt	$765,894	
Present value of repayment of incremental debt	950,149	
Total		1,716,043
Net present value of refunding		$2,747,207

a. This is Term 1 from the discussion of Equation 20.4.

This is approximately the same as our previous result. Since the coupon rate of interest on the incremental debt is 6 percent and the bond discount rate is also 6 percent, the value of the bond is its par value. Hence the sum of Terms 2 and 3 in Equation 20.4 is equal to ΔB. Hence when the refunding costs are financed entirely by the ΔB, Equation 20.4 can be simplified to:

NPV of Refunding

$$\text{NPV} = \sum_{t=1}^{N} \frac{(1-T)(r-r_1)B}{[1+(1-T)r_1]^t} - (1-T)\text{RC}. \tag{20.5}$$

Interest savings on new issue[a]	$4,463,250
Less: Present value of after-tax refunding costs = $(1 - T)RC = \Delta B$	1,716,000
NPV of refunding	$2,747,250

a. In this calculation, the first line is equal to Term 1 of Equation 20.4; and the second line compares with the sum of Terms 2 and 3 in the same equation.

Thus an overview of the refunding analysis is:

Benefits:
Interest savings from the lower interest rate
Costs:
1. After-tax call premium to retire existing bonds
2. After-tax flotation costs on new bond issue
3. After-tax benefits from unamortized flotation costs on the old bond issue (a negative cost)

The sum of these costs is the total after-tax refunding costs expressed as $(1 - T)$RC. The NPV of refunding is the interest savings less the total after-tax refunding costs.

Alternatively, we can measure the costs of refunding by the financing required to cover those costs: The NPV of refunding equals the present value of interest savings less the present value of interest on incremental debt less the present value of incremental debt repayment less equity financing used. If all incremental financing is by debt, the last term drops out. If the after-tax cost of debt is the discount factor, the interest on incremental debt plus debt repayment equal the incremental debt (ΔB), which also equals $(1 - T)$RC. The NPV of refunding can then be simplified to the present value of interest savings less incremental debt or the after-tax refunding costs.

One final point must be mentioned. Since the refunding operation is advantageous to the firm, it must be disadvantageous to bondholders; they must give up their 12 percent bond and reinvest in one yielding 10 percent. This points out the danger of the call provision to bondholders and explains why, at any given time, bonds without a call provision command higher prices than callable bonds.

Effects of Leverage—The Modigliani-Miller Propositions

When the amount of leverage employed by a firm is relatively low, the debt it issues may be considered virtually riskless or risk-free debt. If so, the Modigliani and Miller propositions apply. The MM theory provides a formulation of some very simple relationships for the cost of capital and valuation. The final section of the previous chapter on common stock financing set forth a case that illustrated a general framework for analyzing financing alternatives. Here another case is presented to illustrate the circumstances under which the MM relations may be applied in evaluating choices between alternative forms of financing.

The Robinson Company is considering two alternative financial structures. Its total assets at book value are $500,000. The two alternative financial structures it is considering are:

	Financial Structure	
	No Leverage	20% Leverage
Debt	0	$100,000
Equity	$500,000	400,000

If debt is used, it will bear an interest cost of 10 percent before taxes. The applicable corporate tax rate is 40 percent. The income statements under the two alternative forms of leverage would appear as follows:

Income Statements

	No Leverage	20% Leverage
Sales	$1,000,000	$1,000,000
Total costs	850,000	850,000
Earnings before interest and taxes (EBIT) = $\overline{X}$	$ 150,000	$ 150,000
Interest expense at 10 percent	0	10,000
Income before taxes	$ 150,000	$ 140,000
Taxes at 40 percent	60,000	56,000
Net income	$ 90,000	$ 84,000

Sales, total costs, and earnings before interest and taxes are the same whether the firm is levered or unlevered. The interest expense for the levered firm is a deduction before the tax rate is applied. For the levered firm, the $10,000 of interest expense has the effect of reducing the taxes paid by the firm from $60,000 to $56,000 so that the after-tax cost of interest is only $6,000 (this is due to the tax savings of $4,000).

In addition to the above data, we could obtain from the newspaper the current market price per share of the common stock of the Robinson Company. The Robinson Company, which is now unlevered, has 10,000 shares of stock outstanding with a market value of $60 per share. We now have all the information we need to apply the Modigliani and Miller (MM) propositions. MM's Proposition I states that the cost of capital of an unlevered firm is given by Equation 20.6.

$$k_u = \frac{\overline{X}(1 - T)}{V_u} = \frac{\$150{,}000(0.6)}{\$600{,}000} = \frac{\$90{,}000}{\$600{,}000} = 0.15 = 15\%. \quad \text{MMI (20.6)}$$

The cost of capital for an unlevered firm is equal to its after-tax net operating income (EBIT) divided by the value of the unlevered firm. This is both the cost of equity capital and the overall cost of capital for the unlevered firm since equity provides its total financing.

We next consider the value of the levered firm. MM's Proposition II provides a relationship to determine the cost of equity capital for a levered firm. It is presented in Equation 20.7:

$$k_s = k_u + (k_u - k_b)(1 - T)\frac{B}{S}. \quad \text{MMII (20.7)}$$

We make use of the cost of capital of the unlevered firm already calculated. The cost of equity capital of the levered firm is equal to the cost of capital of the unlevered firm plus a risk adjustment. The risk adjustment is the difference between the cost of capital of the unlevered firm and the cost of debt, multiplied by $(1 - T)$ and weighted by the leverage ratio at market values. To apply this equation for the cost of equity capital, we need to determine the market value of equity of the levered firm. MM have established the following relationship between the value of a levered firm and the value of an unlevered firm:

$$V_L = V_u + TB. \quad (20.8)$$

Equation 20.8 says that the value of the levered firm is equal to the value of the unlevered firm plus an upward adjustment for the tax shelter effect of the interest expense which is, of course, related to the amount of debt outstanding. For our example of the Robinson Company, we would have the data in Equation 20.8a:

$$\begin{aligned} V &= \$600{,}000 + 0.4\ (\$100{,}000) \\ &= \$640{,}000. \end{aligned} \quad (20.8a)$$

Thus the value of the levered firm would be \$640,000. This represents an increase in the value of the firm by almost 7 percent, with virtually no increase in the riskiness of the debt. The value of equity for the levered firm is shown in Equation 20.9.

$$\begin{aligned} S &= V_L - B \\ &= \$640{,}000 - \$100{,}000 \\ &= \$540{,}000. \end{aligned} \quad (20.9)$$

The value of equity is the total value of the firm less the value of debt. The dollar amount for the Robinson case is \$540,000. We can now calculate the cost of equity capital as shown in Equation 20.7a:

$$\begin{aligned} k_s &= 0.15 + (0.15 - 0.10)(0.6)(10/54) \\ &= 0.15 + 0.0055556 \\ &= 0.1556 = 15.56\%. \end{aligned} \tag{20.7a}$$

The leverage of the Robinson Company measured as the ratio of debt to the book value of total assets is 20 percent; measured by the ratio of debt to the market value of the firm, leverage is 15.625 percent; measured by the ratio of debt to the market value of equity, leverage is 18.5 percent. The last measure is used in MM II to calculate a cost of equity for Robinson of 15.56 percent.

Next we calculate the overall, or weighted, cost of capital for the Robinson Company. The simplest method of calculating the firm's weighted cost of capital is shown by Equation 20.10:

$$k = \frac{\overline{X}(1 - T)}{V} = \frac{\$150{,}000(0.6)}{\$640{,}000} = \frac{\$90{,}000}{\$640{,}000} = 14.06\%. \tag{20.10}$$

The result is a weighted cost of capital of 14.06 percent. This is almost 1 percentage point (84 basis points) below the cost of capital for the unlevered firm.

There are two other methods of calculating the firm's weighted cost of capital. These provide some insights on the relationships involved and at the same time give us a check on the computations. Equation 20.11 sets forth the weighted cost of capital in terms of the weighted cost of each component.

$$\begin{aligned} k &= k_s(S/V) + k_b(1 - T)(B/V) \\ &= 0.1555556(54/64) + 0.10(0.6)(10/64) \\ &= 0.1555556(0.84375) + 0.06(0.15625) \\ &= 0.13125 + 0.009375 \\ &= 0.1406 = 14.06\%. \end{aligned} \tag{20.11}$$

We observe the same result of 14.06 percent when we utilize the weighted cost of capital formula explicitly. A third formula for calculating the weighted average cost of capital is set forth in Equation 20.12:

$$k = k_u(1 - TL) = k_u[1 - T(B/V)]. \tag{20.12}$$

This third formula states that the cost of capital for the levered firm is equal to the cost of capital for the unlevered firm times one minus the tax rate multiplied by the debt to value ratio. Since the cost of debt is not shown explicitly, this formula may seem strange. However, Equation 20.12 is derived from 20.11, so the cost of debt is included implicitly.

$$\begin{aligned} k &= 0.15[1 - 0.4(10/64)] \\ &= 0.15[1 - 0.4(0.15625)] \\ &= 0.15(1 - 0.0625) \\ &= 0.15(0.9375) \\ &= 0.1406 = 14.06\%. \end{aligned}$$

Again we obtain the same result of 14.06 percent.

Under the assumptions of the MM conditions the relationship between the cost of capital and valuation is simple and straightforward.[15] For companies with debt to equity ratios already in the range of 50 percent or more, further increases in debt would probably cause both the cost of debt capital and the cost of equity capital to rise in a curvilinear way rather than in the linear relationship implied by MM Proposition II. Risky debt, whose cost rises with leverage, implies that bankruptcy costs are considered to be substantial. As a consequence, real losses will occur if the firm goes bankrupt. If there are substantial losses when the firm goes bankrupt, these additional losses are not eliminated by diversification. Diversification can average out declines in values if additional losses do not have to be taken into consideration. Hence, if there are bankruptcy costs and risky debt, it is likely that at some leverage level the costs of debt and of equity begin to rise at an increasing rate.

From a practical standpoint, the role of the MM propositions can be determined from the statement of the facts of the case. When the leverage ratio of a firm is low—such as we observe in companies like Kellogg, Kodak, and Du Pont—the sale of debt can take place on very favorable terms. The additional debt carries a very low risk and is likely to receive a high quality rating—that is, to be rated an Aaa security. The debt will carry the lowest interest rate prevailing on a prime quality issue. The issuance of the debt will not increase the risk of the common stock equity. The use of debt will move the firm toward a more optimal capital structure. When we evaluate the financing alternatives, given the facts of the case, the use of the debt alternative is chosen. We will predictably find that the cost of capital of the firm will be decreased and its value will be increased.

On the other hand, when the debt ratio of the firm is already high (and sometimes when the outlook for the industry and for the firm are uncertain), a realistic formulation of the financing alternatives will be something like the following pattern. If the firm were to use more debt, the quality rating of the debt would continue low or decline even further. The cost of the debt would be high and the restrictions included in the debt indentures likely to be severe. A realistic assessment of the effects on the required returns on equity would have to estimate that they would rise at an increasing rate with increases in leverage. The cost of equity would not follow MM's Proposition II, but would be curvilinear upward. As a consequence, the use of additional debt would cause the cost of capital of the firm to rise and its value to fall. The indicated market value of the equity would also fall.

The use of equity under the circumstances described would lower the opportunity cost of debt. It would lower the required return on equity perhaps even more than in proportion to the decrease in leverage (the relative increase in equity). The use of equity would be likely to lower the firm's cost of capital and to increase its market value. The indicated market value of equity

15. It is also assumed that the EBIT of the firm remains at the same average level and there is no underlying growth element to take into account.

would also be likely to rise. Thus the use of equity financing would be indicated.

The existence of the two polar case examples still does not make the choice among financing alternatives perfunctory or mechanical. At least six additional factors complicate the analysis:

1. What is the fundamental outlook for the economy, the industry, and the firm? What is the outlook for the sales and operating earnings of the firm?
2. To what extent does the firm already have a high ratio of operating leverage?
3. To what degree is the financial leverage ratio of the firm in a borderline area for which neither the MM conditions nor the non-MM conditions clearly apply?
4. What are the prospective financing needs of the firm in the future, and how do they interact with the degree of uncertainty in the sales and operating income outlook for the firm?
5. Where are we in the timing of costs of financing alternatives? Are the costs of debt high and capital availability tight, as in early 1980? Is it better to wait to obtain long-term debt? (What appears to be cyclically high may turn out to be an intermediate level with reference to the longer term trends for financing costs.)
6. Related to the secular, or long-term, trends in debt costs is the impact of fundamental economic factors such as the inflation rate and the longer term strength of the U.S. dollar in relation to the values of the other major currencies.

Items 5 and 6 of the above list are interrelated. If high inflation rates persist in the U.S., the costs of debt money will continue to rise over the long term. For example, suppose the inflation rate were expected to be 8 percent per annum and interest rates would be about 4 percent without inflation. Nominal interest rates on long-term debt would be about 12 percent, the level experienced in early 1980. Suppose, however, that the inflation rate were 15 to 18 percent per annum, the rates experienced in late 1979 and early 1980, but the rates on long-term bonds observed in the market reflected expectations that the inflation rate would be brought down to 7 to 8 percent. The persistence of inflation rates of 15 to 18 percent would cause the financial markets to revise their expectations of the rates of future inflation upward. It is in this sense that the persistence of higher than currently expected rates of inflation will cause long-term debt interest rates to continue to rise.

But a continued rise in future interest costs would make it desirable to borrow "now rather than later." At least two factors are involved. A continued high rate of inflation means that the "real" cost of debt will continue to fall. Alternatively, we may say that the cost of debt will continue to rise in the future. In some sense we are trying to outsmart the financial markets. We are making the judgment that the future rate of inflation expected or anticipated by us is higher than the anticipated rate of inflation expressed in current market rates on long-term debt.

Given a firm that is operating on the borderline of leverage between the MM world and the non-MM world, the choice among financing alternatives will not be mechanical. A substantial amount of judgment will be involved. Particularly important will be the outlook for the sales and operating earnings of the company. If in a case involving choices among financing alternatives, we could agree on a forecast of the sales and operating earnings of the firm, the choice of the financing alternative is likely to follow. Although the other factors would have to be taken into account, they are likely, even as a group, to be dominated by the outlook for the sales and operating earnings of the firm under future states of the world.

Thus choices among financing alternatives remain a formidable challenge to financial executives and their companies even though the criteria and variables to be taken into account can be well specified. Because of these complexities, we have covered financing decisions in two stages. In Chapters 15 through 17, we developed the general framework for determining the firm's financial structure. In Chapters 18 through 22, we apply these general principles to specific financing decisions which involve the additional variables and details outlined above. Because many complex factors are involved, special methods of financing, such as leasing and the use of convertibles and other forms of options (treated in the following chapters), are employed.

Summary

A *bond* is a long-term promissory note. A *mortgage bond* is secured by real property. An *indenture* is an agreement between the firm issuing the bond and the numerous bondholders, represented by a *trustee.*

Secured long-term debt differs with respect to (1) the priority of claims, (2) the right to issue additional securities, and (3) the scope of the lien provided. These characteristics determine the amount of protection provided to the bondholder by the terms of the security. Giving investors more security will induce them to accept a lower yield but will restrict the future freedom of action of the issuing firm.

The main classes of unsecured bonds are (1) *debentures,* (2) *subordinated debentures,* and (3) *income bonds.* Holders of debentures are unsecured general creditors. Subordinated debentures are junior in claim to bank loans. Income bonds are similar to preferred stock in that interest is paid only when earned.

The characteristics of long-term debt determine the circumstances under which it will be used when alternative forms of financing are under analysis. The cost of debt is limited, but it is a fixed obligation. Bond interest is an expense deductible for tax purposes. Debt carries a maturity date and may require sinking fund payments to prepare for extinguishing the obligation. Indenture provisions are likely to include restrictions on the freedom of action of the firm's management.

The nature of long-term debt encourages its use under the following circumstances:

1. Sales and earnings are relatively stable.
2. Profit margins are adequate to make leverage advantageous.
3. A rise in profits or the general price level is expected.
4. The existing debt ratio is relatively low.
5. Common stock price-earnings ratios are low in relation to the levels of interest rates.
6. Control considerations are important.
7. Cash flow requirements under the bond agreement are not burdensome.
8. Restrictions of the bond indenture are not onerous.

Even if seven of the eight factors favor debt, the remaining factor can swing the decision to the use of equity capital. The list of factors is thus simply a checklist of things to be considered when deciding on bonds versus stock; the actual decision is based on a judgment about the relative importance of the several factors.

The characteristics of preferred stock vary with the requirements of the situation under which it is used. However, certain patterns tend to remain. Preferred stocks usually have priority over common stocks with respect to earnings and claims on assets in liquidation. Preferred stocks are usually cumulative; they have no maturity but are sometimes callable. They are typically nonparticipating and offer only contingent voting rights.

The advantages to the issuer are limited dividends and no maturity. These advantages may outweigh the disadvantages of higher cost and nondeductibility of the dividends as an expense for tax purposes. But their acceptance by investors is the final test of whether they can be sold on favorable terms.

Companies sell preferred stock when they seek the advantages of financial leverage but fear the dangers of the fixed charges on debt in the face of potential fluctuations in income. If debt ratios or the cost of common stock financing are relatively high, the advantages of preferred stock are reinforced.

The use of preferred stock has declined significantly since the advent of the corporate income tax because preferred dividends are not deductible for income tax purposes, while bond interest payments are deductible. In recent years, however, there has been a strong shift back to a new kind of preferred stock—convertible preferred, used primarily in connection with mergers. If the stockholders of the acquired company receive cash or bonds, they are required to pay capital gains taxes on any gains they realize. If convertible preferred stock is given to the selling stockholders, this constitutes a tax-free exchange of securities. The selling stockholders can obtain a fixed income security and at the same time postpone the payment of capital gains taxes.

If a bond or preferred stock issue was sold when interest rates were higher than they are at present, and if the issue is callable, it may be profitable to call the old issue and refund it with a new, lower-cost issue. An analysis similar to capital budgeting is required to determine whether a refunding operation should be undertaken.

The NPV of refunding can be written in two alternative formulations:

$$\text{A.}\quad \begin{bmatrix}\text{NPV}\\ \text{of refunding}\end{bmatrix} = \overset{(1)}{\begin{bmatrix}\text{Present value of}\\ \text{interest savings}\end{bmatrix}} - \overset{(2)}{\begin{bmatrix}\text{Present value}\\ \text{of after-tax}\\ \text{refunding costs}\end{bmatrix}}$$

$$\text{NPV} = \sum_{t=1}^{N} \frac{(1-T)(r-r_1)B}{[1+(1-T)r_1]^t} = (1-T)\text{RC},$$

or we may write:

$$\text{B.}\quad \begin{bmatrix}\text{NPV}\\ \text{of}\\ \text{refunding}\end{bmatrix} =$$

$$\overset{(1)}{\begin{bmatrix}\text{Present}\\ \text{value of}\\ \text{interest}\\ \text{savings}\end{bmatrix}} - \overset{(2)}{\begin{bmatrix}\text{Present}\\ \text{value of}\\ \text{interest}\\ \text{on incremental}\\ \text{debt}\end{bmatrix}} - \overset{(3)}{\begin{bmatrix}\text{Present}\\ \text{value of}\\ \text{repayment}\\ \text{of incremental}\\ \text{debt}\end{bmatrix}} - \overset{(4)}{\begin{bmatrix}\text{Equity}\\ \text{financing employed}\end{bmatrix}}$$

$$\text{NPV} = \sum_{t=1}^{N} \frac{(1-T)(r-r_1)B}{[1+(1-T)r_1]^t} - \sum_{t=1}^{N} \frac{(1-T)r_1\Delta B}{[1+(1-T)r_1]^t} - \frac{\Delta B}{[1+(1-T)r_1]^N}$$
$$- [(1-T)\text{RC} - \Delta B].$$

The last three terms of Expression B are the financing counterpart to the after-tax refunding costs expressed in the last term of Expression A. Some further simplifications can be made. If all incremental financing is by debt, the last term drops out of Expression B. If the after-tax coupon on the new debt is equal to the discount rate used, the present value of interest costs on the incremental debt plus the present value of repayment of the incremental debt, Terms 2 and 3, total to ΔB. Thus ΔB is also equal to $(1 - T)$RC.

Questions

20.1 Explain what is meant by the term *yield to maturity* in reference to (a) bonds and (b) preferred stocks. Is it appropriate to talk of a yield to maturity on a preferred stock that has no specific maturity date?

20.2 Explain why bonds with longer maturities sometimes experience wider price movements from a given change in interest rates than do shorter maturity bonds. Answer first in words and then mathematically.

20.3 A sinking fund is set up in one of two ways:

a. The corporation makes annual payments to the trustee, who invests the proceeds in securities (frequently government bonds) and uses the accumulated total to retire the bond issue on maturity.

b. The trustee uses the annual payments to retire a portion of the issue each year, either calling a given percentage of the issue by a lottery and paying a specified price per bond or buying bonds on the open market, whichever is cheaper.

Discuss the advantages and disadvantages of each procedure from the viewpoint of both the firm and the bondholders.

20.4 Since a corporation often has the right to call bonds at will, do you believe individuals should be able to demand repayment at any time they so desire? Explain.

20.5 What are the relative advantages and disadvantages of issuing a long-term bond during a recession versus during a period of prosperity?

20.6 Missouri Pacific's $4\frac{3}{4}$ percent income bonds due in 2020 are selling for $770, while the company's $4\frac{1}{4}$ percent first mortgage bonds due in 2005 are selling for $945. Each has a $1,000 par value. Why do the bonds with the lower coupon sell at a higher price?

20.7 When a firm sells bonds, it must offer a package of terms acceptable to potential buyers. Included in this package are such features as the issue price, the coupon interest rate, the term of maturity, and sinking fund provisions. The package itself is determined through a bargaining process between the firm and the investment bankers who handle the issue. What particular features would you, as a corporate treasurer, be especially interested in having, and which would you be most willing to give ground on, under each of the following conditions:

a. You believe that the economy is near the peak of a business cycle.

b. Long-run forecasts indicate that your firm may have heavy cash inflows in relation to cash needs during the next five to ten years.

c. Your current liabilities are presently low, but you anticipate raising a considerable amount of funds through short-term borrowing in the near future.

20.8 Bonds are less attractive to investors during periods of inflation because a rise in the price level reduces the purchasing power of the fixed interest payments and of the principal. Discuss the advantages and disadvantages to a corporation of using a bond whose interest payments and principal would increase in direct proportion to increases in the price level (an inflation-proof bond).

20.9 If preferred stock dividends are passed for several years, the preferred stockholders are frequently given the right to elect several members of the board of directors. In the case of bonds that are in default on interest payments, this procedure is not followed. Why does the difference exist?

20.10 Preferred stocks are found in almost all industries, but one industry is the really dominant issuer of preferred shares. What is this industry, and why are firms in it so disposed to using preferred stock?

20.11 If the corporate income tax were abolished, would this raise or lower the amount of new preferred stock issued?

20.12 Investors buying securities have some expected or required rate of return in mind. Which would you expect to be higher—the required rate of return (before taxes) on preferred stocks or that on common stocks?

20.13 Do you think the before-tax required rate of return is higher on very high grade preferred stocks or on bonds in the following instances:

a. for individual investors?
b. for corporate investors?

20.14 For purposes of measuring a firm's leverage, should preferred stock be classified as debt or as equity? Does it matter if the classification is being made (a) by the firm itself, (b) by creditors, or (c) by equity investors?

20.15 A firm is seeking a term loan from a bank. Under what conditions would it want a fixed interest rate, and under what conditions would it want the rate to fluctuate with the prime rate?

Problems

20.1 The Camden Company has two issues of bonds outstanding. Both bear coupons of 7 percent, and the effective yield required on each is 12 percent. Bond A has a maturity of ten years and Bond B a maturity of twenty years. Both pay interest annually.
a. What is the price of each bond?
b. If the effective yield on each bond rises to 14 percent, what is the price of each bond?
c. Explain why the price of one bond falls more than the price of the other when the effective yield rises.

20.2 The Lytes Company has two issues of bonds outstanding. Both bear coupons of 10 percent, and the effective yield required on each is 18 percent because of the uncertain future of the company. Bond C has a maturity of twenty years and Bond D a maturity of thirty years. Both pay interest annually.
a. What is the price of each bond?
b. If the effective yield on each bond rises to 24 percent, what is the price of each bond?
c. Explain why the price of one bond falls more than the price of the other when the effective yield rises.
d. Compare the results in this problem with the results in the previous problem.

20.3 What will be the yield to maturity of a perpetual bond with a $1,000 par value, an 8 percent coupon rate, and a current market price of $800? of $1,000? of $1,200? Assume interest is paid annually.

20.4 Assuming that a bond has four years remaining to maturity and that interest is paid annually, what will be the yield to maturity on the bond with a $1,000 maturity value, an 8 percent coupon interest rate, and a current market price of $825? of $1,107?
a. Would you pay $825 for the bond if your required rate of return for securities in the same risk class was 10 percent ($k_b = 10\%$)? Explain.

20.5 a. The bonds of the Stanroy Corporation are perpetuities bearing a 9 percent coupon. Bonds of this type yield 8 percent. The par value of the bonds is $1,000. What is the price of the Stanroy bonds?
b. Interest rate levels rise to the point where such bonds now yield 12 percent. What is the price of the Stanroy bonds now?
c. Interest rate levels drop to 9 percent. At what price do the Stanroy bonds sell?
d. How would your answers to Parts a, b, and c change if the bonds had a definite maturity date of nineteen years?

20.6 Three years ago your firm issued some eighteen-year bonds with 10.5 percent coupon rates and a 10 percent call premium. You have called these bonds. The bonds originally sold at their face value of $1,000.

a. Compute the realized rate of return for investors who purchased the bonds when they were issued.

b. Given the rate of return in Part a, did investors welcome the call? Explain.

20.7 Carson Electronics, a leading manufacturer in its field, is planning an expansion program. It has estimated that it will need to raise an additional $100 million. Carson is discussing with its investment banker the alternatives of raising the $100 million through debt financing or through selling additional shares of common stock.

The prevailing cost of Aaa debt is 8 percent, while the prevailing cost of Baa debt is 9.6 percent. New equity would be sold at $10 per share. The corporate tax rate is 40 percent. Below are the industry's financial ratios, followed by Carson's balance sheet and income statement:

Electronics Industry Financial Ratios

Current ratio: 2.1 times
Sales to total assets: 1.8 times
Current debt to total assets: 30%
Long-term debt to net worth: 40%
Total debt to total assets: 50%
Coverage of fixed charges: 7 times
Net income to sales: 5%
Return on total assets: 9%
Net income to net worth: 12%

Carson Electronics Balance Sheet as of December 31, 1980 (Millions of Dollars)

Assets		Liabilities		
Total current assets	$ 600	Total current liabilities	$200	
Net fixed assets	400	Long-term debt (at 8%)	100	
		Total debt		$ 300
		Common stock, par value $1		100
		Additional paid-in capital		200
		Retained earnings		400
Total assets	$1,000	Total claims on assets		$1,000

Carson Electronics Income Statement for Year Ended December 31, 1980 (Millions of Dollars)

Total revenues	$2,000
Net operating income	208
Interest expense	8
Net income before taxes	$ 200
Income taxes (at 40%)	80
Net income to equity	$ 120

a. Estimate Carson Electronics' cost of equity capital by using the security market line. The risk-free rate is 6 percent, the expected return on the market is 11 percent, and the beta based on Carson's present leverage is 1.2.
b. What is the value of Carson's total equity? What is its indicated price per share?
c. On the basis of a cost of debt of 8 percent and the cost of equity that you have calculated, determine the weighted average cost of capital for Carson at the present time. (The company has no short-term interest bearing debt.)
d. If Carson finances its expansion by the use of debt, calculate the new financial structure and coverage relationships, and present your conclusion on whether the new debt issue will be risky or relatively risk-free. (Assume that the same percentage of net operating income is earned on the increase in assets as was earned on the total assets before the financing.)
e. If Carson finances with debt, the cost of debt will be 8 percent, while the cost of equity will reflect the rise in beta to 1.25. If the company finances with equity, the cost of debt will be 8 percent, while the cost of equity will reflect a drop in beta to 1.19. Compare the cost of equity under the two methods of financing.
f. Under each of the two methods of financing, what will be the total value of the equity, and what will be the new value per share of common stock?
g. Under the same assumptions as in the preceding questions, calculate the value of the firm under the two methods of financing.
h. Compare the weighted cost of capital under the two methods of financing.
i. Summarize your recommendation about which form of financing Carson should employ for raising the additional $100 million.

20.8 In late 1978 the Coaltown Gas & Electric Company sought to raise $6 million for expansion of facilities and services. The company could have sold additional debt at 9 percent, preferred stock at 8.84 percent, or common stock at $50 a share. Growth in earnings and dividends was expected to be 4.5%. How should the company have raised the money? Relevant financial information is provided below:

Public Utilities Financial Ratios

Current ratio: 1.0 times
Interest earned (before taxes): 4.0 times
Sales to total assets: 0.3 times
Average collection period: 28.0 days
Current debt/total assets: 5–10%
Long-term debt/total assets: 45–50%
Preferred/total assets: 10–15%
Common equity/total assets: 30–35%
Earnings before interest and taxes to total assets: 8.9%
Profits to common equity: 12.1%

Coaltown Gas & Electric Company Balance Sheet as of July 31, 1978 (Thousands of Dollars)

Assets		Liabilities	
Cash	$ 750	Current liabilities	$ 3,000
Receivables	1,500	Long-term debt (at 8%)	30,000
Materials and supplies	1,200	Preferred stock (at 10%)	3,000
Total current assets	$ 3,450	Common stock, $25 par value	11,250
Net property	56,550	Capital surplus	6,600
		Retained earnings	6,150
Total assets	$60,000	Total claims	$60,000

Coaltown Gas & Electric Company Income Statement for Year Ended July 31, 1978 (Thousands of Dollars)

Operating revenues	$18,900
Operating expenses	12,000
Earnings before interest and taxes	$ 6,900
Interest deduction	2,400
Earnings before taxes	$ 4,500
Income taxes (at 40%)	1,800
Earnings after taxes	$ 2,700
Preferred dividends	300
Net income available to common	$ 2,400
Earnings per share =	$5.33
Expected dividends per share =	$4.25

20.9 The Ellis Corporation plans to expand assets by 25 percent. It can finance the expansion with straight debt or with common stock. The interest rate on the debt would be 12 percent. Ellis's current balance sheet and income statement follow.

Ellis Corporation Balance Sheet as of December 31, 1980 (Thousands of Dollars)

Assets		Liabilities	
		Debt (at 10%)	$300
		Common stock, $1 par (100,000 shares outstanding)	100
		Retained earnings	400
Total assets	$800	Total claims	$800

Ellis Corporation Income Statement for Year Ended December 31, 1980 (Thousands of Dollars)

Sales	$2,300
Total costs (excluding interest)	2,070
Net operating income	$ 230
Debt interest	30
Income before taxes	$ 200
Taxes (at 50%)	100
Net income	$ 100

Earnings per share: $\frac{\$100{,}000}{100{,}000} = \$1$

Price-earnings ratio = 10[a]

Market price = P-E × EPS = 10 × 1 = $10

a. The P-E ratio is the market price per share divided by earnings per share. It represents the amount of money an investor is willing to pay for $1 of current earnings. The higher the riskiness of a stock, the lower its P-E ratio, other things held constant.

If Ellis Corporation finances the $200,000 expansion with debt, the rate on the incremental debt will be 12 percent, and the price-earnings ratio of the common stock will drop to nine times. If the expansion is financed with equity, the new stock will sell for $8 per share, the rate on debt will be 10 percent, and the price-earnings ratio will remain at ten times. (The opportunity cost of debt is 12 percent. However, use the 10 percent rate on the debt already on the balance sheet, because this is the rate actually being paid.)

a. Assume that net income before interest and taxes (EBIT) is 10 percent of sales. Calculate EPS at sales levels of $0, $600,000, $2,400,000, $2,800,000 $3,000,000, $3,600,000, and $4,800,000 for financing with (1) debt and (2) common stock. Assume no fixed costs of production.
b. Make a companion chart for EPS and indicate the crossover point in sales (that is, where EPS using bonds equals EPS using stock).
c. Using the price-earnings ratio, calculate the market value per share of common stock for each sales level for both the debt and the equity financing.
d. Using data from Part c, plot market value per share against level of sales and indicate the crossover point.
e. If the firm follows the policy of seeking to maximize (1) EPS or (2) market price per share, which form of financing should be used?
f. The probability estimates of future sales are: 5 percent chance of $0; 10 percent chance of $600,000; 20 percent chance of $2,400,000; 30 percent chance of $2,800,000; 20 percent chance of $3,000,000; 10 percent chance of $3,600,000; and 5 percent chance of $4,800,000. Calculate expected values for EPS, market price per share, the standard deviation, and the coefficient of variation for each alternative.
g. What other factors should be taken into account in choosing between the two forms of financing?
h. Would it matter if the presently outstanding stock were all owned by the final decision maker—the president—and that this represented that individual's entire net worth? Would it matter if the president were compensated entire-

ly by a fixed salary? if the president had a substantial number of stock options?

20.10 a. A manufacturing firm with $60 million of assets judges that it is at the beginning of a three-year growth cycle. It has a total debt to assets ratio of 16 percent, and it expects sales and net earnings to grow at a rate of 10 percent a year and stock prices to rise 30 percent a year over the three-year period. The firm will need $6 million at the beginning of the three-year period and another $3 million by the middle of the third year. It is at the beginning of a general business upswing, when money and capital costs are what they generally are after about a year of recession and at the beginning of an upswing. By the middle of the third year, money and capital costs will show their characteristic pattern near the peak of an upswing. How should the firm raise the $6 million and the $3 million?

b. An aerospace company with sales of $25 million a year needs $5 million to finance expansion. It has a debt to total assets ratio of 65 percent; and its common stock, which is widely held, is selling at a price-earnings ratio of twenty-five times. It is comparing the sale of common stock and convertible debentures. Which do you recommend? Explain.

c. A chemical company has been growing steadily. To finance a growth of sales from $40 million a year to $50 million over a two-year period, it needs $2 million in additional equipment. When additional working capital needs are taken into account, the total additional financing required during the first year is $5 million. Profits will rise by 50 percent after the first ten months. The stock is currently selling at twenty times earnings. The company can borrow on straight debt at 7½ percent or with a convertibility or warrant "sweetener" for ¾ percent less. The present debt to total assets ratio is 25 percent. Which form of financing should it employ?

20.11 During the years 1970–1974, the Kellogg Company had made gross plant and equipment additions of $185 million. Further expansion would require additional capital expansion outlays. To finance its continued expansion, Kellogg was considering alternative methods of raising $100 million of additional funds. The matter had been under continued study and in the summer of 1975, it was decided that the financing would take place in early autumn. The following alternatives were under consideration: One was 8⅝ percent notes of ten-year maturity. Redemption at 100 percent would be permitted as a whole or in part after October 1, 1982. A second was 9 percent debentures that would mature in 2005. Sinking fund payments of $2 million per year would be required beginning in 1985 and could be used for redemption of the bonds at 110 percent in 1985, declining by 1 percentage point a year until 100 percent was reached. A third alternative was to issue common stock. After declining to $10 in 1974, the price of the stock had recovered by mid-1975 to $14.50; and it was contemplated that an issue could be sold to net $14 per share. Relevant financial information follows.

Kellogg Company and Subsidiary Companies Consolidated Statements of Earnings (Dollars in Thousands except per Share Amounts)

	Year Ended December 31,				
	1970	1971	1972	1973	1974
Net sales	$614,412	$677,051	$699,221	$828,408	$1,009,818
Interest and other income	4,130	3,753	5,238	7,099	10,829
	618,542	680,804	704,459	835,507	1,020,647
Costs and expenses:					
Cost of goods sold	374,817	419,963	436,482	539,587	701,471
Selling, general and administrative expense	140,047	147,630	148,566	164,385	175,789
Interest expense	2,188	1,459	1,498	3,388	4,256
	517,052	569,052	586,546	707,360	881,516
Earnings before income taxes	101,490	111,752	117,913	128,147	139,131
Estimated income taxes:					
Current	51,900	55,800	54,600	61,100	60,500
Net deferred	—	900	2,800	2,000	6,600
	51,900	56,700	57,400	63,100	67,100
Net earnings	49,590	55,052	60,513	65,047	72,031
Dividends on preferred stock	89	86	86	84	83
Amount earned on common stock	$ 49,501	$ 54,966	$ 60,427	$ 64,963	$ 71,948
Earnings per share of common stock	$.68	$.76	$.83	$.89	$.98
Dividends per share of common stock	$.45	$.50	$.52	$.54	$.59
Ratio of earnings to fixed charges	34.82	46.97	49.64	30.79	28.64
Rentals included in fixed charges	$727	$920	$800	$700	$602

Sources: Quarterly and annual reports.

Kellogg Company and
Subsidiary Companies
Consolidated Balance Sheets
(Dollars in Thousands)

	December 31, 1974	June 30, 1975 (Unaudited)
Current assets:		
Cash, including certificates of deposit of $15,323 in 1974 and $32,629 in 1975	$ 17,761	$ 34,159
United States Government securities, at cost (approximate market)	11,001	6,500
Accounts receivable, less allowances of $633 in 1974 and $957 in 1975	62,002	100,300
Inventories:		
Raw materials and supplies	84,151	71,507
Finished goods and materials in process	51,796	50,824
Prepaid taxes and other expenses	15,479	18,108
Total current assets	242,190	281,398
Property, plant, and equipment	247,162	264,721
Other Assets:		
Excess of cost over net assets of companies acquired	19,021	19,021
Other investments	1,144	1,067
Patents, trade-marks and goodwill	1	1
Total assets	$509,518	$566,208
Current Liabilities:		
Accounts payable	$ 42,117	$ 44,304
Loans payable	26,595	29,752
Accrued salaries and wages	5,166	5,500
Estimated income taxes	14,358	24,759
Other current liabilities	35,844	44,788
Total current liabilities	124,080	149,103
Long-term loans	10,316	9,711
Deferred income taxes	22,092	25,163
Shareholders' Equity:		
3½% cumulative preferred stock, $100 par value—		
Authorized and issued in 1974, 81,763 shares less 58,241 in Treasury (78,013 less 54,491 in 1975)	2,352	2,352
Common stock, $.50 par value—		
Authorized 80,000,000 shares; issued 73,592,074 in 1974 and 73,612,444 in 1975	36,796	36,806
Capital in excess of par value	19,771	19,999
Retained earnings	294,111	323,074
Total shareholders' equity	353,030	382,231
Total liabilities and shareholders' equity	$509,518	$566,208

Sources: Quarterly and annual reports.

a. The risk-free rate was 6 percent, the expected return on the market was 11 percent, and Kellogg's beta was 1.01 reflecting its present target leverage ratio of 10 percent *(B/V)*. What was Kellogg's cost of equity capital?
b. On the basis of the cost of equity capital that you have computed, and given a cost of debt of 8 percent, what was Kellogg's weighted average cost of capital? (T = 47 percent.)
c. Based on the cost of capital calculated and the target leverage ratio of 10 percent, what would have been the cost of capital of Kellogg if it were unlevered and its tax rate were 47 percent?
d. What was the theoretical value of the Kellogg Company as an unlevered firm? Use the following financial parameters: $\bar{X}$ = \$173.2 million, T = 47%, r = 0.2, b = 0.55, N = 10.
e. Using the $V_L = V_u + TB$ relationship, what were the amounts of V_L and B based on the target leverage ratio of 10 percent?
f. Kellogg's present financial structure at book values was:

Debt	\$100 at 6 percent
Equity	400
Total assets	\$500

Kellogg was considering increasing its target leverage ratio by financing its current \$100 million investment program with debt at 8 percent. Assume that V_u remained unchanged since the additional debt was to be used to finance growth already reflected in the investment rate, b = 0.55. If Kellogg financed the \$100 million expansion by the use of debt, calculate the new book financial structure and coverage relationships and present your judgment as to whether the new debt issue would have been risky or relatively risk-free. Recall that $\bar{X}$ = \$173.2 million and the additional net operating income on the incremental capital would represent a 20 percent rate.
g. What would the new beta be under debt financing with a new target leverage ratio, L^* = 20%?
h. Assume that V_u remained unchanged with the \$100 million additional capital because the b = 0.55 incorporated the investment growth taking place. What were the new V_L, L, and S under the debt and equity financing alternatives?
i. Under the same assumptions as in the preceding questions, calculate the new market value per share of the common stock under the two alternative methods of financing. Note that 73.6 million shares of common stock were outstanding before the financing. The new equity would be sold at \$14.00 per share.
j. Compare the increase in indicated stock price value with the increase in risk if the target leverage ratio was increased by selecting the debt financing.

20.12 The Rover Company has a \$30,000,000 long-term twenty-year bond issue outstanding which has an additional fifteen years to maturity and bears a coupon interest rate of 11.5 percent. The interest payments are made semiannually. Financial market conditions have given the firm the opportunity of refinancing the debt with another fifteen-year bond but at a lower rate of 10 percent. The firm plans to use all debt financing for the proposed bond refunding project. The relevant data on the old issue and on the new refunding issue are summarized below:

Face amount	$30,000,000	$31,301,000
Interest rate	$r_0 = 11.5\%$	$r_1 = 10\%$
Life of bond	20 years	15 years
Maturity date	August 10, 1993	August 10, 1993
Flotation costs[a]	$600,000	—
Net proceeds of sale	$29,400,000	—
Date issued	August 14, 1973	August 10, 1979
Redemption date	August 10, 1978	—
Call price	$105	—

a. Flotation costs on both the old and new issue are 2.0 percent of gross proceeds.

The firm's applicable corporate tax rate is 40 percent. The after-tax cost of debt is used as the discount factor in the analysis. Based on the data provided, evaluate the planned refunding issue.

Selected References

Ang, James S. "The Intertemporal Behavior of Corporate Debt Policy." *Journal of Financial and Quantitative Analysis* 11 (November 1976), pp. 555–566.

———. "The Two Faces of Bond Refunding." *Journal of Finance* 30 (June 1975), pp. 869–874.

Ang, James S., and Patel, Kiritkumar A. "Empirical Research on Capital Markets Bond Rating Methods: Comparison and Validation." *Journal of Finance* 30 (May 1975), pp. 631–640.

Benson, George J. "The Impact of Maturity Regulation on High Interest Rate Lenders and Borrowers." *Journal of Financial Economics* 4 (January 1977), pp. 23–49.

Bierwag, G. O. "Measures of Duration." *Economic Inquiry* 16 (October 1978), pp. 497–507.

———. "Immunization, Duration, and the Term Structure." *Journal of Financial and Quantitative Analysis* 12 (December 1977), pp. 701–742.

Bierwag, G. O.; Kaufman, George G.; and Khang, Chulsoon. "Duration and Bond Portfolio Analysis: An Overview." *Journal of Financial and Quantitative Analysis* 13 (November 1978), pp. 671–681.

Bildersee, John S. "Some New Bond Indexes." *Journal of Business* 48 (October 1975), pp. 506–525.

Black, Fischer, and Cox, John C. "Valuing Corporate Securities: Some Effects of Bond Indenture Provisions." *Journal of Finance* 31 (May 1976), pp. 351–367.

Bloch, Ernest. "Pricing a Corporate Bond Issue: A Look Behind the Scenes." *Essays in Money and Credit.* New York: Federal Reserve Bank of New York, 1964, pp. 72–76.

Bodie, Zvi, and Taggart, Robert A. "Future Investment Opportunities and the Value of the Call Provision on a Bond." *Journal of Finance* 33 (September 1978), pp. 1187–1200.

Boquist, John A.; Racette, George A.; and Schlarbaum, Gary G. "Duration and Risk Assessment for Bonds and Common Stocks." *Journal of Finance* 30 (December 1975), pp. 1360–1365.

Brown, Bowman. "Why Corporations Should Consider Income Bonds." *Financial Executive* 35 (October 1967), pp. 74–78.

Bullington, Robert A. "How Corporate Debt Issues are Rated." *Financial Executive* 42 (September 1974), pp. 28–37.

Caks, John. "Corporate Debt Decisions: A New Analytical Framework." *Journal of Finance* 33 (December 1978), pp. 1297–1315.

———. "The Coupon Effect on Yield to Maturity." *Journal of Finance* 32 (March 1977), pp. 103–115.

Cooper, I. A. "Asset Changes, Interest-Rate Changes, and Duration." *Journal of Financial and Quantitative Analysis* 12 (December 1977), pp. 701–723.

Donaldson, Gordon. "In Defense of Preferred Stock." *Harvard Business Review* 40 (July–August 1962), pp. 123–136.

———. "New Framework for Corporate Debt Policy." *Harvard Business Review* 40 (March–April 1962), pp. 117–131.

Dyl, Edward A., and Joehnk, Michael D. "Sinking Funds and the Cost of Corporate Debt." *Journal of Finance* 34 (September 1979), pp. 887–893.

———. "Effect of Latest IRS Regulations on Advance Refundings." *Financial Management* 6 (Summer 1977), pp. 71–72.

———. "Competitive versus Negotiated Underwriting of Public Utility Debt." *Bell Journal of Economics* 7 (Autumn 1976), pp. 680–689.

Ederington, Louis H. "Negotiated versus Competitive Underwritings of Corporate Bonds." *Journal of Finance* 31 (March 1976), pp. 17–26.

———. "Uncertainty, Competition, and Costs in Corporate Bond Underwriting." *Journal of Financial Economics* 2 (March 1975), pp. 71–94.

———. "The Yield Spread on New Issues of Corporate Bonds." *Journal of Finance* 29 (December 1974), pp. 1531–1543.

Elsaid, Hussein H. "The Function of Preferred Stock in the Corporate Financial Plan." *Financial Analysts' Journal* (July–August 1969), pp. 112–117.

Everett, Edward. "Subordinated Debt—Nature and Enforcement." *Business Lawyer* 20 (July 1965), pp. 953–987.

Fischer, Donald E., and Wilt, Glenn A., Jr. "Non-convertible Preferred Stock as a Financing Instrument, 1950–1965." *Journal of Finance* 23 (September 1968), pp. 611–624.

Fisher, Lawrence. "Determinants of Risk Premiums on Corporate Bonds." *Journal of Political Economy* 67 (June 1959), pp. 217–237.

Gritta, Richard D. "The Impact of Lease Capitalization." *Financial Analysts' Journal* 30 (March–April 1974), pp. 47–52.

Grove, M. A. "On 'Duration' and the Optimal Maturity Structure of the Balance Sheet." *Bell Journal of Economics and Management Science* 5 (Autumn 1974), pp. 696–709.

Guzzardi, Walter, Jr. "The Bomb IBM Dropped on Wall Street." *Fortune,* November 19, 1979, pp. 52–57.

Hickman, W. B. *Corporate Bonds: Quality and Investment Performance,* Occasional Paper 59. New York: National Bureau of Economic Research, 1957.

Ingersoll, Jonathan E.; Skelton, Jeffrey; and Weil, Roman L. "Duration and Security Risk." *Journal of Financial and Quantitative Analysis* 13 (November 1978), pp. 627–650.

Jarrow, Robert A. "The Relationship between Yield, Risk, and Return of Corporate Bonds." *Journal of Finance* 33 (September 1978), pp. 1235–1240.

Jen, Frank C., and Wert, James E. "The Deferred Call Provision and Corporate Bond Yields." *Journal of Financial and Quantitative Analysis* 3 (June 1968), pp. 157–169.

———. "The Effects of Call Risk on Corporate Bond Yields." *Journal of Finance* 22 (December 1967), pp. 637–652.

———. "The Value of the Deferred Call Privilege." *National Banking Review* 3 (March 1966), pp. 369–378.

Joehnk, Michael D.; Fogler, H. Russell; and Bradley, Charles E. "The Price Elasticity of Discounted Bonds: Some Empirical Evidence." *Journal of Financial and Quantitative Analysis* 13 (September 1978), pp. 559–566.

Johnson, Ramon E. "Term Structures of Corporate Bond Yields as a Function of Risk of Default." *Journal of Finance* 22 (May 1967), pp. 313–345.

Johnson, Robert W. "Subordinated Debentures: Debt That Serves as Equity." *Journal of Finance* 10 (March 1955), pp. 1–16.

Kelly, Paul E. "New Financing Techniques on Wall Street." *Financial Executive* 44 (November 1974), pp. 30–43.

Khang, Chulsoon. "Bond Immunization When Short-Term Interest Rates Fluctuate More than Long-Term Rates." *Journal of Financial and Quantitative Analysis* 14 (December 1979), pp. 1085–1090.

Lanstein, Ronald, and Sharpe, William F. "Duration and Security Risk." *Journal of Financial and Quantitative Analysis* 13 (November 1978), pp. 653–668.

Lindvall, John R. "New Issue Corporate Bonds, Seasoned Market Efficiency and Yield Spreads." *Journal of Finance* 32 (September 1977), pp. 1057–1067.

Litzenberger, Robert H., and Rutenberg, David P. "Size and Timing of Corporate Bond Flotations." *Journal of Financial and Quantitative Analysis* 8 (January 1972), pp. 1343–1359.

Livingston, Miles. "Taxation and Bond Market Equilibrium in a World of Uncertain Future Interest Rates." *Journal of Financial and Quantitative Analysis* 14 (March 1979), pp. 11–27.

Mayor, Thomas H., and McCoin, Kenneth G. "The Rate of Discount in Bond Refunding." *Financial Management* 3 (Autumn 1974), pp. 54–58.

Morris, James R. "A Model for Corporate Debt Maturity Decisions." *Journal of Financial and Quantitative Analysis* 11 (September 1976), pp. 339–358.

———. "On Corporate Debt Maturity Strategies." *Journal of Finance* 31 (March 1976), pp. 29–37.

Pinches, George E. "Financing with Convertible Preferred Stock, 1960–1967." *Journal of Finance* 25 (March 1970), pp. 53–63.

Pinches, George E., and Mingo, Kent A. "The Role of Subordination and Industrial Bond Ratings." *Journal of Finance* 30 (March 1975), pp. 201–206.

———. "A Multivariate Analysis of Industrial Bond Ratings." *Journal of Finance* 28 (March 1973), pp. 1–18.

Pinches, George E., and Singleton, J. Clay. "The Adjustment of Stock Prices to Bond Rating Changes." *Journal of Finance* 33 (March 1978), pp. 29–44.

Pye, Gordon. "The Value of Call Deferment on a Bond: Some Empirical Results." *Journal of Finance* 22 (December 1967), pp. 623–636.

———. "The Value of the Call Option on a Bond." *Journal of Political Economy* 74 (April 1966), pp. 200–205.

Racette, George A., and Lewellen, Wilbur G. "Corporate Debt Coupon Rate Strategies." *National Tax Journal* 29 (June 1976), pp. 165–178.

Reilly, Frank K., and Joehnk, Michael D. "The Association between Market-Determined Risk Measures for Bonds and Bond Ratings." *Journal of Finance* 31 (December 1976), pp. 1387–1403.

Scholes, Myron, and Williams, Joseph. "Estimating Betas from Nonsynchronous Data." *Journal of Financial Economics* 5 (December 1977), pp. 309–327.

Scott, James H., Jr. "Bankruptcy, Secured Debt, and Optimal Capital Structure: Reply." *Journal of Finance* 34 (March 1979), pp. 253–260.

Shapiro, Eli, and Wolf, Charles R. *The Role of Private Placements in Corporate Finance.* Boston: Division of Research, Graduate School of Business Administration, Harvard University, 1972.

Shiller, Robert J., and Modigliani, Franco. "Coupon and Tax Effects on New and Seasoned Bond Yields and the Measurement of the Cost of Debt Capital." *Journal of Financial Economics* 7 (September 1979), pp. 297–318.

Smith, Clifford W., and Warner, Jerold B. "On Financial Contracting: An Analysis of Bond Covenants." *Journal of Financial Economics* 7 (June 1979), pp. 117–161.

———. "Bankruptcy, Secured Debt, and Optimal Capital Structure: Comment." *Journal of Finance* 34 (March 1979), pp. 247–252.

Sprecher, C. Ronald. "A Note on Financing Mergers with Convertible Preferred Stock." *Journal of Finance* 26 (June 1971), pp. 683–686.

Stevenson, Richard A. "Retirement of Non-callable Preferred Stock." *Journal of Finance* 25 (December 1970), pp. 1143–1152.

Van Horne, James C. "Behavior of Default-Risk Premiums for Corporate Bonds and Commercial Paper." *Journal of Business Research* 7 (December 1979), pp. 301–313.

———. "Implied Fixed Costs in Long-Term Debt Issues." *Journal of Financial and Quantitative Analysis* 8 (December 1973), pp. 821–833.

Warner, Jerold B. "Bankruptcy, Absolute Priority, and the Pricing of Risky Debt Claims." *Journal of Financial Economics* 4 (May 1977), pp. 239–276.

Weinstein, Mark I. "The Seasoning Process of New Corporate Bond Issues." *Journal of Finance* 33 (December 1978), pp. 1343–1354.

White, William L. "Debt Management and the Form of Business Financing." *Journal of Finance* 29 (May 1974), pp. 565–577.

Winn, Willis J., and Hess, Arleigh, Jr. "The Value of the Call Privilege." *Journal of Finance* 14 (May 1959), pp. 182–195.

Wishner, Maynard I. "Coming: Significantly Larger Roles for Secured Corporate Financing." *Financial Executive* 45 (May 1977), pp. 18–23.

Ziese, Charles H., and Taylor, Roger K. "Advance Refunding: A Practitioner's Perspective." *Financial Management* 6 (Summer 1977), pp. 73–76.

Appendix A to Chapter 20

Refunding Decisions

Since 1974 many articles have appeared on bond refunding, as indicated by the Selected References to this appendix. These articles —and the current broad interest in refunding—were stimulated by characteristics of the economy during the 1970s. Interest rates were relatively low through most of the 1960s. The yield on Aaa corporate bonds was in the 4.5 percent region until after the mid-1960s. During the same period the rates on 4 to 6 months prime commercial paper were below 4 percent. With the onset of inflation after 1966, interest rates began to rise.

In the effort to use monetary policy to control the rising level of inflation, interest rates were pushed in the late 1960s to levels that appeared to be extremely high; they reached a peak just before the recession of 1970–1971. Both long-term and short-term rates approximated 8 percent by 1970. In the effort to counter the recession, monetary policy was subsequently eased. By 1972 the rate on 4 to 6 months prime commercial paper had fallen to 4.7 percent, almost half the peak level it had reached in early 1970.

The years of the late 1970s saw a resurgence of inflationary pressures, a tightening of monetary policy, and again a rise in interest rates. By early 1980 the corporate Aaa bond rate was 13 percent. The rate on 4 to 6 months prime commerical paper was 17.5 percent, and the prime rate charged by banks reached 20 percent. By the end of May 1980, the prime rate was 14 percent, the commercial paper rate 10 percent, and the rate on Aaa bonds was below 11 percent.

Overview

The widely fluctuating interest rates gave rise to opportunities for bond refunding. Bonds sold at high interest rates in the late sixties and early seventies provided opportunities for refunding at lower interest rates in the mid-1970s. The resumption of the sharp rise in interest rates caused bonds sold at lower interest levels to go to a discount by the late 1970s. This raised questions about the profitability of advanced refunding of discount bonds.

Interest rate fluctuations in which interest rates go either lower or higher are said to provide opportunities for bond refunding. Lower interest rates may provide opportunities for interest rate savings. Higher interest rates may provide opportunities for buying in bonds at a discount. Before becoming immersed in the details of the following analysis, we should like first to present as an overview some general principles that should be kept in mind as a framework for the subsequent detailed computations.

In the absence of special characteristics or restrictions, neither falling interest rates nor rising interest rates provide an obvious basis for savings to corporate financial managers. Lower or higher interest rates simply represent the costs of funds at a particular time and without special restrictions provide no opportunities for gains or losses. What makes refunding at lower interest rates advantageous is the call option that is inserted in corporate bond indentures. For example, if the bond is issued at a 9 percent interest rate and if interest rates subsequently fall to 6 percent, a noncallable perpetual bond issued at par would sell at 150 at the lower 6 percent interest yield basis. If the company has a call option which permits it to buy in the bond at 105, for example, the firm can achieve interest savings with a substantial present value.

On the other hand, if the market had priced out accurately the value of the call privilege, then the bond refunding would not represent a net gain. In such a case, the bond refunding would represent only the interest savings that the company woud have to realize in order to be compensated for the higher yield it was required to offer on callable bonds.

With respect to bonds that sell at a discount because interest rates have risen substantially, there is no special privilege analogous to the call option. The firm simply goes into the market and buys its bonds at a discount because the going yield is higher than the coupon rates paid on its existing bonds. One attractive feature to business firms is that the difference between the value of the bond shown on its books and the market price at which the bonds are purchased can be recorded as a realized profit from the standpoint of reporting income. The firm is thus able to report higher income than it otherwise would. However, from a cash flow standpoint this is a disadvantage, not an advantage. The reported profit is subject to income taxation. The gain is simply a paper gain. It has not produced an increment of positive cash flows for the company. The net effect of reporting the income and the taxation of it is to reduce the cash flows for the firm, not to increase them. Thus unless the taxation can be avoided, net cash flows are reduced by buying in the discount bonds.

Analysis of Refunding When Interest Rates Have Fallen

Bond refunding which takes place when interest rates have fallen may yield future cash benefits to the firm as the result of the reduction in bond interest payments. Once the contractual terms under which the new bonds will be sold have been established, the interest saving is known with certainty. Therefore, it is generally agreed that the discount rate should be the cost of debt. However, disagreement has arisen on whether the before-tax cost of debt or the after-tax cost of debt should be used, and this is a central question to be addressed in the materials which follow.

The net present value from a bond refunding can be expressed logically by Equation 20A.1.

$$\text{NPV} = \overset{(1)}{\sum_{t=1}^{N} \frac{(1-T)(r-r_1)B}{(1+r_1)^t}} - \overset{(2)}{\sum_{t=1}^{N} \frac{(1-T)r_1\Delta B}{(1+r_1)^t}} - \overset{(3)}{\frac{\Delta B}{(1+r_1)^N}} - \overset{(4)}{[(1-T)\text{RC} - \Delta B]}, \tag{20A.1}$$

where:

T = Corporate income tax rate
RC = Cost of refunding
r = Coupon rate on old issue
r_1 = Coupon rate on new issue
B = Par value of debt
N = Remaining years to maturity on the old issue

The four numbered terms on the right-hand side of the equation represent the following:

1. Present value of after-tax interest savings on the old bond issue.
2. Present value of interest that will be paid on incremental debt.
3. Present value of repayment of the incremental debt at maturity.
4. Present value of equity issued.

The sense of each of the terms can also be readily explained. In Term 1, the difference in the expression $(r - r_1)$ is the interest savings, which is multiplied times the value of the old bonds and discounted on an after-tax basis to arrive at the present value of the savings (PVS). In the second term, the cost of whatever increase in debt is used to finance the refunding costs is also discounted on an after-tax basis. The third term is the present value of the incremental debt. In the fourth term, we start with the after-tax refunding costs and deduct the incremental debt. The difference must be the amount of external equity financing utilized. We have not thus far discussed the discount factor used in the present value calculations; we shall do that in the following analysis.

We begin by simplifying the second term, with the results shown in Equation 20A.2.

$$\sum_{t=1}^{N} \frac{(1-T)r_1\Delta B}{(1+r_1)^t} = \frac{(1-T)(r_1)\Delta B}{(1+r_1)} \sum_{t=0}^{N-1} \frac{1}{(1+r_1)^t} = \frac{(1-T)r_1\Delta B}{(1+r_1)} \times \frac{1 - \frac{1}{(1+r_1)^N}}{1 - \frac{1}{(1+r_1)}} = (1-T)\Delta B\,[1 - (1+r_1)^{-N}]. \tag{20A.2}$$

First, we factored a $1/(1 + r_1)$ from the denominator. We were then able to evaluate the denominator, using a standard geometric series format to arrive at the results shown. Having the second term in this simplified form permits the equation to be simplified still further. By multiplying through and regrouping terms, we arrive at the results shown in Equation 20A.3.

$$\begin{aligned} \text{NPV} &= \text{PVS} - \Delta B(1 - T)[1 - (1 + r_1)^{-N}] - \Delta B(1 + r_1)^{-N} \\ &\quad - [(1 - T)\text{RC} - \Delta B] \\ &= \text{PVS} - \Delta B + \Delta B(1 + r_1)^{-N} + T\Delta B[1 - (1 + r_1)^{-N}] - \Delta B(1 + r_1)^{-N} \\ &\quad - [(1 - T)\text{RC}] + \Delta B \\ &= \text{PVS} + T\Delta B[1 - (1 + r_1)^{-N}] - (1 - T)\text{RC}. \end{aligned} \tag{20A.3}$$

If the net present value expression is to be greater than zero, then the after-tax refunding costs must be exceeded by the sum of the other terms in the expression. To show this relationship, we formulate the inequality shown in Equation 20A.4.

$$\sum_{t=1}^{N} \frac{(1 - T)(r - r_1)B}{(1 + r_1)^t} + T\Delta B[1 - (1 + r_1)^{-N}] > (1 - T)\text{RC}. \tag{20A.4}$$

Thus far the analysis has been within the framework of debt with a finite time to maturity. If we let N go to infinity, Equation 20A.4 becomes 20A.5:

$$\frac{(1 - T)(r - r_1)B}{r_1} + T\,\Delta B > (1 + T)\text{RC}. \tag{20A.5}$$

The first term represents the standard capitalization of an infinite stream. In the second term the value of $1/(1 + r_1)^N$ becomes zero.

Additionally, if the total after-tax refunding costs are financed by debt so that we have $\Delta B = (1 - T)\text{RC}$, we obtain Equation 20A.6.[1]

$$\begin{gathered} \frac{(1 - T)(r - r_1)B}{r_1} > (1 - T)\text{RC} - T(1 - T)\text{RC} = \frac{(1 - T)(r - r_1)B}{r_1} > \\ (1 - T)\text{RC}(1 - T) = \frac{(1 - T)(r - r_1)B}{(1 - T)r_1} > (1 - T)\text{RC}. \end{gathered} \tag{20A.6}$$

The result in 20A.6 is the same as that obtained by Ahron Ofer and Robert Taggart, Jr., (see the Selected References for their 1977 article) when all new financing is by the incremental debt.

The significance of this result is that if the refunding costs are financed entirely by debt, the incremental debt generates a tax shelter on the full amount of the financing. Hence the relevant cost becomes the after-tax cost of debt.

Myron J. Gordon argued in 1974 for the use of the before-tax cost of debt as the discount factor. However, his proof is flawed by the use of the valuation model for risky returns in his analysis of nonrisky returns. Also, when bonds

1. Gene Laber, "Implications of Discount Rates and Financing Assumptions for Bond Refunding Decisions," *Financial Management* 8 (Spring 1979), pp. 7–12.

are used to finance the refunding costs, additional tax shelter is achieved so that the discount rate is the after-tax rate on the refunding bonds.

In a 1980 comment, Miles Livingston criticizes the Ofer and Taggart results as well as equivalent textbook procedures developed under the same financing assumptions. To view the nature of the criticism, first define the gain in the value of shareholders' equity as the excess of the gains from refunding over the after-tax refunding costs, as shown in Equation 20A.7.

$$\frac{(1 - T)(r - r_1)B}{(1 - T)r_1} - (1 - T)\text{RC} = \Delta S. \tag{20A.7}$$

Next cancel the $(1 - T)$ expressions in the first term and separate the elements of the numerator.

$$\left(\frac{rB}{r_1} - B\right) - (1 - T)(\text{RC}) = \Delta S. \tag{20A.8}$$

Livingston argues that the gain from refunding appears to be the market value of the old bond less the par value of the new bond. But he objects that the old bond cannot sell for more than its call price plus other (relatively small) refunding costs. Technically, Livingston is correct. But the $B(r - r_1)/r_1$ term still measures the value of the interest "saving" from refunding the old bond. The original r and the new r_1 on callable bonds are higher than the rates on noncallable bonds since the issuer must compensate investors for the call option.

Refunding When Interest Rates Have Risen

We next consider the situation where interest rates have risen substantially above the coupon rates on the firm's outstanding bonds. For example, suppose that Firm F earlier had sold ten perpetual bonds at 6 percent, but the prevailing yield on such bonds is now 10 percent. The old bonds now sell for \$600 each. Firm F can retire the bonds at \$6,000, reporting a profit of \$4,000. The interest paid on the old bonds is \$600. The total interest on the \$6,000 of new bonds issued at 10 percent to buy up the old bonds would also be \$600. Thus Firm F experiences no change in interest costs. If the gain of \$4,000 is taxed at, say, 40 percent the net cash flow to the firm is reduced by \$1,600. Thus from a pure cash flow standpoint, all that has really happened is that the firm has an additional cash outflow required by the amount of taxes it has to pay on the increase in reported income.

The Internal Revenue Code provides that a corporation may elect to have excluded from gross income the gain when it buys its own bonds at a discount.[2] But if a corporation does make this election, the basis of the property against which the obligations were issued is reduced by the amount of the gain.[3] This may more than offset the advantage of not reporting the gain from

2. Internal Revenue Code, Secs. 108(a); 1.108(a)–1.
3. Ibid., Secs. 1017; 1.1017–1.

the repurchase of the discount bond, since the depreciation basis is reduced and the basis for determining the gain or loss on a subsequent sale is also reduced. Thus it is difficult to envisage how the negative effects of the tax payments on the actual cash flows of the firm can be avoided.

A superior strategy would be to buy a bond of the same quality at par that pays 10 percent. The interest income will just cancel with the interest expense of the old bond, but there will be no tax liability. From a cash flow standpoint, the firm avoids the $1,600 cash tax payment.

An article in *Business Week* of November 12, 1979, described the very active operations of investment bankers in arranging for helping clients buy up bonds at a discount. The context of this presentation was that the firms were going to have to make purchases for bond sinking funds in one, two, three, or five years anyhow: In other words, the firms had decided that it was a good strategy to make anticipatory purchases since when the purchases would have to be made in subsequent years, the bonds might not be at such deep discounts. The bonds could be purchased at a saving and meet future sinking fund requirements as they became effective.

We believe that this analysis also requires qualification. By buying its own bonds at a discount, a firm would have reported profits and taxable income. The basis for the anticipatory bond purchases appears to be the expectation that interest rates would be lower in the future. If the firm really believed that interest rates were going to be lower, it could buy bonds of equal quality (or a portfolio of bonds), then hold them until it was required to purchase bonds for its own sinking fund. If interest rates fell in the meantime, the firm would have realized capital gain on the bonds that it had purchased. It would have an equal paper loss on its own bonds that it did not purchase. At the same time, it would be receiving a higher yield on the bonds that it purchased at the market when interest rates were higher. Furthermore, it would have obtained protection against a rise in the required yield on its own bonds through quality deterioration. But the fundamental point is that at a minimum it would defer the taxes on the capital gain involved in the interest rate change by buying bonds other than its own.

These general observations provide the foundation for a key to understanding some of the literature in this area. James S. Ang made a 1975 presentation in which he sought to demonstrate that refunding was not only advantageous when current interest rates fall below interest rates at issue. He argued that it might also be profitable when current interest rates rise above the interest rate at issue. Single-period and multi-period models were used along with the hypothetical application using dynamic programming.

However, in their 1978 article cited in the Selected References to this appendix, Thomas H. Mayor and Kenneth G. McCoin demonstrate—following the general logic set forth in this analysis—that refunding when interest rates have risen cannot be profitable unless implementation costs are negative. Implementation costs are measured by brokerage commissions plus the difference between the average purchase price and the current market price.

Implementation costs cannot be reasonably assumed to be negative. In the multi-period model, refunding when interest rates have risen again depends upon very extreme assumptions. First, implementation costs are assumed to be very small. Second, implicit in the analysis is that interest rates will subsequently fall and the firm will realize a capital gain from the interest rate change. This second assumption then means that the firm is able to forecast future interest rates correctly and part of the gain from refunding is to buy the bonds when interest rates are high and sell them when interest rates are lower. If the firm is able to forecast future interest rates, it does not have to engage in refunding to make a profit. It will simply buy bonds when interest rates are high and sell them when interest rates have fallen.

This general result for refunding criteria when interest rates have risen can be made more explicit with reference to the general points made by employing the framework developed by A. J. Kalotay in a 1978 article. The most general expression for the advanced refunding of discounted debt is set forth by Kalotay in Equation 20A.9, shown below:

$$\text{NPV} = -p + \sum_{t=1}^{N} \frac{(1-T)r}{[1+(1-T)r]^{t}} + \frac{1}{[1+(1-T)r_1]^{N}} - \sum_{t=0}^{M} \frac{T(1-p)}{M+1} \times \frac{1}{[1+(1-T)r_1]^{k}} - (1-T)\text{RC}'. \tag{20A.9}$$

The symbols are the same as defined earlier with the exception of p and M; p is the price at which the discounted bond can be purchased, expressed as a decimal ratio of its par value. M is the number of years over which the taxable gain can be amortized. The second term on the right-hand side of the equation is the discounted interest payments. The third term is the discounted principal payment. The fourth term is represented by the tax obligations associated with the gain $(1-p)$. The RC' term represents other refunding costs that have not been explicitly dealt with to this point. In Equation 20A.10 the same equation is rewritten with the summation expressions carried out.

$$\text{NPV} = -p + \frac{r}{r_1}\{1-[1+(1-T)r_1]^{-N}\} + [1+(1-T)r_1]^{-N} - \frac{T(1-p)}{M+1} \times \left\{\frac{[1+(1-T)r_1]-[1+(1-T)r_1]^{-(M-1)}}{(1-T)r_1}\right\} - (1-T)\text{RC}'. \tag{20A.10}$$

The nature of the expressions in the above equation can be shown by using illustrative values for the variables involved. Let $p = 0.57$, $r = 0.0425$, $r_1 = 0.11$, $N = 18$, $\text{RC}' = 0.02$, $T = 0.5$, and $M = 18$. Under the assumptions in the illustration, the value of the discounted interest payments and the discounted principal payments was 0.62, while the purchase price of the bond was assumed to be 0.57. This represented a gain of 0.05. The taxable income, however, is the difference between the par value of the bond at 1 and the purchase price of 0.57. Thus the taxable gain is 0.43. The present value of the tax obligations then turns out to be minus 0.14. The difference between the 0.05 gain from buying a bond with a value of 0.62 at 0.57 is offset by the additional tax obligations of 0.14. The result is a negative 10 percent (−0.57 + 0.24 + 0.38 − 0.14 − 0.01 = −0.10).

Kalotay emphasizes that profitable refunding when interest rates have risen is probably plausible only if for some reason there are no tax obligations or if the tax obligations are amortized over an extremely long period of time. To illustrate this, Kalotay takes the extreme case where the firm discounts interest payments and principal payments at the after-tax cost of debt while the individual investor in the market uses the before-tax rate of interest as the discount factor. This results in an even lower value of p. Under the numerical values previously assumed, the value of p becomes 0.48. Or, alternatively, the underlying determinants of p are shown in Equation 20A.11. Suppose:

$$p = \sum_{t=1}^{N} \frac{r}{(1 + r_1)^t} + \frac{1}{(1 + r_1)^N} = \frac{r}{r_1}[1 - (1 + r_1)^{-N}] + \frac{1}{(1 + r_1)^N}. \qquad (20A.11)$$

When these underlying determinants of p are substituted in Equation 20A.10, we obtain Equation 20A.12:

$$\text{NPV} = \left(1 - \frac{r}{r_1}\right)\{[1 + (1 - T)r_1]^{-N} - (1 + r_1)^{-N}\} - \left(1 - \frac{r}{r_1}\right) \qquad (20A.12)$$
$$[1 - (1 + r_1)^{-N}]\left(\frac{T}{M + 1}\right)\left\{\frac{1 + (1 - T)r_1 - [1 + (1 - T)r_1]^{-M}}{(1 - T)r_1}\right\}.$$

Furthermore, it is assumed in Equation 20A.12 that other refunding costs, the final expression in Equation 20A.9, are negligible and can be dropped. Using the numerical values previously assumed plus the assumption that p is determined by the before-tax cost of debt, the NPV becomes a negative 4 percent (−0.48 + 0.24 + 0.38 − 0.17 − 0.01 = −0.04). Kalotay comments that the assumption that p is determined by discounting at the before-tax cost of debt is more favorable to the refunding decision at higher interest rates. Yet under plausible relationships the NPV is still negative.

The thrust of the logic set forth above and the concrete framework presented by Kalotay is this: To initiate the possibility of favorable refunding requires that the price at which the bond can be purchased be lower than the appropriately discounted interest payments plus the discounted principal payment. Second, the difference between the par value of the bond and its purchase price is taxable income. Profitable refunding requires either that this differential is for some reason not taxable or, alternatively, that the amortization period for the taxable income be extremely long.

Conclusions

We reiterate our general conclusions. When declines in the general level of interest rates have occurred, the call privilege appears to provide an opportunity for reducing interest expenses. But if the call privilege had been correctly priced, then on average, the exercise of this option simply compensates the firm for the higher interest rates that it paid by having the call provision in the indenture of the bonds it sold. The firm paid a higher interest rate differential that it can recoup only by exercising the option it has purchased. The refunding operation then is required to "balance the books" in some sense.

The other face of bond refunding is considered when interest rates have risen. Unless the taxes on the gain from buying back the bonds can be avoided, the net cash flow effects are negative. The absolute amount of interest costs would be essentially unchanged. Therefore, unless the taxes can be avoided without other disadvantages, the effects of refunding when interest rates have risen would appear to be unfavorable. The conclusion seems to be that bond refunding has but one face, not two.

Selected References

Ang, James S. "The Two Faces of Bond Refunding: Reply." *Journal of Finance* 33 (March 1978), pp. 354–356.

———. "The Two Faces of Bond Refunding." *Journal of Finance* 30 (June 1975), pp. 869–874.

Bierman, Harold. "The Bond Refunding Decision." *Financial Management* 1 (Summer 1972), pp. 22–29.

———. "The Bond Refunding Decision as a Markov Process." *Management Science* 12 (August 1966), pp. 545–551.

Bierman, Harold, and Barnea, Amir. "Expected Short-Term Interest Rates in Bond Refunding." *Financial Management* 3 (Spring 1974), pp. 75–79.

Bowlin, Oswald D. "The Refunding Decision: Another Special Case in Capital Budgeting." *Journal of Finance* 21 (March 1966), pp. 55–68.

Boyce, W. M., and Kalotay, A. J. "Tax Differentials and Callable Bonds." *Journal of Finance* 34 (September 1979), pp. 825–838.

Emery, Douglas R. "Overlapping Interest in Bond Refunding: A Reconsideration." *Financial Management* 7 (Summer 1978), pp. 19–20.

Johnson, Rodney, and Klein, Richard. "Corporate Motives in Repurchases of Discounted Bonds." *Financial Management* 3 (Autumn 1974), pp. 44–49.

Kalotay, A. J. "On the Advanced Refunding of Discounted Debt." *Financial Management* 7 (Summer 1978), pp. 7–13.

Kolodny, Richard. "The Refunding Decision in Near Perfect Markets." *Journal of Finance* 29 (December 1974), pp. 1467–1477.

Laber, Gene. "The Effect of Bond Refunding on Shareholder Wealth: Comment." *Journal of Finance* 34 (June 1979), pp. 795–799.

———. "Implications of Discount Rates and Financing Assumptions for Bond Refunding Decisions." *Financial Management* 8 (Spring 1979), pp. 7–12.

———. "Repurchases of Bonds through Tender Offers: Implications for Shareholder Wealth." *Financial Management* 7 (Summer 1978), pp. 7–13.

Livingston, Miles. "Bond Refunding Reconsidered: Comment." *Journal of Finance* 35 (March 1980), pp. 191–196.

———. "The Effect of Bond Refunding on Shareholder Wealth: Comment." *Journal of Finance* 34 (June 1979), pp. 801–804.

Mayor, Thomas H., and McCoin, Kenneth G. "Bond Refunding: One or Two Faces?" *Journal of Finance* 33 (March 1978), pp. 349–353.

———. "The Rate of Discount in Bond Refunding." *Financial Management* 3 (Autumn 1974), pp. 54–58.

Ofer, Ahron R., and Taggart, Robert A., Jr. " 'Bond Refunding Reconsidered': Reply." *Journal of Finance* 35 (March 1980), pp. 197–200.

———. "Bond Refunding: A Clarifying Analysis." *Journal of Finance* 32 (March 1977), pp. 21–30.

Sibley, A. M. "Some Evidence on the Cash Flow Effects of Bond Refunding." *Financial Management* 3 (Autumn 1974), pp. 50–53.

Weingartner, H. Martin. "Optimal Timing of Bond Refunding." *Management Science* 13 (March 1967), pp. 511–524.

Yawitz, Jess B., and Anderson, James A. "The Effect of Bond Refunding on Shareholder Wealth: Reply." *Journal of Finance* 34 (June 1979), pp. 805–809.

———. "The Effect of Bond Refunding on Shareholder Wealth." *Journal of Finance* 32 (December 1977), pp. 1738–1746.

Appendix B to Chapter 20

Floating-Rate Notes

When inflation forces interest rates to high levels, borrowers are reluctant to commit themselves to long-term debt. Yield curves are typically inverted at such times, with short-term interest rates higher than long-term. One factor is that borrowers would rather pay a premium for short-term funds than lock themselves into high long-term rates for two or three decades.

Two risks are faced by those who defer long-term borrowing in hope that interest rates will soon fall. First, there is no assurance that rates will not rise even higher and remain at unexpectedly high levels for an indefinite period. If long-term rates rise to 15 percent, for example, debt that looked expensive at 12 percent will seem like a bargain to a borrower who passed it up in the hope of waiting out the rate crisis. Second, the short-term money may simply become unavailable.

The floating-rate note (FRN) was developed to decrease the risks of interest rate volatility at high levels.[1] In an FRN, the coupon rate varies at a given percentage above prevailing risk-free rates, which are determined by short- or long-term Treasury bill yields. The FRN rate is typically either fixed or guaranteed to exceed a stated minimum for an initial period, then adjusted at specified intervals to movements in the Treasury rates.

History of the FRN

FRN's were first issued in the United States by Citicorp, in 1974. The rate was set at a minimum of 9.7 percent for ten months, then adjusted semiannually to 1 percent above the current three-month Treasury bill rate. Other firms followed Citicorp's lead. These early issues carried rates based on T-bill yields and most allowed investors to "put" the FRN to the issuer at face value after a given date.[2] Initial rates on the notes were well below the going rate on such short-term borrowing as commercial paper. In July 1974, the rate on three-month prime commercial paper was 11.9 percent, while Treasury bills of comparable maturity were yielding 7.6 percent. Because interest rates

1. See the excellent survey by Kenneth R. Marks and Warren A. Law, "Hedging against Inflation with Floating-Rate Notes," *Harvard Business Review* 58 (March–April 1980), pp. 106–112.
2. Remember that a *call* gives the holder the option to buy at a specified price. For example, a security may be selling for $50, but I may have a call to buy it for $45. By symmetry, a *put* gives the owner the option to sell the security to the issuer at a specified price. For example, a bond may have a market price of $900, but I may own a put to sell the bond to the issuing corporation for $1,050.

were generally expected to decline, borrowers hoped that FRN's would also cost less over the life of the notes than fixed-rate long-term debt.

Rates declined as predicted during the following two years, justifying the use of FRN's rather than fixed-rate debentures. Many holders exercised their put options when other investments became more profitable, however, a situation which forced the borrowers to seek new funds after just a few years.

When borrowers began to issue FRN's again in 1978, the put option was far less common. For that reason, and because high-yield certificates were newly available from savings institutions, the second round of FRN's was less well-suited to individual investors. Institutional investors found FRN's a valuable hedge against declines in the value of their bond portfolios, however. Because FRN's carry rates that vary with the market, their value tends to stay stable near the original price.

Strategies for Volatile Markets

The volatility of interest rates during 1979–1980 again made decision making difficult for both borrowers and lenders. During one two-week period in October 1979, long-term Treasury bond yields rose 100 basis points from already high levels. In such a market, borrowers may avoid long-term debt in the expectation that interest rates will soon peak and begin to fall. With inflation continuing to rise, however, and with uncertainty about Federal Reserve moves and a probable recession, no one in late 1979 could be sure that interest rates would not continue their climb toward new record heights. But between March 28, 1980, and May 9, 1980, a period just slightly over one month, the yields on long-term Treasury securities fell 264 basis points.

The trend of innovations during the environment of rising interest rates during 1979 is indicated by the characteristics of individual issues that were offered. An FRN by Continental Illinois Corporation in April could be converted by the holder before May 1986 into fixed-rate 8.5 percent debentures; for the first time, a debt issue was convertible into another debt issue.

Additional new features appeared in the Gulf Oil Corporation issue of $250 million in May. It was the second issue by a nonfinancial corporation, with Standard Oil (Indiana) first in 1974. The issue by Gulf was a thirty-year maturity with a coupon floating 35 basis points above the rate on the thirty-year constant maturity U.S. Treasury bond series published by the Federal Reserve Board. A *drop-lock* feature provided that the security would convert to a fixed rate of $8^3/_8$ percent if the yield on the Treasury bond series fell to 8 percent or below for three consecutive days.

In the Mellon National Corporation issue sold in June 1979, holders have the option to convert to fixed rate debentures with a coupon of $8^1/_2$ percent. Mellon also has the right at its option to convert the securities to fixed-rate debentures whose rate would be the higher of $8^1/_2$ percent or 65 basis points above the rate on Treasury bonds at that time.

In late 1979, borrowers sought to devise ways to shield themselves against further interest rate increases while taking advantage of possible rate reductions. IBM found one solution in its twenty-five-year debenture offered in October 1979. Terms called for sinking fund payments beginning after the sixth year, with an option to boost the payments by 150 percent and a low call price of $102.50 at the first call date. The effect of these provisions was both to protect IBM against immediate interest rate increases and to allow early repayment if rates should fall within the first six years.

In the same month, Georgia-Pacific offered eight-year floating-rate notes designed to accomplish the same objectives. The interest rate on this more complicated offering was set at 12 percent for the first six months, at the higher of 12 percent or 75 basis points above the Treasury bill rate for the next six months, and then at spreads declining from 75 to 50 points above T-bills, with a minimum rate of 6 percent. Additional provisions allowed Georgia-Pacific to convert the notes to longer term debentures during a stated period, with rates fixed at the higher of $8^1/_2$ percent or at least 40 points above long-term Treasury bond yields at the time of conversion. The purchaser also could exercise the right to convert the notes to $8^1/_2$ percent debentures at any time before maturity and could put the notes to Georgia-Pacific at face value after five years. Thus the Georgia-Pacific floating rate notes were puttable, callable, and convertible.

Characteristics of FRN's

The terms of FRN's are not fixed by law; a variety of features has been employed by issuing companies during the relatively short period FRN's have been available. Typical characteristics are:

1. *Convertibility.* Either to common stock or to fixed-rate notes or to both, at either the issuer's option, the holder's option, or both. The note may state particular dates or time periods when conversion is allowed and may set other conditions, such as a given Treasury bill rate at the time of conversion. The rate on the fixed-rate note may be preset or may depend on Treasury rates at conversion.
2. *Put option.* This feature allows the holder to redeem the note at face value, generally at stated times or under other given conditions.
3. *Minimum rate.* This feature prevents the note rate from floating below a stated minimum.
4. *Drop-lock rate.* If the note rate has dropped to a stated rate, it becomes locked at that rate until maturity.
5. *Sinking fund provision.* Permits the issuer to repay stated portions of the principal amount before maturity.
6. *Declining spread.* The spread between the note rate and the Treasury rate decreases by given amounts at specified times.
7. *Declining minimum rate.* The minimum rate decreases in a similar manner.
8. *Call option.* The issuer has the right to call the note, usually at a moderate premium, and sometimes within a short time after issuance.

Since certain features benefit the issuer while others favor potential buyers, the choice of terms for a particular offering influences the market value of the note. For example, convertibility at the issuer's option gives the issuer control over the cost of debt should Treasury rates remain at high levels; lenders will charge a premium for this right. Conversely, convertibility by the holder allows lenders to lock into higher rates of return if Treasury rates begin to fall. Lenders will accept a lower mark-up, or spread, over Treasury rates in return for this option. One important consideration for issuers is the complexity of the offering. If the FRN includes too many options, investors may conclude they are unable to evaluate it accurately and reduce the amount they are willing to pay.

Advantages for Issuers

The floating-rate note makes it possible for borrowers to obtain long-term funds when interest rates are generally high without locking into high rates for the entire life of the loan. The cost of debt will automatically fall when Treasury rates drop, and the issuer-convertibility features can be included as a hedge against the possibility that Treasury rates may continue to rise.

FRN's are particularly useful for financial institutions, which often hold a large percentage of assets bearing floating-rate returns. These institutions can issue FRN's to establish a constant spread between their return on investments and cost of debt. Nonfinancial companies whose revenues tend to vary more than their costs with the rate of inflation can also use FRN's to stabilize their cost-revenue spread. Capital-intensive companies, whose depreciation expenses vary little with inflation, are one example.

Advantages for Lenders

FRN's give investors two important guarantees during periods of high and unpredictable inflation:

1. Returns on investment will follow changes in Treasury rates.
2. Because FRN rates vary with the market, the market value of the note will remain relatively stable.

The convertibility and minimum rate features found in most FRN's give investors additional assurance and flexibility in an unstable investment environment.

Costs

When yield curves are inverted, the immediate costs of issuing FRN's based on short-term Treasury rates can be higher than ordinary fixed-rate long-term borrowing. In such periods, however, FRN's have tended to remain less expensive initially than short-term bank loans or commercial paper.

The long-term cost of selling FRN's depends on the movement of interest rates during the life of the notes. Borrowers issue FRN's when they expect current high rates to decline significantly within a short time and then remain at lower levels. If this occurs, the total cost of funding with FRN's falls below the cost for long-term fixed rate notes. When rates have declined, the issuer can use the issuer-convertibility feature to ensure that total FRN costs remain low despite possible future rate increases.

While most FRN's have been tied to short-term T-bill rates, a few have been based on long-term Treasury bonds. One advantage of long-term-based FRN's is that long-term rates vary less than short-term rates. Borrowers may be willing to pay a premium for greater predictability of costs.

Floating-rate notes provide another illustration of the flexibility of financial markets and instruments. The increased volatility of fluctuations in interest rates has brought forth debt instruments with new types of provisions. Additional new efforts by lenders to achieve protection against inflation include a provision that the principal will also float—that it will be tied to the value of real assets such as oil or silver. Other inflation hedges by lenders include claims on equity such as warrants, convertibility into common stock, or add-on contingent interest fees based on some measure of company performance such as sales or income. Such hedges are added to a fixed interest rate that will be lower than it would otherwise have to be to provide protection against uncertain inflation. Thus the lender trades off some inflation protection against some near-term interest income.

21
Lease Financing

Firms are generally interested in using buildings and equipment. One way of obtaining their use is to buy them, but an alternative is to lease them. Prior to the 1950s, leasing was most often associated with real estate—land and buildings—but today it is possible to lease virtually any kind of fixed asset. We estimate that from 15 to 20 percent of all new capital equipment put in use by business each year is leased.[1] *In a number of respects, leasing is similar to borrowing. However, while debt or equity financing, as part of a general pool of financing sources, cannot be associated with specific assets, leasing is typically identified with individual assets.*

Leasing simultaneously provides for the acquisition of assets and their financing. Its advantage over debt is that the lessor has a better position than a creditor if the user firm experiences financial difficulties. If the lessee does not meet the lease obligations, the lessor has a stronger legal right to take back the asset, because the lessor still legally owns it. A creditor, even a secured creditor, encounters costs and delays in recovering assets that have been directly or indirectly financed. Since the lessor has less risk than other financing sources used in acquiring assets, the riskier the firm seeking financing, the greater the reason for the supplier of financing to formulate a leasing arrangement rather than a loan. The relative tax positions of lessors and users of assets may also affect the lease versus own decision.

Types of Leases

Leases take several different forms, the most important of which are sale and leaseback, service or operating leases, and straight financial leases. These three major types of leases are described below.

1. See also Peter Vanderwicken, "The Powerful Logic of the Leasing Boom," *Fortune*, November 1973, p. 136.

Sale and Leaseback

Under a sale and leaseback arrangement, a firm owning land, buildings, or equipment sells the property to a financial institution and simultaneously executes an agreement to lease the property back for a certain period under specific terms.

Note that the seller, or *lessee,* immediately receives the purchase price put up by the buyer, or *lessor.* At the same time, the seller-lessee retains the use of the property. This parallel is carried over to the lease payment schedule. Under a mortgage loan arrangement, the financial institution receives a series of equal payments just sufficient to amortize the loan and to provide the lender with a specified rate of return on investment. Under a sale and leaseback arrangement, the lease payments are set up in the same manner. The payments are sufficient to return the full purchase price to the financial institution in addition to providing it with some return on its investment.

Operating Leases

Operating, or service, leases include both financing and maintenance services. IBM is one of the pioneers of the service lease contract. Computers and office copying machines, together with automobiles and trucks, are the primary types of equipment covered by operating leases. The leases ordinarily call for the lessor to maintain and service the leased equipment, and the costs of this maintenance are either built into the lease payments or contracted for separately.

Another important characteristic of the service lease is that it is frequently not fully amortized. In other words, the payments required under the lease contract are *not* sufficient to recover the full cost of the equipment. Obviously, however, the lease contract is written for considerably less than the expected life of the leased equipment, and the lessor expects to recover the cost either in subsequent renewal payments or on disposal of the equipment.

A final feature of the service lease is that it frequently contains a cancellation clause giving the lessee the right to cancel the lease and return the equipment before the expiration of the basic agreement. This is an important consideration for the lessee, who can return the equipment if technological developments render it obsolete or if it simply is no longer needed.

Financial Leases

A strict financial lease is one that does not provide for maintenance services, is not cancellable, and is fully amortized (that is, the lessor contracts for rental payments equal to the full price of the leased equipment). The typical arrangement involves the following steps:

1. The firm that will use the equipment selects the specific items it requires and negotiates the price and delivery terms with the manufacturer or distributor.
2. Next, the user firm arranges with a bank or leasing company for the latter to buy the equipment from the manufacturer or distributor, simultaneous-

ly executing an agreement to lease the equipment from the financial institution. The terms call for full amortization of the financial institution's cost, plus a return on the lessor's investment. The lessee generally has the option to renew the lease at a reduced rental on expiration of the basic lease, but does not have the right to cancel the basic lease without completely paying off the financial institution.

Financial leases are almost the same as sale and leaseback arrangements, the main difference being that the leased equipment is new and the lessor buys it from a manufacturer or a distributor instead of from the user-lessee. A sale and leaseback can thus be thought of as a special type of financial lease.

Internal Revenue Service Requirements for a Lease

The full amount of the annual lease payments is deductible for income tax purposes—provided the Internal Revenue Service agrees that a particular contract is a genuine lease and not simply an installment loan called a lease. This makes it important that the lease contract be written in a form acceptable to the IRS. Following are the major requirements for bona fide lease transactions from the standpoint of the IRS:

1. The term must be less than thirty years; otherwise the lease is regarded as a form of sale.
2. The rent must represent a reasonable return to the lessor—in the range of 7 to 12 percent on the investment.
3. The renewal option must be bona fide, and this requirement can best be met by giving the lessee the first option to meet an equal bona fide outside offer.
4. There must be no repurchase option; if there is, the lessee should merely be given parity with an equal outside offer.

Accounting for Leases

In November 1976, the Financial Accounting Standards Board issued its Statement of Financial Accounting Standards No. 13, *Accounting for Leases.* Like other FASB statements, the standards set forth must be followed by business firms if their financial statements are to receive certification by auditors. FASB Statement No. 13 has implications both for the utilization of leases and for their accounting treatment. The elements of FASB Statement No. 13 most relevant for financial analysis of leases are summarized below.

For some types of leases, this FASB statement requires that the obligation be capitalized on the asset side of the balance sheet with a related lease obligation on the liability side. The accounting treatment depends on the type of lease. The classification is more detailed than the two categories of operating and financial leases described above.

From the standpoint of the lessee:
1. Capital leases
2. Operating leases (all leases other than capital leases)

From the standpoint of the lessor:
1. Sales-type leases
2. Direct financing leases
3. Leveraged leases
4. Operating leases (all leases other than the first three)

A lease is classified in Statement No. 13 as a capital lease if it meets one or more of four Paragraph 7 criteria:

1. The lease transfers ownership of the property to the lessee by the end of the lease term.
2. The lease gives the lessee the option to purchase the property at a price sufficiently below the expected fair value of the property that the exercise of the option is highly probable.
3. The lease term is equal to 75 percent or more of the estimated economic life of the property.
4. The present value of the minimum lease payments exceeds 90 percent of the fair value of the property at the inception of the lease. The discount factor to be used in calculating the present value is the implicit rate used by the lessor or the lessee's incremental borrowing rate, whichever is lower. (Note that the lower discount factor represents a higher present value factor and therefore a higher calculated present value for a given pattern of lease payments. It thus increases the likelihood that the 90 percent test will be met and that the lease will be classified as a capital lease.)

From the standpoint of the lessee, if a lease is not a capital lease, it is classified as an operating lease. From the standpoint of the lessor, four types of leases are defined: (1) sales-type leases, (2) direct financing leases, (3) leveraged leases, and (4) operating leases representing all leases other than the first three types. Sales-type leases and direct financing leases meet one or more of the four Paragraph 7 criteria and both of the Paragraph 8 criteria, which are:

1. Collectibility of the minimum lease payments is reasonably predictable.
2. No important uncertainties surround the amount of unreimbursable costs yet to be incurred by the lessor under the lease.

Sales-type leases give rise to profit (or loss) to the lessor—the fair value of the leased property at the inception of the lease is greater (or less) than its cost of carrying amount. Sales-type leases normally arise when manufacturers or dealers use leasing in marketing their products. Direct financing leases are leases other than leveraged leases for which the cost-of-carrying amount is equal to the fair value of the leased property at the inception of the lease. Leveraged leases are direct financing leases in which substantial financing is provided by a long-term creditor on a nonrecourse basis with respect to the general credit of the lessor.

Accounting by Lessees

For operating leases, rentals must be charged to expense over the lease term, with disclosures of future rental obligations in total as well as by each of the following five years. For lessees, capital leases are to be capitalized and shown on the balance sheet both as a fixed asset and a noncurrent obligation. Capitalization represents the present value of the minimum lease payments minus that portion of lease payments representing executory costs such as insurance, maintenance, and taxes to be paid by the lessor (including any profit return in such charges). The discount factor is as described in Paragraph 7(4) —the lower of the implicit rates used by the lessor and the incremental borrowing rate of the lessee.

The asset must be amortized in a manner consistent with the lessee's normal depreciation policy for owned assets. During the lease term, each lease payment is to be allocated between a reduction of the obligation and the interest expense to produce a constant rate of interest on the remaining balance of the obligation. Thus, for capital leases, the balance sheet includes the items in Table 21.1.

In addition to the balance sheet capitalization of capital leases, substantial additional footnote disclosures are required for both capital and operating leases. These include a description of leasing arrangements, an analysis of leased property under capital leases by major classes of property, a schedule by years of future minimum lease payments (with executory and interest costs broken out for capital leases), and contingent rentals for operating leases.

FASB Statement No. 13 sets forth requirements for capitalizing capital leases and for standardizing disclosures by lessees for both capital leases and operating leases. Lease commitments therefore do not represent "off–balance sheet" financing for capital assets, and standard disclosure requirements

Table 21.1

Company X Balance Sheet

Assets	December 31, 1980	December 31, 1981	Liabilities	December 31, 1980	December 31, 1981
			Current:		
Leased property under capital leases, less accumulated amortization	XXX	XXX	Obligations under capital leases	XXX	XXX
			Noncurrent:		
			Obligations under capital leases	XXX	XXX

make general the footnote reporting of information on operating leases. Hence, the argument that leasing represents a form of financing that lenders may not take into account in their analysis of the financial position of firms seeking financing will be even less valid in the future than it is now.

It is unlikely that sophisticated lenders were ever fooled by off–balance sheet leasing obligations. However, the capitalization of capital leases and the standard disclosure requirements for operating leases will make it easier for general users of financial reports to obtain additional information on firms' leasing obligations. Hence, the requirements of FASB Statement No. 13 are useful. Probably, the extent of use of leasing will remain substantially unaltered, since the particular circumstances that have provided a basis for its use in the past are not likely to be greatly affected by the increased disclosure requirements.

Cost Comparison between Leasing and Owning for Financial Leases

We next consider the framework for the analysis of the cost of owning with the cost of leasing. The form of leasing to be analyzed initially will be a pure financial lease which is fully amortized, noncancellable, and without provision for maintenance services.

In concept, the first screening test is whether, from a capital budgeting standpoint, the project passes the investment hurdle rate. The second question is then whether leasing or some other method of financing is the least expensive method of financing the project.

Alternatively, it could be argued that we do not know what the cost of capital (and therefore the investment screening rate) is until we have determined the least expensive method of financing. Having determined this method, we can determine the applicable investment screening hurdle rate for the decision of whether to undertake the project from a capital budgeting standpoint.

To lay a foundation for the leasing versus owning cost comparison, the lessor's point of view will first be considered. The leasing company, or lessor, could be a commercial bank, a subsidiary of a commercial bank, or an independent leasing company. These various types of leasing companies are considered to be providing financial intermediation services of essentially the same kind. Each form of financial intermediary is considered to be providing a product, which represents a form of debt financing to the company that uses the equipment. Since the product that is being sold by the financial intermediary is a debt instrument, the income to that intermediary is considered to be a return on debt which earns the intermediary's cost of capital. This is equivalent to the judgment that the financial intermediary's cost of capital, composed of both debt and equity capital, is approximately equal to the rate charged on the debt (or equivalent) instruments that comprise its assets (the assets of the lessor in our analysis).

We can then proceed to calculate the required lease-rental charge that must be made by the lessor to obtain a fair rate of return for a lending position. To illustrate the analysis, assume the following data:

I_0 = Cost of an asset = \$20,000

Dep = Annual economic and tax depreciation charge

k_b = Before-tax cost of debt = 8%

T = Lessor's corporate tax rate = 40%

N = Economic life and tax depreciation life of the asset = 5 years

NPV_{LOR} = Net present value of the lease-rental income from the assets to the lessor

With the above facts, the equilibrium lease rental rate in a competitive market of lessors can be calculated. What has been posed is a standard capital budgeting question: What cash flow return from the use of an asset will earn the applicable cost of capital? The investment, or cost of the capital budgeting project, is $-I$. The return is composed of two elements: the cash inflow from the lease rental and the tax shelter from depreciation. The discount factor is the lessor's weighted cost of capital which, as we have indicated, will be equal to the applicable rate on debt instruments of the risk of the cash flows involved. As Stewart C. Myers, David A. Dill, and Alberto J. Bautista have pointed out, the weighted cost of capital of the financial intermediary is:

$$k_L = k_u(1 - \lambda T). \tag{21.1}$$

For the financial intermediary, the lambda is the ratio of debt per dollar of assets leased to the sum of lease payments and tax shields generated. With respect to the user of the asset, the underlying assumption is that the firm borrows lambda times the value of the various tax shields and reduces its borrowing by lambda times the value of the lease payments. For the data assumed in the example, we would therefore have for the cost of capital of the lessor the amount shown in Equation 21.1a. Here we postulate that the all-equity financing rate for the lessor (k_{uL}) is 8.57 percent and lambda is 0.75.

$$\begin{aligned} k_L &= k_{uL}(1 - \lambda T) \\ &= 8.57\% \,[1 - 0.75(0.4)] \\ &= 6\%. \end{aligned} \tag{21.1a}$$

The after-tax weighted cost of capital to the lessor is 6 percent. We can verify the lessor's cost of capital computation:

$$\begin{aligned} k_L &= k_b(1 - T)(B/V) + k_s(S/V) \\ k_s &= k_u + (k_u - k_b)(B/S)(1 - T) \\ &= 0.0857 + (0.0857 - 0.08)(3)(0.6) \\ &= 0.0857 + 0.01026 \\ &= 0.096. \\ k_L &= 0.08(0.6)(0.75) + (0.96)(0.25) \\ &= 0.036 + 0.024 \\ &= 0.06. \end{aligned}$$

The uniform annual lease-rental required by the lessor can now be determined, therefore, by Equation 21.2:

$$\begin{aligned} NPV_{LOR} &= -I_0 + \sum_{t=1}^{N} \frac{L_t(1-T) + T\text{Dep}_t}{(1+k)^t} \\ &= -I_0 + \text{PVIFA}(6\%, 5 \text{ years})[L_t(1-T) + T\text{Dep}_t], \end{aligned} \tag{21.2}$$

where:

L_t = Periodic lease payment

Dep_t = Amount of depreciation expense in period t = \$4,000 using straight line depreciation

We can now solve for the equilibrium lease-rental rate required by the lessor by utilizing the data inputs we have provided, as shown in Equation 21.2a:

$$\begin{aligned} 0 &= -\$20{,}000 + (4.2124)[0.6L_t + 0.4(\$4{,}000)] \\ L_t &= \$5{,}246. \end{aligned} \tag{21.2a}$$

Presented with a lease-rental rate of \$5,246, the user firm takes this amount as an input in making a comparison of the cost of leasing with the cost of owning. The analysis of the possible benefits of leasing as compared with owning involves the analysis of the following cash flows:

1. A cash savings equal to the dollar amount of the investment outlay, I, which the firm does not have to incur if it leases.
2. A cash flow amounting to the present value of the after-tax lease dollars which must be paid out, $\text{PV}[L_t(1-T)]$.
3. The present value of the opportunity cost of the lost depreciation tax shield, $\text{PV}(T\text{Dep}_t)$.
4. The present value of the *change* in the interest tax shield on debt which is displaced by the lease financing, $\text{PV}[T\Delta(k_bB_t)]$.

These four terms are presented in Equation 21.3:

$$\text{NPV(lease)} = I_0 - \text{PV}[L_t(1-T)] - \text{PV}[T\text{Dep}_t] + \text{PV}[T\Delta(k_bB_t)]. \tag{21.3}$$

We shall assume that from the standpoint of the user firm, debt and lease financing are perfect substitutes. Therefore, the fourth term in Equation 21.3 will be zero because for every dollar of extra tax shield provided by the lease there is the reduction of a dollar of debt tax shield due to the displacement of debt.

Since both the lease payments and the foregone depreciation tax shields are risk-free, they can be discounted at the cost of debt. Since the debt cost is deductible to the user firm, the after-tax cost of debt is utilized. We can therefore substitute the numbers from our example into Equation 21.3 to obtain Equation 21.3a:

$$\begin{aligned}\text{NPV(lease)} &= I - \text{PVIFA}(6\%, 5\text{ years})[L_t(1 - T)] - \text{PVIFA}(6\%, 5\text{ years})\\ &\quad [T\text{ Dep}_t]\\ &= 20{,}000 - 4.2124(5{,}246)(1 - 0.4) - 4.2124(0.4)(4{,}000)\\ &= 20{,}000 - 13{,}259 - 6{,}740 \qquad \text{(21.3a)}\\ &= 20{,}000 - 19{,}999 \cong 0.\end{aligned}$$

This result can also be expressed as the cost of owning versus the cost of leasing. The first and last terms on the right-hand side of the equation represent the cost of owning. The second term is the cost of leasing.

$$\text{Cost of owning} = I - \text{PVIFA}(6\%, 5\text{ years})[T\text{Dep}_t] = 20{,}000 - 6{,}740 = 13{,}260.$$

$$\text{Cost of leasing} = \text{PVIFA}(6\%, 5\text{ years})[L_t(1 - T)] = 13{,}259.$$

Thus there is equilibrium between the lessor market and the user market. The lessor earns its cost of capital, which determines the lease-rental charge that it must make. At this lease-rental rate, the user is indifferent between owning or leasing the asset.

Note that in determining the lessor's cost of capital we started with the cost of equity that would be applicable to the debt instrument portfolio, or lease portfolio, of the financial intermediary. Given lambda as the appropriate leverage ratio for the lessor, we arrived at the after-tax cost of capital of the lessor. When this is placed on a before-tax basis, it represents the cost of debt borrowing or the implicit capital cost in the lease financing contract. All the required conditions for an indifference result in the leasing market and the user market are obtained.

We have found that the present value of the cost of leasing and the cost of owning is $13,260. We next make a capital budgeting analysis to determine whether the project that requires the use of the asset should be undertaken. We determine that the net benefits of the project are $6,500 per year. These net cash flows are the same whether the firm owns or leases the asset. The flows are capitalized at an assumed 12 percent cost of capital of the project. The present value of the benefits of the project will be:

$$\text{GPV} = \text{PVIFA}(12\%, 5\text{ years})[\$6{,}500(0.6)] = 3.6048(\$3{,}900) = \$14{,}059.$$

The net present value of the project will be the GPV less the PV of costs, or $14,059 − $13,260, which equals $799. The project has a positive NPV and therefore should be accepted.

Next, we shall consider the use of accelerated depreciation. Appendix C of this book provides in convenient form the present value of depreciation for the sum-of-years'-digits and the double declining balance methods of depreciation over a range of values of the cost of capital. In the present example, the sum-of-years'-digits method of depreciation will be illustrated with the after-tax cost of capital of 6 percent for five years. The depreciation factor of 0.875 can be read directly from the table. Then Equation 21.2 can be solved for the uniform annual lease-rental rate required by the lessor:

$$0 = -\$20{,}000 + 4.2124(0.6L_t) + 0.4(\$20{,}000)(0.875)$$
$$4.2124(0.6)L_t = \$20{,}000 - \$7{,}000$$
$$2.5274L_t = \$13{,}000$$
$$L_t = \$5{,}144.$$

The resulting uniform annual lease-rental charge required by the lessor in order to earn its cost of capital of 6 percent is $5,144. Note that this is lower than the lease-rental of $5,246 required for the lessor to earn the cost of capital when straight line depreciation was used. The reason is that with accelerated depreciation, the tax shelter comes in larger amounts in the earlier years, when the present value factors are higher. Thus, since the amount of tax shelter is increased, and since under competitive conditions the lease-rental moves to the level at which lessors earn their cost of capital, the lease-rental is reduced.

With accelerated depreciation, the lower required rental rate will be used in computing the cost of leasing:

$$\text{Cost of leasing} = \text{PVIFA}(6\%, 5 \text{ years})[\$5{,}144(0.6)]$$
$$= 4.2124(\$3{,}086.4) \cong \$13{,}000.$$

The cost of owning should also use accelerated depreciation. It becomes:

$$\text{Cost of owning} = I - [0.4(\$20{,}000)(0.875)]$$
$$= \$20{,}000 - \$7{,}000 = \$13{,}000.$$

The costs of leasing or owning decline from $13,260 to $13,000. The NPV from the project rises from $799 to $1,059. The increased NPV from the project results from the more favorable larger tax shelters provided by the accelerated depreciation. Given competition among the lessors, this results in a lower rental rate and a higher net present value of using the asset, regardless of whether the use is achieved through leasing (renting) or through buying and owning. But again, assuming competitive financial markets, the terms on which leasing versus owning are available to the user firm result in no advantage to one form of acquiring the use of the assets as compared with another. Only when some form of friction in the markets results in more favorable terms to lessees than to user-owners is there an advantage to leasing (and vice versa).

Alternative Computation Procedures in the Leasing Analysis

Thus far we have made the leasing versus owning analysis using compact equations. The same results can be obtained when the flows are tabulated by years. To illustrate, we shall use the same data as in the previous example. The cost of the asset is $20,000, and the required lease-rental rate is calculated to be $5,246 under straight line depreciation. The earlier analysis treated leasing and borrowing as substitutes; so under the owning analysis, the $20,000 is assumed to be borrowed at a 10 percent before-tax cost of debt by the user of the asset.

It is assumed that the loan of $20,000 is paid off at a level annual amount that covers annual interest charges plus amortization of the principal. The amount is an annuity that can be determined by the use of the present value of an annuity formula, shown in Equation 21.4:

$$\$20{,}000 = \sum_{t=1}^{N} \frac{a_t}{(1 + k_b)^t}$$

$$a_t = \frac{\$20{,}000}{(\text{PVIFA})(10\%, 5\text{ years})} \tag{21.4}$$

$$a_t = \frac{\$20{,}000}{3.7908} = \$5{,}276.$$

Solving Equation 21.4 for the level annual annuity results in $5,276, which represents the principal plus interest payments set forth in Column 3 of Table 21.2. The sum of these five annual payments is shown to be $26,380, which represents repayment of the principal of $20,000 plus the sum of the annual interest payments. The interest payments of each year are determined by multiplying Column 2, the balance of principal owed at the end of the year, by 10 percent, the assumed cost of borrowing. The sum of the annual interest payments does, in fact, equal the total interest of $6,380 obtained by deducting the principal of $20,000 from the total of the five annual payments shown in Column 3.

A schedule of cash outflows for the borrow-own alternative is then developed to determine the present value of the after-tax cash flows. This is illustrated in Table 21.3.

The analysis of cash outflows begins with a listing of the loan payments, as shown in Column 2. Next, the annual interest payments from Table 21.2 are listed in Column 3. Since straight line depreciation is assumed, the annual depreciation charges are $4,000 per year, as shown in Column 4. The tax shelter to the owner of the equipment is the sum of the annual interest plus depre-

Table 21.2

Schedule of Debt Payments

End of Year (1)	Balance of Principal Owed at End of Year (2)	Principal plus Interest Payments (3)	Annual Interest 10% × (2): (4)	Reduction of Principal (5)
1	$20,000	$5,276	$2,000	$ 3,276
2	16,724	5,276	1,672	3,604
3	13,120	5,276	1,312	3,964
4	9,156	5,276	916	4,360
5	4,796	5,276	480	4,796
Totals		$26,380	$6,380	$20,000

Table 21.3

Costs of Owning

End of Year (1)	Loan Payment (2)	Annual Interest (3)	Depreciation (4)	Tax Shield: [(3) + (4)]0.4 (5)	Cash Flows after Taxes: (2) − (5) (6)	Present Value Factor (at 6%) (7)	Present Value of Costs (8)
1	$ 5,276	$2,000	$ 4,000	$ 2,400	$ 2,876	0.9434	$ 2,713
2	5,276	1,672	4,000	2,269	3,007	0.8900	2,676
3	5,276	1,312	4,000	2,125	3,151	0.8396	2,646
4	5,276	916	4,000	1,966	3,310	0.7921	2,622
5	5,276	480	4,000	1,792	3,484	0.7473	2,603
Totals	$26,380	$6,380	$20,000	$10,552	$15,828		$13,260

ciation multiplied by the tax rate. The amounts of the annual tax shield are shown in Column 5. Column 6 is cash flow after taxes, obtained by deducting Column 5 from Column 2.

Since the cost of borrowing is 10 percent, its after-tax cost with a 40 percent tax rate is 6 percent. The present value factors at 6 percent are listed in Column 7. They are multiplied by the after-tax cash flows to obtain Column 8, the present value of the after-tax costs of owning the asset.

The costs of leasing the asset can be obtained in a similar manner, as shown in Table 21.4. The uniform annual lease payments are shown in Column 2. By multiplying 0.6 times the Column 2 figures, the after-tax cost of leasing is obtained and shown in Column 3. The present value factors for 6 percent are listed in Column 4 and multiplied times the figures in Column 3. Column 5 presents the after-tax costs of leasing by year, which total to $13,260.

The result is the same as for the costs of owning. Thus in formulating the problem to make the positions of the lessors and users symmetrical, the indif-

Table 21.4

Costs of Leasing

End of Year (1)	Lease Payments (2)	After-Tax: 0.6 × (2) (3)	Present Value Factor (at 6%) (4)	Present Value of Costs: (3) × (4) (5)
1	$ 5,246	$ 3,147.6	0.9434	$ 2,970
2	5,246	3,147.6	0.8900	2,802
3	5,246	3,147.6	0.8396	2,643
4	5,246	3,147.6	0.7921	2,493
5	5,246	3,147.6	0.7473	2,352
Totals	$26,230	$15,738.0		$13,260

ference result between the costs of owning and the costs of leasing is obtained. A number of factors could change this result: differences in costs of capital, differences in applicable tax rates or useability of tax subsidies, differences in patterns of payments required under leasing versus owning, and so on. But in order to measure the effects of factors which cause the costs of leasing and owning to be different, it is helpful to start with an equality relation to understand better what is causing a divergence.

Use of an Internal Rate of Return Analysis

A related approach to analyzing the cost of leasing versus other sources of financing utilizes the internal rate of return. In this approach, the cost of leasing is the internal rate of return or discount rate that equates the present value of leasing payments—net of their tax shields plus the tax shields for depreciation and the investment tax credit that would be obtained if the asset were purchased—with the cost of the asset. In this method the cost of leasing includes not only the after-tax lease payments but the investment tax credit foregone and the depreciation tax deductions that otherwise would have been obtained if the asset had been purchased.

The cost of the asset avoided by leasing is treated as a cash inflow, while the costs of leasing just described are treated as cash outflows. A column of cash flows after taxes is calculated; it begins with a positive figure—the cost of the asset avoided—and then moves to negative figures representing the costs of leasing. A rate of discount that equates the negative cash flows with the positive cash flows in the column (6 percent in our example) is determined.

The discount rate is taken as a measure of the after-tax cost of lease financing. In the procedure, this after-tax cost is then compared with the after-tax cost of debt financing. In our example, the after-tax cost of debt financing is 6 percent, so the 6 percent after-tax cost of leasing is the same.

One of the advantages claimed for the approach is that it avoids the problem of having to determine a discount rate. However, this claim is illusory. The internal rate of return approach to the leasing comparison is fundamentally no different from the after-tax cost of debt method described in the previous section. Hence the internal rate of return analysis is equivalent to the earlier, more general, framework presented for analyzing the lease versus purchase decision.

Cost Comparison for Operating Leases

Under an operating lease the lessor must bear the risk involved in the use of the asset. Operating leases are virtually equivalent to having the lessor own the equipment and operate it. In these circumstances the required rate of return is not the rate on a portfolio of assets of borrowed funds. Rather, it is the weighted average cost of capital for a project of the same operating risk and applicable capital structure for the use to which the assets are placed. Assume that the optimal capital structure for a project of this type is 50 percent debt and that at the optimal capital structure the weighted average cost of capital for a project of this risk is 12 percent. We then pose the question of what the cash flows (the lease rental) will have to be on average to yield a 12 percent return on capital to the lessor. This is stated by Equation 21.5:

$$\text{NPV}_{LOR} = -I + \sum_{t=1}^{N} \frac{F_t(1-T) + T\text{Dep}_t}{(1+k)^t} \tag{21.5}$$

where NPV_{LOR} = Present value to lessor

$F_t = L_t$ = Required lease rental to lessor (where $\text{NPV}_{LOR} = 0$)

k = Weighted average cost of capital

Inserting the data from our analysis, we evaluate Equation 21.5 in Equation 21.5a:

$$\begin{aligned} 0 &= -\$20{,}000 + \text{PVIFA}(12\%, 5 \text{ years})[F_t(1-0.4) \\ &\quad + 0.4(\$4{,}000)] \frac{\$20{,}000}{3.6048} - \$1{,}600 = 0.6F_t \\ &\frac{\$3{,}948}{0.6} = \$6{,}580 = F_t. \end{aligned} \tag{21.5a}$$

Thus where the risk of the project is involved, the applicable cost of capital for the lessor is the cost of capital applicable to the project. Similarly, from a capital budgeting standpoint as viewed by the user of the asset, the same risk-adjusted rate of return on the project is required. If 12 percent is appropriate for the lessor, 12 percent is applicable for the user (assuming that the lessor and user have the same tax rate).

The net present value of owning is calculated in a standard capital budgeting procedure. The present value of the net after-tax cash inflows is compared with the investment required. In the analysis, the weighted cost of capital appropriate to the risk of the use of the asset is used as the discount factor. The formulation, with the related calculations, is shown in Equation 21.6. The before-tax net cash inflows are \$7,417 per year—that is, actual F_t is now given as \$7,417.

NPV of owning

$$\begin{aligned} \text{NPV} &= -I_0 + \sum_{t=1}^{N} \frac{F_t(1-T)}{(1+k)^t} + \sum_{t=1}^{N} \frac{T\text{Dep}_t}{(1+k)^t} \\ &= -I_0 + \text{PVIFA}(12\%, 5 \text{ years})[F_t(1-T) + T\text{Dep}_t] \\ &= -\$20{,}000 + 3.6048(\$4{,}450) + (3.6048)\$1{,}600 \\ &= -\$20{,}000 + \$16{,}041 + \$5{,}768 \\ &= \$1{,}809. \end{aligned} \tag{21.6}$$

The net present value calculation of leasing is performed. It relates the present value of the net after-tax cash inflows to the present value of the cost of leasing. The same weighted cost of capital is used as the discount factor, as indicated by Equation 21.7. (Again the result is an NPV of $1,809.)

NPV of leasing

$$\begin{aligned} \text{NPV} &= \sum_{t=1}^{N} \frac{F_t(1-T)}{(1+k)^t} - \sum_{t=1}^{N} \frac{L_t(1-T)}{(1+k)^t} \\ &= \text{PVIFA}(12\%, 5 \text{ years})[F_t(1-T) - L_t(1-T)] \\ &= 3{,}6048(\$4{,}450) - 3.6048(\$6{,}580)(0.6) \\ &= \$16{,}041 - \$14{,}232 \\ &= \$1{,}809. \end{aligned} \quad (21.7)$$

We can also calculate the net advantage to leasing *(NAL)* versus owning by subtracting Equation 21.6 from Equation 21.7. (Alternatively, a negative *NAL* result would indicate that it would be more advantageous for the user to own rather than lease the asset.) In the subtraction, the term for the present value of the net after-tax cash flows drops out, so we are comparing the cost of leasing with the cost of owning only. As Equation 21.8 shows, the net advantage to leasing is zero, illustrating the initial indifference result:

NAL

$$\begin{aligned} \text{NAL} &= I_0 - \sum_{t=1}^{N} \frac{T\,\text{Dep}_t}{(1+k)^t} - \sum_{t=1}^{N} \frac{L_t(1-T)}{(1+k)^t} \\ &= \$20{,}000 - \$5{,}768 - \$14{,}232 \\ &= 0. \end{aligned} \quad (21.8)$$

A large number of factors potentially affect one or more of the critical variables in the lease versus purchase analysis. But we think it both theoretically correct and necessary from a practical standpoint to be able to identify what is causing the cost of leasing to be higher or lower than the cost of owning. In the following section, we can consider some additional variables that may have an impact on the lease versus purchase decision.

Additional Influences on the Leasing versus Owning Decision

A number of other factors can influence the user firm's costs of leasing versus owning capital assets. These include: (1) different costs of capital for the lessor versus the user firm, (2) financing costs higher in leasing, (3) differences in maintenance costs, (4) the benefits of residual values to the owner of the assets, (5) the possibility of reducing obsolescence costs by the leasing firms, (6) the possibility of increased credit availability under leasing, (7) more favorable tax treatment, such as more rapid write-off, and (8) possible differences in the ability to utilize tax reduction opportunities. A number of arguments exist with respect to the advantages and disadvantages of leasing, given these factors. Many of the arguments carry with them implicit assumptions; thus their applicability to real world conditions is subject to considerable qualifications.

Different Costs of Capital for the Lessor versus the User Firm

If the lessor has a lower cost of capital than the user, the cost of leasing is likely to be lower to the user than the cost of owning. But is it realistic to assume that the cost of capital would be different? To answer this question, the basic risks involved in using capital assets must be considered. It has been demonstrated that two broad types of risks are present.

One risk is that an asset's economic depreciation will vary in some systematic way with the level of the economy from the rate of depreciation expected when the lease rental rate is determined. That is, the risk is that the agreed upon lease payments, which are based on expected depreciation, will be insufficient to cover the subsequent realized depreciation. This risk is borne by the owner, whether it is a leasing firm or a user-buyer.

The other risk is associated with F_t, the uncertain future net cash flows to be derived from employing the capital services of the asset. This risk is borne by the leasing company if the lease contract is cancellable at any time with no penalty, borne by the user firm if the lease contract is noncancellable over the life of the asset, and shared by them under any contractual arrangement between these two extremes. But competitive capital markets will ensure that the implicit discount rate in the leasing arrangement, as negotiated, will reflect the allocation of the risks under the particular sharing arrangement specified. Under the standard price equals marginal cost condition of competitive markets, it is the project's cost of capital that is the relevant discount rate. Hence it is difficult to visualize why the risk in use of a capital asset will be different whether the asset is owned by a leasing company or by the user firm.[2]

Another possibility is that the user firm may have a lower cost of capital than the leasing company. This possibility has been evaluated as follows: "It is true that such a company, looking only at the conventional formulas, might find it profitable to buy rather than rent. But it would find it even more profitable, under those circumstances, to enter the leasing business."[3] This would eliminate any divergence.

Under competitive market conditions, it is unlikely that the disequilibrium conditions implied by the different costs of capital will long persist. The supply of financial intermediaries of the leasing kind will either increase or decrease to restore equilibrium in the benefits to a user firm from leasing versus owning an asset.

2. Merton H. Miller and Charles W. Upton, "Leasing, Buying, and the Cost of Capital Services," *Journal of Finance* 31 (June 1976), pp. 761–786.

3. Ibid., p. 767.

Financing Costs Higher in Leasing

A similar view is that leasing always involves higher implicit financing costs. This argument is also of doubtful validity. First, when the nature of the lessee as a credit risk is considered, there may be no difference. Second, it is difficult to separate the money costs of leasing from the other services embodied in a leasing contract. If, because of its specialized operations, the leasing company can perform nonfinancial services such as maintenance of the equipment at a lower cost than the lessee or some other institution can perform them, then the effective cost of leasing may be lower than the cost of funds obtained from borrowing or other sources. The efficiencies of performing specialized services may thus enable the leasing company to operate by charging a lower total cost than the lessee would have to pay for the package of money plus services on any other basis.

Differences in Maintenance Costs

Another argument frequently encountered is that leasing may be less expensive because no explicit maintenance costs are involved. But this is because the maintenance costs are included in the lease-rental rate. The key question is whether the maintenance can be performed at a lower cost by the lessor or by an independent firm that specializes in performing maintenance on capital assets of the type involved. Whether the costs will differ if supplied by one type of specialist firm rather than another is a factual matter, depending on the industries and particular firms involved.

Residual Values

One important point that must be mentioned in connection with leasing is that the lessor owns the property at the expiration of the lease. The value of the property at the end of the lease is called the *residual value.* Superficially, it appears that where residual values are large, owning is less expensive than leasing. However, even this apparently obvious advantage of owning is subject to substantial qualification. On leased equipment, the obsolescence factor may be so large that it is doubtful whether residual values will be of a great order of magnitude. If these values appear favorable, competition between leasing companies and other financial sources, as well as competition among leasing companies themselves, will force leasing rates down to the point where the potentials of residual values are fully recognized in the leasing contract rates. Thus, the existence of residual values is unlikely to result in materially lower costs of owning.

However, in decisions about whether to lease or to own land, the obsolescence factor is involved only to the extent of deterioration in areas with changing population or use patterns. In a period of optimistic expectations about land values, there may be a tendency to overestimate their rates of increase. As a consequence, the current purchase of land may involve a price so high that the probable rate of return on owned land will be relatively small. Under this condition, leasing may well represent the more economical way of obtaining the use of land. Conversely, if the probable increase in land values is not fully reflected in current prices, it will be advantageous to own the land.

Thus it is difficult to generalize about whether residual value considerations are likely to make the effective cost of leasing higher or lower than the cost of owning. The results depend on whether the individual firm has opportunities to take advantage of over-optimistic or over-pessimistic evaluations of future value changes by the market as a whole and whether the firm or market is correct on average.

Obsolescence Costs

Another popular notion is that leasing costs will be lower because of the rapid obsolescence of some kinds of equipment. If the obsolescence rate on equipment is high, leasing costs must reflect that rate. Thus, in general terms, it can be argued that neither residual values nor obsolescence rates can basically affect the cost of owning versus leasing.

However, it is possible that certain leasing companies are well equipped to handle the obsolescence problem. For example, the Clark Equipment Company is a manufacturer, reconditioner, and specialist in materials handling equipment, with its own sales organization and system of distributors. This may enable Clark to write favorable leases for equipment. If the equipment becomes obsolete to one user, it may be satisfactory for other users with different materials handling requirements, and Clark is well situated to locate the other users. The situation is similar in computer leasing.

This illustration indicates how a leasing company, by combining lending with other specialized services, may reduce the social costs of obsolescence and increase effective residual values. By such operations the total cost of obtaining the use of such equipment is reduced. Possibly other institutions that do not combine financing and specialist functions (such as manufacturing, reconditioning, servicing, and sales) may, in conjunction with financing institutions, perform the overall functions as efficiently and at as low a cost as do integrated leasing companies. However, this is a factual matter depending on the relative efficiency of the competing firms in different lines of business and different kinds of equipment.

Increased Credit Availability

Two possible situations that give leasing an advantage to firms seeking the maximum degree of financial leverage may exist. First, it is frequently stated that firms wishing to purchase a specific piece of equipment can obtain more money for longer terms under a lease arrangement than under a secured loan agreement. Second, leasing may not have as much of an impact on future borrowing capacity as does borrowing to buy the equipment.

This point is illustrated by the balance sheets of two hypothetical firms, A and B, in Table 21.5. Initially, the balance sheets of both firms are identical, with both showing debt ratios of 50 percent. Next, each company decides to acquire assets costing \$100. Firm A borrows \$100 to make the purchase, so an asset and a liability go on its balance sheet, and its debt ratio is increased to 75 percent. Firm B leases the equipment. The lease may call for fixed charges as high as or even higher than the loan, and the obligations assumed under the lease can be equally or more dangerous to other creditors; but the fact that its reported debt ratio is lower may enable Firm B to obtain additional credit

Table 21.5

Balance Sheet Effects of Leasing

Before Asset Increase Firms A and B				After Asset Increase Firm A				Firm B			
		Debt	$ 50			Debt	$150			Debt	$ 50
		Equity	50			Equity	50			Equity	50
Total assets	$100	Total	$100	Total assets	$200	Total	$200	Total assets	$100	Total	$100

from other lenders. The amount of the annual rentals is shown as a note to Firm B's financial statements, so credit analysts are aware of it; but evidence suggests that many of them will still give less weight to Firm B's lease than to Firm A's loan.

This illustration indicates quite clearly a weakness of the debt ratio. If two companies are being compared, and if one leases a substantial amount of equipment, then the debt ratio as calculated here does not accurately show their relative leverage positions.[4]

Rapid Write-Off

If the lease is written for a period that is much shorter than the depreciable life of the asset, with renewals at low rentals after the lessor has recovered costs during the basic lease period, then the deductible depreciation is small in relation to the deductible lease payment in the early years. In a sense, this amounts to a very rapid write-off, which is advantageous to the lessee. However, the Internal Revenue Service disallows the deductibility of lease payments that provide for an unduly rapid amortization of the lessor's costs and have a relatively low renewal or purchase option.

Differences in Tax Rates or Tax Subsidies

An advantage to leasing or to buying may occur when the tax rates of lessors and user firms are different. But even here unambiguous predictions are not always possible. The effects of differential taxes depend upon the relationships among earnings from the capital assets and their interactions with differential tax rates and tax subsidies.

But the inability of a user firm to utilize tax benefits such as the investment tax credit or accelerated depreciation may make it advantageous for it to enter a lease arrangement. In this situation, the lessor (a bank or a leasing

4. Three comments are appropriate here. First, financial analysts sometimes attempt to reconstruct the balance sheets of firms such as B by capitalizing the lease payments—that is, estimating the value of both the lease obligation and the leased assets and transforming B's balance sheet into one comparable to A's. Second, as indicated in Chapter 7, lease charges are included in the fixed charge coverage ratio; and this ratio is approximately equal for Firms A and B, thereby revealing the true state of affairs. Thus it is unlikely that lenders will be fooled into granting more credit to a company with a lease than to one with a conventional loan having terms similar to those of the lease. Third, FASB Statement No. 13 provides for including capital leases in the firm's balance sheet.

company) can utilize the credit, and competition with other lessors may result in lower leasing rates.

For example, the investment tax credit (discussed in Chapter 3) can be taken only if the firm's profits and taxes exceed a certain level. If a firm is unprofitable, or if it is expanding so rapidly and generating such large tax credits that it cannot use them them all, then it may be profitable for it to enter a lease arrangement. In this situation, the lessor (a bank or leasing company) can take the credit and give the lessee a corresponding reduction in lease charges. In recent years, railroads and airlines have been large users of leasing for this reason, as have industrial companies faced with similar situations. Anaconda, for example, financed most of the cost of a $138 million aluminum plant built in 1973 through a lease arrangement.[5] Anaconda had suffered a $365 million tax loss when Chile expropriated its copper mining properties, and the carry-forward of this loss would hold taxes down for years. Thus the firm could not use the tax credit associated with the new plant. By entering a lease arrangement, the company was able to pass the tax credit on to the lessors, who in turn gave it lower lease payments than would have existed under a lōan arrangement. Anaconda's financial staff estimated that financial charges over the life of the plant would be $74 million less under the lease arrangement than under a borrow-and-buy plan.

Incidentally, the Anaconda lease was set up as a leveraged lease.[6] A group of banks and Chrysler Corporation provided about $38 million of equity and were the owner-lessors. They borrowed the balance of the required funds from Prudential, Metropolitan, and Aetna—large life insurance companies. The banks and Chrysler received not only the investment tax credit but also the tax shelter associated with accelerated depreciation on the plant. Such leveraged leases, often with wealthy individuals seeking tax shelters acting as owner-lessors, are an important part of the financial scene today and help explain why leasing has reached a total volume of over $100 billion.

Summary

Leasing has long been used in connection with the acquisition of equipment by railroad companies. In recent years, it has been extended to a wide variety of equipment.

The most important forms of lease financing are: (1) sale and leaseback, in which a firm owning land, buildings, or equipment sells the property and simultaneously executes an agreement to lease it for a certain period under specific terms; (2) service leases or operating leases, which include both financing and maintenance services, are often cancellable and call for payments under the lease contract that may not fully recover the cost of the

5. Vanderwicken, "Powerful Logic of the Leasing Boom," pp. 136–140.

6. Technically, a *leveraged lease* is one in which the financial intermediary (a bank or other lessor) uses borrowed funds to acquire the assets it leases.

equipment; and (3) financial leases, which do not provide for maintenance services, are not cancellable, and do fully amortize the cost of the leased asset during the basic lease contract period.

To understand the possible advantages and disadvantages of lease financing, the cost of leasing an asset must be compared with the cost of owning it. In the absence of major tax advantages and other "market imperfections," there should be no advantage to either leasing or owning an asset when the project's weighted cost of capital is used as the discount factor in the analysis. But when the cost of debt is used as the discount factor, the "indifference result" is not obtained. The conceptual reason for using the cost of capital rather than the cost of debt in analyzing leasing versus owning is that any form of debt requires an equity base that should be taken into account in determining the applicable discount factor. (However, because of the widespread use of the cost of debt as the discount factor, this procedure is also illustrated.)

The recommended procedure is to first use the cost of capital to obtain the result of no advantage to either leasing or owning. Then a wide range of factors that may influence the indifference result can be introduced. These possible influences include tax differences, differences in maintenance costs, different costs of capital for the lessor and the user firm, differences in obsolescence, and differences in the contractual positions in leasing versus other forms and sources of financing. Whether these other factors will actually give an advantage or disadvantage to leasing depends on the facts and circumstances of each transaction analyzed.

Questions

21.1 Discuss this statement: The type of equipment best suited for leasing has a long life in relation to the length of the lease, is a removable, standard product that could be used by many different firms, and is easily identifiable. In short, it is the kind of equipment that could be repossessed and sold readily. However, we would be quite happy to write a ten-year lease on paper towels for a firm such as Eastman Kodak or Owens-Illinois.

21.2 Leasing is often called a hedge against obsolescence. Under what conditions is this actually true?

21.3 Is leasing in any sense a hedge against inflation for the lessee? For the lessor?

21.4 One alleged advantage of leasing is that it keeps liabilities off the balance sheet, thus making it possible for a firm to obtain more leverage than it otherwise could. This raises the question of whether both the lease obligation and the asset involved should be capitalized and shown on the balance sheet. Discuss the pros and cons of capitalizing leases and related assets.

Problems

21.1 a. The Clarkton Company produces industrial machines, which have five-year lives. Clarkton is willing to either sell the machines for $30,000 or to lease them at a rental that, because of competitive factors, yields an after-tax return to Clarkton of 6 percent—its cost of capital. What is the company's competitive lease rental rate? (Assume straight line depreciation, zero salvage value, and an effective corporate tax rate of 40 percent.)

b. The Stockton Machine Shop is contemplating the purchase of a machine exactly like those rented by Clarkton. The machine will produce net benefits of $10,000 per year. Stockton can buy the machine for $30,000 or rent it from Clarkton at the competitive lease rental rate. Stockton's cost of capital is 12 percent, its cost of debt 10 percent, and T = 40 percent. Which alternative is better for Stockton?

c. If Clarkton's cost of capital is 9 percent and competition exists among lessors, solve for the new equilibrium rental rate. Will Stockton's decision be altered?

21.2 The Nelson Company is faced with the decision of whether it should purchase or lease a new forklift truck. The truck can be leased on an eight-year contract for $4,978.22 a year, or it can be purchased for $26,000. The salvage value (Z_N) of the truck after eight years is $2,000. The company uses straight line depreciation. The discount rate applied is its after-tax cost of debt. The company can borrow at 15 percent and has a 40 percent marginal tax rate and a 12 percent cost of capital.

a. Analyze the lease versus purchase decision using the firm's after-tax cost of debt as the discount factor.

b. Discuss your results.

21.3 The Bradley Steel Company seeks to acquire the use of a rolling machine at the lowest possible cost. The choice is either to lease one at $21,890 annually or to purchase one for $54,000. The company's cost of capital is 14 percent, its cost of debt is 10 percent, and its tax rate is 40 percent. The machine has an economic life of six years and no salvage value. The company uses straight line depreciation. The discount rate applied is the after-tax cost of debt. Which is the less costly method of financing?

21.4 The Scott Brothers Department Store is considering a sale and leaseback of its major property, consisting of land and a building, because it is thirty days late on 80 percent of its accounts payable. The recent balance sheet of Scott Brothers is as shown:

Scott Brothers Department Store Balance Sheet as of December 31, 19X0 (Thousands of Dollars)

Assets		Liabilities	
Cash	$ 288	Accounts payable	$1,440
Receivables	1,440	Bank loans (at 8%)	1,440
Inventories	1,872	Other current liabilities	720
Total current assets	$3,600	Total current debt	$3,600
Land	1,152	Common stock	1,440
Building	720	Retained earnings	720
Fixtures and equipment	288		
Net fixed assets	2,160		
Total assets	$5,760	Total claims	$5,760

Profit before taxes is $36,000; after taxes, $20,000. Annual depreciation charges are $57,600 on the building and $72,000 on the fixtures and equipment. The land and building could be sold for a total of $2.8 million. The annual net rental will be $240,000.

a. How much capital gains tax will Scott Brothers pay if the land and building are sold? (Assume all capital gains are taxed at the capital gains tax rate; that is, disregard such items as recapture of depreciation, tax preference treatment, and so on.)
b. Compare the current ratio before and after the sale and leaseback if the after-tax net proceeds are used to clean up the bank loans and to reduce accounts payable and other current liabilities.
c. If the lease had been in effect during the year shown in the balance sheet, what would Scott Brothers' profit for that year have been?
d. What are the basic financial problems facing Scott Brothers? Will the sale and leaseback operation solve them?

Selected References

Athanasopoulos, Peter J., and Bacon, Peter W. "The Evaluation of Leveraged Leases." *Financial Management* 9 (Spring 1980), pp. 76–80.

Axelson, Kenneth S. "Needed: A Generally Accepted Method for Measuring Lease Commitments." *Financial Executive* 39 (July 1971), pp. 40–52.

Beechy, Thomas H. "Quasi-Debt Analysis of Financial Leases." *Accounting Review* 44 (April 1969), pp. 375–381.

Bower, Richard S. "Issues in Lease Financing." *Financial Management* 2 (Winter 1973), pp. 25–34.

Bower, Richard S.; Herringer, Frank C.; and Williamson, J. Peter. "Lease Evaluation." *Accounting Review* 41 (April 1966), pp. 257–265.

Brigham, Eugene F. "The Impact of Bank Entry on Market Conditions in the Equipment Leasing Industry." *National Banking Review* 2 (September 1964), pp. 11–26.

Doenges, R. Conrad. "The Cost of Leasing." *Engineering Economist* 17 (Fall 1971), pp. 31–44.

Dyl, Edward A., and Martin, Stanley A., Jr. "Setting Terms for Leveraged Leases." *Financial Management* 6 (Winter 1977), pp. 20–27.

Fawthrop, R. A., and Terry, Brian. "The Evaluation of an Integrated Investment and Lease-Financing." *Journal of Business Finance and Accounting* 3 (Autumn 1976), pp. 79–112.

———. "Debt Management and the Use of Leasing Finance in UK Corporate Financing Strategies." *Journal of Business Finance and Accounting* 2 (Autumn 1975), pp. 295–314.

Ferrara, William L. "Should Investment and Financing Decisions Be Separated?" *Accounting Review* 41 (January 1966), pp. 106–114.

Ferrara, William L., and Wojdak, Joseph F. "Valuation of Long-Term Leases." *Financial Analysts' Journal* 25 (November–December 1969), pp. 29–32.

Findlay, M. Chapman, III. "A Sensitivity Analysis of IRR Leasing Models." *Engineering Economist* 20 (Summer 1975), pp. 231–241.

———. "Financial Lease Evaluation: Survey and Synthesis." Paper presented at the Eastern Finance Association Meetings, Storrs, Connecticut, April 12, 1973.

Gant, Donald R. "A Critical Look at Lease Financing." *Controller* 29 (June 1961), pp. 274–277, 311–312.

———. "Illusion in Lease Financing." *Harvard Business Review* 37 (March–April 1959), pp. 121–141.

Gaumnitz, Jack E., and Ford, Allen. "The Lease or Sell Decision." *Financial Management* 7 (Winter 1978), pp. 69–74.

Gordon, Myron J. "A General Solution to the Buy or Lease Decision: A Pedagogical Note." *Journal of Finance* 29 (March 1974), pp. 245–250.

Hamel, H. G. "Leasing in Industry." *Studies in Business Policy.* No. 127. New York: National Industrial Conference Board, 1968.

Honig, Lawrence E., and Coley, Stephen C. "An After-Tax Equivalent Payment Approach to Conventional Lease Analysis." *Financial Management* 4 (Winter 1975), pp. 18–27.

Johnson, Robert W., and Lewellen, Wilbur G. "Analysis of the Lease-or-Buy Decision." *Journal of Finance* 27 (September 1972), pp. 815–823.

Keller, Thomas F., and Peterson, Russell J. "Optimal Financial Structure, Cost of Capital, and the Lease-or-Buy Decision." *Journal of Business Finance and Accounting* 1 (Autumn 1974), pp. 405–414.

Kim, E. Han; Lewellen, Wilbur G.; and McConnell, John J. "Sale-and-Leaseback Agreements and Enterprise Valuation." *Journal of Financial and Quantitative Analysis* 13 (December 1978), pp. 871–883.

Knutson, Peter H. "Leased Equipment and Divisional Return on Capital." *NAA Bulletin* 44 (November 1962), pp. 15–20.

Law, Warren A., and Crum, M. Colyer. *Equipment Leasing and Commercial Banks.* Chicago: Association of Reserve City Bankers, 1963.

Levy, Haim, and Sarnat, Marshall. "Leasing, Borrowing, and Financial Risk." *Financial Management* 8 (Winter 1979), pp. 47–54.

Lewellen, Wilbur G.; Long, Michael S.; and McConnell, John J. "Asset Leasing in Competitive Capital Markets." *Journal of Finance* 31 (June 1976), pp. 787–798.

Long, Michael S. "Leasing and the Cost of Capital." *Journal of Financial and Quantitative Analysis* 12 (November 1977), pp. 579–598.

Martin, John D.; Anderson, Paul F.; and Keown, Arthur J. "Lease Capitalization and Stock Price Stability: Implications for Accounting." *Journal of Accounting, Auditing and Finance* 2 (Winter 1979), pp. 151–164.

Miller, Merton H., and Upton, Charles W. "Leasing, Buying, and the Cost of Capital Services." *Journal of Finance* 31 (June 1976), pp. 761–786.

Moyer, Charles R. "Lease Evaluation and the Investment Tax Credit: A Framework for Analysis." *Financial Management* 4 (Summer 1975), pp. 39–44.

Myers, John H. *Reporting of Leases in Financial Statements.* New York: American Institute of Certified Public Accountants, 1962.

Myers, Stewart C.; Dill, David A.; and Bautista, Alberto J. "Valuation of Financial Lease Contracts." *Journal of Finance* 31 (June 1976), pp. 799–819.

Nantell, Timothy J. "Equivalence of Lease versus Buy Analyses." *Financial Management* 2 (Autumn 1973), pp. 61–65.

Nelson, A. Thomas. "Capitalized Leases—The Effect on Financial Ratios." *Journal of Accountancy* 116 (July 1963), pp. 49–58.

Ofer, Ahron R. "The Evaluation of the Lease versus Purchase Alternatives." *Financial Management* 5 (Summer 1976), pp. 67–72.

Olsen, Robert A. "Lease vs. Purchase or Lease vs. Borrow: Comment." *Financial Management* 7 (Summer 1978), pp. 82–83.

Perg, Wayne F. "Leveraged Leasing: The Problem of Changing Leverage." *Financial Management* 7 (Autumn 1978), pp. 47–51.

Roberts, Gordon S., and Gudikunst, Arthur C. "Equipment Financial Leasing Practices and Costs: Comment." *Financial Management* 7 (Summer 1978), pp. 79–81.

Roenfeldt, Rodney L., and Osteryoung, Jerome S. "Analysis of Financial Leases." *Financial Management* 2 (Spring 1973), pp. 74–87.

Sartoris, William L., and Paul, Ronda S. "Lease Evaluation—Another Capital Budgeting Decision." *Financial Management* 2 (Summer 1973), pp. 46–52.

Schachner, Leopold. "The New Accounting for Leases." *Financial Executive* 46 (February 1978), pp. 40–47.

Schall, Lawrence D. "The Lease-or-Buy and Asset Acquisition Decisions." *Journal of Finance* 29 (September 1974), pp. 1203–1214.

Uttal, Bro. "The Lease Is Up on Itel's Lavish Living." *Fortune,* October 8, 1979, pp. 106–109, 113–114, 116, 119.

Vancil, Richard F. "Lease or Borrow: Steps in Negotiation." *Harvard Business Review* 39 (November–December 1961), pp. 238–259.

———. "Lease or Borrow: New Method of Analysis." *Harvard Business Review* 39 (September–October 1961), pp. 122–136.

Vancil, Richard F., and Anthony, Robert N. "The Financial Community Looks at Leasing." *Harvard Business Review* 37 (November–December 1959), pp. 113–130.

22

Warrants and Convertibles

Thus far the discussion of long-term financing has dealt with the nature of common stock, preferred stock, various types of debt, and leasing. It has also explained how offering common stock through the use of rights can facilitate low-cost stock flotations. This chapter will show how the financial manager, through the use of warrants and convertibles, can make the company's securities attractive to an even broader range of investors. Therefore, it is important to understand the characteristics of these two types of securities.

Warrants

A *warrant* is an option to buy a stated number of shares of stock at a specified price. For example, Trans Pacific Airlines has warrants outstanding that give the warrant owners the right to buy one share of TPA stock at a price of $22 for each warrant held. Warrants generally expire on a certain date (TPA's warrants on December 1, 1983), although some have perpetual lives.

Formula Value of a Warrant

Warrants have a calculated, or formula, value and an actual value, or price, that is determined in the marketplace. The formula value is found by use of the following equation:

$$\text{Formula value} = \left(\begin{array}{c}\text{Market price of}\\\text{common stock}\end{array} - \begin{array}{c}\text{Option}\\\text{price}\end{array}\right) \times \left(\begin{array}{c}\text{Number of shares each}\\\text{warrant entitles owner}\\\text{to purchase}\end{array}\right).$$

For instance, a TPA warrant entitles the owner to purchase one share of common stock at $22 a share. If the market price of the common stock is $64.50, the formula price of the warrant is obtained as follows:

$$(\$64.50 - \$22) \times 1.0 = \$42.50.$$

The formula gives a negative value when the stock is selling for less than the option price. For example, if TPA stock is selling for $20, the formula value of the warrants is $-\$2$. Since this makes no sense, the formula value is defined as zero when the stock is selling for less than the option price.

Table 22.1

Formula and Actual Values of TPA Warrants at Different Market Prices

	Value of Warrant		
Price of Stock	Formula Price	Actual Price	Premium
$ 0.00	$ 0.00	Not available	—[a]
22.00	0.00	$ 9.00	$9.00
23.00	1.00	9.75	8.75
24.00	2.00	10.50	8.50
33.67	11.67	17.37	5.70
52.00	30.00	32.00	2.00
75.00	53.00	54.00	1.00
100.00	78.00	79.00	1.00
150.00	128.00	Not available	—[a]

a. Cannot be calculated.

Actual Price of a Warrant

Generally, warrants sell above their formula values. When TPA stock was selling for $64.50, the warrants had a formula value of $42.50 but were selling at a price of $46.87. This represents a premium of $4.37 above the formula value.

A set of TPA stock prices, together with actual and formula warrant values, is given in Table 22.1 and plotted in Figure 22.1. At any stock price below $22, the formula value of the warrant is zero; beyond $22, each $1 increase in the price of the stock brings with it a $1 increase in the formula value of the war-

Figure 22.1

Formula and Actual Values of TPA Warrants at Different Common Stock Prices

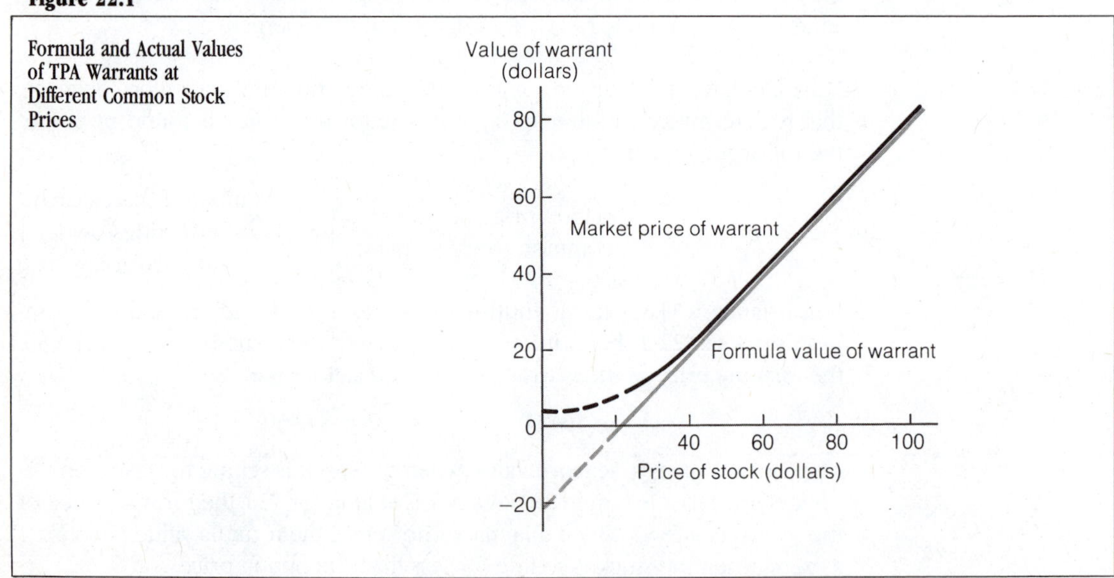

rant. The actual market price of the warrant lies above the formula value at each price of the common stock. Notice, however, that the premium of market price over formula value declines as the price of the common stock increases. For example, when the common sold for $22 and the warrants had a zero formula value, their actual price, and the premium, was $9. As the price of the stock rises, the formula value of the warrants matches the increase dollar for dollar, but for a while the *market price* of the warrant climbs less rapidly and the premium declines. The premium is $9 when the stock sells for $22 a share, but it declines to $1 by the time the stock price has risen to $75 a share. Beyond this point the premium seems to be constant.

Why does this pattern exist? The answer lies in the speculative appeal of warrants; they enable a person buying securities to gain a high degree of personal leverage. To illustrate: Suppose TPA warrants always sell for exactly their formula value, and suppose you are thinking of investing in the company's common stock at a time when it is selling for $25 a share. If you buy a share and the price rises to $50 in a year, you will make a 100 percent capital gain. However, if you buy the warrants at their formula value ($3 when the stock sells for $25), your capital gain will be $25 on a $3 investment, or 833 percent. At the same time, your total loss potential with the warrant is only $3, while the potential loss from the purchase of the stock is $25. The huge capital gains potential, combined with the loss limitation, is clearly worth something—and the exact amount it is worth to investors is the amount of the premium.[1]

But why does the premium decline as the price of the stock rises? The answer is that both the leverage effect and the loss protection feature decline at high stock prices. For example, if you are thinking of buying TPA stock at $75 a share, the formula value of the warrants is $53. If the stock price doubles to $150, the formula value of TPA warrants goes from $53 to $128. The capital gain on the stock is still 100 percent, but the gain on the warrant declines from 833 percent to 142 percent. Moreover, the loss potential on the warrant is much greater when it is selling at high prices. These two factors—the declining leverage impact and the increasing danger of losses—explain why the premium diminishes as the price of the common stock rises.

In the past, warrants have generally been used by small, rapidly growing firms as sweeteners when selling either debt or preferred stocks. Since such firms are frequently regarded by investors as highly risky, their bonds can be sold only if they are willing to accept extremely high rates of interest and very restrictive indenture provisions, to offer warrants, or to make the bonds convertible. In April 1970, however, AT&T raised $1.57 billion by selling bonds with warrants. This was the largest financing of any type ever undertaken by a business firm, and it marked the first use of warrants by a large, strong cor-

1. However, a $3 decline in the stock price produces only a 12 percent loss if the stock is purchased but a 100 percent loss if the warrant is bought and it declines to its formula value.

poration.[2] It can safely be anticipated that other large firms will follow AT&T's lead.[3]

Giving warrants along with bonds enables investors to share in the company's growth if it does, in fact, grow and prosper; therefore, investors are willing to accept a lower bond interest rate and less restrictive indenture provisions. A bond with warrants has some characteristics of debt and some of equity. It is a hybrid security that provides the financial manager with an opportunity to expand the mix of securities, appealing to a broader group of investors and possibly lowering the firm's cost of capital.

Warrants can also bring in additional funds. The option price is generally set 15 to 20 percent above the market price of the stock at the time of the bond issue. If the firm does grow and prosper, and if its stock price rises above the option price at which shares can be purchased, warrant holders will surrender their warrants and buy stock at the stated price. There are several reasons for this:

1. Warrant holders will surrender warrants and buy stock if the warrants are about to expire with the market price of the stock above the option price.
2. Warrant holders will surrender and buy as just mentioned if the company raises the dividend on the common stock. No dividend is earned on the warrant, so it provides no current income. However, if the common stock pays a high dividend, it provides an attractive dividend yield. This induces warrant holders to exercise their option to buy the stock.
3. Warrants sometimes have stepped-up option prices. For example, Textron issued warrants with an exercise price of $10 per share until May 1, 1979, and then $11.25 until the expiration date of the warrants on May 1, 1984.

One desirable feature of warrants is that they generally bring in additional funds only if such funds are needed. If the company grows and prospers, causing the price of the stock to rise, the warrants are exercised and bring in needed funds. If the company is unsuccessful and cannot profitably employ additional money, the price of its stock will probably not rise sufficiently to induce exercise of the options.

Convertibles

Convertible securities are bonds or preferred stocks that are exchangeable into common stock at the option of the holder and under specified terms and conditions. The most important of the special features relates to how

2. It is interesting to note that before the AT&T issue, the New York Stock Exchange had a policy against listing warrants. The NYSE's stated policy was that warrants could not be listed because they were "speculative" instruments rather than "investment" securities. When AT&T issued warrants, however, the exchange changed its policy and agreed to list warrants that met certain specifications.
3. In fact, the number of warrant issues listed on the New York Stock Exchange stood at eleven at the end of 1979. See *1980 Fact Book* (New York: New York Stock Exchange, 1980), p. 33.

many shares of stock a convertible holder receives by converting. This feature is defined as the *conversion ratio,* and it gives the number of shares of common stock the holder of the convertible receives on surrender of the security. Related to the conversion ratio is the *conversion price*—the effective price paid for the common stock when conversion occurs. In effect, a convertible is similar to a bond with an attached warrant.

The relationship between the conversion ratio and the conversion price is illustrated by Adams Electric Company convertible debentures, issued at their $1,000 par value in 1975. At any time prior to maturity on July 1, 1995, a debenture holder can turn in the bond and receive in its place 20 shares of common stock; therefore, the conversion ratio is 20 shares for 1 bond. The bond has a par value of $1,000, so the holder is giving up this amount on conversion. Dividing the $1,000 by the 20 shares received gives a conversion price of $50 a share:

$$\text{Conversion price} = \frac{\text{Par value of bond}}{\text{Shares received}} = \frac{\$1{,}000}{20} = \$50.$$

The conversion price and conversion ratio are established at the time the convertible bond is sold. Generally, these values are fixed for the life of the bond, although sometimes a stepped-up conversion price is used. Litton Industries' convertible debentures, for example, were convertible into 12.5 shares until 1972, and they can be exchanged into 11.76 shares from 1972 until 1982 and into 11.11 shares from 1982 until they mature in 1987. The conversion price thus started at $80 and will rise to $85, then to $90. Litton's convertibles, like most, are callable at the option of the company.

Another factor that may cause a change in the conversion price and ratio is a standard feature of almost all convertibles—the clause protecting the convertible against dilution from stock splits, stock dividends, and the sale of common stock at low prices (as in a rights offering). The typical provision states that no common stock can be sold at a price below the conversion price and that the conversion price must be lowered (and the conversion ratio raised) by the percentage amount of any stock dividend or split. For example, if Adams Electric had a two-for-one split, the conversion ratio would automatically be adjusted to forty and the conversion price lowered to $25. If this protection were not contained in the contract, a company could completely thwart conversion by the use of stock splits and dividends. Warrants are similarly protected against dilution.

Like warrant option prices, the conversion price is characteristically set from 15 to 20 percent above the prevailing market price of the common stock at the time the convertible issue is sold. Exactly how the conversion price is established can best be understood after examining some of the reasons that firms use convertibles.

Advantages of Convertibles

Convertibles offer advantages to corporations as well as to individual investors. The most important of these advantages are discussed below.

A Sweetener When Selling Debt. A company can sell debt with lower interest rates and less restrictive covenants by giving investors a chance to share in potential capital gains. Convertibles, like bonds with warrants, offer this possibility.

The Sale of Common Stock at Higher than Prevailing Prices. Many companies actually want to sell common stock, not debt, but feel that the price of the stock is temporarily depressed. Management may know, for example, that earnings are depressed because of a strike but that they will snap back during the next year and pull the price of the stock up with them. To sell stock now would require giving up more shares to raise a given amount of money than management thinks is necessary. However, setting the conversion price 15 to 20 percent above the present market price of the stock will require giving up 15 to 20 percent fewer shares when the bonds are converted than would be required if stock was sold directly.

Notice, however, that management is counting on the stock's price rising above the conversion price to make the stock actually attractive in conversion. If the stock price does not rise and conversion does not occur, then the company is saddled with debt.

How can the company be sure that conversion will occur when the price of the stock rises above the conversion price? Characteristically, convertibles have a provision that gives the issuing firm the opportunity of calling the convertible at a specified price. Suppose the conversion price is $50, the conversion ratio is twenty, the market price of the common stock has risen to $60, and the call price on the convertible bond is $1,050. If the company calls the bond (by giving the usual notification of twenty days), bondholders can either convert into common stock with a market value of $1,200 or allow the company to redeem the bond for $1,050. Naturally, bondholders prefer $1,200 to $1,050, so conversion occurs. The call provision therefore gives the company a means of forcing conversion, provided that the market price of the stock is greater than the conversion price.

Low-Cost Capital during a Construction Period. Another advantage from the standpoint of the issuer is that a convertible issue can be used as a temporary financing device. During the years 1946 through 1957, AT&T sold $10 billion of convertible debentures. By 1959, about 80 percent of these convertible debentures had been converted into common stock. AT&T did not want to sell straight debt in that amount because its financial structure would have been unbalanced. On the other hand, if it had simply issued large amounts of common stock periodically, there would have been price pressure on its stock because the market is slow to digest large blocks of stock.

By using convertible debentures, which provided for a lag of some six to nine months before they were convertible into common stock, AT&T received relatively cheap money to finance growth. Transmission lines and telephone exchange buildings must first be built to provide the basis for installing phones. While AT&T was building such installations, these investments were not earning any money. Therefore, it was important for the company to minimize the cost of money during the construction period. After six to nine months had elapsed and the installations had been translated into telephones that were bringing in revenues, AT&T was better able to pay the regular common stock dividend.

Disadvantages of Convertibles

From the standpoint of the issuer, convertibles have one possible disadvantage. Although the convertible bond does give the issuer the opportunity to sell common stock at a price 15 to 20 percent higher than it could otherwise be sold, if the stock greatly increases in price, the issuer may find that it would have been better off if it had waited and simply sold the common stock. Further, if the company truly wants to raise equity capital, and if the price of the stock declines after the bond is issued, then it is stuck with debt.

Analysis of Convertible Debentures

A convertible security is a hybrid, having some of the characteristics of common stocks and some of bonds or preferred stocks.[4] Investors expect to earn an interest yield as well as a capital gains yield. Moreover, the corporation recognizes that it incurs an interest cost and a potential dilution of equity when it sells convertibles. This section will develop a theoretical model to combine these two cost components and then will discuss the conditions under which convertibles should be used.

Since an investor who purchases a convertible bond expects to receive interest plus capital gains, the total expected return is the sum of these two parts. The expected interest return is dependent primarily on the bond's coupon interest rate and the price paid for the bond, while the expected capital gains yield is dependent basically on (1) the relationship between the conversion price and the stock price at the time of issue and (2) the expected growth rate in the price of the stock. These two yield components will now be discussed.

Think of the graph in Figure 22.2 as showing the *ex ante,* or expected, relationships, starting now at Year $t = 0$ and projecting events into the future. (The symbols used in Figure 22.2 and the remainder of this chapter are listed in Table 22.2.)

The analysis of convertibles will be organized around four major aspects:

1. Conversion value.
2. Straight bond value.
3. Expected market value.
4. Expected rate of return.

4. For further analysis of the issues treated in this section, see E. F. Brigham, "An Analysis of Convertible Debentures: Theory and Some Empirical Evidence," *Journal of Finance* 21 (March 1966), pp. 35–54.

Figure 22.2

Model of a Convertible Bond

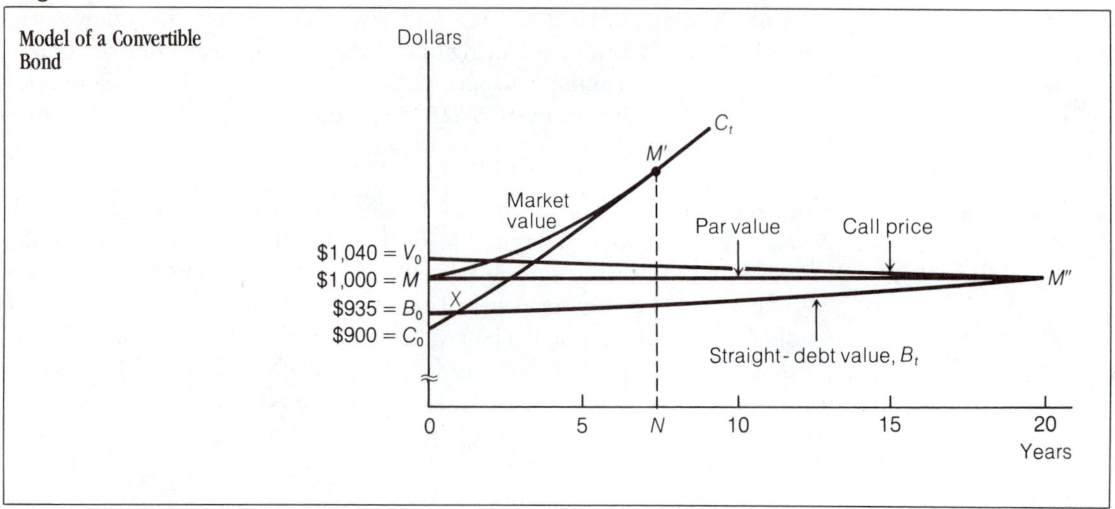

Conversion Value

The hypothetical bond is a new issue that can be purchased for M = $1,000; this initial price is also the par (and maturity) value. The bond is callable at the option of the corporation, with the call price originating at V_0 = $1,040, somewhat above par, and declining linearly over the twenty-year term to maturity to M'' = $1,000 at maturity.

At any point in time, the bond can be converted to stock; the value of the stock received on conversion is defined as the *conversion value* of the bond. The original conversion value (C_0) is established by multiplying the market price of the stock at the time of issue by the number of shares into which the bond can be converted (the conversion ratio). The stock price is expected to grow at a certain rate *(g),* causing the conversion value to rise at this same rate. This establishes the curve C_0C_t, which shows the expected conversion value at each point in time. All of this is expressed by Equation 22.1:

$$C_t = p_0(1 + g)^t\#. \tag{22.1}$$

The initial conversion value of the bond, when $t = 0$, is simply $45 × 20, or $900. One year later it is expected to be $45(1.04)(20) = $936; after two years it is expected to rise to $973.44; and so on. Thus the expected conversion value curve, is a function of the expected growth in the price of the stock.

Straight Debt Value

In addition to its value in conversion, the bond also has a straight debt value, B_t, defined as the price at which the bond would sell in any year t if it did not have the conversion option. At each point in time, B_t is determined by Equation 22.2:

$$B_t = \sum_{j=1}^{t^*} \frac{c}{(1 + k_b)^j} + \frac{M''}{(1 + k_b)^{t^*}}. \tag{22.2}$$

Table 22.2

Summary of Symbols Used in Chapter 22

B_t = Straight debt value of a bond at time t
c = Dollars of interest paid each year ($40)
C_N = Conversion value = $p_0(1 + g)^N\#$
C_t = Conversion value at time t
g = Expected rate of growth of the stock's price = 4 percent
j = Time subscript from 1 to t^*
k_b = Market rate of interest on equivalent risk, nonconvertible debt issues (4.5%)
k_c = Internal rate of return, or expected yield, on the convertible
M = Price paid for the bond
M' = Market value of the convertible bond when its conversion value becomes equal to its market value
M'' = Maturity value
N = Number of years bond is expected to be held
$\#$ = Conversion ratio, or number of shares received on conversion = 20
p_c = Conversion price = $M/\#$
p_0 = Current market price of the stock = $45
t^* = Number of years remaining until maturity
T = Marginal corporate income tax rate
V_0 = Original call price of an option
X = Point at which the bond's conversion value rises above its straight debt value.

Equation 22.2 is used to calculate the bond value, B_t, from each point t to the maturity date. To illustrate the use of the equation, B_t will be calculated at $t = 0$ and $t = 8$. First, note that $t = 0$ is the point in time when the bond is issued, while $t = 8$ means the bond is 8 years old and has 12 years remaining to maturity. So, for B_0, the summation term refers to an annuity of $40 per year for $t^* = 20 - 0 = 20$ years; while for B_8, the summation represents an annuity of $t^* = 20 - 8 = 12$ years:

$$B_0 = \sum_{j=1}^{20} \frac{\$40}{(1.045)^j} + \frac{\$1,000}{(1.045)^{20}}$$

$$= \$40(13.0079) + \$1,000(0.4146)$$
$$= \$520.32 + \$414.60 = \$934.92.$$

$$B_8 = \sum_{j=1}^{12} \frac{\$40}{(1.045)^j} + \frac{\$1,000}{(1.045)^{12}}$$

$$= \$40(9.1186) + \$1,000(0.5897)$$
$$= \$364.74 + \$589.70 = \$954.44.$$

Thus B_t rises over time, and $B_{20} = \$1,000$.[5]

5. In Equation 22.2, bond values are calculated at the beginning of each period, just after the last interest payment has been made. Most bonds (convertible and nonconvertible alike) are actually traded on the basis of a basic price, determined as in Equation 22.2, plus interest accrued since the last payment date. Thus, a person who bought this bond a few days before the end of Year 20 would pay approximately $1,000 plus $40 accrued interest, and the invoice from the broker would indicate these two components. Also, technically semi-annual compounding should be used. However, we have used annual compounding here to focus on issues related to convertibility.

Expected Market Value

The convertible will never sell below its value as a straight bond. If it did, investors interested in buying debt instruments would see it as a bargain, start buying the bonds, and drive their value up to B_t. Similarly, the convertible can never sell below its conversion value. If it did, investors interested in the stock would buy the bonds, convert, and obtain shares at a bargain price; but they would drive the price of the convertible up to C_t in the process. Thus the lines C_0C_t and B_0M'' in Figure 22.2 serve as floors below which the market price of the bond cannot fall. The higher of these two floors dominates, with the discontinuous curve B_0XC_t forming the *effective market value floor*.

Ordinarily, convertibles sell at premiums over their bond and conversion value floors. For the illustrated bond, the expected market value is represented in Figure 22.2 by the curve MM', which lies above the effective floor (B_0XC_t) over most of the range but converges with B_0XC_t in Year *N*. The rationale behind this price action is developed in the following two sections.

Why the Market Value Exceeds the B_0XC_t Floor. The spread between MM' and B_0XC_t, which represents the premium marginal investors are willing to pay for the conversion option, can be explained in several ways.[6] First, since the convertible bond can be converted into common stock if the company prospers and the stock price rises, it usually commands a premium over its value as straight debt (that is, the right of conversion has a positive value). Second, the convertible bond usually commands a premium over its conversion value because investors are able to reduce their risk exposure by holding convertibles. To illustrate: Suppose someone buys the hypothetical bond for $1,000. At the time, it is convertible into 20 shares of stock with a market price of $45, giving a conversion value of $900. If the stock market turns sharply down and the stock price falls to $22.50 per share, the stock investor will suffer a 50 percent loss in value. The price of a convertible bond, however, will fall from $1,000 to the bond value floor (B_0M'' in Figure 22.2), which is at least $935. Hence, holding the convertible entails less risk than holding common stock, and this too causes convertibles to sell at a premium above their conversion value.[7]

Why the Market Value Approaches the Conversion Value. The MM' curve in Figure 22.2 rises less rapidly than the C_0C_t curve, indicating that the market value approaches the conversion value as the conversion value increases.

6. Marginal investors, often called "the market," are defined as those just willing to hold the bond at its going price. These investors are, in fact, the ones who actually determine the level of the bond's price.

7. Two institutional factors may also contribute to convertible premiums. First, margin requirements are typically lower for convertibles than for stock; thus investors can speculate with less money in the convertible market than in the stock market. Second, certain institutional investors, such as life insurance companies, have more freedom to invest in convertibles than in stocks; so if these institutions want to invest in stocks to a greater extent than their regulators permit, they can expand stock holdings "through the back door" with convertibles.

This is caused by three separate factors. First, and probably most important, the bondholders realize that the issue is callable; if it is in fact called, they have the option of either surrendering for redemption or converting. In the former case, they receive the call price; in the latter, they receive stock with a value designated by C_t. If the market price of the bond is above both these values, the holder is in danger of a potential loss in wealth in the event of a call; this fact prevents wide spreads between MM' and B_0XC_t whenever the market value exceeds the call price.

The second factor driving MM' toward C_0C_t is related to the loss protection characteristic of convertibles. Barring changes in the interest rate on the firm's straight debt securities, the potential loss on a convertible is equal to the spread between MM' and B_0M''. Since this spread increases at high conversion values, the loss potential also increases, causing the premium attributable to the loss protection to diminish.

The third factor causing the gap between MM' and C_0C_t to close has to do with the relationship between the yield on a convertible and that on the common stock for which it can be exchanged. The yield on most common stocks consists of two components: a dividend yield and an expected capital gain yield. (The next section will show that convertibles also have two yield components, one from interest payments and one from capital gains.) After some point, the expected capital gain is the same for both instruments, but the current yield on the bond declines in comparison with that on the common stock because dividends on stocks whose prices are rising are typically also rising, while interest payments are fixed. This causes the gap between MM' and C_0C_t to close and would eventually lead to a negative premium except for the fact that voluntary conversion occurs first.

Expected Rate of Return on a Convertible

The purchaser of a convertible generally expects the price of the stock to rise, the conversion value to rise with the stock, and the conversion to take place after some period of time, say N years. Thus the purchaser expects first to receive a series of interest payments of $\$c$ per year for N years and then to have stock with a value equal to $C_N = p_0(1 + g)^N\#$. The expected rate of return on the convertible, k_c, is found by solving for it in Equation 22.3:

$$M = \sum_{t=1}^{N} \frac{c}{(1 + k_c)^t} + \frac{C_N}{(1 + k_c)^N}. \tag{22.3}$$

The equation is purely definitional; it simply states that if an investor pays M dollars for a convertible bond, holds it for N years, and receives a series of interest payments plus a terminal value, then the return on the investment will be equal to k_c.[8]

8. Three simplifications are made in this analysis. First, taxes are ignored. Second, the problem of reinvestment rates is handled by assuming that all reinvestment is made at the internal rate of return. Third, it is assumed that bondholders do not hold stock after conversion; they cash out, as do institutional investors precluded from holding common stock.

The *ex ante* yield on a convertible (k_c) is probabilistic—dependent on a set of variables subject to probability distributions and hence itself a random variable. It is possible, however, to define each of the determinants of k_c in terms of its mean expected value; $E(g)$, for example, is the expected value of the growth rate in the stock's price over N years. For simplicity, $E(g)$ and other random variables are shortened to g, C_N, and so on. With the variables defined in this manner, it is possible to work sequentially to determine C_N from Equation 22.5, developed shortly, then to use C_N in Equation 22.3 to find a value of k_c (the return on a convertible bond) that makes Equation 22.3 hold. The determinants of C_N are (1) the corporation's policy in regard to calling the bond to force conversion; or (2) the investor's decision to hold the bond until it is called, to sell it, or to convert voluntarily. Corporate call policy and investor cash-out policy are therefore examined in the next two sections.

Corporate Call Policy. Corporations issuing convertible bonds generally have policies regarding just how far up the C_0C_t curve they will allow a bond to go before calling to force conversion. These policies range from calling as soon as the company is "sure" conversion will take place (this generally means a premium of about 20 percent over the par value) to never calling at all. If the policy is never to issue a call, however, the firm generally relies on the dividend-interest differential to cause voluntary conversion.

It is apparent that call policy has a direct influence on the expected number of years a convertible will remain outstanding and therefore on the value of C_N found by Equation 22.3. Naturally, expectations about call policy influence the expected rate of return on a convertible bond. Because of this, the issuing firm must take investor expectations into account. A policy in the apparent short-run interest of the corporation may penalize the investor with such a low effective actual yield that the firm will have difficulties when it subsequently attempts to market additional securities.[9] (This point is illustrated in one of the problems at the end of the chapter.)

Investor Cash-Out Policy. Investor cash-out policy is similar to corporate call policy in that it sets a limit on how far up the C_0C_t curve investors are willing to ride. The decision is influenced by the interest-dividend relationship, by investors' aversion to risk (recall that risk due to a stock price decline increases as one moves up the C_0C_t curve), and by investors' willingness to hold securities providing low current yields. In general, it appears that investors are willing to ride higher up C_0C_t, given the dividend-interest relationship, than the firm is willing to let them ride; hence, corporate call policy generally supersedes investor cash-out policy.

9. Some firms seek to encourage *voluntary conversion* rather than call to force conversion. One way of doing this is to include a provision for periodic stepped-up conversion prices; for example, Litton Industries' conversion price goes up every three years (so the number of shares received upon conversion goes down), and this stimulates voluntary conversion at the step-up date provided the conversion value of the bond is above the straight debt value. In addition, voluntary conversion occurs when the dividend yield on stock received on conversion exceeds the interest yield on the convertibles.

As already discussed, the path of the conversion value curve is traced out by Equation 22.1:

$$C_t = p_0(1 + g)^t\#. \tag{22.1}$$

Recognizing that $\# = M/p_c$, where p_c is defined as the initial conversion price of the shares, Equation 22.1 can be rewritten as:

$$C_t = \frac{p_0}{p_c}(1 + g)^t M. \tag{22.4}$$

Setting Equation 22.4 equal to the C_N defined by corporate policy (in this case, $1,200 if a 20 percent premium is used) results in:

$$C_N = \frac{p_0}{p_c}(1 + g)^N M = \$1{,}200 \tag{22.5}$$

$$\$1{,}200 = \frac{\$45}{\$50}(1.04)^N\$1{,}000 = \$900(1.04)^N$$

$$\frac{\$1{,}200}{\$900} = 1.333 = (1.04)^N.$$

The 1.333 is the CVIF for the compound sum of $1 growing at 4 percent for N years. In the 4 percent column of Table A.1 at the end of the book, the factor 1.333 lies between the seventh and eighth years, so $N \approx 7\frac{1}{2}$ years.

This value of N (rounded to eight years for simplicity), together with the other known data, can now be substituted into Equation 22.3:

$$M = \sum_{t=1}^{N} \frac{c}{(1 + k_c)^t} + \frac{p_0(1 + g)^N\#}{(1 + k_c)^N}$$

$$\$,1000 = \sum_{t=1}^{8} \frac{c}{(1 + k_c)^t} + \frac{\$45(1.04)^8 20}{(1 + k_c)^8}$$

$$= \$40(\text{PVIFA}) + \$1{,}232(\text{PVIF}).$$

Using the interest factors for 6 percent:

$$\begin{aligned} \text{PV} &= \$40(6.2098) + \$1{,}232(0.6274) \\ &= \$248 + \$773 = \$1{,}021 > \$1{,}000. \end{aligned}$$

Therefore, k_c is a little larger than 6 percent. Using interest factors for 7 percent:

$$\text{PV} = \$239 + \$717 = \$956 < \$1{,}000.$$

Thus, k_c is between 6 and 7 percent. We interpolate $k_c = 6.3$ percent, so someone purchasing this convertible for $1,000 can expect to obtain a return of 6.3 percent on the investment.

The relationship among the coupon, purchase price, and investor cash-out policy determines the return on an investment in a convertible security. This represents the cost of convertible debt. The required return or cost of convertible debt is composed of two parts. One is the interest return based on the coupon on the convertible debt. This is typically lower than the return on straight debt. The second component of return is based on the expected rise in the price of the common stock into which a conversion may be made. This component of return carries risk associated with a security junior to straight debt. Hence, the required return on convertibles would on average be higher than the cost of straight debt.

Decisions on the Use of Warrants and Convertibles

The Winchester Company, an electronic circuit and component manufacturer with assets of $12 million, illustrates a situation where convertibles are useful. Winchester's profits were depressed as a result of its heavy expenditures on research and development for a new product. This situation had held down the growth rate of earnings and dividends; the price-earnings ratio was only 18 times, as compared with an industry average of 22. At the then current $2 earnings per share and P-E of 18, the stock was selling for $36 a share. The Winchester family owned 70 percent of the 300,000 shares outstanding, or 210,000 shares. It wanted to retain majority control but could not buy more stock.

The heavy R & D expenditures had resulted in the development of a new type of printed circuit that management believed would be highly profitable. To build and equip new production facilities, $5 million was needed; and profits would not start to flow into the company for some eighteen months after construction on the new plant was started. Winchester's debt amounted to $5.4 million, or 45 percent of assets—well above the 25 percent industry average. Debt indenture provisions restricted the company from selling additional debt unless the new debt was subordinate to that outstanding.

Investment bankers informed J. H. Winchester, Jr., the financial vice-president, that subordinated debentures could not be sold unless they were convertible or had warrants attached. Convertibles or bonds with warrants could be sold with a 5 percent coupon interest rate if the conversion price or warrant option price was set at 15 percent above the market price of $36—that is, at $41 a share. Alternatively, the investment bankers were willing to buy convertibles or bonds with warrants at a $5\frac{1}{2}$ percent interest rate and a 20 percent conversion premium, or a conversion (or exercise) price of $43.50. If the company wanted to sell common stock directly, it could net $33 a share.

Which of the alternatives should Winchester have chosen? If common stock were to be used, the company would have to sell over 151,000 shares ($5 million divided by $33). Combined with the 90,000 shares held outside the family, this would amount to 241,000 shares versus the Winchester holdings of 210,000; thus the family would lose majority control if common stock were to be sold.

If the 5 percent convertibles or bonds with warrants were to be used and the bonds converted or the warrants exercised, 122,000 new shares would have been added. Combined with the old 90,000, the outside interest would then be 212,000, so again the Winchester family would lose majority control. However, if the $5\frac{1}{2}$ percent convertibles or bonds with warrants were to be used, then, after conversion or exercise, only 115,000 new shares would be created. In this case the family would have 210,000 shares versus 205,000 for outsiders; absolute control would be maintained.

In addition to assuring control, using the convertibles or warrants also would benefit earnings per share in the long run. The total number of shares would be less because fewer new shares would have to be issued to get the $5 million; thus earnings per share would be higher. Before conversion or exercise, however, the firm would have a considerable amount of debt outstanding. Adding $5 million would raise the total debt to $10.4 million against new total assets of $17 million, so the debt ratio would be over 61 percent versus the 25 percent industry average. This could have been dangerous. If delays were encountered in bringing the new plant into production, if demand did not meet expectations, if the company experienced a strike, if the economy went into a recession, the company would be extremely vulnerable because of the high debt ratio.

Under these circumstances, Winchester decided to sell the $5\frac{1}{2}$ percent convertible debentures. Two years later, earnings climbed to $3 a share, the P-E ratio went to 20, and the price of the stock rose to $60. The bonds were called, but conversion of course occurred. After conversion, debt amounted to approximately $5.5 million against total assets of $17.5 million (some earnings had been retained), so the debt ratio was down to a more reasonable 31 percent.

Convertibles were chosen rather than bonds with warrants for the following reason. If a firm has a high debt ratio and its near-term prospects are favorable, it can anticipate a rise in the price of its stock and thus be able to call the bonds and force conversion. Warrants, on the other hand, have a stated life; and even if the price of the firm's stock rises, the warrants may not be exercised until near their expiration date. If, subsequent to the favorable period (during which convertibles can be called), the firm encounters less favorable developments and the price of its stock falls, the warrants may lose their value and may never be exercised. The heavy debt burden will then become aggravated. Therefore, the use of convertibles gives the firm greater control over the timing of future capital structure changes. This factor is of particular importance to the firm if its debt ratio is already high in relation to the risks of its line of business.

Reporting Earnings if Convertibles or Warrants Are Outstanding

Firms with convertibles or warrants outstanding are required to report earnings per share in two ways: (1) *primary EPS,* which in essence is earnings available to common stock divided by the number of shares actually outstanding, and (2) *fully diluted EPS,* which shows what EPS would be if all warrants had been exercised or convertibles converted prior to the reporting date. For firms with large amounts of option securities outstanding, there can be a substantial difference between the two EPS figures. The purpose of the provision is, of course, to give investors more information on the firm's profit position.

Summary

Both warrants and convertibles are forms of options used in financing business firms. Their use is encouraged by an economic environment combining prospects of both boom or inflation and depression or deflation. The senior position of the securities protects against recessions, and the option feature offers the opportunity for participation in rising stock prices.

Both the convertibility privilege and warrants are used as sweeteners. The option privileges they grant can make it possible for small companies to sell debt or preferred stock that otherwise cannot be sold. For large companies, the sweeteners result in lower costs of the securities sold. In addition, the options provide for the future sale of the common stock at prices higher than can be obtained at present. The options thereby permit the delayed sale of common stock at more favorable prices.

We focused on three central quantitative relationships conveyed by the first three equations developed in the chapter:

The conversion value

$$C_t = p_0(1 + g)^t \#. \tag{22.1}$$

The straight debt value

$$B_t = \sum_{j=1}^{t^*} \frac{c}{(1 + k_b)^j} + \frac{M''}{(1 + k_b)^{t^*}}. \tag{22.2}$$

The expected return on a convertible

$$M = \sum_{t=1}^{N} \frac{c}{(1 + k_c)^t} + \frac{C_N}{(1 + k_c)^N}. \tag{22.3}$$

In using Equation 22.3, the values of all terms are known except for k_c, which is obtained as the solution to the equation.

The conversion of bonds by their holders does not ordinarily bring additional funds to the company. However, the exercise of warrants does provide such funds. The conversion of securities results in reduced debt ratios, and the exercise of warrants strengthens the equity position but leaves the debt or preferred stock on the balance sheet. In comparing convertibles to senior securities carrying warrants, a firm with a high debt ratio should choose convertibles, while a firm with a moderate or low debt ratio should probably employ warrants.

Questions

22.1 Why do warrants typically sell at prices greater than their formula values?

22.2 Why do convertibles typically sell at prices greater than their formula values (the higher of the conversion value or straight debt value)? Would you expect the percentage premium on a convertible bond to be more or less than that on a warrant? (The percentage premium is defined as the market price minus the formula value, divided by the market price.)

22.3 What effect does the trend in stock prices (subsequent to issue) have on a firm's ability to raise funds (a) through convertibles and (b) through warrants?

22.4 If a firm expects to have additional financial requirements in the future, would you recommend that it use convertibles or bonds with warrants? Why?

22.5 Evaluate the following statement: Issuing convertible securities represents a means by which a firm can sell common stock at a price above the existing market.

22.6 Why do corporations often sell convertibles on a rights basis?

Problems

22.1 A convertible bond has a face value of $1,000 and a 10 percent coupon rate. It is convertible into stock at $50; that is, each bond can be exchanged for twenty shares. The current price of the stock is $43 per share.

a. If the price per share grows at 6 percent per year for five years, what will the approximate conversion value be at the end of five years?

b. If dividends on the stock are presently $2 per share, and if these also grow at 6 percent per year, will bondholders convert after five years, or will they tend to hold on to their bonds? Explain.

c. If the bonds are callable at a 10 percent premium, about how much would you lose per bond if the bonds were called before you converted? (Assume the same conversion value as in Part a above, at the end of five years.)

22.2 Warrants attached to a bond entitle the bondholder to purchase one share of stock at $10 per share. Compute the approximate value of a warrant if:

a. The market price of the stock is $9 per share.

b. The market price of the stock is $12 per share.

c. The market price of the stock is $15 per share.

d. Each warrant entitles you to purchase two shares at $10, and the current price of the stock is $15 per share.

22.3 The Garnet Lumber Company's capital consists of 24,000 shares of common stock and 8,000 warrants, each good for buying 3 shares of common at $30 a share. The warrants are protected against dilution (that is, the subscription price is adjusted downward in the event of a stock dividend or if the firm sells common stock at less than the $30 exercise price). The company issues rights to buy 1 new share of common for $25 for every 4 shares. With the stock selling rights on at $35, compute:

a. The theoretical value of the rights before the stock sells ex rights.

b. The new subscription price of the warrants after the rights issue.

22.4 The Ironhill Manufacturing Company was planning to finance an expansion in the summer of 1980. The principal executives of the company agreed that an industrial company such as theirs should finance growth by means of common stock rather than debt. However, they felt the price of the company's common stock did not reflect its true worth, so they were desirous of selling a convertible security. They considered a convertible debenture but feared the burden of fixed interest charges if the common stock did not rise in price to make conversion attractive. They decided on an issue of convertible preferred stock.

The common stock was selling at $48 a share. Management projected earnings for 1981 at $3.60 a share and expected a future growth rate of 12 percent a year. It was agreed by the investment bankers and management that the common stock would sell at 13.3 times earnings, the current price-earnings ratio.

a. What conversion price should be set by the issuer?
b. Should the preferred stock include a call price provision? Why?

22.5 Quality Photocopy has the following balance sheet:

Balance Sheet 1

Current assets	$125,000	Current debt (free)	$ 50,000
Net fixed assets	125,000	Common stock, par value $2	50,000
		Retained earnings	150,000
Total assets	$250,000	Total claims	$250,000

a. The firm earns 15 percent on total assets before taxes (with a 40 percent tax rate); 25,000 shares are outstanding. What are earnings per share?
b. If the price-earnings ratio for the company's stock is 16 times, what is the market price of the company's stock?
c. What is the book value of the company's stock?
d. Sales and financing needs of the firm are expected to double in the next few years. The firm decides to sell debentures to meet these needs. It is undecided, however, whether to sell convertible debentures or debentures with warrants. The new balance sheet is as follows:

Balance Sheet 2

Current assets	$250,000	Current debt	$100,000
Net fixed assets	250,000	Debentures	150,000
		Common stock, par value $2	50,000
		Retained earnings	200,000
Total assets	$500,000	Total claims	$500,000

The convertible debentures will pay 7 percent interest and will be convertible into 40 shares of common stock for each $1,000 debenture. The debentures with warrants will carry an 8 percent coupon and entitle each holder of a $1,000 debenture to buy 25 shares of common stock at $50. Assume that convertible debentures are sold and that all are later converted. Show the new balance sheet, disregarding any changes in retained earnings.

Balance Sheet 3

		Current debt	______
		Debentures	______
		Common stock, par value $2	______
		Paid-in capital	______
		Retained earnings	______
Total assets	______	Total claims	______

e. Complete the firm's income statement after the debentures have all been converted:

Income Statement 1

Net income after all charges except debenture interest and before taxes (15% of total assets)	______
Debenture interest	______
Taxable income	______
Federal income tax (at 40%)	______
Net income after taxes	______
Earnings per share after taxes	______

f. Assume that instead of convertibles, debentures with warrants were issued. Assume further that the warrants were all exercised. Show the new balance sheet figures:

Balance Sheet 4

		Current debt	______
		Debentures	______
		Common stock, par value $2	______
		Paid-in capital	______
		Retained earnings	______
Total assets	______	Total claims	______

g. Complete the firm's income statement after the debenture warrants have all been exercised:

Income Statement 2

Net income after all charges except debenture interest and before taxes	______
Debenture interest	______
Taxable income	______
Federal income tax	______
Net income after taxes	______
Earnings per share after taxes	______

22.6 The Printomat Company has grown rapidly during the past five years. Recently its commercial bank has urged the company to consider increasing permanent financing. Its bank loan under a line of credit has risen to $175,000, carrying 15 percent interest. Printomat has been thirty to sixty days late in paying trade creditors.

Discussions with an investment banker have resulted in the suggestion to raise $350,000 at this time. Investment bankers have assured the company that the following alternatives will be feasible (ignoring flotation costs):

—Sell common stock at $7.

—Sell convertible bonds at a 7 percent coupon, convertible into common stock at $8.

—Sell debentures at a 7 percent coupon, each $1,000 bond carrying 125 warrants to buy common stock at $8.

Additional information is given in the company's balance sheet and income statement, which follow:

Printomat Company Balance Sheet

		Current liabilities	$315,000
		Common stock, par $1	90,000
		Retained earnings	45,000
Total assets	$450,000	Total liabilities and capital	$450,000

Printomat Company Income Statement

Sales	$900,000
All costs except interest	807,000
Gross profit	$ 93,000
Interest	26,000
Profit before taxes	$ 67,000
Taxes (at 40%)	27,000
Profit after taxes	$ 40,000
Shares	90,000
Earnings per share	$0.44
Price-earnings ratio	17 times
Market price of stock	$7.48

Larry Anderson, the president, owns 70 percent of Printomat's common stock and wishes to maintain control of the company; 90,000 shares are outstanding.

a. Show the new balance sheet under each alternative. For the second and third listed alternatives, show the balance sheet after conversion of the debentures or exercise of warrants. Assume that half the funds raised will be used to pay off the bank loan and half to increase total assets.

b. Show Anderson's control position under each alternative, assuming that he does not purchase additional shares.

c. What is the effect on earnings per share of each alternative if it is assumed that profits before interest and taxes will be 20 percent of total assets?

d. What will be the debt ratio under each alternative?

e. Which of the three alternatives would you recommend to Anderson? Explain.

22.7 Continental Chemical Company is planning to raise \$25 million by selling convertible debentures. Its stock is currently selling for \$50 per share (P_0 = \$50). The stock price has grown in the past, and is expected to grow in the future, at the rate of 6 percent per year. Continental's current dividend is \$4.50 per share, so investors appear to have an expected (and required) rate of return of 15 percent ($k = D/P_0 + g$ = \$4.50/\$50 + 6%) on investments as risky as the company's common stock. Continental's tax rate is 40 percent.

Continental recently sold nonconvertible debentures that yield 10 percent. Investment bankers have informed the treasurer that she can sell convertibles at a lower interest yield; they have offered her these two choices:

A. P_c = \$55.55 (# = 18)
C = \$70 (7% coupon yield)
M = \$1,000
25-year maturity

B. P_c = \$58.82(# = 17)
C = \$80 (8% coupon yield)
M = \$1,000
25-year maturity

In each case, the bonds are not callable for two years; but thereafter they are callable at \$1,000. Investors do not expect the bonds to be called unless C_t = \$1,354; but they do expect the bonds to be called if C_t = \$1,354.

a. Determine the expected yield on Bond A and on Bond B.
b. Do the terms offered by the investment bankers seem consistent? Which bond would an investor prefer? Which would Continental's treasurer prefer?
c. Suppose the company decided on Bond A but wanted to step up the conversion price from \$55.55 to \$58.82 after ten years. Should this stepped-up conversion price affect the expected yield and the other terms on the bonds?
d. Suppose, contrary to investors' expectations, Continental called the bonds after two years. What would the *ex post* (after-the-fact) effective yield be on Bond A? Would this early call affect the company's credibility in the financial markets?
e. Sketch out a rough graph similar to Figure 22.2 for Continental. Use the graph to illustrate what would happen to the wealth position of an investor who bought Continental bonds the day before the announcement of the unexpected two-year call.
f. Suppose the expected yield on the convertible had been less than that on straight debt (actually, it was higher). Would this appear logical? Explain.

22.8 The Seaboard Development Company plans to sell a 5 percent coupon, 25-year convertible bond on January 1, 1981, for \$1,000. The bond is callable at \$1,050 in the first year, and the call price declines by \$2 each year thereafter. The bond may be converted into 14 shares of stock that now (January 1, 1980) sells for \$60 per share. The stock price is expected to increase at a rate of 10 percent each year. Nonconvertible bonds with the same degree of risk would yield 12 percent. Investors expect Seaboard to call the convertibles if and when the conversion value exceeds the call price by 40 percent.

a. Graph a model that represents investors' expectations for the bond. Include as points on the graph B_0 and B_5; C_0, C_5, and C_{10}; and the call price at $t = 0$ and $t = 5$. Approximate the other points, and also the market price line.
b. What rate of return do investors appear to be expecting on the bond? Is this expected rate reasonable in view of the rate on Seaboard's straight (nonconvertible) bonds? If not, what does this suggest about (1) probable success of the issue, (2) the wisdom of the company's use of convertibles with the terms given above, and (3) possible changes in the terms if your answer to (1) is that the bonds would probably not sell?

22.9 The Piper Company plans to issue convertible debt with an 8 percent coupon and $1,000 par value. The convertible will have a twenty-year life, but management hopes that future developments will make it advantageous to call the issue at an earlier date.
a. Straight debt with equal risk, coupon, and maturity is selling with a market rate of interest of 12 percent. Determine the straight debt value at time zero and at the end of Years 1 and 2. Use these three points plus the maturity value to graph the straight debt value of the convertible.
b. At time zero the conversion value of the bond is $790 since the initial price of the common stock is $79 and the conversion ratio is 10. The stock is expected to appreciate at a rate of 15.0% per year. Graph the conversion value of the bond C_t on the same graph.
c. What is the minimum price the convertible can sell for at Year 0, 1, 2, and 3, assuming the stock value increases as predicted?
d. Assume that the bond is expected to be called when the conversion value of the bond reaches 140 percent of par value, and that the bonds sell originally at par value. On the graph, locate the maturity conversion value M' and C_t and draw a curve between the issue price M and M' with curvature similar to C_t.
e. In what year is the debt expected to be called?
f. Assume the call price at Year 0 is $1,050, decreasing by $2.50 a year. Show the call price of debt on the same graph. What would the debt holders do if the bond was called at Year 1, 2, or 3?
g. What return on their investment is earned by purchasers of the convertible bonds at their issuance if the bonds are called in four years?

Selected References

Alexander, Gordon J., and Stover, Roger D. "The Effect of Forced Conversion on Common Stock Prices." *Financial Management* 9 (Spring 1980), pp. 39–45.

———. "Pricing in the New Issue Convertible Debt Market." *Financial Management* 6 (Fall 1977), pp. 35–39.

Alexander, Gordon J.; Stover, Roger D.; and Kuhnau, David B. "Market Timing Strategies in Convertible Debt Financing." *Journal of Finance* 34 (March 1979), pp. 143–155.

Bacon, Peter W., and Winn, Edward L., Jr. "The Impact of Forced Conversion on Stock Prices." *Journal of Finance* 24 (December 1969), pp. 871–874.

Baumol, William J.; Malkiel, Burton G.; and Quandt, Richard E. "The Valuation of Convertible Securities." *Quarterly Journal of Economics* 80 (February 1966), pp. 48–59.

Bierman, Harold, Jr. "Convertible Bonds as Investments." *Financial Analysts' Journal* 36 (March–April 1980), pp. 59–61.

Black, Fischer. "Fact and Fantasy in the Use of Options." *Financial Analysts' Journal* 31 (July–August 1975), pp. 36–41.

Black, Fischer, and Scholes, Myron. "The Valuation of Option Contracts and a Test of Market Efficiency." *Journal of Finance* 27 (May 1972), pp. 399–417.

Bond, F. M. "Yields on Convertible Securities: 1969–1974." *Journal of Business Finance and Accounting* 3 (Summer 1976), pp. 93–114.

Brennan, M. J., and Schwartz, E. S. "Convertible Bonds: Valuation and Optimal Strategies for Call and Conversion." *Journal of Finance* 32 (December 1977), pp. 1699–1715.

Brigham, Eugene F. "An Analysis of Convertible Debentures: Theory and Some Empirical Evidence." *Journal of Finance* 21 (March 1966), pp. 35–54.

Chen, Andrew H. Y. "A Model of Warrant Pricing in a Dynamic Market." *Journal of Finance* 25 (December 1970), pp. 1041–1059.

Cretien, Paul D., Jr. "Premiums on Convertible Bonds: Comment." *Journal of Finance* 25 (September 1970), pp. 917–922.

Dawson, Steven M. "Timing Interest Payments for Convertible Bonds." *Financial Management* 3 (Summer 1974), pp. 14–16.

Duvel, David Tell. "Premiums on Convertible Bonds: Comment." *Journal of Finance* 25 (September 1970), pp. 923–927.

Frank, Werner G., and Kroncke, Charles. "Classifying Conversions of Convertible Debentures over Four Years." *Financial Management* 3 (Summer 1974), pp. 33–42.

Frank, Werner G., and Weygandt, Jerry J. "Convertible Debt and Earnings per Share: Pragmatism vs. Good Theory." *Accounting Review* 45 (April 1970), pp. 280–289.

Frankle, A. W., and Hawkins, C. A. "Beta Coefficients for Convertible Bonds." *Journal of Finance* 30 (March 1975), pp. 207–210.

Galai, Dan, and Schneller, Mier I. "Pricing of Warrants and the Value of the Firm." *Journal of Finance* 33 (December 1978), pp. 1333–1342.

Hayes, Samuel L., III. "New Interest in Incentive Financing." *Harvard Business Review* 44 (July–August 1966), pp. 99–112.

Hettenhouse, G. W., and Puglisi, D. J. "Investor Experience with Options." *Financial Analysts' Journal* 31 (July–August 1975), pp. 53–58.

Horrigan, James O. "Some Hypotheses on the Valuation of Stock Warrants." *Journal of Business Finance and Accounting* 1 (Summer 1974), pp. 239–247.

Leabo, Dick A., and Rogalski, Richard J. "Warrant Price Movements and the Efficient Market Model." *Journal of Finance* 30 (March 1975), pp. 163–177.

Loy, L. David, and Toole, Howard R. "Accounting for Discounted Convertible Bond Exchanges: A Survey of Results." *Journal of Accounting, Auditing and Finance* 3 (Spring 1980), pp. 227–243.

Melicher, Ronald W., and Hoffmeister, J. Ronald. "The Issue Is Convertible Bonds." *Financial Executive* 45 (November 1977), pp. 46–50.

Pilcher, C. James. *Raising Capital with Convertible Securities.* Ann Arbor, Mich.: Bureau of Business Research, University of Michigan, 1955.

Pinches, George E. "Financing with Convertible Preferred Stocks, 1960–1967." *Journal of Finance* 25 (March 1970), pp. 53–64.

Poensgen, Otto H. "The Valuation of Convertible Bonds." Part 1. *Industrial Management Review* 6 (Fall 1965), pp. 77–92. "The Valuation of Convertible Bonds." Part 2. *Industrial Management Review* 7 (Spring 1966), pp. 83–98.

Reback, Robert. "Risk and Return in Option Trading." *Financial Analysts' Journal* 31 (July–August 1975), pp. 42–52.

Rush, David F., and Melicher, Ronald W. "An Empirical Examination of Factors Which Influence Warrant Prices." *Journal of Finance* 29 (December 1974), pp. 1449–1466.

Samuelson, Paul A., and Merton, Robert C. "A Complete Model of Warrant Pricing That Maximizes Utility." *Industrial Management Review* 10 (Winter 1969), pp. 17–46.

Schwartz, Eduardo S. "The Valuation of Warrants: Implementing a New Approach." *Journal of Financial Economics* 4 (January 1977), pp. 79–94.

Shelton, John P. "The Relation of the Price of a Warrant to the Price of Its Associated Stock." *Financial Analysts' Journal* 23 (May–June 1967), pp. 143–151; and (July–August 1967), pp. 88–99.

Smith, C. W. "Option Pricing: A Review." *Journal of Financial Economics* 3 (January–March 1976), pp. 3–52.

Soldofsky, Robert M. "Yield-Rate Performance of Convertible Securities." *Financial Analysts' Journal* 27 (March–April 1971), pp. 61–65.

Sprecher, C. Ronald. "A Note on Financing Mergers with Convertible Preferred Stock." *Journal of Finance* 26 (June 1971), pp. 683–686.

Stone, Bernell K. "Warrant Financing." *Journal of Financial and Quantitative Analysis* 11 (March 1976), pp. 143–154.

Walter, James E., and Que, Agustin V. "The Valuation of Convertible Bonds." *Journal of Finance* 28 (June 1973), pp. 713–732.

Weil, Roman L., Jr.; Segall, Joel E.; and Green, David, Jr. "Premiums on Convertible Bonds." *Journal of Finance* 23 (June 1968), pp. 445–464.

———. "A Reply to Premiums on Convertible Bonds: Comment." *Journal of Finance* 25 (September 1970), pp. 931–933.

Appendix A to Chapter 22

The Option Pricing Model (OPM)

Introduction to Options

Options are contracts that give their holder the right to buy (or sell) an asset at a predetermined price, called the *striking* or *exercise price,* for a given period of time. For example, on December 6, 1976, a call option on Dow Chemical common stock gave its holder the right to buy one share of common at an exercise price of \$45 until July 1977. The price of a share of Dow was \$39½ and the call option sold for \$1.75. This would be referred to as an *out-of-the-money option*—the exercise price was more than the current price of the common stock. An *in-the-money option* has an exercise price that is less than the current price of the common stock. An option to buy the Dow common stock at \$35 when the common was selling at \$39½ would be an in-the-money option; it would sell for (39½ − 35) = \$4½ plus the premium of about \$1.75, or at about \$6.25.

In recent years option pricing models (OPM) have been derived which enable us to treat the variables discussed in Chapter 22 and in this appendix with numerical solutions.[1] These models are applicable to a wide range of option-type contracts, including the warrants and convertibles discussed in Chapter 22.

The considerable increase in interest in options and option pricing has been associated with the development of new options markets and important new theoretical developments. In April 1973, organized trading in call options began on the Chicago Board Options Exchange (CBOE), followed by call option trading on the American Stock Exchange (AMEX options); the path-breaking paper by Fischer Black and Myron Scholes appeared at about the same time. In addition to deriving the general equilibrium option pricing equation as well as conducting empirical tests, Black and Scholes suggested other implications of option pricing that have significance for many other important aspects of business finance.

Black and Scholes observed that option pricing principles can be used to value other complex contingent claim assets, such as the equity of a levered

1. F. Black and M. Scholes, "The Pricing of Options and Corporate Liabilities." *Journal of Political Economy* 81 (May–June 1973), pp. 637–654; Black and Scholes, "The Valuation of Option Contracts and a Test of Market Efficiency," *Journal of Finance* 27 (May 1972), pp. 399–417; R. C. Merton, "Theory of Rational Option Pricing," *Bell Journal of Economics and Management Science* 4 (Spring 1973), pp. 141–183.

firm. From this viewpoint, the shareholders of a firm have a call that gives them the right to buy back the firm from the bondholders by paying the face value of the bonds at maturity or exercising other alternatives for buying the bonds. A number of important applications of the option pricing model were then made. As observed by Clifford Smith in his comprehensive review article, "the model is also applied by Merton (1974) to analyze the effects of risk on the value of corporate debt; by Galai and Masulis (1976) to examine the effect of mergers, acquisitions, scale expansions, and spin-offs on the relative values of the debt and equity claims of the firm; by Ingersoll (1976) to value the shares of dual purpose funds; and by Black (1976) to value commodity options, forward contracts, and future contracts."[2]

Because of the large number of additional areas on which the option pricing models provide new insights, it is useful to develop an understanding of the basic ideas involved. First, some of the fundamental characteristics of the use of options will be developed. Second, some of the basic relationships will be developed in an intuitive way as a background for the presentation and application of the Black and Scholes option pricing model.

The Use of Call Options

The underlying nature of options can be explained most concretely by comparing four alternative strategies with regard to gains or losses from fluctuations in the price of the stock. Consider 100 shares of stock whose current price is $50 per share. The results of four alternative investment positions are depicted in Figure 22A.1. An investor who buys the stock and holds it (has a long position in the stock) gains or loses if the stock increases or decreases in price. For a $10 rise or fall in the stock price, the investor gains or loses $10 per share, or plus or minus 20%. (Brokerage costs, taxes, and other factors not central to the main issues under analysis here are not taken into consideration.) This is a simple relationship that is used as the benchmark for comparison with the other possible strategies.

Next we consider the alternative of buying a call that gives an option to buy the stock at $50 for six months. A rough indication of the price (a pricing formula is presented later) would be $300 for the call, or $3 per share of the 100 shares of stock under consideration. Assume that the stock rises to $60 near the end of the six-month period. The value of the call would be $10 since it enables a purchase of a share of stock worth $60 for $50. As will be shown in the option pricing formula, since we have assumed that this opportunity becomes available only just before the end of the six-month option period, very little premium will be added to the difference between the stock value S and the exercise price of the call X_0. The net gain will be the $10 less the $3 price paid for the call, or $7. If the stock declines by $10, the holder of

2. Clifford W. Smith, Jr., "Option Pricing: A Review," *Journal of Financial Economics* 3 (January–March 1976), p. 5.

the option would simply not exercise it; to do so would be to lose more than the $3 per share the investor had paid for the call. Treating the $3 as the investment, the buyer of the call either gains 233 percent or loses 100 percent.

A third position is that a call is sold without owning the stock (a *naked call*). The seller receives the $3 per call (the brokerage house holds the $300 and will require additional deposits if the stock rises in value). If the stock increases in price to $60 just before the end of the expiration of the call option, the option will be worth $10. It will cost the seller of the naked option $10 to supply the stock or to balance off the option position held, so there is a net loss of $7. If the stock declines in value to $40, the option will have no value and the seller will have netted $3.

The percentage gain or loss cannot be meaningfully calculated since it will depend upon how the investment position of the seller of the naked option is defined. Should it be an estimate of some contingent liability of the seller? Or should we infer some estimate of this person's investment worth, which enables trading in naked options? Since there is no clear number for the seller's investment position, we shall not attempt to measure the individual's percentage gain or loss. We can observe that the seller's upside gain is limited to the selling price of the option. However, there is no downside limit on the seller's loss since the rising price of the stock will increase the price of the option it will be necessary to buy in order to balance the options the seller has sold or increase without limit the price of the stock it will be necessary for the seller to buy to satisfy the just-sold call. Obviously, one would not sell a naked call until having judged that the probability of a decline in the price of the stock was very high.

The fourth and final position we consider is the sale of a call by an investor who already owns the 100 shares of the stock (the sale of a *covered call*). Since the investor already owns the stock, we may view the sale of the call as a sale of the stock at $53 if the price of the stock rises to $60 or as a shift in the individual's investment basis for the stock to $47 if the price of the stock declines to $40. Thus a rise in the price of the stock to $60 represents a gain of $3 ÷ $50 = 6 percent, and a decline to $40 represents a loss of $7 ÷ $50 = 14 percent.

Each of the four alternative strategies is depicted graphically in Figure 22A.1. The results of the four strategies are summarized in Table 22A.1. Buying a call greatly magnifies the possible percentage gains and losses. Selling a naked call results in a pattern that is a mirror image of buying a call. Selling a covered call limits the upside percentage gain and reduces somewhat the downside percentage loss. Note that since the seller of a naked call is hurt most by a substantial rise in the price of the stock and the seller of a covered call is hurt most by a substantial decline in the price of the stock, divergent views of the price prospects of the stock may still result in the sale of calls on the stock. Thus transactions in calls may magnify gains or losses or dampen gains or losses, depending upon the investor's position and chosen strategy.

Figure 22A.1

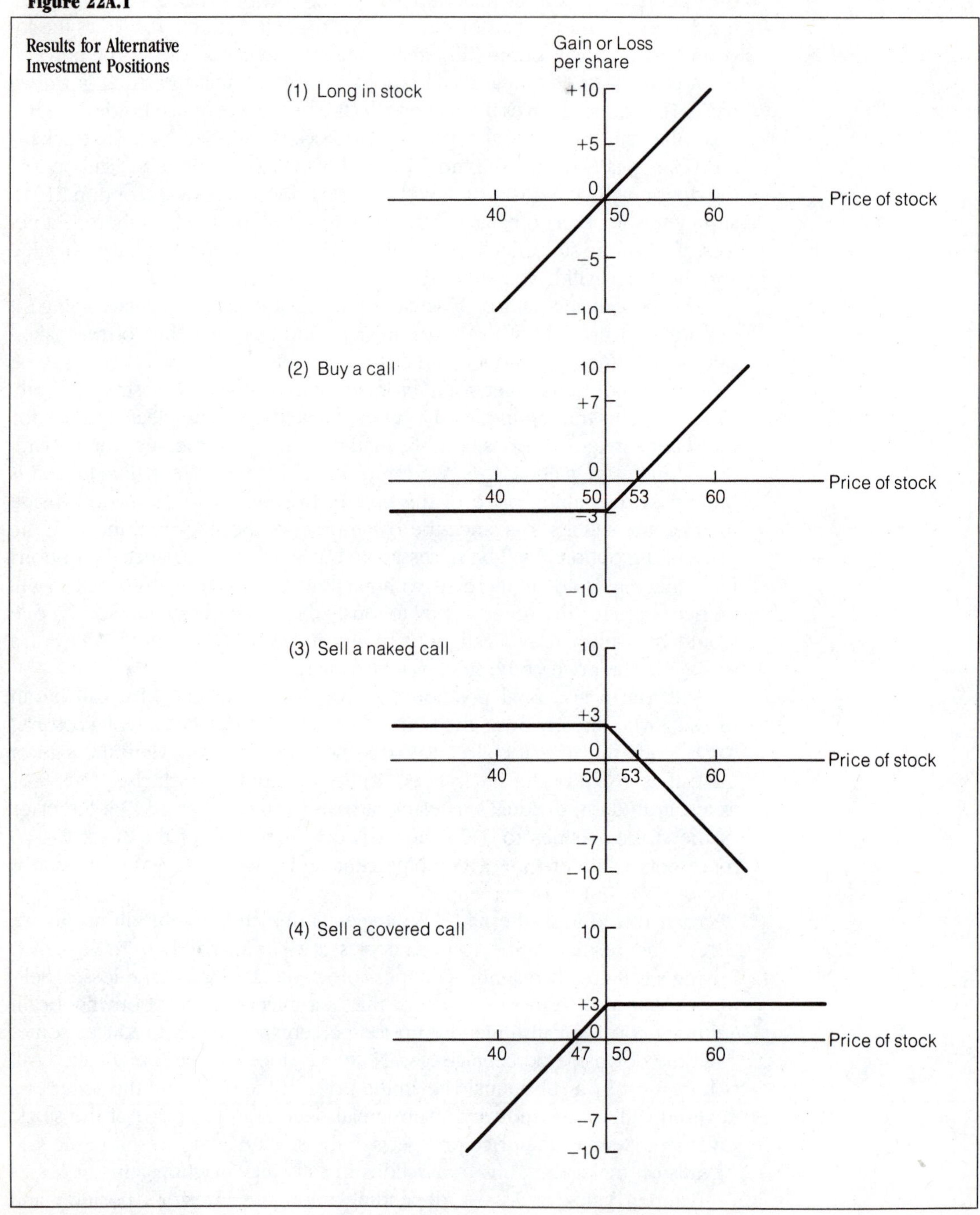
Results for Alternative Investment Positions
Gain or Loss per share
(1) Long in stock
+10
+5
0
-5
-10
40
50
60
Price of stock
(2) Buy a call
10
+7
0
-3
-10
40
50
53
60
Price of stock
(3) Sell a naked call
10
+3
0
-7
-10
40
50
53
60
Price of stock
(4) Sell a covered call
10
+3
0
-7
-10
40
47
50
60
Price of stock

Table 22A.1

Results of Four Alternative Investment Strategies Involving Options

	Gain or (Loss) Per Share with Change in Stock Price			
	Stock Price Increases by $10		Stock Price Decreases by $10	
	Amount	Percent	Amount	Percent
1. Long in stock	$10	20	($10)	(20)
2. Buy a call	$ 7	233	($ 3)	(100)
3. Sell a naked call	($ 7)	[a]	$ 3	[a]
4. Sell a covered call	$ 3	6	($ 7)	(14)

a. Depends upon the definition of the investment made.

Basic Price Relations

With this background on the mechanics of option trading and its implications, we can begin the analysis of the determinants of option prices. An intuitive approach to option pricing is to consider the terminal call price under certainty.[3] Let C^* be the terminal call price, S^* be the terminal stock price, and X_0 be the exercise price of the option. The following relationship will obtain:

$$C^* = S^* - X_0.$$

This is similar to the simple warrant formula. The call price will be equal to the difference between the stock price and the exercise price, or zero if the exercise price is greater than the stock price. Thus if the terminal stock price just before the expiration of a call is $60 and the exercise price of the option is $50, the terminal call price, C^*, will be $10. In an equilibrium world of certainty, the return to all assets is equal to the rate, r. Hence the terminal values of the stock price and option price may be written:

$$S_0{}^* = S_0e^{rt} \text{ and } C_0{}^* = C_0e^{rt}.$$

Substituting, we have

$$\begin{aligned} C_0e^{rt^*} &= e^{rt^*} S_0 - X_0 \\ C_0 &= e^{-rt^*} [e^{rt^*} S_0 - X_0] \\ C_0 &= e^{-rt^*}e^{rt^*} S_0 - e^{-rt^*}X_0 \\ C_0 &= S_0 - e^{-rt^*}X_0. \end{aligned}$$

Thus the value of a call is equal to the price of the stock less the exercise price discounted at r over the time of its remaining maturity period. This expression differs from the Black-Scholes pricing equation only in the multiplica-

3. Based on the presentation in Smith, "Option Pricing."

tion of each of the terms on the right-hand side of the equation, S_0 and X_0, by probability factors. These probability terms reflect the uncertainty about the terminal prices of the stock. With this background, we can now turn to the Black-Scholes option pricing model.

Calculations of Options Values

In the Black-Scholes model, the derivation is based on the creation of a perfect hedge by simultaneously being long (short) in the underlying security and holding an opposite, short (long) position on a number of options. The return on a completely hedged position will then be equal to the risk-free return on the investment in order to eliminate arbitrage opportunities. A call option that can be exercised only on some future maturity date can then be evaluated by the following expressions:[4]

$$C_0 = S_0 N\,(\text{dist. 1}) - X_0 e^{-R_F t^*} N\,(\text{dist. 2}) \qquad (22A.1)$$

$$\text{dist. 1} = \frac{ln(S_0/X_0) + [R_F + (\sigma^2/2)]t^*}{\sigma\sqrt{t^*}} \qquad (22A.2)$$

$$\text{dist. 2} = \text{dist. 1} - \sigma\sqrt{t^*} \qquad (22A.3)$$

where:

C_0 = Option price or value of the option
S_0 = Current value of the underlying asset
X_0 = Exercise or striking price of the option
$N(\cdot)$ = Standardized normal cumulative probability density function
R_F = Riskless interest rate
σ^2 = Instantaneous rate of variance of percentage returns
t^* = Time to maturity or duration of the option[5]

The application of these expressions follows readily from the material we have previously set forth in Appendix A to Chapter 14. For example, the $N(\cdot)$ expressions were treated in Table 14A.3 and the corresponding Figure 14A.4, both dealing with cumulative probability distributions. Some specific numerical examples will illustrate the application of equations 22A.1 through 22A.3.

Suppose we are valuing a warrant to purchase a share of common stock. The following facts could be directly observed or estimated from market data:

4. This is called a *European Option.* It is not unnatural to use a formula for the value of a European call option that can be exercised only at the maturity date of the option. R. C. Merton, in a purely probabilistic formulation for nondividend paying stocks, demonstrated that it is always advantageous to delay exercising a call option until the latest possible date, its maturity.
5. Equations 22A.1 through 22A.3 can also be combined into one equation:

$$C_0 = S_0 \cdot N\left[\frac{ln(S_0/X_0) + (R_F + \sigma^2/2)t^*}{\sigma\sqrt{t^*}}\right] - e^{-R_F t^*} X_0\, N\left[\frac{ln(S_0/X_0) + (R_F - \sigma^2/2)t^*}{\sigma\sqrt{t^*}}\right]$$

$$S_0 = \$10$$
$$X_0 = \$10$$
$$t^* = 4 \text{ years}$$
$$R_F = 6\%$$
$$\sigma^2 = 9\%$$

The value of S could be read from the financial quotation page of a current newspaper. X_0 and t^*, the exercise price of a warrant and its maturity, respectively, are shown on the face of the warrant certificate. The risk-free rate can be estimated from the rates on short-term U.S. Treasury bills. The rate of variance can be estimated by taking the daily prices of the stock for one year, from which a variance of prices could be calculated.[6] We can now proceed to make the calculations as shown in Equations 22A.1a, 22A.2a, and 22A.3a.

$$C_0 = 10\,N(\text{dist. }1) - 10e^{-0.06(4)}\,N(\text{dist. }2) \tag{22A.1a}$$

$$\text{dist. }1 = \frac{ln(10/10) + [0.06 + (0.09/2)]4}{0.3(2)} \tag{22A.2a}$$

$$= \frac{(0.105)4}{0.6} = 0.7$$

$$\text{dist. }2 = 0.7 - 0.3(2) = 0.1 \tag{22A.3a}$$

$$C_0 = 10(0.758) - 10(0.787)(0.5398)$$
$$= 7.58 - 4.25$$
$$= \$3.33.$$

First, we calculate the value of the cumulative distribution function as shown in Equation 22A.2a. It should be noted that the logarithm is the natural logarithm. The *ln* of 10/10 or 1, the first term in the numerator, is zero. The value of dist. 1 is found to be 0.7. We use Appendix D at the end of this book to find the value of 0.7 in the z column. We find a value of 0.2580. This represents the shaded area in Figure 22A.2.

Since the formula calls for the cumulative distribution, we add the total area under the left-hand tail of the distribution, which has a value of 0.5000 exactly. Thus the value of dist. 1 equals 0.758, which is used in Equation 22A.1a. Because dist. 2 is related to dist. 1 by a simple relationship, we place 0.7 in 22A.2a to obtain a dist. 2 value of 0.1. In Table D at the end of the text, we find a value of 0.0398 to which we add 0.5 to obtain 0.5398 to use in Equation 22A.1a.

The evaluation of the $e^{-.06(4)}$ term involves continuous compounding. In Appendix A to Chapter 4 we described how Appendix Table B of natural logarithms at the end of this book could be used to perform continuous com-

6. The model presented here assumes no dividend payments, so that dividends would be ignored in calculating the variance of the percentage value changes. This is precisely correct for non-cash-dividend paying stocks but only approximately correct for others.

Figure 22A.2

Graph of an Appendix D Value

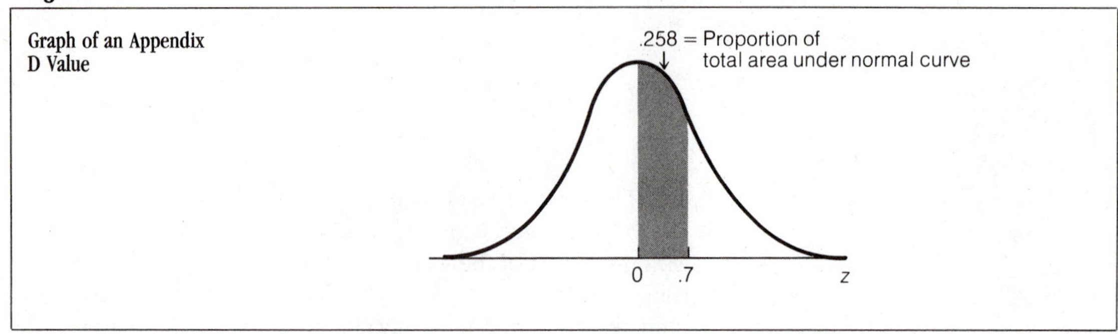

pounding. Looking in Appendix B for 0.24 and interpolating, we obtain 1.27125 for the future sum. We take the reciprocal to obtain the present value factor of 0.786627 or 0.787 used in Equation 22A.1a.[7] Performing the remaining calculations, we obtain $3.33 for the option price.

Next let us assume that the current price of the stock is $20 rather than $10. We now utilize Equations 22A.2b, 22A.3b, and 22A.1b.

$$\text{dist. } 1 = \frac{ln(20/10) + 0.42}{0.6} = \frac{0.693 + 0.42}{0.6} = 1.86. \quad \textbf{(22A.2b)}$$

$$\text{dist. } 2 = 1.86 - 0.6 = 1.26. \quad \textbf{(22A.3b)}$$

$$\begin{aligned} C_0 &= 20\,N\,(\text{dist. } 1) - 10e^{-0.06(4)}\,N\,(\text{dist. } 2) \\ &= 20(0.9686) - 10(0.787)(0.8962) \quad \textbf{(22A.1b)} \\ &= \$12.32. \end{aligned}$$

Proceeding as described before, we now obtain $12.32 as the value of the option. Thus we are enabled to derive the relationship for the predicted market value of the option as depicted in Figure 22.1. We will utilize another set of data to derive the values shown in Table 22A.2 to develop the lines shown in Figure 22A.3 for the indicated market price of a warrant as a function of the following key variables:

S_0 = Price of the stock; varies from $2 to $60

t^* = Duration of the warrant; 4 or 9 years

X_0 = Exercise price of $20

Factors Influencing Options Values

A number of relationships can be observed from the patterns in Table 22A.2 and Figure 22A.3. The higher the price of the stock, the greater the value of the option for fixed values of the other variables. The longer the maturity of the option, the higher its value. Line A of the figure represents the maximum

7. We could obtain an approximate result by using Table A.2 for the present value factors with annual compounding.

Table 22A.2

Relations between the Values of an Option for a Range of Values of Stock Price and Option Maturity[a]

t^* (1)	S_0 (2)	Change (Percent) (3)	N(dist. 1) (4)	N(dist. 2) (5)	C_0 (6)	Change (Percent) (7)	Ratio—Percent Change in Option Price to Percent Change in Stock Price (8)
4	2		0.0000[b]	0.0000[b]	$ 0.00[b]		
4	10		0.3246	0.1457	0.95		
4	20	100	0.7580	0.5398	6.66	601	6.0
4	30	50	0.9156	0.7811	15.17	128	2.6
4	40	33	0.9683	0.8953	24.64	62	1.9
4	60	50	0.9943	0.9733	44.34	80	1.6
9	10		0.6103	0.2676	$ 2.98		
9	20	100	0.8531	0.5596	10.54	254	2.5
9	30	50	0.9332	0.7257	19.53	85	1.7
9	40	33	0.9656	0.8212	29.05	49	1.5
9	60	50	0.9884	0.9147	48.64	67	1.3

a. For X_0 = \$20, $R_F = 0.06$, and $\sigma^2 = 0.09$.
b. These values approach zero.

value of the option, since it cannot be worth more than the stock. Line B represents the minimum value of the option, corresponding to the formula value of the warrant given in Figure 22.1. Its value cannot be negative and will be no less than the formula value of an option given in Chapter 22.

The longer the maturity of the option, the closer it moves toward Line A, its maximum value. Conversely, the shorter the maturity of a warrant, the closer it moves toward its minimum value, Line B. In Figure 22.1, the market price of the TPA warrants is shown to be close to the formula value of a warrant that corresponds to Line B of Figure 22A.3. Hence it is likely that the remaining maturity of the TPA warrants is relatively short.

When the stock price is substantially higher than the exercise price, the option will have a high value and is almost certain to be exercised. The value of the option we have been computing can also be approximated by calculating the current price of a pure discount bond with a face value equal to the exercise price of the option and a maturity equal to the maturity of the option.[8] This current price is deducted from the current stock value to give the value of the option. For example, for a current stock value of \$60, an interest rate of 6 percent, and an option maturity of four years,

$$C_0 = 60 - 20e^{-0.24} = 60 - 20(0.7866) = 60 - 15.73 = 44.27.$$

This result for the value of the option differs only slightly from the result of \$44.34 which we obtained using the option pricing model (OPM). The option

8. The probability factors will approximate 1.

Figure 22A.3

The Relation between Option Value and Stock Price for a Given Exercise Price of the Option

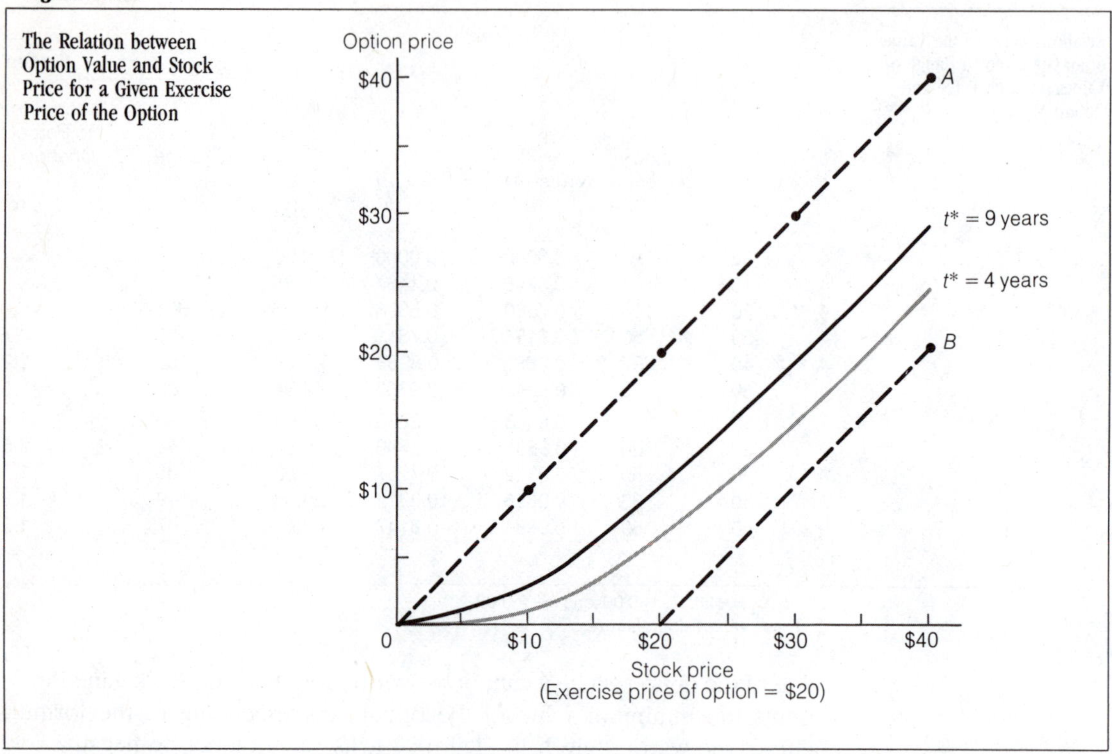

has a high value and is likely to be exercised. On the other hand, if the price of the stock is considerably less than the exercise price of the option, such as the $2 value in Table 22A.2, the option will have no value and will be likely to expire without being exercised.

We observe also that the curves depicting the value of an option as the stock price varies are concave from above and lie below the 45° line drawn from the origin (Line A). For an option of given maturity, any percentage change in the stock price will result in a larger percentage change in the option value. This is demonstrated by the percentage change columns in Table 22A.2 and by Column 8 of the same table, which presents the ratio of the percent change in the option price to the percent change in the stock price. For the longer maturity, the volatility of the option price is reduced somewhat. Also, at higher stock prices for a given maturity, the volatility of the option prices relative to the stock price changes is reduced.

Thus the use of the option pricing models enables us to observe some fundamental patterns in the relationships between stock prices and the related option values. These relationships depend on the level of stock prices, the duration and exercise price of the option, the risk-free interest rate, and the variance of the percentage returns on the stock values.

The Pricing of Corporate Securities

The option pricing model also provides additional insights on the nature of debt and equity in a firm.[9] Since the debt has a maturity, the equity of a firm can be regarded as a European call option on the total value of the firm. The shareholders of the firm have an option to buy back the firm from the bondholders at an exercise price equal to the face value of the bonds at time N, the maturity date of the bonds. If the value of the firm, V_N, is above the face value of the bonds, the equity will have a positive value. If the value of the firm is below the face value of the bonds, the value of the equity is zero; but it cannot become negative because of the limited liability nature of the equity. The limited liability feature of corporate equity helps explain why the corporate form has facilitated raising large amounts of equity funds. The shareholders have protection against a decline in the firm's value below C_0 (the face value of the bonds, the option exercise price) and have a right to the differential in the firm's value above C_0.

The OPM enables us to price out the value of the equity, given the value of the debt, or C_0, the option exercise price. It also enables us to analyze the effect of the riskiness of the firm's investment or production programs (the firm's degree of operating leverage) on the interests and positions of the shareholders in relationship to the creditors. A numerical example will illustrate the ideas involved.

Let us begin by pricing the value of the equity. Assume the following: The current value of the firm, V_0, is \$3,000,000; the face value of the debt, C_0, is \$1,000,000, and has a remaining maturity of four years. In the notation, S_0 takes the place of C_0 and C_0 takes the place of X_0. The variance of the percentage returns on the value of the firm (σ^2) is 0.01, and R_F is equal to 5 percent. By using the OPM we can calculate the indicated market value of the firm's equity, S_0. First we calculate the two distribution functions:

$$\text{dist. } 1 = \frac{ln\,3 + (0.05 + 0.005)4}{0.1(2)} = \frac{1.0986 + 0.22}{0.2} = \frac{1.3186}{0.2} = 6.593.$$

$$N\,(\text{dist. } 1) \cong 1$$
$$\text{dist. } 2 = 6.593 - 0.2 = 6.393$$
$$N(\text{dist. } 2) \cong 1.$$

Second, we calculate the value of the common stock:

$$S_0 = \$3{,}000{,}000(1) - \$1{,}000{,}000(1)e^{-0.2} = \$3{,}000{,}000 - \$818{,}731$$
$$= \$2{,}181{,}269.$$

Given that the value of the firm is \$3,000,000 and the calculated value of the equity shares is \$2,181,269, the indicated market value of the debt is \$818,731.

9. R. C. Merton, "On the Pricing of Corporate Debt: The Risk Structure of Interest Rates," *Journal of Finance* 29 (May 1974), pp. 449–470; D. D. Galai and R. W. Masulis, "The Option Pricing Model and the Risk Factor of Stock," *Journal of Financial Economics* 3 (January–March 1976), pp. 53–81.

We can now investigate the effects of the firm's changing the riskiness of its investment program. Assume that the firm takes on more risky investments so that the variance rises to a 0.16 level. We can now recalculate the values of the equity and debt under the assumption that the value of the firm remains at \$3,000,000. We begin with the distribution functions:

$$\text{dist. } 1 = \frac{(1.0986) + (0.05 + 0.08)4}{0.4(2)} = \frac{1.0986 + 0.52}{0.8} = \frac{1.6186}{0.8} = 2.0233.$$

$$N(\text{dist. } 1) = 0.9785$$
$$\text{dist. } 2 = 2.0233 - 0.8 = 1.2233$$
$$N(\text{dist. } 2) = 0.8894.$$

We can next calculate the value of the equity in the firm by the OPM.

$$\begin{aligned} S_0 &= \$3{,}000{,}000(0.9785) - \$1{,}000{,}000(0.8894)(0.81873) \\ &= \$2{,}935{,}500 - \$728{,}178 \\ &= \$2{,}207{,}322. \end{aligned}$$

The market value of the debt therefore drops to \$792,678. Hence, increasing the riskiness of the firm's production operations increases the value of the equity and reduces the value of the debt. Thus the OPM indicates some inherent divergence of interests between the shareholders and the creditors of the firm. Since the shareholders possess voting control of the firm, they may take actions that may be adverse to the interests of the creditors. It is for such reasons that various *me first rules* are written into the bond indentures representing restrictions on what the firm (through actions of the controlling group, the shareholders, and its designated managerial group) may or may not do.[10] This is for the purpose of protecting the position of the creditors of the firm.

The OPM thus enables us to quantify a number of relations for which we formerly were unable to obtain solutions without making *ad hoc* assumptions about critical variables. In contrast the OPM model provides a logical and internally consistent framework for valuing options and pricing out corporate securities. In addition, all of the elements of the OPM model are measurable by marketplace data. Thus the OPM provides us with new insights on how to value options and new insights on the relative positions of the equity holders and the creditors of the firm. The OPM has been put to considerable practical applications by financial houses during recent years. In addition, it opens up new interesting theoretical paths, many of which remain to be explored fully, especially in the areas of further large-scale empirical testing of a number of aspects of the options pricing model.

10. Eugene F. Fama and Merton H. Miller, *The Theory of Finance* (New York: Holt, Rinehart and Winston, 1972), pp. 150–170.

Problems

22A.1 The common stock of Alpo Company sells for $10 per share. Warrants to purchase the stock at a price of $8 are also available. The warrants have four years to maturity. The instantaneous variance of returns on the common stock is 16 percent. The risk-free rate is 10 percent.

a. Using the option pricing model, determine the value of a warrant.
b. What would be the value of the warrant if the maturity were nine years? Why does the value of the warrant change with the change in maturity?

22A.2 The Monarch Company is currently valued at $500,000. Seventy percent of current value is the face value of debt, all of which will mature in four years. The variance of percentage returns is 56.25 percent. The risk-free rate is 10 percent.

a. Determine the market value of the equity.
b. Determine the market value of the debt.

22A.3 Itex Distributing Company is currently valued at $4,000,000. Twenty percent of current value is the face value of debt, all of which matures in four years. The variance of percentage returns is 42.25 percent. The risk-free rate is 10 percent.

a. Determine the value of the equity.
b. Determine the value of the debt.

22A.4 Stacy Johnston plans to invest in the newly issued call option of the Remington Corporation. The call option has an exercise price of $50 and a maturity date three months from now. The stock price is $32, the instantaneous variance of the stock price is 0.64, and the risk-free rate is 8 percent. What is the value of the call option?

23A.5 The Perry Company has a market value of $25,000,000 and outstanding debt of $16,000,000, which matures in 9 years. The variance of the firm's rate of return is 0.49. The firm pays no cash dividends and pays out the interest at maturity only. If the rate of inflation is expected to rise by 4 percent (thus raising the riskless nominal interest rate from 6 percent to 10 percent), use the OPM to determine which class of Perry's security holders benefits from the rise in R_F.

22A.6 The Lansing Corporation has $30 million outstanding debt which will mature in one year. In the market, the firm has a current value of $100,000,000. The total risk of Lansing's assets is $\sigma = 1.44$. The expected market rate of return is 15 percent. The riskless rate is 10 percent. The beta of Lansing's equity is 1.4, and the beta of its debt is 0.3.

a. Determine the market value of the firm's debt and equity.
b. Determine the cost of debt and equity capital (assuming a world without taxes).

22A.7 The Sandvik Company and the Weller Corporation have the same market value of $75 million. Both firms have the following identical parameters:

$D_S = D_W =$ $25 million	Face value of debt
$T_S = T_W = 4$ years	Maturity of debt
$\sigma_S = \sigma_W = 0.36$	Instantaneous standard deviation
$R_F = 0.11$	Risk-free rate

a. What is the initial market value of debt and equity for Sandvik and Weller?
b. The correlation between the two firms' cash flows is 0.5. If the two firms merge, the surviving firm will be worth $150 million. What will the market value of debt and equity in the merged firm be? If there were no other merger effects, would shareholders agree to the merger?

Selected References

Black, Fisher. "The Pricing of Commodity Contracts." *Journal of Financial Economics* 3 (January–March 1976), pp. 167–179.

Brennan, M. J. "The Pricing of Contingent Claims in Discrete Time Models." *Journal of Finance* 34 (March 1979), pp. 53–68.

Chiras, Donald P., and Manaster, Steven. "The Information Content of Option Prices and a Test of Market Efficiency." *Journal of Financial Economics* 6 (June–September 1978), pp. 213–234.

Cornell, Bradford. "Using the Option Pricing Model to Measure the Uncertainty Producing Effect of Major Announcements." *Financial Management* 7 (Spring 1978), pp. 54–59.

Cox, John C., and Ross, Stephen A. "A Survey of Some New Results in Financial Option Pricing Policy." *Journal of Finance* 31 (May 1976), pp. 383–402.

———. "The Valuation of Options for Alternative Stochastic Processes." *Journal of Financial Economics* 3 (January–March 1976), pp. 145–166.

Cox, John C.; Ross, Stephen A.; and Rubinstein, Mark. "Option Pricing: A Simplified Approach." *Journal of Financial Economics* 7 (September 1979), pp. 229–263.

Dimson, Elroy. "Option Valuation Nomograms." *Financial Analysts' Journal* 33 (December 1977), pp. 71–75.

———. "Instant Option Valuation." *Financial Analysts' Journal* 33 (May–June 1977), pp. 62–69.

Fischer, Stanley. "Call Option Pricing When the Exercise Price Is Uncertain, and the Valuation of Index Bonds." *Journal of Finance* 33 (March 1978), pp. 169–176.

Galai, Dan. "A Proposal for Indexes for Traded Call Options." *Journal of Finance* 34 (December 1979), pp. 1157–1172.

———. "Empirical Tests of Boundary Conditions for CBOE Options." *Journal of Financial Economics* 6 (June–September 1978), pp. 187–211.

———. "Tests of Market Efficiency of the Chicago Board Options Exchange." *Journal of Business* 50 (April 1977), pp. 167–197.

Galai, D., and Masulis, R. W. "The Option Pricing Model and the Risk Factor of Stock." *Journal of Financial Economics* 3 (January–March 1976), pp. 53–82.

Geske, Robert. "The Valuation of Compound Options." *Journal of Financial Economics* 7 (March 1979), pp. 63–81.

———. "The Pricing of Options with Stochastic Dividend Yield." *Journal of Finance* 33 (May 1978), pp. 617–625.

———. "The Valuation of Corporate Liabilities as Compound Options." *Journal of Financial and Quantitative Analysis* 12 (November 1977), pp. 541–552.

Hayes, Samuel L., III, and Tennenbaum, Michael E. "The Impact of Listed Options on the Underlying Shares." *Financial Management* 8 (Winter 1979), pp. 72–76.

Ingersoll, Jonathan E., Jr. "A Contingent-Claims Valuation of Convertible Securities." *Journal of Financial Economics* 4 (May 1977), pp. 289–322.

———. "A Theoretical and Empirical Investigation of the Dual Purpose Funds: An Application of Contingent-Claims Analysis." *Journal of Financial Economics* 3 (January–March 1976), pp. 83–124.

Klemkosky, Robert C., and Resnick, Bruce G. "Put-Call Parity and Market Efficiency." *Journal of Finance* 34 (December 1979), pp. 1141–1155.

Latane, Henry A., and Rendleman, Richard J., Jr. "Standard Deviations of Stock Price Ratios Implied in Option Prices." *Journal of Finance* 31 (May 1976), pp. 369–381.

MacBeth, James D., and Merville, Larry J. "An Empirical Examination of the Black-

Scholes Call Option Pricing Model." *Journal of Finance* 34 (December 1979), pp. 1173–1186.

Margrabe, William. "The Value of an Option to Exchange One Asset for Another." *Journal of Finance* 33 (March 1978), pp. 177–198.

Merton, Robert C. "An Analytic Derivation of the Cost of Deposit Insurance and Loan Guarantees: An Application of Modern Option Pricing Theory." *Journal of Banking and Finance* 1 (June 1977), pp. 3–11.

———. "Option Pricing When Underlying Stock Returns Are Discontinuous." *Journal of Financial Economics* 3 (January–March 1976), pp. 125–144.

———. "On the Pricing of Corporate Debt: The Risk Structure of Interest Rates." *Journal of Finance* 29 (May 1974), pp. 449–470.

Merton, Robert C.; Scholes, Myron S.; and Gladstein, Mathew L. "The Return and Risk of Alternative Call Option Portfolio Investment Strategies." *Journal of Business* 51 (April 1978), pp. 183–242.

Murray, Roger F. "A New Role for Options." *Journal of Financial and Quantitative Analysis* 14 (November 1979), pp. 895–899.

Rendleman, Richard J., Jr., and Bartter, Brit J. "Two-State Option Pricing." *Journal of Finance* 34 (December 1979), pp. 1093–1110.

Roenfeldt, Rodney L.; Cooley, Philip L.; and Gombola, Michael J. "Market Performance of Options on the Chicago Board Options Exchange." *Journal of Business Research* 7, no. 1 (1979), pp. 95–107.

Roll, Richard. "An Analytic Valuation Formula for Unprotected American Call Options on Stocks with Known Dividends." *Journal of Financial Economics* 5 (November 1977), pp. 251–258.

Rubinstein, M. E. "The Valuation of Uncertain Income Streams and the Pricing of Options." *Bell Journal of Economics* 7 (Autumn 1976), pp. 407–425.

Schmalensee, Richard, and Trippi, Robert R. "Common Stock Volatility Expectations Implied by Option Premia." *Journal of Finance* 33 (March 1978), pp. 129–147.

Scholes, Myron. "Taxes and the Pricing of Options." *Journal of Finance* 31 (May 1976), pp. 319–322.

Part Seven
Integrated Topics in Managerial Finance

In the final four chapters, we take up important topics that bring together materials from a number of earlier sections of the book. Chapter 23 discusses the growth of firms through mergers and holding companies and seeks to explain the factors behind these developments. Chapter 24 considers the causes and possible remedies when firms encounter financial difficulties.

In Chapter 25, we apply many of the topics and concepts developed more generally in earlier chapters to the specific circumstances of a small firm. Finally, in Chapter 26 we extend the framework of financing into its international dimensions. A number of aspects of international business finance have been treated throughout the book, but in this final chapter, we add some important areas of international business finance.

23

External Growth: Mergers and Holding Companies

Growth is vital to the well-being of a firm. Without it, the business cannot attract able management because it cannot give recognition by way of promotions; nor can it offer challenging, creative activity. And without able executives, the firm is likely to decline and die. Much of the previous material dealing with analysis, planning, and financing has a direct bearing on the financial manager's potential contribution to the firm's growth. This chapter focuses on strategies for promoting growth.

Some Perspectives on Merger Activity

Merger activity has played an important part in the growth of U.S. firms, and financial managers are required both to appraise the desirability of prospective mergers and to participate directly in evaluating the companies involved in them.[1] Consequently, it is essential that the study of financial management provide the background necessary for effective participation in merger negotiations and decisions.

Financial managers also need to be aware of the broad significance of mergers. Despite the heightened merger activities in the 1920s, again after World War II, and during the 1960s, recent merger movements have neither approached the magnitude nor had the social consequences of those that took place from 1890 to 1905. During this period, more than two hundred major combinations were effected, resulting in the concentration that has characterized the steel, tobacco, and other important industries. Regardless of the business objectives and motives of merger activity, its social and economic consequences must also be taken into account.

While the merger movement of the 1960s peaked in the last two years of that decade, it resumed in 1977 and 1978. In 1977 there were 2,224 mergers, in which 99 of the acquired firms had assets of $10 million or more.[2] While

1. As we use the term, *merger* means any combination that forms one economic unit from two or more previous ones. For legal purposes there are distinctions among the various ways these combinations can occur, but the emphasis here is on fundamental business and financial aspects of mergers or acquisitions.
2. U.S. Department of Commerce, Bureau of the Census, *Statistical Abstract of the United States*, (Washington, D.C.: Government Printing Office, 1979), p. 574.

Table 23.1

Twelve Major Mergers in 1976–1977

Acquiring Company	Acquired Company	Value of Transaction (in Millions)
General Electric	Utah International	$2,170
Atlantic Richfield	Anaconda	536
R. J. Reynolds	Burmah Oil & Gas	520
J. Ray McDermott	Babcock & Wilcox	510
Gulf Oil	Kewanee Industries	440
Getty Oil	Mission; Skelly Oil	356
Champion International	Hoerner Waldorf	351
Pepsico	Pizza Hut	313
Continental Group	Richmond	293
Nestlé	Alcon Laboratories	268
Marathon Oil	Pan Ocean Oil	265
ITT	Carbon Industries	264
Total		$6,286

Source: "The Great Takeover Binge," *Business Week,* November 14, 1977, p. 177.

the replacement costs of fixed assets have continued to rise with inflation, market values of existing companies are often below book values based on historical costs. Companies seeking to add capacity can do so by buying other companies at market prices well below the current replacement costs of the assets acquired. Also, the decline in the international value of the U.S. dollar makes acquisition of U.S. companies by foreign companies "cheap" when expressed in foreign currencies whose value has risen compared to the U.S. dollar.

A sharp increase in tender offers has occurred. In making a tender offer, acquiring firms offer directly to the stockholders to buy their stock at a premium price above current market price. The total $20 billion value of 1969 mergers was closely approached or exceeded during both 1977 and 1978. Illustrative of the larger mergers in recent years are the twelve listed in Table 23.1.

This increased merger activity has given rise to proposals for new laws to limit mergers. Senate Bill S.600 was introduced in March 1979, its aim to prohibit acquisitions by the largest 200 corporations. Shortly thereafter S.1256 was introduced, with the purpose of preventing the eighteen largest oil companies from making any acquisitions outside the petroleum industry. These proposals were stimulated by data indicating that merger activity, particularly conglomerate mergers, was taking place in large numbers. For example, Figure 23.1 indicates that by 1977 the total value of acquisitions in very large mergers had exceeded the peak levels of activity observed during the height of the earlier conglomerate merger movement in the late 1960s.

Figure 23.2 presents data on the total purchase price of mergers and acquisitions for the period 1972 through 1978. The total merger activity reached over $20 billion by 1977 and well over $30 billion by 1978.

Table 23.2 presents data on the value of assets acquired by mergers over

Figure 23.1

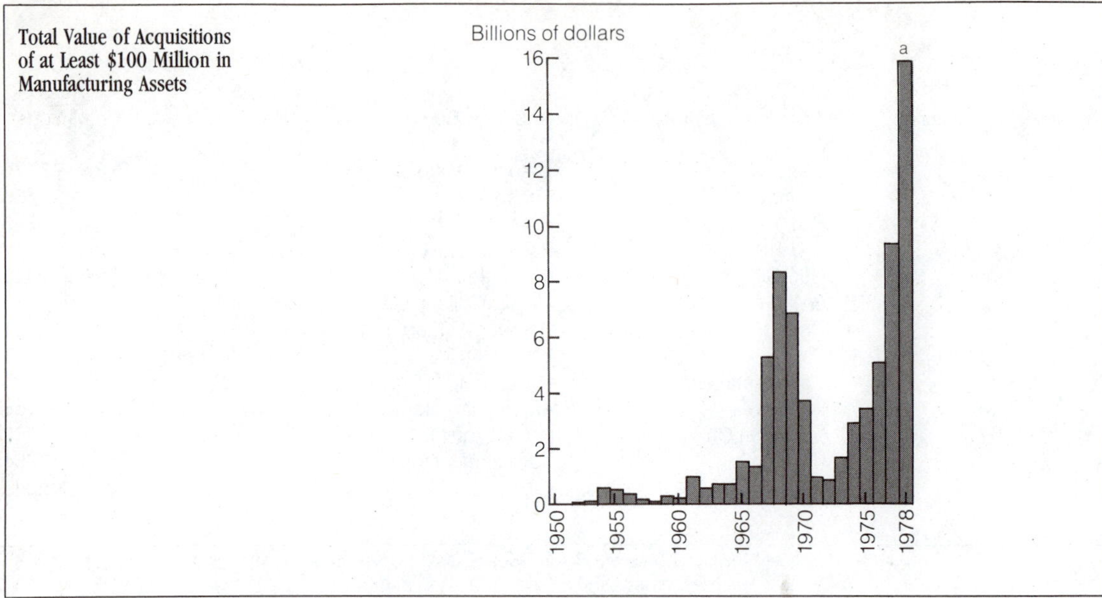

a. 1978 includes mergers still pending as of January 1, 1979.
Source: Senator Edward M. Kennedy, Opening Statement, Hearings before the Subcommittee on Antitrust, Monopoly and Business Rights of the Committee on the Judiciary, United States Senate, Ninety-sixth Congress, Part 1, March 8, 1979 (Washington, D.C.: Government Printing Office, 1979), p. 3. Based on data developed by the Federal Trade Commission.

Figure 23.2

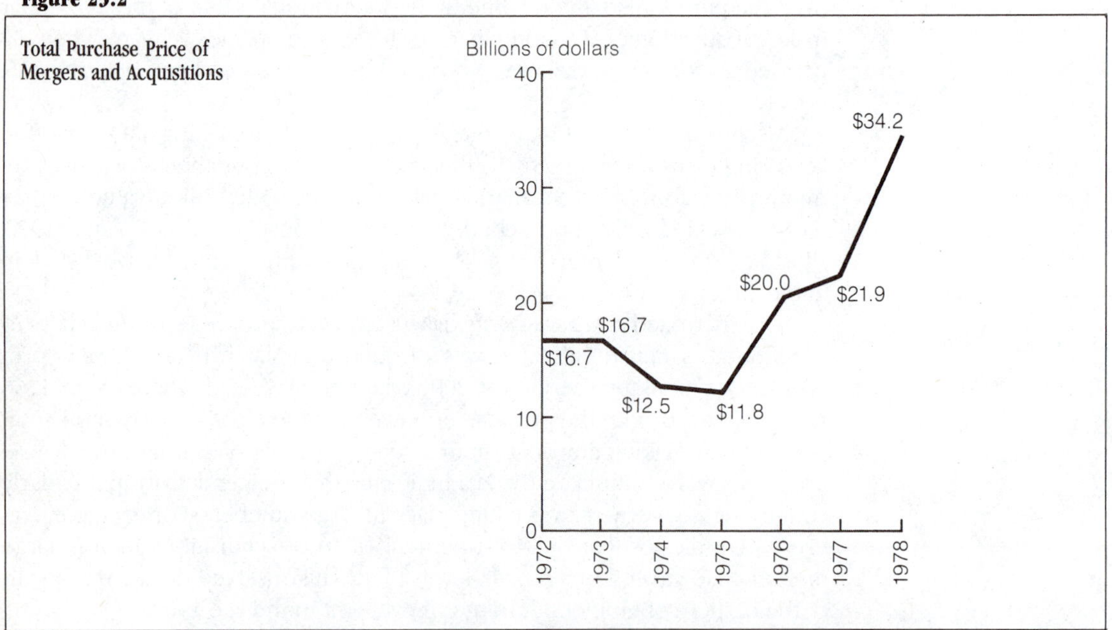

Source: Senator Edward M. Kennedy, Opening Statement, Hearings before the Subcommittee on Antitrust, Monopoly and Business Rights of the Committee on the Judiciary, United States Senate, Ninety-sixth Congress, Part 1, March 8, 1979 (Washington, D.C.: Government Printing Office, 1979), p. 2. Based on data developed by the Federal Trade Commission.

Table 23.2

Mergers in Manufacturing and Mining (Large Companies)

	1950	1954	1955	1958	1960	1962	1963	1965	1966	1967	1968	1969	1970	1971	1972	1973	1974	1975	1976	1977
Number	5	37	67	42	51	65	54	64	76	138	174	138	91	59	60	64	62	59	81	99
Assets acquired, all large companies (billions of dollars)	0.2	1.5	2.2	1.2	1.7	2.7	3.2	3.7	4.4	9.0	13.8	12.2	6.6	3.1	2.7	3.6	5.1	5.5	6.9	9.6

Source: John Shenefield, Statement to Hearings before the Subcommittee on Antitrust, Monopoly and Business Rights of the Committee on the Judiciary, United States Senate, on S. 600, March 8, 1979 (Washington, D.C.: Government Printing Office, 1979), p. 93. Based on data developed by the Federal Trade Commission.

the period 1950 through 1977. A comparison can be made between the data in Figure 23.2, which presents totals in terms of purchase values, and that of Table 23.2, which presents totals measured by the book value of assets acquired. The ratios of purchase price to book values range from 2 to 5 times. Thus substantial premiums were often involved in the acquisitions.

Table 23.3

Large Acquisitions in Manufacturing and Mining by Firms Ranked among the 200 Largest Manufacturing Firms in 1975, by Year, 1948–1977[a] (Millions of Dollars)

Year	Value of Assets Acquired	Value of Assets Acquired in 1977 Dollars[b]
1948	$ 63.2	$ 159.1
1949	45.3	115.2
1950	20.0	50.3
1951	160.1	373.5
1952	195.0	445.1
1953	457.9	1,037.6
1954	919.9	2,074.0
1955	1,148.7	2,599.6
1956	1,246.5	2,779.4
1957	693.4	1,492.8
1958	682.1	1,429.5
1959	687.9	1,430.3
1960	789.4	1,615.3
1961	1,480.7	2,999.7
1962	1,205.6	2,415.0
1963	1,871.7	3,704.4
1964	1,075.7	2,101.5
1965	1,815.7	3,486.9
1966	1,929.5	3,603.1
1967	5,252.8	9,533.8
1968	7,717.1	13,440.9
1969	6,054.5	10,008.3
1970	3,260.2	5,087.8
1971	960.6	1,437.3
1972	739.1	1,070.5
1973	1,767.0	2,409.6
1974	1,874.6	2,303.7
1975	2,592.0	2,918.2
1976	2,809.1	2,990.3
1977	5,236.9[c]	5,236.9
Total	$54,752.2	$90,349.6

a. Acquired firms with assets of $10 million or more.
b. Adjusted to 1977 dollars on the basis of the Consumer Price Index.
c. Preliminary.
Sources: Federal Trade Commission, Bureau of Economics, *Statistical Report on Mergers and Acquisitions* (Washington, D.C.: Government Printing Office, November 1977), Table 22; "Fortune Directory of the 500 Largest Industrial Corporations," *Fortune,* August 1961, May 15, 1976, and May 8, 1978.

terms of constant, 1977 dollars. The previous peak in merger activity, as measured by the value of assets acquired, was the nearly $8 billion book value of assets acquired in 1968. By 1977 the magnitude of merger activity appeared to be approaching the levels of the late sixties. However, when the final column of the table, which is in constant dollars, is analyzed, a different picture emerges. In 1977 dollars, the volume of merger activity in 1968 peaked at over $13 billion. In constant dollars, the magnitude of merger activity in the late seventies appears to have been less than half the size of the merger activity of the late 1960s.

One of the concerns about current merger activity is that the share of the largest 200 U.S. firms is increasing unduly. Data on this issue are in Table 23.4.

When ranked by assets, including those related to international activities, the share of the top 200 firms increased from 55 percent of all manufacturing in 1960 to 61 percent by 1977. When international activity is excluded, the share of the largest 200 rises from 56 percent to 58 percent. When the measurement is based on sales, the share of the largest 200 is somewhat lower. When the ranking is made by value added in the manufacturing activity of the largest firms, the share of all manufacturing drops to 43 percent for the latest year for which we have data and has been relatively stable since the 41 percent share in 1963. It is of interest that the share of value added did not increase appreciably during the conglomerate merger movement of the late 1960s. The last column of Table 23.4 relates the share of the largest 200 U.S. firms to all nonfinancial corporations, not just manufacturing. The share measured by assets declines from 40.5 percent in 1960 to slightly under 40 percent by 1975. One explanation for the difference when the share is related to all nonfinancials relates to the conglomerate nature of mergers during the 1960s and 1970s. To the extent that manufacturing companies acquire

Table 23.4

Share of Largest 200 U.S. Firms on Various Bases

	Manufacturing				All Nonfinancial
	Including International		Excluding International		Including International
	Ranked by Assets	Ranked by Sales	Ranked by Assets	Ranked by Value Added	Ranked by Assets
1958	55.0	46.4		38	
1960	55.4	47.3			40.5
1962	55.2	47.0		40	
1965	55.4	47.5	56.7		40.1
1966	55.6	47.1		42	40.5
1970	60.0	51.9	60.4	43	40.6
1972	58.4	51.5	60.0	43	39.8
1975	59.4	55.1			39.9
1977	61.1	56.6	58.4		

Source: Statement by J. Fred Weston in Hearings before the Subcommittee on Antitrust, Monopoly and Business Rights of the Committee on the Judiciary, United States Senate, on S. 600, April 25, 1979 (Washington, D.C.: Government Printing Office, 1979), p. 542. Based on various publications.

Table 23.5

Share of Total Value Added by Manufacture Accounted for by the 50 and 100 Largest Identical Manufacturing Companies: 1954 to 1970

Company Rank Group in 1954	Percent of Value Added by Manufacture in Each Year Accounted for by the Largest Companies in 1954						
	1970	1967	1966	1963	1962	1958	1954
Largest 50 companies	19	20	21	21	21	20	21
Largest 100 companies	26	27	27	28	27	27	27

Source: U.S. Department of Commerce, Bureau of the Census, *Historical Statistics of the United States from Colonial Times to 1970,* Part 2 (Washington, D.C.: Government Printing Office, 1975), p. 686.

nonmanufacturing assets, nonmanufacturing activity is included in the numerator but related to a denominator defined by manufacturing assets only. When the denominator includes nonmanufacturing as well as manufacturing, then the conglomerate nature of the merger activity does not involve inflating the numerator without changing the denominator.

Another perspective on the position of large firms is provided by Table 23.5. The previous tables and materials related the largest firms to total manufacturing or to total nonfinancial corporations by using whatever firms were the largest in any particular year. Thus the largest 200 firms, as measured in the previous tables, do not represent the same list of firms. It is a changing list that varies according to whatever individual firms succeeded in being among the largest in a particular year. In Table 23.5 specific groups of 50 and 100 firms are followed from 1954 through 1970. For this fixed group of companies, the largest 50 accounted for 21 percent of all value added in 1954. By 1970 this share had declined to 19 percent. Similarly, the largest 100 companies' share declined from 27 percent in 1954 to 26 percent in 1970.

Thus overall, the share of the largest 200 firms to all nonfinancial assets has been stable at about 40 percent since 1960. But there has been a frequently changing list of whatever firms were the largest in the individual years. It appears that any group of large firms that is held identical is unable to maintain, even with merger activity, its share of all manufacturing or all nonfinancial corporation assets over a sustained period of years.

Mergers versus Internal Growth

Many of the objectives of size and diversification can be achieved either by internal growth or by external growth through acquisitions and mergers. In the post–World War II period, many firms achieved considerable diversification through external acquisition. Some financial reasons for utilizing external acquisition instead of internal growth to achieve diversification are discussed in the following section.

Financing

Sometimes it is possible to finance an acquisition when it is not possible to finance internal growth. Building a large steel plant, for example, involves a large investment. Steel manufacturing capacity can be acquired more cheaply in a merger through an exchange of stock than it can be obtained by buying the facilities outright. Sellers are often more willing to accept the purchaser's stock in payment for the facilities sold than are investors in a public offering, and the use of stock reduces cash requirements for the acquisition of assets.

Market Capitalization Rates

While it is not strictly an operating factor, the fact that the earnings of larger economic units are frequently capitalized at lower rates and hence produce higher market values has stimulated many mergers. The securities of larger firms have better marketability; these firms are more able to diversify and thus reduce risks, and they are generally better known. All these factors lead to lower required rates of return and higher price-earnings ratios. As a result, the market value of consolidated firms may be greater than the sum of their individual values, even if there is no increase in aggregate earnings. To illustrate: Three companies may each be earning $1 million and selling at ten times earnings, for a total market value of $30 million. When these companies combine, the new company may obtain a stock exchange listing or may take other action to improve the price of its stock. If so, the price-earnings ratio may rise to fifteen, in which case the market value of the consolidated firm will be $45 million.[3]

A major reason for the increase in takeovers in 1976–1977 is that the replacement values of corporate assets have been rising with inflation while inflation has depressed real earnings, the result being lower stock prices. It has been estimated that by the late 1970s the replacement costs of corporate net assets (for nonfarm, nonfinancial corporations) were about 25 percent higher than the market values of the corporate securities representing ownership of the corporate assets.[4] Because selling prices of products have been based on the historical costs of assets, the prospective returns on new investments at current, higher replacement costs have been unattractively low. With the market values of other companies substantially below their replacement costs, acquisitions provide the opportunity of higher returns than would be earned by investments in physical assets either in the firm's own line of business or in new areas.

Taxes

Without question, the high level of taxation was a factor stimulating merger activity in the postwar period. Studies have indicated that taxes appear to have been a major reason for the sale of about one-third of the firms acquired by merger. In some cases, inheritance taxes precipitated these sales; in others, the advantage of buying a company with a tax loss provided the motivation.

3. The market capitalization rate is related to the cost of equity, as discussed in Chapter 16. A lower capitalization rate results in a lower cost of capital. Therefore, the same actions that raise the market value of the equity also lower the firm's cost of new capital.
4. "The Great Takeover Binge," *Business Week,* November 14, 1977, p. 179.

Terms of Mergers

For every merger actually consummated, a number of other potentially attractive combinations fail during the negotiating stage. Negotiations may be broken off when it is revealed that the companies' operations are not compatible or when the parties are unable to agree on the merger terms. The most important of these terms is the price to be paid by the acquiring firm.

Effects on Price and Earnings

A merger carries the potential for either favorable or adverse effects on earnings, on market prices of shares, or on both. Previous chapters have shown that investment decisions should be guided by the effects on market values, and these effects should in turn be determined by the probable effects on future earnings and dividends. Future events are difficult to forecast, however, so both stockholders and managers attribute great importance to the immediate effects on earnings per share of a contemplated merger. Company directors will often state, "I do not know how the merger will affect the market price of the shares of my company, because so many forces influencing market prices are at work. But the effect on earnings per share can be seen directly."

An example will illustrate the effects of a proposed merger on earnings per share and thus suggest the kinds of problems likely to arise. Assume the following facts for two companies:

	Company A	Company B
Total earnings	$20,000	$50,000
Number of shares of common stock	5,000	10,000
Earnings per share of stock	$4	$5
Price-earnings ratio per share	15 times	12 times
Market price per share	$60	$60

Suppose the firms agree to merge, with B, the surviving firm, acquiring the shares of A by a one-for-one exchange of stock. The exchange ratio is determined by the market prices of the two companies. Assuming no increase in earnings, the effects on earnings per share are shown in the following tabulation:

	Shares of Company B Owned after Merger	Earning per Share	
		Before Merger	After Merger
A's stockholders	5,000	$4	$4.67
B's stockholders	10,000	5	4.67
Total	15,000		

Since total earnings are $70,000, and since a total of 15,000 shares will be outstanding after the merger has been completed, the new earnings per share will be $4.67. Earnings will increase by 67 cents for A's stockholders, but they will decline by 33 cents for B's.

The effects on market values are less certain. If the combined company sells at Company A's price-earnings ratio of 15, the market value per share of the new company will be $70. In this case, shareholders of both companies will have benefited. This result comes about because the combined earnings are now valued at a multiplier of 15, whereas prior to the merger one portion of the earnings was valued at a multiplier of 15 and another portion at a multiplier of 12. If, on the other hand, the earnings of the new company are valued at B's multiplier of 12, the indicated market value of the shares will be $56, and the shareholders of each company will have suffered a $4 dilution in market value.

Because the effects on market value per share are less certain than those on earnings per share, the impact on earnings per share tends to be given great weight in merger negotiations. The following analysis thus emphasizes effects on earnings per share while recognizing that maximizing market value is a valid rule of investment decisions.

As shown below, if a merger takes place on the basis of earnings, neither earnings dilution nor earnings appreciation will take place:

	Shares of Company B Owned after Merger	Earnings per Old Share	
		Before Merger	After Merger
A's stockholders	4,000	$4	$4
B's stockholders	10,000	5	5
Total	14,000		

It is clear that the equivalent earnings per share after the merger are the same as before the merger.[5] The effect on market values, however, will depend on whether the 15-times multiplier of A or the 12-times multiplier of B prevails.

Of the numerous factors affecting the valuation of the constituent companies in a merger, all must ultimately be reflected in the companies' earnings per share, or market price. Hence, all the effects on the earnings position or wealth position of stockholders are encompassed by the above example.

5. On the basis of earnings, the exchange ratio is 4:5. That is, Company A's shareholders receive four shares of B stock for each five shares of A stock they own. Earnings per share of the merged company are $5. But, since A's shareholders now own only 80 percent of the number of their old shares, their equivalent earnings per *old* share are the same $4. For example, if one of A's stockholders formerly held 100 shares, that person will own only 80 shares of B after the merger; and the total earnings will be 80 × $5 = $400. Dividing the $400 total earnings by the number of shares formerly owned, 100, gives the $4 per *old* share.

Quantitative Factors Affecting Terms of Mergers

Five factors have received the greatest emphasis in arriving at merger terms: (1) earnings and the growth of earnings, (2) dividends, (3) market values, (4) book values, and (5) net current assets. Analysis is typically based on the per share values of the foregoing factors. The relative importance of each factor and the circumstances under which each is likely to be the most influential determinant in arriving at terms will vary. The nature of these influences is described below.

Earnings and Growth Rates. Both expected earnings and capitalization rates as reflected in P-E ratios are important in determining the values that will be established in a merger. The analysis necessarily begins with historical data on the firms' earnings; their past growth rates, probable future trends, and variability are important determinants of the earnings multiplier, or P-E ratio, that will prevail after the merger.

The ways in which future earnings growth rates affect the multiplier can be illustrated by extending the preceding example. First, high P-E ratios are commonly associated with rapidly growing companies. Since Company A has the higher P-E ratio, it is reasonable to assume that its earnings will grow more rapidly than those of Company B. Suppose A's expected growth rate is 10 percent and B's is 5 percent. Looking at the proposed merger from the viewpoint of Company B and its stockholders, and assuming that the exchange ratio is based on present market prices, it can be seen that B will suffer a dilution in earnings when the merger occurs. However, B will be acquiring a firm with more favorable growth prospects; hence, its earnings after the merger should increase more rapidly than before. In this case, the new growth rate is assumed to be a weighted average of the growth rates of the individual firms—weighted by their respective total earnings before the merger. In the example, the new expected growth rate is 6.43 percent.

With the new growth rate it is possible to determine just how long it will take Company B's stockholders to regain the earnings dilution—that is, how long it will take earnings per share to revert back to their position before the merger. This can be determined graphically from Figure 23.3.[6] Without the merger, B will have initial earnings of $5 a share, and these earnings will grow at a rate of 5 percent a year. With the merger, earnings will drop to $4.67 a share, but the rate of growth will increase to 6.43 percent. Under these conditions, the earnings dilution will be overcome after five years; from the fifth year on, B's earnings will be higher, assuming the merger is consummated.

This same relationship can be developed from the viewpoint of the faster

6. The calculation could also be made algebraically by solving for N in the following equation:

$$E_1(1 + g_1)^N = E_2(1 + g_2)^N,$$

where:

E_1 and E_2 = Earnings before and after the merger, respectively
g_1 and g_2 = Growth rates before and after the merger, respectively
N = Breakeven number of years

Figure 23.3

Effect of Merger on Future Earnings

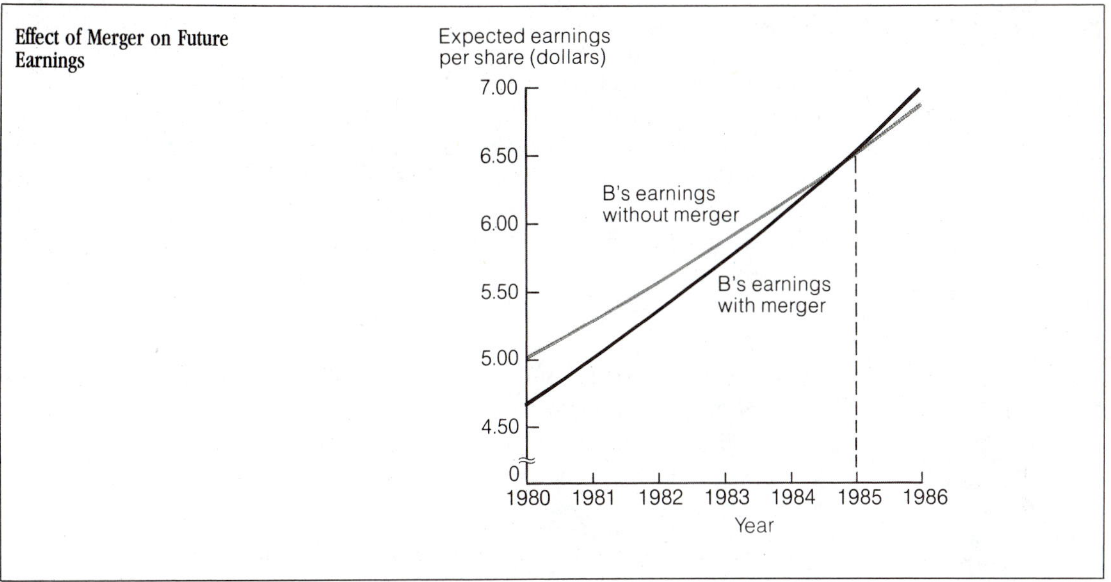

growing firm, for which there is an immediate earnings increase but a reduced rate of growth. Working through the analysis shows the number of years before the earnings accretion will be eroded.

It is apparent that the critical variables are (1) the respective rates of growth of the two firms; (2) their relative sizes, which determine the actual amount of the initial earnings per share dilution or accretion, as well as the new weighted average growth rate; (3) the firms' P-E ratios; and (4) the exchange ratio. These factors interact to produce the resulting pattern of earnings per share for the surviving company. It is possible to generalize the relationships somewhat; for the immediate purposes, it is necessary simply to note that in the bargaining process the exchange ratio is the variable that must be manipulated in an effort to reach a mutually satisfactory earnings pattern.[7]

7. Certain companies, especially the conglomerates, are reported to have used mergers to produce a "growth illusion" designed to increase the prices of their stocks. When a high P-E ratio company buys a low P-E ratio company, the earnings per share of the acquiring firm rise *because* of the merger. Thus mergers can produce growth in reported earnings for the acquiring firm. This growth by merger in turn can cause the acquiring firm to keep its high P-E ratio. With this ratio, the conglomerates can seek new low P-E merger candidates and thus continue to obtain growth through mergers. The chain is broken if (1) the merger activity slows, or (2) the P-E ratio of the acquiring firm falls. In 1968 and 1969 several large conglomerates reported profit declines caused by losses in certain of their divisions. This reduced the growth rate in EPS, which in turn led to a decline in the P-E ratio. A change in tax laws and antitrust suits against some conglomerate mergers also made it more difficult to consummate favorable mergers. These factors, along with tight money and depressed conditions in some industries, caused a further reduction in the P-E ratio and compounded the firms' problems. The net result was a drastic revaluation of conglomerate share prices, with such former favorites as LTV falling from a high of $169 to $7.50 and Litton Industries from $115 to $6.75.

Dividends. Because they represent the actual income received by stockholders, dividends can influence the terms of merger. As Chapter 17 suggests, however, dividends are likely to have little influence on the market price of companies with a record of high growth and high profitability. Some companies have not yet paid cash dividends, but they nonetheless command market prices representing a high multiple of current earnings. However, for utility companies and for companies in industries where growth rates and profitability have declined, the dollar amount of dividends paid can have a relatively important influence on the market price of the stock. Dividends can therefore influence the terms on which these companies will be likely to trade in a merger.[8]

Market Values. The price of a firm's stock reflects expectations about its future earnings and dividends, so current market values are expected to have a strong influence on the terms of a merger. However, the value placed on a firm in an acquisition is likely to exceed its current market price for a number of reasons:

1. If the company is in a depressed industry, its stockholders are likely to overdiscount the dismal outlook for the company. This will result in a very low current market price.
2. The prospective purchaser may be interested in the company for the contribution that it will make to the purchaser's company. Thus the acquired company may be worth more to an informed purchaser than it is in the general market.
3. Stockholders are offered more than current market prices for their stock as an inducement to sell.

For these reasons, the offering price is usually in the range of 10 to 20 percent above the market price before the merger announcement.

Book Value per Share. Book value is generally considered to be relatively unimportant in determining the value of a company, since it represents only the historical investments made in the company—investments that may have little relation to current values or prices. At times, however, especially when it substantially exceeds market value, book value may well have an impact on merger terms. Book value is an index of the amount of physical facilities made available in the merger. Despite a past record of low earning power, it is always possible that, under effective management, a firm's assets may once again achieve normal earning power, in which case the market value of the company will rise. Because of the potential contribution of physical proper-

8. If a company that does not pay dividends on its stock is seeking to acquire a firm whose stockholders are accustomed to receiving dividends, the exchange can be on a convertibles for common stock basis. This will enable the acquired firm's stockholders to continue receiving income.

ties to improved future earnings, book value may have an influence on actual merger terms.

Net Current Assets per Share. Net current assets (current assets minus current liabilities) per share are likely to have an influence on merger terms because they represent the amount of liquidity that can be obtained from a company in a merger. In the postwar textile mergers, net current assets were very high, and this was one of the characteristics making textile companies attractive to the acquiring firms. By buying a textile company, often with securities, an acquiring company was in a position to look for still other merger candidates, paying for new acquisitions with the just-acquired liquidity. Similarly, if an acquired company is debt-free, the acquiring firm may be able to borrow the funds required for the purchase, using the acquired firm's assets and earning power to pay off the loan after the merger or to provide security for renewing or even increasing the borrowing.[9]

Relative Importance of Quantitative Factors. Attempts have been made to determine statistically the relative weights assigned to each of the above factors in actual merger cases. These attempts have been singularly unsuccessful. In one case, one factor seems to dominate; in another, some other determinant appears most important. This absence of consistent patterns among the quantitative factors suggests that qualitative forces are also at work.

Qualitative Influences: Synergy

Sometimes the most important influence on the terms of a merger is a business consideration not reflected at all in historical quantitative data. A soundly conceived merger is one in which the combination produces what may be called a *synergistic,* or "two-plus-two-equals-five," effect. By the combination, more profits are generated than could be achieved by the sum of the individual firms operating separately.

To illustrate: In the merger between Merck and Company and Sharp and Dohme, it was said that each company complemented the other in an important way. Merck had a good reputation for its research organization; Sharp and Dohme had an effective sales force. The combination of these two pharmaceutical companies added strength to both. Another example is the merger between Carrier Corporation and Affiliated Gas Equipment. The merger enabled the combined company to provide a complete line of air-conditioning and heating equipment. The merger between Hilton Hotels and Statler Hotels led to economies in the purchase of supplies and materials. One Hilton executive estimated that the savings accruing simply from the combined management of the Statler and Hilton hotels in New York amounted to $700,000 a year. The bulk of the savings was in laundry, food, advertising, and administrative costs.

9. By the same token, a firm seeking to *avoid* being acquired may reduce its liquid position and use up its borrowing potential.

The qualitative factors may also reflect other influences. The merger or acquisition may enable a company that lacks general management ability to obtain it from the other company. Another factor may be the acquisition of a technically competent scientific or engineering staff if one of the companies has fallen behind in the technological race. In such a situation, the company needing the technical competence possessed by the other firm may be willing to pay a substantial premium over previous levels of earnings, dividends, market values, or book values of the acquired firm.

The purpose of the merger may be to develop a production capability a firm does not possess. Some firms are strong in producing custom-made items with high performance characteristics; yet on entering new markets, these firms must make use of mass production techniques. If a firm has had no such experience, this skill may have to be obtained by means of a merger. Another firm may need to develop an effective sales organization. For example, some of the companies previously oriented to the defense market, such as those in aerospace, found that they had only a limited industrial sales organization; merger was the solution to the problem.

The foregoing are the kinds of qualitative considerations that may have an overriding influence on the actual terms of merger, and the value of such contributions is never easy to quantify. The all-encompassing question, of course, is how the factors will affect the contribution of each company to future earnings per share in the combined operation. The historical data and qualitative considerations described, in addition to judgment and bargaining, combine to determine merger terms.

Case Study of the Mobil-Marcor Merger

The June 11, 1979, issue of *Forbes* characterizes the Mobil acquisition of Marcor (which owned Montgomery Ward and the Container Corporation) as a "$1.5 billion mistake." As evidence, the article cites comparative returns on equity for 1976–1978 for Ward which averaged about 9 percent and for Container at over 10 percent except for a write-off in 1978 which brought its return down to 2.4 percent. These returns are contrasted with Mobil's over 13.5 percent return per year in the oil business.

However, Ward averaged a 4.9 percent return on equity in 1970–1972 before Mobil started buying into Marcor in 1973. For the years 1973–1978, Ward averaged over a 7 percent return on average equity, representing a strong upward trend in profitability, at the same time growing at a faster rate than Sears, Roebuck, its long-time competitor. For the years 1973–1978, Container earned a 10.2 percent return on average equity even with the substantial write-off in 1978.

In another perspective, the average net income of Ward and Container for 1973–1978 was $127.4 million. If received in dividends by Mobil, the after-tax amount, using the 85 percent dividend exclusion rate and a 48 percent marginal corporate tax rate, is $118.2 million. After-tax interest expense on the $673 million, 8.5 percent debentures used in the Marcor purchase is $29.7 million, leaving after-tax net income available to Mobil of $88.5 million. On the investment of $819 million cash plus equity paid by Mobil, this represents a 10.8 percent return.

These returns are not so high as Mobil's recent returns from oil industry operations. But the returns from oil industry operations are subject to great uncertainties. In foreign operations, Mobil is now dependent on decisions of the host countries. Domestic operations are subject to price controls, government regulations, new taxes, and a hostile political environment which could produce punitive legislation and regulations. For an after-tax debt cost of $30 million per year, Mobil is adding close to $100 million to consolidated net income, with a favorable upward trend in the growth and profitability of its Ward operations.

Basically, both retailing and containers can potentially earn at the average for all industry. This is also what oil investments have been earning over an extended time period. Taking the considerable future uncertainties of the oil industry into account, the Marcor investment represented an attempt to add stability to Mobil's overall earnings by diversification.

Financial Accounting Policies in Mergers

After merger terms have been agreed upon, the financial manager must be familiar with the accounting principles for recording the financial results of the merger and for reflecting the initial effect on the earnings of the surviving firm. The financial statements of the survivor in a merger must follow the SEC's regulations. These regulations follow the recommendations of professional accounting societies on combinations, but interpretations of actual situations require much financial and economic analysis.

On August 2, 1970, the eighteen-member Accounting Principles Board (APB) of the American Institute of Certified Public Accountants issued Opinion 16, dealing with guidelines for corporate mergers, and Opinion 17, dealing with goodwill arising from mergers. The recommendations, which became effective October 31, 1970, modify and elaborate previous pronouncements on the pooling of interests and purchase methods of accounting for business combinations. For reasons that will become clear later in this section, corporate managements generally prefer pooling. Six broad tests are used to determine whether the conditions for the pooling of interest treatment are met. If all of them are met, then the combination is, in a sense, a merger among equals, and the *pooling of interests* method can be employed. The six tests are:

1. The acquired firm's stockholders must maintain an ownership position in the surviving firm.
2. The basis for accounting for the assets of the acquired entity must remain unchanged.

3. Independent interests must be combined, each entity must have had autonomy for two years prior to the initiation of the plan to combine, and no more than 10 percent ownership of voting common stock can be held as intercorporate investments.
4. The combination must be effected in a single transaction; contingent payouts are not permitted in poolings but can be used in purchases.
5. The acquiring corporation must issue only common stock with rights identical to its outstanding voting common stock in exchange for substantially all the voting common stock of the other company (*substantially* is defined as 90 percent).
6. The combined entity must not intend to dispose of a significant portion of the assets of the combining companies within two years after the merger.

In contrast, a *purchase* involves (1) new owners, (2) an appraisal of the acquired firm's physical assets and a restatement of the balance sheet to reflect these new values, and (3) the possibility of an excess or deficiency of consideration given up vis-à-vis the book value of equity. Point 3 refers to the creation of goodwill. In a purchase, the excess of the purchase price paid over the book value (restated to reflect the appraisal value of physical assets) is set up as goodwill, and capital surplus is increased (or decreased) accordingly. In a pooling of interests, the combined total assets after the merger represent a simple sum of the asset contributions of the constituent companies.

In a *purchase,* if the acquiring firm pays more than the acquired net worth, the excess is associated either with tangible depreciable assets or with goodwill. Asset write-offs are deductible, but goodwill written off is not deductible for tax purposes, even though the new recommendations require that goodwill be written off over some reasonable period but no longer than forty years. This requires a write-off of at least 2.5 percent a year of the amount of goodwill arising from a purchase. Therefore, if a merger is treated as a purchase, reported profits will be lower than if it is handled as a pooling of interests. This is one of the reasons that pooling is popular among acquiring firms.

Previous to the issuance of APB Opinion 16, another stimulus to pooling was the opportunity to dispose of assets acquired at depreciated book values, selling them at their current values, and recording subsequent profits on sales of assets. Opinion 16 attempted to deal with this practice by the requirement that sales of major portions of assets not be contemplated for at least two years after the merger has taken place. For example, suppose Firm A buys Firm B, exchanging stock worth $100 million for assets worth $100 million but carried at $25 million. After the merger, A could, before the change in rules, sell the acquired assets and report the difference between book value and the purchase price, or $75 million, as earned income. Thus mergers could be used in still another way to create an illusion of profits and growth.

Financial Treatment of a Purchase

The financial treatment of a purchase can best be explained by use of a hypothetical example.[10] The Mammoth Company has just purchased the Petty Company under an arrangement known as a *purchase.* The facts are as given in Table 23.6, which also shows the financial treatment. The illustration conforms to the general nature of a purchase. Measured by total assets, the Mammoth Company is twenty times as large as Petty, while its total earnings are fifteen times as large. The terms of the purchase are one share of Mammoth for two shares of Petty, based on the prevailing market value of their shares of common stock. Thus, in terms of Mammoth's stock, Mammoth is giving to Petty's stockholders $30 of market value and $7 of book value for each share of Petty stock. Petty's market value is $30 a share, its book value is $3 a share,

Table 23.6

Financial Treatment of a Purchase

	Mammoth Company	Petty Company	Adjustments Debit	Adjustments Credit	Pro Forma Balance Sheet
Assets					
Current assets	$ 80,000	$ 4,000			$ 84,000
Other assets	20,000	2,000			22,000
Net fixed assets	100,000	4,000			104,000
Goodwill			$54,000		54,000
Total assets	$200,000	$10,000			$264,000
Liabilities and Net Worth					
Current liabilities	$ 40,000	$ 4,000			$ 44,000
Long-term debt	20,000				20,000
Common stock	40,000	1,000	1,000	4,000	44,000
Capital surplus	20,000			56,000	76,000
Retained earnings	80,000	5,000	5,000		80,000
Total liabilities and net worth	$200,000	$10,000	$60,000	$60,000	$264,000
Explanation					
Par value per share, common stock	$4	$0.50			
Number of share outstanding	10,000	2,000			
Book value per share	$14	$3			
Total earnings	$30,000	$2,000			
Earnings per share	$3	$1			
Price-earnings ratio	20 times	30 times			
Market value per share	$60	$30			

10. The material in this section is technical and is generally covered in accounting courses.

and the fair value of the equity is $6,000.[11] The total market value of Mammoth paid for Petty is $60,000. The goodwill involved can be calculated as follows:

Value given by Mammoth	$60,000
Fair value of net worth of Petty purchased	6,000
Goodwill	$54,000

The $54,000 goodwill represents a debit in the adjustments column and is carried to the pro forma balance sheet. The pro forma balance sheet is obtained by simply adding the balance sheets of the constituent companies, together with adjustments.

A total value of $60,000 has been given by Mammoth for a book value of $6,000. This amount represents, in addition to the debt, a payment of $1,000 for the common stock of Petty, $5,000 for the retained earnings, and $54,000 for goodwill. The corresponding credit is the 1,000 shares of Mammoth given in the transaction at their par value of $4 a share, resulting in a credit of $4,000. The capital surplus of Mammoth is increased by $56,000 ($60,000 paid minus $4,000 increase in common stock). The net credit to the net worth account is $54,000, which balances the net debit to the asset accounts. When these adjustments are carried through to the pro forma balance sheet, total assets are increased from the uncombined total of $210,000 to a new total of $264,000. Total tangible assets, however, still remain $210,000.

The effects on earnings per share for stockholders in each company are shown below:

Total earnings (before write-off of goodwill)	$32,000
Amortization of goodwill	1,350
Total net earnings	$30,650
Total shares	11,000
Earnings per share	$2.79
For Petty shareholders:	
New earnings per share	$1.40
Before-purchase earnings per share	1.00
Accretion per share	$0.40
For Mammoth shareholders:	
Before-purchase earnings per share	$3.00
New earnings per share	2.79
Dilution per share	$0.21

11. Under purchase accounting, the acquiring company "should allocate the cost of an acquired company to the assets acquired and liabilities assumed" (APB Opinion No. 16, p. 318, par. 87). A specific procedure is set forth. First, all identifiable assets acquired should be assigned a portion of the cost of the acquired company, normally equal to their fair (market or appraised) values at date of acquisition. Second, the excess of the cost of the acquired company over the sum of the amounts assigned to net assets should be recorded as goodwill. The sum of fair market values assigned may exceed the cost of the acquired company. If so, values otherwise assignable to noncurrent assets should be reduced by a proportionate part of the excess. If noncurrent assets are reduced to zero and some excess still remains, it should be set up as a deferred credit.

Total earnings represent the combined earnings of Mammoth and Petty. Mammoth believes that the value reflected in goodwill will be permanent, but under APB Opinion 17, it is required to write off the goodwill account over a maximum of forty years. The annual charge of $1,350 is the goodwill of $54,000 divided by 40. The total amount of net earnings is therefore $30,650.

The total shares are 11,000 because Mammoth has given one share of stock for every two shares of Petty previously outstanding.[12] The new earnings per share are therefore $2.79. The calculation of earnings accretion or dilution proceeds on the same principles as the calculations set forth earlier. The results require two important comments, however.

Although the earnings accretion per share for Petty is 40 cents, the earnings dilution per share for Mammoth is relatively small, only 21 cents a share. The explanation is that the size of Mammoth is large in relation to that of Petty. This example also illustrates a general principle: When a large company acquires a small one, it can afford to pay a high multiple of earnings per share of the smaller company. In the present example, the price-earnings ratio of Petty is 30, whereas that of Mammoth is 20. If the acquiring company is large in relation to the acquired firm, it can pay a substantial premium and yet suffer only small dilution in its earnings per share.

It is, however, unrealistic to assume that the same earnings on total assets will result after the merger. After all, the purpose of the merger is to achieve something that the two companies could not have achieved alone. When Philip Morris & Company purchased Benson & Hedges (the maker of Parliament, a leading filter-tip brand), it was buying the ability and experience of Benson & Hedges. By means of this merger, Philip Morris was able to make an entry into the rapidly growing filter cigarette business more quickly than it could otherwise have done. The combined earnings per share were expected to rise.

In the Mammoth-Petty illustration, the earnings rate on the tangible assets of Mammoth is 15 percent and on the tangible assets of Petty 20 percent. Assume that the return on total tangible assets of the combined companies rises to 20 percent. The 20 percent of tangible assets of $210,000 equals $42,000; less the amortization of goodwill over forty years at $1,350 per year, the total is $40,650 net earnings. With the same total shares of 11,000 outstanding, the new earnings per share will be $3.70. Thus there will be an accretion of 85 cents for the Petty shareholders and an accretion of 70 cents for the Mammoth shareholders.

This illustrates another general principle: If the purchase of a small company adds to the earnings of the consolidated enterprise, earnings per share may increase for both participants in the merger. Even if the merger results in an initial dilution in earnings per share of the larger company, it may still be advantageous. The initial dilution can be regarded as an investment that

12. After the one-for-two exchange, Petty shareholders have only half as many shares as before the merger.

will have a payoff at some future date in terms of increased growth in earnings per share of the consolidated company.

Treatment of Goodwill

In a purchase, goodwill is likely to arise; since it represents an intangible asset, its treatment is subject to the exercise of judgment. It will therefore be useful to set out a few generalizations on good practice in the treatment of goodwill.

1. When goodwill is purchased, it should not be charged to surplus immediately on acquisition. Instead it should be written off against income and should go through the income statement. Since goodwill is to be written off against income, it is not appropriate to write it off entirely on acquisition, because this will be of such magnitude that distortion of earnings for that year will result.
2. The general view is not to write off purchased goodwill by charges to capital surplus. Purchased goodwill is supposed to represent and to be reflected in a future rise of income. It should therefore be written off against income rather than against capital surplus.
3. When goodwill is purchased, an estimate should be made of its life. Annual charges based on the estimated life should then be made against income to amortize the goodwill over the estimated period of its usefulness.
4. Intangibles must be written off over a maximum of forty years, according to APB Opinion 17.

When goodwill is purchased, it should be treated like any other asset. It should be written off to the extent that the value represented by any part of it has a limited life, as is likely to be the situation. In a free enterprise economy, the existence of high profits represented by superior earning power attracts additional resources into that line of business. The growth of capacity and the increase in competition are likely to erode the superior earning power over time.

Financial Treatment of Pooling of Interests

When a business combination is a pooling of interests rather than a purchase, the accounting treatment is simply to combine the balance sheets of the two companies. Goodwill will not ordinarily arise in the consolidation.

The financial treatment can be indicated by another example, which reflects the facts as they are set forth in Table 23.7. In order to focus on the critical issues, the balance sheets are identical in every respect. However, a difference in the amount and rate of profit after interest of the two companies is indicated.

Book value per share is $10. The amount of profit after interest and taxes is $42,000 for Company A and $21,000 for Company B. Earnings per share are therefore $3.50 and $1.75, respectively. The price-earnings ratio is 18 for A and 12 for B, so the market price of stock is $63 for A and $21 for B. The net working capital per share is $4.17 in each instance. The dividends per share are $1.75 for A and $0.875 for B.

Table 23.7

Financial Treatment of Pooling of Interests

	Company A	Company B	Net Adjustments on A's Books: Debit	Net Adjustments on A's Books: Credit	Acquiring Company A's New Balance Sheets and Earnings if the Exchange Basis is: Earnings 2/1	Price 3/1
Current assets	$100,000	$100,000			$200,000	$200,000
Fixed assets	100,000	100,000			200,000	200,000
Total assets	$200,000	$200,000			$400,000	$400,000
Current liabilities	$ 50,000	$ 50,000			$100,000	$100,000
Long-term debt	30,000	30,000			60,000	60,000
Total debt	80,000	80,000			160,000	160,000
Common stock, par value $5	60,000	60,000	$30,000[a]		90,000	
			$20,000[b]			100,000
Capital surplus	50,000	50,000		$30,000[a]	130,000	
				$20,000[b]		120,000
Retained earnings	10,000	10,000			20,000	20,000
Total claims on assets	$200,000	$200,000			$400,000	$400,000
			Ratios A/B			
Number of shares of stock	12,000	12,000			18,000	16,000
Book value	$10	$10	1.0			
Amount of profit after interest and taxes	$42,000	$21,000			$63,000	$63,000
Earnings per share	$3.50	$1.75	2.0		$3.50	$3.94
Price-earnings ratio	18	12				
Market price of stock	$63	$21	3.0			
Net working capital per share	$4.17	$4.17	1.0			
Dividends per share	$1.75	$0.875	2.0			
Shareholders' new EPS:						
Company A					$3.50	$3.94
Company B					$1.75	$1.31

a. 2/1 ratio basis.
b. 3/1 ratio basis.

Assume that the terms of the merger will reflect either (1) earnings or (2) market price per share. In both cases it is assumed that A is the acquiring and surviving firm. If A buys B on the basis of earnings, it exchanges half a share of A's common stock for one share of B's common stock. The total number of shares of A's common stock that will be outstanding after the acquisition is 18,000, of which 6,000 will be held by the old stockholders of B. The new earnings per share in the now larger Firm A will be the total earnings of $63,000 divided by 18,000, which equals $3.50 per share. Thus the earnings for A remain unchanged. The old shareholders of B now hold half a share of A for each share of B held before the acquisition. Hence, their equivalent earnings per share from their present holdings of A shares are $1.75, the same as before the acquisition. The stockholders of both A and B have experienced no earnings dilution or accretion.

When the terms of exchange are based on market price per share, the terms of acquisition will be the exchange of one-third share of A stock for one share of B stock. The number of A shares is increased by the 4,000 exchanged for the 12,000 shares of B. The combined earnings of $63,000 are divided by 16,000 shares to obtain an increase in A's earnings per share to $3.94, which represents an earnings accretion of 44 cents per share for the A shareholders. The old B shareholders now hold one-third share of A for each share of B held before the acquisition. Their equivalent earnings are now $3.94 divided by 3, or $1.31, representing an earnings dilution of 44 cents per share.

The adjustment to the common stock account in surviving Firm A's balance sheet reflects the fact that only 6,000 shares of A are used to buy 12,000 shares of B when the acquisition is made on the basis of earnings. The decrease of 6,000 shares times the par value of $5 requires a net debit of $30,000 to the common stock account of A ($60,000 + $60,000 − $30,000 = $90,000), with an offsetting increase of $30,000 in the capital surplus account of Firm A ($50,000 + $50,000 + $30,000 = $130,000). When the exchange is made on the basis of market values, only 4,000 shares of A are needed to acquire the 12,000 shares of B. Hence, the net decrease in the common stock account of A is $20,000, with an offsetting increase of the same amount in A's capital surplus.

The general principle is that when the terms of merger are based on the market price per share, and the price-earnings ratios of the two companies are different, earnings accretion and dilution will occur. The company with a higher P-E ratio will have earnings accretion; the company with the lower P-E ratio will suffer earnings dilution. If the sizes of the companies are greatly different, the effect on the larger company will be relatively small, whether in dilution or accretion. The effect on the smaller company will be relatively large.

Holding Companies

In 1889, New Jersey became the first state to pass a general incorporation law permitting corporations to be formed for the sole purpose of owning the stocks of other companies. This law was the origin of the holding company. The Sherman Act of 1890, which prohibits combinations or collusion in restraint of trade, gave an impetus to holding company operations as well as to outright mergers, because companies could do as one company what they were forbidden to do as separate companies.

Many of the advantages and disadvantages of holding companies are no more than the advantages and disadvantages of large-scale operations already discussed in connection with mergers and consolidations. Whether a company is organized on a divisional basis or with the divisions kept as separate companies does not affect the basic reasons for conducting a large-scale, multiproduct, multiplant operation. However, the holding company form of large-scale operations has different advantages and disadvantages from those of completely integrated divisionalized operations.

Advantages of Holding Companies

Control with Fractional Ownership. Through a holding company operation, a firm can buy 5, 10, or 50 percent of the stock of another corporation. Such fractional ownership may be sufficient to give the acquiring company effective working control of or substantial influence over the operations of the company in which it has acquired ownership. Working control is often considered to entail more than 25 percent of the common stock, but it can be as low as 10 percent if the stock is widely distributed. Also, control on a very slim margin can be held through friendship with large stockholders outside the holding company group. Sometimes holding company operations represent the initial stages of transforming an operating company into an investment company, particularly when the operating company is in a declining industry. When an industry's sales begin to decline permanently and the firm begins to liquidate its operating assets, it may use the liquid funds to invest in industries having a more favorable growth potential.

Isolation of Risks. Because the various operating companies in a holding company system are separate legal entities, the obligations of any one unit are separate from those of the other units. Catastrophic losses incurred by one unit are therefore not transmitted as claims on the assets of the other units.

Although this is the customary generalization of the nature of a holding company system, it is not completely valid. In extending credit to one of the units of a holding company system, an astute financial manager or loan officer will require a guarantee or a claim on the assets of all the elements in the system. To some degree, therefore, the assets in the various elements are joined. The advantage remains to the extent that catastrophes occurring to one unit are not transmitted to the others.

Approval Not Required. A holding company group that seeks to obtain effective working control of a number of companies may quietly purchase a portion of their stock. The operation is completely informal, and the permission or approval of the stockholders of the acquired company or companies is not required. Thus the guiding personalities in a holding company operation are not dependent on negotiations and approval of the other interest groups in order to obtain their objectives. This feature of holding company operations has, however, been limited somewhat by recent SEC actions described later in the chapter.

Disadvantages of Holding Companies

Partial Multiple Taxation. Provided the holding company owns at least 80 percent of a subsidiary's voting stock, Internal Revenue Service regulations permit the filing of consolidated returns, in which case dividends received by the parent are not taxed. However, if less than 80 percent of the stock is owned, returns cannot be consolidated, although 85 percent of the dividends received by the holding company can be deducted. With a tax rate of 46 percent, this means that the effective tax on intercorporate dividends is 6.9 percent. This partial double taxation somewhat offsets the benefits of holding company control with limited ownership, but whether the penalty of 6.9 percent of dividends received is sufficient to offset the advantages is a matter that must be decided in individual situations.[13]

Ease of Enforced Dissolution. In the case of a holding company operation that falls into disfavor with the U.S. Department of Justice, it is relatively easy to require dissolution of the relationship by disposal of stock ownership; for instance, in the late 1950s Du Pont was required to dispose of its 23 percent stock interest in General Motors Corporation, acquired in the early 1920s. Because there was no fusion between the corporations, there were no difficulties, from an operating standpoint, in requiring the separation of the two companies. However, if complete amalgamation had taken place, it would have been much more difficult to break up the company after so many years, and the likelihood of forced divestiture would have been reduced.

Risks of Excessive Pyramiding. Financial leverage effects in pyramiding magnify profits if operations are successful, but they also magnify losses. The greater the degree of pyramiding, the greater the degree of risk involved in any fluctuations in sales or earnings. This potential disadvantage of pyramiding operations through holding companies is discussed in the next section.

Leverage in Holding Companies

The problem of excessive leverage is worthy of further note, for the degree of leverage in certain past instances has been truly staggering. For example, in the 1920s, Samuel Insull and his group controlled electric utility operating companies at the bottom of a holding company pyramid by a one-twentieth of 1 percent investment. As a ratio, this represents 1/2,000. In other words, $1 of capital at the top holding company level controlled $2,000 of assets at the operating level. A similar situation existed in the railroad field. It has been stated that Robert R. Young, with an investment of $254,000, obtained control of the Allegheny system, consisting of total operating assets of $3 billion.

The nature of leverage in a holding company system and its advantages and disadvantages are illustrated by the hypothetical example developed in Table 23.8.[14] As in the previous example, although this case is hypothetical, it illustrates actual situations. Half of the operating company's Class B common stock is owned by Holding Company 1; in fact, it is the only asset of

13. The 1969 Tax Reform Law also empowers the Internal Revenue Service to prohibit the deductibility of debt issued to acquire another firm where the following conditions hold: (1) the debt is subordinated to a "significant portion" of the firm's other creditors; (2) the debt is convertible or has warrants attached; (3) the debt/assets ratio exceeds 67 percent; and (4) on a pro forma basis, the times interest earned ratio is less than 3. The IRS can use discretion in invoking this power.

14. Corrections in computations were supplied by Dr. Narendra C. Bhandari, University of Baltimore.

Table 23.8

Leverage in a Holding Company System

Operating Company			
Total assets	$2,000,000	Debt	$1,000,000
		Preferred stock	150,000
		Common stock: Class A[a]	650,000
		Common stock: Class B	200,000
	$2,000,000		$2,000,000
Holding Company 1			
Class B common stock of operating company	$100,000	Debt	$ 50,000
		Preferred stock	10,000
		Common stock: Class A[a]	30,000
		Common stock: Class B	10,000
	$100,000		$100,000
Holding Company 2			
Class B common stock of Holding Company 1	$5,000	Debt	$2,000
		Preferred stock	1,000
		Common stock: Class A[a]	1,000
		Common stock: Class B	1,000
	$5,000		$5,000

a. Class A common stock is nonvoting.

Holding Company 1. Holding Company 2 holds as its total assets half of the Class B common stock of Holding Company 1. Consequently, $1,000 of Class B common stock of Holding Company 2 controls $2 million of assets at the operating company level. Further leverage could, of course, have been postulated in this situation by setting up a third company to own Class B common stock of Holding Company 2.

Table 23.9 shows the results of holding company leverage on gains and losses at the top level. In the first column, it is assumed that the operating company earns 12 percent before taxes on its $2 million of assets; in the second column it is assumed that the return on assets is 8 percent. The operating and holding companies are the same described in Table 23.8.

A return of 12 percent on the operating assets of $2 million represents a total profit of $240,000. The debt interest of $40,000 is deducted from this amount, and the 50 percent tax rate applies to the remainder. The amount available to common stock after payment of debt interest, preferred stock dividends, and an 8 percent return to the nonvoting Class A common stock is $40,500. Assuming a $40,000 dividend payout, Holding Company 1, on the basis of its 50 percent ownership of the operating company, earns $20,000. If the same kind of analysis is followed through, the amount available to Class B common stock in Holding Company 2 is $4,455. This return is on an investment of $1,000, and it represents a return on the investment in Class B common stock of Holding Company 2 of about 445 percent. The power of leverage in a holding company system can indeed be great.

On the other hand, if a decline in revenues causes the pre-tax earnings to

Table 23.9

Results of Holding Company Leverage on Gains and Losses

	Earnings before Interest and Taxes at 12%	at 8%
Operating Company		
Earnings before interest and taxes	$240,000	$160,000
Less interest on debt (at 4%)	40,000	40,000
Earnings after interest	$200,000	$120,000
Less tax (at 50%)	100,000	60,000
After-tax earnings available for stockholders	$100,000	$ 60,000
Less: Preferred stock (at 5%)	7,500	7,500
Common stock (at 8%)	52,000	52,000
Earnings available to Class B common stock	$ 40,500	$ 500
Dividends to Class B common stock (by management decision)	40,000	500
Transferred to retained earnings	$ 500	$ 0
Holding Company 1		
Earnings before interest and taxes (received from the operating company)	$ 20,000	$ 250
Less 85% of dividends received	17,000	212
Intercorporate dividends subject to tax, before interest	$ 3,000	$ 38
Less interest on debt (at 4%)	2,000	2,000
Before-tax earnings	$ 1,000	[a]
Less tax (at 50%)	500	0
After-tax earnings	$ 500	$ 0
Amount of untaxed dividend	$ 17,000	[b]
After-tax earnings available to stockholders	$ 17,500	$ 0
Less: Preferred stock (at 5%)	500	0
Class A common stock (at 8%)	2,400	0
Earnings available to Class B common stock	$ 14,600	$ 0
Less dividends to Class B common stock (by management decision)	10,000	0
Transferred to reserves	$ 4,600	$ 0
Holding Company 2		
Earnings before interest and taxes (received from Holding Company 1)	$ 5,000	
Less 85% of dividends received	4,250	
Intercorporate dividends subject to tax, before interest	$ 750	
Less interest on debt (at 4%)	80	
Before-tax earnings	$ 670	
Less tax (at 50%)	335	
After-tax earnings	$ 335	
Amount of untaxed dividends	4,250	
After-tax earnings available to stockholders	$ 4,585	
Less: Preferred stock (at 5%)	50	
Class A common stock (at 8%)	80	
Earnings available to Class B common stock	$ 4,455	
Percentage return on Class B common stock	445.5%	

a. Loss.
b. The available amount ($250) is used up by part of the interest charges.

drop to 8 percent of the total assets of the operating company, the results will be disastrous. The amount earned under these circumstances will be $160,000. After deducting the bond interest, the amount subject to tax will be $120,000, and the tax will be $60,000. The after-tax but before-interest earnings will be $100,000. The total prior charges will be $99,500, leaving $500 available to Class B common stock. If all earnings are paid out in dividends to Class B common stock, the earnings of Holding Company 1 will be $250. This is not enough to meet the debt interest. The holding company system will thus be forced to default on the debt interest of Holding Company 1 and, of course, Holding Company 2.

This example illustrates the potential for tremendous gains in a holding company system. It also illustrates that a small earnings decline on the assets of the operating companies will be disastrous.

Tender Offers

In a tender offer, one party—generally a corporation seeking a controlling interest in another corporation—asks the stockholders of the firm it is seeking to control to submit, or tender, their shares in exchange for a specified price. The price is generally stated as so many dollars per share of acquired stock, although it can be stated in terms of shares of stock in the acquiring firm. Tender offers have been used for a number of years, but the pace greatly accelerated after 1965 and peaked in 1976 and 1977.

If one firm wishes to gain control over another, it typically seeks approval for the merger from the other firm's management and board of directors. An alternative approach is the bear hug: In this approach, a company mails a letter to the directors of the takeover target announcing the acquisition proposal and requiring the directors to make a quick decision on the bid. If approval cannot be obtained, the acquiring company can appeal directly to stockholders by means of the tender offer, unless the management and directors of the target firm hold enough stock to retain control. The technique of going directly to the shareholders has been called a Saturday night special. The term implies that a gun has been aimed at the directors, since, if the shareholders respond favorably to the tender offer, the acquiring company will gain control and have the power to replace the directors who have not cooperated in their takeover efforts.

During 1967, congressional investigations were conducted to obtain information that could be used to legislate controls over tender offers. The reasons for the investigations were (1) the frequency of tender offers, (2) the thought that the recent merger trend was leading to too much concentration in the economy, and (3) the feeling that tender offers were somehow unfair to the managements of the firms acquired through this vehicle. A law placing tender offers under full SEC jurisdiction became effective on July 29, 1968. Disclosure requirements written into the statute include the following:

1. The acquiring firm must give the management of the target firm and the SEC thirty days' notice of its intentions to make the acquisition.
2. When substantial blocks are purchased through tender offers or through

> open market purchases—that is, on the stock exchange—the beneficial owner of the stock must be disclosed, together with the name of the party putting up the money for the transaction. Usually the stock is in the "street" name of the brokerage house that acts on behalf of the real (beneficial) owner.

In addition to the new powers granted to the SEC to require disclosure of takeover intentions, certain tactics to prevent takeover can be used by the intended target. More than thirty states have adopted antitakeover laws that can delay tender offers so that an alternative can be pursued. The takeover target may also utilize other legal tactics, such as court suits alleging that antitrust laws and other regulatory guidelines are being violated. Such tactics may forestall a takeover. For example, when Anderson, Clayton, & Co. made a bid for Gerber Products Co., the latter instituted a number of legal suits. After five months of legal maneuvers on both sides, Anderson, Clayton dropped its bid in September 1977. In another case, because Marshall Field threatened antitrust actions and announced its own acquisition program, Carter, Hawley, Hale dropped its 1978 takeover attempt. The Hart-Scott-Rodino Act of 1976, amending the antitrust laws, contains a provision that requires premerger notification to the FTC of large mergers. This provision became effective in July 1978.

As a consequence of the disclosure requirements in connection with intended tender offers, competition among bidders in takeover efforts may cause the acquisition price to rise well above the market price of the stock before the initial tender offer. This can be illustrated by a few examples.

The first example is Tenneco's acquisition of Kern County Land Company. Kern was a relatively old, conservatively managed company whose assets consisted largely of oil properties and agricultural land, together with some manufacturing subsidiaries. Many informed investors believed that Kern's assets had a potential long-run value in excess of its current market price. Occidental Petroleum, a relatively aggressive company, investigated Kern's assets and decided to make a tender offer for the company. At that time, Kern's market price on the New York Stock Exchange was about $60 a share, while the price Occidental decided to offer Kern's stockholders was $83.50 a share. According to Kern's management, Occidental's management got in touch with them over a weekend and informed them that the tender offer would be made the following Monday.

Because Occidental's published statements indicated that it felt Kern's undervalued position was partly the result of an unimaginative management, Kern's management anticipated being replaced in the event that Occidental effected the takeover. Naturally, they resisted the takeover. Kern's president wrote a letter to stockholders condemning the merger and published the letter as an advertisement in the *Wall Street Journal.* His position was that Kern's stock was certainly valuable and that it was worth more than had been offered by Occidental Petroleum.

How would Kern County's stockholders react to this exchange? In the first place, the stock had been selling at about $60 a share, and now they were offered $83.50 a share. With this differential, stockholders would certainly accept the tender unless Kern's management could do something to keep the price above $83.50. What Kern did was to obtain "marriage proposals" from a number of other companies. Kern's management reported to the newspapers—while Occidental's tender offer was still outstanding—that it had received a number of proposals calling for the purchase of Kern's stock at a price substantially in excess of $83.50.

The offer Kern's management finally accepted—and presumably the one giving Kern's stockholders the highest price—was from Tenneco Corporation. Tenneco offered one share of a new $5.50 convertible preferred stock for each share of Kern's stock. At the time of Tenneco's offer, the market value of this convertible preferred was estimated at about $105 a share. Further, Kern's stockholders would not have to pay capital gains tax on this stock at the time of the exchange. (Had they accepted Occidental's offer, the difference between $83.50 and the cost of their stock would be taxable income to Kern's stockholders.) According to newspaper reports, Tenneco planned to keep Kern's existing management after the merger was completed. When the Kern-Tenneco merger was completed, Tenneco owned the Kern stock and thus became a holding company, with Kern being one of its operating subsidiaries.

If the takeover company bids too low initially, it may stimulate a bidding contest. But if it makes the initial bid at a substantial premium over the prevailing market price of the takeover target, it may be criticized by its stockholders for having paid an excessive amount. Both situations have occurred, so a difficult challenge is posed in formulating the right takeover bid. Examples are provided by dramatic episodes that occurred during 1977.

United Technologies (UT) bid $42 per share in March 1977 for Babcock & Wilcox (BW), whose common stock was then selling for less than $35 per share. UT is a producer of aircraft engines, rocket motors and engines, automotive and space equipment, helicopters, elevators, escalators, and other industrial equipment. BW was mainly in steam generating equipment, such as the massive boilers used in both fossil fuel and nuclear powered turbine generator systems. In addition, it produced pollution control equipment and other equipment for the handling and transfer of heat. UT's 1976 sales were $5.2 billion, while BW's 1976 sales were $1.7 billion. Shortly after UT's tender offer, J. Ray McDermott & Co. (JRM) entered the contest. JRM, smaller than either of the other two companies, with sales of $1.2 billion in 1976, was mainly in the engineering, fabrication, and installation of facilities for the production of oil and gas. By May 1977, JRM announced that it had bought nearly 9 percent of BW's stock on the open market. BW proceeded to take legal action against both takeover rivals. In August 1977, UT upped its bid for BW to $48. Shortly thereafter, JRM bid $55, which the BW directors urged its shareholders to accept. A complicated series of counterbids ensued, with

JRM winning the competition for a final price of $65 a share, nearly double the pre-tender market price.

In an example of a bid that might have been too high, Kennecott Copper was motivated by the fear of becoming a takeover target itself. In accordance with a requirement by the FTC of divestiture of Peabody Coal, Kennecott had agreed to a sale to a group of companies for $1.2 billion to be paid in installments. Since Kennecott was in the process of becoming cash rich as it received installment payments for the purchase price, it wanted to utilize the cash. It sought to avoid being acquired by a company that might use debt to buy Kennecott and then use the cash flowing into Kennecott to pay off the debt. Kennecott is an integrated producer of metals (mainly copper) and mineral products with 1976 sales of slightly under $1 billion.

Eaton Corporation (formerly Eaton Yale & Towne), with 1976 revenues of $1.8 billion, had, in early November 1977, made an offer of $47 per share for the stock of the Carborundum Company, then selling at $33.25 per share. Eaton produces locks and other security systems as well as automotive parts and components. Carborundum, a leading producer of carbon products, other abrasives, and refractory and electric products, had 1976 revenues of $614 million. In mid-November 1977, Kennecott made an offer to Carborundum of $66 per share. On November 17, 1977, it was announced that the directors of both companies had unanimously approved the offer. Some stockholders stated that they were stunned by this "squandering of Kennecott's cash." Others praised Kennecott for avoiding the "ridiculous newspaper auction that marked the Babcock & Wilcox battle." The reader is invited to judge the appropriateness of the $66 price paid by Kennecott.

The Economic Setting of Current Merger Activity

It is of interest to consider some of the factors in the economic environment that have stimulated an increase in merger activity. After a period of relative stability in the price level between 1958 and 1966, the United States has experienced persistent inflation, with the Wholesale Price Index increasing at almost 10 percent per year since 1965. Also, the rate of growth and productivity in the economy has fallen from $3\frac{1}{2}$ or 4 percent to under 2 percent per annum since the onset of inflation after 1965. This unfavorable economic performance is partially explained by the sharp rise in the prices of energy and other raw materials. In addition, the general political and economic environment in the world has become uncertain. The greater uncertainty of the economic environment has caused a rise in the risk component of discount factors. Data on the factors involved here are presented in Table 23.10. Two measures of risk premiums are presented. One is the earnings price ratios on common stock compared with the yield on government securities. This differential increased by 1.25 percentage points between the period of the early 1960s and the mid-1970s. Another measure of risk is the Baa bond yield rate

Table 23.10

Rise in the Risk Component of Discount Factors

	Earnings to Price Ratios on Common Stock (Percent)	Yield on Treasury Securities (Percent)	Yield on Baa Corporate Bonds (Percent)
1960–1964	5.43	4.03	5.00
1974–1978	10.45	7.80	9.66

	1960–1964	1974–1978	Change
E-P ratios minus yield on government securities	1.40	2.65	+1.25
Baa bond yield minus yield on government bonds	0.97	1.86	+0.89
	Average		+1.07

Source: President's Council of Economic Advisers, *Economic Report of the President* (Washington, D.C.: Government Printing Office, January 1979), pp. 258, 285.

as compared with the yield on government bonds. This differential rose by almost a percentage point in the same period.

Regardless of whether profitability has decreased during the period of inflation or whether risk premiums have increased or some combination of the two have been operating together, there is less disagreement on the result. What appears definitely to have occurred is a significant shift in the ratio of market values to replacement values of nonfinancial corporations during the period of inflation. This ratio has been referred to as *Tobin's q-ratio.* During the period of price stability in the years 1958 to 1965, the q-ratio rose from 0.681 in the first quarter of 1958 to 1.140 during the fourth quarter of 1965. Thereafter it began to decline during the period of inflation. By 1977 the q-ratio had fallen well below 0.69. The rise in the q-ratio during the period 1958 to 1965 represented an increase of over 67 percent. The ratio then experienced a decline of a comparable order of magnitude. The main explanatory influence in the movement of the q-ratio is, of course, the changes in the market values that make up in the numerator of the ratio. The decline in the q-ratio would be consistent with a decline in real earnings rates, a rise in the required yields on equities, or some combination of both that may have appeared during the period of inflation.

The data suggest the rough approximation that the ratio of the market value of the assets of nonfinancial corporations to their replacement values fell to about 70 percent in 1977–1978. These relationships provide some background for perspectives on the current merger movement. In short, the period of inflation has brought about a significant disparity between prospective returns from new real investments versus prospective returns from investments that represent purchases of other companies. Prospective net present values from new investments appear to be negative. Prospective net present values from purchases of other companies appear to be positive. Many articles in the financial press have observed that a basic reason for the current merger activity stems from the divergence between prospective returns from internal investments compared with prospective returns from acquisitions: It is cheaper to buy another company to obtain physical assets than to buy the physical assets directly. Still this is a somewhat unsatisfactory line of reasoning because it does not provide a good explanation of how such a disparity can persist between prospective returns in asset markets and prospective returns in the financial markets in which the mergers take place.

Summary

Growth is vital to the well-being of a firm. Without it the firm cannot attract able management because it cannot give recognition in promotions and challenging creative activity. Mergers have played an important part in the growth of firms, and since financial managers are required both to appraise the desirability of a prospective merger and to participate in evaluating the respective companies involved in it, the chapter has been devoted to the terms of merger decisions.

The most important term to be negotiated in a merger arrangement is the price the acquiring firm will pay for the acquired one. The most important *quantitative* factors influencing the terms of a merger are (1) current earnings, (2) current market prices, (3) book values, and (4) net working capital. Qualitative considerations may suggest that *synergistic,* or "two-plus-two-equals-five," effects may be present to an extent sufficient to warrant paying more for the acquired firm than the quantitative factors suggest. Recently, the current replacement values of corporate assets have exceeded the market values of related corporate securities.

In mergers, one firm disappears. However, an alternative is for one firm to buy all or a majority of the common stock of another and to run the acquired firm as an operating subsidiary. When this occurs, the acquiring firm is said to be a *holding company.* A number of advantages arise when a holding company is formed, among them:

1. It may be possible to control the acquired firm with a smaller investment than necessary for a merger.
2. Each firm in a holding company is a separate legal entity, and the obligations of any unit are separate from the obligations of the other units.
3. Stockholder approval is required before a merger can take place. This is not necessary in a holding company situation.

There are also some disadvantages to holding companies, among them:

1. If the holding company does not own 80 percent of the subsidiary's stock and does not file consolidated tax returns, it is subject to taxes on 15 percent of the dividends received from the subsidiary.
2. The leverage effects possible in holding companies can subject the company to magnification of earnings fluctuations and related risks.

3. The antitrust division of the U.S. Department of Justice can much more easily force the breakup of a holding company situation than it can bring about the dissolution of two completely merged firms.

Questions

23.1 What are some of the potential benefits that can be expected by a firm that merges with a company in a different industry?

23.2 Distinguish between a holding company and an operating company. Give an example of each.

23.3 Which appears to be riskier—the use of debt in the holding company's capital structure or the use of debt in the operating company's capital structure? Explain.

23.4 Is the public interest served by an increase in merger activity? Give both pro and con arguments.

23.5 Is the book value of a company's assets considered the absolute minimum price to be paid for a firm? Explain. Is there any value that qualifies as an absolute minimum? Explain.

23.6 Discuss the situation where Midwest Motors calls off merger negotiations with American Data Labs because the latter's stock price is overvalued. What assumption concerning dilution is implicit in the above situation?

23.7 There are many methods by which a company can raise additional capital. Can a merger be considered a means of raising additional equity capital? Explain.

23.8 A particularly difficult problem regarding business combinations has been whether to treat the new company as a purchase or as a pooling of interests.

a. What criteria can be used to differentiate between these two forms of business combinations?

b. As a stockholder in one of the firms, would you prefer a purchase or a pooling arrangement? Explain.

c. Which combination would you prefer if you were a high-ranking manager in one of the firms?

23.9 Are the negotiations for merger agreements more difficult if the firms are in different industries or in the same industry? If they are about the same size or quite different in size? If the ages of the firms are about the same or if they are very different? Explain.

23.10 How would the existence of long-term debt in a company's financial structure affect its valuation for merger purposes? Could the same be said for any debt account regardless of its maturity? Explain.

23.11 During the merger activity of 1976–1980, cash was used by the acquiring company to a much greater extent than during the height of the conglomerate merger activity during 1967–1969. What are some reasons for the relatively greater use of cash in the acquisitions of the most recent period?

Problems

23.1 The Brunner Company has agreed to merge with the Powell Company. The shareholders of Powell have agreed to accept half a share of Brunner for each of their Powell shares. The new company will have a P-E ratio of 40. Following is additional information about the merging companies.

	Brunner	Powell
P-E ratio	56	7
Shares outstanding	2,500,000	500,000
Earnings	$1,750,000	$700,000
Earnings per share	$.70	$1.40
Market value per share	$39.20	$9.80

a. After Brunner and Powell merge, what will the new price per share be?
b. Calculate the dollar and percent accretion in EPS for Brunner.
c. Calculate the dollar and percent dilution in EPS for Powell.
d. What is the effect on market price for each?

23.2 The Morris Company has agreed to merge with the Kingston Company. The following is information about the two companies prior to their merger:

	Kingston	Morris
Total earnings	$1,000,000	$750,000
Shares outstanding	1,000,000	250,000
P-E ratio	20 times	18 times

a. The Kingston Company will buy the Morris Company with a 4-for-1 exchange of stock. Combined earnings will remain at the premerger level. What will be the effect on EPS for premerger Kingston stockholders?
b. What will be the effect on EPS for the Morris Company stockholders?
c. Assuming that Kingston has been growing at 20 percent a year and Morris at 5 percent, what is the expected growth rate? (There are no synergistic effects.)

23.3 Melton Company and Kelly Company merge on the basis of market values. Melton Company acquires Kelly Company with a three-for-one exchange of stock. Following are data for the two companies:

	Melton	Kelly
Total earnings	$100,000,000	$1,000,000
Shares outstanding	80,000,000	800,000
Expected growth rate in earnings	10%	25%
P-E ratio	8 times	24 times

a. What is the new EPS for the premerger Melton and Kelly stockholders?
b. If Melton's P-E ratio rises to 15, what is its new market price?
c. What merger concept does this problem illustrate?

23.4 Hempler Company merges with Rider Company on the basis of market values. Hempler pays one share of convertible preferred stock with a par value of $100 and an interest rate of 6 percent (convertible into Hempler's common stock at two shares) for each four shares of Rider Company. Following are more data:

	Hempler	Rider
Total earnings	$1,000,000	$400,000
Common shares outstanding	200,000	80,000
Expected growth rate in earnings	18%	6%
Dividends per share	$1.80	$1.80
P-E ratio	12 times	6 times
Dividend yield	3%	6%

a. Is the dividend return to Rider shareholders changed?
b. 1. What are the new EPS and market price of Hempler if the P-E ratio remains at 12 times?
   2. What are the new EPS and market price on a fully diluted basis?
c. Why might Rider Company shareholders agree to the acquisition?

23.5 You are given the following balance sheets:

Rocky Mountain Services Company Consolidated Balance Sheet (Millions of Dollars)

Cash	$1,500	Borrowings	$1,125
Other current assets	1,125	Common stock	1,875
Net property	1,875	Retained earnings	1,500
Total assets	$4,500	Total claims on assets	$4,500

White Lighting Company Balance Sheet (Millions of Dollars)

Cash	$375	Net worth	$750
Net property	375		
Total assets	$750	Total net worth	$750

a. The holding company, Rocky Mountain, buys the operating company, White Lighting, with "free" cash of $750 million. Show the new consolidated balance sheet for Rocky Mountain after the acquisition.
b. Instead of buying White Lighting, Rocky Mountain buys Conner Company with free cash of $1.125 billion. Conner's balance sheet follows:

Conner Company Balance Sheet (Millions of Dollars)

Cash	$ 750	Borrowings	$ 750
Net property	1,125	Net worth	1,125
Total assets	$1,875	Total claims on assets	$1,875

Show the new consolidated balance sheet for Rocky Mountain after acquisition of Conner.

c. What are the implications of your consolidated balance sheets for measuring the growth of firms resulting from acquisitions?

23.6 Southern Realty Company is a holding company owning the entire common stock of Bryant Company and Sunther Company. The balance sheet as of December 31, 1980, for each subsidiary is identical with the following one:

Balance Sheet as of December 31, 1980 (Millions of Dollars)

Current assets	$ 7.50	Current liabilities	$ 1.25
Fixed assets, net	5.00	First mortgage bonds (at 9%)	2.50
		Preferred stock (at 7%)	2.50
		Common stock	5.00
		Retained earnings	1.25
Total assets	$12.50	Total claims on assets	$12.50

Each operating company earns $1.183 million annually before taxes and before interest and preferred dividends. A 40 percent tax rate is assumed.

a. What is the annual rate of return on each company's net worth (common stock plus retained earnings)?

b. Construct a balance sheet for Southern Realty Company based on the following assumptions: (1) The only asset of the holding company is the common stock of the two subsidiaries, carried at par (not book) value. (2) The holding company has $1.2 million of 8 percent coupon debt and $2.8 million of 6 percent preferred stock.

23.7 To meet its growth objectives, Proxmore Manufacturing is planning to expand by acquisition. It has two potential candidates, Apex Corporation and Allied Engineering. The latest balance sheet for Proxmore and the latest income statements for Apex and Allied are given below, along with certain other statistical information. Both Apex and Allied have debt of $50 million, at a before-tax cost of 10 percent. Assume that the weighted average cost of capital is 10 percent for Proxmore, 8 percent for Apex, and 12 percent for Allied. Assume also that the effective tax rate for all three companies is 40 percent.

Proxmore Manufacturing Balance Sheet as of December 31, 1980 (Thousands of Dollars)

Current assets	$125,000	Current liabilities	$ 50,000
Net fixed assets	150,000	Long-term debt (at 10%)	75,000
		Common equity	150,000
Total	$275,000	Total	$275,000

Income Statement for the Year Ending December 31, 1980 (Thousands of Dollars)

	Apex	Allied
NOI	$20,000	$30,000
Interest on debt (at 10%)	5,000	5,000
Earnings before taxes	15,000	25,000
Less tax at 40%	6,000	10,000
Net income	$ 9,000	$15,000

	NOI	EPS	Growth Rate (Percent)	Market Price	Shares Outstanding
Proxmore	$30M	$3.00	6.0	$45	5,000,000
Apex	20M	4.50	7.5	50	2,000,000
Allied	30M	5.00	2.0	42	3,000,000

a. Based on the above information, determine an appropriate price for Proxmore to pay for each acquisition candidate. Proxmore uses its own weighted average cost of capital in computing the value of an acquisition candidate by capitalizing NOI after tax.

b. Compute the price of each acquisition candidate, using each candidate's own weighted average cost of capital as the capitalization rate.

c. Which capitalization rate is most appropriate in determining the value of an acquisition candidate?

d. Given that Proxmore is forced to make a tender offer for the common stock of each of the two candidates at 20 percent above their current market value, compute the following:
   1. The exchange ratio based on a stock offering.
   2. Proxmore's new earnings growth rate for next year after the acquisition of each company—Apex and Allied.
   3. Proxmore's new EPS following each acquisition.

e. Chart Proxmore's growth in EPS for the next ten years with and without each acquisition to illustrate the dilution effect of the purchase price computed in Part d.

23.8 You are given the following data on two companies:

	Company I	Company II	Adjustments	Consolidated Statement
Current assets	$56,000	$56,000		______
Fixed assets	34,000	34,000		______
Total assets	$90,000	$90,000		______
Current liabilities	$31,000	$31,000		______
Long-term debt	19,000	19,000		______
Total debt, 5%[a]	$50,000	$50,000		______
Common stock, par value $4	24,000	24,000	______	______
Capital surplus	11,000	11,000	______	______
Retained earnings	5,000	5,000	______	______
Total claims on assets	$90,000	$90,000		______

			Ratios	
1. Number of shares of stock	6,000	6,000		1. ______
2. Book value per share	______	______	1. ______	2. ______
3. Amount of profit before interest and taxes[b]	$24,583	$12,917		3. ______
4. Earnings per share	______	______	2. ______	4. ______
5. Price-earnings ratio	22.6	12		
6. Market price of stock	______	______	3. ______	
7. Working capital per share	______	______	4. ______	
8. Dividends per share, 50% payout	______	______	5. ______	
9. Exchange ratio	______	______	6. ______ (I/II)	
10. Equivalent earnings per old share	______	______		

a. Average rate on interest bearing and non–interest bearing debt combined.
b. Assume a 40 percent tax rate.

a. In your judgment, what would be a reasonable basis for determining the terms at which shares in Company I and in Company II would be exchanged for shares in a new company, III? What exchange ratio would you recommend and why?
b. Use the market price of stock relation as the basis for the terms of exchange of stock in the old company for stock in the new company (two shares of III for one share of I, and one-half share of III for one share of II). Then complete the calculations for filling in all the blank spaces, including the adjustments for making the consolidated statement. Treat this problem as a situation that the SEC and accountants would refer to as a pooling of interests.

23.9 The Vertical Company has just purchased the Horizontal Company under an arrangement known as a purchase. The purchase was made by stock in a settlement based exactly on the indicated market prices of the two firms. The data on the two companies are given below.

a. Fill in the blank spaces and complete the adjustments and pro forma balance sheet columns and show the journal entries for the stock purchase. Give an explanation for your entries.
b. Calculate earnings dilution or accretion for both companies on the assumption that total earnings are unchanged.
c. Calculate the earnings dilution or accretion on the assumption that the return on combined tangible assets rises to 20 percent after interest and taxes.
d. Comment on your findings.

	Vertical	Horizontal	Adjustments Debits	Adjustments Credits	Pro Forma Balance Sheet
Current assets	$ 450,000	$ 7,000			
Other assets	150,000	5,000			
Fixed assets	400,000	8,000			
Intangibles (goodwill)					
Total assets	$1,000,000	$20,000			
Current liabilities	$ 200,000	$ 8,000			
Long-term debt	150,000				
Common stock	200,000	2,000			
Capital surplus	150,000				
Retained earnings	300,000	10,000			
Total claims	$1,000,000	$20,000			
Par value	$4.00	$0.50			
Number of shares	______	______			
Total earnings available to common	$ 125,000	$ 8,000			
Book value	______	______			
Earnings per share	______	______			
Price-earnings ratio	10 times	25 times			
Market value per share	______	______			

23.10 Every merger agreement is subject to negotiation between the companies involved. One significant indicator of the compensation received by the acquired company is the market price of each company's stock in relation to the merger terms. Some actual merger data are given in the table.

Calculate the percent premium, or discount, received by the acquired company, using market prices as the criteria. Compare the results of your calculations on the basis of the stock prices of the two previous quarters with that of your results on the basis of the prices immediately preceding the merger. Which is the proper measure of the actual discount or premium received: the one indicated by the earlier stock prices or the one indicated by the stock prices immediately preceding the merger? Explain.

Company		Terms	Market Price Two Quarters before Merger		Market Price Immediately Preceding Merger	
			A	B	A	B
1	A Celanese Corporation B Champlain Oil	2 shares of Celanese for every 3 shares of Champlain	62	34	67	42
2	A Cities Service Company B Tennessee Corporation	0.9 shares (2.25 pref.) for each Tenn. Corp. share (common)	65	48	61	55
3	A Ford Motor Company B Philco Corporation	1 share of Ford for every 4½ shares of Philco	81	22	113	25
4	A General Telephone B Sylvania Electric	Share-for-share basis	52	46	69	69

Selected References

Adler, Michael, and Dumas, Bernard. "Optimal International Acquisitions." *Journal of Finance* 30 (March 1975), pp. 1–19.

Alberts, William W., and Segall, Joel E., eds. *The Corporate Merger.* Chicago: University of Chicago Press, 1966.

Appleyard, A. R., and Yarrow, G. K. "The Relationship between Take-over Activity and Share Valuation." *Journal of Finance* 30 (December 1975), pp. 1239–1249.

Austin, Douglas V. "The Financial Management of Tender Offer Takeovers." *Financial Management* 3 (Spring 1974), pp. 37–43.

Belkaoui, Ahmed. "Financial Ratios as Predictors of Canadian Takeovers." *Journal of Business Finance and Accounting* 5 (Spring 1978), pp. 93–107.

Boczar, Gregory E. "Market Characteristics and Multibank Holding Company Acquisitions." *Journal of Finance* 32 (March 1977), pp. 131–146.

Bradley, James W., and Korn, Donald H. "Acquisition and Merger Trends." *Financial Analysts' Journal* 33 (November–December 1977), pp. 65–70.

Brenner, Menachem, and Downes, David H. "A Critical Evaluation of the Measurement of Conglomerate Performance Using the Capital Asset Pricing Model." *Review of Economics and Statistics* 61 (May 1979), pp. 292–296.

Buckley, Adrian. "A Review of Acquisition Valuation Models—A Comment." *Journal of Business Finance and Accounting* 2 (Spring 1975), pp. 147–152.

Cheney, Richard E. "Remedies for Tender-Offer Anxiety." *Financial Executive* 43 (August 1975), pp. 16–19.

———. "What's New on the Corporate Takeover Scene." *Financial Executive* 40 (April 1972), pp. 18–21.

Conn, Robert L., and Nielsen, James F. "An Empirical Test of the Larson-Gonedes Exchange Ratio Determination Model." *Journal of Finance* 32 (June 1977), pp. 749–759.

Davey, Patrick J. "Defenses against Unnegotiated Cash Tender Offers." *Conference Board Report No. 726.* New York: Conference Board, 1977, pp. 1–29.

Dodd, Peter, and Ruback, Richard. "Tender Offers and Stockholder Returns: An Empirical Analysis." *Journal of Financial Economics* 5 (December 1977), pp. 351–373.

Ellert, James C. "Mergers, Antitrust Law Enforcement and Stockholder Returns." *Journal of Finance* 31 (May 1976), pp. 715–732.

Firth, Michael. "The Profitability of Takeovers and Mergers." *Economic Journal* 89 (June 1979), pp. 316–328.

———. "Synergism in Mergers: Some British Results." *Journal of Finance* 33 (May 1978), pp. 670–672.

Folz, David F., and Weston, J. Fred. "Looking Ahead in Evaluating Proposed Mergers." *NAA Bulletin* 43 (April 1962), pp. 17–27.

Franks, J. R.; Broyles, J. E.; and Hecht, M. J. "An Industry Study of the Profitability of Mergers in the United Kingdom." *Journal of Finance* 32 (December 1977), pp. 1513–1525.

Gahlon, James M., and Stover, Roger D. "Diversification, Financial Leverage, and Conglomerate Systematic Risk." *Journal of Financial and Quantitative Analysis* 14 (December 1979), pp. 999–1013.

Gaskill, William J. "Are You Ready for the New Merger Boom?" *Financial Executive* 42 (September 1974), pp. 38–41.

Gort, Michael. *Diversification and Integration in American Industry.* Princeton, N.J.: Princeton University Press, 1962.

Gort, Michael, and Hogarty, Thomas E. "New Evidence on Mergers." *Journal of Law and Economics* 13 (April 1970), pp. 167–184.

Goudzwaard, Maurice B. "Conglomerate Mergers, Convertibles, and Cash Dividends." *Quarterly Review of Economics and Business* 9 (Spring 1969), pp. 53–62.

Haugen, Robert A., and Langetieg, Terence C. "An Empirical Test for Synergism in Merger." *Journal of Finance* 30 (June 1975), pp. 1003–1014.

Hayes, Samuel L., III, and Taussig, Russell A. "Tactics in Cash Takeover Bids." *Harvard Business Review* 45 (March–April 1967), pp. 135–148.

Hexter, Richard M. "How to Sell Your Company." *Harvard Business Review* 46 (May–June 1968), pp. 71–77.

Higgins, Robert C., and Schall, Lawrence D. "Corporate Bankruptcy and Conglomerate Merger." *Journal of Finance* 30 (March 1975), pp. 93–113.

Hogarty, Thomas F. "The Profitability of Corporate Mergers." *Journal of Business* 44 (July 1970), pp. 317–327.

Kelly, Eamon M. *The Profitability of Growth through Mergers.* University Park, Pa.: Pennsylvania State University, 1967.

Kim, E. Han, and McConnell, John J. "Corporate Merger and the Co-insurance of Corporate Debt." *Journal of Finance* 32 (May 1977), pp. 349–363.

Kitching, John. "Winning and Losing with European Acquisitions." *Harvard Business Review* 52 (March–April 1974), pp. 124–136.

Kummer, Donald R., and Hoffmeister, J. Ronald. "Valuation Consequences of Cash Tender Offers." *Journal of Finance* 33 (May 1978), pp. 505–516.

Langetieg, Terence C. "An Application of a Three-Factor Performance Index to Measure Stockholder Gains from Merger." *Journal of Financial Economics* 6 (December 1978), pp. 365–384.

Larson, Kermit D., and Gonedes, Nicholas J. "Business Combinations: An Exchange-Ratio Determination Model." *Accounting Review* 44 (October 1969), pp. 720–728.

Lee, Li Way. "Co-insurance and Conglomerate Merger." *Journal of Finance* 32 (December 1977), pp. 1527–1537.

Lev, Baruch, and Mandelker, Gershon. "The Microeconomic Consequences of Corporate Mergers." *Journal of Business* 45 (January 1972), pp. 85–104.

Lewellen, Wilbur G. "A Pure Financial Rationale for the Conglomerate Merger." *Journal of Finance* 26 (May 1971), pp. 521–537.

Lorie, J. H., and Halpern, P. "Conglomerates: The Rhetoric and the Evidence." *Journal of Law and Economics* 13 (April 1970), pp. 149–166.

MacDougal, Gary E., and Malek, Fred V. "Master Plan for Merger Negotiations." *Harvard Business Review* 48 (January–February 1970), pp. 71–82.

Mandelker, Gershon. "Risk and Return: The Case of Merging Firms." *Journal of Financial Economics* 1 (December 1974), pp. 303–336.

Mason, R. Hal, and Goudzwaard, Maurice B. "Performance of Conglomerate Firms: A Portfolio Approach." *Journal of Finance* 31 (March 1976), pp. 39–48.

Mead, Walter J. "Instantaneous Merger Profit as a Conglomerate Merger Motive." *Western Economic Review* 7 (December 1969), pp. 295–306.

Melicher, Ronald W. "Financing with Convertible Preferred Stock: Comment." *Journal of Finance* 25 (March 1971), pp. 144–147.

Melicher, Ronald W., and Harter, Thomas R. "Stock Price Movements of Firms Engaging in Large Acquisitions." *Journal of Financial and Quantitative Analysis* 7 (March 1972), pp. 1469–1475.

Melicher, Ronald W., and Rush, David F. "Evidence on the Acquisition-Related Performance of Conglomerate Firms." *Journal of Finance* 29 (March 1974), pp. 141–149.

Mueller, Dennis C. "The Effects of Conglomerate Mergers: A Survey of the Empirical Evidence." *Journal of Banking and Finance* 1 (December 1977), pp. 315–347.

———. "A Theory of Conglomerate Mergers." *Quarterly Journal of Economics* 83 (November 1969), pp. 643–659.

Reid, Samuel Richardson. *Mergers, Managers, and the Economy.* New York: McGraw-Hill, 1968.

Reinhardt, Uwe E. *Mergers and Consolidations: A Corporate-Finance Approach.* Morristown, N.J.: General Learning Press, 1972.

Reum, W. Robert, and Steele, Thomas A., III. "Contingent Payouts Cut Acquisition Risks." *Harvard Business Review* 48 (March–April 1970), pp. 83–91.

Rockwell, Willard F., Jr. "How to Acquire a Company." *Harvard Business Review* 46 (May–June 1968), pp. 121–132.

Salter, Malcolm S., and Weinhold, Wolf A. "Diversification via Acquisition: Creating Value." *Harvard Business Review* 56 (July–August 1978), pp. 166–176.

Shad, John S. R. "The Financial Realities of Mergers." *Harvard Business Review* 47 (November–December 1969), pp. 133–146.

Shick, Richard A. "The Analysis of Mergers and Acquisitions." *Journal of Finance* 27 (May 1972), pp. 495–502.

Shick, Richard A., and Jen, Frank C. "Merger Benefits to Shareholders of Acquiring Firms." *Financial Management* 3 (Winter 1974), pp. 45–53.

Shrieves, Ronald E., and Stevens, Donald L. "Bankruptcy Avoidance as a Motive for Merger." *Journal of Financial and Quantitative Analysis* 14 (September 1979), pp. 501–515.

Silberman, Irwin H. "A Note on Merger Valuation." *Journal of Finance* 23 (June 1968), pp. 528–534.

Smith, Keith V., and Weston, J. Fred. "Further Evaluation of Conglomerate Performance," *Journal of Business Research* 5 no. 1 (1977), pp. 5–14.

Sprecher, C. Ronald. "A Note on Financing Mergers with Convertible Preferred Stock." *Journal of Finance* 26 (June 1971), pp. 683–686.

Stapleton, R. C. "The Acquisition Decision as a Capital Budgeting Problem." *Journal of Business Finance and Accounting* 2 (Summer 1975), pp. 187–202.

Troubh, Raymond S. "Purchased Affection: A Primer on Cash Tender Offers." *Harvard Business Review* 54 (July–August 1976), pp. 79–91.

Vancil, Richard F., and Lorange, Peter. "Strategic Planning in Diversified Companies." *Harvard Business Review* 53 (January–February 1975), pp. 81–90.

Weston, J. Fred. *The Role of Mergers in the Growth of Large Firms.* Berkeley: University of California Press, 1953.

Weston, J. Fred, and Mansinghka, Surendra K. "Tests of the Efficiency of Conglomerate Firms." *Journal of Finance* 26 (September 1971), pp. 919–936.

Weston, J. Fred, and Peltzman, Sam, eds. *Public Policy toward Mergers.* Pacific Palisades, Calif.: Goodyear, 1969.

Weston, J. Fred; Smith, Keith V.; and Shrieves, Ronald E. "Conglomerate Performance Using the Capital Asset Pricing Model." *Review of Economics and Statistics* 54 (November 1972), pp. 357–363.

Woods, Donald H., and Caverly, Thomas A. "Development of a Linear Programming Model for the Analysis of Merger/Acquisition Situations." *Journal of Financial and Quantitative Analysis* 4 (January 1970), pp. 627–642.

Wyatt, Arthur R., and Kieso, Donald E. *Business Combinations: Planning and Action.* Scranton, Pa.: International Textbook, 1969.

24
Reorganization and Bankruptcy

Thus far the text has dealt with issues associated mainly with the growing, successful enterprise. Not all businesses are so fortunate, however; so this chapter will examine financial difficulties—their causes and their possible remedies. The material is significant for the financial manager of successful, as well as potentially unsuccessful, firms. The successful firm's financial manager must know the firm's rights and remedies as a creditor and must participate effectively in efforts to collect from financially distressed debtors. The financial manager of a less successful firm must know how to handle the firm's affairs if financial difficulties arise. Such understanding can often mean the difference between loss of ownership of the firm and rehabilitation of the firm as a going enterprise.

In the United States a new bankruptcy law was enacted by Congress in 1978 to become effective October 1, 1979. A major change in the new bankruptcy law is to provide for combining the procedures of Chapters X and XI from previous bankruptcy laws into a single procedure. To understand the new bankruptcy law therefore requires a review of the previous procedures, which were modified and combined.

Some dramatic major bankruptcies have occurred in recent years. Most notable was the huge Penn Central Company, which involved total assets at the end of 1969 of almost $7 billion and total debts outstanding of over $4 billion. The W. T. Grant bankruptcy was also of substantial magnitude, involving $1.2 billion of assets. A number of bankruptcies have raised questions of impropriety. Illustrative is the Equity Funding Company bankruptcy, which involved writing up fictitious life insurance.

The instabilities of the early 1970s involved large commercial banks as well as nonfinancial enterprises. The Franklin National Bank, which failed in 1974, had reached an asset size of $5 billion and was the twentieth largest of the nation's more than 14,000 FDIC-insured banks. In the same year, the Beverly Hills Bancorp went into bankruptcy. Earlier, the U.S. National Bank of San Diego had to be taken over by the FDIC, and questions of fraud were raised in connection with its prior management. Even large foreign banks ran into difficulties in 1974. The failure of Bankhaus I. D. Herstatt, one of Germany's largest private banks, sent shock waves through the international money markets.

Failure

Failure can be defined in several ways, and some failures do not necessarily result in the collapse and dissolution of a firm.

Economic Failure

Failure in an economic sense usually signifies that a firm's revenues do not cover its costs. It can also mean that the rate of earnings on its historical cost of investment is less than the firm's cost of capital. It can even mean that the firm's actual returns have fallen below its expected returns. There is no consensus on the definition of failure in an economic sense.

Financial Failure

Although *financial failure* is a less ambiguous term than *economic failure,* it has two generally recognized aspects. A firm can be considered a failure if it cannot meet its current obligations as they fall due, even though its total assets may exceed its total liabilities. This is defined as *technical insolvency.* A firm is a failure, or *bankrupt,* if its total liabilities exceed a fair valuation of its total assets (that is, if the "real" net worth of the firm is negative).

Hereafter, when the word *failure* is used, it will mean both technical insolvency and bankruptcy.

Causes of Failures

Different studies assign the causes of failure to different factors. Dun & Bradstreet compilations assign these causes as follows.

Cause of Failure		Percentage of Total
Lack of experience in the line		15.6
Lack of managerial experience		14.1
Unbalanced experience in sales, finance, production, and the like		22.3
Management incompetence		40.7
Fraud		0.9
Disaster		0.9
Neglect		1.9
Reason unknown		3.6
	Total	100.0

Source: Data from *The Business Failure Record, 1974* (New York: Dun & Bradstreet, 1975), p. 12. Used by permission of Dun & Bradstreet.

A number of other studies of failures can be generalized into the following groups.[1]

Cause of Failure	Percentage of Total
Unfavorable industry trends	20
Management incompetence	60
Catastrophes	10
Miscellaneous	10

Both classifications include the effects of recessions but place the resulting failures in the category of managerial incompetence. This method is logical; managements should be prepared to operate in environments in which recessions occur and should frame their policies to cope with downturns as well as to benefit from business upswings. Managements also should anticipate unfavorable industry trends.

A number of financial remedies are available to management when it becomes aware of the imminence or occurrence of insolvency. These remedies are described in subsequent sections.

The Failure Record[2]

How widespread is business failure? Is it a rare phenomenon, or does it occur fairly often? In recent times, about ten thousand to twelve thousand firms a year have failed, but they represent less than one-half of 1 percent of all business firms. The failure rate rises during recession periods, when the economy is weakened and credit is tightened. (Among the large and well-known companies that went bankrupt during the 1970s were the Penn Central Transportation Company, Dolly Madison Industries, Four Seasons Nursing Centers, King Resources Company, Farrington Manufacturing Company, and W. T. Grant.)

Often, mergers or government intervention are arranged as alternatives to outright bankruptcy. Thus, in recent years, the Federal Home Loan Bank System has arranged the mergers of several very large "problem" savings and loan associations into sound institutions, and the Federal Reserve System has done the same thing for banks. Several government agencies, principally the U.S. Department of Defense, arranged to bail out Lockheed in 1970 to keep it from failing. The merger of Douglas Aircraft and McDonnell in the late 1960s was designed to prevent Douglas's failure. Similar instances could be cited

1. See studies referred to in A. S. Dewing, *The Financial Policy of Corporations*, Vol. 2 (New York: Ronald Press, 1953), Chapter 28.
2. This section draws from Edward I. Altman, *Corporate Bankruptcy in America* (Lexington, Mass.: Heath Lexington Books, 1972), pp. 19–24.

for the securities brokerage industry in the late 1960s and early 1970s. In 1980, a loan guarantee was made by the federal government to keep credit flowing to Chrysler Corporation in the effort to keep it in business.

Why do government and industry seek to prevent the bankruptcy of larger firms? Three of the many reasons are (1) to prevent an erosion of confidence (in the case of financial institutions), (2) to maintain a viable supplier, and (3) to avoid disrupting a local community. Also, bankruptcy is an expensive process, so even when the public interest is not at stake, private industry has strong incentives to prevent it.

Extension and Composition

Extension and composition are discussed together because they both represent voluntary concessions by creditors. *Extension* postpones the date of required payment of past-due obligations. *Composition* voluntarily reduces the creditors' claims on the debtor. Both are intended to keep the debtor in business and to avoid court costs. Although creditors must absorb a temporary loss, the debtor's recovery is often greater than if one of the formal procedures had been followed; and the hope is that a stable customer will emerge.

Procedure

A meeting of the debtor and the creditors is held. At the meeting, the creditors appoint a committee consisting of four or five of the largest creditors and one or two of the smaller ones. The meeting is typically arranged and conducted by an adjustment bureau associated with the local credit managers' association or by a trade association.

After the first meeting, if it is judged that the case can be worked out, the bureau assigns investigators to make an exhaustive report. The bureau and the creditors' committee use the facts of the report to formulate a plan for adjustment of the claims. Another meeting between the debtor and the creditors is then held in an attempt to work out an extension or composition, or a combination of the two. Subsequent meetings may be required to reach final agreements.

Necessary Conditions

At least three conditions are usually necessary to make an extension or a composition feasible:

1. The debtor must be a good moral risk, in the sense of seeking to honor obligations and not diverting the business's assets to personal use and advantage.
2. The debtor must show ability to make a recovery.
3. General business conditions must be favorable to recovery.

Extension

Creditors prefer an extension because it provides for payment in full. The debtor buys current purchases on a cash basis and pays off the past-due balance over an extended time. In some cases, creditors may agree not only to extend the time of payment but also to subordinate existing claims to new debts incurred in favor of vendors extending credit during the period of the extension.

Of course, the creditors must have faith that the debtor will solve the problems. But because of the uncertainties involved, they will want to exercise controls over the debtor while waiting for their claims to be paid. For example, the creditors' committee may insist that an assignment of assets be executed, to be held in escrow in case of default. If the debtor is a corporation, the committee may require that stockholders transfer their stock certificates into an escrow account until the repayment called for under the extension has been completed. The committee may also designate a representative to countersign all checks, and it may obtain security in the form of notes, mortgages, or assignment of accounts receivable.

Composition

In a composition, a pro rata cash settlement is made. Creditors receive from the debtor a uniform percentage of the obligations—in cash. The cash received is taken as full settlement of the debt, even though the ratio may be as low as 10 percent. Bargaining occurs between the debtor and the creditors over the savings that result from avoiding bankruptcy: administration costs, legal fees, investigating costs, and so on. In addition to avoiding these costs, the debtor avoids the stigma of bankruptcy and thus may be induced to part with most of the savings that result from avoiding the bankruptcy.

Combination Settlement

Often the bargaining process results in a compromise involving both an extension and a composition. For example, the settlement may provide for a cash payment of 25 percent of the debt and six future installments of 10 percent each. Total payment thereby aggregates to 85 percent. Installment payments are usually evidenced by notes, and creditors also seek protective controls.

Appraisal of Voluntary Settlements

The advantages of voluntary settlements are informality and simplicity. Investigative, legal, and administrative expenses are held to a minimum. The procedure is the most economical and results in the largest return to creditors.

One possible disadvantage is that the debtor is left in control of the business. This situation may involve legal complications or erosion of assets still operated by the debtor. However, numerous controls are available to give the creditors protection.

A second disadvantage is that small creditors may take a nuisance role in that they may insist on payment in full. As a consequence, settlements typically provide for payment in full for claims under $50 or $100. If a composition is involved, and all claims under $50 are paid, all creditors will receive a base of $50 plus the agreed-on percentage of the balance of their claims.

Reorganization in General

Reorganization is a form of extension or composition of the firm's obligations. However, the legal formalities are much more involved than the procedures thus far described. Regardless of the legal procedure followed, reorganization processes have several features in common:

1. The firm is insolvent either because it is unable to meet cash obligations as they come due or because claims on the firm exceed its assets. Hence, some modifications in the nature or amount of the firm's obligations must be made. A scaling down of terms or amounts must be formulated. This procedure may represent scaling down fixed charges or converting short-term debt into long-term debt.
2. New funds must be raised for working capital and for property rehabilitation.
3. The operating and managerial causes of difficulty must be discovered and eliminated.

The procedures involved in effecting a reorganization are highly legalistic and, in fact, thoroughly understood only by attorneys who specialize in bankruptcy and reorganization. This section will therefore discuss only the general principles involved.

In essence, a reorganization is a composition, a scaling down of claims. In any composition, two conditions must be met:

1. The scaling down must be fair to all parties.
2. In return for the sacrifices, successful rehabilitation and profitable future operation of the firm must be feasible.

These are the standards of fairness and feasibility, which are analyzed further in the next section.

Financial Decisions in Reorganization

When a business becomes insolvent, a decision must be made whether to dissolve the firm through liquidation or to keep it alive through reorganization. Fundamentally, this decision depends on a determination of the value of the firm if it is rehabilitated versus the value of the sum of the parts if it is dismembered.

Liquidation values depend on the degree of specialization of the capital assets used in the firm and, hence, their resale value. In addition, liquidation itself involves costs of dismantling, including legal costs. Of course, successful reorganization also involves costs. Typically, better equipment must be installed, obsolete inventories must be disposed of, and improvements in management must be made. Often the greater indicated value of the firm in reorganization compared with its value in liquidation is used to force a compromise agreement among the claimants, even when they feel that their relative position has not been treated fairly in the reorganization plan.

Both the SEC and the courts are called upon to determine the fairness and feasibility of proposed plans of reorganization.[3] In developing standards of fairness in connection with such reorganizations, the courts and the SEC have adhered to two precedent-setting court decisions.[4]

Standards of Fairness

The basic doctrine of fairness states that claims must be recognized in the order of their legal and contractual priority. Junior claimants such as common stockholders can participate only to the extent that they make an additional cash contribution to the reorganization of the firm.

Carrying out this concept of fairness involves the following steps:

1. An estimate of future sales must be made.
2. An analysis of operating conditions must be made so that the future earnings on sales can be estimated.
3. A determination of the capitalization rate to be applied to these future earnings must be made.
4. The capitalization rate must be applied to the estimated future earnings to obtain an indicated value of the company's properties.
5. Provision for distribution to the claimants must be made.

Example of Reorganization and Standards of Fairness

The meaning and content of these procedures can be set out by the use of an actual example of reorganization—that of R. Hoe and Company, Inc.[5] The company was incorporated in 1909 and went public in 1924. Principally involved in the production of printing presses and saws and other woodcutting products, the company operated successfully until after 1965.[6]

At that point sales began growing at an accelerating rate. The rapid growth of sales and profits was accompanied by a rise in the price of Hoe common stock from $2 per share in 1965 to $48 per share in 1968. But the rapid sales growth put a strain on the company's working capital. To remedy this, the firm issued new common stock in 1967 and 1968. In April 1969 it arranged additional financing in the form of a loan at high interest from James Talcott, Inc.

By this point the situation had already begun to deteriorate. Despite the new capital, Hoe continued having difficulty meeting its obligations. Not long after the loan from Talcott, the American Stock Exchange (ASE) suspended trading of Hoe stock because the company had failed to file audited financial statements for the previous year on a timely basis. Subsequently, Hoe reported a decline in earnings for 1968 and a loss for the first quarter of 1969.

3. The federal bankruptcy laws specify that reorganization plans be worked out by court-appointed officials and be reviewed by the SEC.
4. Case v. Los Angeles Lumber Products Co., 308 U.S. 106 (1939) and Consolidated Rock Products Co. v. du Boise, 213 U.S. 510 (1940). *Securities and Exchange Commission, Seventeenth Annual Report* (Washington, D.C.: Government Printing Office, 1951), p. 130.
5. This material is based on the *Securities and Exchange Commission Corporate Reorganization Release No. 319,* September 8, 1976.
6. The early presses were made of wood, and R. Hoe began to manufacture saws to cut the wood.

Table 24.1

R. Hoe and Company, Inc., Balance Sheet as of December 31, 1975 (Thousands of Dollars)

Assets		Liabilities	
Cash and equivalent	$ 3,139	Current liabilities	$ 483
Receivables	925	Debts granted administration status	148
Inventory	3,476	Priority claims (taxes and wages)	390
Net plant	1,307	Unsecured claims	8,719
Investment in Wood Industries, Inc.	633	Total liabilities	$ 9,740
Other assets unrelated to saw division operations	826		
		Class A stock (436,604 shares, $15 liquidating value)	6,549
		Dividends in arrears on Class A stock	5,392
		Common stock (1,933,462 shares outstanding)	781
		Retained earnings deficit	−12,156
		Total stockholder equity	566
Total assets	$10,306	Total liabilities and equity	$10,306

Trade creditors reacted by demanding payment on past-due accounts before shipping new supplies. The withdrawal of trade credit resulted in Hoe filing a petition on July 7, 1969, to reorganize under Chapter X of the Bankruptcy Act.

The bankruptcy trustee who was appointed was forced to deal with some urgent problems. Immediate working capital needs to continue the saw operation were met by renegotiation of contracts with printing press customers. The press operation was based on job orders from customers; but, because of the bankruptcy, no new orders were being received. By October 18, 1974, the trustee had formulated and then filed with the court a reorganization plan that was subsequently analyzed by the SEC. By court order, in 1975 the press business was sold for stock and notes to Wood Industries (a public company), and the loan from Talcott was settled for about $1 million.

Table 24.1 shows the R. Hoe balance sheet as of December 31, 1975—after settlement of the court orders. The trustee proposed an internal plan of reorganization under which Hoe would continue to operate the saw manufacturing business. New capitalization would consist only of 2.87 million shares of common stock. The plan was based on a valuation of the firm at $15,095,000, payable to all creditors and to Class A stockholders. The valuation and plan are detailed in Table 24.2

All priority claims and trustee fees were to be paid in full with cash. Unsecured claims consisting primarily of current liabilities that existed prior to bankruptcy would receive one share of common stock for each $5 of claims. Class A stockholders would receive one share for each 1.523 shares of existing stock. Common stockholders would receive nothing, since the value of

Table 24.2

R. Hoe and Company, Inc., Trustee Valuation and Plan (Thousands of Dollars)

Valuation

Going concern value of saw division		$ 9,688
Excess cash		2,609
Excess inventory		—
Nonoperating assets at present value		1,958
Value of tax-free carry-forward		2,840
Gross amount available for claims		$17,095
Less trustee administrative costs		−2,000
Available for claims after trustee costs		$15,095
Priority claims paid in cash:		
Debts granted administrative status	$390	
Priority claims	148	
Interest on priority claims	215	
Total paid in cash		753
Available for remainder of claims		$14,342

Plan (Remainder of Claims Based on Shares Valued at $5)

		New Shares		
	Amount of Claims	Number of Shares	Value	Percent of Shares
Unsecured claims	$ 8,719			
Interest on unsecured claims	4,190			
Total	$12,909	2,581,800	$12,909	90
Class A stockholders (436,604 shares)	11,941	286,600	1,433	10
Total value	$24,850	2,868,400	$14,342	100

the firm was insufficient to meet creditors' claims, and Class A stock had a liquidation preference of $15 per share plus dividends in arrears.

In evaluating the proposal from the standpoint of fairness, the Securities and Exchange Commission began with an analysis of the prospective value of the company (Table 24.3). The SEC evaluated it at $2.3 million higher than the trustee had—primarily because of differences in beliefs about working capital needs and the going concern value of the firm. To determine going concern value, the trustee had used a P-E ratio of 11.7; but the SEC felt 12 would be more appropriate. The SEC also estimated future annual income at slightly higher than the trustee's estimate—$900,000 compared to $875,000.

Because of these differences, the SEC felt that the trustee's plan did not meet the standard of fairness. It therefore proposed an amended plan, under which the allocation to Class A stockholders would be increased, and unsecured creditors would receive one share of new common stock for each $5 value of claims (a total of 2.58 million shares)—the same as under the trustee's plan. (See Table 24.4.) The allocation to Class A stockholders was increased because of the SEC's higher estimated value of the firm. Under the

Table 24.3

R. Hoe and Company, Inc., SEC Evaluation of Fairness (Thousands of Dollars)

Valuation	Trustee Valuation	SEC Valuation
Going concern value of saw division	$9,688	$10,800
Excess cash	2,609	3,475
Excess inventory	—	1,000
Nonoperating assets at present value	1,958	1,536
Value of tax loss carry-forward	2,840	2,470
Gross amount available for claims	$17,095	$19,281
Less trust administration costs	2,000	1,848
Net value	$15,095	$17,433

new plan, Class A stockholders would receive one share for each 0.579 shares of their Class A stock. Again, common stockholders would receive nothing, since the value of the firm was insufficient to meet even the preferential claims.

Standard of Feasibility

The primary test of feasibility is that the fixed charges on the income of the corporation after reorganization are amply covered by earnings or, if a value is established for a firm that is to be sold, that a buyer can be found at that price. Adequate coverage of fixed charges for a company that is to continue in operation generally requires an improvement in earnings, a reduction of fixed charges, or both.

Among the actions that will have to be taken to improve the earning power of the company are the following:

1. Where the management has been inefficient and inadequate for the task, new talents and abilities must be brought into the company.
2. If inventories have become obsolete, they must be disposed of and the operations of the company streamlined.

Table 24.4

SEC Amended Plan (Thousands of Dollars)

		New Shares		
	Amount of Claim	Number of Shares	Value	Percent of Shares
Unsecured claims:				
Principal	$ 8,719			
Interest	4,190			
Total	$12,909	2,581,800	$12,909	77
Class A stockholders:				
436,604 shares	$11,941	754,200	$ 3,771	23
Total value	$24,850	3,336,000	$16,680	100

Note: Priority claims of $753,000 were to be paid as per the trustee's plan.

3. Sometimes the plant and the equipment of the firm must be modernized before it can operate and compete successfully on a cost basis.
4. Reorganization may also require an improvement in production, marketing, advertising, and other functions to enable the firm to compete successfully.
5. It is sometimes necessary to develop new products so the firm can move from areas where economic trends have become undesirable into areas where the growth and stability potential is greater.

Application of Feasibility Tests

Referring again to R. Hoe and Company, the SEC observed that the company's failure had come about as the result of management attempts to expand the company faster than prudent working capital management would permit. With the sale of the printing press division by court order in 1975, the firm was left with the profitable saw division.

In the SEC's judgment, the critical element in the viability of the saw division was sufficient cash to carry out the SEC's plan and to provide adequate working capital. Under this plan, it was hoped that Hoe would emerge from Chapter X with normal current liabilities incident to its business and a simple and conservative capital structure, consisting only of current liabilities and common stock. Based on the December 31, 1975, balance sheet in Table 24.1, cash and equivalents would be $3,139,000 minus the $753,000 paid to priority claims, or a total of $2,386,000. This is nearly five times the $483,000 level of then-current liabilities.

The case study of R. Hoe and Company is a description of Chapter X proceedings. Proceedings under Chapter X were developed for large corporations with public investors in the bonds and common stock of the firm. In summary, a petition may be filed by the corporation to bring about a reorganization, or the petition can be filed by three or more creditors with claims aggregating $5,000 or over. A trustee, whose functions have been described, must be appointed by the court if liabilities involved exceed $250,000. The absolute priority rule must be followed so that senior creditors must be fully compensated before junior creditors and stockholders.

From the creditors' viewpoint, Chapter X proceedings are very inflexible and time-consuming. The operating control of the debtor firm is placed in a court-appointed trustee who sometimes does not have the technical knowledge to operate the debtor company successfully. Thus, creditors will suffer losses if the debtor company loses customers and operating efficiency under the trustee arrangement.

Chapter XI Proceedings

In contrast, Chapter XI proceedings are more flexible and informal. Chapter XI proceedings were devised for use with small corporations, partnerships, or individuals in cases involving no public participation in the financing or ownership of the firm. In Chapter XI proceedings, the debtor automatically receives the status of debtor in possession. Even after a bankruptcy referee is appointed by the court, the referee may grant an order of continuance which enables the debtor to continue operating the business. The referee can enjoin the creditors from legal action to recover debts by obtaining preference over other creditors and by property foreclosure. Payment schedules are worked out between the debtor and creditors, presented to the refereee for approval, and ultimately paid out to the creditors. From the creditors' standpoint, Chapter XI proceedings are much less time-consuming. The debtors in possession have the opportunity to remain in control of the business, in the hope that they will be more successful than outsiders in reviving the firm and repaying its debts. Creditors are able to exert influence on the debtors. The creditors may even continue to grant credit to the debtor in helping the indebted firm achieve profitability again.

The New Bankruptcy Law

Under the bankruptcy law that became effective in 1979, Chapters X and XI are blended into a single procedure. Cases can be initiated on either a voluntary or involuntary basis. Involuntary petitions must be commenced only under Chapter VII, which deals with liquidation, or Chapter XI, which deals with reorganization. The debtor company remains in possession of its business and continues to operate it unless the court orders otherwise. Under a Chapter VII liquidation case, the court may appoint an interim trustee to operate the business to avoid loss. The debtor, however, may regain possession from the trustee by filing an appropriate bond as required by the court. The trustee has very broad powers and discretion if so authorized by the court. The trustee may retain or replace management as well as augment management with additional professionals. The trustee may also obtain additional financing on an unsecured credit basis.

The consolidated approach under the new bankruptcy law eliminates disputes over whether Chapter X or XI will be used. This speeds up the proceedings, reduces costs, and (it is hoped) shortens the time until the firm is operating profitably again. Since the debtor remains in control of the operations of the business, informal negotiations between the debtor company, the creditors, and the stockholders become more feasible. The absolute priority rule is relaxed under the new law. Negotiations may provide for a restructuring of debt involving rescaling (reducing the amount of obligations that will have to be paid) or time extensions (postponing the required payment dates for all or part of the obligations). Hence, claims from unsecured creditors and stockholders have an increased probability of realizing cash or receiving some contingent claims on the reorganized companies. If it can be established that claimants will receive as much as they would under a straight liquidation program, a reorganization plan can be approved by a vote of the parties who would be affected by it.

Since management will continue to be in control, the debtor and the large prime creditors will dominate the reorganization. Sometimes this means institutions such as banks and insurance companies will dominate the proceedings. It is said that the SEC loses a strong weapon under the new consolidated procedure. Formerly, the threat to convert a Chapter XI to a Chapter X made debtors and large creditors willing to make concessions to avoid such a conversion. Under the new bankruptcy law, the SEC can still sue to have a trustee appointed. However, to be successful in such a suit apparently will require demonstrating management incompetence.

Overall, the new bankruptcy law with respect to business firms provides for greater flexibility in the procedures. Greater flexibility avoids rigid processes that can often be very expensive and time-consuming. On the other hand, greater flexibility may provide opportunities for increased leverage by some of the parties involved, and this may be to the detriment of other parties. Until we have more actual experience with the new bankruptcy law, it is not possible to make a definitive evaluation of its effectiveness.

Liquidation Procedures

Liquidation of a business occurs when the firm is worth more dead than alive. Assignment is a liquidation procedure that does not go through the courts, although it can be used to achieve full settlement of claims on the debtor. Bankruptcy is a legal procedure, carried out under the jurisdiction of special courts, in which a firm is formally liquidated and creditors' claims are completely discharged.

Assignment

Assignment (as well as bankruptcy) takes place when the debtor is insolvent and the possibility of restoring profitability is so remote that the enterprise should be dissolved. Assignment is a technique for liquidating a debt and yielding a larger amount to the creditors than is likely to be achieved in formal bankruptcy.

Technically, there are three classes of assignments: (1) common-law assignment, (2) statutory assignment, and (3) assignment plus settlement.

Common-Law Assignment. Common law provides for an assignment whereby a debtor transfers the title to assets to a third person, known as an assignee or trustee. This person is instructed to liquidate the assets and to distribute the proceeds among the creditors on a pro rata basis.

Typically, an assignment is conducted through the adjustment bureau of the local credit managers' association. The assignee may liquidate the assets through a bulk sale—a public sale through an auctioneer. The auction is preceded by advertising so there will be a number of bids. Liquidation may also be by a piecemeal auction sale conducted on the premises of the assignor by a competent, licensed auctioneer. On-premises sales are particularly advantageous in the liquidation of large machine shops of manufacturing plants.

The common-law assignment, as such, does not discharge the debtor's obligations. If a corporation goes out of business and does not satisfy all its claims, there will still be claims against it; but in effect the corporation has ceased to exist. The people who have been associated with it can organize another corporation free of the debts and obligations of the previous one. Under a common-law assignment, the assignee, in drawing up the checks to pay the creditors, should write on each check the requisite legal language to make the payment a complete discharge of the obligation. The legal requirements for this process are technical and best carried out with the aid of a lawyer, but a statement that endorsement of the check represents acknowledgment of full payment for the obligation is essential.

Statutory Assignment. Statutory assignment is similar in concept to common-law assignment. Legally, it is carried out under state statutes regulating assignment; technically, it requires more formality. The debtor executes an instrument of assignment, which is recorded and thereby provides notice to all third parties. The proceedings are handled under court order; the court appoints an assignee and supervises the proceedings, including the sale of the assets and the distribution of the proceeds. As with the common-law assignment, debtors are not automatically discharged from the balance of the obligations. They can discharge themselves, however, by printing the requisite statement on the settlement checks.

Assignment Plus Settlement. Both the common-law and the statutory assignment may take place with recognition and agreement beforehand by the creditors that it will represent a complete discharge of obligation. Normally, the debtor communicates with the local credit managers' association. The association's adjustment bureau arranges a meeting of all the creditors, and a trust instrument of assignment is drawn up. The adjustment bureau is designated to dispose of the assets, which are sold through regular trade channels, by bulk sales, by auction, or by private sales. The creditors typically leave all responsibility for the liquidation procedure with the assignee —the adjustment bureau.

Having disposed of the assets and obtained funds, the adjustment bureau then distributes the proceeds pro rata among the creditors, designating on the check that this is in full settlement of the claims on the debtor. Ordinarily, a release is not agreed upon before the execution of the assignment. Instead, after full examination of the facts, the creditors' committee usually recommends granting a release following the execution of the assignment. If releases are not forthcoming, the assignor can, within four months of the date of the assignment, file a voluntary petition in bankruptcy. In this event, the assignment is terminated and the assignee must account for the assets, report to the trustee and the referee in bankruptcy, and deliver to the trustee all assets in the estate. (Usually, by that time, assets have been reduced to cash.)

Assignment has substantial advantages over bankruptcy. Bankruptcy through the courts involves much time, legal formalities, and accounting and legal expenses. Assignment saves the costs of bankruptcy proceedings, and it may save time as well. Furthermore, an assignee usually has much more flexibility in disposing of property than does a bankruptcy trustee. Assignees may be more familiar with the normal channels of trade; and since they take action quickly, before the inventories become obsolete, they may achieve better results.

Bankruptcy

Although the bankruptcy procedures need improvement, the Federal Bankruptcy Acts represent some major achievements:

1. They provide safeguards against fraud by the debtor during liquidation.
2. Simultaneously, they provide for an equitable distribution of the debtor's assets among the creditors.
3. Insolvent debtors can discharge all their obligations and start new businesses unhampered by a burden of prior debt.

Prerequisites for Bankruptcy

The debtor can file a voluntary petition of bankruptcy; but if an involuntary petition is to be filed, three conditions must be met:

1. The total debts of the insolvent must be $1,000 or more.
2. If the debtor has fewer than twelve creditors, any single creditor can file the petition if the amount owed is $500 or more. If there are twelve or more creditors, the petition must be signed by three or more of them, each having provable total claims of at least $500.
3. Within the four preceding months, the debtor must have committed one or more of the following six acts of bankruptcy.

Acts of Bankruptcy

The six acts of bankruptcy can be summarized briefly:

1. *Concealment or Fraudulent Conveyance.* Concealment constitutes the hiding of assets with intent to defraud creditors. Fraudulent conveyance is transfer of property to a third party without adequate consideration and with intent to defraud creditors.
2. *Preferential Transfer.* A preferential transfer is the transfer of money or assets by an insolvent debtor to a creditor, giving that creditor a greater portion of the claim than other creditors would receive on liquidation.
3. *Legal Lien or Distraint.* If an insolvent debtor permits any creditor to obtain a lien on the property and fails to discharge the lien within thirty days, or if the debtor permits a landlord to distrain (to seize property that has been pledged as security for a loan) for nonpayment of rent, that person has committed an act of bankruptcy. By obtaining a lien, creditors can force an insolvent but obdurate debtor into bankruptcy.
4. *Assignment.* An act of bankruptcy likewise exists if a debtor makes a general assignment for the benefit of creditors. Again, this enables creditors who have become distrustful of the debtor in the process of assignment

to transfer the proceedings to a bankruptcy court. As a matter of practice, creditors in common-law assignments typically require that a debtor execute a formal assignment document to be held in escrow and to become effective if informal and voluntary settlement negotiations fail. In the event of failure, the assignment becomes effective, and the creditors have the right to bring the case into bankruptcy court.

5. *Appointment of Receiver or Trustee.* If an insolvent debtor permits the appointment of a receiver or a trustee to take charge of the property, the debtor has committed an act of bankruptcy. In this event, the creditors can remove a receivership or an adjustment proceeding to a bankruptcy court.
6. *Admission in Writing.* A debtor who admits in writing an inability to pay the debts and a willingness to be judged bankrupt has committed an act of bankruptcy. The reason for this sixth act of bankruptcy is that debtors are often unwilling to engage in voluntary bankruptcy because it carries the stigma of avoidance of obligations. Sometimes, therefore, negotiations with a debtor reach an impasse. Admission in writing is one of the methods of forcing the debtor to commit an act of bankruptcy and of moving the proceedings into a bankruptcy court, where the debtor will no longer be able to reject all plans for settlement.

Adjudication and the Referee

On the filing of the petition of involuntary bankruptcy, a subpoena is served on the debtor. There is usually no contest by the debtor, and the court adjudges the debtor bankrupt. On adjudication, the case is transferred by the court to a referee in bankruptcy, generally a lawyer appointed for a specified term by the judge of the bankruptcy court to act in the judge's place after adjudication.

In addition, on petition of the creditors, the referee in voluntary proceedings or the judge in involuntary proceedings can appoint a receiver, who serves as the custodian of the debtor's property until the appointment of a trustee. This arrangement was developed because a long period elapses between the date of the filing of a petition in bankruptcy and the election of a trustee at the first creditors' meeting. To safeguard the creditors' interests during this period, the court, through either the referee or the judge, can appoint a receiver in bankruptcy, who has full control until the trustee is appointed.

First Creditors' Meeting: Election of Trustee

At the first meeting of the creditors, a trustee is elected. If different blocks of creditors have different candidates for trustee, the election may become drawn out. Frequently, the trustee will be the adjustment bureau of the local credit managers' association. At this first meeting the debtor may also be examined for the purpose of obtaining necessary information.

Subsequent Procedures

The trustee and the creditors' committee act to convert all assets into cash. The trustee sends a letter to people owing the debtor money, warning that all past-due accounts will result in instant suit if immediate payment is not made. Appraisers are appointed by the courts to set a value on the property. With the advice of the creditors' committee and authorization of the referee, the merchandise is sold by approved methods. As in an assignment, auctions may be held.

Without the consent of the court, property cannot be sold at less than 75 percent of the value set by the court-appointed appraisers. Cash received from the disposition of the property is used first to pay all expenses associated with the bankruptcy proceedings, and then any remaining funds are paid to the claimants.

Final Meeting and Discharge

The trustee who has completed the liquidation and has sent out all the claimants' checks makes an accounting, which is reviewed by the creditors and the referee. The bankruptcy is then discharged, and the debtor is released from all debts.

If the hearings before the referee indicate the probability of fraud, the FBI is required to undertake an investigation. If fraud was not committed and the bankruptcy is discharged, the debtor is again free to engage in business. Since business is highly competitive in many fields, the debtor will probably not have great difficulty in obtaining credit again. Under the National Bankruptcy Act, however, a debtor cannot be granted a discharge more often than once every six years.

Priority of Claims on Distribution of Proceeds

The order of priority of claims in bankruptcy is as follows:

1. Costs of administering and operating the bankruptcy estate.
2. Wages due workers if earned within three months prior to the filing of the petition in bankruptcy, the amount not to exceed $600 per person.
3. Taxes due federal, state, county, or any other government agencies.
4. Secured creditors, with the proceeds of the sale of specific property pledged for a mortgage.
5. General or unsecured creditors—the claim consisting of the remaining balances after payment to secured creditors from the sale of specific property and including trade credit, bank loans, and debenture bonds. Holders of subordinated debt fall into this category, but they must turn over required amounts to the holders of senior debt.
6. Preferred stockholders.
7. Common stockholders.

An example will illustrate how this priority of claims works out. The balance sheet of a bankrupt firm is shown in Table 24.5. Assets total $90 million, and claims are those indicated on the right-hand side of the balance sheet. The subordinated debentures are subordinated to the notes payable to commercial banks.

Assume that the firm's assets are sold. These assets, shown in the balance sheet, are greatly overstated; they are worth much less than the $90 million at which they are carried. The following amounts are realized on liquidation:

Table 24.5

Bankrupt Firm Balance Sheet (Millions of Dollars)

Current assets	$80.0	Accounts payable	$20.0
Net property	10.0	Notes payable (due bank)	10.0
		Accrued wages (1,400 at $500 each)	0.7
		U.S. taxes	1.0
		State and local taxes	0.3
		Current debt	$32.0
		First mortgage	$ 6.0
		Second mortgage	1.0
		Subordinated debentures[a]	8.0
		Long-term debt	$15.0
		Preferred stock	$ 2.0
		Common stock	26.0
		Capital surplus	4.0
		Retained earnings	11.0
		Net worth	$43.0
Total assets	$90.0	Total claims	$90.0

a. Subordinated to $10 million notes payable to the First National Bank.

Current assets	$28,000,000
Net property	5,000,000
Total assets	$33,000,000

The order of priority of payment of claims is shown by Table 24.6. Fees and expenses of administration are typically about 20 percent of gross proceeds, and in this example they are assumed to be $6 million. Next in priority are wages due workers, which total $700,000. The total amount of taxes to be paid is $1.3 million. Thus far, the total of claims paid from the $33 million is $8 million. The net proceeds of $5 million from the sale of fixed property is then paid on the first mortgage, leaving $20 million available to the general creditors.

The claims of the general creditors total $40 million. Since $20 million is available, each claimant will receive 50 percent of the claim before the subordination adjustment. This adjustment requires that the holders of subordinated debentures turn over to the holders of the notes to which they are subordinated all amounts received until the notes to which they are subordinated are satisfied. In this situation, the claim of the holders of notes payable is $10 million, but only $5 million is available; the deficiency is therefore $5 million. After transfer of $4 million by the holders of subordinated debentures, there remains a deficiency of $1 million, which will be unsatisfied. Note that 90 percent of the bank claim will be satisfied, whereas only 50 percent of other unsecured claims will be satisfied. These figures illustrate the usefulness of the subordination provision to the security to which the subordination is made. Since no other funds remain, the claims of the holders of preferred and common stocks are completely wiped out.

Table 24.6

Bankrupt Firm's Order of Priority of Claims (Millions of Dollars)

Distribution of Proceeds on Liquidation

1. Proceeds of sales of assets	$33.0
2. Fees and expenses of administration of bankruptcy	6.0
3. Wages due workers earned three months prior to filing of bankruptcy petition	0.7
4. Taxes	1.3
5. Available after priority payments	$25.0
6. First mortgage, paid from sale of net property	5.0
7. Available to general creditors	$20.0

Claims of General Creditors

Class of Creditor	Claim (1)	Application of 50 Percent (2)	After Subordination Adjustment (3)	Percentage of Original Claims Received (4)
Unsatisfied portion of first mortgage	$1.0	$0.5	$0.5	92
Unsatisfied portion of second mortgage	1.0	0.5	0.5	50
Notes payable	10.0	5.0	9.0	90
Accounts payable	20.0	10.0	10.0	50
Subordinated debentures	8.0	4.0	0	0
	$40.0	$20.0	$20.0	56

Notes:

1. Column 1 is the claim of each class of creditor. Total claims equal $40 million.
2. Line 7 in the upper section of the table shows that $20 million is available. This sum divided by the $40 million of claims indicates that general creditors will receive 50 percent of their claims shown in Column 1.
3. The debentures are subordinated to the notes payable; $4 million is transferred from debentures to notes payable in Column 3.
4. Column 4 shows the results of dividing the Column 3 figure by the original amount given in Table 24.5 except for first mortgage, where $5 million paid on sale of property is included. The 56 percent total figure includes the first mortgage transactions, that is: ($20,000,000 + $5,000,000) ÷ ($40,000,000 + $5,000,000) = 56%.

The order of priority can be altered by special subordination agreements. For example, in the W. T. Grant bankruptcy during the mid-1970s, the commercial banks had agreed to subordinate their loans to the amounts payable to trade creditors in order to induce suppliers of W. T. Grant to continue the flow of merchandise to the company. As a consequence, of the $400 million that appeared to be realizable from W. T. Grant, the order of priority seemed to be the following. First in line were the holders of the $24 million worth of senior debentures. Second, because of an unusual lien arrangement, came trade creditors, with $110 million owed. Third were the banks, which subordinated to the trade creditors $300 million of their $640 million loan to Grant, along with an additional $90 million loaned after the filing for reorganization. Next came junior debenture holders, with claims of $94 million. Last in line were the holders of unsecured debt, including $300 million in landlord claims and utility bills. In addition, it was estimated that administrative costs of the reorganization would total $30 million. There was also an unresolved Internal Revenue Service claim of $60 million plus interest. Further, there would be legal fees estimated to run into the millions that would assume a priority status.[7]

Studies of the proceeds in bankruptcy liquidations reveal that unsecured creditors receive, on the average, about 15 cents on the dollar. Consequently, where assignment to creditors is likely to yield more, assignment is to be preferred to bankruptcy.

Summary

The major cause of a firm's failure is incompetent management. Bad managers should, of course, be removed as promptly as possible; if failure has occurred, a number of remedies are open to the interested parties.

The first question to be answered is whether the firm is better off dead or alive—whether it should be liquidated and sold off piecemeal or rehabilitated. Assuming the decision is made that the firm should survive, it must be put through what is called a reorganization. Legal procedures are always costly, especially in the case of a business failure. Therefore, if it is at all possible, both the debtor and the creditors are better off if matters can be handled on an informal basis rather than through the courts. The informal procedures used in reorganization are (1) extension, which postpones the date of settlement, and (2) composition, which reduces the amount owed.

If voluntary settlement through extension or composition is not possible, the matter is thrown into the courts. If the court decides on reorganization rather than liquidation, it will appoint a trustee (1) to control the firm going through reorganization and (2) to prepare a formal plan of reorganization. The plan, which must be reviewed by the SEC, must meet the standards of fairness to all parties and feasibility in the sense that the reorganized enterprise will stand a good chance of surviving instead of being thrown back into the bankruptcy courts.

The application of standards of fairness and feasibility can help determine the probable success of a particular plan for reorganization. The concept of fairness involves the estimation of sales and earnings and the application

7. "Dividing What's Left of Grant's," *Business Week,* March 1, 1976, p. 21.

of a capitalization rate to the latter to determine the appropriate distribution to each claimant.

The feasibility test examines the ability of the new enterprise to carry the fixed charges resulting from the reorganization plan. The quality of management and the company's assets must be assured. Production and marketing may also require improvement.

Finally, where liquidation is treated as the only solution to the debtor's insolvency, the creditors should attempt procedures that will net them the largest recovery. Assignment of the debtor's property is the cheaper and the faster procedure. Furthermore, there is more flexibility in disposing of the property and thus larger returns. Bankruptcy provides formal procedures in liquidation to safeguard the debtor's property from fraud and to assure equitable distribution to the creditors. The procedure is long and cumbersome. Moreover, the debtor's property is generally poorly managed during bankruptcy proceedings unless the trustee is closely supervised by the creditors.

Questions

24.1 Discuss this statement, giving both pros and cons: A certain number of business failures is a healthy sign. If there are no failures, this is an indication (a) that entrepreneurs are overly cautious, hence not as inventive and as willing to take risks as a healthy, growing economy requires; (b) that competition is not functioning to weed out inefficient producers; or (c) that both situations exist.

24.2 How can financial analysis be used to forecast the probability of a given firm's failure? Assuming that such analysis is properly applied, will it always predict failure? Explain.

24.3 Why do creditors usually accept a plan for financial rehabilitation rather than demand liquidation of the business?

24.4 Would it be possible to form a profitable company by merging two companies, both of which are business failures? Explain.

24.5 Distinguish between a reorganization and a bankruptcy.

24.6 Would it be a sound rule to liquidate whenever the liquidation value is above the value of the corporation as a going concern? Discuss.

24.7 Why do liquidations usually result in losses for the creditors or the owners, or both? Would partial liquidation or liquidation over a period of time limit their losses? Explain.

24.8 Are liquidations likely to be more common for public utility, railroad, or industrial corporations? Why?

Problems

24.1 The financial statements of the Hamilton Publishing Company for 1978 are shown below:

Hamilton Publishing Company Balance Sheet, as of December 31, 1978 (Thousands of Dollars)

Current assets	$130,000	Current liabilities	$ 53,000
Investments	40,000	Advance payments for subscriptions	78,000
Net fixed assets	200,000	Reserves	8,000
Goodwill	14,000	$8 preferred stock, $100 par (1,500,000 shares)	150,000
		$9 preferred stock, no par (100,000 shares, callable at $110)	11,000
		Common stock, $1.50 par (8,000,000 shares)	12,000
		Retained earnings	72,000
Total assets	$384,000	Total claims	$384,000

Hamilton Publishing Company Income Statement for Year Ended December 31, 1978 (Thousands of Dollars)

Operating income		$194,400
Operating expenses		174,800
Earnings before income tax		19,600
Income tax (at 40 percent)		7,840
Income after taxes		11,760
Dividends on $8 preferred stock	$12,000	
Dividends on $9 preferred stock	900	12,900
Income available for common stock		−$1,140

A recapitalization plan is proposed in which each share of $8 preferred stock will be exchanged for a share of $2 preferred (stated value $20), plus $80 of stated principal in 8 percent subordinated income debentures with par value $1,000. The $9 preferred will be retired from cash.

a. Show the pro forma balance sheet (in thousands of dollars) giving effect to the recapitalization and showing the new preferred at its stated value and the common stock at par value.
b. Present the pro forma income statement (in thousands of dollars).
c. How much does the firm increase income available to common stock by the recapitalization?
d. How much less are the required pre-tax earnings after the recapitalization compared to before the change? (Required earnings are the amount necessary to meet fixed charges, debenture interest, and preferred dividends.)
e. How is the debt to net worth position of the company affected by the recapitalization?
f. Would you vote for the recapitalization if you were a holder of the $8 preferred stock?

24.2 The Accurate Instrument Company produces precision instruments. The company's products, designed and manufactured according to specifications set out by its customers, are highly specialized. Declines in sales and increases in development expenses in recent years resulted in a large deficit at the end of 1978 (see the balance sheet and income statement which follow):

Accurate Instrument Company Balance Sheet as of December 31, 1978 (Thousands of Dollars)

Current assets	$375	Current liabilities	$450
Fixed assets	375	Long-term debt (unsecured)	225
		Capital stock	150
		Retained earnings (deficit)	−75
Total assets	$750	Total claims	$750

Accurate Instrument Company Sales and Profits, 1975–1978 (Thousands of Dollars)

Year	Sales	Net Profit after Tax before Fixed Charges
1975	$2,625	$262.5
1976	2,400	225.0
1977	1,425	−75.0
1978	1,350	−112.5

Independent assessment led to the conclusion that the company would have a liquidation value of about $600,000. As an alternative to liquidation, management concluded that a reorganization was possible with the investment of an additional $300,000. Management was confident of the company's eventual success and stated that the additional investment would restore earnings to $125,000 a year after taxes and before fixed charges. The appropriate multiplier to apply is eight times. Management is negotiating with a local investment group to obtain the additional $300,000. If the funds are obtained, the holders of the long-term debt will be given half the common stock in the reorganized firm in place of their present claims.

Should the creditors agree to the reorganization, or should they force liquidation of the firm?

24.3 During the past several months, the American Industrial Products Company has had difficulty meeting its current obligations. Attempts to raise additional working capital have failed. To add to AIP's problems, its principal lenders, the First National Bank and the General Insurance Company, have been placing increased pressure on it because of its continued delinquent loan payments and apparent lack of fiscal responsibility.

The First National Bank is first mortgage holder on AIP's production facility and has a $1 million, unsecured revolving loan with AIP that is past due and on which certain restrictive clauses have been violated. The General Insurance Company is holding $5 million of AIP's subordinated debentures, which are subordinate to the notes payable.

Because of the bank's increasing concern for the long-term future of AIP, it has attached $750,000 of AIP's deposits. This action has forced the company into either reorganization or bankruptcy.

General Insurance has located a large manufacturing company that is interested in taking over AIP's operations. This company has offered to assume the $8 million mortgage, pay all back taxes, and pay $4.3 million in cash for the company.

AIP's estimated sales for 1978 are $20 million, its estimated earnings are $1,294,000, and its capitalization factor is 10 times. The company's balance sheet as of December 31, 1978, follows:

American Industrial Products Company Balance Sheet as of December 31, 1978 (Thousands of Dollars)

Assets		Liabilities	
Current assets	$ 3,000	Accounts payable	$ 2,000
Net property, plant, and equipment	12,000	Taxes	200
Other assets	2,800	Notes payable to bank	250
		Other current liabilities	1,350
		Total current liabilities	$ 3,800
		Mortgage	8,000
		Subordinated debentures	5,000
		Common stock	1,000
		Paid-in capital	2,000
		Retained earnings	−2,000
Total assets	$17,800	Total liabilities and stockholders' equity	$17,800

a. Given all the data and the fact that AIP cannot be reorganized internally, show the effect of the reorganization plan on claims of AIP's creditors.
b. Based on the information in the paragraph preceding the balance sheet, test for the standard of fairness.
c. Comment on the actions of the bank in offsetting AIP's deposits.
d. Do you feel the bank and the insurance company were right in not advancing AIP additional money?

Selected References

Altman, Edward I. *Corporate Bankruptcy in America.* Lexington, Mass.: Heath Lexington Books, 1971.

———. "Railroad Bankruptcy Propensity." *Journal of Finance* 26 (May 1971), pp. 333–346.

———. "Corporate Bankruptcy Potential, Stockholder Returns and Share Valuation." *Journal of Finance* 24 (December 1969), pp. 887–900.

———. "Equity Securities of Bankrupt Firms." *Financial Analysts' Journal* 25 (July–August 1969), pp. 129–133.

———. "Financial Ratios, Discriminant Analysis and the Prediction of Corporate Bankruptcy." *Journal of Finance* 23 (September 1968), pp. 589–609.

Beaver, William H. "Market Prices, Financial Ratios, and the Prediction of Failure." *Journal of Accounting Research* 6 (Autumn 1968), pp. 179–192.

Bulow, J. I., and Shoven, J. B. "The Bankruptcy Decision." *Bell Journal of Economics* 9 (Autumn 1978), pp. 437–456.

Calkins, Francis J. "Corporate Reorganization under Chapter X: A Post-Mortem." *Journal of Finance* 3 (June 1948), pp. 19–28.

———. "Feasibility in Plans of Corporate Reorganizations under Chapter X." *Harvard Law Review* 61 (May 1948), pp. 763–781.

Edmister, Robert O. "An Empirical Test of Financial Ratio Analysis for Small Business Failure Prediction." *Journal of Financial and Quantitative Analysis* 7 (March 1972), pp. 1477–1493.

Ferguson, D. A. "Preferred Stock Valuation in Recapitalizations." *Journal of Finance* 13 (March 1958), pp. 48–69.

Gordon, Myron J. "Towards a Theory of Financial Distress." *Journal of Finance* 26 (May 1971), pp. 347–356.

Green, Steven J. "Bankruptcy: Help or Hindrance?" *Financial Executive* 43 (December 1975), pp. 30–35.

Harris, Richard. "The Consequences of Costly Default." *Economic Inquiry* 16 (October 1978), pp. 477–496.

Johnson, Craig G. "Ratio Analysis and the Prediction of Firm Failure." *Journal of Finance* 25 (December 1970), pp. 1166–1168. See also Edward A. Altman, "Reply." *Journal of Finance* 25 (December 1970), pp. 1169–1172.

Miller, Danny. "Common Syndromes of Business Failure." *Business Horizons* 20 (December 1977), pp. 43–53.

Murray, Roger F. "The Penn Central Debacle: Lessons for Financial Analysis." *Journal of Finance* 26 (May 1971), pp. 327–332.

Pye, Gordon. "Gauging the Default Premium." *Financial Analysts' Journal* 30 (January–February 1974), pp. 49–52.

Stapleton, R. C. "Some Aspects of the Pure Theory of Corporate Finance: Bankruptcies and Take-overs: Comment." *Bell Journal of Economics* 6 (Autumn 1975), pp. 708–710.

Stiglitz, Joseph E. "Some Aspects of the Pure Theory of Corporate Finance; Bankruptcies and Take-overs: Reply." *Bell Journal of Economics* 6 (Autumn 1975), pp. 711–714.

——— "Some Aspects of the Pure Theory of Corporate Finance: Bankruptcies and Take-overs." *Bell Journal of Economics and Management Science* 3 (Autumn 1972), pp. 458–482.

Van Horne, James C. "Optimal Initiation of Bankruptcy Proceedings." *Journal of Finance* 31 (June 1976), pp. 897–910.

Walter, James E. "Determination of Technical Insolvency." *Journal of Business* 30 (January 1957), pp. 30–43.

Warner, Jerold B. "Bankruptcy Costs: Some Evidence." *Journal of Finance* 32 (May 1977), pp. 337–347.

Weston, J. Fred. "The Industrial Economics Background of the Penn Central Bankruptcy." *Journal of Finance* 26 (May 1971), pp. 311–326.

25

Financial Management in the Small Firm

Small business is a key element of the U.S. economy. First, of the approximately 8.5 million firms in the U.S., about 8.0 million are defined by the U.S. government as "small." Thus, small businesses are quantitatively important. Second, and of perhaps even greater significance, small businesses often serve as the vehicle through which ideas for new products and services make their way to the consuming public. Many of the large electronics firms of the 1970s were new, small businesses in the 1950s. Third, the very existence of small businesses, and the fact that new ones are continually being started, provides continuous stimulation to competition in the economy.

In some respects, there is no need to study small business finance as a separate topic—the same general principles apply to large and small firms alike. However, small firms face a somewhat different set of problems than larger businesses, and the goals of a small firm are likely to be oriented toward the aspirations of an individual entrepreneur rather than toward investors in general. Also, the characteristics of the money and capital markets create both problems and opportunities for small firms, and a special governmental agency, the Small Business Administration, exists to help small firms with their financing problems. For all these reasons, a chapter focusing directly on the small firm is useful in a book on financial management.

Life Cycle of the Firm

The life cycle of an industry or firm is often depicted as an S-shaped curve, as shown in Figure 25.1. The four stages in the life cycle are described as follows:

1. *Experimentation period.* Sales and profits grow slowly following the introduction of a new product or firm.
2. *Exploitation period.* The firm enjoys rapid growth of sales, high profitability, and acceptance of the product.

Figure 25.1

Hypothetical Life Cycle of a Typical Firm

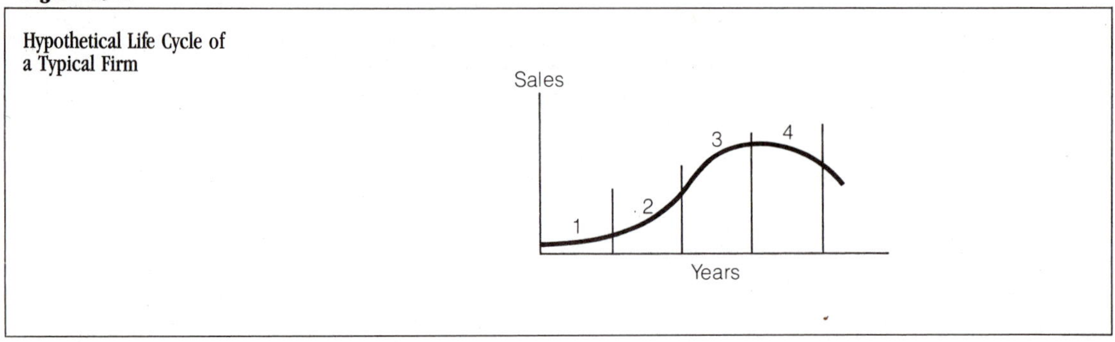

3. *Maturity.* The rate of growth of sales begins to slow down; growth is dependent in large part upon replacement demand.
4. *Decline.* The firm faces the appearance of substitute products, technological and managerial obsolescence, and saturation of demand for its goods.

Although it is an oversimplification, Figure 25.1 provides a useful framework for analysis. The hypothesis represented by the four-stage life-cycle concept is based on a number of assumptions. It assumes competent management in the growth periods and insufficient management foresight prior to the decline phase. Obviously, one of management's primary goals is to prolong Phase 2, completely forestalling Phase 4; a great many firms are apparently successful in this endeavor.

The life cycle is substantially influenced by the form of organization a firm chooses—corporations have potentially long lives, while proprietorships obviously have finite lives. We shall discuss other aspects of the firm's life later, giving special attention to the financing forms employed at each stage.

Small Firms in Traditional Small Business Industries

As noted above, some firms are small because the nature of the industry dictates that small enterprises are more efficient than large ones, while other firms are small primarily because they are new companies—either new entrants to established industries or entrepreneurial enterprises in developing industries. Since these two types of small firms face fundamentally different situations, they have vastly different problems and opportunities. Accordingly, it is useful to treat the two classes separately. We first discuss the small firm in the traditional small business industry, then consider the small firm with growth potential.

Characteristics of Traditional Small Firms

The industries or segments of industries in which small businesses predominate exhibit three common characteristics: (1) a localized market, (2) low capital requirements, and (3) relatively simple technology. Because these characteristics lead to heavy dependence on one person, problems often arise:

1. The manager may not possess the full range of skills required: A good salesperson is not necessarily able to handle employees well; a new business may have at the head a manager who does not yet understand the need for adequate accounting records, financial control systems, and the like.
2. In a small business with only one leader, the control system tends to be informal, direct, and personal; it often lacks formal, standardized controls. If the business grows, the span of responsibilities may become excessive for the entrepreneur.
3. Because of the entrepreneur's preoccupation with the pressing problems of day-to-day operations, planning for the future is often inadequate, so changes in the economic environment or competitive shifts can have severe impacts on the small firm.
4. A relatively high degree of managerial training, experience, and breadth are necessary, yet often lacking; preoccupied with the present, the characteristic small-firm entrepreneur simply does not plan for management succession. Dun & Bradstreet data on business failures indicate that a larger proportion of failures is caused by the lack of experienced management than by any other factor.

Profitability of Small Firms

The problems of a small business may be illustrated by some representative numbers. Most small independent "Mom and Pop" grocery stores have sales of less than $500 per day, but let us assume that a particular store is doing relatively well and has sales of $500 per day. Assume also that the store is open 365 days a year, so its sales for the year total $182,500. According to the *Statement Studies* of the Robert Morris Associates, grocery retailers have a profit margin on sales of about 1 percent after taxes: if our small firm makes 2 percent on sales—to include salaries—that would represent a total profit of only $3,650 for the year. The proprietors of small grocery stores typically work ten to twelve hours per day, six to seven days a week. Making calculations on the conservative side at ten hours a day for six days a week implies sixty hours of work a week. Assuming a two-week vacation, this would be fifty weeks in the year times sixty hours for a total of 3,000 hours. Three thousand hours divided into $3,650 yields about $1.22 per hour. This is well below the now-prevailing minimum wage for unskilled workers and does not include a return on invested capital.

The owners may suffer even more problems. The average net worth turnover ratio for retail grocery stores is fifteen times per year, so on sales of $182,500 the owner would probably need about $12,000 of his or her own capital. An owner will not usually have this much initial capital. As a consequence, the typical small firm incurs an inordinate amount of trade credit. It has a weak current ratio, it is slow in paying its bills, and if it is inefficient, what little capital it has is quickly eroded. For reasons such as these, one-third to one-half of all retail firms are discontinued within their first two years of life: The infant mortality rate is high indeed among small businesses!

In the face of these discouraging statistics, why do people open their own businesses? The reasons vary. One is the hope that they will beat the statistics and will be successful—any community, large or small, has a group of very successful owners of small businesses who, while perhaps not millionaires, can afford $100,000 homes, country clubs, and trips to Europe, not to mention sending their children to college in style. A second reason is the freedom of making one's own decisions, even if the price of this freedom is high. Third, a person may not regard time spent working in his or her own firm as drudgery; there is a wide variety of tasks to be performed in running a small enterprise, and the work can be both interesting and challenging.

Financing the Traditional Small Firm

The typical small business, even the successful one, cannot look to the general capital markets for funds. If the firm owns any real property, it may be able to obtain a mortgage from a bank or a savings and loan. Equipment may perhaps be purchased under a conditional sales contract or be leased. After the business has survived a few years, bank financing may be available on a seasonal basis, but not for permanent growth. Trade credit will, typically, represent the bulk of outside financing (that is, funds not supplied by the owner) available to the firm.

Financial ratio analysis must be of major and overriding importance to the small firm. Such analysis, on a regular basis, is essential to ascertain whether the firm is operating with the requisite managerial efficiency. Whereas a larger, stronger firm may have the financial strength to fall below its industry standards and still recover, the small firm has a smaller margin for error. Thus, anyone interested in a small firm is well advised to look at trends in its financial ratios and to compare them with industry standards.

Working capital management is of overwhelming importance for most small firms. Because the amount of funds available is limited, liquidity is crucial. Trade credit appears to be an easy way of obtaining funds, yet even trade credit is obtained on terms that generally call for payment within thirty days. Since inventories typically represent a large percentage of total assets, a small firm's inventory policy must also be stressed. Large firms usually offer credit, so to meet competition, small firms may also have to extend credit. The large firm is likely to have an established credit department, but how does the small firm evaluate credit risks? What volume of accounts receivable can be built up without endangering both the solvency and the liquidity of the business? All of these are critical questions for the manager of a small business.

Current liability management is also important for the small firm. Although trade credit is relatively easy to obtain, it is often very costly. If discounts are available but not taken, the effective interest expense of such credit can be extremely high—as we know, not taking discounts on terms of 2/10, net 30 implies a 37 percent interest rate. Also, there is a temptation to be a perpetually slow payer, but this involves dangers: Suppliers may refuse any credit whatever, or they may quote higher prices.

As the volume of operations becomes larger, the increased flow of funds through the firm may give the proprietor a false sense of affluence. Such a person may move to a larger home with a spacious yard and pool and buy the latest model car. Since the business is growing, the owner feels the firm can afford to take on more debt. But the owner may be bleeding the business or, at least, removing retained earnings that are really needed to finance growth.

Many traditional small-business industries are today being conducted under franchise arrangement. Franchising represents a device whereby the training and experience required for a particular line of business are sold to the proprietor on a rental contract basis. Sometimes the franchise also includes a valuable trademark or calls for the supply of some key item. The franchiser may, through bulk buying, be able to sell supplies to the franchisee at lower costs than otherwise would be available. But, as many erstwhile franchise operators know, obtaining a franchise is not necessarily the road to riches—in many such arrangements, the owner of the franchised operation may be required to pay an excessive price for the trademark, specialty inputs and supplies, or managerial advice.

In summary, three areas of finance are of the utmost importance to firms in traditional small business industries. First, the proprietor of the traditional small business must rely on internal financing (retained earnings) to a greater extent than would the management of a larger firm. Second, to survive in the long run, the small business owner must be a somewhat better player of a relatively standardized game, in which financial ratio analysis can help the firm to excel. Third, working capital management is critical to the small entrepreneur; a small business owner who fails here will not remain solvent, and the firm will go out of business.

The Small Firm with Growth Potential

The second broad category of small business is the small firm with potential for substantial growth. Typically, such a firm has developed a new product or an innovative way of providing an old service: The electronics industry is a good example of the former, while franchised hamburgers and other food operations illustrate the latter. In this section, we discuss the financial aspects of such firms from inception until the business has matured enough to go public. The significant financial aspects of each stage of the firm's life cycle will be set out as a guide to the establishment and development of the new small business enterprise.

State 1: Experimentation Period

As indicated above and shown in Figure 25.1, the first stage of a firm's life cycle involves experimentation and simply getting itself firmly entrenched. During this period, management must lay the foundation for future growth, realizing that growth occurs either because the firm can increase its share of the market or because of industry expansion. Market share expansion is difficult because of the reaction of existing firms, and even if the industry is growing, management must recognize that every product and industry has a life cycle. Hence, supernormal growth, for whatever cause, will continue for only a finite period.

Even though the prospects of growth in an industry are favorable, there will be fluctuations. In addition, managers must be aware of the sales-to-capacity situation in the industry. For example, one of the most favorable growth industries in recent decades has been that of pleasure boats, which has generally grown at about the same rate as the growth in the population with incomes of over $12,000 per annum—10 to 12 percent per year. However, for a number of years capacity grew at a 20 percent rate, so after a point individual firms experienced the problem of excess capacity in spite of the favorable growth.

Particularly in new industries, it is important that the firm identify the techniques needed to succeed in the line of business. When the auto industry was maturing, dealership organizations and the availability of repair parts and service were the critical factors to the success of individual firms. In the computer industry, a backup of software, of marketing, and of maintenance service personnel was vital. In the aerospace industry, the essentials were technological capability and cost control.

Like the owner of a firm in a traditional small business industry, a growth industry entrepreneur must have a knowledge not only of a product and industry, but also of the standard administrative tools essential for effective management in any line of business. Financial planning and control processes are especially important. Financial ratio analysis should be used to develop standards for determining the broad outlines of the balance sheet and the income statement, as well as for guidelines to help isolate developing problem areas.

It is especially important for a small firm that expects growth to plan for it. Initially, such planning will emphasize the expansion of existing operations; later in the firm's life cycle, it must consider possible movements into new product lines. A basic decision that must be made, whatever type of expansion occurs, is choosing the degree to which production operations will be automated, requiring large fixed costs in the production process but providing great overall efficiency. Standard financial operating leverage, or breakeven analysis, can be employed to measure how changing sales levels will affect the firm's risk and return characteristics. If its forecasts of future sales are optimistic, the firm may make larger investments in fixed assets and choose more highly automated productive processes. As a consequence, its fixed costs will be higher, but its variable costs will be lower. At high operating levels, its total costs per unit will be lower than those of a firm with a smaller ratio of fixed costs to total costs, putting the firm into a strong position in relation to its rivals. However, if volume should fall to low levels, a firm with high operating leverage will face greater risks of bankruptcy.

Stage 2: Exploitation and Rapid Growth Period

After the firm's inception, a successful firm with growth potential will enter Stage 2 of its financial cycle. Here, the firm has achieved initial success—it is growing rapidly and is reasonably profitable. Cash flows and working capital management have become increasingly important. Also, at this stage the firm will have an extraordinary need for additional outside financing; this is shown in Table 25.1, which compares rapid and moderate growth firms. The growth company (Firm 1) expands from $800,000 in sales to $1.2 million in one year; Firm 2 grows by the same amount, but over a four-year period. The percentages in parentheses following the asset-liability accounts indicate the assumed relationships between asset items and the spontaneous sources of funds, which we discussed in Chapter 8 in the section on the percent of sales forecasting method. Note also that profits are assumed to be 6 percent of sales during the year, and that all earnings are retained. Let us further assume that notes payable are increased to cover the financing required—notes payable function as the balancing item. If the firm grows by 50 percent in one year, notes payable almost double. However, if the firm grows from $800,000 to $1.2 million over a four-year period, then notes payable not only

Table 25.1

Financial Effects of Different Rates of Growth (Thousands of Dollars)

	Firm 1		Firm 2				
	Year 1	Year 2	Year 1	Year 2	Year 3	Year 4	Year 5
Sales	$800	$1,200	$800	$900	$1,000	$1,100	$1,200
Current assets (30%)	240	360	240	270	300	330	360
Fixed assets (20%)	160	240	160	180	200	220	240
Total assets	$400	$ 600	$400	$450	$ 500	$ 550	$ 600
Accounts payable (10%)	80	120	80	90	100	110	120
Notes payable	96	172	96	79	56	27	(8)
Other accruals (3%)	24	36	24	27	30	33	36
Current liabilities	$200	$ 328	$200	$196	$ 186	$ 170	$ 148
Common stock	100	100	100	100	100	100	100
Retained earnings[a]	100	172	100	154	214	280	352
Net worth	$200	$ 272	$200	$254	$ 314	$ 380	$ 452
Total claims	$400	$ 600	$400	$450	$ 500	$ 550	$ 600
Key Ratios							
Current ratio (times)	1.2	1.1	1.2	1.4	1.6	1.9	2.4
Debt ratio (percentage)	50	55	50	44	37	31	25
Sales to total assets (times)	2	2	2	2	2	2	2
Profit to net worth (percentage)	24.0	26.5	24.0	21.3	19.1	17.4	15.9

a. Profit is 6 percent of sales; retained earnings are equal to profit plus retained earnings from the previous year.

do not increase at all, but they can actually be paid off. Hence, current liabilities decline from \$200,000 to \$148,000, while net worth increases from \$200,000 to \$452,000.

There is considerable doubt whether the growth firm could actually obtain short-term bank loans of the amount required. Such a large amount of short-term bank financing would cause its current ratio to drop to 1.1, and its debt ratio to rise to 55 percent. This situation develops even with the very favorable 24 percent rate of return on net worth. If the profit rate were lower, the firm's financing problem would be even more serious. When the firm uses four periods to achieve the same amount of growth, the financial ratios indicate a less risky situation. The current ratio never declines—it actually improves over the period. The debt ratio drops from 50 to 25 percent, which is very low compared with the average for all manufacturing firms.

If the rapid growth firm continues to grow at the 50 percent rate, the situation will further deteriorate, and it will become increasingly clear that the firm requires additional equity financing. The debt ratio will become much too high, yet the firm may well be reluctant to bring in additional outside equity money because the original owners are unwilling to share control. At this juncture, some financial pitfalls should be recognized and avoided. These are illustrated by the actual experiences of two individual small business owners who explained to the authors the difficulties they encountered. In one instance, the former owner of a firm described the problems that occurred after he obtained additional funds to support growth. He originally owned 100 percent of his company, but the firm needed capital. When two potential suppliers of the necessary funds each requested 30 percent ownership, the founder of the enterprise agreed, figuring that he would still have control with 40 percent, the largest block of the common stock. However, the two new equity owners joined forces, interfered with the creative management of the company, and caused it to fail. It may seem that this was a rather elementary error, since a person in business might be expected to look ahead to exactly this kind of move. However, production in new businesses tends to consume owner interest, and it is not uncommon for innovative entrepreneurs to fail as financial managers when more than one owner enters and changes the balance of power.

It is also an error to incur debt with an unrealistically short maturity. The former owner of another small firm borrowed on one- and two-year terms, but he failed to realize that if his firm continued to grow at a rapid rate, its needs for financing would increase, not decrease. Subsequently, he simply could not meet his debt maturities. It was convenient to borrow funds that were critically needed for growth on a relatively short-term basis, but when he was unable to make payments as the loans matured, he was forced to give up the controlling share of the equity. Thus, failure to plan properly again caused the founder to lose control of his company.

Risks in the Small Business. Risk is encountered at every stage in a small firm's development. In previous chapters, we have seen that risk results from the impacts of economic conditions, labor problems, competitive pressures, and so on. All firms face such risks, but they are magnified in small businesses. In traditional small-firm industries, entry is easy, competitive pressures drive profit margins to low levels, and there is little margin for error in allowing for adverse developments or managerial mistakes.

For small growth firms, the problem is compounded still further. These firms are typically entering new areas about which little information is available. There may be great potential, but large risks are also involved, and for every glowing success story there are many instances of failure. Further, even after an innovative growth firm has been established, there are continued pressures because of the financial problems noted above. Also, its demonstrated success will stimulate imitators, so its projections must take into account the influx of new firms and the likelihood of a declining market share and increased competitive pressures. Furthermore, high profits may lead to excess capacity, causing problems for every firm in the industry. For all these reasons, the small, rapidly growing firm faces a precarious existence, even when the product-market opportunities upon which it was conceived are sound.

Venture Capital Financing. Small firms that have growth potential face greater risks than almost any other type of business, and their higher risks require special types of financing. This has led to the development of specialized venture capital financing sources. Some venture capital companies are organized as partnerships; others are more formal corporations termed *investment development companies.*[1] The American Research and Development Corporation, one of the first investment development companies, is widely traded in the financial markets; it and other publicly owned investment companies permit individuals and institutions, such as insurance companies, to participate in the venture capital market. Other venture capital companies represent the activities of individuals or partnerships. From time to time the operations of these individual companies are described in the financial press. Notable examples are Arthur Rock and Charles Allen.[2]

When a new business makes an application for financial assistance from a venture capital firm, it receives a rigorous examination. Some development companies use their own staffs for this investigation, while others depend on a board of advisers acting in a consultative capacity. A high percentage of applications is rejected, but if the application is approved, funds are provided. Venture capital companies generally take an equity position in the firms they finance, but they may also extend debt capital. However, when loans are

1. Under the Investment Company Act of 1940, investment development companies are defined as closed-end, nondiversified investment companies. Closed-end investment companies are like mutual funds, but they differ in that they are under no obligation to buy back the shares they have issued.
2. See "Venture Capitalist with a Solid Intuition," *Business Week,* May 30, 1970, p. 102, for an article on Arthur Rock and "Meet Charlie Allen," *Wall Street Journal,* August 4, 1970, for an article on Charles Allen.

made, they generally involve convertibles or warrants or are tied in with the purchase of stock by the investment company.

Venture capital companies perform a continuing and active role in the enterprise. Typically, they do not insist on voting control, but they usually have at least one member on the board of directors of the new enterprise. The matter of control has *not* been one of the crucial considerations in investment companies' decisions to invest—indeed, if the management of a small business is not sufficiently strong to make sound decisions, the venture capital firm is not likely to be interested in the first place. However, the investment company does want to maintain continuous contact, provide management counsel, and monitor the progress of its investment.

Another distinctive contribution of the venture capital firm stems from its ownership by wealthy individuals. (Lawrence Rockefeller, for example, is a leading venture capitalist.) For tax reasons, such people are interested in receiving their income in the form of capital gains rather than current income. They are, therefore, in a position to take larger risks. If they lose on the venture, the net after-tax loss is only a portion of the investment since they are in high personal income tax brackets. For example, a $100,000 loss "costs" only $25,000 for an investor who is in the 75 percent state-plus-federal tax bracket.[3] Their gains, if any, are in the form of capital gains; they are therefore taxed at a rate lower than the rate on ordinary personal income. Thus, for the wealthy individual, the odds are in favor of making higher risk investments.

Another source of venture capital has been developed in recent years—large, well established business firms.[4] A number of large corporations have invested both money and various types of know-how to start or to help develop small business firms. The owner of the small firm is usually a specialist, frequently a technically-oriented person who needs both money and help in such administrative services as accounting, finance, production, and marketing. The small firm's owner contributes entrepreneurship, special talents, a taste for risk taking, and "the willingness to work 18 hours a day for peanuts." A number of major corporations have found that there is a mutual advantage for this form of venture capital investment.

Another important source of venture capital financing for small business is the Small Business Investment Company (SBIC). The Small Business Investment Company Act of 1958 empowered the Small Business Administration (SBA) to license and regulate SBICs and to provide them with financial assistance. A minimum of $150,000 in private capital is required for the licensing of an SBIC, and this amount can be doubled by selling subordinated debentures to the SBA (at interest rates generally below prevailing market rates).

In their operations, SBICs have followed two policies similar to invest-

3. Special tax provisions make it possible to offset more than the regular $1,000 of ordinary income by capital losses if the losses are on small businesses as defined by the tax code.
4. "Venture Capital, Corporation Style," *Forbes*, August 1, 1970, pp. 41–42.

ment development or venture capital companies. First, their investments are generally made by the purchase of convertible securities or bonds with warrants, thus giving the SBICs a residual equity position in the companies to which funds are provided. Second, SBICs emphasize management counsel, for which a fee is charged.[5]

By the end of the 1970s, there were over 300 SBICs with total resources of more than $1.1 billion. In addition, during the year 1971, Public Law 92-213 amended the Small Business Investment Company Act and clarified the SBA's authority to guarantee debentures issued by the SBICs, thus providing the SBIC industry with an expanded source of funding at interest rates somewhat below prevailing market levels.

The SBICs benefit from the aura of government sponsorship and the availability of long-term subordinated debt on attractive terms. Also, the spectacular success of one investment can assure the prosperity of an SBIC or other venture capital company.[6] When SBICs first appeared in the 1950s, these advantages gave rise to very optimistic expectations about SBICs' stock market values. Beginning in 1961, however, investors' appraisals of SBIC common stocks plunged, as it became clear that SBICs were not a guaranteed road to riches. To find and finance successful small businesses requires much work and considerable risks. There was indeed a weeding out of the weaker firms, and since the mid-1960s SBICs have achieved steady progress.

Stage 3: Growth to Maturity

Going Public. With good management, the right economic conditions, and sufficient financing either from a venture capital company or from a government agency, the firm will move into Stage 2, the period of rapid growth. Here the increasing financing requirements will put pressure on the firm to raise capital from the public equity markets. At this point, a full assessment of the critical step of going public must be made.

Going public represents a fundamental change in life-style in at least four respects: (1) The firm moves from informal, personal control to a system of formal controls, and the need for financial techniques such as ratio analysis and the Du Pont system of financial planning and control greatly increases. (2) Information must be reported on a timely basis to the outside investors, even though the founders may continue to have majority control. (3) The firm must have a breadth of management in all the business functions if it is to operate its expanded business effectively. (4) The publicly owned firm typically draws on a board of directors to help formulate sound plans and policies; the board should include representatives of the public owners and other external interest groups to aid the management group in carrying out its broader responsibilities.

5. The larger SBICs have staffs similar to those of holding companies or conglomerates; these staffs provide assistance, for a fee, to the firms in which the SBICs have invested.

6. American Research and Development Company, for example, made over $100 million on the investment of a few thousand dollars in Digital Equipment.

The valuation process is particularly important at the time the firm goes public: At what price will stock be sold to new outside investors? In analyzing the investment value of the small and growing firm, some significant differences in capital costs between large and small firms should be noted:

1. It is especially difficult to obtain reasonable estimates of the cost of equity capital for small, privately owned firms.
2. Because of the risks involved, the required rate of return tends to be high for small firms. However, portfolio effects from a pooling of risks can reduce this factor somewhat.
3. Tax considerations are generally quite important for privately owned companies that are large enough to consider going public, as the owner-managers are probably in the top personal tax brackets. This factor can cause the effective after-tax cost of retained earnings to be considerably lower than the after-tax cost of new outside equity.
4. Flotation costs for new security issues, especially new stock issues, are much higher for small than for large firms. This factor, as well as tax considerations, causes the marginal cost of capital curve for small firms to rise rapidly once retained earnings have been exhausted.

The timing of the decision to go public is also especially important, because small firms are more affected by variations in money market conditions than larger companies. During periods of tight money and high interest rates, financial institutions, especially commercial banks, find that the quantity of funds demanded exceeds the supply available at legally permissible and conventionally acceptable rates. One important method employed to ration credit is to raise credit standards. During tight money periods, both a stronger balance sheet record and a longer and more stable record of profitability are required in order to qualify for bank credit. Since financial ratios for small and growing firms tend to be less strong, such firms bear the brunt of credit restraint. Obviously, the small firm that goes public and raises equity capital before a money squeeze is in a better position to ride it out. This firm has already raised some of its needed capital, and its equity cushion enables it to present a stronger picture to the banks, thus helping it to obtain additional capital in the form of debt.

The SEC has made a number of changes to make it easier for small firms to sell their stock to the public. Under Regulation A offerings, a firm is not required to meet standard SEC securities registration requirements. In 1978, the SEC raised the dollar ceiling for Regulation A offerings from $500,000 to $1.5 million. In late May 1979, the SEC announced that underwriters of Regulation A stock offerings will be able to use a preliminary offering circular as a sales tool, rather than waiting until a final offering circular has been cleared by the SEC staff. Securities firms had told the SEC that their inability to use the preliminary circular had hampered their ability to make firm underwriting commitments for such issues.

Also in May 1979, the SEC announced that a new and simplified registration form would be available to smaller firms with assets of less than $1 million and fewer than 500 shareholders. Such firms will be permitted to raise up to $5 million in the public market by using a new S-18 simplified registration form instead of the standard S-1. The companies may also register the sale at any of the commission's nine regional offices rather than in Washington only. This will enable them to use their local accounting and legal firms, holding down costs.

Small Business Administration

To help small firms obtain capital, the federal government set up the Small Business Administration (SBA).[7] The SBA operates a number of different programs. One was discussed before in connection with the formation and growth of SBICs. Another, the "Business Loan Program," provides funds for construction, machinery, equipment, and working capital.[8] Loans under this program, which are available only when small businesses are unable to obtain funds on reasonable terms from private sources, are of two types: direct loans and participation loans. In a direct loan, the SBA simply makes a loan to a small business borrower. In a participation loan, the SBA lends part of the funds, while a bank or other private lending institution advances the balance. Under a participation loan, a portion of the funds advanced by the private party may be guaranteed by the SBA. The maximum amount the SBA may lend to any borrower is $350,000; this maximum applies to either a direct loan or to the SBA's portion of a participation loan.

Since SBA loans or guarantees are advantageous to the business recipient, the definition of what constitutes a small business is important. Actually, the definition varies somewhat, depending upon the industry. Any manufacturing concern is defined as small if it employs up to 250 people, while it is defined as large if it employs more than 1,000 people. Within this range, the SBA has different standards for different industries. A wholesale firm is classified as

7. The SBA also helps small companies obtain a share of government contracts, and it administers training programs of various types designed to help small entrepreneurs.
8. In addition to the Business Loan Program, the SBA administers a number of other programs, including the following: (1) Equal Opportunity Loan Program, designed specifically for disadvantaged persons who wish to start or expand an existing business, (2) Development Company Loan Program, which is used to help attract businesses to geographic areas in need of economic stimulation, (3) Displaced Business Loan Program, designed to help small businesses which are forced to relocate because of urban renewal or similar events, (4) Disaster Loan Program, designed to aid both businesses and homeowners who suffer losses as a consequence of some natural disaster, (5) Lease Guarantee Program, designed to help small businesses to obtain rental space in the commercial real estate market, (6) Revolving Line-of-Credit Program designed to aid small building contractors, (7) Surety Bonding Program, designed to aid small businesses that must post performance bonds when seeking contracts, and (8) Minority Enterprise SBIC Program, which is designed to stimulate SBICs whose clients are minority-owned firms.

small if its annual sales are $5 million or less. Most retail businesses and service firms are defined as small if their total annual receipts are less than $1 million.[9]

Summary

The key factors relating to small business financing are summarized briefly in Table 25.2, which sets forth the financing patterns at the firm's four stages of development. In its formative stage, the new, small firm must rely most heavily on personal savings, trade credit, and government agencies. During its period of rapid growth, internal financing will become an important source of meeting its financing requirements, although continued reliance will be placed on trade credit. At this stage, its record of accomplishment also makes it possible to obtain bank credit to finance seasonal needs; and if the loan can be paid off on an amortized basis over two or three years, the firm may qualify for a term loan as well. If it has the potential for really strong growth, the firm may also be able to attract equity from a venture capital company.

A particularly successful firm may reach the stage where going public becomes feasible—this leads to access to the broader money and capital markets, and it represents a true coming-of-age for the small firm. Even at this point, however, the firm must look ahead, analyzing its products and their prospects. Because every product has a life cycle, the firm must be aware that without the development of new products, growth will cease, and eventually the firm will decline. Accordingly, as product maturity approaches, the firm must plan for the possibility of share repurchases, mergers, or other longer-term strategies. The best time to look ahead and plan for this is while the firm has energy, momentum, and a high price-earnings ratio.

In our coverage of small business financing, the major emphasis has been on providing a framework for analyzing financial needs and opportunities

Table 25.2

Financing Patterns at Four Stages of a Firm's Development

Stage	Financing Pattern
1. Formation	Personal savings, trade credit, government agencies
2. Rapid growth	Internal financing, trade credit, bank credit, venture capital
3. Growth to maturity	Going public, money and capital markets
4. Maturity and industry decline	Internal financing, share repurchase, diversification, mergers

9. A great deal of additional information on the SBA and its various programs may be obtained directly from the Small Business Administration, Washington, D.C., or from regional SBA offices.

as the characteristics of the firm and its industry evolve. While this type of analysis cannot replace mature judgment, it can certainly aid such judgment and help financial managers of small businesses maximize their contributions to the successful development of small business enterprises.

Questions

25.1 A friend of yours has just developed a new product and plans to start a business to produce it. One of his goals is to maintain absolute control, but his own capital is limited. What are some of the ways he can reduce the amount of his initial outlay while still obtaining the use of an efficiently large plant?

25.2 Assume that you are starting a business of your own of the traditional small business type. Develop an outline of the kinds of decisions you will have to make in establishing and financing the small enterprise.

25.3 What are some sources of information on the past performance of a firm you are thinking of buying?

25.4 What is a voting trust? Why is it used?

25.5 What influence does each of the following have on possible divergences between the goals and objectives of the managers who control a corporation and those of its stockholders?

a. Profit sharing plans.
b. Executive compensation schemes.
c. Employee stock option plans.

Problems

25.1 Susan Smith, a liberal arts student, decided to leave her university at the end of her second year in order to open one of the simplest of retail trade establishments, a grocery store specializing in health foods.

Although Smith had received an allowance from home and had worked a bit at summer jobs, she had managed to save only a little over $1,000. After talking with some of her friends in business administration at the university, Smith recognized that she had to consider such things as location, potential flow of customer traffic, and present and potential competition. Also, she realized that it would be necessary to analyze the alternatives of buying a building or renting a store and buying or renting the equipment and fixtures she would need—counters, shelving, cash register, and the like. The store space she had in mind had not been occupied by a grocery before, so it lacked shelves and counters.

a. Should Smith buy or rent the store facilities?
b. How should she acquire the equipment and fixtures?
c. What kinds of questions is she likely to face with regard to choice of product line?
d. For planning purposes, assume sales per day of $100, $300, and $500, and a profit ratio of net income before taxes to sales of 4 percent. What are her earnings per hour before taxes, assuming that she works 10 hours per day, seven days a week, for 50 weeks per year?
e. With a sales to net worth ratio of 15 times, what investment on her part is indicated at each level of sales? Comment on how she can raise the funds if sev-

eral years are required to reach each alternative level of sales, and also comment upon the implications of her taking withdrawals from the business.

f. What additional questions must Smith face if she sells on credit?

g. What are the critical problems likely to be if sales start at $500 per day?

25.2 The Hollywood Plastics Company was formed by Fred Thatcher and John Watson in 1972 while they were both employed by the Universal Plastics Company. At that time, they had foreseen a great opportunity in the future of the plastics industry, especially in the Southern California area. Therefore, after several detailed discussions, they decided to start their own firm.

Now in 1982, after ten years of fast growth in both sales and profits, Hollywood Plastics has become one of the most successful plastics producers in Southern California. To realize the firm's full growth potential, Thatcher, the president of Hollywood Plastics, considered it necessary for the firm to acquire financing beyond what Hollywood Plastics could achieve under its present form and method of operations. Thus, the idea of going public has been brought up. Through HPC's correspondent bank, Security First National, Thatcher was brought into contact with a number of venture capital sources, as well as several investment bankers. They all asked for a report that would cover Hollywood Plastics' background and present a five-year forecast of sales and earnings.

Thatcher had asked his close friend, Kent Brown, an outstanding finance professor at Cal State, to help him develop the report. As an expert in the finance field, Brown utilized a wide range of tools encompassing most of the topics in modern managerial finance to prepare the report.

The first segment of the report contained a statement of Hollywood Plastics' product concept. An excerpt from the statement is given below:

The products of Hollywood Plastics consist primarily of the following items: modubox systems for industrial users, trays and cases for the school market, duro nesting boxes for the produce and food markets, duro tote boxes for hospitals, airline service trays, display fixtures, instrument cases, instrument housings, rocket engine closures and other custom parts.

Most of the products and customers served by Hollywood Plastics are growing rapidly. In addition, Hollywood Plastics has a number of advantages that will enable the company to continue to increase its penetration of these markets. It has the rights and patents to various box design features and has product names which have been copyrighted. Even more important, Hollywood Plastics continues to be the leader in the development of new ideas for materials handling systems. In the food and hospital industries, sanitation requirements are increasingly requiring the substitution of plastic products for wood containers.

The school market has been only scratched, and Hollywood Plastics is beginning to supply the manufacturers of school equipment with boxes and trays.

The advantages of Hollywood Plastics' product line are continuing to lead to the substitution of its products for older materials. As a consequence, the replacement of older materials in industries whose total growth is low should result in tremendous further growth for Hollywood Plastics.

Hollywood Plastics has developed customer recognition and loyalty both by the quality of its products and by a ten-year program of national advertising, including full-page advertisements in *Modern Materials Handling Magazine, Western Materials Handling,* etc. This advertising program has strengthened the position of the company, as has its strong national distribution system, which utilizes 200 distributors.

The sales growth figures that Brown developed are based on his analysis of Hollywood Plastics' product lines and the prospective growth in each of its product areas. Because of Hollywood Plastics' rapid growth rate, Brown used a semi-logarithmic chart. Brown's projections are shown in the first figure in this problem.

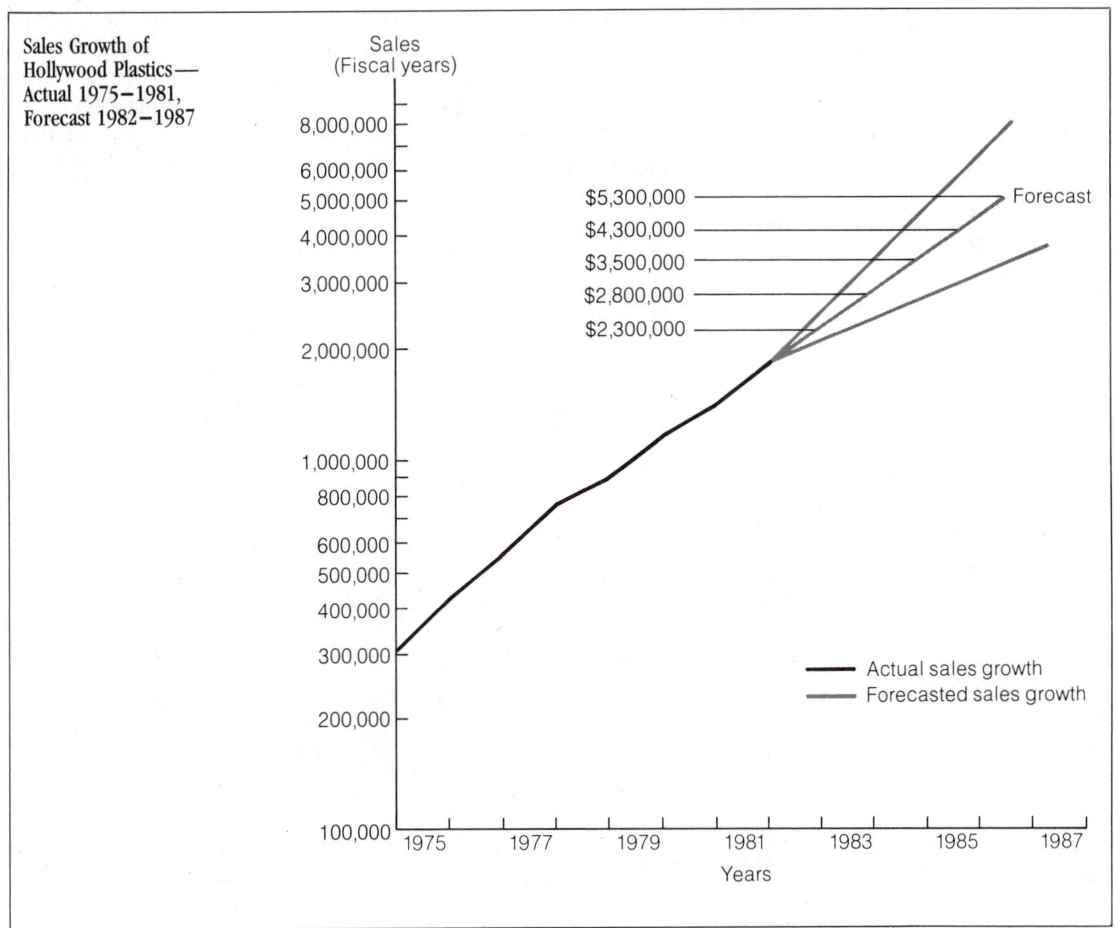

Sales Growth of Hollywood Plastics—Actual 1975–1981, Forecast 1982–1987

Brown also developed some basic financial relations that he used as the foundation for pro forma balance sheets, income statements, and profitability relations as determined by the sales forecast. One of Brown's three tables in this problem presents abbreviated income statements for each of the past five years, with each element of the income statement shown both in absolute terms and as a percentage of net sales. Another table gives historical balance sheets for

Hollywood Plastics between 1977 and 1981. A related breakeven chart is set forth in a figure. The historical balance sheet and income statement (and breakeven analysis) are used to construct the projected financial statements to make possible the analysis and valuation involved in the firm's going public. The following questions indicate the kind of analysis that is required for taking the firm public.

a. From the data in the income statements, plot a scatter diagram of the relationship of each of the following items to sales: (1) cost of goods sold, (2) selling expenses, and (3) general and administrative expenses.
b. Using the following equations: Cost of goods sold = \$6,000 + 0.70 (Sales); Selling expense = \$10,000 + 0.12 (Sales); General and administrative expenses = \$5,000 + 0.10 (Sales); and federal income tax = 0.5 (Net income before tax), set forth a pro forma income statement forecast for Hollywood Plastics for the years 1982 through 1987 including a percentage analysis as shown in the income statements for 1977 through 1981. Assume the forecast sales levels are \$1,776,000 for 1982, \$2,234,000 for 1983, \$2,801,000 for 1984, \$3,482,000 for 1985, \$4,290,000 for 1986, and \$5,247,000 for 1987.

Hollywood Plastics Co.
Balance Sheet, 1977–1981
(Thousands of Dollars)

Assets	1977	1978	1979	1980	1981
Cash	8	1	8	15	35
Accounts receivable	44	69	86	102	165
Inventories	41	59	72	109	86
Total current assets	93	129	166	226	286
Gross fixed assets	50	75	98	129	156
Less: Depreciation	31	58	68	79	100
Net fixed assets	19	17	30	50	56
Total assets	112	146	196	276	342
Liabilities					
Notes payable	19	16	12	24	3
Accounts payable	43	61	81	100	122
Accruals	13	24	30	45	68
Total current liabilities	75	101	123	169	193
Long-term debt	12	4	11	15	11
Capital stock (par value \$.50)	22	22	30	30	30
Retained earnings	3	19	32	62	108
Total net worth	25	41	62	92	138
Total liabilities and net worth	112	146	196	276	342

c. From the balance sheet table data, plot six scatter diagrams to show the relationship to sales of the following items: accounts receivable, inventory, total fixed assets before depreciation, total assets, accounts payable, and total long-term liabilities. Fit regression lines where possible.
d. Using the following equations: Accounts receivable = 0.12 (Sales); Total fixed assets before depreciation = \$15,000 + 0.1 (Sales); Inventories = \$2,800 + 0.086 (Sales); Accounts payable = \$9,400 + 0.078 (Sales); Cash = 0.04 (Sales);

Income Statement, Fiscal Years 1977–1981 (Thousands of Dollars)

	1977		1978		1979		1980		1981	
	Amount	Percent	Amount	Percent	Amount	Percent	Amount	Percent	Amount	Percent
1. Sales (net)	$403	100.0	$560	100.0	$853	100.0	$1,169	100.0	$1,407	100.0
2. Less: Cost of goods sold	310	76.9	397	70.9	598	70.1	821	70.2	1,000	71.1
3. Gross profit	93	23.1	163	29.1	255	29.9	348	29.8	407	28.9
4. Selling expenses	54	13.4	92	16.4	120	14.1	187	16.0	205	14.6
5. Administrative and general expenses	38	9.4	51	9.1	105	12.3	113	9.7	118	8.4
6. Subtotal	92	22.8	143	25.5	225	26.4	300	25.7	323	23.0
7. Profit from operations	1	0.2	20	3.6	30	3.5	48	4.1	84	6.0
8. Other income	9	2.2	4	0.7	6	0.7	3	0.3	—	—
9. Net income before federal income tax	10	2.4	24	4.3	36	4.2	51	4.4	84	6.0
10. Federal income tax	1	0.2	8	1.4	13	1.5	21	1.8	39	2.8
11. Net income	$ 9	2.2	$ 16	2.9	$ 23	2.7	$ 30	2.6	$ 45	3.2

Accruals = 0.08 (Sales); and Annual depreciation = 0.1 (Gross fixed assets), make a forecast of the balance sheets for 1982 through 1987. If more financing is needed, increase notes payable as an adjusting item. If excess cash is available from operations, first pay off notes payable and then create an additional asset account entitled "Cash Available from Operations" (marketable securities.)

e. Using the data you arrived at in Part d, calculate financial ratios. Perform a financial ratio analysis for the years 1977 through 1981 and on a projected basis for 1982 to 1987 on the following ratios: (1) current ratio, (2) average collection period, (3) current liability/total assets, (4) long-term debt/total assets, (5) total debt/total assets, (6) net profits/sales, (7) net profits/total assets, and (8) net profits/net worth. From these ratios, comment on the past financial position of Hollywood Plastics and on the prospects for the forecasted years, 1982 through 1987.

f. The second figure shown in this problem is a breakeven analysis for Hollywood Plastics. Comment on the pattern indicated by the analysis set forth.

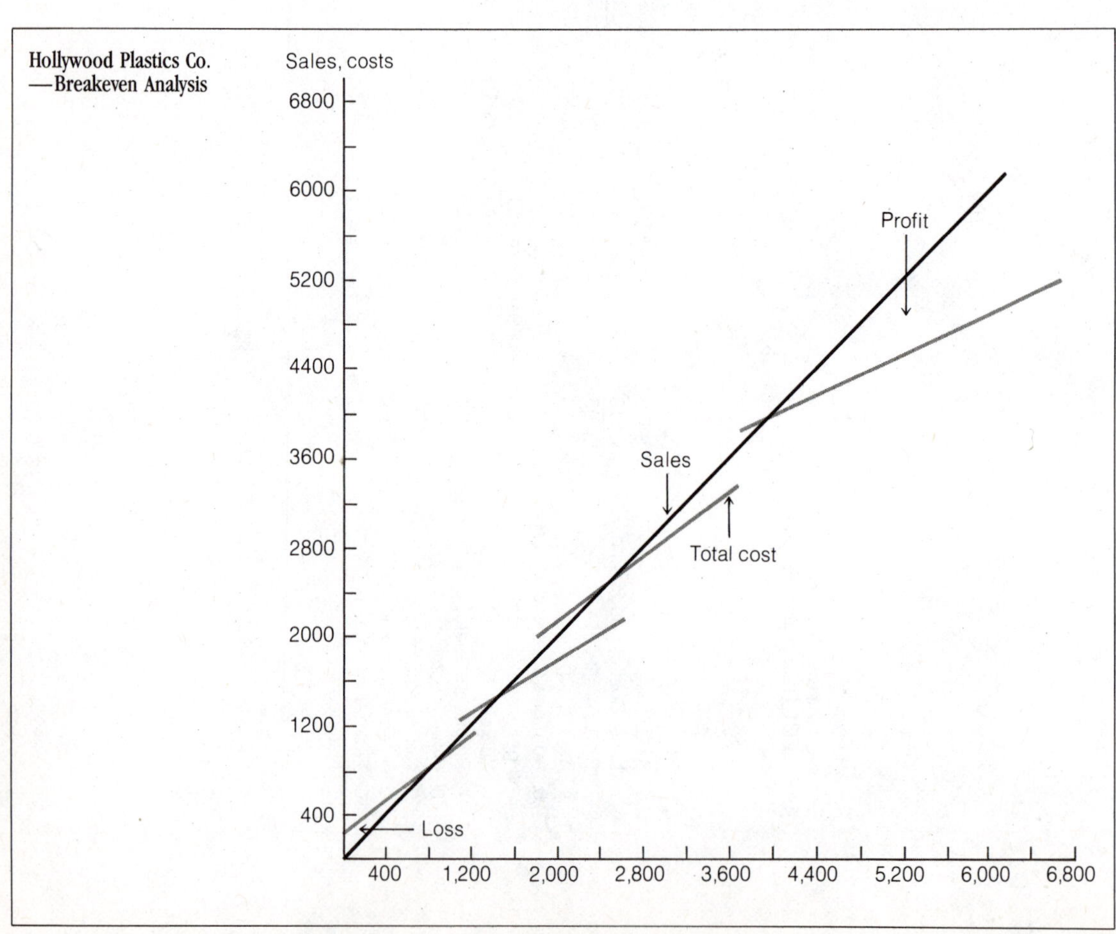

Hollywood Plastics Co. —Breakeven Analysis

g. From the data in the balance sheet table, develop a sources and uses of funds statement for Hollywood Plastics for the five-year period 1977 through 1981.
h. Using the method for calculating the value of a company with a supernormal growth period discussed in Chapter 17, set forth a total value for Hollywood Plastics when a cost of capital of 20 percent is used. (Some justification for the 20 percent cost of capital is set forth in the table titled "Factors Affecting Valuation of Hollywood Plastics.") Use the projected net income figures you have developed, assuming a dividend payout of 50 percent and assuming that from 1988 on, dividends will grow at a normal rate of 10 percent per annum.
i. The investment bankers actually sold 40,000 shares at net proceeds of $400,000. Discuss this implied valuation of the company in comparison with your calculation under Part h above.
j. Based on data on costs of flotation by size of issue, indicate what you think might be appropriate compensation to the investment bankers for taking this company public.

Factors Affecting Valuation of Hollywood Plastics

A. Product-Market Characteristics

1. Hollywood Plastics is the originator of many materials handling systems and continues to be the leader in the development of new products and uses.
2. Companies in the food and hospital fields are increasingly substituting the products of Hollywood Plastics for older and less sanitary materials they have been using in the past.
3. Five of the six markets in which products are sold are strong growth areas.

B. General Valuation Factors

1. Strong national distribution with 200 distributors.
2. Can support sales growth to $5 million without expansion of plant.

C. Additional Valuation Items

1. Current earnings underestimated by approximately $30,000 per year based on immediate write-off of tooling expense.
2. Current value of net worth estimated by Kent Brown to be approximately $1,000,000 based on appraisal of individual asset items and cash balances.
3. Selling power built up by ten-year advertising program has capital value.

Selected References

Archer, S. H., and Faerber, L. G. "Firm Size and the Cost of Externally Secured Equity Capital." *Journal of Finance* 21 (March 1966), pp. 69–83.

Brigham, Eugene F., and Smith, Keith V. "The Cost of Capital to the Small Firm." *Engineering Economist* 13 (Fall 1967), pp. 1–26.

Casey, William J. *Chairman's Report of the SBA Task Force on Venture and Equity Capital for Small Business.* Washington, D.C.: U.S. Small Business Administration, January 1977, pp. 1–21.

Davis R. D. "Small Business in the Next Decade." *Advanced Management Journal* 31 (January 1966), pp. 5–8.

Garvin, W. J. "Small Business Capital Gap: The Special Case of Minority Enterprise." *Journal of Finance* 26 (May 1971), pp. 445–457, 466–471.

Gilmore, F. F. "Formulating Strategy in Smaller Companies." *Harvard Business Review* 49 (May 1971), pp. 71–81.

Guttentag, J. M., and Herman, E. S. "Do Large Banks Neglect Small Business?" *Journal of Finance* 21 (September 1966), pp. 535–538.

Korbel, John. "Micro-Analytic Model of the Generation and Application of Savings in Small Business." *Review of Economics and Statistics* 47 (August 1965), pp. 279–286.

Martin, Dawson. "Can Edge Act Companies Have a Venture Capital Strategy?" *Columbia Journal of World Business* 4 (November–December 1969), pp. 73–80.

McConkey, D. D. "Will Ecology Kill Small Business?" *Business Horizons* 15 (April 1972), pp. 61–69.

Pfeffer, Irving, ed. *The Financing of Small Business.* New York: Macmillan, 1967.

Rossiter, Bruce G., and Miller, Gene I. "Financing the New Enterprise." In *The Treasurer's Handbook,* edited by J. Fred Weston and Maurice B. Goudzwaard. Homewood, Ill.: Dow Jones–Irwin, 1976, pp. 861–900.

Rubel, S. M. "Important Changes Occur in Venture Capital Industry." *Bankers Monthly* 87 (May 1970), pp. 24–25.

Steiner, George. "Approaches to Long-Range Planning for Small Business." *California Management Review* 10 (Fall 1967), pp. 3–16.

Walker, Ernest W., and Petty, J. William II. "Financial Differences between Large and Small Firms." *Financial Management* 7 (Winter 1978), pp. 61–74.

Wheelright, S. C. "Strategic Planning in the Small Business." *Business Horizons* 14 (August 1971), pp. 51–58.

White, L. T. "Management Assistance for Small Business." *Harvard Business Review* 43 (July 1965), pp. 67–74.

26

International Business Finance

International financial developments are having an increased effect on people because all parts of the world are now more closely linked together than ever before. Communications throughout the world take place within a matter of minutes or even seconds. Jet airplanes can take people anywhere within a matter of hours. Realignment of the relative values of different countries' currencies is continually occurring. These international financial developments have been helpful to some and harmful to others. Although the relationships are complex, the fundamentals presented here will provide a basis for understanding the new opportunities and threats that result from the increasingly dynamic international environment.

Changes in Relative Monetary Values in Recent Years

The changes in currency values that have taken place since 1965 are set forth in Table 26.1, which compares the values in relation to the U.S. dollar for two countries whose currencies have increased in strength and two whose currencies have declined in strength over recent years. In August 1971 the major countries of the world departed from a policy of fixed exchange rates. But even before this formal recognition of realignment in currency values, changes had already been taking place. For years the ratio of the Japanese yen to the U.S. dollar was 360 to 1. By mid-1978 the number of yen required to equal one dollar had dropped to 186. The value of the yen in relation to the dollar increased by 86 percent from 1965 to 1978 and then fell back to a 68 percent increase. The value of the German mark was four marks to the dollar, but by mid-1980 it had dropped to less than two marks to the dollar. Thus the dollar value of the mark increased from approximately 25 cents to 57 cents—an increase of over 100 percent.

For Mexico and Brazil, however, the changes have been in the opposite direction. During the 1960s the Mexican peso was worth 8 cents, and its ratio

This chapter utilizes materials developed jointly with Bart W. Sorge in J. Fred Weston and Bart W. Sorge, *International Managerial Finance* (Homewood, Ill.: Richard D. Irwin, 1972); and J. Fred Weston and Bart W. Sorge, *Guide to International Financial Management* (New York: McGraw-Hill, 1977).

Table 26.1

Number of Foreign Currency Units per U.S. Dollar

	1965	1970	1971	1972	1973	1974	1975	1976	1977	1978	1979	June 17, 1980
Japan X	360.90	357.60	314.80	302.00	280.00	300.95	305.15	292.80	240.00	194.60	239.70	215.45
E	0.00277	0.00280	0.00318	0.00331	0.00357	0.00332	0.00328	0.00342	0.00417	0.00514	0.00417	0.00464
Index	100	101	115	119	129	120	118	123	151	186	151	168
W. Germany X	4.00	3.65	3.27	3.20	3.70	2.41	2.62	2.36	2.11	1.83	1.73	1.76
E	0.2500	0.2740	0.3058	0.3125	0.2703	0.4149	0.3817	0.4237	0.4739	0.5464	0.5780	0.5682
Index	100	110	122	125	108	166	153	169	190	219	231	227
Mexico X	12.50	12.50	12.50	12.50	12.50	12.50	12.50	20.00	22.70	22.72	22.80	22.83
E	0.08	0.08	0.08	0.08	0.08	0.08	0.08	0.05	0.0441	0.0440	0.0439	0.0438
Index	100	100	100	100	100	100	100	63	55	55	55	55
Brazil X	0.89	2.47	5.64	6.22	6.22	7.44	9.07	12.35	16.05	20.92	42.53	51.45
E	1.1236	0.4049	0.1773	0.1608	0.1608	0.1344	0.1103	0.0810	0.0623	0.0478	0.0235	0.0194
Index	100	36	16	14	14	12	10	7	6	4	2	2

X = Number of LCs (foreign currency units) per dollar.
E = Value of one LC (foreign currency unit) in dollars.
Index: 1965 = 100.
Sources: International Monetary Fund, *International Financial Statistics*, monthly issues, and "Foreign Exchange," *Wall Street Journal*, June 18, 1980, p. 40.

to the U.S. dollar was 12.5 to 1. In 1976 the peso was allowed to float against the dollar, and by mid-1978 the ratio of the peso to the dollar had moved to 22.85. Thus the value of the peso had shrunk to slightly over 4 cents, a decline of almost 50 percent from its previous value. For years Brazil has had a policy of periodically adjusting the value of its cruzeiro. Through these successive adjustments, in early 1980 the value of the cruzeiro in relation to the dollar was only 2 percent of what it had been in 1965.

Thus changes in currency values in relation to the dollar have been very substantial—and in both directions. Almost every business firm has experienced some of the effects of these changes on its operations. Its inputs may include imported materials, and its products may be exported or become part of an exported product. Some large companies have earned more than half their profits abroad. Even for smaller companies it is not uncommon to find that, if international sales can be developed to about one-fourth of total sales, then earnings from foreign sales or operations are likely to be as high as 40 to 50 percent of total earnings. International operations often enable the smaller firm to achieve better utilization of its investment in fixed plant and equipment.

The Development of an International Firm

A firm generally develops its international activities through an evolutionary process. Different areas of each firm are engaged in international activities in different degrees. The steps in the progression from a domestic to a multinational firm may differ among individual firms, but a general pattern can be observed. The existence of the development of a strong competitive product for domestic sales is a prerequisite for international operations. A firm must have a management team capable of developing and producing a strong, quality product to be able to cope with the many new environmental factors and uncertainties that will be encountered in international operations. A firm that cannot make it in the domestic market is even less likely to make it in the international market. Furthermore, a firm that is successful on a domestic basis is more likely than others to be able to obtain the financing required to achieve involvement in international operations.

Importing raw materials or parts may bring international exposure to the firm, since import contacts create interest in potential outlets for foreign sales. Exporting through brokers is a recommended first step if the firm's sales personnel have little experience in export sales and if the goods sold require a knowledge of foreign markets. A firm that exports large industrial machines may attempt to make sales directly since it is dealing with buyers whose needs it fully understands. But a firm selling a nondurable consumer good, such as a food product, needs to develop an understanding of the purchase habits and requirements of the consumers in foreign countries. It may also have to make use of a complex and different form of distribution system. Hence its first step is likely to be through brokers.

When a satisfactory volume of sales has been achieved, the firm may establish a foreign branch sales office, which will enable it to achieve more direct contacts overseas and to keep in closer touch with foreign market developments. The foreign sales office also locates technical service personnel closer to the firm's customers, a procedure that enables them to respond promptly when needed.

For a number of reasons, a firm may subsequently begin to consider establishing a production operation abroad. For example, before the U.S. automobile market became receptive to small cars, companies such as General Motors and Ford began producing more compact cars in foreign countries, where higher gasoline prices and narrower streets and roads created a much earlier market for such cars.

However, because of strong controls by some foreign governments, licensing often has to precede foreign sales as well as foreign production operations. Where licensing is essential because of foreign government regulations, its advantages and disadvantages must be evaluated. One of the advantages is that it can shift a wide range of problems from the domestic firm to its foreign licensee. Another advantage is that since the domestic firm is not required to make an additional investment, the net cash flows from licensing may represent a very high return on the incremental investment to the U.S. firm. From the long-term point of view, however, licensing has serious disadvantages. A firm producing highly technical products involving unique manufacturing processes may have to impart confidential know-how or information to the licensee, which can become a competitor when the license expires. For this reason a firm may seek to work out a partial ownership position with the licensee so that it can continue to participate in the long-term profits from the operation.

Joint venture is another form of participation in foreign operations that may precede the establishment of foreign subsidiaries. Indeed, it may be required by government regulations and restrictions. For example, some countries do not permit foreign firms to engage in manufacturing operations, limiting them to joint ventures as minority investors. Joint ventures can be of value in helping obtain the local goodwill and support necessary for the success of the operation. They also enable smaller firms to expand abroad with a small investment and to share the risk with foreign investors. But joint ventures can also produce conflicts of interest and a possible loss of control for the U.S. firm.

Ultimately, the U.S. firm may seek to establish wholly-owned manufacturing branch plants or subsidiaries abroad, since administration and control are easier without the complication of local partners, and maximum security of business methods and know-how is achieved. Wholly-owned manufacturing facilities are possible in most developed countries and in some developing countries.

The development of international operations is shown in Table 26.2, which indicates how a firm progresses from export and import sales activi-

Table 26.2

The Development Process for Multinational Operations

1. Development of a strong product for domestic sales
2. Importation of some products
3. Use of export brokers
4. Direct export selling
5. Branch sales office abroad
6. Licensing
7. Licensing with joint venture
8. Joint venture
9. Wholly-owned manufacturing subsidiary
10. Multinational management organization
11. Multinational ownership of equity securities

ties to become an international company financed by sales of equity as well as by debt issues in countries throughout the world. However, this sequence is not always followed. A small firm with limited international experience that sells to countries characterized by considerable uncertainty may be limited to export and import activity. On the other hand, a large firm with well-established products in the United States, with long experience in international operations, and with a broad range of experienced management personnel may ultimately have wholly-owned foreign subsidiaries. Even before a firm is established abroad, it may finance abroad. After it is established abroad, its equity shares are likely to be widely owned by foreign nationals, particularly in countries where it conducts business operations.

Now that the methods by which a firm can become involved in international operations have been sketched, some of the specific decision areas will be dealt with. Although many business firms do not regard themselves as involved in international operations, they are nevertheless affected by international developments—developments that affect their cost of labor (for example, if prices of imports rise, the U.S. cost of living will rise, triggering wage increases) and material inputs, the prices of the products sold, and the sources of competition in the sale of products. The most pervasive influence, however, is that of fluctuating foreign exchange rates.

Impact of Exchange Rate Fluctuations

A fundamental difference between international business finance and domestic business finance is that international transactions and investments are conducted in more than one currency. For example, when a U.S. firm sells goods to a French firm, the U.S. firm usually wants to be paid in dollars and the French firm usually expects to pay in francs. Because of the existence of a foreign exchange market in which individual dealers and many banks trade, the buyer can pay in one currency and the seller can receive payment in another.

Since different currencies are involved, a rate of exchange must be established between them. The conversion relationship of the currencies is expressed in terms of their price relationship. If foreign exchange rates did not fluctuate, it would make no difference whether firms dealt in dollars or any other currency. However, since exchange rates do fluctuate, firms are subject to exchange rate fluctuation risks if they have a net asset or net liability position in a foreign currency. When net claims exceed liabilities in a foreign currency, the firm is said to be in a "long" position, because it will benefit if the value of the foreign currency rises. When net liabilities exceed claims in regard to foreign currencies, the firm is said to be in a "short" position, because it will gain if the foreign currency declines in value.

Expressing Foreign Exchange Rates

The foreign exchange rate represents the conversion relationship between currencies and depends on demand and supply relationships between the two currencies. The foreign exchange rate is the price of one currency in terms of another. Exchange rates may be expressed in dollars per foreign currency unit or units of foreign currency per dollar. An exchange rate of $.50 to FC1 shows the value of one foreign currency unit in terms of the dollar. We shall use E_0 to indicate the spot rate and E_f to indicate the forward rate at the present time and E_1 to indicate the actual future spot rate corresponding to E_f. An exchange rate of FC2 to $1 shows the value of the dollar in terms of the number of foreign currency units it will purchase. We will use the symbol X with corresponding subscripts to refer to the exchange rate expressed as the number of foreign currency units per dollar.

Measuring the Percentage of Devaluation or Revaluation

Assume that there has been a devaluation of the French franc from 3 per U.S. dollar to 4 per U.S. dollar. This can be expressed as the percentage change in the number of French francs required to purchase 1 U.S. dollar ($= D_{fd}$).

For example, where $X_0 = 3$ and $X_1 = 4$,

$$\% \text{ change} = (X_1 - X_0)/X_0 = (4 - 3)/3 = 1/3, \text{ or } 33\tfrac{1}{3}\% = D_{fd}.$$

There has been an increase of 33⅓ percent in the number of French francs required to equal one U.S. dollar.

To show the percentage change in the dollar value of the franc ($= D_{df}$),

$$E_0 = \frac{1}{X_0} = \frac{1}{3} \text{ and } E_1 = \frac{1}{X_1} = \frac{1}{4}.$$

Now the percentage change is given by

$$\begin{aligned}\% \text{ change} = (E_0 - E_1)/E_0 &= \left(\frac{1}{X_0} - \frac{1}{X_1}\right) / \frac{1}{X_0} \\ &= (1/3 - 1/4)/(1/3) = [(4 - 3)/12]/(1/3) = 1/4 = 25\% = D_{df}.\end{aligned}$$

There has been a 25% decrease in the value of the franc in terms of the U.S. dollar.

Summary of Exchange-Rate Relationships
D_{fd} is the change in value in terms of LC/$.

$$D_{fd} = \frac{X_1 - X_0}{X_0} = \frac{\frac{1}{E_1} - \frac{1}{E_0}}{\frac{1}{E_0}} = \frac{E_0}{E_1} - 1 = \frac{E_0 - E_1}{E_1}.$$

D_{df} is the change in value in terms of $/LC.

$$D_{df} = \frac{E_0 - E_1}{E_0} = \frac{\frac{1}{X_0} - \frac{1}{X_1}}{\frac{1}{X_0}} = \frac{X_0}{X_0} - \frac{X_0}{X_1} = \frac{X_1 - X_0}{X_1}.$$

Because of the risks of exchange rate fluctuations, transactions have developed in a forward, or futures, foreign exchange market. This market enables a firm to hedge in an attempt to reduce the risk. Individuals also speculate by means of transactions in the forward market. Forward contracts are normally for a thirty-, sixty-, or ninety-day period, although special contracts for longer periods can be arranged by negotiation.

The cost of this protection is the premium or discount of the forward contract over the current spot rate, which varies from 0 to 2 or 3 percent per year for currencies that are considered reasonably stable. For currencies undergoing devaluation in excess of 4 to 5 percent per year, the required discounts may be as high as 15 to 20 percent per year. When it is probable that future devaluations may exceed 20 percent per year, forward contracts are usually unavailable.

The magnitude of the premium or discount required depends on the forward expectations of the financial communities of the two countries involved and on the supply and demand conditions in the foreign exchange market. Since members of the financial communities are usually well-informed about the expected forward exchange values of their respective currencies, the premiums or discounts quoted are very closely related to the probable occurrence of changes in the exchange rates. As a result, the forward market is chiefly used as protection against *unexpected* changes in the foreign exchange value of a currency.

Three basic relationships will be treated:

1. Consistent foreign exchange rates
2. The Fisher effect
3. The interest rate parity theorem

Consistent Foreign Exchange Rates

Equilibrating transactions take place when exchange rates are not in proper relationship with one another. This will be illustrated by some examples with unrealistically rounded numbers that make the arithmetic of the calculations simple. The right direction of analysis will be obtained if the reader remembers the general maxim that arbitrageurs will seek to sell high and to buy low. First we will indicate the consistency of spot rates. Suppose the dollar value of the pound is $2 in New York City and $1.90 in London. The following adjustment actions would take place: In New York City sell £190 for $380. Pounds are sold in New York because the pound value is high there. In London sell $380 for £200. In London the dollar value is high in relation to the pound. Thus £190 sold in New York City for $380 can be used to buy £200 in London, a gain of £10. The sale of pounds in New York causes their value to decline and the purchase of pounds in London causes their value to rise until no further arbitrage opportunities remain. The same foreign exchange prices, assuming minimal transporation costs, would have to obtain in all locations.

The relations between two individual localities can be generalized across all countries. This is referred to as consistent cross rates. It works in the following fashion: Assume that the equilibrium relation between the dollar and the pound is $2 to £1 and that the dollar to franc rate is $.25 to fr. 1. Now, suppose that in New York City £.10 = fr. 1. The following adjustment process would take place. Sell $200 for £100 used to obtain fr. 1,000. The fr. 1,000 will buy $250. This is a $50 profit over the initial $200. Sell dollars for pounds and pounds for francs, since the pound is overvalued with respect to both the dollar to pound and dollar to franc relationships. Dollars will fall in relation to the pound and the pound will fall in relation to the franc until consistent cross rates obtain. If the relation were fr. 1 = £.125, consistent cross rates would obtain. Check using the following relation:

$$\$1 = £.5$$
$$£1 = \text{fr. } 8.00$$
$$\text{fr. } 1 = \$.25.$$

The product of the right-hand sides of the three relationships must equal 1. Check thus: 0.5 × 8 × 0.25 = 1. We have thus established consistency between foreign exchange rates.

The Fisher Effect

The Fisher effect holds for the relationship between interest rates and the anticipated rate of inflation. While it can also be regarded as purely a relationship for a domestic economy, it is utilized in developing some of the international relationships we will consider. The Fisher effect states that nominal interest rates rise to reflect the anticipated rate of inflation. The Fisher effect can be stated in a number of forms, as shown below:

$$\frac{P_0}{P_1} = \frac{1 + r}{1 + R_n}$$

$$1 + r = (1 + R_n)\frac{P_0}{P_1}$$

$$r = \left[(1 + R_n)\frac{P_0}{P_1}\right] - 1$$

$$R_n = \left[(1 + r)\left(\frac{P_1}{P_0}\right)\right] - 1$$

where:

P_0 = Initial price level
P_1 = Subsequent price level
$\frac{P_1}{P_0}$ = Rate of inflation
$\frac{P_0}{P_1}$ = Relative purchasing power of the currency unit
r = Real rate of interest
R_n = Nominal rate of interest

While the Fisher effect can be stated in a number of forms, its basic import can be conveyed by a simple numerical example. Over a given period of time, if the price index is expected to rise by 10 percent and the real rate of interest is 7 percent, then the current nominal rate of interest is:

$$R_n = [(1.07)(1.10)] - 1$$
$$= 17.7 \text{ percent.}$$

Similarly if the nominal rate of interest is 12 percent and the price index is expected to rise by 10 percent over a given time period, the current real rate of interest is:

$$r = \left[1.12\left(\frac{100}{110}\right)\right] - 1$$
$$= 1.018 - 1 = 0.018 = 1.8 \text{ percent.}$$

The Interest Rate Parity Theorem (IRPT)

The interest rate parity theorem is an extension of the Fisher effect to international markets. It holds that the ratio of the forward and spot exchange rates will equal the ratio of foreign and domestic gross interest rates. The formal statement of the interest rate parity theorem can be expressed as follows:

$$\frac{X_f}{X_0} = \frac{1 + R_{f0}}{1 + R_{d0}} = \frac{E_0}{E_f}$$

where:

X_f = Current forward exchange rate expressed as FC units per \$1
E_f = Current forward exchange rate expressed as dollars per FC1
X_0 = Current spot exchange rate expressed as FC units per \$1
E_0 = Current spot exchange rate expressed as dollars per FC1
R_{f0} = Current foreign interest rate
R_{d0} = Current domestic interest rate

Thus if the foreign interest rate is 15 percent while the domestic interest rate is 10 percent and the spot exchange rate is $X_0 = 10$, the predicted current forward exchange rate will be:

$$X_f = \frac{1 + R_{f0}}{1 + R_{d0}}(X_0) \qquad \textit{For 90 days:}$$

$$= \frac{1.15}{1.10}(10) \qquad X_f = \frac{1.0375}{1.025}(10)$$

$$= 10.45. \qquad = 10.122.$$

Thus the indicated foreign forward rate is 10.45 units of foreign currency per $1. Thus the foreign forward rate is at a discount of 4.5 percent on an annual basis. If the time period of a transaction is ninety days, we have to rework the problem, first changing the interest rates to a quarterly basis. The discount on the ninety-day forward rate would now be 1.22 percent on the quarterly basis, since the ninety-day forward rate would be 10.122.

Alternatively, the example could be formulated for the effect on interest rates of expected changes in future foreign exchange rates. Here is a dynamic relationship that needs to be recognized: If the foreign exchange rate is expected to rise over a period of time, relative interest rates will reflect the rate of change expected in the foreign exchange rates. This is illustrated in Figure 26.1.

The figure shows that as the value of the foreign currency falls (the exchange rate expressed in the number of foreign currency units per dollar rises), the ratio of foreign interest rates to domestic interest rates rises. At the inflection point of the rise in the expected number of foreign currency units per dollar, the ratio of foreign interest rates to domestic interest rates peaks. When the expected ratio of the foreign currency to the domestic currency levels off, then the former ratio of gross foreign interest rates to gross domestic interest rates is reestablished.

We could also use the interest rate parity theorem to express the results in terms of the interest rate parities required for given relationships between

Figure 26.1

Illustration of the Interest Rate Parity Theorem

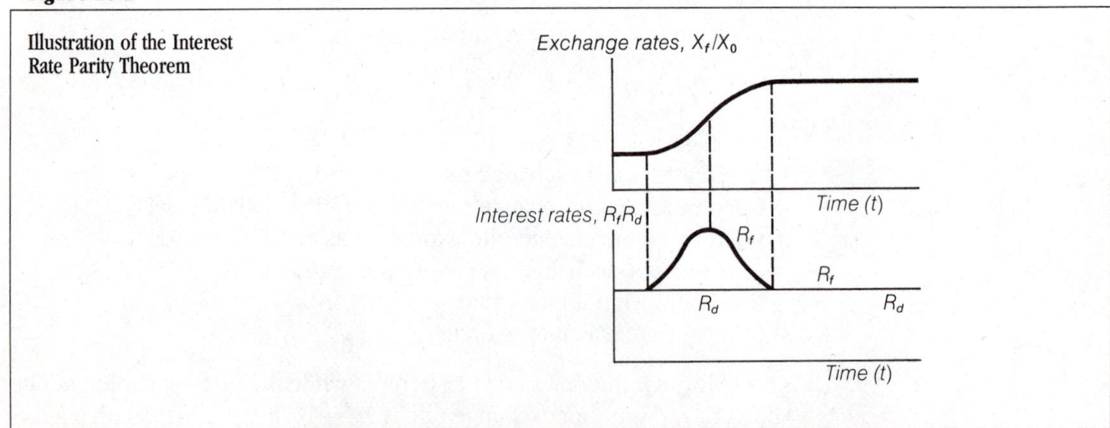

spot and future exchange rates. The transactions that result in interest rate parity are referred to as covered interest arbitrage. The basic facts of an arbitrage outflow situation are:

U.S. interest rate = 5%

German interest rate = 7%

Spot exchange rate $1 = DM4

Forward exchange rate discount = 1%

The following arbitrage transaction will take place. In New York, borrow $100,000 for ninety days ($\frac{1}{4}$ year) at 5 percent. The loan repayment at the end of ninety days is $100,000 [1 + (0.05 × $\frac{1}{4}$)] = $101,250. At the spot exchange rate, convert the $100,000 loan into DM400,000. In Germany, invest the DM400,000 for ninety days at 7 percent. Receive at the end of ninety days DM400,000 [1 + (0.07 × $\frac{1}{4}$)] = DM407,000.

A covering transaction is also made. To insure against adverse changes in the spot rate during the ninety-day investment period, sell investment proceeds forward. Since the forward exchange rate discount is 1 percent, then 4[1 + (0.01 × $\frac{1}{4}$)] = DM4.01 is required to exchange for $1, in ninety days (forward). Sell investment proceeds forward; that is, contract to receive DM407,000 ÷ 4.01 = $101,496.

$$\begin{aligned}\text{Arbitrage profits} &= \text{Investment receipts} - \text{Loan payments} \\ &= \$101{,}496 - \$101{,}250 \\ &= \$246.\end{aligned}$$

The arbitrage transaction increases the *demand* for currency in New York and increases the *supply* of funds in Germany. This raises the interest rate in New York and lowers it in Germany, thus narrowing the differential. The covering transaction increases the supply of German forward exchange, while the arbitrage investment action increases the demand for spot funds. Both forces tend to increase the forward exchange discount. The interest rate differential decreases and the forward rate discount increases until both are equalized.

An arbitrage inflow takes place when the forward exchange rate discount exceeds the interest rate differential. The basic facts are now:

U.S. interest rate = 5%

German interest rate = 6%

Spot exchange rate DM4 = $1

Forward exchange rate discount = 2%

The arbitrage transaction involves borrowing in the foreign country. In Germany, borrow DM400,000 for ninety days at 6 percent. The loan repayment at the end of ninety days is DM400,000 [1 + (0.06 × $\frac{1}{4}$)] = DM406,000. At the spot exchange rate, convert the DM400,000 loan into $100,000. In New York, invest the \$100,000 for ninety days at 5 percent. Receive at the end of ninety days \$100,000 $[1 + (0.05 \times 1/4)] =$ \$101,250.

Again, a covering transaction would be made. To insure coverage for the loan repayment, buy DM406,000 forward. At a 2 percent forward exchange rate discount, it costs DM4$[1 + (0.02 \times 1/4)] =$ DM4.02 to buy \$1 forward. Thus, to repay DM400,000 requires DM406,000 ÷ 4.02 = \$100,995.

$$\begin{aligned} \text{Arbitrage profits} &= \text{Investment receipts} - \text{Loan repayments} \\ &= \$101{,}250 - \$100{,}995 \\ &= \$255. \end{aligned}$$

The arbitrage transaction increases the *demand* for DM and increases the *supply* of dollars. The U.S. interest rate decreases and the German rate rises; thus the differential increases. Covering transactions increase the spot supply of DM, thus decreasing the premium on forward DM. The interest rate differential and the forward exchange rate discount decrease until both rates are equalized.

As a result of the covered interest arbitrage transactions of the types described, the relationships depicted by the interest rate parity theorem would obtain. This relationship determines the home-currency cost that would be involved when a purchase or sale is made and a future payment or receipt is involved.

Risk Position of the Firm in Foreign Currency Units

The risk position of a firm in relation to possible fluctuations in foreign exchange rates can be clarified by referring to expected receipts or obligations in foreign currency units. If a firm is expecting receipts in foreign currency units (if it is "long" in the foreign currency units), its risk is that the value of the foreign currency units will fall (devaluing the foreign currency in relation to the dollar). If a firm is expecting to have obligations in foreign currency units (if it is "short" in the foreign currency units), its risk is that the value of the foreign currency will rise and it will have to buy the currency at a higher price.

Methods of Dealing with the Risk of a Decline in Foreign Currency Values

A brief example will illustrate methods of taking protective action against a decline in the value of a foreign currency. On September 1, 1980, the USP Company makes a sale of goods to a foreign firm; it will receive LC 380,000 (payment in local or foreign currency units) on December 1, 1980. The USP Company has incurred costs in dollars and wishes to make definite the amount of dollars it will receive on December 1. It is considering three alternatives to deal with the risk of exchange rate fluctuation. The first alternative is to enter the forward market to sell LC 380,000 for dollars at the ninety-day forward rate quoted on September 1, 1980. The company can then utilize the LC 380,000 it receives on December 1, 1980, to pay for the dollars it has contracted to buy at the ninety-day forward rate. Under this arrangement the company will receive a definite amount in dollars in December as determined by the forward rate on September 1.

The second alternative is to borrow now from a foreign bank the LC amount such that the principal plus interest will equal what the company will be receiving on December 1. The interest rate paid is 28 percent. By borrowing, the company will receive the LCs immediately, and with them it can immediately purchase dollars at the September spot rate. It can then invest the dollars received in the United States at an 8 percent interest rate. When the company receives the LC 380,000 in December, it can use the funds to liquidate the local currency loan incurred in September. (The effective tax rate in both countries is 40 percent.)

The third alternative is to make no attempt to cover the exchange risk involved in waiting the three months for receipt of the LC 380,000. Under this alternative, the USP Company will convert the LC 380,000 into dollars at whatever spot rate prevails on December 1, 1980.

The three alternatives will be analyzed for a pattern of actual spot and forward exchange rates on September 1, 1980, and the expected spot rate on December 1, 1980. First to be considered is the pattern of rates characteristic of countries subject to currency devaluation:

	September 1, 1980
Spot rate of foreign currency units per $1	LC 1.90
Ninety-day forward rate	LC 2.00
	December 1, 1980
Expected future spot rate	LC 2.10

The three alternatives can now be analyzed. The first alternative involves entering a forward contract in which the USP Company sells LC 380,000 for dollars at a rate of 2 LC to $1. Therefore, the company has contracted to receive $190,000. At the spot rate, it would have received $200,000, so a reduction of expected sales revenue of $10,000 has been incurred, providing a tax shelter of $4,000. Thus total receipts and taxes saved amounts to $194,000.

Under the second alternative, the USP Company borrows LC from a bank in the foreign country; the amount of LC plus interest equals the LC 380,000 that will be received in December. The company will have to pay interest at 28 percent on the loan obtained from the foreign bank. Since the loan is for ninety days, or one-fourth of a year, the 28 percent is divided by 4 to obtain 7 percent, which is then multiplied by $(1 - T)$, for a total of 4.2 percent, the after-tax interest rate. Since

$$1.042\,X = \text{LC } 380{,}000,$$
$$X = \text{LC } 364{,}683.$$

At the spot exchange rate, the proceeds from the LC 364,683 divided by 1.90 equal $191,938; and this amount can be invested in the U.S. to earn an 8 percent annual rate for ninety days, or 2 percent times $(1 - T)$, which equals 1.2 percent. The proceeds of $191,938 times 1.012 equal $194,241. On December 1, 1980, USP will receive the LC 380,000, which it will use to repay the LC 380,000 principal plus interest on its LC loan.

Under the third alternative, on December 1, 1980, the LC 380,000 will be converted into dollars at the spot rate then in effect. This represents LC 380,000 divided by 2.10, or $180,952. The expected $180,952 involves a reduction in taxable sales revenue of $19,048, so net proceeds with the tax shelter are $180,952 plus 0.4 ($19,048), which equals $188,571.

The net proceeds received under the three alternatives are:

1. Sell LC in forward market for dollars	$194,000
2. Borrow LC and repay from LC received in future	194,241
3. Receive dollars based on spot rate when LC funds received	188,571

Under the assumptions of this example, the second alternative provides the greatest amount of funds. But different degrees of uncertainty are associated with each of the three alternatives. The dollars to be received under the first two alternatives are certain, while those under the third are not.

Before the fact, it is not possible to state definitely which alternative will yield the largest number of dollars on December 1, 1980. It depends on the future level of the spot rate on that date. Suppose that the actual spot rate on that December 1 turns out to be exactly what it was on September 1, 1980. In this situation, the first two alternatives will be unchanged, but for the third alternative, 380,000 divided by 1.90 equals $200,000—making it the best choice. But under the original assumptions, the third alternative was the worst choice. Thus doing nothing under the new set of assumed data turns out to be the best course of action, although it is clearly the riskiest. The use of the forward market or borrowing and investing through the money markets will sometimes yield lower net proceeds than taking no protective actions whatsoever will do, but having an unprotected position with respect to foreign exchange rate fluctuations is the greatest risk.

Using the forward market or borrowing is a form of insurance taken out to protect against unexpected fluctuations in foreign exchange rates. Like other forms of insurance, the protection involves a cost. But the situation is similar to that of buying fire insurance on your house. You could save the money if you could be sure that a fire were not going to occur. If you have paid fire insurance for several years and no fire has occurred, you could have saved money by not buying the fire insurance. But you paid the money to protect against the loss that would have taken place if the unexpected fire had occurred. Similarly, the cost of forward hedging or borrowing is a form of insurance premium paid to avoid even larger losses.

Protection against Rising Values of Foreign Currencies

When a foreign currency is rising in value, the U.S. firm has a risk exposure if it is in a short position with respect to the foreign currency. This means that if the firm has payments to be made in foreign currency units or has liabilities outstanding that are expressed in such units, a rise in the value of the foreign currency unit will require that more dollars be used to buy it after it has risen in value. Or, to put it another way, if the firm has future obligations that are expressed in foreign currency units, its risk exposure is from the potential rise in the value of those units.

To illustrate: On September 1, 1980, the INT Corporation made a purchase of goods from a foreign firm that will require the payment of LC 380,000 on December 1 of the same year. The corporation wishes to make definite the amount of dollars it will need to pay the LC 380,000 on that date. The foreign firm is in a country whose currency has been rising in relation to the dollar in recent years. The tax rate in both countries is 40 percent. The observed pattern of foreign exchange rates is as follows:

	September 1, 1980
Spot rate of foreign currency units per $1	LC 2.10
Ninety-day forward rate	LC 2.00
	December 1, 1980
Expected future spot rate	LC 1.90

The INT Corporation considers the three alternatives discussed earlier to deal with the risk of exchange rate fluctuations. However, the *direction* of actions is now different. The first alternative is to enter the forward market to *buy* LC 380,000 for dollars at the ninety-day forward rate in effect on September 1, 1980. The corporation can then utilize the LC 380,000 it will receive under the forward contract on December 1, 1980, to meet the obligation it has incurred to make a payment of LC 380,000 on that date.

The second alternative is to borrow an amount in dollars to exchange into LCs to buy foreign securities that, with interest, will equal LC 380,000 on December 1, 1980. The interest rate paid in the United States is 12 percent; the interest earned in the foreign country is 8 percent.

The third alternative is to make no attempt to cover the risk involved in waiting for three months to pay the foreign currency obligation in the amount of LC 380,000. Under this alternative, the corporation will need sufficient dollars to equal LC 380,000 at whatever spot rate prevails on December 1, 1980.

The effects of the three alternatives can be analyzed. The first alternative involves entering a forward contract in which the INT Corporation buys LC 380,000 for dollars at a rate of LC 2 to $1. Therefore, the corporation will spend $190,000 to meet the future foreign currency obligation in the amount of LC 380,000. At the spot rate, it would have had to make a payment of 380,000 divided by 2.10, or $180,952, which is $9,048 less than the $190,000. This increase in expenses represents a tax shelter, at the 40 percent tax rate, of $3,619. The $190,000 expended on the forward contract minus the tax shelter of $3,619 is equal to $186,381, which represents the net after-tax costs of meeting the foreign currency obligation of LC 380,000 due on December 1, 1980.

Under the second alternative, the INT Corporation borrows dollars from a bank in the United States in an amount which, with foreign income, will total LC 380,000 when the foreign obligation becomes due on December 1, 1980. The amount it borrows is:

$$
\begin{aligned}
(2.10)\,(1 + [0.08 \div 4]0.6)X &= \text{LC } 380{,}000 \\
(2.10)\,(1.012)X &= \text{LC } 380{,}000 \\
2.1252X &= \text{LC } 380{,}000 \\
X &= \$178{,}807.
\end{aligned}
$$

Adding the interest expense, the total cost is 1.018 ($178,807) = $182,026.

Under the third alternative, on December 1, 1980, the LC 380,000 will be obtained by the use of dollars converted into the foreign currency at the spot rate then in effect. This will represent LC 380,000 divided by 1.90, or $200,000. However, under the September 1 spot rate, INT Corporation will have needed a dollar outlay of only $180,952 (LC 380,000 divided by 2.10). Therefore, the firm will have incurred an opportunity loss of $19,048, which will result in a tax shelter of 0.4($19,048), or $7,619.20. Hence, the after-tax costs are $192,381.

The amount of dollars to be paid under the three alternatives are:

1. Buy LC in forward market	$186,381
2. Borrow in the United States and invest in foreign country	182,026
3. Pay dollars for LC based on expected future spot rate	192,381

Under the assumptions of this example, the second alternative involves the smallest outlay in dollars to meet the LC 380,000 obligation due on December 1, 1980. The dollars that will have to be paid under the first and second alternatives are certain; under the third alternative, the total proceeds are uncertain. Before the fact, it is not possible to state definitely which alternative will cost the least amount of dollars to meet the obligation due on December 1,

1980. It depends on the future level of the spot rate on that date. For example, suppose that the actual spot rate on December 1 turns out to be exactly what it was on September 1. In that case the net cost of using the third alternative for arranging to meet the future LC obligation will be dollars based on the December 1, 1980, spot rate of LC 2.10—$180,952.

The third alternative is best here, while under the original assumptions it was the worst. But again, taking no protective action is clearly the riskiest method.

Monetary Balance

Firms must take protective actions not only in regard to future expected receipts or obligations but also against a long or short position in foreign currencies resulting from the balance sheet position of their foreign subsidiaries. In the example of USP Company, the sale of the goods for LC 380,000 represented an account receivable for the three months until the obligation was paid. Suppose, however, that the number of LCs per $1 had risen from 1.90 to 2.00. At 1.90 LCs per $1, the account receivable would have been worth $200,000 in U.S. currency. But at the lower value of the LCs, 2 LC to $1, the account receivable would have been worth only $190,000. This represents a before-tax loss of $10,000 in the dollar value of the receivables.

Conversely, in the INT Corporation example, the firm had an account payable of LC 380,000. If the change in the LC value had been an upward one, from LC 2.00 to LC 1.90 per $1, the firm would have had a loss because the accounts payable expressed in dollars would have increased by $10,000. Hence the concept of monetary balance comes into consideration. *Monetary balance* involves avoiding either a net receivable or a net payable position. Monetary assets and liabilities are those items whose value, expressed in local currency, does not change with devaluation or revaluation. To illustrate:

Monetary Assets	Monetary Liabilities
Cash	Accounts payable
Marketable securities	Notes payable
Accounts receivable	Tax liability reserve
Tax refunds receivable	Bonds
Notes receivable	Preferred stock
Prepaid insurance	

What is referred to as a firm's monetary position is another way of stating the firm's position with regard to real assets. For example, the basic balance sheet equation can be written as follows:

$$\text{Monetary assets} + \text{Real assets} = \text{Monetary liabilities} + \text{Net worth.}$$

Consider the following pattern of relationships:

	Monetary Assets	+	Real Assets	=	Monetary Liabilities	+	Net Worth
Firm A: Monetary creditor	$6,000		$4,000		$4,000		$6,000
Firm B: Monetary debtor	4,000		6,000		6,000		4,000

Firm A is a monetary creditor because its monetary assets exceed its monetary liabilities; its net worth position is negative with respect to its investment coverage of net worth by real assets. In contrast, Firm B is a monetary debtor because it has monetary liabilities that exceed its monetary assets; its net worth coverage by investment in real assets is positive. Thus the monetary creditor can be referred to as a firm with a negative position in real assets and the monetary debtor as a firm with a positive position in real assets. From the foregoing we can see that the following relationships are equivalent:

Firm A	(Long position in foreign currency)	≡	Monetary creditor	≡	Monetary assets exceed monetary liabilities	≡	Negative position in real assets	≡	Balance of receipts in foreign currency less obligations in foreign currency is *positive.*
Firm B	(Short position in foreign currency)	≡	Monetary debtor	≡	Monetary liabilities exceed monetary assets	≡	Positive position in real assets	≡	Balance of receipts in foreign currency less obligations in foreign currency is *negative.*

Thus, if Firm A has a long position in a foreign currency, on balance it will be receiving more funds in foreign currency, or it will have a net monetary asset position that exceeds its monetary liabilities in that currency. The opposite holds for Firm B, which is in a short position with respect to a foreign currency. Hence the analysis with respect to a firm with net future receipts or net future obligations can be applied also to a firm's balance sheet position. A firm with net receipts is a net monetary creditor. Its foreign exchange rate risk exposure has a net receipts position in a foreign currency that is vulnerable to a decline in value.

Conversely, a firm with future net obligations in foreign currency is in a net monetary debtor position. The foreign exchange risk exposure it faces is the possibility of an increase in the value of the foreign currency. The alternative methods of protection against foreign exchange fluctuations discussed earlier apply to the short or long balance sheet position a firm may have with respect to foreign currency.

In addition to the specific actions of hedging in the forward market or borrowing and lending through the money markets, other business policies can help the firm achieve a balance sheet position that minimizes the foreign exchange rate risk exposure to either currency devaluation or currency revaluation upward. Specifically, in countries whose currency values are likely to fall, local management of subsidiaries should be encouraged to follow these policies:

1. Never have excessive idle cash on hand. If cash accumulates, it should be used to purchase inventory or other real assets.
2. Attempt to avoid granting excessive trade credit or trade credit for extended periods. If accounts receivable cannot be avoided, an attempt should be made to charge interest high enough to compensate for the loss of purchasing power.
3. Wherever possible, avoid giving advances in connection with purchase orders unless a rate of interest is paid by the seller on these advances from the time the subsidiary—the buyer—pays them until the time of delivery, at a rate sufficient to cover the loss of purchasing power.
4. Borrow local currency funds from banks or other sources whenever these funds can be obtained at a rate of interest no higher than U.S. rates adjusted for the anticipated rate of devaluation in the foreign country.
5. Make an effort to purchase materials and supplies on a trade credit basis in the country in which the foreign subsidiary is operating, extending the final date of payment as long as possible.

The opposite policies should be followed in a country where a revaluation upward in foreign currency values is likely to take place. All these policies are aimed at a monetary balance position in which the firm is neither a monetary debtor nor a monetary creditor. Some firms take a more aggressive position. They seek to have a net monetary debtor position in a country whose exchange rates are expected to fall and a net monetary creditor position in a country whose exchange rates are likely to rise. Since exchange rate risk protection, as well as the conduct of international operations, requires international financing, this topic is considered next.

FASB Statement No. 8 is the governing guideline for U.S. based multinational firms as they translate the financial statements of foreign subsidiaries denominated in foreign currencies into U.S. dollars. This statement became effective for all fiscal years beginning on or after January 1, 1976. It defines the objective of translation to be to measure and express (1) in dollars and (2) in conformity with U.S. generally accepted accounting principles the assets, liabilities, revenues, or expenses that are measured or denominated in a foreign currency.

Forward Contracts. There are two components of the forward contract to account for, the gain or loss when the transaction is completed and the discount or premium in the use of the forward contract. Accounting for each depends on the use of the forward contract. If the contract is for an identifiable foreign currency commitment, then the gain or loss and the discount or premium are deferred. A forward contract used to hedge a definite commitment will not result in book entries until the sale occurs. To qualify, the transaction must satisfy all of the following requirements: (1) The life of the forward contract is equal to or greater than the life of the commitment involved. (2) The contract is for the currency of the commitment. (3) The commitment has been finalized and cannot be cancelled.

If the contract is to hedge an exposed asset or liability position, the gain or loss is recognized as of the balance sheet date, while the discount or premium is amortized over the life of the contract. The premium (discount) or the gain (loss) is defined as follows:

Premium (Discount)

Let F_0 be the amount of the contract in LC,
E_0 be the spot rate at the time of the contract, and
E_f be the forward rate.

Then the premium (discount) $= F_0(E_f - E_0)$.

Gain (loss)

Let E_1 be the spot rate at the first date a statement is prepared.
Gain (loss) $= F_0(E_0 - E_1)$.
Let E_2 be the spot rate at the end of the forward contract.
Gain (loss) $= F_0(E_1 - E_2)$.

We will now illustrate the application of these FASB Statement No. 8 rules for the two major types of contracts.

Contract Used to Cover an Identifiable Foreign Currency Commitment

U.S. based Magnum Engineering is building a plant for a U.S. firm and buys components from a manufacturer in England. The price is £400,000 on the delivery date, January 31, 1980. To hedge possible exchange-rate fluctuations of the pound sterling, Magnum buys a ninety-day forward contract on November 1, 1979, for £400,000 at the rate £1 = \$2. Magnum's fiscal year ends December 31.

1. Assume the spot exchange rates shown below. Make the journal entries to record the transaction. What is the cost of the components to be added to the cost of the plant?

November 1, 1979	£1 = \$2.10
December 31, 1979	£1 = \$2.00
January 31, 1980	£1 = \$1.95

Under FASB Statement No. 8, the forward contract is a hedge against a specific identifiable commitment. The journal entries to record the transactions would be:

		Debit	Credit
11/1/79, 12/31/79 No entry			
1/31/80 Cost of equipment inventory		$800,000	
Cash to complete the forward contract			$800,000
Equipment inventory account:			
Cash payment to English firm	$780,000		
Loss on forward contract	20,000		
Cost of equipment inventory	$800,000		

If the firm had not purchased a forward contract, the £400,000 could have been purchased at £1 = $1.95, or $780,000, instead of $800,000 under the forward contract.

2. Alternatively assume that the spot rates were rising as follows. How would the transactions be recorded?

November 1, 1979	£1 = $2.10
December 31, 1979	£1 = $2.10
January 31, 1980	£1 = $2.15

The new accounting entries would be:

		Debit	Credit
11/1/79, 12/31/79 No entry			
1/31/80 Cost of equipment inventory		$800,000	
Cash to complete the forward contract			$800,000
Equipment inventory account:			
Cash payment to English firm	$860,000		
Gain on forward contract	(60,000)		
Cost of equipment inventory	$800,000		

For this type of transaction the effect is to fix the cost of the equipment at the time of purchase of the forward contract regardless of subsequent fluctuations in exchange rates.

The next major category covered by FASB Statement No. 8 is in connection with a forward contract used with an exposed net asset or net liability position. The previous material demonstrates that if a firm is in an exposed foreign exchange position, there will be some costs to obtain protection against that exposure. Even rearranging the firm's pattern of payments and receipts or monetary assets and liabilities will represent a departure from normal operations and therefore will involve some costs. If the forward market is used or if borrowing is used, there will be some costs; but the amount of the costs can be made definite. If the firm does not take actions to make the amount of these costs definite, then at the time of making any financial reports, current FASB Statement No. 8 reporting regulations require that its gains or losses on its foreign exchange exposure be reported. If the firm has not taken protective actions with regard to its foreign exchange exposure, wide swings in earnings may be a consequence. However, if a firm has taken protective actions, FASB regulations simply provide for the systematic amortization over appropriate time periods of the costs incurred in achieving the hedged position. Apparently some confusion has arisen on this point through the error of considering only the reporting requirements on the hedged position without adding in the exposed net assets or net liability position of the firm being protected. The principles involved may be illustrated by the following example.

U.S. based Globalcorp's subsidiary in Country X is in a net monetary creditor position of FC300,000. High inflation in Country X is putting devaluation pressure on the FC in terms of the dollar, and Globalcorp sells a ninety-day forward contract of FC300,000 on November 1, 1979, at the forward rate of FC1 = \$.09. Globalcorp's fiscal year corresponds to the calendar year. These are the relevant foreign exchange rates:

		Assumptions A	B	C	D	E
November 1, 1979						
Spot rate	E_0 = LC1 =	\$.11	\$.11	\$.11	\$.11	\$.11
90-day forward rate	E_f = LC1 =	.09	.09	.09	.09	.09
December 31, 1979						
Spot rate	E_1 = LC1 =	.10	.11	.10	.12	.05
January 31, 1980						
Spot rate	E_2 = LC1 =	.09	.15	.05	.10	.11

The premium (discount) to be amortized over the life of the contract is:

$$\text{Premium (discount)} = F_0(E_f - E_0) = \$300{,}000\ (0.9 - 0.11)$$
$$= (\$6{,}000).$$

On December 31, 1979, the amount of the discount on the forward contract to be amortized is \$4,000 regardless of the actual spot rate on that date. Hence, Globalcorp spent \$4,000 to protect against the loss that would otherwise have occurred due to the decline in the dollar value of the foreign currency in the future. For example, under Assumption A, the translation loss would have been \$3,000, so the "gain" from avoiding this potential loss is a positive \$3,000, as shown in Column 3 of Table 26.3. The total benefit from

Table 26.3

FASB Reporting Requirements on a Hedging Contract

Assumptions (1)	Amortized Portion of Forward Contract Premium (Discount) $(2/3)F_0(E_f - E_0)$ (2)	Opportunity Gain (Loss) on December 31, 1979 $F_0(E_0 - E_1)$ (3)	Total Gain (Loss) on December 31, 1979 (2) + (3) (4)	Remainder of Forward Contract Premium (Discount) $(1/3)F_0(E_f - E_0)$ (5)	Opportunity Gain (Loss) January 31, 1980 $F_0(E_1 - E_2)$ (6)	Total Gain (Loss) on January 31, 1980 (5) + (6) (7)	Total Gain (Loss) November 1, 1979–January 31, 1980 (4) + (7) (8)
A	($4,000)	$ 3,000	($ 1,000)	($2,000)	$ 3,000	$ 1,000	$ 0
B	(4,000)	0	(4,000)	(2,000)	(12,000)	(14,000)	(18,000)
C	(4,000)	3,000	(1,000)	(2,000)	15,000	13,000	12,000
D	(4,000)	(3,000)	(7,000)	(2,000)	6,000	4,000	(3,000)
E	(4,000)	18,000	14,000	(2,000)	(18,000)	(20,000)	(6,000)

the hedged position is shown in Column 4 as the ($4,000) plus the gain or loss avoided. The same logic applies to the January 31, 1980, position. Hence, Column 8 of Table 26.3 simply sums the net gains or losses that were recorded for the two months ending December 31, 1979, and for the subsequent one month ending on January 31, 1980.

In Table 26.4 the actual translation gain or loss is added to the gain or loss from the hedging position as calculated in Table 26.3. The actual translation loss on December 31, 1979, is $F_0(E_1 - E_0)$ and on January 31, 1980, is measured by $F_0(E_2 - E_1)$. The overall gain or loss at each accounting date, therefore, is the amortized portion of the cost of hedging. FASB Statement No. 8 formulates the measurement of the gain or loss in Table 26.3, so that when added to the actual translation gain or loss from the exposed position, the overall loss is limited to the discount from establishing the hedged position in the forward market.

Table 26.4 demonstrates that at each reporting date the amortized net gain or loss from the use of the hedging operation is recorded. Since the term of the hedge is three months and two months have expired by the end of the year, two-thirds of the cost of establishing the hedge is charged to operations as of the end of the year. The remaining one-third is charged to operations at the end of the remaining third month. Table 26.4 underscores the principle that the use of the hedge fixes the net final cost of the exposed position to the discount between the current spot rate and the current forward rate. Numerous complaints have been made that FASB Statement No. 8, paragraph 25, introduces unreal fluctuations into income statement results. These comments fail to take into consideration the gains or losses from translation of the financial statements. When combined with gains or losses on the forward contract, the net results are as shown in Table 26.4 and represent the amortiza-

Table 26.4

Overall Gain or (Loss) from Hedging an Exposed Position

December 31, 1979			January 31, 1980			
Gain or (Loss) on Hedging Contract	Translation Gain or (Loss)	Overall Gain or (Loss)	Gain or (Loss) on Hedging Contract	Translation Gain or (Loss)	Overall Gain or (Loss)	Overall Gain or (Loss) from Hedging and Translation November 1, 1979–January 31, 1980
(1)	(2)	(3)	(4)	(5)	(6)	(7)
($ 1,000)	($ 3,000)	($4,000)	$ 1,000	($ 3,000)	($2,000)	($6,000)
(4,000)	0	(4,000)	(14,000)	12,000	(2,000)	(6,000)
(1,000)	(3,000)	(4,000)	13,000	(15,000)	(2,000)	(6,000)
(7,000)	3,000	(4,000)	4,000	(6,000)	(2,000)	(6,000)
14,000	(18,000)	(4,000)	(20,000)	18,000	(2,000)	(6,000)

tion of the cost of hedging. Three principles are illustrated. One is that the expected inflation rate is already reflected in the forward exchange rates. The second is that hedging in the forward market involves a discount representing a cost. The third is that the amount of the discount in the forward market limits the amount of the loss. The use of hedging does not avoid the loss from the future expected inflation. It establishes the amount of the loss and prevents the loss from being larger or smaller.

Translation of Financial Statements

When the parent company's ownership of a subsidiary exceeds 50 percent and the contribution of the subsidiary is substantial in relation to that parent company, the subsidiary is likely to consolidate its financial statements into those of the parent. When consolidation takes place, the statements of the foreign subsidiary must be translated from the local currency of account into the currency used by the parent.

A number of alternative principles of translation of financial statements from one currency into another have developed over time. The current-noncurrent approach translates current assets and liabilities at current exchange rates. Other accounts are translated at historical exchange rates. The monetary-nonmonetary approach discussed above translates monetary items at current exchange rates and nonmonetary items at historical exchange rates. The temporal method was first introduced in Accounting Research Study Number 12 of the American Institute of Certified Public Accountants in 1972. It was also adopted in FASB Statement No. 8 in 1976.

The temporal method modifies the monetary-nonmonetary approach in considering the valuation basis of assets and liabilities. For example, inventories valued on the last-in-first out (LIFO) principle are likely to be carried on the balance sheet at historical costs since the most recent movements into inventories are charged to the income statement. Hence, historical foreign exchange rates would be applied to the inventories carried at historical costs. This would coincide with the monetary-nonmonetary translation approach. On the other hand, if inventory valuation is based on the first-in-first-out (FIFO) principle, the balance sheet will reflect inventories acquired at the most recent dates. Hence, the temporal method would translate the balance sheet inventory account at current exchange rates rather than historical exchange rates when first-in-first-out inventory accounting is used. The foregoing concepts can be clarified by use of an illustrative case.

The Forsub Company, S.A., a subsidiary of the Multinat Company, a U.S. firm, is operating in an inflationary country. The first column of Table 26.5 presents its balance sheet expressed in local currency units. A year ago the exchange rate of the host country's currency was LC4 per $1. It is now LC5 per $1. The host government permits write-up of assets on an annual basis. This is accomplished every January in line with the rate of inflation during the prior year. For this reason, the proper historical exchange rate is the one in

Table 26.5

Alternative Methods of Currency Translation (in Millions)

Forsub Company, S. A. Balance Sheet as of December 31, 1980	In Local Currency Accounts	Translation: Current-Noncurrent Method Exchange Rate	Amount	Monetary-Nonmonetary Method Exchange Rate	Amount	Temporal Method Exchange Rate	Amount
Cash	LC 400	5	$ 80	5	$ 80	5	$ 80
Accounts receivable	1,000	5	200	5	200	5	200
Inventory[a]	2,000	5	400	4	500	5	400
Total current assets	3,400		$ 680		$ 780		$ 680
Investments, nonmonetary	1,200	4	$ 300	4	$ 300	4	$ 300
Gross plant and equipment	10,000	4	2,500	4	2,500	4	$2,500
Reserve for depreciation	4,000	4	1,000	4	1,000	4	1,000
Net plant and equipment	6,000	4	1,500	4	1,500	4	1,500
Total assets	LC 10,600		$2,480		$2,580		$2,480
Accounts payable	LC 400	5	$ 80	5	$ 80	5	$ 80
Notes payable	600	5	120	5	120	5	120
Accruals	400	5	80	5	80	5	80
Total current liabilities	1,400		280		280		280
Bonds outstanding	1,600	4	400	5	320	5	320
Common stock	4,000	4	1,000	4	1,000	4	1,000
Retained earnings	3,600	4	900	4	900	4	900
Revaluation account			(100)		80		(20)
Total liabilities and capital	LC 10,600		$2,480		$2,580		$2,480

a. Assuming the FIFO method of inventory accounting.

effect at the beginning of the year. For the sake of simplicity, it is assumed that the firm uses an average rate of LC4.5 per $1 for profit and loss statement purposes.

First, we shall illustrate translation by the current-noncurrent method and then by the monetary-nonmonetary method. The relationship to the temporal method will then be indicated.

Note that the revaluation account is negative under the current-noncurrent and temporal methods but is positive under the monetary-nonmonetary method. While the revaluation account serves as a balancing figure for the balance sheet, it can also be independently derived as follows.

Under the monetary-nonmonetary approach, the net monetary position (NMP) of the firm is equal to monetary assets (MA) less monetary liabilities (ML).

$$\begin{aligned} \text{NMP} &= \text{MA} - \text{ML} \\ &= 400 + 1{,}000 - (400 + 600 + 400 + 1{,}600) \\ &= 1{,}400 - 3{,}000 = -1{,}600. \end{aligned}$$

This net monetary liability position is favorable under the existing conditions of devaluation. The change of the monetary assets and liabilities in terms of the U.S. dollar due to translation is therefore calculated as:

$$\begin{aligned} \text{Change} &= \text{NMP}\left(\frac{1}{X_1} - \frac{1}{X_0}\right) \\ &= -\ 1{,}600\left(\frac{1}{5} - \frac{1}{4}\right) \\ &= -\ 1{,}600\left(-\ \frac{1}{20}\right) = +80. \end{aligned}$$

This represents a net gain of $80 million in net worth dollar value due to the decrease in the dollar value of the monetary liabilities, and it results in this amount being added to the revaluation reserve. The revaluation account can likewise be determined for the current-noncurrent approach.

$$\begin{aligned} \text{Net current position} &= \text{CA} - \text{CL} \\ &= 3{,}400 - 1{,}400 \\ &= 2{,}000. \\ \text{Change} &= \text{NCP}\left(\frac{1}{X_1} - \frac{1}{X_0}\right) \\ &= 2{,}000\left(\frac{1}{5} - \frac{1}{4}\right) \\ &= -100. \end{aligned}$$

The temporal method takes into account the valuation basis of the assets. Forsub uses the FIFO method of inventory accounting. Under this method, the oldest inventories are charged out first, and the balance sheet values will reflect the most current inventory cost. Hence the market current exchange rate would be used for translation. In this way the temporal method modifies the monetary method. Under the temporal method the exposure is $20 million, shown as a negative amount in the revaluation account.

If LIFO had been the method of inventory accounting, the balance sheet value of inventory would reflect historical costs. Hence the historical exchange rate would be applicable for translation. Under these circumstances, the temporal method would give the same result as the monetary-nonmonetary method for the facts of this particular case.

Translation of the profit and loss statement for the foreign subsidiary is

Table 26.6

Income Statement for the Year Ended December 31, 1980 (in Millions)

			Exchange Rate		Dollar Amount
Sales, net		LC 5,400	4.5		$1,200
Cost of sales:					
Inventory charge-outs[a]	LC 400		4	100	
Depreciation	600		4	150	
Other costs	2,025		4.5	450	
Cost of sales		3,025			700
Gross operating profit		2,375			$ 500
Selling, general and administrative expense		900	4.5		200
Net operating profit		1,475			$ 300
Interest expense		200	5		40
Earnings before taxes		1,275			$ 260
Income taxes at 40 percent		510	5		102
Earnings after taxes		LC 765			$ 158

a. Assuming the FIFO method of inventory accounting.

presented in Table 26.6. Sales, selling, general and administrative expenses, and other costs are translated at the average exchange rate in effect during the year, 4.5 foreign currency units to the dollar. Inventory charge-outs are translated at the historical exchange rate, since the FIFO method of inventory accounting is employed. Depreciation is translated at the historical exchange rate that is used to translate the plant and equipment account to which the depreciation item relates. Interest expense is translated at the average rate of 4.5 because, like other categories of revenues and costs, it is developing over the entire period covered by the income statement. Note that where exchange rates are not shown for an item (as in the subtotals), the dollar amount is found merely by summing or subtracting the translated cost and revenue figures. Also, the 40 percent tax rate is applied to the LC earnings before taxes and then translated at the appropriate exchange rate, resulting in a slightly lower than 40 percent rate on earnings expressed in dollars.

Among the alternative methods of financial translation, we believe that accounting practice has been moving in the right direction. The current-noncurrent approach called for translation of long-term debt at the old exchange rates. This procedure involved a logical error because the long-term debt obligation was expressed in foreign currency units. With fluctuations in exchange rates, the current dollar value in relation to the foreign currency has changed from the historical dollars received; therefore, a gain or loss has actually taken place. The temporal method recommended by FASB Statement No. 8 represents a logical extension of the monetary rule. This method of international financial translation provides internally consistent and meaningful financial results.

International Financing

The general principles affecting financing decisions are the same for international financing as for domestic financing. However, the variables affecting international financing decisions are expanded, and the number of financing methods and sources is increased. The forms and sources of financing are similar in the different countries of the world, but important differences provide new pitfalls and additional opportunities. A wider range of alternatives must be evaluated in both quantitative and qualitative terms in choosing among alternative sources, forms, and localities of international financing. Financing in an international setting makes use of the increasingly important international financing markets—the Eurocurrency and Eurobond markets. The facilities of private lending institutions are augmented substantially by international lending agencies, national development banks, and other government agencies performing important functions in financing operations and projects.

Some financing operations are distinctive to international business finance. A form of commercial bank financing widely used in Europe is represented by overdrafts. An overdraft agreement permits a customer to draw checks up to some specified maximum limit in excess of the checking account balance. In contrast to U.S. practice, European overdrafts are provided for in previous loan agreements and have widespread use in normal banking relations.

Another form of financing—one that was until recent years much more widespread in Europe than in the United States—is the use of discounted *trade bills* in both domestic and foreign transactions. The increased use of bankers acceptances in the United States has been associated with the growth of the movement of goods in international trade.

A third variation from U.S. financing practices found in Europe is the broad participation of commercial banks in medium- and long-term lending activities. In Europe, commercial banks carry on considerable activities of the kind that would be described as investment banking operations in the United States. This difference results from a legal requirement in the United States. The Banking Act of 1933 required the divestiture of investment banking operations by commercial banks.

A fourth practice distinctive to international financing relates to arbi-loans and link financing, both of which represent forms of equalizing the supply of and demand for loanable funds in relation to sensitive interest rate levels among different countries. Under *arbi-loans,* or international interest arbitrage financing, a borrower obtains loans in a country where the supply of funds is relatively abundant. The borrowed funds are then converted into another foreign currency needed by the firm. Simultaneously, the borrower enters into a forward exchange contract to protect itself on the reconversion of the new foreign currency into the original foreign currency that will be required at the time the loan must be repaid. Commercial banks are typically involved in arbi-loan transactions both as lenders and as intermediaries in the foreign exchange trading.

In *link financing,* the commercial banks take an even more direct role. A lender bank in the U.S., for example, deposits funds with a bank in Mexico, the borrower's country, where interest rates are higher. This deposit may be earmarked for the specified borrower. The lender, of course, is expected to hedge its position in the foreign exchange markets, since it will be repaid in the currency of the country in which the bank deposit was made. The U.S. bank receives a rate that provides an interest differential after all additional expenses, such as the cost of hedging, are taken into consideration. The Mexican bank receives a commission for handling the transaction.

Expanding Role of U.S. Commercial Banks and Investment Bankers

Commercial banks have long performed an important role in export and import financing. They have increased the number of their foreign branches and have expanded their foreign operations and lending activities. They have also participated in consortiums with foreign merchant banks (banks that specialize in business lending) and investment banks for the conduct of all forms of international financing services.

Through their Edge Act corporations, by which they can make equity investments, commercial banks have participated for many years in the financing of international operations. Edge Act subsidiaries were provided for by amendments in 1916 and 1919 to the Federal Reserve Act of 1913. The amendments give U.S. commercial banks the authority to enter international markets and engage in certain operations that are prohibited in the United States. Edge Act subsidiaries can conduct all forms of international banking; they can issue or confirm letters of credit, finance foreign trade, engage in spot and foreign exchange transactions, and so on. Through these foreign banking subsidiaries and affiliates, direct investments in the form of both debt and equity can be made in commercial and industrial firms.

U.S. investment banking firms have actively participated in arranging Eurocurrency financing, mainly for their U.S. customers. They have developed joint participation activities with foreign merchant banks and with foreign investment banking houses. They have established offices in foreign countries and have participated in international underwriting groups that have developed the Eurobond market.

Commercial banks have become especially active in international project financing. This type of financing involves large investment projects, usually joint ventures between government and private enterprise that are financed by international and government sources as well as by private sources, often through a Eurodollar bank syndicate. International project financing is characterized by large investments for development activities such as the opening of a new mine, major drilling or exploration, or the establishment of a major chemical or pharmaceutical complex. Normally, there is more than one major equity owner of the project company itself. The equity owners collectively possess or arrange for the requisite operating, technical, marketing, and financial strengths needed for the project's success.

International project financing generally involves relatively high debt leverage. Since the projects provide output for international markets, debt is issued in several currencies. The sources of debt are commercial banks, export credit agencies, suppliers, product purchasers, international lending agencies, regional or national development banks, and local governments.

International investment bankers serve as project financial advisers, fitting together the various types of financing needed to meet the project's requirements. Each transaction typically includes various covenants related directly to the characteristics of the project.[1]

The Eurodollar System

The Eurodollar system, which operates as an international money market, was developed in the early 1950s as banks accepted interest bearing deposits in currencies other than their own. Most of the early activity occurred in Europe, where the predominant foreign currency used was the dollar (whose stability gave it the status of an international currency). Since the system is now worldwide, including many different currencies, it is often called the *Eurocurrency system.*

The flow process of the Eurodollar market can be illustrated as follows. A European firm holds a dollar deposit in a New York bank. It can hold the dollars in the form of a dollar deposit claim on its European bank by drawing a check on the New York bank and making a deposit in the European bank. The European bank can in turn make loans to other customers. Except for holding fractional reserves against its dollar deposit liabilities, the European bank has served as an intermediary in transferring the dollar balances in the United States from its depositors to its borrowers. Yet its depositors still hold claims in dollars.

The Eurobanks, including the foreign branches of many U.S. banks, accept Eurodollar deposits and lend out these funds. The transactions involve large amounts, and the spread between the interest rates on loans and the interest paid on deposits is usually small. This is a fast-action market in which most transactions are arranged over the phone or through cables, with the confirming documents sent later by mail.

Eurodollar loans are typically in multiples of $1 million and have maturities ranging from thirty days to five to seven years. If the borrower is known to the bank, a loan of less than a year can be arranged quickly. Eurodollar loans are typically unsecured, but there may be restrictions of other kinds placed on the borrowing activities of the firm receiving the loan. One form of Eurodollar loan is the floating rate revolving loan, sometimes referred to as a revolver or a roll-over credit. The rate on the loan is quoted as the percentage above the London interbank offer rate (LIBO), and it reflects the rates on liquid funds that move among the money markets of the developed nations. The floating rate provision dampens borrowing based on speculation on fu-

1. For a more complete discussion, see Robert L. Huston, "Project Financing," in *The Treasurer's Handbook,* ed. J. Fred Weston and Maurice B. Goudzwaard (Homewood, Ill.: Dow Jones–Irwin, 1976).

ture interest rates. Prime borrowers typically pay from three-fourths of 1 percent over the LIBO (for seven- to eight-year maturities) to three-eighths of 1 percent over the LIBO (for five-year maturities). Lines of credit are typically established for a given period not to exceed twelve months and can be renegotiated at the end of the period. There is usually a commitment fee of one-fourth of 1 percent to one-half of 1 percent on the unused portion of the line of credit. The Eurocurrency system contributes to increasing and redistributing the world supply of international reserves or liquid resources. It represents an important addition to the development of a competitive and unified international money market.

Eurobonds represent the longer-term range of maturities in the Eurocurrency market. They are offered for sale in more than one country through international syndicates of underwriting and selling banks, and they are typically denominated in a strong currency, such as the German mark. The U.S. dollar continues to be used, despite fluctuations in its value, because it is a principal transaction currency. A large pool of Eurodollars is also available. Sometimes Eurobonds are denominated for repayment in multiple currencies. The creditor can request payment of the interest and principal in any predetermined currency at a previously established parity.

Convertible Eurobonds were stimulated by the entry of U.S. firms into financing through the Eurobond market. The convertible Eurobonds of U.S. firms have the advantage of carrying relatively low interest rates. Also, the market is broad so that larger amounts can be sold. This represents a method of internationalizing the ownership of the common stock of U.S. multinational corporations that have large direct investments and operations in foreign countries. For the foreign investors the convertible Eurobonds have the advantage of a fixed rate of interest plus potential capital gains.

The Eurobond market has helped internationalize the local character of the capital markets in individual European countries by underwriting the sales of their securities to investors in a number of European countries. The market contributes to the international financial adjustment process by stimulating the outflow of funds from countries with balance of payments surpluses (such as Germany).

An Example of International Financing

A case will illustrate the decision-making process in selecting among alternative currencies to use in financing long-term bonds.[2] Worldcorp operates throughout the world, with facilities in many countries. It is planning a joint venture that includes building a new plant in West Germany. To help meet its financing requirements, Worldcorp is considering an issue of bonds with a ten-year maturity in the equivalent amount of $50 million. Worldcorp is evaluating two alternatives:

2. This presentation is based on W. R. Folks, Jr., and R. Advani, "Raising Funds with Foreign Currency," *Financial Executive* 48 (February 1980), pp. 44–49.

1. A dollar issue at 11 percent annual coupon issued at par, with issuing expenses of 2.5 percent of face value.
2. A Deutsche mark (DM) issue at 8 percent annual coupon issued at 99 with additional issuing expenses of 2.5 percent of face value. (Therefore, total flotation expense is 3.5 percent of face value.)

The initial exchange rate is DM1 = U.S. $0.5701. The treasurer of Worldcorp forecasts the DM to rise in value in relation to the U.S. dollar by 4.13 percent per year for the ten-year life of the bond. Worldcorp's applicable tax rate is 46 percent. To make the comparison between the two alternatives, we first analyze the DM borrowing. We need four items: the net proceeds of the loan in dollars, the annual interest expense in dollars, tax savings from the issuing expenses, and after-tax repayment of principal in dollars at the end of ten years.

The Net Proceeds in Dollars. Flotation expense is 3.5 percent of the face amount or 0.035 × $50,000,000 = $1,750,000. The net proceeds are $50,000,000 less $1,750,000 = $48,250,000.

Annual Interest Expense in Dollars. The amount borrowed is $50,000,000, which, expressed in DM by dividing by the current exchange rate of 0.5701, is DM87,703,912. The interest rate on the DM loan is 8 percent, which is multiplied times the DM87,703,912 to obtain DM7,016,313. This is expressed in dollars by multiplying by 0.5701 to obtain $4 million, or $2,160,000 after tax. This after-tax interest expense expressed in dollars increases at the rate of the forecast of the rise in the DM value in relation to the dollar, which is 4.13 percent per year.

Tax Savings from the Issuing Expenses. The issuing expenses in dollars are $1,750,000 or $175,000 per year. This represents a tax shelter of 0.46 × $175,000, which equals $80,500 per year.

After-Tax Repayment of Principal. The net repayment of the principal amount borrowed involves several factors. The value of the DM in dollars is now 0.5701. Its value is expected to grow in relation to the dollar at a rate of 4.13 percent per year. The compound value of one dollar at 4.13 percent in ten years is $(1.0413)^{10}$, which equals 1.49885. Multiplied by 0.5701, this gives the tenth year exchange rate of 0.8545 used in the following calculations:

Repayment of principal = DM87,703,912 at 0.8545 =	$74,942,993
Original principal = DM87,703,912 at 0.5701 =	50,000,000
Exchange loss	$24,942,993
Tax savings at 0.46	11,473,777
After-tax exchange loss	$13,469,216

The net repayment of principal is \$74,942,993 less \$11,473,777 = \$63,469,216.

We now have the basic inputs for determining the after-tax cost of borrowing in DM. It is obtained by solving for r_a (the after-tax interest cost) in the following equation:

$$\$48{,}250{,}000 = \sum_{t=1}^{10} \frac{(0.54)(\$4{,}000{,}000)(1.0413)^t}{(1 + r_a)^t} - \sum_{t=1}^{10} \frac{\$80{,}500}{(1 + r_a)^t} + \frac{\$63{,}469{,}216}{(1 + r_a)^{10}}.$$

The solution is 7.55 percent, which we can verify as follows:

$$\begin{aligned}
\$48{,}250{,}000 &= \$2{,}160{,}000 \times \left(\frac{1.0413}{1.0755}\right)\left[\text{CVIFA}\left(\frac{1.0413}{1.0755} - 1, 10 \text{ years}\right)\right] \\
&\quad - \text{PVIFA}(7.55\%; 10 \text{ years}) \times \$80{,}500 \\
&\quad + \text{PVIF}(7.55\%; 10 \text{ years})\ \$63{,}469{,}216 \\
&= \$2{,}160{,}000(0.9682)\text{CVIFA}(-3.18\%; 10 \text{ years}) \\
&\quad - \text{PVIFA}(7.55\%; 10 \text{ years}) \times \$80{,}500 \\
&\quad + \text{PVIF}(7.55\%; 10 \text{ years})\$63{,}469{,}216 \\
&= \$2{,}160{,}000(0.9682)(8.68385) - (6.84844) \times \$80{,}500 \\
&\quad + (0.482943) \times \$63{,}469{,}216 \\
&= \$18{,}160{,}640 - \$551{,}299 + \$30{,}652{,}014 \\
&\cong \$48{,}261{,}355.
\end{aligned}$$

Thus at an after-tax cost of 7.55 percent, the net proceeds in dollars is equal to the present value of the after-tax interest costs (less the tax savings from the issuing costs) plus the present value of the net repayment of principal.

We next compare the cost of borrowing in DM with the cost of borrowing in dollars. We need the same four basic information inputs.

Net Proceeds in Dollars. Issuing expenses are 2.5 percent of \$50,000,000 = \$1,250,000. Net proceeds are therefore \$48,750,000.

Interest Costs in Dollars. The interest expense is 0.11 times \$50,000,000 times (1 − 0.46), which equals \$2,970,000 each year.

Tax Savings from the Issuing Expenses. Issuing expenses per year are \$125,000. The tax shelter is 0.46 times this amount, which equals \$57,500.

After-Tax Repayment of Principal. This is simply the present value of \$50,000,000 to be paid ten years hence.

The equation to test for the after-tax cost is:

$$\begin{aligned}
\$48{,}750{,}000 &= \$2{,}912{,}500(\text{PVIFA } r_a\%, 10 \text{ years}) \\
&\quad + \$50{,}000{,}000(\text{PVIF } r_a\%, 10 \text{ years}).
\end{aligned}$$

The solution is 6.17 percent, which can be verified as follows:

$$\begin{aligned}
\$48{,}750{,}000 &= \$2{,}912{,}500(7.3012) + \$50{,}000{,}000(0.5495) \\
&= \$21{,}264{,}745 + \$27{,}475{,}000 \\
&\cong \$48{,}739{,}745.
\end{aligned}$$

We find that the after-tax cost of using dollar bonds is 6.17 percent, while the after-tax cost of using bonds denominated in DM is 7.55 percent. Several issues are raised by this result. First, the difference is not of great magnitude. Second, the difference reflects the forecast of the future rise in the foreign exchange value of the DM in relation to the dollar. This forecast could be in error. The current interest rate differential on dollars versus DM implies a smaller rise in the exchange value of the DM in relation to the dollar than the 4.13 percent per annum. This forecast by the treasurer of Worldcorp implies that full interest rate parity is not reflected in the current dollar versus DM borrowing rates and that the "market is wrong." While the market is never wrong, it does change its mind, sometimes frequently.

Of course, a wide range of economic and political factors in the U.S. and in West Germany could change the interest parity relation and relative dollar and DM exchange rates over the ten-year life of the loan. The choice among the two alternative sources of financing is subject to uncertainty and error. One set of considerations for the treasurer is to judge the most likely direction of error. Is the most likely possibility that the DM will rise in value in relation to the dollar at a rate even higher than the 4.13 percent forecast? If so, this is a further reason for borrowing in dollars.

Or, alternatively, suppose that Worldcorp has large amounts of future receipts that will be made in DM—particularly near the tenth year maturity of the bond. If so, Worldcorp would be at least partially hedged with respect to a DM bond issue. On the other hand, Worldcorp may already have future exposure to a rise in the value of the DM in relation to the dollar. This would be a further reason for using the dollar as the denomination of the bond issue rather than the DM.

Working Capital Management in International Enterprise

International cash management involves minimizing the exposure of foreign-located funds to foreign exchange rate risk and avoiding prohibitions on the movement of funds from one country to another. Funds denominated in a foreign currency, particularly that of developing countries, are potentially subject to a decrease in value in terms of the home currency. The financial manager who hopes to avoid foreign exchange rate risk and prohibitions against the international movement of funds must continually assess political and economic trends in the countries of operation in order to anticipate changes that can have a detrimental effect.

The general principles that apply to the management of cash on an international basis are very similar to those used successfully by many firms on a domestic basis. Multinational firms try to speed up the collection of cash by having bank accounts in the banking system of each country. In many countries, customers pay their bills by requesting their bank or postal administration to deduct the amount owed from their account and to transfer it to the other firm's account.

Multinational commercial banks, particularly those that have branches or affiliates in a large number of countries, can be very helpful to multinational firms. Several of the larger U.S. multinational commercial banks have foreign departments whose sole purpose is to help U.S. multinational firms solve their problems of international cash management. An international bank can speed the flow of funds of a multinational firm and thereby decrease the exposure of these funds to foreign exchange rate risk. It can suggest the routing of the transfers as well as the national currency to be used. While in the United States the average time between the initiation and completion of a financial transaction is two to three days, the time interval for foreign transactions can be as long as two or three weeks. The long delays unnecessarily tie up large amounts of funds and should be avoided. In this area, the multinational commercial banks are particularly helpful, since they can transfer funds from one country to another (provided government restrictions do not interfere) on a same-day basis if they have branches or affiliates in the two countries involved.

Increasingly, the arena for business finance is the global market. At the start of each day, the corporate treasurer determines whether to borrow or to lend in the international financial market. The investment decisions are made in both domestic and foreign countries.

The financial manager of the multinational corporate enterprise must consider the form and extent of protection against currency fluctuations on sales and purchases. If the firm has surplus cash, the financial manager must compare the returns from investing in the domestic money market with those from investing in the international market. Similarly, if short-term financing needs arise, the manager must make comparisons between domestic and foreign financing sources. Among the considerations are the advantages and disadvantages of using the impersonal international financial market versus those of developing long-term financing relations with international commercial banks or financial groups in the U.S., London, Paris, Zurich, Bonn, and Tokyo.

Summary

A firm generally develops its international activities through an evolutionary process. First, it needs to develop a strong competitive product for domestic sales. Then it may start to export through a broker. When foreign sales increase, it may open a foreign branch sales office. Finally, it may establish a wholly-owned manufacturing plant or subsidiary in the foreign country. If the foreign government places restrictions on foreign investments or imports, licensing or joint ventures may be the only feasible ways of doing business in the foreign country.

International business transactions are conducted in more than one currency. If a firm is expecting receipts in foreign currency units, its risk is that the value of the foreign currency units will fall. If it has obligations to be paid in foreign currency units, its risk is that the value of the foreign currency will rise. To reduce foreign exchange risk, firms can engage in transactions in the forward foreign exchange market. They can also borrow at current spot exchange rates the amount of local currency needed for future transactions. These two forms of hedging are essentially insurance and therefore involve costs.

Firms also take protective action against long or short positions in foreign currencies resulting from the balance sheet position of their foreign subsidiaries. Monetary assets and liabilities are those items whose value, expressed in local currency, does not change with devaluation or revaluation. A firm seeks to have a net monetary creditor position in a country whose exchange rates are expected to rise and a net monetary debtor position in a country whose exchange rates are expected to fall. A monetary debtor position can be created by investing all excess cash, granting as little trade credit as possible, avoiding advances, and borrowing funds. A monetary creditor position can be developed by holding cash or cash equivalents, such as foreign securities, and by having receivables due in the foreign currency.

International financing broadens the range of fund sources. These sources include international and government institutions, Eurocurrency and Eurobond markets, overdrafts from European banks, discounted trade bills, and arbi-loans and link financing. Edge Act subsidiaries permit commercial banks to enter international markets and engage in operations from which they are prohibited in the United States. U.S. commercial banks and investment banking firms have become very active in international financing and related services.

International cash management involves minimizing exposure of foreign-located funds to exchange rate risks and avoiding restrictions on the movement of funds from one country to another. International banks provide many services that facilitate effective international working capital management by multinational firms.

Questions

26.1 What has been the impact of advances in the technology of transportation and communication on international trade and finance?

26.2 Why is the ratio of foreign earnings to a firm's total earnings likely to be greater than the ratio of its foreign sales to total sales?

26.3 If a firm has difficulty developing a product that will sell in the local domestic market, is it likely to have greater success in a foreign market? Explain.

26.4 What are the advantages and disadvantages to a firm of licensing the production of its products to foreign firms?

26.5 What are the pros and cons of engaging in a joint venture rather than establishing a wholly-owned foreign subsidiary?

26.6 What are monetary assets and liabilities (as contrasted with "real" or nonmonetary assets and liabilities)?

26.7 What are arbi-loans and link financing?

26.8 What are some of the services provided by U.S. commercial banks to firms engaged in international operations or financing?

26.9 What are some of the services provided by U.S. investment banking firms to U.S. business firms engaged in international operations or financing?

26.10 What is the Eurocurrency system, and what economic functions does it perform?

26.11 Describe some major characteristics of Eurodollar loans.

26.12 In what respects are domestic working capital management and international working capital management similar and different?

26.13 What services can the multinational commercial bank perform to help the U.S. multinational operating firm solve its problems of international cash management?

26.14 What are some of the reasons that U.S. firms engage in financing abroad?

Problems

26.1 The Whitley Company's subsidiary has monetary assets of LC 800,000 and monetary liabilities of LC 1,000,000. Calculate the gain or loss of the parent under the following two states of the world:

a. There has been a devaluation; the local currency has dropped from 20 LC per $1 to 25 LC per $1.

b. There has been a revaluation; the local currency has appreciated from 20 LC per $1 to 15 LC per $1.

26.2 The Ravel Company exports a substantial amount of cosmetics each year and therefore has a great part of its assets invested in LC receivables. Monetary assets are LC 30,000,000, while monetary liabilities are LC 10,000,000. Calculate any gains or losses under the following two states of the world:

a. There is a revaluation from 4 LC per $1 to 3 LC per $1.

b. There is a devaluation from 4 LC per $1 to 5 LC per $1.

26.3 The Ajax Company's international transfer of funds amounts to about $2 million monthly. Presently, the average transfer time is ten days. It has been proposed that the transfer of funds be turned over to one of the larger international banks, which can reduce the transfer time to an average of two days. A charge of one-half of 1 percent of the volume of transfer has been proposed for this service. In view of the fact that the firm's opportunity cost of funds is 12 percent, should this offer be accepted?

26.4 The MNC Corporation has a number of subsidiaries located in various Asian countries. These subsidiaries collect the equivalent of $500,000 each month, and the funds are transferred to the company's cash center in Hong Kong. The average transfer time has been fourteen days. An international bank, eager to solicit business from MNC, has offered to handle the transfer of these funds at a guaranteed average transfer time of not more than two days. The company's opportunity cost is 15 percent.

a. How much is this service worth to the company?

b. What are the advantages and disadvantages of the arrangement?

26.5 Davidson International's principal manufacturing plant in Europe is located in Paris. In-transfer and temporarily idle funds have been routed to and through this office. However, since forward market quotations on the French franc have been weakening lately, the manager of the international division is planning to reroute temporarily idle cash funds to the office of the company's German subsidiary. The company has been protecting itself by entering into forward ninety-day contracts to purchase dollars with French francs at an annual discount of 5 to 6 percent. By comparison, ninety-day forward contracts can be obtained to buy dollars with West German marks at a premium in relation to the present spot rate of 1.5 percent. Short-term interest rates in France are 7.5 percent and in West Germany approximately 7 percent.

a. Should West Germany become the transfer center of the firm's international funds flow? What would be the cost or benefit of any change that might be suggested?
b. What requirements for an international financial center are considered important in locating a cash concentration center in a particular city? Why?

26.6 A U.S. manufacturing company has imported industrial machinery at a price of DM5.0 million. The machinery will be delivered and paid for in six months. For planning purposes, the American company wants to establish what the payment (in dollars) will be in six months. It decides to use the forward market to accomplish its objective. The company contacts its New York bank, which provides the quotations given below. The bank states that it will charge a commission of 1/4 percent on any transaction.

	DM	Swiss Franc	$
Six-month Eurocurrency rates (% per annum) denominated in the following currencies	9.40	5.85	16.10
Spot exchange rates (currency/Swiss franc)	1.0561	—	0.5990

a. Does the American company enter the forward market to go long or short of forward DM?
b. What is the number of DM/$? What is the dollar value of the Deutsche mark?
c. What is the equilibrium forward rate for the Deutsche mark expressed as DM/$?
d. What price in dollars can the American company establish by using the forward market in Deutsche marks?

26.7 A West German company buys industrial machinery from a U.S. company at a price of $20 million. The machinery will be delivered and paid for in six months. The German company seeks to establish its cost in Deutsche marks. It decides to use the forward market to accomplish its objective. The company contacts its Bonn bank, which provides the quotations listed below. The bank states that it will charge a commission of 1/4 percent of any transaction.

	DM	£	$
Six-month Eurocurrency rates (% per annum) denominated in the following currencies	9.40	17.90	16.10
Spot exchange rates (currency/U.K.£)	4.0185	—	2.2793

a. Does the German company enter the forward market to go long or short of forward dollars?
b. What is the number of DM/$? What is the dollar value of the Deutsche mark?
c. What is the equilibrium forward rate for the Deutsche mark expressed as $/DM?
d. Does the commission increase or decrease the dollar value of the Deutsche mark?
e. What price in Deutsche marks can the Germany company establish by using the forward market in dollars?

26.8 The Kory Company has made a sale of construction equipment to a foreign firm and will receive LC 11,000,000 on May 31, 19X9. The company has incurred all of its expenses in dollars and needs to know the definite dollar amounts that it will receive on May 31, 19X9. The effective tax rate in both countries is 40 percent, and the expected future spot rate is 12 LC per dollar. The director of finance at Kory Company is considering three options to deal with the foreign exchange risk:

a. To enter the forward market to sell LC 11,000,000 for dollars at the ninety-day forward rate quoted on March 1, 19X9, which is 11 LC per dollar. Under this arrangement the Kory Company will receive a definite amount in dollars in May as determined by the forward rate on March 1, 19X9.
b. To borrow on March 1, 19X9, from a foreign bank an amount in local currency (LC) plus interest that will equal the amount the Kory Company will be receiving on May 31, 19X9. The interest rate on the loan would be 32 percent. By borrowing, the company will receive LCs and, with the LCs received, can immediately purchase dollars at the March 1, 19X9, spot rate, which is LC 10 per dollar. The dollars received can be invested in the United States at an interest rate of 12 percent. When the company receives the LC 11,000,000 on May 31, 19X9, it can liquidate the local currency loan plus interest.
c. To make no attempt to cover the exchange risk involved in waiting the three months for receipt of the LC 11,000,000. Under the third alternative, the company will convert the LC 11,000,000 into dollars at the spot rate of LC 12 per dollar that is expected to prevail on May 31, 19X9.

Which alternative should be chosen?

26.9 Rework Problem 26.8 assuming a foreign interest rate of 60 percent. Which alternative is the most attractive now? Explain.

26.10 On March 1, 19X9, the Burrows Company bought from a foreign firm electronic equipment that will require the payment of LC 900,000 on May 31, 19X9. The spot rate on March 1, 19X9, is LC 10 per dollar; the expected future spot rate is LC 8 per dollar; and the ninety-day forward rate is LC 9 per dollar. The U.S. interest rate is 12 percent, and the foreign interest rate is 8 percent. The tax rate for both countries is 40 percent. The Burrows Company is considering three alternatives to deal with the risk of exchange rate fluctuations:

a. To enter the forward market to buy LC 900,000 at the ninety-day forward rate in effect on March 1, 19X9.
b. To borrow an amount in dollars to buy the LC at the current spot rate. This money is to be invested in government securities of the foreign country; with the interest income, it will equal LC 900,000 on May 31, 19X9.
c. To wait until May 31, 19X9, and buy LCs at whatever spot rate prevails at that time.

Which alternative should the Burrows Company follow in order to minimize its cost of meeting the future payment in LCs? Explain.

Selected References

Adler, Michael. "The Cost of Capital and Valuation of a Two-Country Firm: Reply." *Journal of Finance* 32 (September 1977), pp. 1354–1357.

———. "The Cost of Capital and Valuation of a Two-Country Firm." *Journal of Finance* 29 (March 1974), pp. 119–132.

Albach, Horst, "The Development of the Capital Structure of German Companies." *Journal of Business Finance and Accounting* 2 (Autumn 1975), pp. 281–294.

Aliber, Robert Z. *Exchange Risk and Corporate International Finance.* New York: Wiley, 1978.

Anderson, Gerald L. "International Project Financing." *Financial Executive* 45 (May 1977), pp. 40–45.

Aubey, Robert T., and Lombra, Raymond E. "The Use of International Currency Cocktails in the Reduction of Exchange Rate Risk." *Journal of Economics and Business* 29 (Winter 1977), pp. 128–134.

Baker, James C., and Bates, Thomas H. *Financing International Business Operations.* Scranton, Pa.: Intext Educational Publishers, 1971.

Bowditch, Richard L., and Burtle, James L. "The Corporate Treasurer in a World of Floating Exchange Rates." In *The Treasurer's Handbook,* edited by J. Fred Weston and Maurice B. Goudzwaard. Homewood, Ill.: Dow Jones–Irwin, 1976, pp. 84–112.

Calderon-Rossell, Jorge R. "Covering Foreign Exchange Risks of Single Transactions." *Financial Management* 8 (Autumn 1979), pp. 78–85.

Christofides, N.; Hewins, R. D.; and Salkin, G. R. "Graph Theoretic Approaches to Foreign Exchange Operations." *Journal of Financial and Quantitative Analysis* 14 (September 1979), pp. 481–500.

Cornell, Bradford. "Relative Price Changes and Deviations from Purchasing Power Parity." *Journal of Banking and Finance* 3 (September 1979), pp. 263–279.

———. "Determinants of the Bid-Ask Spread on Forward Foreign Exchange Contracts." *Journal of International Business Studies* 9 (Fall 1978), pp. 33–41.

———. "Spot Rates, Forward Rates and Exchange Market Efficiency." *Journal of Financial Economics* 5 (August 1977), pp. 55–65.

Cornell, Bradford, and Dietrich, J. Kimball. "The Efficiency of the Market for Foreign Exchange under Floating Exchange Rates." *Review of Economics and Statistics* 60 (February 1978), pp. 111–120.

Davis, Steven I. "How Risky Is International Lending?" *Harvard Business Review* 55 (January–February 1977), pp. 135–143.

Denis, Jack, Jr. "How to Hedge Foreign Currency Risk." *Financial Analysts' Journal* 32 (January–February 1976), pp. 50–54.

Dufey, Gunter. "Corporate Finance and Exchange Rate Variations." *Financial Management* 1 (Summer 1972), pp. 51–57.

Eiteman, David K., and Stonehill, Arthur I. *Multinational Business Finance.* 2d ed. Reading, Mass.: Addison-Wesley, 1979.

Elliott, J. W. "The Expected Return to Equity and International Asset Prices." *Journal of Financial and Quantitative Analysis* 13 (December 1978), pp. 987–1002.

Feiger, George, and Jacquillat, Bertrand. "Currency Option Bonds, Puts and Calls on Spot Exchange and the Hedging of Contingent Foreign Earnings." *Journal of Finance* 34 (December 1979), pp. 1129–1139.

Feinschreiber, Robert. "The Foreign Tax Credit under Siege." *Financial Executive* 47 (October 1979), pp. 56–62.

Folks, William R., Jr. "Optimal Foreign Borrowing Strategies with Operations in Forward Exchange Markets." *Journal of Financial and Quantitative Analysis* 13 (June 1978), pp. 245–254.

———. "Decision Analysis for Exchange Risk Management." *Financial Management* 1 (Winter 1972), pp. 101–112.

Folks, William R., Jr., and Advani, Ramesh. "Raising Funds with Foreign Currency." *Financial Executive* 48 (February 1980), pp. 44–49.

Folks, William R., Jr., and Stansell, Stanley R. "The Use of Discriminant Analysis in Forecasting Exchange Rate Movements." *Journal of International Business Studies* 6 (Spring 1975), pp. 33–50.

Fowler, D. J. "Transfer Prices and Profit Maximization in Multinational Enterprise Operations." *Journal of International Business Studies* 9 (Winter 1978), pp. 9–26.

Franck, Peter, and Young, Allan. "Stock Price Reaction of Multinational Firms to Exchange Realignments." *Financial Management* 1 (Winter 1972), pp. 66–73.

Geweke, John, and Feige, Edgar. "Some Joint Tests of the Efficiency of the Markets for Forward Foreign Exchange." *Review of Economics and Statistics* 61 (August 1979), pp. 334–341.

Giddy, Ian H. "Exchange Risk: Whose View?" *Financial Management* 6 (Summer 1977), pp. 23–33.

———. "An Integrated Theory of Exchange Rate Equilibrium." *Journal of Financial and Quantitative Analysis* 11 (December 1976), pp. 883–892.

Goldberg, Michael A., and Lee, Wayne Y. "The Cost of Capital and Valuation of a Two-Country Firm: Comment." *Journal of Finance* 32 (September 1977), pp. 1348–1353.

Goodman, Stephen H. "Foreign Exchange-Rate Forecasting Techniques: Implications for Business and Policy." *Journal of Finance* 34 (May 1979), pp. 415–427.

Hackett, John T. "New Financial Strategies for the MNC." *Business Horizons* 15 (April 1975), pp. 13–20.

Hagemann, Helmut. "Anticipate Your Long-Term Foreign Exchange Risks." *Harvard Business Review* 55 (March–April 1977), pp. 81–88.

Hawkins, R. G.; Mintz, N.; and Provissiero, M. "Government Takeovers of U.S. Foreign Affiliates." *Journal of International Business Studies* 7 (Spring 1976), pp. 3–16.

Imai, Yutaka. "Exchange Rate Risk Protection in International Business." *Journal of Financial and Quantitative Analysis* 10 (September 1975), pp. 447–456.

Jucker, James V., and de Faro, Clovis. "The Selection of International Borrowing Sources." *Journal of Financial and Quantitative Analysis* 10 (September 1975), pp. 381–407.

Kohlhagen, Steven W. "A Model of Optimal Foreign Exchange Hedging without Exchange Rate Projections." *Journal of International Business Studies* 9 (Fall 1978), pp. 9–19.

Lee, Wayne Y., and Sachdeva, Kanwal S. "The Role of the Multinational Firm in the Integration of Segmented Capital Markets." *Journal of Finance* 32 (May 1977), pp. 479–492.

Lessard, Donald R., ed. *International Financial Management, Theory and Application.* New York: Warren, Gorham & Lamont, 1979.

———. "World, National, and Industry Factors in Equity Returns." *Journal of Finance* 29 (May 1974), pp. 379–391.

Lieberman, Gail. "A Systems Approach to Foreign Exchange Risk Management." *Financial Executive* 46 (December 1978), pp. 14–19.

Logue, Dennis E., and Oldfield, George S. "Managing Foreign Assets When Foreign Exchange Markets Are Efficient." *Financial Management* 16 (Summer 1977), pp. 16–22.

Logue, Dennis E.; Sweeney, Richard James; and Willett, Thomas D. "Speculative Behavior of Foreign Exchange Rates during the Current Float." *Journal of Business Research* 6 (May 1978), pp. 159–174.

Meadows, Edward. "How the Euromarket Fends Off Global Financial Disaster." *Fortune,* September 24, 1979, pp. 122–124, 128, 130, 135.

Mehra, Rajnish. "On the Financing and Investment Decisions of Multinational Firms in the Presence of Exchange Risk." *Journal of Financial and Quantitative Analysis* 13 (June 1978), pp. 227–244.

Nehrt, Lee Charles. *The Political Climate for Private Foreign Investment.* New York: Praeger, 1970.

Ness, Walter L., Jr. "A Linear Programming Approach to Financing the Multinational Corporation." *Financial Management* 1 (Winter 1972), pp. 88–100.

Obersteiner, Erich. "Should the Foreign Affiliate Remit Dividends or Reinvest?" *Financial Management* 2 (Spring 1973), pp. 88–93.

Petty, J. William II, and Walker, Ernest W. "Optimal Transfer Pricing for the Multinational Firm." *Financial Management* 1 (Winter 1972), pp. 74–87.

Quinn, Brian S. "The International Bond Market for the U.S. Investor." *Columbia Journal of World Business* 14 (Fall 1979), pp. 85–90.

Remmers, Lee; Stonehill, Arthur; Wright, Richard; and Beekhuisen, Theo. "Industry and Size as Debt Ratio Determinants in Manufacturing Internationally." *Financial Management* 3 (Summer 1974), pp. 24–32.

Robbins, Sidney M., and Stobaugh, Robert B. "Financing Foreign Affiliates." *Financial Management* 1 (Winter 1972), pp. 56–65.

Rodriguez, Rita M. "FASB No. 8: What Has It Done to Us?" *Financial Analysts' Journal* 33 (March–April 1977), pp. 40–47.

———. "Management of Foreign Exchange Risk in the U.S. Multinationals." *Journal of Financial and Quantitative Analysis* 9 (November 1974), pp. 849–857.

Rodriguez, Rita M., and Carter, E. Eugene. *International Financial Management.* 2d ed. Englewood Cliffs, N.J.: Prentice-Hall, 1979.

Rogalski, Richard J., and Vinso, Joseph D. "Price Level Variations as Predictors of Flexible Exchange Rates." *Journal of International Business Studies* 8 (Spring–Summer 1977), pp. 71–81.

Rolfe, Sidney E., and Damm, Walter, eds. *The Multinational Corporation in the World Economy.* New York: Praeger, 1970.

Sangster, Bruce F. "International Funds Management." *Financial Executive* 45 (December 1977), pp. 46–52.

Schwab, Bernhard, and Lusztig, Peter. "Apportioning Foreign Exchange Risk through the Use of Third Currencies: Some Questions on Efficiency." *Financial Management* 7 (Autumn 1978), pp. 25–30.

Senbet, Lemma W. "International Capital Market Equilibrium and the Multinational Firm Financing and Investment Policies." *Journal of Financial and Quantitative Analysis* 14 (September 1979), pp. 455–480.

Severn, Alan K., and Meinster, David R. "The Use of Multicurrency Financing by the Financial Manager." *Financial Management* 7 (Winter 1978), pp. 45–53.

Shapiro, Alan C. "Payments Netting in International Cash Management." *Journal of International Business Studies* 9 (Fall 1978), pp. 51–58.

———. "Financial Structure and Cost of Capital in the Multinational Corporation."

Journal of Financial and Quantitative Analysis 13 (June 1978), pp. 211–226.

———. "Capital Budgeting for the Multinational Corporation." *Financial Management* 7 (Spring 1978), pp. 7–16.

———. "Defining Exchange Risk." *Journal of Business* 50 (January 1977), pp. 37–39.

———. "International Cash Management—The Determination of Multicurrency Cash Balances." *Journal of Financial and Quantitative Analysis* 11 (December 1976), pp. 893–900.

———. "Exchange Rate Changes, Inflation, and the Value of the Multinational Corporation." *Journal of Finance* 30 (May 1975), pp. 485–502.

———. "Evaluating Financing Costs for Multinational Subsidiaries." *Journal of International Business Studies* 6 (Fall 1975), pp. 25–32.

Solnik, Bruno. "International Parity Conditions and Exchange Risk: A Review." *Journal of Banking and Finance* 2 (October 1978), pp. 281–293.

———. "Testing International Asset Pricing: Some Pessimistic Views." *Journal of Finance* 32 (May 1977), pp. 503–517.

———. "The International Pricing of Risk: An Empirical Investigation of the World Capital Market Structure." *Journal of Finance* 29 (May 1974), pp. 365–378.

Starr, Danforth W. "Opportunities for United States Corporate Borrowers in the International Bond Markets." *Financial Executive* 47 (June 1979), pp. 50, 52–59.

Stehle, Richard. "An Empirical Test of the Alternative Hypotheses of National and International Pricing of Risky Assets." *Journal of Finance* 32 (May 1977), pp. 493–502.

Sterling, J. F., Jr. "A New Look at International Lending by American Banks." *Columbia Journal of World Business* 14 (Fall 1979), pp. 61–70.

Stonehill, Arthur, et al. "Financial Goals and Debt Ratio Determinants: A Survey of Practice in Five Countries." *Financial Management* 4 (Autumn 1975), pp. 27–41.

Vinso, Joseph D., and Rogalski, Richard J. "Empirical Properties of Foreign Exchange Rates." *Journal of International Business Studies* 9 (Fall 1978), pp. 69–79.

Voupel, James W., and Curhan, Joan P. *The Making of Multinational Enterprise.* Boston: Harvard Business School, Division of Research, 1969.

Weston, J. Fred, and Sorge, Bart W. *International Managerial Finance.* Homewood, Ill.: Richard D. Irwin, 1972, pp. xv and 388.

———. *Guide to International Financial Management.* New York: McGraw-Hill, 1977.

Part Eight

Appendix Tables

Appendix A Interest Tables

Table A.1

Compound Sum of \$1 CVIF = $(1 + r)^N$

Period	1%	2%	3%	4%	5%	6%	7%	8%	9%	10%	12%	14%	15%	16%	18%	20%	24%	28%	32%	36%
1	1.0100	1.0200	1.0300	1.0400	1.0500	1.0600	1.0700	1.0800	1.0900	1.1000	1.1200	1.1400	1.1500	1.1600	1.1800	1.2000	1.2400	1.2800	1.3200	1.3600
2	1.0201	1.0404	1.0609	1.0816	1.1025	1.1236	1.1449	1.1664	1.1881	1.2100	1.2544	1.2996	1.3225	1.3456	1.3924	1.4400	1.5376	1.6384	1.7424	1.8496
3	1.0303	1.0612	1.0927	1.1249	1.1576	1.1910	1.2250	1.2597	1.2950	1.3310	1.4049	1.4815	1.5209	1.5609	1.6430	1.7280	1.9066	2.0972	2.3000	2.5155
4	1.0406	1.0824	1.1255	1.1699	1.2155	1.2625	1.3108	1.3605	1.4116	1.4641	1.5735	1.6890	1.7490	1.8106	1.9388	2.0736	2.3642	2.6844	3.0360	3.4210
5	1.0510	1.1041	1.1593	1.2167	1.2763	1.3382	1.4026	1.4693	1.5386	1.6105	1.7623	1.9254	2.0114	2.1003	2.2878	2.4883	2.9316	3.4360	4.0075	4.6526
6	1.0615	1.1262	1.1941	1.2653	1.3401	1.4185	1.5007	1.5869	1.6771	1.7716	1.9738	2.1950	2.3131	2.4364	2.6996	2.9860	3.6352	4.3980	5.2899	6.3275
7	1.0721	1.1487	1.2299	1.3159	1.4071	1.5036	1.6058	1.7138	1.8280	1.9487	2.2107	2.5023	2.6600	2.8262	3.1855	3.5832	4.5077	5.6295	6.9826	8.6054
8	1.0829	1.1717	1.2668	1.3686	1.4775	1.5938	1.7182	1.8509	1.9926	2.1436	2.4760	2.8526	3.0590	3.2784	3.7589	4.2998	5.5895	7.2058	9.2170	11.703
9	1.0937	1.1951	1.3048	1.4233	1.5513	1.6895	1.8385	1.9990	2.1719	2.3579	2.7731	3.2519	3.5179	3.8030	4.4355	5.1598	6.9310	9.2234	12.166	15.916
10	1.1046	1.2190	1.3439	1.4802	1.6289	1.7908	1.9672	2.1589	2.3674	2.5937	3.1058	3.7072	4.0456	4.4114	5.2338	6.1917	8.5944	11.805	16.059	21.646
11	1.1157	1.2434	1.3842	1.5395	1.7103	1.8983	2.1049	2.3316	2.5804	2.8531	3.4785	4.2262	4.6524	5.1173	6.1759	7.4301	10.657	15.111	21.198	29.439
12	1.1268	1.2682	1.4258	1.6010	1.7959	2.0122	2.2522	2.5182	2.8127	3.1384	3.8960	4.8179	5.3502	5.9360	7.2876	8.9161	13.214	19.342	27.982	40.037
13	1.1381	1.2936	1.4685	1.6651	1.8856	2.1329	2.4098	2.7196	3.0658	3.4523	4.3635	5.4924	6.1528	6.8858	8.5994	10.699	16.386	24.758	36.937	54.451
14	1.1495	1.3195	1.5126	1.7317	1.9799	2.2609	2.5785	2.9372	3.3417	3.7975	4.8871	6.2613	7.0757	7.9875	10.147	12.839	20.319	31.691	48.756	74.053
15	1.1610	1.3459	1.5580	1.8009	2.0789	2.3966	2.7590	3.1722	3.6425	4.1772	5.4736	7.1379	8.1371	9.2655	11.973	15.407	25.195	40.564	64.358	100.71
16	1.1726	1.3728	1.6047	1.8730	2.1829	2.5404	2.9522	3.4259	3.9703	4.5950	6.1304	8.1372	9.3576	10.748	14.129	18.488	31.242	51.923	84.953	136.96
17	1.1843	1.4002	1.6528	1.9479	2.2920	2.6928	3.1588	3.7000	4.3276	5.0545	6.8660	9.2765	10.761	12.467	16.672	22.186	38.740	66.461	112.13	186.27
18	1.1961	1.4282	1.7024	2.0258	2.4066	2.8543	3.3799	3.9960	4.7171	5.5599	7.6900	10.575	12.375	14.462	19.673	26.623	48.038	85.070	148.02	253.33
19	1.2081	1.4568	1.7535	2.1068	2.5270	3.0256	3.6165	4.3157	5.1417	6.1159	8.6128	12.055	14.231	16.776	23.214	31.948	59.567	108.89	195.39	344.53
20	1.2202	1.4859	1.8061	2.1911	2.6533	3.2071	3.8697	4.6610	5.6044	6.7275	9.6463	13.743	16.366	19.460	27.393	38.337	73.864	139.37	257.91	468.57
21	1.2324	1.5157	1.8603	2.2788	2.7860	3.3996	4.1406	5.0338	6.1088	7.4002	10.803	15.667	18.821	22.574	32.323	46.005	91.591	178.40	340.44	637.26
22	1.2447	1.5460	1.9161	2.3699	2.9253	3.6035	4.4304	5.4365	6.6586	8.1403	12.100	17.861	21.644	26.186	38.142	55.206	113.57	228.35	449.39	866.67
23	1.2572	1.5769	1.9736	2.4647	3.0715	3.8197	4.7405	5.8715	7.2579	8.9543	13.552	20.361	24.891	30.376	45.007	66.247	140.83	292.30	593.19	1178.6
24	1.2697	1.6084	2.0328	2.5633	3.2251	4.0489	5.0724	6.3412	7.9111	9.8497	15.178	23.212	28.625	35.236	53.108	79.496	174.63	374.14	783.02	1602.9
25	1.2824	1.6406	2.0938	2.6658	3.3864	4.2919	5.4274	6.8485	8.6231	10.834	17.000	26.461	32.918	40.874	62.668	95.396	216.54	478.90	1033.5	2180.0
26	1.2953	1.6734	2.1566	2.7725	3.5557	4.5494	5.8074	7.3964	9.3992	11.918	19.040	30.166	37.856	47.414	73.948	114.47	268.51	612.99	1364.3	2964.9
27	1.3082	1.7069	2.2213	2.8834	3.7335	4.8223	6.2139	7.9881	10.245	13.110	21.324	34.389	43.535	55.000	87.259	137.37	332.95	784.63	1800.9	4032.2
28	1.3213	1.7410	2.2879	2.9987	3.9201	5.1117	6.6488	8.6271	11.167	14.421	23.883	39.204	50.065	63.800	102.96	164.84	412.86	1004.3	2377.2	5483.8
29	1.3345	1.7758	2.3566	3.1187	4.1161	5.4184	7.1143	9.3173	12.172	15.863	26.749	44.693	57.575	74.008	121.50	197.81	511.95	1285.5	3137.9	7458.0
30	1.3478	1.8114	2.4273	3.2434	4.3219	5.7435	7.6123	10.062	13.267	17.449	29.959	50.950	66.211	85.849	143.37	237.37	634.81	1645.5	4142.0	10143.
40	1.4889	2.2080	3.2620	4.8010	7.0400	10.285	14.974	21.724	31.409	45.259	93.050	188.88	267.86	378.72	750.37	1469.7	5455.9	19426.	66520.	*
50	1.6446	2.6916	4.3839	7.1067	11.467	18.420	29.457	46.901	74.357	117.39	289.00	700.23	1083.6	1670.7	3927.3	9100.4	46890.	*	*	*
60	1.8167	3.2810	5.8916	10.519	18.679	32.987	57.946	101.25	176.03	304.48	897.59	2595.9	4383.9	7370.1	20555.	56347.	*	*	*	*

*CVIF > 99,999

Table A.2

Present Value of $1
PVIF = $(1 + r)^{-N}$

Period	1%	2%	3%	4%	5%	6%	7%	8%	9%	10%	12%	14%	15%	16%	18%	20%	24%	28%	32%	36%
1	.9901	.9804	.9709	.9615	.9524	.9434	.9346	.9259	.9174	.9091	.8929	.8772	.8696	.8621	.8475	.8333	.8065	.7813	.7576	.7353
2	.9803	.9612	.9426	.9246	.9070	.8900	.8734	.8573	.8417	.8264	.7972	.7695	.7561	.7432	.7182	.6944	.6504	.6104	.5739	.5407
3	.9706	.9423	.9151	.8890	.8638	.8396	.8163	.7938	.7722	.7513	.7118	.6750	.6575	.6407	.6086	.5787	.5245	.4768	.4348	.3975
4	.9610	.9238	.8885	.8548	.8227	.7921	.7629	.7350	.7084	.6830	.6355	.5921	.5718	.5523	.5158	.4823	.4230	.3725	.3294	.2923
5	.9515	.9057	.8626	.8219	.7835	.7473	.7130	.6806	.6499	.6209	.5674	.5194	.4972	.4761	.4371	.4019	.3411	.2910	.2495	.2149
6	.9420	.8880	.8375	.7903	.7462	.7050	.6663	.6302	.5963	.5645	.5066	.4556	.4323	.4104	.3704	.3349	.2751	.2274	.1890	.1580
7	.9327	.8706	.8131	.7599	.7107	.6651	.6227	.5835	.5470	.5132	.4523	.3996	.3759	.3538	.3139	.2791	.2218	.1776	.1432	.1162
8	.9235	.8535	.7894	.7307	.6768	.6274	.5820	.5403	.5019	.4665	.4039	.3506	.3269	.3050	.2660	.2326	.1789	.1388	.1085	.0854
9	.9143	.8368	.7664	.7026	.6446	.5919	.5439	.5002	.4604	.4241	.3606	.3075	.2843	.2630	.2255	.1938	.1443	.1084	.0822	.0628
10	.9053	.8203	.7441	.6756	.6139	.5584	.5083	.4632	.4224	.3855	.3220	.2697	.2472	.2267	.1911	.1615	.1164	.0847	.0623	.0462
11	.8963	.8043	.7224	.6496	.5847	.5268	.4751	.4289	.3875	.3505	.2875	.2366	.2149	.1954	.1619	.1346	.0938	.0662	.0472	.0340
12	.8874	.7885	.7014	.6246	.5568	.4970	.4440	.3971	.3555	.3186	.2567	.2076	.1869	.1685	.1372	.1122	.0757	.0517	.0357	.0250
13	.8787	.7730	.6810	.6006	.5303	.4688	.4150	.3677	.3262	.2897	.2292	.1821	.1625	.1452	.1163	.0935	.0610	.0404	.0271	.0184
14	.8700	.7579	.6611	.5775	.5051	.4423	.3878	.3405	.2992	.2633	.2046	.1597	.1413	.1252	.0985	.0779	.0492	.0316	.0205	.0135
15	.8613	.7430	.6419	.5553	.4810	.4173	.3624	.3152	.2745	.2394	.1827	.1401	.1229	.1079	.0835	.0649	.0397	.0247	.0155	.0099
16	.8528	.7284	.6232	.5339	.4581	.3936	.3387	.2919	.2519	.2176	.1631	.1229	.1069	.0930	.0708	.0541	.0320	.0193	.0118	.0073
17	.8444	.7142	.6050	.5134	.4363	.3714	.3166	.2703	.2311	.1978	.1456	.1078	.0929	.0802	.0600	.0451	.0258	.0150	.0089	.0054
18	.8360	.7002	.5874	.4936	.4155	.3503	.2959	.2502	.2120	.1799	.1300	.0946	.0808	.0691	.0508	.0376	.0208	.0118	.0068	.0039
19	.8277	.6864	.5703	.4746	.3957	.3305	.2765	.2317	.1945	.1635	.1161	.0829	.0703	.0596	.0431	.0313	.0168	.0092	.0051	.0029
20	.8195	.6730	.5537	.4564	.3769	.3118	.2584	.2145	.1784	.1486	.1037	.0728	.0611	.0514	.0365	.0261	.0135	.0072	.0039	.0021
25	.7798	.6095	.4776	.3751	.2953	.2330	.1842	.1460	.1160	.0923	.0588	.0378	.0304	.0245	.0160	.0105	.0046	.0021	.0010	.0005
30	.7419	.5521	.4120	.3083	.2314	.1741	.1314	.0994	.0754	.0573	.0334	.0196	.0151	.0116	.0070	.0042	.0016	.0006	.0002	.0001
40	.6717	.4529	.3066	.2083	.1420	.0972	.0668	.0460	.0318	.0221	.0107	.0053	.0037	.0026	.0013	.0007	.0002	.0001	*	*
50	.6080	.3715	.2281	.1407	.0872	.0543	.0339	.0213	.0134	.0085	.0035	.0014	.0009	.0006	.0003	.0001	*	*	*	*
60	.5504	.3048	.1697	.0951	.0535	.0303	.0173	.0099	.0057	.0033	.0011	.0004	.0002	.0001	*	*	*	*	*	*

*The factor is zero to four decimal places.

Table A.3

Sum on an Annuity of $1 Per Period for N Periods:

$$CVIFA = \sum_{t=1}^{N} (1 + r)^{t-1}$$

$$= \frac{(1 + r)^N - 1}{r}.$$

Number of Periods	1%	2%	3%	4%	5%	6%	7%	8%	9%	10%	12%	14%	15%	16%	18%	20%	24%	28%	32%	36%
1	1.0000	1.0000	1.0000	1.0000	1.0000	1.0000	1.0000	1.0000	1.0000	1.0000	1.0000	1.0000	1.0000	1.0000	1.0000	1.0000	1.0000	1.0000	1.0000	1.0000
2	2.0100	2.0200	2.0300	2.0400	2.0500	2.0600	2.0700	2.0800	2.0900	2.1000	2.1200	2.1400	2.1500	2.1600	2.1800	2.2000	2.2400	2.2800	2.3200	2.3600
3	3.0301	3.0604	3.0909	3.1216	3.1525	3.1836	3.2149	3.2464	3.2781	3.3100	3.3744	3.4396	3.4725	3.5056	3.5724	3.6400	3.7776	3.9184	4.0624	4.2096
4	4.0604	4.1216	4.1836	4.2465	4.3101	4.3746	4.4399	4.5061	4.5731	4.6410	4.7793	4.9211	4.9934	5.0665	5.2154	5.3680	5.6842	6.0156	6.3624	6.7251
5	5.1010	5.2040	5.3091	5.4163	5.5256	5.6371	5.7507	5.8666	5.9847	6.1051	6.3528	6.6101	6.7424	6.8771	7.1542	7.4416	8.0484	8.6999	9.3983	10.146
6	6.1520	6.3081	6.4684	6.6330	6.8019	6.9753	7.1533	7.3359	7.5233	7.7156	8.1152	8.5355	8.7537	8.9775	9.4420	9.9299	10.980	12.135	13.405	14.798
7	7.2135	7.4343	7.6625	7.8983	8.1420	8.3938	8.6540	8.9228	9.2004	9.4872	10.089	10.730	11.066	11.413	12.141	12.915	14.615	16.533	18.695	21.126
8	8.2857	8.5830	8.8923	9.2142	9.5491	9.8975	10.259	10.636	11.028	11.435	12.299	13.232	13.726	14.240	15.327	16.499	19.122	22.163	25.678	29.731
9	9.3685	9.7546	10.159	10.582	11.026	11.491	11.978	12.487	13.021	13.579	14.775	16.085	16.785	17.518	19.085	20.798	24.712	29.369	34.895	41.435
10	10.462	10.949	11.463	12.006	12.577	13.180	13.816	14.486	15.192	15.937	17.548	19.337	20.303	21.321	23.521	25.958	31.643	38.592	47.061	57.351
11	11.566	12.168	12.807	13.486	14.206	14.971	15.783	16.645	17.560	18.531	20.654	23.044	24.349	25.732	28.755	32.150	40.237	50.398	63.121	78.998
12	12.682	13.412	14.192	15.025	15.917	16.869	17.888	18.977	20.140	21.384	24.133	27.270	29.001	30.850	34.931	39.580	50.894	65.510	84.320	108.43
13	13.809	14.680	15.617	16.626	17.713	18.882	20.140	21.495	22.953	24.522	28.029	32.088	34.351	36.786	42.218	48.496	64.109	84.852	112.30	148.47
14	14.947	15.973	17.086	18.291	19.598	21.015	22.550	24.214	26.019	27.975	32.392	37.581	40.504	43.672	50.818	59.195	80.496	109.61	149.23	202.92
15	16.096	17.293	18.598	20.023	21.578	23.276	25.129	27.152	29.360	31.772	37.279	43.842	47.580	51.659	60.965	72.035	100.81	141.30	197.99	276.97
16	17.257	18.639	20.156	21.824	23.657	25.672	27.888	30.324	33.003	35.949	42.753	50.980	55.717	60.925	72.939	87.442	126.01	181.86	262.35	377.69
17	18.430	20.012	21.761	23.697	25.840	28.212	30.840	33.750	36.973	40.544	48.883	59.117	65.075	71.673	87.068	105.93	157.25	233.79	347.30	514.66
18	19.614	21.412	23.414	25.645	28.132	30.905	33.999	37.450	41.301	45.599	55.749	68.394	75.836	84.140	103.74	128.11	195.99	300.25	459.44	700.93
19	20.810	22.840	25.116	27.671	30.539	33.760	37.379	41.446	46.018	51.159	63.439	78.969	88.211	98.603	123.41	154.74	244.03	385.32	607.47	954.27
20	22.019	24.297	26.870	29.778	33.066	36.785	40.995	45.762	51.160	57.275	72.052	91.024	102.44	115.37	146.62	186.68	303.60	494.21	802.86	1298.8
21	23.239	25.783	28.676	31.969	35.719	39.992	44.865	50.422	56.764	64.002	81.698	104.76	118.81	134.84	174.02	225.02	377.46	633.59	1060.7	1767.3
22	24.471	27.299	30.536	34.248	38.505	43.392	49.005	55.456	62.873	71.402	92.502	120.43	137.63	157.41	206.34	271.03	469.05	811.99	1401.2	2404.6
23	25.716	28.845	32.452	36.617	41.430	46.995	53.436	60.893	69.531	79.543	104.60	138.29	159.27	183.60	244.48	326.23	582.62	1040.3	1850.6	3271.3
24	26.973	30.421	34.426	39.082	44.502	50.815	58.176	66.764	76.789	88.497	118.15	158.65	184.16	213.97	289.49	392.48	723.46	1332.6	2443.8	4449.9
25	28.243	32.030	36.459	41.645	47.727	54.864	63.249	73.105	84.700	98.347	133.33	181.87	212.79	249.21	342.60	471.98	898.09	1706.8	3226.8	6052.9
26	29.525	33.670	38.553	44.311	51.113	59.156	68.676	79.954	93.323	109.18	150.33	208.33	245.71	290.08	405.27	567.37	1114.6	2185.7	4260.4	8233.0
27	30.820	35.344	40.709	47.084	54.669	63.705	74.483	87.350	102.72	121.09	169.37	238.49	283.56	337.50	479.22	681.85	1383.1	2798.7	5624.7	11197.9
28	32.129	37.051	42.930	49.967	58.402	68.528	80.697	95.338	112.96	134.20	190.69	272.88	327.10	392.50	566.48	819.22	1716.0	3583.3	7425.6	15230.2
29	33.450	38.792	45.218	52.966	62.322	73.639	87.346	103.96	124.13	148.63	214.58	312.09	377.16	456.30	669.44	984.06	2128.9	4587.6	9802.9	20714.1
30	34.784	40.568	47.575	56.084	66.438	79.058	94.460	113.28	136.30	164.49	241.33	356.78	434.74	530.31	790.94	1181.8	2640.9	5873.2	12940.	28172.2
40	48.886	60.402	75.401	95.025	120.79	154.76	199.63	259.05	337.88	442.59	767.09	1342.0	1779.0	2360.7	4163.2	7343.8	22728.	69377.	*	*
50	64.463	84.579	112.79	152.66	209.34	290.33	406.52	573.76	815.08	1163.9	2400.0	4994.5	7217.7	10435.	21813.	45497.	*	*	*	*
60	81.669	114.05	163.05	237.99	353.58	533.12	813.52	1253.2	1944.7	3034.8	7471.6	18535.	29219.	46057.	*	*	*	*	*	*

*CVIFA > 99.999.

Table A.4

Present Value of an Annuity of $1 Per Period for N Periods:

$$PVIFA = \sum_{t=1}^{N} \frac{1}{(1+r)^t}$$

$$= \frac{1 - \frac{1}{(1+r)^N}}{r}$$

Number of payments	1%	2%	3%	4%	5%	6%	7%	8%	9%	10%	12%	14%	15%	16%	18%	20%	24%	28%	32%
1	0.9901	0.9804	0.9709	0.9615	0.9524	0.9434	0.9346	0.9259	0.9174	0.9091	0.8929	0.8772	0.8696	0.8621	0.8475	0.8333	0.8065	0.7813	0.7576
2	1.9704	1.9416	1.9135	1.8861	1.8594	1.8334	1.8080	1.7833	1.7591	1.7355	1.6901	1.6467	1.6257	1.6052	1.5656	1.5278	1.4568	1.3916	1.3315
3	2.9410	2.8839	2.8286	2.7751	2.7232	2.6730	2.6243	2.5771	2.5313	2.4869	2.4018	2.3216	2.2832	2.2459	2.1743	2.1065	1.9813	1.8684	1.7663
4	3.9020	3.8077	3.7171	3.6299	3.5460	3.4651	3.3872	3.3121	3.2397	3.1699	3.0373	2.9137	2.8550	2.7982	2.6901	2.5887	2.4043	2.2410	2.0957
5	4.8534	4.7135	4.5797	4.4518	4.3295	4.2124	4.1002	3.9927	3.8897	3.7908	3.6048	3.4331	3.3522	3.2743	3.1272	2.9906	2.7454	2.5320	2.3452
6	5.7955	5.6014	5.4172	5.2421	5.0757	4.9173	4.7665	4.6229	4.4859	4.3553	4.1114	3.8887	3.7845	3.6847	3.4976	3.3255	3.0205	2.7594	2.5342
7	6.7282	6.4720	6.2303	6.0021	5.7864	5.5824	5.3893	5.2064	5.0330	4.8684	4.5638	4.2883	4.1604	4.0386	3.8115	3.6046	3.2423	2.9370	2.6775
8	7.6517	7.3255	7.0197	6.7327	6.4632	6.2098	5.9713	5.7466	5.5348	5.3349	4.9676	4.6389	4.4873	4.3436	4.0776	3.8372	3.4212	3.0758	2.7860
9	8.5660	8.1622	7.7861	7.4353	7.1078	6.8017	6.5152	6.2469	5.9952	5.7590	5.3282	4.9464	4.7716	4.6065	4.3030	4.0310	3.5655	3.1842	2.8681
10	9.4713	8.9826	8.5302	8.1109	7.7217	7.3601	7.0236	6.7101	6.4177	6.1446	5.6502	5.2161	5.0188	4.8332	4.4941	4.1925	3.6819	3.2689	2.9304
11	10.3676	9.7868	9.2526	8.7605	8.3064	7.8869	7.4987	7.1390	6.8052	6.4951	5.9377	5.4527	5.2337	5.0286	4.6560	4.3271	3.7757	3.3351	2.9776
12	11.2551	10.5753	9.9540	9.3851	8.8633	8.3838	7.9427	7.5361	7.1607	6.8137	6.1944	5.6603	5.4206	5.1971	4.7932	4.4392	3.8514	3.3868	3.0133
13	12.1337	11.3484	10.6350	9.9856	9.3936	8.8527	8.3577	7.9038	7.4869	7.1034	6.4235	5.8424	5.5831	5.3423	4.9095	4.5327	3.9124	3.4272	3.0404
14	13.0037	12.1062	11.2961	10.5631	9.8986	9.2950	8.7455	8.2442	7.7862	7.3667	6.6282	6.0021	5.7245	5.4675	5.0081	4.6106	3.9616	3.4587	3.0609
15	13.8651	12.8493	11.9379	11.1184	10.3797	9.7122	9.1079	8.5595	8.0607	7.6061	6.8109	6.1422	5.8474	5.5755	5.0916	4.6755	4.0013	3.4834	3.0764
16	14.7179	13.5777	12.5611	11.6523	10.8378	10.1059	9.4466	8.8514	8.3126	7.8237	6.9740	6.2651	5.9542	5.6685	5.1624	4.7296	4.0333	3.5026	3.0882
17	15.5623	14.2919	13.1661	12.1657	11.2741	10.4773	9.7632	9.1216	8.5436	8.0216	7.1196	6.3729	6.0472	5.7487	5.2223	4.7746	4.0591	3.5177	3.0971
18	16.3983	14.9920	13.7535	12.6593	11.6896	10.8276	10.0591	9.3719	8.7556	8.2014	7.2497	6.4674	6.1280	5.8178	5.2732	4.8122	4.0799	3.5294	3.1039
19	17.2260	15.6785	14.3238	13.1339	12.0853	11.1581	10.3356	9.6036	8.9501	8.3649	7.3658	6.5504	6.1982	5.8775	5.3162	4.8435	4.0967	3.5386	3.1090
20	18.0456	16.3514	14.8775	13.5903	12.4622	11.4699	10.5940	9.8181	9.1285	8.5136	7.4694	6.6231	6.2593	5.9288	5.3527	4.8696	4.1103	3.5458	3.1129
25	22.0232	19.5235	17.4131	15.6221	14.0939	12.7834	11.6536	10.6748	9.8226	9.0770	7.8431	6.8729	6.4641	6.0971	5.4669	4.9476	4.1474	3.5640	3.1220
30	25.8077	22.3965	19.6004	17.2920	15.3725	13.7648	12.4090	11.2578	10.2737	9.4269	8.0552	7.0027	6.5660	6.1772	5.5168	4.9789	4.1601	3.5693	3.1242
40	32.8347	27.3555	23.1148	19.7928	17.1591	15.0463	13.3317	11.9246	10.7574	9.7791	8.2438	7.1050	6.6418	6.2335	5.5482	4.9966	4.1659	3.5712	3.1250
50	39.1961	31.4236	25.7298	21.4822	18.2559	15.7619	13.8007	12.2335	10.9617	9.9148	8.3045	7.1327	6.6605	6.2463	5.5541	4.9995	4.1666	3.5714	3.1250
60	44.9550	34.7609	27.6756	22.6235	18.9293	16.1614	14.0392	12.3766	11.0480	9.9672	8.3240	7.1401	6.6651	6.2492	5.5553	4.9999	4.1667	3.5714	3.1250

Appendix B Natural Logarithms of Numbers between 1.0 and 4.99

N	0	1	2	3	4	5	6	7	8	9
1.0	0.00000	.00995	.01980	.02956	.03922	.04879	.05827	.06766	.07696	.08618
.1	.09531	.10436	.11333	.12222	.13103	.13976	.14842	.15700	.16551	.17395
.2	.18232	.19062	.19885	.20701	.21511	.22314	.23111	.23902	.24686	.25464
.3	.26236	.27003	.27763	.28518	.29267	.30010	.30748	.31481	.32208	.32930
.4	.33647	.34359	.35066	.35767	.36464	.37156	.37844	.38526	.39204	.39878
.5	.40547	.41211	.41871	.42527	.43178	.43825	.44469	.45108	.45742	.46373
.6	.47000	.47623	.48243	.48858	.49470	.50078	.50682	.51282	.51879	.52473
.7	.53063	.53649	.54232	.54812	.55389	.55962	.56531	.57098	.57661	.58222
.8	.58779	.59333	.59884	.60432	.60977	.61519	.62058	.62594	.63127	.63658
.9	.64185	.64710	.65233	.65752	.66269	.66783	.67294	.67803	.68310	.68813
2.0	0.69315	.69813	.70310	.70804	.71295	.71784	.72271	.72755	.73237	.73716
.1	.74194	.74669	.75142	.75612	.76081	.76547	.77011	.77473	.77932	.78390
.2	.78846	.79299	.79751	.80200	.80648	.81093	.81536	.81978	.82418	.82855
.3	.83291	.83725	.84157	.84587	.85015	.85422	.85866	.86289	.86710	.87129
.4	.87547	.87963	.88377	.88789	.89200	.89609	.90016	.90422	.90826	.91228
.5	.91629	.92028	.92426	.92822	.93216	.93609	.94001	.04391	.94779	.95166
.6	.95551	.95935	.96317	.96698	.97078	.97456	.97833	.98208	.98582	.98954
.7	.99325	.99695	.00063[a]	.00430[a]	.00796[a]	.01160[a]	.01523[a]	.01885[a]	.02245[a]	.02604[a]
.8	1.02962	.03318[a]	.03674	.04028	.04380	.04732	.05082	.05431	.05779	.06126
.9	.06471	.06815	.07158	.07500	.07841	.08181	.08519	.08856	.09192	.09527
3.0	1.09861	.10194	.10526	.10856	.11186	.11514	.11841	.12168	.12493	.12817
.1	.13140	.13462	.13783	.14103	.14422	.14740	.15057	.15373	.15688	.16002
.2	.16315	.16627	.16938	.17248	.17557	.17865	.18173	.18479	.18784	.19089
.3	.19392	.19695	.19996	.20297	.20597	.20896	.21194	.21491	.21788	.22083
.4	.22378	.22671	.22964	.23256	.23547	.23837	.24127	.24415	.24703	.24990
.5	.25276	.25562	.25846	.26130	.26413	.26695	.26976	.27257	.27536	.27815
.6	.28093	.28371	.28647	.28923	.29198	.29473	.29746	.30019	.30291	.30563
.7	.30833	.31103	.31372	.31641	.31909	.32176	.32442	.32708	.32972	.33237
.8	.33500	.33763	.34025	.34286	.34547	.34807	.35067	.35325	.35584	.35841
.9	.36098	.36354	.36609	.36864	.37118	.37372	.37624	.37877	.38128	.38379
4.0	1.38629	.38879	.39128	.39377	.39624	.39872	.40118	.40364	.40610	.40854
.1	.41099	.41342	.41585	.41828	.42070	.42311	.42552	.42792	.43031	.43270
.2	.43508	.43746	.43984	.44220	.44456	.44692	.44927	.45161	.45395	.45629
.3	.45862	.46094	.46326	.46557	.46787	.47018	.47247	.47476	.47705	.47933
.4	.48160	.48387	.48614	.48840	.49065	.49290	.49515	.49739	.49962	.50185
.5	.50408	.50630	.50851	.51072	.51293	.51513	.51732	.51951	.52170	.52388
.6	.52606	.52823	.53039	.53256	.53471	.53687	.53902	.54116	.54330	.54543
.7	.54756	.54969	.55181	.55393	.55604	.55814	.56025	.56235	.56444	.56653
.8	.56862	.57070	.57277	.57485	.57691	.57898	.58104	.58309	.58515	.58719
.9	.58924	.59127	.59331	.59534	.59737	.59939	.60141	.60342	.60543	.60744

a. Add 1.0 to indicated figure.

Appendix C Tables of Accelerated Depreciation Factors

Sum-of-Years'-Digits Method (SYD) at Different Costs of Capital

Period	6%	8%	10%	12%	14%	15%	16%
1	—	—	—	—	—	—	—
2	—	—	—	—	—	—	—
3	0.908	0.881	0.855	0.831	0.808	0.796	0.786
4	0.891	0.860	0.830	0.802	0.776	0.763	0.751
5	0.875	0.839	0.806	0.775	0.746	0.732	0.719
6	0.859	0.820	0.783	0.749	0.718	0.703	0.689
7	0.844	0.801	0.761	0.725	0.692	0.676	0.661
8	0.829	0.782	0.740	0.702	0.667	0.650	0.635
9	0.814	0.765	0.720	0.680	0.643	0.626	0.610
10	0.800	0.748	0.701	0.659	0.621	0.604	0.587
11	0.786	0.731	0.683	0.639	0.600	0.582	0.565
12	0.773	0.715	0.665	0.620	0.581	0.562	0.545
13	0.760	0.700	0.648	0.602	0.562	0.543	0.526
14	0.747	0.685	0.632	0.585	0.544	0.525	0.508
15	0.734	0.671	0.616	0.569	0.527	0.508	0.491
16	0.722	0.657	0.601	0.553	0.511	0.492	0.475
17	0.711	0.644	0.587	0.538	0.496	0.477	0.460
18	0.699	0.631	0.573	0.524	0.482	0.463	0.445
19	0.688	0.618	0.560	0.510	0.468	0.449	0.432
20	0.677	0.606	0.547	0.497	0.455	0.436	0.419

Double Declining Balance Method (DDB) at Different Costs of Capital

Period	6%	8%	10%	12%	14%	15%	16%
1	—	—	—	—	—	—	—
2	—	—	—	—	—	—	—
3	0.920	0.896	0.873	0.851	0.831	0.821	0.811
4	0.898	0.868	0.840	0.814	0.789	0.777	0.766
5	0.878	0.843	0.811	0.781	0.753	0.739	0.727
6	0.858	0.819	0.783	0.749	0.718	0.704	0.689
7	0.840	0.796	0.756	0.720	0.687	0.671	0.656
8	0.821	0.774	0.731	0.692	0.657	0.641	0.625
9	0.804	0.753	0.708	0.667	0.630	0.614	0.597
10	0.787	0.733	0.685	0.643	0.605	0.588	0.571
11	0.771	0.714	0.664	0.620	0.582	0.564	0.547
12	0.755	0.696	0.644	0.599	0.559	0.541	0.524
13	0.740	0.678	0.625	0.579	0.539	0.521	0.504
14	0.725	0.661	0.607	0.560	0.520	0.501	0.484
15	0.711	0.645	0.590	0.542	0.502	0.483	0.466
16	0.697	0.630	0.573	0.526	0.485	0.466	0.450
17	0.684	0.615	0.558	0.510	0.469	0.451	0.434
18	0.671	0.601	0.543	0.495	0.454	0.436	0.419
19	0.659	0.587	0.529	0.480	0.440	0.422	0.405
20	0.647	0.574	0.515	0.467	0.427	0.409	0.392

Appendix D Table of Areas under the Normal Curve

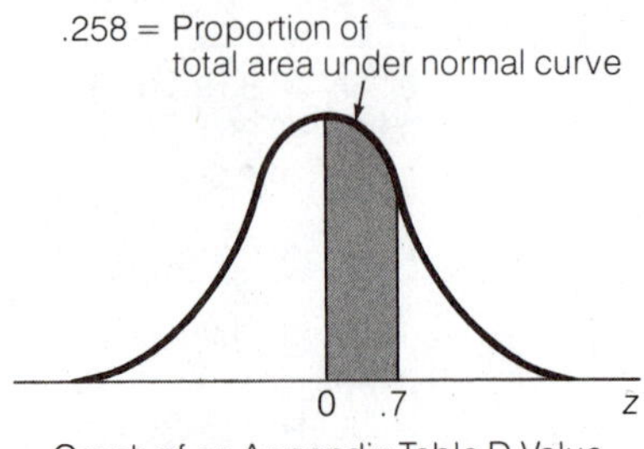

Graph of an Appendix Table D Value

z	.00	.01	.02	.03	.04	.05	.06	.07	.08	.09
0.0	.0000	.0040	.0080	.0120	.0160	.0199	.0239	.0279	.0319	.0359
0.1	.0398	.0438	.0478	.0517	.0557	.0596	.0636	.0675	.0714	.0753
0.2	.0793	.0832	.0871	.0910	.0948	.0987	.1026	.1064	.1103	.1141
0.3	.1179	.1217	.1255	.1293	.1331	.1368	.1406	.1443	.1480	.1517
0.4	.1554	.1591	.1628	.1664	.1700	.1736	.1772	.1808	.1844	.1879
0.5	.1915	.1950	.1985	.2019	.2054	.2088	.2123	.2157	.2190	.2224
0.6	.2257	.2291	.2324	.2357	.2389	.2422	.2454	.2486	.2517	.2549
0.7	.2580	.2611	.2642	.2673	.2704	.2734	.2764	.2794	.2823	.2852
0.8	.2881	.2910	.2939	.2967	.2995	.3023	.3051	.3078	.3106	.3133
0.9	.3159	.3186	.3212	.3238	.3264	.3289	.3315	.3340	.3365	.3389
1.0	.3413	.3438	.3461	.3485	.3508	.3531	.3554	.3577	.3599	.3621
1.1	.3643	.3665	.3686	.3708	.3729	.3749	.3770	.3790	.3810	.3830
1.2	.3849	.3869	.3888	.3907	.3925	.3944	.3962	.3980	.3997	.4015
1.3	.4032	.4049	.4066	.4082	.4099	.4115	.4131	.4147	.4162	.4177
1.4	.4192	.4207	.4222	.4236	.4251	.4265	.4279	.4292	.4306	.4319
1.5	.4332	.4345	.4357	.4370	.4382	.4394	.4406	.4418	.4429	.4441
1.6	.4452	.4463	.4474	.4484	.4495	.4505	.4515	.4525	.4535	.4545
1.7	.4554	.4564	.4573	.4582	.4591	.4599	.4608	.4616	.4625	.4633
1.8	.4641	.4649	.4656	.4664	.4671	.4678	.4686	.4693	.4699	.4706
1.9	.4713	.4719	.4726	.4732	.4738	.4744	.4750	.4756	.4761	.4767
2.0	.4772	.4778	.4783	.4788	.4793	.4798	.4803	.4808	.4812	.4817
2.1	.4821	.4826	.4830	.4834	.4838	.4842	.4846	.4850	.4854	.4857
2.2	.4861	.4864	.4868	.4871	.4875	.4878	.4881	.4884	.4887	.4890
2.3	.4893	.4896	.4898	.4901	.4904	.4906	.4909	.4911	.4913	.4916
2.4	.4918	.4920	.4922	.4925	.4927	.4929	.4931	.4932	.4934	.4936
2.5	.4938	.4940	.4941	.4943	.4945	.4946	.4948	.4949	.4951	.4952
2.6	.4953	.4955	.4956	.4957	.4959	.4960	.4961	.4962	.4963	.4964
2.7	.4965	.4966	.4967	.4968	.4969	.4970	.4971	.4972	.4973	.4974
2.8	.4974	.4975	.4976	.4977	.4977	.4978	.4979	.4979	.4980	.4981
2.9	.4981	.4982	.4982	.4983	.4984	.4984	.4985	.4985	.4986	.4986
3.0	.4987	.4987	.4987	.4988	.4988	.4989	.4989	.4989	.4990	.4990

Appendix E Answers to Selected End-of-Chapter Problems

We present here some partial answers to selected end-of-chapter problems. For the most part, the answers given are only the final answers (or answers at intermediate steps) to the more complex problems. Within limits, these answers will be useful to see if the student is on the right track toward solving the problem. The primary limitation, which must be kept in mind, is that some questions may have more than one solution, depending upon which of several equally plausible assumptions are made in working the problem. Also, many of the problems involve some verbal discussion as well as numerical calculations. We have not presented any of this discussion material here.

2.1 a. (1) 25% gain, (2) 31.4% gain, (3) 40% gain; b. (1) 23% loss, (2) 37.2% loss, (3) 56.1% loss.

2.2 a. (1) 34.5% loss, (2) 49.3% loss, (3) 69% loss; b. (1) 16.5% gain, (2) 23.6% gain, (3) 33% gain.

3.1 a. $12,250; b. 30%; c. 20.42%.

3.2 a. $10,750; b. 30%; c. 19.55%.

3.3 a. $28,820; b. 22.17%; c. 46%.

3.4 a. Marginal tax rate = 17%, average tax rate = 17%; c. Marginal tax rate = 46%, average tax rate = 44.08%.

3.5 Tax liability—1974: 0; 1975: 0; 1976: $5,250; 1977: $15,250; 1978: ($20,500).

3.6 a. (1) 1979: $10,183; 1980: $19,629; 1981: $30,424; (2) 1979: $7,901; 1980: $11,451; 1981: $15,451.

3A.2 a. (1) $1,000; (2) Year 1: $1,777.80; Year 2: $1,555.60; Year 3: $1,333.30; Year 4: $1,111.10; Year 5: $888.90; Year 6: $666.70; Year 7: $444.40; Year 8: $222.20; (3) Year 1: $2,000.00; Year 2: $1,600.00; Year 3: $1,333.30; Year 4: $1,066.70; Year 5: $666.70; Year 6: $533.30; Year 7: $400.00; Year 8: $400.00; (4) Year 1: $2,125.00; Year 2: $1,593.75; Year 3: $1,195.31; Year 4: $896.48; Year 5: $672.36; Year 6: $505.70; Year 7: $505.70; Year 8: $505.70; b. Declining balance method highest, straight line method lowest.

4.2 8.94 million tons.

4.3 9 years.

4.4 a. $3,494.35; b. $29,854.89.

4.5 9%.

4.6 10%.

4.7 12%.

4.8 16%.

4.9 a. Year 1: $248,000; Year 2: $307,520; Year 3: $381,320; Year 4: $472,840; Year 5: $586,320; Year 6: $727,040.

4.10 a. Year 1: $1.10; Year 2: $1.21; Year 3: $1.33; Year 4: $1.46; Year 5: $1.61; Year 6: $1.77; b. $6.00.

4.11 a. $875.39; b. $1,000.01; c. $1,297.58.

4.12 $8,414.41.

4.13 $59,238.20.

4.14 a. 12%; b. $748.51; c. $906.15.

4.15 Investment 1: a. 8%; b. $1,259.71; c. 8%; d. 8%; Investment 2: a. 8%; b. $1,244.52; c. 7.56%; d. 7.56%.

5.1 $E(R_M) = 9\%$, $\text{Var}(R_M) = 0.01$, $\sigma_M = 0.10$, $\bar{R}_F = 6\%$.

5.2 $E(R_M) = 16\%$, $\text{Var}(R_M) = 0.01$, $\sigma_M = 0.10$.

5.3 a. 0.17; b. 0.0029; c. 0.0539; d. 0.3171.

5.4 a. 0.1625; b. 0.01871875; c. 0.1368; d. 0.8418; e. 0.01243752; f. 0.97342124.

5.5 a. $\bar{R}_a = 0.17$, $\bar{R}_b = 0.116$; b. $\text{Cov}(R_a R_b) = 0.00508$, $\rho_{\text{ab}} = 0.592$; c. 0.1565; d. 0.095.

6.1 a. $800; b. $1,600.

6.2 a. $777.95; b. $914.82.

6.3 $90.

6.4 10%.

6.5 Percentage price change: A, 7.58% decrease; B, 12.29% decrease.

6.6 Percentage price change: C, 12.13% decrease; D, 11.56% decrease.

6.7 a. 11.11%; b. 13.17%; c. 9%; d. 9%.

6.8 Bond 1: 6.7%; Bond 2: 5.4%.

6.9 a. $21.43 million; b. $32.7 million.

6.10 a. $58.45 million; b. $114.70 million.

7.1 Debt = $30,000, Total assets = $90,000, Sales = $180,000, Cash + Accounts receivable = $36,000, Accounts receivable = $14,795, Cost of goods sold = $126,000, Inventories = $36,000.

7.2 a. Debt/Assets = 46%, Average collection period = 51 days, Profit/Net worth = 7.3%.

7.3 a. Current ratio = 2, Times interest earned = 1.88, Sales/Total assets = 1.82.

7.4 a. Quick ratio = 1.5, Inventory turnover = 5.2, Profit margin on sales = 3%, Return on total assets = 4.65%.

7.5 a. 1979: Current ratio = 0.6, Average collection period = 49.5 days, Return on net worth = 5.4%, Debt ratio = 48%.

7.6 Fixed charge coverage = (2.0); 5-year compounded growth in sales = 8.61%, 5-year compounded growth in dividends per share = (8.20%).

8.1 Outside financing required, $262,500.

8.2 Total assets = $80 million, Cash = $3 million, Total current assets = $40 million, Change in retained earnings = $3.6 million, Notes payable = $6.9 million.

8.3 Additional financing needed, $150,000.

8.5 b. $1,214,400; d. External funds needed: (1) $1,041,600; $1,387,200; (2) $1,444,800; $1,099,200; (3) $1,099,200.

8.6 a. 12.4%; b. 22%; c. 3.2%; d. 13%; e. 19%.

8.8 a. Total sources = $351.

8.9 a. Total sources = $519.

9.1 b. 13,750 units; c. Operating leverage at 12,000 units = −6.86, at 18,000 units = 4.24

9.2 b. 6,000 units; c. Operating leverage at 5,000 units = −5, at 8,000 units = 4.
9.3 a. (1) 63,750 units; b. (2) 7.78; c. (3) $175,500.
9.4 b. $130; c. $25,000.
9.6 a. Total loans outstanding, April 1982 = $72,000.
10.3 b. A = 5.827%, B = 5.827%, C = 6.128%, D = 6.903%.
10.4 a. Aggressive, 6%; Average, 7.1%; Conservative, 15%.
11.1 a. 21.28%.
11.2 a. $2,450,000; b. $196,000; c. $16,333.
11.3 a. $1 million; b. 4 days.
11.6 Change in profitability: Category 3, $55,380.82; Category 4, $14,671.24; Category 5, $1,627.42.
11.7 a. 12,000 units; b. 15 orders; c. 13,600 units.
11.9 b. 100 orders per year; c. 15,000 units; d. 41.42%; e. 41.42%.
12.1 a. 24.58%; b. 14.90%; c. 22.58%; d. 24.83%; e. 12.29%.
12.2 Select alternative 3; Effective rate = 14.86%.
12.3 a. Trade discount; Effective rate = 14.90%.
12.4 Select field warehousing; Total cost = $49,375.
12.5 a. (1) 57% of short-term financing, (2) 34% of total debt, (3) 29% of total financing.
12.6 a. $300,000.
12.7 Line of credit cost = $3,416.67; Trade discount foregone cost = $4,000; Commercial paper net cost = $3,436.07.
12.8 a. Bank loan: $136,986; Factored accounts receivable: $114,943.
12.9 a. $320,000; b. 60 days; *Factoring:* c. $260,520; d. $68,880; e. 26.44%; *Receivables Financing:* c. $249,600; d. $38,400; e. 15.38%.
12.10 b. Total dollar costs = $252,360 = 26.37%.
13.1 a. NPV = $100,338; b. IRR = 18%; c. Yes.
13.2 a. NPV = $24,306; b. Cash flow = $28,000; c. Yes.
13.3 b. NPV = $23,490.
13.4 a. NPV = $17,235; b. NPV = $20,477.
13.5 NPV = $44,166.
13.6 a. $720,000; b. ΔF = $182,000; c. $200,000.
13.7 a. ΔF = $46,200, NPV = $70,317.20; b. ΔF = $31,200, NPV = $733.70; c. NPV = $5,752.80.
13.8 a. ΔF = $3,340, NPV = ($1,251,59), reject; b. ΔF = $3,180, NPV = $58.66, accept; c. NPV = $2,458.66, accept; d. ΔF = $4,080, NPV = $6,188.47, accept.
13.9 a. Orchard: NPV at 0% = $70,000, NPV at 6% = $31,810, NPV at 10% = $11,980, NPV at 20% = ($24,150); b. Orchard IRR = 12.86%, Mining IRR = 15.78%.
13.10 a. NPV = $341; b. NPV = $9,148.
13.11 a. ΔF = $626, NPV = ($243); b. NPV = ($183.36).
13.12 a. 28%.
13A.1 b. IRR_a = 17.5%, IRR_b = 15.5%; e. IRR $\cong$ 26%.
13A.2 Electric powered machine; IRR $\approx$ 24%, NPV = $3,158, Return on incremental investment $\approx$ 32.9%.
13A.3 Machine H; $NPV_\infty(H)$ = $67,400.
13A.4 a. Project A: NPV = $10,692, IRR = 24%; Project B: NPV = $13,705, IRR = 18%.
13A.5 a. Project E: NPV_∞ = $4,677.95, IRR = 17.3%; Project F: NPV_∞ = $1,503.08, IRR = 13.69%.
13A.6 Choose project C; PI_c = 1.5943, $NPV_\infty(C)$ = $2,734.

13A.7 a. Cash flow = \$20,500, NPV = \$6,413.85, accept; b. NPV = (\$1,427.30), reject.
13A.8 NPV = (\$630), reject project.
13A.9 NPV = \$67,939, accept project.
13A.10 a. NPV = \$8,711; b. NPV = (\$1,779).
13A.11 a. $IRR_a{}^*$ = 19.8%, $IRR_b{}^*$ = 20.5%, $NPV_a{}^*$ = \$5,841.71, $NPV_b{}^*$ = \$6,295.50; c. Reinvestment rate = 15.8%.
13A.12 a. NPV = (\$185,070); b. NPV = \$660,940.
14.1 a. Expected NPV = \$10,179, Expected IRR = 14.4%; b. Probability = 0.7.
14.2 a. Project A expected cash flow = \$4,500, Project B expected cash flow = \$5,100; b. NPV_a = \$6,691.05, NPV_b = \$7,749.18.
14.4 a. Expected NPV = (\$8,470); b. Expected NPV = (\$8,470); c. 2%; d. 12%; e. 41%.
14.5 a. CV_a = 0.242, CV_b = 0.421; b. R_a = 8.42%, R_b = 10.21%; c. NPV_a = \$569.20, NPV_b = \$3,279.
14.6 $R_a{}^*$ = 8%, $R_b{}^*$ = 10%, $R_c{}^*$ = 14%.
14.7 a. Required return = 15%; b. NPV = \$211.32.
14.8 a. Based on coefficient of variation, $R_a{}^*$ = 14%, $R_b{}^*$ = 18%; Based on security market line, $R_a{}^*$ = 15%, $R_b{}^*$ = 12%.
14.9 a. Lambda = 5; b. V_j = \$3,000; c. R_j = 10%.
14.10 a. $\overline{R}_M = 10\%$, $\sigma_M = 0.2$, $\overline{R}_1 = 20\%$, $\sigma_1 = 0.424$, $\overline{R}_2 = 10\%$, $\sigma_2 = 0.349$, $\rho_{1M} = 0.943$, $\rho_{2M} = 0.344$, $\rho_{12} = 0.027$; b. $w_1 = 40\%$, $w_2 = 60\%$, $\overline{R}_p = 14\%$, $\sigma_p = 0.274$.
14.11 a. Risk index: Year 0, 1.00; Year 1, 0.9465; Year 5, 0.7593; Year 10, 0.5766; Year 20, 0.3326; Year 30, 0.1918.
14.12 a. V_j = \$2,000; b. V_j = \$2,000.
14.13 a. Choose Project Q; b. Choose Project Q.
14A.1 b. Mean = 15; c. Standard deviation = \$2.933 million; d. CV = 0.1955; e. 36.7%; f. 24.8%.
14A.2 a. Expected gain = \$6,500; b. Expected loss = (\$2,500).
14B.1 a. NPV = \$34; b. $\sigma \cong 271$; c. 44.83%; d. 55%; e. 50%; f. 1.02; g.0.
14B.2 a. NPV = \$357; b. $\sigma \cong 572$; c. 73%; d. 0.
14B.3 a. 70%; b. 10%; c. 4%; d. 90%; e. 14%.
14C.1 a. PV of savings = \$4,648.00, PV of abandonment = \$4,698.13; b. PV of savings = \$4,822.30.
14C.2 a. NPV = \$2,717, σ = \$1,420; b. NPV = \$2,762, σ = \$1,360.
14C.3 a. Sale after 5 years, NPV = \$2,379; Sale after 10 years, NPV = \$3,535; Sale after 15 years, NPV = \$1,993; d. NPV = \$2,099; e. NPV = \$1,993.
14D.1 Correlation coefficient = 0: a. $w_i = 0.80$, $w_j = 0.20$; b. $E(R_p) = 12.6\%$, $\sigma_p = 4.47\%$; Correlation coefficient = −1: a. $w_i = 0.67$, $w_j = 0.33$; b. $E(R_p) = 12.99\%$, $\sigma_p = 0$; Correlation coefficient = −0.5: a. $w_i = 0.71$, $w_j = 0.29$; b. $E(R_p) = 12.87\%$, $\sigma_p = 3.32\%$; Correlation coefficient = +0.5: a. $w_i = 1$, $w_j = 0$; b. $E(R_p) = 12\%$, $\sigma_p = 5\%$.
14D.3 a. 28% in *i,* 72% in *j;* b. Minimum risk portfolio: $\overline{R}_p = 8.28\%$, $\sigma_p = 2.47\%$; d. 55% in *i,* 45% in *j.*
14D.4 a. $w_d = 84.28\%$, $w_c = 15.72\%$; b. *100% in C:* $E(R_p) = 8\%$, $\sigma_p = 10.84\%$; *100% in D:* $E(R_p) = 6\%$, $\sigma_p = 2.97\%$; *Minimum variance portfolio:* $E(R_p) = 6.31\%$, $\sigma_p = 2.21\%$; e. 4.55%.
15.1 B/TA = 0: k_s = 12%; B/TA = 10%: k_s = 12.7%; B/TA = 30%: k_s = 14.6%; B/TA = 50%: k_s = 16.8%; B/TA = 60%: k_s = 16.5%.
15.2 B/TA = 0: k_s = 10.5%, σ = 5.4%, CV = 0.514; B/TA = 10%: k_s = 11.2%, σ = 5.8%, CV = 0.518; B/TA = 30%: k_s = 12.7%, σ = 7.6%, CV = 0.598; B/TA =

50%: k_s = 14%, σ = 10.8%, CV = 0.771; B/TA = 60%: k_s = 13.1%, σ = 13.7%, CV = 1.046.

15.3 B = 0: EPS = \$1.20, Share price = \$10.00, Book equity leverage = 0%, Market equity leverage = 0%; B = \$1,000,000: EPS = \$1.27, Share price = \$10.58, Book equity leverage = 10%, Market equity leverage = 9.5%; B = \$5,000,000: EPS = \$1.64, Share price = \$10.25, Book equity leverage = 48.58%, Market equity leverage = 47.97%.

15.4 B/S = 0.4: a. β_j = 0.99; b. k_s = 10.95; B/S = 0.8: a. β_j = 1.18; b. k_s = 11.90%; B/S = 1.0: a. β_j = 1.28; b. k_s = 12.40%; B/S = 1.2: a. β_j = 1.38; b. k_s = 12.90%; B/S = 1.6: a. β_j = 1.57; b. k_s = 13.85%.

15.5 a. At sales = \$2,000: $EPS_{\text{Debt financing}}$ = \$2.76; $EPS_{\text{Stock financing}}$ = \$2.58; b. Expected $EPS_{\text{Debt financing}}$ = \$3.16; Expected $EPS_{\text{Stock financing}}$ = \$2.90.

15.6 a. (1) OL = 1.5, (2) FL = 1.45, (3) CLE = 2.18; b. *Bond financing:* (1) EPS = \$1.23, (2) CLE = 3.90; *Stock financing:* (1) EPS = \$1.38, (2) CLE = 2.91.

15.7 b. Crossover point is at Sales of \$1,460.00, EPS of \$1.376.

16.1 k_e = 17%.

16.2 a. k_s = 18%; b. k_j^* = 13.2%.

16.3 $k_b(1 - T)$ = 6%.

16.4 a. YTM = 11%; b. 10.87%.

16.5 11%.

16.6 12%.

16.7 a. k_s = 14%; b. \$43.56; c. 14%.

16.8 a. \$25 million; b. \$15 million; c. 14.7%; d. 10.99%.

16.9 15.84%.

16.10 12.2%

16.11 a. Structure 1: Weighted cost = 12%; Structure 2: 10.56%; Structure 4: 9.96% (lowest); Structure 6: 12.30%; Structure 8: 14.21%.

16.12 a. \$30 million; b. \$15 million; c. Internal, \$3 million; External, \$12 million; e. \$6 million.

16.13 a. At \$8,000,000 and \$16,000,000; b. MCC below first break = 11.95%, MCC between first and second breaks = 12.62%, MCC above second break = 13.9%.

16A.1 a. PV = \$13,717; b. Total proceeds = \$9,385.

16A.2 Present value of proceeds: a. \$13,952; b. \$9,846; c. \$8,428; d. \$16,624; e. \$11,500.

16B.1 a. V_U = \$12 million, V_L = \$16 million.

16B.2 a. k_u = 18%, k_s = 22.8%; b. k_u = 18%, k = 14.4%.

16B.3 a. V_a = \$4.2 million, V_b = \$3 million; b. k_a = 7.1%, k_b = 17.5%.

16B.4 a. 10%; b. 12.5%.

16C.1 a. $\overline{R}_M$ = 10%; b. Var(R_M) = 1%; c. $E(R_j) = R_F + \lambda \text{Cov}(R_j, R_M)$; d. Cov($R_j$,$R_M$) = 2.15%; e. $\overline{R}_j$ = 15%; f. $E(R_j)$ = 14.6%.

16C.2 a. $\overline{R}_M$ = 12%; b. Var(R_M) = 1.8%; d. 10%; e. Cov(R_j,R_M) = 2.1%; f. $E(R_j)$ = 12.9%.

16C.3 a. V_j = 56; b. R_j^* = 17.85%.

16C.4 a. R_i = 5% + β_i5%; b. 13.75%; c. Required rate of return on a new division = 17.5%.

16C.5 a. $\overline{R}_M$ = 0.10, Var(R_M) = 0.023; b. $\overline{R}_a$ = 0.10, Cov(R_a,R_M) = 0.043, β_a = 1.87, R_a^* = 13.5%; $\overline{R}_b$ = 0.10, Cov(R_b,R_M) = 0.018, β_b = 0.78, R_b^* = 9.1%.

16C.6 Expected return on project = 12%, Cost of capital = 9.6%.

16D.1 b. p_1 = 0.10, p_2 = 0.20.

16D.2 b. p_1 = 0.5305, p_2 = 0.4533.

16D.3 Optimum leverage = $3,000.
16D.4 Choose plan X; Value of firm = $1,810.
17.1 External equity needed = $1,220,000.
17.2 $2,760,000.
17.3 $11.11.
17.5 a. $1,237,500; b. $2,025,000; c. $3,250,000; d. $2,250,000; e. $4,750,000.
17.6 35%.
17.7 Capital stock balance = $1 million, Retained earnings balance = $1.5 million.
17.10 b. $12.00; c. $352 a share.
17.11 b. $33.6 million.
17.13 b. Between $19.20 and $28.80 per share.
17.14 $42.42.
17.15 $31 million.
17.16 a. $36.9 million; b. $52.32 million.
17.17 a. $67 million; b. $113.43 million.
18.1 11.5%.
18.2 13.6%.
18.4 Compensation costs as a percent of proceeds: (1) 10.4%; (2) 3.8%; (3) 0%; Other expenses as a percent of proceeds: (1) 4.89%; (2) 0.90%; (3) 0.13%.
19.1 $3.00.
19.2 a. $2.50.
19.3 a. $6.00.
19.4 a. $6.00; b. Total assets = $32,370.
19.5 At $25 per share: a. (1) 200,000 shares, (2) 0.5 rights, (3) $3.15, (4) $47.25, (5) $1.76.
19.6 c. Shares required to elect 1 director = 45,456; e. 2 directors.
20.1 a. Bond A = $717.51, Bond B = $626.56; b. Bond A = $634.83, Bond B = $536.42.
20.2 a. Bond C = $571.77, Bond D = $558.68; b. Bond C = $424.53, Bond D = $417.61.
20.3 a. 10%; b. 8%; c. 6.67%.
20.4 At $825, YTM = 14%, At $1,107, YTM = 5%.
20.5 a. $1,125; b. $750; c. $1,000.
20.6 a. 13.8%.
20.7 a. 12%; b. Value of equity = $1,000, Price per share = $10; c. 11.27%; e. Cost of equity under debt financing = 12.25%, Cost of equity under equity financing = 11.95%; g. Value of the firm under debt financing = $1,248, Value of the firm under equity financing = $1,208.
20.9 a. Sales level of $2,400,000: (1) EPS = $.93, (2) EPS = $.84; b. Breakeven sales = $1,500; f. Bond financing: $\overline{EPS}$ = $1.02, σ_{EPS} = 0.5319, CV_{EPS} = 0.5215, $E(p)$ = $9.18, σ_p = 4.7871, CV_p = 0.5215.
20.11 a. 11.05%; b. 10.4%; c. 10.913%; d. $1,356; e. V_L = $1,423, B = $143; g. β_L = 1.08; h. *Debt:* V_L = $1,450, B = $200, S = $1,250; *Equity:* V_L = $1,403, B = $100, S = $1,303; i. *Debt:* $16.98; *Equity:* $16.14.
20.12 NPV of refunding = $1,345,623.
21.1 a. $7,870; c. $8,854.
21.2 a. NAL = $1,822.38.
21.3 NAL = ($28,286.10).

21.4 a. Capital gains tax = $278,400; b. Before: 1:1; After: 3:1; c. ($31,200).

22.1 a. $1,150.80; c. $50.80.

22.2 b. $2.00; c. $5.00; d. $10.00.

22.3 a. $2.00; b. $28.00.

22.5 a. $.90; b. $14.40; c. $8.00 per share; d. Common stock = $62,000, Paid-in capital = $138,000; e. EPS after taxes = $1.45; f. Debentures = $150,000, Common stock = $57,500, Paid-in capital = $180,000, Total assets = $687,500; g. EPS after taxes = $1.90.

22.6 *Original:* b. 70%; c. $0.44; d. 70%; *Alternative 1:* b. 45%; c. $0.54; d. 22%; *Alternative 2:* b. 47%; c. $0.56; d. 22%; *Alternative 3:* b. 47%; c. $0.77, d. 50%.

22.7 a. Bond A: 10.65%; Bond B: 11%.

22.8 b. 11.12%.

22.9 a. B_0 = $701.25, B_1 = $705.36, B_2 = $709.98; c. Year 0 = $790.00, Year 1 = $908.50, Year 2 = $1,044.78, Year 3 = $1,201.49; e. During Year 4; g. 15.9%.

22A.1 a. $5.335; b. $7.323.

22A.2 a. $353,031; b. $146,969.

22A.3 a. $3,506,672; b. $493,328.

22A.4 $1.18.

22A.6 a. Market value of debt = $20.774 million, Market value of equity = $79,226 million; b. Cost of debt = 11.5%, Cost of equity = 17%.

22A.7 a. Market value of debt = $15.9591 million, Market value of equity = $59.0409 million; b. Market value of equity = $117.897 million.

23.1 a. $35.60; b. 27% accretion; c. 68% dilution.

23.2 a. 12.5% decline; b. 16.7% increase; c. 13.5%.

23.3 b. $18.45.

23.4 b. (1) EPS = $6.40, Market price = $76.80; (2) EPS = $5.83, Market price = $69.96.

23.5 a. Total assets = $4,500; b. Total assets = $5,250.

23.6 a. 6.4%.

23.7 *Apex:* a. $120 million; b. $150 million; d. (1) Exchange rate = 1.33, (2) 6.6%, (3) $3.13 a share; *Allied:* a. $180 million; b. $150 million; d. (1) Exchange rate = 1.12, (2) 4.0%, (3) $3.59 a share.

23.9 b. Horizontal: $2.58 accretion; Vertical: $.21 dilution; c. Horizontal: $5.04 accretion; Vertical: $1.02 accretion.

23.10 Two quarters before merger: (1) 20%, $6.92 premium; (2) 22%, $10.50 premium; (3) 18%, $18.00 discount; (4) 13%, $6.00 premium; Immediately preceding merger: (1) 5%, $2.22 premium; (2) 0.2%, $0.10 discount; (3) No change; (4) No change.

24.1 c. $5.1 million increase; d. $6.9 million less.

25.1 d. $.40; $1.20; $2.00; e. $2,333; $7,000; $11,667.

26.1 a. $2,000 gain; b. $3,333.33 loss.

26.2 a. $1,666,666 gain; b. $1 million loss.

26.4 a. 0.5%.

26.6 b. DM/$ = 1.7631, $/DM = 0.5672; c. 1.7084 DM/$; e. $2,934,100.

26.7 b. DM/$ = 1.7630, $/DM = 0.5672; c. $.5853; d. Decreases; e. DM 34,258,308.

26.8 a. Net proceeds = $1,040,000; b. Net proceeds = $1,068,511; c. Net proceeds = $989,999.60.

26.10 a. Cost = $96,000; b. Cost = $90,533.60; c. Cost = $103,500.

Glossary

A

Abandonment Value The amount that can be realized by liquidating a project before its economic life has ended.

Accelerated Depreciation Depreciation methods that write off the cost of an asset at a faster rate than the write-off under the straight line method. The three principal methods of accelerated depreciation are: (1) sum-of-years'-digits, (2) double declining balance, and (3) units of production.

Accruals Continually recurring short-term liabilities. Examples are accrued wages, accrued taxes, and accrued interest.

Aging Schedule A report showing how long accounts receivable have been outstanding.

Amortization The repayment of the principal amount of a loan in installments during the life of the loan.

Annuity A series of payments of a fixed amount for a specified number of years.

Arbitrage The process of selling overvalued and buying undervalued assets so as to bring about an equilibrium where all assets are properly valued. One who engages in arbitrage is called an arbitrageur.

Arrearage Overdue payment; frequently, omitted dividends on preferred stocks.

Assignment A relatively inexpensive way of liquidating a failing firm that does not involve going through the courts.

B

Balloon Payment The final payment on a partially amortized debt, scheduled to be larger than all preceding payments.

Bankers Acceptance A promissory note by a business debtor arising out of a business transaction; a bank, by endorsing, assumes the obligation of payment at the due date. The debtor has a deposit at the bank that will be charged for the amount plus interest.

Bankruptcy A legal procedure for formally liquidating a business, carried out under the jurisdiction of courts of law.

Beta Coefficient Measures the extent to which the returns on a given investment move with the stock market.

Bond A long-term debt instrument.

Book Value The accounting value of an asset. The book value of a share of common stock is equal to the net worth (common stock plus retained earnings) of the corporation divided by the number of shares of stock outstanding.

Breakeven Analysis An analytical technique for studying the relationship among fixed cost, variable cost, and profits.

Budget Projected financial statements used to compare with actual performance to stimulate improvements in the use of company resources in a planning and control process.

Business Risk The risk resulting from the nature of the products sold by the firm and from the degree of operating leverage employed.

C

Call (1) An option to buy (or "call") an asset at a specified price within a specified period. (2) The process of redeeming a bond or preferred stock issue before its normal maturity.

Call Premium The amount in excess of par value that a company must pay when it calls a security.

Call Price The price that must be paid when a security is called. The call price is equal to the par value plus the call premium.

Capital Asset An asset with a life of more than one year that is not bought and sold in the ordinary course of business.

Capital Asset Pricing Model (CAPM) A theory of asset pricing in which the return of an asset or security is the risk-free return plus a risk premium based on the excess of the return on the market over the risk-free rate multiplied by the asset's systematic risk (which cannot be eliminated by diversification).

Capital Budgeting The process of planning expenditures on assets whose returns are expected to extend beyond one year.

Capital Gains Profits on the sale of capital assets held for twelve months or longer.

Capital Losses Losses on the sale of capital assets.

Capital Market Line (CML) A graphical representation of the relationship between risk and the required rate of return on an efficient portfolio.

Capital Markets Financial transactions involving instruments with maturities greater than one year.

Capital Rationing A situation where a constraint is placed on the total amount of capital investments during a particular period.

Capital Structure The permanent long-term financing of the firm represented by long-term debt, preferred stock, and net worth (net worth consists of capital, capital surplus, and retained earnings). Capital structure is distinguished from *financial structure,* which includes short-term debt plus all other accounts.

Capitalization Rate A discount rate used to find the present value of a series of future cash receipts; sometimes called *discount rate.*

Carry-Back; Carry-Forward For income tax purposes, losses that can be carried back or forward to reduce average taxable income.

Cash Budget A schedule showing cash flows (receipts, disbursements, and net cash) for a firm over a specified period.

Cash Cycle The length of time between the purchase of raw materials and the collection of accounts receivable generated in the sale of the final product.

Certainty Equivalents The amount of cash (or rate of return) that someone would require *with certainty* to make the recipient indifferent between this certain sum (or rate of return) and a particular uncertain, risky sum (or rate of return).

Certificate of Deposit (CD) A form of savings deposit which cannot be withdrawn before its maturity date. However, CD's are negotiable and are sold in an active secondary market before their maturity date.

Characteristic Line A linear least-squares regression line that shows the relationship between an individual security's return and returns on the market. The slope of the characteristic line is the beta coefficient.

Chartists Technical stock market analysts who believe that observations of the historical pattern of price or returns behavior can lead to trading rules for achieving superior performance.

Chattel Mortgage A mortgage on personal property (not real estate). A mortgage on equipment would be a chattel mortgage.

Coefficient of Variation (CV) Standard deviation divided by the mean.

Collateral Assets that are used to secure a loan.

Combined Leverage Effect (CLE) The combination of financial and operating leverage which indicates the effect on EPS of a given change in sales.

Commercial Paper Unsecured, short-term promissory notes of large firms. The rate of interest on commercial paper is typically somewhat below the prime rate of interest.

Commitment Fee The fee paid to a lender for a formal line of credit.

Compensating Balance A required minimum checking account balance that a firm must maintain with a commercial bank. The required balance is generally equal to 15 to 20 percent of the amount of loans outstanding. Compensating balances raise the effective rate of interest on bank loans.

Composition An informal method of reorganization that voluntarily reduces creditors' claims on the debtor firm.

Compound Interest An interest rate that is applicable when interest in succeeding periods is earned not only on the initial principal but also on the accumulated interest of prior periods. Compound interest is contrasted to *simple interest,* in which returns are not earned on interest received.

Conditional Sales Contract A method of financing new equipment by paying it off in installments over a one-to-five-year period. The seller retains title to the equipment until payment has been completed.

Consol Bond A perpetual bond issued by England in 1814 to consolidate past debts; by extension, any perpetual bond.

Consolidated Tax Return An income tax return that combines the income statement of several affiliated firms.

Continuous Compounding (Discounting) As opposed to discrete compounding, interest is added continuously rather than at discrete points in time.

Contribution Margin The difference between sales price per unit and variable costs per unit.

Conversion Price The effective price paid for common stock when the stock is obtained by converting either convertible preferred stocks or convertible bonds. For example, if a $1,000 bond is convertible into 20 shares of stock, the conversion price is $50 ($1,000/20).

Conversion Ratio or Conversion Rate The number of shares of common stock that may be obtained by converting a convertible bond or share of convertible preferred stock.

Convertibles Securities (generally bonds or preferred stocks) that are exchangeable at the option of the holder for common stock of the issuing firm.

Correlation Coeffficient Measures the degree of relationship between two variables.

Cost of Capital The discount rate that should be used in the capital budgeting process or in valuation computations.

Coupon Rate The stated rate of interest on a bond.

Covariance (Cov) The correlation between two variables multiplied by the standard deviation of each variable:

$$\text{Cov} = \rho_{xy}\sigma_x\sigma_y.$$

Covenant Provisions contained in loan agreements. Covenants are designed to protect the lender and include such items as limits on total indebtedness, restrictions on dividends, minimum current ratio, and similar provisions.

Cumulative Dividends A protective feature on preferred stock that requires all past preferred dividends to be paid before any common dividends are paid.

Cumulative Voting A method of voting for corporate directors which permits multiple votes for a single director. This can enable a minority group of shareholders to obtain some voice in the control of the company.

Cut-Off Point In the capital budgeting process, the minimum rate of return on acceptable investment opportunities.

D

Debenture A long-term debt instrument that is not secured by a mortgage on specific property.

Debt Ratio Total debt divided by total assets or total debt divided by net worth.

Decision Tree A device for setting forth graphically the pattern of relationship between decisions and probability factors.

Default The failure to fulfill a contract. Generally, default refers to the failure to pay interest or principal on debt obligations.

Degree of Leverage The percentage increase in operating income or net income resulting from a given percentage increase in sales. The degree of leverage may be calculated for financial leverage, operating leverage, or both combined.

Devaluation The process of reducing the value of a country's currency stated in terms of other currencies; for example, the British pound might be devalued from $2.30 for one pound to $2.00 for one pound.

Discount Rate The interest rate used in the discounting process; sometimes called *capitalization rate.*

Discounted Cash Flow Techniques Methods of ranking investment proposals. Included are (1) internal rate of return method, (2) net present value method, and (3) profitability index or benefit/cost ratio.

Discounting The process of finding the present value of a series of future cash flows. Discounting is the reverse of compounding.

Discounting of Accounts Receivable Short-term financing where accounts receivable are used as security for the loan. Also called assigning accounts receivable.

Dividend Yield The ratio of the current dividend to the current price of a share of stock.

Du Pont System A system of planning and control that emphasizes analysis of investments and cost elements for their effects on return on investment, asset turnover, and profit margins.

E

EBIT Acronym for *earnings before interest and taxes.* Also, net operating income (NOI).

Economical Ordering Quantity (EOQ) The optimum size of order which results in the least cost of purchasing and holding inventories.

Edge Act Corporations Subsidiaries of U.S. banks which can conduct all forms of international banking, including investing in the equities of other companies.

Efficient Market Hypothesis The theory that historical data on prices or returns plus other publicly available data are already reflected in current prices of assets or securities and cannot be used to earn above-average returns.

Efficient Portfolio A portfolio which provides the highest expected return for a given level of risk, or the lowest amount of risk for a given level of expected return.

EPS Acronym for *earnings per share.*

Equity (S) The net worth of a business, consisting of capital stock, capital (or paid-in) surplus, earned surplus (or retained earnings), and occasionally, certain net worth reserves. *Common equity* is that part of the total net worth belonging to the common stockholders. *Total equity* would include preferred stockholders. The terms *net worth* and *common equity* are frequently used interchangeably.

Eurocurrency Refers to bank deposits in one country denominated in the currency of another country—for example, U.S. dollar deposits in a French bank.

Ex Dividend Date The date on which the right to the current dividend no longer accompanies a stock. (For listed stock, the ex dividend date is four working days prior to the date of record.)

Exchange Rate The rate at which one currency can be exchanged for another—for example, $2.30 for one British pound.

Excise Tax A tax on the manufacture, sale, or consumption of specified commodities.

Exercise Price The price that must be paid for an asset when an option is exercised.

Expected Return The mean value of the probability distribution of possible returns.

Ex Rights The date on which stock purchase rights are no longer transferred to the purchaser of the stock.

Extension An informal method of reorganization in which the creditors voluntarily postpone the date of required payment on past-due obligations.

External Funds Funds acquired through borrowing or by selling new common or preferred stock.

F

Factoring A method of financing accounts receivable under which a firm sells its accounts receivable (generally without recourse) to a financial institution (the factor).

Federal Funds Deposits of member banks in the Federal Reserve Bank to meet reserve requirements. Sales of federal funds represent loans from one member bank to another, usually for overnight or over a weekend.

Field Warehousing A method of financing inventories in which a "warehouse" is established at the place of business of the borrowing firm.

Financial Accounting Standards Board (FASB) A private (nongovernment) agency which functions as an accounting standards-setting body.

Financial Intermediation Financial transactions which bring savings surplus units together with savings deficit units so that savings can be redistributed into their most productive uses.

Financial Lease A lease that does not usually provide for maintenance services, which is not cancellable, and which is fully amortized over its life.

Financial Leverage The ratio of total debt to total assets or of total debt to equity. There are other measures of financial leverage, especially those which relate cash inflows to required cash outflows.

Financial Markets Transactions in which the creation and transfer of financial assets and financial liabilities take place.

Financial Risk That portion of total corporate risk, over and above basic business risk, that results from using debt.

Financial Structure The entire right-hand side of the balance sheet—the way in which a firm is financed.

Fisher Effect The excess of nominal interest rates over real (purchasing-power-adjusted) interest rates, reflecting the rate of anticipated inflation.

Fixed Charges Costs that do not vary with the level of output, especially fixed financial costs such as interest, lease payments, and sinking fund payments.

Flexible Budget *See* Variable Budget.

Float The amount of funds tied up in checks that have been written but are still in process and have not yet been collected.

Floating Exchange Rates Exchange rates may be fixed by government policy ("pegged") or allowed to "float" up or down in accordance with supply and demand. When market forces are allowed to function, exchange rates are said to be floating.

Flotation Cost The cost of issuing new stocks or bonds.

Forward Contract A purchase or sale at a price specified now, with the transaction to actually take place at some future date. Can apply to commodities, foreign currencies, Treasury bills, and so on.

Fully-Diluted EPS Shows what earnings per share would be if all warrants had been exercised or convertibles converted prior to the reporting date.

Funded Debt Long-term debt.

Funding The process of replacing short-term debt with long-term securities (stocks or bonds).

G

General Purchasing Power Reporting A proposal by the FASB that the current values of nonmonetary items in financial statements be adjusted by a general price index.

Going-Concern Value The amount received when a firm is sold as an operating business. The excess over liquidating value is the value of the management organization operating the firm.

Goodwill Intangible assets of a firm established by the excess of the price paid for the going concern over its book value.

H

Holder-of-Record Date The date on which a company closes its stock transfer books and makes up a list of the stockholders as of that date, to receive a future dividend payment.

Holding Company A corporation operated for the purpose of owning the common stocks of other corporations.

Hurdle Rate In capital budgeting, the minimum acceptable rate of return on a project; if the expected rate of return is below the hurdle rate, the project is not accepted. The hurdle rate should be the marginal cost of capital.

I

Improper Accumulation Earnings retained by a business for the purpose of enabling stockholders to avoid personal income taxes.

Income Bond A bond that pays interest only to the extent that income is actually earned by a company.

Incremental Cash Flow Net cash flow attributable to an investment project.

Incremental Cost of Capital The weighted cost of the increment of capital raised during a specified time period.

Indenture A formal agreement between the issuer of a bond and the bondholders.

Insolvency The inability to meet maturing debt obligations.

Interest Factor (IF) Numbers found in compound interest and annuity tables.

Interest Rate Parity Theorem States that the ratio of domestic forward to spot exchange rates expressed in foreign currency units per one domestic currency unit will equal the ratio of one plus foreign to one plus domestic interest rates.

Internal Financing Funds available from the normal operations of the firm; internal financing is approximately equal to retained earnings plus depreciation.

Internal Rate of Return (IRR) The rate of return on an asset investment. The internal rate of return is calculated by finding the discount rate that equates the present value of future cash flows to the cost of the investment.

Intrinsic Value A valuation arrived at by the application of data inputs to a valuation theory or model. The resulting value may be compared with the prevailing market price.

Investment Banker A firm which underwrites and distributes new issues of securities.

Investment Tax Credit Business firms can deduct as a credit against their income taxes a specified percentage of the dollar amount of new investments in each of certain categories of assets.

L

Legal List A list of securities in which mutual savings banks, pension funds, insurance companies, and other fiduciary institutions are permitted to invest.

Leverage Factor The ratio of debt to total assets or debt to equity.

Lien A lender's claim on assets that are pledged for a loan.

Line of Credit An arrangement whereby a financial institution (bank or insurance company) commits itself to lend up to a specified maximum amount of funds during a specified period.

Liquidating Value The amount that could be realized if an asset or group of assets (the entire assets of a firm, for example) are sold separately from the organization that has been using them.

Liquidity Refers to a firm's cash position and its ability to meet maturing obligations.

Listed Securities Securities traded on an organized security exchange.

Lock-Box Plan A procedure used to speed up collections and to reduce negative float.

M

Margin—Profit on Sales The *profit margin* is the percentage of net income to sales.

Margin—Securities Business The buying of stocks or bonds on credit, known as *buying on margin.*

Marginal Cost The cost of an additional unit. The marginal cost of capital is the cost of additional funds.

Marginal Efficiency of Capital A schedule showing the internal rate of return on investment opportunities.

Marginal Revenue The increase in revenue produced by selling additional units.

Market Portfolio The total of all investment opportunities available.

Merger Any combination that forms one company from two or more previously existing companies.

Money Market Financial markets in which funds are borrowed or lent for short periods (that is, less than one year). (The money market is distinguished from the capital market, which is the market for long-term funds.)

Monte Carlo Method A sensitivity analysis of the effects of using random combinations of probabilities applicable to two or more factors that affect the outcomes of business decisions.

Mortgage A pledge of designated property as security for a loan.

N

Net Present Value (NPV) Method The NPV is equal to the present value of future returns, discounted at the marginal cost of capital, minus the present value of the cost of the investment.

Net Worth The capital and surplus of a firm—capital stock, capital surplus (paid-in capital), earned surplus (retained earnings), and, occasionally, certain reserves. For some purposes, preferred stock is included; generally, net worth refers only to the common stockholders' position.

NOI Acronym for *net operating income,* same as EBIT; symbol X is also used.

Nominal Interest Rate The contracted or stated interest rate, undeflated for price level changes.

Normal Probability Distribution A symmetrical, bell-shaped probability function.

O

Objective Probability Distributions Probability distributions determined by relative frequencies.

Operating Lease A lease in which the lessee has the option of cancelling the lease before maturity without default. In contrast, a financial lease provides for a full payment of the lessor's projected investment and return over the life of the lease.

Operating Leverage The extent to which fixed costs are used in a firm's operation. Breakeven analysis is used to measure the extent to which operating leverage is employed.

OPM *See* Option Pricing Model.

Opportunity Cost The rate of return on the best *alternative* investment that is available. It is the highest return that will *not* be earned if the funds are invested in a particular project. For example, the opportunity cost of *not* investing in Bond A yielding 8 percent might be 7.99 percent, which could be earned on Bond B.

Option A contract that gives the holder the right to buy (or sell) an asset at a predetermined price for a given period of time.

Option Pricing Model (OPM) The risk-free rate, the current value of the asset, the variance of returns, the exercise price, and the duration of an option are expressed in a formula from which the value of the option can be calculated.

Ordinary Income Income from the normal operations of a firm. Ordinary income specifically excludes income from the sale of capital assets.

Organized Security Exchanges Formal organizations having tangible, physical locations. Organized exchanges conduct an auction market in designated (listed) investment securities. The New York Stock Exchange is an example of an organized exchange.

Overdraft System A system where a depositor may write checks in excess of his balance, with his bank automatically extending a loan to cover the shortage.

Oversubscription Privilege In a rights offering, gives subscribing stockholders the right to buy, on a pro rata basis, all shares not taken in the initial offering.

Over-the-Counter Market All facilities that provide for trading in unlisted securities; that is, those not listed on organized exchanges. The over-the-counter market is typically a telephone market, with most business conducted by phone.

P

Par Value The nominal value of a stock or bond.

Payback Period The length of time required for the net revenues of an investment to return the cost of the investment.

Payout Ratio The percentage of earnings paid out in the form of dividends.

Pegging A market stabilization action taken by the manager of an underwriting group during the offering of new securities. The manager does this by continually placing orders to buy at a specified price in the market.

Perpetual Bond A bond which pays interest annually into perpetuity.

Perpetuity A stream of future payments expected to continue forever.

Pledging of Accounts Receivable Short-term borrowing from financial institutions where the loan is secured by accounts receivable. The lender may physically take the accounts receivable but typically has recourse to the borrower; also called *discounting of accounts receivable.*

Pooling of Interest An accounting method for combining the financial statements of firms that merge. Under the pooling-of-interest procedure, the assets of the merged firms are simply added to form the balance sheet of the surviving corporation.

Portfolio Combining assets to reduce risk by diversification.

Portfolio Effect The extent to which the variation in returns on a combination of assets (a portfolio) is less than the simple average of the variations of the individual assets.

Portfolio Theory Deals with the selection of optimal portfolios, those portfolios that provide the highest possible return for any specified degree of risk.

Preemptive Right A provision contained in the corporate charter and bylaws that gives holders of common stock the right to purchase on a pro rata basis new issues of common stock (or securities convertible into common stock).

Present Value (PV) The value today of a future payment, or stream of payments, discounted at the appropriate discount rate.

Price-Earnings Ratio (P-E) The ratio of price to earnings. Faster growing or less risky firms typically have higher P-E ratios than either slower growing or riskier firms.

Price-Level Adjustment A restatement of a financial statement to adjust for the effects of general or specific price-level changes; for example, inflation.

Primary EPS Earnings available to common stock divided by the number of shares actually outstanding, disregarding any unexercised warrants or unconverted convertibles.

Prime Rate The rate of interest commercial banks charge borrowers with the highest credit ratings.

Private Placement Financing directly from the source of funds without the use of an intermediary such as an investment banker.

Pro Forma A projection. A pro forma financial statement shows how financial statements will look under specified assumptions. Pro forma statements may reflect historical relations or future projections.

Profit Center A unit of a firm with divisions that have identifiable cash flows and investments on which a rate of return on investment or other performance measures can be calculated.

Profit Margin The ratio of net income to sales.

Profit Planning *See* Breakeven Analysis.

Profitability Index (PI) The present value of future returns divided by the present value of the investment outlay.

Progressive Tax A tax that requires a higher percentage payment on higher incomes. The personal income tax in the United States, which rises from a rate of 14 percent on the lowest increments of income to 70 percent on the highest increments, is progressive.

Prospectus Information provided on a new security issue to provide a record of representations by the issuer to the prospective buyer.

Proxy A document giving one person the authority or power to act for another. Typically, the authority in question is the power to vote shares of common stock.

Purchase Accounting A method of accounting that allows for a firm's goodwill value in a transaction (the premium, or discount, over the book value) to be set up as an asset of the surviving firm.

Pure (or Primitive) Security A security that pays off $1 if one particular state-of-the-world occurs and pays off nothing if any other state-of-the-world occurs.

Put An option to sell a specific security at a specified price within a designated period.

R

Rate of Return The internal rate of return on an investment.

Recourse Arrangement A term used in connection with accounts receivable financing. If a firm sells its accounts receivable to a financial institution under a recourse agreement and if the accounts receivable cannot then be collected, the selling firm must repurchase the account from the financial institution.

Rediscount Rate The rate of interest at which a bank may borrow from a Federal Reserve Bank.

Refunding Sale of new debt securities to replace an old debt issue.

Regression Analysis A statistical procedure for predicting the value of one variable (dependent variable) on the basis of knowledge about one or more other variables (independent variables).

Reinvestment Rate The rate of return at which cash flows from an investment are reinvested. The reinvestment rate may or may not be constant from year to year.

Reorganization When a financially troubled firm goes through reorganization, its assets are restated to reflect their current market value, and its financial structure is restated downward to reflect reductions on the asset side of the statement. Under a reorganization, the firm continues in existence; this is contrasted to bankruptcy, in which the firm is liquidated and ceases to exist.

Replacement Cost Accounting A requirement under SEC Release No. 190 (1976) that large companies disclose the replacement costs of inventory items and depreciable plant. Superceded by similar provisions in FASB Statement No. 33, issued in 1979.

Required Rate of Return The rate of return necessary to avoid a decline in the value of a security.

Residual Value The value of leased property at the end of the lease term.

Retained Earnings That portion of earnings not paid out in dividends. The figure that appears on the balance sheet is the sum of the retained earnings for each year throughout the company's history.

Right A short-term option to buy a specified number of shares of a new issue of securities at a designated subscription price.

Rights Offering A securities flotation offered to existing stockholders.

Risk The degree of dispersion of future returns from their average expected value. Measured by the variance, standard deviation, or coefficient of variation of possible future returns.

Risk-Adjusted Discount Rates The discount rate applicable for a particular risky (uncertain) stream of income; the riskless rate of interest plus a risk premium appropriate to the level of risk attached to the particular income stream.

Risk-Free Rate Generally the return on short-maturity U.S. Treasury securities, on which there is little likelihood of variability or default.

Risk Premium The difference between the required rate of return on a particular risky asset and the rate of return on a riskless asset with the same expected life.

Risk-Return Trade-off Function *See* Security Market Line.

S

Safety Stock An amount added to inventory holdings as a precautionary measure in the face of uncertainty as to delivery times and usage rates, and the cost of stock-outs.

Sale and Leaseback An operation whereby a firm sells land, buildings, or equipment to a financial institution and simultaneously executes an agreement to lease the property back for a specified period under specific terms.

Salvage Value The value of a capital asset at the end of a specified period. It is the current market price of an asset being considered for replacement in a capital budgeting problem.

Securities and Exchange Commission (SEC) A federal government agency with which a registration statement must be filed on new issues of securities and which supervises the operation of securities exchanges and related aspects of the securities business.

Securities, Junior Securities that have lower priority in claims on assets and income than other, senior, securities. For example, preferred stock is junior to debentures, but debentures are junior to mortgage bonds. Common stock is the most junior of all corporate securities.

Securities, Senior Securities having claims on income and assets that rank higher than certain other, junior, securities. For example, mortgage bonds are senior to debentures, but debentures are senior to common stock.

Security Agreement A standardized document or form which includes a description of the specific assets pledged for the purpose of a secured loan.

Security Market Line (SML) The relationship between the required return on a security and the product of its risk times a normalized market measure of risk. Risk-return relationships for individual securities or investments.

Selling Group A group of securities brokers or dealers formed for the purpose of distributing a new issue of securities; part of the investment banking distribution process.

Sensitivity Analysis Simulation analysis in which the values of causal variables are changed to determine the degree to which the results are related to the behavior of individual variables.

Short Selling Selling a security that is not owned by the seller at the time of the sale. The seller borrows the security from a brokerage firm and must at some point repay the brokerage firm by buying the security on the open market.

Simulation Analysis of relationships by making assumptions in a model about the values of some of the variables and observing the effects on outcomes or results.

Sinking Fund Periodic payments which at the applicable interest rate will accumulate to a target amount of funds desired for such purposes as reducing or completely paying off an obligation.

Small Business Administration (SBA) A government agency organized to aid small firms with their financing and other problems.

Spontaneous Financing Financing (for example, trade credit) which arises from ordinary business transactions.

Standard Deviation (σ) A statistical term that measures the variability of a set of observations from the mean of the distribution.

State-Preference Model (SPM) An approach to dealing with uncertainty by describing what will happen in each of a set of alternative future states-of-the-world.

Stock Dividend A dividend paid in additional shares of stock rather than in cash. It involves a transfer from retained earnings to the capital stock account.

Stock Split An accounting action to increase the number of shares outstanding; for example, in a 3-for-1 split, three new shares are issued for each one formerly held.

Subjective Probability Distributions Probability distributions formulated by judgments not completely based on empirical evidence such as relative frequencies.

Subordinated Debenture A bond having a claim on assets only after specified senior claims have been paid off.

Subscription Price The price at which a security may be purchased in a rights offering.

Synergy The improved performance of a firm that has resulted from a merger is greater than would be the simple sum of the individual pre-merger entities; derives from the interdependency of the activities of the firms.

Systematic Risk That part of a security's risk that cannot be eliminated by diversification.

T

Tangible Assets Physical assets (as opposed to intangible assets such as goodwill and the stated value of patents).

Tender Offers An offer to buy the stock of a firm at a specified price. Sometimes the offer is submitted for approval to the board of directors of the target company; or the offer may be made directly to the shareholders of the company.

Term Loan A loan generally obtained from a bank or an insurance company with a maturity greater than one year. Term loans are generally amortized; periodic repayments are made to reduce the outstanding amount of the loan over its life.

Term Structure of Interest Rates The relationship between interest rates and loan maturity.

Terminal Value The value of an asset at a future time. The value of an asset today is the present value of its terminal value discounted at the appropriate rate.

Trade Credit Interfirm debt arising through credit sales and recorded as an account receivable by the seller and as an account payable by the buyer.

Transfer Price The price used within a firm to record the "sale" of products or assets by one division to another.

Treasury Stock Common stock that has been repurchased by the issuing firm.

Trust Receipt An instrument acknowledging that the borrower holds certain goods in trust for the lender. Trust receipt financing is used in connection with the financing of inventories for automobile dealers, construction equipment dealers, appliance dealers, and other dealers in expensive durable goods.

Trustee The representative of bondholders who acts in their interest and facilitates communication between them and the issuer. Typically these duties are handled by a department of a commercial bank.

U

Underwriting (1) The entire process of issuing new corporate securities. (2) The insurance function of bearing the risk of adverse price fluctuations during the period in which a new issue of stock or bonds is being distributed.

Underwriting Syndicate A syndicate of investment firms formed to spread the risk associated with the purchase and distribution of a new issue of securities. The larger the issue, the more firms typically are involved in the syndicate.

Unlisted Securities Securities that are traded in the over-the-counter market.

Unsystematic Risk That part of a security's risk associated with random events; unsystematic risk can be eliminated by proper diversification.

Utility Theory A body of theory dealing with the relationships among money income, utility (or satisfaction), and the willingness to accept risks.

V

Value Additivity Principle Neither fragmenting cash flows nor recombining them will affect the resulting values of the cash flows.

Variable Budget A system whereby budget projections of inflows and outflows have different relationships at different levels of activity of the unit.

Venture Capital Financing of a firm when its future outlook is highly uncertain. An example is the financing of a new small firm before it has established a performance record.

W

Warrant A long-term option to buy a stated number of shares of common stock at a specified price. The specified price is generally called the *exercise price.*

Weighted Cost of Capital A weighted average of the component costs of debt, preferred stock, and common equity. Also called the composite cost of capital.

Working Capital Refers to a firm's investment in short-term assets—cash, short-term securities, accounts receivable, and inventories. *Gross working capital* is defined as a firm's total current assets. *Net working capital* is defined as current assets minus current liabilities.

Y

Yield The rate of return on an investment; the internal rate of return.

Yield to Maturity Based on a bond's coupon and price, the rate of return that is expected if a bond is held to maturity.

Index

Summary of Key Formulas in Managerial Finance
(Symbols are defined inside front cover)

I. Compound Interest

A. Basic Relations

1a. Compound sum:

$$S_N = P_0(1 + r)^N$$

1b. Present value:

$$P_0 = S_N(1 + r)^{-N}$$

2a. Sum of annuity:

$$S_{r,N} = [(1 + r)^N - 1]/r$$

2b. Present value of annuity:

$$P_{r,N} = [1 - (1 + r)^{-N}]/r$$

B. Bond Valuation

1. Valuation of a perpetual bond:

$$B = \frac{c}{r}$$

2. Valuation of bond of finite maturity:

$$B = \sum_{t=1}^{N} \frac{c_t}{(1 + r)^t} + \frac{M}{(1 + r)^N}$$

II. Capital Budgeting Relations

A. Basic Capital Budgeting Relation—NPV

$$\text{NPV} = \sum_{t=1}^{N} \frac{F_t}{(1 + k)^t} - \text{I}$$

B. Internal Rate of Return (R)

$$\text{NPV} = \sum_{t=1}^{N} \frac{F_t}{(1 + R)^t} - \text{I} = 0$$

C. Profitability Index

$$\text{PI} = \frac{\text{PV benefits}}{\text{cost}}$$

$$= \frac{\sum_{t=1}^{N} \frac{F_t}{(1 + k)^t}}{\text{I}}$$

D. Equivalent Annual Annuity Factor

$$a = 1/\text{PVIFA}_{(k,N)}$$

III. Return and Risk

A. Portfolios

1. Expected return on a portfolio:

$$E(R_p) = w_1R_1 + w_2R_2 \ldots w_nR_n$$

2. Standard deviation of a portfolio (two-asset case):

$$\sigma_p = (w_a^2\sigma_a^2 + w_b^2\sigma_b^2 + 2w_a w_b \rho_{ab} \sigma_a \sigma_b)^{1/2}$$

3. Portfolio weights to minimize $\boldsymbol{\sigma_p}$ (two-asset case):

$$w_a = \frac{\sigma_b^2 - \rho_{ab}\sigma_a\sigma_b}{\sigma_a^2 + \sigma_b^2 - 2\rho_{ab}\sigma_a\sigma_b}$$

B. CAPM Relationships

1. Security Market Line (SML):

$$\bar{R}_j = R_F + \lambda\text{Cov}(\tilde{R}_j,\tilde{R}_M)$$

$$\lambda = \frac{\bar{R}_M - R_F}{\sigma_M^2}$$

2. $\bar{R}_j = R_F + (\bar{R}_M - R_F)\beta_j$

where:

$$\beta_j = \text{Cov}(\tilde{R}_j,\tilde{R}_M)/\sigma_M^2$$

3. CAPM valuation (certainty equivalent form):

$$V_j = \frac{E(X_j) - \lambda\text{Cov}(X_j,\tilde{R}_M)}{R_F}$$

IV. Cost of Capital Relationships

A. Cost of Equity Capital

$$k_s = k_u + (k_u - k_b)(B/S)(1 - T)$$

$$k_s = R_F + \lambda\text{Cov}(R_u,R_M)\left[1 + \frac{B(1 - T)}{S}\right]$$

B. Weighted Cost of Capital

1. $k_u = \dfrac{E(X)(1 - T)}{V_u}$ $\qquad k = \dfrac{E(X)(1 - T)}{V_L}$

2. $k = k_b(1 - T)\dfrac{B}{V} + k_s\dfrac{S}{V}$

3. $k = k_u[1 - T(B/V)]$

C. Influence of Tax Subsidy on Value

$$V = V_u + BT$$